Emerging Technologies of the 21st Century

Emerging Technologies of the 21st Century

Edited by
AJIT KUMAR ROY
National Consultant (Impact Assessment) for
East and North East Region of India
National Agricultural Innovation Project (World Bank Funded)
KAB-2, PUSA, New Delhi-110012
Ex. Consultant (Statistics), College of Fisheries
Central Agricultural University
Lembucherra, Tripura West
Ex. Computer Specialist, SAARC Agricultural Information Centre
Dhaka, Bangladesh
Ex Pr. Head, Social Science, CIFA, ICAR, Bhubaneswar
Ex Co-ordinator, Bioinformatics Centre, CIFA, ICAR, Bhubaneswar

NEW INDIA PUBLISHING AGENCY
New Delhi – 110 034

NEW INDIA PUBLISHING AGENCY
101, Vikas Surya Plaza, CU Block, LSC Market
Pitam Pura, New Delhi 110 034, India
Phone: + 91 (11)27 34 17 17 Fax: + 91(11) 27 34 16 16
Email: info@nipabooks.com
Web: www.nipabooks.com

Feedback at feedbacks@nipabooks.com

ISBN : 978-93-83305-33-9

Composed, Designed and Printed at Jai Bharat Printing Press, Delhi

DEDICATION

The book is dedicated to my late parents,
my wife, sons and daughter in laws &
future generations of my family to come.

PREFACE

Global technology revolution is leading to social, economic, political, and personal change throughout the world. Like the agricultural and industrial revolutions of the past, this technology revolution has the potential to transform human quality of life and lifespan, transform work and industry, reshuffle wealth, shift power among nations and within nations. It is believed that various technologies including information technology, biotechnology, nanotechnology, and materials technology have the potential for significant and dominant global effects. New digital technologies open the door on changes in learning and teaching that go much deeper than anything we have experienced in history. It is believed that life in the coming days will be revolutionized by the growing effect of multidisciplinary technology across all dimensions of life: social, economic, political, and personal. *Against this backdrop, it is attempted to bring together a compilation in the form of a Book broadly on various emerging technologies applied in the disciplines covering Basic and Applied Sciences, in the form a book entitled **"Emerging Technologies of the 21st Century"***

All the forty two *Book chapters constitute the following focus areas like Biotechnology, Bioinformatics, Nanotechnology, Expert System Neural Network, Applied Technologies, Database,Modeling,Analytics and Business Intelligence Software, IPR & Social Issues*. Chapters on *Emerging digital technologies, Information and communication Technology Tools, skill and technologies for 21st century Education, Big data, Business intelligence soft wares, GIS, IPR and Knowledge/Patenting/ Indigenous and Traditional Knowledge Management (KM) challenges are also included in the book.*

It is expected that the book will be very much useful because with the emergence of new technologies and application through software tools are becoming very important in the 21st Century society. The compilation of all important chapters could not have been possible without the contributions of expert professionals from India and abroad working in various research institutes and universities. The editor express deep sense of gratitude to all of them.

—Ajit Kumar Roy

About the Editor

Born in 1946, **Sri Ajit Kumar Roy** obtained his M.Sc. degree in Statistics. Sri Roy joined Agricultural Research Service (ARS) of Indian Council of Agricultural Research (ICAR) as Scientist in 1976. Presently National Consultant(Impact Assessment),for East & north Eastern States if India, National Agricultural Innovation Project(world bank funded).

Prof. Roy has been engaged in R & D activities in social science, IT, bioinformatics, statistics and economics for the last 45 years. He was deputed by Govt. of India to take up the assignment of Computer Specialist at SAARC Agricultural Information Centre (SAIC), Dhaka, Bangladesh for over 3 years. He has in his credit fifteen books, eight technical manuals, many e-publications, (published by SAIC and CIFA), and over ninety research publications covering the areas of statistics, economics, bioinformatics and ICT applications in aquaculture/fisheries/ agriculture research of in journals of National & International repute. He has retired from active service as Head, Social Science Section, Central Institute of Freshwater Aquaculture CIFA, ICAR, Bhubaneswar.As coordinator of BTIS Project engaged in development of the informatics based infrastructure of Bioinformatics Centre on Aquaculture at CIFA, Bhubaneswar. He has organized many workshops on application of ICT in fisheries/agriculture research. As Principal Scientist and Head, Social Science Section, CIFA, Bhubaneswar, he was involved in research in the area of application of Bioinformatics, Statistics and Econometrics in fisheries and aquaculture research. As Consultant(Statistics) he was involved in teaching, research and consultancy at Central Agricultural University, Manipur for two and half years. Some of his latest publications listed below have revolutionized R&D activities in the areas of Social Science Research in Aquaculture/Fisheries. i) Information and knowledge Management Tools Techniques,NIPA,*101 Vikas Surya Plaza, Pitampura, New Delhi.xiv+684(ISBN:978-93-81450-62-8)* ii) *Applied Computational Biology and Statistics in Biotechnology and Bioinformatics. NIPA, 101 Vikas Surya Plaza, Pitampura, New Delhi,.xiv+1138(ISBN: 9789380235929).iii)* Modeling, Forecasting, Artificial Neural Network and Expert system in Fisheries & Aquaculture, Daya Publishing House, New Delhi,xv+239p(ISBN:1081-7035-571-0) 2009 iv)Applied Bioinformatics, Statistics and Economics in Fisheries Research. NIPA, Pitampura, New Delhi, XII+606 p. *(ISBN: 81-89422-86-3),2008 v)* Socio and Techno Economic Aspect of Aquaculture in Kolleru Lake, Andhra Pradesh, India, Central Institute of Freshwater Aquaculture, Bhubaneswar, XXI+154 p. *(ISBN : 978-81-904422-1-3),2008.vi)*Evaluation and Impact Assessment of Technologies and Developmental Activities in Agriculture, Fisheries and Allied Fields,NIPA.101 Vikas Surya Plaza, Pitampura, New Delhi.xiv+510p. vii) Fisheries Resource and Production Statistics *of* NE States of India—An Analytical Value Added Presentation, Narendra Publishing House, Delhi (India), (ISBN: 978 - 93 - 80428 - 95 - 6), 313p.

Contents

Section 2 : Nanotechnology

Section 3 : Expert System Neural Network

Section 6 : IPR & Social Issues

Section 1
Biotechnology

CHAPTER - 1

The Green Revolution : Clean Energy and Fuel Directly From Algae Production Systems

Enzo Alibrandi
CEO Manager – TERRAQUA, Aquaculture and Aquarist Technician
E-mail: terraquaworld@gmail.com

1. INTRODUCTION

Increasingly, in recent years, we hear of new technologies for the production of clean energy or, as they say now in common usage, from renewable energy sources, there are many sources of renewable energy, but certainly the ones that deserve special attention are those derived from algae. Today, thanks to innovative systems called photobioreactors, you have a way to start producing, though unfortunately still a small part, the amount of clean energy from algae and various biological processes that develop. The photobioreactor is one of the most innovative systems of the 21st century, and is paving the way for a new concept of energy utilization , although the fossil fuel (oil of course) continues to lead the way, even if you are aware of the drastic and continuous decrease the world's resources. Although still under investigation, but there are many aspects that allow, thanks to special engineering studies , already now create systems suitable for the production of energy directly from algae , while biofuels obtained from the latter, there are several studies and tests , which aim to further lower production costs, in order to bring them at par or even below the threshold of current fossil fuels. In addition, these photo bioreactors, allow to produce, under controlled conditions, products and raw materials from the algae for food and non-food market, often providing a viable substitute, nutritious and natural, to all those raw materials that are harmful to human health and animals, especially in the food and health sectors.

2. VARIETY OF ALGAE AND THEIR USE THROUGH PHOTO BIOREACTORS AND OTHER TYPES OF PLANTS

With in these technological systems such as photobioreactors or similar, it is possible to produce various types of algae. However, there are, according to recent studies, some types of algae more likely to develop certain types of products and/or services, including biofuels. Several species of algae can be produced both in photobioreactors as well as also in less complex systems, such as tanks in reinforced or VTR, still, in controlled environments such as laboratories. Below is a brief overview will be made of the most important species of algae, especially from the point of view of their use in the technology, energy and food.

2.1 Spirulina

Spirulina (Arthrospiraplatensis) is a blue-green microalgae (part of the group of blue-green algae). The spirulina, thanks to its many properties, isused in the food and pharmaceutical field, allowing the production of food supplements, pharmaceuticals and cosmetics, also thanks to the presence of essential oils and vitamins often rare in other types of products. In the energy field, spirulina can also be used for the production of clean energy for electricity and heating a practical example can be found in Hamburg, where he built the first building energy algae. Regarding biofuels, Spirulina, is not currently used, as it produces a low photosynthetic, thus not allowing gas exchange such as to generate the various processes of energy required to produce biofuel or green oil.

Production technology used

For the production of spirulina are used in most cases, tanks of about 80-100 m^2, which allow a total daily production of about 1200 kg of seaweed. Such technology is very common and easy to produce, with very low costs in terms of management. Even photo bioreactors are used for the production of spirulina algae even if it is better than the first type of production, which allows the use of the tanks even in outdoor spaces and under direct sunlight, a suitable condition for the physiological processes of the algae.

2.2 Dunaliella, Chlorella, Neochloris

These three types of algae are currently the most suitable for the production of biofuels is that of clean energy. Recent studies have shown that these species have a particularly high content of oils, such as to allow an industrial production in many cases. These algae are among others also used for human food, thanks to the presence of significant percentages of protein and vitamins.

Production technology used

For the production of clean energy and biofuels, these algae are produced in large plants photo bioreactors, with a length of about 80 meters. And, thanks to such systems, it is possible to obtain a density productive enough to justify any investment in this technology. Photo bioreactors are carried out, in order to exploit solar energy to trigger so the various production processes required for the production from algae.

3. SYSTEMS AND TECHNOLOGIES FOR THE PRODUCTION OF ENERGY AND BIOFUELS FROM ALGAE

As described above, there are different types of algae, or less suitable for the production of clean energy and biofuel. All of these types of algae and microalgae, are selected for the production through the use of various technological systems and their production, also happens to be used in some particular systems or in certain areas, such as the aqueous treatment.

3.1 Photobioreactors

Photobioreactors, both the closed and open type , are currently one of the most advanced technological solutions for the production of energy from algae. Photobioreactors are cropping systems, closed or open , optimal for the growth of micro-organisms that depend on sunlight or artificial light , such as microalgae, cyanobacteria, photosynthetic bacteria .

From the fews trains grown in recent decades it has gone to the current more than 50,000 , many of them used for the production of substances of great quality and value : antifungal , antibacterial, antiviral , products for the pharmaceutical, nutrition, cosmetics.

The basic function of photobioreactors ,which are similar to the fermenters used by the pharmaceutical industry for the growth of heterotrophic organisms, is to ensure a controlled process in which it is possible to produce microbial biomass and / or metabolites .

They differ from fermenters because they also require an adequate supply of light energy. They can be classified as indoor or outdoor photobioreactors . The first are small, they are often the prototypes and their lighting is kind of artificial lamps of various types, while for outdoor photobioreactors, which require large spaces, lighting depends on the solar radiation, and are are particularly affected by day-night cycles. More specifically, it is called photo bioreactors when referring to structures in which the crop is not in contact with the atmosphere or with other types of contaminants, dust, other micro-organisms , etc. The closed photo bioreactorsmay be aerobic or anaerobic , and require advanced technologies, especially for the control of all process parameters such as pH, temperature, hydrodynamics, cell concentration, carbon dioxide, oxygen, replenishment of nutrients etc. The construction materials have to be very transparent and resistant, not be toxic, chemical stability and have, if possible, have a reduced cost. Just the economic factor is often a cause of distrust systems using closed photobioreactors for example, the production of hydrogen or biofuels, as the possibility of a future development to industrial level must pass through the economics ustainability. In the open photobioreactors the growth of microorganisms occurs mainly in large tanks or ponds, but in these environments is rather limited ability to control crop and their degree of purity. For these reasons, before moving on to the stages of production of large volumes, it is convenient to precede them by the steps of laboratory and closed photo bioreactors.

3.2 Raceways

The tanks raceways are used for the production of algae or microalgae, both outdoors and indoors. Surely the predominant factor that still allows the use of these systems is certainly their cost-effectiveness, since they are used in fiber glass or plastic tanks for the production, this also adds a significant reduction in operating costs of these same plants as well as the need to invest more content than the photobioreactors. The tanks are referred to as " raceways "in that they have an oval shape, with a central support on which is placed a motorized paddle aerator, which constantly stirs the water the crops, thus favoring the oxygenation and gas exchange. One of the major defects in the use of such tanks is to not have a complete control of the factors that determine optimal production of algae, especially if it is of algae for the production of raw green (pure oil). Therefore, this type of system is particularly used to initiate a productive activity in the field of biofuels, bearing in mind that , in this type of system, with time, you will need to integrate systems in photo bioreactor, even in a partial way.

CONCLUSIONS

The 21st Century is characterized by a considerable progress, constantly increasing, relative to technology and biotechnology, in order to reduce consumption, to live better the community and at the same time protecting the environment and future generations. Biotechnology created from algae are definitely the future given that, at present, in the world, are becoming more apparent the various uses and outcomes associated with algae, both in the energy field and in other fields of application. Of course, again, is much work to be done, especially in some sectors, such as biofuels from algae, but we are definitely on the right track. If you succeed in trovarte a solution to reduce the production costs of algae in photobioreactors, reduce the cost of the latter is in the realization that in management, then you will open a door to the future, thus finally eliminating all possible sources of pollution.

❑❑❑

CHAPTER - 2

The Role of Next Generation Sequencing in Shaping the Future of Life Sciences Research in the 21st Century

Upendra Kumar Devisetty
Department of Plant Biology LSA, 1 Shields Avenue, University of California Davis, Davis, USA
E-mail: udevisetty@ucdavis.edu
Lekkala Devudu Naidu
Assistant Professor (O.G.)
Area : Nano-Technology
Affiliation : Department of Chemical Engineering, School of Bioengineering Kattankulathur Campus, SRM University
E-mail: demudunaidu.k@ktr.srmuniv.ac.in

1. INTRODUCTION

The key global challenges facing the mankind in the 21st century are food, water, energy security, environment, combating cancer, and infectious diseases. Solving these challenges requires concerted efforts using modern scientific and technological advances in multiple disciplines. One such technology that has revolutionized life science research is "next-generation sequencing". The NGS technology has brought an enormous technological shift in DNA sequencing through dramatic high-throughput and a precipitously dropping cost of raw sequence data. NGS technologies changed the dynamics and pace of genomic research in humans, animals, plants and microbes largely due to their rapid, inexpensive and highly accurate sequencing capabilities. The capillary electrophoresis based sequencing technology pioneered by Sanger and Coulson (Sanger, Nicklen, & Coulson, 1977) has been completely replaced by NGS since its emergence in 2005. The first commercially available NGS platform GS20 was developed by 454 Life Sciences and since then several NGS technologies including Illumina, ABI SOLiD, as well as single molecular sequencing technology of Helicos and Pacific Biosciences (Metzker, 2010). The main principle of NGS involves the DNA molecules, which are sequenced in a massively parallel fashion in flow cells. Because of this highly parallelized process, each single molecule is individually sequenced and can be counted among the total millions and millions of sequences generated. NGS technologies have increased high-throughput capacity and reduced sequencing costs, which makes it possible for these technologies to perform sequencing of whole genomes of many species including cancer cells. To date, whole-genome sequencing of many non-model species from microbes, plants to animals have been done (http://www.genomenewsnetwork.org/resources/sequenced_genomes/genome_guide_index.shtml). Besides genome sequencing, current NGS applications include targeted resequencing, epigenetics and metagenomics. Since this technology has been impacting several biological fields, this review will attempt to provide an overview and important features of various NGS platforms currently in market, applications, bioinformatics tools, current limitations and future promises that this technology hold.

2. OVERVIEW OF NGS TECHNOLOGIES

Popular commercial platforms that are based on this sequencing technology can be broadly divided into four main categories: sequencing by synthesis, sequencing by ligation, single-molecule sequencing and nanopore sequencing technologies. Sequencing methods by synthesis and ligation can be considered as second generation NGS platforms, and single-molecule and nanopore sequencing methods can be considered as third generation and fourth generation NGS platforms respectively. Good reviews of these sequencing technologies has been provided elsewhere (Mardis, 2008; Metzker, 2010), although capacity and read length have increased since the publication of these reviews. Because of this, all biological disciplines that depend on DNA sequence data have been fundamentally transformed and as the costs and capabilities of NGS technologies continue to improve, whole new fields of biology are being opened up, allowing scientists to analyze a variety of datasets for the identification of new mutations and deeper exploration of the functional principles governing the function of genes, genomes and cells.

2.1 Sequencing by Synthesis

The idea of sequencing by synthesis has been around for a while and is the basis for several NGS technologies. In this method, DNA is fragmented to appropriate size, attached to adapter sequences, and then clonally amplified to increase the fluorescent or chemical signals. Templates are then separated and immobilized in preparation for flow-cell cycles. The three platforms in this group are Roche/454, Illumina and Ion Torrent. Though each of these use different chemistry, all use sequential washes of nucleotides along with varying chemistries for fluorescent or chemical detection of nucleotide incorporation. They also differ in length of the reads generated and methods of amplification and immobilization of templates.

2.1.1 Roche/454 GS FLX pyrosequencing

In March 2007, Roche Diagnostics announced their acquisition 454 Life sciences for US$154.9 million. This is the first commercially introduced NGS technology and is based on pyrosequencing method (Margulies, Melman, & Shanzer, 2005). 454 sequencing uses a large-scale parallel pyrosequencing system (http://www.my454.com) utilizes an enzyme cascade to produce light from a pyrophosphate released during nucleotide incorporation in order to sequence DNA. Briefly, the sheared fragments are attached to microbeads and amplified in an emulsion-based PCR. These microbeads are further distributed to a fiber optic slide (PicoTiterPlate™), where the four dNTPs are added in turns. The sequence of DNA is determined by analyzing the fluorescence emitted by the activity of luciferase enzyme during the process of template extension by a single nucleotide addition.

2.1.2 Illumina genome analyzer

Initially developed by Solexa, Illumina bought out Solexa in 2006. The Illumina Genome Analyzer (http://www.illumina.com) uses solid-phase bridge amplification and proprietary reversible terminator reaction technology for fast, accurate and high-throughput sequencing. Briefly the sheared DNA fragments that contain 5′- 3′ adapters are immobilized in a 8-channel microfabricated flow cell. Then the DNA molecules are first attached to primers on a slide and then bridge amplified so that local colonies are formed. DNA is sequenced using all four fluorescently labeled nucleotides to sequence millions of clusters on the flow cell.

2.1.3 Ion Torrent system

The Ion Torrent system (http://www.iontorrent.com) is unique among all NGS technologies in which the detection for sequencing is not based on fluorescent dyes but rather measuring pH change as the result of the release of H^+ ion upon nucleotide incorporation during a natural polymerase reaction using an ion sensor located underneath the micro machined wells in a semiconductor chip, each containing a different DNA template. According to Ion Torrent patent applications, field transistors were used to measure the change in pH in microwell structures. By sequentially adding nucleotides, the machine is able to detect which nucleotides were incorporated in the growing DNA strand. Although this method greatly reduces the cost of DNA sequencing, there are several limitations such as shorted fragment lengths, high frequency of errors and challenges during sequencing homopolymer regions.

2.2 Sequencing by Ligation

Sequencing by ligation uses the mismatch sensitivity of DNA ligase to determine the sequence of nucleotides in a given DNA strand. The methods under sequencing by ligation use oligonucleotide probes of differing lengths, which are labeled with fluorescent tags depending on the nucleotides to be determined. The fragmented DNA templates are primed with a short, known anchor sequence, which allows the probes to hybridize. DNA ligase is added to the flow cell and joins the fluorescently labeled probe to the primer and template. Fluorescence imaging is performed to determine which probe was incorporated. This process is repeated several times using different sets of probes to query the DNA template and assess the sequence of nucleotides.

2.2.1 Life technologies SOLiD™

SOLiD (Sequencing by Oligonucleotide Ligation and Detection) is a NGS technology developed by Life Technologies/Applied Biosystems (http://www.appliedbiosystems.com). Libraries of DNA fragments are prepared first from the sample and are used to prepare clonal bead populations similar to that of 454 sequencing and the clonal bead populations are covalently bound to a slide by 3′ modification of the beads. During sequencing reaction step, a fluorescently labeled di-base probe hybridizes to the complementary sequence adjacent to primed template and DNA ligase enzyme then joins the dye-labeled probe to the primer. After all the non-ligated probes are washed off, fluorescence is imaged to identify the nucleotides incorporated at first and second base.

2.3 Single-Molecule Sequencing

Single-molecule sequencing (SMS) or third generation sequencing circumvents some of the issues facing second-generation sequencing. Using chemiluminiscence, SMS methods produce a detectable signal of nucleotide incorporation during DNA sequencing from a single DNA molecule, thus eliminating the need for DNA template amplification. Thus SMS methods provide several benefits over NGS methods, such as simplified sample preparation, use of low or degraded starting material (Orlando *et al.*, 2011) and the avoidance of PCR biases and errors introduced during template amplification steps. In addition these methods can be used to sequence RNA directly thus removing biases created during cDNA fragmentation and amplification processes (Ozsolak *et al.*, 2009). Two of the leading SMS technologies are Heliscope and Pacific Biosciences.

2.3.1 Heliscope™ single molecule sequencer (Helicos)

The Helicos was the first commercially available SMS technology in the market (Harris *et al.*, 2008). The basic principle of the Helicos sequencer relies on "true single molecule sequencing" (tSMS) technology. The tSMS technology begins with DNA fragmentation and addition of polyA tail to the generated DNA fragments followed by hybridization of DNA fragments to polyT oligonucleotides, which are attached to the flow cell and concurrently sequenced in parallel reactions. The sequencing cycle consists of DNA extension with one out of four fluorescently labeled nucleotides, followed by nucleotide detection with the Heliscope sequencer. Subsequently chemical cleavage of fluorophores allows the next cycle of DNA elongation to begin with another nucleotide, which enables the determination of the DNA sequence. The Heliscope can sequence up to 28Gb in single sequencing reaction and takes about 8 days (http://www.helicosbio.com).

2.3.2 Pacific biosciences

Recently Pacific Biosciences released their PacBio RS SMS platform (http://www.pacificbiosciences.com), which offers real-time sequencing from single polymerase DNA molecules. The process utilizes DNA polymerase molecules bound to 50nm-wide nanophotonic structures in an array slide called the zero mode waveguide (ZMW). The ZMW spatially restricts the volume of nucleotides and light emissions to a small area surrounding the DNA polymerase. The polymerase synthesizes DNA from a template using four fluorescently labelled nucleotides within the ZWMs and thus sequencing requires no amplification of DNA template ahead. Fluorescence imaging then allows the sequence of nucleotides to be determined. Though this method generates DNA sequence reaching in the tens of thousands of base pairs, it has limitations such as degradation of polymerase by laser excitation and generation of the highest raw error rates of NGS methods (~15%).

2.4 Nanopore DNA Sequencing

In contrast to all other sequencing technologies mentioned above, nanopore DNA sequencing technology differs in that the DNA sequencing is devoid of labeling and detection. This technique was developed based on studies of translocation of DNA through various artificial nanopores. At the forefront of developing nanopore technology is Oxford Nanopore Technologies (http://

www.nanoporetech.com). The basic idea is that a strand of molecule either DNA or RNA can be directly analyzed, as it passes through a nanopore, which is an alpha-hemolysin, pore covalently attached to a cyclodextrin molecule – the binding site for nucleotides. The principle of this sequencing method lies in the modulation of ionic current through the pore as a DNA molecule traverses it, revealing characteristics and parameters of the molecule. A potential advantage of using nanopore technology is the speed at which the DNA/RNA molecule traverses through the pore, potentially enabling fast DNA sequencing.

3. APPLICATIONS OF NEXT-GENERATION SEQUENCING

Since the introduction of NGS technologies in 2005, the past several years have seen a dramatic increase in the growth of NGS. The NGS market has reached $170 million in 2012 and expected to reach $580 million in 2018 with an impressive compound annual growth rate of 22.7% (http://www.lifesciences.frost.com). The field of molecular biology has undergone complete transformation as a result of NGS, which provides higher accuracy, higher throughput and more applications than any other technology. To date, the power of high-throughput NGS technologies is not restricted to high-throughput resequencing of DNA samples to discover and genotype variants but is also being extensively being utilized for other biological components such as RNA, proteins as well as protein-nucleic acid interactions in complex systems. The abundance of NGS data, its qualitative and quantitative nature, and its applicability to any organism, has enabled researchers to tailor NGS to wide variety of applications including (1) whole genome sequencing and reduced representation sequencing for comprehensive discovery of mutations and polymorphisms in individual human genomes; (2) mapping of structural rearrangements such as copy number variations (CNV), balanced translocation breakpoints and chromosomal inversions; (3) genome-wide mapping of DNA-protein interactions by deep sequencing of DNA fragments (ChIP-Seq); (4) large-scale analysis of DNA methylation by deep sequencing of bisulfite-treated DNA (BS-Seq); (5) large-scale gene expression studies where short-gun libraries derived from mRNA or small RNAs are deeply sequenced (RNA-Seq) and many others.

3.1 Genomic Applications

3.1.1 Genome sequencing and targeted resequencing

Recent technological advances in genomic science have enabled scientists to routinely generate unprecedented amounts of genomic sequence data from almost any species, opening the floodgates for study of genome content in non-model organisms (Rokas & Abbot, 2009). The main reason for these changes has been the emergence of NGS technologies. Whole genome sequencing and targeted resequencing is an important application of NGS is for the identification of causal alleles for disease susceptibility. Genome sequencing using NGS started with sequencing of bacterial genomes using 454 technology. With the decreasing the cost of sequencing, a large number of organisms were sequenced making these technologies a sufficiently commonplace. As of 2012, according to Genomes Online Database (http://www.genomesonline.org), a total of 3920 bacterial and 854 eukaryotic genomes have been sequenced. There are two different approaches for sequencing a genome, *de novo* sequencing and resequencing. De novo sequencing is done in the absence of reference genome and resequencing is done to characterize the genetic diversity within the species or between closely related species.

3.1.2 Detecting Genetic variation and genomic rearrangements

The knowledge and availability of genetic markers can serve as valuable tools to assess genetic diversity both within and between species, for the production of high-resolution genetic maps, genotyping segregating populations, marker-trait association studies, marker-assisted selection and map-based cloning (Edwards & Batley, 2004). In the last three decades, a number of PCR-based DNA fingerprinting methods such as RFLP (Restriction Fragment Length Polymorphism), RAPD (Random Amplified Polymorphic DNA), AFLP (Amplified Fragment Length Polymorphism), SSR (Simple Sequence Repeats), Diversity Arrays Technologies (DArT) and SNP (Single Nucleotide Polymorphisms) (Agarwal, Shrivastava, & Padh, 2008) have been developed and extensively used in marker development. However, it still remains a daunting task to identify highly polymorphic and closely linked molecular markers for a target trait for molecular marker-assisted selection since most of these methods are labor-intensive and time-consuming. Sometimes faster analysis of genetic variations should uncover new drug targets and pathways even in advanced stages of cancer that mutate beyond initial therapies. The NGS technology provides a powerful resource for detecting large numbers of genetic variants within a short amount of time. Using NGS, several marker development methods such as reduced-representation libraries (RRLs) (Luca, Hudson, Witonsky, & Di Rienzo, 2011), complexity reduction of polymorphic sequences (CRoPS) (van Orsouw *et al.*, 2007) were reported in humans and crops. Though the applicability of NGS for marker detection can be partially limited by the reference sequence available for a particular species under investigation, however NGS provides a extremely useful resources for marker detection in both model and non model species with or without a reference sequence. NGS technologies such as the Illumina Genome Analyzer (GA), the Roche/454 FLX system and the AB SOLiD system have significantly improved throughput and dramatically reduced the cost of SNP detection compared to capillary-based electrophoresis methods (Shendure, Mitra, Varma, & Church, 2004). As more and more genomes have been sequenced using NGS technologies, there has been a rapid increase in genetic markers detected.

Genomic structural variants are widespread polymorphisms and along with SNPs contribute to phenotypic variation with in population. In fact, structural variants accounts for more differences between human genomes than the more extensively studied SNP differences (Pang *et al.*, 2010). The different classes of structural variants include interchromosomal translocations (fusion of two non-homologous chromosomes) and copy number variation (which mainly includes insertions, deletions, duplications, inversions, recurring mobile elements and other rearrangements, usually defined as those covering 50 or more base pairs). Though many structural variants are inherited, however somatically acquired variants could play an important role in the onset and progression of cancer (Redon *et al.*, 2006),(Sebat *et al.*, 2004). Other conditions including autism, schizophrenia and Crohn's disease have all been associated with structural variation and so uncovering structural variation will be absolutely necessary for understanding the origin of these diseases. NGS has led to the development of several algorithms for detecting structural variation using multiple NGS platforms.

3.1.3 Nucleotide degradation pattern identification

Understanding the nature of DNA damage and the processes that promote DNA degradation is of interest to researchers studying on aging, cancer, forensics and evolution (Hoeijmakers, 2009). However studies involving chemical degradation of DNA have largely been restricted to classic kinetic experiments, where *in vitro* measurement-series of DNA decay at changing temperatures and pH values are assumed to reflect cellular conditions. Now, NGS technology provide a means to directly assess these complex processes through massively parallel sequencing of DNA molecules from fossils that were preserved at a variety of conditions for up to several hindered thousands of years. For example complete genomes from ancient individuals and extinct species have recently been sequenced (Miller *et al.*, 2008) (Rasmussen *et al.*, 2010). This information has shed light on the evolutionary history of extinct mammal lineages and provided new perspectives on human evolution (Reich *et al.*, 2010).

3.1.4 Genotyping by sequencing

During the last decade, a variety of techniques such as single base extension assays or microarrays were employed for genotyping of humans, a we are a species with low genetic diversity (about one substitution per thousand nucleotides) (W. H. Li & Sadler, 1991), as well as maize (Tenaillon, Hufford,

Gaut, & Ross-Ibarra, 2011) and Drosophila (Yang *et al.*, 2009) (more than one substitution per thousand nucleotides). However most of these techniques require invariant primer binding sites in order to obtain consistent results. Unfortunately such invariant regions are often difficult to find in case of maize (Gore *et al.*, 2009). In addition, the presence of large-scale structural variation can also complicates DNA sequence alignment. Even though abundant diversity is a challenge to assays that rely on scoring fixed positions, it is advantageous to direct sequencing approaches, because sequencing efficiency of genotyping scales directly with genetic diversity. With the advent of high-throughput NGS and technical improvement such as bar-coding of the DNA samples, the multiplexing of different genetic materials in single sequencing run has been enabled opening the area of genotyping by sequencing (GBS). The GBS approach is mainly suitable for population studies, characterization of germplasm, genetic improvement and trait mapping in diverse organisms. The main advantage of GBS compared to other methods is its technical simplicity and the public availability of bioinformatics pipelines.

3.2 Transcriptomic Applications

3.2.1 RNA sequencing

The application of NGS methods that enable massive-scale cDNA sequencing (termed RNA-Seq), generates a wealth of information beyond that is obtained from genomic DNA sequencing (Wang, Gerstein, & Snyder, 2009). For example, for research into somatic mutations in cancer (The Cancer Genome Atlas (http://cancergenome.nih.gov/)), RNA-Seq has the advantage of enriching for changes in coding sequences, which likely effect function, compared to genome sequencing. Though chromosomal rearrangements can be detected by DNA sequencing, RNA-Seq is a powerful resource to identify those rearrangements that lead to chimeric transcripts are more likely to have functional consequences in cancer (Maher, Kumar-Sinha, *et al.*, 2009),(Maher, Palanisamy, *et al.*, 2009). RNA-Seq provides an enormous amount of information at multiple levels of the transcription of the genome as it yields sequence and splicing patterns leading to the detection of novel transcripts and isoforms (Maher, Kumar-Sinha, *et al.*, 2009),(Q. Zhao *et al.*, 2009) and sequence alterations. Direct sequencing of cDNA offers an alternative approach for high-throughput transcriptome analysis (Wang, *et al.*, 2009), it provides precision in measuring transcriptome data (B. Li, Ruotti, Stewart, Thomson, & Dewey, 2010) and its higher resolution improves detection of novel transcripts, differential allele expression, alternative splice variants, and post-transcriptional modifications as well as uncovering the role of regulatory factors in controlling the expression of those genes, such as transcription factors and non-coding RNAs.

3.2.2 Whole exome sequencing

One of the widely used applications of RNA Sequencing is Whole Exome Sequencing (WES), which is a new and efficient approach to studying the genetic basis of a phenotype (Mamanova *et al.*, 2010). The technique consists of selective capture and sequencing of protein-coding regions of all genes in the genome (i.e., the 'whole exome'). Even though only 1-2% of the entire human genome constitutes the whole exome, 85% of all DNA mutations occur in protein coding regions with large effects on disease-related traits. WES has been successful in elucidating the genetic causes of many human diseases, starting from single gene disorder to more complex genetic disorders such as quantitative traits and cancer (Ng *et al.*, 2010) (Bras & Singleton, 2011). Therefore, combining NGS technologies with cDNA sequencing not only reduces the cost of whole genome sequencing, but is also an efficient way to discover many of the mutations that underlie rare and common human diseases.

3.2.3 Genome annotation: characterizing transcriptome structure

A well genome annotation is essential for functional studies. Gene prediction, within the process of genome annotation, is a complex process and is usually carried out by integrating multiple sources of evidence such as cDNA, proteins in closely related species, *de novo* predictions of *in-silico* gene models (Brent, 2008) and expressed sequence tags (ESTs). The Genome annotation based on gene prediction programs, that rely on ESTs and/or homology can only detect protein-coding regions and does not contain information regarding tissue, condition and environment specific expression patterns, especially if they are poorly conserved. It has been estimated that most ESTs miss 20-40% of transcripts that (a) are either novel transcripts; (b) are transcribed under certain tissue, environmental and treatment conditions or (c) that have highly specific expression patterns (Brent, 2008). RNA-Seq can be used for detection of novel transcribed genes, novel exons that are missing from the genome annotation and correction of functional and structural annotation of gene models. Determining the function of these novel transcripts/isoforms is a very interesting research challenge and opportunity for future functional genomics research.

3.2.4 Gene regulatory analysis

The characterization of gene expression in cells through the measurement of mRNA levels has been of interest to researchers in terms of spatial and temporal gene expression. Even though it has been shown that a strong correlation does not always exists between the abundance of mRNA and its related protein because of post transcriptional gene regulation events such as RNA interference (Greenbaum, Colangelo, Williams, & Gerstein, 2003), measurement of mRNA concentration is still considered a standard technique in determining how the transcriptional machinery of the cell is effected in the presence of external signals. The most common application of RNA-Seq is the identification of those genes that show differential gene regulation under certain treatments or conditions. Gene expression patterns hold important information regarding the specific functions of particular cell or tissue types or biological pathways.

3.2.5 Single nucleotide variation identification

Transcriptome sequence based SNPs have been analyzed in many plants and animals using different NGS platforms (Barbazuk, Emrich, Chen, Li, & Schnable, 2007). The discovered coding SNPs are a valuable resource for gene-specific studies and also will enable researchers to use these as molecular markers for genotyping mapping populations and also fine mapping of regions of interest.

3.2.6 Coexpression networks

Coexpression networks are data-derived representations of genes behaving in a similar way across tissues and developmental conditions. The main purpose of coexpression networks lies in the ability to infer functions of previously unknown genes and RNA-Seq can be successfully used to infer this kind of analysis in specific pathways based on Pearson correlation, both in plants (Giorgi, Del Fabbro, & Licausi, 2013) and animals (Iancu *et al.,* 2012).

3.2.7 Fusion gene detection

Fusion genes have gained significant attention recently because of their role in cancer (Maher, Kumar-Sinha, *et al.,* 2009). Fusion genes are caused by different structural modifications in the genome. RNA-Seq with its ability to analyze whole transcriptome in an unbiased fashion is an attractive tool to find fusion gene events in cancer. RNA-Seq reports multiple and potentially novel combinations of genes, providing an ideal starting point for further experimental validations.

3.2.8 Transcriptome assembly

For non-model organisms with no available genome sequence, transcriptome assembly offers a cost-effective method of characterizing the gene set. Currently there are two basic approaches for transcriptome assembly using RNA-Seq technologies: assemble-then-align (*de novo*) – the direct assembly of sequenced reads into transcripts without the need of reference and align-then-assemble (reference-based) – assembly of transcripts by first mapping to a reference genome (Haas & Zody, 2010). Both methods have advantages and disadvantages. For example, alignment-first methods are computationally less demanding, tolerate sequencing errors, detect repeats through alignment, and group transcripts by genomic proximity, however these methods are completely dependent on a reference genome and assume that transcripts are collinear with the genome, and mismatched genome alignment or genome assembly errors can lead to errors in transcriptome prediction. In the case of assemble-first methods, these are not dependent on reference genome and therefore can define transcripts not present in the reference as well as defining non-collinear transcripts and trans-spliced transcripts that result from chromosomal rearrangements. However these methods will perform poorly on low expressed genes, and can produce chimeras and misassemblies due to repeats.

3.2.9 Small RNA sequencing

Many classes of small RNA (sRNAs), such as micro RNA (miRNA), piwi-interacting RNA (piRNA) and small interfering RNA (siRNA) have been reported to play a significant role in post-translational gene regulation of gene expression. Small RNA sequencing using NGS has now become routine for both sRNA discovery and sRNA profiling since it can sequence the entire complement of sRNA with high integrity and sensitivity compared to traditional Sanger sequencing. It has been reported that miRNA signature can serve as biomarker for diseases, tissues or cell development and has been used for drug development (Calin & Croce, 2006).

3.3 Epigenetic Applications

3.3.1 Genome-wide identification of protein-DNA interaction

Much of gene regulation occurs at the level of transcriptional control, and the binding sites of transcription factors are associated with regulation of gene expression. Experimental identification of these binding sites has been one of the widely studied areas of molecular biology. Chromatin immunoprecipitation (ChIP) has emerged as the major technique of identification these protein-DNA interactions. Early sequencing protocols for probing transcription factor DNA-binding sequences used Sanger sequencing. However, because of complex cloning steps and cost of, this method limited the depth of sampling to less than necessary for a thorough investigation. Chromatin immunoprecipitation sequencing (ChIP-Seq) enabled an unprecedented view of genome-wide in vivo protein-DNA interactions because of the depth of sampling and lower cost of sequencing. ChIP-Seq reports the identification of DNA-binding sites for the transcription factors effectively in terms of impressive quality of the data and the large variation in the number of DNA-binding sites for these factors. The method briefly consists of enriching the DNA associated with a transcription factor or histone modification of interest using ChIP followed by massively parallel sequencing of the DNA and mapping of these reads back to the genome (G. Robertson *et al.*, 2007). NGS-based methods allowed widespread application of genomic ChIP profiling, replacing, the earlier microarray techniques. ChIP-Seq can be used to accurately survey interaction between protein, DNA and RNA, permitting the interpretation of regulation events central to many biological processes and disease states. ChIP-Seq not only provides clear indications of transcription factor binding sites at high resolution but also genome-wide mapping of histone marks.

3.3.2 Evaluating the DNA methylome

DNA methylation is the process in which a methyl group is added to the C5 carbon residue (4mC) of cytosines by DNA methyltransferases (Law & Jacobsen, 2010). DNA cytosine methylation is a central epigenetic modification used by higher eukaryotic organisms and is involved in several key physiological processes such as regulation of gene expression, X-chromosome inactivation, imprinting and silencing of germline specific genes and repetitive elements (K. D. Robertson, 2005). Patterns of methylation are stably maintained through somatic cell division and can be inherited across generations. These patterns are sometimes perturbed in important human diseases such as cancer. Understanding of how methylation patterns are maintained is therefore of great importance in medical sciences. Bisulfite conversion of genomic DNA combined with NGS (BS-Seq) is becoming a widely used method to measure the methylation state of whole genome and can be used to generate base pair resolution of the methylome (Laurent *et al.*, 2010).

3.4 Bioinformatics – Tools and Strategies for NGS Data Analysis

NGS technologies have increasingly becoming widespread and have begun to revolutionize every field of biological sciences. The growing number of robust applications and the increasingly steadily falling cost of generating NGS data suggest that these technologies will continue to evolve, open new applications in the biological sciences and poses serious pressure on the bioinformatics community to come up with the statistical methods and software systems to analyze such data. In addition, given the huge amount of data that is produced, developing a sound data storage solution is essential to successful application of this technology. In all, NGS requires the development of computational tools and methods that can analyze and store the resulting datasets more efficiently.

During the past several years, a large number of new software applications, algorithms, data storage systems and recently cloud computing stratagies have been developed to deal with this kind of data.

The tools for bioinformatics data analysis of NGS can be broadly divided into methods for quality control of raw sequence data, alignment, assembly, variant detection, variant annotation, and visualization. A detailed review of bioinformatics tools for data analysis was done elsewhere (Pabinger *et al.*, 2013).

3.4.1 Preprocessing (Quality assessment)

The first step in analysis after the completion of a sequencing run is to evaluate the quality of the raw reads and either trim or remove reads that do not meet a certain quality score. The raw reads generated by sequencing platforms are filled with sequence artifacts such as base calling error, poor quality reads and adapter and primer contamination (Dai *et al.*, 2010). Since many downstream analysis tools are not capable of removing the low-quality reads, it is necessary to filter out bad reads to avoid drawing wrong biological conclusions from the data. A variety of tools have been developed to perform the various stages of quality assessment. They include NGSQC tool kit, PRINSEQ, FastQC, and FASTX-Tool kit.

3.4.2 Read alignment

After the data has been processed to keep good quality reads, reads are usually aligned to an existing reference genome. Read alignment considered as an important challenge presented by NGS technologies, because of the order of data produced by machine per day. With the emergence of such data, researchers have realized that traditional tools for aligning Sanger reads are not sufficient for this kind of data. For this reason, over the last few years, many read alignment tools have been developed to align several millions of reads back to an existing reference genome. These new tools use the many advantages specific to each of the sequencing technologies. For instance, short sequence length of Solexa, SOLiD and Helicos reads, the low insertions and deletion error rate of Illumina reads and the bi-base coding of SOLiD reads. The most prevalent alignment tools are Bowtie, BWA, MAQ, Novoalign, and SOAP.

3.4.3 De novo assembly

Tools that allow for the de novo assemblies of short read assemblies are necessary when a reference genome doe not exist or when a novel genome is required. The *de novo* approaches particularly concentrates on grouping of reads into significant contiguous sequences or contigs. These contigands are assembled into scaffolds and chromosomes to reconstruct the original genomic

DNA for novel species. In the last two years, several algorithms have been developed for the *de novo* assembly. *De novo* assembly tools include Velvet, Abyss, SOAPdenovo. All these programs are based on de Bruijn graph structure and differ in how they treat errors and read-pair information.

3.4.4 Variant detection

After assembling the reads, the next step in NGS data analysis pipeline is to use tools to detect genetic variants such as SNP and indels. Tools for genome-wide variant identification can be divided into four categories – germline callers, somatic callers, CNV identification and SV identification. The detection of germline mutations is important for finding causes of rare diseases. For example, most of the cancer studies focus on the identification of somatic mutations by comparing sequencing results of tumor to normal tissue. The most popular tool for variant detection, GATK processes re-alignment insertions/deletions (indels), performs base quality recalibration and calls genotypes. Other tools that can detect variants include SAMtools, VarScan, and SomaticSniper.

3.4.5 Structural variation detection

Structural variation generally implies a large DNA alteration in the range of 1kb to 3Mb in length. The discovery of SVs is gradually changing our understanding of the human genotype. A powerful software module for structural variation detection is BreakDancer and it provides genome-wide screening of large structural variants and detects indels by integrating evidence from several samples and libraries. Other tools include VariationHunter, SVDetect, and PEMer.

3.4.6 Variant annotation

With the increasing amount of data generated by NGS experiments, the possibility of predicting the functional impact of the variants is becoming increasingly important. Computer aided annotation enables scientists to filter and prioritize potential disease-causing variations for further analysis. Each of the available tools implements different method independently for variant annotation and most of them focus on the annotation of SNPs. Most popular among them are ANNOVAR, SIFT, and SNPeff.

3.4.7 Visualization

The visualization and validation of generated results is one of the most important and challenging steps in all NGS data analysis workflows. Visual representation of data can be tremendously important for the interpretation of obtained results. Therefore, tools for visualization should support all above steps and in addition should be user-friendly, intuitive and responsive. The tools for visualization can be grouped into 3 different types: tools supporting interpretation of de novo or resequencing experiments; genome browsers that allow users to browse mapped experimental data in combination with different types of annotation tools and finally comparative viewers that facilitate the comparison of sequences from multiple individuals. Tools that allow for the visualization of the alignment or assembly of short read data include include IGV, IGB, and SAMtools, MaqView.

4. BOTTLENECKS AND COMPUTATIONAL CHALLENGES OF NGS DATA ANALYSIS

Advances in the field of NGS have resulted in greatly accelerated production of huge sequence data. This poses immediate challenges for database maintenance in terms of data mining, sequence analysis and storage. The computational power of desktop computers is not sufficient for the analysis and storage of today's NGS data sets. Despite the rapid development of computers consistently in terms of processing speed, data analyses lags behind data storage and maintenance requirements for the large amount of sequence data produced by high-throughput NGS techniques (Shendure & Ji, 2008). In addition to computing power and software tools, a big challenge is the storage of the generated data. Researchers are reluctant to discard raw sequence data since improved algorithms may help extract further information in future. Long term archiving of these large amounts of data is not a trivial task and it is clear that the NGS community is facing a storage problem. A researcher who wants to use NGS technology today needs extensive IT and high-performance infrastructure for analyzing and storing of both sequenced and analyzed data. However, this kind expertise and facilities are not available to every research group.

In order to reach effective conclusions quickly and efficiently, the techniques of parallel computation using virtualization of the resources have appeared and are collectively termed as "cloud computing". The collective resources include hardware, software, and working platform can be available and provided in the form of virtual machines (VMs). The VMs completely eliminated the need to build or administer local infrastructure and the computational workload is shifted to the provider, which implements required hardware and software upgrades over time. In addition, cloud computing offers machines with different hardware and software capabilities and specifications and users can select and configure VMS to meet their different computational needs. The major advantage of using cloud computing is that it can provide storage and computation cheaply (both up-front costs and on-going costs) compared to earlier technologies (such as Grid Computing, Distributed system, and Utility Computing) which previously were employed in large datacenters. In recent years, cloud computing has emerged as a viable option to quickly and easily acquire the computational resources for large-scale data analyses (Stein, 2010) (Shanker, 2012). A considerable enthusiasm now exists within the bioinformatics community for the use of cloud computing for NGS data analyses (http://genomebiology.com/series/cloudcomputing) and several cloud-based bioinformatics applications and resources have been developed to address the challenges of working with huge volumes of NGS data. The application of bioinformatics and computational tools to complement the results obtained from wet lab experiments provides a means to refine these results and their predictions. Therefore it is of paramount importance in research and development studies to achieve reduced time consumption in computational activities, despite exponentially growing datasets. Cloud computing has provided a means to address this problem and a number of pipelines cloud computing based pipelines for high-throughput NGS data analysis have been applied in the field of genomics and other biological research and development sectors (S. Zhao *et al.*, 2013) (Nagasaki *et al.*, 2013). New cloud computing tools and algorithms are consistently being developed and successfully implemented to manage the huge datasets and analyze them more efficiently in lesser time.

5. CONCLUSIONS AND FUTURE PERSPECTIVES OF NGS

Over the past several years, next generation sequencing technologies have catapulted in prominence, with increasingly widespread adoption of several platforms. Common characteristics extend beyond the technologies themselves, to the quantity and quality of data that are generated, such that all raise a similar set of new challenges for experimental design, data analysis and interpretation. The continued erosion of sequencing costs by several magnitudes, coupled with open source software and tools for data analysis, and data storage is increasing the extent to which individual researcher can pursue projects at a scale previously accessible to only major genome centers. Advances in DNA-sequencing technology coupled with novel, efficient computational analysis tools, have made it possible to analyze sequencing-based experimental data on an unprecedented scale. Key areas of research and development that will benefit from NGS include food security (e.g plant and animal breeding, disease diagnostics and management), industrial biotechnology (e.g drug discovery) and medicine (molecular diagnostics, personalized medicine and nutrition). The progress made so far through NGS breakthroughs could ultimately help towards improving crop productivity, disease prevention, making personalized genome services, personalized medicines and other applications in future. The third and fourth generation sequencing technologies are currently being developed intensively and would help the genome research more affordable than any time before.

REFERENCES

Agarwal, M., Shrivastava, N., & Padh, H. (2008). Advances in molecular marker techniques and their applications in plant sciences. Plant Cell Reports, 27(4), 617-631. doi: 10.1007/s00299-008-0507-z

Barbazuk, W. B., Emrich, S. J., Chen, H. D., Li, L., & Schnable, P. S. (2007). SNP discovery via 454 transcriptome sequencing. [Research Support, Non-U.S. Govt Research Support, U.S. Gov't, Non-P.H.S. Validation Studies]. The Plant Journal : For Cell and Molecular Biology, *51*(5), 910-918. doi: 10.1111/j.1365-313X.2007.03193.x

Bras, J. M., & Singleton, A. B. (2011). Exome sequencing in Parkinson's disease. [Research Support, N.I.H., Intramural Research Support, Non-U.S. Govt Review]. Clinical Genetics, *80*(2), 104-109. doi: 10.1111/j.1399-0004.2011.01722.x

Brent, M. R. (2008). Steady progress and recent breakthroughs in the accuracy of automated genome annotation. [Research Support, N.I.H., Extramural Research Support, Non-U.S. Gov't Review]. Nature Reviews. Genetics, *9*(1), 62-73. doi: 10.1038/nrg2220

Calin, G. A., & Croce, C. M. (2006). MicroRNA signatures in human cancers. [Research Support, N.I.H., Extramural Research Support, Non-U.S. Gov't Review]. Nature Reviews. Cancer, 6(11), 857-866. doi: 10.1038/nrc1997

Dai, M., Thompson, R. C., Maher, C., Contreras-Galindo, R., Kaplan, M. H., Markovitz, D. M., . Meng, F. (2010). NGSQC: cross-platform quality analysis pipeline for deep sequencing data. [Research Support, N.I.H., Extramural Research Support, Non-U.S. Gov't]. BMC genomics, 11 Suppl 4, S7. doi: 10.1186/1471-2164-11-S4-S7

Edwards, D., & Batley, J. (2004). Plant bioinformatics: from genome to phenome. [Review]. Trends in biotechnology, 22(5), 232-237. doi: 10.1016/j.tibtech.2004.03.002

Giorgi, F. M., Del Fabbro, C., & Licausi, F. (2013). Comparative study of RNA-seq- and microarray-derived coexpression networks in Arabidopsis thaliana. [Comparative Study Research Support, Non-U.S. Gov't]. Bioinformatics, 29(6), 717-724. doi: 10.1093/bioinformatics/btt053

Gore, M. A., Chia, J. M., Elshire, R. J., Sun, Q., Ersoz, E. S., Hurwitz, B. L., . . . Buckler, E. S. (2009). A first-generation haplotype map of maize. [Research Support, U.S. Gov't, Non-P.H.S.]. Science, 326(5956), 1115-1117. doi: 10.1126/science.1177837

Greenbaum, D., Colangelo, C., Williams, K., & Gerstein, M. (2003). Comparing protein abundance and mRNA expression levels on a genomic scale. [Comparative Study Research Support, U.S. Gov't, P.H.S. Review]. Genome Biology, 4(9), 117. doi: 10.1186/gb-2003-4-9-117

Haas, B. J., & Zody, M. C. (2010). Advancing RNA-Seq analysis. [Comment News]. Nature Biotechnology, 28(5), 421-423. doi: 10.1038/nbt0510-421

Harris, T. D., Buzby, P. R., Babcock, H., Beer, E., Bowers, J., Braslavsky, I., . . . Xie, Z. (2008). Single-molecule DNA sequencing of a viral genome. [Research Support, N.I.H., Extramural Research Support, Non-U.S. Gov't]. Science, 320(5872), 106-109. doi: 10.1126/science.1150427

Hoeijmakers, J. H. (2009). DNA damage, aging, and cancer. [Review]. The New England Journal of medicine, 361(15), 1475-1485. doi: 10.1056/NEJMra0804615

Iancu, O. D., Kawane, S., Bottomly, D., Searles, R., Hitzemann, R., & McWeeney, S. (2012). Utilizing RNA-Seq data for de novo coexpression network inference. [Comparative Study Research Support, N.I.H., Extramural Research Support, Non-U.S. Gov't Research Support, U.S. Gov't, Non-P.H.S.]. Bioinformatics, 28(12), 1592-1597. doi: 10.1093/bioinformatics/bts245

Laurent, L., Wong, E., Li, G., Huynh, T., Tsirigos, A., Ong, C. T., . . . Wei, C. L. (2010). Dynamic changes in the human methylome during differentiation. [Research Support, N.I.H., Extramural Research Support, Non-U.S. Gov't]. Genome Research, 20(3), 320-331. doi: 10.1101/gr.101907.109

Law, J. A., & Jacobsen, S. E. (2010). Establishing, maintaining and modifying DNA methylation patterns in plants and animals. [Research Support, N.I.H., Extramural Review]. Nature Reviews. Genetics, 11(3), 204-220. doi: 10.1038/nrg2719

Li, B., Ruotti, V., Stewart, R. M., Thomson, J. A., & Dewey, C. N. (2010). RNA-Seq gene expression estimation with read mapping uncertainty. [Research Support, Non-U.S. Gov't]. Bioinformatics, 26(4), 493-500. doi: 10.1093/bioinformatics/btp692

Li, W. H., & Sadler, L. A. (1991). Low nucleotide diversity in man. [Research Support, U.S. Gov't, P.H.S.]. *Genetics, 129*(2), 513-523.

Luca, F., Hudson, R. R., Witonsky, D. B., & Di Rienzo, A. (2011). A reduced representation approach to population genetic analyses and applications to human evolution. [Research Support, N.I.H., Extramural Research Support, Non-U.S. Gov't]. Genome Research, 21(7), 1087-1098. doi: 10.1101/gr.119792.110

Maher, C. A., Kumar-Sinha, C., Cao, X., Kalyana-Sundaram, S., Han, B., Jing, X., . . . Chinnaiyan, A. M. (2009). Transcriptome sequencing to detect gene fusions in cancer. [Research Support, N.I.H., Extramural Research Support, Non-U.S. Gov't Research Support, U.S. Gov't, Non-P.H.S.]. Nature, 458(7234), 97-101. doi: 10.1038/nature07638

Maher, C. A., Palanisamy, N., Brenner, J. C., Cao, X., Kalyana-Sundaram, S., Luo, S., . . . Chinnaiyan, A. M. (2009). Chimeric transcript discovery by paired-end transcriptome sequencing. [Research Support, N.I.H., Extramural Research Support, Non-U.S. Gov't Research Support, U.S. Gov't, Non-P.H.S.]. Proceedings of the National Academy of Sciences of the United States of America, 106(30), 12353-12358. doi: 10.1073/pnas.0904720106

Mamanova, L., Coffey, A. J., Scott, C. E., Kozarewa, I., Turner, E. H., Kumar, A., . . . Turner, D. J. (2010). Target-enrichment strategies for next-generation sequencing. [Research Support, N.I.H., Extramural Research Support, Non-U.S. Gov't Review]. Nature Methods, 7(2), 111-118. doi: 10.1038/nmeth.1419

Mardis, E. R. (2008). Next-generation DNA sequencing methods. [Review]. Annual review of genomics and human genetics, 9, 387-402. doi: 10.1146/annurev.genom.9.081307.164359

Margulies, D., Melman, G., & Shanzer, A. (2005). Fluorescein as a model molecular calculator with reset capability. [Evaluation Studies Research Support, Non-U.S. Gov't]. Nature Materials, 4(10), 768-771. doi: 10.1038/nmat1469

Metzker, M. L. (2010). Sequencing technologies - the next generation. [Research Support, N.I.H., Extramural Review]. Nature Reviews. Genetics, 11(1), 31-46. doi: 10.1038/nrg2626

Miller, W., Drautz, D. I., Ratan, A., Pusey, B., Qi, J., Lesk, A. M., . . . Schuster, S. C. (2008). Sequencing the nuclear genome of the extinct woolly mammoth. [Research Support, N.I.H., Extramural Research Support, Non-U.S. Gov't]. Nature, 456(7220), 387-390. doi: 10.1038/nature07446

Nagasaki, H., Mochizuki, T., Kodama, Y., Saruhashi, S., Morizaki, S., Sugawara, H., . . . Nakamura, Y. (2013). DDBJ read annotation pipeline: a cloud computing-based pipeline for high-throughput analysis of next-generation sequencing data. [Research Support, Non-U.S. Gov't]. DNA research : an international journal for rapid publication of reports on genes and genomes, 20(4), 383-390. doi: 10.1093/dnares/dst017

Ng, S. B., Buckingham, K. J., Lee, C., Bigham, A. W., Tabor, H. K., Dent, K. M., . . . Bamshad, M. J. (2010). Exome sequencing identifies the cause of a mendelian disorder. [Research Support, N.I.H., Extramural Research Support, Non-U.S. Gov't]. Nature Genetics, 42(1), 30-35. doi: 10.1038/ng.499

Orlando, L., Ginolhac, A., Raghavan, M., Vilstrup, J., Rasmussen, M., Magnussen, K., . . . Willerslev, E. (2011). True single-molecule DNA sequencing of a pleistocene horse bone. [Research Support, Non-U.S. Gov't]. Genome Research, 21(10), 1705-1719. doi: 10.1101/gr.122747.111

Ozsolak, F., Platt, A. R., Jones, D. R., Reifenberger, J. G., Sass, L. E., McInerney, P., . . . Milos, P. M. (2009). Direct RNA sequencing. Nature, 461(7265), 814-818. doi: 10.1038/nature08390

Pabinger, S., Dander, A., Fischer, M., Snajder, R., Sperk, M., Efremova, M., . . . Trajanoski, Z. (2013). A survey of tools for variant analysis of next-generation genome sequencing data. Briefings in Bioinformatics. doi: 10.1093/bib/bbs086

Pang, A. W., MacDonald, J. R., Pinto, D., Wei, J., Rafiq, M. A., Conrad, D. F., . . . Scherer, S. W. (2010). Towards a comprehensive structural variation map of an individual human genome. [Research Support, Non-U.S. Gov't]. Genome Biology, 11(5), R52. doi: 10.1186/gb-2010-11-5-r52

Rasmussen, M., Li, Y., Lindgreen, S., Pedersen, J. S., Albrechtsen, A., Moltke, I., . . . Willerslev, E. (2010). Ancient human genome sequence of an extinct Palaeo-Eskimo. [Historical Article Research Support, Non-U.S. Gov't Research Support, U.S. Gov't, Non-P.H.S.]. Nature, 463(7282), 757-762. doi: 10.1038/nature08835

Redon, R., Ishikawa, S., Fitch, K. R., Feuk, L., Perry, G. H., Andrews, T. D., . . . Hurles, M. E. (2006). Global variation in copy number in the human genome. [Research Support, Non-U.S. Gov't]. Nature, 444(7118), 444-454. doi: 10.1038/nature05329

Reich, D., Green, R. E., Kircher, M., Krause, J., Patterson, N., Durand, E. Y., . . . Paabo, S. (2010). Genetic history of an archaic hominin group from Denisova Cave in Siberia. [Research Support, N.I.H., Extramural Research Support, Non-U.S. Gov't Research Support, U.S. Gov't, Non-P.H.S.]. Nature, 468(7327), 1053-1060. doi: 10.1038/nature09710

Robertson, G., Hirst, M., Bainbridge, M., Bilenky, M., Zhao, Y., Zeng, T., . . . Jones, S. (2007). Genome-wide profiles of STAT1 DNA association using chromatin immunoprecipitation and massively parallel sequencing. [Research Support, Non-U.S. Gov't]. Nature Methods, 4(8), 651-657. doi: 10.1038/nmeth1068

Robertson, K. D. (2005). DNA methylation and human disease. [Research Support, U.S. Gov't, P.H.S.Review]. Nature Reviews. Genetics, 6(8), 597-610. doi: 10.1038/nrg1655

Rokas, A., & Abbot, P. (2009). Harnessing genomics for evolutionary insights. [Research Support, Non-U.S. Gov't Research Support, U.S. Gov't, Non-P.H.S. Review]. Trends in Ecology & Evolution, 24(4), 192-200. doi: 10.1016/j.tree.2008.11.004

Sanger, F., Nicklen, S., & Coulson, A. R. (1977). DNA sequencing with chain-terminating inhibitors. Proceedings of the National Academy of Sciences of the United States of America, 74(12), 5463-5467.

Sebat, J., Lakshmi, B., Troge, J., Alexander, J., Young, J., Lundin, P., . . . Wigler, M. (2004). Large-scale copy number polymorphism in the human genome. [Research Support, Non-U.S. Gov't Research Support, U.S. Gov't, Non-P.H.S. Research Support, U.S. Gov't, P.H.S.]. Science, 305(5683), 525-528. doi: 10.1126/science.1098918

Shanker, A. (2012). Genome research in the cloud. [Review]. Omics : a journal of integrative biology, 16(7-8), 422-428. doi: 10.1089/omi.2012.0001

Shendure, J., & Ji, H. (2008). Next-generation DNA sequencing. Nature Biotechnology, 26(10), 1135-1145. doi: 10.1038/nbt1486

Shendure, J., Mitra, R. D., Varma, C., & Church, G. M. (2004). Advanced sequencing technologies: methods and goals. [Review]. Nature Reviews. Genetics, 5(5), 335-344. doi: 10.1038/nrg1325

Stein, L. D. (2010). The case for cloud computing in genome informatics. Genome Biology, 11(5), 207. doi: 10.1186/gb-2010-11-5-207

Tenaillon, M. I., Hufford, M. B., Gaut, B. S., & Ross-Ibarra, J. (2011). Genome size and transposable element content as determined by high-throughput sequencing in maize and Zea luxurians. [Comparative Study Research Support, Non-U.S. Gov't]. Genome Biology and Evolution, 3, 219-229. doi: 10.1093/gbe/evr008 van Orsouw, N. J., Hogers, R. C., Janssen, A., Yalcin, F., Snoeijers, S., Verstege, E., . . . van Eijk, M. J. (2007). Complexity reduction of polymorphic sequences (CRoPS): a novel approach for large-scale polymorphism discovery in complex genomes. [Research Support, Non-U.S. Gov't]. PloS one, 2(11), e1172. doi: 10.1371/journal.pone.0001172

Wang, Z., Gerstein, M., & Snyder, M. (2009). RNA-Seq: a revolutionary tool for transcriptomics. [Review]. Nature reviews. Genetics, 10(1), 57-63. doi: 10.1038/nrg2484

Yang, Y., Xu, S., Xia, L., Wang, J., Wen, S., Jin, P., & Chen, D. (2009). The bantam microRNA is associated with drosophila fragile X mental retardation protein and regulates the fate of germline stem cells. [Research Support, N.I.H., Extramural Research Support, Non-U.S. Gov't]. PLoS genetics, 5(4), e1000444. doi: 10.1371/journal.pgen.1000444

Zhao, Q., Caballero, O. L., Levy, S., Stevenson, B. J., Iseli, C., de Souza, S. J., . . . Strausberg, R. L. (2009). Transcriptome-guided characterization of genomic rearrangements in a breast cancer cell line. [Research Support, Non-U.S. Gov't]. Proceedings of the National Academy of Sciences of the United States of America, 106(6), 1886-1891. doi: 10.1073/pnas.0812945106

Zhao, S., Prenger, K., Smith, L., Messina, T., Fan, H., Jaeger, E., & Stephens, S. (2013). Rainbow: a tool for large-scale whole-genome sequencing data analysis using cloud computing. BMC Genomics, 14, 425. doi: 10.1186/1471-2164-14-425

❑❑❑

CHAPTER - 3

Various Platforms for Massively Parallel DNA Sequencing (Next Generation Sequencing)

Mamta Singh[1] & Anindya Sundar Barman[2]
[1]Assistant Professor, Department of Fish Genetic & Reproduction
College of Fisheries (Central Agricultural University)
Lembucherra, Tripura (West) 799210
Email: mamta0131@gmail.com
[2]Assistant Professor
Department of Fish Genetic & Reproduction
College of Fisheries (Central Agricultural University)
Lembucherra, Tripura (West) 799210
Email: barman.anindya@gmail.com

INTRODUCTION

Massively Parallel DNA sequencing also known as next-generation sequencing, revolutionize the genomics and transcriptomics research as their effects are increasingly widespread. A new generation of non-Sanger-based sequencing technologies has delivered on its promise of sequencing DNA at unprecedented speed, thereby enabling impressive scientific achievements and novel biological applications. Before the next generation sequencing, the Sanger's enzymatic di-deoxy chain termination was used for nucleotide sequencing from last 30 years with various original improvements. Sanger enzymatic di-deoxy chain termination technique first described in 1977 and the Maxam and Gilbert chemical degradation method described in the same year, which was used in sequence cases which could not easily be resolved with the Sanger technique. The two laboratories where the first automated DNA sequencers were produced, simultaneously, were those of Leroy Hood at Caltech, commercialized by Applied Biosystems, and Wilhelm Ansorge at the European Molecular Biology Laboratory EMBL and commercialized by Pharmacia-Amersham, later General Electric (GE) Healthcare. The Sanger method was used in the first automated fluorescent project for sequencing of a genome region, in which sequence determination of the complete gene locus for the HPRT gene was performed using the EMBL technique; in that project the important concept of paired-end sequencing was also introduced for the first time.

When the international community decided on determination of the whole human genome sequence, the goal triggered the development of techniques allowing higher sequencing throughput. In Japan, the work on fluorescent DNA sequencing technology by the team of H. Kambara (http://www.hitachi.com/rd/fellowkambara.html) in the Hitachi laboratories resulted in the development after 1996 of a high-throughput capillary array DNA sequencer. Two companies, ABI (commercializing the Kambara system) and Amersham (Taking over and developing further the system setup in the US by the Molecular Dynamics company), commercialized automated sequencing using parallel analysis in systems of up to 384 capillaries at that time. As the users and developers of the DNA sequencing techniques realized, the great limitations of the Sanger sequencing protocols for even larger sequence output were the need for gels or polymers used as sieving separation media for the fluorescently labeled DNA fragments, the relatively low number of samples which could be analyzed in parallel and the difficulty of total automation of the sample preparation methods. These limitations initiated efforts to develop techniques without gels, which would allow sequence determination on very large numbers (i.e. millions) of samples in parallel. One of the first developments of such a technique was at the EMBL (at that time one of the two world leaders in DNA sequencing technology) from 1988 to 1990. A patent application by EMBL described a large-scale DNA sequencing technique without gels, extending primers in 'sequencing-by-synthesis, addition and detection of the incorporated base', proposing and describing the use of the so-called 'reversible terminators' for speed and efficiency. The first step of the technique consisted in detecting the next added fluorescently labeled base (reversible terminator) in the growing DNA chain by means of a sensitive CCD camera. This was performed on a large number of DNA samples in parallel, attached either to a planar support or to beads, on DNA chips, minimizing reaction volumes in a miniaturized micro system. In the next step the terminator was converted to a standard nucleotide and the dye removed from it. This cycle and the process were repeated to determine the next base in the sequence. The principle described in the patent application is in part very similar to that used today in the so-called next-generation devices, with many additional original developments commercialized by Illumina-Solexa, Helicos and other companies.

Platforms for Next generation DNA Sequencing

There are several platform are available for massively parallel sequencing with some advantages and disadvantages when compared to each others. In this chapter four most widely used next generation sequencing platforms are discussed i.e. the Roche/454 FLX (www.454.com/enablingtechnology/the-system.asp), the Illumina/ Solexa Genome Analyzer (www.illumina.com/pages.ilmn?ID=203), and the Applied Biosystems SOLiD$_{TM}$ System (www.marketing.appliedbiosystems.com/images/Product/SolidKnowledge/flash/102207/solid) & Life technologies Ion torrent (www.lifetechnologies.com/us/en/home/brands/ion-torrent.htmlý).

Roche/454 FLX pyrosequencer

In pyrosequencing, each incorporation of a nucleotide by DNA polymerase results in the release of pyrophosphate, which initiates a series of downstream reactions that ultimately produce light by the firefly enzyme luciferase. The amount of light produced is proportional to the number of nucleotides incorporated (up to the point of detector saturation). In this approach (Figure 1), the library fragments are mixed with a population of agarose beads whose surfaces carry oligonucleotides complementary to the 454-specific adapter sequences on the fragment library, so each bead is associated with a single fragment. Each of these fragment : bead complexes is isolated into individual oil : water micelles that also contain PCR reactants, and thermal cycling (emulsion PCR) of the micelles produces approximately one million copies of each DNA fragment on the surface of each bead. These amplified single molecules are then sequenced en masse. First the beads are arrayed into a picotiter plate (PTP) that holds a single bead in each of several hundred thousand single wells, which provides a fixed location at which each sequencing reaction can be monitored. Enzyme containing beads that catalyze the downstream pyrosequencing reaction steps are then added to the PTP and the mixture is centrifuged to surround the agarose beads. On instrument, the PTP acts as a flow cell into which each pure nucleotide solution is introduced in a stepwise fashion, with an imaging step after each nucleotide incorporation step. The PTP is seated opposite a CCD camera that records the light emitted at each bead. The first four nucleotides on adapter fragment adjacent to the sequencing primer added in library construction correspond to the sequential flow of nucleotides into the flow cell. This strategy allows the 454 base-calling software to calibrate the light emitted by a single nucleotide incorporation. However, the calibrated base calling cannot properly interpret long stretches (>6) of the same nucleotide, so these areas are prone to base insertion and deletion errors during base calling. By contrast, because each incorporation step is nucleotide specific, substitution errors are rarely encountered in Roche/454 sequence reads. The FLX instrument currently provides 100 flows of each nucleotide during an 8-h run, which produces an average, read length of 250 nucleotides. These raw reads are processed by the 454 analysis software and then screened by various quality filters to remove poor-quality sequences, mixed sequences and sequences without the initiating TCGA sequence. The resulting reads yield 100 Mb of quality data on average. Downstream of read processing, an assembly algorithm can assemble FLX reads. Although shorter than reads derived from capillary sequencers, FLX reads are of sufficient length to assemble small genomes such as bacterial and viral genomes to high quality and contiguity.

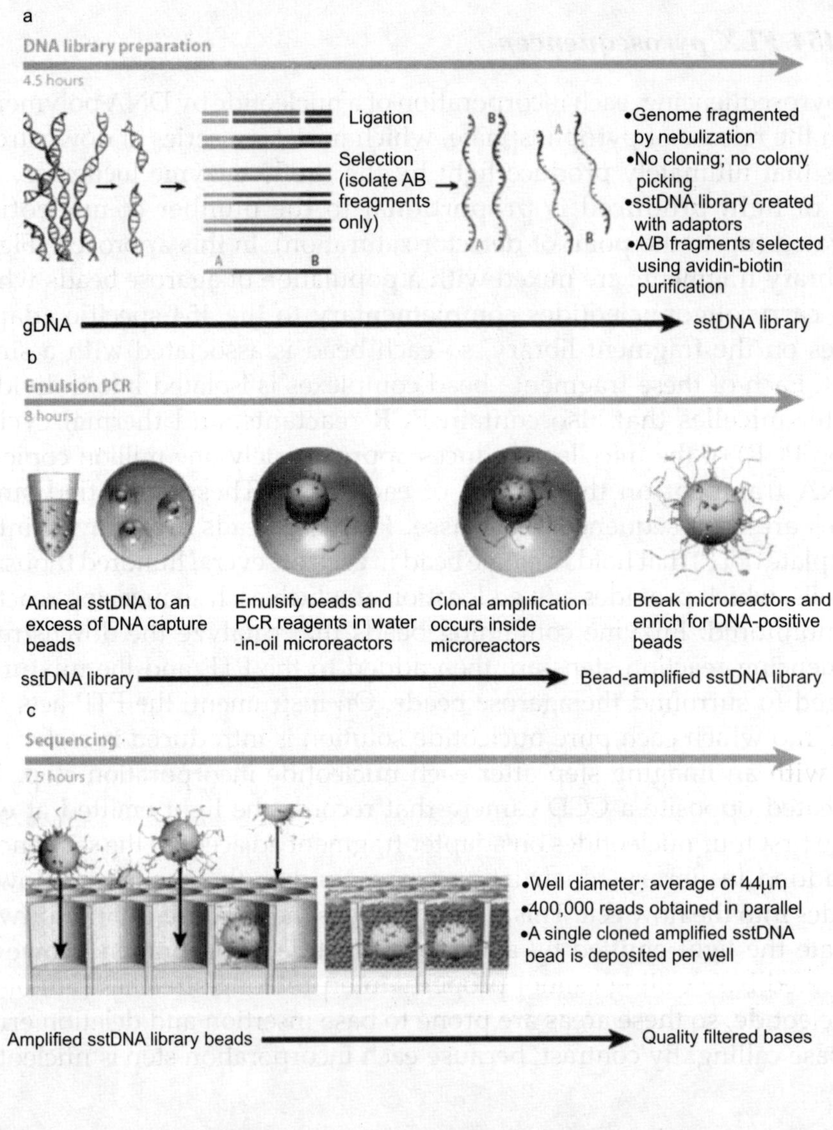

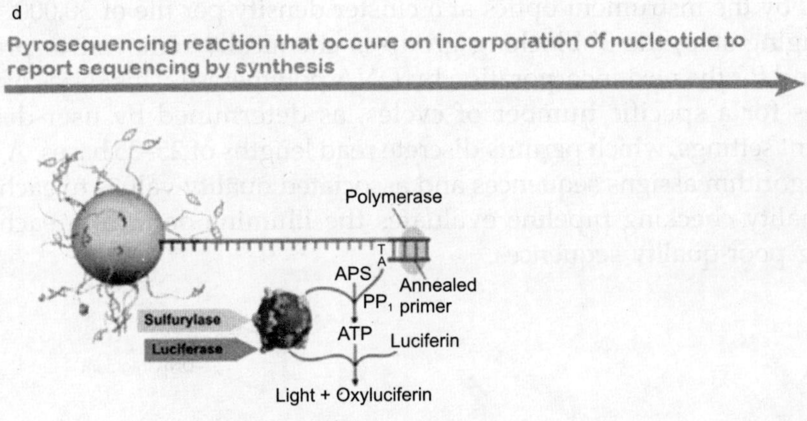

Fig. 1 : The method used by the Roche/454 sequencer to amplify single-stranded DNA copies from a fragment library on agarose beads. A mixture of DNA fragments with agarose beads containing complementary oligonucleotides to the adapters at the fragment ends are mixed in an approximately 1:1 ratio. The mixture is encapsulated by vigorous vortexing into aqueous micelles that contain PCR reactants surrounded by oil, and pipetted into a 96-well microtiter plate for PCR amplification. The resulting beads are decorated with approximately 1 million copies of the original single-stranded fragment, which provides sufficient signal strength during the pyrosequencing reaction that follows to detect and record nucleotide incorporation events. sstDNA, single-stranded template DNA (Images adapted from Mardis, 2008 and http://www.454.com).

Illumina Genome Analyzer

The single molecule amplification step for the Illumina Genome Analyzer starts with an Illumina-specific adapter library, takes place on the oligo-derivatized surface of a flow cell, and is performed by an automated device called a Cluster Station. The flow cell is an 8-channel sealed glass micro fabricated device that allows bridge amplification of fragments on its surface, and uses DNA polymerase to produce multiple DNA copies, or clusters, that each represents the single molecule that initiated the cluster amplification. A separate library can be added to each of the eight channels, or the same library can be used in all eight, or combinations thereof. Each cluster contains approximately one million copies of the original fragment, which is sufficient for reporting incorporated bases at the required signal intensity for detection during sequencing. The Illumina system utilizes sequencing by- synthesis approach in which all four nucleotides are added simultaneously to the flow cell channels, along with DNA polymerase, for incorporation into the oligo-primed cluster fragments (Figure 2). Specifically, the nucleotides carry a base-unique fluorescent label and the 3′-OH group is chemically blocked such that each incorporation is a unique event. An imaging step follows each base incorporation step, during which each flow cell lane is imaged in three 100-tile segments by the instrument optics at a cluster density per tile of 30,000. After each imaging step, the 3′ blocking group is chemically removed to prepare each strand for the next incorporation by DNA polymerase. This series of steps continues for a specific number of cycles, as determined by user-defined instrument settings, which permits discrete read lengths of 25–35 bases. A base-calling algorithm assigns sequences and associated quality values to each read and a quality checking pipeline evaluates the Illumina data from each run, removing poor-quality sequences.

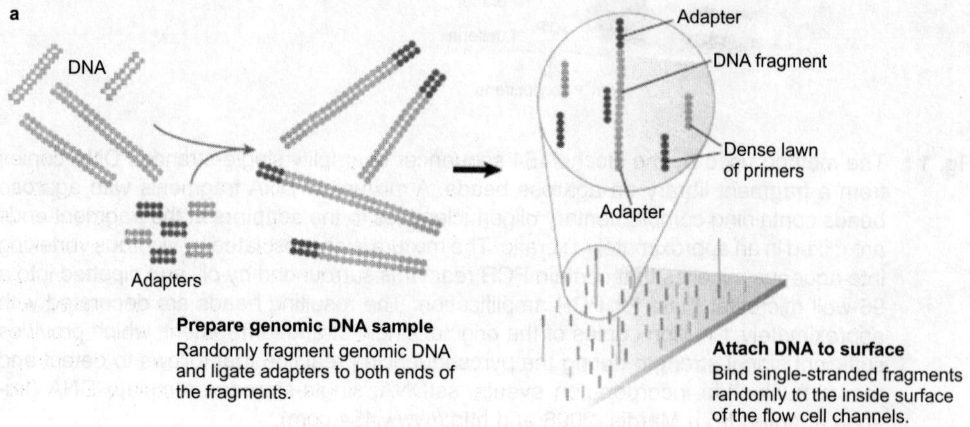

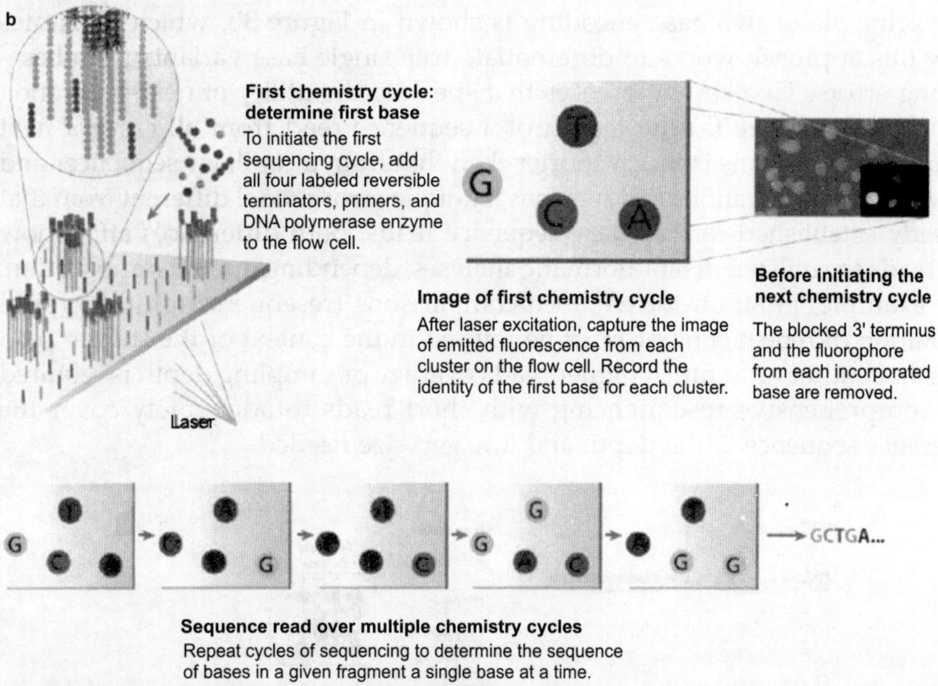

Fig. 2 : The Illumina sequencing-by-synthesis approach. Cluster strands created by bridge amplification are primed and all four fluorescently labeled 3'-OH blocked nucleotides are added to the flow cell with DNA polymerase. The cluster strands are extended by one nucleotide. Following the incorporation step, the unused nucleotides and DNA polymerase molecules are washed away, a scan buffer is added to the flow cell, and the optics system scans each lane of the flow cell by imaging units called tiles. Once imaging is completed, chemicals that effect cleavage of the fluorescent labels and the 3'-OH blocking groups are added to the flow cell, which prepares the cluster strands for another round of fluorescent nucleotide incorporation (Images adapted from Mardis, 2008).

Applied Biosystems SOLiD Sequencer

The SOLiD platform uses an adapter-ligated fragment library similar to those of the other next-generation platforms, and uses an emulsion PCR approach with small magnetic beads to amplify the fragments for sequencing. Unlike the other platforms, SOLiD uses DNA ligase and a unique approach to sequence the amplified fragments, as illustrated in Figure 3a. Two flow cells are processed per instrument run, each of which can be divided to contain different libraries in up to four quadrants. Read lengths for SOLiD are user defined between 25–35 bp, and each sequencing run yields between 2–4 Gb of DNA sequence data. Once the reads are base called, have quality values, and low-quality sequences have been removed, the reads are aligned to a reference genome to enable a second tier of quality evaluation called two-base encoding.

The principle of two-base encoding is shown in Figure 3b, which illustrates how this approach works to differentiate true single base variants from base-calling errors. Two key differences that speak to the utility of next-generation sequence reads are (a) the length of a sequence read from all current next generation platforms is much shorter than that from a capillary sequencer and (b) each next generation read type has a unique error model different from that already established for capillary sequence reads. Both differences affect how the reads are utilized in bioinformatic analyses, depending upon the application. For example, in strain-to-reference comparisons (resequencing), the typical definition of repeat content must be revised in the context of the shorter read length. In addition, a much higher read coverage or sampling depth is required for comprehensive resequencing with short reads to adequately cover the reference sequence at the depth and low gap size needed.

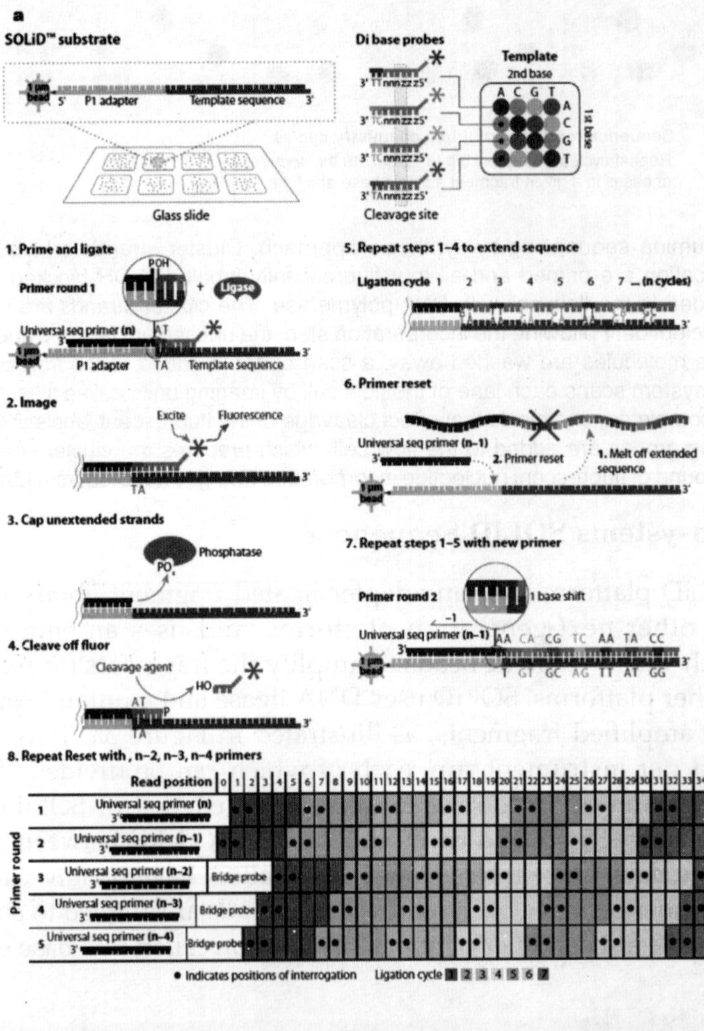

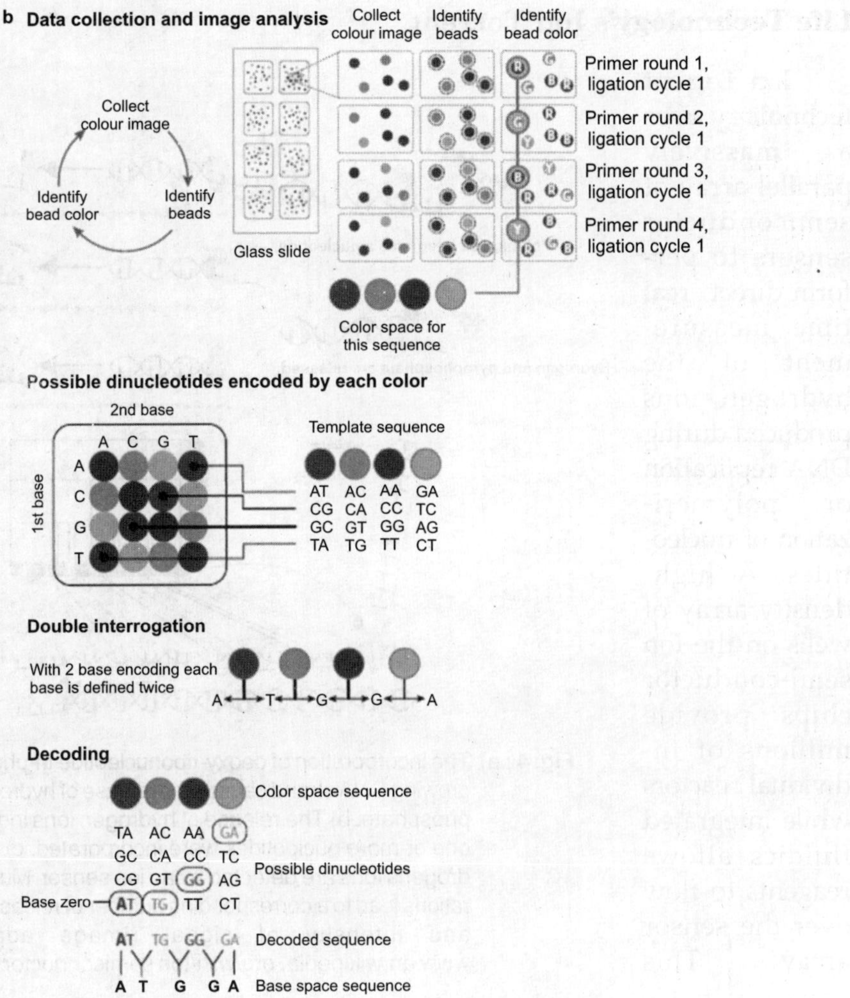

Fig. 3 : (a) The ligase-mediated sequencing approach of the Applied Biosystems SOLiD sequencer. DNA fragments for SOLiD sequencing are amplified on the surfaces of 1-ìm magnetic beads to provide sufficient signal during the sequencing reactions, and are then deposited onto a flow cell slide. Ligase-mediated sequencing begins by annealing a primer to the shared adapter sequences on each amplified fragment, and then DNA ligase is provided along with specific fluorescent labeled 8mers, whose 4th and 5th bases are encoded by the attached fluorescent group. Each ligation step is followed by fluorescence detection, after which a regeneration step removes bases from the ligated 8mer (including the fluorescent group) and con comitantly prepares the extended primer for another round of ligation. (b) Principles of two-base encoding. Because each fluorescent group on a ligated 8mer identifies a two-base combination, the resulting sequence reads can be screened for base-calling errors versus true polymorphisms versus single base deletions by aligning the individual reads to a known high-quality reference sequence (Images adapted from Mardis, 2008).

Life Technology's Ion Torrent

Ion Torrent technology uses a massively parallel array of semiconductor sensors to perform direct real time measurement of the hydrogen ions produced during DNA replication or polymerization of nucleotides. A high-density array of wells on the Ion semi-conductor chips provide millions of individual reactors while integrated fluidics allows reagents to flow over the sensor array. This unique combination of fluidics, micro-machining, and semiconductor technology enable the direct translation of genetic information (DNA) to digital information (DNA sequence) rapidly generating large quantities of high quality data. A micro-well containing a template DNA strand to be sequenced is flooded with a single species of dNTP. If the introduced dNTP is complementary to the leading template nucleotide, it is incorporated into the growing complementary strand. This causes the release of a hydrogen ion that triggers an ISFET ion sensor, which indicates that a reaction has occurred. If homopolymer repeats are present in the template sequence, multiple dNTP molecules will be incorporated in a single cycle. This leads to a corresponding number of released hydrogens and a proportionally higher electronic signal. This technology differs from other sequencing technologies in that no modified nucleotides or optics are used. Ion semiconductor sequencing may also be referred to as Ion Torrent sequencing,

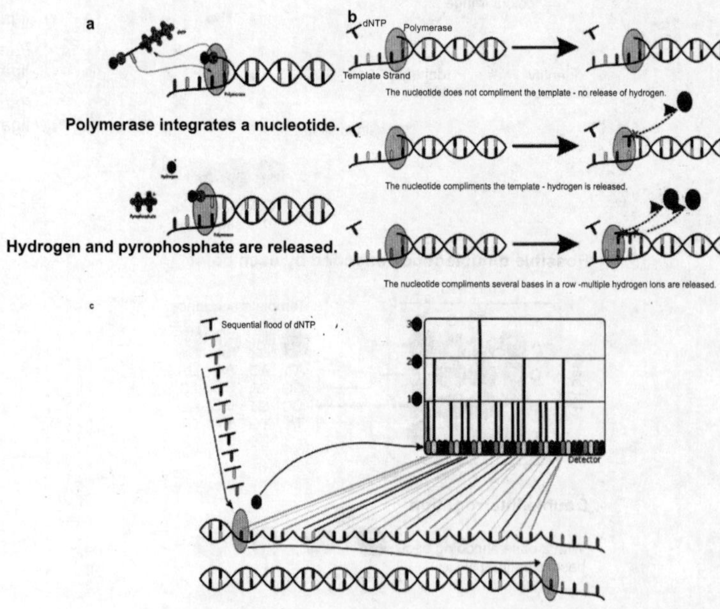

Fig. 4 : a) The incorporation of deoxy-ribonucleotide tri-phosphate into a growing DNA strand causes the release of hydrogen and pyrophosphate. b) The release of hydrogen ions indicates if zero, one or more nucleotides were incorporated. c) Released hydrogens ions are detected by an ion sensor. Multiple incorporations lead to a corresponding number of released hydrogens and intensity of signal (Image adapted from www.en.wikipedia. org/wiki/Ion semiconductor sequencing).

pH-mediated sequencing, silicon sequencing, or semiconductor sequencing.

The major benefits of ion semiconductor sequencing are rapid sequencing speed and low upfront and operating costs. This has been enabled by the avoidance of modified nucleotides and optical measurements. Because the system records natural polymerase-mediated nucleotide incorporation events, sequencing can occur in real-time. In reality, the sequencing rate is limited by the cycling of substrate nucleotides through the system. Ion Torrent Systems Inc., the developer of the technology, claims that each incorporation measurement takes 4 seconds and each run takes about one hour, during which 100-200 nucleotides are sequenced. If the semiconductor chips are improved the number of reads per chip should increase.

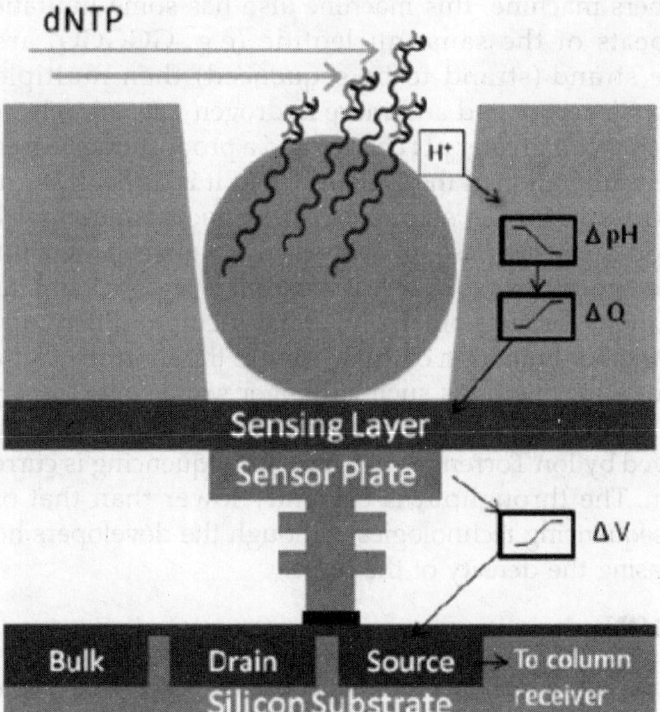

Fig. 5 : Cross-section of single well of an Ion torrent sequencing chip. The well houses Ion sphere particles containing DNA template. When a nucleotide incorporates, a proton release and the pH of the well changes, a sensing layer detects the change in pH and translates the chemical signal to a digital signal (Image adapted from www3.appliedbiosystems.com/cms/groups/ applied_markets_ marketing/ documents/ general documents/cms_094273).

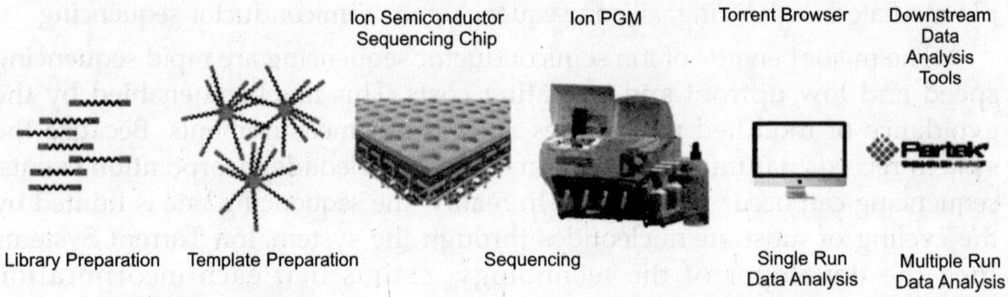

Fig. 6 : Schematic representation of Ion Torrent sequencing workflow (Image adapted from www3.appliedbiosystems.com/cms/groups/applied_markets_marketing/documents/general documents/cms_094273)

Like others machine, this machine also has some limitations. If homopolymer repeats of the same nucleotide (e.g. GGGGG) are present on the template strand (strand to be sequenced) then multiple introduced nucleotides are incorporated and more hydrogen ions are released in a single cycle. This results in a greater pH change and a proportionally greater electronic signal. This is a limitation of the system in that it is difficult to enumerate long repeats. This limitation is shared by other techniques that detect single nucleotide additions such as pyrosequencing. Signals generated from a high repeat number are difficult to differentiate from repeats of a similar but different number; e.g., homo repeats of length 7 are difficult to differentiate from those of length 8. Another limitation of this system is the short read length compared to other sequencing methods such as Sanger sequencing or pyrosequencing. Longer read lengths are beneficial for de novo genome assembly. The read length achieved by Ion Torrent semiconductor sequencing is currently 400 base pairs per run. The throughput is currently lower than that of other high-throughput sequencing technologies, although the developers hope to change this by increasing the density of the chip.

CONCLUSION

It is important to recognize the significant impacts that implementation of these platforms in a production sequencing environment has depends on informatics and bioinformatics infrastructures. The massively parallel scale of sequencing implies a similarly massive scale of computational analyses that include image analysis, signal processing, background subtraction, base calling, and quality assessment to produce the final sequence reads for each run. In every case, these analyses place significant demands on the information technology (IT), computational, data storage, and laboratory information management system (LIMS) infrastructures extant in a sequencing center, thereby adding to the overhead required for high-throughput data production.

This aspect of next-generation sequencing is at present complicated by the dearth of current sequence analysis tools suited to shorter sequence read data; existing data analysis pipelines and algorithms must be modified to accommodate these shorter reads. In many cases, and certainly for new applications of next-generation sequencing, entirely new algorithms and data visualization interfaces are being devised and tested to meet this new demand. Therefore, the next-generation platforms are effecting a complete paradigm shift, not only in the organization of large-scale data production, but also in the downstream bioinformatics, IT, and LIMS support required for high data utility and correct interpretation. This paradigm shift promises to radically alter the path of biological inquiry, as the following review of recent endeavors to implement next generation sequencing platforms and accompanying bioinformatics-based analyses serves to substantiate.

REFERENCE

Ansorge, W. *et al.* (1986) A non-radioactive automated method for DNA sequence determination. J. Biochem. Biophys. Methods 13, 315–323

Ansorge, W. *et al.* (1987) Automated DNA sequencing: ultrasensitive detection of fluorescent bands during electrophoresis. Nucleic Acids Res. 15, 4593–4602

Ansorge, W., EMBL Heidelberg (1991), Process for sequencing nucleic acids without gel sieving media on solid support and DNA chips (Verfahren zur Sequenzierung von Nukleinsauren ohne Gele). German Patent Application DE 41 41 178 A1 and Corresponding Worldwide Patent Applications.

Edwards, A. *et al.* (1990) Automated DNA sequencing of the human HPRT locus. Genomics 6, 593–608

Maxam, A.M. and Gilbert, W. (1977) A new method for sequencing DNA. Proc. Natl. Acad. Sci. U. S. A. 74, 560–564

Mardis, E. R. (2008) Next-Generation DNA Sequencing Methods. Annu. Rev. Genomics Hum. Genet., 9:387–402.

Schuster, S.C. *et al.* (2008) Method of the year, next-generation DNA sequencing. Functional genomics and medical applications. Nat. Methods 5, 11–21

Sanger, F. *et al.* (1977) DNA sequencing with chain-terminating inhibitors. Proc. Natl. Acad. Sci. U. S. A. 74, 5463–5467

Smith, L.M. *et al.* (1986) Fluorescence detection in automated DNA sequence analysis. Nature 321, 674–679

❑❑❑

CHAPTER - 4

Next Generation Sequencing Technologies: Relevance in Post Genomic Era

Anil Kumar and Shivani Tyagi
School of Biotechnology, Devi Ahilya University, Khandwa Road, Indore-452001, India
E-mail: ak_sbt@yahoo.com

INTRODUCTION

DNA sequencing is a process of deciphering the complete order of nucleotide in the DNA molecule with precision. Over the past few years, there has been a shifting from the automated Sanger's method of sequencing to next generation technologies. There was a milestone in the year 2003 for the researchers when fine sequence of human genome project was declared complete. The project was completed in 13 years with nearly $3 billion expenditure and more than 20,000 researchers and technicians took part in it all over the Globe. DNA sequence determination is performed using dideoxy chain termination technology (Ronaghi, 2001). The dideoxy sequencing method was developed by Frederick Sanger and his colleagues (Sanger *et al.*, 1977) and is called as First-generation sequencing technology. Since early 2000s, there became drastic improvements in the sequencing technologies from Sanger's method used for Human genome project to Next Generation Sequencing (NGS) technologies used these days. The change in technologies not only reduced the expenditure to the minimal but also involved minimum use of human resource and time. High –throughput sequencing technologies are increasingly being used to address varied range of biological objectives. It provides a promising approach to increase the scale, robustness and efficiency of the results of whole genome within few hours and minimum expense. Key players in the field of NGS are 454 GX Flex Roche, Solexa Illumina, SOLiD ABI (Applied Biosystems), ViSiGen biotechnologies, Helicose Biosciences and Polonater systems. There are three methods that hold the research are sequencing by hybridization

(Drmanac *et al.*, 1989; Khrapko *et al.*, 1989), pyrosequencing (Ronaghi et al, 1996 ; Ronaghi *et al.*, 1998) and parallel signature sequencing (Brenner *et al.*, 2000). Basically, a combinatorial strategy is used in newer technologies like template preparation, sequencing, imaging, genome alignment and its assembly. Influx of NGS in market has changed the view of researchers and their approach in basic, clinical and applied areas. Also, it has changed the dominion of experiments beyond just knowing the base order in DNA sequence. One of the classical example is gene expression studies done using micro-arrays and has now been shifted to seq-based methods which can easily quantify and identify the transcripts without its prior knowledge of gene (Wold and Myers, 2008; Wang *et al.*, 2009). Now it is possible to sequence whole genome of an organism that can be used for comparative and evolutionary studies that was being considered to be much difficult few years ago.

The application of the protocol is dependent on the technologies being used by these systems (Table 1). The uses of NGS tools are restricted to whole genome, transcriptome, chip –seq, RNA profiling and metagenomics but at present, NGS has found a new way in forensics and clinical diagnostics also (http://www.fortmilltimes.com/2013/10/10/3017107/research-and-markets-next-generation.html). Combination of specific protocols differentiates one technology from another and determines the data production using those platforms. This would provide challenge in data output and inference deduction from the data.

Table 1: Technologies being used for NGS by various manufacturers.

System	Technology
Roche 454 GS FLX	Pyrosequencing
SOLiD ABI	Sequencing by ligation
SOLEXA Illumina	Sequencing by synthesis
Polonater	Sequencing by ligation
Helicose BioSciences	Nanopore sequencing
ViSiGen Biotechnologies	Single-molecule sequencing

Table 2: Comparative analysis of the cost of sequencing per base.

System	Cost/ Mbp	Cost/instrument	Paired end	Read Length
Solexa	~$2	$430,000	Yes	36 bp
SOLiD	~$2	$591,00	Yes	35 bp
454	~$60	$500,000	Yes	250 bp
Polonator	~$1	$155,000	Yes	13 bp
HeliScope	~$1	$1,350,000	Yes	30 bp

Sequencing was started in late 1980s where Slab Gel sequencers using radioactive isotopes were used manually; later fluorescence chemistry took over and used to give 10 kbp/ 4hours. Capillary sequencers were in late 1990s and used to give 50 kbp/ 1hour run. Massive parallel pyrosequencing in 2005 gave 20 MB/5hours run, whereas, in 2007, there was sequencing by synthesis giving 1GB/5days run and single molecule sequencing in 2010 gave 100 GB/5days run. Using these high-throughput technologies, human genome can be read in 15 minutes. The massively parallel sequencing technologies produce high throughput data per run with minimum cost (Table 2). Genomic DNA, RNA, BAC colonies, small RNA, PCR Products, ChIP DNA, mRNA and FFPE RNA can be used as sample type in these instruments. However, the chemistry of NGS varies with different protocols. There are two ways used for template preparation such as; clonally amplified DNA from single DNA molecule and single DNA template. A common step among NGS technologies is the attachment of template on immobilized solid support. This will allow billions of reactions to occur simultaneously.

The era of NGS in 21st century has brought large scale data retrieval which has been used for data resources and also in population/ cohorts studies to understand disease markers, mutations and also in the study of complex diseases like autism and cancer. There are a number of projects running these days like **ENCODE project** (Encyclopedia of DNA elements) which was launched by The National Human Genome Research Institute (NHGRI) in 2003 to identify functional elements in human genome (Maher, 2012) . There are two components of the project- pilot phase and technology development phase. Also the primary assays used in the project are DNase 1 hypersensitivity, ChIP-seq, DNA methylation assays and RNA-seq. Similarly, the **1000 Genome project** was launched in 2008 with the support of Wellcome Trust Sanger Institiute, Beijing Genomics Institute, NHGRI and National Institutes of Health (NIH). The objective of the project is to find genetic variations having frequencies of at least 1% in the under study population which will support association studies (Durbin *et al.*, 2010). Secondary goal of the project is to go for genotyping studies for probe selection which will support recombination and mutation studies.

The Human Microbiome Project (HMP) has been started to catalog microorganism found in the human body which has been supported by the NIH and launched in 2008. The major goals include association of diseases and change in human microbiome in order to prepare data repository, to prepare reference set of microbiome and its ethical, legal and social implications (Barbara *et al.*, 2012). Role of microbiome in large number of diseases in digestive tract, childhood disorders and reproductive organs was studied using HMP data.

Exome Sequencing Project (ESP) has been launched by The National Heart, Lung, and Blood Institute (NHLBI) to identify various new genes involved in complex heart, lung and blood disorders. This is the major project to study Human coding genetic variations (Bamshad *et al.*, 2011). The technology used is deep whole exome re-sequencing using nearly 7000 individuals. The project teams included in the project are Blood count/ hematology project team, Blood pressure project team, Anthropometry project team, Lipids project team, Early MI project team, Lung study team, Stroke study team, Subclinical / Quantitative traits project team and Personal genomics project team.

Therefore, next generation sequencing technology is much relevant and can be exploited for many applications in this post genomic era of 21st century.

Chemistry of Next Generation Sequencing (NGS)

Sequencing by synthesis (SBS)- This technology uses four fluorescently labeled nucleotides that support both paired end and single read libraries and provides high resolution and efficient genome sequencing. Characterization of complete genome can be achieved by combining short inserts and long reads. During sequencing, deoxyribonucleotide get attached to newly synthesized chain. The dideoxynucleotides work as terminators for polymerization, this means now after each ddNTP incorporation and subsequent termination, the base is imaged and read. After termination, the base is cleaved by enzymatic treatment to allow incorporation of next base. Incorporation bias is not a problem in this system because all the reversible terminator-bound deoxyribonucleotides are separate and single in number. Signal intensity is based on the base call of a particular nucleotide. This technology lies around massive quantity of sequence and reads in parallel. It has been developed by Solexa and based on reversible dye terminators and bridge PCR. In reversible dye terminators, 3′-end has a protection group which is changed by hydroxyl group during DNA chain complementation. In Bridge amplification or bridge PCR, the primers are attached on the solid surface through covalent binding (Bing *et al.*, 1996) and one primer has a cleavable site. There is no need of emulsions and beads for the amplification. Amplification temperature for the PCR is kept constant at 60^{0}C and formamide is used as denaturating agent. Pre-amplified library is denatured and loaded onto the channels in neutral solution and DNA molecules get attached to the PCR primers on the flow cell. Hybridized DNA library and primers get elongated using extension mix (Buffers, dNTPs and Taq polymerase). After extension, the original library is denatured using formamide while the extended molecule bends and hybridizes to other PCR primer forming a bridge like structure. Again, there will be extension of hybridized primer. But there are two major disadvantages namely surface amplification is lesser efficient than amplification in solution and duplex DNA has high probability of re-association than hybridizing with PCR primer (Fig. 1).

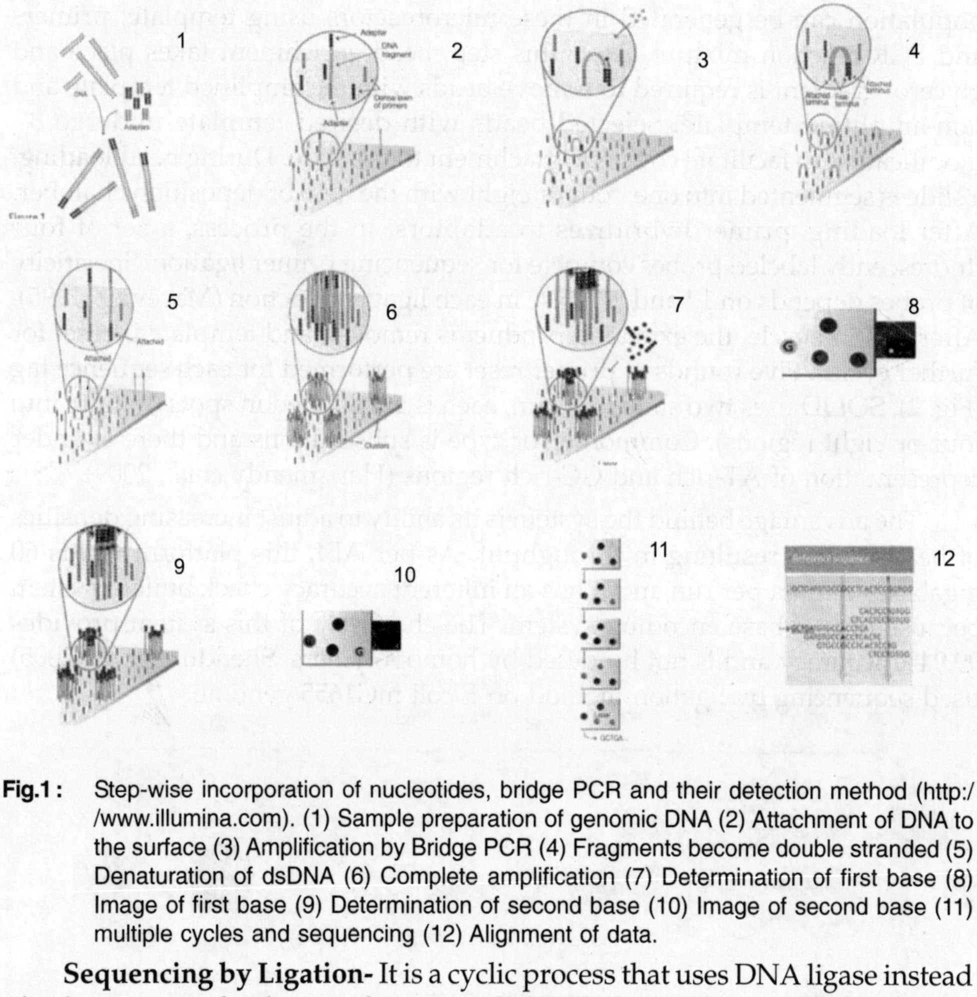

Fig.1 : Step-wise incorporation of nucleotides, bridge PCR and their detection method (http://www.illumina.com). (1) Sample preparation of genomic DNA (2) Attachment of DNA to the surface (3) Amplification by Bridge PCR (4) Fragments become double stranded (5) Denaturation of dsDNA (6) Complete amplification (7) Determination of first base (8) Image of first base (9) Determination of second base (10) Image of second base (11) multiple cycles and sequencing (12) Alignment of data.

Sequencing by Ligation- It is a cyclic process that uses DNA ligase instead of polymerase and either one-base-encoded probe or two-base-encoded probes. SOLiD (Sequencing by Oligonucleotide Ligation and Detection) is trademark product of Applied Biosystems that works on the principle of emulsion PCR (ePCR) and sequencing by ligation. This method uses two-base-encoded probes which provide advantage of improved accuracy in detection of SNVs (Single nucleotide variants) and base calling. The process starts with the preparation of library that includes sequencing –fragment type or mate-paired type. The template is sheared by sonication or physical disruption using Covaris S2 or HydroShear, respectively. Sheared template is end-repaired, purified and ligated to the universal adaptors (P1 and P2) to obtain library. The P1 and P2 adaptors are used for amplification purpose and then size selection is done using PAGE gels or Agarose gel. This is followed by ePCR for bead enrichment. In ePCR, there is a need of microreactors composed of water-in-oil phase. Clonal bead population can be generated in these microreactors using template, primers and PCR reaction mixture. After this step, bead enrichment takes place and glycerol gradient is required to remove beads with the amplified template and non-amplified template. Selected beads with desired template undergo 3'-modification to facilitate covalent attachment to the slide. During bead loading, a slide is segmented into one, four or eight with the help of deposition chamber. After loading, primer hybridizes to adaptors. In the process, a set of four fluorescently labeled probes compete for sequencing primer ligation. Specificity of probes depends on 1st and 2nd base in each ligation reaction (Macevicz ,1995). After ligation cycle, the extended product is removed and template is reset for further cycles. Five rounds of primer reset are performed for each sequence tag (Fig. 2). SOLiD uses two slides per run, each is partitioned in spots (mainly into four or eight regions). Common error type is substitutions and there is under representation of AT-rich and GC-rich regions (Harismendy *et al.*, 2009).

The advantage behind the system is its ability to adjust increasing densities of beads /slide resulting in throughput. As per ABI, this platform yields 60 gigabases of data per run and it has an inherent accuracy check built in system because of two base encoding system. The chemistry of this system provides 99.94% accuracy and is not hindered by homopolymers. Shendure *et al.* (2005) used sequencing by ligation method on E.coli mG1655 genome.

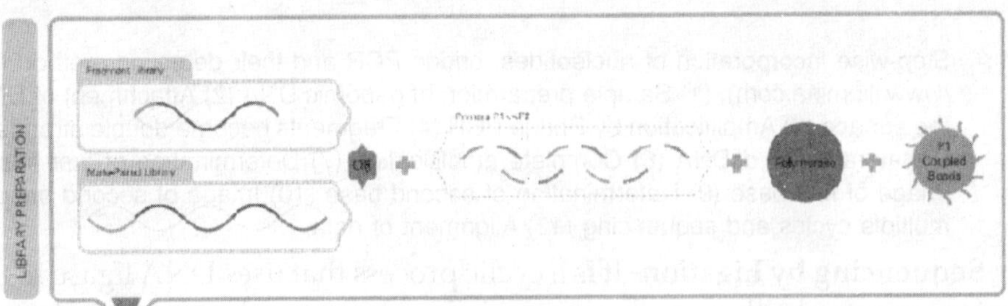

1.

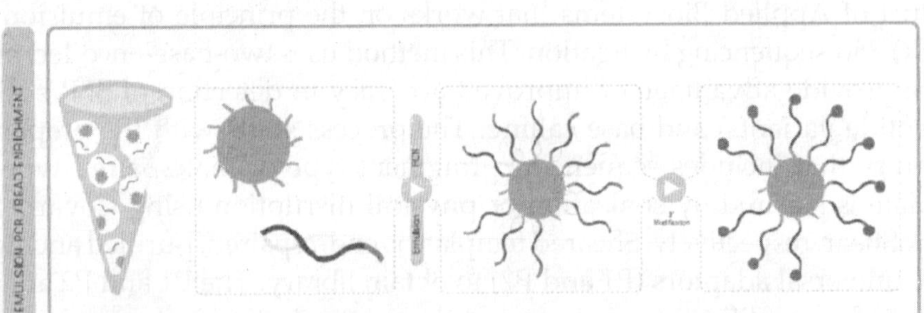

2.

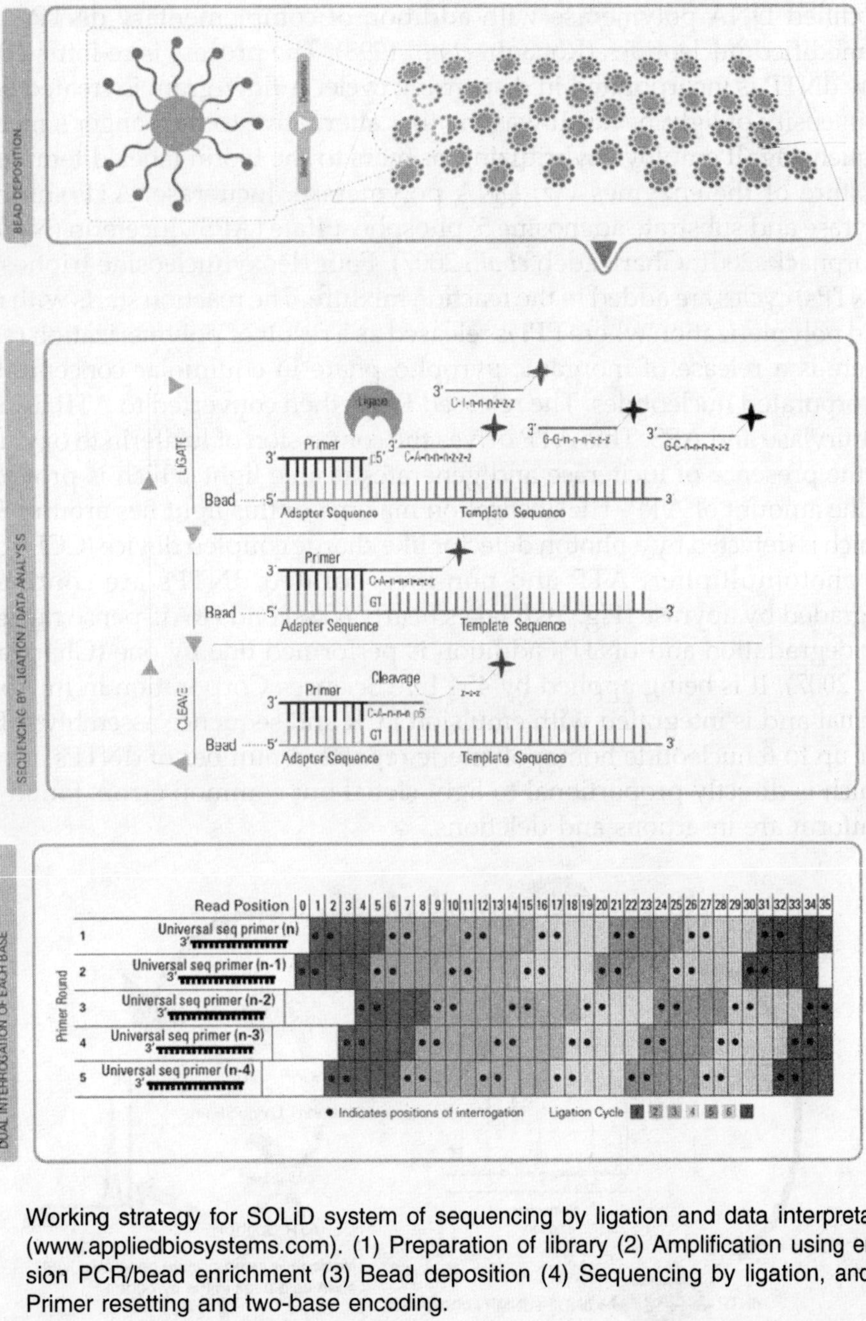

3.

4.

5.

Fig. 2: Working strategy for SOLiD system of sequencing by ligation and data interpretation (www.appliedbiosystems.com). (1) Preparation of library (2) Amplification using emulsion PCR/bead enrichment (3) Bead deposition (4) Sequencing by ligation, and (5) Primer resetting and two-base encoding.

Pyrosequencing- It is non-electrophoretic and bioluminescence method that relies on the principle of sequencing by synthesis and detects a pyrophosphate (PPi) release on nucleotide incorporation in the growing chain and suitable for 100 bp read (Gharizadeh *et al.,* 2003a). Pyrosequencing uses modified DNA polymerase with addition of complementary dNTPs instead of modified nucleotides (Ronaghi *et al.*, 1998). The process is re-initiated when new dNTP is incorporated in dispensing cycle. A flow-gram is created because of intensity of light peaks. It was the first alternative to the Sanger's method of sequencing. It employs hybridizing primers to the biotin labeled template and mixture of the enzymes viz; DNA polymerase, luciferase, ATP sulfurylase, apyrase and substrate adenosine 5′ phosphosulfate (APS), luceferin (Nyren and Skarpnack, 2001; Gharizadeh *et al.*, 2007). Four deoxynucleoside triphosphates (dNTPs) cycles are added in the reaction mixture. The reaction starts with nucleic acid polymerization where PPi is released as a result of polymerization reaction. There is a release of inorganic pyrophosphate in equimolar concentration of incorporated nucleotides. The released PPi is then converted to ATP using ATP sulfurylase and APS. This ATP drives the conversion of luciferin to oxyluciferin in the presence of luciferase and generates visible light which is proportional to the amount of ATP. The absorption maxima of this light lies around 560 nm which is detected by a photon detector like charge coupled device (CCD) camera or photomultiplier. ATP and non-incorporated dNTPs are continuously degraded by apyrase (Fig. 3). It takes nearly 65 seconds to dispense nucleotides for degradation and dNTPs addition is performed one by one (Gharizadeh *et al..*, 2007). It is being applied by 454 Life Sciences Corporation in microfluidic format and is integrated with emulsion PCR and sequence assembly software. For up to 6 nucleotide homopolymeric repeats, a number of dNTPs are added which is directly proportional to light signal but common errors found in this platform are insertions and deletions.

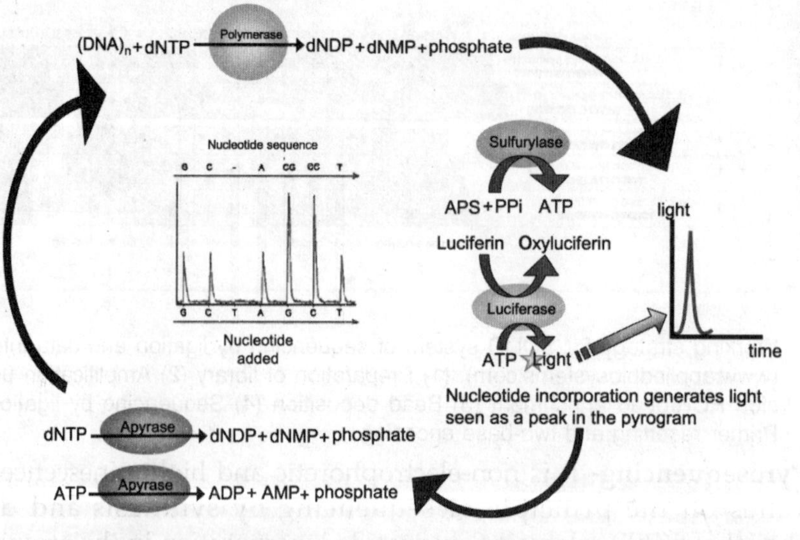

Fig. 3 : Workflow of pyrosequencing and its data analysis (http://www.454.com)

Nanopore sequencing- It is a technique which utilizes a small hole of 1 nanometer in internal diameter made by etching hole in silicone piece or porous transmembrane proteins which can act as nanopores. The Ion-beam method is used to make smaller holes. Graphene is being used these days as solid-state nanopore (Garaj *et al.*, 2010; Chan, 2005) (Fig. 4). The principle of the technology lies in the difference of current magnitude when something passes through the ions. When a nanopore is immersed in a conducting fluid having set voltage, electric current is generated due to conduction. The amount of current is altered and is dependent on the size and shape of the nanopore. There are two types of nanopores namely Alpha hemolysin and MspA. Bacterial Alpha hemolysin (aHL) is a nanopore that causes lysis of RBCs. The pore size is nearly 10 nm with two 5 nm distinct sections. Upper larger section is consisted of vestibule like structure while lower section has three recognition sites (R1, R2, R3) which is capable to discriminate between bases (Stoddart *et al.*, 2009; Purnell *et al.*, 2008). The MspA pore (*Mycobacterium smegmatis* porin A) is an improvement of aHL having goblet structure with thick rim and bottom diameter of 1.2 nm (Faller *et al.*, 2004). It has a negative core that restricts single stranded DNA. Natural nanopre is improved by replacing 3 negatively charged aspartic acids with neut-ral aspargine. The electric current across the membrane is 10 times more than aHL (Butler *et al.*, 2008). The detection of DNA sequence is done using solid-state nanopores and fluorescence with two or four color systems. Probes have fluorophore and quencher at the start and end of the template. The upstream fluorophore will fluoresce when dsDNA is translocated via solid state nanopore and consequently stripped off (McNally *et al.*, 2010 ; Soni *et al.*, 2010). Two colors system has a capacity of 50 to 250 bp/sec/pore whereas there is capacity of above 500bp/ sec/pore with four colors system.

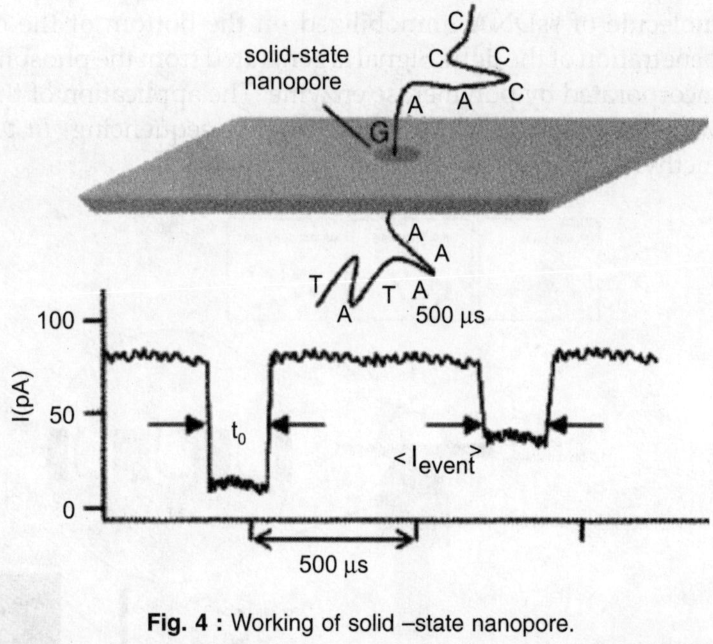

Fig. 4 : Working of solid –state nanopore.

Single-molecule real time (SMRT) sequencing- This technology harnesses natural replication process for accurate and efficient sequencing developed by Pacific Biosciences. The most successful and efficient technology that holds the market these days is real time sequencing method. Unlike other methods of reversible terminators, real time does not stop DNA synthesis process and involves imaging of continuous process of incorporation of dye labeled nucleotides (Metzker ,2009).

Single molecule detection utilizes zero-mode waveguide (ZMW) to which DNA polymerase is affixed at the bottom with the template. ZMW creates illuminated observation to detect single nucleotide (Fig 5). It has 70 nm diameter and 100 nm depth (Korlach *et al.,* 2008). The optical field of the light decays exponentially when it passes through a chamber. The illumination of ZMW is nearly 20 zeptoliters ($20X10^{-21}$ liters). Four florescent dyes are used to attach four DNA nucleotides. During incorporation, n of nucleotide by DNA polymerase, the fluorescent tag is detached and diffuses out of the detection area of ZMW and respective base call is made (Levene *et al.*, 2003). A chip with many ZMW is used which contains an active DNA polymerase and single molecule of ssDNA immobilized on the bottom of the chip to facilitate the penetration of the light. Signal is generated from the phosphor-linked nucleotide incorporated by polymerase enzyme. The application of the technology is very wide such as in *de novo* sequencing, re-sequencing, *In vitro* diagnostics and methylation studies.

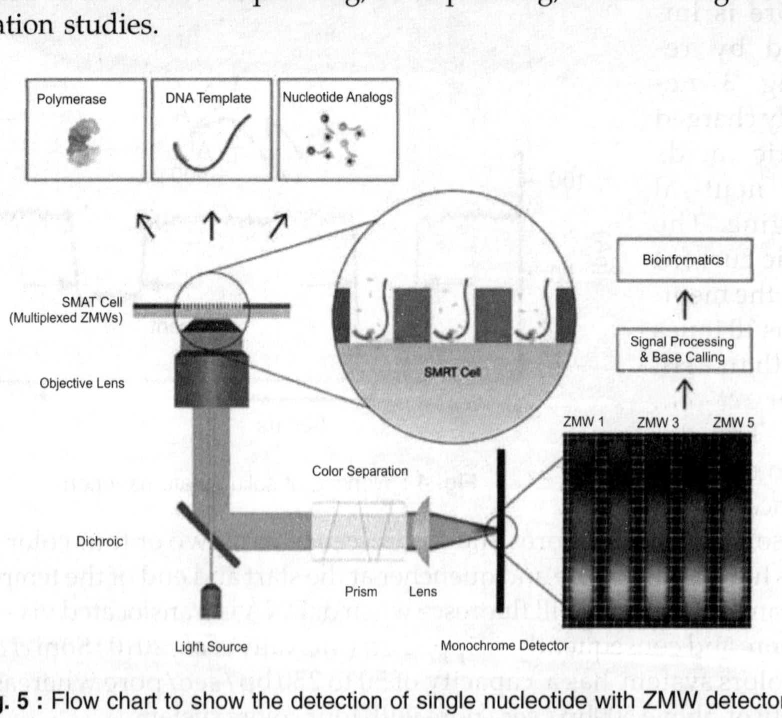

Fig. 5 : Flow chart to show the detection of single nucleotide with ZMW detectors.

Chromatin immunoprecipitation sequencing (ChIP)- DNA and protein association is fundamental interaction which is responsible for regulation of gene expression, transcription and replication by controlling the availability of DNA. ChIP is a technique useful for the study of biological interaction of DNA-Protein complexes (Solomon *et al.*, 1988). The protocol requires isolated and lysed nuclei followed by fragmentation of DNA. Besides, DNA binding protein specific antibody is used to immunoprecipitate the complex of DNA-Protein. Cross linking between DNA and protein is reversed and fragmented DNA is ligated with P1 and P2 adaptors for its amplification using emulsion PCR or bridge PCR for library creation. These amplified products are then used on different next generation platforms like Illumina, Roche or Applied Biosystem for sequencing. Previously, the application of ChIP was confined to examination of specific gene by southern blotting and qPCR (quantitative PCR) but recent advances have shifted the studies to genome-wide studies of DNA-protein interaction. Ren and co-workers in 2000 for the first time reported this technology. The main disadvantage is its low signal-to-noise ratio and also it needs replicates for authentic data and its interpretation to support putative binding sites.

Ion PGM from Ion Torrent- It is a Personal Genome Machine (PGM) that uses semiconductor sequencing technology. The technology was launched by Ion Torrent in 2010. There is a release of proton on incorporation of nucleotide into DNA strand by polymerase enzyme. Consequently there will a change in pH which is then detected by PGM. The chip is flooded with nucleotide one after the other and if there is incorrect nucleotide, there will not be any change in voltage and if there is incorporation of two nucleotides then the voltage is increased and detected as double. The detection does not require florescence and scanning of camera. This makes the platform lesser expensive and smaller in size. It enables 200 bp reads in 2 hours and the sample preparation takes 6 hours for 8 samples simultaneously. Its application revolves around identification of microbial pathogens. A particular type of *E.coli* has been studied for its antibiotic resistance by whole genome sequencing. It was appeared to be a hybrid of entero aggregative *E.coli* and entero-hemorrhagic *E.coli* (Chin *et al.*, 2011).

Imaging and Data Analysis- Sequencing strategy of clonally amplified and single molecule template is very different. Clonal amplification gives population of identical templates. Upon imaging, it is observed that a consensus of probes are added to the identical templates for a particular cycle. This is in great demand on the efficiency and incomplete extension of template results in dephasing of lagging strand while leading strand dephasing occurs due to multiple nucleotide addition in a given cycle. Fluorescence noise increases because of signal dephasing resulting in base-calling errors and short reads.

Dephasing has no effect on single –molecule template but deletion errors might owe quenching effects and no signal will be detected because of no probe. For detection purposes, barcodes are being used .They not only minimise the complexity and confusion in interpreting bulk data, but also avoid interference with adaptor probes. Essentially 13:4 SECDED design is used which is a 7- base indexing design. Genetic algorithm is used for base-balance collection. Poisson distribution is used to allocate reads within the genes. High frequency genes are lesser nosy than low abundance genes. The problem of noise can be dealt, by increasing the read length or number of reads. Number of bioinformatics tools like alignment, base calling. SNP detection (Fig. 6), de novo assembly and Genome browsing or annotation can be used as tools of analyse data.

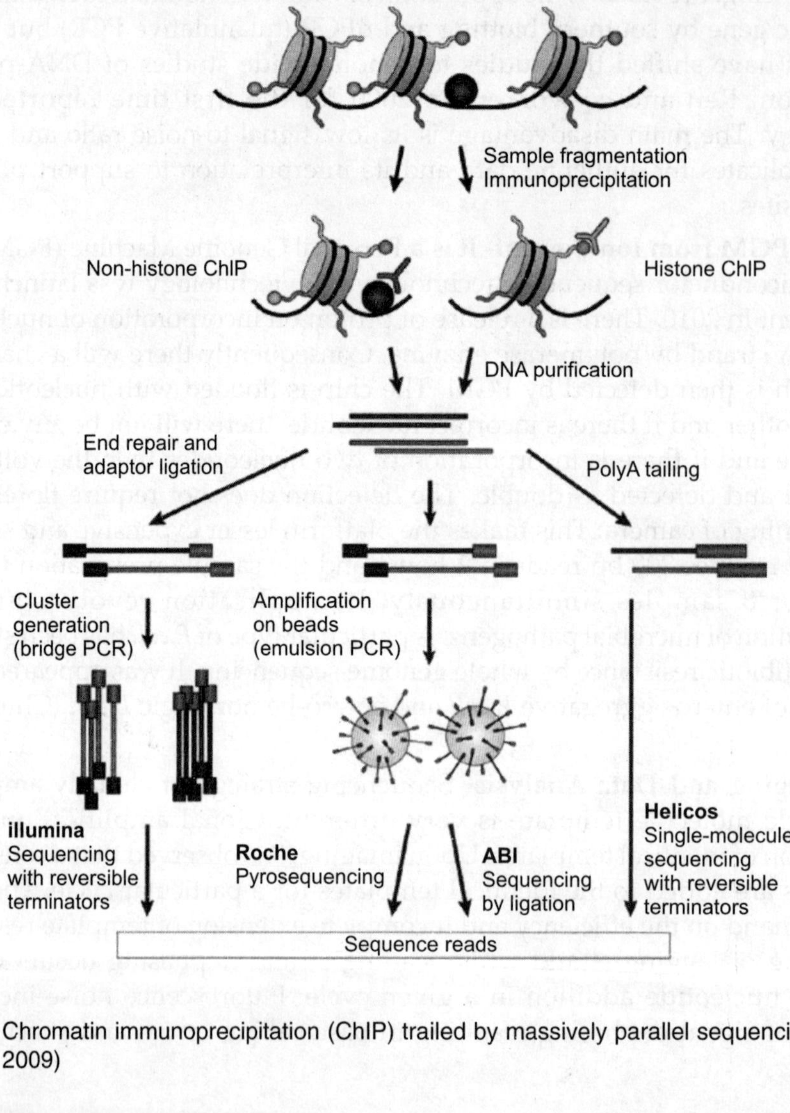

Fig. 6 : Chromatin immunoprecipitation (ChIP) trailed by massively parallel sequencing. (Park, 2009)

Multiplexing is used which is a method to analyse multiple biological samples in one sample. Barcodes play important role in multiplexing as these are unique and it is easy to track the sample after the run. MAQ (Li *et al.*, 2008) or ELAND (Bentley *et al.*, 2008) tools are used to align the reads to check for the sequence variation. Bentley and colleagues in 2008 reported 99.5 % concordance of SNVs (Single nucleotide variants) using these tools while 2.5% rate of getting false positive results.

Fig. 7 : Sequencing data giving an impression of SNP detection (in red) using reference sequence as control.

Roche 454 was the first group in collaboration with Gibbs and colleagues to use NGS for whole human genome. Diploid genome of J.D. Watson was compared with the reference genome (Wheeler *et al.*, 2008) and approximately 3.3 million SNVs were identified accounting for substantial fraction of total sequence variants and many having the potential of causing disease (Iafrate *et al.*, 2004). National Human Genome Research Institute has granted nearly $100 million for the development of Next Generation Technologies since 2004. Many companies like IBM, Oxford Nanopore technologies, LaserGen Inc. and Intelligent Bio-Systems are at various stages of its commercialization and development. NGS technologies are not only useful for sequencing genomes for disease prediction but also to characterize the evolutionary relations with the ancestor. The current future of the technology is to obtain high quality sequence data from DNA, isolated from single cell which could be a breakthrough in the cancer genomics. The field of sequencing using NGS is fast growing making the era worth for genomic studies.

Applications of NGS - The NGS has taken a new step towards the inexpensive, robust, accurate and efficient research. Genome wide studies of many organisms have flooded the databases with the numerous information. The study of areas like metagenomics, exomics , transcriptomics and epigenomics are now possible using upgraded sequencing technologies. These studies are providing information of basic research and also of its application. The information gathered and compiled is now being used in crop improvement for its yield, diagnostics, prognostics, livestock, cancer therapies and other complex disorders. Beijing Researchers across the World are primarily focussing on translating genomic data into breeding and association studies so that it can be used in agriculture, medicine, clinical treatments and drug discoveries.

Mate –pair library sequencing is beneficial for *de novo* sequencing because this decreases gap regions and extends scaffold length. Reinhardt *et al.* in 2009 developed a method for *de novo* assembly of genome from sequencing data of short read technology. Genome assembly is possible without reference sequence and one sample yields N50 scaffold size of 531,821 bp and by scaffolds over 100,000bp, > 75% of predicted genome coverage is possible.

In *de novo* sequencing, an insert of a size below 800 bp called as short fragment library is applied in re-sequencing research. Primary genetic sequence is generated of a particular organism followed by a detailed genetic analysis (Goldberg *et al.*, 2006).

Four of the organisms mentioned in Table 3 have been sequenced using NGS independently and in combination with Sanger's method (Velasco *et al..*, 2007; DiGuistini *et al.*, 2009; Huang *et al.*, 2009; Li *et al.*, 2010). Sanger's method in combination with pyrosequencing was used to sequence heterozygous grape genome.

Table 3: *De-novo* sequencing of genomes using next generation sequencing technologies

Organism	Common name	Genome size	Platform	Depth	Reference
Vitis *vinifera*	Grape	500	Sanger and 454	11X	Velasco *et al*, 2007
Cucumic *sativus*	Cucumber	367	Sanger and Solexa	72.2X	Huang *et al*, 2009
Grosmannia *clavigera*	Blue stain fungus	32.5	Sanger, solexa nd 454	50X	DiGuistini *et al*, 2009
Ailuropoda *melanoleuca*	Panda	246	Solexa	56X	Li *et al.*, 2010

A sequence of whole genome and a set of mapped marker loci have been generated. To assemble the genome sequence of larger eukaryotic genome, long Sanger method and short sequencing by synthesis approach was used for the first time (Velasco *et al.*, 2007). With its high accuracy, long read lengths, efficiency and robustness, capillary electrophoresis based sequencing has become a standard technology for de-novo sequencing (Imelfort and Edwards, 2009 ; Turner *et al.*, 2009a). However, if the cost is calculated then, de novo assembly is very expensive and time taking. In contrast, NGS holds market for high-throughput data as it is inexpensive per base pair and reduces the time for collating the data. A combination method of whole –genome sequencing and copy number analysis is applied for mutation identification studies (Skovgaard *et al.*, 2011). Mills and colleagues in 2011 constructed a map of genomic structural variants (SV) on the basis of whole genome DNA using SOLiD platform. The 22,025 deletions and 6,000 SVs, insertions and tandem duplications were found in the map. The whole genome re-sequencing is undoubtedly an effective way for the study of functional genes but is highly expensive and needs fine expertise for massive data interpretation. So target region sequencing is a better option to combat the problem and microarray capture of target region sequencing can be used for the purpose. Fehniger et al in 2010 used Illumina GA and SOLiD from ABI to define miRNA trasncriptome using resting and cytokine-activated primary murine natural killer cells (NK cells). The bioinformatics tools were used to identify 302 known and 21 novel libraries of NK cells.

To study mRNA expression, RNA-seq is being used these days. The sample preparation is same as that of transcriptome sequencing. Transcriptome by far is a complete set of transcripts residing in a cell (Jacquier, 2009). The basic understanding of trascriptome is vital for interpretation of functional units of the genome and also to reveal molecular components of the cells and tissues to understand the insight of disease and development. The study of transcriptomics gives transcriptional structure of the genes, splicing patterns and post-transcriptional modifications, quantification of expression of each transcript under different physiological and diseased conditions. Besides, it is easy to catalog all the transcripts in context of cell type and species basis. RNA-seq approach is used for transcriptome profiling which uses deep sequencing technology (Wang *et al.*, 2009). Conventional Sanger's method detects nearly 60% of transcripts in a particular cell and fails to cover long transcripts and poorly expressed transcripts (Brent, 2008). This gap of information can be dealt with the use of next generation technologies. A wasp Polistes metricus is a classical example, where 454 sequencing technology was used to generate 391,157 EST (expressed sequence tag) which read from the brain transcriptome (Toth *et al.*, 2007). The read were aligned with the ESTs of honeybee , and *Apis mellefera* was used as reference to annotate the transcript of the wasp. There was 39% match and therefore observed a strong correlation between expression levels of the two species. Illumina and SOLiD particularly produces short reads which are useful for gene expression profiling. RNA-seq was done to monitor yeast vegetative growth (Nagalakshmi *et al.*, 2008) and mouse embryonic stem cell differentiation (Cloonan *et al.*, 2008). RNA-seq has made better resolvability of start and ends of most transcripts. It has high resolution and sensitivity, because of that, many novel transcribed regions and splicing isoforms of known genes are mapped. These novel regions suggested that there is high transcriptomic complexity than what was known earlier. Small RNA analysis is an application of NGS to discover novel small RNAs and their profiling. Till date , 454 technologies have been used to study small RNA profiles of the moss *Physcomitrella patens* (Axtell *et al.*, 2006), *Triticum aestivum* (Yao *et al.*, 2007) , the unicellular alga *Chlamydomonas reinhardtii* (Zhao *et al.*, 2007), Marek disease virus (Burnside *et al.*, 2006), and some primates (Berezikov *et al.*, 2006). Deeper small RNA libraries can be generated using the higher throughput of Illumina and SOLiD technologies. Illumina sequencing has been used to identify 334 known and 104 novel miRNA genes expressed in embryonic cells (Morin *et al.*, 2008b). Besides, small RNA profiling has been reported in *Xenopus tropicalis* (Armisen *et al.*, 2009),*Gossypium hirsutum* L. (Pang *et al.*, 2009) and *Caenorhabditis elegans* embryo (Stoeckius *et al.*, 2009).

CONCLUSION

Next generation sequencing technology has been exploited to enable important applications in human genetics such as SNP detection, heterozygosity and microbiome detection. It has given a chance for large scale data retrieval with minimal cost. The data coverage, efficiency and quality are far better than the methods opted earlier. NGS has a range of applications in finding new variations, complex disease markers, evolutionary studies and role of non coding RNA in health sector. The expected development in NGS is to obtain good-quality data from single cell genome which would be helpful in cancer studies. Because of the everyday advancements in NGS technologies, this has become a golden period for the genomic studies. The NGS technology has much relevance in this post genomic era.

ACKNOWLEDGEMENTS

The authors acknowledge the facilities of the Department of Biotechnology, Ministry of Science and Technology, Government of India, New Delhi (DBT) under the Bioinformatics sub centre in the preparation of this manuscript.

REFERENCE

Armisen, J., Gilchrist, M.J. , Wilczynska, A. , Standart, N. , and Miska, E.A . 2009. Abundant and dynamically expressed miRNAs, piRNAs, and other small RNAs in the vertebrate Xenopus tropicalis . Genome Res. 19 : 1766 – 1775 .

Axtell, M.J., Jan, C., Rajagopalan, R., and Bartel, D.P. 2006. A two- hit trigger for siRNA biogenesis in plants. Cell. 127: 565 – 577.

Bamshad, M.J., Ng. SB., Bigham, A.W., Tabor, H.K., Emond, M.J., Nickerson, D.A., and Shendure, J . 2011. Exome sequencing as a tool for Mendelian disease gene discovery. Nature Reviews Genetics. 11(12): 745-755

Barbara, A., Nelson, Karen, E., Pop, Mihai, Creasy, Heather, H., Giglio, Michelle, G., Huttenhower, Curtis, Gevers, Dirk, Petrosino, Joseph, F. *et al.* 2012. A framework for human microbiome research .Nature. 486 (7402): 215–221.

Bentley, D. R. *et al.* 2008. Accurate whole human genome sequencing using reversible terminator chemistry.Developers from Illumina/Solexa and colleagues report details on their reversible terminator platform and demonstrate the technology by sequencing a flow-sorted X chromosome and the genome from a Yoruban male. Nature 456: 53–59.

Berezikov, E., Thuemmler, F., Van, Laake, L.W., Kondova, I. , Bontrop, R. , Cuppen, E. , and Plasterk, R.H . 2006. Diversity of microRNAs in human and chimpanzee brain. Nat Genet. 38: 1375 – 1377.

Bing, D. H., Boles, C., Rehman, F. N., Audeh, M., Belmarsh, M., Kelley, B., and Adams, C. P. 1996. Bridge amplification: a solid phase PCR system for the amplification and detection of allelic differences in single copy genes. Genetic Identity Conference Proceedings, Seventh International Symposium on Human Identification.

Brent, M.R. 2008. Steady progress and recent breakthroughs in the accuracy of automated genome annotation. Nat Rev Genet. 9: 62 – 73.

Butler, T. Z., Pavlenok, M., Derrington, I., Niederweis, M., and Gundlach, J. 2008. Single-molecule DNA detection with an engineered MspA protein nanopore. Proc. Natl. Acad. Sci. 106 (9): 20647-20652.

Chan, E.Y. 2005. Single Nucleotide Polymorphisms (SNPs): Detection, Interpretation, and Applications Advances in sequencing technology. 3:13–40.

Chin, C.S., Sorenson, J., Harris, J.B., *et al.* 2011. The origin of the Haitian cholera outbreak strain. New England Journal of Medicine. 364(1):33–42.

Cloonan, N. , Forrest, A.R.R. , Kolle, G. , Gardiner, B.B.A. , Faulkner, G.J. , Brown, M.K. , Taylor, D.F. , Steptoe, A.L. , Wani, S. , Bethel, G. , *et al.* 2008.Stem cell transcriptome profiling via massive – scale mRNA sequencing. Nat Methods. 5: 613 – 619.

DiGuistini, S. , Liao, N.Y. , Platt, D. , Robertson, G. , Seidel, M. , Chan, S.K. , Docking, T.R. , Birol, I. , Holt, R.A. , Hirst, M. , *et al.* 2009 . De novo genome sequence assembly of a filamentous fungus using Sanger, 454 and Illumina sequence data. Genome Biol. 10(9): R94.

Durbin, R. M., Abecasis, D. L., Altshuler, R. M., Auton, G. A. R., Brooks, D. R., Durbin, A., Gibbs, A. G., Hurles, F. S., McVean, F. M., Donnelly, P., Egholm, M., Flicek, P., Gabriel, S. B., Gibbs, R. A., Knoppers, B. M., Lander, E. S., Lehrach, H., Mardis, E. R., McVean, G. A., Nickerson, D. A., Peltonen, L., Schafer, A. J., Sherry, S. T., Wang, J., Wilson, R. K., Gibbs, R. A., Deiros, D., Metzker, M., Muzny, D., Reid, J. 2010. A map of human genome variation from population-scale sequencing. Nature. 467 (7319): 1061–1073

Faller, M. *et al.* 2004 .The structure of a mycobacterial outer-membrane channel. Science.303 (5661):1189-1192.

Garaj, S., Hubbard, W., Reina, A., Kong, J., Branton, D., and Golovchenko, J. 2010. Graphene as a sub-nanometer trans-electrode membrane. Nature. 467 (7312): 190–193.

Gharizadeh, B., Ghaderi, M. and Nyren, P. 2007. Pyrosequencing technology for short DNA sequencing and whole genome sequencing. Technology. 47: 129-132.

Gharizadeh, B., Ohlin, A., Molling, P., Backman, A., Amini, B., Olcen, P. and Nyren, P. 2003a. Multiple group-specific sequencing primers for reliable and rapid DNA sequencing. Mol. Cell Probes.17: 203-210.

Goldberg, S.M.D. , Johnson, J. , Busam, D. , Feldblyum, T. , Ferriera, S. , Friedman, R. , Halpern, A. , Khouri, H. , Kravitz, S.A ., Lauro, F.M. *et al.* 2006 . A Sanger/pyrosequencing hybrid approach for the generation of high - quality draft assemblies of marine microbial genomes. Proc Natl Acad Sci U S A. 103: 11240 – 11245.

Harismendy, O. *et al.* 2009. Evaluation of next generation sequencing platforms for population targeted sequencing studies. Genome Biol. 10(3): R32

Huang, S. , Li, R. , Zhang, Z. , Li, L. , Gu, X. , Fan, W. , Lucas, W.J. , Wang, X. , Xie, B. , Ni, P. , *et al.* 2009 . The genome of the cucumber, Cucumis sativus L. Nat Genet. 41: 1275 – 1281.

Iafrate, A. J. *et al.* 2004. Detection of large-scale variation in the human genome. Nature Genet. 36: 949–951.

Imelfort, M. and Edwards, D. 2009. De novo sequencing of plant genomes using second - generation technologie . Brief Bioinform . 10 : 609 – 618 .

Jacquier, A. 2009. The complex eukaryotic transcriptome: Unexpected pervasive transcription and novel small RNAs. Nat Rev Genet. 10: 833 – 844.

Korlach, P.J., Marks, R.L., Cicero, J.J., Gray, D.L., Murphy, D.B., Roitman, T.T., Pham, G.A., Otto, M., and Foquet, S.W. 2008. Turner, Selective aluminum passivation for targeted immobilization of single DNA polymerase molecules in zero-mode waveguide nanostructures. PNAS. 105: 1176-1181.

Levene, M.J., Korlach, J., Turner, S.W., Foquet, M., Craighead, H.G., and Webb, W.W. 2003. Zero-Mode waveguides for Single-Molecule Analysis at high concentrations. Science. 299: 682-686.

Li, R. , Fan, W. , Tian, G. , Zhu, H. , He, L. , Cai, J. , Huang, Q. , Cai, Q. , Li, B., Bai, Y. , *et al.* 2010 . The sequence and de novo assembly of the giant panda genome. Nature. 463: 311 – 317.

Li, H., Ruan, J. and Durbin, R. 2008. Mapping short DNA sequencing reads and calling variants using mapping quality scores. Genome Res. 18:1851–1858.

Macevicz, S. C.1995. US Patent. 5750341.

Maher, B. 2012. "ENCODE: The human encyclopaedia". Nature 489 (7414): 46–48.

McNally, B., Singer, A., Yu, Z., Sun, Y., Weng, Z., and Meller, A. 2010. Optical recognition of converted DNA nucleotides for single molecule DNA sequencing using nanopore arrays. Nano Lett. 10 (6): 2237-2244.

Metzker, M. L. 2009. Sequencing in real time. Nature Biotech. 27: 150–151.

Mills, R.E., Walter, K., Stewart, C., *et al.* 2011. Mapping copy number variation by population-scale genome sequencing. Nature. 470(7332) :59–65.

Morin, R.D. , O'Connor, M.D. , Griffith, M. , Kuchenbauer, F. , Delaney, A. , Prabhu, A.L. , Zhao, Y. , McDonald, H. , Zeng, T. , Hirst, M. , *et al.* 2008b . Application of massively parallel sequencing to microRNA profi ling and discovery in human embryonic stem cells. Genome Res. 18: 610 – 621.

Nagalakshmi, U. , Wang, Z. , Waern, K. , Shou, C. , Raha, D. , Gerstein, M. , and Snyder, M . 2008. The transcriptional landscape of the yeast genome defi ned by RNA sequencing. Science. 320: 1344 – 1349.

Nyren, P. and Skarpnack, S.E. 2001. Method of sequencing DNA based on the detection of the release of pyrophosphate and enzymatic nucleotide degradation. U.S. Patent 6258568. http://ip.com/patent/US6258568.

Pang, M. , Woodward, A.W. , Agarwal, V. , Guan, X. , Ha, M. , Ramachandran, V. , Chen, X. , Triplett, B.A. , Stelly, D.M. , and Chen, Z.J . 2009. Genome - wide analysis reveals rapid and dynamic changes in miRNA and siRNA sequence and expression during ovule and fi ber development in allotetraploid cotton (Gossypium hirsutum L.) . Genome Biol . 10 : R122 .

Park, P. J. , 2009. ChIP–seq: advantages and challenges of a maturing technology .Nature Reviews Genetics. 10: 669-680.

Purnell, R., Mehta, K., and Schmidt, J. 2008. Nucleotide identification and orientation discrimination of DNA homopolymers immobilized in a protein nanopore. Nano Letters. 8(9): 3029-3034.

Reinhardt, J.A., Baltrus, D.A., Nishimura, M.T., Jeck, W.R., Jones, C.D., and Dangl, J.L. 2009. De novo assembly using low-coverage short read sequence data from the rice pathogen Pseudomonas syringae pv. oryzae. Genome Research.19(2) :294–305

Ren, B., Robert, F., Wyrick, J.J., Aparicio, O, Jennings, E.G., *et al.* 2000. Genome-wide location and function of DNA binding proteins. Science. 290: 2306–2309.

Ronaghi, M., Uhlén, M. and Nyrén, P. 1998. A sequencing method based on real-time pyrophosphate. Science. 281: 363–365.

Shendure, J. *et al.* 2005. Accurate multiplex polony sequencing of an evolved bacterial genome. Science. 309: 1728–1732.

Skovgaard, O., Bak, M., Løbner-Olesen, A., *et al.* 2011. Genome-wide detection of chromosomal rearrangements, indels, and mutations in circular chromosomes by short read sequencing. Genome Research. 21(8) :1388–1393

Solomon, M.J., Larsen, P.L. and Varshavsky, A. 1988. Mapping protein-DNA interactions in vivo with formaldehyde: evidence that histone H4 is retained on a highly transcribed gene. Cell 53:937–947.

Soni, G., Singer, A., Yu, Z., Sun, Y., McNally, B., and Meller, A. 2010. Synchronous optical and electrical detection of biomolecules traversing through solid-state nanopores. Rev. Sci. Instru. 81: 014301-014307.

Stoddart, D., Heron, A., Mikhailova, E., Maglia, G., and Bayley, H. 2009. Single-nucleotide discrimination in immobilized DNA oglionucleoties with a biological nanopore. Proc. Natl. Acad. Sci. USA. 106: 7702–7707.

Toth, A.L. , Varala, K. , Newman, T.C. , Miguez, F.E. , Hutchison, S.K. , Willoughby, D.A. , Simons, J.F. , Egholm, M. , Hunt, J.H. , Hudson, M.E. , *et al.* 2007. Wasp gene expression supports an evolutionary link between maternal behavior and eusociality. Science. 318: 441 – 444.

Turner, D.J., Keane, T.M., Sudbery, I., and Adams, D.J. 2009a. Next - generation sequencing of vertebrate experimental organisms . Mamm Genome. 20: 327 – 338 .

Velasco, R. , Zharkikh, A. , Troggio, M. , Cartwright, D.A. , Cestaro, A. , Pruss, D. , Pindo, M. , Fitzgerald, L.M. , Vezzulli, S. , Reid, J. , *et al.* 2007 . A high quality draft consensus sequence of the genome of a heterozygous grapevine variety. PLoS One. 2(12) : e1326 .

Wang, Z., Gerstein, M. and Snyder, M. 2009. RNA-Seq: a revolutionary tool for transcriptomics. Nature Rev. Genet. 10: 57–63.

Wheeler, D. A. *et al.* 2008. The complete genome of an individual by massively parallel DNA sequencing. Nature. 452: 872–876.

Wold, B. and Myers, R. M. 2008. Sequence census methods for functional genomics. Nature Methods. 5:19–21.

Yao, Y., Guo, G., Ni, Z. , Sunkar, R. , Du, J. , Zhu, J.K. , and Sun, Q . 2007. Cloning and characterization of microRNAs from wheat (Triticum aestivum L.) . Genome Biol. 8(6) : R96.

Zhao, T., Li, G., Mi, S., Li, S., Hannon, G.J. , Wang, X.J. , and Qi, Y . 2007. A complex system of small RNAs in the unicellular green alga Chlamydomonas reinhardtii . Genes Dev. 21: 1190 – 1203.

❑❑❑

CHAPTER - 5

Next Generation Sequencing: A Way to Accelerate the Upcoming Epigenetic Research

Shailja Dwivedi and Afroz Alam*
Department of Bioscience and Biotechnology
Banasthali Vidyapith, Tonk-304 022 (India)
E-mail: Afrozalamsafvi@gmail.com

ABSTRACT

Genomics is a relatively new scientific discipline, having DNA sequencing as its core technology. As technology has improved the cost and scale of genome characterization over sequencing's 40-year history, the scope of investigation has commensurately broadened. Demand has never been greater for revolutionary technologies that deliver fast, inexpensive and accurate genome information. This challenge has catalyzed the development of next-generation sequencing (NGS) technology. Over the past few years, massively parallel DNA sequencing platforms have become widely available, reducing the cost of DNA sequencing by over two orders of magnitude, and democratizing the field by putting the sequencing capacity of a major genome center in the hands of individual investigators. These new technologies are rapidly evolving, and near-term challenges include the development of strong protocols for generating sequencing libraries, building effective new approaches to data-analysis, and often a rethinking of experimental design. Next-generation DNA sequencing has the potential to dramatically accelerate biological and biomedical research, by enabling the comprehensive analysis of genomes, transcriptomes and interactomes to become inexpensive, routine and widespread, rather than requiring significant production-scale efforts. This article explains the methods, advantages and disadvantages of methods and softwares of Next Generation Sequencing with its impact and applications on genomics and other related field of biology.

INTRODUCTION

The field of DNA sequencing technology development has a rich and diverse history (Inaki *et al.*, 2011; Sanger, 1988). However, the overwhelming majority of DNA sequence production to date has relied on some version of the Sanger biochemistry (Sanger, 1988). Over the past five years, the incentive for developing entirely new strategies for DNA sequencing (Sanger *et al.*, 1977) has emerged on at least four levels, undeniably reinvigorating this field. First, in the wake of the Human Genome Project (HGP), there are few remaining avenues of optimization through which significant reductions in the cost of conventional DNA sequencing can be achieved. Second, the potential utilities of short-read sequencing has been tremendously strengthened by the availability of whole genome assemblies for *Homo sapiens* and all major model organisms, as these effectively provide a reference against which short reads can be mapped. Third, a growing variety of molecular methods have been developed, whereby a broad range of biological phenomena can be assessed by high-throughput DNA sequencing (e.g., genetic variation, RNA expression, protein-DNA interactions and chromosome conformation). And fourth, general progress in technology across disparate fields, including microscopy, surface chemistry, nucleotide biochemistry, polymerase engineering, computation, data storage and others, have made alternative strategies for DNA sequencing increasingly practical to realize. Here, we review the current crop of next-generation DNA sequencing platforms: how they work, their relative strengths and limitations, and its current and emerging applications. We briefly discuss related developments in this field, such as new software tools and front-end methods for isolating arbitrary genomic subsets. We emphasized that the DNA sequencing technology field has become a quickly moving target and will make a very frequent technology of 21st century. As this technology helps to develop human genome project also can be help in many different fields of biological sciences (Bernstein *et al*, 2012; Boyle *et al*, 2012; Taiwo *et al.*, 2012).

HISTORY

(Deoxyribonucleic acid) DNA was demonstrated as the genetic material by Oswald Theodore Avery in 1944. Its double helical strand structure composed of four bases was determined by James D. Watson and Francis Crick in 1953, leading to the central dogma of molecular biology. In most cases, genomic DNA defined the species and individuals, which makes the DNA sequence fundamental to the research on the structures and functions of cells and the decoding of life mysteries (Church and Gilbert, 1984). DNA sequencing technologies could help biologists and health care providers in a broad range of applications such as molecular cloning, breeding, finding pathogenic genes, and comparative and evolution studies. In 1977, Frederick Sanger developed DNA sequencing technology which was based on chain-termination method (also known as Sanger sequencing), and Walter Gilbert developed another sequencing technology based on chemical modification of DNA and subsequent cleavage at specific bases. Because of its high efficiency and low radioactivity, Sanger sequencing was adopted as the primary technology in the "first generation" of laboratory and commercial sequencing applications (http://en.wikipedia.org/wiki/DNA-sequencing/). At that time, DNA sequencing was laborious and radioactive materials were required. After years of improvement, Applied Bio-systems introduced the first automatic sequencing machine (namely AB370) in 1987, adopting capillary electrophoresis which made the sequencing faster and more accurate. AB370 could detect 96 bases one time, 500 K bases a day, and the read length could reach 600 bases. The current model AB3730xl can output 2.88 M bases per day and read length could reach 900 bases since 1995. Emerged in 1998, the automatic sequencing instruments and associated software using the capillary sequencing machines and Sanger sequencing technology became the main tools for the completion of human genome project in 2001 (Collins *et al.*, 2003). This project (Next generation sequencing) greatly stimulated the development of powerful novel sequencing instrument to increase speed and accuracy, while simultaneously reducing cost and manpower. Not only this, X-prize also accelerated the development of next-generation sequencing (NGS) (Fujimoto *et al.*, 2012).

The NGS technologies are different from the Sanger method in aspects of massively parallel analysis, high throughput, and reduced cost. Although NGS makes genome sequences handy, the followed data analysis and biological explanations are still the bottle-neck in understanding genomes. Following the human genome project, '454' was launched by 454 in 2005, and Solexa released Genome Analyzer the next year, followed by (Sequencing by Oligo Ligation Detection) SOLiD provided from Agencourt, which are three most typical massively parallel sequencing systems in the next-generation sequencing (NGS) that shared good performance on throughput, accuracy, and cost compared with Sanger sequencing. These founder companies were then purchased by other companies: in 2006 Agencourt was purchased by Applied Biosystems, and in 2007, 454 were purchased by Roche, while Solexa was purchased by Illumina. After years of evolution, these three systems exhibit better performance and their own advantages in terms of read length, accuracy, applications, consumables, man power requirement and informatics infrastructure, and so forth.

Global advantages of second-generation or cyclic-array strategies, relative to Sanger sequencing, include the following:

- *In vitro* construction of a sequencing library, followed by *in vitro* clonal amplification to generate sequencing features, circumvents several bottlenecks that restrict the parallelism of conventional sequencing (that is, transformation of *E. coli* and colony picking).
- Array-based sequencing enables a much higher degree of parallelism than conventional capillary-based sequencing. As the effective size of sequencing features can be on the order of 1μm, hundreds of millions of sequencing reads can potentially be obtained in parallel by rastered imaging of a reasonably sized surface area.
- Because array features are immobilized to a planar surface, they can be enzymatically manipulated by a single reagent volume. Although micro liter scale reagent volumes are used in practice, these are essentially amortized over the full set of sequencing features on the array, dropping the effective reagent volume per feature to the scale of pico-liters or femtoliters. Collectively, these differences translate into dramatically lower costs for DNA sequence production.

Technologies Used in Next Generation Sequencing

To study about the methods used in next generation sequencing it's very necessary to know that which technologies were used in the first generation sequencing and how the technologies of next generation sequencing were developed. As we described about a very little in history about the first generation sequencing methods now here detail is described-

First Generation sequencing

Sanger method

Since the early 1990s, DNA sequence production has almost exclusively been carried out with capillary-based, semi-automated implementations of the Sanger biochemistry (Sanger, 1988). In high-throughput production pipelines, DNA to be sequenced is prepared by one of two approaches: first, for shotgun *de novo* sequencing, randomly fragmented DNA is cloned into a high-copy-number plasmid, which is then used to transform *Escherichia coli;* or second, for targeted re-sequencing, PCR amplification is carried out with primers that flank the target. The output of both approaches is an amplified template, either as many 'clonal' copies of a single plasmid insert present within a spatially isolated bacterial colony that can be picked, or as many PCR amplicons present within a single reaction volume. The sequencing biochemistry takes place in a 'cycle sequencing' reaction, in which cycles of template denaturation, primer annealing and primer extension are performed. The primer is complementary to known sequence immediately flanking the region of interest. Each round of primer extension is stochastically terminated by the incorporation of fluorescently labeled di de oxy nucleotides (ddNTPs). In the resulting mixture of end-labeled extension products, the label on the terminating ddNTP of any given fragment corresponds to the nucleotide identity of its terminal position. Sequence is determined by high-resolution electrophoretic separation of the single-stranded, end-labeled extension products in a capillary based polymer gel. Laser excitation of fluorescent labels as fragments of discreet lengths exit the capillary, coupled to four-color detection of emission spectra, provides the readout that is represented in a Sanger sequencing 'trace'. Software translates these traces into DNA sequence, while also generating error probabilities for each base-call (Ewing and Green, 1998; Ewing, 1998). The approach that is taken for subsequent analysis, for example, genome assembly or variant identification depends on precisely what is being sequenced and why? Simultaneous electrophoresis in 96 or 384 independent capillaries provides a limited level of parallelization.

After three decades of gradual improvement, the Sanger biochemistry can be applied to achieve read-lengths of up to ~1,000 bp, and per-base 'raw' accuracies as high as 99.999%. In the context of high-through-put shotgun genomic sequencing, Sanger sequencing costs on the order of $0.50 per kilobase.

Next Generation Sequencing

Five platforms for massively parallel DNA sequencing read production are in reasonably widespread use at present: 454 sequencing (used in the 454 Genome Sequencers, Roche Applied Science; Basel), Solexa technology (used in the Illumina (San Diego) Genome Analyzer), the SOLiD platform (Applied Biosystems; Foster City, CA, USA), the Polonator (Dover/Harvard) and the HeliScope Single Molecule Sequencer technology (Helicos; Cambridge, MA, USA).

> **Emulsion PCR (ePCR):** method for DNA amplification that uses water in oil emulsion to isolate single DNA molecules in aqueous microreactors

The concept of cyclic-array sequencing can be summarized as the sequencing of a dense array of DNA features by iterative cycles of enzymatic manipulation and imaging-based data collection15 (Shendure, 2005). Two reports in 2005 described the first integrated implementations of cyclic-array strategies that were both practical and cost-competitive with conventional sequencing (McKernan, 2006), and other groups have quickly followed (Berezikov, 2006).

Sequencing technologies include a number of methods that are grouped broadly as template preparation, sequencing and imaging, and data analysis.

The unique combination of specific protocols distinguishes one technology from another and determines the type of data produced from each platform. These differences in data output present challenges when comparing platforms based on data quality and cost. Although quality scores and accuracy estimates are provided by each manufacturer, there is no consensus that a 'quality base' from one platform is equivalent to that from another platform There are two methods used in preparing templates for NGS reactions: clonally amplified templates originating from single DNA molecules, and single DNA molecule templates. These methods are classified as cyclic reversible termination (CRT), single-nucleotide addition (SNA) and real-time sequencing. Sequencing by ligation (SBL), an approach in which DNA polymerase is replaced by DNA ligase, is also described. Imaging methods coupled with these sequencing strategies range from measuring bioluminescent signals to four-color imaging of single molecular events. The voluminous data produced by these NGS platforms place substantial demands on information technology in terms of data storage, tracking and quality control (Rausch *et al.*, 2012).

Template preparation

Current methods involve randomly breaking genomic DNA into smaller sizes from which either fragment templates or mate-pair templates are created. A common theme among NGS technologies is that the template is attached or immobilized to a solid surface or support. The immobilization of spatially separated template sites allows thousands to billions of sequencing reactions to be performed simultaneously.

Clonally amplified templates

Emulsion PCR (ePCR): method for DNA amplification that uses water in oil emulsion to isolate single DNA molecules in aqueous microreactors

Most imaging systems have not been designed to detect single fluorescent events, so amplified templates are required. The two most common methods are emulsion PCR (ePCR) (Eid *et al.*, 2009) and solid-phase amplification (Collins, 2003). ePCR is used to prepare sequencing templates in a cell-free system, which has the advantage of avoiding the arbitrary loss of genomic sequences –a problem that is inherent in bacterial cloning methods. A library of fragment or mate-pair targets is created, and adaptors containing universal priming sites are ligated to the target ends, allowing complex genomes to be amplified with common PCR primers. After ligation, the DNA is separated into single strands and captured onto beads under conditions that favour one DNA molecule per bead. After the successful amplification and enrichment of ePCR beads, millions can be immobilized in a polyacrylamide gel on a standard microscope slide (Polonator) (Sjoblom *et al.*, 2006), chemically crosslinked to an aminocoated glass surface (Life/APG; Polonator) (Kloosterman *et al.*, 2011) or deposited into individual PicoTiterPlate (PTP) wells (Roche/454) (Lu *et al.*, 2007) in which the NGS chemistry can be performed. Solid-phase amplification can also be used to produce randomly distributed, clonally amplified clusters from fragment or mate-pair templates on a glass slide. High-density forward and reverse primers are covalently attached to the slide, and the ratio of the primers to the template on the support defines the surface density of the amplified clusters. Solid-phase amplification can produce 100–200 million spatially separated template clusters (Illumina/Solexa), providing free ends to which a universal sequencing primer can be hybridized to initiate the NGS reaction.

Single-molecule templates

Although clonally amplified methods offer certain advantages over bacterial cloning, some of the protocols are cumbersome to implement and require a large amount of genomic DNA material (3–20 μg). The preparation of single-molecule templates is more straightforward and requires less starting material (<1 μg). More importantly, these methods do not require PCR, which creates mutations in clonally amplified templates that masquerade as sequence variants. AT-rich and GC-rich target sequences may also show amplification bias in product yield, which results in their underrepresentation in genome alignments and assemblies. Quantitative applications, such as RNA–seq5, perform more effectively with non-amplified template sources, which do not alter the representational abundance of mRNA molecules. Before the NGS reaction is carried out, single molecule templates are usually immobilized on solid supports using one of at least three different approaches. In the first approach, spatially distributed individual primer molecules are covalently attached to the solid support (Hardin *et al.*, 2000). The template, which is prepared by randomly fragmenting the starting material into small sizes (for example, ~200–250 bp) and adding common adaptors to the fragment ends, is then hybridized to the immobilized primer. In the second approach, spatially distributed single- molecule templates are covalently attached to the solid support (Hardin *et al.*, 2000) by priming and extending single-stranded, single-molecule templates from immobilized primers. A common primer is then hybridized to the template. In either approach, DNA polymerase can bind to the immobilized primed template configuration to initiate the NGS reaction. Both of the above approaches are used by Helicos BioSciences. In a third approach, spatially distributed single polymerase molecules are attached to the solid support (Eid *et al.*, 2009), to which a primed template molecule is bound. This approach is used by Pacific Biosciences (Eid *et al.*, 2009) and is described in patents from Life/visiGen (Hardin *et al.*, 2000) and LI-COR Biosciences (Williams, 1998). Larger DNA molecules (up to tens of thousands of base pairs) can be used with this technique and, unlike the first two approaches; the third approach can be used with real-time methods, resulting in potentially longer read lengths.

Sequencing and Imaging

There are fundamental differences in sequencing clonally amplified and single-molecule templates. Clonal amplification results in a population of identical templates, each of which has undergone the sequencing reaction. Upon imaging, the observed signal is a consensus of the nucleotides or probes added to the identical templates for a given cycle. This places a greater demand on the efficiency of the addition process, and incomplete extension of the template ensemble results in lagging-strand dephasing. The addition of multiple nucleotides or probes can also occur in a given cycle, resulting in leading-strand dephasing. Signal dephasing increase fluorescence noise, causing base-calling errors and shorter reads (Erlich *et al.*, 2008), because dephasing is not an issue with single-molecule templates, the requirement for cycle efficiency is relaxed. Single molecules, however, are susceptible to multiple nucleotide or probe additions in any given cycle. Here, deletion errors will occur owing to quenching effects between adjacent dye molecules or no signal will be detected because of the incorporation of dark nucleotides or probes. In the following sections, sequencing and imaging strategies that use both clonally amplified and single-molecule templates are discussed.

> **16S metagenic sequencing**
>
> A common amplicon sequencing application is comparing the bacterial 16S rRNA gene, a widely used method for studying phylogeny and taxonomy. This method has been used to evaluate bacterial diversity in many environments, allowing researchers to characterize microbiomes from samples that in parallels, is uniquely suited to this application. The ability to pool samples and obtain high sequence coverage during a single run allows NGS to identify rarer varients that are missed, or too expensive to identify using CE based sequencing approaches.

Cyclic reversible termination

As the name implies, CRT uses reversible terminators in a cyclic method that comprises nucleotide incorporation, fluorescence imaging and cleavage. In the first step, a DNA polymerase, bound to the primed template, adds or incorporates just one fluorescently modified nucleotide, which represents the complement of the template base. The termination of DNA synthesis after the addition of a single nucleotide is an important feature of CRT. Following incorporation, the remaining unincorporated nucleotides are washed away. Imaging is then performed to determine the identity of the incorporated nucleotide. This is followed by a cleavage step, which removes the terminating/ inhibiting group and the fluorescent dye. Additional washing is performed before starting the next incorporation step.

The key to the CRT method is the reversible terminator, of which there are two types: 32 blocked and 32 unblocked. The use of a dideoxynucleotide, which acts as a chain terminator in Sanger sequencing, provided the basis for the initial development of reversible blocking groups attached to the 32 end of nucleotides (Metzker, 1994). Blocking groups, such as 32 -*O*-allyl- 22 -deoxyribonucleoside triphosphates (dNTPs) (32) and 32 -*O*-azidomethyl-dNTPs (Guo *et al.*, 2008), have been successfully used in CRT. 32 -blocked terminators require the cleavage of two chemical bonds to remove the fluorophore from the nucleobase and restore the 32 -OH group.

Sequencing by ligation

SBL is another cyclic method that differs from CRT in its use of DNA ligase (Tomkinson *et al.*, 2011) and either one-base-encoded probes or two-base-encoded probes. In its simplest form, a fluorescently labeled probe hybridizes to its complementary sequence adjacent to the primed template. DNA ligase is then added to join the dye-labeled probe to the primer. Non-ligated probes are washed away, followed by fluorescence imaging to determine the identity of the ligated probe36. The cycle can be repeated either by using cleavable probes to remove the fluorescent dye and regenerate a 52 -PO_4 group for subsequent ligation cycles or by removing and hybridizing a new primer to the template.

Shendure and colleagues (Sjoblom *et al.*, 2006.) used the SBL method to sequence the *Escherichia coli* mG1655 genome.SBL method is being used on the Polonator instrument. Life/APG has commercialized their SBL platform called support oligonucleotide ligation detection (SOLiD) (Williams, 1998).

Single-nucleotide addition: pyrosequencing

Pyrosequencing is a non-electrophoretic, bioluminescence method that measures the release of inorganic pyrophosphate by proportionally converting it into visible light using a series of enzymatic reactions (Ronaghi *et al.*, 1996; Ronaghi *et al.*, 1996). Unlike other sequencing approaches that use modified nucleotides to terminate DNA synthesis, the pyrosequencing method manipulates DNA polymerase by the single addition of a dNTP in limiting amounts. Upon incorporation of the complementary dNTP, DNA polymerase extends the primer and pauses. DNA synthesis is reinitiated following the addition of the next complementary dNTP in the dispensing cycle. The order and intensity of the light peaks are recorded as flowgrams, which reveal the underlying DNA sequence.

Margulies and colleagues (Margulies *et al.*, 2005) described the first NGS platform to integrate pyrosequencing using their PTP device. Commercialized by Roche/454, the instrument uses DNA templates prepared by emPCR, with 1–2 million beads deposited into PTP wells.

Real-time sequencing

The next technology method to hit the commercial sector is likely to be real-time sequencing, and Pacific Biosciences is currently leading this effort (Eid, J. *et al.*, 2009). Unlike reversible terminators, real-time nucleotides do not halt the process of DNA synthesis. Simply put, the method of real-time sequencing involves imaging the continuous incorporation of dye-labelled nucleotides during DNA synthesis (Metzker ML. 2009). With the Pacific Biosciences platform, single DNA polymerase molecules are attached to the bottom surface of individual zero-mode waveguide detectors (Zmw detectors) (Leamon, 2003) that can obtain sequence information while phospholinked nucleotides are being incorporated into the growing primer strand (Eid *et al.*, 2009)

Next Generation Sequencing Platforms

The following sections aim to introduce the reader to the primary features of most widely used next-generation platforms.

Charge-coupled device (CCD): a capacitor array used in optical scanners to capture images

Roche/454 pyrosequencing

This next-generation sequencer was the first to achieve commercial introduction (in 2004) and uses an alternative sequencing technology known as pyrosequencing. In pyrosequencing, each incorporation of a nucleotide by DNA polymerase results in the release of pyrophosphate, which initiates a series of downstream reactions that ultimately produce light by the firefly enzyme luciferase. The amount of light produced is proportional to the number of nucleotides incorporated (up to the point of detector saturation). In the Roche/ 454 approach, the library fragments are mixed with a population of agarose beads whose surfaces carry oligonucleotides complementary to the 454-specific adapter sequences on the fragment library, so each bead is associated with a single fragment. Each of these fragment: bead complexes is isolated into individual oil: water micelles that also contain PCR reactants, and thermal cycling (emulsion PCR) of the micelles produces approximately one million copies of each DNA fragment on the surface of each bead. These amplified single molecules are then sequenced en masse. First the beads are arrayed into a picotiter plate (PTP; a fused silica capillary structure) that holds a single bead in each of several hundred thousand single wells, which provides a fixed location at which each sequencing reaction can be monitored. Enzyme containing beads that catalyze the downstream pyrosequencing reaction steps are then added to the PTP and the mixture is centrifuged to surround the agarose beads. On instrument, the PTP acts as a flow cell into which each pure nucleotide solution is introduced in a step wise fashion, with an imaging step after each nucleotide incorporation step. The PTP is seated opposite a CCD camera that records the light emitted at each bead. The first four nucleotides (TCGA) on the adapter fragment adjacent to the sequencing primer added in library construction correspond to the sequential flow of nucleotides into the flow cell. This strategy allows the 454 base-calling software to calibrate the light emitted by a single nucleotide incorporation. However, the calibrated base calling cannot properly interpret long stretches (>6) of the same nucleotide (homo-polymer run), so these areas are prone to base insertion and deletion errors during base calling. By contrast, because each incorporation step is nucleotide specific, substitution errors are rarely encountered in Roche/454 sequence reads.

Illumina Genome Analyzer

> **Bridge amplification:** allows the generation of *in situ* copies of a specific DNA molecule on an oligo-decorated solid support

Commonly referred to as 'the Solexa', this platform has its origins in work by Turcatti and colleages (Fedurco M, *et al.*, 2006) and the merger of four companies—Solexa (Essex, UK), Lynx Therapeutics (Hayward, CA, USA), Manteia Predictive Medicine (Coinsins, Switzerland) and Illumina. The single molecule amplification step for the Illumina Genome Analyzer starts with an Illumina-specific adapter library, takes place on the oligo-derivatized surface of a flow cell, and is performed by an automated device called a Cluster Station. The flow cell is an 8-channel sealed glass micro-fabricated device that allows bridge amplification of fragments on its surface, and uses DNA polymerase to produce multiple DNA copies, or clusters, that each represents the single molecule that initiated the cluster amplification. A separate library can be added to each of the eight channels, or the same library can be used in all eight, or combinations thereof. Each cluster contains approximately one million copies of the original fragment, which is sufficient for reporting incorporated bases at the required signal intensity for detection during sequencing.

The Illumina system utilizes sequencing by- synthesis approach in which all four nucleotides are added simultaneously to the flow cell channels, along with DNA polymerase, for incorporation into the oligo-primed cluster fragments. Specifically, the nucleotides carry a base-unique fluorescent label and the 3′-OH group is chemically blocked such that each incorporation is a unique event. An imaging step follows each base incorporation step, during which each flow cell lane is imaged in three 100-tile segments by the instrument optics at a cluster density per tile of 30,000. After each imaging step, the 3′ blocking group is chemically removed to prepare each strand for the next incorporation by DNA polymerase. This series of steps continues for a specific number of cycles, as determined by user-defined instrument settings, which permits discrete read lengths of 25–35 bases. A base-calling algorithm assigns sequences and associated quality values to each read and a quality checking pipeline evaluates the Illumina data from each run, removing poor-quality sequences.

Applied Biosystems SOLiD™ Sequencer

This platform has its origins in the system described by J.S. and colleagues (Shendure *et al.*, 2005) in 2005 and in work by McKernan and colleagues (McKernan *et al.*, 2006) at Agencourt Personal Genomics (Beverly, MA, USA) (acquired by Applied Biosystems (Foster City, CA, USA) in 2006).

The SOLiD platform uses an adapter-ligated fragment library similar to those of the other next-generation platforms, and uses an emulsion PCR approach with small magnetic beads to amplify the fragments for sequencing. Unlike the other platforms, SOLiD uses DNA ligase and a unique approach to sequence the amplified fragments. Two flow cells are processed per instrument run, each of which can be divided to contain different libraries in up to four quadrants. Read lengths for SOLiD are user defined between 25–35 bp, and each sequencing run yields between 2–4 Gb of DNA sequence data. Once the reads are base called, have quality values, and low-quality sequences have been removed, the reads are aligned to a reference genome to enable a second tier of quality evaluation called two-base encoding.

Two key differences that speak to the utility of next-generation sequence reads are (*a*) the length of a sequence read from all current next generation platforms is much shorter than that from a capillary sequencer and (*b*) each next generation read type has a unique error model different from that already established for capillary sequence reads. Both differences affect how the reads are utilized in bio-informatics analyses, depending upon the application. For example, in strain-to-reference comparisons (resequencing), the typical definition of repeat content must be revised in the context of the shorter read length. In addition, a much higher read coverage or sampling depth is required for comprehensive resequencing with short reads to adequately cover the reference sequence at the depth and low gap size needed.

HeliScope

The Helicos sequencer (Harris *et al.*, 2008), based on work by Quake's Group (Braslavsky *et al.*, 2003), also relies on cyclic interrogation of a dense array of sequencing features. However, a unique aspect of this platform is that no clonal amplification is required. Instead, a highly sensitive fluorescence detection system is used to directly interrogate single DNA molecules via sequencing by synthesis. Template libraries, prepared by random fragmentation and poly-A tailing (that is, no PCR amplification), are captured by hybridization to surface-tethered poly-T oligomers to yield a disordered array of primed single-molecule sequencing templates.

At each cycle, DNA polymerase and a single species of fluorescently labeled nucleotide are added, resulting in template-dependent extension of the surface-immobilized primer-template duplexes. After acquisition of images tiling the full array, chemical cleavage and release of the fluorescent label permits the subsequent cycle of extension and imaging. As described in a recent report (Harris *et al.*, 2008), several hundred cycles of single-base extension (that is, A, G, C, T, A, G, C, T) yield average read-lengths of 25 bp or greater.

Notable aspects of this system include the following. First, like the 454 platform, the sequencing is asynchronous, as some strands will fall ahead or behind others in a sequence-dependent manner. Second, no terminating moiety is present on the labeled nucleotides. As with the 454 system, therefore, homo-polymer runs are an important issue. Third, the raw sequencing accuracy can be substantially improved by a two-pass strategy in which the array of single-molecule templates (here with adaptors at both ends) is sequenced as described above, and then fully copied. As the newly synthesized strand is surface-tethered, the original template can be removed by denaturing. Sequencing primed from the distal adaptor then yields a second sequence for the same template, obtained in the opposite orientation. Positions that are concordant between the two reads have *phred*-like quality scores approaching (Braslavsky *et al.*, 2003).

Advantage and disadvantage of different approaches

In terms of costs, limitations and practical aspects of implementation, clear differences between conventional sequencing and the second-generation platforms determine which general strategy represents the best option for any given project. The applications of conventional sequencing (that is, Sanger) have grown diverse, and for small-scale projects in the kilobase-to-megabase range, this will likely remain the technology of choice for the immediate future. This is a consequence of its greater 'granularity' (that is, the ability to efficiently operate at either small or large production scales) relative to the new technologies. Even so, it is clear that despite limitations relative to Sanger sequencing (e.g., in terms of read-length and accuracy), large-scale projects will quickly come to depend entirely on next-generation sequencing. As an example of the advantages of the new platforms, consider that large-scale resequencing studies for identifying germlines variation or somatic mutations have relied on Sanger-based resequencing approaches, that in turn are reliant on one-at-a-time PCR amplification of each targeted region (Stahlhut Espinosa *et al.*, 2006, Zhao *et al.*, 2007) a recent informal survey of the overall cost to conventionally sequence 100 genes from 100 samples, assuming each gene has an average of 10 exons, quoted estimates from noncommercial genome centers and commercial sequence service providers ranged from $300,000 to over $1,000,000. Clearly, this cost is beyond the range of most individual laboratories. In addition to reducing the per-base cost of sequencing by several orders of magnitude, second-generation instruments have fewer infrastructure requirements; instead, the principle challenge is downstream data management.

Genome sequencing in cancer

High-throughput sequencing of cancer genomes has been a major factor in the understanding of the genetics of this complex disease. Exome sequencing, RNA sequencing, paired end sequencing and whole-genome sequencing of cancer genomes have led to a dramatic increase in the number of known recurrent somatic alterations, such as mutations, amplifications, deletions and translocations (Bass *et al.*, 2011; Salzman *et al.*, 2011; Fujimoto *et al.*, 2012).A recent example, using paired-end sequencing, Inaki *et al.* (2011) discovered that approximately half of all structural rearrangements in breast cancer genomes result in fusion transcripts, where single segmental tandem duplication spanning multiple genes is a major source. They estimated that 44% of these fusion transcripts are potentially translated, and found a novel RPS6KB1 VMP1 fusion gene that is recurrent in a third of breast cancer samples analyzed, with potential association with prognosis. Simultaneously, Hillmer *et al.* (2011) applied paired-end sequencing on cancer and non-cancer human genomes, and found that non-cancer genomes contain more inversion, deletions and insertions, whereas cancer genomes are dominated by duplications, translocations and complex rearrangements. Recent works from Korbel et al and others have found that cancer genomes lacking p53 often contain genomic regions that undergo extensive rearrangements called 'chromothripsis', suggestive of complex chromosome shattering and rejoining in a single event (Nowell, 1976; Korbel *et al.*, 2007; Stratton *et al.*, 2009; Kloosterman *et al.*, 2011; Stephens *et al.*, 2011; Tubio and Estivill, 2011; Rausch *et al.*, 2012).

There are important differences among the second-generation platforms themselves (Table 1). Some applications (e.g., resequencing) may be more tolerant of short read-lengths than others (e.g., *de novo* assembly). The cost of sequencing varies greatly between the second-generation platforms, and as consumers, we hope for more competition between dealers than was the case with conventional sequencing in the past decade. Comparisons of 'per-base' costs can be helpful but occasionally misleading, as, for example, more accurate bases may be worth more than less accurate bases.

Table 1: Second-generation DNA sequencing technologies

Instrument	Feature generation	Sequencing by synthesis	Cost per megabase	Paired Ends?	1° error modality	Read-length	Ref.
452	Emulsion PCR	Polymerase (pyrose-quencing)	~$60-$500,000	Yes	Indel	250 bp	40,11
Solexa	Bridge PCR	Polymerase (reversible terminators)	~$2-$430,000	Yes	Subst	36 bp	3,16
SOLiD	Emulsion PCR	Ligase (octamers with two-base encoding)	~$2-$591,000	Yes	Subst	35 bp	58,41
Polonator	Emulsion PCR	Ligase (nonamers)	~$1-$155,000	Yes	Subst	13 bp	58,11
Heloscope	Single molecule	Polymerase (asynchronous extensions)	~$1-$1,350,000	Yes	Del	30 bp	18,5

Software for NGS

The diversity and rapid evolution of next-generation sequencing technology is posing challenges for bioinformatics in areas including sequence quality scoring, alignment, assembly and data release. These are discussed in more detail below.

Sequence quality

The topic of sequence quality scoring has become an area of intense interest, given the relatively low quality of raw data from the new sequencing platforms, and the various context dependent error distributions associated with different sequencing by synthesis biochemistries. As second-generation sequencing matures and the range of biological and clinical problems to which it is applied expands, it will be critical to have clear metrics in place for data quality, reliability, reproducibility and biological relevance. Given the nascent state of the field, there is an opportunity to establish an early consensus of standardized benchmarks for comparing current and newly introduced platforms, and, it is hoped, avoid the dilemmas of data comparison that have occurred in the past

Chromatin immune-precipitation (ChIP): chemical cross linking of DNA and proteins, and immune-precipitation using a specific antibody to determine DNA:protein associations in vivo

Serial analysis of gene expression (SAGE): measures the quantitative expression of genes in an mRNA population sample by generating SAGE tags that are then sequenced

Noncoding RNA (ncRNA): any native RNA that is transcribed but not translated into a protein

microRNA (miRNA): 21–23-base RNA molecules that participate in RNA induced silencing of gene expression

with multi-vendor genomic technologies, such as microarrays. Multiple applications will benefit from standardized quality metrics. This might include metrics to quantify the general quality of *de novo* sequence assemblies; metrics for the confidence associated with individual read alignments to a reference; metrics for confidence in raw and consensus base-calls for improved polymorphism and mutation discovery; and general quality control and assurance metrics for large-scale sequencing projects.

Examples of areas that should be systematically evaluated in assessered sequencing data quality with new sequencing platforms include: (i) technical reproducibility; (ii) distribution of estimated accuracies for raw base-calls (e.g., *phred*-like scores); (iii) systematic error patterns in raw or consensus sequence data; (iv) bias and skewing of true ratios in tag-counting applications.

Software and bioinformatics tools for data analysis

Even at this early stage of commercial availability, a variety of software tools are available for analyzing next-generation sequencing data as-Cross_match, ELAND, Exonerate, MAQ, Mosaik, RMAP, SHRiMP, SOAP, SSAHA2, SXOligoSearch, ALLPATHS, Edena, Euler-SR, SHARCGS, SHRAP, SSAKE, VCAKE, Velvet, PyroBayes, PbShort, ssahaSNP Their functions fit into several general categories, including: (i) alignment of sequence reads to a reference; (ii) base-calling and/or polymorphism detection; (iii) *de novo* assembly, from paired or unpaired reads; and (iv) genome browsing and annotation.

Next generation sequencing and its impact on genomics

Genomics is a relatively new scientific discipline, having DNA sequencing as its core technology. As technology has improved the cost and scale of genome characterization over sequencing's 40-year history, the scope of inquiry has commensurately broadened. Massively parallel sequencing has proven revolutionary, shifting the paradigm of genomics to address biological questions at a genome-wide scale. Sequencing now empowers clinical diagnostics and other aspects of medical care, including disease risk, therapeutic identification, and prenatal testing. Next-generation sequencing technologies have had an incredible impact on our knowledge of human genetic diseases over a very short time frame. Whether this trend will continue rests on a variety of issues, some quite complex. For example, the size of whole-human-genome data sets remains large, and this poses significant challenges for data download and storage and for computational infrastructure. Data privacy of human subjects is paramount but is increasingly difficult to control, raising concerns in the public that may inhibit consent by individuals to participate in genetic studies. Ethical aspects overshadow the return of information to study participants and individuals seeking genetic diagnosis due to our remaining ignorance about the pathologic and functional consequences of variation in the human genome. The next few years will determine which applications of NGS are incorporated into the clinical diagnostic setting, many of which may benefit patients but yet may not be covered by insurers. Even as this scenario plays out, it is undoubtedly the case that NGS will continue to be a revolutionary force in basic biomedical and biological genomics inquiry for some time to come.

Single-cell sequencing in embryonic stem cell developmental biology

Previously, transcriptome analyses and whole-genome sequencing required a large number of cells, which made it inherently difficult to study gene expression or genomic variation within rare totipotent and pluripotent cell populations or within early embryos consisting of only a limited number of cells. How so many cell types can be derived from each pluripotent stem cell, and how each stem cell 'knows' how to behave differently, has been an area of intense research. Indeed, within early animal embryos, each cell is likely to express specific transcriptional programs that define its eventual developmental fate (Gage and Verma, 2003; Sylvester and Longaker, 2004).

With the emergence of technologies that allow single-cell expression analysis, expression programs in 64-cell human blastocysts were determined resulting in the identification of distinct markers uniquely expressed in the different cell types of the blastocyst (Guo *et al.*, 2008). Single-cell RNA sequencing enabled an even more in-depth and comprehensive analysis of the stem cell transcriptome at a genome-wide manner. With such capabilities, Tang *et al.* (2009) identified over 1500 previously unknown splice junctions that could be critical for oogenesis.

Further comprehensive analysis of complex biological systems using single-cell approaches will undoubtedly provide new insights. It will likely reveal the myriad of underlying biological states that exist (e.g., cell cycle) as well as the role that stochastic events have in the formulation of complex cellular and developmental processes.

Applications of next generation sequencing

The past several years have seen an accelerating flurry of publications in which next-generation sequencing is applied for a variety of goals Important applications include: (i) full-genome resequencing or more targeted discovery of mutations or polymorphisms (ii) mapping of structural rearrangements, which may include copy number variation, balanced translocation breakpoints and chromosomal inversions; (iii) 'RNA-Seq', analogous to expressed sequence tags (EST) or serial analysis of gene expression (SAGE), where shotgun libraries derived from mRNA or small RNAs are deeply sequenced; the counts corresponding to individual species can be used for quantification over a broad dynamic range, and the sequences themselves can be used for annotation (e.g., splice junctions and transcript boundaries); (iv) large-scale analysis of DNA methylation, by deep sequencing of bisulfite-treated DNA; (v) 'ChIP-Seq', or genome-wide mapping DNA-protein interactions, by deep sequencing of DNA fragments pulled down by chromatin immune-precipitation. Over the next few years, the list of applications will undoubtedly grow, as will the sophistication with which existing applications are carried out.

Discovering non coding RNA

One of the most exciting areas of biological research in recent years has been the discovery and functional analysis of noncoding RNA (ncRNA) systems in different organisms. First described in plants, ncRNAs are providing new insights into gene regulation in animal systems as well, as recognized by the awarding of the Nobel Prize in Medicine and Physiology to Andrew and Mello in 2006. Perhaps the most profound impact of next-generation sequencing technology has been on the discovery of novel ncRNAs belonging to distinct classes in an extraordinarily diverse set of species (Axtell MJ, *et al.*, 2007; Berezikov *et al.*, 2006, Brennecke *et al.*, 2007; Houwing *et al.*, 2007,Kasschau *et al.*, 2007; Lu *et al.*, 2007; Ruby *et al.*, 2006; Zhao *et al.*, 2007). In fact, this approach has been responsible for the discovery of ncRNA classes in organisms not previously known to possess them (Ruby *et al.*, 2006). These discoveries are being coupled with an ever-expanding comprehension of the functions embodied by these unique RNA species, including gene regulation by a variety of mechanisms. In this regard, studying the roles of specific microRNAs (miRNAs) in cancer is helping to uncover certain aspects of the disease (Calin *et al.*, 2007; Stahlhut Espinosa and Slack, 2006). Noncoding RNA discovery is best accomplished by sequencing because the evolutionary diversity of ncRNA gene sequences makes it difficult to predict their presence in a genome with high certainty by computational methods alone. The unique structures of the processed ncRNAs pose difficulties for converting them into next-generation sequencing libraries, but remarkable progress has already been made in characterizing these molecules. With these barriers dissolving, the high capacity and low cost of next-generation platforms ensure that discovery of ncRNAs will continue at a rapid pace and that sequence variants with important functional impacts will also be determined. Because the readout from next-generation sequencers is quantitative, ncRNA characterization will include detecting expression level changes that correlate with changes in environmental factors, with disease onset and progression, and perhaps with complex disease on onset or severity, for example. Importantly, the discovery and characterization of ncRNAs will enhance the annotation of sequenced genomes such that, especially in model organisms and humans, the impact of mutations will become more broadly interpretable across the genome.

Future Possibilities

As this article has described, the advent and widespread availability of next-generation sequencing technology has ushered in an era in which DNA sequencing will become a more universal readout for an increasingly wide variety of front-end assays. However, more applications of next-generation sequencing, beyond those covered here, are yet to come. For example, genome resequencing will likely be used to characterize strains or isolates relative to high-quality reference genomes such as C. elegans, Drosophila, and human. Studies of this type will identify and catalog genomic variation on a wide scale, from single nucleotide polymorphisms (SNPs) to copy number variations in large sequence blocks (>1000 bases). Ultimately, resequencing studies will help to better characterize, for example, the range of normal variation in complex genomes such as the human genome, and aid in our ability to comprehensively view the range of genome variation in clinical isolates of pathogenic microbes, viruses, etc.

Epigenomic variation, as an extension of genome resequencing applications, also will be investigated using next-generation sequencing approaches that enable the ascertainment of genome-wide patterns of methylation and how these patterns change through the course of an organism's development, in the context of disease, and under various other influences. Perhaps the most exciting possibility engendered by the ability to use DNA sequencing to rapidly read out experimental results is the enhanced potential to combine the results of different experiments correlative analyses of genome-wide methylation, histone binding patterns, and gene expression, for example owing to the similar data type produced. The power in these correlative analyses is the power to begin unlocking the secrets of the cell.

CONCLUSION

Since 2004, the National Human Genome Research Institute has awarded more than $100 million for the development of NGS technologies (Schloss, 2008), and these awards have facilitated much of the progress in NGS to date, as well as several commercial developments. Many companies, including IBM, Oxford Nanopore Technologies, Intelligent Bio-Systems, LaserGen Inc. and NABsys, have NGS technologies at various stages of development and commercialization.

The production of billions of NGS reads has also challenged the infrastructure of existing information technology systems in terms of data transfer, storage and quality control, computational analysis to align or assembly read data, and laboratory information management systems for sample tracking and process management. Advances in bioinformatics are ongoing, and improvements are needed if these systems are to keep pace with the continuing developments in NGS technologies.

NGS technologies have an impressive range of applications, and more are being developed. In addition to the applications described above, NGS technologies are being used to characterize the evolutionary relationships of ancient genomes (Green *et al.*, 2006, Briggs, 2009), and to elucidate the role of noncoding RNAs in health and disease (Ponting *et al.*, 2009). In the not too distant future, it is foreseeable that NGS technologies could be used to obtain high-quality sequence data from a genome isolated from a single cell, which would be a substantial breakthrough, particularly for cancer genomics. For this to occur, advances will be needed in techniques for efficiently isolating intact long DNA molecules and in NGS methods for accurately reading the sequence content of these molecules. The field of NGS development and applications is a fast-moving area of research, which makes this an exciting time for genomic studies.

ACKNOWLEDGEMENTS

Authors are thankful to Prof. Aditya Shastri, Vice Chancellor, Banasthali Vidyapith (Rajasthan) and Prof. Vinay Sharma, Dean, Faculty of Science and Technology, for providing necessary facilities.

REFERENCES

Axtell MJ, Snyder JA, Bartel DP. 2007. Common functions for diverse small RNAs of land plants. Plant Cell 19:1750-69.

Bass AJ, Lawrence MS, Brace LE, Ramos AH, Drier Y, Cibulskis K, Sougnez C, Voet D, Saksena G, Sivachenko A, Jing R, Parkin M, Pugh T, Verhaak RG, Stransky N, Boutin AT, Barretina J, Solit DB, Vakiani E, Shao W *et al.*, 2011. Genomic sequencing of colorectal adenocarcinomas identifies a recurrent VTI1A-TCF7L2 fusion. Nat Genet 43: 964-968.

Bentley DR. 2006. Whole-genome re-sequencing. Curr. Opin. Genet. Dev. 16, 545-552.

Berezikov E, Thuemmler F, van Laake LW, Kondova I, Bontrop R, 2006. Diversity of microRNAs in human and chimpanzee brain. Nat. Genet. 38:1375-77.

Bernstein BE, Birney E, Dunham I, Green ED, Gunter C, Snyder M. 2012. An integrated encyclopedia of DNA elements in the human genome. Nature 489: 57-74.

Boyle AP, Hong EL, Hariharan M, Cheng Y, Schaub MA, Kasowski M, Karczewski KJ, Park J, Hitz BC, Weng S, Cherry JM, Snyder M. 2012. Annotation of functional variation in personal genomes using regulomedb. Genome Res 22: 1790-1797.

Braslavsky I, Hebert B, Kartalov E & Quake SR. 2003 Sequence information can be obtained from single DNA molecules. Proc. Natl. Acad. Sci. USA 100, 3960-3964.

Brennecke J, Aravin AA, Stark A, Dus M, Kellis M. 2007. Discrete small RNA-generating loci as master regulators of transposon activity in Drosophila. Cell 128:1089-103.

Briggs AW. 2009. Targeted retrieval and analysis of five Neandertal mtDNA genomes. Science 325, 318-321.

Calin GA, Liu CG, Ferracin M, Hyslop T, Spizzo R. 2007. Ultraconserved regions encoding ncRNAs are altered in human leukemias and carcinomas. Cancer Cell 12:215-29.

Canard, B. & Sarfati, R. 1994. DNA polymerase fluorescent substrates with reversible 3?-tags. Gene 148, 1-6.

Carthew, RW & Sontheimer EJ. 2009 Origins and mechanisms of miRNAs and siRNAs. Cell 136, 642-655.

Church GM and Gilbert W. 1984. "Genomic sequencing," Proceedings of the National Academy of Sciences of the United States of America, vol. 81, no. 7, pp. 1991-1995. http://en.wikipedia.org/wiki/DNA_sequencing/.

Dressman D, Yan H, Traverso G, Kinzler KW & Vogelstein B. 2003. Transforming single DNA molecules into fluorescent magnetic particles for detection and enumeration of genetic variations. Proc. Natl. Acad. Sci. USA 100, 8817-8822 (t 20).

Eid, J. *et al.*, 2009. Real-time DNA sequencing from single polymerase molecules. Science 323, 133-138.

Erlich Y, Mitra PP, dela Bastide M, McCombie WR & Hannon G J. 2008. Alta-Cyclic: a self-optimizing base caller for next-generation sequencing. Nature Methods 5, 679-682.

Ewing B & Green P. 1998. Base-calling of automated sequencer traces using phred. II. Error probabilities. Genome Res. 8, 186-194.

Ewing B, Hillier L, Wendl MC & Green P. 1998. Base-calling of automated sequencer traces using phred. I. Accuracy assessment. Genome Res. 8, 175-185.

Fedurco M, Romieu A, Williams S, Lawrence I & Turcatti G BTA. 2006. A novel reagent for DNA attachment on glass and efficient generation of solid-phase amplified DNA colonies. Nucleic Acids Res. 34, e22. (t 22)

Collins F S, Morgan M and Patrinos A. 2003. "The Human Genome Project: lessons from large scale biology," Science, vol. 300, no. 5617, pp. 286-290. http://genomics.xprize.org/

Fujimoto A, Totoki Y, Abe T, Boroevich KA, Hosoda F, Nguyen HH, Aoki M, Hosono N, Kubo M, Miya F, Arai Y, Takahashi H, Shirakihara T, Nagasaki M, Shibuya T, Nakano K, Watanabe-Makino K, Tanaka H, Nakamura H, Kusuda J. 2012. Whole genome sequencing of liver cancers identifies etiological influences on mutation patterns and recurrent mutations in chromatin regulators. Nat Genet 44: 760-764.

Gage FH and Verma IM. 2003. Stem cells at the dawn of the 21st century - Introduction. Proc Natl Acad Sci USA 100: 11817-11818

Green RE, rause J, Ptak SE, Briggs AW, Ronan MT, Simons JF, Du L, Egholm M, Rothberg JM,Paunovic M & Pääbo S. 2006. Analysis of one million base pairs of Neanderthal DNA. Nature 444, 330-336.

Guo G, Huss M, Tong GQ, Wang C, Li Sun L, Clarke ND, Robson P. 2010. Resolution of cell fate decisions revealed by single-cell gene expression analysis from zygote to blastocyst. Dev Cell 18: 675-685.

Guo J, Xu N, Li Z, Zhang S, Wu J, Kim DH, Sano Marma M, Meng Q, Cao H, Li X, Shi S, Yu L, Kalachikov S, Russo JJ, Turro NJ, Ju J. 2008. Four-color DNA sequencing with 3?-O-modified nucleotide reversible terminators and chemically cleavable fluorescent dideoxynucleotides. Proc. Natl Acad. Sci. USA 105, 9145-9150.

Hardin S, Gao X, Briggs J, Willson R & Tu SC. 2000. Methods for real-time single molecule sequence determination. US Patent 7,329,492.

Harris, T.D. *et al.*, 2008. Single-molecule DNA sequencing of a viral genome. Science 320, 106-109.

Hillmer AM, Yao F, Inaki K, Lee WH, Ariyaratne PN, Teo ASM,Woo XY, Zhang Z, Zhao H, Chen JP, Zhu F, So JBY, Salto-Tellez M, Poh WT, Zawack KFB, Nagarajan N, Gao S, Li G, Kumar V, Lim HPJ *et al.*, 2011. Comprehensive long-span paired-end-tag mapping reveals characteristic patterns of structural variations in epithelial cancer genomes. Genome Res 21: 665-675.

Houwing S, Kamminga LM, Berezikov E, Cronembold D, Girard A, *et al.,* 2007. A role for Piwi and piRNAs in germ cell maintenance and transposon silencing in zebrafish. Cell 129:69-82.

Hutchison CA, III. 2007. DNA sequencing: bench to bedside and beyond. Nucleic Acids Res. 35, 6227-6237.

Inaki K, Hillmer AM, Ukil L, Yao F, Woo XY, Vardy LA, Zawack KFB, Lee CWH, Ariyaratne PN, Chan YS, Desai KV, Bergh J, Hall P, Putti TC, Ong WL, Shahab A, Cacheux-Rataboul V, Karuturi RKM, Sung W-K, Ruan X *et al.,* 2011. Transcriptional consequences of genomic structural aberrations in breast cancer. Genome Res 21: 676-687.

Ju J, Kim DH, Bi Li, Meng Q, Bai X, Li Z, Li X, Marma MS, Shi S, Wu J, Edwards JR, Aireen Romu A, and Turro NJ. 2006. Four-color DNA sequencing by synthesis using cleavable fluorescent nucleotide reversible terminators. Proc. Natl. Acad. Sci. USA 103, 19635-19640 (2006).

Kasschau KD, Fahlgren N, Chapman EJ, Sullivan CM, Cumbie JS, *et al.,* 2007. Genome-wide profiling and analysis of Arabidopsis siRNAs. PLoS Biol. 5:e57.

Kim JB, Porreca GJ, Song L, Greenway SC, Gorham JM, Church GM, Seidman CE, Seidman JG. 2007. Polony multiplex analysis of gene expression (PMAGE) in mouse hypertrophic cardiomyopathy. Science 316, 1481-1484.

Kloosterman WP, Hoogstraat M, Paling O, Tavakoli-Yaraki M, Renkens I, Vermaat JS, van Roosmalen MJ, van Lieshout S, Nijman IJ, Roessingh W, van't Slot R, van de Belt J, Guryev V, Koudijs M, Voest E, Cuppen E. 2011. Chromothripsis is a common mechanism driving genomic rearrangements in primary and metastatic colorectal cancer. Genome Biol 12: R103.

Korbel JO, Urban AE, Affourtit JP, Godwin B, Grubert F, Simons JF, Kim PM, Palejev D, Carriero NJ, Du L, Taillon BE, Chen Z, Tanzer A, Saunders ACE, Chi J, Yang F, Carter NP, Hurles ME, Weissman SM, Harkins TT *et al.,* 2007. Paired-end mapping reveals extensive structural variation in the human genome. Science 318: 420-426.

Leamon, JH. 2003. A massively parallel PicoTiterPlate based platform for discrete picoliter-scale polymerase chain reactions. Electrophoresis 24,3769-3777.

Levene MJ. *et al.* Levene MJ, Korlach J, Turner SW, Foquet M, Craighead HG, Webb WW. 2003. Zero-mode waveguides for single molecule analysis at high concentrations. Science 299, 682-686.

Lu C, Meyers BC, Green PJ. 2007. Construction of small RNA cDNA libraries for deep sequencing. Methods 43:110-1.

Margulies, M. *et al.,* 2005. Genome sequencing in microfabricated high-density picolitre reactors. Nature 437, 376-380.

McKernan K, Blanchard A, Kotler L & Costa G. 2006. Reagents, methods, and libraries for bead-based sequencing. US patent application 20080003571.

Metzker ML, Raghavachari R, Richards S , Jacutin SE, Civitello A , Burgess K , and Gibbs RA. 1994. Terminarion of DNA synthesis by novel 3?-modified deoxyribonucleoside triphosphates. Nucleic Acids Res. 22, 4259-4267.

Metzker ML. 2009. Sequencing in real time. Nature Biotech. 27, 150-151.

Mitra RD & Church GM. 1999. In situ localized amplification and contact replication of many individual DNA molecules. Nucleic Acids Res. 27, e34.

Mitra RD, Shendure J, Olejnik J, Edyta Krzymanska O. & Church GM. 2003. Fluorescent in situ sequencing on polymerase colonies. Anal. Biochem. 320, 55-65.

Nowell PC. 1976. Clonal evolution of tumor-cell populations. Science 194: 23-28.

Ponting CP, Oliver PL & Reik W. 2009. Evolution and functions of long noncoding RNAs. Cell 136, 629-641.

Pop M & Salzberg SL. 2008. Bioinformatics challenges of new sequencing technology. Trends Genet. 24, 142-149.

Rausch T, Jones David TW, Zapatka M, Stu¨tz Adrian M, Zichner T, Weischenfeldt J, Ja¨ger N, Remke M, Shih D, Northcott Paul A, Pfaff E, Tica J, Wang Q, Massimi L, Witt H, Bender S, Pleier S, Cin H, Hawkins C, Beck C *et al.*, 2012. Genome sequencing of pediatric medulloblastoma links catastrophic dna rearrangements with TP53 mutations. Cell 148: 59-71.

Ronaghi M, Karamohamed S, Pettersson B, Uhlén M & Nyrén P. 1996. Real-time DNA sequencing using detection of pyrophosphate release. Anal. Biochem. 242, 84-89.

Ronaghi M, Uhlén M & Nyrén P. 1998. A sequencing method based on real-time pyrophosphate. Science 281, 363-365.

Ruby JG, Jan C, Player C, Axtell MJ, Lee W, *et al.*, 2006. Large-scale sequencing reveals 21U RNAs and additional microRNAs and endogenous siRNAs in C. elegans. Cell 127:1193-207.

Salzman J, Marinelli RJ, Wang PL, Green AE, Nielsen JS, Nelson BH, Drescher CW, Brown PO. 2011. ESRRA-C11orf20 is a recurrent gene fusion in serous ovarian carcinoma. PLoS Biol 9: e1001156.

Sanger F, Air GM, Barrell BG, Brown NL, Coulson AR, Fiddes CA, Hutchison CA, Slocombe PM, Smith M. 1977. Nucleotide sequence of bacteriophage phi X174 DNA. Nature 265,687-695.

Sanger F. 1988. Sequences, sequences, and sequences. Annu. Rev. Biochem. 57, 1-28.

Schloss, J. A. 2008. How to get genomes at one ten-thousandth the cost. Nature Biotech. 26, 1113-1115.

Shendure J, Mitra RD, Varma C & Church GM. 2004. Advanced sequencing technologies: methods and goals. Nat. Rev. Genet. 5, 335-344.

Shendure J, Porreca1 GJ Reppas NB, Lin X, McCutcheon JP, Rosenbaum AM, Wang MD, Zhang K, Mitra RD, Church GM. 2005. Accurate multiplex polony sequencing of an evolved bacterial genome. Science 309, 1728-1732.

Sjoblom, T. *et al.*, 2006. The consensus coding sequences of human breast and colorectal cancers. Science 314, 268-274.

Stahlhut Espinosa CE, Slack FJ. 2006. The role of microRNAs in cancer. Yale J. Biol. Med. 79:131-40.

Stephens PJ, Greenman CD, Fu B, Yang F, Bignell GR, Mudie LJ, Pleasance ED, LauKW, Beare D, Stebbings LA, McLaren S, Lin M-L, McBride DJ, Varela I, Nik-Zainal S, Leroy C, Jia M, Menzies A, Butler AP, Teague JW*et al.*, 2011. Massive genomic rearrangement acquired in a single catastrophic event during cancer development. Cell 144: 27-40.

Stratton MR, Campbell PJ, Futreal PA. 2009. The cancer genome. Nature 458: 719-724.

Sylvester KG, Longaker MT. 2004. Stem cells - review and update. Arch Surg 139: 93-99.

Taiwo O, Wilson GA, Morris T, Seisenberger S, ReikW, Pearce D, Beck S, Butcher LM. 2012. Methylome analysis using MeDIP-seq with low DNA concentrations. Nat Protoc 7: 617-636.

Tang F, Barbacioru C, Wang Y, Nordman E, Lee C, Xu N, Wang X, Bodeau J, Tuch BB, Siddiqui A, Lao K, Surani MA. 2009. mRNA-Seq whole-transcriptome analysis of a single cell. Nat Meth 6: 377-382.

Tomkinson AE, Vijaya kumar S, Pascal JM & Ellenberger T. 2006. DNA ligases: structure, reaction mechanism, and function. Chem. Rev. 106, 687-699.

Tubio JMC and Estivill X. 2011. Cancer: when catastrophe strikes a cell. Nature 470: 476-477.

Turcatti, G, Romieu A, Fedurco M & Tairi AP. 2008. A new class of cleavable fluorescent nucleotides: synthesis and optimization as reversible terminators for DNA sequencing by synthesis. Nucleic Acids Res. 36, e25.

Valouev A, Ichikawa J, Tonthat T, Stuart J, Ranade S, Peckham H, Zeng K, Malek JA, Costa G, McKernan K, Sidow A, Fire A, Johnson SM. 2008. A high-resolution, nucleosome position map of C. elegans reveals a lack of universal sequence-dictated positioning. Genome Res. 18, 1051-1063.

Williams JGK. 1998. System and methods for nucleic acid sequencing of single molecules by polymerase synthesis. US Patent 6,255,083.

Wood, L.D. *et al.*, 2007. The genomic landscapes of human breast and colorectal cancers. Science 318, 1108-1113.

Zhao T, Li G, Mi S, Li S, Hannon GJ, *et al.*, 2007. A complex system of small RNAs in the unicellular green alga Chlamydomonas reinhardtii. Genes Dev. 21:1190-203.

❑❑❑

CHAPTER - 6

Proteins in Plant Defence System : An Overview

Arpita Singh, Sujoy Saha, Ruchi Garg, Atul K. Pandey & A. B. Rai
Indian Institute of Vegetable Research, Varanasi (U.P.)-221305

INTRODUCTION

Plants are rich source of nutrients for most of the organisms including microbes' arthropods and vertebrates. There are various biotic *viz.* insects, weeds and pathogens and abiotic factors *viz.* temperature, humidity, salinity etc. that causes harm to plants. For yield loss due to pest EIL (Economic injury levels) calculation is important (Stern *et al*, 1959). EIL calculation will define economic damage (yield losses equal to management costs) in calculable terms. Since plants are sessile they cannot move to avoid the menace of these factors, but they have developed a unique way of structural, chemical, and protein-based defences which are specifically designed to detect and inhibit invading organisms before they are able to cause extensive damage. In response to the incitations by the pathogens some genes are activated which in turn codes for defence proteins (Grennan, 2006). Understanding how plants defend themselves from pathogens and herbivores is essential in order to protect our livelihood and nutritional security. In addition to proteins, plant anatomy and some of the ecological relationship also plays an important role in plant defense mechanism. Induction of plant resistance against fungi and bacteria was reported in 1900.

Plant Defenses

Plants unlike mammals lack adaptive immune system so they rely on innate immune system of each cell and gets signals from the infection sites (Dangl & Jones, 2001; Ausubel, 2005; Chisholm *et al.* 2006). Various biotic and abiotic stresses induce biochemical and physiological changes in plants system that prevents various pathogen invasions. These changes include physical strengthening of the cell wall (through lignification, suberization and callose deposition) or accumulation of phenolic compounds, phytoalexins and pathogenesis-related (PR) proteins (Bowles, 1990). Generally, plants evolved with two types viz. continuous and inducible defense mechanism. Continuous defense also called as constitutive or structural defense, always exists in plant include pre-formed structures (cell walls, waxy epidermal cuticles and bark) which provides protection as well as rigidity and strength to plants. Inducible or chemical defense is found at the site of injury, related with production of toxic substances and cell suicide. These toxic releases or secretions are known as defense related proteins or pathogenesis related proteins (PR proteins). Since production of these proteins requires high energy and nutrient requirement, they are produced exclusively only when the pathogen is detected by the plants. The induction of these PR proteins is connected with Systemic Acquired Resistance (SAR), which is analogous to innate immune system. Induction of these proteins is usually triggered by some biochemical like Salicylic acid (White, 1979) and ethephon (an ethylene-releasing compound) (Vera and Conejero, 1988) and are responsible for various metabolic changes. It has been very well examined in tobacco where successful establishment of Systemic acquired resistance (Malamy *et al.*, 1990) was due to production of endogenous salicylic acid. Salicylic acid is important in stress signal transduction pathway. Beside these, several defense actions like mimicry, camonflage, thigmonastic movements, leaf shedding and colour changes (Williams & Lawrence, 1981; Raven *et al.*, 2005), have been reported.

(a) Constitutive/Structural defense

Plants morphology and chemical composition are constitutive resistance properties (Stahl 1888; Fraenkel 1959). Apart from providing shape and strength, cell wall is the main line of defence against bacterial and fungal pathogen. It acts as an external barrier for pathogen invasion as well as gets stimulated to release some defense chemicals rapidly when the cell detects potential pathogens. Cell wall also contains pectins, which form hydrated gel, that helps in cementing neighbouring cells together and act as barrier for many soft rot pathogens as they target pectin to break cell (like in vegetables and fruits which becomes mushy and brown).

Other protective structures like lignin (in woody plants, highly impermeable to pathogens), cutin, suberin and waxes (fatty substances) are also found to act as defense structures (Heil & Bostock, 2002; Dow *et al.*, 2000). Trichomes (leaf hairs) are specialized epidermal cells on plant parts and provide both physical and chemical protection against insect pests as well as Lestivores. In potato and tomato, aphids are repelled by glandular trichomes (Pare & Tumlinson, 1999). In woody plants, the periderm replaces the epidermis on stems and roots. Outer bark (phellem) is a preformed structural barrier that contains high amounts of water-resistant suberin and prevents many pathogens and insects from reaching the living cells. Thorns and spines are modified structures that protect plants from grazing vertebrates.

(b) Chemical defense

In chemical defense, chemicals are released in response to infection. These chemicals are categorised into two types of metabolites i.e. Primary metabolite and secondary metabolite. Primary metabolites like sugars, proteins amino acids and nucleic acids, are produced by all plant cells that are directly involved in growth, physiological development and basic cell metabolism (Manuel *et al.*, 1985). Secondary metabolites are those substances which are not directly involved in growth or reproduction but they are often involved with plant defense. These compounds are usually terpenoids, phenolics, alkaloids and proteins.

Terpenoids (terpenes) are the largest class of secondary metabolites occurring in all plants and the simplest terpenoid is isoprene (C_5H_8). It is a volatile gas (hydrocarbon) emitted during photosynthesis in large quantities by leaves that may protect cell membranes from damage caused by high temperature or light. Monoterpenoids and sesquiterpenoids are essential oils, which are highly volatile compounds that contribute as insect toxins and protect the plant against fungal or bacterial attack. Citronella an essential oil isolated from lemon grass (*Cymbopogon citratus*) it contains high limonoid levels and has become a popular insect repellent due to its low toxicity in humans and biodegradable properties. Pyrethrins are monoterpenoid esters which act as insect neurotoxins (produced by chrysanthemum plants). The insecticides permethrin and cypermethrin are actually synthetic analogues of pyrethrins, called pyrethroids. Pine tree resin contains monoterpenoids alpha- and beta-pinene, which are also potent insect repellents.

Phenolics

Phenolics are the largest group of secondary metabolites, exhibiting defense action against pathogens. Their production in plants is mainly linked with shikimic acid and malonic acid pathways. For example Flavonoids, anthocyanins, phytoalexins, tannins, lignin, and furanocoumarins. Phytoalexins (isoflavonoids) are pathogen specific and possess both antibiotic and antifungal properties. These properties mainly target disrupting cellular structure and metabolism.

Tannins are water-soluble flavonoid polymers mainly produced by plants and stored in vacuoles. It is toxic to insects because it inactivates certain protein as it bind to salivary proteins and digestive enzymes including trypsin and chymotrypsin.

Lignins are branched heterogeneous polymer mainly present in secondary cell walls of plants. Lignin serves as an excellent physical barrier to pathogens as it is insoluble, rigid, and virtually indigestible.

Furanocoumarins are produced by a wide variety of plants in response to pathogen or herbivore attack.

Alkaloids such as caffeine (an alkaloid found in coffee (*Coffea arabica*), tea (*Camellia sinensis*), and cocoa (*Theobroma cacao*) is toxic to both insects and fungi. "Nicotine produced in the roots of tobacco plants (*Nicotiana tabacum*) are released when herbivores graze on the leaves and break open the vacuoles. Atropine, a neurotoxin and cardiac stimulant produced by the deadly nightshade plant (*Atropa belladonna*) is a secondary metabolite of plants and serves as a drug with a wide variety of effects. It is used for dilation of the pupils, as a pain reliever, muscle relaxer, and anti-inflammatory, and to treat menstrual problems, peptic ulcer disease, histaminic reaction, and motion sickness (Ebadi, 2007).

Antifungal proteins/ proteins or PR proteins and their types

Several anti fungal proteins viz. Pathogensesis-related (PR) proteins (Van Loon, 1989), proteinase inhibitors (Ryan, 1990), thionins (Bohlmann and Apel, 1991), permatins (Vigers *et al.*, 1991), ribosome-inactivating proteins (RIP) (Sinclair *et al.*, 1994) and lipid transfer proteins (LTP) (Terras *et al.*, 1992b) have been reported to play a key role in plant defense. Thaumatin-like (TL) proteins, defensins, cyclophilin-like protein, glycine/histidine-rich proteins killer proteins (killer toxins) also have a significant role in the activity of pathogens in plants (Agrawal *et al.*, 2000). Nomenclature of these proteins is based upon either mode of action, (e.g., glucanases), their structure (e.g., cysteine rich), or their similarity to a known "type" protein.

In many pathogenic fungi, chitin and β-1, 3-glucan are the major structural component of the cell walls and these antifungal proteins degrades the cell wall. During infection period, the rate of accumulation of these antifungal proteins increases.

Many proteins found in plants confer disease resistance and are Resistance Pathogen related called as (R) proteins or (PR) proteins. (PR) proteins are proteins produced in plants in the event of a pathogen attack (Loon, 1985). The production and release of these PR proteins by the plants in response to stress or invading pathogen (fungi, viruses) is of great importance. These PR proteins may be phytoalexins, antimicrobial peptides, and small proteins e.g., thionins (Bloch *et al*, 1998; Florach & Stiekema, 1994), defensins (Broekaert *et al.*,1995) hevein-like proteins, and knottin-like peptides (Segura *et al.* 1993) and up-regulate a number of antimicrobial proteins. These proteins were first discovered in tobacco (*Nicotiana tabacum*) plants reacting hypersensitively to tobacco mosaic virus infection (Gianinazzi *et al.*, 1970; Van Loon and Van Kammen, 1970). They detect the disease causing microorganisms like bacteria, virus, and fungi by specific pathogen effector molecules during infection cycle. Effectors molecules are generally pathogen proteins evolved for spread of pathogen life cycle in order to suppress the host. PR proteins play a major role in exploiting plant diseases either in either of two ways, induction of proteins by biotic or abiotic agents or over expressing of these proteins (transgenic plants). Many more or less closely related PR proteins have been detected in several plant species (Carr and Klessig, 1989; Bol and Linthorst, 1990; Bowles, 1990; Linthorst, 1991; White and Antoniw, 1991).

Properties and types of PR proteins

Generally in plants, PR proteins are of low molecular weight, acid-soluble, and protease-resistant proteins (Leubner & Meins, 1999; Neuhaus, 1999) possessing similar functions. The intercellular spaces are abundant with acidic PR proteins, whereas, basic PR proteins are predominantly located in the vacuole (Legrand *et al.*, 1987; Niki *et al.*, 1998; Van Loon & Van Strien, 1999).

Classification of the PR proteins is based on molecular mass, isoelectric point, localization and biological activity (Van Loon 1985). It is classically divided initially into 5 families' viz. PR-1, 2, 3, 4 & 5 and the division is based on serological and amino acid sequence analyses (Van Loon, 1985). These five families of PR-proteins are again categorised into two subclasses basd upon their isoelectric points:

- a basic subclass [located in vacuole of plant cell] and
- an acidic subclass [located in the extracellular space] Kitajima & Sato, 1999).

Recent studies shows that PR-proteins are categorized into 17 families depending upon their properties and functions including β-1,3-glucanases, chitinases, thaumatin-like proteins, peroxidases, ribosome-inactivating proteins, defenses, thionins, nonspecific lipid transfer proteins, oxalate oxidase, and oxalate-oxidase-like proteins (Van Loon & Van Strien, 1999)

PR-1 proteins

These types of proteins have molecular mass of ~15 to 17 kDa and show homology to the super family of cysteine-rich proteins. PR-1 proteins have been reported in rice, wheat, maize, tobacco, *Arabidopsis thaliana* and barley, (Agrawal *et al.*, 2000; Bryngelsson *et al.*, 1994; Molina *et al.*, 1999; Muradov *et al.*, 1993; Rauscher *et al.*, 1999). PR-1 protein accumulates in higher level after infection. It has been found that at micromolar level, PR-1 proteins have antifungal activity against various fungal pathogens like *Phytophthora infestans*, *Uromyces fabae* and *Erysiphe graminis* (*Niderman et al.*, 1995).

PR-2 proteins (β-glucanses)

PR-2 proteins are β-glucanases and possess *in vitro* (1, 3) β-*endoglucanase* activity. These proteins are reported in a wide variety of plants, including tobacco, *A. thaliana*, peas, grains, and fruits (Cote *et al.*,1991; Kim & Hwang, 1997; Rezzonico *et al.*, 1998) and depending upon their amino acid sequence analysis they are classified into three classes (Table-1) (Beffa & Meins,1996; Cote *et al.*, 1991; Leah *et al.*, 1991; Linthorst *et al.*, 1990; Meins *et al.*, 1992; Nielsen *et al.*,1997; Payne *et al.*,1990).

Table 1 : Nature, size, and location of PR-2 proteins

S. No.	Types	Nature	Size	Location in plant cell
1.	Class I	basic proteins	~ 33 kDa	plant vacuole
2.	Class II	Acidic	36 kDa	Extracellular
3.	Class III	Acidic	36 kDa	Extracellular

The major difference between class I proteins and the other two classes is that class I proteins are preproproteins (inactive proteins n protein precursor). (Alberts, 2002). These are processed into enzymatically active forms by post translational methods. These proteins are active against a wide number of fungi, including human and plant pathogens (e.g., *Rhizoctonia solani*, *C. albicans*, and *Aspergillus fumigatus*) at micromolar levels. β-1, 3-glucanases catalyze the cleavage of the β-1, 3-glucosidic bonds in β-1, 3-glucan or callose (Simmons, 1994), which is another important structural component of the cell walls of pathogenic fungi (Wessels & Sietsma, 1981; Adams, 2004). The structural (1,3)β-glucan which is present particularly at the hyphal apex of filamentous molds, gets hydrolyzed by the anti fungal (1,3)β-glucanases of PR-2 proteins of plant. This is because the enzyme gets most of its substrate (glucan) in fungal cell wall and thereby weakens the cell wall resulting in cell lysis. Production of oligosaccharide elicitors, which elicit the production of other PR proteins or low molecular weight antifungal compounds, such as phytoalexins is another indirect effect of β-1, 3-glucanases in plant defense.

PR-3 proteins (chitinases)

PR-3 proteins have molecular mass between 26 and 43 kDa (Nielsen *et al.*, 1997; Watanabe *et al.*, 1999) and chitinase falls in this group. Chitin is the major structural component of fungal cell walls and also of the exoskeleton of arthropods (Bartnicki-Garcia, 1968). In plants, chitinases are generally endo-chitinase. Endochitinases cleave cell wall chitin polymers in situ, resulting in a weakened cell wall and rendering fungal cells osmotically sensitive(Jach *et al.*,1995). There are two types of chitinases known, class I (located in vacuole) and class III (outside the cell) (Neuhaus, 1996). Chitin is generally degraded by these endochitinases and inhibits fungal growth (Broekaert, 1988; Schlumbaum, 1986). On the basis of their primary structures, plant chitinases have been classified into seven classes and among them class I chitinases have the highest antifungal activity due to the presence of a chitin-binding domain (Sela-Buurlage *et al.*, 1993). In transgenic plants, induction of chitinase was found to be higher. Transgenic plants showed delayed development of disease symptoms. One of the excellent example found in rice where chitinase gene was transformed, which shows increased resistance against fungus *Rhizoctonia solani* (sheath blight of rice) (Datta *et al.*, 2001).

PR-4 (chitin-binding) proteins

PR-4 proteins have molecular mass of 13-14.5 kDa and are also called as chitin-binding proteins. Sources of PR-4 proteins are mostly potato, tobacco, barley, tomato and they are classificed into two groups. (Friedrich *et al.*, 1991, Hejgaard *et al.*, 1992, Koo *et al.*,1998; Ponstein *et al* .,1994] Van Damme,1999). Class I proteins and Class II proteins.

- Class I are from the super family of chitin binding lectins and posses those amino acid sequence similar to chitin-binding polypeptide known as hevein (Friedrich *et al.*, 1991; Kouzuma *et al.*, 2000; Van Damme,1999)
- Class II proteins lack the chitin-binding hevein.

The two categories of PR-4 proteins also exhibit antifungal activity against *Trichoderma harzianum*, *Fusarium culmorum*, *F. graminearum*, and *B. cinerea*. There are some examples of non PR-4 chitin binding proteins and peptides which are actually not PR proteins like antifungal protein 1 (AFP1 found in Streptomyces tendae, 9.8 kDa) (Bormann, 1999), tachystatins (Kawabata *et al.*, 1996; Osaki *et al.*, 1999), penaeidins (Destoumieux *et al.*, 1997; Destoumieux *et al.*, 2000a; Destoumieux *et al.*, 2000b). But they act in the same way by binding to cell wall and disrupting polarity and thereby inhibit fungal pathogens.

PR-5 (Thaumatin like proteins-TL Proteins)

PR-5 proteins carry similar amino acid sequence like thaumatin protein and hence called as TL proteins. Major sources of TL proteins are *A. thaliana*

(Hu *et al.*, 1995, 1997), corn (Huynh *et al.*, 1992; , Roberts *et al.*, 1990),, soybeans, rice, wheat, tobacco (Koiwa *et al.*, 1997), tomato (Singh *et al.*,1987), pumpkin (Cheong *et al.*,1997), beans (Ye *et al.*, 1999), barley (Hejgaard *et al.*, 1991) and flax (Borgmeyer *et al.*, 1992).

Defensins

Defensins are a group of low-molecular-mass cysteine rich oligomeric proteins found in fungi (Lacadena *et al.*, 1995), insects (Lamberty, 1999) and plants (Broekaert *et al.*, 1995, Bull *et al.*, 1992). They were first isolated from the endosperm of barley (*Hordeum vulgare*) and wheat (*Triticum aestivum*). Fungal defensins ranges from 45-54 amino acids and are positively charged (Almeida *et al.*, 2000; Alves *et al.*, 1994). Defensins are classified into four groups (Segura *et al.*, 1998) (Table-2)

Table 2 : Classification of defensin

S. No.	Group	Function
1.	Group I (morphogenic defensins) changes in susceptible fungi	Causes morphological
2.	Group II (nonmorphogenic group) but do not cause morphological changes	inhibit fungal growth
3.	Group III	inhibit α-amylases in vitro
4.	Group IV	antifungal specificity and structure

Studies reported that defensin obtained from radish (Rs-AFP2) or dahlia (DM-AMP1), when applied on *Neurospora crassa* hyphae caused efflux of potassium ions and calcium uptake through binding to specific cell membrane receptors (Thevissen *et al.*; 1999; 2000). These are highly active and inhibit large number of plant fungal pathogens like *Botrytis cinerea, Alternaria brassicola, Fusarium. culmorum, Fusarium oxysporum, Fusarium. solani.*

Cyclophilin

Cyclophilins are found in vast group of organisms (bacteria, fungi, plants and animals). This protein is highly conserved groups and serves as intracellular receptors for cyclosporine (Ostoa-Saloma *et al.*, 2000). Protein called Mungin exhibited similarity with cyclophilin, was isolated from mung bean (*Phaseolus mungo*) and inhibited α- and β-glucosidases in vitro. Mungin, a 18 kDa proteins showed antifungal activity against *Rhizoctonia solani*, *Fusarium oxysporum*, *Botrytis. cinerea*, and *Coprinus comatus* (Ye *et al.*, 2000).

Glycine/histidine-rich proteins

The mode of action of these proteins mainly secreted by insects is yet to be understood, and they are highly rich in glycine/histidine. The most common human pathogen inhibited by this protein is *Candida albicans* (Dae-Hee *et al.*, 1998).

Ribosome-inactivating proteins (RIPs)

RIPs are actually RNA N-glycosidase that usually depurinate rRNA which results in ribosome damage leading to the arrest of protein synthesis (Table 3)(Barbieri *et al.*, 1993, Ferreras *et al.*, 1995; Hwu *et al.*, 2000, Langer *et al.*, 1996; Pu *et al.*, 1996, Taylor & Irvin, 1990). These RIPs have anti fungal activity as it is capable of inhibiting protein synthesis of bacteria, fungi, and plant both *in vitro* and *in vivo* (Iglesias *et al.*, 1993). Major sources of RIPs are Mirabilis expansa (Vivanco *et al.*, 1999), *Pisum sativum* (Lam *et al.*, 1998, Ye *et al.*, 2000) *Momordica charantia* (Leung *et al.*, 1997), and *Ricinus communis* (Arias *et al.*, 1994).

Table 3 : Classification of Ribosome inactivating proteins

S. No.	Types	Size (Mol. Mass)	Binding chain
1.	Type 1	11 to 30 kDa	single-chain N-glycosidases
2.	Type 2	~60 kDa	two chains, a cell binding lectin (B chain) and an N glycosidase (A chain),
3.	Type 3		four chains organized as two dimers of type 2 RIPs

Lipid Transfer Proteins (LTPs)

Lipid transfer proteins have a molecular weight of ~8.7 kDa and composed of ~90 amino acids stabilized by four disulfide bonds with a central tunnel-like hydrophobic cavity. These are small proteins and have been isolated from mammals, plants, fungi, and bacteria (Cammue *et al.*, 1995; Coutos-Thevenot *et al.*, 1993; Molina *et al.*, 1993; Nielsen *et al.*, 1996; Segura *et al.*, 1993; Tassin *et al.*, 1998;, Torres-Schumann *et al.*, 1992). The main function of LTPs is to transfer phospholipids between membranes. The mode of action of LTPs is not known but they are effective against a number of bacteria and fungi in in vitro.

Protease inhibitors

Examples of protease inhibitors are serine and cysteine. Serine (e.g., trypsin and chymotrypsin) and cysteine proteases have potent activity against plant and animal pathogens and emerged as a class of antifungal proteins.

Studies revealed that the serine protease inhibitors inhibited α-amylase activity of insects but not of bacteria (Schimoler-O'Rourke *et al.*, 2001)

Other proteins

Many other proteins are known with antifungal activity although their mode of action is not known *viz.* Viridin & Snakin-1. Viridin (molecular mass of 65kDa) isolated from the culture medium of Trichoderma viride and is reported to be active against sensitive fungi at 6 μ (Hao *et al.*, 1999, 2000) whereas Snakin-1 (6.9 kDa) isolated from potato is active at 10 μ (Segura *et al.*, 1999).

Role of Lectins

Plant lectins are defined as all plant proteins that possess at least one non catalytic domain that binds reversibly to a specific mono- or oligosaccharide. On the basis of overall structure, three major types of lectins are distinguished, namely "merolectins," "hololectins," and "chimerolectins", The discovery of first plant lectin was based on the binding of the castor bean lectin to glycoconjugates on the membranes of human red blood cells, So it is clear that lectin receptors must be present in the plant itself. The only plant protein, lectins are capable of recognizing and binding glycoconjugates present on the surface of microorganisms (i.e. bacteria and fungi). Some of the, main properties like stability under unfavourable conditions, stability over a wide range of pH, ability to withstand heat and resistant to animal and insect proteins, provides major support in favour of defense action of plant lectins and their close resemblance with other pathogenesis related proteins like protease inhibitors, chitinases and glucanases, RIPs, amylase inhibitors, antifungal proteins and thionin.

It is well known that whole plant is exposed to continuous threat of diseases and pests, though there are some parts that are most likely to attacked by predators and need extra protection. For e.g. seeds and resting storage organs which lack active defence system, are the most attractive sites for predators and parasites and are actively destroyed by them. On the contrary, plant system which is attacked by pest or insect can survive because it possesses passive defense system to protect their organs and seeds. Lectin accumulation in those parts supports the protective role of lectin.

In thorn apple (*Datura stramonium*), the movement of motile bacteria at the air water interface is blocked by seed lectin (Broekaert and Peumans, 1986). This block is generally related with the specific release of lectin from the seed coat and seed epidermis. This lectin prevents invasion of harmful bacteria through chemotactic movement of soil bacteria.

Transgenic plants and PR-proteins

It is known that pathogen invades the plant and tries to establish successfully in the host system. Though PR proteins are present but once pathogen gets entry, it tries to degrade the PR proteins rapidly. So in order to manage diseases, overproduction of these PR proteins in the early stages of infection cycle is required so that pathogen may be eliminated before its establishment. Thus PR proteins must be present in intracellular spaces where pathogen starts growing initially.PR proteins are present in intracellular (vacuoles) spaces and extracellular spaces but only vacoular PR proteins have anti fungal activity (Woloshuk *et al.,* 1991). So it is important that degradation of PR proteins must be checked and the plants should be induced to secrete basic chitinases and glucanase from apoplast region at an early stage. So a vacoular PR protein has to be targeted so that they may come out and growth can be checked. Genetic engineering emerged as a solution for combating this problem. It enables new way of disease management by incorporating various ways. For example, plants or bacteria possessing genes coding for enzymes like glucanase, chitinase, their transfer into host plant and expression of those genes results in breakdown of glucan or chitin (essential components of cell wall). With the introduction of plant genes, innate plant defense mechanism becomes active by releasing proteinase inhibitors, phytoalexins which play an important role in plant defense. Hypersensitive reaction is another mechanism through which plant can stop further infection at its infection site.

Proteins and signal induction

Plant defense is mediated through various signalling pathways which depend on interaction of several genes or proteins. Ubiquitin and Salicylic acid play a role in the resistance to pathogens by inducing the production of pathogenesis related proteins and has central role in cell signalling. It regulates several processes including protein degradation and immunological responses. The main functions of ubiquitin is to target proteins for destruction, is also useful in signaling pathways, hormone release, apoptosis, and translocation of materials throughout the cell. If there is any disturbance in ubiquitination, plant's immune system gets weakened due to invasion and successful establishment of pathogens and increases the accumulation of other harmful molecule (Trujillo & Shirasu., 2010). The plant signalling pathways are mainly controlled by negative feedback pathways and they are regulated by the de-ubiquitination enzymes, degradation of transcription factors, and the activation of transcription factors (Sadanandom *et al.,* 2012).

CONCLUSION

The potency of the PR proteins which are induced by plants after infection is a major system of defense against pathogen. Fungal cell wall degradation, pore formation, cellular ribosome damage and inhibition of DNA synthesis and infection cycle are the multi prolonged approaches adopted by the protective PR proteins to save the plants. The antifungal proteins are currently being used by agribusiness that helps in generating modified plants or transgenic plant which possess resistance against a wide range of microorganisms that may cause severe damage to crops. As chemicals continue to pose a threat to environment and ecology, these proteins will be the new to researches regarding crop production and sustainable production.

REFERNCES

Ausubel, F. M. Are innate immune signaling pathways in plants and animals conserved? Nature Immunol. 6, 973-979 (2005).

Agrawal G K, Jwa N S, Rakwal R. A novel rice (Oryza sativa L.) acidic PR1 gene highly responsive to cut, phytohormones, and protein phosphatase inhibitors. Biochem Biophys Res Commun. 2000;274:157-165.

Alberts, Bruce (2002). Molecular biology of the cell. New York: Garland Science. p. 760.

Adams DJ. Fungal cell wall chitinases and glucanases. Microbiology. 2004; 150: 2029-2035.

Almeida M S, Cabral K M, Zingali R B, Kurtenbach E. Characterization of two novel defense peptides from pea (Pisum sativum) seeds. Arch Biochem Biophys. 2000;378:278-286.

Alves A L, De Samblanx G W, Terras R R, Cammue B P, Broekaert W F. Expression of functional Raphanus sativus antifungal protein in yeast. FEBS Lett. 1994;348:228-232.

Arias F J, Rojo M A, Ferreras J M, Iglesias R, Munoz R, Soriano F, Mendez E, Barbieri L, Girbes T. Isolation and characterization of two new N-glycosidase type-1 ribosome-inactivating proteins, unrelated in amino-acid sequence, from Petrocoptis species. Planta. 1994;194:487-491.

Broekaert WF, Peumans WJ (1986) Lectin release from seeds of Datura stramonium and interference of the Datura strumonium lectin with bacterial motility. In TC Bog-Hansen, E Van Driessche, eds, Lectins, Biology, Biochemistry, Clinical Biochemistry, Vol 5. Walter de Gruyter, Berlin, pp 57-65.

Barbieri L, Batelli M G, Stirpe F. Ribosome-inactivating proteins from plants. Biochim Biophys Acta. 1993;1154:237-282. [Bormann C, Baier D, Horr I, Raps C, Berger J, Jung G, Schwartz H. Characterization of a novel, antifungal, chitin-binding protein Streptomyces tendae Tu901 that interferes with growth polarity. J Bacteriol. 1999; 181:7421-7429.

Broekaert W F, Terras F R, Cammue B P, Osborn R W. Plant defensins: novel antimicrobial peptides as components of host defense system. Plant Physiol. 1995;108:1353-1358.

Borgmeyer J R, Smith C E, Huynh Q K. Isolation and characterization of a 25 kDa antifungal protein from flax seeds. Biochem Biophys Res Commun. 1992; 187:480-487.

Broekaert WF, Van Parijs J, Allen A K, Peumans WJ. Comparison of some molecular, enzymatic and antifungal properties of chitinases from thorn-apple, tobacco and wheat. Physiol. Mol. Plant Pathol. 1988; 33: 319-331.

Bartnicki-Garcia S. Cell wall chemistry, morphogeneseis, and taxonomy of fungi. Ann. Rev. Microbiol. 1968; 22: 87-108.

Bryngelsson T, Sommer-Knudsen J, Gregersen P L, Collinge D B, Ek B, Thordal Christensen H. Purification, characterization, and molecular cloning of basic PR-1-type pathogenesis-related proteins from barley. Mol Plant Microbe Interact. 1994; 7:267-275.

Bowles DJ (1990) Defense-related proteins in higher plants. Annu Rev Biochem 59 873-907

Bol JF, Linthorst JM (1990) Plant pathogenesis-related proteins induced by virus infection. Annu Rev Phytopathol28 113-138

Broekaert W F, Terras F R, Cammue B P, Osborn R W. Plant defensins: novel antimicrobial peptides as components of host defense system. Plant Physiol. 1995;108:1353-1358.

Bloch C, Jr, Patel S U, Baud F, Zvelebil M J, Carr M D, Sadler P J, Thornton J M. 1H NMR structure of an antifungal ?-thionin protein SI?1: similarity to scorpion toxins. Proteins. 1998; 32:334-349.

Bohlmann H and Apel K (1991). Thionins. Annu. Rev. Plant Physiol. Plant Mol. Biol. 42 : 227-240

Bull J, Mauch F, Hertig C, Regmann G, Dudler R. Sequence and expression of a wheat gene that encodes a novel protein associated with pathogen defense. Mol Plant Microbe Interact. 1992;5:516-519.

Chisholm, S. T., Coaker, G., Day, B. & Staskawicz, B. J. Host-microbe interactions: shaping the evolution of the plant immune response. Cell 124, 803-814 (2006).

Carr JP, Klessig DF (1989). The pathogenesis-related proteins of plants. In JK Setlow, eds, Genetic Engineering: Principles and Methods, Vol 11. Plenum Press, New York, pp 65-109.

Cote F, Cutt J R, Asselin A, Klessig D F. Pathogenesis-related acidic ?-1, 3-glucanase genes of tobacco are regulated by both stress and developmental signals. Mol Plant Microbe Interact. 1991; 4:173-181.

Cheong N E, Choi Y O, Kim W Y, Bae I S, Cho M J, Hwang I, Kim J W, Lee S Y. Purification and characterization of an antifungal PR-5 protein from pumpkin leaves. Mol Cells. 1997; 7:214-219.

Cammue B P, Thevissen K, Hendriks M, Eggermont K, Goderis I J, Proost P, Van Damme J, Osborn R W, Guerbette F, Kader J C. A potent antimicrobial protein from onion seeds showing sequence homology to plant lipid transfer proteins. Plant Physiol. 1995;109:445-455.

Coutos-Thevenot P, Jounenne T, Maes O, Guerbette F, Grosbois M, Le Caer J P, Boulay M, Deloire A, Kader J C, Guern J. Four 9-kDa proteins excreted by somatic embryos of grapevine are isoforms of lipidtransfer proteins. Eur J Biochem. 1993;217:885-889.

Dae-Hee K, Lee Y T, Lee Y J, Chung J H, Lee B L, Choi B S, Younghoon L. Bacterial expression of tenecin 3, and insect antifungal protein isolated from Tenebrio molitor, and its efficient purification. Mol Cells. 1998;8:786-789.

Destoumieux D, Bulet P, Loew D, Van Dorsselaer A, Rodriguez J, Bachere E. Penaeidins, a new family of antimicrobial peptides isolated from the shrimp Penaeus vannamei (Decapoda) J Biol Chem. 1997;272:28398 -28406.

Destoumieux D, Munoz M, Bulet P, Bachere E. Penaeidins, a family of antimicrobial peptides from penaeid shrimp (Crustacea, Decapoda) Cell Mol Life Sci. 2000;57:1260-1271.

Destoumieux D, Munoz M, Cosseau C, Rodriguez J, Bulet P, Comps M, Bachere E. Penaeidins, antimicrobial peptides with chitin-binding activity, are produced and stored in shrimp granulocytes and released after microbial challenge. J Cell Sci. 2000; 113:461-469.

Datta K, Tu J, Oliva N, Ona I, Velazhahan R, Mew T W, Muthukrishnan S, Datta SK. Enhanced resistance to sheath blight by constitutive expression of infection-related rice chitinase in transgenic elite indica rice cultivars. Plant Sci. 2001; 160: 405-414.

Dow, M., M.A. Newman, and E. von Roepenack. 2000. The induction and modulation of plant defense responses by bacterial lipopolysaccharides. Annual Review of Phytopathology 38:241-261.

Dangl, J. L. & Jones, J. D. G. Plant pathogens and integrated defence responses to infection. Nature 411, 826-833 (2001).

Ebadi, Manuchair (2007). Pharmacodynamic Basis of Herbal Medicine. CRC Press. p. 203.

Fraenkel GS (1959) The raison d'etre of secondary plant substances: these odd chemicals arose as a means of protecting plants from insects and now guide insects to food. Science 129:1466-1470.

Florach D E, Stiekema W J. Thionins: properties, possible biological roles and mechanisms of action. Plant Mol Biol. 1994;26:25-37.

Friedrich L, Moyer M, Ward E, Ryals J. Pathogenesis-related protein 4 is structurally homologous to the carboxy-terminal domains of hevein, Win-1 and Win-2. Mol Gen Genet. 1991;230:113-119.

Ferreras J M, Iglesias R, Barbieri L, Alegre C, Bolognesi A, Rojo M A, Carbajales M L, Escarmis C, Girbes T. Effects and molecular action of ribosome-inactivating proteins on ribosomes from Streptomyces lividans. Biochim Biophys Acta. 1995;1243:85-93.

Gianinazzi S, Martin C, Vallée JC (1970) Hypersensibilité aux virus, temperatures et protéines solubles chez le Nicotiana Xanthi nc. Apparition de nouvelles macromolécules lors de la répression de Ia synthèse virale. CR Acad Sci Paris 270 2383-2386.

Grennan, A.K. 2006. Plant response to bacterial pathogens. Overlap between innate and gene-for-gene defense response. Plant Physiology 142(3):809-811.

Hao J J, Geng C, Xie W, Gang Z, Liu W.Y., Wang E. Isolation and characterization of viridin, a new 65 KDa autifungla protein from the mould Trichoderma viride. Biolchem. 1999; 380 : 1243-1245.

Hao J J, Ye J Q, Yang Q, Gang Z Z, Liu WY, ang E. A silent autifungal protein (AFP) like gene lacking two in trons in the mould Trichd All me. Viride. Biochem Biophys Acta. 2000; 1475: 119-124.

Heil, M., and R.M. Bostock. 2002. Induced systemic resistance (ISR) against pathogens in the context of induced plant defenses. Annals of Botany (London), 89(5):503-512.

Hejgaard J, Jacobsen S, Bjorn S E, Kragh K M. Antifungal activity of chitin-binding PR-4 type proteins from barley grain and stressed leaf. FEBS Lett. 1992;307:389-392.

Hejgaard J, Jacobsen S, Svendsen I. Two antifungal thaumatin-like proteins from barley grain. FEBS Lett. 1991; 291:127-131.

Hu X, Reddy A S. Nucleotide sequence of a cDNA clone encoding a thaumatin-like protein from Arabidopsis. Plant Physiol. 1995;107:305-306.

Hu X, Reddy A S. Cloning and expression of a PR5-like protein from Arabidopsis: inhibition of fungal growth by bacterially expressed protein. Plant Mol Biol. 1997; 34:949-959.

Huynh Q K, Borgmeyer J R, Zobel J F. Isolation and characterization of a 22 kDa protein with antifungal properties from maize seeds. Biochem Biophys Res Commun. 1992; 182:1-5.

Hwu L, Huang C C, Chen D T, Lin A. The action mode of the ribosome-inactivating protein ?-sarcin. J Biomed Sci. 2000;7:420-428.

Iglesias R, An as F.J., Rojo MA, Escarmis Ci Ferreras. JM, Gnbes T. Molecular action of the type I ribosome-inactivating protein saporians on vicia sativa ribosomes. FEBS Lett. 1993; 325:291-294.

Jach G, Gornhardt B, Mundy J, Logemann J, Pinsdorf E, Leah R, Schell J, Maas C. Enhanced quantitative resistance against fungal disease by combinatorial expression of different barley antifungal proteins in transgenic tobacco. Plant J. 1995; 8:97-109.

Kitajima S, Sato F. Plant pathogenesis-related proteins: molecular mechanisms of gene expression and protein function. J Biochem. 1999; 125:1-8.

Kim Y J, Hwang B K. Isolation of a basic 34 kilo Dalton ?-1,3-glucanase with inhibitory activity against Phytophthora capsici from pepper stems. Physiol Mol Plant Pathol. 1997; 50:103-115.

Kouzuma Y, Inanaga H, Doi-Kawano K, Yamasaki N, Kimura M. Molecular cloning and functional expression of cDNA encoding the cysteine proteinase inhibitor with three cystatin domains from sunflower seeds. J Biochem. 2000;128:161-166.

Kawabata S, Nagayama R, Hirata M, Shigenaga T, Agarwala S L, Saito T, Cho J, Nakajima H, Takagi T, Iwanaga S. Tachycitin, a small granular component in horseshoe crab hemocytes, is an antimicrobial protein with chitin-binding activity. J Biochem. 1996;120:1253-1260.

Koiwa H, Kato H, Nakatsu T, Oda J, Yamada Y, Sato F. Purification and characterization of tobacco pathogenesis-related protein PR-5d, an antifungal thaumatin-like protein. Plant Cell Physiol. 1997;38:783-791.

Lam SS. Wamg J. Ng TB. Pufication and characterization of novel rebosome inactivating proteins, α and β-pisarins, from seeds of the garden pea Pisum sativum. Biochem Biophys Res common. 1998; 253:135-142.

Langer M, Rothe M, Eck J, Mockel B, Zinke H. A nonradioactive assay for ribosome-inactivating proteins. Anal Biochem. 1996;243:150-153.

Leung K C, Meng Z Q, Ho W K. Antigenic determination fragments of ?-momorcharin. Biochim Biophys Acta. 1997;1336:419-424. Lam S S, Wang H, Ng T B. Purification and characterization of novel ribosome inactivating proteins, ?- andn?-pisavins, from seeds of the garden pea Pisum sativum. Biochem Biophys Res Commun. 1998;253:135-142.

Lacadena J, Martinez del Poxo A, Gasset M, Patino B, Campos-Olivas R, Vazquez C, Martinez-Ruiz A, Mancheno J M, Onaderra M, Gavilanes J G. Characterization of the antifungal protein secreted by the mould Aspergillus giganteus. Arch Biochem Biophys. 1995;324:273-281.

Lamberty M, Ades S, Uttenweiler-Joseph S, Brookhart G, Bushey D, Hoffmann J A, Bulet P. Insect immunity. Isolation from the lepidopteran Heliothis virescens of a novel insect defensin with potent antifungal activity. J Biol Chem. 1999;274:9320-9326.

Leah R, Tommerup H, Svendsen I, Mundy J. Biochemical and molecular characterization of three barley seed proteins with antifungal properties. J Biol Chem. 1991; 266:1564-1573.

Legrand M, Kauffmann S, Geoffroy P, Fritig B. Biological function of pathogenesis-related proteins: Four tobacco pathogenesisrelated proteins are chitinases. Proceeding of National Academy of Sciences. 1987; 84: 6750-6754.

Linthorst H J M, Melchers L S, Mayer A, Van Roekel J S C, Cornelissen B J C, Bol J F. Analysis of gene families encoding acidic and basic ?-1,3 glucanases of tobacco. Proc Natl Acad Sci USA. 1990; 87:8756-8760.

Leubner-Metzger G, Meins FJ. Functions and regulation of plant ?-1,3-glucanases (PR-2). In: Datta, S. K., Muthukrishnan, S. eds. Pathogenesis-Related Proteins in Plants. CRC Press, Boca Raton, Florida, p. 77-105; 1999.

Linthorst HJM (1991) Pathogenesis-related proteins of plants. Crit Rev Plant Sci 1 0 123-150.

Loon LC (1985). "Pathogenesis-related proteins". Plant Molecular Biology 4 (2-3):111-116.

Malamy J, Carr JP, Klessig DF, Raskin I (1990) Salicylic acid a likely endogenous signal in the resistance response of tobacco to vira1 infection. Science 250 1002-1004

Manuel, F. Balandrin, James A. Klocke, Eve Syrkin Wurtele, Wm. Hugh Bollinger (1985). Natural Plant Chemicals: Sources of Industrial and Medicinal Materials. Natural plant chemicals: Sources of industrial and medicinal materials. Science 228: 1154-60.

Molina A, Gorlach J, Volrath S, Ryals J. Wheat genes encoding two types of PR-1 proteins are pathogen inducible, but do not respond to activators of systemic acquired resistance. Mol Plant Microbe Interact. 1999; 12:53-58.

Muradov A, Petrasovits L, Davidson A, Scott K J. A cDNA clone for a pathogenesis related protein 1 from barley. Plant Mol Biol. 1993; 23:439-442.

Meins F, Neuhaus J M, Sperisen C, Ryals J. Characterization and analysis of thionin genes. In: Meins F, Boller T, editors; Meins F, Boller T, editors. Genes involved in plant defense. Vienna, Austria: Springer-Verlag; 1992. pp. 245-282.

Molina A, Segura A, Garcia-Olmedo F. Lipid transfer proteins (nsLTPs) from barley and maize leaves are potent inhibitors of bacterial and fungal plant pathogens. FEBS Lett. 1993;16:119-122.

Nielsen K K, Nielsen J E, Madrid S M, Mikkelsen J D. New antifungal proteins from sugar beet (Beta vulgaris L.) showing homology to non-specific lipid transfer proteins. Plant Mol Biol. 1996;31:539-552.

Neuhaus JM, Fritig B, Linthorst H J M, Meins F, Jr F M, Mikkelsen J D, Ryals J. A revised nomenclature for chitinase genes.Plant Mol. Biol. Reporter. 1996; 14: 102-104.

Nielsen K K, Nielsen J E, Madrid S M, Mikkelsen J D. Characterization of a new antifungal chitin-binding peptide from sugar beet leaves. Plant Physiol. 1997; 113:83-91.

Niderman T, Genetet I, Buryere T, Gees R, Stintzi A, Legrand M, Fritig B, Mosinger E. Pathogenesisrelated PR-1 proteins are antifungal. Isolation and characterization of three 14-kilodalton proteins of tomato and of a basic PR-1 of tobacco with inhibitory activity against Phytophthora infestans. Plant Physiol. 1995; 108:17-27.

Niki T, Mitsuhara I, Seo S, Ohtsubo N, Ohashi Y. Antagonistic effect of salicylic acid and jasmonic acid on the expression of pathogenesis-related (PR) protein genes in wounded mature tobacco leaves. Plant Cell Physiol. 1998; 39: 500-507.

Neuhaus JM. Plant chitinases (PR-3, PR-4, PR-8, PR-11). In "Pathogenesis related proteins in plants", eds. Datta, S.K. and Mathukrishnan, S. CRC Press, Boca Raton, pp. 77-105; 1999.

Osaki T, Omotezako M, Nagayama R, Hirata M, Iwanaga S, Kasahara J, Hattori J, Ito I, Sugiyama H, Kawabata S. Horseshoe crab hemocyte-derived antimicrobial polypeptides, tachystatins, with sequence similarity to spider neurotoxins. J Biol Chem. 1999;274:26172-26178.

Ostoa-Saloma P, Carrero J C, Petrossian P, Herion P, Landa A, Laclette J P. Cloning, characterization and functional expression of a cyclophilin of Entamoeba histolytica. Mol Biochem Parasitol. 2000;107:219-225.

Pare, P.W., and J.H. Tumlinson. 1999. Plant volatiles as a defense against insect herbivores. Plant Physiology 121(2):325-331.

Payne G, Ward E, Gaffney T, Goy P A, Moyer M, Harper A, Meins F, Jr, Ryals J. Evidence for a third structural class of ?-1,3-glucanase in tobacco. Plant Mol Biol. 1990; 15:797-808.

Ponstein A S, Bres-Vloemans S A, Sela-Buurlage M B, van den Elzen P J, Meichers L S, Cornelissen B J. A novel pathogen-and wound-inducible tobacco (Nicotiana tabacum) protein with antifungal activity. Plant Physiol. 1994;104:109-118.

Pu Z, Lu B Y, Liu W Y, Jin S W. Characterization of the enzymatic mechanism of ? momorcharin, a novel ribosome-inactivating protein with lower molecular weight of 11,500 purified from the seeds of bitter gourd (Momordica charantia) Biochem Biophys Res Commun. 1996;229:287-294.

Roberts W, Selitrennikoff C P. Zeamatin, an antifungal protein from maize with membranepermeabilizing activity. J Gen Microbiol. 1990;136: 1771-1778.

Rezzonico E, Flury N, Meins F, Jr, Beffa R. Transcriptional down-regulation by abscisic acid of pathogenesis-related ?-1, 3-glucanase genes in tobacco cell cultures. Plant Physiol. 1998; 117:585-592.

Rauscher M, Adam A L, Wirtz S, Guggenheim R, Mendgen K, Deising H B. PR-1 protein inhibits the differentiation of rust infection hyphae in leaves of acquired resistant broad bean. Plant J. 1999; 19:625-633.

Ryan C A (1990). Protease inhibitors in plants: Genes for improving defences against insects and pathogens. Annu. Rev. Phytopathol. 28: 425-449.

Raven, Peter H.; Ray F. Evert, & Susan E. Eichhorn (2005). Biology of Plants. New York: W. H. Freeman and Company. ISBN 0-7167-1007-2

Stern, V. M., Smith, R. F., van den Bosch, R., and Hagen, K. S., The integrated control concept, Hilgardia, 29, 81, 1959.

Stahl E (1888) Planzen und Schnecken: Biologische Studie ¨uber die Schutzmittel der P?anzen gegen Schneckenfrass. Jena Z Naturwiss 22:557-684

Sinclair L J, Carzaniga R, Harris N, Fordham-Skelton A P and Cory R R D (1994). Synthesis and targeting of saponins, type 1 ribosome-inactivating proteins from S. officinalis (Soaport). J.Cellular Biochem., Suppl 18A : p 111 (Abstr.).

Segura A, Moreno M, Garcia-Olmedo F. Purification and antipathogenic activity of lipid transfer proteins (LTPS) from the leaves of Arabidopsis and spinach. FEBS Lett. 1993;332:243-246. [PubMed]

Segura A, Moreno M, Molina A, Garcia-Olmedo F. Novel defensin subfamily from spinach (Spinacia oleracea) FEBS Lett. 1998;435:159-162.

Segura A, Moreno M, Madueno F, Molina A, Garcia-Olmedo F. Snakin-1, a peptide from potato that is active against plant pathogens. Mol Plant Microbe Interact. 1999;12:16-23.

Simmons CR. The physiology and molecular biology of plant 1, 3-?-D-glucanases and 1,3;1,4-?-D-glucanases. Crit. Rev. Plant Sci. 1994; 13: 325-387.

Schlumbaum A, Mauch F, Vogeli U, Boller T. Plant chitinases are potent inhibitors of fungal growth. Nature. 1986; 324: 365-367.

Sela-Buurlage MB, Ponstein AS, Bres-Vloemans SA, Melchers LS, Van Den Elzen PJ M, Cornelissen BJC. Only specific tobacco (Nicotiana tabacum) chitinases and ?-1,3 glucanases exhibit antifungal activity. Plant Physiol. 1993; 101: 857-863.

Singh N K, Bracker C A, Hasegawa P M, Handa A K, Buckel S, Hermodson M A, Pfankoch E, Regnier F E, Bressan R A. Characterization of osmotin. Plant Physiol. 1987; 85:529-536.

Schimoler-O'Rourke R, Richardson M, Selitrennikoff C P. Zeamatin inhibits trypsin and ?-amylase activities. Appl Environ Microbiol. 2001;67:2365-2366.

Sadanandom, Ari; Bailey, Mark; Ewan, Richard; Lee, Jack; Nelis, Stuart (1 October 2012). "The ubiquitin-proteasome system: central modifier of plant signalling". New Phytologist 196 (1): 13-28. doi:10.1111/j.1469- 8137.2012.04266.x (http://dx.doi.org/10.1111% 2Fj.1469-8137.2012.04266.x).

Tassin S, Broekaert W, Marion D, Acland D, Ptak M, Vovelle F, Sodano P. Solution structure of Ace-AMP1, a potent antimicrobial protein extracted from onion seeds. Structural analogies with plant nonspecific lipid transfer proteins. Biochemistry. 1998;37:3623-3637.

Taylor B E, Irvin J D. Depurination of plant ribosomes by pokeweed antiviral protein. FEBS Lett. 1990;273:144-146.

Terras F R G, Schoofs H M E, De Bolle M F C, Van Lewven F, Vanderleyden J, Cammue B P A and Broedaert F (1992b). In vitro antifungal activity of a raddish (Raphanus sativus L.) seed protein homologous to non-specific lipid transfer proteins. Plant Physiol. 100 : 1055-1058

Thevissen K, Terras F T, Broekaert W F. Permeabilization of fungal membranes by plant defensins inhibits fungal growth. Appl Environ Microbiol. 1999;65:5451-5458.

Thevissen K, Osborn R W, Acland D P, Broekaert W F. Specific binding sites for an antifungal plant defensin from Dahlia (Dahlia merckii) on fungal cells are required for antifungal activity. Mol Plant Microbe Interact. 2000;13:54-61.

Torres-Schumann S, Godoy J A, Pintor-Toro J A. A probable lipid transfer protein gene is induced by NaCl in stems of tomato plants. Plant Mol Biol. 1992;18:749-757.

Trujillo, M; Shirasu, K (2010 Aug). "Ubiquitination in plant immunity." Current Opinion in Plant Biology 13 (4): 402-8. PMID 20471305

Vera P, Conejero V. Pathogenesis-related proteins of tomato : p-69 as an alkaline endoproteinase. Plant Physiol. 1988 May;87(1):58 63.

Van Loon L C (1989). Stress proteins in infected plants. In Plant- Microbe Interactions: Molecular and Genetic Perspectives, Vol.3 (Eds., Kosuge T and Nebter E W),.Mc Graw-Hill Publishing Co, New York.

Van Loon LC, Van Kammen A (1970) Polyacrylamide disc electrophoresis of the soluble leaf proteins from Nicotiana tabacum var. 'Samsun" and 'Samsun NN". Changes in protein constitution after TMV infection. Virology 4 0 199-201

Van Loon LC, Van Strien EA. The families of pathogenesis-related proteins, their activities, and comparative analysis of PR-1 type proteins. Physiological and Molecular Plant Pathology. 1999; 55: 85-97.

Van Loon L C. Pathogenesis-related proteins. Plant Mol Biol. 1985;116:111-116.

Van Damme E J, Charels D, Roy S, Tierens K, Barre A, Martins J C, Rouge P, Van Leuven F, Does M, Peumans W J. A gene encoding a hevein-like protein from elderberry fruits is homologous to PR-4 and class V chitinase genes. Plant Physiol. 1999; 119:1547-1556.

Vigers A J, Roberts W K and Selitrennikoff C P (1991). A new family of plant antifungal proteins. Mol. Plant Microbe Interact. 4 : 315-323

Vivanco J M, Savary B J, Flores H E. Characterization of two novel type I ribosome-inactivating proteins from the storage roots of the andean crop Mirabilis expansa. Plant Physiol. 1999;119:1447-1456.

Woloshuk CP, Meuleuhoff EJS, Sela-Buurlage M, van den Elzen PJM, Cornelissen BJC (1991) Pathogen-induced proteins with inhibitory activity toward Phytophthora infestam. Plant Cell 3: 619-628.

Watanabe T, Kanai R, Kawase T, Tanabe T, Mitsutomi M, Sakuda S, Miyashita K. Family 19 chitinases of Streptomyces species: characterization and distribution. Microbiology. 1999; 145:3353-3363.

Wessels JGH, Sietsma JH. Fungal cell wall: a survey, in: W. Tanner, F. A. Loewus (Eds.), Encyclopedia of Plant Physiology, New Series, Plant Carbohydrates II, vol. 13B, Springer-Verlag, p. 352-394; 1981.

White RF, Antoniw JF (1991) Vis-induced resistance responses in plants. Crit Rev Plant Sci 9 443-454

Williams, Kathy S.; Lawrence E. Gilbert (April 1981). "Insects as selective agents on plant vegetative morphology: egg mimicry reduces egg-laying by butterflies". Science 212 (4493): 467-469. Bibcode:1981Sci...212..467W. doi:10.1126/science.212.4493.467. PMID 17802547

White RF (1979) Acetylsalicylic acid (aspirin) induces resistance to tobacco mosaic virus in tobacco. Virology 99 410-412

Ye X Y, Wang H X, Ng T B. First chromatographic isolation of an antifungal thaumatin-like protein from French bean legumes and demonstration of its antifungal activity. Biochem Biophys Res Commun. 1999;263:130-134.

Ye X Y, Ng T B. Mungin, a novel cyclophilin-like antifungal protein from the mung bean. Biochem Biophys Res Commun. 2000;273:1111-1115.

❑❑❑

CHAPTER - 7

Marker Free Plants - A Route for Transgenics from Micro to the Market with Enhanced Biosafety

Shailja Dwivedi and Afroz Alam*
Department of Bioscience and Biotechnology
Banasthali Vidyapith, Tonk-304 022 (India)
**E-mail: Afrozalamsafvi@gmail.com*

ABSTRACT

During the efficient genetic transformation of plants with the gene of interest, some selectable marker genes are also used in order to identify the transgenic plant cells or tissues. Antibiotic and herbicide selective agents and their resistance gene are commonly used to introduce economically valuable genes into crop plants. According to the biosafety authority and consumer view points, the presence of selectable marker genes in released transgenic crops may be transferred to weeds or pathogenic microorganism in the gastrointestinal tract or soil, and will make them resistant to treatment with herbicides or antibiotics, respectively. Sexual crossing also raises the problem of transgene expression because redundancy of transgenes in the genome may trigger homology-dependent gene silencing. The future potential of transgenic technologies for crop improvement depends greatly on our abilities to engineer stable expression of multiple transgenic traits in a predictable fashion and to prevent the transfer of undesirable transgenic material to non-transgenic crops and related species. Therefore the development of efficient marker free transgenic plants system is very essential. That is why many technologies and various approaches designed to timely elimination of transgenes when their function is no longer needed. Due to the limited number of available selectable marker genes, in future the stacking of transgenes will be increasingly desirable. The production of marker-free transgenic plants is now a critical requisite for their commercial deployment and also for engineering multiple and complex trait. Here we describe the current technologies to eliminate the selectable marker genes (SMG) in order to develop marker-free transgenic plants and also discuss the regulation and biosafety concern of genetically modified (GM) crops.

INTRODUCTION

Genetic engineering of plants mostly involves the addition of genetic material (single or multiple genes) that is integrated into a recipient plant, leading to the modification of the plant's genome. The plants with modified genome are known as transgenic plants or genetically modified (GM) plants. A traditional approach to produce transgenic plants is based on the application of constitutively expressed selectable genes which are resistance to antibiotics and herbicides (Angenon *et al.*, 1994) or reporter genes (Herrera-Estrella *et al.*, 1994) for screening of transformed cells. Commonly used selectable markers (such as *npt II* gene of neomycin phosphotransferase and *htp* gene of hygromycin phosphotransferase) genes permit growth of transformed plant or cells in selective medium. Expression of other selectable genes in transgenic plants may give a metabolic advantage to transgenic plants, by accelerating their growth and differentiation. Reporter gene such as *gusA* (*uidA*) of β-glucuronidase or *gfp* of green fluorescent protein, permit a visual screening of transformed plant cells. However, after selection of transformed plants, the presence of marker genes in their genomes becomes useless and their effects become unpredictable or dangerous. Because of cross-pollination and horizontal gene transfer, uncontrolled spreading of selective genes in natural plant populations or horizontal transfer of antibiotic resistance genes to animal and human intestinal microorganisms and a vertical transfer of herbicide resistance genes to weeds is seen as the main problem of genetically modified crop (Goldstein *et al.*, 2005, Upadhyaya *et al.*, 2010). Currently, commercial transgenic plants with selectable antibiotic and herbicide resistance genes occupy vast territories and represent a substantial potential ecological danger. In this connection, the problem arises of novel technology development for creation of transgenic plants devoid of "genetic waste", e.g., selectable markers and reporter genes. In connection with urgent need for the removal of these genes from plants, new methodologies are now developing for the production of marker-free transgenic plants with enhanced biosafety.

Genetic Transformation

Genes of interest are introduced, often by Agrobacterium-mediated transformation, and become integrated at random positions in the genome. Initial experiments involved gene transfer by using *Agrobacterium tumefaciens* (Herrera-Estrella, 1983). Transgenic technologies have enormous potential to improve crops of interest in a relatively precise way (Barampuram and Zhang, 2011). Many different methods of gene transfer has been developed using direct DNA transfer to produce transgenic plant. These methods include particle bombardment (Gan, 1989), chemical treatments and electroporation (Bates, 1994). The transformation of most crop species has been rapidly achieved using various modifications of the technique. However, the methods to introduce foreign DNA in a plant cell, either by *Agrobacterium tumefaciens*, microinjection, particle gun or protoplast transformation, are relatively inefficient (Rakoczy-Trojanowska, 2002). The addition of gene to the desired trait of the plant also requires the use of selection marker genes to select the transformed cells and tissues.

The genetic markers developed for use in plant cells in general have been derived from either bacterial or plant sources and can be divided into two types: selectable and screenable markers.

- Selectable markers are those which allow the selection of transformed cells, or tissue explants, by their ability to grow in the presence of an antibiotic or herbicide, such as Hygromycin, Kanamycin and Glyphosate. In addition to selecting for transformants, such markers can be used to follow the inheritance of a foreign gene in a segregating population of plants.
- Screenable markers encode gene products whose enzyme activity can be easily assayed, allowing not only the detection of transformants but also an estimation of the levels of foreign gene expression in transgenic tissue. Markers such as β-glucuronidase (GUS), luciferase or β-galactosidase allow screening for enzyme activity by histochemical staining or fluorimetric assay of individual cells and can be used to study cell-specific as well as developmentally regulated gene expression.

Selectable Marker Genes

SMG systems and reporter genes are essential to plant genetic engineering and for the development of transgenic crops. These are almost always present in engineered DNA plasmids used for genetic transformation of plant tissue (Lee and Gelvin, 2008). Without them, creation of transgenic crops is not feasible on purely economic and practical terms. These systems allow the relatively straightforward identification and selection of plants that have stably incorporated the marker genes along with the genes of interest. Selectable markers allow the transformed tissue to tolerate an otherwise lethal exposure of an antibiotic or herbicide. Untransformed cells and tissues are killed while the cells carrying the desired gene grow and regenerate into plants. A visible marker gene will display a color characteristic when the transformed tissue is exposed in certain assays. Selectable markers and visible marker reporter genes rarely affect the studied trait of interest, but provide a powerful tool in determining the success of the transformation events or identification of transformation events before the gene of interest (GOI) can be identified in the culture (Sheen *et al.*, 1995). Two main aspects of the marker gene have to be considered. Firstly, its structure (nucleic acid sequence), which will determine factors such as regulation of transcription (constitutive, environmental or developmental expression), rate of transcription, transcript stability and efficiency of translation. Secondly, the gene product is responsible for the dominant expression of a suitable selective phenotype. The selectable functions on most general transformation vectors are prokaryotic antibiotic resistance enzymes that have been engineered to be expressed constitutively in plant cells.

Most commonly used selectable marker genes are-

- *nptII* and *hpt* genes (for resistance to the aminoglycoside antibiotics, kanamycin and hygromycin)
- bar gene (for resistance to herbicide phosphinothricin)

Approximately 50 different selection systems have been developed over the past several years (Sundar and Sakthivel, 2008; Miki and McHugh, 2004). In addition, the existence of marker genes in transgenic crops could evoke additional, lengthy risk assessments for release of crops that contain useful novel traits. Horizontal gene transfer (HGT) is the transfer of genetic material directly to a living cell or an organism followed by its expression. HGT occurs only among unrelated species, such as between plants and microbes, as well as between microorganisms (Thomson, 2001). Transfer of plant DNA into microbial or mammalian cells under normal conditions of dietary exposure would require all of the following events to occur:

1. Removal of the relevant gene from the plant genome, probably as linear fragments.
2. Protection of the gene from nuclease degradation in the plant as well as animal gastrointestinal tract.
3. Uptake of the gene with dietary DNA.
4. Transformation of bacteria or competent mammalian cells.
5. Insertion of the gene(s) into the host DNA by rare repair or recombination events into a transcribable unit; and finally,
6. Continuous stabilization of the inserted gene. In such described way the resistant gene can be transferred to the undesired species of plant or microbe and will be hard to control.

The drawbacks of traditional markers are becoming apparent even in practical research:

- Different marker gene systems are required for the retransformation of plants that have already been genetically modified. However, there are only a few available for each crop species.
- If several marker genes left over from various developmental phases accumulate in a plant, the stability of the genetically engineered trait can be impaired.
- The probability of unforeseen effects (pleiotropic effect) occurring in the plants increases with the number of transferred genes and marker genes because the role of one gene is affected by the other.

Therefore, there is a need for the development of techniques for the efficient production of 'clean' marker-free transgenic plants. Thus, the development of efficient techniques for the removal of selection markers, as well as the directed integration of transgenes at safe locations in the genome, is of great interest to biotech companies. Furthermore, the removal of selectable marker genes will also have a technical advantage, since the number of available selectable marker genes is limiting, and stacking of transgenes will become more and more desirable in the near future. In the next generation of transgenic plants, antibiotic-resistance markers will be the exception rather than the rule. However, there is still a long way to go before sufficient new procedures and strategies.

From transgenic plant to marker free transgenic plant (commercialization)

The plant with modified genome is known as transgenic plant or genetically modified plant. The first successful genetic engineering of a plant was reported in 1983. Broad-leafed plants such as tobacco and tomato were easiest to transform, and reliable transformation of cereals such as rice and maize were not reported until the late 1980s. In 2008, 13.3 million farmers worldwide grew GM crops. Of these, 12.3 million, or 90%, were smallholder, resource-poor farmers in developing countries. In 1996, the transgenic GM crops were released and commercialized in the US, China, Canada, Argentina, Australia and Mexico. The estimated area of the commercial production of GM crops was approximately 52.6 million ha. GM crop was legally accepted and commercialized in only 13 countries by that time (the US, Argentina, Canada, China, South Africa, Australia, Mexico, Bulgaria, Uruguay, Romania, Spain, Indonesia and Germany). The commercial production of GM crops in India and Brazil began in 2002. The increase between 2000 and 2001, in 1 year alone, was 9.4 million ha and represented a 19% increase (http://www. agnet.org/library/eb/526/). By the end of 2001, 52.6 million ha was allotted to transgenic or GM crops and the number of countries growing these crops have since increased dramatically to almost more than double (James 2001). The US and Argentina account for 83.5% of all commercial GM crops planted to date. Together with Canada and China, these four countries accounted for almost 99% of the global GM crop area in 2001 (James, 2001).

In the Latin American continent, Mexico banned GM maize in 1998. Brazil has a moratorium on growing commercial GM crops and is sometimes presented as the country that will supply the world its non-GM soybean (Campolina de and Soares, 2001). However, especially in regions close to Argentina and Paraguay, GM soybean is estimated to occupy 35% of the Brazilian total soybean growing area, albeit illegally (Schuhmacher, 2002). In Asia, India has approved the commercial application of GM cotton in 2002 (James, 2002a, b). In the African continent, South Africa is so far the only country growing commercialized GM crops. Europe and Australasia are not growing substantial number of GM crops.

On a global basis in 2010, a record 15.4 million farmers grew biotech crops in about 1 billion ha. It is interesting to note that over 90% of these, about 14.4 million, were small resource-poor farmers in developing countries (James, 2010).The number of countries growing GM crops has increased to 29 in recent years. This suggests that the GM crops are the fastest adopted technology in the field of agriculture (James, 2010). The benefits and dangers of GM crops are the subject of intense debate. The five key areas of political controversy related to GM crops are food safety, the effect on natural ecosystems, and gene flow into non-GM crops, moral/religious concerns and corporate control of the food supply. Horizontal transfer of antibiotic-resistance genes to animal and human gut bacteria and vertical transfer of herbicide-resistance genes to weedy relatives are perceived as major biosafety concerns in genetically engineered crops (Dale *et al.*, 2002). Selectable marker gene (SMG) elimination is very important for transgene stacking (Francois *et al.*, 2002; Halpin, 2005; Manimaran *et al.*, 2011). SMG elimination enables engineering of a transgenic plant with additional transgenic traits by sequential transformations using the same SMG (Hohn *et al.*, 2001). Only a few SMGs are available for transforming a crop plant. In addition, repeated use of the same promoter and a polyadenylation signal for different SMGs could cause gene silencing in transgene-stacked lines (Matzke *et al.*, 1989). Although the advantage of SMG elimination in transgene stacking by sequential transformation was recognized very early (Yoder and Goldsbrough, 1994), very little progress has been made in this direction.

Methods to eliminate marker gene from nuclear genome

To avoid above described problems with the transgenic plants many methods have been developed for the elimination of selectable marker genes.

Co-Transformation

Co-transformation is a method for production of marker-free transformants based on *Agrobacterium*- or biolistics mediated transformation in which a SMG and gene of interest are on separate constructs. Three approaches are used for co-transformation:

1. Introduction of two TDNAs, in separate *Agrobacterium* strains or (i-b) biolistics introduction of two plasmids in the same tissue.
2. Introduction of two T-DNAs carried by different replicons within the same *Agrobacterium* strain; and
3. Introduction of two T-DNAs located on the same replicon within an *Agrobacterium* (Gelvin, 2003; Afolabi *et al.*, 2005).

In all of these variants, SMGs can subsequently be removed from the plant genome during segregation and recombination that occurs during sexual reproduction by selecting on the transgene of interest and not the SMG in progeny. Therefore, co-transformation methods cannot be used for vegetatively propagated plants (Scutt *et al.*, 2002).

The advantages of co-transformation methods include the high adaptability of conventional, unmodified Agrobacterium-mediated gene transfer methods and easier handling of the binary vectors because the two T-DNA are separated and, hence, target gene TDNA can be handled independently of selectable marker gene T-DNA. This method depends on the co-transformation efficiency and the independent integration of T-DNA into the plant genome. Generally, the co-transformation efficiency is in the range of 30–50%, which is acceptable for practical applications.

In this method SMG can be eliminated from the plant genome at the time of segregation and recombination that occurs during sexual reproduction by selecting on the transgene of interest and not the SMG in progeny. In spite of all these, there are several inevitable limitations. The methods described above are very time consuming and compatible only for fertile plants. The tight linkage between co-integrated DNAs limits the efficiency of co-transformation. Indeed, integration of SMG and the transgene is at indiscriminate event: both the SMG and transgene may integrate in the same loci and that is not feasible for co-transformation. Rao and Veluthambi (2010) reported efficient strategies to employ marker elimination and achieved marker-free transgenic tobacco in the T_0 generation itself.

Multi Auto Transformation

The multi-auto-transformation (MAT) vector system represents a highly sophisticated approach for the removal of nuclear marker genes (Ebinuma *et al.*, 1997). The MAT vector system is a positive selection system that gives the advantage of regeneration to the transgenic cells without killing the non-transgenic cells. It is a unique transformation system that uses morphological changes caused by oncogene [the isopentenyl transferase (*ipt*) gene] or rhizogene (the *rol* gene) of *A. tumefaciens* which control the endogenous levels of plant hormones and the cell responses to plant growth regulators as the selection marker. Expression of the ipt gene causes abnormal shoot morphology called extreme shooty phenotype (ESP), which subsequently reverts into normal shoots with objective transgenes due to the excision of ipt gene by the function of 'hit andrun' cassette system (Ebinuma and Komamine, 2001).

In this MAT system, a chosen GOI is placed adjacent to a multigenic element flanked by RS recombination sites. A copy of the selectable ipt gene from *A. tumefaciens* is inserted between these recombinase sites, together with the yeast R recombinase gene and this entire assembly is situated within a T-DNA element for the Agrobacterium-mediated transformation of plant tissues. In this plant transformation system, neither antibiotic- nor herbicide-resistance genes are necessary as a selection marker. In addition, this system of transformation allows for repeated transformation of genes of interest in a plant (Sugita *et al.*, 2000).

Site Specific Recombination

Recombination is a universal phenomenon that can occur at any place along two homologous DNA molecules. In temperate bacteriophages, there is a second type of recombination called site-specific recombination, which takes place only between defined excision sites in the phage and in the bacterial chromosome. Positions of the site-specific recombination in the bacterial and phage DNA are called the bacterial and phage attachment sites, respectively. Each attachment site consists of three segments. The central segment has the conserved nucleotide sequence that sites the recombination event. A phage protein, an integrase, catalyzes the site-specific recombination events, which lead to physical exchange of DNA. Excision requires the phage enzyme integrase plus an additional phage protein called excisionase. Basically three methods of site recombination are widely used-

- **Cre/lox site-specific recombination system**: The Cre/loxP system consists of two components: (a) two loxP sites each consisting of 34 bp inverted repeats cloned in direct orientation flanking a DNA sequence and (b) the cre gene encoding a 38 kDa recombinase protein that specifically binds to the loxP sites and excises the intervening sequence along with one of the loxP sites. One of the greatest advantages of the Cre/lox system is the specificity of the enzyme for its 34 bp recognition sequence. The cre gene was driven by the heat-inducible promoter (hsp), and the nptII gene is flanked by lox sequences. These inducible site-specific recombination systems can also be applied in vegetatively propagated crop plants for marker gene excision.

- **FLP/FRT recombination system**: In the FLP/frt site specific system of the 2 ìm plasmid of Saccharomyces *cerevisiae,* the FLP enzyme efficiently catalyses recombination between two directly repeated FLP recombination target (frt) sites, eliminating the sequence between them. By controlled expression of the FLP recombinase and specific allocation of the frt sites within transgenic constructs, the system can be applied to eliminate the marker genes after selection.
- **R/RS recombination system**: The MAT vectors consist of yeast site-specific recombination R/RS system to excise the DNA fragment and the *ipt* gene positioned between two directly oriented recombination sites. The R/rs system comprises a R recombinase gene and two rs recombination site sequences. The ipt combined with the (R) gene was placed within two directly-oriented recognition sites to remove it from transgenic cells after transformation. The improved MAT vector is used to generate marker-free transgenic plants efficiently. Such a system can be applied to woody plants or vegetatively propagated species to produce marker-free transgenic plants as well as providing the basis for the development of an inducible plant transformation system.

Transposon based marker method

In the 1940s, Barbara McClintock made an astonishing discovery. She detected two factors of DNA transposition in maize: a Ds (disassociation) element that was located at a chromosome break site and an unlinked genetic factor (Ac) which was required to activate the breakage of chromosome 9. McClintock concluded that such an unstable phenotype resulted from the movement or transposition of Ds (Griffiths *et al.*, 2005). Transposable elements can also be used to produce marker-free transgenic plants. Use of transposable elements for marker gene removal involves several steps:

1. Insertion of the marker gene onto a transposon, a segment of DNA that "hops" around in the plant's genome.
2. Co-transformation with gene of interest; and
3. Segregation of the marker gene.

A MAT vector system containing the *ipt* gene and *Ac* element has been designed so that when tobacco leaf segments were transformed and selected, subsequent excision of the modified *Ac* produced marker-free transgenic tobacco plants without sexual crosses or seed production (Ebinuma *et al.*, 1997). However, there are several drawbacks of using a transposable element system for marker gene removal: (i) different species have variable rates of transposition efficiency; (ii) this method requires labor and time costs for crossing transgenic plants and the selection of the progeny (Ebinuma *et al.*, 2001; Ow *et al.*, 2001) (iii) there is low efficiency of marker-free transgenic plant generation, because of the tendency of transposable elements to reinsert elsewhere in the genome; (iv) imprecise excision; (v) generation of mutations because of insertion and excision cycles; and (vi) genomic instability of transgenic plants because the continuous presence of heterologous transposons [Scutt *et al.*, 2002] decreases efficiency.

Chemical inducible system

In order to initiate the Cre/lox recombination for removal of the marker gene, other novel inducible site-specific recombination systems have been developed. Now several approaches are used to overcome these shortcomings by using some chemical inducers (Yuan *et al.*, 2004; Zhang *et al.*, 2006) or by heat shock (Wang *et al.*, 2005; Cuellar *et al.*, 2006). The chemical-inducible Cre/loxP (CLX) vector system benefits also from a particularly regulated system of chemical induction (Sreekala *et al.*, 2005). The procedure could be used for vegetatively propagated species and may be particularly well adapted to crop species requiring transformation by the regeneration of embryo cultures. â-estradiaol is most commonly used compound for this system.

Heat inducible system

A new binary expression vector based on the 'genetically modified-gene-deletor' system was constructed. In this vector, the gene coding for FLP site-specific recombinase under the control of a heat shock-inducible promoter HSP18.2 from *A. thaliana* and ipt gene as a selectable marker gene under the control of the cauliflower mosaic virus 35S (CaMV 35S) promoter was flanked by two loxP/FRT fusion sequences as recombination sites in direct orientation. Further characterization of the transgenic tobacco plants confirmed the elimination of the *ipt* gene along with gusA in the primary stage. Heat-inducible approach provides a reliable strategy for auto excising a selectable marker gene from calli, shoots or other tissues of transgenic plants after transformation and producing marker-free transgenic plants. The disadvantage of this method is not negotiable. When auto-excision constructs are used, the recombinase can be activated by a chemical compound or by a heat shock in the shoots and seeds or during a subculture step and an extra regeneration step. The latter possibility lengthens the time to obtain marker-free transgenic plants and can introduce (additional) somaclonal variation.

Positive selection system

Some marker genes for positive selection enable the identification and selection of genetically modified cells without injury or death of the non-transformed cell population (negative selection). In this case, the selection marker genes should give the transformed cell the capacity to metabolize some compounds that are not usually metabolized. This fact will give the transformed cells an advantage over the non-transformed ones. The addition of this new compound in the culture medium, as nutrient source during the regeneration process, allows normal growth and differentiation of transformed cells, while non-transformed cells will not be able to grow and regenerate de novo plants.

- **The *gus* gene**: The gus gene codes for the β-glucuronidase enzyme (GUS; EC 3.2.1.31) and was isolated from Escherichia coli. This gene is widely used as a reporter gene in transgenic plants. In this system, the selective agent is a glucuronide derivative of benzyladenine (benzyladenine N-3-glucuronide), an inactive form of the plant hormone cytokinin. This glucuronide present in the selection medium can be hydrolysed by the GUS enzyme produced in the transformed cells, releasing active cytokinin (benzyladenine) in the medium. This cytokinin will be a stimulator for transformed cell regeneration while the non-transformed cell development is arrested. The selective agent (benzyladenine N-3-glucuronide) does not have any effect on the non-transformed cells because the cytokinin is in its inactive form. There are only few reports concerning the successful use of this system in the effective recovery of transgenic plants (Joersbo and Okkels, 1996; Okkels *et al.*, 1997).
- **The manA gene**: The man gene codes for the phosphomannose isomerase enzyme isolated from *Escherichia coli.* In the presence of mannose, the PMI converts mannose-6-phosphate into fructose-6-phosphate in transformed cells that can be immediately incorporated in the plant metabolic pathway. Thus, mannose can be used as the sole carbohydrate source for the transformed cells. Mannose cannot be usually metabolized by non transformed cells and is converted into mannose-6-phosphate by endogenous hexokinase. Therefore, when mannose is added to the culture medium, plant growth may be minimized due to mannose-6-phosphate accumulation. The mannose-6-phosphate toxicity in plant cells was shown to be responsible for

apoptosis, or programmed cell death, through induction of an endonuclease, responsible for DNA laddering (Stein and Hansen 1999). Mannose is a hexose that fills the desirable requirements for a good selection agent: it is (a) soluble in plant culture media, (b) absorbed by plant cells, (c) inexpensive, (d) easily available and (e) safe.

- **The xylA and DOGR1 genes**: A similar positive selection system has been developed using the xylose isomerase gene (xylA) isolated from *Thermoanaerobacterium thermosulfurogenes* or from *Streptomyces rubiginosus,* as selection marker gene (Haldrup *et al.*, 1998a, b). Transgenic plants of potato, tobacco and tomato were successfully selected in xylose-containing media. Recently, the DOGR1 gene encoding 2-deoxyglucose-6-phosphate phosphatase (2-DOG-6-P) was used to develop a positive selection system for tobacco and potato plants (Kunze *et al.*, 2001). DOGR1 gene, which has been isolated from yeast, gives resistance to 2-deoxyglucose (2-DOG) when over expressed in transgenic plants.

Negative selection system

An alternative and potentially more efficient strategy is based on the incorporation of a negative selection step. The use of a negative SMG next to a positive SMG in the same construct is a powerful method to create marker gene-free transgenic plants. In this method, transformed offspring are selected for the absence of negative SMG under the selection pressure of a negative marker gene and the presence of the desired transgene. This negative selection method allows researchers to decrease their search for selectable marker-free transgenic plants without having to resort to copious molecular analyses, *i.e.*, thousands of PCRs (Jeongmoo *et al.*, 2004). Finally, the combination of using a mixture of mechanisms, transient selection, sequential transformation, negative marker genes, P-DNA and a mutated *virD2* gene together should be capable of producing high frequency marker-free transgenic plants by co-transformation methods. Recently, a novel marker gene has been characterized, *dao1*, encoding D-amino acid oxidase that it can be used as for either positive or negative marker, depending on the substrate (Erikson *et al.*, 2004). Therefore, it is possible to apply the negative selection after a positive selection using one marker gene, *dao1*, via changing D-alanine or D-serine to D-isoleucine or D-valine for the substrates.

Auto Excision Strategy

A number of methods to eliminate the selection marker gene form the plant genome are now known. The earlier methods of auto excision such as the heat inducible system and chemical-inducible system are time consuming and the marker gene is eliminated in the next generation after segregation. For the development of marker-free transgenic plants, scientists have developed a novel and ideal method, which eliminates the selection marker gene in a single generation. This method is known as 'auto excision strategy', in which the marker is easily eliminated in the T1 seeds of the transgenic plants (the seeds which is collected from the T_0 plants) (Mlynarova *et al.* 2006). The next generation of the transgenic plants will be marker free.

Using this method the frequency of regenerating marker-free transgenic lines in Arabidopsis is 83–100%. In spite of all the above, auto excision strategy has its limitations: it is successful only in flowering plants. It will not be useful for the vegetatively propogated plants like grapes, potato and banana.

Abiotic stress related gene as selectable marker

It is a well-known fact that various genes encode proteins that protect the plants at the time of several environmental stresses like drought stress, salt stress and oxidative stress. Till date so many genes that are well characterized in *A. thaliana* or in several agronomically important crops can be used for the development of marker-free transgenic plants. Incorporation of such well-characterized genes in to those plants that are salt sensitive, including rice (*Oryza sativa*), maize (*Zea mays*), soybean (*Glycine max*), beans (*Phaseolus vulgaris*) and tomato (*Lycopersicum esculantum*), is a contribution to the agriculture sector for developing transgenic plants (Munns, 2005).

The basic ideas behind this strategy is that plant tissue or the plant senses high Na+ concentration in the soil/media and initiates signal transduction to activate a set of stress responsive genes for salt tolerance. The gene is incorporated into the plant tissue or explants without the selection marker gene. After transformation the tissue will grow under the pressure of salt stress, and explants that grow well without any deformities are selected and grown further in the salt stress medium until the vegetative proliferation of the explants. In the whole experiment there is no need to use the selection marker. The gene itself can be used as selection marker to select the transformed tissue (Zhang *et al.*, 2009a, b). There are following limitations: (i) In case of an unknown gene it will be difficult to use the system. (ii) Screening will be tedious because there will be chances of escape of untransformed calli.

Intra-chromosomal recombination system

Intra-chromosomal recombination in plants (Zubko *et al.*, 2002) is obtained by insertion of SMG between two direct repeats of *attP* that facilitates spontaneous excision. Base composition of the *attP* site sequence is A + T rich, which is conjectured to play a recombination-stimulating role (Muller *et al.*, 1999). Possibly, the formation of a recombination hot spot is caused via the induction of double-strand breaks (DSBs) (Puchta, 2005), but may also reduce of the stability of transgene sequences later on.

The potential advantages are: (i) expression of a heterologous recombinase and sexual reproduction are not necessary; (ii) there is a one step selection procedure for transgenic calli (lengthy propagation two-step time as above might increase the risk of somaclonal variation); (iii) it utilizes a natural nuclear recombination systems present in plants; (iv) the frequency of intra-chromosomal recombination between two homologous sequences in plants might be increased by stimulation of repair systems; and (v) the efficiency of homologous recombination is directly correlated with the size of the homologous regions

Transformation Method not Using Selectable Markers

Above mention methods to eliminate the selectable markers from transgenic plants are very time consuming that is some new methods also have been developed. These methods can direct produce marker free transgenic plants.

Direct Screening by PCR

In this method the transformed explants by Agrobacterium carrying plasmid with desired genes can be screened by PCR. GOI (gene of interest) integration in the genome and their expression were confirmed by the blot analysis of DNA after Southern and by real-time PCR.

The method of marker-free plant detection by PCR is rather simple and does not require much time. It also does not require numerous crosses for segregation of GOI and marker gene in the transgenic plant progeny. However, a great disadvantage of this method is a high probability of false positive results of PCR because of seedling contamination with Agrobacterium abundant in plant tissue intercellular space after transformation. In this connection, the analysis of GOI expression is obligatory required. In addition, this method is suitable only for a limited number of plant species with a high potential of regeneration and transformation. Marker free potato, rice and groundnut development is the example of the success of this method.

Methods of Direct Screening of Transformants by the Presence of GOI Expression Product

The new method of marker free plant generation is based on the direct screening of GOI expression product. The developed strategy of direct screening of Marker free plants on the basis of products of GOI expression has an important advantage as compared with other methods. Transgenic plants detected by this method do not initially contain selectable markers, and therefore their selection does not require laborious operations of their removal. In this case, the time of plant production harboring GOI shortens. This method permits a reduction of long antibiotic or herbicide stress load on plants during transformant screening on selective media. For Agrobacterium mediated plant transformation the vectors with shortened T-DNA may be used and this can reduce the undesired effect of long vector sequences on the density of their packing in the chromatin and thus on GOI expression. In addition, this method does not require the removal of selectable marker genes in then progeny; therefore, it can be used for vegetatively propagated plants and also for woody plants with the long cycle of development.

Marker free plants with desired genes

The various methods to obtain marker-free transgenic plants have proven their utility and are increasingly being deployed to obtain crop plants with agronomically useful genes. One of the crops that have received more attention is rice. Indeed some papers have described the production of marker-free transgenic plants with different genes of interest. Applying the co-transformation / segregation strategy with the use of 'double right border' twin T-DNA vectors Lu *et al.* (2001) obtained marker-free transgenic rice plants harboring a *Rice ragged stunt virus* (RRSV) derived synthetic resistance gene. Another group obtained transgenic rice devoid of selectable marker genes that produce high levels of carotenoids using the same strategy but with two binary vectors in one *Agrobacterium* strain (Parkhi V, 2009). Marker-free rice plants, with improved resistance to *Magnaporthe grisea* were obtained by the expression of the rice pistil predominant chitinase gene using a vector system with two T-DNAs (Hashizume *et al.*, 2006).

Sripriya *et al.* (2008) generated marker-free transgenic plants with improved resistance to sheath blight. A single *A. tumefaciens* strain harbored a cointegrate vector with the *hph* and *gus* genes and a binary vector with the rice chitinase (*chi1*) gene. Selectable marker-free rice plants expressing the *Bacillus thuringiensis* synthetic *cry1B* gene were obtained by transposon mediated repositioning of the GOI (Cotsaftis *et al.*, 2002). The Cry1B expression cassette was flanked by the inverted terminal repeats of the maize *Ac* transposon that permit the repositioning of this cassette in the rice genome. On the other hand, Sengupta *et al.* (2010) have exploited the Cre/*lox* site-specific recombination system to produce selectable marker-free transgenic rice plants with improved resistance to green leafhoppers (*Nephotettix virescens*) and brown planthopper (*Nilaparvata lugens*).

The first commercially available marker-free transgenic plant that was obtained through this system was developed by the company Renessen. They generated the transgenic corn line LY038, from which the *nptII* selectable marker gene, originally present between tandemly oriented *lox* sites, was removed through introduction of the *cre* gene by a sexual cross (Ow, 2007). For the market, this corn line has the name MaveraTM High Value Corn with Lysine. In another report, the production of marker-free transgenic soybean [*Glycine max* (L.) Merr.] is described which produces ã-linolenic acid and stearidonic acid that are important for pharmaceutical and nutraceutical industries (Sato *et al.*, 2004). The expression of a chitinase gene, *ChiC*, on an *ipt*-type MAT (isopentenyl transferase-type multi-auto-transformation) vector, allowed the production of marker-free disease-resistant transgenic potato plants (Khan *et al.*, 2011).

CONCLUSION AND FUTURE PROSPECTS

A substantial argument of the supporters of the genetically modified plant production is an expansion of the area under commercial varieties of transgenic plants. By 2011, the total area occupied by such plants achieved 148 million ha (Clive, 2010). It is stated that plant genetic engineering solves the problems of agriculture by the ways essentially similar to those of classical breeding and genetics, both being based on gene transfer. However, this is true only for potential possibilities of genetic engineering, which are not still completely realized. In the genome of commercial plants, there is a large amount of unnecessary genetic material or simply the genetic debris, which creates serious problems in connection with its possible transfer to the environment and its unpredictable consequences. First of all, this is a problem of transgenic plant biosafety with such obvious drawbacks as the presence in their genomes and constitutive expression of unwanted and potentially dangerous selective genes for resistance to antibiotics and herbicides. At present, the production of marker-free biosafe transgenic plants is possible. Such plants do not experience an additional genetic load, which must improve their productivity.

Fundamental studies of marker-free plants open new perspectives for the fine analysis of plant cell life in pure experiments on plants devoid of non-target genes. The development of methods of marker-free transgenic plants production and creation of the novel generation of such plants is a first step toward the approaching genetic engineering technology to modern breeding process and transgenics would further strengthen the crop improvement program with widespread applications in both fundamental research and biotechnology. Overall, the GM crops are expected to contribute globally to the food security.

ACKNOWLEDGEMENTS

Authors are thankful to Prof. Aditya Shastri, Vice Chancellor, Banasthali Vidyapith (Rajasthan) and Prof. Vinay Sharma, Dean, Faculty of Science and Technology, Banasthali Vidyapith (Rajasthan) for providing necessary facilities.

REFERENCES

Afolabi AS, Worland B, Snape J and Vain P. 2005. Multiple T-DNA co-cultivation as a method of producing marker-free (clean gene) transgenic rice (*Oryza sativa* L.) plant. African J. Biotechnol. 4, 531–540.

Angenon G, Dillen W and van Montagu M. 1994. Antibiotic Resistance Markers for Plant Transformation, Plant Molecular Biology Manual, Gelvin, S.B. and Schilperoort, R.A., Eds., Dordrecht: Kluwer, pp. C1:1–13.

Barampuram S and Zhang ZJ. 2011. Recent advances in plant transformation. Method. Mol. Biol. 701 1–35.

Bates GW. 1994. Genetic transformation of plants by protoplast electroporation. Mol. Biotechnol. 2 135–145.

Campolina de and Soares A. 2001. Campaign overview: for a GMO-free Brazil; in Proceedings of the flipside of genetic engineering (http://wwwgentechdebatnl/news/shownewsasp?itemid).

Clive J. 2010. Global Status of Commercialized Biotech/GM Crops, ISAAA Brief, no. 42.

Cotsaftis O, Sallaud C, Breitler JC, Meynard D, Greco R, Pereira A and Guiderdoni E. 2002. Transposon-mediated generation of marker free rice plants containing a Bt endotoxin gene conferring insect resistance. Mol. Breeding 10: 165-180.

Cuellar W, Gaudin A, Solorzano D, Casas A, Nopo L, Chudalayandi P, Medrano G, Kreuze J and Ghislain M. 2006. Self-excision of the antibiotic resistance gene nptII using a heat inducible Cre-loxP system from transgenic potato. Plant Mol. Biol. 62 71–82.

Dale PJ, Clarke B and Fontes EMG. 2002. Potential for the environmental impact of transgenic crops. Nat. Biotechnol. 20 567–574.

Ebinuma H and Komamine A. 2001. MAT multi-auto-transformation vector system. The oncogenes of Agrobacterium as positive markers for regeneration and selection of marker-free transgenic plants. In Vitro Cell Dev. Biol. Plant 37 103–113.

Ebinuma H, Sugita K, Matsunaga E and Yamakado M. 1997. Selection of marker-free transgenic plants using the isopentenyl transferase gene. Proc. Natl. Acad. Sci. USA 94 2117–2121.

Ebinuma H, Sugita K, Matsunaga E and Endo S *et al.*, 2001. Systems for the removal of a selection marker and their combination with a positive marker. Plant Cell Rep. *20*, 383–392.

Erikson O, Hertzberg M and Nasholm T. 2004. A conditional marker gene allowing both positive and negative selection in plants. Nat. Biotechnol. 22, 455–458.

Francois IEJA, Broekaert WF and Cammue BPA. 2002. Different approaches for multi-transgene-stacking in plants. Plant Sci. 163 281–295.

Gan C. 1989. Gene Gun Accelerates DNA-Coated Particles To Transform Intact Cells. The Scientist 3 25.

Gelvin S B. 2003. *Agrobacterium*-mediated plant transformation: the biology behind the "Gene-Jockeying" tool. Microbiol. Mol. Biol. Rev. *67*, 16–37.

Griffiths AJF, Miller JH, Suzuki DT, Lewontin RC and Gelbart WM (Eds.). 2005. *An Introduction to Genetic Analysis*, 8th edn., Freeman, San Francisco. pp. 424–450.

Goldstein DA, Tinland B, Gilbertson LA, Staub JM, Bannon GA, Goodman RE, McCoy RL and Sil vanovich A. 2005. Human Safety and Genetically Modified Plants: A Review of Antibiotic Resistance Markers and Future Transformation Selection Technologies, J. Appl. Microbiol.vol. 99, pp. 7–23.

Haldrup A, Petersen SG and Okkels FT. 1998a. The xylose isomerase gene from Thermo-anaerobacterium thermosulfurogenes allows effective selection of transgenic plant cells using D-xylose as the selection agent. Plant Mol. Biol. 37 287–296.

Haldrup A, Petersen SG and Okkels FT. 1998b. Positive selection: a plant selection principle based on xylose isom-erase an enzyme used in the food industry. Plant Cell Rep. 18 76–81.

Halpin C. 2005. Gene stacking in transgenic plants—the challenge for 21st century plant biotechnology. Plant Biotechnol. J. 3 141–155.

Hashizume F, Nakazaki T, Tsuchiya T and Matsuda T. 2006. Effectiveness of genotype based selection in the production of marker-free and genetically fixed transgenic lineages: ectopic expression of a pistil chitinase gene increases leaf-chitinase activity in transgenic rice plants without hygromycin-resistance gene. Plant Biotechnol. 23: 349-356.

Herrere-Estrella. 1983. Transfer and expression of foreign genes in plants; Phd thesis (Laboratory of Genetics, Gent University, Belgium).

Herrera-Estrella L, Leon P, Olsson O, and Teeri TH. 1994. Reporter Genes for Plants, Plant Molecular Biology Manual, Gelvin, S.B. and Schilperoort, R.A., Eds., Dordrecht: Kluwer, pp. C2: 1–32.

Hohn B, Levy AA and Puchta H. 2001. Elimination of selection markers from transgenic plants. Curr. Opin. Biotechnol. 12 139–143.

James C. 2001. Global review of commercialized transgenic crops: 2001 ISAAA Briefs no 24: Preview (Ithaca: International Service for the Acquisition of Agri-Biotech Applications) http://wwwisaaaorg/publications/briefs/Brief_24html.

James C. 2002. Global status of commercialized transgenic crops. ISAAA Briefs 27 1–36.

James C. 2002. World-wide deployment of GM crops: aims and results state of the art; in Discourse on genetically modified plants. Bundesministerium fur Verbraucherschutz Ernahrung und Landwirtschaft, Bad Neuenahr, Germany http:// wwwgruenegentechnikde/Doku_Fachtagung/james_englpdf.

James C. 2010. Global status of commercialized biotech/GM crops. ISAAA Brief 42.

Jeongmoo P, Young L, Bong K and Won C. 2004. Co-transformation using a negative selectable marker gene for the production of selectable marker gene-free transgenic plants. Theor. Appl. Genet. *109*, 1562–1567.

Joersbo M and Okkels FT. 1996. A novel principle for selection of transgenic plant cells: positive selection.Plant Cell Rep. 16 219–221.

Khan RS, Nyui VO, Chin DP, Nakamura I and Mii M. 2011. Production of marker-free disease-resistant potato using isopentenyl transferase gene as a positive selection marker. Plant Cell Rep. 30: 587-597.

Kunze I, Ebneth M, Heim U, Geiger M, Sonnewald U and Herbers K. 2001. 2-Deoxyglucose resistance: a novel selection marker for plant transformation. Mol. Breed. 7 221–227.

Lee LY and Gelvin SB. 2008. T-DNABinary Vectors and Systems. Plant. Physiol. 146 325–332.

Lu HJ, Zhou XR, Gong ZX, Upadhyaya NM. 2001. Generation of selectable marker free transgenic rice using double right-border (DRB) binary vectors. Aust. J. Plant. Physiol. 28: 241-248.

Manimaran P, Ramkumar G, Sakthivel K, Sundaram RM, Madhav MS and Balachandran SM. 2011. Suitability of non-lethal marker and marker-free systems for development of transgenic crop plants: Present status and future prospects. Biotechnol. Adv. 29 703–714.

Matzke MA, Primig M, Trnovsky J and Matzke AJM. 1989. Reversible methylation and inactivation of marker genes in sequentially transformed tobacco plants. EMBO J. 8 643–649.

Miki B and Mchugh S. 2004. Selectable marker genes in transgenic plants: applications alternatives and biosafety. J. Biotechnol. 107 193–232.

Mlynarova L, Conner AJ and Nap JPH. 2006. Directed microspore-specific recombination of transgenic alleles to prevent pollen-mediated transmission of transgenes. Plant Biotechnol. J. 4 445–452.

Muller AE, Kamisugi Y, Gruneberg R, Niedenhof I *et al.*, 1999. Palindromic sequences and A+T-rich DNA elements promote illegitimate recombination in Nicotiana tabacum. J. Mol. Biol. *291*, 29–46.

Munns R. 2005. Genes and salt tolerance: bringing them together. New Phytol. 167 645–663.

Okkels FT, Ward J and Joersb M. 1997. Synthesis of cytokinin glucuronides for the selection of transgenic plant cells. Phytochemistry 46 801–804.

Ow DW. 2001. The right chemistry for marker gene removal? Nat. Biotechnol. 2001, 19, 115–116.

Ow DW. 2007. GM maize from site-specific recombination technology, what next? Curr. Opin. Biotechnol. 18: 115-120.

Parkhi V, Kumar V, Sunilkumar G, Campbell LM, Singh NK and Rathore KS. 2009. Expression of apoplastically secreted tobacco osmotin in cotton confers drought tolerance. Mol. Breed. 23: 625-639.

Puchta H. 2000. Removing selectable marker genes: taking the shortcut. Trends Plant Sci. 5, 273–274.

Rakoczy-Trojanowska M. 2002. Alternative methods of plant transformation - a short review. Cell Mol. Biol. Lett. 7 849–858.

Ramana Rao MV and Veluthambi K. 2010. Selectable marker elimination in the T_0 generation by Agrobacterium-mediated co-transformation involving Mungbean yellow mosaic virus TrAP as a non-conditional negative selectable marker and bar for transient positive selection. Plant Cell Rep. 29 473–483.

Sato S, Xing A, Ye X, Schweiger B, Kinney A, Graef G and Clemente T. 2004. Production of ã-Linolenic Acid and Stearidonic Acid in Seeds of Marker-Free Transgenic Soybean. Crop Science 44: 646-652.

Schuhmacher KD. 2002. The importance of genetically modified products in the trade of agricultural goods and foodstuffs; in Dokumentation Diskurs Grune Gentechnik Bundesministerium fur Verbraucherschutz Ernahrung und Landwirtschaft, Berlin, Germany (http://wwwgruenegentechnikde/oku_Anh290102/ Schuhmacher_vortrpdf).

Scutt CP, Zubko E and Meyer P. 2002. Techniques for the removal of marker genes from transgenic plants. Biochimie *84*, 1119–1126.

Sengupta S, Chakraborti D, Mondal HA and Das S. 2010. Selectable antibiotic resistance marker gene-free transgenic rice harbouring the garlic leaf lectin gene exhibits resistance to sap-sucking planthoppers. Plant Cell Rep. 29: 261-271.

Sheen J, Hwang S, Niwa Y, Kobayashi H and Galbraith DW. 1995. Green-fluorescent protein as a new vital marker in plant cells. Plant J. 8 777–784.

Sreekala C, Wu L, Gu K, Wang D, Tian D and Yin Z. 2005. Excision of a selectable marker in transgenic rice *Oryza sativa* L using a chemically regulated Cre/loxP system. Plant Cell Rep. 24 86–94.

Stein JC and Hansen G. 1999. Mannose induces an endonuclease responsible for DNA laddering in plant cells. Plant Physiol. 121 71–79.

Sugita K, Matsunaga E, Kasahara T and Ebinuma H. 2000. Transgene stacking in plants in the absence of sexual crossing. Mol. Breed. 6 529–536.

Sundar IK and Sakthivel N. 2008. Advances in selectable marker genes for plant transformation. J. Plant. Physiol. 165 1698–1716.

Sripriya R, Raghupathy V and Veluthambi K. 2008. Generation of selectable marker free sheath blight resistant transgenic rice plants by efficient co-transformation of a cointegrate vector T-DNA and a binary vector T-DNA in one *Agrobacterium tumefaciens* strain. Plant Cell Rep. 27: 1635-1644.

Thomson J. 2001. Horizontal transfer of DNA from GM Crops to bacteria and to mammalian cells. J. Food Sci. 66 188–193.

Upadhyaya CP, Nookaraju A, Gururani MA, Upadhyaya DC, Kim DH, Chun SC and Park SW. 2010. An Update on the Progress towards the Development of Marker-Free Transgenic Plants, Bot. Stud., vol. 51, pp. 277–292.

Wang Y, Chen B, Hu Y, Li J and Lin Z. 2005. Inducible excision of selectable marker gene from transgenic plants by the Cre/lox site-specific recombination system. Transgenic Res. 14 605–614.

Yoder JI and Goldsbrough AP. 1994. Transformation systems for generating marker-free transgenic plants. Bio/Technology12 263–267.

Yuan Y, Liu YJ and Wang T. 2004. A new cre/lox system for deletion of selectable marker gene. Acta Bot. Sin. 46 862–866.

Zhang Y, Li H, Ouyang B, Lu Y and Ye Z. 2006. Chemical-induced autoexcision of selectable markers in elite tomato plants transformed with a gene conferring resistance to lepidopteran insects. Biotechnol. Lett. 28 1247–1253.

Zhang WJ, Yang SS, Shen XY, Jin YS, Zhao HJ and Wang T. 2009. The salt-tolerance gene rstB can be used as a selectable marker in plant genetic transformation. Mol. Breed. 23 269–277.

Zhang Y, Liu H, Li B, Zhang JT, Li Y and Zhang H. 2009. Generation of selectable marker-free transgenic tomato resistant to drought cold and oxidative stress using the Cre/ loxPDNA excision system. Transgenic Res. 18 607–619.

Zubko E, Scutt C and Meyer P. 2000. Intrachromosomal recombination between attP regions as a tool to remove selectable marker genes from tobacco transgenes. Nat. Biotechnol. *18*, 442–445.

❑❑❑

Chapter - 8

Metabolomics- A Step to Better Future

Manoj Kumar Singh
Director and Research Scientist, Singh Biotech LLP. H.no.-531, MIG-21 Ward No.41, Waidhan, District: Singrauli, Madhya Pradesh-486886,
E-mail: manojksingh85@gmail.com.

Every aspect of the living organism is the sum total result of the metabolism carried out within its cells and in other organisms. Metabolism is the sum total of the chemical reactions occurring in the cell or organism. Metabolism is of two kinds:

1. **Anabolism**- It is also known as constructive metabolism as it involves synthesis of complex substances from the simpler ones, which are required for growth, maintenance and storage in the organism. Example: Formation of starch from glucose.
2. **Catabolism**- It is also known as destructive metabolism as it involves breaking of the complex substances into simpler ones, leading to release of the energy required for performing various activities of living beings. Example: Respiration.

Metabolite is the end product or the intermediate product of a biological pathway. Metabolite can be classified into two types mainly:

a. Primary metabolite

b. Secondary metabolite

Primary Metabolite

Metabolites that are involved in those processes that are basically similar in all the organisms and that are necessary for maintenance and survival known as the Primary Metabolites. The primary metabolites include metabolites involved in the processes of growth (Biosynthesis), energy production, transformation and turnover of cellular components. These are produced mainly during the growth phase of the organism. Examples: Amino acids, DNA, RNA etc.

Secondary Metabolite

Metabolites that do not play any role in any of the important biological function in the life of organisms that produce them are known as the Secondary metabolites. The Secondary Metabolite is produced after the growth phase and especially during the stress periods. Examples: pigments, alkaloids, antibiotics, terpenes etc.

Sources of Metabolites

SOURCES OF METABOLITIES		
ANIMALS	PLANTS	MICROOGANISMS

Animals

a. Animal cell culture

Better understanding at the cellular level and the different conditions required for the growth of the specific tissues through metabolomic study has now made it possible to culture artificial Skin, cartilages and even organs.

Animal cell culture is used to produce important biopharmaceutical metabolites like:

- Virus vaccines eg: polio, rabies, mumps and hepatitis B etc.
- Monoclonal antibodies
- Recombinant proteins eg: Blood clotting factor VIII and IX, Eryhtropoitein
- Human growth hormone
- Interferon and interleukins

b. Genetically modified Animals

Study of metabolites and the metabolic pathways that govern their production has helped in the application of the Genetic engineering into using the whole animal as a bioreactor for the production of those molecules which have medicinal importance and even in the higher production of useful metabolites in the animals especially for higher wool and meat production. Some genetically modified sheep and pigs have been used to secrete blood clotting factor VIII and IX into their milk which is separated from it.

Plants

a. Plant cell culture:

Plants are the source of a large variety of biochemicals, which are metabolites of both primary and secondary metabolisms. But secondary metabolites are of much greater interest since they have impressive biological activities like antimicrobial, antibiotic, insecticidal, hormonal properties and valuable pharmacological and pharmaceutical activities and many are used as flavours, fragrances, colours etc. These secondary metabolites are produced in a very small amount and for their large amount production one will require cutting down many trees/plants but cell culture offers a brilliant alternative. Plant cell suspension is used for biochemicals production in high concentration for example: Berberine from *Coptis japonica*, Taxol from *Taxus spp*. and Ginseng from Ginseng etc.

b. Genetically modified plants

The recombinant DNA technology is used to improve the agronomic, nutritive and stress resistance features in-order to achieve high plant yield. The gene *aroA* isolated from *Salmonella typhimurium* or *E.coli* is inserted into plant for resistance to Glyphosate. The *cry* gene of *B.thuringiensis* is inserted into plants for Insect resistance. Also the gene for beta carotene was inserted into rice to produce vitamin A rich Golden rice for omission of vitamin deficiency diseases among the poor people.

Microorganisms

a. Bacteria

Among the microorganisms bacteria are considered the biggest source of the metabolites used for various human activities and are involved in important natural

They are used for the commercial production of:

- Enzymes eg: alpha amylase, lactase, pectinase, alkaline protease etc.
- Antibiotics eg: Protein antibiotics "Bacteriocins" from *Lactobacillus spp.*
- Organic acids eg: lactic acid, citric acid etc
- Amino acid eg: glutamic acid, lysine etc
- Alcohols
- Biopesticides eg: Use of *Bacillus thuringiensis*
- Biofertilizer eg: Use of *Azotobacter, Rhizobium spp.*

b. Fungi

They are the achlorophyllous, heterotrophic, sporeforming, nonvascular eukaryotic organisms. The fungi in nature through decomposition maintain the nutrient and carbon recycling are also considered as the biosynthetic factories due to their large product range of industrial products like alcohols, fats, citric acid, gluconic acid etc courtesy their fementation property. Also they are the large source of antibiotics like penicillin. The fungi associated with the plant roots are known as the mycorrhizae which not only help in providing the nutrients to the plants also are found to help in the removal of toxic metals from the soil and in land remediation (Khan *et al.*, 2000). Thus, showing function of a biofertilizers, biopesticide and bioremediator.

c. Cyanobacteria

Cyanobacteria are common and natural aquatic organisms present in many surface waters. Cyanobacteria are single-celled microscopic bacteria and can be found in fresh, salt or brackish waters. Cyanobacteria are source of many high value products ranging from sugars, isoprene, ethanol, hydrogen, lipids, and amino acids etc which make it most valuable microorganism (Ducat *et al.*, 2011).

Metabolic pathway study has long been a part of the biotechnology but in its initial stage followed rather crude methodology to study the important metabolites and identify commercially important microbes and plants. Studies of the metabolic pathways not only help in determining the different types of the metabolites present in the organism but also in the study of the important enzymes and their activity. For studying biotic or abiotic stresses on animals, plants or microbes, metabolomics could very easily be applied to large populations, because this approach tends to be of higher throughput and generally lower cost than transcriptomics and proteomics, whilst also providing indications of which area of metabolism may be affected by external perturbation (Hollywood *et al.*, 2006).

Metabolomics is relatively new discipline and techniques for high throughput metabolic profiling are still under development. No single technique is suitable for the analysis of all different types of molecules, so a mixture of techniques is used. Methods such as gas chromatography, high pressure liquid chromatography and capillary electrophoresis are used to separate according to various chemical and physical properties. The molecules then identified using methods such as mass spectrometry. Metabolomics deals with the identification, qualitative and quantitative measurement of the metabolites acting in the biochemical network. It is widely applied advanced microbiological research to understand the metabolic as well as systems behaviors of industrial important microorganisms. It is rapidly becoming possible to measure hundreds or thousands of metabolites in small samples of biological fluids or tissues. This makes it possible to assess the metabolic component of nutritional phenotypes and will allow individualized dietary recommendations (German *et al.*, 2004). Metabolomics due to its focus on the metabolites and their level at different stages is rapidly becoming a favorite Omics used for establishing various disease specific signatures. Metabolic aberrations have been defined in various disease processes either as contributing to the disease, as potential biomarkers, or as therapeutic targets (Mangalam *et al.*, 2013). In diagnosis of Alzheimer Disease, profiling in plasma and CSF could be used to establish metabolic signatures for the purposes of an accurate diagnosis, including the early clinical (e.g., MCI) or preclinical stages, or within individuals to monitor disease progression and therapeutic efficacy (Trushina *et al.*, 2013). Metabolomics involves fewer complexities, is more precise and provides more relevant data compared with other techniques. It has also been proven to be a valuable analytical tool for the identification of secondary metabolites from medicinal plants, particularly for evidence-based development of new phyto-therapeutical agents and Nutraceuticals (Satheeshkumar *et al.*, 2012). Metabolomics is a powerful tool for the assessment of expressed (in vivo or in situ) biological processes, which can be used to investigate microbial activity in different environmental conditions and pollutant abatement (Callaghan *et al.*, 2013).

All the information acquired from the metabolic study is used to construct a metabolome for each organism similar to their genome and proteome. This information of different metabolites and the pathways governing their production is used in the improvement of their quantity and quality. The Figure No. 1 shows the typical scheme for Metabolome analysis and Figure No. 2 shows Application of the Metabolomics.

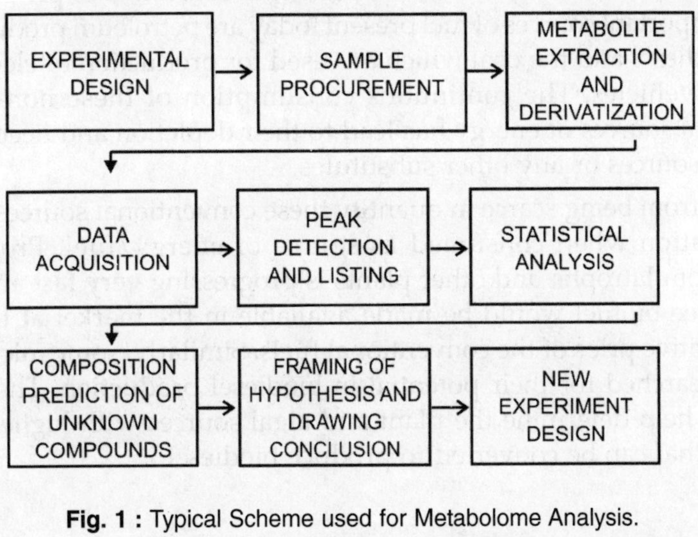

Fig. 1 : Typical Scheme used for Metabolome Analysis.

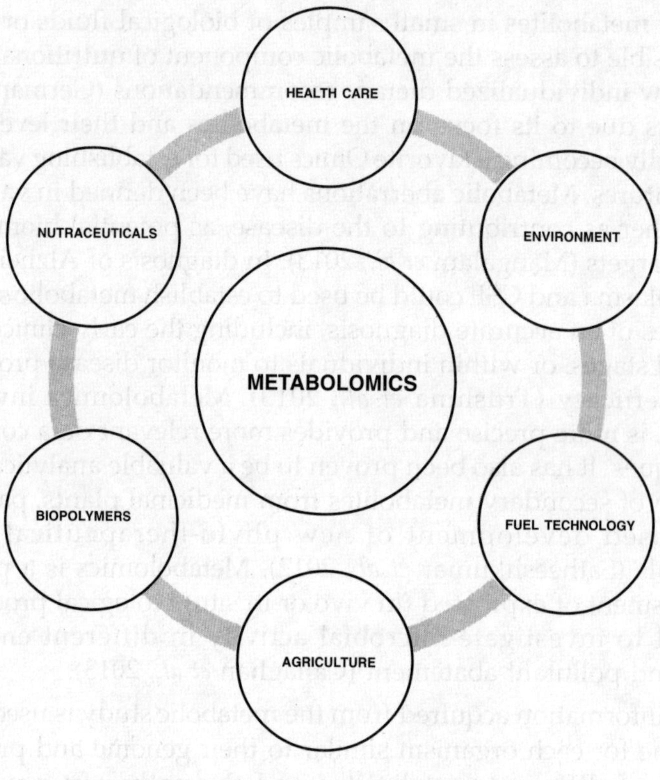

Fig. 2 : Applications of Metabolomics

Fuel Technology

A Fuel is a Substance that can be used or is consumed to produce energy. The most important sources of fuel present today are petroleum products namely petrol and diesel and the coal which are used for production of electricity and to run the vehicles. The continuous consumption of these non-renewable conventional sources of energy has lead to their depletion and need for newer alternative sources or any other substitutes.

Apart from being scarce in quantity these conventional sources produce a lot of pollution when consumed as source of energy/fuel. Production of biodiesel from Jatropha and other plants is progressing very fast and soon the pollution free biofuel would be made available in the market at the cheaper and competitive price of the conventional fuels. Similarly, some microalgae are also been searched for their potential in biodiesel production. The metabolic studies can help determine the plant and algal sources with higher lipid and oil content that can be converted to produce biodiesel.

Environment

Call it a curse or the biggest drawback of the development that it has always affected the environment and that too not in a positive manner but with a negative impact. We humans have failed to realize its importance at the very time but reconcile it after the time has gone away. The enormous growth of industrialization and the use of numerous aromatic compounds in dyestuffs, explosives, pesticides and pharmaceuticals has resulted in serious environmental pollution and has attracted considerable attention continuously over the last two decades. Many aromatic hydrocarbons, nitroaromatic compounds, polycyclic aromatic hydrocarbons, polychlorinated biphenyls, diauxins and their derivatives are highly toxic, mutagenic and/or carcinogenic to natural microflora as well as to higher systems including humans. The increasing costs and limited efficiency of traditional physicochemical treatments of soil have spurred the development of new remediation technologies. Phytoremediation is emerging as an efficient treatment technology that uses plants to bioremediate pollutants from soil environments (Singh *et al.*, 2003) and Plant-Fungus association is a promising combination for the abatement of the land pollution (Khan *et al.*, 2000).

Agriculture

The world population is growing at a very fast face and so is the number of hungry stomachs. The case of hunger and malnutrition is worse in the developing and the underdeveloped countries. With more emphasis on industrialization and development more land is being used for setting up the industries and for the residential purposes. There is a great need for higher yielding and nutrition richness of the crops been grown today due to very high demand and great amount of cases of diseases arising due to improper nutrition. Metabolomics provides the complete knowledge of the metabolites present in the plant as these metabolites are responsible for the defense mechanism, nutritive value, aroma and colours which attract insects for the pollination. Through the application of the metabolomics in the form of metabolic engineering it is now possible to produce plants as crops and vegetables which have higher resistance to drought, pests, C-N interactions etc (Saxena *et al.*, 2013 and Dudareva *et al.*, 2008).

Biopolymers

Polyhydroxy- alkanoates (PHA) are synthesized from acetyl-CoA used as a precursor and are used for the synthesis of biodegradable plastics with thermoplastic properties. Example: Polyhydroxybutyrate (PHB). At present the PHAs are produced by bacterial fermentation, and the cost of biodegradable plastic is quite high than that of synthetic plastics. Genes encoding the enzymes aceto-acetyl CoA reductase (*phbB*) and PHB synthase (*phbC*) involved in the PHB synthesis from the precursor acetyl-CoA have been transferred from the bacterium *Alcaligenes eutrophus* and expressed into the plastids of leaves in *Arabidopsis thaliana*. The Figure No. 3 is showing the pathway for the production of PHB.

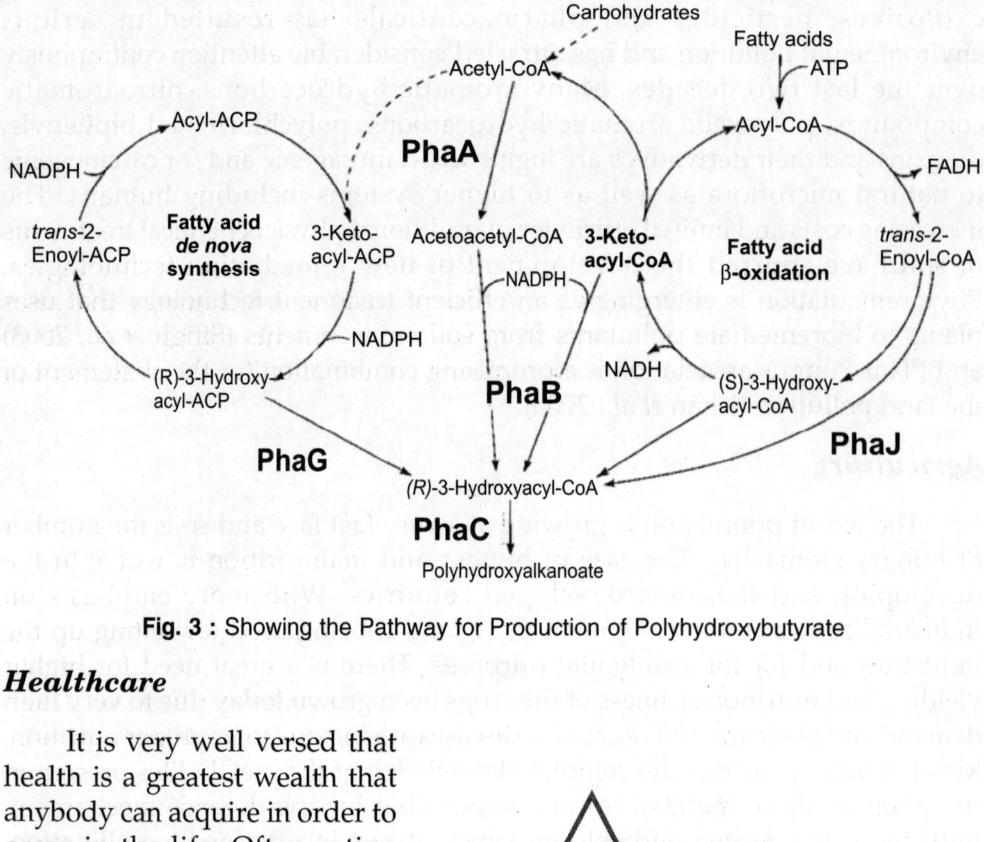

Fig. 3 : Showing the Pathway for Production of Polyhydroxybutyrate

Healthcare

It is very well versed that health is a greatest wealth that anybody can acquire in order to grow in the life. Often eating healthy foods and regular exercise is associated with healthy body. But with ever changing environmental conditions, food habits and pattern of living broadly influence our health. One can never tell when did he/she got ill and how much impact then it will have on them. The various

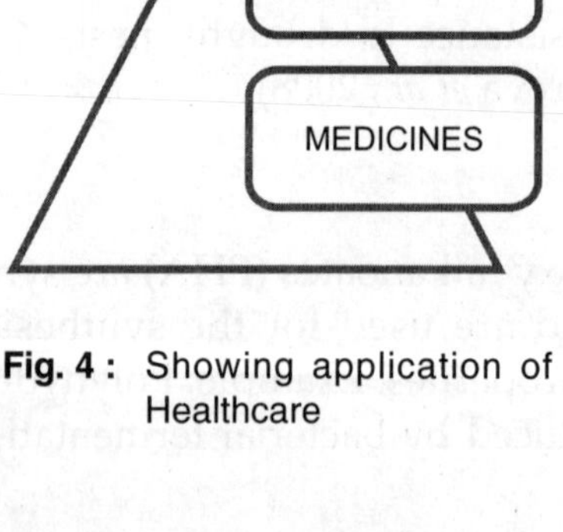

Fig. 4 : Showing application of Metabolomics in Healthcare

metabolites present in the body fluid help in the diagnosis of the disease and bio-active compounds from microbes and plants serve as medicines for various disease treatments. The Figure No. 4 is showing application of Metabolomics in Healthcare.

a. Diagnostics

With more than 90% of all diagnostics clinical assays based on testing for small molecules and 30% of the identified genetic disorders involve diseases of small molecule metabolites. The metabolites study, offer a great advantage to keep a track of one's health and proper diagnosis of the disease. The diseases associated with the metabolic disorders are very good examples of metabolic study and application in the disease management.

b. Medicines

The 21st century witnessed re-emergence of Ayurveda and shifting from chemical based drugs to biopharmaceutical that is biological natural sources of medicines. Herbal drugs have become a major topic of study leading to more and more plant metabolites being evaluated for their potential as antimicrobials and different disease treatments like treating skin diseases (Roopashree *et al.*, 2008). 89% of all the known drugs are small molecules and 50% of all drugs derived from pre-existing metabolites, offer great advantage of metabollomics study.

Nutraceuticals

The food or the food components having both nutritive and medical/health benefit are known as the Nutraceuticals. Various microorganisms and plant sources work as the prebiotics providing important nutrients helpful for the proliferation of the gut bacteria and also as the probiotics providing the required nutrition in their whole form. The *Lactobacillus spp.* present in the curd helps in the utilization of the lactose sugar present in the milk and provides vitamins B1 and B2, some low calorie sugars and Polysaccharides etc. (Hugenholtz *et al.*, 2002). The non-digestible food ingredients like some carbohydrates, proteins and lipids stimulate the absorption of several minerals etc work as prebiotics and certain microbes like *Lactobacillus spp.*, *Aspergillus oryzae* and *Bacillus subtilis* etc are used as Probiotics in which lactic acid produced during the lactose breakdown by Lactobacillus lowering the pH and preventing the growth of other harmful bacteria (Choudhari *et al.*, 2008). The figure no. 5 shows the metabolism of glucose by *Lactobacillus spp.*

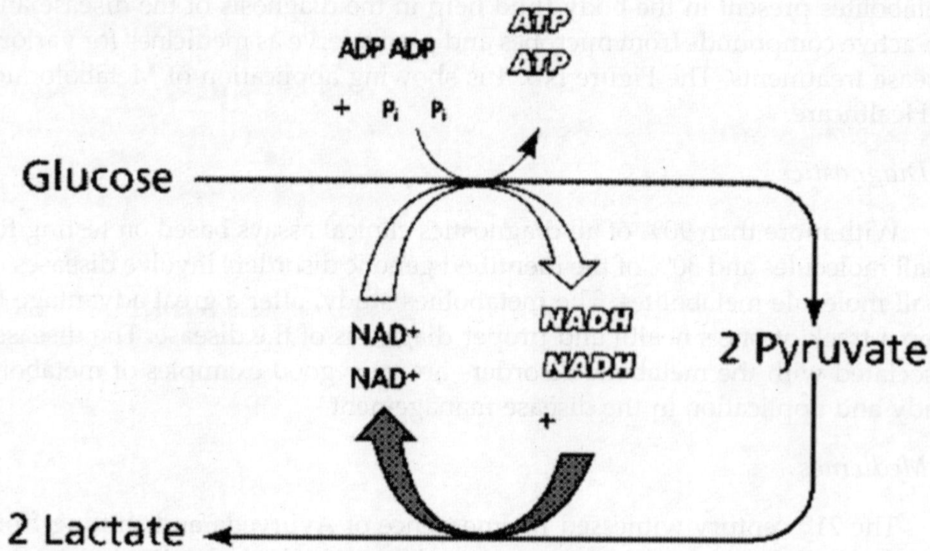

Fig. 5 : Pathway for Glucose metabolism by *Lactobacillus spp.*

Review of Literature

Among the various sources of the commercially beneficial metabolites a new and novel sources have been found in marine and fresh water cyanobacteria. Various studies have suggested that the bioactive compounds present in the marine and fresh water cyanobacteria having ecological roles as allelochemicals, specifically including compounds that may inhibit competing sympatric macrophytes, algae and microbes. These allelochemicals may also play a role in defense against potential predators and grazers, particularly aquatic invertebrates and their larvae. Evidences of allelochemical roles of cyanobacterial toxins, prove the potential for development and application of these compounds as algaecides, herbicides and insecticides (Berry *et al.*, 2008). Although many microorganisms have been used for the bioindustrial generation of valuable metabolites, the productive potential of cyanobacterial species has remained largely unexplored. Cyanobacteria possess several advantages as organisms for bioindustrial processes, including simple input requirements, tolerance of marginal agricultural environments, rapid genetics, and carbon-neutral applications that could be leveraged to address global climate change concerns. The potential of the engineering of cyanobacterial species for the production of valuable bioindustrial compounds, including natural cyanobacterial products (e.g. sugars and isoprene), biofuels (e.g. alcohols, alkanes and hydrogen), and other commodity chemicals is being studied (Ducat *et al.*, 2011).

Onion has been an important vegetable crop grown the world over and has many medicinal values too, thus having nutraceutical importance. With the recent technological advancements in biological sciences and instrumentation, nutraceutical breeding is becoming easier. Metabolomics is a key technology available to plant breeders that can combine with existing technologies to breed healthier plant food. Onions is a widely-grown crop that has tremendous health benefits. The health benefits of onions are due to secondary metabolites. In nature, plants produce secondary metabolites in low quantities. The use of metabolomics to determine production mechanisms of secondary metabolites would help develop onion cultivars that contain high levels of secondary metabolites (Saxena *et al.*, 2013).

The nutritional key role of grain legumes is unquestionable, due to the massive presence of macro and micronutrients. Among these nutrients, proteins play a relevant role in consideration of their amino acid composition which can easily be balanced in the diet. In the frame of a reappraisal of the effects that grain legume components may have on human well-being, widely accepted claims on their beneficial activity in the prevention and treatment of various diseases has been put forward. Specific proteins, and there from peptides, have unequivocally been shown to play a role in plasma lipid and glucose homeostasis, inhibition of hydrolytic enzymes involved in a number of critical physio-pathological phenomena, blood pressure control and immuno-modulation. All these basic functions are more or less directly related to a number of diseases, most of which are typical of the affluent countries, including cardio-vascular diseases, diabetes, cancer, obesity, hypertension, immunity-related diseases. Many efforts and further studies are needed in order to disclose the mechanism(s) underlying the grain legume proteins/peptides effects; to identify and characterise novel biological activities often "hidden" inside the polypeptide chains, to establish clear dose/response relationships in order to calibrate the preparation and use of nutraceutically enhanced foods. As parallel or further steps, the biotechnological approaches can be extremely useful as cognitive tools and in novel more effective biologically active protein molecules design (Duranti *et al.*, 2006). Lactic acid has a nutraceutical value which is regularly comsumed in the form of curd or yogurt etc along with other food and also as a constituent of the cosmetic or health product. Lactic acid bacteria have a relatively simple and well described metabolism where sugar source is mainly converted to lactic acid. Metabolic engineering strategies on the level of sugar metabolism, that leads to either the efficient re-routing of the lactococcal sugar metabolism to nutritional end-products other than lactic acid such as L-alanine, several low-calorie sugars and oligosaccharides or to enhancement of sugar metabolism for complete removal of (undesirable) sugars from food materials. Various metabolic engineering approaches that aim at increasing the flux through complex biosynthetic pathways, leading to the production of the B-vitamins folate and riboflavin are been developed (Hugenholtz *et al.*, 2002). The biosynthetic pathway of L-tartaric acid, the form most commonly encountered in nature, and its catabolic ties to vitamin C, remain a challenge to plant scientists. Vitamin C and L-tartaric acid are plant-derived metabolites with intrinsic human value. In contrast to most fruits during development, grapes accumulate Ltartaric acid, which remains within the berry throughout ripening. Berry taste and the organoleptic properties and aging potential of wines are intimately linked to levels of L-tartaric acid present in the fruit, and those added during vinification. The use of transcript and metabolite profiling to identify candidate cDNAs from genes expressed at developmental times and in tissues appropriate for L-tartaric acid biosynthesis in grape berries. Surveying organic acid content in *Vitis* and related genera have lead to identification of a non-tartrate-forming species in which this gene is deleted. This species accumulates in excess of three times the levels of vitamin C than comparably ripe berries of tartrate-accumulating species, suggesting that modulation of tartaric acid biosynthesis may provide a rational basis for the production of grapes rich in vitamin C (DeBolt *et al.*, 2006). In a research framework proposal it was suggested that integrating the dynamic concentration profile of bioavailable xenobiotic molecules that result from *in vivo* absorption and hepatic and gut bacterial metabolism, as well as the human metabolic response profile will probably address the bottleneck problem in the pharmacological evaluation of multicomponent pharmaceuticals and nutraceuticals, leading to the direct elucidation of the pharmacological and molecular mechanisms of these compounds (Lan *et al.*, 2013).

In an attempt to round up the dominance of *Pseudomonas aeuroginosa* in varied environmental conditions a study was conducted using the metabolic approach, investigating the metabolome profiles of two genetically and morphologically divergent strains, the reference strain PAO1 and the mucoid clinical isolate TBCF10839 in exponential growth and stationary phase in six different carbon sources (cadaverine, casamino acids, citrate, glucose, succinate and tryptone). Both strains exhibited strong similarities in mode of growth; the metabolite patterns were mainly defined by the growth condition. Besides this adaptive response, a basic core metabolism shapes the *P. aeruginosa* metabolome, independent of growth phase, carbon source and genetic background. This core metabolism includes pathways related to the central energy and amino acid metabolism. These consistently utilized metabolic pathways are closely related to glutamate which represents a dominant metabolite in all conditions analysed. This specified adaptation strategy combined with the invariant basic core metabolism may represent a fundamental requirement for the metabolic versatility of this organism (Frimmersdorf *et al.*, 2010).

Metabolomics is a relatively new approach aimed at improved understanding of these metabolic networks and the subsequent biochemical composition of plants and other biological organisms. Analytical tools within metabolomics including mass spectrometry (MS) and nuclear magnetic resonance (NMR) spectroscopy can profile the impact of time, stress, nutritional status, and environmental perturbation on hundreds of metabolites simultaneously resulting in massive, complex data sets. This information, in combination with transcriptomics and proteomics, has the potential to generate a more complete picture of the composition of food and feed products, to optimize crop trait development, and to enhance diet and health. Although much progress has been demonstrated, challenges remain before the complex information generated by metabolomic research can be fully interpreted and applied to an understanding of the biological systems upon which modern agriculture is based (Dixon *et al.*, 2006).

The feasibility of metabolomic fingerprinting approach based on ultra-high performance liquid chromatography quadrupole-time-of-flight mass spectrometry (UHPLC-QTOFMS) was studied to assess its ability to discriminate between maize varieties, and to show the associations between them on the metabolomic level. The non-targeted metabolomic analysis was applied to assess the variability within two varieties grown under different environmental conditions and to characterise the association within a sample set comprising both conventional and transgenic (MON-OO81O-6) maize varieties cultivated under the same environmental conditions (locality). UHPLC-QTOFMS technique demonstrated to hold a great potential in discriminative metabolomics of conventional and Bt transgenic maize varieties. The processing of metabolomic fingerprints (mass spectra) by advanced chemometric methods demonstrated the capability of this approach to classify various maize varieties in both GM and non-GM sample sets (Vaclavik *et al.*, 2013).

Metabolomics is the functional analysis method aimed at acquiring robust and reproducible quantitative information on cellular metabolites. Metabolic fingerprinting is gaining considerable interest across a wide variety of disciplines especially in biomarker discovery for disease prognosis, diagnose and therapy monitoring. Not only will the discovery of the multiple metabolites markers be beneficial for patient stratification and assessing therapeutic intervention but the identification of the key metabolites and their spatial distribution within the tissues will likely lead to a greater understanding of the physiology of the disease process that will serve as a hypothesis generator for novel drug targets (Ellis *et al.*, 2007).

A study reporting the chemical investigation and cytotoxic activity of the secondary metabolites produced by the endophytic fungus *Chaetomium* sp. isolated from *Salvia officinalis* growing in Morocco. This plant was collected from the Beni-Mellal Mountain in Morocco and belongs to the Lamiaceae family and is named in Morocco "Salmia". The endophytic fungus *Chaetomium* sp. was isolated from the tissues of the stem of this plant. The fungal strain was identified by PCR. The crude organic extract of the fungal strain was proven to be active when tested for cytotoxicity against L5178Y mouse lymphoma cells. Chemical investigation of the secondary metabolites showed that cochliodinol is the main component beside isocochliodinol. The structures of the isolated compounds were determined on the basis of NMR analysis (1H, 13C, COSY and HMBC) as well as by mass spectrometry using ESI (Electron Spray Ionisation) as source (Debbab *et al.*, 2009).

In a study aiming to isolate and identify novel active metabolite, Streptomyces aureofaciens CMUAc130 was isolated from the root tissue of Zingiber officinale Rosc. (Zingiberaceae). It was an antagonist of Colletotrichum musae and Fusarium oxysporum, the causative agents of anthracnose of banana and wilt of wheat, respectively. Evidence for the in-vitro antibiosis of S. aureofaciens CMUAc130 was demonstrated by the zone of fungal-growth inhibition. Microscopic observations showed thickness and bulbous structures at the edges of the inhibited fungal hyphae. The culture filtrate and crude extract from this strain were all inhibitory to tested phytopathogenic fungi. The major active ingredients from the culture filtrate of S. aureofaciens CMUAc130 were purified by silica gel-column chromatography and identified to be (i) 5,7-dimethoxy-4-p-methoxylphenylcoumarin and (ii) 5,7-dimethoxy-4-phenylcoumarin by NMR and mass-spectral data, respectively. Bioassay studies showed that compounds (i) and (ii) had antifungal activities against tested fungi, and their MICs were found to be 120 and 150 mg ml"1, respectively (Taechowisan *et al.*, 2005).

In an attempt to find out natural sources of the antibiotic protecting the plants from disease causing pathogens twenty *Pseudomonas fluorescens* strains were isolated from rice growing soil samples and characterized. One of the *P.fluorescens* isolated and identified from the dual culture test. It was fermented for secondary metabolite in a small scale and extracted with ethyl acetate. The isolated metabolite tested against rice fungal pathogens. The structure of the compound was elucidated by high-resolution NMR spectroscopy (Battu *et al.*, 2009).

Metabolic engineering of the volatile spectrum offers enormous potential for plant improvement because of the great contribution of volatile secondary metabolites to reproduction, defense and food quality. Recent advances in the identification of the genes and enzymes responsible for the biosynthesis of volatile compounds have made this metabolic engineering highly feasible. Notable successes have been reported in enhancing plant defenses and improving scent and aroma quality of flowers and fruits. These studies have also revealed challenges and limitations which will be likely surmounted as our understanding of plant volatile network improves (Dudareva *et al.*, 2008).

Plant cells and tissue cultures hold great promise for controlled production of a myriad of useful secondary metabolites on demand. The current yield and productivity cannot fulfill the commercial goal of a plant cell-based bioprocess for the production of most secondary metabolites. A rational approach to molecular plant cell bioprocessing based on the fundamental understanding of metabolic pathways and their regulations is urgently required to stimulate further advances; however, the strategies and technical framework are still being developed. Using anthocyanin biosynthesis as a case study, an integrated postgenomic approach has been proposed. This combines the functional analysis of metabolic pathways for biosynthesis of a particular metabolite from profiling of gene expression and protein expression to metabolic profiling. A global correlation not only can thus be established at the three molecular levels, but also places emphasis on the interactions between primary metabolism and secondary metabolism; between competing and/or complimentary pathways; and between biosynthetic and post-biosynthetic events (Zhang *et al.*, 2004). Fenugreek (Trigonella foenum-graecum L.) has a long and respected history of medicinal uses in Middle East and Persian medicine. The hypocholesterolaemic and hypoglycaemic effects of fenugreek were attributed to its major steroidal sapogenin, diosgenin and its major alkaloid, trigonelline. Metabolic engineering of fenugreek is an effective tool to both increase diosgenin and trigonelline yield and alter those distribution. In this order, there are some possibilities for increasing the diosgenin and trigonelline contained in the seed, either during the growing period by using different cultural techniques or during post harvest treatments by different techniques (enzymes, hormones, etc.) of germination with incubation, different conditions of incubation and fermentation by storage by the use of tissue and cell culture (static or suspension) and by biological manipulation of the steroidal and alkaloid yield (Mehrafarin *et al.*, 2010).

The cost-effective production of biofuels from renewable materials will begin to address energy security and climate change concerns. Ethanol, naturally produced by microorganisms, is currently the major biofuel in the transportation sector. Advanced biofuels, such as long chain alcohols and isoprenoid- and fatty acid-based biofuels, have physical properties that more closely resemble petroleum-derived fuels, and as such are an attractive alternative for the future supplementation or replacement of petroleum-derived fuels. The recent developments in the engineering of metabolic pathways for the production of known and potential advanced biofuels by microorganisms. The focus is on the metabolic engineering of genetically tractable organisms such as *Escherichia coli* and *Saccharomyces cerevisiae* for the production of these advanced biofuels (Pamela *et al.*, 2010).

Elucidating the molecular and biochemical mechanisms of methylotrophy in fresh and marine water cyanobacteria by comparing their genomes functional homologies and metabolomes with Type I, II and X methylotrophs using systems biology approach will provide an insight to understand their methane assimilation capacities in the ecosystem. It is emphasis the genomes of cyanobacteria can have the metabolic capabilities not only for methane, but also other C1 compounds assimilation by finding the genes involved in their metabolomes. The genes with unknown functions are predicted and complied with known functional genes for reconstruction of methane pathway using bioinformatics resources and thereafter, metabolic model of this pathway is developed with experimental as well as hypothetical data using systems biology approach. The resulted exposure will perhaps coincide with experimental data so as to exploit cyanobacteria for producing hydrogen from C1 compounds and for bioremediation purpose (Chellapandi *et al.*, 2010). Phytoremediation of aromatic pollutants aims to degrade them into less toxic/non toxic harmless compounds and limit their further movement by sequestration and accumulation. Deep groundwater contaminants can be treated by irrigation on constructed wetlands. Several plant species, in particular poplar trees, have shown promising potential for phytoremediation of many highly toxic and recalcitrant organic compounds such as PCBs, PAHs, nitroaromatic explosives, etc. This plant-mediated technology could be used as an in situ, non-invasive and aesthetic solution with the additional advantages of versatility and low cost. It can be employed in high-risk contamination zones by planting specific species for preventive measures (Singh *et al.*, 2003).

Metabolic Engineering

The ultimate application of the information obtained from the metabolic pathways studies and generation of metabolome has been identification of the important metabolites and successfully producing or enhancing their production in the same or genetically modified organism through metabolic engineering by coupling with genetic engineering following the given methodology as shown in figure no. 6.

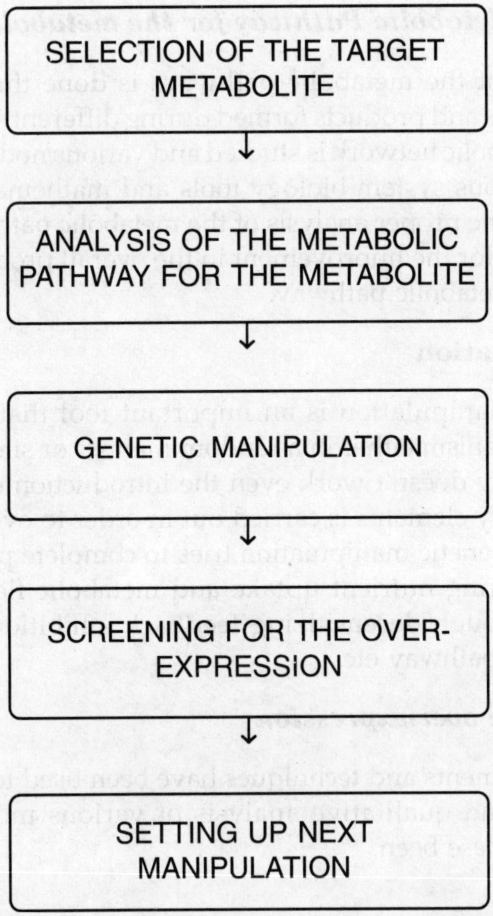

Fig. 6 : Showing different steps of Metabolic Engineering.

Metabolic engineering can be defined as improvement of cellular activities by manipulation of enzymatic, transport and regulatory functions of the cell with the use of recombinant DNA technology.

Selection of the target metabolite

The first step of the metabolic engineering involves identification and selection of the important metabolite having health benefit or any other importance. This can be achieved through searching of the databases, reading of the Published books and other resources. Also it is important to identify the organism through which it can be commercially produced that is in a large amount.

Analysis of the Metabolic Pathway for the metabolite

The analysis of the metabolic pathways is done through study of the different metabolites and products formed during different stages of a metabolic pathway. The metabolic network is studied and various node points are marked out. There are various system biology tools and mathematical and statistical evaluation help in the proper analysis of the metabolic pathway and figure out the correct strategy for the improvement in the overall production of the target metabolite in the metabolic pathway.

Genetic Manipulation

The genetic manipulation is an important tool that is used to induce mutation in the organism either in a random manner or site specific for higher yield. If this strategy doesn't work even the introduction of the heterologous genes and regulatory elements is carried out in order to overproduction of the target metabolite. Genetic manipulation tries to complete partial pathways for new products, altering nutrient uptake and metabolic flow and redirecting metabolic flow through desensitizing feedback inhibition and alteration in protein processing pathway etc.

Screening for the over-expression

Various instruments and techniques have been used for the identification and quantitative and qualitative analysis of various metabolites. The few important among these been:

I. Assay

An assay is an investigative (analytic) procedure in laboratory medicine, pharmacology, environmental biology, and molecular biology for qualitatively assessing or quantitatively measuring the presence or amount or the functional activity of a target entity (the analyte) which can be a drug or biochemical substance or a cell in an organism or organic sample.

Bioassays are typically conducted to measure the effects of a substance on a living organism and are essential in the development of new drugs and in monitoring environmental pollutants. Both are procedures by which the potency or the nature of a substance is estimated by studying its effects on living matter. Bioassay is a procedure for the determination of the concentration of a particular constitution of a mixture. Bioassays are procedures that can determine the concentration of purity or biological activity of a substance such as vitamin, hormone, and plant growth factor. While measuring the effect on an organism, tissue cells, enzymes or the receptor is preparing to be compared to a standard preparation. Bioassays may be qualitative or quantitative. Qualitative bioassays are used for assessing the physical effects of a substance that may not be quantified, such as abnormal development or deformity.

II. LC/MS

Liquid Chromatography (LC) is a separation technique a small volume of liquid sample is injected into a tube packed with a porous particle (stationery phase) and individual components of the sample are separated from one another by a liquid moving under the influence of gravity. The separation is based on various chemical and physical interactions between their molecules and the packing particles. The separated components are collected at the exit of the column and are measured through external measuring instruments like spectrophotometer and Mass spectrometer etc. Before entering the mass spectrometer the sample is converted into ions by an ionizing device. The advanced version of the Liquid chromatography is High Performance Liquid Chromatography (HPLC), in principle both Liquid Chromatography and High Performance Liquid Chromatography are same except the speed, efficiency, sensitivity and ease of operation HPLC is far superior. In HPLC the small amount of liquid sample is injected through a tube packed with tiny particles of 3-5 ìm in diameter , where the individual components of the sample move down the packed tube with a liquid (mobile phase) forced through the column by high pressure applied by a pump. At the end lies a detector which measures the amount of the different components and gives output in the form of a Liquid Chromatogram.

Mass spectrometry is a powerful analytical technique used to identify to quantify metabolites, serving to both separate and to detect metabolites. It measures the masses of individual molecules that have been converted into ion like molecules that are electrically charged. Formation of gas phase sample ions is a prerequisite to the mass sorting and detection processes that occur in a mass spectrometer. Early mass spectrometers required a sample to be in the form of a gas but in modern spectrometers, samples in the form of a liquid solution or embedded in a solid matrix are used (Allwood *et al.*, 2010). The figure no.7 represents the process followed in a Mass spectrometer.

Fig. 7 : Showing the detection of a metabolite in a Mass Spectrometer.

III. NMR spectroscopy

Measures nuclear magnetism or changes in nuclear magnetism in a molecule. NMR spectroscopy measures the absorption of light (radio waves) due to changes in nuclear spin orientation. NMR only occurs when a sample is in a strong magnetic field. Different nuclei absorb at different energies (frequencies). NMR is fully quantitative and highly reproducible method and being the non-destructive it has emerged into a high throughput analysis system with minimal sample preparation and no need for derivatization. Modern NMR spectrometers have a very strong liquid helium-cooled superconducting magnet, because resolution directly depends on magnetic field strength. Less expensive machines using permanent magnets and lower resolution are also available.

Setting up next manipulation

After the screening for the success of the initial manipulation for the over-expression of the target metabolite or molecule, the decision is to go for second manipulation or strategy in case the previous manipulation fails to meet the target.

CONCLUSION

In the conclusion it can be said that metabolomics has emerged as most favored technology for vivid fields of Functional Genomics, Nutraceuticals, Pharmocogenomics and Clinical Research etc. The metabolite study has provided a great opportunity to evaluate metabolites as biomarkers which can be used for Diagnosis and Prognosis of the diseases and their better management. The various advances in the technology of Chromatography, Nuclear Magnetic Resonance and Mass Spectrometry have propelled our potential to study different metabolites both qualitatively and quantitatively. The study of the interaction among the plants and microbes has provided important information on production of different metabolites having properties for disease protection, growth promotion and remediation of various pollutants. Metabolomics has given insight into important secondary metabolites from plants and bacterial sources and also the metabolic pathways governing their production. Metabolic Engineering offers a mixing of information obtained from Metabolomics study with Recombinant DNA Technology to bring about changes at the genetic level for just overproduction of the target metabolite or adding another gene to produce a totally new product. Metabolomics has shown a great potential which can work with other fields of Omics to create a better future.

ACKNOWLEDGEMENT

I would like to thank "SINGH BIOTECH LLP" for providing me the favorable environment for my work and also my friends for their constant encouragement.

REFERENCES

A.G. Khan, C. Kuek, T.M. Chaudhry, C.S. Khoo, W.J. Hayes (2000), Role of plants, mycorrhizae and phytochelators in heavy metal contaminated land remediation, Chemosphere, 41:197-207.

Abdessamad Debbab, Amal Hassan Aly, Ru Angelie Edrada-Ebel, Werner E.G. Müller, Mahjouba Mosaddak, Abdelhak Hakiki, Rainer Ebel, Peter Proksch (2009), Bioactive secondary metabolites from the endophytic fungus *Chaetomium* sp. isolated from *Salvia officinalis* growing in Morocco, Biotechnol. Agron. Soc. Environ.13(2): 229-234.

AK Mangalam, LM Poisson, E Nemutlu, I Datta, A Denic, P Dzeja, M Rodriguez, R Rattan and S Giri (2013), Profile of Circulatory Metabolites in a Relapsing-remitting Animal Model of Multiple Sclerosis using Global Metabolomics, Clin Cell Immunol: 4.

Ashish Saxena and Christopher S Cramer (2013), Metabolomics: A Potential Tool for Breeding Nutraceutical Vegetables, Adv Crop Sci Tech, 1:2.

Avanee Choudhari, Dr. Shilpshri Shinde and Dr. B. N. Ramteke (2008), Prebiotics and Probiotics as Health promoter, Veterinary World, Vol.1(2): 59-61.

Callaghan AV (2013), Metabolomic investigations of anaerobic hydrocarbon-impacted environments, Curr Opin Biotechnol. 24(3):506-15.

Chellapandi, P and Dhivya.C (2010), Overview of Microbial Metabolomics: A Special Insight to Cyanobacterial Methylotrophy, J.Adv.Dev.Res.Vol-1(1): 59-73.

Daniel C. Ducat, Jeffrey C. Way and Pamela A. Silver (2011), Engineering cyanobacteria to generate high-value products, Trends in Biotechnology, Vol. 29, No. 2.

David E llis, Warwick B. Dunn, Julian L. Griffin, J. William Allwood and Royston Goodacre (2007), Metabolic Fingerprinting as a diagnostic tool, Pharmacogenomics,8(9):1243-1266.

Eliane Frimmersdorf,Sonja Horatzek, Anya Pelnikevich, Lutz Wiehlmann and Dietmar Schomburg (2010), How *Pseudomonas aeruginosa* adapts to various environments: a metabolomic approachem, Environmental Microbiology, 12(6), 1734–1747.

Eugenia Trushina, Tumpa Dutta, Xuan-Mai T. Persson, Michelle M. Mielke, Ronald C. Petersen (2013), Identification of Altered Metabolic Pathways in Plasma and CSF in Mild Cognitive Impairment and Alzheimer's Disease Using Metabolomics, Plos One, 8: 5.

German JB, Bauman DE, Burrin DG, Failla ML, Freake HC, King JC, Klein S, Milner JA, Pelto GH, Rasmussen KM, Zeisel SH (2004), Metabolomics in the opening decade of the 21st century: building the roads to individualized health, J Nutr.,134(10):2729-32.

J. William Allwood and Royston Goodacre (2010), An Introduction to Liquid Chromatography–Mass Spectrometry Instrumentation Applied in Plant Metabolomic AnalysesPhytochem. Anal.,21:33–47.

Jeroen Hugenholtz, Wilbert Sybesma, Masja Nierop Groot, Wouter Wisselink, Victor Ladero, Kay Burgess, Douwe van Sinderen, Jean-Christophe Piard, Gerrit Eggink, Eddy J. Smid, Graciela Savoy7, Fernando Sesma7, Tanja Jansen2, Pascal Hols4 & Michiel Kleerebezem (2002), Metabolic engineering of lactic acid bacteria for the production of Nutraceuticals, Antonie van Leeuwenhoek 82: 217–235.

John P. Berry, Miroslav Gantar, Mario H. Perez, Gerald Berry and Fernando G. Noriega (2008), Cyanobacterial Toxins as Allelochemicals with Potential Applications as Algaecides, Herbicides and Insecticides, Mar. Drugs,6,117-146.

Katherine Hollywood, Daniel R. Brison and Royston Goodacre (2006), Metabolomics: Current technologies and future trends, Proteomics, 6:4716–4723.

Lukas Vaclavik, Jaroslava Ovesna, Ladislav Kucera, Jan Hodek, Katerina Demnerova and Jana Hajslova (2013), Application of Ultra-high Performance Liquid Chromatography-Mass Spectrometry (UHPLC-MS) Metabolomic Fingerprinting to Characterise GM and Conventional Maize Varieties, Czech J. Food Sci. Vol. 31,No. 4: 368–375.

Marcello Duranti (2006), Grain legume proteins and nutraceutical properties, Fitoterapia, 77:67-82.

Mehrafarin A., Qaderi A, Rezazadeh Sh., Naghdi Badi H. Noormohammadi Gh., Zand E (2010), Bioengineering of Important Secondary Metabolites and Metabolic Pathways in Fenugreek (Trigonella foenum-graecum L.), Journal of Medicinal Plants, Vol.9:35.

Natalia Dudareva and Eran Pichersky (2008), Metabolic engineering of plant volatiles, Current Opinion in Biotechnology, 19:1–9.

Pamela P., Peralta-Yahya and Jay D. Keasling (2010), Advanced biofuel production in microbes, Biotechnol. J., 5:147–162.

Prasanna Reddy Battu and MS Reddy (2009), Isolation of secondary metabolites from Pseudomonas fluorescens and its Characterization, Asian J. Research Chem. 2(1):26-29.

Richard A. Dixon, David R. Gang,Adrian J. Charlton, Oliver Fiehn, Harry A. Kuiper,Tracey L. Reynolds, Ronald S. Tjeerdema, Elizabeth H. Jeffery,J. Bruce German,William P. Ridley And James N. Seiber (2006), Applications of Metabolomics in Agriculture, J. Agric. Food Chem. 54:8984-8994.

Roopashree TS, Raman Dang, Shobha Rani RH, Narendra C (2008), Antibacterial activity of antipsoriatic herbs: Cassia tora, Momordica charantia and Calendula officinalis, International Journal of Applied Research in Natural Products,Vol. 1(3):20-28.

Satheeshkumar N, Nisha N, Sonali N, Nirmal J, Jain GK, Spandana V (2012), Analytical profiling of bioactive constituents from herbal products, using metabolomics—a review, Nat Prod Commun., 7(8):1111-5.

Seth DeBolt, Douglas R. Cook, and Christopher M. Ford (2006), L-Tartaric acid synthesis from vitamin C in higher plants, PNAS, Vol.103 (14):5608-5613.

Singh, O. V., R. K. Jain (2003), Phytoremediation of toxic aromatic pollutants from soil, Appl Microbiol Biotechnol, 63:128–135.

Thongchai Taechowisan,Chunhua Lu, Yuemao Shen and Saisamorn Lumyong (2005), Secondary metabolites from endophytic Streptomyces aureofaciens CMUAc130 and their antifungal activity, Microbiology, 151: 1691-1695.

Wei Zhang,Chris Franco,Chris Curtin and Simon Conn (2004), To Stretch the Boundary of SecondaryMetabolite Production in Plant Cell-Based Bioprocessing: Anthocyanin as a Case Study, Journal of Biomedicine and Biotechnology,5:264–271.

❑❑❑

CHAPTER - 9

Safe and Effective Stem Cell Therapy Promises to Revolutionise 21st Century Medicine

Arumugasamy Karthiga, Sanjeev Kumar Singh*
Computer Aided Drug Designing and Molecular Modeling Lab, Department of Bioinformatics, Alagappa University, Karaikudi-630 003, Tamil Nadu, India.
**E-mail: skysanjeev@gmail.com*

INTRODUCTION

Scientists have known that certain animals can regenerate missing parts of their bodies. But we can not replace a missing leg or a finger; our bodies are constantly regenerating blood, skin and other tissues. The identity of the powerful cells that allow us to regenerate some tissues was first revealed when experiments with bone marrow in the 1950's established the existence of stem cells in our bodies and led to the development of bone marrow transplantation, a therapy now widely used in medicine. Stem cell therapies are one of the most promising areas of medicine, and many such therapies are now in development by industrial and academic groups. The first successful allogenic stem cell graft in humans using donor bone marrow was undertaken in the USA in 1968 and bone marrow transplantation continues to provide the best example of the clinical use of adult stem cells. Currently, cell therapies are regulated under the US Food and Drug Administration's (FDA's) Good Tissue Practices Final Rule, which uses a tiered system based on the level of risk associated with the cell product. Scientists were able to extract embryonic stem cells from mice in the 1980s, but it wasn't until 1998 that a team of scientists from the University of Wisconsin–Madison became the first group to isolate human embryonic stem cells and keep them.

More recently, Japanese researcher, Shinya Yamanaka, received the 2012 Nobel Prize in Physiology or Medicine for the discovery of induced pluripotent stem cells (iPSCs). Stem cell research is being pursued in the hope of achieving major medical breakthroughs. A few cell products, such as Carticel and skin replacement therapies, have received FDA approval. Both adult and embryonic stem cells may also provide a route for scientists to develop valuable new methods of drug discovery and testing. A number of stem cell therapies exist, but most are at experimental stages or costly, with the notable exception of bone marrow transplantation. Even though, stem cell research has expanded rapidly beyond scientific and ethical concerns, the emerging field of stem cell therapeutics faces structural, commercial and economic challenges. The new era of iPSC-based cell therapy promises the personalized medicine using cells from the patient able to treat cancer, Type 1 diabetes mellitus, Parkinson's disease, Huntington's disease, Celiac disease, Cardiac failure, muscle damage and neurological disorders, and many others. Stem cell therapy is an emerging medicinal technology and investigators are beginning to focus on the potential utility of iPSCs as a tool for drug development, modeling of disease, and transplantation medicine.

Classification of Stem Cell by their Potential Differentiation

Stem cells are categorized by their potential to differentiate into other types of cells. Embryonic stem cells are the most potent since they must become every type of cell in the body (Figure 1).

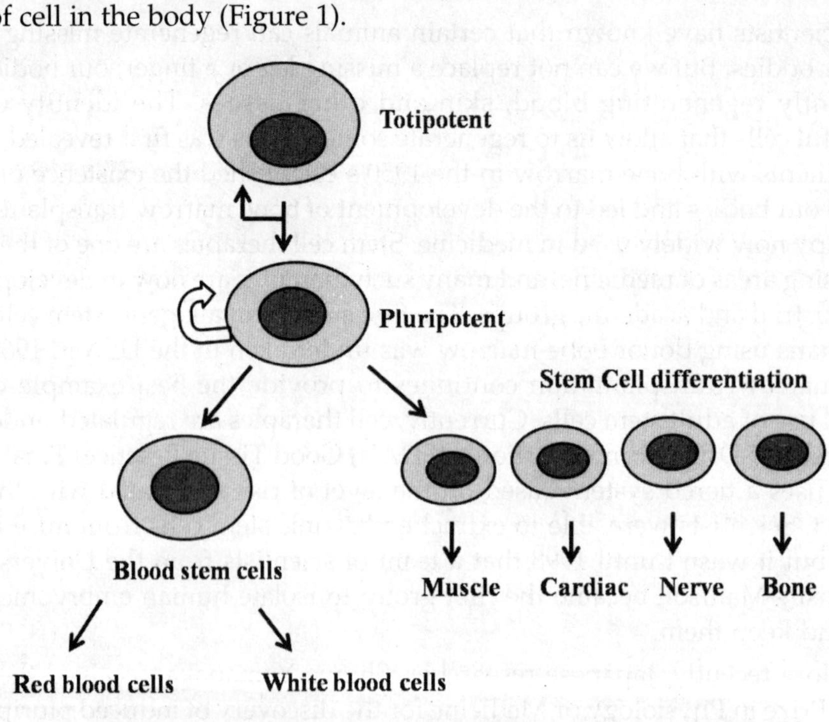

Fig. 1 : Hierarchial of stemcell multiplication and differentiation

- **Totipotent** – A cell can give rise to all the cell types in the body including the entire embryo and placenta; a fertilized egg cell is the only cell that is considered totipotent.
- **Pluripotent** - A pluripotent stem cell is derived from a totipotent stem cell and can make up any type of cell in the body, except those types of cells used to make embryonic tissue (such as the egg). Embryonic stem (ES) cells are an example of this type.
- **Multipotent** - The ability to differentiate into a closely related family of cells only. They have the potential plasticity and can undergo differentiation. The trigger for plasticity is stress or tissue injury which up regulates the stem cells and releases chemo attractants and growth factors. Hematopoietic (adult) stem cells that can become red and white blood cells or platelets are example of multipotency.
- **Unipotent** - the ability to only produce cells of their own type, but have the property of self-renewal required to be labeled a stem cell. Examples include (adult) muscle stem cells.

Stem Cells and their Accessible Sources

Stem cell can be illustrated in cellular level, "a cell that has the capacity both to produce identical daughter cell's self-renewal' and to produce daughters those are fated to differentiate commitment". In mammals, they are come from two main sources

1. Embryonic stem cells - which are isolated from the inner cell mass of blastocysts
2. Adult stem cells - which are found in various tissues (Eg. Bone marrow, Adipose tissue)

EMBRYONIC STEM CELLS

A blastocyst is a pre-implantation embryo that develops 5 days after the fertilization of an egg by a sperm. It contains all the material necessary for the development of a complete human being. The blastocyst consists of an inner cell mass (embryoblast) and an outer cell mass (trophoblast). The outer cell mass becomes part of the placenta, and the inner cell mass is the group of cells that will differentiate to become all the structures of an adult organism. This latter mass is the source of embryonic stem cells - totipotent cells (cells with total potential to develop into any cell in the body).

Sources of Embryonic Stem Cells (ES cells)

In vitro fertilization

The largest potential source of blastocysts for stem cell research is from *in vitro* fertilization (IVF) clinics. The process of IVF requires the retrieval of a woman's eggs via a surgical procedure after undergoing an intensive regimen of fertility drugs, which stimulate the ovaries to produce multiple mature eggs. When IVF is used for reproductive purposes, doctors typically fertilize all of the donated eggs in order to maximize their chance of producing a viable blastocyst that can be implanted in the womb. Because not all the fertilized eggs are implanted, this has resulted in a large bank of "excess" blastocysts are stored in freezers. In normal development, the blastocyst would implant in the wall of the uterus to become the embryo and continue developing into a mature organism. When the blastocyst is used for stem cell research, scientists remove the inner cell mass and place these cells in a culture dish with a nutrient-rich liquid where they give rise to embryonic stem cells (Figure 2).

Fig. 2 : Specialized cell lines derived from blastocyst by *in vitro* fertilization technique (IVF).

Embryonic stem cells seem to be more flexible than stem cells found in adults, because they have the potential to produce every cell type in the human body. They are also generally easier to collect, purify and maintain in the laboratory than adult stem cells. Isolation of stem cells with specific genetic traits necessary for the study of particular diseases.

Nuclear transfer

The process called nuclear transfer offers another potential way to produce embryonic stem cells. In animals, nuclear transfer has been accomplished by inserting the nucleus of an already differentiated adult cell, for example, a skin cell into a donated egg that has its nucleus removed.

This egg, which now contains the genetic material of the skin cell, is then stimulated to form a blastocyst from which embryonic stem cells can be derived. The stem cells that are created in this way are therefore copies or "clones" of the original adult cell because their nuclear DNA matches that of the adult cell.

RNA interference (RNAi)

Another method to test the function of a gene is to use RNA interference (RNAi) to decrease the expression of a gene of interest. In RNAi, small pieces of double-stranded RNA (siRNA; small interfering RNA) are either chemically synthesized and introduced directly into cells, or expressed from DNA vectors. Once inside the cells, the siRNA can lead to the degradation of the messenger RNA (mRNA), which contains the exact sequence as that of the siRNA. mRNA is the product of DNA transcription and normally can be translated into proteins. RNAi can work efficiently in somatic cells, and there has been some progress in applying this technology to human ES cells.

Umbilical Cord Blood

Blood that remains in the placenta and in the attached umbilical cord after childbirth. Cord blood is collected and cryogenically preserves these cells for potential medical use because it contains stem cells, which can be used to treat hematopoietic and genetic disorders. Person's own (autologous) amniotic stem cells can be safely infused back into that individual without being rejected by the body's immune system. They have unique characteristics compared to other sources of stem cells. They are an increasing focus of regenerative medicine research. Research in this area has the potential to revolutionize medicine.

ADULT STEM CELLS

Adult or somatic stem cells exist throughout the body after embryonic development and are found inside of different types of tissue. These stem cells have been found in tissues such as the brain, bone marrow, blood, blood vessels, skeletal muscles, skin, and the liver. They remain in a quiescent or non-dividing state for years until activated by disease or tissue injury. Adult stem cells can divide or self-renew indefinitely, enabling them to generate a range of cell types (**Figure 3**) from the originating organ or even regenerates the entire original organ. It is generally thought that adult stem cells are limited in their ability to differentiate based on their tissue of origin, but there is some evidence to suggest that they can differentiate to become other cell types.

GENETIC MANIPULATION OF ES CELLS

Since establishing human ES cells in 1998, scientists have developed genetic manipulation techniques to determine the function of particular genes, to direct the differentiation of human ES cells towards specific cell types, or to tag an ES cell derivative with a certain marker gene. Several approaches have been developed to introduce genetic elements randomly into the human ES cell genome, including electroporation, transfection by lipid-based reagents, and lentiviral vectors. However, homologous recombination, a method in which a specific gene inside the ES cells is modified with an artificially introduced DNA molecule. This is more precise method of genetic engineering that can modify a gene in a defined way at a specific locus. While this technology is routinely used in mouse ES cells, it has recently been successfully developed in human ES cells, thus opening new doors for using ES cells as vehicles for gene therapy and for creating *in vitro* models of human genetic disorders.

DIFFERENTIATION OF HUMAN ES CELLS

The pluripotency of ES cells suggests possible widespread uses for these cells and their derivatives. The ES cell-derived cells can potentially be used to replace or restore tissues that have been damaged by disease or injury, such as diabetes, heart attacks, Parkinson's disease or spinal cord injury. The differentiation of ES cells also provides model systems to study early events in human development. Because of possible harm to the resulting child, it is not ethically acceptable to experimentally manipulate the post implantation human embryo.

ANIMAL MODEL FOR STEM CELL RESEARCH

Usually mice are act as important *in vivo* experimentation model in stem cell research. Remarkably in many respects they mirror human biology. 99% of mouse genes have an equivalent in humans, making mice ideal for studying function of human genes in health as well as diseases such as cancer, cardiovascular diseases and diabetes. These multifactorial diseases are in part due to mutations in our genes. The sequence of the mouse genome is a key informational tool for understanding the contents of the human genome and a key experimental tool for biomedical research.

APPLICATION OF STEM CELLS

Stem cell research is both an evolution and a revolution in modern biomedicine. Stem cells particularly embryonic stem cells (ES cells) – represent part of the post-genomic technology for delivering on the promises of the human genome sequencing project. Stem cell treatments are a type of intervention strategy that introduces new cells into damaged tissue in order to treat disease or injury.

Tissue Transplantation

Transplantation is the act of transferring cells, tissues, or organs from one site to another. Corneas, skin, bone, cardiovascular tissue (heart valves and veins), the pancreas for islet cells and connective tissue are the most common tissues transplanted.

Major types of transplantation

Autotransplantation

Transplantation of organs, tissues or even proteins from one part of the body to another in the same individual. Tissue transplanted by such "autologous" procedure is referred to as an autograft or autotransplant.

Allotransplantation

An allograft is a transplant of an organ or tissue between two genetically non-identical members of the same species. Most human tissue and organ transplants are allografts.

Xenotransplantation

A transplantation of organ or tissue from one species to another. Xenotransplantion is often an extremely dangerous type of transplant because of the increased risk of non-compatibility, rejection and disease carried in the tissue.

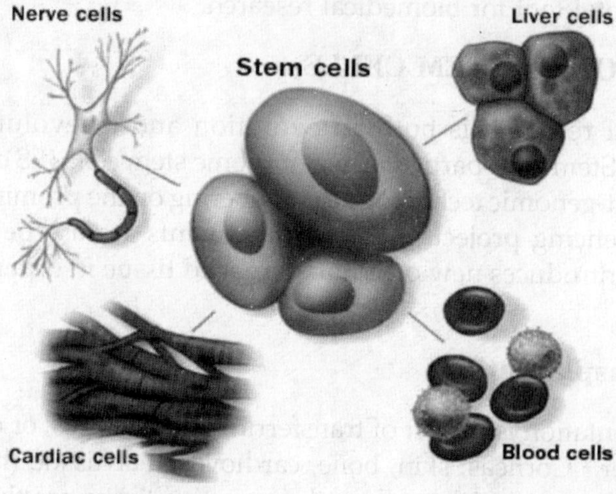

Fig. 3 : Regeneration of desired cell lines from stem cells.

IMPORTANCE OF STEM CELLS IN TRANSPLANTATION

Transplant rejection occurs, when donor's transplanted tissue is rejected by the recipient's immune system. The rejection which destroys the transplanted tissue because of Major Histocompatibility Complex (MHC) that plays a crucial role in immune response and is most important in rejection. Immunological self/nonself recognition is controlled by MHC class I and II MHC genes, which are the most polymorphic loci known in vertebrates. These MHC genes encode cell surface proteins (class I and II MHC molecules) that present small peptide antigens to T cells. Through antigen presentation, MHC molecules control all specific immunological responses, both cell- and antibody-mediated. To overcome this problem stem cell therapy would be used to minimize the transplant rejection."

BONE MARROW TRANSPLANT TO CURE LEUKEMIA

Leukemia is a cancer of white blood cells, or leukocytes. Like other blood cells, leukocytes develop from somatic stem cells. Mature leukocytes are released into the bloodstream, where they work to fight off infections in our bodies. Leukemia results when leukocytes begin to grow and function abnormally, becoming cancerous. These abnormal cells cannot fight off infection, and they interfere with the functions of other organs. In a bone marrow transplant, the patient's bone marrow stem cells are replaced with those from a healthy, matching donor. Chemotherapy is one of the ways to eliminate the abnormal cells, some time it may not work alone, for this stage bone marrow transplant is used. To do this, all of the patient's existing bone marrow and abnormal leukocytes are first killed using a combination of chemotherapy and radiation. Next, a sample of donor bone marrow containing healthy stem cells is introduced into the patient's bloodstream. If the transplant is successful, the stem cells will migrate into the patient's bone marrow and begin producing new, healthy leukocytes to replace the abnormal cells. Human umbilical cord blood has been investigated as an alternative stemcell source to bone marrow for cell transplantation and therapy, because of its haematopoietic and non-haematopoietic (mesen-chymal) components.

ADULT TISSUE AS SOURCE FOR ISLET CELLS

Diabetes is actually a group of diseases characterized by abnormally high levels of the sugar glucose in the bloodstream. This excess glucose is responsible for most of the complications of diabetes, which include blindness, kidney failure, heart disease, stroke, neuropathy, and amputations. Type 1 diabetes, also known as juvenile-onset diabetes, typically affects children and young adults.

Diabetes develops when the body's immune system sees its own cells as foreign body and destroys them. As a result, the islet cells of the pancreas, which normally produce insulin, are destroyed. In the absence of insulin, glucose cannot enter the cell and glucose accumulates in the blood. Type 2 diabetes occurs when the body cannot use insulin effectively. This is called insulin resistance and the result is the same as with type 1 diabetes a buildup of glucose in the blood. Islet cells isolated from human cadavers by adding to the cells' DNA special genes that stimulate cell proliferation. The cell lines are further engineered to express the beta islet cell gene, PDX-1, which stimulates the expression of the insulin gene. Such cell lines have been shown to propagate in culture and can be induced to differentiate to cells, which produce insulin. When transplanted into immune-deficient mice, the cells secrete insulin in response to glucose.

REPAIRING THE DAMAGED HEART

Therapeutic successes in the area of stem cell research have opened up many new avenues for treating cardiovascular diseases, especially with respect to the prevention of the development of cardiac failure due to acute heart attack (acute myocardial infarction caused by sudden and prolonged oxygen starvation) or chronic coronary artery disease (gradual oxygen starvation due to cumulative narrowing of the coronary artery). The delivery of bone marrow-derived stem cells via the coronary artery (intracoronary), the left ventricle (transendocardial) as well as directly into the heart muscle during cardiac bypass surgery (intramyocardial) is being investigated for the treatment of acute heart attack and chronic coronary artery disease. All have been explored in mouse or rat models, and some have been tested in larger animal models, such as pigs. A few small studies have also been carried out in humans, usually in patients who are undergoing open-heart surgery. Several of these have demonstrated that stem cells that are injected into the circulation or directly into the injured heart tissue appear to improve cardiac function and/or induce the formation of new capillaries. The mechanism for this repair remains controversial, and the stem cells likely regenerate heart tissue through several pathways. Although much more research is needed to assess the safety and improve the efficacy of this approach,

IMPLICATIONS FOR CANCER TREATMENT

At present, the cancer treatment is targeted at its proliferation potential. Although current treatments can shrink the size of the tumor, these effects are transient and usually do not improve patient's survival outcomes. The cancer stem cell (CSC) hypothesis represents a truly innovative concept in cancer biology with profound fundamental and clinical implications (Figure 4).

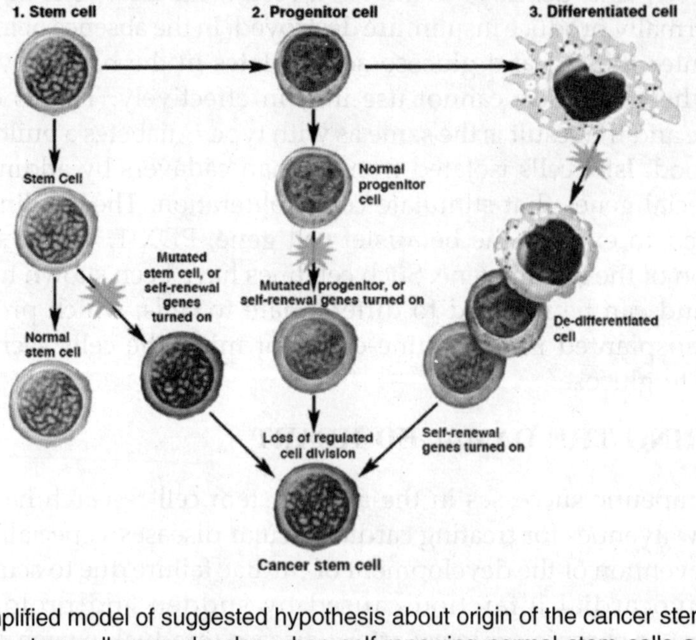

Fig. 4 : A simplified model of suggested hypothesis about origin of the cancer stems cells. The cancer stem cells may develop when self-renewing normal stem cells acquire mutations and are transformed by altering only proliferative pathways. It is also possible that the cancer stem cells originate by multiple oncogenic mutations in the restricted progenitor cells which acquire the capability of self renewal.

Cancer stem cells that retain stem cell properties are highly tumorigenic, and display increased resistance to radiation and chemotherapy. During chemotherapy, most of the primary tumor cells may be destroyed but if cancer stem cells are not eradicated, they become refractory cancer stem cells and may lead to recurrence of tumor. Although the origin of the cancer stem cells is yet to be defined, the hypothesis that cancer stem cells are derived from either the self-renewing normal stem cells or from the progenitor cells that have acquired the ability of self renewal due to mutations. CSCs may come from a rare fusion event between stem cells and other cells.

Cancer therapy has entered in to an exciting new era, with traditional therapies such as chemotherapy, radiotherapy and surgeries on one side while the stem cells on the other hand. The subsequent molecular characterization of the purified stem cells by genomic and proteomic analysis will lay the foundation for the elucidation of the molecular and cellular mechanisms that regulate self renewal and differentiation in homeostasis and cancer.

Apart from their well known role in immunoreconstitution, the stem cells have attracted much attention especially with the new gene technologies such as the gene incorporation into the eukaryotic cells allowing more focused delivery of the anti-cancer agents.

CANCER STEM CELL – SIGNIFICANT DRUG TARGET

The cancer stem cells are relatively quiescent compared to other cancer cells and do not appear to have the hyper-proliferation signals activated such as tyrosine kinase. One approach to target the cancer stem cells may be the identification of the markers that are specific for the cancer stem cells compared to normal stem cells (Table 1). Another clinically relevant inherent property of stem cells is their ability to pump drugs out of the cell through the use of the ATP Binding Cassette (ABC) drug transporters. ABC transporters are special family of membrance proteins which significantly modulate the absorption, metabolism, cellular effectivity and toxicity of pharmacological agents. If these efflux pumps could be inhibited, CSCs could be more susceptible to current or newly designed chemotherapeutic agents used in conjunction.

Table 1: Prospectively identified cancer stem cells and the corresponding markers

Cancer Type	CSC-specific markers	Normal stem-cell marker
Breast	$CD44^+$ / CD24low Lin^-	$CD24^{med}$ $CD49^{fhi}$CD29 CD24 Lin^-
Brain	$CD133^+$	$CD133^+$ Lin^-
Hematopoietic	$CD34^+$ $CD38^-$ $Thy1^-$ Lin^-	$CD34^+$ $CD38^+$ $Thy1^-$$Lin^-$c-$Kit^+$$Thy1^{low}$ Sca1 Lin^+
Prostate	$CD44^+$ / á2â1^{hi} / CD133+	CD133 a2b1^{hi}
Lung	Sca-1^+ / $CD45^-$ / $Pecam^-$	Sca-1^+ $CD34^+$ Lin^-

These advances in our understanding of cancer stem cell biology will open new avenues for the improvement of cancer assessment, prognosis, surveillance, prevention therapy. Combining genetic, cellular and molecular analysis of *in vitro* and *in vivo* CSC experimental models with the prospective detection, purification and analysis of CSCs from surgical specimens and body fluid from cancer patients. The concept of the cancer stem cells may allow new treatment options in the possible cure of the cancer.

Bioinformatics Accelerate Stem Cell Assessment

The development of algorithms for clustering, analysis of the data generated by techniques like microarray, real-time PCR, FACS, immune phenotyping, spectrophotometry, and a host of other molecular biology techniques used in stem cell research provide the identification of stem cell signatures.

Table 2 : Analysis of stem cell signature through bioinformatics tools

Resource	Role	Web link
ORF Finder	Finder for detection of open reading frames	http://www.ncbi.nlm.nih.gov/projects/gorf/
Pfam, ProDom, etc	Analysis of protein motifs to identifysequence motifs characteristic of certain protein families	http://pfam.sanger.ac.uk/search, http://www.toulouse.inra.fr/ prodom.html
TMpred	Transmembrane helices examination	http://www.ch.embnet.org/software/TMPRED_form.html
SignalIP	Analysis of signal peptides, which seeks to differentiate uncleaved signal anchors fromcleaved signal peptides	http://www.cbs.dtu.dk/services/SignalP/
EST	Murine and human expressed sequence tags (ESTs) contigs	http://www.ncbi.nlm.nih.gov/dbEST/
SCDb	Stem Cell Database (StemDB) itself (a measure of internal redundancy) helps in further characterization for the definition of stem ness	http://www.stemdb.org/stemdb/servlets/Navigate?action=main.jsp

Combined with molecular techniques, bioinformatics tools (Table 2) suggested that the state of large sets of molecules such as proteins, nucleic acids and lipids, as well as the position of these molecules within the cells, like the specific patterns of chromatin organization form a stem-cell signature. The stem-cell signature should therefore be determined by systems-biology tools that can identify patterns, rather than by the analysis of individual genes or even multiple gene-product behaviours. The resulting transcriptome and proteome should then be compared, placing special emphasis on the analysis of post-transcriptional and posttranslational modifications and on changes in the trafficking and localization of molecules within cells. Mathematical modeling of the vast amount of data generated from such studies should unravel the constellation of cellular characteristics that determine the stem state.

Structural and functional analysis of different kinds of stem cells done by multiple sequence alignment tools CLUSTAL, T- Coffee, MUSCE. NCBI's Digital Differential Display (DDD) tool is used for comparing EST profiles in order to identify genes with significantly different expression levels, PSORT which predicts the sub cellular location of gene products and proteins.

CHALLENGES IN STEM-CELLS THERAPY

Stem cells have enormous therapeutic potential to treat a vast array of serious diseases. Further, their isolation, expansion, and storage are a very technique-sensitive procedure. When banked, how long can they be safely stored retaining the original stemness is questionable. Now autologous stem cells are ideally suited for a patient as there is no risk of immune rejection, the process is least expensive, and avoids legal and ethical concerns. The cells need to be procured from an autologous source, and isolated and expanded in number before they can be used and hence the process is time consuming. The use of pre-existing allogenic cell lines and cell organ culture removes the problem of harvesting cells from the patients themselves and saves considerable time. But this also have some problem, "Are allogenic stem cells safe in terms of immune suppression and pathogen transmission?" is not yet answered.

Tumorigenesis

Human embryonic stem cell (HESC) is difficult to control the growth and differentiation of the embryonic stem cell posing risk of tumorogenicity and teratoma (benign tumor) formation. While research is on to overcome some of these shortfalls as of now, ESCs are not so far used therapeutically and have only remained an excellent platform for research. Viruses used as vector in re-progmming the adult cells to induced pluripotent stem cell (iPSC). In animal studies, the virus used to introduce the stem cell factors sometimes causes cancers. Researchers are currently investigating non-viral delivery strategies.

Misdirected Growth

The possibility of transplanted stem cells differentiating into the wrong type of tissue is yet another concern regarding therapeutic stem cell use. At present, scientists still know very little about how stem cell differentiation is controlled. The safety of these therapies is evaluated and that caution is displayed before a therapy becomes accepted for use.

Ethical Issues

Some of the social ethical issues have been raised against the stem cell research. Human embryonic stem cell (HESC) research offers much hope for alleviating the human suffering brought on by the ravages of disease and injury. Despite the tremendous therapeutic promise of HESC research, the research has met with heated opposition because the harvesting of HESCs involves the destruction of the human embryo. HESCs are derived *in vitro* around the fifth day of the embryo's development. A typical day-5 human embryo consists of 200-250 cells, most of which comprise the trophoblast, which is the outermost layer of the blastocyst. HESCs are harvested from the inner cell mass of the blastocyst, which consists of 30-34 cells. The derivation of HESC cultures requires the removal of the trophoblast. This process of disaggregating the blastocyst's cells eliminates its potential for further development. Opponents of HESC research argue that the research is morally impermissible because it involves the unjust killing of innocent human beings. Recently, scientists trying to get the embryonic stem cell from the normal adult stem cell line through the nucleus transformation of the oocyte to somatic cell.

STEM CELL THERAPIES IN THE FUTURE

Cord Blood Bank

Many cord blood banks have been established in the United Kingdom, France and many other countries worldwide. Umbilical cord blood can be considered as one of the most abundant sources of non-embryonic stem cells. The umbilical cord blood collection is non-invasive and has no side effects on either the baby or the mother. Intermediate age stage between the embryonic stem cells and the adult stem cell leads to a higher proliferating potential. Pre-clinical trials on animal models showed promising results toward moving into clinical trials. They are an increasing focus of regenerative medicine research. Research in this area has the potential to revolutionize medicine.

Clinical Trials

Today's stem cell therapies usually rely on cells that are donated by another person. This raises the possibility of donor cell rejection by the patient's immune system. Up to date 4769 stem cell based clinical trials are registered globally. In the future, it may be possible for a person to use a sample of his or her own stem cells to regenerate tissue, which would reduce or even eliminate the danger of rejection. Ideally, somatic stem cells would preclude the use of embryonic stem cells for cell therapy, eliminate the ethical objections against stem cell research, and also resolve immunological rejection problems. Some currently going on clinical trials are listed below (Table 3)

Table 3 : Pluripotent stem cells in clinical trials (USA)

Clinical trial stage	Disease target	Cell type
Phase I: 10 patients enrolled 2010-12	Complete subacute thoracic spinal cord injuries	Human embryonic stem cell derivedOligodendrocyte progenitor cells (GRNOPC1)
Phase I/II: 12 patients enrolled 2011	Stargardt's Macular Dystrophy (juvenile macular degeneration)	Retinal Pigment Epithelium derived from humanembryonic stem cells
Phase I/II: 12 patients enrolled 2011-12	Age-related Macular Degeneration	Retinal Pigment Epithelium derived from humanembryonic stem cells

CONCLUSION

The stem cell research is highly active and rapidly-developing research field, still its need more standardized molecular level techniques to characterize the stem cells and their derivatives. Future therapeutic interventions, either directly or as research tools to establish novel models for degenerative disease that will inform drug development. The other great challenge will be to continue to unravel the factors that control the differentiation of human ES cells to specific lineages, so that ES cells can fulfill their tremendous promise in basic human biology, drug screening, and transplantation medicine to develop patient-specific therapies.

REFERENCES

Ali, H., Bahbahani, H. Umbilical cord blood stem cells – potential therapeutic tool forneural injuries and disorders. (2010) Acta neurobiologiae experimentalis, 70: 316–324

Amit, M., Margulets, V., Segev, H., Shariki, K., Laevsky, I., Coleman, R., Itskovitz-Eldor, J. (2003). Human feeder layers for human embryonic stem cells. Biology of reproduction, 68:2150–2156

Bethesda, M.D. (2011). Are stem cells involved in cancer?. In stem cell information: National Institute of Health, U.S. Department of Health and Human Services, chapter 9.

Bhattacharya, B., Miura, T., Brandenberger, R., et al. (2004). Gene expression in human embryonic stem cell lines: unique molecular signature. Blood 103(8):2956:2964

Carpenter, M.K., Vasconcells, J.F., Rao, M.S. (2009). Developing safe therapies from human pluripotent stem cells. Nature Biotechnology 27:7 606-613

Cheng, L., Ramesh, A.V., Nikitin, A.F., Choi, A., Nikitin, A.Y. (2010). Mouse models for cancer stem cell research. Toxicologic Pathology 38: 62-71

Dwyer, R.M., Khan, S., Barry, F.P., Brien, T.O., Kerin, M.J. (2010). Advances in mesenchymal stem cell-mediated gene therapy for cancer. Stem Cell Research & Therapy 1(25):1-7

Fang, D., Nguyen, T.K., Leishear, K. et al. (2005). A Tumorigenic Subpopulation with Stem Cell Properties in Melanomas. Cancer Research 65(20):9328-9337

Fujishiro, S.H., Nakano K., Mizukami Y., et al. (2012). Generation of Naive-Like Porcine-Induced Pluripotent Stem Cells Capable of Contributing to Embryonic and Fetal Development. Stem cells and development 1-10

Gu, Q., Hao, J., Zhao, XY., Li, W., Liu, L., Wang, L., Liu, ZH., Zhou, Q. (2012). Rapid conversion of human ESCs into mouse ESC-like pluripotent state by optimizing culture conditions . Protein Cell 3(1): 71–79

Hentze, H., Graichen, R., Colman, A. (2006). Cell therapy and the safety of embryonic stem cell-derived grafts. Trends in Biotechnology 25:1

Kehat, I., Kenyagin-Karsenti, D., Snir, M., Segev, H., Amit, M. Gepstein, A., Livne, E., Binah, O., Itskovitz-Eldor, J., Gepstein, L. (2001). Human embryonic stem cells can differentiate into myocytes with structural and functional properties of cardiomyocytes. The Journal of Clinical Investigation,108:407-414

Laflamme, M.A., Gold, J., Xu, C., Hassanipour, M., Rosler, E., Police, S., Muskheli, V., Murry, C.E. (2005). Formation of human myocardium in the rat heart from human embryonic stem cells. American Journal of Pathology 167(3):663-671

Lang, M.F., Yang, S., Zhao, C., et al. (2012). Genome-Wide Profiling Identified a Set of miRNAs that are differentially expressed in glioblastoma stem cells and normal neural stem cells. Public Library of Science ONE 7(4):36248

Li, F., Tiede, B., Massague, J., Kang, Y. (2006). Beyond tumorigenesis: cancer stem cells in metastasis. Cell Research, 1-12

Li, M.D., Atkins, H., Bubela, T. (2014). The global landscape of stem cell clinical trials. Regenerative Medicine. 9(1) Doi:10.2217/RME.13.80

Loh, Y.H. Agarwal, S., Park, IH., Urbach, H., Huo, H., Heffiner, G.C., Kim, K., Miller, J.D., Ng, K., Daley G.Q. (2009). Generation of induced pluripotent stem cells from human blood. Blood, 113: 5476-5479

Lui, K.O., Boyd, A.S., Cobbold, S.P., Waldmann, H., Fairchild, P.J. (2010). A role for regulatory T cells in acceptance of ESC-derived tissues transplanted across an Major Histocompatibility Complex Barrier. Stem cells, 28:1905–1914

Matveyenko, A.V., Georgia, S., Bhushan, A., Butler, P.C. (2010). Inconsistent formation and nonfunction of insulin-positive cells from pancreatic endoderm derived from human embryonic stem cells in athymic nude rats. American Journal of Physiology Endocrinology and Metabolism, 299:713–720

Menasche, P. Cell-based Therapy for Heart Disease: (2009). A clinically Oriented perspective. Moleculartherapy, 17(5) 758–766

Mestas, J., Hughes, C.C.W. (2004). Of Mice Not Men: Differences between Mouse and Human Immunology. The Journal of Immunology, 172:2731-2738

Muller, F.J. Laurent, L.C., Kostka, D. et al. (2008). Regulatory networks define phenotypic classes of human stem cell lines. Nature, 455(7211):401-405

Nadig, R.R. (2009). Stem cell therapy – Hype or hope? A review. Journal of Conservative Dentistry 12(4):131-138

Naegele, J.R., Maisano, X., Yang, J., Royston, S., Ribeiro, E. (2010). Recent advancements in stem cell and gene therapies for neurological disorders and intractable epilepsy. Neuropharmacology, 58(6): 855–864

Nikolic, B., Faintuch, S., Goldberg, S.N., Kuo, M.D, Cardella, J.F. (2009). Stem Cell Therapy: A Primer for Interventionalists and Imagers. Journal of Vascular and Interventional Radiolgy, 20:999 –1012

Nir, S.G., Eldor, J.I. (2004). Cell therapy using human embryonic stem cells. Transplant Immunology, 12:203–209

Nunes, V.A., Cavacana, N., Canovas, M., Strauss, B.E., Zatz, M. (2007). Stem cells from umbilical cordblood differentiate into myotubes and express dystrophin in vitro only after exposure to in vivo muscle environment Biology of the cell 99 (4):185-196

Onyshchenko, M.I., Panyutin, I.G., Panyutin, I.V., Neumann, R.D. (2012). Stimulation of cultured H9 human embryonic stem cells with thyroid stimulating hormone does not lead to formation of thyroid-like cells. Stem Cells International, 1-8

Penn, D.J. (2002). Major Histocompatibility Complex (MHC). Encyclopedia of Life Sciences, 1-7

Postovit, L.M., Margaryan, N.V., et al., (2008). Human embryonic stem cell microenvironment suppresses the tumorigenic phenotype of aggressive cancer cells. Proceedings of the National Academy of Science, 105(11):4329 – 4334

Rao, M. (2013). iPSC-based cell therapy: An important step forward. Stem cell Reports. (1)281-282-

Richard, M., Tan, S.P., Tan, S.P., Chan, W.K., Bongso, A. (2004). The transcriptome profile of human embryonic stem cells as defined by SAGE. Stem cell, 22:51-64

Sagar, J., Chaib, B., Sales, K., Winslet, M., Seifalian, A. (2007). Role of stem cells in cancer therapy and cancer stem cells: a review. Cancer Cell International, 7:9

Sato, N., Sanjuan, I.M., Heke, M., Uchida, M., Naef, F., Brivanloua, A.H. (2003). Molecular signature of human embryonic stem cells and its comparison with the mouse. Developmental Biology, 260:404 – 413

Schinker, A.H., Jonker, J.W. (2009). Mammalian drug efflux transporters of the ATP binding cassette (ABC) family: an overview. Advanced Drug Delivery Reviews, 55(1):3–29

Siegel, Andrew. (Spring 2013 Edition). Ethics of Stem cell Research. The Stanford Encyclopedia of Philosophy Edward N. Zalta, editor.

Smith, A. (2009). Design principles of pluripotency. EMBO Molecular Medicine, 1:251–254

Stevens, J.M., Syndercombe-Court, D., Oakervee, H.E., McCloskey, D., Jenner, M.J., Gribben, J.G., Cavenbagh, J.D. (2007). Development of original donor cell leukemia after successful engraftment from a second donor. Blood, 110: 4621-4622

Waterston, R. H., Lindblad-Toh K., Birney, E. et al. (2002). Initial sequencing and comparative analysis of the mouse genome. Nature, 420:520

❑❑❑

CHAPTER - 10

Future Prospects of Plasma Treatment Technology for Disinfection

Waman Paunikar†, Swapnil Sanmukh†, Krishna Khairnar*, Rajshree Chandekar†, Chetan Khapekar†, Naresh Bokade†, Udit Pal‡, Ram Prakash‡, Ghanshyam L Bodhe†

Environmental Virology Cell †CSIR-National Environmental Engineering Research Institute (CSIR-NEERI), Nehru Marg, Nagpur-440020, India

‡CSIR-Central Electronics Engineering Research Institute (CSIR-CEERI), Pilani-333031, India

** Corresponding Author*

1. INTRODUCTION

Dielectric-barrier discharges (DBDs) also referred to as barrier discharges or silent discharges. DBDs have for a long time been regarded as the ozonizer discharge. In 1932 Buss observed that in a plane parallel gap with insulated electrodes air breakdown occurs in a number of individual tiny breakdown channels.[1,2] Recently, it was realised that plasma can be influenced, modelled and optimised for a given application through microdischarges. The most important characteristic of dielectric-barrier discharges is that non-equilibrium plasma conditions can be provided in a much simpler way than with other alternatives like low pressure discharges, fast pulsed high pressure discharges or electron beam injection. Moreover, the DBDs can breakdown most of the gases at about atmospheric pressure in a large number of independent current filaments or microdischarges. The dielectric barrier limits the amount of charge and energy deposited in a microdischarge and distributes the microdischarges over the entire electrode surface. When a dielectric-barrier discharge is operated in rare gases or a rare gas halogen mixture plasma conditions in a microdischarge channel are similar to those in pulsed excimer lasers. Consequently, each microdischarge can act as an intense source of ultraviolet (UV) or vacuum ultraviolet (VUV) radiation. The absorption coefficient of most substances increases at shorter wavelengths. So, in many cases the UV radiation is absorbed in a very thin surface layer. The xenon excimer lamp can induce photo-cleavage of water and oxygen.[2]

In 1979, K. Donohoe obtained a uniform glow discharge with pulsed excitation in a helium/ethylene mixture,[3,4] due to which the term atmospheric pressure glow (APG) was coined. In 1956, for generating uniform glow discharges at atmospheric pressure in helium, air, argon, oxygen and nitrogen by 50 Hz power source, electrode configuration consisting of two metal foils covered with a special metal mesh and ceramic plates were used by Gambling and Edels. Electret dielectrics can accumulate charges on the surface, and are trapped uniformly on the surface by the applied voltage. The charge carriers are ejected spontaneously from the surface leading to homogeneous discharge due to the change in polarity of the electric field exceeding threshold value.[2]

The application of gas plasmas effectively inactivating microorganisms is attracting many researchers.[6] It is known that there are abundant charged particles, chemically reactive species, and UV photons in the plasma discharge, all of which can cause damages of cells, thus achieving inactivation or mutation. From a biological point of view, biochemical impacts are observed when microorganisms are exposed to plasmas, for example, (a) Protein denaturalization, (b) Enzyme deactivation and (c) DNA mutation.

It is reported that atmospheric pressure plasma (APP) discharge has considerable impact on *Escherichia coli* due to the damage of the cell membrane that results in cell lysis.[7] Till date; we are unable to determine the effect of plasma treatment on the biomacromolecules like cell wall and membrane, composed of polysaccharides and membrane-bound proteins. It is necessary to investigate the problem of cell lysis and death, as well as mutation for understanding the mechanism of plasma treatment.

1.1. History of DBD

W. Siemens first introduced DBDs in 1857 for the purpose of ozone generation in air, however G. C. Lichtenberg carried out its first experiment in 1778. At the beginning of the 20th century, research activities were carried out resulting in a better understanding of the DBD and further research contributed towards its various applications.[8-10]

Concerning Public health matters such as multi- and extensive drug-resistant microbes, bioterrorism, etc. there is an urgent need for intensified efforts to prevent transmission of infections using environmental controls. Due to this, ultraviolet germicidal irradiation (UVGI), has received considerable interest. Certain questions regarding efficacy and safety limits the application of UV based technologies for disinfection, despite that UVGI can be safe and highly effective in disinfecting the air, water, and surfaces thereby preventing transmission of a variety of infections. At present, Low-pressure mercury (Hg) discharge lamps are used in UVGI applications and emit shortwave ultraviolet-C (UV-C, 100–280 nanometer) radiation, primarily at 254 nm. However, mercury based lamps can contribute for heavy metal pollution and related health hazards.[10]

Downes and Blunt demonstrated that the ability of sunlight to neutralize bacteria was dependent on intensity, duration, and wavelength, with the shorter wavelengths of the solar spectrum being the most effective.[11-13] UV-C radiation kills or inactivates microbes by damaging their deoxyribonucleic acid (DNA). Initial investigations were devoted to find the wavelength dependence of the germicidal action of light. The principal mode of inactivation occurs when the absorption of a photon forms pyrimidine dimers between adjacent thymine bases and renders the microbe incapable of replicating.

Table 1: History of Research and Development of VUV/UV Dielectric Barrier Discharge and their disinfection efficiency.

Year	Achievement	Reference (s)
1885	Duclaux reported differences in sensitivity to sunlight between different species of bacterial spores	Duclaux *et al.*, 1885.
1892	Geisler showed that UV radiation from sunlight and electric lamps was more effective in killing bacteria than longer wavelength radiation; however, he also noted that the lethal effects of longer wavelength radiation were amplified at increased intensities.	Geisler *et al.*, 1892.
1904-1905	Hertel *et al.*, were the first to show the mutagenic effects of UV radiation	Hertel *et al.*, 1904-1905
1929	Gates published a series of articles providing the first analytical bactericidal action spectrum. Using an Hg arc lamp, Gates produced similarly shaped action spectra for *Staphylococcus aureus* and *Bacillus coli* (*B. coli*), both with peak effectiveness at 265 nm.	Gates, 1929.
1930	Gates publishes analytical bactericidal action spectrum with peak effectiveness at 265 nm, very near the 254 nm output of low-pressure Hg germicidal lamps.	Gates, 1930
1935	Wells and Fair demonstrated that airborne infectious organisms could be effectively killed in a short period of time using aerosolized *E. coli* at 254 nm radiation in controlled conditions.	Wells and Fair, 1935.

Contd...

1934-1955	Well and his colleagues presents the concept of airborne infection via "droplet nuclei" —evaporated droplets containing infectious organisms that can remain suspended in the air for extended durations. Wells and Faird demonstrate the ability of UVGI to efficiently inactivate airborne microorganisms and prove the concept of infection via the airborne route. Wells et. al used upper-room UVGI to prevent the epidemic spread of measles. Overholt *et al.* extended the application of UVGI in hospitals by implementing various configurations of cubicle-like UVGI "light curtains" designed to prevent respiratory cross-infections. Whisler *et al.* evaluated the effect of physical and environmental factors on UVGI efficacy, including humidity and air circulation—two important factors in the performance of UVGI. The Council on Physical Therapy accepted UVGI for disinfecting purposes.Hollaender and Oliphant claimed, that the high UV Germicidal Irradiation for Air Disinfection sensitivity of many agents at about (260 nm) is based on the important function of deoxyribose nucleic acid in biological activities of organisms.	Well and his colleagues, 1932-45; Overholt *et al.*, 1940; Council on Physical Therapy, 1943; Hollaender and Oliphant, 1944; Whisler *et al.*, 1940.
1957–1976	Riley exposes guinea pigs to air originating from an occupied TB ward and proves that TB is spread via the airborne route. Riley *et al.* determine virulent tubercle bacilli and Bacillus Calmette-Guérin (BCG) to be equally susceptible to UVGI and measure the disappearance rate of aerosolized BCG in a model room with and without upper-room UVGI. UVGI effectively inactivated *E. coli* in the ward and prevented rabbits from developing TB. Conversely, exposed rabbits were infected with TB without the use of UVGI. Studies have confirmed both that TB could readily be spread through droplet nuclei and that UVGI could sufficiently inactivate the infected air. Beukers and Berends, 1960; exposed frozen solutions of thymine to UV-C radiation resulting in the formation of thymine dimmers. McLean prevented the spread of influenza in Veterans Hospital TB patients using	Riley *et al.*, 1957–1976; Beukers and Berends, 1960; Hart, 1960; McLean, 1961; Riley and Kaufman 1971

Contd...

	upper-room UVGI during the 1957 pandemic, providing evidence for the airborne transmission of influenza. Riley *et al.* studied the effects on disinfection rates in the lower room from air mixing via convection and a ceiling fan and mathematically modeled it. Riley and Kaufman investigated the effect of relative humidity (RH) on the efficacy of UVGI, with a sharp decline found in the fraction of organisms killed at RH values higher than 60% to 70%.	
1985–1992	UV-C wavelengths are the most biologically active radiation and, ironically, much less dangerous to humans. This is because UV-C radiation is absorbed by the outer dead layer of human skin, while UV-B and UV-A radiation penetrate deeper. The distinction should be made between the biological effect and the penetration depth of UV radiation, a key concept in UVGI safety toward quantitatively examining UVGI efficacy and safety measures for the proper use of UVGI.	Bruls *et al.*, 1984; Chang et al., 1985; Knudson *et al.*, 1986;Clement *et al.*, 1987; Eliasson *et al.*,1987; Iseman, 1992; Nardell, 1993-1995
2001	Studies evaluating various environmental and physical factors on UVGI efficacy (e.g., air mixing and ventilation, humidity, microbial sensitivity, fixture irradiance and configuration, and photore activation) were carried out.	Ko *et al.*, 2001.
2004	Dielectric barrier plays important roles in prevention of arcing and in the so-called non-thermal excitation of the plasma. In addition, dielectric barrier discharge generates uniform discharge plasma at atmospheric pressure.	Roth, 2004.
2007-2008	Plasma based devices have been appreciated for biological sterilization.Cooper *et al.*, studied the effect of plasma on *Bacillus stratosphericus* in three viability states e.g viable, culturable at low plasma dose, and viable but nonculturable (VBNC) at high plasma dose. *B. Stratosphericus* has the potential to turn into VBNC upon plasma application. Yating Studied the effect of atmospheric pressure non-equilibrium plasmas (APNPs) on *N. gonorrhoeae.* APNPs are able to effectively and quickly	Freedman *et al.*, 2007; Gallagher *et al.*, 2007; Muranyi *et al.*, 2007; Avdeev *et al.*, 2007; Matafonova *et al.*, 2008Cooper *et al.*, 2010; Yating *et al.*, 2010Kvam *et al.*, 2012; Maisch *et al.*, 2012 Pan *et al.*, 2013

Contd...

	kill the *N. gonorrhoeae*, and the killing effect is related to the structural damage of cell membrane.The use of nonthermal plasmas for disinfecting multidrug-resistant microbes e.g *Staphylococcus aureus* (MRSA), *Pseudomonas aeruginosa*, and *Candida albicans* in environmental settings and substantiate ongoing clinical applications for plasma devices. In 2012, Maisch *et al.* studied the effect of cold atmospheric plasma for different time intervals or ultraviolet C (UVC) radiation doses on *D. radiodurans. D. radiodurans* was sensitive to the cold atmospheric plasma treatment same as the methicillin-resistant Staphylococcus aureus (MRSA) strain. In contrast, *D. radiodurans* was more resistant than MRSA to UVC radiation treatment. Pan *et al.*, used cold plasma for disinfecting the *E. faecalis* in vitro biofilms in dental root canal treatment.	

1.2. Types of Disinfection Methods

For water treatment technologies various traditional sterilization methods such as thermal sterilization, chemical sterilization and irradiation of UV and gamma rays are presently implemented on a large scale. But during the last decade, plasma based devices have been appreciated for biological sterilization.[54] It has tremendous scope for application in comparison to conventional methods.[59] UV and gamma irradiation generates energetic photons which can cause serious damage to DNA and are harmful for human body.[63] However, most of the traditional sterilization methods are time consuming and are operated in closed space while other methods (like UV irradiation) are harmful to the humans. The plasma based devices can be applied to open space, have very short sterilization time (1 min), generate many reactive species (e.g., ozone, hydroxyl radical and oxygen atom) and have huge advantage over other sterilization systems. The physical process proceeds by positive and negative ions in the discharge's streamer, and chemical process is done by ozone, atomic oxygen, hydroxyl radical, etc.[64]

Some of the traditionally followed sterilisation methods for water treatment application includes:

1. Dry Heat Sterilization[228]
2. Pressurized steam sterilization[60,61]
3. Boiling[221]
4. Chlorine Dioxide [64,65,66,67,68]

5. Bromine Chloride[68,70]
6. Ethylene oxide (EO)[222]
7. Formaldehyde[62,223,224,226,227]
8. Ozone[65, 69,70, 71,72]
9. Ultraviolet Light[73,74,75]
10. Ultrasonics[71, 76, 77,78,127]

1.3. Need for Alternative Disinfection Treatment Technique

The technology of bacterial inactivation using nonthermal plasma produced by gas discharge at atmospheric pressure has received much attention in recent years.[64] Traditional disinfection and sterilization methods have some drawbacks. These methods need long treatment time.[79] Some polymer-based instruments and some extremely costly equipment (e.g., endoscopes) could not be disinfected by autoclaving. Toxic matters such as formaldehyde, ethylene oxide, and glutaric dialdehyde not only harm the human body but also pollute the environment.

Research on plasma sterilization started in 1960s. Since then, extensive researches have been done in plasma sterilization. As compared to incineration and thermal plasma treatment the advantage of using a non-equilibrium discharge is that most of the discharge energy can be utilised to accelerate electrons and generate free radicals.[80] As per the work carried out by Ghomi *et al.*, DBDs may also have advantages over conventional methods when different pollutants have to be treated simultaneously.[80] DBDs are considered especially if pollutant concentrations are low, say in the 10 to 1000 ppm range. The decomposition of greenhouse gases CO, and CH, under different operating conditions are studied over a wide temperature and pressure range using DBD sources. In addition, the handling and DBD treatment of large parts is facilitated at atmospheric pressure. Plasma can be classified in capacitively coupled plasmas (CCPs) and inductively coupled plasmas (ICP) due to the power input. Two types of atmospheric plasma used for biological sterilization includes thermal and non-thermal plasma.[80]

1.3.1. Thermal plasma

As per Ghomi *et al.* and other workers, in thermal plasma, energy flux from electrons to heavy particles equilibrates the energy flux from heavy particles to the environment only when temperature of heavy particle becomes almost equal to the electron temperature.[80,81] Using thermal plasma is limited because of its high temperature (2,000 K up to 10,000 K). This temperature can cauterize and damage the tissue.[82] In the case of contact glow discharges almost all the species in the discharge zone, i.e. anions, cations and neutrals, heat up, so the plasma generated in the reactors can be called hot plasma.[69, 83]

1.3.2. Non-thermal plasma

Non-thermal plasma operates at room temperature; its high efficiency and safety are suitable for medical and biological purposes. DBD is one of the fast and reliable non-thermal plasma that is used widely for sterilization.[54] In silent discharges, pulsed corona discharges, only free electrons gain high energy and the rest of the heavier charges and neutrals remain close to room temperature, and the plasma so generated is called cold plasma or non-equilibrium plasma.[48,69,84,85]

Chlorine is currently being re-evaluated as the standard for disinfection of drinking water and wastewater. Nevertheless, due to the cost of hypochlorite manufacturing and its potential carcinogenic and mutagenic effects [70] to aquatic species [71] there use are also limited. Sterilization or inactivation of pathogenic microorganisms is necessary in the most important fields such as medicine, food industry and agriculture.[116,117,118] In the past years, too much attention has been paid to the electrode structure and to the application conditions at which nonthermal plasma can effectively inactivate microorganisms.[87,88] It is generally considered that the electric field and plasma products (UV radiation, charged particles, and reactive oxygen species (ROS)) are the bactericidal agents.[89] These species in plasma are very complex and the bacterial inactivation using nonthermal plasma is related to many subjects, such as plasma physics, biology, medicine, and disinfection, therefore it remains largely unknown of what mechanisms atmospheric-gas plasmas acted in microbial inactivation.[69]

UV disinfection has rapidly become an alternative to chlorination of wastewater effluents.[85] It has been shown to be both effective and economically competitive with chlorination.[90] It is well known that under high-pressure conditions, nonequilibrium discharges in rare gases or rare-gas/halogen mixtures produce excimers.[84] Excimers do not possess a stable ground state and tend to decay rapidly, releasing in the process radiation in the VUV, UV, or even visible range. Figure 3 shows a typical DBD setup devised and optimised by us for both air and water disinfection studies. The radiation generated by excimer lamps is incoherent but intense and spectrally selective.[91] Ermel and Kurrat showed that plasma reactor enables the generation of plasma-active species at atmospheric pressure without expensive vacuum systems. Active species can include ultraviolet or visible photons, charged particles, including electrons, ions and free radicals, and highly reactive neutral species, such as reactive atoms (oxygen, fluorine, ozone, nitrogen oxides, etc), exited states atoms, and reactive molecular fragments.[91] Emission of UV-light and generation of radicals and charged particles contributes for destruction of microorganisms in plasmas through breaking the strains in the DNA and destroying the shell of a cell by chemical reactions.

In 1857, Siemens used dielectric barrier discharge for the generation of ozone from air or oxygen[243]. Presently, use of dielectric barrier for ozone generation are effective tools as an alternative disinfectant and acceptable because of its powerful oxidation effects [243]. Ozone is effective in deactivating bacteria, viruses, protozoa and endospores. Unlike chlorination, the use of ozone in water disinfection does not leave any residuals in finished water. Ozone decomposes spontaneously during water treatment forming hydroxyl free radicals OH- [244]. Hydroxyl free radical is considered to be one of the most effective oxidizing agents in water that can destroy the cell of microorganisms [245]. As hydroxyl can deteriorate the cell wall or recombine producing hydrogen peroxide (H_2O_2) which is a strong oxidant itself. They can attack and penetrate cell wall of microorganisms causing disorder in the cell physiology and thus resulting in cell death. However, ozonation has disadvantages it can form mutagenic and carcinogenic agents such as bromide in the treated water [245].

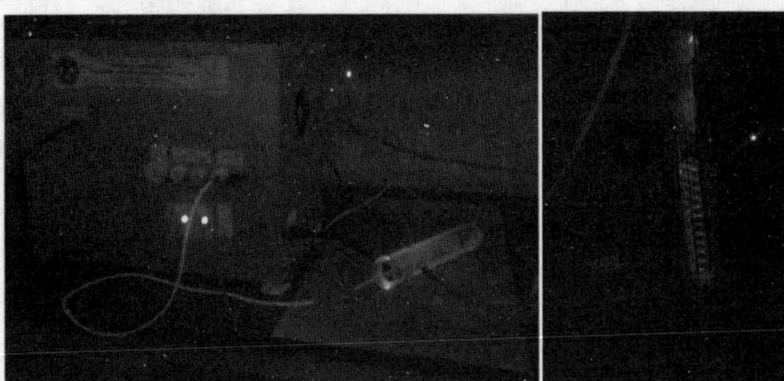

A B

Fig. 3 : Typical DBD setup devised and optimized by CSIR-CEERI for both (A) Air disinfection and (B) Water disinfection studies.

Ozone produced in plasma region is a powerful oxidizer that could destroy microorganisms effectively. Ozone concentration in nature varies between 0.01 ppm to 0.05 ppm, depending on season and geographic location as observed by Ermel and Kurrat.[93] High voltage ozone generators produce ozone/gas mixture, which contains 1 % to 3 % ozone when using dry air, and from 3 % to 6 % ozone when high purity oxygen is used as a feed gas. Experimentally it is proved that high concentration ozone could be an effective air disinfectant, which germicidal effect predicates on irradiation dose and processing time.[94] Due to inherited properties of DBD plasmas to generate active species and UV irradiation the grid arrangement presents a low-cost alternative to conventional disinfection processes. These filaments, also known as microdischarges, are the active regions of a DBD in which active chemical species and UV/VUV radiation can be produced. These microdischarges act as individual discharges which work independently of one another.[93]

In principal, a DBD source is operated on large range of parameters like,

i) Thickness of dielectric layer

ii) Gas gap

iii) Gas pressure etc

The interdependent relationship between all the parameters it is essential to achieve desired radiation (172 nm peak for Xe) for long operation. To improve efficiency of compact sealed-off excimer source, demountable DBD characterization setup of DBD source with optimization of geometrical and electrical parameters is required. Based on optimization parameters, sealed off DBD tubes must be fabricated. Excilamps can be considered as attractive alternatives to mercury lamps and lasers for applications in microbial control technologies because of the absence of elemental mercury, long lifetime, geometric freedom, high photon flux, and moderate operating temperatures.[95] The ultraviolet excimer sources have been developed[57] for inactivation of microorganisms[58] depending on their wavelength and their intensity. Photoinactivation is caused by changing absorption degrees of different biomolecules such as DNA, membranes, or proteins. Phosphors can be used to transform its VUV radiation to visible light. This wavelength conversion is utilized in mercury-free fluorescent lamps.[57]

1.4. Proposed Theories

Theories have been proposed for proper elucidation of mechanisms behind such discharge phenomenon for the initiation of corona discharges in water.[47]

1.4.1. Electronic theory

According to the electronic theories the free electrons accelerate under the applied electric field and may collide with and ionize the ambient molecules, thus producing more free electrons (electron avalanche) and leading to breakdown in water.[105 105] The basic dielectric barrier discharge (DBD) is totally dependent on the electric field applied. If the applied electric field reached to the ignition level, the breakdown will occur and it is known as micro discharge [229-238]. The discharge time of microdischarges is few nanoseconds and it is uniformly distributed over the dielectric surface. The figure 1 can be used to explain the overall discharge behaviour of DBD.

As long as the gap voltage V_g is smaller than the ignition voltage then there is no discharge activity and the device behaves like a series combination of two capacitance namely gap capacitance C_g and dielectric capacitance C_d. The total capacitance C is given as

$$C = (C_d \times C_g) / (C_d + C_g)$$

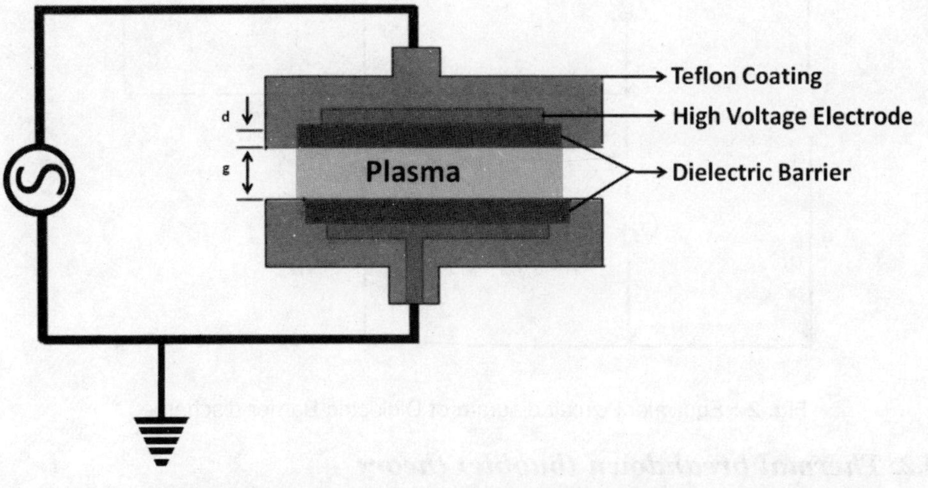

Fig. 1 : Schematic view of the parallel plate geometry of the DBD.

Whenever the gap voltage V_g crosses the ignition voltage level then the micro discharge are initiated. During half cycle the discharge voltage V_d remains approximately constant ($V_d = V_s =$ Const.) and the current flow through discharge gap is maintained by a large number of micro discharge figure 2. The discharge voltage mainly depends on the factors like gas composition, pressure and gas spacing. The microdischarge mechanism active in DBD is self-terminating and works over a large range of supply frequencies with different voltage or current shapes. Figure 1 shows a schematic view of the parallel plate geometry of the DBD used presently in our lab. Upon inelastic collision the free electron may ionize an ambient gas molecule, thus producing more free electrons. The free electrons may repeat the process and thus produce an electron avalanche (streamer).[69,84] The discharge-generated ions traverse the space and accumulate on the dielectric, where they produce a reverse electric field and stop current flow in few nanoseconds. Due to the short duration of the micro-discharge only electrons, being the lightest charged particles, can gain high energy while the rest of the heavier charges and neutrals remain close to room temperature. The energetic electrons, in turn, initiate the plasma chemical reactions that are responsible for the production of free radicals and ions, which ultimately destroy the pollutants.[69]

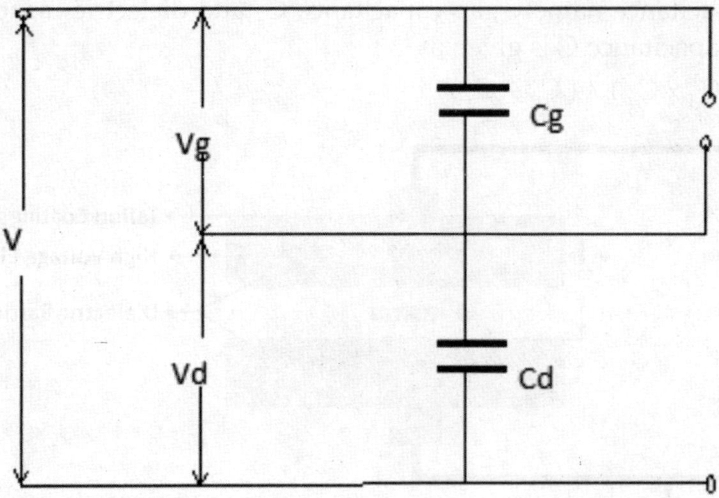

Fig. 2 : Equivalent circuit diagram of Dielectric Barrier discharge

1.4.2. Thermal breakdown (bubble) theory

According to the thermal breakdown (bubble) theories, the current in the high-field region causes heating and vaporization of the liquid, forming bubbles. Gas breakdown occurs within each bubble, causing further heating and growth of the bubble until complete breakdown of the gap occurs. A single streamer has a fraction of a millimetre diameter and can propagate to a distance of more than a centimetre in water.[47,69,105]

A spark discharge provides a more reactive environment than a corona discharge because of its high-energy particles, UV radiation, shockwaves and supercritical water causing temperature mediated transformation (which may reach 14,000–50,000 K) and free radical reactions in and around the plasma channel.[103] As the high-voltage pulse ends, the plasma channel cools and transfers its thermal energy to the surrounding water, resulting in the formation of steam bubbles.[69]

The high-energy electrons produced in electrical discharges result in the excitation, dissociation, electron capture or ionization of the target molecules. These free radicals (OH• in the case of water), play a major role in the destruction of pollutants.[106,107]

1.5. Mechanism of disinfection by DBD

Several mechanisms have been discussed to explain the generation of diffuse DBDs. These include gas pre-ionization by electrons or metastable from previous discharges [112] and interaction between the plasma and the dielectric surfaces.[123] Since atmospheric pressure conditions are most suitable for many DBD applications, the research on the properties of the different discharge modes has focused mainly on atmospheric pressure conditions rather than on the low pressure regime. The bactericidal agents generated by DBD plasma may include UV radiation, charged particles, ROS, etc. Studies have shown that the kinetics of cell death during plasma exposure is not indicative of UV-radiation excitation.[148] It is well known that both plant and animal hosts adopt defense strategies which utilize the ROS reactive oxygen species against the invaded microorganisms.[176] The DBD can create such ROS as oxygen atoms, ozone, metastable oxygen molecules, peroxide, superoxide, and hydroxyl radicals, and all of them are bactericidal.[147] These ROS have strong oxidizability and are prone to act with the bacteria cells. The ROS can oxidize the cell membrane and can cause the leakage of cytoplasm. It is believed that, in the first several seconds with plasma treatment, due to the rupture of cell membrane, the cytoplasm gradually leaks out, resulting in the concentrations of K+, protein, and nucleic acid in bacterial suspension increasing up to a higher value. This is also consistent with the quick death of cells in the first several seconds. However, with the plasma exposure time extended, the leaked protein and nucleic acid will be gradually oxidized by ROS, leading to the decrease of their concentration, but for K+, it cannot be oxidized, and thus, its concentration turns saturated. In this way, the bacteria cells are killed. Therefore, it is concluded that the ROS would play the main role in the inactivation process. A higher discharge power corresponds to more ROS generation and better inactivation effect.[147, 176]

Plasma sterilization could be classified in three mechanisms;

i) The hydroxyl radical can attach to unsaturated fatty acids and induce lipid peroxidation

ii) Oxygen radical can cause DNA oxidation

iii) Oxidation of amino acids can occur followed by protein oxidation

It is reported that fatty acid peroxide was formed by plasma and it altered to the membrane lipids.[124] But sterilization did not proceed by only chemical effect. The charge accumulation on the cell membrane induced electrostatic stress that was responsible for cell rupture.[7] The sterilization mechanism using plasma has been extensively researched but is still unclear. The mechanism of sterilization by DBD effect is not yet completely understood. Electric field and reactive species are effective factors for bacterial inactivation.[59] As observed by Ermel and Kurrat; active species include ultraviolet or visible photons, charged particles such as electrons, ions and free radicals, and highly reactive neutral species, such as reactive atoms (oxygen, fluorine, ozone, nitrogen oxides, etc), exited states atoms, and reactive molecular fragments. Ghomi *et al.* and other workers observed that, collision of heavy ions with microorganism cells can destroy their membrane.[125] The collision of energetic electrons with some atoms and molecules can break some molecular bounds and produce the excited and active particles such as radicals and metastable atoms. [80,126]

1.6. Effect of Sterilization using DBD Reactor

Disinfection of water and wastewater with UV radiation appears to be a potential alternative to chlorine. Low concentrations of chlorine residuals are toxic to aquatic life, [127] and some of the by-products of chlorination have been shown to be mutagenic.[128] Germicidal UV radiation does not produce undesirable by-products and is effective in inactivating a variety of microorganisms.[129]

In addition, effect of electrical sterilization might have been effective if the current flowing through spores increased by adding water. During the period of the exposure to DBD, cell membrane could be breakdown due to high electric field across the membrane.[130] The effect of DBD treatment became weaker with the increase of discharge gap. Addition of NaCl increased effect of sterilization and reached the peak at 4g/l of NaCl. However, sterilization with 8g/l and 10g/l NaCl solution were lower than that that of pure water. When the spores are covered with conductive liquid, they showed to be electrically shielded so that electrical membrane breakdown is eliminated. [131,132]

The experiments carried out to study the effect of sterilization on *Bacillus Subtilis* by dry method indicate that almost all *Bacillus Subtilis* spores were killed by dry method with D-value of about 40 seconds as compared with wet method, which was about 7 seconds. These results suggest that the addition of H_2O increased the effect of sterilization. It is supposed that $OH^\bullet$ radicals were produced from H_2O, and sterilization was effectively done by the $OH^\bullet$ radicals produced in the spore's neighbourhood. Oxidative degradation following VUV photolysis of water, due to its simplicity, has fast become an attractive alternative to other advanced oxidation processes (AOPs).[131,132]

As per Vander Walt, Germicidal effect of UV light for the bacteria Escherichia coli, Salmonella typhi, Shigella sonnei, Streptococcus faecalis, Staphylococcus aureus, and *Bacillus Subtilis* spores are well studied for a 99.9% inactivation of the cultured vegetative bacteria, total coliforms, and standard plate count microorganisms. However, the viruses, the bacterial spores, and the amoebic cysts required about 3-4 times, 9 times, and 15 times, respectively, then the dose required for *E. coli*. These ratios covered a narrower relative dose range than that previously reported for chlorine disinfection of *E. coli*, viruses, spores, and cysts.[45,128,133]

Hence, it is suggested that the doses of UV light necessary to kill pathogens, including viruses, bacteria spores, and protozoa, are much more comparable to the doses of UV light necessary to kill indicator bacteria than is the case for chlorine. As a result, the UV levels necessary to meet coliform standards may be relatively more effective than chlorination in killing pathogens. Because of the difficulties and subtleties of measuring UV dose,[134] many of the dose values reported are not comparable. In general, the VUV process is very simple and has the particular advantage that no chemicals need to be added. The process represents a challenge to other photochemical water treatment processes.[132] Treatment of contaminated surface water, ground water as well as wastewater containing biocidal or nonbiodegradable components is under investigation.

Effect of DBD reactor sterilization has been well studied on the following:

a) Vegetative bacteria [131,134,135,137]

b) Viruses[67,133,138]

c) Bacterial spores and protozoan cysts[139,140 141 142]

1.7. Effects of DBD Plasma

Various work groups had already reported various experimental results and data based on their observation on the effect of DBD plasma on bacterial survival, concentration of membrane bound proteins and intracellular proteins and polysaccharides of cell membrane; which gives novel insights about the role of DBD plasma in microbial disinfection processes.

1.7.1. Bacterial survival

It is reported that after exposure by plasma discharge for 1 min 12-h culture of cells, the activities of the key enzymes in cells, like glycerol dehydrogenase and glycerol dehydratase, were increased by 12% and 62%, respectively. This suggests that plasma improved the activities of key enzymes in cells to lead to the enhancement of viability. Some researchers thought that the electric field may be one of the bacteria inactivation mechanisms.[177] The action of applied electric field on bacteria sterilization was explored, and the voltage was increased by step until the critical discharge voltage.[178] The protein and nucleic acid concentration were measured at wavelength 280 nm and 260 nm respectively by many workers. As the OD value is proportional with the concentration, it reflects the detected concentration indirectly of the considered component. It was observed that, when the exposure time exceeded 10 s, the decreasing rate of protein concentration changed slowly, but the decreasing rate of nucleic acid did not change much.

The UV absorbance at 254 nm was measured, and a small correction for UV light scattering by suspended particles was made.[179] The turbidity of the samples was less than 4 nephelometric turbidity units, so the interference with coliform growth associated with high turbidity was probably minimal.[180] The survival of fecal coliforms was greater than that of total coliforms. This difference could be due either to the differing UV sensitivity of the different groups of species included in the total coliform group or to the effects of the test conditions on the repair of sublethal damage. Sublethal UV damage can be repaired under certain conditions, and bacteria can then form colonies.[134] Growth conditions shortly after UV irradiation can affect the number of these damaged organisms which can recover after plating.[134]

It is recognized, however, that the standard fecal coliform MPN procedure may underestimate the actual population of fecal coliform bacteria under certain conditions.[181-183] The large differences in dose-survival relationships in various UV disinfection studies are probably due to other factors, such as the difficulty in determining UV dose,[184] rather than to the method of enumerating coliforms. The results presented here show that excimer UV radiation is very effective against various types of bacteria in suspension in relatively clear water. It is now well known that the high killing efficacy of UV is not due solely to formation of thymine dimers in the DNA. It is believed that cell lysis plays a major role in the killing process during the duration of the exposure.[185]

Bacteria possess a range of DNA repair systems, permitting rapid recovery from sublethal UV damage.[144] A number of DNA repair enzymes are also induced by oxidative stress in bacteria.[145] They are primarily involved in two types: base excision repair and nucleotide excision repair.[146] The repair mechanisms activated by plasma discharge lead to enhanced survival ratios.[147] Experimental results showed that almost 100% of *S. aureus* and *E. coli* strains were killed in less than 10s and 7s of plasma treatment, respectively. It is concluded that the reactive oxygen species (ROS) in plasma play a dominant role in the inactivation process but not the electric field. It is suggested that the ROS can oxidize the cell membrane and then damage the protein and nucleic acid inside the cells and, thus, kill the bacteria. In the aqueous media there is a need for investigation for clear water and wastewater disinfection application at high initial concentration of *E. coli* and Entercocci. These two microorganisms provide a better assessment of treatment of wastewater efficiency.[56, 148-150]

Laroussi *et al.* found that the plasma exposure produced gross structural damage in the Gram-negative *E. coli*, whereas none was observed in the more structurally robust Gram-positive *Bacillus Subtilis*. The observed reduction in *B. subtilis* cells indicates that the penetration of reactive species through the cell membrane may be possible.[148,149] Yu *et al.* suggested that DBD plasma could lead to pH decrease in the medium, which cannot be enough to inactivate the viable yeast cells, but might contribute to a remarkable rupture of the inactivated cells.[151] Liu showed that different kinds of charged particles in plasma move all along the electric field. Formation of proton layer is an excellent catalyst for hydrolysis reaction because it exhibits strong acidity.[152]

1.7.2. Concentrations of membrane-bound and intracellular proteins

It could be found that the absorbance of cell membrane samples exposed to the DBD plasma in helium increased linearly with the exposure time. The protein concentration in cell supernate increased, whereas the concentration of membrane-bound proteins decreased with plasma exposure. The concentration of membrane-bound proteins decreased remarkably in the first 1 min; whereas the protein concentration in supernate increased observably in the time course from 1 to 2 min. It is suggested that membrane-bound proteins were destroyed by plasma, resulting in damage of the intact cell membrane.[64] This implies that the rapid death of cells might be due to a large release of proteins from cells. As the extension of exposure time in plasma, the color intensities of bands were weakened, and the proteins with large molecular weights (more than 44 kDa) disappeared little by little, whereas the proteins with small molecular weights (less than 20 kDa) increased gradually. This phenomenon indicated that proteins could be decomposed into peptides with low molecular weights by DBD plasma. DBD plasma can effectively decompose the membrane-bound proteins to amino acids.[64,153-155]

1.7.3. Polysaccharides of Cell Membrane

The polysaccharides on the cell wall and membrane can be disintegrated by DBD plasma. There is no doubt that the electrostatic effect is one possibility of the rupture of cells.[149] The concentration of amino acids in cell debris suspension was increased with the exposure time. The disintegration of biomacromolecules on cell wall and membrane promoted the cell rupture and release of cellular contents (e.g., proteins) from the cellular cytoplasm into the extracellular environment continuously. The DBD plasma in helium at atmospheric pressure affect the viability of *K. pneumoniae* and the disintegration of biomacromolecules, e.g., polysaccharides and proteins through a series of complex chemical reactions laid by oxidation and decomposition of proteins and polysaccharides from cell wall and membrane to form amino acids, peptides, maltose, glucose, and acetic acid.[64,154,155]

2. EFFECT OF ULTRAVIOLET-INDUCED MUTATION AND DNA REPAIR

UV light is one of the most practical methods used for disinfection in wastewater treatment systems because it can inactivate bacteria, viruses, Bacterial spores, and oocysts of protozoa.[156,157] Unlike those for other technologies, such as chlorination and ozonation, one of the technological advantages often put forward for UV disinfection is its lack of sensitivity to temperature variations. This independence from temperature would be expected if UV were a simple photochemical reaction.[158]

Severin *et al.* performed a series of batch inactivation studies with bacteria, yeast, and viruses and demonstrated that the effect of temperature on UV inactivation was very small.[159] Abu-ghararah,1994 found that the effect of water temperature on the kinetics of the UV disinfection process in the normal operating range of most treatment plants (20 to 40°C) is not statistically significant.[157,160] However, the physiological effect of inactivation is not well understood and is complicated by the ability of many organisms to repair UV damage inflicted to their nucleic acids. While the infliction of damage is a purely photochemical reaction that occurs in the few seconds while water is exposed to UV radiation in the disinfection channels, the interplay of reactions which eventually lead to inactivation includes some biochemical reactions which can be affected by temperature.[157] The low-pressure mercury lamp emitted at 254 nm is traditionally used for inactivation of microorganisms. This lamp emits near the DNA peak absorption coefficient at 265 nm.[168] This absorption causes damage to DNA by altering nucleotide base paring, particularly photoproducts and thymine dimers formation between adjacent pyrimidine molecules on the same strand of DNA.[169] If the damage remains not repaired, the transcription and the replication of DNA are blocked. UV disinfection inactivates microorganisms through the formation of cyclobutane pyrimidine dimers in their DNA.[161] However, these cyclobutane pyrimidine dimers may be removed via photoreactivation, which allows inactivated microorganisms to recontaminate the water. The formation of a dimer can be reversed by two repair mechanisms:

(a) Photoreactivation and (b) Dark repair.

Studies on photo reactivation is supposed to involve two step mechanisms as suggested by Harm in 1980, initially there is a formation of a complex between a photoreactivation enzyme (PRE) and the dimer to be repaired, which does not require light and is dependent on temperature, pH, and ionic strength.[161,162] Later, the PRE and repaired DNA released through another step. In which restoration of the dimer to its original monomerized form occurs and it is dependent on light energy intensity. This reaction occurs in less than a millisecond. The limiting step of whole reactivation process is the formation of the PRE dimer complex. An extended period of exposure to photoreactivating light would enable the release of PRE, which would then be available to form new complexes as mentioned earlier. The prediction of temperature effects is complicated by the nature of DNA itself and the complexity of reactions, enzymes, and molecules implicated in the inactivation and repair processes. The effect of temperature on the reactivation phase is still little studied. Chan and Killick investigated the effect of salinity and temperature on the reactivation of *Escherichia coli* in a marine environment. They found that the effect of salinity is greater than that of temperature. The information about the influence of temperature on the reactivation process subsequent to inactivation with UV radiation is still not readily available.[163]

The spectrophotometric assay used to measure the activity of photolyase in vitro is based on the principle that thymine monomers absorb strongly at 260 nm while dimers do not.[164-166] In-vivo studies on photolyase and photoreactivation are under study.[167] Studies have found that photoreactivation of *Escherichia coli* following medium-pressure (MP) UV disinfection is lower than that following low-pressure (LP) UV disinfection. [166,170,171] A hypothesized explanation for this is damage to photolyase, because it contains a tryptophan-rich flavin adenine dinucleotide (FAD) cofactor that has a peak absorbance at 280 nm, a wavelength emitted by MP and not LP UV lamps.[161] The oxidation of the flavin adenine dinucleotide in photolyase may have caused the decrease in activity.[166] Currently, no evidence to test the hypothesis, and research on this is limited.[172]

Rahmani *et al.* and others have reported that the damage of membrane to cells of *Escherichia coli* occurs only after irradiation with UV radiation above 305 nm.[173] The proteins show a strong absorption coefficient at 220 nm,[173,43] which is an alternative way to reduce the photoreactivation mechanism. The light dependent photoreactivation mechanism is particularly effective for specific wavelengths ranging from 300 to 500 nm. This mechanism uses a single enzyme called photolyase to repair UV-induced damage in the DNA.[174] The photolyase of *E. coli* is basically specific for repair of pyrimidine dimer. The photoreactivation causes problems particularly for large-scale use of UV inactivation of microorganisms when processing treated wastewater, drinking water, and sewage are exposed to sunlight. In this case, the photo inactivated cells can get out and then photoreactivated by sunlight. One possible solution being applied in practice is to increase the irradiance of UV source to such a high value that the DNA is extensively damaged and the photoreactivation is no longer possible. However, the higher power consumption is still a disadvantage.[175]

2.1. Efficiency of Sterilization

The drinking water industries are interested in including UV light treatment as an alternative to chemical disinfection treatment for disinfecting water supplies. The major driving force to include UV light treatment is the recent discovery of its effectiveness against protozoans, especially *Cryptosporidium* spp.[186,187] Adding UV disinfection capability to existing treatment plants or including it in the construction of new plants can provide additional disinfection credit. UV disinfection has the potential for reducing the use of chlorine and its associated disinfection by-products. Microbes were found to be significantly more resistant to ultra violet germicidal irradiation

UVGI at higher humidity. Good air circulation is requisite for effective upper-room UVGI as humidity tends to increase the strength of a microdischarge, while irradiating the cathode with UV photons tends to decrease it.[2,187] The *H. pylori* is inactivated by UV light to approximately the same degree as other tested gram-negative organisms,[187,188] but, little is known about the survivability of the other organism in this state.

2.2. Applications

2.2.1. Dye decolorization

Dielectric barrier discharge (DBD) can produce ultraviolet light,[189] ozone,[190] and hydroxyl radicals[191] which can be properly fabricated to decolorize azo dye, characterized by having an azo group consisting of two nitrogen atoms (N=N) and are the largest class of dyes used in textile industry.[192] The pH studies shown that DBD plasma could completely decolorized azo dyes at pH range of 3–9 within very short reaction time. The time required for complete decolorization was increased with increasing order of pH. Complete color removal (100 %) from effluents was observed by using Dielectric Barrier Discharge (DBD) Low Temperature Plasma, at dielectric spacing 5mm (all pH) without any other reagent added within 4 min.[189-192] The destruction of Methylene blue and carbon tetrachloride by DC corona discharges between a needle in air and a water layer has been demonstrated.[69,193] The destruction of organic compounds by electrical discharges in water was demonstrated by decolorization of anthraquinone dye.[47,69,103,116-118]

2.2.2. Food processing and medical applications

In the food processing and the medical field, sterilization is one of the most important processes for guaranteeing the safety of food or medical services. Discharge plasma can dissociate H_2O_2 to OH radicals, which are strong oxidants. Recently, OH radicals are used for sterilization of medical instruments, etc. Since OH radical's lifetime is very short, the safety against leak is high. The sterilization using low-pressure discharge plasma to generate OH radicals system has been in practical use. Sterilization using OH radicals produced by atmospheric discharge plasma is also studied.[194]

2.2.3. Industrial applications

The unique features and characteristics of DBDs offer a wide industrial application including ozone generation mainly used in water and gas treatment, excimer lamps, plasma ISAS, etc. The dehydrogenation of benzene and other alkenes takes place in low temperature plasma (LTP). Phenol is usually selected as a model organic compound for such studies.[119,195,196] Tezuka and Iwasaki observed complete oxidation of phenols, vanillic acid, chlorophenols and benzoic acid[120,121] in contact glow discharge electrolysis. The intermediates results in oxidative ring cleavage, which produces new intermediates such as oxalic acid, formic acid, malonic acid, tartaric acid, malic acid, etc. These partial oxidation products further oxidize to simple molecules such as carbon dioxide and water under this conditions.[197] This technique allows mass spectrometric measurements in the positive as well as in the negative mode. Due to low currents, undesired discharges are avoided. This ionization method provides ions from liquids at atmospheric pressure for mass spectrometric measurements. The UV irradiation emitted by the DBD is well known as an efficient source to dissociate compounds and generate radicals.

2.2.4. Applications of Atmospheric pressure plasma

Atmospheric pressure plasma (APP) has been explored for the potential applications in various fields. Some of the important applications includes Printed circuit board (PCB) hole etching,[63] Surface modification of polymers,[198] Air purification,[199] Sterilization,[200] UV curing of photoreactive polymers, Photo-deposition of large area or patterned thin metal or semiconductor films of high- and low-dielectric-constant insulating layers, Photo-assisted low-temperature oxidation of Si, SiGe and Ge, Polymer etching, Microstructuring of polymer surfaces, etc. Plasma jets or plumes at atmospheric pressure are becoming widely used, such as the atmospheric-pressure plasma plume[117] and the plasma needle.[201]

2.2.5. Pollution control

Applications of DBDs for pollution control and for the destruction of poisonous compounds have received growing attention. For the treatment of nitrogen oxides and sulphur oxides in flue gases, decomposition of volatile organic compounds (VOCs) and other pollutants as discussed above in industrial application. Contamination of exhaust air streams with gaseous hydrocarbons or organic solvent vapors occurs in many industrial processes, e. g. in chemical processing, in print and paint shops, in semiconductor processing as well as in soil remediation and water treatment.[202,203] Many hazardous organic molecules are readily attacked by free radicals, electrons or UV photons. These species are initially generated by electron collisions in the microdischarge filaments and subsequently initiate a number of reaction paths generating additional O, OH or HO_2 radicals for decomposing pollutants. The application of electrical discharges for pollution control[202-204] are abatement of acidic gases (SO_x, NO_x),[205] utilization of greenhouse gases (CH4, CO2, etc) and gas to liquid conversion gases pollutants,[197,206] removal of toxic volatile organic compounds (VOCs),[207] Hazardous particulates and Harmful microorganisms.[96]

In the area of water purification, ozone synthesis is an industrially accepted application of electrical discharges.[48,112] When ozone is injected into the exhaust gas,which can be efficiently produced by dielectric barrier discharge (DBD),[190] NO can be easily oxidized to NO_2 without producing any harmful by-products. As compared with the nonthermal plasma process, the reduction of NO_2 back to NO does not occur.[208] The injection of ozone into the ex- haust gas was suggested as a NO oxidation method for improving the selective catalytic reduction (SCR) process at low temperatures.[208] It is reported that injection of ozone produced by the dielectric barrier discharge was able to readily increase the NO_2 content and was also responsible for catalytic reduction of NO_x. On the other hand, at lower temperatures, the NO_x reduction was found to keep increasing with the NO_2 content. In electrohydraulic discharges, the destruction of pollutants may be initiated simultaneously by pyrolysis in a hot plasma channel, free radical oxidation, UV radiation, supercritical water oxidation, etc. The higher rate of pollutant destruction is in spark discharges than in streamer discharges. The addition of O_3 or H_2O_2 accelerates the oxidation of pollutants during electrical discharges because these compounds decompose into free radicals by streamer or spark discharges.[69]

2.2.6. *Surface modification and surface coating*

Plasma treatment of polymer surfaces to promote wettability, printability and adhesion has a long tradition (also known as "corona treatment"). As an additional process the deposition of thin films in DBDs has been investigated.[209] They showed that by using pulsed dielectric-barrier discharges microdischarge properties can be influenced in such a manner that superior surface modification and coatings of excellent quality can be obtained. The treatment of surfaces at low temperature and close to atmospheric pressure is an important advantage for large-scale industrial applications. It is to be expected that coating techniques using vapour or gas phase deposition in DBDs and also the annealing and oxidation of sol-gel films subjected to DBDs will be further developed. Surface treatment with DBDs has a great potential in the near future. [204] It is observed that, DBDs operated in miniature pores of reticulated ceramic foams the internal surface of foam structure can be covered with catalytic coatings. Such close contact between the DBD plasma establishes catalytic activity over a very large specific surface area. Nowadays, DBDs are also used in plasma display panels, high-power CO_2 lasers and excimer UV/VUV lamps.[93]

2.2.7. *UV light inactivation of bacterial biothreat agent*

The possibility of drinking water becoming contaminated with biothreat agents and the efficacy of current disinfection practices for the reduction in viability (inactivation) of biothreat agents [210] have been a great concerned for public health. The use of UV irradiation as a supplemental water disinfection practice is increasing for several reasons, among them improving control of protozoa, such as *Cryptosporidium* spp.,[211] and decreasing disinfection by-products created by chemical disinfectants.[212] As the spores are more resistant to UV but were reported to have similar UV susceptibility.[213] The inactivation results for *Y. pestis*, *F. tularensis*, *Brucella* spp., and *Burkholderia* spp. reflect findings similar to those of other waterborne pathogenic organisms, such as *Escherichia coli*, *Shigella sonnei*, *Yersinia enterocolitica*, and *Campylobacter jejuni*.[213] We can expect a facility following Environmental Protection Agency regulations to remove or inactivate the gram-negative bacteria biothreat agents like *Y. pestis*, *F. tularensis*, *B. mallei*, *B. pseudomallei*, *B. suis*, *B. melitensis Bacillus anthracis* Ames spores, *B. anthracis* 34F2 (Sterne) spores, *Brucella melitensis* ATCC 23456, *B. melitensis* IL195, *Brucella suis* KS528, *B. suis* MO562, *Burkholderia mallei* M9, *B. mallei* M13, *Burkholderia pseudomallei* ATCC 11688, *B. pseudomallei* CA650, *Francisella tularensis* LVS, *F. tularensis* NY98, *Yersinia pestis* A1122, and *Y. pestis* Harbin[46, 69,211,214,211,217,218,219]. Previous work established that bacterial spores are 10 to 50 times more resistant to UV at 254 nm than vegetative cells. [211,215,216]

2.2.8 Water purification by electrical discharges

Electrical discharges in association with intense electric fields, shock waves, UV radiation, O_3, H_2O_2, etc, all of which can contribute for microbial disinfection and are effective sterilizing agent.[69,96] It has been proposed that high-intensity pulsed electric fields without corona or spark discharge activities can be considered as a future technology for the sterilization of food products,[97] as they kill microorganisms without destroying food constituents and its nutritive value. Various factors such as the duration and the peak value of the voltage, the shape of the electrodes, etc [98] determines the sterilization efficiency of a pulsed electric field. Bactericides such as O_3 or H_2O_2 improve its efficiency on small scale.[99] It is proposed that corona or spark discharges under strong electric field improve the sterilization process.[100,69]

Electrical discharges taking place in an air or oxygen environment convert oxygen into ozone. In addition to ozone electrical discharges in air produce a variety of chemically active species, such as $O^{\bullet}$, $OH^{\bullet}$, $N^{\bullet}$, O^{-3}, N^{-2}, N^{-}, OH'', O'', O^{+2}, N^{+2}, N^{+}, O^{+}, etc .[69,84] These species are short lived and decay before ozone enriched air/oxygen gets into water. Electrical discharges in aerated water are also possible and they produce $OH^{\bullet}$, $H^{\bullet}$, $O^{\bullet}$, O_3, H_2O_2, etc.[101] The *in situ* electrical discharges for ozone production in water may provide a means to utilize most of these chemically active species for water cleaning. The synergistic effect of intense electric fields necessary for electrical discharges [97] in combination with conventional disinfectants such as O_3 and H_2O_2 [99] are lethal to different microorganisms found in water. The electrical discharges in water are also reported to produce ultraviolet (UV) radiation and shock waves,[103] which are helpful in the destruction of pollutants.[103] It is clear that electrical discharges are the best and environment friendly next-generation technologies for water treatment and they may prove far more effective than conventional oxidants and disinfectants.[69]

In a dielectric barrier discharge reactor the electrical discharges take place between electrodes where at least one of the electrodes is covered with a thin layer of dielectric material, such as glass or quartz.[48] Upon inelastic collision the free electron may ionize an ambient gas molecule, thus producing more free electrons. The free electrons may repeat the process and thus produce an electron avalanche (streamer).[69,84] The discharge-generated ions traverse the space and accumulate on the dielectric, where they produce a reverse electric field and stop current flow in few nanoseconds. Due to the short duration of the micro-discharge only electrons, being the lightest charged particles, can gain high energy while the rest of the heavier charges and neutrals remain close to room temperature. The energetic electrons, in turn, initiate the plasma chemical reactions that are responsible for the production of free radicals and ions, which ultimately destroy the pollutants.[69]

In both cases of contact glow discharge electrolysis and dielectric barrier discharge reactors, the electrical discharges take place in the gas phase in close proximity to the water surface. They require an intense electric field (>1 MV cm^{-1}) for electrical discharge to take place in water. Such high electric fields are possible by applying high-voltage pulses (15–100 kV) in a pulsed corona discharge[47,99] and are used as effective disinfectants. This is why most of the studies on water treatment are carried out using pulsed corona discharge reactors and the available industrial scale units are also based on this technique.[104] The mechanism of the initiation of corona discharges in water is still not fully understood and research is being carried out to explore these technologies.

2.2.9. *Ozone and water treatment*

The ozone concentration may be increased by increasing the ozone generation reactions and/or by decreasing the ozone destruction reactions. By employing a double discharge surfaces reactor[108] or a hybrid of silent and surface discharges [48,109] may increase the number of sites for ozone generation reactions within the given discharge volume. Porous silica gel packing can also effectively increase the ozone generation efficiency by spreading of an active plasma zone through micro-discharges. The pore size of alumina packing is a critical factor in ozone generation activity,[110] where the dissolved ozone dissociates into $OH^\bullet$ through a cyclic chain mechanisms which is also responsible for the oxidation of aqueous pollutants.[111,112] As it is reported that $OH^\bullet$ (10^7–10^9 M^{-1} s^{-1}) is much more efficient than ozone (10^1–10^7 M"1 s"1) for organic contaminants degradation.[112] Hence, faster conversion rate of ozone into hydroxyl radicals determines the efficiency of pollutant destruction. In advanced oxidation processes (AOPs), UV radiation, H_2O_2,[113] activated carbon,[114] etc, catalyze the O_3 to $OH^\bullet$ conversion. Moreover, the catalytic conversion of ozone into $O^\bullet$ can improve the efficiency of ozonation.[115]

Pulsed corona discharge during ozonation has few advantages; where distributed ozone enriched air/oxygen increase the rate of ozone dissolution in water[47] and generates additional free radicals such as $OH^\bullet$ and $O^\bullet$.[55] The technique of pulsed corona discharges in water during ozonation needs to be investigated as electrical discharges can generate free radicals and neutral active species and may eliminate the need for a separate reactor for ozone generation.[69] In general, the density of the chemically active species increases with an increase in the applied voltage.[117] The mechanism of ozone conversion to free radicals in the ozonation process is due to, Negative polarity of DC voltage [47], Bubbling some gas during the discharges [117] and Using argon instead of oxygen for gas bubbling [116,118].

The reactive species like, $OH^\bullet$, $H^\bullet$ and $O^\bullet$ are produced with gas bubbling,[116-118] whereas, $OH^\bullet$, $H^\bullet$ and H_2O_2 are produced without gas bubbling [100]and their intensity of the former increases with an increase in the rate of gas bubbling. The accumulation of H_2O_2 with time increases the pH of solution slightly.[100]

Spark discharges produce UV radiation and shock waves; they also produce $OH^\bullet$ and H_2O_2 with efficiencies better than those in streamer discharges.[116-117] The production of O_3 with oxygen bubbling indicates that O_3 synthesis takes place from oxygen in the bubbles.[69] Water conductivity plays an important role in the generation of corona discharges and on the production of chemically active species.[47]

As the corona discharge is partial, the discharge current should be transferred by ions present in the solution. Thus, an increase in the water conductivity (above optimum value of 10–80 ìS cm"1) results in a faster compensation of the space charge electric field on the streamer head and a decrease in rate of production of chemically active species.[117] It should be kept in mind that there is a large difference in the discharge in deionized water and in water with a conductivity of 0.5 mS cm"1, which should be expected for wastewater. Free radicals, electrons or UV photons readily attack many hazardous organic chemical. DBDs are used to provide reactive species such as $H^\bullet$, $OH^\bullet$, and $N^\bullet$. These species initially formed by electron collisions; in the microdischarge filaments subsequently provide a number of reaction paths to generate additional $O^\bullet$, $OH^\bullet$ or $HO^\bullet$, radicals. The free radicals can oxidize organic compounds. $OH^{\bullet}$ is primarily responsible for the oxidation of organic compounds, both in the case of ozonation and in the case of electrical discharges in water or above water level.[101,104,119-121] These radicals can subsequently react with hazardous compounds to form non-hazardous or less hazardous substances such as CO, simple acids or, upon addition of ammonia for example, solid salt particles. Further work on the combination of catalyst/adsorbent with electrical discharges for water purification is mandatory because it holds promise in making the processes more effective and cheaper.[69]

3. CONCLUSION

From the above discussion it can be concluded that electrical discharge techniques may prove to be more effective, cheaper and environmentally friendly than conventional water treatment techniques. UV emission from plasma arrangements and effects of irradiation on bacteria organisms is widely investigated.[69] There is a need for further developments in the area of water treatment by electrical discharges. In particular, there is a need to find new and more efficient materials that may be used as catalysts for ozone generation.[69] Further studies are required to clarify the role of the physical and chemical properties of catalyst materials on ozone generation. The application of pulsed high voltages during ozonation may result in better dispersion of ozone in water and faster conversion of ozone into free radicals, which may lower the cost of the ozonation processes. Water treatment by direct electrical discharges is being tested on an industrial scale. Further study on the destruction behaviour of possible water pollutants, including microorganisms and toxic organic compounds from industrial effluents, is mandatory. The identification of breakdown products needs to be carried out to clarify the mechanism of plasma chemical reactions involved. In particular, the studies on the application of suitable catalysts in an electrical discharge reactor have great possibilities to make the process more effective, cheaper and competitive with conventional methods.

Both the electrical discharges in water and above water level have their merits and demerits. Electrical discharges above water level, which is in gas phase, require less energy for the discharge to take place; while electrical discharges in water make a simpler system and produce the chemically active species in water, which can directly attack the aqueous pollutants. Among the types of electrical discharges, pulsed corona discharges are the most often studied and seem to be the most promising for water purification. The growing demand for the cleaning up of raw water and industrial waste water without the use of hazardous chemicals or the generation of secondary pollutants together with the rapid pace of development in the area of electrical discharges for water purification suggest that these techniques may play a major role in the water treatment industry in the future.[69] The studies must be carried out for accurately define the UV dose required to inactivate certain human pathogens, including bacteria, viruses, spores, and cysts, and to evaluate the validity of using coliforms as indicators of UV disinfection efficiency.[220]

ACKNOWLEDGEMENTS

We thankfully acknowledge financial support from Council of Scientific and Industrial Research (CSIR), Govt. of India for Inter Laboratory Project (ILP-0011) and project under 12th five year plan (PSC-0101).

CORRESPONDENCE

Dr. Waman Narayan Paunikar (Scientist and Head, Environmental Virology Cell) (E:mail wn_paunikar@neeri.res.in), Mr. Swapnil Ganesh Sanmukh (Research Scholar) (E:mail swamukh1985in@rediffmail.com), Dr. Krishna Suresh Khairnar (Scientist and Corresponding author) (E:mail k_khairnar@neeri.res.in and kskhairnar@gmail.com), Miss. Rajshree Chandekar (Research Scholar), Mr. Chetan Khapekar (Project Assistant), Mr. Naresh Bokade (Technical officer), Dr. Ghanshyamdas Bodhe (Scientist and Head, Analytical Instrument Division) (E:mail gl_bodhe@neeri.res.in) are affiliated to CSIR-NEERI, Nagpur-440020, Maharashtra, India.

AUTHOR CONTRIBUTIONS

The chapter was written and reviewed by WP, SS, KK and GB. References and literature review were collectively done by SS, RC and CK. Technical suggestions were provided by NB, UP, RP and GB. All authors have given approval to the final version of the manuscript.

FUNDING SOURCES

This work has been carried out as a part of Inter- institutional project ILP-0011 funded by CSIR.

ABBREVIATIONS

APP, Atmospheric pressure plasma DBD, Dielectric Barrie Discharge, UV, Ultraviolet, VUV, Vacuum Ultraviolet, APG, atmospheric pressure glow, UVGI, ultraviolet germicidal irradiation, DNA, Deoxyribose nucleic acid, RH, Relative humidity, BCG, Bacillus Calmette-Guérin, CCPs, capacitively coupled plasmas, ICP, Inductive coupled plasma, ROS, Reactive oxidative species, MV, millivolt, kV, Kilo volt, nm, nanometer, ppm, parts per million, K, Kelvin, AOPs, advanced oxidation processes, DC, Direct Current, µS, micro Siemens, *C*, conductivity, *V*, voltage, *t*, time, *f*, frequency, CFU, colony forming unit, ml, millilitre, kDa, kilo

Dalton, PRE, photoreactivation enzyme, LP, low pressure, MP, medium pressure, FAD, Flavin Adenine Dinucleotide, OD, optical density, PCB, Printed circuit board, VOCs, volatile organic compounds, SCR, selective catalytic reduction.

REFERENCES

Abu-ghararah, Z. J. Environ. Sci. Health Part A 1994, 29, 585–603.

Avdeev, S. M.; Boichenko, A. M.; Sosnin, E. A.; Tarasenko, V. F.; Yakovlenko, S. I. Laser Phys., 2007, 17, 1119– 1123,.

Barratt, P. A.; Baumgartl, A.; Hannay, N.; Vetter, M.; Xiong, F. Water Sci. Technol. 1997, 35, 347–52

Beukers, R.; Berends, W. Biochim Biophys Acta 1960, 41, 550-551.

Biosafety-EMS Disinfectants & Sterilization Methods. Donnelly rev.2008. 1-20

Bissonnette, G. K.; Jazeski, J. J.; McFeters, G. A.; Stuart, D. G. Appl. Microbiol. 1977, 33, 590-595.

Bolton, J. R.; Linden, K. G. J. Environ. Eng. 2003, 129, 209–215.

Braswell, J. R.; Hoadly, A. U. Appl. Microbiol. 1974, 28, 328-329.

Braun D.; Gibalov V.; Pietsch G. Plasma Sources Sci Technol 1992;1:166.

Braun D.; Kuchler U.; Pietsch G. J. J Phys D: Appl Phys 1991;24:564.

Bruls, W. A., Slaper, H., VanderLeun, J. C.; Berrens, L. Photochem Photobiol. 1984, 40, 485-94.

Buss, K. Arch. Elektrotech. 1932, 26, 261-265.

Butler, R. C.; Lund, V.; Carlson, D. A. Appl. Environ. Microbiol. 1987, 53, 375– 378.

Chalmers, I. D.; Zanella, L.; MacGregor, S. J. J. Anal. At. Spectrosc. 1997, 12, 1091–3

Chan, Y. Y.; Killick, E. G. Water Res. 1995, 29, 1373–1377.

Chang, J. C. H.; Osoff, S. F.; Lobe, D. C.; Dorfman, M. H.; Dumais, C. M.; Qualls, R. G.; Johnson, J. D. Appl. Environ. Microbiol. 1985, 49, 1361–1365.

Chang, J. S. 1993 Non-thermal plasma for pollution control NATO ASI Series G ed B M Penetrante and S E Schultheis (Berlin: Springer) Part A, pp 1–32

Chang, J. S. IEICE Trans. Commun. 1996, E79-B, 447–56

Cheremisinoff, N. R.; Cheremisinoff, P. N.; Trattner, R. B. Chemical and Non-Chemical Disinfection. New York: Ann Arbor Pub, 1981.

Choi, J. H., Han, I., Baik, H. K., Lee, M. H., Han, D., Park, J., Lee, I., Song, K. M., Lim, Y. S. Journal of Electrostatics, 2008, DOI:10.1016/j.elstat.2005.04.001

Clements, J. S.; Sato, M.; Davis, R. H. IEEE Trans. Ind. Appl. 1987, 1A-23, 224–35

Connaughton, D. Mater. World 1996,July 4 389–90

Cooper M.; Fridman G.; Fridman A.; Joshi S.G. J Appl Microbiol; 2010; 109, 2039–20

Cotton, C.; Passantino, L. J. Environ. Eng. Sci. 2005, 4, S57–S63.

Council on Physical Therapy. Acceptance of ultraviolet lamps for disinfecting purposes. JAMA 1943; 122, 503-5.

Cui, N. Y., Brown, N. M. D. Appl. Surf. Sci. 2002, 189, 31–38.

Cursons, R. T. M., Brown, T. J., Keys, E. A. Appl Env Micro. 1980, 40, 62.

Demple, B.; Harrison, L. Annu. Rev. Biochem., 1994, 63, 915–948.

Deng, X. T.; Shi, J. J.; Kong, M. G. IEEE Trans. Plasma Sci., 2006, 34, 1310–1316.

Deng, X. T.; Shi, J. J.; Shame, G.; Kong, M. G. Appl. Phys. Lett., 2005, 87, 153 901.1– 153 901.3.

Donnellan, J. E.; Stafford, R. S. Biophysiol. J. 1968, 8, 17-28.
Donohoe, K.G.; Wydeven, T. Appl J. Polymer Sci. 1979, 23, 2591-2601
Downes, A.; Blunt, T. P. Proc. R. Soc. Lond. 1878, 28,199-212.
Downes, A; Blunt, T. P. Nature 1877, 16, 218.
Duclaux, E. Annals of chemistry and physics 1885, 6, 5-59.
Dutka, B. J.; Kuchma S.; Kwan, K. K. Water Air Soil Pollut. 1979, 11, 349-352.
Eliassen, R.; Skrinde, P. T.; Davis, W. B. JAWWA 1958, 50, 1371-1384.
Eliasson B.; Hirth M.; Kogelschatz U.; J Phys D: Appl Phys 1987;20:1421.
Eliasson B.; Kogelschatz U. IEEE Trans Plasma Sci 1991;19(2):309;
Eliasson, B., Hirth, M.; Kogelschatz, U. J. Phys. D: Appl. Phys. 1987, 20, 1421–37
Eliasson, B.; Kogelschatz, U. IEEE Trans. Plasma Sci., 1991, 19, 1063–1077.
Ermel, V.; Kurrat, M. Dielectric Barrier Discharge Arrangement for Air Disinfection (http://www.htee.tubs.de/forschung/veroeffentlichungen/Dielectric_Barrier_Discharge_Ermel.pdf)
Ewart S.L. In: Smith BL. editor. Large Animal Internal Medicine: diseases of horses cattle, sheep and goats. 3rd edition. 2001. St. Louis: Mosby. pp. 1371-1380.
Fridman, G.; Friedman, G.; Gutsol, A.; Shekhter, A. B.; Vasilets, V. N.; Fridman, A. Plasma Process. Polym. 2008, 5, 503–533.
Fridman, G.; Peddinghaus, M.; Balasubramanian, M.; Ayan, H.; Fridman, A.; Gutsol, A.; Brooks, A.; Friedman, G. Plasma Chem Plasma Process 2007, 27, 113–114.
Gallagher, M. J.; Vaze, Jr. N.; Gangoli, S.; Vasilets, V. N.; Gutsol, A. F.; Milovanova, T. N.; Anandan, S.; Murasko, D. M.; Fridman, A. A. IEEE Trans. Plasma Sci., 2007, 35, 1501–1510.
Gambling, W.A.; Edels, H. Brit. J. Appl. Phys. 1956, 7 , 376-379
Gates, F. L. J. Gen. Physiol. 1929, 13, 249-60.
Gates, F. L. J. Gen. Physiol. 1930, 14, 31-42.
Gaunt, L. F.; Beggs, C. B.; Georghiou, G. E. IEEE Trans. Plasma Sci., 2006, 34, 1257–1269.
Geisler, T. To a question on the effect of light on bacteria. Central Journal of Bacteriology and parasites customer. 1892, 11, 161 – 73.
Gherardi, N.; Gouda, G.; Gat, E.; Ricard, A.; Massines, F. Plasma Sources Sci.Technol.2000, 9, 340–6
Ghislaine R.; Laura M.; Thomas C. Am. J. Trop. Med. Hyg., 82(3), 2010, 473–477.
Ghomi H.; Safa N. N.; Ramezani K; Karimi M. Bacterial Inactivation by DBD Plasma in Atmospheric Pressure. Ispc conference, paper (http://www.ispc-conference.org/ispcproc/papers/169.pdf)
Gibalov V. I.; Pietsch G.J. J Phys D: Appl Phys 2000; 33:2618.
Gibalov V.I.; Samoilovich V. G.; Filippov Y. V. Russ J Phys Chem 1981;55:471.
Giese, A.C., Christensen, E., "Effects of Ozone on Organisms", Physiol. Zool., 1954, 27, 101-106.
Glaze, W. H. Environ. Sci. Technol. 1987, 21, 224–30
Glover, J.L.; Bendick, P.J.; Link, W.J.; Plunkett, R.J. Lasers Surg Med. 1982, 2, I01-6.
Goldstein, B.D., McDonagh, E.M., "Effect of Ozone on Cell Membrane Protein Fluorescence I. in vitro Studies Utilizing the Red Cell Membrane", Environ. Res., 1975, 9, 179-186.
Golubovskii, Y. B.; Maiorov, V. A.; Behnke, J.; Behnke, J. F. J. Phys. D: Appl. Phys.2002, 35, 751–61
Green, B. A.; Clausen, E. M.; Litsky, U. Appl. Environ. Microbiol. 1977, 33,1259-1264.

Greene CE. In: Greene CE., editor. Infectious Diseases of the Dog and Cat. 1998. Philadelphia: WB Saunders Company. pp. 673-683.

Halliwell, B.; Gutteridge, J. M. C; Cross C. E. J. Lab. Clin.Med. 1992, 19, 598–620.

Harm, W. Biological effects of ultraviolet radiation. 1980, Cambridge University Press, New York, NY.

Hart, D. JAMA 1960, 172, 1019-28.

Hayashi, D.; Hoeben, W. F. L. M.; Dooms, G.; Van Veldhuizen, E. M.; Rutgers, W. R.; Kroesen, G. M. W. J. Phys. D: Appl. Phys. 2000, 33, 1484-1486.

Hayes, S. L.; White, K. M.; Rodgers, M. R. Assessment of the Effectiveness of Low-Pressure UV Light for Inactivation of Helicobacter pylori. Applied and Environmental Microbiology, 2006, 72, 3763–3765.

Henle, E. S.; Linn, S. J. Biol. Chem. 1997, 272, 19 095–19 098.

Hertel, E. Journal of General Physiology. 1905, 5, 95-122.

Hertel, E. Magazine for General Physiology. 1904, 4, 1 - 43.

Hill, W. F. Jr.; Hamblet F. E.; Benton W. H.; Akin E. W. Appl. Microbiol. 1970, 19, 805-812.

Hockberger, P. E. Photochem. Photobiol. 2002, 76, 561- 79.

Hoeben, W. F. L. M.; van Veldhuizen, E. M.; Rutgers, W. R.; Kroesen, G. M. W. J. Phys. D: Appl. Phys. 1999, 32, L133–7

Hoigne, J. Handbook of Environmental Chemistry vol 5, ed J Hrubec (Berlin: Springer) Part c, 1998, 83–141

Hoigne, J. Water Sci. Technol. 1997, 35, 1–8

Hoigné, J; Bader H. Water Research, 1983. 17(2): p. 173-183.

Hollaender, A.; Oliphant, J. W. J Bacteriol. 1944, 48, 447-54.

Horton, J. P., Horwood, M. P., Phynney, D. E. Sew Indust Waste. 1951, 24, 457.

Hu, J.; Quek, P. H. Effects of UV Radiation on Photolyase and Implications with Regards to Photoreactivation following Low- and Medium-Pressure UV Disinfection. Applied and Environmental Microbiology 2008, 74, 327–328.

Huffman, D. E.; Slifko, T. R.; Rose, J. B. Water Res. 2000, 34, 2491–2498.

Imaizumi, Y.; Takashima, K.; Katsura, S.; Mizuno, A. "Sterilization Using OH radicals Produced by Atmosheric Discharge Plasma," IEEE Conference Record, 2003 IEEE Industry Applications Conference, 2003, 437.

Imlay, J. A. Annu. Rev. Microbiol., 2003, 57, 395–418.

Iseman, M. D. Ann. Intern. Med. 1992, 117, 251-3.

Jagger, J. 1967. Introduction to research in UV photobiology. Prentice-Hall, Inc., Englewood Cliffs, N.J.

Jans, U.; Hoigne, J. Ozone Sci. Eng. 1998, 20, 67–90

Jeffrey DJ. Rev. sci. tech. Off. int. Epiz. 1995, 14(1), 57-74.

Jing X.; Li C.; Honglin W. Chemical Engineering Journal 2008,138.

Johnson, J. D.; Qualls R. G. 1981. Ultraviolet disinfection of secondary effluent: measurement of dose and effects of filtration. Report of EPA project R804770010. Municipal Environmental Research Laboratory, Cincinnati, Ohio.

Jolley, R. L.; Lee, N. E.; Pitt, W. W.; Denton, M. S.; Thompson, J. E.; Hartmann, S. J.; Mashni, C. I. Effects of chlorine, ozone and ultraviolet light on non-volatile organics in wastewater effluents. In: Venosa AD (Ed): Progress in Wastewater Disinfection Technology 1979, EPA-600/9-79-018.

Jong, P. De.; Van Heesch, E. J. M. Milchwissenschaft, 1998, 53 4–8

Jorns, M. S.; G. B. Sancar; Sancar A. Biochemistry 1985, 24:1856– 1861.

Joshi, A. A.; Locke, B. R.; Arce, P.; Finney, W. C. J. Hazard. Mater. 1995, 41, 3–30

Kahn, A. S.; Swerdlow, D. L.; Juranek, D. D. Public Health Rep. 2001, 116, 3–14.

Kanazawa, S.; Kogoma M.; Moriwaki T.; Okazaki S. 8th International Symposium on Plasma Chemistry, Tokyo,1987, 1839-1844

Kanazawa, S.; Kogoma, M.; Okazaki, S.; Moriwaki, T. Nucl. Instrum. Methods in Phys. Res. 1989, B37/38, 842-845

Kelly- Wintenberg, K.; Hodge, A.; Montie, T.C.; Deleanu, L.; Sherman, D.; Roth, J.R.; Tsai, P.; Wadsworth, L. J. Vac. Sci. Technol. A 17, 1999, 1539–1544.

Kelly-Wintenberg, K; Sherman, D. M.; Tsai, P.Y.; Gadri, R. B.; Karakaya, F.; Chen, Z.; Roth, J. R.; Montie, T. C. IEEE Trans. Plasma Sci. 2000, 28, 64–71.

Knudson, G. B. Appl. Environ. Microbiol. 1986, 52, 444–449.

Ko, G.; Burge, H.A.; Nardell, E.A.; Thompson, K.M. Risk Anal 2001, 21,657-73.

Kobayashi, K.; Tomita, Y.; Sanmyo, M. J. Phys. Chem. B 2000, 1049, 6318–26

Kogelschatz U, Eliasson B, Egli W. J Phys IV (France) 1997;C4:47.

Kogelschatz, U. Plasma Chem Plasma Proc. 2003, 23, 1.

Kogelschatz, U.; Eliasson, B.; Egli, W. Journal De Physique IV 1997, 7, C4 , 47-66

Kohn, W.G.; Collins, A.S.; Cleaveland, J.L.; Harte, J.A.; Eklund, K.J.; Malvitz, D.M.; Morb. Mort. Wkly. Rep. (MMWR), 2003, 52, 1–67.

Krasnoperov, L. N.; Krishtopa, L. G.; Bozzelli, J. W. J. Adv. Oxid. Technol. 1997, 2 248–56

Kvam E.; Davis B.; Mondello F.; Garner A. L. Antimicrob Agents and Chemotherapy,2012, Vol 56; 4, p. 2028–2036

Lapresa, G.; Bünning, G.; Franz, J.T.; Hempel, D.C. Bioscope 2 1994, 3, 26-28.

Laroussi, M. IEEE Trans. Plasma Sci. 1996, 24, 1188–1191.

Laroussi, M.; Alexeff, I.; Kang, W.L. IEEE Trans. Plasma Sci. 2000, 28, 184–188.

Laroussi, M.; Mendis, D. A.; Rosenberg, M. New J. Phys. 2003, 5, 41.1–41.10.

LeChevallier, M. W.; Evans T. M.; Seidler R. J. Appl. Environ. Microbiol. 1981, 42,159-167.

Legrini, O.; Oliveros, E.; Braun, A.M. Chem. Rev. 1991, 93, 671-698.

Lichtenberg, G. C. Comment. Soc. Göttingen. 1778, 8, 65-79.

Lindenauer, K. G.; Darby, J. L. Water Res. 1994, 28:805– 817.

Liu, C. J.; Zou J. J. J. Tianjin Univ. 2004, 37, 3, 189–192.

Locas, A.; Demers, J.; Payment, P. Can. J. Microbiol. 2008, 54, 11, 971–975.

Longemann, F. P.; Annee, J. H. J. Water Sci. Technol. 1997, 35353–60

Lungu, C. P., Mustata, I., Bratescu, M., Saito, N., Takai, O. "Active species generation in water by direct electrical discharges" in International Balkan Workshop on Applied Physics, Constanta, Romania, 6-8 July 2009.

Lyons, W.A. Sewage Indust Waste 1951; 23, 9, 1084.

Ma, Y.; Zhang, G.; Shi, X.; Xu, G; Yang, Y. IEEE Transaction on Plasma Science 2008, 36, 4, 1615-1619.

MacFarlane, A. W.; Stanley, R. J. Biochemistry. 2001, 40:15203–15214.

Maisch T.; Shimizu T.; Isbary G.; Heinlin J.; Karrer S.; Klämpfl T. G; Li Y.; Morfill G.; Zimmermann J. L. Appl and Environ Microbiol, 2010, Vol 78; 12; p. 4242–4247

Malik, M. A.; Ghaffar, A.; Malik, S. A. Water puriûcation by electrical discharges Plasma Sources Sci. Technol. 2001, 10, 82–9.

Malik, M. A.; Malik, S. A. Platinum Met. Rev. 1999, 43, 109–13.

Mamane-Gravetz, H.; Linden, K. G. J. Appl. Microbiol. 2005, 98:351–363.

Maris P. Rev. sci. tech. Off. int. Epiz. 1995, 14(1), 47-55.

Matafonova, G. G.; Batoev, V. B.; Astakhova, S. A.; Gómez, M.; Christofi, N. Lett. Appl. Microbiol. 2008, 47, 508– 513.

Matsunga, T.; Hieda, K.; Nikaido, O.; Photochem. Photobiol. 1991, 54, 403–410.

McLean, D. J. ; Giese, A. C. J. Biol. Chem., vol. 1950, 187, 537– 542.

McLean, R.L. Am Rev Respir Dis. 1961, 83, 36-8.

Mendis, D. A.; Rosenberg, M.; Azam F. "IEEE Trans. Plasma Sci. 2000, 28, 1304–1306.

Miller, G.W.; Rice, R.G.; Robson, C.M.; Scullin, R.L.; Kuhn, W.; Wolf, H. An Assessment of Ozone and Chlorine Dioxide Technologies for Treatment of Municipal Water Supplies. EPA-600/ 8-78-018, 1978.

Moisan, M.; Barbeau J.; Crevier M.-C.; Pelletier J.; Philip N.; Saoudi B. Pure Appl. Chem. 2002, 74, 349–358.

Moisan, M.; Barbeau, J.; Moreau, S.; Pelletier, J.; Tabrizian, M.; Yahia, L.H. Int. J. Pharmaceut. 2001, 226, 1–21.

Mok, Y. S. J. Chem. Eng. Japan. 2004, 37, 1337.

Montie, T. C.; Kelly-Wintenberg K.; Roth J. R. IEEE Trans. Plasma Sci. 2000, 28, 41–50.

Morley PS. Vet Clin Food Anim, 2002, 18:133-55.

Morris, E. J. Med. Lab. Technol. 1972, 29:41-47.

Morris, J. C. 1975.Aspects of the quantitative assessment of germicidal efficiency, p. 1 10. J. D. Johnson (ed.), Disinfection- water and wastewater. Ann Arbor Science, Ann Arbor, Mich.

Muranyi, P.; Wunderlich, J.; Heise M. J. Appl. Microbiol. 2007, 103, 1535–1544.

Nardell, E. A. Am J Infect Control. 1995; 23,156-64.

Nardell, E. A. Med Clin North Am. 1993, 77, 1315-34.

National Research Council. 1980. Drinking water and health, vol. II. National Academy Press, Washington, D.C.

Nicholson, W. L.; Galeano, B. Appl. Environ. Microbiol. 2003, 69, 1327–1330.

Nicholson, W. L.; Law, J. F. J. Microbiol. Methods 1999, 35, 13–21.

Nicholson, W. L.; Munakata N.; Horneck G.; Melosh H. J.; Setlow P. Microbiol. Mol. Biol. Rev. 2000, 64, 548–572.

Nomoto, Y.; Ohkubo, T.; Kanazawa, S.; Adachi, T. IEEE Trans. Ind. Appl. 1995, 31, 1458-62.

Oguma, K.; Katayama H., Mitani H., Hirata T.; Ohgaki. S. Appl. Environ. Microbiol. 2001, 67, 4630–4637.

Oguma, K.; Katayama H., Ohgaki. S. Appl. Environ. Microbiol. 2002, 68, 6029–6035.

Ohshima, T.; Sato, K.; Terauchi, H.; Sato, M. J. Electrost. 1997, 42, 159–66

Overholt, R.H.; Betts, R.H. J Thorac Surg. 1940, 9, 520-9.

Painter, R. B. Genetics 1974, 78, 139–148.

Pan J. ; Sun K.; Liang Y.; Sun P; Yang X.; Wang J.; Zhang J.; Zhu W.; Fang J.; Becker K. H., 2013, Basic Research—Technology, Cold Plasma Therapy Vol 39, 1,p. 105-110.

Park, B.J.; Lee, D.H.; Park, J. C.; Lee, I. S.; Lee, K. Y.; Hyun, S.O.; Chun, M. S. Phys. Plasmas 2003, 10, 4539–4544.

Pashaie, B.; Dhali, S. K.; Honea, F.I. Appl Phys 1994, 27.

Payne, G.; Heelis P. F.; Rohrs B. R.; Sancar A. Biochemistry 1987, 26; 7121–7127.

Penetrante, B.M.; Bardsley, J. N.; Hsiao, M. C. Jpn. J. Appl. Phys. 1997, 36 , 5007-5017

Penetrante, B.M.; Schultheis, S.E. (Eds.), Non-Thermal Plasma Techniques for Pollution Control, NATO ASI Series, Vol. G 34, Springer, Berlin, 1993.

Pierce, J. J. Soc. Dyers Color 1994, 110, 131 –133.

Pietsch GJ. Contrib Plasma Phys 2001;41(6):620.

Qualls, R. G.; Chang J. C. H.; Ossoff S. F.; Johnson J. D. Appl. Environ. Microbiol. 1984, 48, 699-701.

Qualls, R. G.; Dorfman M. H.; Hohnson J. D. Water Res. 1989, 23, 317–325.

Qualls, R. G.; Flynn M. P.; Johnson J. D. J. Water Pollut. Control Fed. 1983, 55, 1280-1285.

Qualls, R. G.; Johnson, J. D. Appl. Environ. Microbiol. 1983, 45, 872-877.

Rahmani, B.; Bhosle, S.; Zissis, G. IEEE Trans. Plasma Sci. 2009, 37, 546–550.

Rapson, W. H., Nazar, M. A., Butsky, V. V. Bull. Env. Contam. Tox. 1980, 24, 590-597.

Reed, N. G. The History of Ultraviolet Germicidal Irradiation for Air Disinfection. Public Health Reports. 2010, 125, 15-27

Reinisch, R. F.; Gloria H. R.; Androes, G. M. 1970. Concerning the production of free radicals in protein by ultraviolet light, p. 190. In R. F. Reinisch (ed.), Photochemistry of macromolecules. Plenum Press, New York, NY.

Rice, E. W.; Hoff, J. C. Appl. Environ. Microbiol. 1981, 42, 546-547.

Rice, E. W.; Hoff, J. C.; Schaeffer, F. W. III. Appl. Environ. Microbiol. 1982, 43, 250-251.

Rice, J. K.; Ewell, M. Appl. Environ. Microbiol. 2001, 67:5830– 5832.

Richardson S.D TrAC Trends in Analytical Chemistry, 2003. 22(10): p. 666-684.

Rico, B; Perez, D; Lema, J. M.; Lucas, T. Ozone Sci. Eng. 1997, 19, 471–80

Riley, R.L.; Kaufman, J.E. Appl Microbiol. 1972, 23, 1113-20.

Riley, R.L.; Kaufman, J.E. Arch Environ Health 1971, 22, 551-3.

Riley, R.L.; Knight, M.; Middlebrook, G. Am. Rev. Respir. Dis. 1976, 113,413-8.

Riley, R.L.; Mills, C.C.; Nyka, W.; Weinstock, N.; Storey, P.B.; Sultan, L.U.; et al. Am J Hyg 1959, 70,185-96.

Riley, R.L.; Mills, C.C.; O'Grady, F.; Sultan, L.U.; Wittstadt, F.; Shivpuri, D.N. Am Rev Respir Dis. 1962, 85, 511-25.

Riley, R.L.; O'Grady, F. Airborne infection: transmission and control. New York: The Macmillan Company; 1961.

Riley, R.L.; Permutt, S.; Kaufman, J.E. Arch Environ Health 1971, 23, 35-9.

Riley, R.L.; Wells, W.F.; Mills, C.C.; Nyka, W.; McLean, R.L. Am Rev Tuberc. 1957, 75,420-31.

Robinson, J. W., Ham, M. ; Balaster, A. N. J. Appl. Phys. 1973, 44, 72–5

Roessler, P. F., Severin, B. F. 1996. Ultraviolet light disinfection of water and wastewater, p. 313–366. In C. Hurst (ed.), Modeling disease transmission and its prevention by disinfection. Cambridge Press, Cambridge, United Kingdom.

Rose, L. J.; O'Connell, H. UV Light Inactivation of Bacterial Biothreat Agents. Applied and Environmental Microbiology. 2009, 75, 2987–2990.

Rose, L. J.; Rice E. W.; Jensen B. J.; Murga R.; Peterson A.; Donlan R.; Arduino M. J. Appl. Environ. Microbiol. 2005, 71, 566–568.

Roth, J. R. "Prospective Industrial Applications of the One Atmospheric Glow Discharge Plasma (OAUGDPTM)", IEEE Conference Record, 2004 IEEE Industry Applications Conference, pages 223, October 2004

Roth, J. R., Rahel, J., Dai, X., Sherman D. M. The physics and phenomenology of One Atmosphere Uniform Glow Discharge Plasma (OAUGDP™) reactors for surface treatment applications. 2005, J. Phys. D: Appl. Phys. 38, 555.

Rubin A. J. (ed.), Chemistry of water supply, treatment and distribution. Ann Arbor Science, Ann Arbor, Mich. Grymonpre, D. R.; Finney, W. C. ; Locke, B. R. Chem. Eng. Sci. 1999, 54, 3095–105

Rutala W. A.; Weber D. J. Infect Control Hosp Epidemiol 1998,19, 798-804.

Salcedo, I.; Andrade, J. A.; Quiroga, J. M.; Nebot, E. Photoreactivation and Dark Repair in UV-Treated Microorganisms: Effect of Temperature. Applied and Environmental Microbiology, 2007, 73, 1594–1600.

Sambrook, J.; Russell, D. W. Molecular Cloning a laboratory manual third edition, 1997, 16.54-16.58.

Samoilovich V.; Gibalov V.;, Kozlov K.; Physl chemistry of the barrier discharge, 1997. D. usseldorf: DVS-Verlag GmbH.

Sato, M.; Ohgiyama, T. ; Clements, J. S. IEEE Trans. Ind. Appl. 1996, 32, 106–12

Scarpino, P.V.; Cronier, S.; Zink, M.L.; Brigano, F. A. O.; Hoff, J. C. Effect of particulates of disinfection of Enteroviruses and coliform bacteria in water by chlorine dioxide. Proc AWWA Technol Conf 1977, V 2B-3, 11.

Scott, D.B.M., Lesher, E.C., "Effect of Ozone on Survival and Permeability of Escherichia coli", J. Bacteriol., 1963, 85, 567-576.

Scott, G.I.; Middaugh, D.P.; Crane, A.M.; McGlothin, N.; Watabe, N. Water Chlor Env Impct Hlth. 1980, 3, 501.

Severin, B. F.; Suidan M. T.; Engelbrecht, S. Environ. Sci. Technol. 1983, 17:717–721.

Sharma, A.; Pruden, A.; Stan, O.; Collins, G. J. IEEE Trans. Plasma Sci. 2006, 34, 1290–1296.

Sharma, A. K.; Camaioni, D. M.; Josephson, G. B.; Goheen, S. C. ; Mong, G. M. J. Adv. Oxid. Technol. 1997, 2 , 239–47

Sharma, A. K.; Locke, B. R.; Arce, P.; Finney, W. C. Hazard. Waste Hazard. Mater. 1993,10, 209–19

Siemens W. Ann. Phys. Chem. 1857 (102) 66.

Siemens, W. V. Poggendorff's Annals of Chemistry and Physics 1857,102, 66.

Sladek, R. E. J.; Stoffels, E. J. Phys. D, Appl. Phys. 2005, 38, 1716–1721.

Soloshenko, I. A.; Tsiolko, V. V.; Khomich, V. A.; Shchedrin, A. I.; Ryabtsev, A. V.; Bazhenov, V. Y.; Mikhno, I. L. Plasma Phys. Rep. 2000, 26, 845–853.

Sosnin, E. A.; Avdeev, S. M.; Kuznetzova, E. A.; Lavrent'eva, L. V. Instrum. Exp. Tech. 2005, 48, 663–666.

Sosnin, E. A.; Oppenländer, T.; Tarasenko, V. F. J. Photochem. Photobiol. C. 2006, 7, 145–163.

Steelman, V. M., Urol. Nurs. 1992, 12, 123–127.

Sun, B.; Sato, M.; Clements, J. S. J. Electrost. 1997, 39, 189–202.

Sun, B.; Sato, M.; Clements, J. S. J. Phys. D: Appl. Phys. 1999, 32, 1908–15.

Sun, B.; Sato, M.; Harano, A.; Clements, J. S. J. Electrost. 1998, 43, 115–26

Sun, Y.; Qiu, Y. IEEE Transactions on Plasma Science. 2007, 35, 1496-1500.

Takenaka, Y.; Kuzumoto, M.; Yasui, K.; Yagi, S.; Tagashira, M. IEEE J. Quantum Electron. 1991, 27, 2482-2487.

Tezuka, M.; Iwasaki, M. Plasmas Ions 1999, 1, 23–6

Tezuka, M.; Iwasaki, M. Thin Solid Films 1998, 316, 123–7

U.S. Environmental Protection Agency. 2006. Ultraviolet disinfection guidance manual for the final long term 2 enhanced surface water treatment rule. EPA 815-R- 06-007. U.S. Environmental Protection Agency, Office of Water, Washington, DC.

Viner, A.S.; Lawless, P.A.; Ensor, D.S.; Sparks, L.E. IEEE Trans. Ind. Appl. 1992, 28, 504–512.

Vogt, C.; Regil, S. Controlling trihalomethanes while attaining disinfection. In: Water Disinfection with Ozone, Chloramines or Chlorine Dioxide. Proc. AWWA Sem 20152, 1980.

Wagenaars, E.; Brandenburg, R.; Brok, W. J. M.; Bowden, M. D.; Wagner, H. E. J. Phys. D: Appl. Phys. 2006, 39, 700–711.

Walt, E. V. The effect of ultraviolet light, cavitational flow and ultrasound on protozoan cysts and oocysts, bacteriophages and clostridium (http://www.ewisa.co.za/literature/files/109%20Paper.pdf)

Wang, S.C.; Liu, Y. H. Industrial Electronics, IEEE Transactions. 2008, 55, 142–153.

Wangner, H.E.; Brandenburg, R.; Kozlov, K.V; Sonnenfeld. A.; Michel, P.; Behnke, J.F. Vacuum 2003, 71, 417–436.

Ward, R. W.; DeGraeve G. M. J. Water Pollut. Control. Fed. 1978, 50, 46-60.

Ward, R.W.; DeGraeve, G.M. Water Res Bull 1980, 16:48.

Wells, M.W. JAMA 1945, 129,197-200.

Wells, W.F. Airborne contagion and air hygiene: an ecological study of droplet infections. Cambridge (MA): Harvard University Press; 1955.

Wells, W.F. Am. J. Hyg. 1934, 20,611-8.

Wells, W.F. J. Franklin Inst. 1940, 229,347-72.

Wells, W.F. J. Franklin Inst. 1944, 238,185-93.

Wells, W.F. J. Franklin Inst. 1945, 240,379-95.

Wells, W.F.; Fair, M.G. Science, 1935; 82, 280-1.

Wells, W.F.; Wells, M.W. JAMA, 1936, 107, 1805-9.

Wells, W.F.; Wells, M.W.; Wilder, T.S. Am. J. Hyg. 1942, 35, 97-121.

Whisler, B.A. Iowa State Coll J Sci 1940, 14, 215-31.

Willberg, D. M.; Lang, P. S.; Hochemer, R. H.; Kratel, A.; Hoffman, M. R. Environ. Sci. Technol. 1996, 30, 2526–34

Wright, H.; Gaithuma, D.; Greene, D.; Aieta, M. J. Am. Water Works Assoc. 2006, 98, 81–92.

Xi-lu, W.; Mizuno, A.; Katsura, S. Chin. Phys. Lett. 1998, 15, 41–2.

Xu, X. J.; Zhu D. C. Physics of Gas Discharge. Shanghai, China: Fudan Univ. Press, 1996, 312–314.

Yan, K; Hui, H; Cui, M.; Miao, J.; Wu, X.; Bao, C. ; Li, R. J. Electrost. 1998, 44 17–139.

Yating T.U.; Li X. U.; Ying Y.U. ; Ming T.; Juan L. I.; Hongxiang C. J Huazhong Univ Sci Technol(Med Sci) 2010, 30(2):226-230

Yip, R. W.; Konasewich, D. E. 1972. Ultraviolet sterilization of water-its potential and limitations. Water Poll. Control (Canada) June: 14-18.

Yoshida K.; Tagashira H.; Kitami M. Inst Technol 1986;18:11.

Young, S.B., Setlow, P. Mechanisms of Bacillus subtilis spore resistance to and killing by aqueous ozone. Journal of Applied Microbiology. 2004, 96, 1133–1142.

Yu, H.; Xiu, Z. L.; Ren, C. S.; Zhang, J. L.; Wang, D. Z.; Wang, Y. N.; Ma, T. C. IEEE Trans. Plasma Sci. 2005, 33, 1405–1409.

Yu, Q. S.; Huang, C.; Hsieh, F. H.; Huff, H.; Yixiang D. Journal of Biomedical Materials Research. 2006, 80B, 211-219.

Zelle, M. R.; HoUlaender, A. 1955. Effects of radiation on bacteria, p. 365-430. In A. Hollaender (ed.), Radiation biology, vol. II. McGraw-Hill Book Co., New York.49, 1985.

❑❑❑

CHAPTER - 11

Novel Applications of Bacterial and Algal Viruses in Advancement of Molecular Biology and for Enhancement of Bio-fuel Production

Swapnil Ganesh Sanmukh‡, Krishna Khairnar,* Suresh Khairnar‡ and Waman Narayan Paunikar‡

‡Environmental Virology Cell, National Environmental Engineering Research Institute (CSIR- NEERI), Nehru Marg, Nagpur-440020, Maharashtra (India).

**Corresponding Author*

INTRODUCTION

The field of virology is still not explored extensively. The use of bacterial and algal viruses till date are mostly restricted to areas like phage therapy (Sanmukh *et al.*, 2012), whole genome sequencing, isolation and characterization of lytic enzymes (Paunikar *et al.*, 2011), control of pathogenic multi drug resistant micro-organisms, structure elucidation through electron microscopy as well as NMR spectroscopic methods. Bioinformatics approach is also well explored for the gene annotation, sub cellular localization as well as structure prediction of various unknown as well as unclassified proteins in different viruses (Sanmukh *et al.*, 2010). Our main concern while dealing with most viruses is limited to its classification and characterization but, we forget to reveal its true nature by exploring various budding applications which they may suffice. Moreover, very few viruses are sequenced and their genome is made available at ICTV (International Committee for Taxonomy of Viruses) which makes their information more unclear. Considering all above scenario, we can feel the urgent need for entering into a new area of "Applied Virology". Due to various limitations with respect to funding and possible facility requirements, researchers are not yet optimizing on the applications of viruses for potential molecular biology applications as well as its industrial implementation in cost effective, time efficient and for commercial gain.

The natural ability of viruses can be harnessed to do the most common classification of different viruses for whether they are lytic or lysogenic by as simple and effective technique mostly used to study the toxicity testing of different chemicals, drugs, vaccines as well as other pharmaceutical and biological ingredients i.e. *Comet Assay method*. Normally, comet assay method is used to study the time and dose concentration effect of target compound on the cells (animal or human derived) for the determination of toxic/enhancing/ static effect through the cell lyses/proliferation/cell deformities formations. The comet assay is the widely used method for *in vitro* toxicity testing which is also an alternative to the use of animal models for *in vivo* testing. Since, its inception in 1984 by Ostling & Johansson, it is being frequently modified for wide range of application. Inspite of its wide applicability, unfortunately there's no report of its application in bacteriophages research. Here we present a novel application of comet assay for the detection of bacteriophage mediated bacterial cell lysis. The lytic activity of bacteriophage devours the bacterial cell which results in the release of bacterial genomic material that gets detected by ethidium bromide staining method by the comet assay protocol. The conventional methods in bacteriophage research for studying bacterial lysis by bacteriophages like plaque assay method is time consuming, laborious and costly. The results of the study show that the application of comet assay can be an economical, time saving and less laborious alternative to conventional plaque assay for the detection of bacteriophage mediated bacterial cell lysis.

Moreover, the industrial application of algae is well explored for the generation of clean and renewable energy in the form of "Bio-fuel". This is by far the most extensively researched field for carbon sequestration, bio-fuel precursor extraction from lipids, etc. Various studies have been conducted recently to use microalgal system for the production of algal lipid for biodiesel production. The calorific value of lipid from *Chlorella* sp. has been reported to be higher than most of the other fresh water microalgae making it a potential candidate to be used as biofuel. This is a first report of novel application of microalgal viruses for improving the extraction efficiency of algal lipid for biodiesel production by viral lysis of *Chlorella vulgaris*. The algal lipid extraction efficiency increased by 11.68% in case of *Chlorella* virus treated *C. vulgaris* when compared to *Chlorella* virus untreated *C. vulgaris*. The application of *Chlorella* virus and the viral encoded lytic enzymes for increasing the extraction efficiency of algal lipid will be helpful in optimizing algal biofuel industry in future.

Here, we will discuss two novel methodologies formulate and optimized by National Environmental Engineering Research Institute affiliated to Council of Scientific and Industrial Research (CSIR-NEERI) encompassing the emerging area of "Applied Virology", namely:

A. Simple and effective modification of comet assay for differentiating lytic and lysogenic bacteriophages.

B. Novel application of algal viruses for increasing the extraction efficiency of algal lipids for bio-fuel production.

METHODOLOGY

The two methodologies are described separately for clear understanding of the protocols to be implemented and followed.

A. Simple and Effective Modification of Comet Assay for Differentiating Lytic and Lysogenic Bacteriophages

The Single Cell Gel Electrophoresis assay which is also known as "comet assay" is a sensitive technique for the detection of DNA damage and DNA repair quantitatively and qualitatively in single cells (Olive and Banath, 2006). This method was first developed by Ostling & Johansson in 1984 (Ostling and Johanson, 1984) and later modified for use under alkaline conditions by Singh *et al.* (Singh *et al.*, 1988), producing a sensitive version of the assay which can assess ds-DNA breaks, ss-DNA breaks, detect alkali-labile sites expressed due to strand breaks in DNA and single-strand breaks associated with incomplete excision repair. The assay is also effective in detecting DNA–DNA and DNA–protein crosslinking. The detection of altered DNA migration is dependent on various parameters such as the concentration of agarose in the gel, the pH, temperature and duration of alkaline unwinding and the pH, temperature, voltage, amperage and duration of electrophoresis.

Comet assay has been standardized for evaluation of DNA damage/repair, biomonitoring and genotoxicity testing. The term "comet" refers to the pattern of DNA migration through the electrophoresis gel, which often resembles a comet (Avishai *et al.*, 2002). Electrophoresis at high pH results in structures resembling comets, observed by fluorescence microscopy; the intensity of the comet tail relative to the head reflects the number of DNA breaks. This is followed by visual analysis with staining of DNA and calculating fluorescence to determine the extent of DNA damage. This can be performed by manual scoring or automatically by imaging software (Avishai *et al.*, 2002).

The assay is well established method and has gained wide acceptance as a valuable tool to analyze white blood cells or lymphocytes in human biomonitoring studies (Angerer *et al.*, 2007; Faust *et al.*, 2004; Kassie *et al.*, 2000; Moller, 2006) and various other cells (Szeto *et al.*, 2005; Mussali-Galante *et al.*,

2005; Emri *et al.*, 2004; Graham-Evans *et al.*, 2004; Rojas *et al.*, 2000; Augustowska *et al.*, 2007; Fraser, 2004; Schmid *et al.*, 2007; Singh *et al.*, 2003) with the simultaneous detection of single- and double-stranded breaks (Enciso *et al.*, 2009). It makes feasible the studies related to the fundamental DNA damage and repair (Speit and Hartmann, 2005) and routine genotoxicity testing and assessment of industrial chemicals, biocides, agrochemicals and pharmaceuticals (Moller, 2005).

The assay has been modified by various workers at various steps including lysis and electrophoretic conditions to make it suitable for assessing different types of DNA damage in different cell types (Collins, 2004, Speit and Hartmann, 2005); Moreover, Many researchers have already reported and have reviewed comet assay method with modification for wide applications (Tice, 1995; Fairbairn *et al.*, 1995; Fairbairn *et al.*, 1996; Anderson *et al.*,1998; Rojas *et al.*, 1999; Speit and Hartmann, 1999). We attempt to investigate the capacity of the comet assay to analyze phage lytic activity using a combination of the comet assay with phage mediated lysis (Khairnar *et al.*, 2014).

MATERIALS AND METHOD

Preparation of Slide- On a slide wiped with 70% alcohol, add 200 µl of 1% agarose on both ends of the slide. Gently place cover slips over the agarose. After solidification, remove cover slips. Prepare solution of *E. coli* (ATCC 13706) and coliphage (ATCC 13706 B1) (approximately 20 µl each) in 2 ml eppendorff tube vial for test sample preparation. Simultaneously, prepare control sample without the addition of coliphage (ATCC 13706 B1) in 2 ml Eppendorf tube. Add 1% low melting agarose in the Eppendorf tube to make it 200 µl. Add the mixture of control and test samples at different ends on the agarose coated slide and placed cover slips over it. Allow it to solidify (~5 to 10 minutes). Slide off the cover slip and finally add third layer of 1% agarose (200 µl) over the agarose encapsulated control and test samples. Place coverslips over it allow it to solidify (~5 to 10 minutes). Incubate the slide for 4-6 hours at 37ºC in an incubator. Lysis treatment is not required for this method as prokaryotic cells are lysed by their respective host through their lytic activity (Singh *et al.*, 1988). The detailed procedure is given in flowchart (Figure 3).

Micro gel Electrophoresis- After incubation, place the slide horizontally in an electrophoresis tank. Fill the reservoir with electrophoresis buffer to completely immerse the slide. Carry out the electrophoresis for 15 minutes at 0.8v/cm. After electrophoresis, keep the slide for 10-15 minutes in the electrophoresis buffer to allow the unwinding of the DNA. Remove the slide from electrophoresis tank and add a few drops of the working solution of ethidium bromide on the agarose encapsulated control and test samples. Place the coverslips over slide. Examine the DNA stained slide in fluorescent microscope (LEICA DM 2500) equipped with a 365nm excitation filter and 435nm barrier filter (Singh *et al.*, 1988).

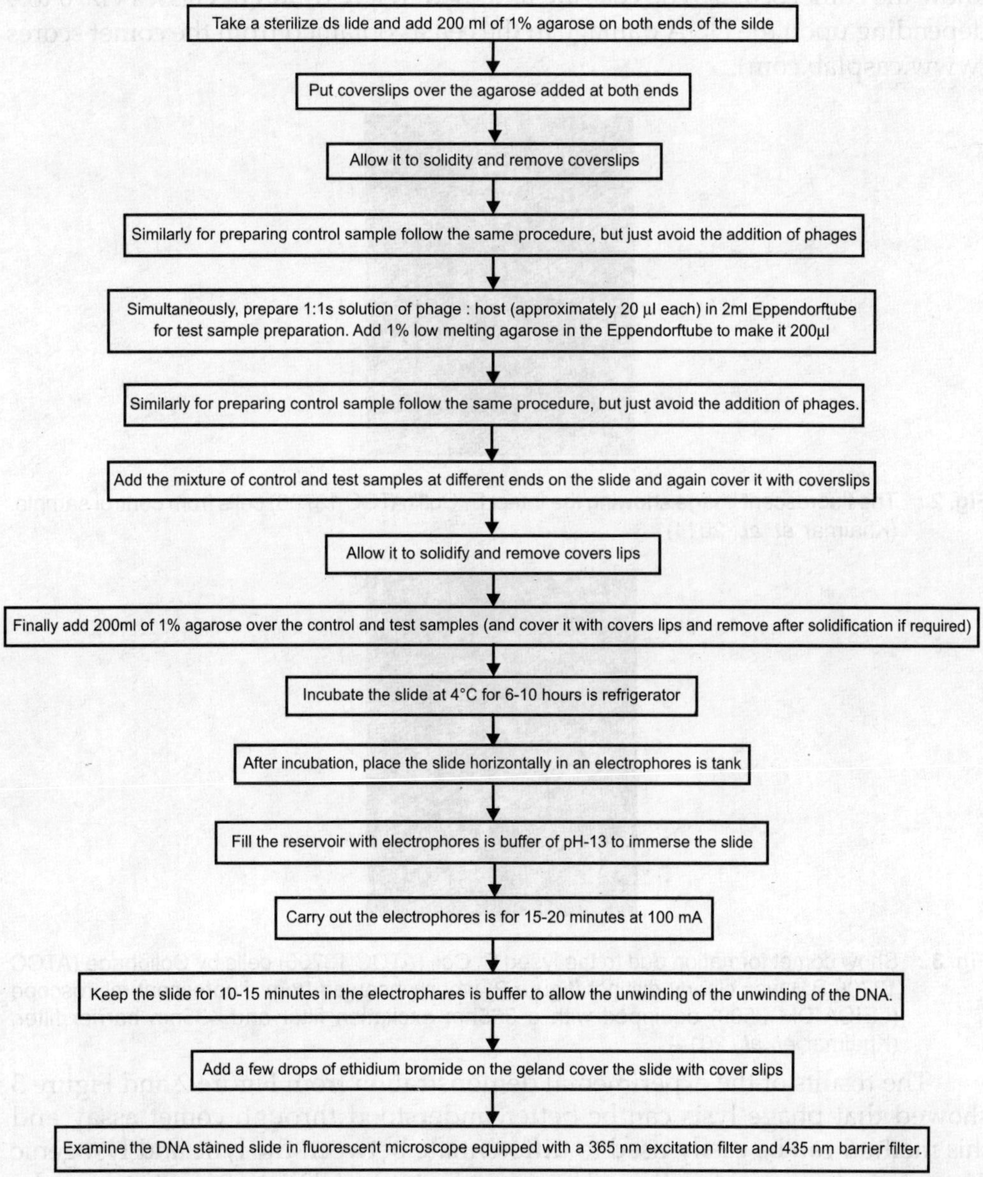

Fig. 1 : Flowchart for modified comet assay procedure for determination and differentiation between lytic and lysogenic phages. (Khairnar *et. al.*, 2014)

Comet analysis and data interpretation- The comets are analysed using the CASP software in which comet images in tiff format are used to estimate the DNA content of individual nuclei and to evaluate DNA damage with respect to the fraction of total DNA content in the comet tail. The length of DNA migration (Comet tail) in these cells was measured by using CASP software to know the comet scores. The cells are assigned to five different classes viz. 0 to 4 depending upon the DNA damage to the cell as obtained from the comet scores (www.casplab.com).

Fig. 2 : The fluorescent image showing the intact E. Coli (ATCC 13706) cells from control sample. (Khairnar *et. al.*, 2014)

Fig. 3 : Show comet formation due to the lysed E. Coli (ATCC 13706) cells by Coliphage (ATCC 13706 B1) was clearly distinct (figure 2) when observed from fluorescent microscope (LEICA DM 2500) equipped with a 365nm excitation filter and 435nm barrier filter. (Khairnar *et. al.*, 2014)

The results of the experimental demonstration from Figure 2 and Figure 3 showed that phage lysis can be better understood through comet assay and this method can be easily used to differentiate between the lytic and lysogenic phages under consideration. The mean extent of DNA migration can be calculated for different bacteria infected with different phages incubated for different time period. The results of each experiment were verified independently. The plaque assay for *E. coli* (ATCC 13706) strains and coliphage (ATCC 13706 B1) under consideration was also carried out to confirm the authenticity of the results obtained and was positive (Figure 4). The CASP software used for interpretation of lysed DNA from bacterial cell validated the lytic activity of the phage and provided a better visualization of lytic event (www.casplab.com).

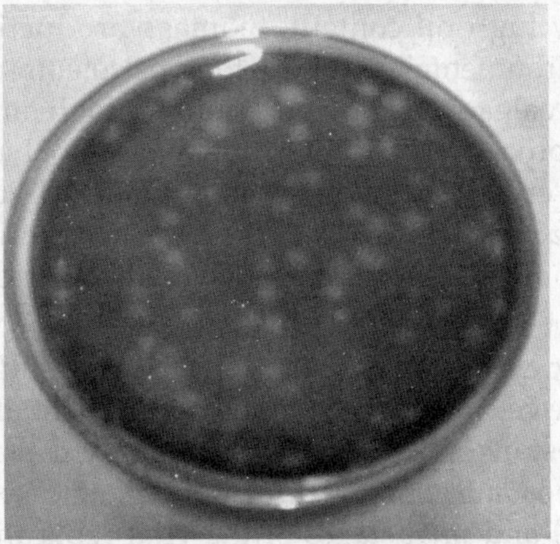

Fig. 4 : Plaque assay results for *E. coli* (ATCC 13706) strains and coliphage (ATCC 13706 B1)

There is a need of various criteria's for determining feasibility of results, certain aspect must be given prime importance which includes like increase or decrease in DNA migration with respect to increasing phage concentration and lysis. In case of positive or negative comet assay response, it is important that the researcher(s) assess the possibility of either increase or decrease in migration related or not related with phage lysis. Statistical methods should not be the only determining factor for identifying a positive response. Reproducibility in independent experiments is considered the strongest evidence for validating positive or negative results. Positive results of the phage lysis test indicate that the phage is lytic and induces DNA damage in bacterial cells. Negative results of the phage lysis test indicate that, the phage is lysogenic and does not induce DNA damage in bacterial cells (Tice, 1005; Tice *et al.*, 1991; Tice *et al.*, 2000).

The possible limitation of this study is that along with bacterial cells, the phages also have genetic material in the form of DNA or RNA, which may be responsible for producing false positive results during the treatment period or incubation period resulting in negative results. Under certain conditions of osmotic and temperature fluctuations, phages also ejects their genomic materials within the media resulting in false positive results or negative results which should be avoided. In due course, with development of expertise in this assay method, modification of study parameters for better resolution of comet can be defined. As the bacterial genome size is quite small more efforts should be taken in better designing and developing this method.

B. Novel Application of Algal Viruses for Increasing the Extraction Efficiency of Algal Lipids for Bio-fuel Production

Microalgae are a promising candidate for biodiesel production. Microalgae have comparatively high oil content, biomass productivity and are more sustainable and environmentally friendly than petroleum-derived fuels (Hu *et al.*, 2008). Some microalgae are known to produce high amounts of lipids and can be applied in bioprocess to produce alternative oils for biodiesel manufacture Ratledge, 2005. Nevertheless, the microalgal biodiesel has not been widely commercialized mainly due to its high costs. The microalgal biodiesel production can be optimized for cost effectiveness and increasing the algal lipid extraction efficiency (Li *et al.*, 2008; Pittman *et al.*, 2011).

In a normal lytic cycle, virus particles attach to the surface of host *Chlorella* cells and degrade the cell wall at the point of attachment; the viral core is then released into the host cytoplasm, leaving an empty capsid on the cell wall. Within 6 to 8 hours post infection, mature viral progenies exit the cells after cell lysis. Both the initial and final stages of the viral replication cycle obviously require cell wall-degrading activities, but little is known about the nature and origin of the enzymes that degrade the cell wall (Van Etten *et al.*, 1991). A common characteristic of virus-sensitive *Chlorella* strains is a rigid cell wall containing uronic acids and glucosamine in addition to other sugars such as glucose, rhamnose, galactose, xylose, arabinose, and mannose (Kapaun *et al.*, 1992; Kapaun and Reisser, 1995).

The exploitation of microalgae for commercial biodiesel production is not yet a commercial reality and still warrants further research and development (Benemann, 2008). Mechanism that could conceptually scaled-up the yield of biodiesel precursors has not yet been demonstrated effectively (Benemann, 2008). Beside the selection of candidate microalgal strains for high production of biodiesel precursors, the present research challenge is also about increasing the extraction efficiency of biodiesel precursors (Sierra*et al.*, 2008). The aim of this study was to increase the extraction efficiency of bio-diesel precursors from algae *Chlorella vulgaris* by using a novel approach like *Chlorella* virus mediated lysis (Sanmukh *et al.*, 2014).

MATERIALS AND METHODS

Isolation and identification of microalgae- Recently, a report has demonstrated that the calorific value of *Chlorella vulgaris* was found to be 28 kJ/g, which was highest among the fresh water microalgae making it a promising candidate to be exploited for alternate fuel (Scragg *et al.*, 2002). Fifteen algal strains were isolated from different aquatic ecosystems in and around Nagpur; out of which one was identified as *C. vulgaris*. The microalga was identified by light microscopy analysis (Leica DM2500 Wien, Austria) and was used for further experimental studies. In addition, the partial sequence of microalgae was amplified and subjected to denovo nucleotide sequencing of 18S rRNA to confirm the microalgal species. The partial nucleotide sequence was subjected to Basic Local Alignment Search Tool (BLAST) (Altschul *et al.*, 1990); it was found that the sequence had 100% and 99% identity with other *C. vulgaris* nucleotide sequences submitted to genbank with accession numbers AB699112.1 and JX185298.1 respectively. The isolated *C. vulgaris* microalgae was propagated in nitrate depleted Bold Basal Media (Rippka, 1988) at 28 ± 2 ^{0}C and light intensity of 350 μmol m^{-2} s^{-1} for a week using a light meter and subsequently sub-cultured (Scragg, 2002). The sub-cultured microalgae strain of isolated *C. vulgaris* in exponential phase was subjected to further study as depicted in the workflow (Fig. 5.).

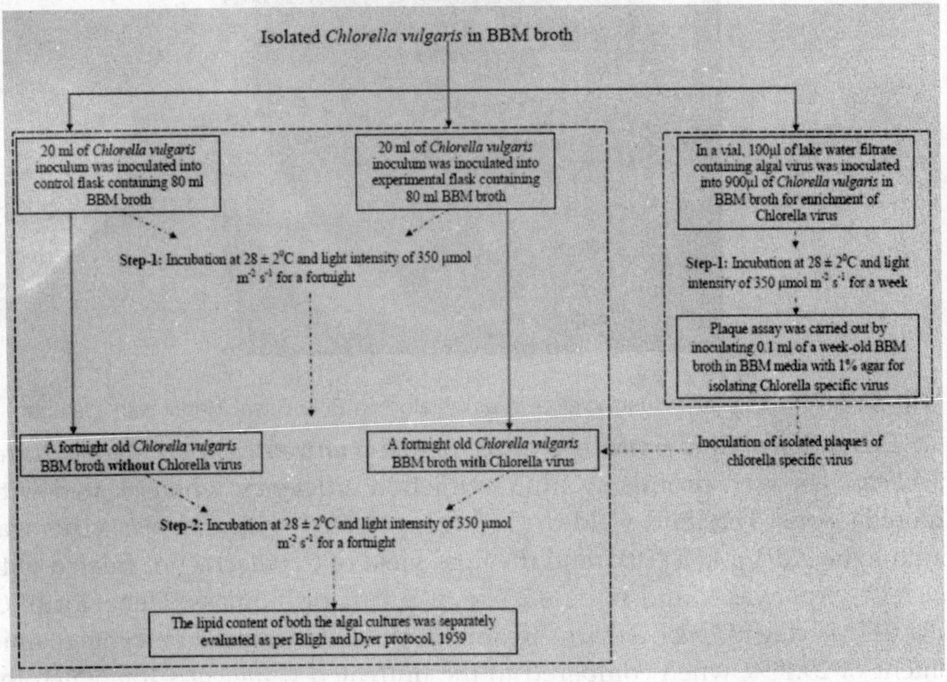

Fig. 5 : Workflow for increasing the extraction efficiency of bio-diesel precursor from algae through application of algal viruses (Sanmukh *et al.*, 2014)

Isolation and enrichment of Chlorella vulgaris specific virus-The surface water sample collected from Ambazari Lake, Nagpur, Maharashtra, India was used for isolation of *C. vulgaris* specific virus. The water sample was filtered through 0.2μm polycarbonate membranes (Millipore, India.); 100 μl of the filtrate was inoculated into 900-μl exponentially growing culture of isolated *C. vulgaris*. The cultures were incubated for a week (Sanmukh *et. al.*, 2014). The virus was isolated from the lysed culture using plaque assay procedure using Bold Basal Media with 1% agar (Fig. 2.). The single plaque was selected for enrichment in exponentially growing *C. vulgaris* culture in Bold Basal Media and was incubated at 28 ± 2 ^{0}C and light intensity of 350 μmol m^{-2} s^{-1} for 1 week (Rippka, 1988).

Extraction of lipid from micro-algal biomass- Extraction and estimation of lipid content from micro-algal biomass with and without algal virus treatment was carried out by following the standard protocol of Bligh and Dyer, 1959 (Bligh and Dyer, 1959). Each experiment was done in triplicate. The mean and standard deviation of the experimental results was calculated using MS-Excel.

Fig. 6 : Chlorella vulgaris specific algal virus isolated on Bold Basal Media with 1% agar.

Extraction of lipid from algal virus treated & untreated microalgal culture- *C. vulgaris* showed promising lipid extraction efficiency when treated with Chlorella virus. The lipid yield of *C. vulgaris* treated with *Chlorella* virus was found to be 0.291 g/g ± 0.017 and the lipid yield of *C. vulgaris* not treated with *Chlorella* virus was found to be 0.257 g/g ± 0.02 of biomass. Henceforth, *C. vulgaris* lysis due to *Chlorella* virus treatment yielded increased percentage lipid content of 29.1 %, when compared to the untreated *C. vulgaris* for which the percentage lipid content was 25.7 %. The result implied that algal lipid extraction efficiency increased by 11.68% in case of *Chlorella* virus treated *C. vulgaris* when compared to *Chlorella* virus untreated *C. vulgaris* (Sanmukh et al., 2014).

This study reports for the first time the application of *Chlorella* virus for increasing algal lipid extraction efficiency from *C. vulgaris*. We found from our results that *Chlorella* virus could be helpful in increasing the extraction efficiency of the algal lipid through viral mediated lysis of *C. vulgaris* under optimum conditions (Sanmukh *et al.*, 2014). We hope that similar approach can be adopted for isolating other viruses against different microalgae for possible exploitation in enhancing algal lipid recovery.

However, this method has some limitations as far as efficiency is concerned such as; development of resistance after frequent use of viruses (*Chlorella* viruses, in this case); lysogenic conversion of the viruses within their specific hosts; and unpredictability of viral lysis event in the culture. The limitations can be minimized; as resistant algal strain can be screened for lytic viruses from environmental samples, which is simple and affordable, lysogen formation may be minimized by maintaining optimum conditions for algal growth. The lysis events can be monitored by microscopic observation of culture after viral addition and incubation for desired period depending upon culture volume. Nevertheless, we think that there is a need to explore fluid dynamics between two fluids for improving the extraction efficiency of algal lipid for ultimately potentiating the biodiesel production. Further algal virus encoded products in the form of formulations can also be employed for efficient lysis of biodiesel producing algae commercially.

CONCLUSIONS

Both the techniques described above represents novel preliminary applications of viruses for the advancement of biotechnology. They both have considerable impact on the traditional methods used for characterizing viruses (Bacteriophages) and increasing the yield of bio-fuel precursors (Lipid extraction). Considering the results and discussion made above both the techniques can be optimized and commercialized for the betterment of areas like molecular biology and bio-energy. The modifications in the methods are presumptive for making them more effective, efficient and economical. Moreover, they have clearly established as the modern techniques for the 21st century and we may hope for their better applications in the near future.

ACKNOWLEDGEMENTS

We thankfully acknowledge financial support from Council of Scientific and Industrial Research (CSIR), Govt. of India for Inter Laboratory Project (ILP-0011) and project under 12th five year plan (PSC-0101).

CORRESPONDENCE

Mr. Swapnil Ganesh Sanmukh (Research Scholar) (E:mail swamukh1985in@rediffmail.com), Dr. Krishna Suresh Khairnar (Scientist and Corresponding author) (E:mail k_khairnar@neeri.res.in and kskhairnar@gmail.com) and Dr. Waman Narayan Paunikar (Scientist and Head)

(E:mail wn_paunikar@neeri.res.in) are affiliated to Environmental Virology Cell (EVC), CSIR-NEERI, Nagpur-440020, Maharashtra, India.

REFERENCES

Altschul S, Gish F, Miller W, Myers W, Lipman DJ. Basic local alignment search tool. J Mol Biol 1990;215: 403–410.

Anderson, D, Yu, TW, McGregor, DB: Comet assay responses as indicators of carcinogen exposure. Mutagenesis, 1998, 13, 539–555.

Angerer J, Ewers U, Wilhelm M: Human biomonitoring: state of the art. Int J Hyg Environ Health. 2007, 210:201–228.

Augustowska K, Magnowska Z, Kapiszewska M, Gregoraszczuk EL: Is the natural PCDD/PCDF mixture toxic for human placental JEG-3 cell line? The action of the toxicants on hormonal profile, CYP1A1 activity, DNA damage and cell apoptosis. Human Exp Toxicol. 2007, 26:407–417.

Avishai N, Rabinowitz C, Moiseeva E, Rinkevich, B: Genotoxicity of the Kishon River, Israel: the application of an in vitro cellular assay. Mutation Research 2002, 518(1): 21–37.

Benemann JR. Opportunities and challenges in algae biofuels production. Algae World. 2008 (http://www.fao.org/uploads/media/algae_positionpaper.pdf)

Bligh EG, Dyer WJ. A rapid method of total lipid extraction and purification. Can J Biochem Physiol 1959;37: 911–917.

Collins AR: The Comet assay for DNA damage and repair principles, applications, and limitations. Mol Biotechnol. 2004, 26:249–260.

Emri G, Schaefer D, Held B, Herbst C, Zieger W, Horkay I, Bayer LC: Low concentrations of formaldehyde induce DNA damage and delay DNA repair after UV irradiation in human skin cells. Exp Dermatol. 2004, 13:305–315.

Enciso M, Sarasa J, Agarwal A, Fernandez JL, Gosalvez J: A two-tailed Comet assay for assessing DNA damage in spermatozoa. Reprod BioMed Online. 2009, 18:609–616.

Fairbairn DW, Olive PL, O'Neill KL: The Comet assay: a comprehensive review. Mutat. Res., 1995, 339, 37–59.

Fairbairn DW, Walburger DK, Fairbairn JJ, O'Neill KL: Key morphologic changes and DNA strand breaks in human lymphoid cells: discriminating apoptosis from necrosis. Scanning, 1996, 18, 407–416.

Faust F, Kassie F, Knasmuller S, Boedecker RH, Mann M, Merschundermann V: The use of the alkaline Comet assay with lymphocytes in human biomonitoring studies. Mutat Res. 2004, 566:209–229.

Fraser L: Structural damage to nuclear DNA in mammalian spermatozoa: its evaluation techniques and relationship with male infertility. Pol J Vet Sci. 2004, 7:311–321.

Graham-Evans B, Cohly HH, Yu H, Tchounwou PB: Arsenic induced genotoxic and cytotoxic effects in human keratinocytes, melanocytes and dendritic cells. Int J Environ Res Public Health. 2004, 1:838–839.

Hu Q, Sommerfeld M, Jarvis E, Ghirardi M, Posewitz M, Seibert M, Darzins A. Microalgal triacylglycerols as feedstocks for biofuel production: perspectives and advances. Plant J 2008; 54: 621–639.

Kapaun E, Loos E, Reisser W. Cell wall composition of virus-sensitive symbiotic chlorella species. Phytochemistry 1992; 31: 3103–3104.

Kapaun E, Reisser W. A chitin-like glycan in the cell wall of a Chlorella sp. (Chlorococcales, Chlorophyceae). Planta 1995; 197: 577-582.

Kassie F, Parzefall W, Knasmuller S: Single cell gel electrophoresis assay: a new technique for human biomonitoring studies. Mutat Res. 2000, 463:13–31.

Khairnar K, Sanmukh S, Chandekar R. Punikar W. A simple and novel modification of comet assay for determination of bacteriophage mediated bacterial cell lysis. J. of virological methods. 203 (2014) : 33-38.

Li Y, Horsman M, Wu N, Lan CQ, Dubois-Calero N. Biofuels from microalgae. Biotechnol Prog 2008; 24: 815–820.

Moller P: Genotoxicity of environmental agents assessed by the alkaline Comet assay. Basic Clin Pharmacol Toxicol. 2005, 96:1–42.

Moller P: The alkaline Comet assay: towards validation in biomonitoring of DNA damaging exposures. Basic Clin Pharmacol Toxicol. 2006, 98:336–345.

Mussali-Galante P, Avila-Costa MR, Pinon-Zarate G, Martinez- Levy G, Rodriguez-Lara V, Rojas-Lemus M, Avila-Casado MC, Fortoul TI: DNA damage as an early biomarker of effect in human health. Toxicol Ind Health. 2005, 21:155–166.

Olive PL, Banath JP: The Comet assay: a method to measure DNA damage in individual cells. Nature Protocols. 2006, 1:23–29.

Ostling O, Johanson KJ: Microelectrophoretic study of radiation-induced DNA damages in individual mammalian cells. Biochem Biophys Res Commun. 1984, 123:291–298.

Paunikar WN, Sanmukh SG, Ghosh TK. Non-specificity of phage enzymes. International Journal of Pharma and Biosciences 2011; 2(2), B546-B552.

Pittman JK, Dean AP, Osundeko O. The potential of sustainable algal biofuel production using wastewater resources. Bioresour Technol. 2011; 102: 17–25.

Ratledge C. Single Cell Oils for the 21st Century, in Single Cell Oils Champaign. AOCS Press, IL, USA 2005.

Rippka R. Isolation and purification of cyanobacteria. Methods Enzymol. 1988; 167: 3–27.

Rojas E, Lopez MC, Valverde M: Single cell gel electrophoresis assay: methodology and applications. J. Chromatogr. B Biomed. Appl., 1999, 722, 225–254.

Rojas E, Valverde M, Lopez MC, Naufal I, Sanchez I, Bizarro P, Lopez I, Fortoul TI, Ostrosky-Wegman P: Evaluation of DNA damage in exfoliated tear duct epithelial cells from individuals exposed to air pollution assessed by single cell gel electrophoresis assay. Mutat Res. 2000, 468:11–17.

Sanmukh S G, Khairnar K., Chandekar R H, Paunikar W N. Increasing the extraction efficiency of algal lipid for biodiesel production : Novel application of algal viruses. Afr. J. Biotechnol. 2014, 13(15) : 1666-1670.

Sanmukh SG, Meshram DB, Paunikar WN, Swaminathan S. Interaction of fishes with pathogenic bacteria and application of phages for their control- a review. Reviews in fish biology and fisheries (2012) DOI 10.1007/s11160-012-9257-7.

Sanmukh SG, Paunikar WN, Ghosh TK & Chakrabarti T. Structure and Function Predictions of Hypothetical Proteins in Vibrio Phages. International Journal of Biometrics and Bioinformatics, 2010, 4(5), 161-175.

Schmid TE, Eskenazi B, Baumgartner A, Marchetti F, Young S, Weldon R, Anderson D, Wyrobek AJ: The effects of male age on sperm DNA damage in healthy non-smokers. Hum Reprod. 2007, 22:180–187.

Scragg AH, Illman AH, Carden A, Shales SW. Growth of microalgae with increased calorific values in a tubular bioreactor. Biomass Bioenerg. 2002; 23: 67–73.

Sierra E, Acien FG, Fernandez JM, Garcýa JL, Gonzalez C, Molina E. Characterization of a flat plate photobioreactor for the production of microalgae. Chem Eng J 2008; 138: 136–147.

Singh NP, McCoy MT, Tice RR, Schneider EL. A simple technique for quantitation of low levels of DNA damage in individual cells. Exp Cell Res. 1988, 175:184–191.

Singh NP, Muller CH, Berger RE: Effects of age on DNA double-strand breaks and apoptosis in human sperm. Fertil Steril. 2003, 80:1420–1430.

Speit G, Hartmann A: The comet assay (single-cell gel test)—a sensitive genotoxicity test for the detection of DNA damage and repair. In Henderson, D.S. (ed.), Methods in Molecular Biology, Vol. 113, DNA Repair Protocols: Eucaryotic Systems. Humana Press, Totowa, NJ, 1999, pp. 203–212.

Speit G, Hartmann A: The Comet assay: a sensitive genotoxicity test for the detection of DNA damage. Methods Mol Biol. 2005, 291:85–95.

Spivak G: The Comet-FISH assay for the analysis of DNA damage and repair. Methods Mol Biol. 2010, 659:129–145.

Szeto YT, Benzie IF, Collins AR, Choi SW, Cheng CY, Yow CM, Tse MMA: A buccal cell model Comet assay: development and evaluation for human biomonitoring and nutritional studies. Mutat Res. 2005, 578:371–381.

Tice RR, Agurell E, Anderson D, Burlinson B, Hartmann A, Kobayashi H, Miyamae Y, Rojas E, Ryu JC, Sasaki YF: The single cell gel/comet assay: guidelines for in vitro and in vivo genetic toxicology testing. Environ. Mol. Mutagen., 2000, 35, 206–221.

Tice RR, Andrews PW, Hirai O, Singh NP: The single cell gel (SCG) assay: an electrophoretic technique for the detection of DNA damage in individual cells. In Witmer, C.R., Snyder, R.R., Jollow, D.J., Kalf, G.F., Kocsis, J.J. and Sipes, I.G. (Eds), Biological Reactive Intermediates IV, Molecular and Cellular Effects and their Impact on Human Health. Plenum Press, New York, NY, pp. 1991, 157–164.

Tice RR: The single cell gel/comet assay: a microgel electrophoretic technique for the detection of DNA damage and repair in individual cells. In Phillips, D.H. and Venitt, S. (Eds), Environmental Mutagenesis. Bios Scientific, Oxford, UK, 1995, pp. 315–339.

Van Etten JL, Lane LC, Meints RH. Viruses and viruslike particles of eukaryotic algae. Microbiol Rev 1991; 55: 586-620.

www.casplab.com

□□□

CHAPTER - 12

Role of Soil Microbes in Sustainable Soil Health and Agricultural Production

M. Manjunath*, S.Saha, V. Venkataravanappa and A. B. Rai.
Division of Crop Protection, Indian Institute of Vegetable Research, Varanasi- 221 305 India.
**E-mail: manjumbl@gmail.com*

INTRODUCTION

Soil is a very important component of the earth's biosphere. It is the basis of agricultural production and also in the maintenance of local, regional and global environmental quality (Glanz 1995). The thin layer of soil covering the surface of the earth represents the difference between survival and extinction for most land-based life (Doran and Parkin 1996). Analysis of soil productive capacity point out human-induced degradation on nearly 40% of the world's agricultural land as a result of soil erosion, atmospheric pollution, widespread soil cultivation, over-grazing, land clearing, salinization and desertification (Oldeman 1994). Degradation and loss of productive agricultural land is definitely one of our most pressing ecological concerns, similar to the other human caused environmental problems like global climate change, depletion of the protective ozone layer and serious reduction in biodiversity (Lal 1998).

Soil Health

Soil health in a broader sense is the capacity of soil to function as a vital living system to sustain biological productivity, promote environmental quality and maintain plant and animal health. Soil health can be inferred by measuring specific soil properties (e.g. organic matter content) and by observing fertility status of soil and also by studying soil microorganisms in their environments, as microbial diversity is intimately related to soil structure and function (Doran and Zeiss 2000).

Diversity and Role of Soil Microorganisms

Knowledge of the biodiversity of microbes in soil is essential to sustain agricultural productivity (Colwell, 1997). Healthy soils maintain a diverse community of soil organisms. It has been estimated that within the top one to three feet of soil as much as 17,000 lbs. fungi and 40 lbs. bacteria exist per acre (Prabhu *et al.,* 2010).

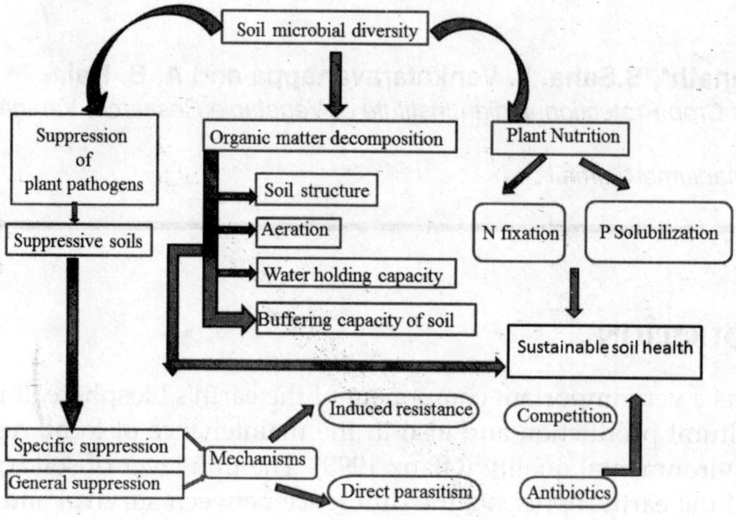

Fig. 1 : Mode of action of soil microorganisms in maintaining soil health

The majority of fungi and bacteria present in soils are considered to be beneficial to crop plants in the following ways;

1. Suppression of pathogenic microorganisms
2. Organic matter decomposition
3. Plant Nutrition

Sustainable Management of Soil-Borne Plant Diseases

Soil-borne diseases result from a reduction in the biodiversity of soil organisms. Harmful fungi and bacteria that parasitize higher plants are generally present in all native soils (Sullivan 2004). Farmers have been using newer and more powerful chemicals in an effort to manage the plant pathogens. This chemical intervention has made things worse over the time. Many pesticides reduce the diversity of soil life, lead to development of resistance among the pathogens and also leaves behind harmful residues in soil and farm produce (Sullivan 2004).

There is an urgent need to reduce the use of pesticides to sustain farm productivity and to maintain environmental quality. To achieve this one of the best alternative is to add the beneûcial soil microorganisms. Beneûcial organisms can be added directly or the soil environment can be made more favourable for them with organic amendments (Sullivan 2004). When organic matter, such as compost, is added to topsoil the natural organic matter content is raised considerably which increases carbon source availability and subsequently stimulates growth of the useful organisms.

Suppressive Soils

A suppressive soil is one in which "the pathogen does not establish or persist, establishes but causes little or no damage, or establishes and causes disease for a while but thereafter the disease is less important, although the pathogen may persist in the soil" (Baker and Cook 1974). Suppressiveness is linked to the types and numbers of soil organisms, fertility level and nature of the soil itself.

Types of Disease Suppression

1. Specific Suppression
2. General suppression

Specific suppression

Specific suppression is the inhibition of particular pathogen due to the activity of individual or certain groups of microorganisms and is transferable between soils. A good example of speciûc suppression is take-all decline resulting from the build-up of fluorescent *Pseudomonas* sp. that produce the antifungal metabolite 2,4-diacetylphloroglucinol and suppression of *Rhizoctonia* sp. by the fungus *Trichoderma* sp. It locates through a chemical released by the pathogen and then attacks it. Beneficial fungal strands entangle the pathogen and release enzymes that dehydrate *Rhizoctonia* sp. cells and ultimately kill them (Sullivan 2004).

General suppression

It is the result of a non-specific increase in the activity of the microbial community. In this case it is the increase in activity of the microbial community as a whole that is important, rather than changes in the activity of a few specific antagonistic organisms. The competition for resources and production of anti-microbial substances reduces the ability of pathogens to grow and infect, resulting in lower disease levels. General suppression is often enhanced by the addition of organic matter, by following certain agronomic practices, because this activity in turn enhances soil microbial activity. No one microorganism is responsible for general suppression and it is due to the activity of total microbial community. It is also referred as non-specific antagonism or biological buffering. This kind of suppression is not transferable between soils.

Mechanisms of Disease suppression

1. Induced resistance
2. Direct parasitism
3. Nutrient competition
4. Direct inhibition through antibiotics secretion

Induced resistance

Ray (1901) and Beauverie (1901) for the first time noticed the pathogen induced resistance in plants. It can be defined as an enhanced expression of natural defence mechanisms of plants against different pathogens provoked by various external factors and manifested upon subsequent inoculation. It is based on expression of latent genetic information present in plant and is not underlined by genome alterations (mutations or introgression of foreign genetic material)-a feature relevant to an important biological safety (Benhamou and Picard 1999; Kuc 2001).

Nowadays, the term induced systemic resistance (ISR) is being used to designate the resistance induced in leaves of plants by inoculation of roots with non-pathogenic rhizobacteria. This novel type of induced resistance was first described in *Arabidopsis* plants, inoculated with the root-colonizing non-pathogenic bacteria *Pseudomonas fluorescens* against the bacterial leaf pathogen *Pseudomonas syringae* pv. Tomato (Pieterse *et al.*, 1998). Rhizobacteria-mediated ISR has also been demonstrated against fungi, bacteria and viruses in *Arabidopsis*, bean, carnation, cucumber, radish, tobacco and tomato (Van Loon *et al.*, 1998). Induced resistance may help to minimise the use of toxic chemicals for disease control and thus could be proposed as an alternative, non-conventional, non-biocidal and ecologically-friendly approach for plant protection and hence for sustainable agriculture.

Direct parasitism

Parasitism of a plant pathogen by other microorganisms is a well known phenomenon. The strains of *Trichoderma* sp. and *Coniothyrium minitans* are parasitic on *Rhizoctonia solani* and *Sclerotinia sclerotiorum* respectively (Chet and Baker 1981; Jones and Stewart 2011). It is due to specific recognition of the antagonist and its target pathogen and a number of cell wall degrading enzymes to enable the parasite to enter the hyphae of the pathogen.

Antibiotics

Antibiosis is one of the mechanism in which one microorganism produces certain secondary metabolites that are toxic to other microorganisms at low concentrations. Rhizospheric microorganisms are known to produce antimicrobial compounds that are effective against certain plant pathogens and pests (Dey *et al.*, 2004; Herman *et al.*, 2008). This phenomena is most common in *Bacillus* sp., *Pseudomonas* sp., *Streptomyces* sp. and *Trichoderma* sp. (Alabouvette *et al.*, 2006). Fluorescent pseudomonads and *Bacillus* species play an active role in suppression of pathogenic microorganisms. Antibiotics produced by beneficial microbes include, 2,4-Diacetyl phloroglucinol, phenazine-1-carboxyclic acid, phenazine-1-carboxamide, pyoluteorin, pyrrolnitrin, oomycinA, viscosinamide, butyrolactones, kanosamine zwittermycin-A, aerugine, rhamnolipids, cepaciamide A, ecomycins, pseudomonic acid, azomycin, antitumor antibiotics FR901463, cepafungins and antiviral antibiotic karalicin. These antibiotics are known to possess antiviral, antimicrobial, insect and mammalian antifeedant, antihelminthic, phytotoxic, antioxidant, cytotoxic, antitumour and plant growth promoting activities. Antagonistic cyanobacteria (*Anabaena variabilis* RPAN59 and *A. oscillarioides* RPAN69) amended compost-vermiculite and compost formulations exhibited 10–15 % lower disease severity of damping off in tomato caused by *Pythium debaryanum, Fusarium oxysporumt sp lycopersici, Fusarium moniliforme* and *Rhizoctonia solani* and 40–50 % higher values than chemical and biological control treatments in terms of fresh weight and height of the plants (Chaudhary *et al.*, 2012).

Composts amended with *Anabaena oscillarioides* C12 and *Bacillus subtillis* B5 and the compost tea preparations are effective in reducing the diseases severity damping off (12.5%) when compared to control 48.1% (Dukare *et al.*, 2011). *Anabaena variabilis* RPAN59 and *A. laxa* RPAN8 inhibited two phytopathogenic fungi i.e., *Fusarium moniliforme* and *F. oxysporum* f.sp *lycopersici* by producing chitosanase and β-1, 4-glucanase enzymes (Prasanna *et al.*, 2013).

Competition

All the soil microorganisms compete with each other for food and space. Any change in environmental conditions such as food supply, temperature, moisture, oxygen supply, etc., can result in changes which cause one or many types of soil microbes to become temporarily dominant over the others. The level of disease suppressiveness is typically related to the level of total microbiological activity in a soil. The larger the active microbial biomass, the greater the soil's capacity to use carbon, nutrients and energy, thus lowering their availability to pathogens. In other words, competition for mineral nutrients is high, as most soil nutrients are tied up in microbial bodies. Competition for space and nutrients generally occurs between rhizosphere and phyllosphere inhabiting microorganisms. The antagonist organisms directly compete with pathogens for these resources. Root inhabiting microorganisms compete for suitable sites at the root surfaces. Competition for nutrients, especially for carbon, is responsible for the inhibition of fungal spore germination i.e., fungistasis in soil (Alabouvette *et al.* 2006). Numbers and diversity of competitors, inhibitors and predators of disease organisms and food sources for these organisms in soil is very important. Increase in the activity of microbial community in the soil will enhance the general suppression of pathogens by raising competition for nutrients.

Organic Matter Decomposition

During the period of Green Revolution chemical fertilizers were heavily used along with improved germplasm and irrigation. Over the last 40 years, mineral fertilizers accounted for an estimated 40 per cent of the increase in food production (Jenkinson 2010). Apart from this, they also carried significant costs to the environment. Today, Asia and Europe have the world's highest rates of mineral fertilizer use per hectare. They also face the greatest problems of environmental pollution resulting from excessive fertilizer use, including soil and water acidification, contamination of surface and groundwater resources and increased emissions of potent greenhouse gases. The N-uptake efficiency in China is only about 26-28 per cent for rice, wheat and maize and less than 20 per cent for vegetable crops (Miao *et al.,* 2011). The remainder is simply lost in the environment.

To avoid all these environmental problems, there is a need to reduce the use of chemicals in agriculture. Organic farming is one of the alternatives because it works in harmony with nature unlike the chemicals. This involves use of more organic matter in place of chemicals. Microorganisms play very important role in organic matter decomposition and recycling of soil nutrients. Dead plant residues and plant nutrients are good source of food for the microbes in the soil. Soil organic matter (SOM) is basically all the organic substances (anything with carbon) in the soil, both living and dead. SOM includes plants, microorganisms (bacteria, fungi, protozoa, blue green algae etc.) and the fresh and decomposing organic matter from plants and animals (Hoorman and Islam 2010).

Soil organic matter (SOM) has two components called the active (35%) and the passive (65%) SOM. Active SOM is composed of the living and dead plant or animal material which is food for microbes and is composed of easily digested sugars and proteins. (Hoorman and Islam 2010). Bacteria are the first microbes to digest new organic plant and animal residues in the soil. These are the smallest and most hardy microbes in the soil, which can survive under harsh conditions. Under the right conditions of heat, moisture and a food source, they can reproduce very quickly. Aerobic bacteria assimilate about 5 to 10 per cent of the carbon while anaerobic bacteria only assimilate 2 to 5 percent, leaving behind many waste carbon compounds and inefficiently using energy stored in the SOM. Bacteria are only 20–30% efficient at recycling carbon, have a high nitrogen content (3 to 10 carbon atoms to 1 nitrogen atom or 10 to 30% nitrogen), a lower carbon content, and a short life span (Hoorman and Islam 2007).

Fungus generally release less carbon dioxide into the atmosphere and are more efficient at converting carbon to form new cells. The fungus generally captures more energy from the SOM as they decompose it, assimilating 40 to 55 per cent of the carbon. Most fungi consume organic matter higher in cellulose and lignin, which is slower and tougher to decompose. The lignin content of most plant residues may be of greater importance in predicting decomposition velocity than the C:N ratio. They have a large surface area and help in the transport of mineral nutrients and water to the plants and are not as hardy as bacteria. Their population levels tend to decline with conventional tillage. Fungi have a higher carbon to nitrogen ratio (10:1 carbon to nitrogen or 10% nitrogen) but are more efficient at converting carbon to soil organic matter. The amount, the type and availability of the organic matter will determine the microbial population and how it evolves. Each individual organism (bacteria, fungus) to has certain enzymes and complex chemical reactions that help the organism to assimilate carbon. As waste products are generated and the original organic residues are decomposed, new microorganisms may take over, feeding on the waste products. The early decomposers generally attack the easily digested sugars and proteins followed by microorganisms that attack the more resistant residues (Hoorman and Islam 2010).

Nitrogen fixation

Soil microorganisms are very important as almost every chemical transformation taking place in soil involves their active contribution. In particular, they play an active role in soil fertility as a result of their involvement in the cycle of nutrients like carbon and nitrogen, which are required for plant growth.

Nitrogen is a very critical nutrient element for plant growth and development. Nitrogen gas (N_2) constitutes nearly 80% of the atmosphere, but in this form nitrogen is not available to plants. Microbes are able to convert nitrogen gas into ammonium ($NH4^+$), through nitrogenase enzyme system, which can be used readily by plants. The genera *Rhizobium*, *Sinorhizobium*, *Mesorhizobium*, *Bradyrhizobium*, *Azorhizobium* and *Allorhizobium* are most efficient and fix about 200 to 250 kg N /ha/yr . All of these bacteria form host-specific symbiosis with leguminous plants, which is initiated by the formation of root or stem nodules via intrinsic signalling systems. The genera *Azotobacter, Azospirillum, Herbaspirillum* are some of the free-living nitrogen-fixing organisms. *Azotobacter* sp. is useful for vegetables, cereals, cotton etc. *Azospirillum* sp. fixes nitrogen in low oxygen environments, being effective for low land rice, sorghum, sugarcane.

Phosphorus solubilization

Fixation of phosphorous is a very common problem in soils. This leads to unavailability of applied phosphatic fertilizer to plants. Some of the microbes like *Bacillus polymyxa, Aspergillus niger, Pseudomonas striata* etc. are very efficient in solubilizing fixed phosphorus. Phosphorus solubilisation occurs through different microbial mechanisms including organic acid production and proton extrusion (Surange, 1995; Dutton and Evans, 1996; Nahas, 1996). Microorganisms solubilize phosphorus by secreting certain metabolites such as organic acids, which through their hydroxyl and carboxyl groups chelate the cation bound to phosphate (Sagoe *et al.*, 1998). Swarnalakshmi *et al.* (2013) reported the combination of cyanobacteria and bacteria (*Anabaena* and *Pseudomonas* biofilm) in enhancing phosphorus uptake by wheat.

CONCLUSION

Maintenance of soil health under intensive cultivation practices is a major challenge. Excessive use of chemical fertilizers and pesticides has led to many problems such as resistance among pathogens, resurgence of minor pests and harmful residues in the farm produce besides polluting soil, air and ground water. In order to achieve sustainable crop yields there is a need to minimize use of chemicals in agriculture by integrating legumes, cover crops and organic residues, manures and composts. Soil microorganisms play very important role in decomposition of organic residues and nutrient recycling, suppression of plant pathogens and also providing plant nutrients through nitrogen fixation and phosphorus solubilisation. Decomposition of organic materials in turn helps in improving soil structure, soil aeration and water holding capacity.

SUMMARY

Soil is a critically important component of the earth's biosphere; it is the basis of agricultural production and also in the maintenance of local, regional and global environmental quality. Degradation and loss of productive agricultural land is undeniably one of our most pressing ecological concerns. The majority of fungi and bacteria present in soils are considered to be beneficial to crop plants. Soil-borne diseases result from a reduction in the biodiversity of soil organisms.The chemical intervention to improve the agricultural production has made things worse over the time. Many pesticides reduce the diversity of soil life, lead to development of resistance among the pathogens and also leaves behind harmful residues in soil and farm produce. There is an urgent need to reduce the use of pesticides to sustain farm productivity. One of the alternatives is to add the beneûcial soil organisms along with the food they need. A soil is considered suppressive when, in spite of favourable conditions for disease to occur, a pathogen either cannot become established, establishes but produces no disease, or establishes and produces disease for a short time and then declines. Microorganisms play important role in organic matter decomposition. Dead plant residues and plant nutrients become food for the microbes in the soil. Soil organic matter (SOM) is basically all the organic substances (anything with carbon) in the soil, both living and dead. SOM includes plants, blue green algae, microorganisms (bacteria, fungi, protozoa, nematodes, beetles, springtails, etc.) and the fresh and decomposing organic matter from plants, animals, and microorganisms. Soil microorganisms are very important as almost every chemical transformation taking place in soil involves their active contribution. In particular, they play an active role in soil fertility as a result of their involvement in the cycle of nutrients like carbon and nitrogen, which are required for plant growth. Nitrogen can be added to soil by incorporating N-fixing legumes and trees into cropping systems. The genera *Rhizobium*, *Sinorhizobium*, *Mesorhizobium*, *Bradyrhizobium*, *Azorhizobium* and *Allorhizobium* are the most efficient and fixes about 200 to 250 kg N /ha/yr. The genera *Azotobacter*, *Azospirillum*, are some of the free-living nitrogen-fixing organisms, useful for vegetables, cereals, cotton low land rice, sorghum, sugarcane etc. The organisms such as *Bacillus polymyxa*, *Aspergillus niger*, *Pseudomonas striata* etc. are involved in solubilizing unavailable phosphorus and making it available to the plants.

ACKNOWLEDGEMENTS

We thank the authorities of the Indian Institute of Vegetable Research, Varanasi, for providing the necessary facilities for preparing this manuscript.

REFERENCES

Aker KF, Cook RJ (1974). Biological control of plant pathogens. San Francisco, U.S.A., W.H. Freeman & Co.

Alabouvette C, Olivain C, Steinberg C (2006) Biological control of plant diseases: the European situation. European Journal of Plant Pathology 114:329–341.

Arias ME, Gonzalez-PereZ JA, Gonzalez-Vila FJ, Ball AS (2005) Soil health—a new challenge for microbiologists and chemists. International Microbiology 8:13-21.

Beauverie J (1901) Essais d'immunisation des végétaux contre les maladies cryptogamiques. CR Acad Sci Paris 133: 107-110.

Benhamou N, Picard K (1999) La résistance induite: une nouvelle stratégie de défense des plantes contre les agents pathogènes. Phytoprotection 80: 137-168.

Bloem J, de Ruiter P, Bouwman LA (1997) Soil food webs and nutrient cycling in agro-ecosystems. In: van Elsas JD, Trevors JT, Wellington HME (ed) Modern soil microbiology. Marcel Dekker, New York, pp. 245-278.

Chaudhary V, Prasanna R, Nain L, Dubey S C, Gupta V, Singh R, Jaggi S, Bhatnagar AK (2012) Bioefficacy of novel cyanobacteria-amended formulations in suppressing damping off disease in tomato seedlings World J Microbiol Biotechnol (2012) 28:3301–3310

Colwell, RR (1997). Microbial biodiversity and biotechnology. In: Reaka-Kudla ML, Wilson DE, Wilson EO (ed) Biodiversity II: Understanding and protecting our biological resources. Joseph Henry Press, University of Washington, Washington, DC, pp. 279-288.

Dey R, Pal KK, Bhatt DM, Chauhan SM (2004) Growth promotion and yield enhancement of peanut (Arachis hypogaea L) byapplication of plant growth promoting rhizobacteria. Microbiological Research 159:371 –394.

Doran JW, Parkin TB (1996) Quantitative indicators of soil quality: a minimum data set. In: Doran JW, Jones AJ (Ed) Methods for Assessing Soil Quality. Soil Science Society of America, Special Publication 49, Madison, WI, pp. 25–37.

Dorana J, Zeiss R (2000) Soil health and sustainability: managing the biotic component of soil quality. Applied Soil Ecology 15: 3–11.

Dukare AS, Prasanna R, Dubey SC, Chaudhary V, Nain L, Singh R, Saxena AK (2011) Evaluating novel microbe amended composts as biocontrol agents in tomato. Crop Protection 30:436-442

FAO (2011). FAOSTAT statistical database (http:// faostat.fao.org/).

Glanz JT (1995) Saving Our Soil: Solutions for Sustaining Earth's Vital Resource. Johnson Books, Boulder, CO, USA.

Herman MAB, Nault BA, Smart CD (2008) Effects of plant growth promoting rhizobacteria on bell pepper production and green peach aphid infestation in New York. Crop Protection 27: 996 – 1002.

Hoorman J, Islam R (2007) Nutrient Recycling with Manure and Cover Crops. 7 Indiana CCA Conference Proceedings: 1-10.

Hoorman J, Islam R (2010) Understanding Soil Microbes and Nutrient Recycling .Agriculture and natural resources 1-5.

Jenkinson DS (2010) Department of Soil Science, Rothamsted Research. Interview with BBC World. 6 November 2010.

Jones EE, Stewart A (2011) Coniothyrium minitans survival in soil and ability to infect sclerotia of Sclerotinia sclerotiorum New Zealand Plant Protection 64: 168-174.

Kögel-Knabner I (2000) Analytical approaches for characterizing soil organic matter. Org Geochem 31: 609-625.

Kuc J (2001) Concepts and direction of induced systemic resistance in plants and its application. European Journal of Plant Pathology 107: 7-12.

Lal R (1998) Basic concepts and global issues: soil quality and agricultural sustainability. In: Lal R (Ed) Soil Quality and Agricultural Sustainability. Ann Arbor Science, Chelsea, MI, USA, pp. 3–12.

Lynch JM, Poole NJ (1979) Microbial ecology: a conceptual approach. John Wiley, New York.

Miao Y, Stewart BA, Zhang FS (2011) Long-term experiments for sustainable nutrient management in China. A review. Agronomy and Sustainable Development (in press)

Oldeman LR (1994). The global extent of soil degradation. In: Greenland DJ, Szabolcs I (Ed) Soil Resilience and Sustainable Land Use. CAB International, Wallingford, Oxon, UK, pp. 99–118.

Pieterse CMJ, van Wees SCM, van Pelt JA, Knoester M, Laan R, Gerrits H, Weisbeek PJ, van Loon LC (1998) A novel signaling pathway controlling induced systemic resistance in Arabidopsis. Plant Cell 10: 1571-1580.

Prabhu V, Ishwarya M, Kayalvizhi SR, Hariprakash R, Balakrishnan, V (2010) Reclamation of Dye Affected Soil at Tirupur Region by Using Vermitechnology, South India. Journal of Ecobiotechnology 2(4): 16-21.

Prasanna R, Chaudhary V, Gupta V, Babu S, Kumar A, Shivay YS, Nain L 2013. Cyanobacteria mediated plant growth promotion and bioprotection against Fusarium wilt in tomato. European Journal of Plant Pathology 136: 337-353

Ray J (1901) Les maladies cryptogamiques des végétaux. Reviews in General Botany 13: 145-151.

Sethi R.R.,Kumar,A., Sharma, S.P., Verma, H.C.(2010).Prediction of water table depth in hard rock basin by using Artificial Neural Network. International Journal of water resources and environmental engineering,2(4), pp.95-102

Shamseldin, A.Y. (1997) Application of a neural network technique to rainfall-runoff modeling. J. Hydrology. 199(3/4), pp. 172-194.

SNNS (1995). User manual, version 4.1, Rep. No. 6/95, Institute for Parallel and Distributed High Performance Systems, University of Stuttgart, Stuttgart, Germany.

Sophocleous, MA (1991). Combining the soil water balance and water table fluctuation methods to estimate natural groundwater recharge: Practical aspects. Journal of Hydrology, 124, pp.229-241.

Sudheer, K. P., Gosain, A. K. and Ramasastri, K. S. (2003). Estimating actual evapotranspiration from limited climatic data using neural computing technique. Journal of Irrigation and Drainage Engineering, 129(3), pp. 214-218

Swarnalakshmi K, Prasanna R, Kumar A, Pattnaik S, Chakravarty K, Shivay YS, Singh R, Saxena AK (2013) Evaluating the influence of novel cyanobacterial biofilmed biofertilizers on soil fertility and plant nutrition in wheat. European Journal of Soil Biology 55 : 107-116.

Tsoukalas, L. H., and Uhrig, R. E. (1996). Fuzzy and neural approach in engineering, Wiley, New York.

Van Loon LC, Bakker PAHM, Pieterse CM (1998) Systemic resistance induced by rhizosphere bacteria. Annual Review of Phytopathology 36: 453-458.

Wang,Y., Traore,S. and Kerh,T.(2008). Neural network approach for estimating reference evapotranspiration from limited climatic data in Burkina Faso. WSEAS Transactions on Computers, 7(6), pp.704-713.

❑❑❑

CHAPTER - 13

Motif Discovery in Biological Macromolecules: Current Trends, Methods, Applications and Future Challenges

Amandeep Kaur Kahlon and Ashok Sharma

Biotechnology Division, CSIR-Central Institute of Medicinal and Aromatic Plants (CIMAP), Kukrail Picnic Spot Road, P.O: CIMAP, Lucknow-226015 (U.P.), India; E-mail: amangenomics@gmail.com; ashoksharma@cimap.res.in

1. INTRODUCTION

Motifs are patterns in biological sequences which can indicate the presence of certain biological characteristics and function. In general, these could represent patterns in any kind of biological sequences such as DNA sequences, RNA sequences and protein sequences. Evolutionary conserved regions (ECRs) are sequences with atleast 100 bp length alongwith minimum 70% identity, which includes most of the protein-coding exons, promoters, enhancers and repressors. ECRs are the preliminary step for finding TFBSs (Transcription factor binding sites) within the raw genome sequences of higher eukaryotes (large sizes of the genomes). DNA sequence motifs are short length, recurring patterns in DNA and are known to be associated with a biological function. These motifs sometimes indicate sequence specific binding sites for proteins such as nucleases and transcription factors (TF). Some sequence motifs are involved in biological processes at RNA level, such as ribosome binding, mRNA processing (splicing, editing, polyadenylation) and transcription termination. Motif identification is important at protein level for biological processes such as protein-subcellular localization, protein membrane, protein-protein interactions, identification of active site of enzyme(s) and post-translational modifications. Motif search is useful in understanding gene function, human disease, drug design, etc. Regulation of splicing in eukaryotes occurs through the coordinated action of multiple splicing factors. Sequence motifs are also useful in the study of genetic regulatory networks and regulatory program of individual genes. (S. Jones *et al.*, 2003). Exons and introns contain numerous putative binding sites for splicing regulatory proteins. On the other hand, splicing is rare and occurs mostly at non-coding RNA in prokaryotes. Experimentally-identified splicing regulatory sequences were analyzed using a computational method based on the natural distribution of nucleotides and splicing regulatory sequences. [A. Goren *et al*, 2010]. Machine learning approaches are used to compile sequential segments and constitute structural features of an interaction site into Hidden Markov Model descriptors. This is applicable in prediciting protein-protein interactions (PPI) and protein-ligand interactions (PLI) using 3D informationof sequences. [D. T. Moore *et al.*, 2008; G. Ciriello and C. guerra, 2008; A Henschel *et al.*, 2007] Evolutionary conserved phylogenetic motifs are detected by expectation-maximization algorithm, Parsimony and likehood [A. M. Moses et al., 2004 and M. C. Suros, 2010]. Although there are various applications of motif discovery in computational biology and depending on the study macromolecules are explored for conserved and functional motifs in DNA, RNA and protein sequences. Certain limitations and challenges still exist in computational biology. Incomplete understanding of biological processes, pathways and diverse mode of action of DNA, RNA and proteins is a major issue in developing efficient computational tools and algorithms. The present chapter was aimed to explore the diverse types of motifs, their applications and methods available for motif discovery, their applications, limitations and future need for more advanced methods.

2. SEQUENCE AND STRUCTURAL MOTIFS

A sequence motif is a nucleotide or amino acid sequence pattern found in similar DNA or protein sequences, respectively. First protein sequence motif were identified as ATP- or GTP- binding motifs with characteristic of very broad range of proteins. For example, walker motif A has the pattern GXXXXGK (T/S); X-can be any amino acid, G-Glycine, K-Lysine, T-threonine, S-serine. {rpteom strictira; ,ptofs sicj as je;ox-turn-helix and zinc finger motifs are able to bind with DNA. [R. Nussi Nov and H. J. Wolfson, 1991; R. G. Brennan and B. W. Mathews, 1989; S. N. Chou *et al.*, 2003; S. Mahony *et al*, 2005] Sequence motifs can be recognized by simple inspection of its primary amino acid sequence of a protein and provides evidence for its biochemical function. For example, protease enzyme of HIV virus was first identified as aspartyl protease with characteristic sequence motif for proteases in its primary sequences.

2.1 DNA motifs and Their Types

A DNA motif is defined as a nucleic acid sequence pattern that has some biological significance such as being DNA binding sites for a regulatory protein, i.e., a transcription factor. [P. D'haeseleer, 2006]. This pattern is short (5 to 20 base-pairs long) and is known to recur in different genes or several times within a gene. Every gene contains regulatory regions and is approx. 100-1000 bp upstream of the transcriptional start site. TFBS (Transcriptional Factor Binding sites) are known as motifs and are located within the regulatory regions of genes. These transcription factors modulate gene expression by binding to a specific location in the particular gene regulatory region (TFBS). These motifs can be located anywhere within the regulatory region of a gene. Variation is also possible across different regulatory regions due to mutations in non-essential bases. Finding the same motif in multiple genes regulatory regions highlights a possible relationship amongst those genes. There is always a lot of sequence variability present with respect to a single motif. The regulatory sequences containing the motifs may sometimes be located very far away from coding regions that they regulate. Hence, it is difficult to determine the portion of the DNA sequence that should be analyzed. The regulatory sequences may sometimes, be present on the opposite strand from the coding sequence they regulate. It was hypothesize that DNA methylation at conserved consensus motifs prevents disorderly transcription factor binding. Genome-wide methylation maps of the human heart and sperm found that all conserved consensus motifs as well as the subset of those that reside outside CpG islands have an aggregate profile of hyper-methylation. Majority of conserved consensus motifs in the human genome are hyper-methylated, whereas biologically proven TFBS with conserved consensus motifs are hypomethylated. [M. K. Choy et al., 2010]. The genes containing helicase motifs may have evolved from a common ancestor [N. Tuteja and R. Tuteja, 2004]. The helix-turn-helix motif is an integral part of the protein-DNA interface with the second α-helix located within the major groove of the DNA.

2.2 RNA motifs and Their Types

RNA motifs prediction helps in Classification of RNA families, in searching new members of a known RNA family along with information on RNA functionality. RNA motifs correspond to the loops (hairpin, internal and junction) and they intersperse the Watson-crick two dimensional helices of RNA structure. They induce compact folding of complex RNA to constitute specific protein and ligand binding sites. They are ordered stacked arrays of non-watson-crick base pairs to build distinctive folding of phosphodiester backbones of the interacting RNA strands. Therefore, it is very essential to first classify its non-watson-crick base pairs geometrically in order to identify and compare motifs at the time of analyzing 3D structure of RNA. Examination of RNA three dimensional structures shows that they are composed of a combination of recurring structural motifs joined by a small number of types of tertiary interaction motifs. These motifs are commonly subgrouped by secondary structure types; double helices, hairpin loops, internal loops, junction loops/

multiloops, interaction of RNA with metal ions, binding motifs, aptamers, tertiary interactions, RNA splicing motifs [D. K. Hendrix et al., 2005; N. B. Leontis and E. Westhof, 2002], small molecules, proteins and other RNAs characterized by a set of recurring motifs [L. A. Chasin, 2007]. The identification and classification of RNA structural motifs is used to trace their evolutionary relationships. These are useful as building blocks in RNA engineering. RNA 3D motifs are well-defined geometric arrangements of interacting nucleotides. Kink-turns are complex RNA motifs with double- and single-stranded components and introduce a signature three-dimensional structure into helical stems and are recurrent architectural RNA elements that are found in Archaea, Prokarya, and Eukarya. K-turn (KT) motifs are functionally diverse and have been identified in rRNAs, mRNAs, and small untranslated RNAs (utRNAs, also called non-proteincoding RNAs. KT motifs serve as protein recognition sites and are able to engage in multiple intermolecular interactions simultaneously [H. Tiedge, 2006].

The kink-turn (k-turn) is a common structural motif in RNA that introduces a tight kink into the helical axis. These k-turns play an important architectural role in RNA structures and serve as binding sites for a number of proteins. A database of structural k-turn motifs in RNA and universal nomenclature for the nucleotide positions in k-turns was devised [K.T. Schroeder et al, 2010], thus avoiding the confusion that could arise from the many different numbering systems used in various crystal structures.

RNA motifs are called recurrent due to their independent occurrence in different, non–homologous places of the same or different RNA molecules while sharing a similar 3D structure. Many of the motifs composing hairpin, internal and junction "loops" and the RNA tertiary interactions they form recur in RNA 3D structure. Hence, a general approach to 3D motif searching must handle all these cases. Recurrent motifs usually share a core of base–paired and –stacked nucleotides arranged in the same way, whereas, differ from each other in the identity of the nucleotides forming each basepair and the number of unpaired bases bulged out or extruded from the motif. By comparing all available examples of recurrent motifs, one can better understand the natural variability within each motif family. Recurrent motifs can be local or composite. Local motifs are composed of nucleotides that belong to the same hairpin (terminal) or internal loop. Terminal loops occur at the ends of individual helices while internal loops are flanked by two helices. Composite motifs are composed of nucleotides from disparate and discontinuous stretches of polynucleotide sequence. The same recurrent motif can occur in local and composite versions. For example, composite instances of sarcin motifs and kink-turn motifs have been identified in the structures of the 5S, 16S, and 23S ribosomal RNAs (rRNA). The internal loop in Helix 95 of 23S rRNA is a local example of the sarcin/ricin motif. A composite version of this motif occurs in the multi–helix junction in Domain 2 of 23S rRNA (Helices 35, 37, 39, 40 and 45). Composite motifs are easy to overlook in visual analyses. They are generally missed by computational approaches that analyze the conformations of successive nucleotides in the RNA chain. Recurrent motifs play similar roles in different RNA molecules or domains. Some play architectural roles, for example forming bends, kinks or branch points, while others serve as anchors for tertiary interactions that compact and stabilize the folded 3D structure of the molecule. Sometimes k-turn motifs mediate RNA–protein or RNA–ligand inter–molecular interactions.

2.3 Protein Motifs and Their Types

Sequence or structural elements conserved among different proteins are called protein motifs [D. Lee *et al.*, 2007]. Cysteine motifs with secondary structures and their bonding states are stored in CMD database. Helix-cap sequence motifs were derived using database helix assignments for proteins of known structure using gibbs sampling approach [E. Kruus et al, 2005]. It is important to identify enzyme active sites or ligand binding sites. Bioinorganic motifs [K. Degtyarenko, 2000] are common structural feature shared by functionally related but not necessarily homologous. They are mainly composed of metal atom(s) and first coordination shell ligands. These are described for possible evolutionary relationships of metalloproteins. Posttranslational modification of proteins with isoprenyl anchors is called prenylation of proteins. The protein prenylation motifs (isoprenyl lipid moieties) are important due to their involvement in mediating protein-membrane and protein-protein interactions [S. Maurer-Stroh and F. Eisenhaber, 2005]. These motifs for carboxy-terminal protein prenylation were refined through analysis of known substrates for farnesyltransferase (FT), geranylgeranyltransferase I (GGT1) and geranylgeranyltransferase II (GGT2) using prenylation prediction suite. This prediction of partially overlapping substrate specificities is important to understand the cellular action of farnesyl transferase inhibitors, anti-cancer and anti-parasite agents. Short-linear motifs (SLiMs) are usually 3 to 10 amino acid residues in length and functionally important in protein-subcellular localization, protein half-life and protein-protein interactions and post-translational modifications [D. S. Lieber et al., 2010 and M. Parras-Molto *et al.*, 2013] [R. Sen *et al.*, 2008].

3.0 TOOLS AND DATABASES

Molecular biology applies the DNA, RNA and protein sequence and structure information for functional analysis. Based on the understanding of these macromolecules, several tools and databases were developed using computational biology approaches. It is important to develop additional tools that can be used for the prediction of functionally relevant features [D. Quest *et al.*, 2008]. Therefore, conservation criteria are widely used for this purpose. The RNA 3D Motif Atlas [A. I. Petrov et al., 2013] aims to combine the best features of the existing methods in an exhaustive and systematic way for continuous updating and archiving. The existing manually curated motif databases are either no longer updated such as SCOR (K. T. Shroeder *et al.*, 2010) or focus only on a limited number of motifs (kink-turn database [P. S. Kloesterman *et al.*, 2004]). There are also several databases that provide extracted loops for download but do not classify them. To find a consensus motif of a set of homologous or functionally related RNA molecules, recent approaches have been limited to simple motifs, require sequence alignment, and make prior assumptions concerning the data set. On the other hand, genetic programming predicts RNA consensus motifs based solely on the data set. GeRNAMo (Genetic programming of RNA Motifs)—predicts the most common motifs without sequence alignment and is capable of dealing with any motif size. If prior knowledge is available, the user can specify other attributes of the motif (e.g., the range of the motif's minimum and maximum sizes), thereby increasing both sensitivity and speed. It was described by experiments using either ferritin iron response element (IRE), signal recognition particle (SRP), or microRNA sequences and showed that the most common motif is found repeatedly. This system offers substantial advantages over previous methods [S. Michal *et al.*, 2007]. FR3D find and score geometrically similar candidate motifs, without regard to the sequential position of their nucleotides in the RNA chain or the identity of their bases [M. Sarver *et al.*, 2008]. DiLiMot [V. Neduva and R. B. Russell, 2006], SLiMDisc (short linear motif discovery)[101] [N.E. Davey et al, 2006] and SLiMFinder [N.E. Davey et al, 2010] can predict motifs enriched in small sets of proteins. However, these are not suitable for large scale data with thousands of proteins and complex protein behaviors. On the other hand, FIRE-pro (finding informative regulatory elements in proteins) facilitates the discovery of short sequence motifs informative of the global behavior of proteins. The use of mutual information provides a universal framework that can be applied to any type of biological data, (discrete or quantitative) and the algorithm can be applied to proteome-scale data from any organism, including humans. The algorithm can simultaneously discover over- and under-represented motifs and has no requirement for an explicit background model. Due to increasingly quantitative nature of proteomics experiments, FIRE-pro was said to be valuable tool for revealing sequence elements and determine diverse protein behavior [D. S. Lieber et al, 2010].

Table 1: Tools/web servers and databases available for motif identification in DNA

DNA motif identification tools and databases	Prediction methods and algorithm	URL	Applications	References
PatSearch	Scans user submitted sequences for any combination of position weight matrices, primary sequence patterns and structural motifs also allowing mismatches and mis-pairings below a user fixed threshold.	http://bighost.area.ba.cnr.it/BIG/PatSearch/	A flexible and fast pattern matcher able to search for specific combinations of oligonucleotide consensus sequences, secondary structure elements and position-weight matrices.	G. Grillo *et al.*, 2003
FootPrinter [85]	Identify best conserved motifs in homologous regions.	http://bio.cs.washington.edu/software.html	For the discovery of regulatory elements in a set of homologous regulatory regions from multiple species.	M. Blanchette and M. Tompa, 2003
ZPicture	Web based sequence alignment and visualization tool generating conservation profiles and identifying ECRs.	http://zpicture.dcode.org	Analysis of large genomic regions of any length from microbes to human.	I. Ovcharenko *et al.*, 2004
PhyMe	Probabilistic algorithm for ab-initio detection of binding site motifs in heterogenous sequences. Realistic model incorporates binding site specificity.	http://edsc.rockefeller.edu/cgi-bin/phyme/download.pl	Handle broader range of species divergence.	S. Sinha *et al.*, 2004

Contd.

WebLogo	Logo generation algorithm process RNA, DNA or protein multiple sequence alignments in FASTA or CLUSTAL formats.	http://weblogo.berkeley.edu/logo.cgi	Graphical representation of an amino acid or nucleic acid multiple sequence alignment consensus sequence.	G. Crooks *et al.*, 2004
CompareProspector	Sequence motif finding algorithm extending Gibbs sampling.	http://www.compareprospector.stanford.edu/	Identify eukaryotic transcription regulatory element.	Y. Liu *et al.*, 2004
CisML	XML (Extensible Markup Language) - based format for sequence motif detection software.	http://zlab.bu.edu/CisML/	A common output format to simplify testing and benchmarking the tools for analyzing transcription factor binding sites to protein motif detection, the exchange of data between laboratories and combining results from multiple tools to take advantage of their different features.	P. M. Haverty and Z. Weng, 2004
SynoR 2005	De novo identification of synonymous regulatory elements (SRE) using known TFBS.	http://synor.dcode.org	Synonymous regulatory elements (SRE) in vertebrate genomes	I. Ovcharenko and M.A. Nobrega,

Contd.

PhyloGibbs	Gibbs-sampling approach.	http://www.biozentrum.unibas.ch/~nimwegen/cgi-bin/phylogibbs.cgi; http://www.imsc.res.in/~rsidd/phylogibbs.	Discovery of regulatory sites in intergenic DNA.	R. Siddharthan *et al.*, 2005
GANN	Genetic algorithm.	http://bioinformatics.org.au/gann	Neural networks for the detection of conserved combinations of features in DNA	R.G. Beiko and R.L. Charlebois, 2005
PHYLOCLUS	Phylogenetic motif discovery and Bayesian clustering algorithm.	http://stat.wharton.upenn.edu/~stjensen/research/phyloclus.html or http://www.fas.harvard.edu/~junliu/phyloclus.html	For predicting co-regulated genes, de novo discovery methods are used to find motifs conserved by evolution and then a Bayesian hierarchical clustering model is used to cluster these motifs, thereby grouping together genes that are putatively co-regulated.	S. T. Jensen *et al.*, 2005
Gemoda	Generic motif discovery algorithm (Gemoda) for sequential data.	http://web.mit.edu/bamel/ gemoda	Discovery of motifs in amino acids sequences, a new solution to the (l,d)-motif problem in DNA sequences and the discovery of conserved protein substructures.	K. L. Jensen *et al.*, 2006
PRIORITY	De novo DNA motif discovery tool.	http://www.cs.duke.edu/	Recognize binding sites of three structural	L. Narlikar *et al.*, 2006

Contd.

			classes of transcription factors.	
oPOSSUM	The transcription factor binding site models have been updated to include new profiles from the JASPAR database.	http://www.cisreg.ca/oPOSSUM/	Applicable for orthology assignment, transcription start site (TSS) determination and sequence alignment; for the analysis of over represented combinations of motifs in human mouse genes, yeast and worms.	S. J. H. Sui *et al.*, 2007
Tree Gibbs Sampler (TGS)	Software for identifying motifs by simultaneously using the motif over representation property and the motif evolutionary conservation property.	https://compbio.iupui.edu/xiaomanli/LiSoftware/retrieve.	Useful for the extraction of regulatory elements in multiple genomes of both closely related and distant species.	X. Cai *et al.*, 2007
MATLIGN	Tool aligns and evaluates the similarity of motifs using a combination of scoring functions and hierarchical clustering.	http://ekhidna.biocenter.helsinki.fi/poxo/matlign	For post-processing large collections of DNA sequence Motifs.	M. Kankainen and A. Loytynoja, 2007
HeliCis	De novo detection of DNA motifs with periodic spacing.	http://lymphomics.wall.gu.se/helicis	This can detect weak periodic patterns which are not easily discovered using a sequential approach.	E. Larsson *et al.*, 2007

Contd.

STAMP	Directly accepts the output files from 12 supported motif-finders, enabling quick interpretation of motif-discovery analyses.	http://www.benoslab.pitt.edu/stamp	Exploring DNA-binding motif similarities.	S. Mahony *et al.*, 2007
Melina II	Web-based tool for promoter analysis. Melina II shows potential DNA motifs in promoter regions with a combination of several available programs, Consensus, MEME, Gibbs sampler, MDscan and Weeder, as well as several parameter settings.	http://melina.hgc.jp.	Predictive algorithms to find potential motifs from promoter regions.	T. Okumura *et al.*, 2007
rMotifGen	User-defined, randomly generated or created scoring matrix (PSSM).	http://bioinformatics.louisville.edu/brg/rMotifGen/	For creating random DNA or amino acid sequences with a variable number of motifs.	E. C. Rouchka and C. T. Hardin, 2007 [30]
PhyloCon	Wang and Stormo algorithm	http://www.stormo.wustl.edu/PhyloCon/?	Incorporates multiple species data.	T. Wang, 2007
Scan2S	Regular expression-based motif-scanning algorithm with optional secondary structure constraints.	http://physiology.med.cornell.edu/go/scan2s	Enabled the search of sequence databases using long flexible motifs with optional secondary structure constraints, to detect restriction	M. Y. Niv *et al.*, 2008

Contd.

			endonucleases of GATC and CCGG specificities.	
c-REDUCE	Correlation-based algorithm Regulatory Element Detection Using Correlation with Expression called conservation-REDUCE (c-REDUCE).	http://www.osti.gov/c-REDUCE	Account for variability at a motif position inferred from evolutionary information. Tested on ChIP-chip data for yeast transcription factors and on gene expression data in Drosophila.	K. Kechris and H. Li, 2008
CSMET(Conditional Shadowing via Multi-resolution Evolutionary Trees)	Context-dependent probabilistic graphical model.	http://www.sailing.cs.cmu.edu/csmet/	Comparative genomic motif detection.	P. Ray *et al.*, 2008
MicrobesOnline	Comparative genome browser based on phylogenetic trees for every gene family as well as a species tree.	http://www.microbesonline.org	To identify co-regulated genes, MicrobesOnline can search for genes based on their expression profile, and provides tools for identifying regulatory motifs and seeing if they are conserved.	P. S. Dehal *et al.*, 2010
DOOR(Database for prokaryotic operons)	Computationally predicted operons of all the sequenced prokaryotic genomes.	http://csbl1.bmb.uga.edu/OperonDB	Finds desired operons and associated information, prediction of cis-regulatory motifs and operons for RNA genes.	F. Mao *et al.*, 2009

Contd.

MotifMap	Procedure for identifying regulatory sites, with high levels of conservation across different species, using a new scoring scheme, the Bayesian branch length score (BBLS).	http://motifmap.ics.uci.edu	Human genome-wide map of candidate regulatory motif sites. This provides a systematic view of gene regulation in the genome.	X. Xie *et al.*, 2009
MEME	Meme motif discovery algorithm.	http://meme.nbcr.net/meme/	Useful for both DNA and protein sequences to identify motifs.	T. L. Bailey *et al.*, 2009
ECM Finder (Evolutionary Conserved Motif)	Regular expression.	http://jookimlab.lsu.edu/	Transcription factor binding site (TFBS) prediction.	K. Kang *et al.*, 2009
COMPASSS (Complex Pattern of Sequence Search Software)	Wu and Manber, 1994 algorithm	http://www.steanolandi.eu/; http://www.compasss.sourceforge.net/	For mining complex motifs in whole genomes.	G. Maccari *et al.*, 2010
CompleteMOTIFs [79] (cMOTIFs)	Comprehensive web tool for ChIP-seq data analysis.	http://cmotifs.tchlab.org	Helps to identify novel or known TFBS of interest as well as possible co-factor binding sites.	L. Kuttippurathu *et al.*, 2011
FIMO (Find Individual Motif Ocurrences)	Tool for scanning DNA or protein sequences with position-specific scoring matrices.	http://meme.sdsc.edu.	The program computes a log-likelihood ratio score for each position in a given sequence database, uses established dynamic programming methods to convert this score to a P-value and then	C. E. Grant *et al.*, 2011

Contd.

			applies false discovery rate analysis to estimate a q-value for each position in the given sequence.	
Magma (Multiple Aligner of Genomic Multiple Alignments)	Magma algorithm for multi-gene, multi-species computational motif discovery	http://stormo.wustl.edu/	Identifies motifs conserved across species and occur in several locations within the reference genome.	N. E. Ihuegbu *et al.*, 2012
MISCORE [25] (Mis-match based matrix similarity scores)	For finding DNA regulatory motifs in promoter sequences. Motif signal modeling power and computational efficiency for candidate motif characterization, evaluation and selection.	http://www.latrobe.edu.au/MISCORE	Automatically filter out some repetitive k-mers from a motif model due to the introduction of the compositional complexity in the function. Capabilities to separate and recognize functional DNA motifs and its instances from non-functional ones.	D. Wang and S. Tapan, 2012
qPMS7 (Quorum Planted Motif Search)	Fast algorithm for Finding (l,d)-Motifs in DNA and protein sequences.	http://pms.engr.uconn.edu/downloads/qPMS7.zip	Algorithm qPMS7 is faster than other existing algorithms, especially for large values of l and d. It is applicable in DNA and protein sequences.	H. Dinh *et al.*, 2012
TFBSshape	Motif database for DNA	http://rohslab.cmb.usc.	Used to compare,	L. Yang *et al.*, 2014

Contd.

	shape features of transcription factor binding sites	edu/TFBSshape/	qualitatively and quantitatively, the DNA binding specificities of closely related TFs and uncover differential DNA binding specificities that are not apparent from nucleotide sequence alone.	
DRIMust (Discovering Rank Imbalanced Motifs)	The DRIMust algorithm is based on the minimum hypergeometric statistical framework and uses suffix trees for an efficient enumeration of motif candidates.	http://drimust.technion.ac.il/	Combines efficient search on large ranked lists with rigorous P-value assessment for the detected motifs. De novo motif discovery in DNA, RNA or Protein sequences.	L. Leibovich *et al.*, 2013
Non-B DB v2.0	Database of predicted non-B DNA-forming motifs.	http://nonb.abcc.ncifcrf.gov	Catalogs predicted non-B DNA-forming sequence motifs, including Z-DNA, G-quadruplex, A-phased repeats, inverted repeats, mirror repeats, direct repeats and their corresponding subsets in several genomes.	R. Z. Cer *et al.*, 2013
MotifLab	General workbench for analyzing regulatory	http://www.motiflab.org	For motif analysis in genomic data and	K. Klepper and F. Drablos, 2013

Contd.

	sequence regions, transcription factor binding sites and cis-regulatory modules.		analyse data objects by allowing users to integrate popular motif discovery tools and graphical representation of results.	
Dispom	denovo motif discovery tool combines searching for differentially abundant motifs, inferring their positional distributions and adjusts the motif lengths for de-novomotif discovery.	http://www.jstacs.de/index.php/Dispom	For finding binding sites of DNA-binding proteins that are differentially abundant in a set of target regions compared to a set of control regions.	J. Grau *et al.*, 2013

Table 2: Tools/web servers and databases available for motif identification in RNA

DNA motif identification tools and databases	Prediction methods and algorithm	URL	Applications	References
RNAMotif	RNA structural motifs search algorithm on nucleotide sequence database of prokaryotic and eukaryotic genomes.	ftp.scripps.edu/pub/macke/rnamotif-version.tar.gz.	Capable of finding sequences containing any of the secondary structure element: single strands, duplexes (both antiparallel and parallel), pseudoknots, triplexes, quadruplexes.	T. J. Macke *et al.*, 2001
SCOR	Structural Classification of RNA database.	http://scor.lbl.gov	Manual classification of RNA structural	P. S. Klosterman *et al.*, 2004

Contd.

			motifs based on recorded literature, computation and observation.	
GPRM	Genetic programming algorithm.	http:// www.cs.bgu.ac.il/	Find structural motifs in RNA.	Y. J. Hu, 2003
RNAProfile	Algorithm applicable to detect RNA motifs globally conserved in a set of sequences or motifs appearing in a small subset of them.	ftp://www.pesolelab.it/pub/(current version 2.0)	Capable of characterizing and discovering known regulatory motifs in mRNA and more complex motifs in non-coding RNA.	G. Pavesi *et al.*, 2004
CMfinder	Covariance model RNA motif finding algorithm.	http://bio.cs.washington.edu/yzizhen/CMfinder/	To obtain highly accurate covariance models of known RNA motifs based on small numbers of related sequences, which identified homologs in deeply-diverged species.	Z. Yao, 2006
FR3D	MATLAB program implementing geometric search algorithm.	http://rna.bgsu.edu/FR3D	User supplied 3D structure of a query motif in RNA to find and score geometrically similar candidate motifs.	M. Sarver *et al.*, 2008
GeRNAMo	Evolutionary computation and genetic programming algorithm to predict	http://www.cs.bgu.ac.il/	Predicts the most common motifs without sequence alignment and capable	S. Michal *et al.*, 2007

Contd.

	RNA consensus motifs using data sets.		with any motif size.	
Locomotif	Dynamic programming algorithm.	http://bibiserv.techfak.unibielefeld.de/locomotif	Graphical motif description to RNA motif search.	J. Reeder *et al.*, 2007
SFmap	COS (WR) algorithm (conservation of score weighted rank), which computes similarity scores for a given regulatory motif based on information derived from its sequence environment and its evolutionary conservation.	http://sfmap.technion.ac.il	For predicting putative splicing factor binding sites in genomic data.	I. Paz *et al.*, 2010
k-turn	Structural database for k-turn motifs in RNA.	http://www.dundee.ac.uk/biocentre/nasg/kturn/index.php.	The k-turn provides a simple model system for the study of RNA folding, RNA structure and function.	K. T. Schroeder *et al.*, 2010
RNApromo	Stochastic content-free grammers (SCFGs) based algorithm finds local motifs in a set of unaligned RNAs and probabilistic inference algorithm refines the predicted motif using statistical estimation.	http:// www.genei.weizmann.ac.il/	Predicts putative motifs in sets of mRNAs for common post-transcriptional regulation.	M. Rabani *et al.*, 2011 and M. Rabani et al., 2008
RNA Bricks	Database of RNA 3D motifs and their interactions. The	http://iimcb.genesilico.pl/rnabricks	Identification of local structural similarities among evolutionarily	G. Chojnowski *et al.*, 2014

Contd.

	database is also equipped with an algorithm for 3D motif search and comparison.		related and unrelated RNA molecules. Identify motifs with modified ribonucleotide residues at specific positions.	
RNA 3D Motif Atlas	Database for structure modeling and prediction of RNA 3D motifs.	http://rna.bgsu.edu/motifs	For automated classification of internal and hairpin loop RNA 3D motifs.	A. I. Petrov *et al.*, 2013

Table 3 : Tools/web servers and databases available for motif identification in protein

Protein motif identification tools and databases	Prediction methods and algorithm	URL	Applications	References
PRINTS	Database of protein motif fingerprints	http://ncbi.nlm.nih.gov; ftp.embl-heidelberg.de	Analysis of protein sequences with improved diagnostic reliability over single-motif methods by virtue of the mutual context provided by motif neighbours.	T. K. Attwood *et al.*, 1994
PRATT	Knuth-Morris-Pratt string searching algorithm (KMP algorithm)	http://www.web.expasy.org/pratt/	Discover patterns conserved in a set of protein sequences.	I. Jonassen *et al.*, 1995
LOCK 2	Structural superposition algorithm	http://fold.stanford.edu/LOCK	Capable of detecting distant structural homologies.	A. P. Singh and D. L. Brutlag, 1997

Contd.

FingerPRINTScan	Method classsifies the sequences with distant evolutionary relationships using PRINTS database.	http://www.bioinf.man.ac.uk/fingerPRINTScan/	Identifies unknown gene or protein as a member of known family.	P. Scordis *et al.*, 1999
EMOTIF	Database of more than 170000 of highly specific and sensitive protein sequence motifs.	http://motif.stanford.edu/emotif/	To identify and classify divergent sequences due to representation of critical positions conserved in evolution.	J. Y. Huang and D. L. Brutlag, 2001
MBA (fold assignment method)	Uses information present in the occurrences of motifs in the probe sequence and target annotation to combine it with a conventional sequence /structure score.	http://www.doe-mbi.ucla.edu/mba	Generate a motif-fold compatibility motif-based fold assignment score combined with the sequence-based information to obtain the final MBA score.	L. Salwinski and D. Eisenberg, 2001
FoldMiner	Structural motif discovery algorithm	http://fold.stanford.edu/FoldMiner	Detect global and local motifs in a database of proteins without the need for multiple structure or sequence alignments.	J. Shapiro and D. Brutlag, 2004
3MATRIX and 3MOTIF	a web-based sequence motif visualization system that displays sequence motif information in 3D form.	http://3matrix.stanford.edu; http://3motif.stanford.edu	Properties of motifs such as sequence conservation and solvent accessible surface area are also displayed in the visualizations, using carefully chosen color shading schemes.	S. P. Bennette *et al.*, 2003

Contd.

MyHits	The MyHits server includes a collection of tools to generate graphical representations of sequence alignments and their annotated features.	http://myhits.isb-sib.ch	The annotation of protein sequences and to the analysis of their domains and signatures.	M. Pagni *et al.*, 2004
IMOTdb	Database of 854488 motifs corresponding to 60849 protein structural domains and 22648 protein structural entries.	http://caps.ncbs.res.in/imotdb/	Spatially interacting motifs in single protein structures as well as among distantly related protein structures that belong to a superfamily.	A. Bhaduri *et al.*, 2004 [1]
Phylomat	user-friendly data-mining tool for the phylogenomic analysis	http://alg.ncsa.uiuc.edu/pmat	Phylogenomic analysis of conserved sequence motifs/domains in annotated proteomes.	W. V. Graham *et al.*, 2004
Motif Scan	Scans motifs in a sequence	http://myhits.isb-sib.ch/cgi-bin/motif_scan	Finds all known motifs in a protein sequence.	M. Pagni *et al.*, 2004
QuasiMotiFinder	MSA of homologous query proteins against original PROSITE signatures.	http://quasimotifinder.tau.ac.il/	Average evolutionary conservation of the signature in the query proteins significantly reduces the rate of FP and FN compared with simple pattern search.	R. Gutman *et al.*, 2005
MINER	Sliding sequence window algorithm	http://pmap.csupomona.edu/MINER/	Ideal for functional site prediction in	D. La and D. R. Livesay, 2005

Contd.

	and partition metric algorithm.		protein sequences.	
PrePS (Prenylation Prediction Suite)	Evaluation of evolutionary motif conservation and carboxy-terminal protein prenylation.	http://mendel.imp.univie.ac.at/sat/PrePS	To predict partially overlapping substrate specificities for understanding cellular action of farnesyl transferase inhibitors, anticancer and anti-parasite agents.	S. Maurer-Stroh and F. Eisenhaber, 2005
MotifProp	Graph-based propagation algorithm to detect more subtle similarity relationships than pairwise comparison methods.	http://www.cs.columbia.edu/compbio/motifprop	Useful or discovering conserved structural components in remote homologies.	R. Kuang *et al.*, 2005
InterProScan	Combine different protein signature recognition methods from InterPro.	http://www.ebi.ac.uk/interpro/	Functional analysis of proteins and classification of proteins into domains, families and important sites.	E. Quevillon *et al.*, 2005
DILIMOT	Discovery of linear motifs	http://dilimot.embl.de	Identify linear protein functional motifs such as protein interactions, post-translational modifications.	V. Neduva and R. B. Russell, 2006
SLiMDisc (short, linear motif discovery)	TEIRESIAS algorithm.	http://www.bioinformatics.ucd.ie/shields/software/slimdisc/	Short, linear motif discovery without evolutionary descent among protein sequences.	N. E. Davey *et al.*, 2006

Contd.

ScanProsite	Scans against the PROSITE signature database, "unspecific" signatures with a high probability of occurrence.	http://www.expasy.org/tools/scanprosite/	Detects PROSITE signature matches in protein sequences.	E. de Castro *et al.*, 2006
CoSMoS	Regular Expression based method.	http://www.biology.lsa.umich.edu/cosmos	To rapidly identify highly conserved sequence motifs in all proteins encoded in E. coli genome.	X. I. Liu *et al.*, 2006
MegaMotifBase	Structural motifs database of proteins	http://www.hsls.pitt.edu/	Provides tree-dimensional orientation of protein structural motifs via graphic and spatial orientation matrices.	G. Pugalenthi *et al.*, 2008
MALISAM (Manual Alignments For Structurally Analogous Motifs)	First database with pairs of structural analogs and their alignments.	http://prodata.swmed.edu/malisam	Application in protein-folding studies for the similarities between analogs from folding and packing constraints rather than evolutionary relatedness.	H. Cheng *et al.*, 2008
MSDmotif	MSDmotif database contains integrated details about sequence, structure, the relative position and the neighbour environment of many motif types.	http://www.ebi.ac.uk/msd-srv/msd motif	Application for querying the PDB for ligands, binding sites, small 3D structural and sequence motifs and the underlying database.	A. Golovin and K. Henrick, 2008
Multiple motif	It can be used to develop	www.chem.ucla.edu/files	Scan the proteome and	T. C. Petrossian and S. G.

Contd.

scanning program	a putative list of enzymes for any type of protein that has one or more motifs conserved at variable spacings.	/MotifSetup.Zip	score different combinations of the top fitting sequences for each motif. The program takes into account the conserved number of amino acids between the motifs.	Clarke, , 2009
ELM	Database currently covering 146 known motifs, with annotation that includes >1300 experimentally reported instances.	http://elm.eu.org/	Exploratory tool for suggesting new candidates of known linear motifs in proteins of interest.	C. M. Gould *et al.*, 2010
FIRE-Pro	Algorithm calculates correlation between motif profile and protein behavior profile using mutual information.	http://tavazoielab.princeton.edu/FIRE-pro.	Discover protein motifs from large-scale proteomics datasets.	D. S. Lieber *et al.*, 2010
SLiMFinder	SLiMBuild algorithm and SLiMChance algorithm.	http://bioware.ucd.ie/slimfinder.html.	De novo motif discovery identifying statistically over-represented motifs in a set of protein sequences for evolutionary relationship.	N. E. Davey *et al.*, 2010
Sub-HMM	Automated method for identifying conserved protein motifs by creating sub-HMMs from	http://subhmm.ucr.edu	For identifying proteins that share only short sequence similarities.	K. Horan *et al.*, 2010

Contd.

	custom or existing profile HMM data sets.			
SALAD database	Database for comparing protein sequences and can provide valuable hints for biological analysis.	http://salad.dna.affrc.go.jp/salad/	Graphical viewer that displays a motif pattern diagram linked to the resulting bootstrapped dendrogram for each protein group.	M. Mihara *et al.*, 2010
GOmotif	PROSITE and regular expression formatted motifs is taken as input and search the gene ontology annotated protein database using motif search tools.	http://www.gomotif.ca	Identify the possible biological role of protein sequence motifs.	F. Bristow *et al.*, 2011
FurinDB	Database includes experimentally verified furin cleavage sites, substrates, species, experimental methods, original publications of experiments and associated drugs targeting furin substrates.	http://www.nuolan.net/substrates.html	Applicable for understanding the molecular evolution and relationships between sequence motifs, 3D structures, cellular functions and physical properties required by furin for cleavage and for elucidating the molecular mechanisms.	S. Tian *et al.*, 2011
MoDiPath	SLiM Database grouped according to the KEGG pathway database.	http://www.biocomputing.it/modipath.	Identifies over-represented SLiMs in KEGG pathways in different organisms, and uses functional	A. Sayadi *et al.*, 2011

Contd.

			and structural annotation to assess their plausibility.	
CMD	Database of bonding states of cysteine motifs with secondary structures of proteins.	http://birg4.fbb.utm.my/cmd/	Information about the bonded, free cysteine residues, and their motifs that allows in-depth characterization of the sequence motif composition.	H. Bostan *et al.*, 2012
Minimotif Miner 3.0	Database for identifying new minimotifs in protein queries.	http://minimotifminer.org; http://mnm.engr.uconn.edu) of disease.	Predict new functions in proteins and causes	T. Mi *et al.*, 2012

4.0 METHODS AND ALGORITHMS

4.1 DNA Motif Discovery Methods

The amount of non-coding DNA is vast and that the methods for predicting functional transcription factor binding sites tend to produce results with a high percentage of false positives. Hence, finding regions significantly enriched in binding sites is difficult. A novel method was developed for predicting regulatory regions in DNA sequences, to find the evolutionary conservation of regulatory elements between species without assuming that the order of motifs is preserved across species [B. Wilczynski *et al.*, 2009]. A novel heuristic algorithm, TFBSGroup (http://bioinformatics.bioengr.uic.edu/TFBSGroup/), is able to identify nearly exact matches for long and weak (*l*, *d*) motifs in DNA sequences under the ZOMOPS constraint [C. Jia *et al*, 2013]. Sequential Monte Carlo motif identification algorithm (BAMBI) is based on a position weight matrix model that does not require additional constraints and is able to estimate motif properties such as length, logo, number of instances and their locations solely on the basis of primary nucleotide sequence data [G.H. Jajamovich et al, 2011].

DIMDom algorithm (DIscovering Motifs with DOMain knowledge) nu EM (Expectation-Maximization) appriach. Expectation step first finds the over-represented patterns in the DNA sequence. thereafter, maximization step predicts the class of binding site patterns on the basis of motif matric with the maxinum log likelihood. This step further modifies the motif matrix according to the predicted class. The binding sites with domain knowledge help to find the motif more quickly as compared with the MEME algorithm [H. C. M. Leung, et al, 2007].

Accurate prediction of DNA secondary structure and hybridization using dynamic programming algorithms requires a database of thermodynamic parameters for several motifs including Watson-Crick base pairs, internal mismatches, terminal mismatches, terminal dangling ends, hairpins, bulges, internal loops, and multibranched loops [J. S. Lucia and D. Hicks, 2004; J Shi *et al.*, 2011].

M.K. Das, 2007 classified the DNA motif finding algorithms into three major classes: 1) Finding motifs using promoter sequences from coregulated genes from a single genome; 2) Using orthologous promoter sequences of a single gene from multiple species through phylogenetic footprinting method; and 3) combination approach using promoter sequences of coregulated genes along with phylogenetic footprinting. Algorithms based on promoter sequences of coregulated genes are word-based algorithms, probabilistic algorithm, ensemble algorithm, machine learning techniques and others. The standard method used for phylogenetic footprinting constructs a global multiple alignment of the orthologous promoter sequences. Thereafter, identify the conserved region in the alignment using a tool such as CLUSTAL W. However, if the species are too closely related, the sequence alignment is obvious but uninformative, since the functional elements are not sufficiently better conserved than the surrounding non-functional sequence. On the other hand, if they are too distantly related, it is difficult or impossible to find an accurate alignment. [G. Badr *et al.*, 2013; P. Monsieurs *et al.* 2006; P.P. Kuksa and V. Pavlovic., 2010; R. Chauhan and P. Agarwal, 2012; R. Gordan et al., 2010]. To overcome this problem, motif finding algorithms such as MEME, Consensus, Gibbs sampler have been used for phylogenetic footprinting. These algorithms do not consider phylogenetic relationship of the given sequences and consider that input sequences are independent. Therefore, the data sets containing closely related species will have high weight for reported motifs. Even if these methods were modified to weigh the input sequences unequally, this would still not help in finding the information in an arbitrary phylogenetic tree. To overcome this problem, Blanchette and Tompa designed an algorithm for motif finding from phylogenetic footprinting using dynamic programming to find most parsimonious k-mer from each of the input sequences where k is the motif length [M. Blanchette and M. Tompa, 2003]. Is PHYLONET algorithm of systematically identifies phylogenetically conserved motifs by analyzing all the promoter sequences of related genomes and produces a network of regulatory sites for the organism. Statistical significance of motifs is estimated by Karlin-Altschul statistics. PhyloScan algorithm combines the evidence from matching sites found in orthologous data from several related species with evidence from multiple sites within an intergenic region to detect regulons. A new Gibbs sampling algorithm detected motif-encoding regions in sequences and optimally partitions them into distinct motif models. This was applied to find bacterial outer membrane protein repeats [A.F. Neuwald *et al*, 1995]. Among the three scanning algorithms, the MONKEY algorithm was found to have the highest accuracy for predicting yeast TFBSs [J. Hawkins *et al.*, 2009].

Discriminant analysis is a powerful statistical pattern recognition method for DNA sequence motif finding, such as splice site prediction, exon/introns prediction,translational start site prediction, polyadenylation site prediction and promoter prediction. Under this method, linear discriminant analysis (LDA) and quadratic discriminant analysis (QDA) methods were reported [M. Q. Zhang, 2000]. PairMotif, was proposed for planted (l, d) motif search (PMS) to effectively reduce both candidate motifs and scanned l-mers. Multiple pairs of lmers with relatively large distances were selected from input sequences to restrict the search space. Comparisons with several recently proposed algorithms show that PairMotif requires less storage space and runs faster on most PMS instances. Among the algorithms, only PairMotif can solve the weak instance within 10 hours. Moreover, the performance of PairMotif is stable over the sequence length, to identify motifs in longer sequences. The experimental results demonstrate the validity of the proposed algorithm [Q. Yu *et al.*, 2012].

4.2 RNA motif Discovery Methods

New grammar based method for RNA motifs search a sequence database for RNA structures with known functional sites (motifs). This applies the nested grammars to simultaneously integrate secondary structure, primary structure and biologically verified constraints[D. Quest et al, 2008]. RNAProfile algorithm is useful for finding conserved secondary structure motifs in unaligned RNA sequences [G. Pavesi *et al*, 2004].

RCrane helps crystallographers to place phosphates and bases into electron density this automatically predicts and builds the detailed all-atom structure of the traced nucleotides [K. S. Keating and A. M. Pyle, 2012].

GeRNAMo (Genetic programming of RNA Motifs), an evolutionary computation system searches for a common motif amongst the given data set of RNA sequences. GeRNAMo does not perform any sequence alignment. Furthermore, the genetic programming helps the system to explore the search space of motif structures in a reasonable amount of time. GeRNAMo [S. Michal *et al.*, 2007] was tested on various data sets with a known common motif, as well as on RNA data sets that do not have any known relations among them. GPRM was specifically designed to identify common secondary structure elements within a set of homologous or functionally related RNA sequences. GPRM operates on a population of possible RNA structure elements. GPRM utilizes genetic programming to explore the search space of RNA secondary structure elements [Y. J. Hu, 2003]. It has been tested on some datasets to verify other prediction systems as well as pseudoknots. MATLAB program, FR3D search 3D structure of a query motif and find and score geometrically similar candidate motifs. This does not consider to the sequential position of their nucleotides in the RNA chain or identity of their bases. This algorithm finds all candidate motifs whose geometric discrepancy with respect to query motif falls below a user specified cutoff discrepancy.

This technique can be applied to RMSD searches. Candidate motifs identified geometrically may be further screened symbolically to identify particular basepair types or base–stacking arrangements, sequence continuity or nucleotide identity constraints. The search algorithms have been optimized to allow users to search the non–redundant RNA 3D structure database on their personal computer in short duration. The geometric discrepancy takes into account the general shape of the candidate motif and the orientations of its bases [M. Sarver *et al.*, 2008]. RNA motif discovery algorithms [J. Gorodkin et al., 1997] were classified into two main classes: enumerative approaches and heuristics approaches. In enumerative approaches, the search space is exhaustively explored in order to discover overrepresented motifs. Algorithms in this class can be further divided into: dynamic programming-based approaches (DP), data structures-based approaches (DS), and graph-based approaches (GB). On the other hand, in heuristic approaches, only promising regions of the search are explored. Examples of algorithms in this class include: Expectation maximization and evolutionary algorithms. In addition, there are other heuristics specifically designed to tackle the motif discovery problem [G. Badr et al, 2013].

4.3 Protein Motif Discovery Methods

For the calculation of positional conservation in a protein sequence alignment, AL2CO program was developed. Three different approaches are implemented in the program, entropy, variance and matrix score based algorithms to define the conservation index [J. Pei and N. V. Grishin, 2001]. SLiMScape is an protein short linear motif plugin of cytoscape [K. T. O'Brien *et al.*, 2013].Knowledge about local protein sequence motifs is important for the analysis of biologically significant conserved regions of protein sequences. These conserved regions can potentially determine the diverse conformation and activities of proteins [I. Jonassen *et al.*, 2001; J. Glasgow *et al.*, 2010; N. J. Mulder and /R. Apweiler, 2001; S. Kt *et al.*, 2008; S. Ren *et al.*, 2008]. In this work, recurring sequence motifs of proteins are explored with an improved K-means clustering algorithm on a new dataset. The structural similarity of these recurring sequence clusters to produce sequence motifs is studied in order to evaluate the relationship between sequence motifs and their structures. In this apprach new greedy initialization method was proposed for the K-means algorithm to improve traditional K-means clustering techniques. The new initialization method tries to choose well separated initial points with the potential to form high-quality clusters. This improved K-means algorithm satisfactorily increased the percentage of sequence segments belonging to clusters with high structural similarity. Careful comparison of sequence motifs obtained by the improved and traditional algorithms also suggests that the improved K-means clustering algorithm may discover some relatively weak and subtle sequence motifs, which are undetectable by the traditional K-means algorithms. Experimental results also indicated that the improved K-means algorithm generated more detailed sequence motifs [W. Zhong *et al*, 2005]. Clustering approaches (Numerical clustering, Bayesian statistical clustering and Conceptual clustering) method depends on quantitative attributes such as inter-atomic, inter-residue distances, bond and torsion angles. Distance metrics are used to measure similarity or dissimilarity among data points and functional criteria measure the quality of the data partition. Non-clustering approaches includes graph-matching, feature selection and empirical folding of proteins. [T. Lin *et al.*, 2011]

5.0 APPLICATIONS

Eight drug resistant genes, beta-lactamase, metallo-beta-lactamase, vanB, mecA, norA, qacA, qacB and qacC of *Staphylococcus aureus* strain Mu50 were studied and their phylogenetic motifs were identified to predict evolutionary conserved functional residues. These motifs were further validated through domain search to locate their site and functionality in protein sequences [A.K. Kahlon *et al*, 2012]. The identification of structurally and functionally conserved residues in drug resistant target proteins could help in search of probable candidate drugs in future.

Calmodulin (CaM) is known for its cellular calcium sensor activity and is vital for many enzymes, cell cycle, ion channels and cellular signaling processes. Due to high degree of conservation in amino acid sequences of calmodulin among vertebrates suggested its functional importance to maintain interaction with a diverse family of CaM binding proteins. Three sequence motifs were identified for CaM interaction with a variety of CaM target proteins. Among these motifs, one is calcium independent (IQ motif) and other two are calcium dependent binding motifs (1-8-14 and 1-5-10 motifs). Although sequence diversity was seen among different binding regions but these three recognition motifs exist for most of the CaM binding proteins. Calcium independent CaM binding site in neuromodulin and neurogranin contains consensus sequence IQ motif (IQXXXRGXXXR) and is similar to IQ motif of cardiac myosin. This motif was identified in GTP binding receptors binding parathyroid hormone (PTH) and PTH related peptide, vasoactive intestinal peptide, glucagon-like peptide and are associated with calcium homeostasis, contraction and other neuronal effects. Calcium dependent CaM binding motifs were reported such as calcineurin, nitric oxide synthase, skeletal muscles, smooth muscles, α-fodrin, heat shock protein, calcium dependent protein kinase (CDPK) of *Arabidopsis thaliana*, soyabean, maize and other kinases in yeast and mouse, adenylyl cyclase of *Bordetella pertussis* and *Bacillus anthracis*. The inner hydrophobic residues at positions 5 and 8 of calcium dependent CaM binding proteins are highly conserved and may help to interact with hydrophobic patches of the COOH- and NH2-terminal domains of CaM for the binding process. They emphasized further structural evaluation of region of CaM binding proteins with CaM and their role in cellular function [A.R. Rhoads and F. Friedberg, 1997].

Phylogenetic motifs in 11 candidate genes involved in type 2 diabetes mellitus were reported to have functional importance due to evolutionary conservedness. The phylogenetic motif profiling approach identified key functional residues in sulfonylurea receptor, calpain10 enzyme, glucagon receptor, glucokinase, glucose transporter, transcription factor HNF4A, insulin receptor, potassium channel KCNJ11, lipoprotein lipase, transcription factor PPARG, regulatory subunit of phosphorylating enzyme. [A. Sharma *et al*, 2007], [D. La and D. R. Livesay, 2005; D. La *et al.*, 2005]

The B-class genes APETALA3 (AP3) and PISTILLATA (PI) in Arabidopsis thaliana and their orthologs in other species were used to study the development of petals and stamens in angiosperm flowers. Evolutionary analysis indicated that B-class genes have undergone multiple gene duplication events in angiosperms. Despite conservation over a wide evolutionary distance, the function of C-terminal motifs is not well understood. It was found that truncated forms of AP3 and PI, which lack the conserved C-terminal motifs, function to direct floral organ identity specification in Arabidopsis plants. It was concluded that the euAP3 and PI-derived motifs of AP3 and the PI motif of PI are not essential for floral organ identity function of AP3 and PI in Arabidopsis [E. Piwarzyk *et al*, 2007].

The knowledge about antibody scaffold helped to uncover unique and unpredictable positioning of the inhibitory loops to bind and inhibit protease function. The identification of a human inhibitory recombinant antibody A11 validated the reverse binding motif approach for using antibodies for selective inhibition of protease targets in cancer [E.L. Schneider *et al*, 2012].

The KEPE motif appeared to be restricted to the metazoan lineage and has three length variants—short, medium and long. This do not appear to interchange after screening human proteome using a regular expression based on the C/EBP motif [F. Diella *et al*, 2009].

Unmethylated cytosine-guanosine (CpG) sequences were reported as immunostimulatory component of microbial DNA and toll-like receptor 9 was identified as the receptor involved in CpG recognition. These CpG motifs of bacterial DNA are important for intestinal homeostasis and protects from intestinal inflammation through induction of regulatory mechanism in healthy organism. However, in chronic intestinal inflammation through induction of Th1 responses CpG/TLR9 interaction exacerbates inflammation of intestine [F. Obermeier *et al*, 2010].

The highly conserved amino acids glutamic acid/aspartic acid–arginine–tyrosine (i.e., the E/DRY motif) has a functional role with respect to regulating heptahelical G protein-coupled receptors PCR conformational states. It is considered that glutamic acid/aspartic acid maintains the receptor in its ground state because mutations frequently induce constitutive activity (CA). This hypothesis has been confirmed by the rhodopsin ground-state crystal structure and through computational modeling approaches. However, some class A

GPCRs are resistant to CA and suggested alternative roles for the glutamic acid/aspartic acid residue and the E/DRY motif. They proposed two different subgroups of receptors within class A GPCRs that make different use of the E/DRY motif, independent of the G protein type (Gs, Gi, or Gq) to which the receptor couples. In phenotype 1 receptors, non-conservative mutations of the glutamic acid/aspartic acid–arginine residues, also increase affinity for agonist binding, retain G protein coupling, and retain an agonist-induced response. Whereas, in second phenotype receptors, the E/DRY motif is more directly involved in governing receptor conformation and G protein coupling/recognition. Hence, mutations of the glutamic acid/aspartic acid residues do not induce CA. Thus, it is essential to study the rhodopsin ground-state model of conformational activation to explore the role of this highly conserved triplet in GPCR activation and function [G. E. Rovati *et al*, 2007].

Motif based tools were found useful on evolutionary analysis of multipartite single-stranded DNA viruses [H. L. Wang et al, 2013].

To find a statistically significant association between cis-regulatory motifs and functional gene sets, computational framework was developed to include a new statistical score for motif scanning, and use of different scores for predicting targets of different motifs. The recently sequenced genome of the jewel wasp, *Nasonia vitripennis* (a solitary species) was used along with the existing knowledge of motifs and gene annotations in fruitfly genome. Hence, applied the framework to find motifs associated with socially regulated gene sets in the honeybee, *Apis mellifera*, after comparisons with Nasonia, to identify honeybee-specific associations [J. Kim *et al*, 2010].

Finding significant nucleotide sequence motifs in prokaryotic genomes can be divided into three types of tasks: (1) supervised motif finding, where a sample of motif sequences is used to find other similar sequences in genomes; (2) unsupervised motif finding, which typically relates to the task of finding regulatory motifs and protein binding sites and (3) exploratory motif finding, which aims to identify potential functionally significant sequence motifs as those that are unusual in some statistical sense [J. Mrazek, 2009].

Structural homology of Gα proteins identified bifunctional structural motif at the N-terminal of these proteins. Structural motif is more widely applicable as a membrane-targeting and palmitoylation-determining signal. Homology models of all the different human Gá paralogs were generated using automated homology modeling, and the electrostatic potential of these proteins was calculated and visualized. A basic, positively charged, structural motif in the N-termini of heterotrimeric G proteins was identified. They presented the possibilities available for experimentalists to discover structural motifs that are not readily observed by analysis of the linear sequence [M. Kosloff *et al*, 2002].

Four conserved motifs among the RNA dependent polymerase encoding elements were identified in RNA viruses [O. Poch *et al.*, 1989].

The inactive protein precursors synthesized in the secretory pathway undergo proteolytic cleavage by furin to produce biologically active proteins. Furin has two main sub-cellular locations, trans-golgi network and cell surface. In the trans-golgi network, furing performs cleavage to activate host substrates such as extracellular matrix proteins, signaling peptides, growth factors, serum proteins, cell surface transmembrane receptors and ion channels. On the cell surface, it cleaves pathogenic substrates to activate bacterial toxins and viral fusion peptides. Furin cleavage of functional proteins leads to wide range of human diseases such as carcinogenesis, neurological disorders and pathogenic infections. Knowledge of furin cleavage site is important to elucidate molecular meachanisms, onset and progression of human diseases [S.Tian *et al*, 2011].

Monoubiquitylation is a regulatory signal to alter the activity, location or structure of a protein. Monoubiquitin signals are recognized by ubiquitin-binding proteins to transmit the regulatory information conferred by monoubiquitylation. The ubiquitin-binding motif (CUE motif) is an evolutionarily conserved monoubiquitin-binding domain and was required to mediate intramolecular monoubiquitylation [S.C.Shih *et al*, 2003].

Multiple motif scanning program was developed to scan the *Saccharomyces cerevisiae* proteome for Class I *S*-adenosylmethionine-dependent methyltransferases. This program considers the conserved number of amino acids between the motifs and output of the program contained ranked list of proteins that can be used to identify new methyltransferases and to reevaluate the assignment of previously identified putative methyltransferases [T. C. Petrossian and S. G. Clarke, 2009].

The majority of membrane enveloped viruses bud from infected cells after taking control over host ESCRT machinery to escape from host immune response. The knowledge of proline rich motifs (PRMs) recognition in the ESCRT pathway seems to be compatible with antiviral development. The P(S/T) AP motif is known as the major late domain of HIV-1, HTLV-1, Ebola, and many other characterized viruses. PPXY late domains of many viruses such as Rous sarcoma, Marburg, Ebola, and Rabies viruses recruit the Nedd4 family ligases WWP1, WWP2 and prickle to the site of virus budding. The LYPXnL motif, (where n=1 or 3) is another example of a Pro-containing ESCRT interacting sequence first discovered as a viral late domain. [X. Ren and J.H. Hurley, 2011].

Several areas of potentially great significance are currently emerging from the study of RNA structure and RNA structural motifs. These include RNA engineering and design, nanotechnology, the association of RNA structure with human disease and its treatment through drug design, siRNA, antisense, and ribozyme technology. Further more, the evolution of RNA and RNA motifs, their mutation patterns, and the conservation and identification of functional non-coding RNAs (ncRNAs) in genomic sequences [G. Pavesi et al., 2004].

6.0 LIMITATIONS

The methods for predicting functional transcription factor binding sites tend to produce results with a high percentage of false positives. This makes the problem of finding regions significantly enriched in binding sites difficult [B. Wilczynski *et al.*, 2009].

There are problems associated with SLiMs identification with low support with many motifs. Certain motifs which have low support and low information content are almost indistinguishable from random noise in most datasets. It is therefore important to reduce the search space by restricting the input to only those proteins (with emphasis on relevant regions of proteins) that are likely to contain the SLiM of interest. This reduction of search space has the greatest impact on reduction of false positives. These can be small scale analyses, such as probing a group of proteins which share a function, sub-cellular location or interacting partner. There can be large, genomic scale analyses, such as surveys of entire protein–protein interaction databases or GO term analysis.

Despite great efforts spent on RNA structural motif recognition and classification, there are several issues that remain unsolved. The first problem is that the molecular environment of the RNA structure models available in PDB is not given importance. Information about contacts between symmetry mates in a crystal is often ignored, despite its influence on local features of RNA structure and in some cases even on the global fold of the RNA. Large structures containing RNA molecules (e.g. the ribosome), models are split into several PDB files but may not be independent. Using the maximum resolution of diffraction data as a measure of structure quality but crystal structure model quality is a local property and must be locally validated. RNA Bricks database resolved these issues. This database provides information about local environments of the collected motifs, including contacts with other RNA motifs, proteins, metal ions, water molecules or small molecule ligands. RNA Bricks also stores data on contacts between symmetry mates in crystals and between molecules from split PDB entries (i.e. in huge structures divided into multiple files, due to the PDB file format restrictions). A unique feature of RNA Bricks is the availability of three structure-quality scores with single nucleotide resolution. These may be used to select most reliable subsets of stored RNA structures and motifs. This also implemented an algorithm for PDB-wide structure based searches.

7.0 FUTURE CHALLENGES

Different algorithmic strategies are used for assessing overrepresented binding sites in the sequences but limited success in higher eukaryotes. Failure of de novo motif discovery approaches [U. Keich and P. A. Pevzner, 2002; V. X. Jin *et al.*, 2009; W. Hugo *et al.*, 2010; W. B. Langdon and A. P. Harrison, 2009; Y. tomital *et al.*, 2008] to accurately detect motifs is due to statistical problems due to fixed size of co-regulated gene clusters also failure in detection of motifs do not necessarily signifies that unfound motifs are not active biologically. Prior knowledge enhances the motif discovery and is necessary too. Large molecular signalling networks due to advancement of system biology are increasingly mapped out. However understanding their dynamical behaviours have become the new challenge in biological research. Similar to the way engineers learn how electrical circuits function, biologists need to first discover and understand small network motifs and recurring sub-networks before undertaking the task of making sense of more complex biological networks [Q. Zhang *et al*, 2013].

8.0 CONCLUSION

Motif finding remains still a challenge for biologists and computer scientists due to incomplete understanding of system biology and biological processes or pathways in organisms. The discovery and characterization of these network motifs known as ultra-sensitive response motifs will continue to help bring systems-level perspectives to the quantitative investigation of existing and newly discovered biochemical pathways and about their attendant cellular outcomes [Q. Zhang *et al.*, 2013]. Researchers have developed and applied many different approaches in motif discovery and the progress made in this area of research is very encouraging. Performance comparison of different motif finding tools and identification of the best tools/algorithms have proven to be a difficult task. This is due to diverse and complex algorithms and motif models.

ACKNOWLEDGEMENTS

The authors acknowledge Department of Biotechnology (DBT), New Delhi, India for financial support under BTISnet programme.

REFERENCES

A. Bhaduri, G. Pugalenthi, N. Gupta and R. Sowdhamini. iMOT: an interactive package for the selection of spatially interacting motifs. Nucleic Acids Research 2004, 32: W602–W605.

A. Golovin and K. Henrick. MSDmotif: exploring protein sites and motifs. BMC Bioinformatics 2008, 9: 312.

A. Sayadi, L. Briganti, A. Tramontano and A. Via. Exploiting publicly available biological and biochemical information for the discovery of novel short linear motifs. PLoS ONE 2011, 6: e22270.

A.F. Neuwald, J.S. Liu and C.E. Lawrence. Gibbs motif sampling: Detection of bacterial outer membrane protein repeats. Protein Science 1995, 4: 1618-1632.

A. Goren, E. Kim, M. Amit, K. Vaknin, N. Kfir, O. Ram and G. Ast. Overlapping splicing regulatory motifs—combinatorial effects on splicing. Nucleic Acids Research 2010, 38: 3318-3327.

A. Henschel, C. Winter, W. K. Kim and M. Schroeder. Using structural motif descriptors for sequence-based binding site prediction. BMC Bioinformatics 2007, 8: S5.

A.I. Petrov, C.L. Zirbel and N. B. Leontis. Automated classification of RNA 3D motifs and the RNA 3D Motif Atlas. RNA 2013, 19: 1327-1340.

A. K. Kahlon, M. P. Darokar and A. Sharma. Probing the evolutionary conserved regions within functional site of drug-resistant target proteins of *Staphylococcus aureus*: *In silico* phylogenetic motif profiling approach. Indian Journal of Biochemistry and Biophysics 2012, 49: 442-450.

A. M. Moses, D. Y. Chiang and M. B. Eisen. Phylogenetic motif detection by expectation-maximization on evolutionary mixtures. Pacific Symposium on Biocomputing 2004, 9: 324-335.

A.P. Singh and D. L. Brutlag. Hierarchical protein structure superposition using both secondary structure and atomic representations. Proc. Int. Conf. Intell. Syst. Mol. Biol. 1997, 5: 284–293.

A.R. Rhoads and F. Friedberg. Sequence motifs for calmodulin recognition. The FASEB Journal 1997, 11: 331-340.

A. Sharma, T. Rastogi, M. Bhartiya, A. K. Shasany and S. P. S. Khanuja. Type 2 diabetes mellitus: phylogenetic motifs for predicting protein functional sites. Journal of Biosciences 2007, 32: 999-1004.

B. Wilczynski, N. Dojer, M. Patelak and J. Tiuryn. Finding evolutionarily conserved cis-regulatory modules with a universal set of motifs. BMC Bioinformatics 2009, 10: 82.

C.E. Grant, T.L. Bailey and W. S. Noble. FIMO: scanning for occurrences of a given motif. Bioinformatics 2011, 27: 1017–1018.

C. Jia, M.B. Carson and J. Yu. A fast weak motif-finding algorithm based on community detection in graphs. BMC Bioinformatics 2013, 14: 227.

C.M. Gould, F. Diella, A. Via, P. Puntervoll, C. Gemund, S. Chabanis-Davidson, S. Michael, A. Sayadi, J. C. Bryne, C. Chica, M. Seiler, N. E. Davey, N. Haslam, R. J. Weatheritt, A. Budd, T. Hughes, J. Pas, L. Rychlewski, G. Trave, R. Aasland, M. Helmer-Citterich, R. Linding and T.J. Gibson. ELM: the status of the 2010 eukaryotic linear motif resource. Nucleic Acids Research 2010, 38: D167–D180.

D. La and D.R. Livesay. Predicting functional sites with an automated algorithm suitable for heterogeneous datasets. BMC Bioinformatics 2005, 6: 116.

D. La, B. Sutch and D.R. Livesay. Predicting protein functional sites with phylogenetic motifs. Proteins: Structure, Function and Bioinformatics 2005, 58: 309-320.

D. Lee, O. Redfern and C. Orengo. Predicting protein function from sequence and structure. Nature Reviews Molecular Cell Biology 2007, 8: 995-1005.

D.K. Hendrix, S.E. Brenner and S.R. Holbrook. RNA structural motifs: building blocks of a modular biomolecule. Quarterly Reviews of Biophysics 2005, 38: 221–243.

D. La and D.R. Livesay. MINER: software for phylogenetic motif identification. Nucleic Acids Research 2005, 33: W267-W270.

D. Quest, K. Dempsey, M. Shafiullah, D. Bastola and H. Ali. MTAP: The motif tool assessment platform. BMC Bionformatics 2008, 9: S6.

D. S. Lieber, O. Elemento and S. Tavazoie. Large-scale discovery and characterization of protein regulatory motifs in eukaryotes. PLOS ONE 2010, 5: e14444.

D.T. Moore, B.W. Berger and W.F. DeGrado. Protein-protein interactions in the membrane: Sequence, structural, and biological motifs. Structure 2008, 16: 991–1001.

D. Wang and S. Tapan. MISCORE: a new scoring function for characterizing DNA regulatory motifs in promoter sequences. BMC Systems Biology 2012, 6: S4.

E. de Castro, C.J.A. Sigrist, A. Gattikar, V. Bulliard, P.S. Langendijk-Genevaux, E. Gasteiger, A. Bairoch and N. Hulo. ScanProsite: detection of PROSITE signature matches and ProRule-associated functional and structural residues in proteins. Nucleic Acids Research 2006, 34: W362-W365.

E. Larsson, P. Lindahl and P. Mostad. HeliCis: a DNA motif discovery tool for colocalized motif pairs with periodic spacing. BMC Bioinformatics 2007, 8: 418.

E. Piwarzyk, Y. Yang and T. Jack. Conserved C-terminal motifs of the Arabidopsis proteins APETALA3 and PISTILLATA are dispensable for floral organ identity function. Plant Physiology 2007, 145: 1495–1505.

E. Quevillon, V. Silventoinen, S. Pillai, N. Harte, N. Mulder, R. Apweiler and R. Lopez. InterProScan: protein domains identifier. Nucleic Acids Research 2005, 33: W116-W120.

E.C. Rouchka and C. T. Hardin. rMotifGen: random motif generator for DNA and protein sequences. BMC Bioinformatics 2007, 8: 292.

E. Kruus, P. Thumfort, C. Tang and N. S. Wingreen. Gibbs sampling and helix-cap motifs. Nucleic Acids Research 2005, 33: 5343–5353.

E. L. Schneider, M. S. Lee, A. Baharuddin, D. H. Goetz, C. J. Farady, M. Ward, C. I. Wang, C. S. Craik. A reverse binding motif that contributes to specific protease inhibition by antibodies. J Mol Biol 2012, 415: 699-715.

F. Diella, S. Chabanis, K. Luck, C. Chica, C. Ramu, C. Nerlov and T. J. Gibson. KEPE—a motif frequently superimposed on sumoylation sites in metazoan chromatin proteins and transcription factors. Bioinformatics 2009, 25: 1-5.

F. Mao, P. Dam, J. Chou, V. Olman and Y. Xu. DOOR: a database for prokaryotic operons. Nucleic Acids Research 2009, 37: D459–D463.

F. Obermeier, C. Hofmann and W. Falk. Inflammatory bowel diseases: When natural friends turn into enemies—The importance of CpG motifs of bacterial DNA in intestinal homeostasis and chronic intestinal inflammation. International Journal of Inflammation 2010, doi:10.4061/2010/641910.

F. Bristow, R. He and G. V. Domselaar. GOmotif: A web server for investigating the biological role of protein sequence motifs. BMC Bioinformatics 2011, 12: 379.

G. Badr, I. A. Turaiki, H. Mathkour. Classification and assessment tools for structural motif discovery algorithms. BMC Bioinformatics 2013, 14:S4.

G. Chojnowski, T. Walen and J. M. Bujnicki. RNA Bricks—a database of RNA 3D motifs and their interactions. Nucleic Acids Research, 2014, 42:D123-31.

G. Ciriello and C. Guerra. A review on models and algorithms for motif discovery in protein-protein interaction networks. Briefings in Functional Genomics and Proteomics 2008, 7: 147-156.

G. E. Rovati, V. Capra and R. R. Neubig. The highly conserved DRY motif of class A G protein-coupled receptors: Beyond the ground state. Mol Pharmacol 2007, 71: 959–964.

G. Grillo, F. Licciulli, S. Liuni, E. Sbisa and G. Pesole. PatSearch: a program for the detection of patterns and structural motifs in nucleotide sequences. Nucleic Acids Research 2003, 31: 3608–3612.

G. Maccari, F. Gemignani and S. Landi. COMPASSS (COMplex Pattern of Sequence Search Software), a simple and effective tool for mining complex motifs in whole genomes. Bioinformatics 2010, 26: 1777-1778.

G. Pavesi, G. Mauri, M. Stefani and G. Pesole. RNAProfile: an algorithm for finding conserved secondary structure motifs in unaligned RNA sequences. Nucleic Acids Research 2004, 32: 3258-3269.

G. Pugalenthi, P. N. Suganthan, R. Sowdhamini and S. Chakrabarti. MegaMotifBase: a database of structural motifs in protein families and superfamilies. Nucleic Acids Research 2008, 36: D218–D221.

G. E. Crooks, G. Hon, J. M. Chandonia, and S. E. Brenner. WebLogo: A sequence logo generator. Genome Research 2004, 14:1188–1190.

G.H. Jajamovich, X. Wang, A. P. Arkin, M. S. Samoilov. Bayesian multiple-instance motif discovery with BAMBI: inference of recombinase and transcription factor binding sites. Nucleic Acids Research 2011, 39: e146.

H. Dinh, S. Rajasekaran, J. Davila. qPMS7: A Fast Algorithm for Finding (l, d)-Motifs in DNA and Protein Sequences. PLoS ONE 2012, 7: e41425.

H. Tiedge. K-turn motifs in spatial RNA coding. RNA Biol. 2006, 3: 133–139.

H. Bostan, N. Salim, Z. A. Hussein, P. Klappa and M. S. Shamsir. CMD: A database to store the bonding states of cysteine motifs with secondary structures. Advances in Bioinformatics Vol. 2012, doi: 10.1155/2012/849830.

H. C. M. Leung, F. Y. L. Chin and B. M. Y. Chan. Discovering motifs with transcription factor domain knowledge. Pacific Symposium on Biocomputing 2007, 12: 472-483.

H. Cheng, B. H. Kim and N. V. Grishin. MALISAM: a database of structurally analogous motifs in proteins. Nucleic Acids Research 2008, 36: D211–D217.

H. L. Wang, C. H. Chang, P.H. Lin, H. C. Fu, C.Y. Tang, H. H. Yeh. Application of motif based tools on evolutionary analysis of multipartite single-stranded DNA viruses. PLoS ONE 2013, 8: e71565.

I. Jonassen, I. Eidhammer, D. Conklin and W.R. Taylor. Structure motif discovery and mining the PDB. Bioinformatics 2001, 18: 362-367.

I. Jonassen, J. F. Collins and D. G. Higgins. Finding flexible patterns in unaligned protein sequences. Protein Science 1995, 4: 1587-1595.

I. Ovcharenko and M. A. Nobrega. Identifying synonymous regulatory elements invertebrate genomes. Nucleic Acids Research, 2005, 33:W403–W407.

I. Ovcharenko, G. G. Loots, R. C. Hardison, W. Miller and L. Stubbs. zPicture: dynamic alignment and visualization tool for analyzing conservation profiles. Genome Res. 2004, 14: 472-477.

I. Paz, M. Akerman, I. Dror, I. Kosti and Y. M. Gutfreund. SFmap: a web server for motif analysis and prediction of splicing factor binding sites. Nucleic Acids Research 2010, 38: W281–W285.

J. Glasgow, E. Steeg and S. Fortier. Motif discovery in protein structure databases. Book Chapter "Pattern discovery in molecular biology: Tools, techniques and applications" by Jason Wang, Bruce Shapiro and Dennis Sha sha (Eds.), Oxford University press. (2010)

J. Gorodkin, L. J. Heyer and G. D. Stormo. Finding the most significant common sequence and structure motifs in a set of RNA sequences. Nucleic Acids Research 1997, 25: 3724–3732.

J. Grau, J. Keilwagen, A. Gohr, I. A. Paponov, S. Posch, M. Seifert, M. Strickert and I. Grosse. Dispom: a discriminative de-novo motif discovery tool based on jstacs library. J Bioinform Comput Biol 2013, 11: 1340006.

J. Kim, R. Cunningham, B. James, S. Wyder, J. D. Gibson, O. Niehuis, E. M. Zdobnov, H. M. Robertson, G. E. Robinson, J. H. Werren, S. Sinha. Functional characterization of transcription factor motifs using cross-species comparison across large evolutionary distances. PLoS Comput Biol 2010, 6: e1000652.

J. Mrazek. Finding sequence motifs in prokaryotic genomes- a brief practical guide for a microbiologist. Briefings in Bioinformatics 2009, 10: 525-536.

J. Pei and N. V. Grishin. AL2CO: Calculation of positional conservation in a protein sequence alignment. Bioinformatics 2001, 17: 700-712.

J. Reeder, J. Reeder and R. Giegerich. Locomotif: from graphical motif description to RNA motif search. Bioinformatics 2007, 23: i392-i400.

J. Shapiro and D. Brutlag. FoldMiner: Structural motif discovery using an improved superposition algorithm. Protein Science 2004, 13: 278-294.

J. Hawkins, C. Grant, W. S. Noble and T. L. Bailey. Assessing phylogenetic motif models for predicting transcription factor binding sites. Bioinformatics 2009, 25: i339–i347.

J. S. Lucia and D. Hicks. The thermodynamics of DNA structural motifs. Annu. Rev. Biophys. Biomol. Struct. 2004, 33:415–40.

J. Shi, W. Yang, M. Chen, Y. Du, J. Zhang and K. Wang. AMD, an automated motif discovery tool using stepwise refinement of gapped consensuses. PLoS ONE 2011, 6: e24576.

J. Y. Huang and D. L. Brutlag. The EMOTIF database. Nucleic Acids Research, 2001, 29: 202-204.

K. Degtyarenko. Bioinorganic motifs: towards functional classification of metalloproteins. Bioinformatics 2000, 16: 851-864.

K. Horan, C. R. Shelton and T. Girke. Predicting conserved protein motifs with Sub-HMMs. BMC Bioinformatics 2010, 11: 205.

K. Klepper and F. Drablos. MotifLab: a tools and data integration workbench for motif discovery and regulatory sequence analysis. BMC Bioinformatics 2013, 14: 9.

K. Kang, J. H. Chung and J. Kim. Evolutionary Conserved Motif Finder (ECMFinder) for genome-wide identification of clustered YY1- and CTCF-binding sites. Nucleic Acids Research 2009, 37: 2003–2013.

K. Kechris and H. Li. c-REDUCE: Incorporating sequence conservation to detect motifs that correlate with expression. BMC Bioinformatics 2008, 9: 506.

K. L. Jensen, M. P. Styczynski, I. Rigoutsos and G. N. Stephanopoulos. A generic motif discovery algorithm for sequential data. Bioinformatics 2006, 22: 21-28.

K. S. Keating and A. M. Pyle. RCrane: semi-automated RNA model building. Acta Crystallographica 2012, D68: 985–995.

K. T. O'Brien, N. J. Haslam and D. C. Shields. SLiMScape: a protein short linear motif analysis plugin for cytoscape. BMC Bioinformatics 2013, 14:224.

K. T. Schroeder, S. A. Mcphee, J. Ouellet and D. M. J. Lilley. A structural database for k-turn motifs in RNA. RNA 2010, 16: 1463-1468.

L. Kuttippurathu, M. Hsing, Y. Liu, B. Schmidt, D. L. Maskell, K. Lee, A. He, W. T. Pu and S. W. Kong. CompleteMOTIFS: DNA motif discovery platform for transcription factor binding experiments. Bioinformatics 2011, 27: 715-717.

L. Leibovich, I. Paz, Z. Yakhini and Y. Mandel-Gutfreund. DRIMust: a web server for discovering rank imbalanced motifs using suffix trees. Nucleic Acids Research, 2013, 1–6. doi:10.1093/nar/gkt407.

L. Narlikar, R. Gordon, U. Ohler and A. J. Hartemink. Informative priors based on transcription factor structural class improve de novo motif discovery. Bioinformatics 2006, 22: e384-e392.

L. Salwinski and D. Eisenberg. Motif-based fold assignment. Protein Science 2001, 10: 2460-2469.

L. A. Chasin. Searching for splicing motifs. Alternative Splicing in the Post genomic Era, edited by Benjamin J. Blencowe and Brenton R. Graveley. ©2007 Landes Bioscience.

L. Yang, T. Zhou, I. Dror, A. Mathelier, W. W. Wasserman, R. Gordan and R. Rohs. TFBSshape: a motif database for DNA shape features of transcription factor binding sites. Nucleic Acids Research 2014, 42: D148-55.

M. Blanchette and M. Tompa. FootPrinter: a program designed for phylogenetic footprinting. Nucleic Acids Research 2003, 31: 3840-3842.

M. Csuros. Count: evolutionary analysis of phylogenetic profiles with parsimony and likelihood. Bioinformatics 2010, 26: 1910-1912.

M. Kankainen and A. Loytynoja. MATLIGN: a motif clustering, comparison and matching tool. BMC Bioinformatics 2007, 8: 189.

M. Mihara, T. Itoh and T. Izawa. SALAD database: a motif-based database of protein annotations for plant comparative genomics. Nucleic Acids Research 2010, 38: D835–D842.

M. Pagni, V. Loannidis, L. Cerutti, M. Zahn-Zabal, C. V. Jongeneel and L. Falquet. MyHits: a new interactive resource for protein annotation and domain identification. Nucleic Acids Research 2004, 32: W332–W335.

M. Parras-Molto, F. J. Campos-Laborie, J. Garcia-Dieguez, M. R. Rodriguez-Grinolo and A. J. Perez-Pulido. Classification of protein motifs based on subcellular localization uncovers evolutionary relationships at both sequence and functional levels. BMC Bioinformatics 2013, 14:229.

M. Rabani, M. Kertesz and E. Segal. Computational prediction of RNA structural motifs involved in post-transcriptional regulatory processes. PNAS 2008, 105: 14885–14890.

M. Rabani, M. Kertesz and E. Segal. Computational prediction of RNA structural motifs involved in post-transcriptional regulatory processes. Methods in Molecular Biology 2011, 714: 467-479.

M. K. Choy, M. Movassagh, H. G. Goh, M. R. Bennett, T. A. Down, R. S. Y. Foo. Genome-wide conserved consensus transcription factor binding motifs are hyper-methylated. BMC Genomics 2010, 11:519.

M. K. Das and H. K. Dai. A survey of DNA motif finding algorithms.BMC Bioinformatics 2007, 8: S21.

M. Kosloff, N. Elia and Z. Selinger. Structural homology discloses a bifunctional structural motif at the N-termini of Gá proteins. Biochemistry 2002, 41: 14518-14523.

M. Q. Zhang. Discriminant analysis and its application in DNA sequence motif recognition. Briefings in Bioinformatics 2000, 1: 331-342.

M. Sarver, C. L. Zirbel, J. Stombaugh, A. Mokdad, N. B. Leontis. FR3D: Finding local and composite recurrent structural motifs in RNA 3D structures. Journal of Mathematical Biology 2008, 56: 215-252.

M. Y. Niv, L. Skrabanek, R. J. Roberts, H. A. Scheraga and H. Weinstein. Identification of GATC- and CCGG- recognizing Type II REases and their putative specificity-determining positions using Scan2S—a novel motif scan algorithm with optional secondary structure constraints. Proteins 2008, 71: 631–640.

N. Tuteja and R. Tuteja. Unraveling DNA helicases: Motif, structure, mechanism and function. European Journal of Biochemistry 2004, 271: 1849–1863.

N. B. Leontis and E. Westhof. The annotation of RNA motifs. Comparative and Functional Genomics 2002, 3: 518–524.

N. E. Davey, D. C. Shields and R. J. Edwards. SLiMDisc: short, linear motif discovery, correcting for common evolutionary descent. Nucleic Acids Research 2006, 34: 3546-3554.

N. E. Davey, N. J. Haslam, D. C. Shields and R. J. Edwards. SLiMFinder: a web server to find novel, significantly over-represented, short protein motifs. Nucleic Acids Research 2010, 38: W534-W539.

N. E. Ihuegbu, G. D. Stormo and J. Buhler. Fast, sensitive discovery of conserved genome-wide motifs. Journal of Computational Biology 2012, 19: 139-147.

N. J. Mulder and R. Apweiler. Tools and resources for identifying protein families, domains and motifs. Genome Biology 2001, 3: 1-8.

O. Poch, I. Sauvaget, M. Delarue and N. Tordo. Identification of four conserved motifs among the RNA dependent polymerase encoding elements. The EMBO Journal 1989, 8:3867-3874.

P. D'haeseleer. What are DNA sequence motifs? Nature Biotechnology 2006, 24: 423-425.

P. Monsieurs, G. Thijs, A. A. Fadda, S. C. J. D. Keersmaecker, J. Vanderleyden, B. D. Moor and K. Marchal. More robust detection of motifs in coexpressed genes by using phylogenetic information. BMC Bioinformatics 2006, 7:160.

P. Scordis, D. R. Flower and T. K. Attwood. FingerPRINTScan: intelligent searching of the PRINTS motif database. Bioinformatics 1999, 15: 799-806.

P. M. Haverty and Z. Weng. CisML: an XML-based format for sequence motif detection software. Bioinformatics 2004, 20: 1815-1817.

P. P. Kuksa and V. Pavlovic. Efficient motif finding algorithms forlarge-alphabet inputs. BMC Bioinformatics 2010, 11:S1.

P. Ray, S. Shringarpure, M. Kolar, E. P. Xing. CSMET: Comparative genomic motif detection via multi-resolution phylogenetic shadowing. PLoS Comput Biol 2008, 4: e1000090.

P. S. Dehal, M. P. Joachimiak, M. N. Price, J. T. Bates, J. K. Baumohl, D. Chivian, G. D. Friedland, K. H. Huang, K. Keller, P. S. Novichkov, I. L. Dubchak, E. J. Alm and A. P. Arkin. MicrobesOnline: an integrated portal for comparative and functional genomics. Nucleic Acids Research 2010, 38: D396–D400.

P. S. Klosterman, D. K. Hendrix, M. Tamura, S. R. Holbrook and S. E. Brenner. Three-dimensional motifs from the SCOR, structural classification of RNA database: extruded strands, base triples, tetraloops and U-turns. Nucleic Acids Research 2004, 32: 2342-2352.

Q. Yu, H. Huo, Y. Zhang, H. Guo. PairMotif: A new pattern-driven algorithm for planted (l, d) DNA motif search. PLoS ONE 2012, 7: e48442.

Q. Zhang, S. Bhattacharya and M. E. Andersen. Ultrasensitive response motifs: basic amplifiers in molecular signaling networks. Open Biol 2013, 3: 130031.

R. Chauhan and P. Agarwal. A Review: Applying Genetic Algorithms for Motif Discovery. International Journal of Computer Technology and Applications 2012, 3: 1510-1515.

R. Gordan, L. Narlikar and A. J. Hartemink. Finding regulatory DNA motifs using alignment-free evolutionary conservation information. Nucleic Acids Research 2010, 38: e90.

R. Gutman, C. Berezin, R. Wollman, Y. Rosenberg and N. Ben-Tal. QuasiMotiFinder: protein annotation by searching for evolutionarily conserved motif-like patterns. Nucleic Acids Research 2005, 33: W255–W261.

R. Kuang, J. Weston, W. S. Noble and C. Leslie. Motif-based protein ranking by network propagation. Bioinformatics 2005, 21: 3711-3718.

R. Nussinov and H. J. Wolfson. Efficient detection of three-dimensional structural motifs in biological macromolecules by computer vision techniques. Proceedings of National Academy Sciences USA 1991, 88:10495-10499.

R. Siddharthan, E. D. Siggia and E. V. Nimwegen. PhyloGibbs: A Gibbs sampling motif finder that incorporates phylogeny. PLoS Computational Biology 2005, 1: e67.

R. G. Beiko and R. L. Charlebois. GANN: Genetic algorithm neural networks for the detection of conserved combinations of features in DNA. BMC Bioinformatics 2005, 6: 36.

R. G. Brennan and B. W. Matthews. The Helix-Turn-Helix DNA Binding Motif. The Journal of Biological Chemistry 1989, 264: 1903-1906.

R. Z. Cer, D. E. Donohue, U. S. Mudunuri, N. A. Temiz, M. A. Loss, N. J. Starner, G. N. Halusa, N. Volfovsky, M. Yi, B. T. Luke, A. Bacolla, J. R. Collins and R. M. Stephens. Non-B DB v2.0: a database of predicted non-B DNA-forming motifs and its associated tools. Nucleic Acids Research 2013, 41: D94–D100.

S. Jones, J. A. Barker, I. Nobeli and J. M. Thornton. Using structural motif templates to identify proteins with DNA binding function. Nucleic Acids Research 2003, 31: 2811-2823.

S. Ke, X. H. F. Zhang and L. A. Chasin. Positive selection acting on splicing motifs reflects compensatory evolution. Genome Research 2008, 18: 533-543.

S. Mahony and P. V. Benos. STAMP: a web tool for exploring DNA-binding motif similarities. Nucleic Acids Research 2007, 35:W253–W258.

S. Mahony, A. Golden, T. J. Smith and P. V. Benos. Improved detection of DNA motifs using a self-organized clustering of familial binding profiles. Bioinformatics 2005, 21: i283-i291.

S. Maurer-Stroh and F. Eisenhaber. Refinement and prediction of protein prenylation motifs. Genome Biology 2005, 6:R55.

S. Michal, T. Ivry, O. Schalit-Cohen, M. Sipper and D. Barash. Finding a common motif of RNA sequences using genetic programming: The GeRNAMo system. IEEE/ACM Transactions on Computational Biology and Bioinformatics 2007, 4: 596-610.

S. Ren, V. N. Uversky, Z. Chen, A. K. Dunker and Z. Obradovic. Short linear motifs recognized by SH2, SH3 and Ser/Thr Kinase domains are conserved in disordered protein regions. BMC Genomics 2008, 9:S26.

S. Sinha, M. Blanchette and M. Tompa. PhyME: A probabilistic algorithm for finding motifs in sets of orthologous sequences. BMC Bioinformatics 2004, 5: 170.

S. Tian, Q. Huang, Y. Fang and J. Wu. FurinDB: A Database of 20-residue Furin cleavage site motifs, substrates and their associated drugs. International Journal of Molecular Sciences 2011, 12: 1060-1065.

S. C. Shih, G. Prag, S. A. Francis, M. A. Sutanto, J. H. Hurley and L. Hicke. A ubiquitin-binding motif required for intramolecular monoubiquitylation, the CUE domain. The EMBO Journal 2003, 22: 1273-1281.

S. Gupta, J. A. Stamatoyannopoulos, T. L. Bailey and W. S. Noble. Quantifying similarity between motifs. Genome Biology 2007, 8: R24.

S. H. Chou, K. H. Chin and A. H. J. Wang. Unusual DNA duplex and hairpin motifs. Nucleic Acids Research 2003, 31: 2461-2474.

S. J. H. Sui, D. L. Fulton, D. J. Arenillas, A. T. Kwon and W. W. Wasserman. oPOSSUM: integrated tools for analysis of regulatory motif over-representation. Nucleic Acids Research 2007, 35: W245–W252.

S. P. Bennette, L. Lu and D. L. Brutlag. 3MATRIX and 3MOTIF: a protein structure visualization system for conserved sequence motifs. Nucleic Acids Research 2003, 31: 3328-3332.

S. Ren, G. Yang, Y. He, Y. Wang, Y. Li and Z. Chen. The conservation pattern of short linear motifs is highly correlated with the function of interacting protein domains. BMC Genomics 2008, 9:452.

S. T. Jensen, L. Shen and J. S. Liu. Combining phylogenetic motif discovery and motif clustering to predict co-regulated genes. Bioinformatics 2005, 21: 3832-3839.

T. Lin, R. F. Murphy, Z. Bar-Joseph. Discriminative motif finding for predicting protein subcellular localization. IEEE/ACM Transactions on Computational Biology and Bioinformatics 2011, 8: 441-451.

T. Mi, J. C. Merlin, S. Deverasetty, M. R. Gryk, T. J. Bill, A. W. Brooks, L. Y. Lee, V. Rathnayake, C. A. Ross, D. P. Sargeant, C. L. Strong, P. Watts, S. Rajasekaran and M. R. Schiller. Minimotif Miner 3.0: database expansion and significantly improved reduction of false-positive predictions from consensus sequences. Nucleic Acids Research 2012, 40: D252-D260.

T. C. Petrossian and S. G. Clarke. Multiple motif scanning to identify methyltransferases from the yeast proteome. Molecular and Cellular Proteomics 2009, 8: 1516–1526.

T. J. Macke, D. J. Ecker, R. R. Gutell, D. Gautheret, D. A. Case and R. Sampath. RNAMotif, an RNA secondary structure definition and search algorithm. Nucleic Acids Research 2001, 29: 4724-4735.

T. K. Attwood, M. E. Beck, A. J. Bleasby and D. J. Parry-Smith. PRINTS: A database of protein motif fingerprints. Nucleic Acids Research 1994, 22: 3590-3596.

T. L. Bailey, M. Boden, F. A. Buske, M. Frith, C. E. Grant, L. Clementi, J. Ren, W. W. Li and W. S. Noble. MEME Suite: tools for motif discovery and searching. Nucleic Acids Research 2009, 37: W202–W208.

T. Okumura, H. Makiguchi, Y. Makita, R.Yamashita and K. Nakai. Melina II: a web tool for comparisons among several predictive algorithms to find potential motifs from promoter regions. Nucleic Acids Research 2007, 35: W227–W231.

T. Wang. Using PhyloCon to identify conserved regulatory motifs. Current Protocols in Bioinformatics. 2007, 19: 2.12.1-2.12.29.

U. Keich and P. A. Pevzner. Subtle motifs: Defining the limits of motif finding algorithms. Bioinformatics 2002, 18: 1382-1390.

V. Neduva and R. B. Russell. DILIMOT: Discovery of linear motifs in proteins. Nucleic Acids Research 2006, 34: W350-W355.

V. X. Jin, J. Apostolos, N. S. V. R. Nagisetty and P. J. Farnham. W-ChIPMotifs: a web application tool for de novo motif discovery from ChIP-based high-throughput data. Bioinformatics 2009, 25: 3191-3193.

W. Hugo, F. Song, Z. Aung, S. K. Ng and W. K. Sung. SLiM on Diet: finding short linear motifs on domain interaction interfaces in Protein Data Bank. Bioinformatics 2010, 26: 1036-1042.

W. V. Graham, D. K. Tcheng, A. L. Shirk, M. S. Attene-Ramos, M. E. Welge and H. R. Gaskins. Phylomat: An automated protein motif analysis tool for phylogenomics. Journal of Proteome Research 2004, 3: 1289-1291.

W. Zhong, G. Altun, R. Harrison, P.C. Tai and Y. Pan. Improved K-Means Clustering Algorithm for Exploring Local Protein Sequence Motifs Representing Common Structural Property. IEEE Transactions on Nanobioscience 2005, 4: 255-265.

W. B. Langdon and A. P. Harrison. Evolving DNA motifs to predict GeneChip probe performance. Algorithms for Molecular Biology 2009, 4: 6.

X. Cai, H. Hu and X. S. Li. Tree Gibbs Sampler: identifying conserved motifs without aligning orthologous sequences. Bioinformatics 2007, 23: 2013-2014.

X. Ren and J. H. Hurley. Proline-rich regions and motifs in trafficking: From ESCRT interaction to viral exploitation. Traffic 2011, 12: 1282–1290.

X. I. Liu, N. Korde, U. Jakob and L. I. Leichert. CoSMoS: Conserved sequence motif search in the proteome. BMC Bioinformatics 2006, 7:37.

X. Xie, P. Rigor and P. Baldi. MotifMap: a human genome-wide map of candidate regulatory motif sites. Bioinformatics 2009, 25:167–174.

Y. Liu, X. S. Liu, L. Wei, R. B. Altman and S. Batzoglou. Eukaryotic regulatory element conservation analysis and identification using comparative genomics. Genome Research 2004, 14: 451-458.

Y. J. Hu. GPRM: a genetic programming approach to finding common RNA secondary structure elements. Nucleic Acids Research 2003, 31: 3446-3449.

Y. Tomita, R. Kato, M. Okochi and H. Honda. A motif detection and classification method for peptide sequences using genetic programming. Journal of Bioscience and Bioengineering 2008, 106: 154-161.

Z. Yao, Z. Weinberg and W. L. Ruzzo. CMfinder—a covariance model based RNA motif finding algorithm. Bioinformatics 2006, 22: 445-452.

❑❑❑

CHAPTER - 14

Emerging Application of Proteomics in Realms of Aquaculture Nutrition, Health and Flesh Quality Management

Arun B. Patel
Associate Professor & Head, Department of Aquaculture, College of Fisheries, CAU, Lembucherra, Tripura-799210

1 INTRODUCTION

Aquaculture has been growing at higher rate than any other animal food-producing sector globally with Asia dominating the production. Considering the higher consumer demand for aquatic animal food, coupled with stagnating harvest from capture fisheries the rapid growth of aquaculture is expected to continue in the future. For instance, the global production of farmed food fish including finfishes, crustaceans, molluscs, amphibians (frogs), aquatic reptiles (except crocodiles) and other aquatic animals such as sea cucumbers, sea urchins, sea squirts and jellyfishes was 59.9 million metric tones (mmt), up by 7.5 percent from 55.7 mmt in 2009 (FAO, 2012). Asia accounted for 89 percent of world aquaculture production by volume in 2010 with China alone accounting for more than 60 percent of global aquaculture production volume in 2010. The other major producers in Asia are India (4.65 mmt), Viet Nam (2.67 mmt), Indonesia (2.30 mmt), Bangladesh (1.31mmt), Thailand (1.29 mmt), Myanmar (0.85mmt), the Philippines (0.74 mmt) and Japan (0.72 mmt). Further, in light of increasing population pressure on land, intensification of aquaculture practices has been taking place and now two-third of all food fish production aquaculture is achieved with artificial feeding (FAO, 2012). In recent years it also has become apparent that aquaculture production is vulnerable to adverse impacts of diseases and environmental conditions as farmed organisms are susceptible to a wide range of factors that can pose a major threat to a thriving aquaculture industry with considerable economical repercus-sions. For instance, in 2010, aquaculture in China suffered production losses of 1.7 million tonnes caused by natural disasters, diseases and pollution. Disease outbreaks virtually wiped out marine shrimp farming production in Mozambique in 2011 (FAO, 2012). In addition, impacts of culture environment, and harvest and post-harvest handlings on flesh quality are also increasingly becoming important issues.

Therefore, one of the main objectives of aquaculture is to produce fish with an optimal growth rate and health status in sustainable manner. From a physiological point of view, fish growth is a complex process that apart from genetic background depends on other mutually interdependent processes, such as development, nutrition, metabolism and physiological stress. Since growth is a physiological process with multiple tissue contributions (e.g. liver, intestine, pan-creas and muscle), a multidisciplinary approach is required in order to have a complete view of all the factors contributing to growth. Furthermore, as consumers become more and more aware about the production methods and get concerned with issues of ethical production, animal treatment and welfare, and environment-friendly production systems as well as sustainability, these may affect their buying choices. It is to be considered that the culture environment in which a fish is reared and then in a manner it is slaughtered may have an impact upon both production and flesh quality. These factors have led to considerable interest both in indices of good welfare and in development of production systems or technologies that promote it. Balancing current productivity standards with higher disease and stress resistance, feed efficiency to lower environmental impact, ability to use more sustainable fish ingredients (e.g. vegetable proteins and oils) are increasingly being important more than ever before.

The present chapter is an attempt to review the potential application of proteomics in the realms of abovementioned themes like aquaculture nutrition, health and flesh quality management for a better elucidation of different physiological mechanisms and responses with an objective of contributing to the optimization of aquaculture production with sustainability perspectives.

2. PROTEOMICS IN AQUACULTURE

During the last decade proteomics has emerged as a powerful tool towards deepening the understanding of aquaculture organisms' biology and functional networks that govern the process of growth in fish. The resultant understandings may potentially help aquaculture to achieve the goal of sustainable high productivity of a better quality product. Notably, compared to genomics, proteomics provides not only information at a mechanistic level but can also capture changes in protein activity measured as post-translational modifications (PTMs). As is established, the transcriptome does not account for the post-transcriptional and post-translational regulation of protein expression and most studies reveal a poor correlation between protein expression and changes in transcript level (Pandey & Mann, 2000). The proteome can then provide relevant information of an organism's physiological state that is missed by the transcriptome. Interpretation of proteomic data requires availability of information on genomic DNA and expressed RNAs, however as reviewed by Rodrigues *et al.* (2012), there is a general paucity of information at the genome level in most of the 541 species or species groups of aquatic animals being currently utilized in aquaculture including 327 fish species (FAO, 2012). Full genomes are still only available for some model species such as zebra fish, stickleback, medaka, coelacanth, fugu and Tetraodon, although more focus is being given lately to studying the genomes of commercial species (like tilapia, cod and salmon). As a result, proteomic studies on aquaculture species still face great deal of challenges at the level of protein identification. Nevertheless, recent developments in genome sequencing technologies have brought down the cost associated with full genome sequencing from hundreds of thousands to thousands of dollars, suggesting that the availability of genomic and EST data on aquaculture organisms will not remain a bottleneck in aquaculture proteomics for long (Rodrigues *et al.*, 2012).

3. PROTEOMIC TECHNOLOGIES

The proteomic technologies that have been employed to obtain data regarding teleost fishes and invertebrate species may be broadly categorized into gel-based or gel-free approaches. The common workflow in both approaches includes: 1) sample preparation; 2) protein separation and quantification; and, 3) Protein identification and characterization, albeit with certain differences. A brief description follows:

I. Gel Based Approach

a. **Sample preparation:** First of all, protein from a given bodily fluid, organ, tissue or cell extract is extracted through solublization in appropriate solvents like aqueous buffer and organic solvents so as to target all or a specific subset of the proteins of interest. Besides buffering agents, commonly used aqueous extraction buffers often contain detergents, chaotropes (structure-brakers), reducing agents and protease inhibitors, ensuring that enzymatic activity is halted during extraction and that intra and inter-molecular interactions between proteins are minimized, preventing aggregation. To improve protein separation and identification, several procedures may be employed. Sample fractionation based on chromatography, electrophoresis, differential solubility and/or (ultra) centrifugation is often employed as sample pre-processing prior to proteome analysis, simplifying protein extracts and/or improving the dynamic range of a protein mixture.

b. **Protein separation and quantification.** The two most important analytical techniques in proteomics are two-dimensional gel electrophoresis (2-DE) and mass spectrometry (MS). Due to the central role that these two methods have in proteomic studies, most experiments are broadly classified as either "gel-based proteomics" or "gel-free proteomics", depending on whether 2-DE is used for protein separation and quantification or not. So far, 2-DE is the most common strategy for protein separation and quantification of hundreds (and sometimes thousands) of different proteins from a single extract taking advantage of the fact that the isoelectric point of a protein is mostly uncorrelated to its molecular weight. This is mostly due to the facts that they are generally less expensive than purely MS-based approaches and information on small post-translational modifications (PMTs) and highly homologous isoforms can often be obtained directly.

c. **Protein identification and characterization** immunostaining methods have been employed for protein identification after 2-DE, however, in recent years the overwhelming majority of gel-based proteomic studies rely on digestion of detected proteins and analysis of the resulting peptides by MS for their identification and characterization since it does not rely on specific antibodies against every single protein to be identified. Further, usually only low number of proteins are present on a single 2-DE spot, and hence, the results obtained can be quite reliable.

II. Gel Free Approach

The gel-free strategies are becoming increasingly popular, since they generally allow higher analytical throughput and generally deeper proteome coverage than gel-based methods. Its popularity is also being furthered by the continuous improvement and cost-reduction of MS-based methods. In contrast to the usual "top-down" approach of gel-based proteomic studies, where proteins are separated and quantified before being digested and identified, most gel-free studies employ a "bottom-up" approach where, proteins are digested from the start and analyses (separation, quantification, charac-terization) are done at the peptide level. The information on protein abundance/identity is inferred from the obtained information on peptide abundance/identity, using computational tools. However, it is important to bear that the protein identifications depend not only on the quality of spectra, but also on the quality of the sequence database used. It also must be added that the dynamic and complex nature of the proteome provides several intrinsic challenges during interpretation of proteomic results regardless of the methods employed. The fact that most proteins display post-translational modifications (PTMs) further adds to the proteomes' com-plexities and is increasingly seen as essential to study, given the biologically important roles some of these PTMs are known to have.

4. APPLICATION OF PROTEOMICS IN NUTRITION

It is important to consider that with increasing global population on the limited earth surface area, intensification of culture practices is unavoidable and almost two-third of aquaculture production is now coming from feed based culture systems. It is contended that augmentation of suitable feed and feed resources is one of the most important challenges pertaining to sustainable growth of aquaculture. In this regard, it has been considered crucial to lower the use of fish meal which is mostly dependent on finite marine origin resources through partial to complete replacement with alternative and more sustainable plant-origin ingredients. However, despite of great advances in recent years as a sustainable fish feed resources, plant origin plants have elicited inferior growth performance and feed efficiency when compared with fish meal. The mechanisms behind the inferior growth response have not been fully understood. Similarly, physiological mechanisms elicited due to other nutritional and allied factors such as starvation on one hand and supplementation with bioactive compounds on the other are also not well understood. The proteomic approach has been successfully implemented in nutritional studies with fish for better elucidation of physiological and/or metabolic mechanisms and capacities (Martin *et al.,* 2001, Kolditz *et al.,* 2007). For instance, proteome analysis has identified a number of metabolic pathways sensitive to plant protein substitution in rainbow trout liver, for example, pathways involved in cellular protein degradation, fatty acid break-down, and NADPH metabolism (Martin *et al.,* 2003, Vilhelmsson *et al.,* 2004). Adaptation of rainbow trout to a diet with a partial (30%) substitution of fish meal with soybean meal for 12 weeks resulted in unaltered growth rates but increased protein catabolism and turnover, accompanied by changes in the abundance of 33 structural proteins (e.g. keratin and tubulin), lipid binding proteins (e.g. apolipo-protein A) and heat shock proteins, which are indicative of a stress response (Mitch *et al.,* 1999). In a subsequent trial, rainbow trout was fed a fishmeal-free diet and showed a significant reduction in growth rate and changes in 30 protein spots namely, several proteins involved in primary energy metabolism (production of NADPH, ATP, etc.) increased their abundance in liver, as well as two proteasome subunits, indicative of an increase in protein degradation (Mitch *et al.,* 1999).

Similarly, replacement of fish oil in fish feed added to supply both energy and n-3 fatty acids is also becoming scarce. Hepatic proteome has been analyzed to investigate metabolic changes induced by the absence of fish oil in trout diets (Kolitz *et al.*, 2007). Fish fed the fish oil free diet exhibited lower growth rate and body fat deposition and 105 differentially expressed hepatic proteins. The 13 identified proteins supported that fish oil suppression increased fatty acid transport, de novo lipid synthesis and fatty acid desaturation, while decreasing fatty acid catabolism. Several proteins involved in glycolysis, amino acid catabolism and energy production were up-regulated, showing a shift in nutrient utilization for energy production. Overall, changes in protein abundance in the livers of fish fed diets containing plant protein sources suggest that these fish have higher energy demands than fish fed fish meal-based diets. It is also important to bear in mind that genetic background of the studied fish also has important impacts on proteome level responses.

Another area in which proteomic studies show a high potential is in elucidation of interaction between specific nutrients or feed additives and the immune system. An optimal dietary supply of indispensable amino acid supply is of paramount importance to fish growth. Lysine (Lys) is an indispensable amino acid (AA) and is generally the first limiting AA in most vegetable proteins used in fish feeds. Lys availability may thus limit protein synthesis and accretion, and growth of fish. Metabolic effects of various dietary Lys imbalance levels were examined by 2D-proteomics using zebrafish as model (Gomez-Requeni et al. 2011). Comparative proteomic analysis of whole-body zebrafish showed 45 spots differentially expressed. Twenty-nine of these proteins were identified revealing proteins involved in muscle growth, energy and lipid metabolism, eye lens differentiation, chaperone activity and apoptosis. Lys deficiency was accompanied by a down-regulation of muscle proteins and up-regulation of proteins associated to fasting, energy deficit, growth arrest and apoptosis. Additionally, it was found that excess Lys was accompanied by an up-regulation of proteins related to glycolysis, steroidogenesis and sexual maturation.

A comparative proteomic approach was used to assess the protein expression profile in the liver of 34 days old pikeperch larvae fed diets varying in their phospholipid (PL) contents (Hamza *et al.*, 2010). From the 56 protein spots with a differential intensity associated to dietary changes, 11 proteins were un-ambiguously identified by LC-MS/MS tandem mass spectrometry. Results showed that under high PL intake, the glycolytic pathway was down-regulated due to the under-expression of the fructose biphosphate aldolase B and the phosphoglucomutase 1, while propionyl coenzyme A carbox-ylase (a gluconeogenic enzyme) was also under-expressed. A high dietary PL level increased the expression of sarcosine dehydrogenase, an enzyme involved in methionine metabolism, along with vinculin, a structural protein. In the larvae fed with the lowest dietary PL content, over-expression of both glutathione S-transferase M, glucose regulated protein 75 might indicate a cellular stress, while the under-expression of peroxiredoxin-1 might indicate a lower defence against oxidative stress (Hamza *et al.,* 2010).

In other proteomic studies, dietary nucleotides supplementation caused differential expression of muscle metabolic proteins including glyceraldehyde-3-phosphate dehydrogenase, creatine kinase, adenylate kinase, nucleoside diphosphate kinase, and triosephosphate isomerase (Kevanshockooh *et al.,* 2012). In addition to metabolic enzymes, troponin-T-1 as a structural protein was found to increase in abundance in fish fed the nucleotide supplemented feeds. Similarly, the intake of maslinic acid, a triterpene used as a feed additive to stimulate growth and protein turnover rates, was found to regulate gilthead seabream hepatic proteins involved in the metabolism of glucose, lipids, amino acids, and purines, as well as in detoxification and xenobiotics, oxidative stress, immune system, protein synthesis, protein folding, signaling, and cytoskeleton formation (Rufino-Palomares *et al.,* 2011).

On the other hand, proteomic studies have indicated that nutrient deprivation or starvation elicited 24 differentially expressed proteins in fishes including on one hand enolase and cytochrome C oxidase, and cathepsin D on the other, most likely related to the higher energy requirements and protein degradation, respectively, that takes place during fasting (Martin *et al.,* 2001). More recently, starvation (15 days) and resumption of feeding (7 days) of zebra fish expressed 18 identified proteins indicating that starvation resulted in reduction in glycolysis and increase in gluconeogenesis, while resumption of feeding caused these activities to return to normal levels (Enyu & Shu-Chien, 2011). Expression pattern of several proteins related to fatty acid and amino acid metabolism also suggested the utilization of non-carbohydrate resources for energy during starving conditions. Proteins with chaperoning and antioxidative roles such as glucose-regulated protein, paraxonase and heat-shock protein were also increased in starved conditions. A proteomic approach with zebrafish also indicated that high-caloric intake was related to a decrease in oxygen-binding activity, namely heme binding proteins (Jury *et al.,* 2008).

Thus it may be evident that proteomics holds great promise for discoveries in elucidation of physiological mechanism in nutrition research. Integrated with other advanced technologies (genomics, transcriptomics, metabolomics, and bioinformatics) and systems biology, proteomics will greatly facilitate the discovery of key proteins that function to regulate metabolic pathways and whose synthesis, degradation, and modifica-tions are affected by specific nutrients or other dietary factors. This will aid in rapidly enhancing our knowledge of the complex mechanisms responsible for nutrient utilization, identifying new biomarkers for nutritional status and disease progression, and designing a contemporary paradigm for dietary prevention and intervention of disease.

5. PROTEOMICS IN FISH HEALTH AND WELFARE IN AQUACULTURE

Farmed aquatic species are susceptible to a wide range of pathogens (bacteria, virus, parasites and fungus) responsible for disease and losses with significant impact on not only the volume but also the quality of production (Hill, 2005). Similarly, a broad range of pollutants, contaminants and drugs may also be used either inadvertently or by choice to increase productivity that may have impacts on health status of fishes. Therefore, an effective health management program in aquaculture industry should cover several steps, from up-to-date information on health status, reducing exposure and spread of pathogens and management of drugs or chemicals (Hill, 2005).

The proteomics technologies can play a major role in health management in aquaculture, since it can assist in both the diagnosis of disease as well as the development of new vaccines. For that matter, a recent study elucidated the molecular mechanisms of iridoviral pathogenesis which is responsible for 30% (adult fish) to 100% (fry) mortality in cultured grouper and has the ability of inducing an advanced cytopathic effect in a grouper cell line (Zhou *et al.*, 2011). On the other hand, Dumetz (2008) has reported a number of novel candidate proteins for developing vaccines against flavobacteriosis infection in aquaculture, using 2-DE and LC-MS/MS techniques. Furthering the effort in this direction, Huan & Wang (2011) reported anti-Vibrio immune response of Zhikong scallop (*Chlamys farreri*) through proteomics tech-niques. The results of their study also indicated that molecular chaperons and the antioxidant system are the key elements in the anti-Vibrio immune response of hepatopancreas of *C. farreri*.

The proteomics has also been demonstrated to be an effective tool for evaluating toxic effects of different contaminants such as biotoxin, pharmaceuticals, horomones and etc. in aquaculture species (Eidem *et al.*, 2006, Nzoughet *et al.*, 2009, Silvestre *et al.*, 2010). There are also some studies correlating environmental sources of stress in aquaculture including hypoxia (Jiang *et al.*, 2009), anoxia (Wulff et al. 2008), hyperoxygenation (Salas-Leiton *et al.*, 2009), and temperature (Addis *et al.*, 2010) as well as stress induced by management practices like high stocking densities (Provan et al. 2006) with proteome changes in several tissues (Rodrigues *et al.*, 2012). Most of these proteomic studies to elucidate effect of metals, biotoxins and other environmental toxicants on the proteome of fish have focused on the liver which has been found to generally display increased signs of oxidative stress, changes in immune/ inflammatory effectors, as well as induction of transporters and detoxification enzymes.

In addition to direct health and toxic impacts in aquaculture as mentioned above, proteomics may play important role in stress management in aquaculture organisms which are also exposed to various kinds of suboptimal situations related with aquaculture management, fish handling, crowding, harvesting and slaughter stress. These events usually induce cellular adaptations mediated (among others) by oxygen sensing systems characterized by the induction of cytoprotection systems (including increased expression of chaperones, detoxification enzymes, protein turnover and antioxidant proteins) as well as adaptive changes in energy homeostasis and cell cycle control. Furthermore, the effect of these physiological stressors has slightly different effects on the organism's distinct organs such as the release of epinephrine and glucocorticoids (like cortisol) into the blood-stream. Whether the fish would be able to cope with the oxidative stress or not is determined by prior state of the cell, as well as the type, intensity and duration of exposure to these types of oxidative stress indicating that cellular response is context-dependent (Ellis *et al.*, 2012).

Comparative proteomic studies in fish so far has indicated that although most types of stress broadly induce changes in terms of energy metabolism, cytoskeletal dynamics and expression of cytoprotective proteins across most organs, there are specific particularities in cellular responses depending on cellular/tissue type (Ellis *et al.*, 2012). For example, in energy-bound organs, like brain and muscles, changes in energy metabolism have been demonstrated to be quite evident particularly at the level of glycolysis/carbohydrate metabo-lism and phosphotransfer networks (Smith *et al.*, 2009). Liver tissue also displays energy metabolism shifts in response to stress, but at a much deeper level, reflecting its essential role in physiolog-ical detoxification and energy management. This suggests that proteomic studies on fish welfare may benefit from holistic approaches, covering several organs and using complementary measures of health and stress status, which provide the necessary contextual information for correctly interpreting observed changes as adaptive or maladaptive.

Finally, this may be stated that although welfare biomarker discovery and validation is still a big challenge, it is clear that proteomics provides untargeted information which is invaluable to meaningfully understand fish welfare and work towards a sustainable and ethical aquaculture, and hence, the use of proteomics in aquaculture research is increasingly seen as, not only relevant, but essential.

6. QUALITY OF PRODUCED FISH

The influence of ante mortem aquaculture and allied parameters including feed composition (Baron *et al.*, 2009, D'Souza et al. 2006, Johnsen *et al.*, 2011), temperature (Gines et al. 2004) and stress (Bjornevik & Solbakken, 2010) as well as post *mortem* parameters especially storage temperature and time (Stein *et al.*, 2005) on flesh quality is well established. Flesh quality in the present context is implied to describe either the "eating quality" or the "technological quality" indicating flesh's suitability for certain products, production processes and types of storage conditions. However, underlying mechanisms responsible for a certain quality in aquaculture species are not well understood (Rodrigues *et al.*, 2012). The proteomics can be employed to gather knowledge at a molecular level of the involved mechanisms. Further, it can be combined with other techniques like transcriptomics for comprehensive elucidation of underlying mechanisms as reported by Kolditz et al. (2008) in which they observed that rainbow trout *(Oncorhynchus* mykiss) showed changes in liver metabolism to manage fat allocation in the muscle of a fish fed a high energy/high fat diet lower level of expressions of proteins involved in intra-cellular lipid transport, the respiratory chain, glycolysis/gluconeogenesis and amino-acid metabolism when compared to fish fed with a low energy diet. Therefore, the found proteins could be used as quality markers to prevent excess muscle fat accumulation (Kolditz *et al.*, 2008). On the other hand, Morzel et al. (2006), observed modification in protein expression in rainbow trout (Oncorhynchus mykiss) in white muscle as induced by a pre-slaughter crowding (>50 kg/m^3 for 15 min) indicating a rapid increase in energy demand or structural protein. Similar findings have been reported for other fishes including Atlantic salmon (Veiseth, et al. 2010) and gilthead seabream (Alves, 2010).

In another proteomic study dealing with impacts of temperature during chilled storage revealed greatest alteration in muscle protein pattern of sea bass at the highest storage temperature with clear degradation of particularly myosin heavy chain and glyceraldehydes-3-phosphate dehydrogenase and decreased abundance of nucleoside diphosphate kinase B during storage but in a temperature independent manner (Terova *et al.*, 2011). However, also at a low chilling temperature (1 °C) several proteins changed in abundance during storage, although to a lesser extent. It is to be noted that these changes are associated with changes in muscle texture which is one of the very important quality aspects.

A proteomics driven understanding of quality could lead to the inclusion of quality as a breeding parameter together with the parameters health, growth, and feed conversion which are primarily used today. The perspective in this respect is to find correlations between protein expression in a tissue and the eating or technological quality of this tissue. This would open up for a biomarker guided selective breeding directed towards a better and less variable quality. Moreover, when the quality related biomarkers are combined with biomarkers relating to production parameters such as diet, feeding regime, temper-ature and handling procedures (stressors) it constitutes a strong tool for design of fish having certain product specific properties.

7. CONCLUSION

The current limitations aside proteomics appear to be a powerful tool for elucidating important physiological mechanisms pertaining to emerging areas of nutrition, health, welfare and flesh quality through identifying important proteins. Proteomics has undoubtedly been demonstrated to have potential to provide a comprehensive measure of response of aquaculture fish or shellfish species to an external stimulus and / or stressors. Integration of proteomic technology with others like transcriptomics or metabolomics may be an important area of future research in the area as a wider visions as well as a validation of results can be obtained in this manner. Similarly, areas like proteogenomics might become a powerful approach in identifying protein biomarkers and to study genome variations through correlating proteomic data with the genomic and transcriptomic data. This may enable identification of novel genes that are missed by gene prediction programme. It is also contended that one of the most important challenges of proteomics is that annotation of the proteomes of species commonly used in aquaculture has so far been achieved only for very few species. Nevertheless, it is also anticipated that the use of de novo sequencing approaches might overcome this issue in the near future.

REFERENCES

Addis MF, Cappuccinelli R, Tedde V, Pagnozzi D, Porcu MC, Bonaglini E, et al. 2010. Proteomic analysis of muscle tissue from gilthead sea bream (Sparus aurata, L.) farmed in offshore floating cages. Aquaculture ;309:245–52

Alves RN, Cordeiro O, Silva TS, Richard N, de Vareilles M, Marino G, et al. 2010. Metabolic molecular indicators of chronic stress in gilthead seabream (Sparus aurata) using comparative proteomics. Aquaculture; 299:57–66.

Baron CP, Hyldig G, Jacobsen C. 2009. Does Feed Composition Affect Oxidation of Rainbow Trout (Oncorhynchus mykiss) during Frozen Storage? J Agric Food Chem ;57: 4185–94.

Bjornevik M, Solbakken V. 2010. Preslaughter stress and subsequent effect on flesh quality in farmed cod. Aquacult Res;41: 467–74.

D'Souza N, Skonberg DI, Stone DAJ, Brown PB. 2006 Effect of soybean meal-based diets on the product quality of rainbow trout fillets. J Food Sci 2006;71:S337–42.

Dumetz F, Duchaud E, Claverol S, Orieux N, Papillon S, Lapaillerie D, et al. 2008. Analysis of the Flavobacterium psychrophilum outer-membrane subproteome and identification of new antigenic targets for vaccine by immunomics. Microbiology-Sgm, 154:1793–801.

Eidem JK, Kleivdal H, Kroll K, Denslow N, van Aerle R, Tyler C, et al. Development and validation of a direct homologous quantitative sandwich ELISA for fathead minnow (Pimephales promelas) vitellogenin. Aquat Toxicol;78: 202–6.

Ellis T, Yildiz HY, López-Olmeda J, Spedicato MT, Tort L,Øverliand Ø 2012. Cortisol and finfish welfare. Fish Physiol Biochem;3 8:163–88.

Enyu YL, Shu-Chien AC. 2011. Proteomics analysis of mitochondrial extract from liver of female zebrafish undergoing starvation and refeeding. Aquacult Nutr., 17:E413–23.

FAO, 2009. The state of world fisheries and aquaculture. Rome, Italy: Food and Agriculture Organization of the United Nations.

FAO, 2012. The state of world fisheries and aquaculture. Rome, Italy: Food and Agriculture Organization of the United Nations.

Fernandes JM, Molle G, Kemp GD, Smith VJ. 2004. Isolation and characterisation of oncorhyncin II, a histone H1-derived antimicrobial peptide from skin secretions of rainbow trout, Oncorhynchus mykiss. Dev Comp Immunol;28:127–38.

Fernandes JM, Saint N, Kemp GD, Smith VJ. 2003. Oncorhyncin III: a potent antimicrobial peptide derived from the non-histone chromosomal protein H6 of rainbow trout, Oncorhynchus mykiss. Biochem J;373:621–28.

Gines R, Valdimarsdottir T, Sveinsdottir K, Thorarensen H. 2004. Effects of rearing temperature and strain on sensory characteristics, texture, colour and fat of Arctic charr (Salvelinus alpinus). Food Qual Preference; 15:177–85.

Gomez-Requeni P, de Vareilles M, Kousoulaki K, Jordal AE, Conceicao LE, Ronnestad I. 2011. Whole body proteome response to a dietary lysine imbalance in zebrafish Danio rerio. Comp Biochem Physiol Part D Genomics Proteomics;6:178–86.

Hamza N, Silvestre F, Mhetli M, Khemis IB, Dieu M, Raes M, et al. 2010. Differential protein expression profile in the liver of pikeperch (Sander lucioperca) larvae fed with increasing levels of phospholipids. Comp Biochem Physiol Part D Genomics Proteomics;5:130–7.

Hill B. 2005. The need for effective disease control in international aquaculture. Dev Biol (Basel), 21:3–12.

Huan P, Wang H. B L. 2011. Comparative proteomic analysis of challenged Zhikong scallop (Chlamys farreri): A new insight into the anti-Vibrio immune response of marine bivalves. Fish Shellfish Immunol; 31:1186–92.

Jiang H, Li F, Xie Y, Huang B, Zhang J, Zhang C, et al. 2009. Comparative proteomic profiles of the hepatopancreas in Fenneropenaeus chinensis response to hypoxic stress. Proteomics ;9:3353–67.

Johnsen CA, Hagen O, Adler M, Jonsson E, Kling P, Bickerdike R, et al. 2011. Effects of feed, feeding regime and growth rate on flesh quality, connective plasma hormones in farmed Atlantic salmon (Salmo salar L.). Aquaculture;318: 343–54.

Jury DR, Kaveti S, Duan ZH, Willard B, Kinter M, Londraville R. 2008. Effects of calorie restriction on the zebrafish liver proteome. Comp Biochem Physiol Part D Genomics Proteomics;3:275–82.

Keyvanshokooh S, Tahmasebi-Kohyani A. 2012. Proteome modi-fications of fingerling rainbow trout (Oncorhynchus mykiss) muscle as an effect of dietary nucleotides. Aquaculture;324–325:79–84.

Kolditz C, Lefevre F, Borthaire M, Medale F. 2007. Transcriptome and proteome analysis of changes induced in trout liver by suppression of dietary fish oil. FASEB J ; 21:A1402–3.

Kolditz CI, Paboeuf G, Borthaire M, Esquerre D, SanCristobal M, Lefevre F, et al. 2008. Changes induced by dietary energy intake and divergent selection for muscle fat content in rainbow trout (Oncorhynchus mykiss), assessed by transcriptome and proteome analysis of the liver. BMC Genomics ;9:506.

Martin SA, Vilhelmsson O, Medale F, Watt P, Kaushik S, Houlihan DF. 2003. Proteomic sensitivity to dietary manipulations in rainbow trout. Biochim Biophys Acta;1651:17–29.

Martin SAM, Cash P, Blaney S, Houlihan DF. 2001. Proteome analysis of rainbow trout (Oncorhynchus mykiss) liver proteins during short term starvation. Fish Physiol Biochem;24:259–70.

Mitch WE, Bailey JL, Wang X, Jurkovitz C, Newby D, Price SR. 1999. Evaluation of signals activatıng ubiquitin-proteasome proteolysis in a model of muscle wasting. Am J Physiol Cell Physiol;276:C1132–8.

Morzel M, Chambon C, Lefevre F, Paboeuf G, Laville E. 2006. Modifications of trout (Oncorhynchus mykiss) muscle proteins by preslaughter activity. J Agric Food Chem;54: 2997–3001.

Noga EJ, Ullal AJ, Corrales J, Fernandes JM. 2011. Application of antimicrobial polypeptide host defenses to aquaculture: Exploitation of downregulation and upregulation responses. Comp Biochem Physiol Part D Genomics Proteomics;6: 44–54.

Nzoughet JK, Hamilton JT, Botting CH, Douglas A, Devine L, Nelson J, et al. 2009. Proteomics identification of azaspiracid toxin biomarkers in blue mussels, Mytilus edulis. Mol Cell Proteomics;8:1811–22.

Pandey A, Mann M, 2000. Proteomics to study genes and genomes. Nature, 405:837–46.

Provan F, Bjornstad A, Pampanin DM, Lyng E, Fontanillas R, Andersen OK, et al. 2006. Mass spectrometric profiling - a diagnostic tool in fish? Mar Environ Res;62:S105–8 Suppl.

Rodrigues Pedro M., Silva, Tomé S. Silva, Dias Jorge Dias, Jessen Flemming 2012. Proteomics in aquaculture: Applications and trends• Journal of Proteomics 75: 4325–4345.

Rufino-Palomares E, Reyes-Zurita FJ, Fuentes-Almagro CA, de la Higuera M, Lupianez JA, Peragon J. 2011. Proteomics in the liver of gilthead sea bream (Sparus aurata) to elucidate the cellular response induced by the intake of maslinic acid. Proteomics, 11:3312–25.

Salas-Leiton E, Canovas-Conesa B, Zerolo R, Lopez-Barea J, Canavate JP, Alhama J. 2009. Proteomics of juvenile senegal sole (Solea senegalensis) affected by gas bubble disease in hyperoxygenated ponds. Mar Biotechnol (NY) ;11: 473–87.

Silvestre F, Huynh TT, Bernard A, Dorts J, Dieu M, Raes M, et al. 2010. A differential proteomic approach to assess the effects of chemotherapeutics and production management strategy on giant tiger shrimp Penaeus monodon. Comp Biochem Physiol Part D Genomics Proteomics;5:227–33.

Smith RW, Cash P, Ellefsen S, Nilsson GE. 2009. Proteomic changes in the crucian carp brain during exposure to anoxia. Proteomics;9:2217–29.

Stien LH, Hirmas E, Bjornevik M, Karlsen O, Nortvedt R, Rora AMB, et al. 2005. The effects of stress and storage temperature on the colour and texture of pre-rigor filleted farmed cod (Gadus morhua L.). Aquacult Res;36:1197–206.

Terova G, Addis MF, Preziosa E, Pisanu S, Pagnozzi D, Biosa G, et al. 2011. Effects of postmortem storage temperature on sea bass (Dicentrarchus labrax) muscle protein degradation: Analysis by 2-D DIGE and MS. Proteomics;11:2901–10.

Veiseth-Kent E, Grove H, Faergestad EM, Fjaera SO. 2010. Changes in muscle and blood plasma proteomes of Atlantic salmon (Salmo salar) induced by crowding. Aquaculture;309: 272–9.

Vilhelmsson OT, Martin SA, Medale F, Kaushik SJ, Houlihan DF. 2004. Dietary plant-protein substitution affects hepatic metabolism in rainbow trout (Oncorhynchus mykiss). Br J Nutr;92:71–80.

Wulff T, Jessen F, Roepstorff P, Hoffmann EK. 2008. Long term anoxia in rainbow trout investigated by 2-DE and MS/MS. Proteomics;8:1009–18.

Zhou S, Wan Q, Huang Y, Huang X, Cao J, Ye L, et al. 2011. Proteomic analysis of Singapore grouper iridovirus anvelope proteins and characterization of a novel envelope protein VP088. Proteomics, 11:2236–48.

❑❑❑

Section 2
Nanotechnology

CHAPTER - 15

Application of Nanotechnology for Plant Disease Management

Majumder D, Tariang J. and Maibam N.
[1]*School of Crop Protection, College of Post-Graduate Studies, Central Agricultural University, Umiam, Meghalaya -793 103, India*

INTRODUCTION

Plant diseases caused by microbial plant pathogens and sub microscopic entities including virus and viroids induce both quantitative and qualitative losses of high magnitude in yields. The extent of loss may range from slight to 100% depending on the susceptibility/resistant level of the cultivars and prevailing favourable environmental conditions (Narayanasamy, 2011). With the introduction of high yielding cultivars, adoption of modern production techniques such as high input agronomic practices, changes in cultural practices, free movement of planting materials and changes in weather conditions over the years have led to increase in pest and disease problems, several of which have become major constraints in their successful cultivation (Gupta and Thind, 2006). The challenge is how to feed the growing population by producing more on a stagnant or shrinking landscape; with lesser input cost and with lesser hazards to the eco-system. The detection and management of diseases prior to economic loss will help to minimize the yield loss of the crops. Physical and chemical techniques have been applied either alone or in combination with certain cultural practices to enhance the effectiveness of reducing pathogen inoculums and consequent reduction in disease incidence. Disease management technologies, such as bacteriophages and systemic acquired resistance (SAR) inducers, have been under investigation for several years as alternatives to Cu bactericides against bacterial plant pathogens (Ocsoy *et al.*, 2013). In between, nanotechnology has proved its place in agricultural sciences and related industries, as an interdisciplinary technology and a pioneer in solve problems and lacks (Mousavi *et al.*, 2011). Nanotechnology has many applications in all stages of production, processing, storing, packaging and transport of agricultural products. In recent years, nanotechnology has been increasingly applied to the development of novel antimicrobials for the management of plant pathogens affecting agricultural crops (Ocsoy *et al.*, 2013). New technology such as nanoscale platforms, biological sensors, miniature detection devices and nano sensors could play a significant role in the future pathogen detection and disease management (Kamel A, 2013). Fluorescent silica nanoprobes have potential for rapid diagnosis of plant diseases (Banik and Sharma, 2011). Nanotechnology offers a great opportunity to develop new products to detect and manage plant diseases with the aid of the nanoparticles and nanosensors. Although the idea of nanotechnology producing nanoscale objects and carrying out nanoscale manipulations, has been around for quite some time, the birth of the concept is usually linked to a speech by Rachard Feyman at the December 1959 meeting of the American physical society where he asked "What would happen if we could arrange the atoms one by one the way we want them?" (Kumar, 2009). Nanotechnology has many applications in all stages of production, processing, storing, packaging and transport of agricultural products.

Food security has always been the biggest concern of mankind. Almost 60% of the country's population depends on agriculture. Diseases are the major limiting factor for crop productivity and with the rising population and increase in the mouths to feed in India there is a need for development of new technologies to solve this problem without hampering the environment. We have observed in this current 21st century the common practise adopted by farmers is the use of chemicals for quick management of the diseases attacking their crops. The present study is to emphasize on the development of the potentials of the application of nanotechnology in diagnosing or detecting some of the worlds major diseases. New technology to combat disease epidemics and nanosensor networks to continuously monitor the health of plants could be developed. Recent researches suggests nanotechnology could hold the answer.

NANOTECHNOLOGY

Nanotechnology is the technology that deals with materials at nanoscale level having unique properties than their macroscopic or bulk counter parts and has promised applications in various fields of science (Soheyla *et al.*, 2012). The term "Nanotechnology" was first used by Norio Taniguchi in 1974, a researcher at the University of Tokyo referring to the ability of engineering materials at nanoscale (Davies and Jones, 2010). The prefix "nano" is derived from the Greek word meaning "dwarf". In more technical terms, the word "nano" means 10^{-9} or one billionth of something. The word nanotechnology is generally used when referring to materials with the size of 0.1 to 100 nanometres, however, it is also inherent that these materials should display different properties from bulk (or micrometric and larger) materials as a result of their size. These differences include physical strength, chemical reactivity, electrical conductance, magnetism and optical effects (Prasanna, 2007).

Studies have been conducted using nanosized particles to control major fungal and bacterial plant pathogens such as *Pythium ultimum, Magnaporthe grisea, Colletotrichum gloeosporioides, Botrytis cinerea, Rhizoctonia solani,* as well as *Bacillus subtilis, Azotobacter chrococuum, Rhizobium tropici, Pseudomonas syringae* and *Xanthomonas campestris* pv. *vesicatoria* (Park *et al.*, 2006). DNA-Directed Silver Nanoparticles on Graphene Oxide has been used as an antibacterial against *Xanthomonas perforans,* causing bacterial spot of tomato and results in significant reduction in disease with no phytotoxicity (Ocsoy *et al.*, 2013).

Nanotechnology in Agriculture

Nanotechnology has the potential to revolutionize the agricultural and food industry with new tools for the molecular treatment of diseases, rapid disease detection, enhancing the ability of plants to absorb nutrients etc. Smart sensors and smart delivery systems will help the agricultural industry to combat viruses and other crop pathogens (Mousavi, 2011). Nanotechnology envisage nanostructured catalysts to be available in the near future which will increase the efficiency of pesticides and herbicides, allowing lower doses to be used. Nanotechnology will also protect the environment indirectly through the use of alternative (renewable) energy supplies and filters or catalysts to reduce pollution and clean-up existing pollutants.

The application of nanotechnology to the agricultural and food industries was first addressed by a United States Department of Agriculture Road map published in September 2003. An agricultural methodology widely used in USA, Europe and Japan, which efficiently utilises modern technology for crop management, is called Controlled Environment Agriculture (CEA). CEA is an advanced and intensive form of hydroponically-based agriculture. Plants are grown within a controlled environment so that horticultural practices can be optimized. The computerized system monitors and regulates localised environments such as fields of crops. CEA technology, as it exists today, provides an excellent platform for the introduction of nanotechnology to agriculture. With many of the monitoring and control systems already in place, nanotechnological devices for CEA that provide "scouting" capabilities could tremendously improve the grower's ability to determine the best time of harvest for the crop, the vitality of the crop and food security issues, such as microbial or chemical contamination (Joseph, 2006).

Impact of nanotechnology in agriculture

Impact of nanotechnology in agriculture can be discussed as follows:

1. Food security for growing population
2. Large cultivable areas

3. Shrinkage of cultivable lands
4. Minimises wastage of inputs
5. Minimises wastage of products
6. Perishability or low shelf life
7. Diseases and calamities
8. Packaging limitations
9. Increase productivity in cultivable areas
10. Technology limitations
11. Impact on Environment
12. Skill limitations

1. Food security for growing population

The use of nanotechnology in agriculture and food industry can revolutionize the sector with new tools for disease detection, targeted treatment, enhancing the ability of plants to absorb nutrients, fight diseases and withstand environmental pressures and effective systems for processing, storage and packaging.

2. Large cultivable areas

Bringing more areas under cultivation by nanotechnology enabled environmental monitoring and management including cost effective water management through applications of nano science. Use of nanotechnology in agriculture can thus change the land use pattern substantially.

3. Shrinkage of cultivable lands

The remedy is to enhance productivity through nanotechnology driven precision farming and to maximize the output and minimize inputs through better monitoring and targeted action.

4. Minimizes wastage of inputs

Nanotechnology enabled sensors and smart delivery systems will help the agricultural industry to combat viruses and other crop pathogens. In the near future, nano structured catalysts will be available which will increase the efficiency of pesticides and herbicides, allowing lower doses to be used.

5. Minimizes wastage of products

Precision farming makes use of computers, global satellite positioning systems and remote sensing devices to measure highly localised environmental conditions thus, determining whether crops are growing at maximum efficiency or precisely identifying the nature and location of problems with the goal to maximise output (i.e. crop yields) while minimising input (i.e. fertilisers, pesticides, herbicides, etc) through monitoring environmental variables and applying targeted action. Precision farming through use of nanotechnology applications can help to reduce agricultural waste and thus keep environmental pollution to a minimum.

6. Perishability or low shelf life

The use of nanotechnology in sensing applications will ensure food safety and security, as well as technology applications which alert the customers and shopkeepers when a food is nearing the end of its shelf-life. Nanotechnology based new antimicrobial coatings and dirt repellent plastic bags are a remarkable improvement in ensuring the safety and security of packaged food.

7. Diseases and calamities

The union of biotechnology and nanotechnology in sensors will create equipment of increased sensitivity, allowing an earlier response to environmental changes and diseases.

8. Packaging limitations

Silver nanoparticles kill pathogens, bacteria, viruses and fungus and are used as a good and safe packaging pot. Such nanotechnology based packaging materials are 100 times more secure than the normal one for the storage of juices, milk and other agri-products. Nanotechnology products in packaging food products thus offer immense potential.

Food packaging films in the name of "hybrid system" films have enormous number of silicate nano particles. They massively reduce the entrance of oxygen and other gases and the exit of moisture, thus preventing food from spoiling or drying.

Nanotechnology can provide solutions for modifying the permeation behavior of foils, increasing barrier properties (mechanical, thermal, chemical, and microbial) and improving mechanical and heat-resistance properties. Other nanotechnology devices may include developing active antimicrobial and antifungal surfaces and sensing as well as signalling microbiological and biochemical changes

9. Increase productivity in cultivable areas

Precision farming with nanotechnology application here makes farming more targeted and scientific. Precision farming makes use of computers, global satellite positioning systems, and remote sensing devices to measure various parameters. Accurate information through applications of nanotechnology for real time monitoring of soil conditions, environmental changes and diseases and plant health issues.

10. Technology limitations

Various devices designed through application of nanotechnology which include biosensor for the detection of pesticides, herbicides, insecticide, viruses, microbe will bridge this gap to a great extent.

Smart packaging developed by applying nano science concepts & technology would be able to repair small holes/tears, respond to environmental conditions (e.g. temperature and moisture changes), and alert the customer if the food is contaminated.

11. Impact on environment

Nanotechnology will also help to protect the environment indirectly through the use of alternative (renewable) energy supplies and filters or catalysts to reduce pollution and clean-up existing pollutants.

Nanotechnology Research also aims to proper use of water, pesticides and fertilizers more efficiently. This Nanotechnology application will help to reduce pollution and to make agriculture more environmentally friendly. Thus, the use of nanotechnology in agriculture will lead to a real breakthrough in this sector.

12. Skill limitations

Nanotechnology applications have the potential to produce easy-to-handle devices which reduce the dependence on human skills on many fronts thus reducing the human risk.

Developments in the Agricultural Sector due to Nanotechnology (Anonymous, 2006)

Scientists are working on various technologies to develope fertiliser and pesticide delivery systems, which can respond to environmental changes. The ultimate aim is to tailor these products in such a way that they will release their cargo in a controlled manner (slowly or quickly) in response to different signals e.g. magnetic fields, heat, ultrasound, moisture, etc.

New research also aims to make plants use water, pesticides and fertilizers more efficiently to reduce pollution and to make agriculture more environmentally friendly. Smaller companies are forming alliances with major players such as LG, BASF, Honeywell, Bayer, Mitsubishi and DuPont to make complete plant health monitoring systems in the next 10 years using nanotechnologies

One of the world's largest agrochemical corporations, Syngenta, is using nanoemulsions in its pesticide products. One of its successful growth regulating products is the Primo MAXX plant growth regulator, which if applied prior to the onset of stress such as heat, drought, disease or traffic can strengthen the physical structure of turfgrass and allow it to withstand ongoing stresses throughout the growing season. Another encapsulated product from Syngenta delivers a broad control spectrum on primary and secondary insect pests of cotton, rice, peanuts and soybean, marketed under the name Karate ZEON is a quick release microencapsulated product containing the active compound lambda-cyhalothrin (a synthetic insecticide based on the structure of natural pyrethrins) which breaks open on contact with leaves. In contrast, the encapsulated product "gutbuster" only breaks open to release its contents when it comes into contact with alkaline environments, such as the stomach of certain insects.

Nanotechnology can also be used to clean ground water. The US company Argonide is using 2 nm diameter aluminium oxide nanofibres (NanoCeram) as a water purifier. Filters made from these fibres can remove viruses, bacteria and protozoan cysts from water. Similar projects are taking place elsewhere, particularly in developing countries such as India and South Africa.

Altairnano's Nanocheck contains lanthanum nanoparticles that absorb phosphates from aqueous environments. Applying these in ponds and swimming pools effectively removes available phosphates and as a result prevents the growth of algae. The company expects this product to benefit commercial fish ponds which spend huge amounts of money to remove algae.

Research at Lehigh University in the US shows that an ultrafine, nanoscale powder made from iron can be used as an effective tool for cleaning up contaminated soil and groundwater- a trillion-dollar problem that encompasses more than 1000 still-untreated Superfund sites (uncontrolled or abandoned places where hazardous waste is located) in the United States, some 150,000 underground storage tank releases and a huge number of landfills, abandoned mines and industrial sites. The iron nanoparticles catalyse the oxidation and breakdown of organic contaminants such as trichloroethene, carbon tetrachloride and dioxins to simpler carbon compounds which are less toxic. This could pave the way for a nano-aquaculture, which would be beneficial for a large number of farmers across the world. Other research at the Centre for Biological and Environmental Nanotechnology (CBEN) has shown that nanoscale iron oxide particles are extremely effective at binding and removing arsenic from groundwater (something which affects the water supply of millions of people in the developing world, and for which there is no effective existing solution).

In Thailand, Chiang Mai University's Nuclear Physics laboratory has come up with a new rice white-grained variety from a traditional purple coloured rice variety called 'Khao Kam' through the usage of nanotechnology. The word 'Kam' means deep purple and the rice variety is known for its purple stem, leaves and grains. Using nanotechnology scientist changed the colour of the leaves and stems of Khao Kam from purple to green and the grain became whitish. The research involves drilling a nano-sized hole through the wall and membrane of the rice in order to insert a nitrogen atom. The hole is drilled using a particle beam (a stream of fast moving particles, not unlike a lightning bolt) and the nitrogen atom is shot through the hole to stimulate rearrangement of the rice DNA. This newly derived organism through the change at the atomic level is designated as Atomically Modified Organisms (AMOs).

Application of Nanotechnology in Plant Pathology

Nanotechnology is a promising technique in plant pathology either by providing controlled delivery of functional molecules or as diagnostic tool for disease detection, which is an important step for developing strategies for plant disease management (Sharon *et al.*, 2010). In crop sciences, nanotechnology can be used for the production of nanocapsules for delivery of pesticides, fertilizers, and other agrochemicals (Jha *et al.*, 2011). Application of nanotechnology in plant pathology with new molecular and cellular biology tools are expected to provide disease prevention and treatment in plants e.g. disease diagnosis, disease monitoring, smart treatment delivery systems at a nanoscale that serve as carriers and provide board chemical detection and decision taking ability for self regulation. These smart systems deliver precise quantities of drugs or nutrients or other agrochemicals are required which can monitor and minimize pesticide and antibiotic use.

Today, application of agricultural fertilizers, pesticides, antibiotics, and nutrients is typically by spray or drench application to soil or plants or through feed or injection systems to animals. Delivery of pesticides is ether provided as "preventative" treatment or is provided once the disease causing organism has multiplied and symptoms are evident in the plant. In this context, nanotechnologies offer a great opportunity to develop new products against pests. Nanoscale devices are envisioned that would have the capability to detect and treat an infection, nutrient deficiency or other health problem long before symptoms were evident at the macro-scale.

Application of nanotechnology for detecting plant pathogens

Plant pathogens and pests are of the major factors limiting crop productivity. A need for detecting plant disease at an early stage so that tons of food can be protected from the possible outbreak has tempted Nanotechnologists to look for a nanosolution for protecting the food and agriculture from bacteria, fungus and viral agents. Nanosensor provide a rapid response and real-time processing with accurate, quantitative, reliable, reproducible, robust, specific and stable results. Plant pathogens can be detected with the help of nanosensors and biosensors. A detection technique that takes less time and that can give results within a few hours, that is simple, portable and accurate and does not require any complicated technique for operation so that even a simple farmer can use the portable system. Nanosensors work through a variety of methods such as by the use of nanoparticles to fluoresce different colours or by magnetic materials which can selectively attach themselves to pathogens. A sensor employing either infrared light or magnetic materials can then note the presence of even any number of different bacteria and other pathogens. Another advantage of nanosensors is that they can access into the tiny crevices where the pathogens often hide. Thus nanotechnology may reduce the time to detect the presence of microbial pathogens from 2 to 7 days down to a few hours, minutes or even seconds. Also, If an autonomous nano-sensors linked into a GPS system for real-time monitoring can be distributed throughout the field to monitor soil conditions and crop, would be of great help. The union of biotechnology and nanotechnology in sensors will create equipment of increased sensitivity, allowing an earlier response to environmental changes and diseases. A biosensor is composed of a biological component, such as a cell, enzyme or antibody, linked to a tiny transducer; a device powered by one system that then supplies power to a second system. The biosensors detect changes in cells and molecules that are then used to measure and identify the test substance, even if there is a very low concentration of the tested material. When the substance binds with the biological component, the transducer produces a signal proportional to the quantity of the substance. If there is a large concentration of bacteria in a particular plant, biosensor will produce a strong signal indicating that the plant is infected with bacterial pathogen. These nano-based diagnostic kits not only increase the speed of detection but also increase the power of the detection.

Nanoparticles in plant disease managements

1. Nano carbon

Carbon nanotubes (CNT) are allotropes of carbon whose nanostructure is cylindrical in shape. These nanotubes have many applications, especially in the fields of nanotechnology, electronics, and architecture. Often used as thermal conductors, these nanotubes also host unique electrical properties and are surprisingly strong. Recently scientists (Khodakovsky *et al.*, 2000) have reported that when they planted tomato seeds in a soil that contained carbon nanotubes these CNTs could not only penetrate into the hard coat of germinating tomato seeds but also exerted growth enhancing effect. They envisaged that the enhanced growth was due to increased water uptake caused by penetration of CNT. This could be a boon for using CNT as vehicle to deliver desired molecules into the seeds during germination that can protect them from the diseases. Since it is growth promoting, it will not have any toxic or inhibiting or adverse effect on the plant.

2. Nano silver

Nano silver is the most studied and utilized nanoparticle for bio-system. It has long been known to have strong inhibitory and bactericidal effects as well as a broad spectrum of antimicrobial activities. Application of silver in management of plant diseases has been tested by Jo *et al*. (2009) with reference to two fungal pathogens of cereals viz. *Bipolaris sorokiniana* (spot blotch of wheat) and *Magnaportha* grisea (rice blast). In vitro assays indicated that silver both in ionic and nanoparticle forms inhibited colony growth of both the pathogens but more sensitive in *M. grisea* as compared to *B. Sorokiniana*. Silver nanoparticles, which have high surface area and high fraction of surface atoms, have high antimicrobial effect as compared to the bulk silver. Kim *et al*. (1998) studied the antifungal effectiveness of colloidal nano silver (1.5 nm average diameter) solution, against rose powdery mildew caused by *Diplocarpon rosae*. It is a very wide spread and common disease of both green house and outdoor grown roses. It causes leaf distortion, leaf curling, early defoliation and reduced flowering. Double capsulized nano silver was prepared by chemical reaction of silver ion with aid of physical method, reducing agent and stabilizers. They were highly stable and very well dispersive in aqueous solution. The nano silver colloidal solution of concentration of 5000 ppm was diluted in 10 ppm of 500 kg and sprayed at large area of 3306 m^2 polluted by rose powdery mildew. Two days after the spray more than 95% of rose powdery mildew faded out and did not recur for a week. Nano silver colloid is a well dispersed and stabilized silver nanoparticle solution and is more adhesive on bacteria and fungus, hence are better fungicide. No wonder that maximum patents are filed for 'Nano silver for preservation and treatment of diseases in agriculture field.' This popularity of nano silver has caused concern about regulating and classifying the nano silver as pesticide (Anderson, 2009). In May 2008, the International Center for Technology Assessment (ICTA) submitted a petition to EPA requesting that it regulate nano-silver used in products as a pesticide under the Federal Insecticide, Fungicide and Rodenticide Act (FIFRA). Silver is now an accepted agrochemical replacement. It eliminates unwanted microorganisms in planter soils and hydroponics systems. It is being used as several other plant diseases. Moreover, silver is an excellent plant-growth stimulator. There are literally thousands of other essential uses for this odourless, nearly tasteless and colourless, powerful, non-toxic disinfectant and healing agent.

3. Nano silica-silver composite

Silicon (Si) is known to be absorbed into plants to increase disease resistance and stress resistance (Brecht *et al.*, 2003; Ma *et al.*, 2001). Aqueous silicate solution used to treat plants, is reported to exhibit excellent preventive effects on pathogenic microorganisms causing powdery mildew or downy mildew in plants. Moreover, it promotes the physiological activity and growth of plants and induces disease and stress resistance in plants (Garver *et al.*, 1998; Kanto *et al.*, 2004). But, since silica has no direct disinfection effects on pathogenic microorganisms in plants, it does not exhibit any effect on established diseases. Further, the effects of silica significantly vary with the physiological environment and thus, they are not registered as an agricultural chemical. As mentioned above silver is known as a powerful disinfecting agent. It kills unicellular microorganisms by inactivating enzymes having metabolic functions in the microorganisms by oligodynamic action (Kim *et al.*, 1998) and is known to exhibit superb inhibitory effects on algal growth also. Silver in an ionic state exhibits high antimicrobial activity (Kim *et al.*, 1998; O'Neill *et al.*, 2003; Thomas and McCubin, 2003). However, ionic silver is unstable due to its high reactivity and thus gets easily oxidized or reduced into a metal depending on the surrounding media and it does not continuously exert antimicrobial activity. Silver in the form of a metal or oxide, is stable in the environment, but because of its low antimicrobial activity it is used in relatively increased amount, which is not very desirable. A new composition of nano-sized silica-silver for control of various plant diseases has been developed by Park *et al.* (2006) which consisted of nano-silver combined with silica molecules and water soluble polymer, prepared by exposing a solution including silver salt, silicate and water soluble polymer to radioactive rays. It showed antifungal activity and controlled powdery mildews of pumpkin at 0.3 ppm in both field and greenhouse tests. The pathogens disappeared from the infected leaves 3 days after spray and the plants remained healthy thereafter. Park *et al.* (2006) also studied the 'effective concentration' of nanosized silica-silver on suppression of growth of many fungi and found that, *P. ultimum, M. grisea, C. gloeosporioides, B. cinere* and *R. solani* showed 100% growth inhibition at 10 ppm of the nanosized silica-silver. Whereas, B. *subtilis, A. chrococuum, R. tropici, P. syringae* and *X. compestris pv. vesicatoria* showed 100% growth inhibition at 100 ppm. They have also reported chemical injuries caused by a higher concentration of nanosized silica-silver on cucumber and pansy plant, when they were sprayed with a high concentration of 3200 ppm.

4. Nano Alumino-Silicate

Leading chemical companies are now formulating efficient pesticides at nano scale. One of such effort is use of alumino-silicate nanotubes with active ingredients. The advantage is that alumino-silicate nanotubes sprayed on plant surfaces are easily picked up in insect hairs. Insects actively groom and consume pesticide-filled nanotubes. They are biologically more active and relatively more environmentally-safe pesticides.

5. *Mesoporous silica nanoparticles*

Mesoporous silica nanoparticles can deliver DNA and chemicals into plants creating a powerful new tool for targeted delivery into plant cells (Wang *et al.*, 2002). Lin's research group has developed porous, silica nanoparticles systems that are spherical in shape and the particles have arrays of independent porous channels. The channels form a honeycomb-like structure that can be filled with chemicals or molecules. These nanoparticles have a unique "capping" strategy that seals the chemical inside. They have also demonstrated that the caps can be chemically activated to pop open and release the cargo inside the cells where it is delivered. This unique feature provides total control for timing the delivery. Plant cells have rigid cell wall. Hence, to penetrate it they had to modify the surface of the particle with a chemical coating. It has been successfully used to introduce DNA and chemicals in to arabidopsis, tobacco and corn plants. The other advantage is that with the mesoporous nanoparticles, one can deliver two biogenic species at the same time. Therefore, it plays an important role in genetic manipulation of plants, minimized the chemical and residue problem and delivery of chemicals at target site in plants.

6. *Nanoemulsion*

The term 'nanoemulsion' has been widely used to describe the complex systems consisting of oil phase, surfactant and water, which are optically isotropic and kinetically stable colloidal solution with droplet size in the range of 20-200 nm . Currently, nanoemulsion are becoming the subject of many studies due to their wide range of particle sizes in nanoscale and this has contributed to more branches of potential uses and applications. Nanoemulsion was characterized for particle size viscosity, surface morphology and refractive index. Nanoparticles suspensions very often present a physicochemical instability during their storage. In order to overcome this lack of stability and facilitate the handling of these colloidal systems, the water elimination from the aqueous dispersions to obtain a dry solid form appears as the most promising strategy. Nanoemulsions, as non-equilibrium systems, present characteristics and properties which depend not only on composition but also on the preparation method. Nanoemulsions can encapsulate functional ingredients within their droplets, which can facilitate a reduction in chemical degradation.

7. *Nano copper*

Nano copper was reported to be highly effective in controlling bacterial diseases viz. Bacterial blight of rice (*Xanthomonas oryzae pv. oryzae*) and leaf spot of mung (*X. Compestris pv. phaseoli*) as reported by Gogoi *et al.*, 2009. Several non-pathogenic fungi such as *Trichoderma* species are known biocontrol agents and their biomass is utilised in different commercial formulations meant for multifarious applications in agriculture.

Nanotechnology uses for insect-pest management

Today, the major problem in the agricultural pest management is the development of suitable agents which can kill insects physically. Hence, nanosilica mediated gene delivery in plants and pests control have got more emphasis. White fly (*Trialeurodes vaporarium*), an important pest has become possible to control by electrostatically spraying of amorphous silica. Coconut mite *(Dermanyssus gallinae)* is causing havoc throughout India. There are no remedies at present. However nanosilica have shown excellent efficacy against this mite. In studies of plants, these nanosilicas did not show any adverse effect on the plant physiology, fish and silkworm physiology. Control of granary weevil *Sitophilus granarius* and mustard beetle *Phaedon cochleariae* cab be achieved by the application of silica based materials Fossil Shield Ò90.0s, AdvasanÒ and BiobeckÒPA910. Many other Coleopteran granary insects, viz. *S. oryza*, and *Tribolium* sp. that bore the finished cereals and beans can effectively be managed by application of Surface Functionalized FS nanosilica. This nano-structured silica kills arthropod pests based on physicosorption of lipid from insect cuticle. Admixture experiments with silica and different synthetic pesticides show that some of them are having synergistic effect and can be applied in combination in pet management programme. Immunity in beneficial insects can be developed using nanosilica. This was observed in case of *Bombyx mori* where grasserie disease caused by nuclear polyhedrosis virus (NPV) could be controlled with the help of lipophilic amorphous silica nanoprticles (LASN)-live *Bombyx mori* NPV conjugate as drug. The International Agency for Research on Cancer (IARC) has rated amorphous silica dust as non-carcinogenic. USDA also considers amorphous silica as safe for anthropogenic use.

Nanotechnology materials and devices for biomolecular detection

Advances in nanotechnology and nanosciences are having a significant impact on the field of diagnostics, where a number of nanoparticle-based assays have been introduced for biomolecular detection (Fortina *et al.*, 2005; Gaspar *et al.*, 2007; Jain, 2007). The promise of increasing sensitivity and speed, reduced cost and labour makes nanodiagnostics an appealing alternative to current molecular diagnostic techniques. New synthesis, fabrication and characterization methods for nanomaterials, which have dimensions that range from 1 to 100 nm, have evolved to a point that deliberate modulation of their size, shape and composition is possible, thereby allowing control of their properties. Along with these advances has come the ability to tailor their binding affinities for various biomolecules (proteins, nucleic acids, and microbial pathogens) through surface modification and engineering (Rosi and Mirkin, 2005). Each of these capabilities allows the design of materials that can potentially be implemented into new bio-diagnostic assays that can compete favourably with the current molecular diagnostic methodologies. In this section, the most promising nanomaterials and their use in the detection of nucleic acids and microbial pathogens will be highlighted.

1. Quantum dots

QDs are 2-8 nm in diameter, roughly spherical (some QDs have rod like structures), fluorescent, crystalline particles of semiconductors whose excitons are confined in all the three spatial dimensions. QDs have emerged as important tool for detection of specific biological marker in medical field with extreme accuracy. They have been used in cell labelling, cell tracking, *in vivo* imaging and DNA detection (Sharon *et al.*, 2010). Their potential application in diverse fields can be attributed to the property of quantum confinement. In 1998, the first use of QDs for biological detection and about its photochemical properties was reported (Bruchez *et al.*, 1998; Chan and Nie, 1998). Diagnostics using colloidal QDs has got tremendous hoist from this milestone finding. QDs are robust and very stable light emitters and can be broadly tuned through size variations. In the past two years, wide range of protocols for bio-conjugating QDs (Wang *et al.*, 2002; Guo *et al.*, 2003) have been developed in diverse areas of applications such as cell labeling (Wu *et al.*, 2000), cell tracking (Park *et al.*, 2002), in vivo detection (Taylor *et al.*, 1984; Xu *et al.*, 2003). Diagnosis of a disease in its very early stage can play important role in treatment. Due to phenomenal advancement in nanotechnology, QDs have emerged as pivotal tool for detection of a particular biological marker with extreme accuracy. QDs being very photo-stable and optically sensitive can be used as labelling and can be easily traced with ordinary equipment. Early detection of diseases using quantum dots is proved to be boon.

2. FloDots

In addition to QDs, luminescent dye-doped silica nanoparticles (FloDots), which consist of luminescent organic or inorganic dye molecules dispersed inside a silica matrix, have also been developed for ultra-sensitive bioanalysis and diagnostics (Tapec *et al.*, 2002; Yao *et al.*, 2006). Owing to the silica matrix shielding effect, the doped dye molecules are protected from environmental oxygen, enabling the fluorescence to be constant and thus providing an accurate measurement for bioanalysis (Tapec *et al.*, 2002). Moreover, the silica matrix provides a versatile substrate for surface immobilization and various bio-recognition molecules, including oligonucleotides and antibodies, have been conjugated to FloDots (Santra *et al.*, 2001; Hilliard *et al.*, 2002; Tapec *et al.*, 2002).

FloDots have been used successfully for the detection of DNA hybridization and in immunoassays. Using FloDots functionalized with oligonucleotides as labels for chip-based sandwich DNA assays, Zhao *et al.* (2003) reported a detection limit of 1 fM target DNA. The high sensitivity of the assay can be ascribed to the fact that each FloDot has the fluorescence intensity of thousands of dye molecules; therefore, each gene hybridization is reported by thousands of fluorophores.

Although the use of FloDots represents an improvement over conventional fluorophore-based assays, they remain somewhat limited by the fundamental drawbacks of conventional fluorophores, including broad adsorption and emission profiles, which ultimately limit multiplexing capabilities (Rosi and Mirkin, 2005).

3. *Gold nanoparticles*

Metal nanoparticles such as gold, silver and iron, constitute one of the most researched branches of nanotechnology due to their electronic, optical, catalytic, and thermal properties (Guo and Wang, 2007; Theron *et al.*, 2008). Among these, gold nanoparticles are intensively used in a variety of colorimetric and fluorescence biodetection assays (Penn *et al.*, 2003; Thaxton *et al.*, 2006; Gaspar *et al.*, 2007). Specific focus has been directed at colloidal gold nanoparticles ranging from 3 to 100 nm in size, since they are rather stable and their properties can be easily tailored by chemical modification of their surfaces (Mirkin and Taton, 2000; Sandström *et al.*, 2003). Gold nanoparticle-based probes have been used in the identification of pathogenic bacteria in a chipbased system (Taton *et al.*, 2000). The assay consists of a capture DNA strand immobilized on a glass chip that recognizes the DNA of interest. A separate sequence on the captured target strand is then labelled with an oligonucleotide- functionalized gold nanoparticle probe. After catalytic reduction of silver onto the gold nanoparticle surfaces to amplify the target signal, the capture strand/ target/ nanoparticle sandwich is visualized with a flatbed scanner. The target DNA was detected at concentrations of 50 fM, which represents a nearly 100-fold increase in sensitivity over traditional fluorescence-based assays. The assay depends upon the target-selective binding of gold nanoparticle probes to consecutive regions of a target DNA sequence in solution, followed by transfer to an evanescently illuminated glass microscope slide for light scattering measurements. Whereas the gold particle probes scatter orange light in the presence of target, the probes scatter green light if the target is absent, whilst the target concentration is quantified by measuring the intensity of scattered light.

Despite its widespread use in nucleic acid hybridization assays, the use of gold nanoparticles for detection of bacterial pathogens in immunoassays has only recently been described (Lin *et al.*, 2005). The assay comprises detection of organism-specific antigens with biotinylated polyclonal antibodies after which gold particles functionalized with a secondary antibiotin antibody are added and the particles are then visualized under a dark-field stereomicroscope.

4. Nanofabrication

Nanofabrication techniques have been used in creating artificial plant parts such as stomata and xylem vessel which are then used to study the infection process and behaviour of pathogens inside host plant for example *Uromyces appendiculatus* (fungus causing rust disease of bean), *Colletotrichum graminicola* (fungus causing anthracnose in corn) and *Xyllela fastidiosa* (xylem limited bacterium causing pierce's disease of grape vine (Meng *et al.*, 2005).

5. Magnetic nanoparticles

In contrast to gold nanoparticles and QDs, magnetic nanoparticles have not been used in many biological applications. Nevertheless, advances in the synthesis of monodispersed magnetic nanoparticles ranging in size from 2 to 20 nm Park *et al.* (2004) and Sun *et al.* (2004), has provided a basis from which to explore applications of magnetic nanoparticles in diagnostics. Magnetic nanoparticles are produced from materials that can be strongly attracted by magnets or be magnetized (Safarik and Safarikova, 2002). They can be prepared in the form of single domain or superparamagnetic (Fe3O4), greigite (Fe3S4), maghemite (ã-Fe2O3) and various types of ferrites (MeO•Fe2O3, where Me = Ni, Co, Mg, Zn, Mn, etc.). Bound to biorecognition molecules, magnetic nanoparticles can be used to facilitate the separation, purification and concentration of different biomolecules (Richardson *et al.*, 2001; Yang *et al.*, 2004; Gu *et al.*, 2006). To do so, biorecognition molecules such as antibodies can be immobilized on the surface of magnetic nanoparticles through covalent or electrostatic interactions (Gupta and Gupta, 2005). After reacting these magnetic nanoparticles with sample solutions, targeted molecules can be bound by or captured on the surface of these magnetic nanoparticles. By applying a magnetic field, these nanoparticles can subsequently be concentrated and separated from the bulk solution and identified.

Despite the promise shown by biofunctional magnetic nanoparticles, some challenges regarding their widespread use have yet to be overcome. In addition to requiring a robust surface chemistry to attach bioactive molecules onto magnetic nanoparticles without laborious synthetic efforts, more precise control of the numbers and orientations of the molecules on the surfaces of magnetic nanoparticles is also required (Gu *et al.*, 2006).

6. Carbon nanotubes

Since their discovery, carbon nanotubes (CNTs) have attracted great attention as nanoscale building blocks for micro and nanodevices. CNTs can be divided essentially into single-walled carbon nanotubes (SWCNTs) and multi-walled carbon nanotubes (MWCNTs) based on the principle of hybridized carbon atom layers in the walls of CNTs. Whereas SWCNTs have diameters ranging from 0.3 to 3 nm, the MWCNTs are composed of a concentric arrangement of many cylinders and can reach diameters of up to 100 nm (Iijima and Ichihashi, 1993; Balasubramanian and Burghard, 2006).

CNTs are considered to be ideal for use in biosensors for detecting individual biomolecules and other biological agents. Not only do they have high surface-to-volume and surface- to-weight ratios, but they are also conducting, act as electrodes, and can be derivatives with functional groups that allow immobilization of biomolecules (Davis *et al.*, 2003; Balasubramanian and Burghard, 2005; Sinha *et al.*, 2006). The use of nano-size electrodes based on CNTs has the potential to greatly improve the sensitivity in recognizing DNA hybridization events. Li *et al.* (2003), developed DNA microarrays containing sensing pads constructed from MWCNTs and built into a matrix within a silicon nitride template. The upper (open) ends of the tubes act as nanoelectrodes and are functionalized with ssDNA probes. Target DNA that hybridizes to the ssDNA probe on the ends of the electrically conductive MWCNTs is detected using an electrochemical method that relies on guanine oxidation. The hybridization of less than a few attomoles of oligonucleotide targets was demonstrated. In an alternative approach, CNTs coated with alkaline phosphatise enzymes was used for the detection of amplified DNA (Wang *et al.*, 2004). This assay employs a magnetic microparticle modified with oligonucleotides that are complementary to one-half of the target DNA sequence, and alkaline phosphatase-coated carbon nanotubes that are modified with oligonucleotides that are complementary to the other half of the target DNA sequence. Binding of the target DNA promotes the formation of a magnetic microparticle/target/carbon nanotube sandwich, which is magnetically separated from the assay medium. After separation, the enzyme substrate á-naphthyl phosphate is added to the mixture, resulting in formation of á-naphthol product that is ultimately detected at a CNT modified electrode via chronopotentiometric stripping. This method detected target DNA at concentrations as low as 54 aM (Wang *et al.*, 2004). While CNTs currently are not as easily functionalized as QDs or nanoparticles, they offer the distinct advantage of rapid, real-time detection and may thus become viable options as nanostructured biodiagnostic devices (Rosi and Mirkin, 2005).

In addition to challenges at the fabrication level (e.g., production of pure and uncontaminated nanotubes is costly, continuous growth of defect-free CNTs to macroscopic lengths is difficult to obtain and dispersion of CNTs onto a polymer matrix is very difficult) (Sinha *et al.*, 2006), another important issue related to the use of CNTs is their toxicity (Oberdorster *et al.*, 2007). Although results suggest that chemically modifying CNTs can reduce their cytotoxicity to a certain extent (Sayes *et al.*, 2006), more research is required to address the effect of CNTs on biological systems, as well as information related to safety issues.

7. Nanowires

A nanowire is a structure, with the diameter of the order of a nanometer (10^{-9} meters). It can also be defined as the ratio of the length to width being greater than 20. Alternatively, nanowires can be defined as structures that have a thickness or diameter constrained of tens of nanometre or less an unconstrained length. It have been explored as signal transduction motifs in the electrical detection of DNA, proteins and microbial pathogens (Patolsky *et al.*, 2006). Nanowire sensors operate on the basis that the change in chemical potential accompanying a target binding event can act as a field-effect gate upon the nanowire, thereby changing its conductance. The ideal nanowire sensor is a lightly doped, high-aspect ratio, single-crystal nanowire with a diameter between 10 and 20 nm (Cheng *et al.*, 2006). Recently, detailed protocols for fabrication of silicon nanowire devices, including their covalent modification with biorecognition molecules, have been described (Patolsky *et al.*, 2006). Real-time, label-free detection of DNA has been demonstrated by Hahm and Lieber (2004) using silicon nanowires functionalized with peptide nucleic acid (PNA). The conductance of the PNA-functionalized silicon nanowire bridging two electrodes was measured in the presence of target DNA and mutant DNA with three consecutive base deletions. Introduction of target DNA into the assay caused a rapid and immediate change in conductance, while the effect of mutant DNA was negligible. Furthermore, the conductance changes scale with target concentration, and target DNA at concentrations as low as 10 fM were detected (Hahm and Lieber, 2004). Semiconducting silicon nanowires have also been used for the electrical detection of viruses in solutions (Patolsky *et al.*, 2004).

In addition to silicon nanowires, metallic multi-striped nanowires have also shown great promise as potential platforms for multiplex immunoassays (Nicewarner-Pena *et al.*, 2001). These nanowires are built through submicrometer layering of different metals, e.g., gold, silver and nickel, by melectrodeposition within a porous alumina template. Due to the permutations in which the metals can be deposited, a large number of unique yet easily identifiable encoded nanowires can be fabricated. The multi-striped nanowires, when coated with target-specific antibodies, were reported to efficiently and accurately allow multiplex detection of bacterial pathogen (Tok *et al.*, 2006).

Nanowires are set apart from other available nanobiotechnologies due to several key features such as direct, label-free, real-time electrical signal transduction, as well as ultrahigh sensitivity, exquisite selectivity and the potential for integration of addressable arrays (Rosi and Mirkin, 2005). However, an intrinsic limitation of nanowires is that the detection sensitivity depends on solution ionic strength. Consequently, for samples with a high ionic strength, diagnostics will require a desalting step before analysis to achieve the highest sensitivity (Zheng *et al.*, 2005). Furthermore, a practical constraint might be that the synthesis and fabrication of nanowire biosensor devices require some technologies that are not common to most laboratories (Patolsky *et al.*, 2006).

8. Nanocantilevers

Nanocantilevers, which are typically made of silicon, silicon nitride or silicon oxide, require only minute changes in compressive or tensile surface stress on either their upper surface or lower surface to cause measurable deflection of the cantilever and are capable of converting biomolecular recognition reactions into micromechanical motion. Consequently, nanocantilevers offer an opportunity for the development of highly sensitive, miniature and label-free detection systems (Thundat and Majumder, 2003; Hansen and Thundat, 2005; Carrascosa *et al.*, 2006).

Direct, label-free detection of DNA typically involves the use of silicon cantilevers with a thin gold coating on the top surface that is functionalized with thiolated capture DNA strands. Binding of the capture DNA strands with the introduced target DNA causes deflection of the cantilever, which can be measured accurately using optical detection methods. Using this approach, Fritz *et al.* (2000) demonstrated the hybridization of complementary oligonucleotides with a detection limit of 10 nM and showed that a single mismatch between two 12-mer oligonucleotides is clearly detectable. Similarly, promising results were obtained by Hansen *et al.* (2001) with a 10-mer oligonucleotide.

Despite being in its early days, cantilevers provide an opportunity for label-free, real-time measurements in fluids in a single-step reaction and can potentially serve as a powerful platform for sensitive, multiplexed detection of biomolecules. Although cantilevers can be microfabricated by standard low-cost silicon technology, leading to a decrease in production costs and allowing the possibility of integrating multiple functional devices onto the same platform (Dhayal *et al.*, 2006), some challenges must be overcome before cantilever array sensors can come into widespread use. These challenges relate especially to methods for detecting nanoscale motion and the development of immobilization techniques that can efficiently transduce the stress involved in biochemical interaction to the cantilever substrate (Cheng *et al.*, 2006).

Potential risks of nanoparticles

Public and private spending on nanotech R&D is accelerating and over 700 new products have already come to the market but, a growing number of scientific studies and government reports have recently warned that engineered nanoparticles could pose unique risks to human health and the environment due to their size and quantum properties. Nanotech products have come to market in the absence of public awareness and regulatory oversight. Only a limited number of toxicological studies made on engineered nanoparticles as a class are more toxic due to their smaller size. When reduced to the nano-scale, particles have a larger surface area that can make them more chemically reactive. As particle size decreases and reactivity increases, a substance that may be inert at larger scales, can assume hazardous characteristics at the nano-scale. One concern is that the increased reactivity of nanoparticles could harm living tissue, perhaps by giving rise to "free radicals" that may cause inflammation, tissue damage or growth of tumours. Nanoparticles can be inhaled, ingested or pass through the skin. Once in the blood stream, nanoparticles can elude the body's immune system such as the blood-brain barrier. Ironically, the very same properties that make engineered nanoparticles so attractive for the development of targeted drug delivery systems-namely, their mobility in the bloodstream and ability to penetrate cell membranes-could also be qualities that make them dangerous.

CONCLUSION

Nanotechnology for the control of plant diseases is a promising technique in plant pathology either by providing controlled delivery of functional molecules or as diagnostic tool for disease detection, an important step in plant disease treatment (Sharon *et al.* 2010). The benefits of nanotechnology are huge but so is the potential to misuse it. Chemical weapons produced from nanoparticles could be even more harmful due to the fact that the smaller a particle, the greater its impact either positively or negatively. Increased toxicity on some nanoparticles due to their increased surface area. Carbon nanotubes have been shown to induce tumours in studies on laboratory animals. Also, nanoparticles of copper, titanium oxide, silicon oxide and cobalt have a toxic and inflammatory effect on certain cells. A study in 2005 at Rice University confirmed that certain nanoparticles are bactericidal and as bacteria are the foundations of many ecosystems, their misuse could be disastrous. The safety of this technology and its application on plants have the potential for its destructive use. All of the above needs careful monitoring to reduce the risks and maximize the benefits. Scientists need to be more careful about promoting their science and they need media training so that they can manage the way their science is promoted. As with all emerging technologies, a successful future for nanotechnology will only be acheived through open sharing of ideas and research findings, through a testing of the capability boundaries and frank discussion of fears and failings. Nanosensors can be linked to a GPS system for real-time monitoring of disease, and distributed throughout the field to monitor soil conditions and crop health. Nano-Phytopathology can be applied as a tool to understand plant-pathogen interactions, which will provide new methods for crop protection.

REFERENCES

Anderson C B. 2009. Regulating nanosilver as a pesticide. Environmental Defense Fund, February 12.

Anonymous. 2006. European Nanoforum Report May 2006. Nanotechnology in agriculture and food.

Balasubramanian K and Burghard M. 2005. Chemically functionalized carbon nanotubes. Small 1(2) : 180–192.

Balasubramanian K and Burghard M. 2006. Biosensors based on carbon nanotubes. Anal. Bioanal Chem. 385: 452–468.

Banik S and Sharma P. 2011. Plant pathology in the era of nanotechnology. Indian Phytopath. 64(2): 120-127.

Brecht M, Datnoff L, Nagata R and Kucharek T . 2003. The role of silicon in suppressing tray leaf spot development in St. Augustine grass. Publication in University of Florida. 1-4.

Bruchez M, Moronne M, Gin P, Weiss S and Alivisatos A P. 1998. Semiconductor nanocrystals as fluorescent biological labels. Science. 281:2013–6.

Carrascosa L G, Moreno M, Álvarez M and Lechuga L M. 2006. Nanomechanical biosensors: A new sensing tool Trends. Anal. Chem. 25:196–206.

Chan W C W and Nie S M. 1998. Quantum Dot Bioconjugates for Ultrasensitive Nonisotopic. Detection Science. 281(5685):2016 -2018.

Cheng M M C, Cuda G, Bunimovich Y L, Gaspari M, Heath J R, Hill H D, Mirkin C A, Nijdam A J, Terracciano R, Thundat T and Ferrari M. 2006. Nanotechnologies for biomolecular detection and medical diagnostics. Curr. Opin. Chem. Biol. 10:11–19.

Davis J J, Coleman K S, Azamian B R, Bagshaw C B and Green M L H. 2003. Chemical and biochemical sensing with modified single walled carbon nanotubes. Chem. Eur. J. 9:3732-3739.

Davies J and Jones L. 2010. The Use of Nanotechnology for the Detection and Treatment of Cholera. Research paper based on Pathology lectures at Medlink/Vetlink. pp. 1-8.

Dhayal B, Henne W A, Doorneweerd D D, Reifenberger R G and Low P S. 2006. Detection of Bacillus subtilis spores using peptide-functionalized cantilever arrays. J. Am. Chem. Soc. 128:3716–3721.

Fortina P, Kricka L J, Surrey S and Grodzinski P. 2005. Nanobiotechnology: The promise and reality of new approaches to molecular recognition. Trends Biotechnol. 23:168–173.

Fritz J, Baller M K, Lang H P, Royhuizen H, Vettiger P, Meyer E, Guntherodt H J, Gerber C and Gimzewski J K. 2000. Translating biomolecular recognition into nanomechanics. Science. 288:316–318.

Garver T L W, Thomas B J, Robbins M P and Zeyen R J. 1998. Phenyalanine ammonia-lyase inhibition, autofluorescence, and localized accumulation of silicon, calcium and manganese in oat epidermis attacked by the powdery mildew fungus Blumeria graminis (DC) speer. Physiol. Mol. Plant Pathol. 52:223-243.

Gaspar J F, Baptista P V and Rueff J. 2007. Gold nanoparticle-based systems in Genetics. Curr. Pharmacogen. 5:39–47.

Gogoi R, Dureja P and Singh P K. 2009. Nanoformulations a safer and effective option for agrochemicals. Indian Farming. 59(8): 7-12.

Gu H, Xu K, Xu C and Xu B. 2006. Biofunctional magnetic nanoparticles or protein separation and pathogen detection. Chem. Commun. 9: 941–949.

Guo W Z, Li J J, Wang Y A, Peng X G. 2003. Conjugation Chemistry and Bioapplications of Semiconductor Box Nanocrystals Prepared via Dendrimer Bridging. Chem. Mater. 15:3125–33.

Guo S and Wang E. 2007. Synthesis and electrochemical applications of gold nanoparticles. Anal Chim. Acta. 598:181–192.

Gupta A K and Gupta M. 2005. Synthesis and surface engineering of iron oxide nanoparticles for biomedical applications. Biomaterials. 26:3995–4021.

Gupta S K and Thind T S. 2006. Disease Problems in Vegetable Production. Scientific Publishers, Jodhpur, India. p.1.

Hahm J I and Lieber C M. 2004. Direct ultrasensitive electrical detection of DNA and DNA sequence variations using nanowire nanosensors. Nano. Lett. 4: 51–54.

Hansen K M and Thundat T. 2005. Microcantilever biosensors Methods. 37:57-64.

Hansen K M, Ji H F, Wu G, Datar R, Cote R, Majumdar A and Thundat T. 2001. Cantilever-based optical deflection assay for discrimination of DNA single-nucleotide mismatches. Ana.l Chem. 73:1567–1571.

Hilliard L R, Zhao X and Tan W. 2002. Immobilization of oligonucleotides onto silica nanoparticles for DNA hybridization studies. Anal. Chim. Acta. 470:51–56.

Iijima S and Ichihashi T. 1993. Single-shell carbon nanotubes of 1-nm diameter. Nature. 363:603–605.

Jain K K. 2007. Applications of nanobiotechnology in clinical diagnostics. Clin. Chem. 53:2002–2009.

Jha Z, Behar N, Sharma SN, Chandel G. Sharma D K and Pandey M P. 2011. Nanotech-nology : Prospects of Agricultural Advancement. Nano Vision (2) : 88-100.

Jo Y K, Kim B H and Jung G. 2009. Antifungal activity of silver ions and nanoparticles of phytopathogenic fungi. Plant Dis.93:1037-1043.

Joseph T and Morrison M. 2006. Nanotechnology in Agriculture and Food. In: Nanoforum Report. pp. 2-14.

Kamel A. ABD-Eslam 2013. Nanoplatforms for Plant Pathogenic Fungi Management. Fungal Genomics and Biology.2: 2-3

Kanto T, Miyoshi A, Ogawa T, Maekawa K and Aino M. 2004. Suppressive effect of potassium silicate on powdery mildew of strawberry in hydroponics. J. Gen. Plant Pathol. 70:207-211.

Khodakovsky A, Schroder P and Sweldens W. 2000. Progressive geometry compression in Siggraph . Computer Graphics Proceedings. 271–278.

Kim T N, Feng Q L, Kim J O, Wu J, Wang H, Chen G C and Cui F Z. 1998. Antimicrobial effects of metal ions (Ag+, Cu2+, Zn2+) in hydroxyapatite. J. Mater. Sci. Mater. Med. 9: 129-134.

Kumar R. 2009. Nanotechnology In Agriculture. In: Agropedia. http://agropedia.iitk.ac.in/content/nanotechnology-agriculture

Li J, Ng H T, Cassell A, Fan W, Chen H, Ye Q, Koehne J, Han J and Meyyappan M. 2003. Carbon nanotube nanoelectrode array for ultrasensitive DNA detection. Nano. Lett. 3:597–602.

Lin F Y H, Sabri M, Alirezaie J, Li D and Sherman P M. 2005. Development of a nanoparticle-labeled microfluidic immunoassay for detection of pathogenic microorganisms. Clin. Diag. Lab. Immunol. 12:418–425.

Ma J F, Goto S, Tami K and Ichii M. 2001. Role of root hairs and lateral roots in silicon uptake by rice. Plant Physiol. 127:1773-1780.

Meng Y, Li Y, Galvani, C D, Hao G, Turner J N, Burr T J and Hoch H C. (2005). Upstream Migration of Xylella fastidiosa via Pilus-Driven Twitching Motility. J. Bacteriol.187: 5560-67.

Mirkin C A and Taton T A. 2000. Semiconductors meet biology. Nature. 405:626–627.

Mousavi R S and Rezaei M. 2011. Nanotechnology in Agriculture and Food Production. J. Appl. Environ. Biol. 1(10):414-419.

Narayanasamy P. 2011. Crop Disease Management: Principles and Practices. New India Publishing Agency Pitam Pura, New- Delhi. 3-4.

Nicewarner P S R, Freeman R G, Reiss B D, He L, Pena D J, Walton I D, Cromer R, Keating C D and Natan M J. 2001. Submicrometer metallic barcodes. Science. 294:137-141.

O'Neill M, Vine M G, Beezer G, Bishop A E, Hadgraft A H, Labetoulle J, Walkeer M and Bowler P G. 2003. Antimicrobial properties of silver containing wound dressings: a microcalorimertic study. Int. J. Pharm. 263:61-68.

Oberdorster G, Stone V and Donaldson K. 2007. Toxicology of nanoparticles: A historical perspective. Nanotoxicol. 1:2–25.

Ocsoy I, Paret M. L, Ocsoy M. A. , Kunwar S. , Chen T. , You M and Tan W. 2013. Nanotechnology in Plant Disease Management: DNA-Directed Silver Nanoparticles on Graphene Oxide as an Antibacterial against Xanthomonas perforans. ACSNANO. 7(10): 8972–8980.

Park S J, Taton T A and Mirkin C A. 2002. Array-based electrical detection of DNA with nanoparticle probes. Science. 295:1503.

Park J I, Kim M G, Jun Y W, Lee J S, Lee W R and Cheon J. 2004. Characterization of superparamagnetic "core-shell" nanoparticles and monitoring their anisotropic phase transition to ferromagnetic "solid solution" nanoalloys. J. Am. Chem. Soc. 126:9072–9078.

Park H J, Sung H K, Hwa J K and Seong H C. 2006. A new composition of nanosized silica-silver for control of various plant diseases. Plant Pathol. J. 22(3): 295-302.

Patolsky F, Zheng G, Hayden O, Lakadamyali M, Zhuang X and Lieber C M. 2004. Electrical detection of single viruses. Proc. Natl. Acad. Sci. USA. 101:14017–14022.

Patolsky F, Zheng G and Lieber C M. 2006. Fabrication of silicon nanowire devices for ultrasensitive label-free real-time detection of biological and chemical species. Nature Protocols. 1:1711–1724.

Penn S G, He L and Natan M J. 2003. Nanoparticles for bio-analysis. Curr. Opin. Chem. Biol. 7: 609–615.

Prasanna, B.M., 2007. Nanotechnology in agriculture. ICAR National Fellow, Division of Genetics, I.A.R.I., New Delhi–110012.

Richardson J, Hawkins P and Luxton R. 2001. The use of coated paramagnetic particles as a physical label in a magnetoimmunoassay. Biosens Bioelectron 16:989-993.

Rosi N L and Mirkin C A. 2005. Nanostructures in Biodiagnostics. Chem. Rev. 105: 1547–62.

Safarik I and Safaríkova M. 2002. Magnetic nanoparticles and biosciences. Monatsh. Chem. 133:737–759.

Sandstrom P, Boncheva M and Akerman B. 2003. Nonspecific and thiol-specific binding of DNA to gold nanoparticles. Langmuir. 19:7537–7543.

Santra S, Zhang P, Wang K, Tapec R and Tan W. 2001. Conjugation of biomolecules with luminophore-doped silica nanoparticles for photostable biomarkers. Anal. Chem. 73: 4988–4993.

Sayes C M, Liang F, Hudson J L, Mendez J, Guo W, Beach J M, Moore V C, Doyle C D, West J L, Billups W E, Ausman K D and Colvin V L. 2006. Functionalization density dependence of single-walled carbon nanotubes cytotoxicity in vitro. Toxicol. Lett. 161:135–142.

Sharon M, Choudhary A K, Kumar R. 2010. Nanotechnology in agricultural diseases and food safety. J. of Phytology. 2:83-92.

Sinha N, Ma J and Yeow J T W. 2006. Carbon nanotube-based sensors. J. Nanosci. Nanotechnol. 6:573–590.

Soheyla H, Hamed B, Eshrat G F and Farzaneh N. 2012. Green synthesis of copper oxide nanoparticles using Penicillium aurantiogriseum, Penicillium citrinum and Penicillium Waksmanii. Digest J. Nanomaterials and Biostructures. 7(3):999-1005.

Sun S H, Zeng H, Robinson D B, Raoux S, Rice P M, Wang S X, Li G X. 2004. Monodisperse MFe2O4. (M = Fe Co Mn). nanoparticles. J. Am. Chem. Soc. 126:273–279.

Taylor M A, Wise S K and McIntosh A M. 1984. Selective detection of Mycoplasma hyorhinis using cloned genomic DNA fragments. Infect. Immun. 47:827-830

Thomas S and McCubin P. 2003. A comparison of the antimicrobial effects of four silver containing dressings on three organisms. J. Wound Care. 12:101-107.

Tapec R, Zhao X J and Tan W. 2002. Development of organic dye-dopedsilica nanoparticles for bioanalysis and biosensors. J. Nanosci. Nanotechnol. 2:405–409.

Taton T A, Mirkin C A and Letsinger R L. 2000. Scanometric DNA array detection with nanoparticle probes. Science. 289: 1757–1760.

Thaxton C S, Georganopoulou D G and Mirkin C A. 2006. Gold nanoparticle probes for the detection of nucleic acid targets. Clin. Chim. Acta. 363:120–126.

Theron J, Walker J A and Cloete T E. 2008. Nanotechnology and water treatment: Applications and emerging opportunities. Cri.t Rev. Microbiol. 34: 43–69.

Thundat T and Majumdar A. 2003. Microcantilevers for physical chemical and biological sensing In: Sensors and Sensing in Biology and Engineering Barth F G, Humphrey J A C and Secomb T W, eds, Springer-Verlag, New York. 338–355.

Tok J B, Chuang F Y, Kao M C, Rose K A, Pannu SS, Sha M Y, Chakarova G, Penn S G and Dougherty G M. 2006. Metallic striped nanowires as multiplexed immunoassay platforms for pathogen detection. Angew. Chem. 45: 6900–6904.

Wang Y, Li J J, Chen H Y and Peng X G. 2002. Stabilization of inorganic nanocrystals by organic dendrons. J. Am. Chem. Soc. 124: 2293-8.

Wang J, Liu G and Jan M R. 2004. Ultrasensitive electrical biosensing of proteins and DNA: Carbon-nanotube derived amplification of the recognition and transduction events. J. Am. Chem. Soc. 126:3010–3011.

Xu Y, Wolfgang J, Jian T and A. R. W. McKellar W R A. 2003. Spectroscopic Studies of Quantum Solvation in ^{4}HeN-N_2O Clusters. Phys. Rev. Lett. 91(16) 3401.

Yang H H, Zhang S Q, Chen X L, Zhuang Z X, Xu J G and Wang X R. 2004. Magnetite-containing spherical silica nanoparticles for biocatalysis and bioseparations. Anal. Chem. 76:1316-1321.

Yao G, Wang L, Wu Y, Smith J, Xu J, Zhao W, Lee E and Tan W. 2006. FloDots: Luminescent nanoparticles. Anal. Bioanal. Chem. 385:518–524.

Zhao X, Tapec-Dytioco R, Wang K and Tan W. 2003. Efficient collection of trace amounts of DNA/mRNA molecules using genomagnetic nano-capturers. Anal. Chem. 75:3476–3483.

Zheng G, Patolsky F, Cui Y, Wang W U and Lieber C M. 2005. Multiplexed electrical detection of cancer markers with nanowire sensor arrays. Nature Biotechnol. 23:1294–1301.

❑❑❑

CHAPTER - 16

Use of Nanotechnology for Improving Water Quality

Amitava Rakshit , Sumit Rai and Avinash Rai
[1]*Department of Soil Science and Agricultural Chemistry, Institute of Agricultural Science Banaras Hindu University, UP-221005, India*
Email: amitavar@bhu.ac.in

ABSTRACT

Nanomaterials will potentially play an important role in water quality. Production and applications of nanomaterials in industry are increasing. Furthermore, there are a handsome number of marketed nanomaterial-based consumer products. Therefore, how nanomaterials diagnose and function and how they perturb normal biological systems all become a top concern. In recent years, researchers are actively engaged in such investigations and discussions. At the same time, technologies and methods are developed to make more targeting nanoparticles for use in water.

Key words: Nanomaterial, Applications,Water quality

1. THE PRESENT REALITY

Lack of drinking water and sanitation kills about 4,500 children a day (WHO,2012). In the 21st century, many countries are entering an era of severe water shortage. Increasing competition among agricultural, industrial, and domestic users will lead to clashes and significant increases in the real cost of water. According to the latest report of the United Nations Children's Fund Joint Monitoring Programme for Water Supply and Sanitation (2010), over 2.6 billion people were living without access to improved sanitation facilities, and nearly 900 million people were not receiving their drinking-water from improved water sources. 3.3 million people die from water-related health problems each year and 46% of people on earth do not have water piped to their homes. It is estimated that around 37.7 million Indians are affected by waterborne diseases annually, 1.5 million children are estimated to die of diarrhoea alone and 73 million working days are lost due to waterborne disease each year. The resulting economic burden is estimated at $600 million a year. Further providing drinking water to more than 700 million people residing in the rural areas of India in about 1.42 million habitations spread over 15 diverse ecological regions is an enormous challenge. The health burden of poor water quality is enormous. The problems of chemical contamination is also prevalent in India with about 2.17 lakh quality affected habitations in the country with more than half of the habitations affected with excess iron (1,18,088). This is followed by fluoride (31,306), salinity (23,495) nitrate (13,958) arsenic (5,029) in that order. There are about 25000 habitations affected with multiple problems. About 66 million populations are at risk due to excess fluoride in 200 districts of 17 states.

2. IMPROVING WATER QUALITY IS A MAJOR CONCERN

Problems relating to water quality can generally be divided into four categories. The first one concerns biological contaminants such as bacteria and pathogenic organisms. Inadequate handling of human excreta is the main cause of this type of water contamination. The second category relates to pollution that arises from different types of land use and management and includes sediments, nutrients and chemical products for pest control. The third type relates chemical compounds that are by-products of different kinds of industrial production and are also emitted by the use of these products. The pollutants in this category vary significantly and include both organic and inorganic compounds and have a high degree of industrial processing in common. The forth category contains what is often referred to as emerging pollutants and include pharmaceuticals, xenobiotics and endocrine disruptors. These substances are biologically highly active and can have significant effects on humans and on the environment even at low doses.

Improving water quality is consistently ranked as a top environmental concern in most of the recently conducted public opinion surveys. Achieving universal access is an important long-term goal but how to accelerate health gains against this long-term backdrop and especially amongst the most affected populations is an important challenge for acceptance in present changing socio-cultural people's beliefs and behaviours, and achieving sustainability and affordability in the provision of safe water. Many different low-cost interventions and strategies at the household and community level have been developed, described and evaluated on the basis of various criteria for household and community use in developed and developing countries. Public awareness to the current water crisis is rising around the world. However, for supporting increasing domestic, tourist and industrial demand and sustaining growing future generations across the globe, new integrated water production, purification, distribution and reuse systems have to be considered, able to solve in principle problems of water quantity and quality, environmental protection, reduction of energy consumption and water cost, is the application of nanotechnology. The unique and novel properties of nanoparticles make them well suited for treating water. Nanotechnology offers an opportunity to refine and optimise current techniques, and to provide new and novel methods of purifying water. Our main objective is to review a comprehensive discussion on application of nanotechnology to water quality improvement .

3. PROGRESS MADE TO DATE

Water of adequate quality and quantity is central to the integrity of the environment. It is essential to our life support enterprises, even to our ability to ensure we have sufficient drinking water to supply our needs. Generally water treatment plants clean water effectively using a variety of possible techniques using the principle of chemistry, physics or microbiology (Pendergast and Hoek, 2011). In general the methods used include physical processes such as filtration, sedimentation, and distillation, biological processes such as slow sand filters or biologically active carbon, chemical processes such as flocculation and chlorination and the use of electromagnetic radiation such as ultraviolet light.

A number of chemical methods are used for water treatment at point-of-use or entry and for community water systems. These methods can be grouped into several main categories with respect to their purpose and the nature of the technology. The main categories to consider here are: (1) chemical pre-treatments by coagulation-flocculation or precipitation prior to sedimentation or filtration, (2) adsorption process, (3) ion exchange processes and (4) chemical disinfection processes. All of these processes can contribute to microbial reductions from water, but the chemical disinfection processes are specifically intended to inactivate pathogens and other microbes in water. Therefore, chemical disinfection processes appropriate for household water treatment in the developing world will be the focus of attention in this section of the report.

Although alum and iron salts are the most widely used chemical coagulants for community drinking water treatment, other coagulants have been and are being used to coagulate water at point of use, including alum potash, crushed almonds or beans and the contents of moringa (*Moringa oleifera)* and strychnos(*Strychnos nux-vomica)* seeds(Verma and Rakshit,2011). Generally these methods are difficult to optimize without training and equipment and the cost involved are moderate to high. Further of the Earth's water, 97.5% is saline and not readily available for consumption or use. While it can be desalinated, the energy required to desalinate it is often prohibitive in terms of cost and energy sources may not be readily available. Other freshwater resources including ground sources or surface water and water originating in other sources such as rain, snow and fog, as well as water contained in vegetation. It is also a matter of great concern that approximately 60% of global freshwater resources are contained in water basins which cross international boundaries , leading to issues of contamination across borders and to possibilities of conflict and dispute leading to make the issue more complicated.

4. NANOTECHNOLOGY COULD BE AN ANSWER

Water treatment technologies seek to remove solid and other contaminants, or to neutralise them, and many treatments have a long history of use in systems for producing water for domestic, industrial and agricultural use. Water resource management is an important element in the conservation of water and in optimising its use. Methods for identifying the amount of contamination in water and determining its suitability for use, as well as those for ascertaining how much water is needed and where, aid good water management. While the situation is grim, recent advances strongly indicate that many of the current water quality problems can be addresses and potentially resolved using nanotechnology (Figure 1). For instance, recent advances show that many of the current problems involving water quality can be addressed using nanosorbents, nanocatalysts, bioactive nanoparticles, nanostructured catalytic membranes, and nanoparticle enhanced filtration.

Nanotechnology is gaining greater use in water systems. It is envisaged as being particularly efficient for three key purposes: treatment and remediation, sensing and detection, and pollution prevention. Established techniques for water treatment can have drawbacks which nanotechnology may help to address. Some methods use chemicals, are energetically costly, can be difficult to implement and manage, require substantial investments in term of funds, human capital and infrastructures, are not sufficiently adapted to local expertise and situations and may depend on having large infrastructures. New technologies, and especially nanotechnology using nanosorbents, nanocatalysts, bioactive nanoparticles, nanostructured catalytic membranes, and nanoparticle enhanced filtration, are expected to provide solutions which could help in the future in addressing this range of issues.

Nanotechnology is generally used in areas where there is a need to address contaminants at the molecular level. In several cases , nanotechnology has been in use as a conventional water treatment technique for many years although the term nanotechnology was not in common use when the products and systems were introduced. Many nanotechnology developments for water purification are enhancements of conventional technologies, while others under development offer novel approaches.

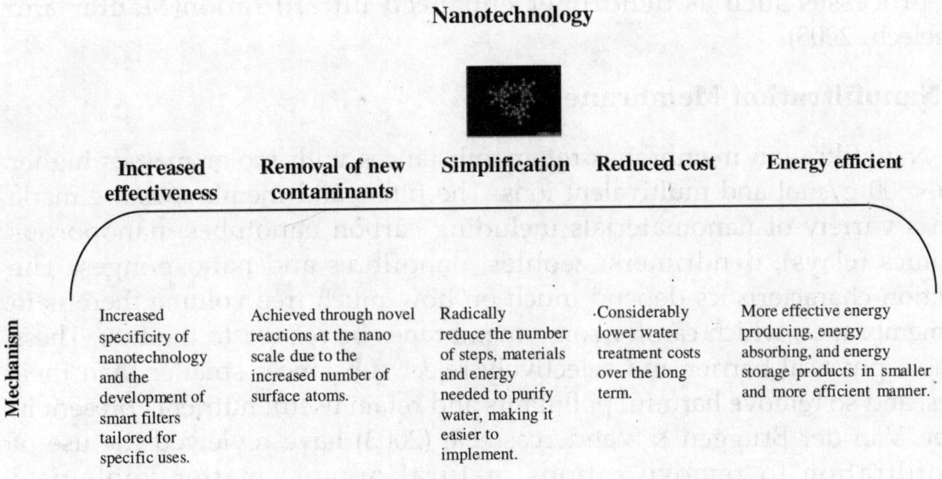

Fig. 1 : Benefits of nanotechnology in water science

5. NANOFORMULATIONS USED IN IMPROVING WATER QUALITY

The ability to remove toxic compounds from surface, subsurface and other environments that are very difficult to access in situ, and doing so rapidly, efficiently and within reasonable costs is the ultimate goal for any water quality project. Innovative use of nanoparticles with huge potential is vital as well as useful. Nanotechnology is having a wider coverage in different applications in water science (Cloete *et al.*, 2010).It is being used to develop small and portable sensors with enhanced capabilities for detecting biological and chemical contaminants at very low concentration levels in the environment, including in water. Ultimately, nanotechnology has the potential to contribute towards the development of low–cost portable filters, purifiers and other techniques could positively impact rural communities and informal settlements located close to industrial areas, where the accessible water is heavily contaminated. It can be further used in desalination of sea water by removing the salt from seawater, another large sustainable source of potable water could be provided significantly more cheaply than existing techniques.New, more efficient and cost-effective techniques could be applied to protect the environment alongside industrial practices. For example, nanotechnology may be used by the mining industry to prevent the contamination of groundwater from inactive mines by cleaning of acid mine drainage sources.

Below, we highlight the results of selected nanomaterials as separation and reactive media for water purification with the development of novel water-purification functional materials *viz*. nanosorbents, redox and catalytically active nanoparticles, nanostructured membranes andbioactive active nanoparticles and processes such as dendrimer enhanced ultrafiltration(Mauter and Elimelech, 2008).

5.1 Nanofiltration Membranes

Nanofiltration membranes retain substances with molar masses higher than <300 g/mol and multivalent ions. The filters and membranes are made from a variety of nanomaterials including carbon nanotubes, nanoporous ceramics (clays), dendrimers, zeolites, nanofibres and nanosponges. The retention characteristics depend much on how much free volume there is in the membranes, which can for some membranes be related to the flux. These act as a physical barrier and selectively reject substances smaller than their pores, and so remove harmful pollutants and retain useful nutrients present in water. Van der Bruggen & Vandercasteele (2003) have reviewed the use of nanofiltration to remove cations, natural organic matter, biological contaminants, organic pollutants, nitrates and arsenic from groundwater and surface water. Favre-Reguillon *et al.* (2003) showed that nanofiltration can be used to remove minute quantities of U(VI) from seawater. Mohsen *et al.* (2003) have evaluated the use of nanofiltration to desalinate water. They found that nanofiltration in combination with reverse osmosis could effectively render brackish water potable. Peltier *et al.* (2003) demonstrated an improvement in water quality for a large water distribution system using nanofiltration. Substantial reductions in the quantities of both organic and biological contaminants (e.g., bacteria and viruses) were achieved using this process. Nanomaterials are providing novel opportunities to develop more efficient and cost effective nanostructured and reactive membranes for water purification and desalination. Srivastava *et al.* (2004) recently reported the successful fabrication of carbon nanotube filters. These new filtration membranes consist of hollow cylinders with radially aligned carbon nanotube walls. Srivastava *et al.* (2004) showed that the filters were effective at removing bacteria (Escherichia coli and Staphylococus aureus) and Poliovirus sabin 1 from contaminated water. The carbon nanotube filters are readily cleaned by ultrasonication and autoclaving. DeFriend *et al.* (2003) reported the successful fabrication of alumina UF membranes using alumina (A-alumoxanes) nanoparticles (7–25 nm). The pore-size, and molecular weight cut-off (MWCO) of the membranes depend to a large extent on the 'uniformity' of the alumina nanoparticles. The new UF membranes, which have MWCO between 1000–10,000 Da and average pore diameter of 4 nm, showed selectivity toward a number of synthetic dyes (e.g., Direct Red 81, Direct Blue 71 and Direct Yellow 71). DeFriend *et al.* (2003) also showed that the selectivity and permeate flux through the UF membranes can be increased by doping the alumina nanoparticles with Fe, Mn and La. Stanton *et al.* (2003) have fabricated novel NF membranes by deposition of 4.5–5.0 layer pairs of poly(styrene sulfonate)/poly(allylamine hydrochloride) onto porous alumina. The new NF membranes exhibit high water flux, high retention of divalent cations [Ca(II) and Mg(II)] and Cl)/SO_4^{2-}) selectivity ratios up to 80. Note that Hollman & Bhattacharaya (2004) have also prepared novel membranes with enhanced metal ion retention and permeate flux by deposition of multilayers of charged polypeptides [poly(9Lglutamic acid) or poly(L-lysine)] inside the pores of functionalized polycarbonate track-etched membranes (thickness = 10 lm and pore diameter = 200 nm). Finally, we would like to highlight the successful preparation of reactive membranes by incorporation of bimetallic Fe0/ Pt0 nanoparticles into cellulose acetate films by Meyer *et al.* (2004). The embedded metal domains of the membranes have an average diameter of 24 nm and were found to be very effective at reducing TCE with ethane as the only observed by-product.

5.2 Nanocatalysts and Magnetic Nanoparticles

Nanocatalysts are particles with catalytic properties that can chemically break down pollutants. Their use mitigates the extensive cost of transporting them elsewhere. This, in turn, has the potential for treating contaminants at very low levels, especially where the current treatment techniques are ineffective or very expensive. Magnetic nanoparticles have large surface areas relative to their mass and easily bind with chemicals. Their ability to bind with contaminants, such as arsenic or oil, which can be easily removed using a magnet, makes them an appealing solution for water treatment. Nanoparticles have great potential as water-purification catalysts and redox active media due their large surface areas and their size and shapedependent optical, electronic and catalytic properties (Obare & Meyer, 2004). During the last decade, titanium dioxide (TiO_2) nanoparticles have emerged as promising photocatalysts for water purification (Adesina, 2004). TiO2 nanoparticles are very versatile; they can serve both as oxidative and reductive catalysts for organic and inorganic pollutants. The removal of total organic carbon from waters contaminated with organic wastes was greatly enhanced by the addition of TiO2 nanoparticles in the presence of ultraviolet light as shown by Chitose *et al.* (2003). Kabra *et al.* (2004) have recently reviewed the utilization of photocatalysts in the treatment of water contaminated by organic and inorganic pollutants. They documented the successful use of TiO_2 nanoparticles to (i) degrade organic compounds (e.g. chlorinated alkanes and benzenes, dioxins, furans, PCBs, etc.) and (ii) reduce toxic metal ions [e.g., Cr(VI), Ag(I) and Pt(II)] in aqueous solutions under UV light. The synthesis of visible light-activated TiO2 nanoparticles has attracted considerable interest (Asahi *et al.*, 2001; Bae & Choi, 2003; Adesina, 2004; Obare & Meyer, 2004). One of the most cited studies in the field is that published by

Ashasi *et al.* (2001). They synthesized N-doped TiO_2 nanoparticles that were capable of photodegrading methylene blue under visible light. Bae & Choi (2003) have synthesized visible light-activated TiO_2 nanoparticles based on TiO_2 modified by ruthenium-complex sensitizers and Pt deposits. The Pt/TiO_2/RuIIL3 nanoparticles drastically enhanced the rate of reductive dehalogenation of trichloroacetate and carbon tetrachloride in aqueous solutions under visible light. Nanoscale zero valent iron (Fe0) and bimetallic Fe0 particles have emerged as effective redoxmedia for the detoxification of organic and inorganic pollutants in aqueous solutions. These nanomaterials (10–100 nm) have larger surface areas and reactivity than bulk Fe0 particles (Schrick *et al.*, 2002; Zhang, 2003; Nurmi *et al.*, 2005). Zhang (2003) has given an overview of the synthesis, characterization and use of nanoscale Fe0 particle and Fe0/Pd0, Fe0 /Pt0, Fe0/Ag0, Fe0/Ni0 and Fe0/Co0 in environmental remediation. These nanoparticles can reduce a variety of organic pollutants (e.g., chlorinated alkanes and alkenes, chlorinated benzenes, pesticides, organic dyes, nitro aromatics, PCBs) and inorganic anions (e.g., nitrates) in aqueous solutions to less toxic and recalcitrant by-products. Fe0 and bimetallic Fe0 nanoparticles have also been successfully used to reduce redox active metal ions such as Cr(VI) to less toxic and mobile Cr(III) species (Zhang, 2003). The immobilization of metalloporphyrinogens in soil–gel matrices has also been successfully used to prepare redox and catalytically active nanoparticles for the reductive dehalogenation of chlorinated organic compounds (PCE, TCE and carbon tetrachloride) in aqueous solutions (Dror *et al.*, 2005).

5.3 Nanosorbents

Nanosorbents are nanoscale particles from organic or inorganic materials that have a high affinity to absorb substances. Nanosorbents have applications in air or water purification, and also in remediation of groundwater or wastewater treatment processes. One of the most prominent examples of a conventional sorbent for environmental application is activated carbon. This conventional material is cost effective in application and thus widespread for water purification. However, nanostructured sorbents offer the opportunity of an even greater sorption capacity and may be designed to target specific contaminants. Different carbon based materials and metal oxides are under investigation to address a variety of contaminants. However, most potential nanosorbents are in the state of research; very few applications are market ready and will require both translation from lab to field scale plus appropriate safety testing. Nanoparticles can also be functionalized with various chemical groups to increase their affinity towards target compounds (Savage and Diallo, 2005). The unique properties of nanoparticles to develop high capacity and selective sorbents for metal ions and anions have been investigated for the sorption of Pb(II), Cu(II) and Cd(II) onto multiwalled carbon nanotubes (MWCNTs) (Li *et al.* 2003). It has been reported maximum sorption capacities of 97.08 mg/g for Pb(II), 24.49 mg/g for Cu(II) and 10.86 mg/g for Cd(II) at room temperature, pH 5.0 and metal ion equilibrium concentration of 10 mg/l. Li *et al.* (2003) also found that the metal–ion sorption capacities of the MWCNTs were 3–4 times larger than those of powder activated carbon and granular activated carbon, two commonly used sorbents in water purification. The sorption of Pb(II) onto chitosan nanoparticles (40–100 nm) prepared by ionic gelation of chitosan and tripolyphosphate. The phosphate-functionalized chitosan nanoparticles have a maximum Pb(II) sorption capacity of 398 mg/g. (Qi & Xu, 2004). Peng *et al.* (2005) have recently developed a novel sorbent with high surface area (189 m2/g) consisting of cerium oxide supported on carbon nanotubes (CeO_2-CNTs). They showed that the CeO_2-CNT particles are effective sorbents for As(V). Deliyanni *et al.* (2003) have also synthesized and characterized a novel As(V) sorbent consisting of akaganeite [b-FeO(OH)] nanocrystals. In addition, Lazaridis *et al.* (2005) have shown that nanocrystalline akaganeite is also an effective sorbent for Cr(VI).Zeolites are effective sorbents and ion-exchange media for metal ions. NaP1 zeolites ($Na_6Al_6\ Si_{10}O_{32}$, $12H_2O$) have a high density of Na ion exchange sites (Savage and Diallo 2005). They can be inexpensively synthesized by hydrothermal activation of fly ash with low Si/Al ratio at 150°C in 1.0–2.0 M NaOH solutions (Moreno *et al.*, 2001). NaP1 zeolites have been evaluated as ion exchange media for the removal of heavy metals from acid mine wastewaters (Moreno *et al.*, 2001). Alvarez-Ayuso *et al.* (2003) reported the successful use of synthetic NaP1 zeolites to remove Cr(III), Ni(II), Zn(II), Cu(II) and Cd(II) from metal electroplating wastewaters. Self-assembled monolayers on mesoporous supports (SAMMS) are providing novel opportunities to develop more effective sorbents for toxic metal ions (Yantasee *et al.*, 2003), anions (Kelly *et al.*, 2001) and radionuclides (Fryxell *et al.*, 2005; Lin *et al.*, 2005). These sorbents are made via surfactant templated synthesis of mesoporous ceramics. This produces nanoporous ceramic oxides with very large surface areas (±1000 m2/g) and high density of sorption sites that can be functionalized to increase their selectivity toward target pollutants. Carbonaceous nanomaterials can serve as high capacity and selective sorbents for organic solutes in aqueous solutions. Mangun *et al.* (2001) have synthesized nanoporous activated carbon fibers (ACFs) with an average pore-size of 1.16 nm and surface areas ranging from 171 to 483 m^2/g. They measured the sorption of benzene, toluene, pxylene and ethylbenzene onto the ACFs at 20°C. Mangun *et al.* (2001) found that the sorption isotherms are adequately described by a Freundlich equation. In all cases, the ACFs had much higher organic sorption equilibrium constants than granular activated carbon. Peng *et al.* (2003) have evaluated the sorption of 1,2-dichlorobenzene (DCB) onto CNTs. They found that it takes only 40 min for DCB sorption onto the CNTs to reach equilibrium with a maximum sorption capacity of 30.8 mg/g. Li *et al.* (2004) reported that MWCNTs were better sorbents of volatile organic compounds than carbon black in aqueous solutions. Fugetsu *et al.* (2004) have successfully encapsulated MWCNTs inside cross-linked alginate vesicles. The caged MWCNTs showed high sorption capacity and selectivity for four watersoluble dyes (acridine orange, ethidium bromide, eosin bluish and orange G). Zhao & Nagy (2004) have synthesized hybrid inorganic–organic nanosorbents by incorporation of sodium dodecyl sulphate (SDS) into magnesium–aluminum layered double hydroxides (LDHs). They reported that the SDS functionalized Mg/Al LDHs had higher sorption capacity for chlorinated alkenes [tetrachloroethylene (PCE) and trichloroethylene (TCE)] in aqueous solutions than organoclays. Fullerenes can also serve as sorbents for polycyclic aromatic compounds (PAHs) such as naphthalene (Cheng *et al.*, 2004). Finally, we would like to point out the recent synthesis and characterization of amphiphilic polyurethane nanoparticles that can sorb PAHs (e.g., naphthalene) and increase their bioavailability in aqueous solutions (Tungittiplakorn *et al.*, 2004, 2005).

5.4 Nanofibres

Nanofibers are defined as fibers with diameters less than 100 nanometers. They can be produced by interfacial polymerization, electrospinning, and forcespinning. The most frequently mentioned ceramic materials with nanofiber morphology are titanium dioxide (TiO_2), silicon dioxide (SiO_2), zirconium dioxide (ZrO_2), aluminum oxide (Al_2O_3), lithium titanate ($Li_4Ti_5O_{12}$), titanium nitride (TiN) or platinum (Pt). The use of nanofibres, such as those fabricated by electrospinning, offers one potential solution for the present obstacles to reliable water treatment. The small pore size, high specific surface area and high porosity of electrospun nanofibre webs can be utilised to separate solid impurities from the liquid phase through filtration, ensuring good quality drinking water.

5.5 Bioactive Nanoparticles

A variety of strong oxidants (e.g., chlorine) are used as disinfectants for pathogens (e.g., bacteria and viruses) in water treatment. Because these compounds tend to generate toxic disinfection byproducts such as trihalomethanes, haloacetic acids and aldehydes, alternative disinfectants are critically needed to comply with the Stage 1 Disinfection Byproduct Rule of the 1996 Safe Drinking Water Act Amendments (USEPA, 1998b). The mechanisms by which disinfectants such as chlorine inactivate waterborne pathogens include (1) impairment of pathogen cellular function by destruction of major constituents (e.g., cell wall), (2) interference with the pathogen cellular metabolic processes, and (3) inhibition of pathogen growth by blockage of the synthesis of key cellular constituents (e.g., DNA, coenzymes and cell wall proteins) (USEPA, 1999). Nanomaterials are also providing unprecedented opportunities to develop chlorine-free biocides. Stoimenov *et al.* (2002) showed that MgO nanoparticles are very effective biocides against Grampositive and Gram-negative bacteria (Escherichia coli and Bacillus megaterium) and bacterial spores (Bacillus subtillus). Characterization of the interactions of the nanoparticles with the bacteria by atomic force microscopy (AFM), transmission electron microscopy (TEM), and laser confocal microscopy showed considerable changes in the integrity of the cell membranes, resulting in the death of the bacteria in most cases (2002). Because Ag(I) and silver compounds have been used as antimicrobial compounds in various biomedical products and applications, several investigators have begun evaluating the use of silver nanoparticles as biocides. Sondi & Salopek- Sondi (2004) have prepared stable Ag nanoparticles of narrow size distribution by reducing silver nitrate solutions with ascorbic acid in the presence of Daxad 19 (sodium salt of a highmolecular- weight naphthalene sulfonate formaldehyde condensate) as stabilizing agent. They found that Ag nanoparticles were effective biocides against Escherichia coli. Son *et al.* (2004) reported that cellulose acetate (CA) fibers with embedded Ag nanoparticles (prepared by direct electrospinning of a CA solution with silver nitrate followed by photoreduction) were also effective biocides against Gram-positive and Gram-negative bacteria including *Staphylococcus aureus*, *Escherichia coli*, *Klebsiella pneumonia* and *Pseudomonas aeruginosa*.

5.6 Dendrimer Enhanced Ultrafiltration

RO membranes have pore sizes of 0.1-1.0 nm and thus are very effective at retaining dissolved inorganic and organic solutes with molar mass below 1000 Da (Zeman & Zydney, 1996). NF membranes, on the other hand, are very effective at removing hardness (e.g., multivalent cations) and organic solutes with molar mass between 1000–3000 Da (e.g., natural organic material) (Zeman & Zydney, 1996). However, high pressures are required to operate both RO and NF membranes. Conversely, UF membranes require lower pressure (200–700 kPa). Unfortunately, they are not very effective at removing dissolved organic and inorganic solute with molar mass below 3000 Da. Advances in macromolecular chemistry such as the invention of dendritic polymers are providing unprecedented opportunities to develop effective UF processes for purification of water contaminated by toxic metal ions, radionuclides, organic and inorganic solutes, bacteria and viruses. Dendritic polymers, which include random hyperbranched polymers, dendrigraft polymers, dendrons and dendrimers, are relatively monodispersed and highly branched macromolecules with controlled composition and architecture consisting of three components: a core, interior branch cells and terminal branch cell (Fre´chet & Tomalia, 2001). Dendritic polymers exhibit many features that make them particularly attractive as functional materials for water purification. These 'soft' nanoparticles, with sizes in the range of 1–20 nm, can be used as high capacity and recyclable watersoluble ligands for toxic metal ions, radionuclides and inorganic anions (Ottaviani *et al.*, 2000; Birnbaum *et al.*, 2003; Diallo *et al.*, 2004). Dendritic polymers can also be used as (i) recyclable unimolecular micelles for recovering organic solutes from water (Arkas *et al.*, 2003) and (ii) scaffolds and templates for the preparation of redox and catalytically active nanoparticles. Dendritic polymers have also been successfully used as delivery vehicles or scaffolds for antimicrobial agents such as Ag(I) and quaternary ammonium chlorides (Balogh *et al.*, 2001; Chen & Cooper, 2002).A dendrimer-enhanced ultrafiltration (DEUF) process has been developed for recovering metal ions from aqueous solutions (Diallo *et al.*, 2004). As a proof-of-concept study, Diallo *et al.* (2005) tested the feasibility of using DEUF and poly(amidoamine) (PAMAM) dendrimers with ethylene diamine (EDA) core and terminal NH_2 groups to recover Cu(II) ions from aqueous solutions. On a mass basis, the Cu(II) binding capacities of the PAMAM dendrimers are much larger and more sensitive to solution pH than those of linear polymers with amine groups. Separation of the dendrimer-Cu(II) complexes from solutions can be achieved simply by UF membranes with the appropriate MWCO. The metal ion laden dendrimers can be regenerated by decreasing the solution pH to 4.0 (Diallo *et al.*, 2004); thus enabling the recovery of the bound Cu(II) ions and recycling of the dendritic polymer. PAMAM dendrimers have a very low tendency to foul commercially available regenerated cellulose (RC) membranes (Diallo *et al.*, 2004). They also have much smaller intrinsic viscosities than linear polymers with the same molar mass because of their globular shape (Fre´chet & Tomalia, 2001). Thus, comparatively smaller operating pressure and energy consumption could be achieved withdendritic polymers in tangential/cross-flow UF systems typically used in water purification. Other applications of DEUF to water purification are discussed by Diallo *et al.* (2004).

5.7 Aquaporins

These natural proteins that transport water through cell walls are embedded in organic membranes and with a high permeation rate(0.7-700 litres per second per gram) depending on the hydrostatic and/or osmotic pressure.

Aquaporin act as water channel which selectively allow water molecules to pass through in single file the transport of ions ,protons, hydroxyl ions is abrogated by electrostatic tuning mechanism. Smaller molecules are also restricted passage because their electrochemical properties do not fit. Potential applications are freshwater purification, desalination and industrial wastewater recycling. The production of aquaporin biomimetic membrane prototypes was a complex, multi-stage procedure. It required the concentration of protein within vesicles or concentration of vesicles within the active layer to be optimised within strict experimental protocols.

6. CHALLENGES AND RESEARCH NEEDS

Although nanotechnology enabled water treatment processes have shown great promise in laboratory studies, their readiness for commercialization varies widely. Some are already on the market, while others require significant research before they can be considered for full scale applications. Their future development and commercialization face a variety of challenges including technical hurdles, cost-effectiveness, and potential environmental and human risk. The technical challenges are still quite fundamental on one hand regarding the development of the nanosorbent and on the other hand regarding the system setup. Novel nanoparticles must fulfil a variety of requirements at the same time to be economicallyand societally beneficial, specificity, high sorption capacity and cost level. Scaling up the production is challenging especially for carbon based materials.Again since the water industry is very conservative, new nanomaterials systems should ideally be compatible with existing systems meaning thatit must be possible to integrate the materials cost effectively into existing systems. At the same time safety issues of nanomaterials are a major concern.The system setup must ensure that the nanomaterials are removed entirely to avoid the release of nanoparticles to the environment and to drinking water as well as to safe costs by regenerating the nanosorbents. There are two major research needs for full-scale applications of nanotechnology in water/ wastewater treatment. First, the performance of various nanotechnologies in treating real natural and waste waters needs to be tested (Pan and Xing, 2008). Future studies need to be done under more realistic conditions to assess the applicability and efficiency of different nanotechnologies as well as to validate nanomaterial enabled sensing technologies. Secondly, the long-term efficacy of these nanotechnologies is largely unknown as most lab studies were conducted for relatively short period of time. Research addressing the long-term performance of water and wastewater treatment nanotechnologies is in great need. As a result, side-by-side comparison of nanotechnology enabled systems and existing technologies is challenging. Despite the superior performance, the adoption of innovative technologies strongly depends on the cost effectiveness and the potential risk involved. The current cost of nanomaterials is prohibitively high with few excep tions such as nano-TiO2, nanoscale ion oxide, and polymeric nanofibers. There are currently two approaches to address the cost issue. One proposed approach is to use low purity nano- materials without significantly compromising efficiency as much of the production cost is related to separation and purification (Qu *et al.*, 2013). Alternatively, the cost-effectiveness can be improved by retaining and reusing nanomaterials. Nanomaterials possess unique challenges for risk assessment and management as they are small particles instead of molecules or ions for which risk assessment framework and protocols are already in place. Better understanding and mitigating potential hazards associated with the use of nanomaterials in water treatment will lead to broader public acceptance, which is crucial for new technology adoption. The compatibility between aforementioned nanotechnologies and current water and wastewater treatment processes and infrastructure also needs to be addressed. Most treatment plants and distribution systems in developed countries are expected to remain in place for decades to come. As a result, it is important to be able to implement nanotechnology with minimal changes to existing infrastructure in the near term. In the meantime, nanotechnology enabled treatment pro- cesses can be employed in places where water treatment infrastructure does not exist or in POU devices (Yang and Xing, 2010).

7. CONCLUDING REMARKS

The use different nanomaterials for water treatment are gaining momentum globally. The unique properties of nanomaterials and their conjoining ability with current treatment technologies has shown great prospect in revolutionizing the quality of water. Although most of nanotechnologies discussed above are still in the laboratory research stage, some of them made their way to even commercialization but still it has not been used in large scale. The challenges faced by wastewater treatment nanotechnologies are important like technical barriers, high cost, and potential environmental and human risk. So to find out the better way out from these problems, a collaborative work between research institutions, industry, government, and other stakeholders is essential and improving nanotechnology by carefully steering its direction while avoiding unintended consequences can continuously provide robust solutions to water treatment challenges, both incremental and revolutionary. The cost of new nano-water technologies is likely to be a factor limiting its adoption in many countries. In developing countries, inability to pay for these technologies may require a change in aid and international funding strategies, for example redirection or increase of funds. However, the issue of reluctance to adopt a new behaviour and concern over health and safety would remain and may only be resolved over time. In developed countries, a reluctance to pay for new developments in water treatment may be effectively addressed through education and communication.

8. REFERENCES

Adesina A.A., 2004. Industrial exploitation of photocatalysis progress, perspectives and prospects. Catal. Surv. Asia 8(4), 265–273.

Alvarez-Ayuso E., A. Garcia-Sanchez & X. Querol, 2003. Purification of metal electroplating waste waters using zeolites. Water Res. 37, 4855–4862.

Aorkas M., D. Tsiourvas & C.M. Paleos, 2003. Functional dendrimeric "nanosponges" for the removal of polycyclic aromatic hydrocarbons from water. Chem. Mater 15(14), 2844–2847.

Asahi R., T. Morikawa, T. Ohwaki, K. Aoki & Y. Taga, 2001. Visible-light photocatalysis in nitrogen-doped titanium oxides. Science 293(5528), 269–271.

Bae E. & W. Choi, 2003. Highly enhanced photoreductive degradation of perchlorinated compounds on dye-sensitized metal/TiO2 under visible light. Environ. Sci. Technol. 37(1), 147–152.

Balogh L., D.R. Swanson, D.A. Tomalia, G.L. Hagnauer & A.T. McManus, 2001. Dendrimer-silver complexes and nanocomposites as antimicrobial agents. Nano Lett. 1(1), 18–21.

Birnbaum E.R., K.C. Rau & N.N. Sauer, 2003. Selective anion binding from water using soluble polymers. Sep. Sci. Technol. 38(2), 389–404.

Chen C.Z.S. & S. Cooper, 2002. Interactions between dendrimer biocides and bacterial membranes. Biomaterials 23(16), 3359–3368.

Cheng X., A.T. Kan & M.B. Tomson, 2004. Naphthalene Adsorption and Desorption from Aqueous C60 Fullerene. J. Chem. Eng. Data. 49, 675–683.

Chin, S.S., Chiang, K., Fane, A.G., 2006. The stability of polymeric membranes in a TiO2 photocatalysis process. Journal of Membrane Science 275 (1-2), 202-211.

Chitose N., S. Ueta & T.A. Yamamoto, 2003. Radiolysis of aqueous phenol solutions with nanoparticles. 1. Phenol degradation and TOC removal in solutions containing TiO2 induced by UV, gamma-ray and electron beams. Chemosphere 50(8), 1007–1013.

Cloete, T.E., Kwaadsteniet, M.d., Botes, M., Lopez-Romero, J.M., 2010. Nanotechnology in Water Treatment Applications.Caister Academic Press.

DeFriend K.A., M.R. Wiesner & A.R. Barron, 2003. Alumina and aluminate ultrafiltration membranes derived from alumina nanoparticles. J. Membr. Sci. 224(1–2), 11–28.

Deliyanni E.A., D.N. Bakoyannakis, A.I. Zouboulis & K.A. Matis, 2003. Sorption of As(V) ions by akagane´ite-type nanocrystals. Chemosphere 50(1), 155–163.

Diallo M.S., S. Christie, P. Swaminathan, L. Balogh, X. Shi, W. Um, C. Papelis, W.A. Goddard III & J.H. Johnson Jr., 2004. Dendritic chelating agents 1. Cu(II) binding to ethylene diamine core poly(amidoamine) dendrimers in aqueous solutions. Langmuir 20, 2640–2651.

Dror I., D. Baram & B. Berkowitz, 2005. Use of nanosized catalysts for transformation of chloro-organic pollutants. Environ. Sci. Technol. 39(5), 1283–1290.

Favre-Reguillon A., G. Lebuzit, J. Fooz & A. Guy, 2003. Selective concentration of uranium from seawater by nanofiltration. Ind. Eng. Chem. Res. 42, 5900–5904.

Fre´chet J.M.J. & D.A. Tomalia, (Eds.). 2001. Dendrimers and Other Dendritic Polymers. New York: Wiley and Sons.

Fryxell G.E., Y. Lin, S. Fiskum, J.C. Birnbaum, H. Wu, K. Kemner & S. Kelly, 2005. Self-assembled monolayers on mesoporous supports. Environ. Sci. Technol. 39(5), 1324–1331.

Fugetsu B., S. Satoh, T. Shiba, T. Mizutani, Y.B. Lin, N. Terui &. Al. 2004. Caged multiwalled carbon nanotubes as the adsorbents for affinity-based elimination of ionic dyes. Environ. Sci. Technol. 38, 6890–6896.

Kabra K., R. Chaudhary & R.L. Sawhney, 2004. Treatment of hazardous organic and inorganic compounds through aqueous phase photocatalysis: A review. Ind. Eng. Chem. Res. 43(24), 7683–7696.

Kelly S.D., K.M. Kemmer, G.E. Fryxell, J. Liu, S.V. Mattigod & K.F. Ferris, 2001. X-ray-absorption fine-structure spectroscopy study of the interactions between contaminant tetrahedral anions and self-assembled monolayers on mesoporous supports. J. Phys. Chem. B. 105(27), 6337–6346.

Lazaridis N.K., D.N. Bakoyannakis & E.A. Deliyanni, 2005. Chromium(VI) sorptive removal from aqueous solutions by nanocrystalline akaganeite. Chemosphere 58(1), 65–73.

Li Q.L, D.X. Yuan & Q.M. Lin, 2004. Evaluation of multiwalled carbon nanotubes as an adsorbent for trapping volatile organic compounds from environmental samples. J. Chromatogr. 1026, 283–288.

Li, Y.H., Ding, J., Luan, Z.K., Di, Z.C., Zhu, Y.F., Xu, C.L., Wu, D.H. and Wei, B.Q. (2003) Competitive adsorption of Pb2+, Cu2+ and Cd2+ ions from aqueous solutions by multiwalled carbon nanotubes. Carbon 41(14), 2787–2792.

Lin Y., S.K. Fiskum, W. Yantasee, H. Wu, S.V. Mattigod, E. Vorpagel, G.E. Fryxell, K.N. Raymond & J. Xu, 2005. Incorporation of hydroxypiridinone ligands into self-assembled monolayers on mesoporous supports for selective actinide sequestration. Environ. Sci. Technol. 39(5), 1332–1337.

Mangun C.L., Z.R Yue, J. Economy, S. Maloney, P. Kemme & D. Cropek, 2001. Adsorption of organic contaminants from water using tailored ACFs Carbon. Chem. Mater. 13, 2356– 2360.

Mauter, M.S., Elimelech, M., 2008. Environmental applications of carbon-based nanomaterials. Environmental Science and Technology 42 (16), 5843e5859.

Meyer D.E., K. Wood, L.G. Bachas & D. Bhattacharyya, 2004. Degradation of chlorinated organics by membrane-immobilized nanosized metals. Environ. Prog. 23(3), 232–242.

Mohsen M.S., J.O. Jaber & M.D. Afonso, 2003. Desalination of brakish water by nanofiltration and reverse osmosis. Desalination 157(1), 167–167.

Moreno N., X. Querol & C. Ayora, 2001. Utilization of zeolites synthesized from coal fly ash for the purification of acid mines water. Environ. Sci. Technol. 35, 3526–3534.

Nurmi J.T., P.G. Tratnyek, V. Sarathy, D.R. Baer, J.E. Amonette, K. Pecher, C. Wang, J.C. Lineham, D.W. Matson, R.L. Penn & M.D. Driessen, 2005. Characterization and properties of metallic iron nanoparticles: spectroscopy, electrochemistry, and kinetics. Environ. Sci. Technol. 39(5), 1221–1230.

Obare S.O. & G.J. Meyer, 2004. Nanostructured materials for environmental remediation of organic contaminants in water. J. Environ. Sci. Health A. 39(10), 2549–2582.

Ottaviani M.F., P. Favuzza, M. Bigazzi, N.J. Turro, S. Jockusch & D.A. Tomalia, 2000. A TEM and EPR investigation of the competitive binding of uranyl ions to starburst dendrimers and liposomes: Potential use of dendrimers as uranyl ion sponges. Langmuir 16(19), 7368–7372.

Pan, B., Xing, B.S., 2008. Adsorption mechanisms of organic chemicals on carbon nanotubes. Environmental Science and Technology 42 (24), 9005-9013.

Peltier S., E. Cotte, D. Gatel, L. Herremans & J. Cavard, 2003. Nanofiltration improvements of water quality in a large distribution system. Water Sci. Tech.: Water Supply 3, 193–200.

Pendergast, M.M., Hoek, E.M.V., 2011. A review of water treatment membrane nanotechnologies. Energy & Environmental Science 4 (6), 1946-1971.

Peng X., Z. Luan, J. Ding, Z. Di, Y. Li & Tian,B. 2005. Ceria nanoparticles supported nanotubes for the removal of arsenate from water. Mater. Lett. 59, 399–403.

Qi L. & Xu,Z.2004. Lead sorption from aqueous solutions on chitosan nanoparticles. Colloid. Surf. A. 251(1–3), 183–190.

Qu, M., Wu,-J., Zhao, G. and Zhang Y. 2013. Nanostructioned Siolgaces, Coatings and Films : Fabrication, Characterization and application. Journal of Nanomaterials. 1-2.

Savage, N. and Diallo, M.S. 2005. Nanomaterials and water purification: Opportunities and challenges. Journal of Nanoparticle Research 7: 331–342.

Schrick B., J.L. Blough, A.D. Jones & T.E. Mallouk, 2002. Hydrodechlorination of trichloroethylene to hydrocarbons using bimetallic nickel-iron nanoparticles. Chem. Mater. 14(12), 5140–5147.

Son W.K., J.H. Youk, T.S. Lee & W.H. Park, 2004. Preparation of antimicrobial ultrafine cellulose acetate fibers with silver nanoparticles. Macromol. Rapid Commun. 25(18), 1632–1637.

Sondi I. & B. Salopek-Sondi, 2004. Silver nanoparticles as antimicrobial agent: A case study on E-coli as a model for Gram-negative bacteria. J. Coll. Interf. Sci. 275(1), 177–182.

Srivastava A., O.N. Srivastava, S. Talapatra, R. Vajtai & P.M. Ajayan, 2004. Nature Mater. 3(9): 610–614.

Stanton B.W., J.J. Harris, M.D Miller & M.L. Bruening, 2003. Ultrathin, multilayered polyelectrolyte films as nanofiltration membranes. Langmuir 19(17), 7038–7042.

Stoimenov P.K., R.L. Klinger, G.L. Marchin & K.J. Klabunde, 2002. Metal oxide nanoparticles as bactericidal agents. Langmuir 18(17), 6679–6686.

Tungittiplakorn W., C. Cohen & L.W. Lion, 2005. Engineered polymeric nanoparticles for bioremediation of hydrophobic contaminants. Environ. Sci. Technol. 39(5), 1354–1358.

Tungittiplakorn W., L.W. Lion, C. Cohen & J.Y. Kim, 2004. Engineered polymeric nanoparticles for soil remediation. Environ. Sci. Technol. 38(5), 1605–1610.

US Environmental Protection Agency, 1999. Alternative disinfectants and oxidants guidance manual. EPA Office of Water Report 815-R-99-014.

US Environmental Protection Agency. 1998. Microbial and disinfection by-product rules. Federal Register 63(241), 69389–69476.

Vander Bruggen B. & C. Vandecasteele, 2003. Removal of pollutants from surface water and groundwater by nanofiltration overview of possible applications in the drinking water industry. Environ. Pollut. 122, 435–445.

Verma, D.K. and Rakshit, A.2011. Water purification using indigenous method. International Journal of Agriculture Environment & Biotechnology: 4(3): 283-284.

WHO, 2012. Progress on Drinking Water and Sanitation. 2012 Update.

Yang, K., Xing, B.S., 2010. Adsorption of organic compounds by carbon nanomaterials in aqueous phase: Polanyi theory and its application. Chemical Reviews 110 (10), 5989e6008.

Yantasee W., Y. Lin, G.E. Fryxell, B.J. Busche & J.C. Birnbaum, 2003. Removal of heavy metals from aqueous solution using novel nanoengineered sorbents: Self-assembled carbamoylphosphonic acids on mesoporous silica. Separ. Sci. Technol. 38(15), 3809–3825.

Zeman L.J. & A.L. Zydney, 1996. Microfiltration and Ultrafiltration. New York: Marcel Dekker principles and applications.

Zhang W.-X., 2003. Nanoscale iron particles for environmental remediation. J. Nanopart. Res. 5, 323–332.

Zhao H.T. & K.L. Nagy, 2004. Dodecyl sulfate-hydrotalcite nanocomposites for trapping chlorinated organic pollutants in water. J. Coll. Interf. Sci. 274(2), 613–624.

❑❑❑

Section 3
Expert System Neural Network

CHAPTER - 17

Artificial Neural Network with Application to Forecasting in Limited Data Situation

H.C.Verma[1], R.R.Sethi[2], Deepak Kumar Verma[3]

[1]vermahc@hotmail.com, Central Institute for Subtropical Horticulture(ICAR), Rehmankhera, PO-Kakori, Lucknow-226101, Uttar Pradesh, India.

[2]ranurani@yahoo.com, Directorate of Water Management (ICAR), Bhubaneswar-751023, Orissa, India

[3]dbiotech88@gmail.com, Dr. M.C. Saxena Group of Colleges, Lucknow, Uttar Pradesh,India.

INTRODUCTION

Artificial Neural Network (ANN) is a branch of the field in computer science known as "Artificial Intelligence (AI)". The field goes by many names, such as connectionism, parallel distributed processing, neuro-computing, machine learning, and artificial neural networks. A tremendous growth in interest of this computational mechanism has occurred since Rumelhart(1986) rediscovered a mathematically rigorous theoretical framework neural network. Traditional (physically-based) modeling of physical processes tries to explain the underlying processes. On the contrary, the data-driven models are based on a limited knowledge of the modeling process and rely on the data describing input and output characteristics. Data-driven models are based on pure relationships between input and output data and not the physical principle linking input and output. They offer real advantages over conventional methods, including the ability to handle large amounts of dynamic, non-linear or noisy data and such tools can be especially useful when the underlying relationship are not fully understood. Data-driven modeling uses results from such overlapping fields as data mining, artificial neural networks, rule-based type approaches such as expert systems, fuzzy logic concepts, and machine learning systems.

Artificial neural networks are suited to problems where relationships between the variables to be modeled are not well understood. Mathematically, an ANN may be treated as a universal approximator. The ability to learn and generalize 'Knowledge' from sufficient data pairs make it possible for ANN to solve large-scale complex problems such as non-linear modeling, pattern recognition, classification, control and others – all of which find application in water resources management today. Since the early nineties, ANNs have been successfully used in water management area such as rainfall-runoff modeling, stream flow prediction, groundwater modeling, water quality, hydrologic time series, and reservoir operation.

Architecture and Mathematical Representation of ANN

Artificial Neural network is an information processing paradigm inspired by biological nervous systems, such as our brain, and simulates human neural system. A NN consists of a large number of processing elements, called *neurons*. Each neuron has an internal state, called its activation or and distribute it to the hidden layers. These hidden layers do all the necessary computation and output the results to the output layer, which outputs the data to the user. There are many types of networks - ranging from simple Boolean networks (Perceptions), to complex self-organizing networks.

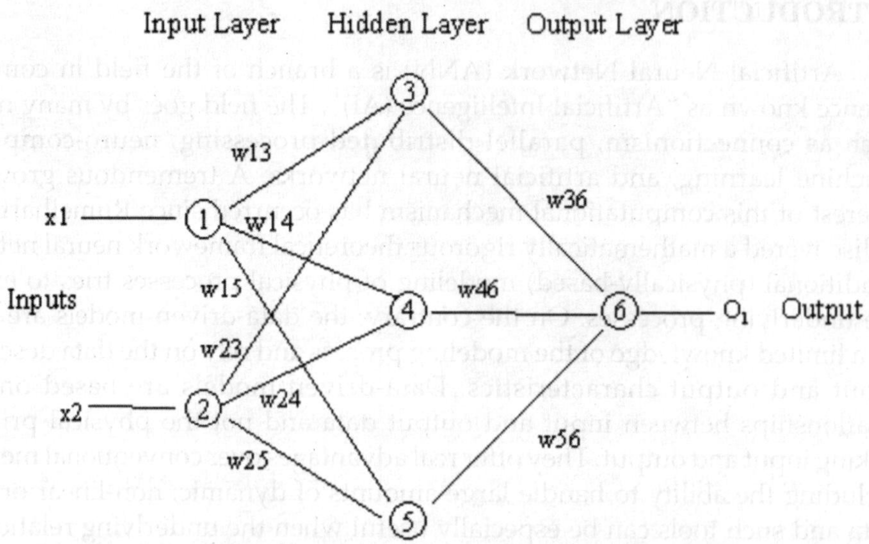

Fig. 1 : Configuration of Feedforward Three-Layer ANN

A neural network (NN) is characterized by :

- *Architecture* - its pattern of connections between the neurons.

- *Learning Algorithm* - its method of determining the weights on the connections.
- *Activation function* - which determines its output.

A schematic diagram of a typical jth node (neuron) of neural network is displayed in Fig.2. Here $x_1, x_2, x_3.....x_n$ are the n inputs to the neuron 'j' and forms an input vector $X=(x_1, x_2, x_3.....x_n)$ which is also called input pattern. The sequence of weights leading to the node forms a vector $W_j = (w_{1j}, w_{2j}, w_{3j}, ...w_{nj})$, where w_{ij} represents the connection weight from the ith node in preceding layer to this node. Here the total input I received by node 'j' is -

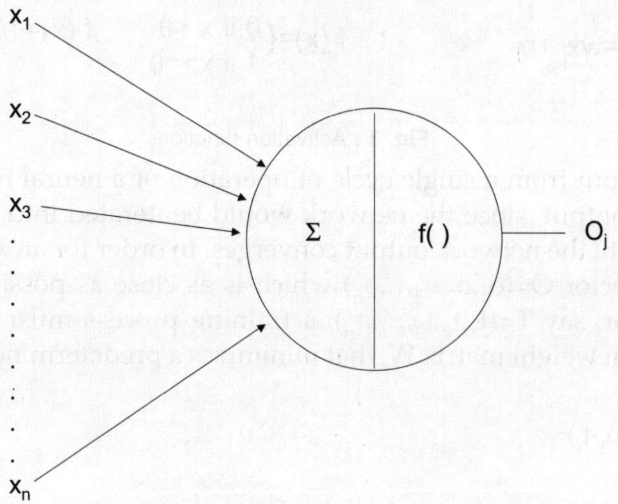

Fig. 2 : Schematic diagram of a neuron 'j'

$$I = \sum_{i=1}^{n} w_{ij}.x_i \tag{1}$$

e.g. in Fig.1, the value passed from neuron 3 to neuron 6 is = f(w13* value of neuron 1+ w23* value of neuron 2)

To generate the final output O_j, the sum is passed on to non-linear filter f(.) called Activation/Transfer/Squash function.

$$O_j = f(I-\theta) \tag{2}$$

Where, θ is threshold value. The transfer functions do the final mapping of the activations of the output neurons into the network output. The neuron calculates a weighted sum of inputs and compares it to a threshold. If the sum is higher than the threshold, the output is set to 1, otherwise to 0. There are different forms of f(.) used in eq. (2) as shown in Fig.3 .

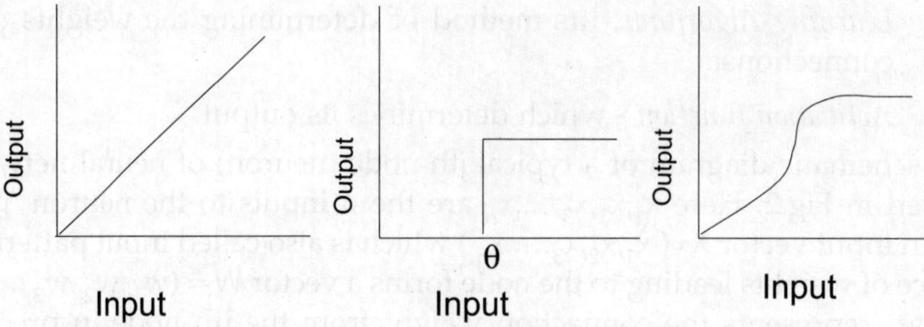

Linear function: $f(x)=wx_j+b$

Step function: $f(x)=\begin{cases}0 & \text{if } x<\theta\\ 1 & \text{if } x>=\theta\end{cases}$

Sigmoid function: $f(x)=1/(1+e^{-x})$

Fig. 3 : Activation functions

The output from a single cycle of operation of a neural network may not be the final output, since the network would be iterated into further cycles of operation until the network output converges. In order for an ANN to generate an output vector $O=(o_1,o_2,o_3....o_n)$ which is as close as possible to the target output vector, say $T=(t_1,t_2,t_3,.....t_n)$, a training process must be employed to find optimum weight matrix W, that minimizes a predetermined error function E given by

$$E=\sum_{p}\sum_{n}(o_i-t_i)^2 \qquad (3)$$

Where, n= no. of output nodes and p= no. of training(input/output) patterns.

Neural Network Models

Over the years, several Neural Network systems have evolved. The following are some of the systems that have gained significance:

- Perceptron
- ADALINE and MADALINE
- Multi-Layer Feedforward Network (MLFF)
- Radial Basis Function (RBF)
- Time Delay Neural Network TDNN)
- Recurrent Neural Network (RNN)
- Hopefield network

- Adoptive Resonence Theory (ART)
- Fuzzy Associative Memory (FAM)
- Bidirectional Associative Memory (BAM)
- Self Organizing Feature Maps (SOFM)

Network Learning and Training

The learning in NN is the process of mapping a set of inputs to a desired set of output, either with or without an explicit training process. Neural networks "learn" from experience/examples, just like children learn to recognise dogs from examples of dogs. The system learns new knowledge by adjusting connection weights. Training is an external process but learning is a desired process that takes place internal to the network. There are two types of learning processes:

i) Supervised learning

In this method, both the inputs and the outputs are provided. The network then processes the inputs and compares its resulting outputs against the desired outputs. Errors are then calculated, causing the system to adjust the weights, which control the network. The ANN models that use unsupervised learning are Feedforward Backpropagation network, Redial Basis Function networks and Perceptrons.

ii) Unsupervised learning

In this method, no training data is provided. The hidden neurons must find a way to organize them without help from the outside. This is often referred to as self-organization or adoption. It is most suitable for clustering and classification problems. The models that use unsupervised learning are Kohonen Self-Organizing Feature Map, Hopefield network, Bi-directional Associative Memory, Fuzzy Associative Memory and ART1.

Supervised and unsupervised learning methods, which are most popular forms of learning, have found expression through various rules. Some of the widely used rules are: Hebb's rule, Gradient descent rule and delta rule.

Feedforward Backpropagation Network

Backpropagation is a supervised learning algorithm and is mainly used by Multi-Layer-Perceptrons to change the weights connected to the net's hidden neuron layer(s). The backpropagation algorithm uses a computed output error to change the weight values in backward direction. To get this net error, a forward propagation phase must have been done before. It is called Feedforward

Backpropagation Network (Fig.1). While propagating in forward direction, the neurons are being activated using the sigmoid activation function.

The backpropagation algorithm works as follows:

1. Perform the forward propagation phase for an input pattern and calculate the output error.
2. Change all weight values of each weight matrix using the formula weight (old) + learning rate * output error * output (neurons i) * output (neurons i+1) * (1 - output (neurons i+1)).
3. Go to step 1.
4. The algorithm ends, if all output patterns match their target patterns

The first input pattern is propagated through the net. The same procedure is used for the next input pattern, but then with the changed weight values. After the forward and backward propagation of the second pattern, one learning step is complete and the net error can be calculated by adding up the squared output errors of each pattern. By performing this procedure repeatedly, this error value gets smaller and smaller. The algorithm is successfully finished, if the net error is zero or approximately zero.

Developing an ANN Model

There is no fixed rule for developing NN but some steps that can be followed are briefly described below:

i. *Determination and preparation of model inputs:* Input data selection and preparation are the most time-consuming tasks of neural network. A neural network is only as good as the input data used to train it. Once the most appropriate raw input data has been selected, it must be prepossessed. Transformation and normalization are two widely used preprocessing methods. Transformation involves manipulating raw input data to reduce its dimensionality (reducing number of input variables), while normalization is a transformation performed on input data to distribute the data evenly and scale it (mostly in the range of –1 to 1 to 0 to 1) into an acceptable range for the network. Some simple preprocessing methods include computing differences between or taking ratio of inputs. This reduces number of inputs to the network and helps it learn more easily.

ii. *Networks selection:* It involves selection of network model, number and size of hidden layers and initial weight matrix. Trail-and-error method is used to select network parameters to obtain the best model.

iii. *Networks training and cross training:* Much of the process of determining the best parameters for a given application is trail and error. It needs to start with a network topology and initial weight, and train the network on your training data set. When the network reaches the satisfactory minimum error, save the weights

iv. *Network testing/validation:* The trained network is applied on test data set to find the error on this data set. If it is not satisfactory the training process needs to be repeated again with different set of initial weights. If the error is not satisfactory then you need to re-enter the design phase or the train and test phase.

Example of ANN Application: ANN Model for prediction of water table depth in a hard rock basin in limited data situation

The objectives of this study were to determine the factors that influence and control the water table fluctuation in a specific geomorphologic situation, to develop a forecasting model and examine its potential in predicting water table depth using limited data. Prediction of region specific water table fluctuation would certainly guide the way towards conceiving, designing and taking scientific measures to ensure sustainable groundwater management. Analysis of change in groundwater table depth, groundwater flow directions within the watershed showed that the influencing factors of rainfall, groundwater draft from nearby structures and the resulting fluctuation in groundwater table depth were well correlated in a specific geological situation. Models for prediction of water table depth were developed based on artificial neural networks (ANNs). The study employed multilayer feedforward neural network with backpropagation learning method to develop the model. The neural networks with different numbers of hidden layer neurons were developed using 4 years (2005-2008) monthly rainfall, potential evapotranspiration (PET), and water table depth from nearby influencing wells data as input and one month ahead water table depth as output. The best model was selected based on the root mean square error (RMSE) of prediction using independent test data set. The results of the study clearly showed that ANN can be used to predict water table depth in a hard rock aquifer with reasonably good accuracy even in case of limited data situation.

Odisha as a whole has a huge balance of groundwater resources with a wide scope for its development (Pati, 2009). But, due to presence of hard rock areas and many associated problems with complex hydrological system it has not been exploited to the desirable levels. Present study area was focused in the Nayagarh block located in Nayagarh district of Odisha. Monitoring wells have been identified within the Munijhara watershed. It showed that 55% of the wells showed depletion in water table depth during pre-monsoon dry season. This leads to the associated problem of lowering tubewell depth and drying of open dug wells in these areas. The possible reason could be increase in groundwater draft due to population growth, low groundwater recharge etc. As the demand increases it may not be feasible to check the draft of groundwater resources but there is a chance to increase the recharge rate to the aquifer by suitable means. It is necessary to quantify the present rate of groundwater recharge, monitor the change in water table depth and then predict the future trend of water table depth before any intervention. Groundwater development in Nayagarh block is only 15.52% (GEC, 2008). It was observed that water table depth in the dug wells rises up to the ground level during monsoon season, but immediately after rainy season it gets lowered down which indicates the direct relationship between amount of rise in water level and precipitation for different geological formations. In other words factors characterized by a parameter that correlates rise in groundwater level with precipitation for each zone has to be defined properly. Many studies have been conducted in applications of ANNs to hydrology which can be found in the ASCE Task Committee report (ASCE, 2000a, b). Literature showed that feasibility of using artificial neural networks (ANNs) was studied to estimate groundwater level in piezometers in unconfined chalky aquifer of North France (Lallahem *et al.*, 2005), to estimate aquifer parameter values (Balkhair, 2002), to forecast the groundwater level using rainfall, temperature, and stream discharge as inputs (Daliakopoulos *et al.*, 2005), and to evaluate the groundwater level in fractured media (Lallahem *et al.*, 2004). Affandi et al, 2007 compared the capability of an ANN with five different backpropagation (BP) algorithms for estimating groundwater level fluctuation. Seven different types of network architectures and training algorithms were investigated and compared in terms of model prediction efficiency and accuracy. Result showed that accurate predictions were achieved with a standard feedforward neural network trained with the Lavenberg-Marquardt (Daliakopoulos *et al.*, 2005). It is worth mentioning that sufficient lengths of water table depth measurements are usually unavailable in developing countries (Coulibaly *et al.*, 2001). Such countries typically have very few observation wells and lack long-period time-series data due to budget limitations and government policy (Affandia *et al.*, 2007). This necessitates developing models that are capable of forecasting ground water table depth using limited data. In many other areas, the efforts were made to develop neural network based forecasting models with limited data (Aminian *et al.*, 2005; Sudheer *et al.*, 2003; Wang *et al.*, 2008). Keeping it in view, an attempt was made to determine the factors that influence and control the water table fluctuation in a specific geologic situation develop ANN based model and test its potential in predicting ground water table depth with limited climatic and nearby wells data.

MATERIAL AND METHODS

Study Area

The study was carried out in Munijhara micro watershed, which lies between 20^0 05′and 20^0 09′N latitude and 85^0 05′ to 85^0 09′E longitude (Fig.1). The area is located in Nayagarh block of Nayagarh district of Orissa (India), which occupies the central part of Eastern Orissa and is underlain by hard rocks, includes Khondalite-Charnockite suit of rocks and granites rocks. Altitude of the region varies from 80 to 100 m above mean sea level (MSL). Total area of the watershed is 45 km^2 out of which only 2.69 km^2 (6%) area is under forest cover and rest is cultivated, pasture and residential areas. The main drain in the watershed is Munijhara with drainage density of 0.35 km/km^2 and is of third order. Boundaries of watershed make the area a typical geo-hydrological unit with single outlet. Goundwater flow in the watershed coincides with the topographic map of the area. Subsurface lithology (12-15m depth) is dominated by granite and hard rock aquifer (CGWB, 2004). From the field survey, it was observed that groundwater is being abstracted from 166 numbers of tube wells and 450 numbers of open wells for domestic and agricultural purposes. There is also presence of few water storage structures of village ponds and big structures in each village but it often get dried during summer season.

Climatic Condition

Climatically this region is sub humid and receives average annual rainfall of 1449 mm, 80% of which occurs in the monsoon season (June-September). The mean minimum and maximum temperature of this region are 13°C in January and 44°C in May respectively and mean relative humidity is 90%. Except monsoon periods, groundwater is the only source of available resources both for domestic and crop demand throughout the year.

Artificial Neural Networks

Artificial neural network (ANN) is an information processing paradigm inspired by biological nervous systems, such as our brain. It consists of large number of highly interconnected processing elements, called neurons, working together (Tsoukalas and Uhrig, 1997). An ANN consists of input, hidden, and output layers and each layer includes an array of processing elements. A neural network is characterized by its architecture that represents the pattern of connection between nodes, its method of determining the connection weights, and the activation function (Fausett, 1994)

Feedforward Neural Network

The most popular ANN architecture in hydrologic modelling is the feedforward neural network trained with a backpropagation algorithm (ASCE 2000a, b). Feedforward neural networks are among the most common neural networks in use (Mehrotra *et al.*, 1997). Feedforward neural networks have been applied successfully for solving different problems since the advent of the error backpropagation learning algorithm. This network architecture and the corresponding learning algorithm can be viewed as a generalization of the popular least-mean-square (LMS) algorithm (Haykin, 1999). A feedforward neural network consists of an input layer, one or more hidden layers of computation nodes, and an output layer. In feedforward network the input signal propagates through the network in a forward direction, layer by layer. Their main advantage is that they are easy to handle, and can approximate any input/output map, as established by Hornik *et al.* (1989). Backpropagation learning algorithm used gradient descent with momentum term to calculate derivatives of performance cost function with respect to the weight and bias variables of the network. Each variable is adjusted according to the gradient descent with momentum. This is probably the simplest and most common way to train a network (Haykin, 1999). For each step of the optimization, if performance decreases the learning rate is increased.

Training of a feedforward neural network involves two phases. The calculation of the output is carried out, layer by layer, in the forward direction. The output of one layer is the input to the next layer. In the reverse pass, the weights of the output neuron layer are adjusted first since the target value of each output neuron is available to guide the adjustment of the associated weights. The weights in the output and hidden layer neurons can be calculated using eqs. (4) and (5), respectively (Tsoukalas and Uhrig 1996)

$$w(N+1) = w(N) - \eta.\delta.\phi \tag{4}$$

$$w(N+1) = w(N) + \eta.x.\sum_{q=1}^{r} \delta_q \tag{5}$$

Where, *w*=weight; *N*=number of iteration; *x*=input value; *h*=learning rate; ϕ=output; and δ is defined as $2.\varepsilon_q.\partial\phi/\partial I$, *I* being the sum of the weighted inputs, *q*=neuron index of the output layer, and ε_q=error signal. This training method is known as the standard backpropagation training method. Since, it uses a form of gradient descent, it is assumed that the error surface slope is always negative and hence, constantly adjusting weights toward minimum. It is very easy for the training process to get trapped in a local minimum. The problem of the local minima can be avoided by adding a momentum term to the weight change, to permit larger learning rates. The change of weight is then computed as follows:

$$\Delta w(N+1) = -\eta.\delta.\theta + \mu.\Delta w(N) \tag{6}$$

Where, μ=momentum coefficient and Δw (*N*+1) =change of weight during *N* to *N*+1 learning cycles. Therefore, the new value of weight becomes equal to the previous value of the weight plus the weight change, which includes the momentum term. This training method is known as back-propagation with momentum which uses gradient descent with momentum (GDM) algorithm. The feedforward network with a backpropagation-based gradient descent learning rule has been shown to be a good choice for solving problems with non-linear relationship (Haykin, 1999; Shamseldin, 1997; Hsu *et al.*; Bose and Liang, 1996). Therefore in this study, we used feedforward neural network with backpropagation learning algorithm to approximate the relation between input parameters (water table depth in target and nearby influencing well, rainfall and PET) in question, and the resulting output parameter (one month ahead water table depth in target well).

Data sets

Monthly rainfall data during 1993-2007 was collected from different departments of Nayagarh and analyzed to determine the rainfall distribution. Monthly monitoring of fluctuation in water table depth during 2005 to 2008 was carried out in 64 numbers of spatially distributed dug wells in Munijhara watershed of Nayagarh block of Orissa. Out of total selected dug wells, 55%, 25% and 20% of dug wells were located in flood plain, granite gneiss and upland plain respectively. Contour map representing the pre and post monsoon water table fluctuation for the entire watershed was prepared by krigging method. Analysis of change in groundwater table depth, groundwater flow directions within the watershed was carried out. For the purpose of model development, monthly PET data were also collected for period of 2005-2008. Rainfall and PET were directly taken as input variables as these are well known factors that influence the water table depth. However, the nearby wells that have direct influence on the water table depth of target well were determined through a linear cross correlation. In this way, the nearby wells having higher correlation coefficient (>0.80) with the water table depth in target wells were selected as input variables for the models. A total of 4 years monthly data (January, 2005-December, 2008) related to above mentioned variables were used for model development.

Normalization of data

Normalization is a transformation performed on input data to distribute the data evenly and scale it into an acceptable range for the network (mostly in the range of –1 to 1 or 0 to 1). Because the neurons of the middle layer were assigned a sigmoidal activation function that speed-up ANN leaning if input data is in range of –1 to 1 or 0 to 1. Keeping this in view, the normalization was carried out so that the all input data fall in the range of 0 to 1. The following equation was used:

$$x_{norm} = 0.1 + 0.8\left(\frac{x_o - x_{\min}}{x_{\max} - x_{\min}}\right) \tag{7}$$

Where, x_{norm}=normalized value; x_0=original observed value; $x_{\max}$=maximum value; and $x_{\min}$= minimum value.

Model evaluation criteria

Two different criteria viz., Root Mean Square Error (RMSE) and coefficient of determination (R^2) were used in order to evaluate the effectiveness of each network and its ability to make precise predictions.

The Root Mean Square Error (RMSE) was calculated by

$$RMSE = \sqrt{\frac{\sum_{i=1}^{N}(X_i - X_i^{'})^2}{N}} \tag{8}$$

Where X_i is the observed data, $X_i^{'}$ is the calculated data and N is the number of observations. The RMSE can give a quantitative indication of the model error in terms of a dimensioned quantity. An RMSE equal to zero indicates a perfect match between the observed and predicted values.

The R^2 was calculated by

$$R^2 = 1 - \frac{\sum (X_i - X_i^{'})^2}{\sum X_i^2 - \frac{\sum (X_i^{'})^2}{N}} \tag{9}$$

In R^2 efficiency criterion, the best fit between observed and calculated values would have R^2=1.

Network training, validation and testing

Before applying the ANN to the data, the input and output data were normalized to fall in the range of 0 to1. The normalized data set was divided into three subsets for the purpose of training, validation and testing. Out of total 4 years monthly data, 50% and 25% were used for model training and validation, respectively and 25% were used for model test. The training data set was used to train a neural net by minimizing the error of this data set during training. The validation data set was used to determine the performance of a neural network during training. The test set was used for checking the overall performance of a trained and validated network. A total of 9 networks, 3 each for upland plain, flood plain and granite formation were developed and trained using SNNS 4.2 software. For ANN architectures, the numbers of nodes in the input layer were fixed at seven, six and five in case of the models for upland plain, flood plain, and granite zones, respectively with one node in output layer. The numbers of nodes in the hidden layer of different models were varied from 6 to 10. The activation function used was log-sigmoid. Backpropagation algorithm using gradient descent with momentum term was used to train the neural network.. To obtain the best ANN architecture several possibilities were considered in this study. Training and validation data sets were shuffled before training and validation to ensure the randomness during ANNs training and validation. The networks were trained and performances were measured in terms of error rate on training and validation data set simultaneously. Each ANN architecture was trained for different learning rates and momentum values, and error rate on training and validation data set were monitored using error graph module of the software. The training was stopped as soon as validation error rate started stabilizing or increasing because it may lead to network memorization or over training. In this way, by means of trial and error, optimum network parameters viz. learning rate and momentum values were determined for all three networks for each geological formations of the watershed. After training was over, the weights were saved and the trained network was run on test data to evaluate the performance of these networks.

RESULTS AND DISCUSSION

Rainfall Distribution

Rainfall analysis (1993-2007) showed that mean annual and monsoon rainfall of Nayagarh was 1350 and 1131.02 mm respectively. The standard deviation for annual and monsoon (June - October) rainfall were 291.7 and 251.17 with coefficient of variation of 20.87 % and 22.2% respectively (Table 1). Kharif, summer and rabi season contributes 83%, 11% and 4% to mean annual rainfall of the area. High demand of water in rainfed area without irrigation facilities usually met through groundwater. But, status of groundwater development for study area showed that there is an urgent need to recharge groundwater through conservation structures. For construction of water conservation structures there is need to predict the monsoon rainfall of any area.

Table 1 : Rainfall analysis of Nayagarh (1993-2007)

Statistical parameters	Annual rainfall (mm)	Monsoon rainfall (mm)
Mean	1350.13	1131.02
Standard Deviation	291.73	251.17
Coefficient of variance (%)	21.60	22.00
Sample variance	85108.94	63084.94
Kurtosis	-0.52	0.25
Skewness	0.14	0.80
Range	821.9- 1824.1	753.6-1657.4
Confidence Level (95.0%)	161.56	139.09

Water Table Fluctuation

The WTF method requires a very good knowledge of piezometric level throughout the entire basin. This could be achieved owing to a very dense observation network (64 wells in 40 km^2 area) provided mainly defunct or wells used for domestic purposes only where the rate of withdrawal of water is comparatively less. Sophocleous (1991) pointed out that the WTF method could be misleading if the water level fluctuations are confused with those resulting from pumping, barometric, or other causes. Care was taken to avoid any interference from pumping wells to the monitoring wells. Monthly monitoring and analysis of fluctuation in water table depth during 2005 to 2008 of was carried out and contour map was prepared for pre and post monsoon season. It was observed that the groundwater elevation in pre monsoon season was almost similar however there was change in water table elevation in post monsoon season only. Mean water table elevation during June-2008 and November-2008 was 81.9m and 84m respectively, which was the maximum difference in water table depth (2.11m) in last 3 year i.e. 2006 to 2008. The reason can be attributed to more number of total rainy days (85) and maximum amount of rainfall (1187.9mm) received during monsoon 2008.

Relationship of Water Table Fluctuation in Different Geological Formations

Geological and geomorphological area of watershed was extracted using GIS tools from the district resource map of Nayagarh developed by Geological

Survey of India, Bhubaneswar, Orissa (Fig. 1). Geomorphologically the watershed was classified as flood plain (23 km^2) and upland plain (17 km^2). Out of total monitoring wells located in the watershed, 55% wells are in flood plain area and rest 25% and 20% are in granite gneiss and upland plains respectively. Trend of water table fluctuation in different geologic formations and all the possible influencing factors like rainfall, Potential evapotranspiration (PET) and effect of nearby monitoring wells in the specific geomorphologic conditions that may affect the change in water table depths were analyzed. The correlation coefficient between rainfall, PET and water table fluctuation among the monitoring wells located in the flood plain zone was worked out to be 0.88 to 0.98. But, in case of upland plain areas dominated by hard rocks and granite zones, negative correlation between water table fluctuation and rainfall was observed.

Performance of ANN Models

To evaluate the performance of trained ANN models for all the three geological formations, we run the trained and validated networks using independent test dataset. Two statistical indices of performance were computed for the test result: the root mean square error and the coefficient of determination (R^2). Table 2 shows the performance indices of ANN models with different architectures and for different locations using the testing data set. The models giving lowest RMSE value on test data were selected as the best models. In case of upland plain, the model ANN (7-8-1) gave the lowest RMSE value 0.83, hence it is selected as the best model. Similarly, in case of flood plain, the model ANN (6-7-1) gave the lowest RMSE value 0.63, and in granite zone the model ANN (5-6-1) gave lowest RMSE value 1.33. These models were selected as the best models. It is evident from the table that high correlation between observed and predicted result (correlation coefficient in the range of 0.84-0.98) were obtained for the flood plain and upland plain formation using different ANN models but for granite formation, correlation is somewhat lower. To provide a visual interpretation and appreciation of the results, Fig. 3-5 show the variations of observed water table depth and those estimated by ANN (7-8-1) for upland plain formation, ANN (6-7-1) for flood plain formation and ANN(5-6-7) for granite formation areas of watershed, respectively. These figures show good agreement between observed and predicted value of water table depth in monitoring wells located in upland and flood plain areas. While values in the later part of these graphs are slightly underestimated by ANN, earlier values are better modeled by it which represent the water scarce period in this agro climatic region and therefore this type of better prediction accuracy is very much desirable to manage ground water resources more effectively. Among all the models, the prediction accuracy in flood plain and upland plain areas were comparatively better than that of granite zone. The result shows that the RMSE values of all the models for granite formation were quite high, thereby making prediction accuracy relatively low in comparison to flood plain and upland plain. It may be due to less influence of nearby monitoring wells on water table fluctuation in monitoring well in this formation. The RMSE values obtained in this study using limited data were well comparable with some of the similar previous studies that used larger data set (Coulibaly *et al.*, 2001; Daliakopoulos *et al.*, 2005 and Krishna *et al.*, 2008). The results from this study suggest that ANN can provide a reliable method to forecast water table depth with good accuracy even with limited data.

Table 2 : Performance indices of ANN models with different architectures[a]

Geological Formations	ANN Architecture	RMSE(m)	R^2
Upland Plain	ANN(7-8-1)	0.83	0.96
	ANN(7-9-1)	0.89	0.98
	ANN(7-10-1)	0.89	0.95
Flood Plain	ANN(6-7-1)	0.63	0.87
	ANN(6-8-1)	0.67	0.84
	ANN(6-9-1)	0.66	0.82
Granite	ANN(5-6-1)	1.33	0.59
	ANN(5-7-1)	1.82	0.38
	ANN(5-8-1)	1.81	0.36

[a]Based on one year's test data CONCLUSIONS

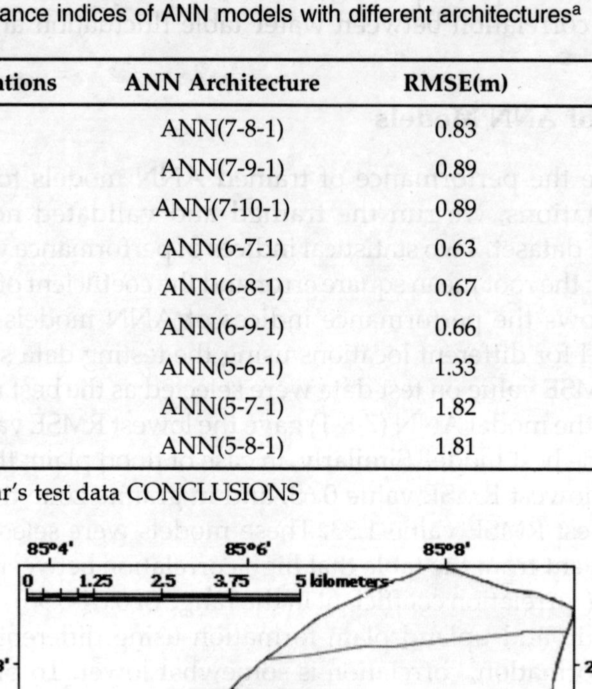

Fig. 4 : Geology and geomorphological map of Munijhara watershed

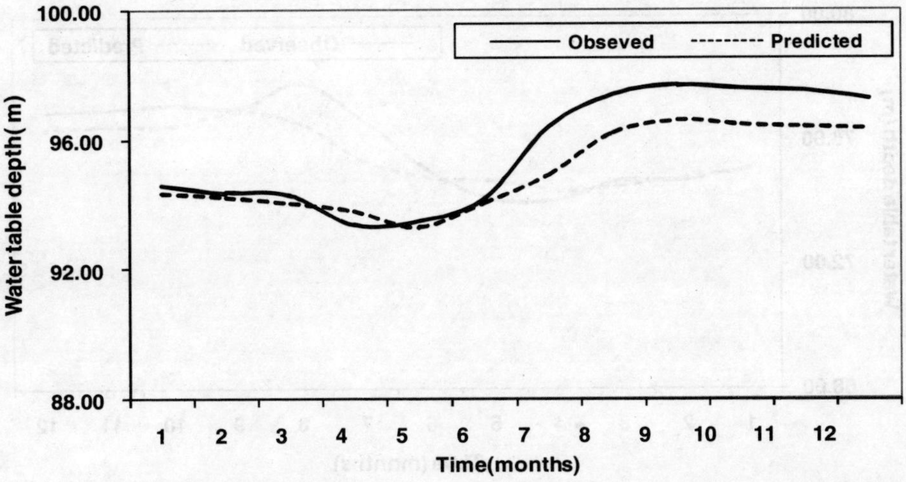

Fig. 5 : Comparison of observed groundwater depths with predicted results using ANN (7-8-1) model for the monitoring well of upland plain geological formation for the period January 2008–December 2008.

In this study the factors that influence and control the water table fluctuation in a specific geologic situation were determined and used to develop ANN models for forecasting one month ahead ground water table depth for different geological formations. The results clearly showed that ANN can be used to predict water table depth in a hard rock aquifer with reasonably good accuracy even in case of limited data situation(Sudheer,K.P.,*et.al.,* 2003). The result of this is in good agreement with previous related studies done with larger length of data. Therefore, it can be concluded that an ANN is an effective tool for forecasting of ground water table depth for the purposes of groundwater management, even though only limited data samples were available. In this study the models were calibrated with limited input data set monitored during study period only, the performance of the model can further be improved with sufficient data sets. It would be interesting to find out how would other architectures and training algorithms of ANN perform in poor data situation. Using other soft computing methods to forecast water table depth can also be an interesting study to pursue.

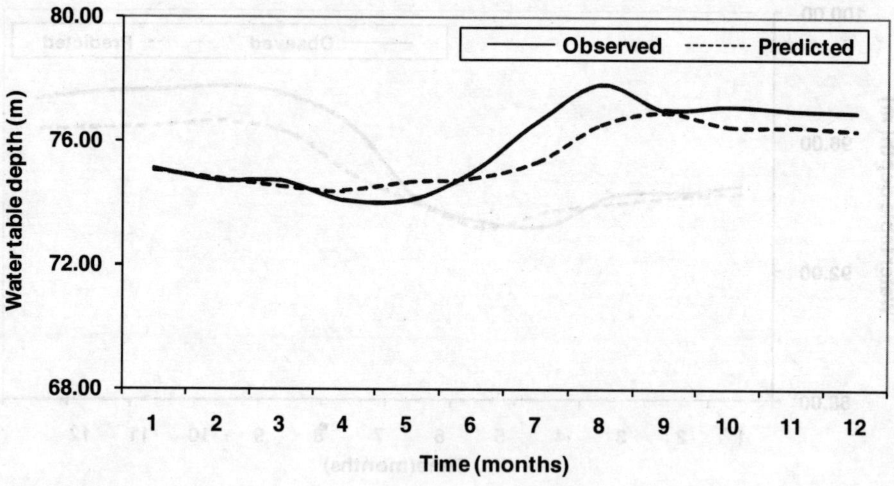

Fig. 6: Comparison of observed groundwater depths with predicted results using ANN (6-7-1) model for the monitoring well of flood plain geological formation for the period January 2008–December 2008.

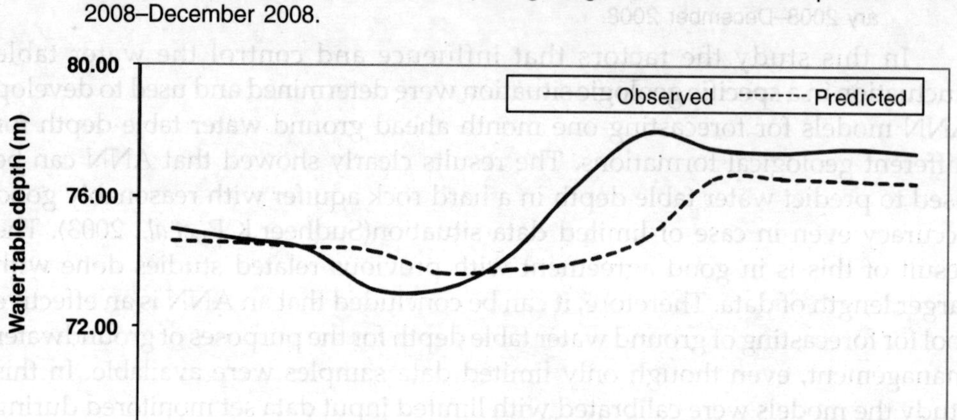

Fig. 7 : Comparison of observed groundwater depths with predicted results using ANN (5-6-1) model for the monitoring well of granite geological formation for the period January 2008–December 2008.

ACKNOWLEDGEMENTS

Authors thank the referees/reviewers for providing their valuable suggestions to improve the quality of the manuscript. .This work was done when first author was posted at Directorate of Water Management, Bhubaneswar.

NOMENCLATURE

The following abbreviations/symbols are used in this paper

PET	=	Potential Evapotranspiration
ANN	=	Artificial Neural Network
GDM	=	Gradient Descent with Momentum
RMSE	=	Root Mean Square Error
R^2	=	Coefficient of determination
GIS	=	Geographical Information System
w	=	weight, the strength of connection between neurons
N	=	number of iteration
x	=	input value
η	=	learning rate
ϕ	=	output
I	=	sum of the weighted inputs
q	=	neuron index of the output layer
ε_q	=	error signal
μ	=	momentum coefficient
Δw (N+1)	=	change of weight during N to N+1 learning cycles
x_{norm}	=	normalized value
x_0	=	original input value
x_{max}	=	maximum of input values
x_{min}	=	minimum of input values
$WTD_t(t)$	=	water table depth in target well at time t
$WTD_i(t)$	=	water table depth in i^{th} (i=1…n) well nearby to target well

REFERENCES

Affandi, Azhar K.,Watanabe, Kunio and Tirtomihardjo, Haryadi. (2007). Application of an artificial neural network to estimate groundwater level fluctuation. Journal of spatial hydrology. 7(2), pp 23-46.

Aminian, K. and Ameri, S. (2005). Application of artificial neural networks for reservoir characterization with limited data. Journal of Petroleum Science and Engineering. 49(3-4), pp. 212-222.

ASCE Task Committee on Application of Artificial Neural Networks in Hydrology (2000a). Artificial neural networks in hydrology-I: Preliminary concepts. Journal of Hydrologic Engineering 5(2), pp 115–123.

ASCE Task Committee on Application of Artificial Neural Networks in Hydrology (2000b). Artificial neural networks in hydrology-II: Hydrologic applications. Journal of Hydrologic Engineering 5(2), pp124–137.

Balkhair, K.S. (2002) Aquifer parameters determination for large diameter wells using neural network approach, Journal of Hydrology, 265, pp118-128.

Bierkens, M. F. P.(1998). Modeling water table fluctuations by means of a stochastic differential equation, Water Resources Research, 34(10), pp 2485– 2499.

Bose, N.K. and Liang, P. (1996). Neural network fundamentals with Graph, Algorithms and Application. New York, N.Y., McGraw-Hill.

CGWB(2004).Central groundwater Board, Ministry of Water Resources, Government of India.

Coulibaly, P., Anctil, F., Aravena, R. and Bobee, B. (2001). Artificial neural network modeling of water table depth fluctuations, Water Resources Research, 37(4), pp 885-896.

Daliakopoulos, Ioannis N., Coulibaly, Paulin, Tsanis, Ioannis K. (2005). Groundwater level forecasting using artificial neural networks. Journal of hydrology. 309, pp 229-240(Elsevier)

Fausett L., "Fundamentals of Neural Networks – Architektures, Algorithms and Application". Prentice Hall Inc., Englewood Cliffs, NJ, 1994.

GEC, Report of the Groundwater Resource Estimation Committee(1997). Ground Water Resource Estimation Committee. Groundwater Resource Estimation Methodology. Ministry of Water Resource, Govt of India.

Haykin, S. (1999). Neural Networks: A Comprehensive Foundation. Second edition. Prentice-Hall, Englewood Cliffs, NJ.

Hornik, K., Stinchcombe, M., White, M., 1989. Multilayer feed forward networks are universal approximators. Neural Networks 2, 359–366.

Hsu,K.,Gupta, H.V. and Sorooshian,S.(1995). Artificial neural network modeling of the rainfall-runoff process. Water Resources Research 31(10), pp.2517-2530

Knotters, M., and De Gooijer, J. G. (1999). TARSO modeling of water table depths, Water Resources Research, 35(3), pp 695–705.

Krishna, B., Satyaji Rao, Y. R. and Vijaya, T. (2008). Modelling groundwater levels in an urban coastal aquifer using artificial neural networks. Hydrological Processes, 22, pp. 1180–1188.

Lallahem, S., Mania, J., Hani, A., Najjar, Y. (2005). On use of neural networks to evaluate groundwater levels in fractured media. Journal of hydrology. 307(1-4), pp 92-111.

Mehrotra, K., Mohan, C.K., Ranka, S., 1997. Elements of Artificial Neural Networks. The MIT Press, Boston. 344 pp.

Pati, G.C. (2009)Groundwater Resource Scenario of Orissa. Proc. of Workshop on Groundwater Scenario and quality in Orissa, Organized by CGWB, Govt. of India, pp.1-8

Shamseldin, A.Y. (1997) Application of a neural network technique to rainfall-runoff modeling. J. Hydrology. 199(3/4), pp. 172-194.

Sethi R.R.,Kumar,A., Sharma, S.P., Verma, H.C.(2010).Prediction of water table depth in hard rock basin by using Artificial Neural Network. International Journal of water resources and environmental engineering,2(4), pp.95-102

SNNS (1995). User manual, version 4.1, Rep. No. 6/95, Institute for Parallel and Distributed High Performance Systems, University of Stuttgart, Stuttgart, Germany.

Sophocleous, MA (1991). Combining the soil water balance and water table fluctuation methods to estimate natural groundwater recharge: Practical aspects. Journal of Hydrology, 124, pp.229-241.

Sudheer, K. P., Gosain, A. K. and Ramasastri, K. S. (2003). Estimating actual evapotranspiration from limited climatic data using neural computing technique. Journal of Irrigation and Drainage Engineering, 129(3), pp. 214-218

Tsoukalas, L. H., and Uhrig, R. E. (1996). Fuzzy and neural approach in engineering, Wiley, New York.

Wang,Y., Traore,S. and Kerh,T.(2008). Neural network approach for estimating reference evapotranspiration fro347m limited climatic data in Burkina Faso. WSEAS Transactions on Computers, 7(6), pp.704-713.

❑❑❑

CHAPTER - 18

Artificial Neural Network Model for Forecasting Future Rainfall Scenario of Jharkhand State of India

H.C.Verma[1], and A.Mishra[2]

[1]Central Institute of Subtropical Horticulture, Rehmankhera, P.O.-Kakori-226101, Lucknow(up).

[2]International Water Management Research Institute (CGIAR), South Africa

[1]vermahc@hotmail.com, Central Institute for Subtropical Horticulture(ICAR), Rehmankhera, PO-Kakori, Lucknow-226101, Uttar Pradesh, India.

[2]atmaram.mishra@cgiar.org, Senior Researcher - Agriculture Water Management, IWMI(CGIAR), South Africa.

INTRODUCTION

There is growing concern in both the scientific community and the general public over the possibility of important climatic changes due to increases in relatively active gases in the atmosphere, a phenomenon commonly referred to as "climate change." In the past century, the activities of a rapidly expanding and industrializing human population have added significant quantities of heat retaining gases to the atmosphere. For example, the Intergovernmental Panel on Climate Change (IPCC) estimates that by 2100 increases in greenhouse gases will likely lead to an increase in temperature of between $I0^0$ C and 3.50^0 C (Houghton *et al.,* 1996) and an increase in sea level of between 13 and 94 cm (Warrick *et al.,* 1996). The IPCC also reports that warmer temperatures will most likely intensify the hydrological cycle, leading to an increase in the precipitation intensity and number of storm events (Houghton *et al.,* 1996). Our results of this study also agree with it.

MATERIALS AND METHODS

The General Circulation Models (GCMs), which are among the most advanced tools for estimating future climate change scenarios, operate on a coarse scale. In this case ,the output from a GCM has to be downscaled to obtain the information relevant to hydrologic studies(Tripathi, *et. al.*, 2006). More recently, downscaling has found wide application in hydroclimatology for scenario construction and simulation/prediction of (i) regional precipitation (Kim *et al.*, 2004); (ii) low-frequency rainfall events (Wilby, 1998) (iii) mean, minimum and maximum air temperature (Kettle and Thompson, 2004); (iv) soil moisture (Georgakakos and Smith, 2001; Jasper *et al.*, 2004)

In this study, two different emission scenarios from two different GCM models viz. IPCC IS92a scenario from second generation GCM and IPCC SRES A1B scenario from third generation GCM were used to predict and compare the future rainfall trends. For this study, the Jharkhand state of eastern region was selected. Monthly global climatic data from an ensemble of 201-year simulations using the IPCC "IS92a" forcing scenario from CCCma were used in which the change in green house gases (GHG) forcing corresponds to that observed from 1900 to 1990 and increases at a rate 1% per year thereafter until year 2100. Similarly, the data from IPCC 20-th Century experiment with CGCM3.1/T47 for years 1900-2000 and IPCC SRES A1B experiment with CGCM3.1/T47 for years 2001-2100, initialized from the end of the 20C3M experiment, were considered for this study. The A1B scenario describes a future world of very rapid economic growth, low population growth after 2050, and the rapid introduction of new and more efficient technologies, convergence among regions, capacity building, and increased cultural and social interactions, with a substantial reduction in regional differences in per capita income and a balance emphasis on all energy sources. For developing data driven model to predict the rainfall, the monthly global climatic data for IS92a and SRES A1B (including 20C3M) scenarios, January 1900 to December 2100 for nine grid points covering the whole Jharkhand state were extracted. The extracted GCM variables include air temperature, specific humidity, geo-potential height, zonal and meridional wind velocities at 200hPa, 500 hPa and 850 hPa pressure levels each, geo-potential height at 1000 hPa and sea level pressure.The global climatic variables were selected from nine grid points covering whole Jharkhand and ranging from 20.41 to 27.83^0 N lat. And 82.50 to 90.00^0 E long for predicting rainfall. The variables of GCM dataset considered are 153 (geo-potential height at 4 different pressure levels, zonal and meridional wind fields, specific humidity and temperature variables for three different pressure levels, and sea level pressure at each of 9 grid points).

These 153 variables were screened to identify the global climatic variables (predictors) that have high correlation with observed precipitation (>0.75). Following above analysis, the total significant variables were reduced to 70 and 49 from 153 variables for IS92A and SRES A1B scenarios respectively. These variables were further processed using principal component analysis and 4 principal components were selected that preserved more than 98% of variance present in them.

Soft computing techniques were used to develop the model to predict the rainfall using global climatic variables (principal components) from GCM as inputs to the model and observed rainfall as output. Three different ANN algorithms were tried to develop the models. The monthly data for 101 years (1900-2000) related to screened global climatic variables and rainfall were used for model development (training, validation and testing). Data were split in three groups: 61 years for model training, 30 years for validation and 10 years for testing. The performance of models was evaluated in terms of correlation coefficient between observed and predicted rainfall and Normalized Mean Square Error (NMSE) of predicted values for test data set. The best models, for which the values of NMSE were 0.26 and 0.24 for IS92A and SRES A1B scenarios respectively, were selected. The correlation coefficient between observed and predicted rainfall for both model was 0.88. The model test result for SRES A1B scenario is shown in figure 1.

RESULTS AND DISCUSSIONS

Using GCM predictors as input, the models were used to predict future monthly rainfall for period 2011-2100. The result was analyzed for three time slices viz. 2011-2040, 2041-2070 and 2071-2100 in terms of average monsoon rainfall (Jun.-Sept) and summer-winter season rainfall (Oct-May) and with respect to the predicted average seasonal rainfall of the baseline period (1961-1990). As per IS92 scenario, the result shows the increasing trend of rainfall for monsoon period by 9.6%, 12.29%, and 15.62% for periods 2011-2040, 2041-2071 and 2071-2100 respectively with respect to baseline period. Similarly, the results revealed increasing trend of average annual rainfall of 16.61%, 27.80% and 57.42% for periods 2011-2040, 2041-2071 and 2071-2100 respectively as compared to baseline period. As per SRES A1B scenario, the result shows the increasing trend of rainfall for monsoon period by 8.35%, 14.21%, and 19.94% for periods 2011-2040, 2041-2071 and 2071-2100 respectively with respect to baseline period. For average annual rainfall, the results revealed increasing trend of 8.44%, 15.43% and 20.66% for periods 2011-2040, 2041-2071 and 2071-2100 respectively as compared to baseline period (Fig.2). Thus, both scenarios indicate the increasing trends in the rainfall for the region but IS92a scenario indicates the higher increase as compared to SRES A1B scenario.

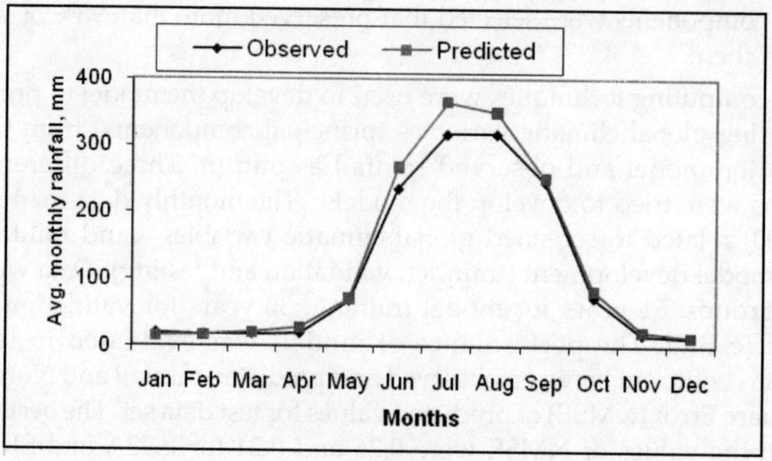

Fig. 1 : Observed vs. predicted average monthly rainfall for model test using SRES A1B scenario

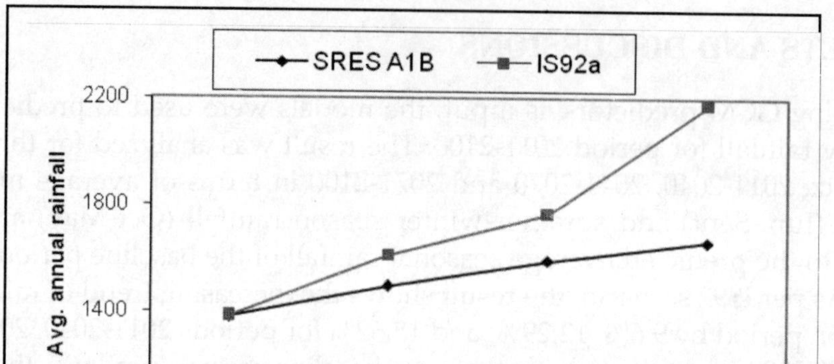

Fig. 2 : Comparison of model predicted average annual rainfall using IS92a and SRES A1B scenarios period (1991-2000)

CONCLUSIONS

The monthly rainfall for Jharkhand is predicted using global climatic variable using two different emission scenarios viz. IPCC IS92a from a second generation GCM and SRES A1B from a third generation GCM. It is found that both scenarios indicate the increasing trends in the annual rainfall for the region but IS92a scenario indicates the higher increase as compared to SRES A1B scenario.

ACKNOWLEDGEMENTS

The authors express their sincere thank to anonymous referees/reviewers for their constructive comments and suggestion on the earlier draft of the chapter..This work was done when authors were posted at Directorate of Water Management(ICAR), Bhubaneswar.

REFERENCES

Denault, Catherine, Millar, Robert G, Lence, Barbara J(2006).Asessment of possible impacts of climate change in urban catchments, Journal of the American Water Resources Association

Georgakakos, K.P., Smith, D.E. (2001). Soil moisture tendencies into the next century for the conterminous United States. Journal of Geophysical Research – Atmospheres 106 (D21), 27367–27382.

Houghton, J.T., L.G. Meira Filho, B.A. Callander, N. Harris, A. Kattenberg, and K. Maskell, 1996. Climate Change 1995: The Science of Climate Change. Contribution of Working Group 1 to the second Assessment Report of the Intergovernmental Panel on Climate Change, Cambridge University Press, Cambridge, United Kingdom.

IPCC, 1992. Leggett, J., Pepper W.J., Swart, R., (Eds.) Climate change 1992, the supplementary report to the IPCC scientific assessment, Intergovernmental Panel on Climate Change IPCC, Cambridge University Press, Cambridge, UK, (Chapter 3).

IPCC, 2001. McCarthy, J.J., Canziani, O.F., Leary, N.A., Dokken, D.J., White, K.S. (Eds.), Climate Change 2001: Impacts, Adaptation and Vulnerability, Contribution of Working Group II to the Third Assessment Report of the Intergovernmental Panel on Climate Change, Cambridge University Press, Cambridge, UK.

Kettle, H., Thompson, R. (2004). Statistical downscaling in European mountains: verification of reconstructed air temperature. Climate Research 26 (2), 97–112.

Kim, M.K., Kang, I.S., Park, C.K., Kim, K.M. (2004). Super ensemble prediction of regional precipitation over Korea. International Journal of Climatology 24 (6), 777–790.

Tripathi ,.S, Srinivas, V.V., Nanjundiah and Ravi S.(2006). Downscaling of precipitation for climate change scenarios: A support vector machine approach, Journal of Hydrology, Elsevier,330 (3-4). pp. 621-640.

Warrick, R.A., C. Le Provost, M.F. Meier, J. Oerlemans, and PL. Woddworth, 1996. Changes in Sea Level. In: Climate Change 1995: The Science of Climate Change. Contribution of Working Group 1 to the second Assessment Report of the Intergovernmental Panel on Climate Change, J.T. Houghton, L.G. Meira Filho, B.A. Callander, N. Harris, A. Kattenberg, and K. Maskell (Editors). Cambridge University Press, Cambridge.United Kingdom, pp. 363-405.

Wilby, R.L.(1998). Modelling low-frequency rainfall events using airflow indices, weather patterns and frontal frequencies.Journal of Hydrology 213 (1–4), 380–392.

❑❑❑

CHAPTER - 19

Web Based Expert System for Identifying Pests and Disease Problems of Rice Crop

B.Sailaja[1], A.P.K.Padma Kumari[2], D.Krishnaveni[3], Shaik N. Meera[4], R.Nagarjuna Kumar[5], S.Gayatri[6] and G.R.Maruthi Sankar[7]

[1]*Directorate of Rice Research, Rajendranagar, Hyderabad-500030.*
E-mail:saila_r@yahoo.com
[2]*Directorate of Rice Research, Rajendranagar, Hyderabad-500030.*
E-mail: appadma @drricar.org
[3]*Directorate of Rice Research, Rajendranagar, Hyderabad-500030.*
E-mail: dkrishnaveni @drricar.org
[4]*Directorate of Rice Research, Rajendranagar, Hyderabad-500030.*
E-mail: shaikmeera@drricar.org
[5]*Central Research Institute for Dryland Agriculture, Hyderabad-500059.*
E-mail: rnagarjunakumar@yahoo.com
[6]*Directorate of Rice Research, Rajendranagar, Hyderabad-500030.*
[7]*Central Research Institute for Dryland Agriculture, Hyderabad-500059.*
E-mail: gmsankar2009@gmail.com

ABSTRACT

Expert systems are very popular computer programs designed to simulate the problem solving behavior of human thinking in a narrow domain. The world has changed into a global village. Information has become a powerful commodity and agricultural production has evolved into a complex business requiring the accumulation and integration of knowledge and information from many diverse sources. Rice is the staple food of over half the world's population. India is the second largest producer and consumer of rice in the world. In order to remain competitive, the modern farmer often relies on agricultural specialists and advisors to provide information for decision making. In order to alleviate this problem, expert systems were identified as a powerful tool with extensive potential in agriculture. Rapid development of web technology benefits our decision-making and various activities in agriculture. With this background, web based rice expert system has been developed for diagnosing pest and disease problems of rice crop.

Key Words: Rice, Expert system, Knowledge, Decision making

INTRODUCTION

Rice is an essential food for more than two billion people in the world. Two thirds of the world's population is living in Asia, where rice is the prime source of daily food. This makes the production of rice an important social, political and economic factor. Biotic stresses including insect pests and diseases play a crucial role in limiting the rice production. Farmers are often faced with pest management decisions, which involve several pests, diseases, weeds and other abiotic stresses. Hence the available technologies like host plant resistance, cultural, chemical, biological, mechanical and physical control methods need to be employed harmoniously to achieve the goals of Integrated Pest Management. However, this demands complex decision making in the light of vast information knowledge base. *The recent advancement in the field of software technology has opened up new challenges as well as opportunities to fulfill increasing needs for up-to-date and precise information.*

"Expert System" *is one of the important application oriented with branches of Artificial Intelligence.* An expert system is a computer program that emulates the decision-making ability of a human expert (Jackson, 1998). It uses a knowledge base of human expertise for problem solving, or to clarify uncertainties where normally one or more human experts would need to be consulted. *In the past decade, a great deal of expert systems had been developed and applied to many fields such as office automation, science, and medicine including agriculture.* The inference engine is an automated reasoning system that evaluates the current state of the knowledge-base, applies relevant rules, and then asserts new knowledge into the knowledge base. The inference engine may also include capabilities for explanation, so that it can explain to a user the chain of reasoning used to arrive at a particular conclusion by tracing back over the firing of rules that resulted in the assertion (Hayes-Roth *et.al.*, 1983).

There are primarily two modes for an inference engine: forward chaining and backward chaining. In forward chaining an antecedent fires and asserts the consequent. Backward chaining is a bit less straight forward. In backward chaining the system looks at possible conclusions and works backward to see if they might be true (http://en.wikipedia.org, 2014).

Earlier, a standalone expert system was developed using MS Access and Visual Basic to aid in the decision making in identifying pest and disease problems of rice crop at farm level (Sailaja *et al.*, 2004). This package is downloadable and can be installed on any desktop. This is not directly accessible in the public domain.

Web-based applications have a much easier path to successful cross-platform compatibility than downloadable software applications. Web-based applications need not to be downloaded, installed and configured. They can indeed utilized by multiple users at the same time Web-based applications are always updated to the last release, without requiring the user to take pro-active action, and without needing to prompt or interfere with user work. An attempt was, therefore, made to develop web based expert system for rice pest and disease management to aid in the management at farm level. In this system, the main emphasis was given to enable users to formulate and acquire answers to questions with confidence.

Development of Expert System

This expert system for rice crop was developed using Microsoft SQL as back end and .Net as front end. Important pest and disease problems of rice crop were analyzed and knowledge base was designed in SQL. Main components of expert system are knowledge base, inference engine and user interface. The process of expert system is depicted in Fig 1.

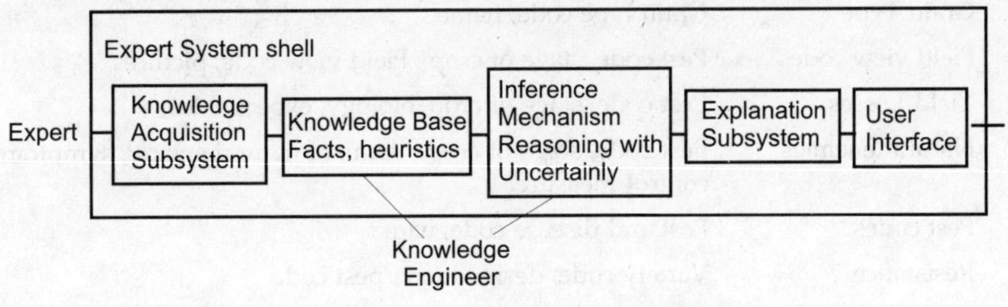

Fig. 1 : Flow diagram of expert system

Knowledge base contains knowledge necessary for understand, formulate and solve problems. It includes two basic elements: one is facts on the problem situation and associated theoretical details on the problem, and the second is the special heuristics, or rules-aided investigation that directs the use of knowledge to solve a specific problem in a particular domain. For developing expert system, knowledge acquisition was done by discussing with subject experts and critically reviewing scientific literature on the management of pathogens and insect pests. Knowledge base was then created by entering these facts and rules in tabular form and in all, 21 tables were designed (Table 1). One-to-one and many-to-one relationships were created among tables.

Table 1: Knowledge base tables designed for the rice pest and disease management

S.No.	Name of the table	Attributes
1.	Pests	Description of pest as shape, colour, appearance, occurrence etc
2.	Diseases	Description of diseases as symptoms, part affected, symptom, colour etc
3.	States	State code, State name
4.	Districts	District code, District name, State code
5.	Eco System	Eco code, Eco system name
6.	Seasons	Season code, Season name, ecocide
7.	Weather	Max temp, Min temp, RH, Rainfall
8.	Season-Climate	Season code,
9.	Biology	Biology,description, behaviour, etl etc.
10.	Control measures	Control code, control name
11.	Cultural control	Pest code, stage of crop, method
12.	Chemical control	Pest code, stage of crop, chemical name, trade, dosage
13.	Varieties	Variety name, parentage,designation , days to 50% flowering, duration,suitable ecosystem, grain type
14.	Grain Type	Grain type code, name
15.	Field view codes	Pest code, stage of crop , Field view code, pictures
16.	Yield Losses	Pest code, stage of crop, biology, expected loss
17.	Natural enemies	Pest code, stage of crop, name of natural enemy, symptoms, control measure.
18.	Pest codes	Pest and disease code, name
19.	Resistance	Variety code, designation , pest code
20.	Soils	Soil type, pH, Depth etc
21.	Crop Stages	Stage code, name, crop age, season, varietal duration

Inference engine is the brain of the expert system. This component is a computer program that provides a methodology for reasoning about any information in the knowledge base. This component provides directions on how to use the system's knowledge by developing the agenda, which then organizes and controls the steps taken to solve problems whenever consultation is performed. An inference mechanism was developed using .net program to conduct formalized reasoning for user's answers and corresponding rules in the knowledge base. Mostly IF… Then, statements were used in this program. Two important inference methods, viz., forward chaining and backward chaining methods were deployed. In general forward chaining method is more suitable to the problems that are loosely defined or with multiple goals. The backward chaining is more suitable for problems in which the goal is well defined and possible solutions are limited. These two methods were appropriately used in this program based on the user's responses. In total there were 16 stored procedures and 23 active server pages (ASPs) designed for developing this application.

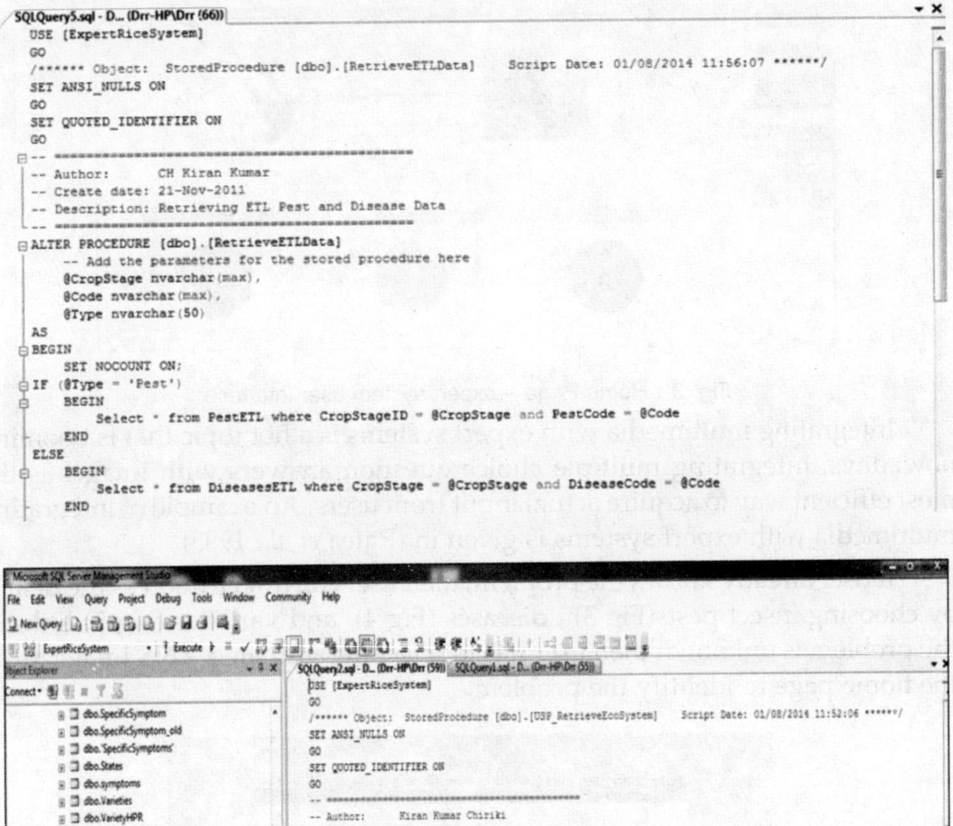

Fig. 2 : Screen shot of ASP page and Stored procedures used for Rice Expert System

User Interface: The home page of Rice Expert System(Fig 3) consists of series of questions and answers to diagnose the problem, to browse directly major pests/diseases/varieties, to access information on better crop protection measures, commonly used pesticides for rice and frequently asked questions.

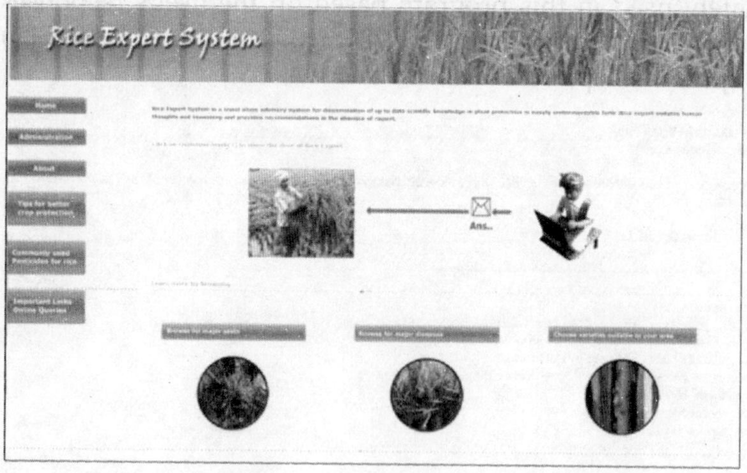

Fig. 3 : Home Page – expert system user interface

Integrating multimedia with expert systems is a hot topic that is booming nowadays. Integrating multiple choice question answers with images is the most efficient way to acquire actual input from users. An example of integrating multimedia with expert systems is given in (Rafea *et al.*, 1995).

If user already knows the problem, then user can directly access the details by choosing insect pests(Fig 3) , diseases (Fig 4) and varieties (Fig 5) links. If the problem is unknown then user has to select the animated **ANS image** from the home page to identify the problem.

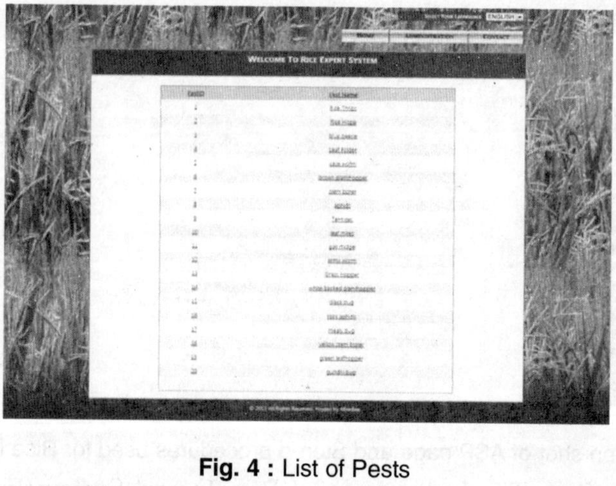

Fig. 4 : List of Pests

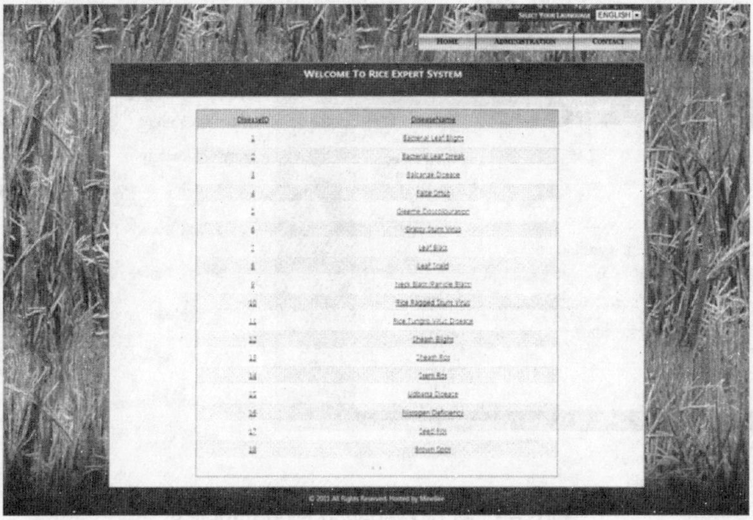

Fig. 5 : List of Diseases

Questionnaire menu of the expert system begins by collecting information about the place followed by ecosystem based on the input provided by the user while selecting through drop down menus. At the second level it collects information on weather followed by crop details as variety duration, crop stage etc. At the third level, questions seek to gather information on the various symptoms in the field that were encountered by the user. Then a series of questions were designed to access the right answer from the knowledge base with regard to either disease or insect pest problems. After the input response from user to questions on the field appearance and symptoms, details screen on disease or insect pest will start appearing. At the final level the engine generates various control measure options as recommendations for controlling the disease or insect pest. The flow questions for insect pests and diseases are shown in the fig 6.

An interface was developed with questionnaire supported by popup menus, list boxes including pictures for each item in the drop down menus and option groups. Each option was aided by appropriate visual colour photographs to help the user for accurately selecting his choice and seek solution. Questions were designed in simple natural language. In this system, knowledge base contains general decision rules that represent the knowledge of experts on pests and diseases. It has 90 rules for identifying insect pests and 105 rules for identifying diseases. For Example flow of questions for identifying StemBorer was shown in the fig 7.

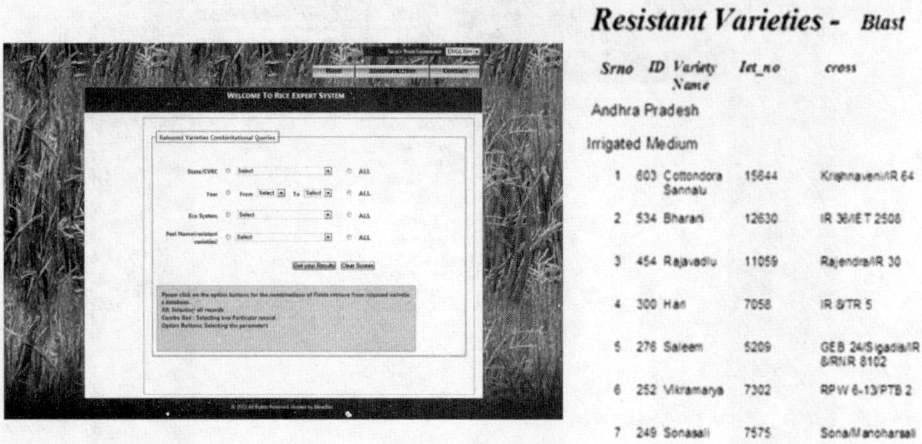

Fig. 6 : List of Released Rice Varieties

Place → Season → Weather → Crop rotation → Variety → Planting method →
Planting dates → Crop stage → Fertiliser use → Field appearance → Presence of insects
Pest details
Part infected → Place of insects → Shape and colour of insects → No of insects per hill
Diseases details
Part infected → Type of symptoms → Shape and colour of lesion → Severity of disease
Recommendations
First level of recommendation → Second level includes chemical and biological control measures → Resistant varieties

Fig. 7 : Flow chart of different processes to diagnose insect pest and diseases

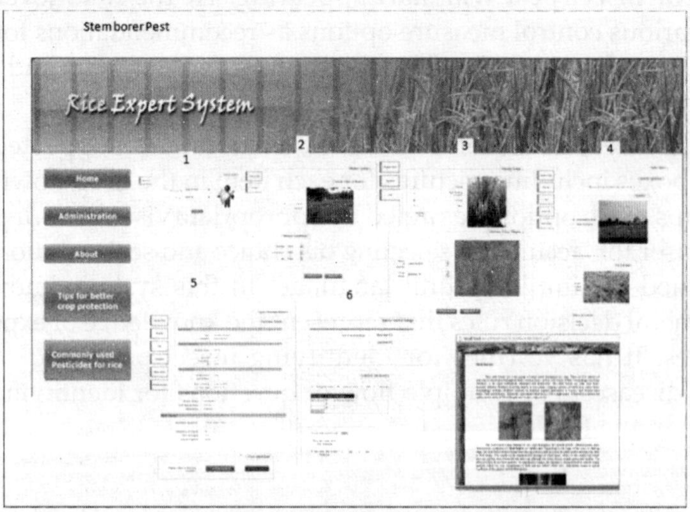

Fig. 8 : Flow questions to diagnose insect pest stem borer

In addition to the pest/disease identification, the system also advises for the nutrient deficiency through PDF files. Rice expert system is not only used for diagnose pest or disease problems but also maintains database of newly arriving problems regarding pests and diseases of rice crop. This data can be further analysed to identify location specific pest/disease problems, movement of pest/diseases etc. Web based expert system is dynamic system to diagnose pest and disease problems at field level without experts advice.

Testing of this system was done involving small clientele group with respect to diseases like leaf blast, rice tungro virus and insect pests like brown planthopper and stem borer. The program will be further upgraded and refined by adding nutrient deficiency module to increase efficiency and effective management. This facility is therefore expected to enhance the performance of farmers and extension personnel, reduce the time required to solve any pathogen or insect pest related problem without waiting for an expert advice, and make farming more efficient and profitable.

REFERENCES

Hayes-Roth, Frederick; Donald Waterman, Douglas Lenat (1983). Building Expert Systems. Addison-Wesley. ISBN 0-201-10686-8.

http://en.wikipedia.org/wiki/Expert_system. Accessed on 8.01.2014.

Jackson, Peter (1998), Introduction To Expert Systems (3 ed.), Addison Wesley, p. 2, ISBN 978-0-201-87686-4.

Nwigbo Stella and Agbo Okechuku Chuks, School of Science Education, Expert system: a catalyst in educational development in Nigeria: "Knowledge-based systems collect the small fragments of human know-how into a knowledge-base which is used to reason through a problem, using the knowledge that is appropriated".

Rafea, A., El-Beltagy, A. (1987). Expert Systems as An Appropriate Technology to SpeedUp Agriculture Desert Development in Egypt. Proceedings of the Second International Desert Development Conference, Harwood Academic Publisher. 47-57.

Sailaja B, Krishnaveni D, Padma Kumari AP and Mishra B. 2004. Developing Computer Expert for Management of Pathogens and Insect Pests in Rice. Indian Journal of Mycology and Plant Pathology, 34 (2): 495-499.

❑❑❑

CHAPTER - 20

Expert System in Agricultural Extension: An Attractive and Efficient Technology for Extension Services

Bishwarup Saha
Assistant Professor, Fisheries Extension, College of Fisheries
Central Agrricultural University
Lembucherra, Tripura.

Sustainable development and environment friendly technologies in agriculture are the need of the time. It is also necessary that these technologies should be able to solve farmers' problems that vary according to his socio-economic and ecological condition. To reach the wide as well as diverse section of our producers, the extension system should be location specific and very fast. The technology must be based on farmer' need, existing resources of farmers, appropriate marketing and should be considered the cost benefit ratio. Sustainable development of producers, efficient technology as well as effective transfer of technology within a short period of time is thus utmost important in recent period. These require larger proportion of human skill combined with electronic information system. In this connection, expert system can be effective in transfer of technology to meet the need of the time. Expert system is the turning point and breaking through of artificial intelligence developing, it is breaking through from generic thinking to special knowledge applying, from theory method to actual system design. Over the years the field of application of expert system has been widening rapidly. Many countries have made expert system in different field, such as: financial decision-making, medical treatment and diagnose, diagnose on breakdown of machinery, chemical engineering, geological prospecting, military affairs, and other agricultural domain. Recently, many researchers in India has been identified the advantage of this system and already developed expert system in several commodities in agricultural crops.

WHAT IS AN EXPERT SYSTEM?

An 'Expert System' is an intelligent computer program that uses knowledge and inference procedures to solve problems that are difficult enough to require human expertise for their solution. The knowledge necessary to perform at such a level plus the inference procedures used can be thought of as a model of the expertise of the best practitioners in the field. (*Daniel Hunt, 1986*)

An expert system is a computer program that represents and reasons with knowledge of some specialist subject with a view to solving problems or giving advice. Jackson (2007)

"Expert System" is an intelligent computer programme that uses knowledge and inference procedure for solving specific problems requiring human expertise for their solution. The knowledge base necessary for performing at such a level plus the inference procedure used can be thought of as a model of the expertise of the best practitioners in the field. This software being a web based expert system for extension, the knowledge and expertise of the agricultural scientists can be easily accessed and utilized by the farmers and extension workers while being at great distances from the location of actual experts in the specific areas.

An expert system is a computing system that is capable of expressing and reasoning about some domain of knowledge. It is an interactive computer- based decision tool that uses both facts and heuristics to solve difficult decision making problems, based on knowledge acquired from an expert.

They will generally build upon the ideas of knowledge representation, production rules, search, and so on, that we have already covered. Intelligent Knowledge Based System (IKBS) is sometimes used as a synonym for Expert System.

Developing an expert system in a specific knowledge domain is quite a difficult task as it requires team of experienced knowledge engineers, programmers as well as domain experts. Agriculture, being a very vast and varied domain of knowledge with over a hundred crops distributed in different geographic regions having varied climatic conditions, building such a team in every domain of knowledge of agriculture is itself a challenging and huge task. Knowledge engineers gather knowledge from domain experts and put it in such a form that system can use for inferring and reasoning using a knowledge representation technique. Programmers then build an online interface so that the end users can use the system over the Internet. First expert system, called DENDRAL, was developed in the early 70's at Stanford University.

Need of Expert System in Agricultural Extension

The following points can reflect the need of expert system in agricultural extension further.

- Many technologies developed by the researchers are remained unused due to many limitations in technology itself combined with inefficient conventional extension system in the country. Therefore, expert system can be effective solution in providing information and helps to convert it into knowledge of the millions of farmers located in different situation at a same time without the present of expert physically.
- Technologies to be effective in the farmer's field should be location specific in nature. Same technology can't be adopted by diverse farmers with different needs and situation. Therefore, expert system is likely to be better solution where one can decide the best suitable option for his/her farm condition from a basket of solutions with considering the available resources.
- At present, farmers are looking forward to sustain their livelihood. They need the enterprises which provide them more economic benefit with considering the cost benefit ratio in his farm condition. Farmers are the master of their own situation. They don't need spoon feeding from research extension system. They just need an efficient system which helps them to take appropriate decision. Therefore there should be a system of intuitive knowledge based system like, expert system of extension that may suggest the appropriate technology in the farmer's field with considering the agro climatic situation of the area coupled with cost benefit ratio.
- Computerization of organization is already proved efficient. Many organizations in India such as railway as well as air reservation, online banking, online trading, medical institution, industries are getting benefit through computerization. Wide array of people has welcomed this system and is also getting benefit through this system. Agriculture is still lagging from the benefit. Therefore, it is assume that computerization of agriculture will do well to farmers.
- In this fast changing scenario, if extension is to move successfully from the concern of production, marketing and economic benefit to the farmers, it has to change its approach from conventional method to electronic method to provide better benefit to the farmers with least input and resources. The expert system of extension, which develops the knowledge based information including decision rules and available on web site, will be able to help the farmers not only in

taking decision to what they should cultivate with maximum profit but also the related queries.

Expert systems can be distinguished from other kinds of AI program because

- They deal with subjects of considerable complexity—subjects that normally require a good deal of human expertise. Provide expert-level solutions to complex problems.
- They must be fast and reliable;
- They must be capable of explaining and justifying solutions be understandable.
- They must be sufficiently flexible that new information may be easily accommodated.

Difference between conventional extension system and expert system of extension

Expert system of extension has multiple of advantage over conventional extension system. Bahal (2004) has identified several comparisons between the two. These are discussed below:

Sl. No.	Conventional Extension System	Expert System in Extension
1.	There is limited possibility to disseminate the same information to all farmers at the same time.	There is possibility to disseminate the same information to all the farmers at the same time.
2.	The farmers need, resources, infrastructure, market facilities etc. are rarely considered while recommending the information.	The farmers need, resources, infrastructure, market facilities etc. are considered while recommending the information.
3.	Information given depends on its availability.	Information is to be chosen what ever is needed and suitable.
4.	Cost benefit analysis is not well calculated	Recommendations depend on well calculated cost benefit analysis.
5.	The farmer can get the information only if extension agent is available.	The farmer can get the information from any Cyber Cafe at any place at any time.
6.	The information may not necessary be helpful in decision making in choosing any commodity or enterprise.	The information provided by expert system taken essentially helpful in decision making while choosing any commodity or enterprise.
7.	The information may not be updated	The information generally updated on day-to-day basis.

Contd.

8.	The extension agents are generally less educated and non technical.	The experts are highly knowledgeable and high-tech.
9.	The working is fragmented, as it is totally manual.	The working is through networking and very compact and interconnected with number of electronic systems.
10.	This system is now getting out dated.	This is recent advancement which suits the already build infrastructure.

Application of expert systems

- Configuration – Assemble proper components of a system in the proper way.
- Diagnosis- Infer underlying problem based on observed evidence.
- Instruction- Intelligent teaching so that a student can ask *why, how,* and *what if* questions just as if a human were teaching.
- Interpretation- Explain observed data.
- Monitoring- Compares observed data to expected data to judge performance.
- Planning- Devise actions to yield a desired outcome.
- Prognosis- Predict the out come of a given situation.
- Remedy- Prescribe treatment for a problem.
- Control- Regulate a process. May require interpretation, diagnosis, monitoring, planning, prognosis, and remedies.
- Newer applications of ES- Credit analysis systems, Pension fund advisors, Automated help desks, Homeland security systems, Market surveillance systems, Business process reengineering systems

Design methodology of expert system

The design methodology of Expert System of Extension is discussed in sequential manner as below:

1. The Expert System of Extension Programme may generally be developed on computer by the team of the experts on different aspect of interest (domain) say particular crops of agriculture. The crop/ commodity or domain may be divided into required areas.
2. The knowledge based information of each item may be collected from relevant and authentic sources. The knowledge based data may be then entered into computer programme. The decision rules need to be developed and entered into the computer language, which can be used as and when required for processing by the clients.

3. Before providing any information to the clients the computer programme ask some basic questions like as name, location, soil type, land holding, family labour, source of irrigation, distance from market etc.
4. Based on these basic information, computer will start making search from the already stored knowledge based information in the hard disk looking the maximum profit to the clients and finally provide a need based information to the clients.
5. Computer programme will provide a number of options in priority order so that clients can choose the best option suitable to him. If the client will follow all the recommendations given in the computer and rest other things remain the same, he is bound to get the expected benefit which he has planned at the outset of the programme.

Architecture of an Expert System

The process of building expert systems is often called knowledge engineering. The knowledge engineer is involved with all components of an expert system as shown in the Figure 1:

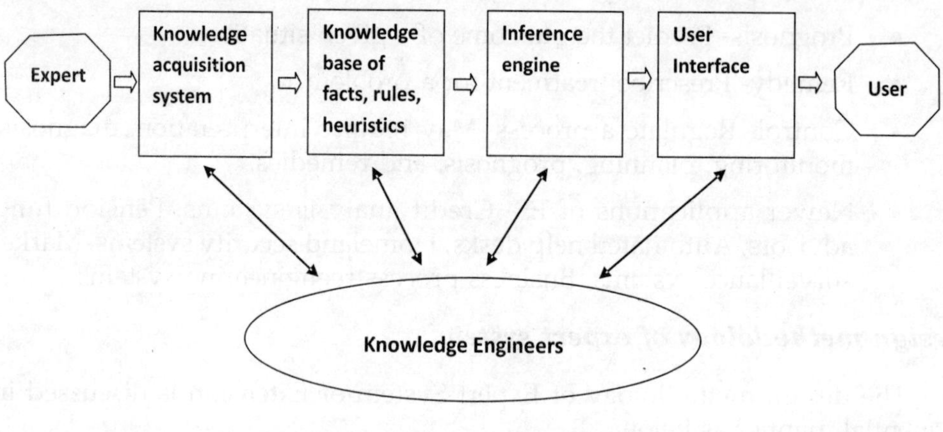

Fig.1 : Architecture of an Expert System

Building expert systems is generally an iterative process. The components and their interaction will be refined over the course of numerous meetings of the knowledge engineer with the experts and users. We shall look in turn at the various components.

Knowledge Acquisition

The knowledge acquisition component allows the expert to enter their knowledge or expertise into the expert system, and to refine it later as and when required. The knowledge engineer, undertaking the knowledge acquisition must convert the acquired knowledge into computer language. The knowledge acquisition process is usually comprised of three principal stages:

1. Knowledge elicitation is the interaction between the expert and the knowledge engineer/program to elicit the expert knowledge in some systematic way.
2. The knowledge thus obtained is usually stored in some form of human friendly intermediate representation.
3. The intermediate representation of the knowledge is then compiled into an executable form (e.g. production rules) that the inference engine can process.

In practice, much iteration through these three stages is usually required.

Knowledge Base

The knowledge base is the core component of any expert system since it contains the relevant knowledge acquired from an expert in the particular field. Knowledge engineer may be the responsible for working with an expert to develop the knowledge base for the system.

The task involved in developing the knowledge base usually consists of following four stages:

1. Knowledge acquisition- Find as much as possible about the problem and domain from books, manuals, etc. In particular, become familiar with any specialist terminology and jargon.
2. Knowledge representation- All types of representation of problems, solutions and knowledge in a rule base. A good coordination between the engineer and expert (usually many times during the course of building the system) is utmost important to find out the technique to solve the problems.
3. Knowledge programming- it captures causal connections from one state to another state. This is antecedent-consequent form of a rule.
4. Knowledge refinement

   The iterative nature of the knowledge acquisition and knowledge base process can be represented in the following diagram (Figure 2):

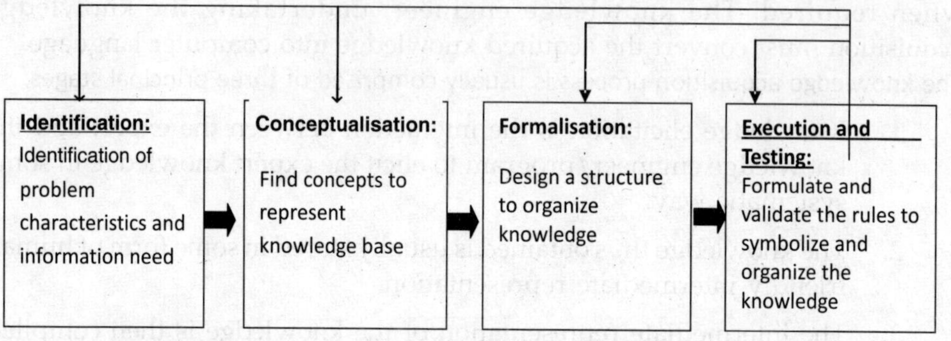

Fig. 2 : Knowledge acquisition and knowledge base process of Expert System

Knowledge identification: the information need of the end users need to be identified and perceived. The knowledge engineer should understand the domain well enough to know which objects and facts need talking about.

Knowledge conceptualization: Primitive concepts and conceptual relations of the problem solution domain need to be identified.

Knowledge formalisation: Designing the structural properties of the conceptual knowledge.

Logical analysis and execution: Decide how to perform reasoning in the problem domain. Work out systematic procedures for implementing and testing the system.

The Inference Engine

We have already looked at production systems, and how they can be used to generate new information and solve problems. However, the heart of an expert system is the reasoning engine or "inference engine". The reasoning engine processes the input statements of the problem statement document.

Match the premise patterns of the rules against elements in the working memory. Generally the rules will be domain knowledge built into the system, and the working memory will contain the case based facts entered into the system, plus any new facts that have been derived from them. The input is usually presented to the reasoning engine in an in-memory tree structure. The major task of the inference engine is to take a problem statement and to match it with set of attributes in the rule base in a rule consequent table. The inference engine uses the results of this match to start retrieving the corresponding rule antecedents.

If there is more than one rule that can be applied, use a conflict resolution strategy to choose one to apply. Activate the chosen rule, which generally means adding/deleting an item to/from working memory. Stop if a terminating condition is reached, or return to step 1.

The User Interface

The Expert System user interface usually comprises of two basic components:

1. The Interviewer Component

   This controls the dialog with the user and/or allows any measured data to be read into the system. For example, it might ask the user a series of questions, or it might read a file containing a series of test results.

2. The Explanation Component

   This gives the system's solution, and also makes the system's operation transparent by providing the user with information about its reasoning process. For example, it might output the conclusion, and also the sequence of rules that was used to come to that conclusion. It might instead explain why it could not reach a conclusion.

   Generally, the Expert system of Extension user inference is designed using the hypertext markup language (HTML), Cascaded Style Sheet (CSS), Java Script, and Java Server Pages (JSP) to allow the user to communicate with the system and access required information through web browser such as Microsoft Internet Explorer or Netscape communicator. The system acts as an extension expert to provide needed information after putting data related to existing condition of the end users/ farmers into the system. The system also helps in dissemination of recent technologies and advancement in the particular field with a generic search capability.

Advantages of expert systems

- The computer can store far more information than a human. It can draw on a wide variety of sources such as stored knowledge from books, case studies to help in diagnosis and advice.
- The computer does not 'forget' or make mistakes.
- Data can be kept up-to-date.
- The expert system is always available 24 hours a day and will never 'retire'.
- The system can be used at a distance over a network. So rural areas or even poorer third world countries have access to experts.

- Provides accurate predictions with probabilities of all possible problems with more accurate advice based on particular agro ecological and socio-personal situation.
- Some people prefer the privacy of talking to a computer.

Limitations / Disadvantages of expert systems

- Over reliance upon computers
- Some 'experts' could loose their jobs or not be given training if computers are available to do the job.
- Lacks the 'human touch'! – lack of personal contact
- Dependent upon the correct information being given. If data or rules wrong the wrong advice could be given.
- Expert systems have no "common sense". They have no understanding of what they are for, nor of what the limits of their applicability are, nor of how their recommendations fit into a larger context.

SUMMARY AND CONCLUSION

In the era of globalization farmers need profitable, location specific technology coupled with very calculated information. Our conventional system of extension could not reach up to the mark because of several problems such as lack of man power, deficiency of public fund, lack of needed oriented as well as location specific technology, poor skill of field level extension worker in extending technology etc. Therefore, expert system of extension can take the lead by overcoming the shortfalls. This system is planned and designed in such a way that it will extend needful, client base, location specific technological information to the huge number of clients at a same time through website even in the remote sector of the country.

Expert system makes use of the concept of 'object oriental' to build up the model of the expert knowledge, the concept mode is constructed according to the relations between the represent objects. This system is developed in computer using internet and web designing. The scientists, suitable technical staff and knowledge engineers sum up the knowledge, experience and method during the whole process. The particular domain of interest is divided into different areas at first for example in aquaculture say; stocking ratio and rate, feed formula, aqua environment, water quality parameter, and disease diagnosis, prevention and cure, marketing etc. The information of each area is collected from relevant and authentic sources from the libraries different research institute, state agricultural universities etc. Efforts are made to collect the information base on per unit input and output for a particular socio-agro-ecological situation. This information collected is converted into knowledge base. The knowledge base is stored in a database. The knowledge base is augmented with the decision rules. These rules are utilized to solve the queries of the farmers.

The programme is made in such a way that it will ask some basic questions from the users at the outset, for example; your login name, your state and district, pond size, sources of stocks, sources of income, total number of family labour, assets, capital availability, market facilities etc. When user put all the relevant data required by the machine, the computer progrmme will automatically start making searches from inbuilt stored knowledge data base considering providing the maximum profit to the farmers in his given situation. Farmers have flexibility to change the options so that he can get and select another better alternative to secure his livelihood. Likewise he can select best option for his particular situation. Users must get expected benefit if follows all the recommendation in a given scenario provided by the computer programme.

Many developed countries in the globe have already identified the prospect of Expert System (ES) in Extension and developed there by. However, developing countries still remained the back bencher in adopting the expert system in agriculture. The ES is already proved as efficient, accurate, and precise and considers the cost benefit ratio. The ES has a better prospect, and can aid decision making of the agricultural production.

ACKNOWLEDGEMENT

This report is based on review of research and popular articles written by distinguishing scientists, academician and policy makers. This report is prepared for the academic purpose. I thankfully acknowledge everyone whose books and articles I read and cited in the manuscript. This report was made possible through the generous support of Dean, College of Fisheries (CAU), Lembucherra, Tripura.

REFERENCES

Bahal, R., Wason, M and Sudeep (2004). Expert system for effective extension. Communication support for sustaining extension services. Department of extension education institute of agricultural sciences, Banaras Hindu University, Varanasi.

Hunt, V.D. (1986). Artificial Intelligence and Expert Systems Sourcebook, New York: Chapman and Hall.

Jackson. P. (2007). Introduction to expert systems, International computer science series, Addison-Wesley Longman, Incorporated.http://books.google.co.in/books/about/Introduction_to_expert_systems. html?id=Q7MmAAAAMAAJ&redir_esc=y

❑❑❑

Section 4
Applied Technologies

CHAPTER - 21

Theory of Supercritical Fluid Extraction and its Global Challenges and Strategies for Control, Utilization of CO_2 for Sustainable Development for entire Chemical Processing

Omprakash H. Nautiyal
Professor of Organic Chemistry/Natural Products Chemistry 102, Shubh Building, Shivalik II, Canal Road, Chhani Jakat Naka, Vadodara 390002, Gujarat, India.
E-mail: opnautiyalus@yahoo.com

ABSTRACT

Supercritical fluid extraction technology specifically employing carbon dioxide as an extracting solvent under supercritical conditions have gained tremendous importance in the commercial applications as well as academic fields. The basic advantage is its operation above pressure and critical temperature. The most convenient things are variations of pressure, temperatures, batch time, flow rate and fractionation of important constituents of essential oils, herbs and petrochemicals. In the recent times most of the researchers have studied the Organic synthesis under supercritical conditions with the improved yield and reaction selectivity. The chapter also describes the thermodynamics also.

1.1 INTRODUCTION

Supercritical fluids (SCFs) are increasingly replacing the organic solvents that are used in industrial purification and re crystallization operations because of regulatory and environmental pressures on hydrocarbon and ozone-depleting emissions. SCF-based processes have helped to eliminate the use of hexane and methylene chloride as solvents. With increasing scrutiny of solvent residues in pharmaceuticals, medical products, and nutraceuticals, and with stricter regulations on VOC and ODC emissions, the use of SCFs is rapidly proliferating in all industrial sectors.

Supercritical fluid extraction (SFE) plants are operating at throughputs of 100,000,000 lbs/yr or more in the foods industry. Coffee and tea are decaffeinated via supercritical fluid extraction and most major brewers in the US and Europe use flavors that are extracted from hops with supercritical fluids. SCF processes are being commercialized in the polymers, pharmaceuticals, specialty lubricants and fine chemicals industries. SCFs are advantageously applied to increasing product performance to levels that cannot be achieved by traditional processing technologies, and such applications for SCFs offer the potential for both technical and economic success.

A supercritical fluid is any substance at at temperature and pressure above its critical point, where distinct liquid and gas phases do not exist. It can diffuse through solids like a gas, and dissolve materials like a liquid. In addition, close to the critical point, small changes in pressure or temperature result in large changes in density, allowing many properties of a supercritical fluid to be "fine-tuned". Supercritical fluids are suitable as a substitute for organic solvents in a range of industrial and laboratory processes. Carbon dioxide and water are the most commonly used supercritical fluids, being used for decaffeination and power generation, respectively.

In addition, there is no surface tension in a supercritical fluid, as there is no liquid/gas phase boundary. By changing the pressure and temperature of the fluid, the properties can be "tuned" to be more liquid- or more gas-like. One of the most important properties is the solubility of material in the fluid. Solubility in a supercritical fluid tends to increase with density of the fluid (at constant temperature). Since density increases with pressure, solubility tends to increase with pressure. The relationship with temperature is a little more complicated. At constant density, solubility will increase with temperature. However, close to the critical point, the density can drop sharply with a slight increase in temperature. Therefore, close to the critical temperature, solubility often drops with increasing temperature, and then rises again.

All supercritical fluids are completely miscible with each other so for a mixture a single phase can be guaranteed if the critical point of the mixture is exceeded. The critical point of a binary mixture can be estimated as the arithmetic mean of the critical temperatures and pressures of the two components.

$T_{c(mix)}$ = (mole fraction A) x T_cA + (mole fraction B) x T_cB.

Justification

Carbon dioxide as supercritical carbon dioxide utilization has become an important global issue due to continuous rise in atmospheric CO_2

concentrations, accelerated growth in the consumption of carbon-based energy globally, depletion of carbon-based energy resources, and low efficiency in current energy systems. The barriers for CO_2 utilization include:

(1) Economy of CO_2 captures, separation, purifying it and transporting to manufacture site;

(2) Energy requirements of CO_2 chemical conversion (plus source and cost of co reactants);

(3) Market size limitations, little investment-incentives and lack of industrial commitments for enhancing CO_2-based chemicals; and

(4) The lack of socio-economical driving forces.

The strategic objectives may include:

(1) Utilization of CO_2 for environmentally-benign physical and chemical processing that adds value to the process;

(2) Utilization of CO_2 to produce industrially useful chemicals and materials that adds value to the products;

(3) Utilization of CO_2 as feasible processing extractent for processing or as a medium for energy recovery and emission reduction; and

(4) Utilization of CO_2 recycling involving renewable sources of energy to conserve carbon resources for sustainable development.

Environmental problems and threat due to emissions of pollutants from combustion of solid, liquid and gaseous fuels in various stationary and mobile energy systems as well as the emissions from manufacturing plants have also become major global problems involving not only the pollutants such as NOx, SOx, and suspending particulate matter, but also the greenhouse gases (GHG) such as carbon dioxide (CO_2) and methane (CH_4). There are increasing concerns for global climate change and thus heightened interest worldwide for reducing the emissions of GHG, particularly CO_2. This will facilitate the researches globally in the field of Synthetic Organic chemistry, CO_2 conversion over heterogeneous catalysis, synthesis gas production from CO_2, processing of polymer synthesis employing SC-CO_2, thermodynamics of chemical reactions and on entire chemical processing and eco friendly processing.

For greater accuracy, the critical point can be calculated using equations of state, such as the Peng-Robinson, or group contribution methods. Other properties, such as density, can also be calculated using equations of state.

Table 1: Critical properties of various solvents (Reid *et al.*, 1987)

Solvent	Molecular weight g/mol	Critical temperature K	Critical pressure MPa (atm)	Critical density g/cm^3
Carbon dioxide (CO_2)	44.01	304.1	7.38 (72.8)	0.469
Water (H_2O) (acc. IAPWS)	18.015	647.096	22.064 (217.755)	0.322
Methane (CH_4)	16.04	190.4	4.60 (45.4)	0.162
Ethane (C_2H_6)	30.07	305.3	4.87 (48.1)	0.203
Propane (C_3H_8)	44.09	369.8	4.25 (41.9)	0.217
Ethylene (C_2H_4)	28.05	282.4	5.04 (49.7)	0.215
Propylene (C_3H_6)	42.08	364.9	4.60 (45.4)	0.232
Methanol (CH_3OH)	32.04	512.6	8.09 (79.8)	0.272
Ethanol (C_2H_5OH)	46.07	513.9	6.14 (60.6)	0.276
Acetone (C_3H_6O)	58.08	508.1	4.70 (46.4)	0.278

Table 2 shows density, diffusivity and viscosity for typical liquids, gases and supercritical fluids.

Table 2 : Comparison of Gases, Supercritical Fluids and Liquids

	Density (kg/m^3)	Viscosity (µPa.s)	Diffusivity (mm^2/s)
Gases	1	10	1-10
Supercritical Fluids	100-1000	50-100	0.01-0.1
Liquids	1000	500-1000	0.001

1.2 PHASE DIAGRAM

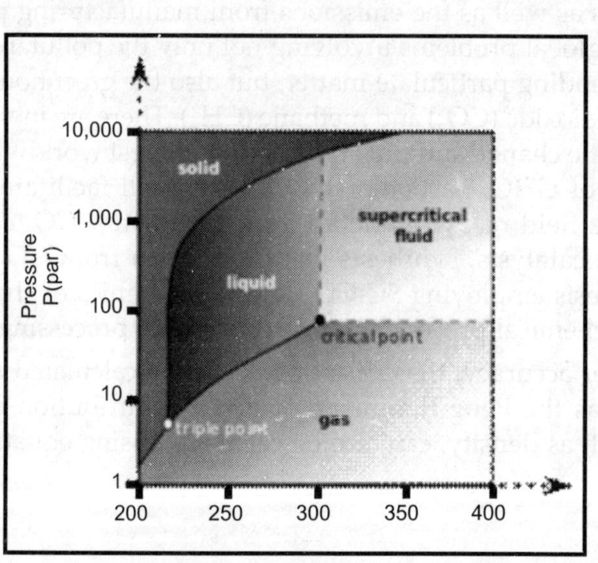

Fig. 1 : Carbon dioxide pressure-temperature phase diagram

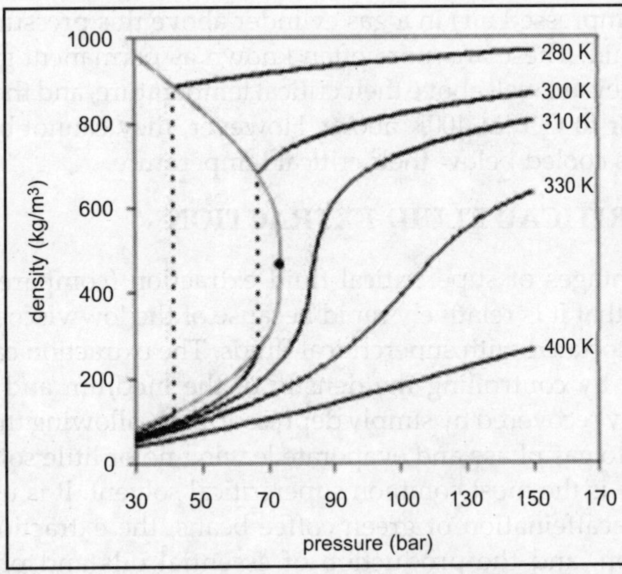

Fig. 2 : Carbon dioxide density-pressure phase diagram

Figures 1 and 2, shows projections of a phase diagram. In the pressure-temperature phase diagram (Fig. 1) the boiling separates the gas and liquid region and ends in the critical point, where the liquid and gas phases disappear to become a single supercritical phase. This can be observed in the density-pressure phase diagram for carbon dioxide, as shown in Figure 2. At well below the critical temperature, e.g., 280K, as the pressure increases, the gas compresses and eventually (at just over 40 bar) condenses into a much denser liquid, resulting in the discontinuity in the line (vertical dotted line). The system consists of 2 phases in equilibrium, a dense liquid and a low density gas. As the critical temperature is approached (300K), the density of the gas at equilibrium becomes denser, and that of the liquid lower. At the critical point, (304.1 K) and 7.38 MPa (73.8 bar), there is no difference in density, and the 2 phases become one fluid phase. Thus, above the critical temperature a gas cannot be liquefied by pressure. At slightly above the critical temperature (310K), in the vicinity of the critical pressure, the line is almost vertical. A small increase in pressure causes a large increase in the density of the supercritical phase. Many other physical properties also show large gradients with pressure near the critical point, e.g. viscosity, the relative permittivity and the solvent strength, which are all closely related to the density. At higher temperatures, the fluid starts to behave like a gas, as can be seen in Figure 2. For carbon dioxide at 400 K, the density increases almost linearly with pressure.

Many pressurized gases are actually supercritical fluids. For example, nitrogen has a critical point of 126.2K (- 147 °C) and 3.4 MPa (34 bar). Therefore, nitrogen (or compressed air) in a gas cylinder above this pressure is actually a supercritical fluid. These are more often known as permanent gases. At room temperature, they are well above their critical temperature, and therefore behave as a gas, similar to CO_2 at 400K above. However, they cannot be liquefied by pressure unless cooled below their critical temperature.

1.3 SUPERCRITICAL FLUID EXTRACTION

The advantages of supercritical fluid extraction (compared with liquid extraction) are that it is relatively rapid because of the low viscosities and high diffusivities associated with supercritical fluids. The extraction can be selective to some extent by controlling the density of the medium and the extracted material is easily recovered by simply depressurizing, allowing the supercritical fluid to return to gas phase and evaporate leaving no or little solvent residues. Carbon dioxide is the most common supercritical solvent. It is used on a large scale for the decaffeination of green coffee beans, the extraction of hops for beer production, and the production of essential oils and pharmaceutical products from plants. A few laboratory test methods include the use of supercritical fluid extraction as an extraction method instead of using traditional solvents.

1.4 SUPERCRITICAL FLUIDS

The critical point (CP) marks the end of the vapor liquid coexistence curve. A fluid is termed supercritical when the temperature and pressure are higher than the corresponding critical values. Above the critical temperature, there is no phase transition in that the fluid can not undergo a transition to a liquid phase, regardless of the applied pressure.

A supercritical fluid (*SCF*) is characterized by physical and thermal properties that are between those of the pure liquid and gas. The fluid density is a

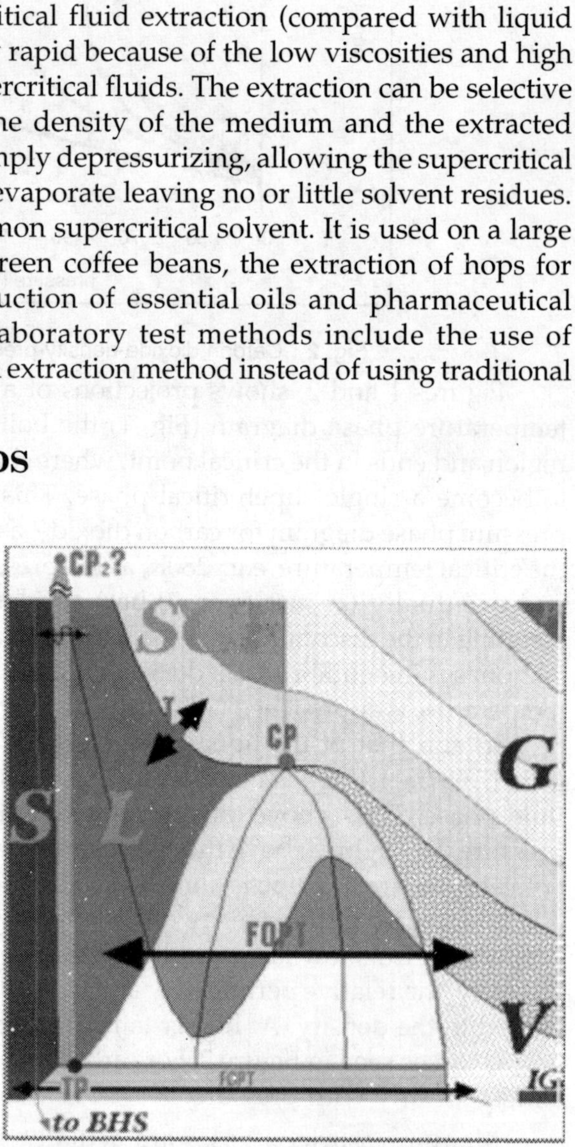

Fig. 3 : Critical point of supercritical fluid

strong function of the temperature and pressure. The diffusivity of SF is much higher than for a liquid and *SCF* readily penetrates porous and fibrous solids. Consequently, SCF can offer good catalytic activity (Figure 3).

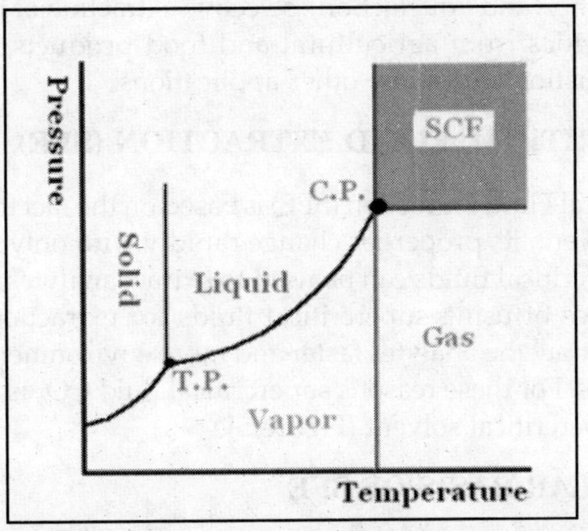

Fig. 4 : triple point of supercritical fluid

1.5 PROPERTIES OF SUPERCRITICAL FLUIDS

- There are drastic changes in some important properties of a pure liquid as its temperature and pressure is increased approaching the thermodynamic critical point. For example, under thermodynamic equilibrium conditions, the visual distinction between liquid and gas phases, as well as the difference between the liquid and gas densities, disappear at and above the critical point. Similar drastic changes exist in properties of a liquid mixture as it approaches the thermodynamic critical loci of the mixture (Figure 4).
- Other properties of a liquid fuel that change widely near the critical region are thermal conductivity, surface tension, constant-pressure heat capacity and viscosity. In comparing a liquid sample with a supercritical fluid (SCF) sample of the same fuel both possessing the same density, thermal conductivity and diffusivity of a SF are higher than the liquid, its viscosity is much lower, while its surface tension and heat of vaporization have completely disappeared. These drastic changes make a supercritical fuel appreciably preferred over that of a liquid fuel with the same density. Further, it is expected that the combustion phenomena resulting from that of a supercritical fuel will be quite different from that of a liquid fuel.

- Applications of SCF include recovery of organics from oil shale, separations of biological fluids, bio separation, petroleum recovery, crude de-asphalting and de waxing, coal processing (reactive extraction and liquefaction), selective extraction of fragrances, oils and impurities from agricultural and food products, pollution control, combustion and many other applications.

1.6 SUPERCRITICAL FLUID EXTRACTION (SFE)

Supercritical Fluid Extraction (SFE) is based on the fact that, near the critical point of the solvent, its properties change rapidly with only slight variations of pressure. Supercritical fluids can be used to extract analytes from samples. The main advantages of using supercritical fluids for extractions is that they are inexpensive, extract the analytes faster and more environmentally friendly than organic solvents. For these reasons supercritical fluid CO_2 is the reagent widely used as the supercritical solvent (Figure 5).

1.7 MOLECULAR BASIS OF SFE

Advantages of SFE

1. SCFs have solvating powers similar to liquid organic solvents, but with higher diffusivities, lower viscosity, and lower surface tension.
2. Since the solvating power can be adjusted by changing the pressure or temperature separation of analytes from solvent is fast and easy.
3. By adding modifiers to a SCF (like methanol to CO_2) its polarity can be changed for having more selective separation power.
4. In industrial processes involving food or pharmaceuticals, one does not have to worry about solvent residuals as you would if a "typical" organic solvent were used.
5. Candidate SCFs are generally cheap, simple and many are safe. Disposal costs are much less and in industrial processes, the fluids can be simple to recycle.
6. SCF technology requires sensitive process control, which is a challenge. In addition, the phase transitions of the mixture of solutes and solvents have to be measured or predicted quite accurately. Generally the phase transitions in the critical region are rather complex and difficult to measure and predict. The research has provided much insight into these phenomena.

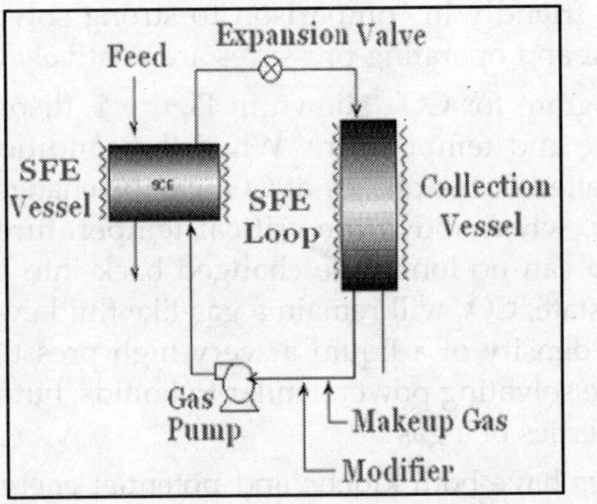

Fig. 5 : Schematic flow of supercritical fluid

1.8 SUPERCRITICAL FLUID APPLICATIONS IN MANUFACTURING AND MATERIALS PRODUCTION

Environmentally friendly supercritical CO_2 and its associated technologies are being used in many applications to replace hazardous solvents, lower costs, and improve efficiencies. Some of the applications requiring a supercritical fluid pump include:

- Supercritical Fluid Extraction (SFE)
- Supercritical Fluid Chromatography (SFC)
- Catalysis/Reaction Feed
- Injection molding and Extrusion
- Particle Formation
- Cleaning
- Electronic Chip Manufacturing
- Plastics Production

Teledyne Isco Syringe Pumps, which are excellent CO_2 pumps or Supercritical Fluid pumps, are used in R&D and production in many of these applications. Syringe pumps are well-suited for use with Supercritical Fluids and can operate at high pressures with great accuracy and reliability.

1.9 THEORY

Supercritical fluids are very dense gases with many properties superior to liquids or solvents. While there are many fluids that can be used in their supercritical state, CO_2 is the one most often used because it is considered environmentally friendly in comparison to strong solvents, and its critical temperature point and operating pressures are relatively easy to work with.

A phase diagram for CO_2, shown in Figure 1, displays the relationship between pressure and temperature. When the conditions of pressure and temperature are altered, the phases of CO_2 can be changed to a solid, gas, or liquid. However, when above the critical temperature, Tc, CO_2 becomes supercritical, and can no longer be changed back into liquid by increasing pressure. In this state, CO_2 will remain a gas-like fluid even though it may be approaching the density of a liquid at very high pressures. Its supercritical properties include solvating power similar to liquids, but with the penetrating or diffusion properties of a gas.

All molecules have both kinetic and potential energy. Kinetic energy is defined as energy of molecular motion, while potential energy is stored energy of an object relative to its position. The potential energy of attraction between molecules is known as the Van der Waal force.

The process of dissolving is directly affected by the Van der Waal force between solvent molecules and solute molecules. Surface tension and viscosity increase as this force makes solvent molecules draw closer together, leading to decreased diffusion and inhibiting the processes of solvating, extraction, and cleaning.

Kinetic energy will overcome the Van der Waal force if the solvent temperature is raised above the critical point, thereby reducing the attraction between the molecules. This lowers surface tension and viscosity, and increases diffusion capability, enabling the solvent to penetrate more deeply into and around small pores and features.

It should be noted that while supercritical CO_2 is excellent for dissolving small, non-polar organic compounds, it is less effective in dissolving many polar or ionic compounds and large polymers (except for fluorinated oligomers). Solvating properties can be improved with the addition of small amounts of other fluids or modifiers. This can include fluids, additives such as ethanol or water, or fluorinated detergents.

1.10 APPLICATIONS

Due to lower toxicity as compared to common organic solvents, and being ubiquitous in nature, CO_2 has high promise in replacing Freon and organic solvents in many industrial manufacturing processes. Even though CO_2 does have some shortcomings, research is currently being done to overcome these problems

1.10.1 Supercritical Fluid Chromatography (SFC)

Chromatography is an analytical technique used in separating chemical mixtures into separate components. SFC uses supercritical CO_2 to replace solvents as the mobile phase in HPLC. Because of supercritical CO_2, advantages in diffusion and performance of the separation columns are improved, with higher resolutions and faster separations.

1.10.2 Catalysis/Reactant Feed

Reactions with supercritical CO_2 may have important applications in fields such as catalysis and polymerization. The use of supercritical CO_2 to replace solvents has the benefit of increasing and controlling reaction kinetics by altering the pressure. Also, there is the possibility of producing unique materials, which would be difficult to do with conventional techniques.

1.10.3 Injection Molding and Extrusion

The presence of CO_2 in plastic melts lowers viscosities thereby decreasing the injection molding pressures required, and/or decreasing the injection times. These advantages will increase the life of molding equipment and increase production rates. Also by lowering the melt temperatures, you can mold thermally labile compounds. CO_2 is also used as an expanding or foaming agent for injection molding or extrusions. Adding air pockets in plastic reduces the amount of material used, decreases shrinkage, warpage and improved tolerances. The use of CO_2 in forming micro cells produces denser foams, making thin wall applications possible.

1.10.4 Particle Formation

Supercritical fluids can be used in the production of powders or micro particles with possible uses in the pharmaceutical industry. With conventional techniques, there is little control over powder properties, such as particle size. By rapidly depressurizing materials dissolved in CO_2, micro particles are produced with drugs or other components of interest embedded in a substrate. This is accomplished by pumping the mixture through a capillary where the CO_2 is vaporized at the outlet, leaving powders behind. This powder has uses such as time released drugs.

1.10.5 Cleaning

Supercritical fluids can be an effective solvent for cleaning many kinds of parts, electronics, plastics, or clothing. With the enhanced wetting and diffusion properties, supercritical CO_2 can improve the cleaning of components with small openings, delicate equipment, or porous materials. It can remove oils, fats, waxes, and other contaminates without damaging the matrix.

1.10.6 Electronic Chip Manufacturing

One possible important industrial application may be in the electronic chip fabrication process. Chip manufacturing creates a large environmental burden. It is estimated that the production of a 2.0g chip consumes at a minimum 72g of chemicals and 1.6Kg of fossil fuels. This gives a 630:1 weight ratio of chemical–fossil fuels and product. In comparison, the manufacturing of a typical automobile has a corresponding ratio of 2:1. Also, in the manufacturing of a 2.0g chip, 32L of water are used during the washing and rinsing steps during photolithography.

Even though water can be recycled, this process requires extra energy. Supercritical CO_2 along with appropriate detergents may eliminate the need for water and reduce energy consumption in the manufacturing process. Due to the low surface-tension of supercritical fluids compared to water, finer surface features and structures can be better cleaned without risk of causing damage.

1.10.7 Plastics Production

Currently, PTFE and other fluoropolymers are being synthesized in refrigerant, and since perfluoro monomers and oligomers are soluble in CO_2, it can replace refrigerant in this application. After the 1986 Montreal Protocol, CO_2 has successfully replaced Freon as a polymer foaming agent. Finally, due to its inertness, CO_2 can be an excellent solvent for reaction involving a strong oxidizing or reducing agent.

The benefits of Supercritical Fluids in Reaction Engineering applications can greatly exceed the initial equipment outlay. Research in reactions involving supercritical fluids, e.g., $SFCO_2$, has shown it possible to obtain the following advantages:

- Better product uniformity
- Faster reaction rates
- Improved selectivity
- Greater energy savings compared to evaporation of traditional bulk solvents
- More environmentally benign
- Non-flammable
- Non-toxic

Teledyne Isco syringe pumps provide accurate pulse less flow and are excellent CO_2 pumps or Supercritical Fluid pumps. They are commonly used in SF reaction engineering research at lab and pilot scales.

Supercritical fluids are very dense gases with many properties superior to liquids or solvents. While there are many fluids that can be used in their supercritical state, CO_2 is the one most often used because it is considered environmentally friendly, and its critical temperature and operating pressures are relatively easy to work with. In the supercritical state, molecular forces that give liquids their particular properties of surface tension, viscosity or slower diffusion are altered. Molecules do not "stick together" as well, so viscosities are lower with higher diffusion rates. Such enhanced properties can be beneficial to the reaction process since mixing is improved thereby improving distribution and enhancing product quality.

A phase diagram for CO_2, shown in Figure 1, displays the relationship between pressure and temperature. When the conditions of pressure and temperature are altered, the phases of CO_2 can be changed to a solid, liquid, or gas. However, when above the critical temperature, TC, CO_2 becomes supercritical, and can no longer be changed back into liquid by increasing the pressure. (Figure 6)

In this state, CO_2 will remain a gas-like fluid even though it may be approaching the density of a liquid at very high pressures. Its supercritical properties include solvating power similar to liquids, the penetrating or diffusion properties of a gas, and a "zero" surface tension.

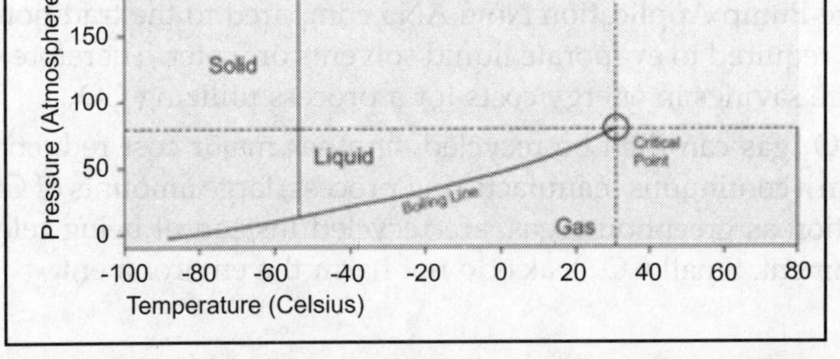

Fig. 6 : Phase Diagram of Carbon Dioxide

CO_2 is a naturally occurring component of our atmosphere. CO_2 is non-toxic in small amounts (consider your own breath), and not a volatile organic compound (VOC), hence not contributing to smog formation. CO_2 is also non-flammable—a great advantage over many conventional liquid solvents.

Supercritical CO_2 has a low viscosity and high diffusivity compared to the usual liquid solvents used as a medium for reactions. Low viscosity and high diffusivity cause the reagents (or soluble catalysts) to rapidly travel to all locations inside a reactor. With uniform conditions throughout the reactor, the reaction process can obtain desirable results: better product uniformity, faster reaction rates, and improved selectivity. It should be noted that, despite all the advantages, $SFCO_2$ is best at dissolving small, non-polar organic compounds, but has difficulty dissolving many polar or ionic compounds, or most large polymers (fluorinated oligomers are an exception). Solvating properties can be improved with the addition of small amounts of other fluids or modifiers. These can include additives such as surfactants, or modifiers such as ethanol or methanol.

After completing supercritical fluid reaction, $SFCO_2$ is depressurized to a gaseous state, and solutes generally precipitate and fall out of solution. That is, the reaction product(s) is no longer soluble in gaseous CO_2. In the manufacture of chemical solids, often the product must be dried after the reaction process to remove solvents.

A large amount of energy is used for drying in these conventional processes. With a reaction process involving $SFCO_2$, the product is left dry after the reaction, and following depressurization; hence no further drying is required. This has also been shown in polymer manufacturing, where by using $SFCO_2$, dry product can be obtained with a resultant significant energy savings.

1.10.8 Syringe Pump Application Note

1.10.8.1 AN5

Syringe Pump Application Note AN5 compared to the traditional drying procedures required to evaporate liquid solvents or water. Therefore, there can be very large savings in energy costs for a process utilizing CO_2.

The CO_2 gas can then be recycled, another major cost reduction. When using CO_2 in a continuous manufacturing process, large amounts of CO_2, which could function as greenhouse gas, are recycled instead of being released into the environment. Small CO_2 leaks do not harm the environment.

1.11 APPLICATIONS USING SUPERCRITICAL CO_2

Catalysis

Homogeneous catalysts are highly active and selective, while heterogeneous catalysts are less active but easier to separate and re-use. In 2006, Liotta, Eckert, Hallett, and Pollet reported techniques for recycling homogeneous catalysts using $SFCO_2$ by changing pressure of the CO_2 in the reaction. This allowed the homogeneity to be turned on and off. Another example comes from Toghiani et al, where $SFCO_2$ was used to oxidize unsaturated fatty acids to make diacids and epoxides. The reaction medium was $SFCO_2$, which was completely oxidized.

1.11.1 Nanotechnology

$SFCO_2$ is becoming an enabling solvent for producing nonmaterial such as aero gels of Al_2O_3, SiO_2, TiO_2, and ZrO_2. These non materials, which often have new and exciting properties such as tunable pore sizes and high surface areas, have applications as biomaterials, and catalysts for fuel cells and solar cells. Also, $SFCO_2$ drying has been widely used to produce aero gels that exhibit a very high specific surface area and maintain the nano architecture due to the zero surface tension.

1.12 PHARMACEUTICALS AND BIOMEDICAL DEVICES

Supercritical fluids have emerged as the green solvents in the pharmaceutical industry for micronization of inhalable medicines, and separation of chiral enantiomers. $SFCO_2$ is also playing a role as a valuable tool in tissue engineering and preparing biomedical devices, as CO_2 is largely anti-bacterial and can be used in producing tissue scaffolds.

1.12.1 Polymerization

Previously, De Simone and coworkers have shown that $SFCO_2$ is a promising alternative medium for free-radical, cationic, and step-growth polymerizations, and continuous processes. The free radical initiator AIBN was shown to have a higher efficiency in $SFCO_2$ than in benzene, due to low viscosity of $SFCO_2$.

1.12.2 Polymer Functionalization and Processing

In 1994 and 1995, Watkins and McCarthy showed how $SFCO_2$ could be used to carry small molecules for fictionalization of a polymer.

1.12.3 Applications - CO_2 as reactant

In some reactions, CO_2 may be consumed, i.e. mitigated. For example, Noyori et al described the use of $SFCO_2$ reacting with hydrogen to make formic acid. It is possible to obtain higher reaction rates and longer catalyst lifetimes using this method.

1.12.4 Implementation

Case 1: Pressure Control

In this example, the pump is used in constant pressure mode. In constant pressure mode, the pump automatically displaces its volume to achieve the pressure requested by the operator. For $SFCO_2$, pressure is directly related to solubility. (Figure 7)

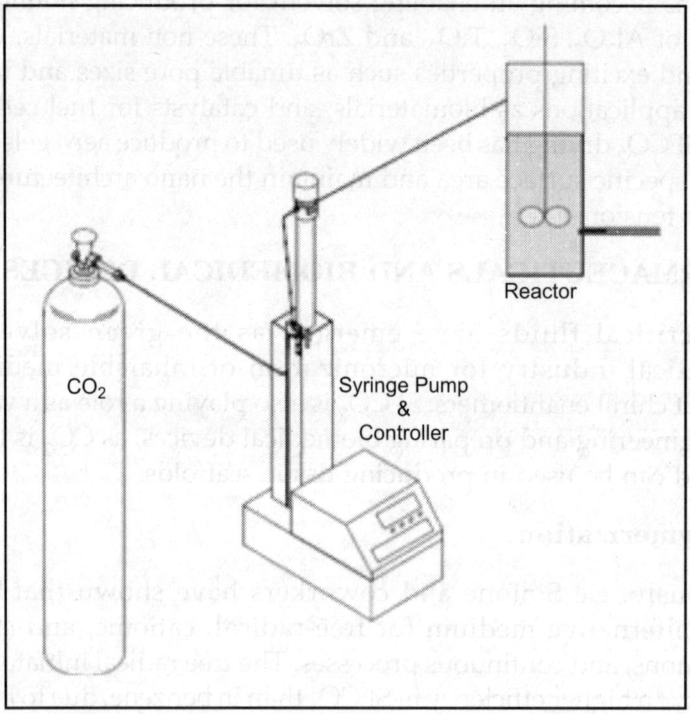

Fig. 7 : $SFCO_2$ density and solubility during reaction

Case 2: Stable Mass Delivery

In this example, the pump is maintained at a constant temperature and is operated in constant flow mode. Steady back pressure is provided by the back pressure device. With known pressure, temperature, and volumetric displacement rate ("flow rate"), the mass of CO_2 delivered to the reactor is predictive.

1.12.5 Syringe Pump Application Note AN5

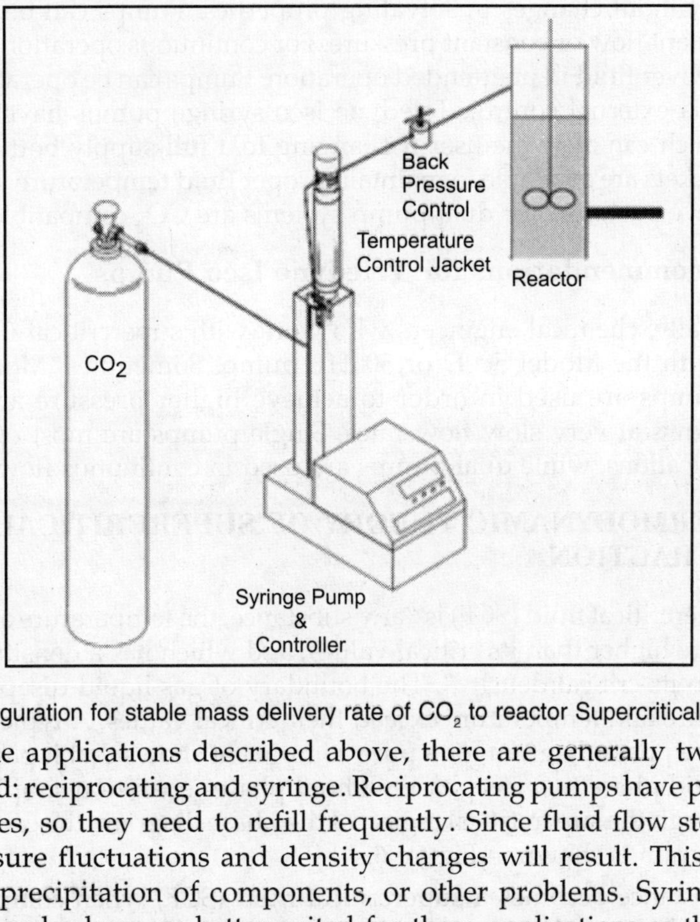

Fig. 8 : Configuration for stable mass delivery rate of CO_2 to reactor Supercritical Fluid Pumps

For the applications described above, there are generally two types of pumps used: reciprocating and syringe. Reciprocating pumps have pistons with short strokes, so they need to refill frequently. Since fluid flow stops during refill, pressure fluctuations and density changes will result. This can cause unwanted precipitation of components, or other problems. Syringe pumps, considered pulse less, are better suited for these applications as the pressure and flow rates can be more accurately controlled. For most supercritical fluid applications, pressure must be maintained, so a constant pressure mode is needed. When pumps compress CO_2, even in the liquid state, heat generated will accumulate in the pump head. If this heat is not removed, incoming CO_2 could be inadvertently heated above the critical point, thereby impacting fill efficiencies. For proper operation, CO_2 pumps must incorporate some means to remove this heat. Not all materials are suitable for use with CO_2, so wetted materials must be checked for compatibility. (Figure 8)

1.12.6 Why Use Teledyne Isco Pumps?

Teledyne Isco syringe pumps are well suited for use with CO_2 and provide the best in accuracy and reliability. Flow rate accuracy is +/- 0.5% or better, and flows are pulse less. Pulse less flow means fluid pressure and density are constant, without changes in solvating properties. Pumps can be operated in either constant flow or constant pressure. For continuous operation, dual pump systems deliver fluid in unattended operation. Pumps can be operated as stand-alone or via external control. Teledyne Isco syringe pumps have a "poor fill alarm" which can alert the user if changing to a full supply bottle is needed. Cooling jackets are available to maintain proper fluid temperature in the pump. Special valve packages for dual pump systems are CO_2 compatible.

1.12.7 Recommendations for Teledyne Isco Pumps

Typically, chemical engineers who work with supercritical fluids choose to work with the Model 500D or 500HL pump. Sometimes, Model 260D or 100DM pumps are used in order to achieve higher pressure and/or more accurate flows at very slow flow rates. Single pumps are most often used in batch applications, while dual pumps are used in continuous flow.

1.13 THERMODYNAMIC THEORY OF SUPERCRITICAL EXTRACTION

A supercritical fluid (SCF) is "any substance, the temperature and pressure of which are higher than its critical values, and which has a density close to or higher than its critical density". The boundary of gas-liquid disappears when both pressure and temperature exceed their critical values. A typical pressure-temperature phase diagram for a pure component shows that it passes directly from a liquid phase to a gas phase without phase separation simply by taking a path through the supercritical region of the phase diagram, the carbon dioxide -phase diagram is shown in Figure 6.

A substance becomes a supercritical fluid (SCF) when compressed to a pressure and elevated to a temperature greater than that of its critical point (see Figure 2.1). The density of gas increases as the pressure increases. As the thermal temperature increases, then the density of the liquid decreases. At the critical point, the density of gas and liquid become identical as the pressure and temperature increase. The difference between gas phase and liquid phase disappears, and a supercritical fluid is formed. Although a supercritical fluid (SCF) is a single phase, it exhibits properties of both liquid phase and gas phase. Supercritical fluid has density and solvating properties similar to a liquid. Solubility increases with density and pressure; thus, SCFs have high viscosity properties closer to gases. These properties promote high mass transfer rates between a solute and a supercritical fluid.

In 1879, Hannay and Hogarth first discovered that solid solubility increased significantly in supercritical fluid by studying the solubility of cobalt (II) chloride, iron (III) chloride, potassium bromide, and potassium iodide in supercritical ethanol (Tc=243°C Tp=63 atm). They also found that decreasing the pressure around critical pressure caused the solutes to precipitate significantly as a "snow". Zhuse reported the first industrial application in 1951. The food and beverage industry was the first to make commercial use of supercritical carbon dioxide extraction.

Replacing conventional organic solvents with SCFs in extraction procedures is a major advancement in today's pollution prevention programs. Supercritical fluid extraction can be used for waste separation and minimization, as well as solvent recycling. Other advantages of supercritical extraction include high efficiency, high extraction rates and greater selectivity. In 1970, Zosel reported the decaffeination of green coffee with carbon dioxide. This was a significant development in supercritical extraction. The application of supercritical carbon dioxide in the food industry is widely used for extraction of organics. Table 2 shows some typical industrial supercritical extraction processes.

Table 2 : Fundamentals and applications of supercritical fluid technology

Application scope	Supercritical fluid	Industrial ConditionT (°C)	Industrial ConditionP (Mpa)
Lemon oil extraction	CO_2	40	30
Nicotine extraction	CO_2	45	30
Hops extraction	CO_2	40	30
Coffee decaffination	CO_2	50~70	15~30
Lipid extraction from bean, sunflower	CO_2	45~55	31.9~40.5
Essence extraction from black pepper	CO_2	90	16.2~22.3
Oil extraction from almond	CO_2	35~75	20.7~62.0
Oil extraction from fennel and cinnamon	CO_2	30~50	150~300
Flavoring extraction from pineapple	CO_2	40	60
Oil extraction from corn	CO_2	40	8~9
Coal extraction/liquidation	Propane	0~40	8~20

The process of supercritical fluid extraction is relatively simple. The extraction system usually consists of an extractor, controller, and pump. A fluid is pumped through the extractor from its storage vessel. The system controller maintains the pressure and temperature. The pressure and temperature are increased to the compound's supercritical conditions in the extractor. A continuous stream of the SCF is supplied to the extractor where it absorbs the contaminant. The solvent and solute stream travel to the expansion vessel. Here, as the pressure decreases, the solubility of the solute decreases and the two components separate. The contaminant is collected and the extracting fluid is recycled back to the storage tank for reuse.

1.14 PROPERTIES OF SUPERCRITICAL FLUIDS

The carbon dioxide pressure-temperature phase diagram, a typical diagram for a pure component, is shown in Figure 4. There are three lines—melting line, boiling line and liquid line. These lines define the regions corresponding to the gas, liquid and solid.

Each line represents the equilibrium state of the gas-liquid, liquid-solid and gas-solid phase. The boiling line starts at the triple point and ends at the critical point. Table 3 gives the Tc, Pc and boiling point for some typical supercritical fluids. Supercritical fluids have the properties of both a liquid and a gas. Supercritical fluids have densities similar to liquids. Therefore, supercritical fluids have a relatively high liquid-like density. In general, the solubility of a compound in a supercritical fluid is related to its vapor pressure and density. Solubility increases with density and pressure, thus, supercritical fluids have a high absorption capacity. Supercritical fluids also have rapid diffusion and low viscosity close to those of gases. The gas-like properties allow for high mass transfer rates between a solute and a supercritical fluid. Table 4 shows the typical values for the density, viscosity, and diffusivity coefficients of a gas, supercritical fluid, and liquid by order of magnitude.

Table 3 : Critical data for selected substances

Gas	Boiling point (K)	Supercritical Temperature Tc (K)	Supercritical pressure Pc (Mpa)
CO_2	194.7	304.2	7.38
C_2H_4	161.4	282.4	5.13
NO	121.4	180	6.48
C_2H_6	184.5	305.4	4.94
$CClF_3$	296.92	28.9	3.71
C_3H_8	231.1	369.8	4.26
H_2O	373.15	647.3	21.83
NH_3	299.81	405.6	11.25
H_2S	212.87	373.5	8.89

Table 4 : Properties of supercritical fluids vs. gases and liquids

	Gas	Supercritical fluid	Liquid
Density (g/cm^3)	10^{-3}	0.1 ~ 1	1
Diffusion coefficient (cm^2/s)	10^{-1}	10^{-3} ~ 10^{-4}	< 10^{-5}
Viscosity (g/cm.s)	10^{-4}	10^{-3}~10^{-4}	10^{-2}

The most important property for a supercritical fluid is the density. The higher the supercritical fluid density the higher is the solubility. This behavior is illustrated in Figure 2. At the low temperature of 310 K, the density changes dramatically around the critical pressure. Above 310 K, the change becomes small with increasing temperature. This means the property of density can be controlled by both pressure and temperature around critical temperature and critical pressure. Reducing the pressure decreases the solubility of the solute very quickly and the solute can be separated very easily by reducing the pressure. (Table 4)

The temperatures normally employed for supercritical fluid are in the range of room temperature to 200°C as shown in Table 4. The materials to be used for supercritical fluid, is more available with lower critical temperature. From Table 4 it was observed that carbon dioxide is a suitable substance for use as a supercritical fluid. Supercritical extraction has high efficiency, high extraction rates and greater selectivity. A major advantage of supercritical carbon dioxide extraction is that conventional organic solvents can be replaced by supercritical carbon dioxide in extraction

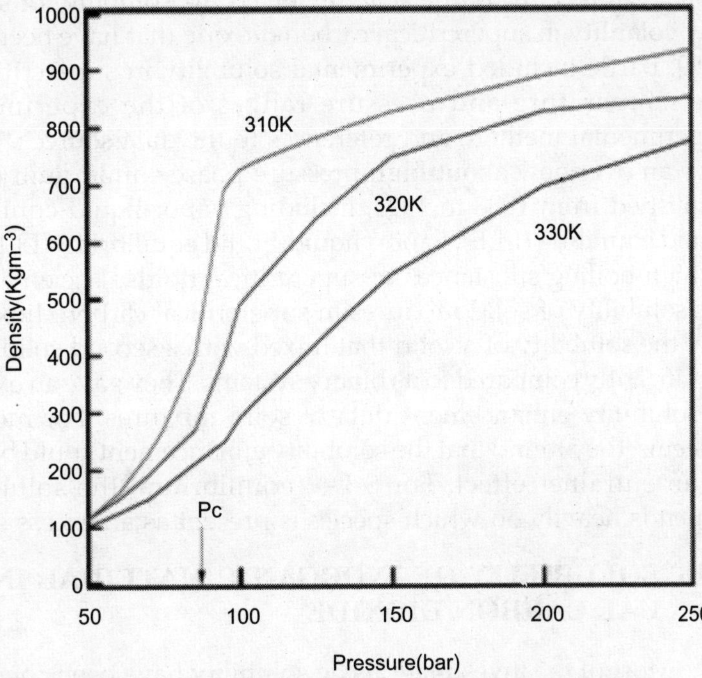

Fig. 9 : Density-pressure isotherms for carbon dioxide

procedures. Its non-toxic and non-combustible properties make it environmentally friendly. This is a major advancement in today's pollution prevention programs. Supercritical carbon dioxide has a higher density than most of the other supercritical fluids. But supercritical carbon dioxide has a lower critical temperature and pressure than most of the others. Therefore, supercritical carbon dioxide extraction energy costs are lower than those of other fluids. (Figure 9)

Supercritical carbon dioxide is also commercially available in high purity. Therefore, supercritical carbon dioxide is a popular and inexpensive solvent used in supercritical extraction.

1.15 SOLUBILITY OF ORGANIC MATERIAL IN SUPERCRITICAL CARBON DIOXIDE

The solubility of solutes in supercritical fluids is very important to establish the technical and economic feasibility of any supercritical fluid extraction process and separation operations. A large number of investigations on solubility have been made in recent years. The experimental data and methods have been reported in several review articles. Knapp *et al.* (1981) reviewed the high-pressure phase-equilibrium data covering the period from 1900 to 1980. Fornari *et al.* (1990) reviewed the phase-equilibrium data covering the period from 1978 to 1987. Bartle *et al.* reviewed the solubility of solids and liquids of low volatility in supercritical carbon dioxide that have been published through 1989. Bartle included experimental solubility in supercritical carbon dioxide, the temperature and pressure ranges of the experimental process, the experimental method, and references to the data sources. Dohrn and Brunner give an overview about high-pressure phase equilibrium data that have been published from 1988 to 1993, including vapor-liquid equilibria (VLE), liquid-liquid equilibria (LLE), vapor- liquid-liquid equilibria (VLLE), and the solubility of high-boiling substances in supercritical fluids. Lucien and Foster reviewed the solubility of solid mixtures in supercritical carbon dioxide. They indicated that the solubility of a solid that mixed with a second solid might be enhanced significantly compared to its binary systems. They gave an extensive compilation of solubility enhancement data of solid mixtures. For most S-V equilibrium systems, they found that the solubility enhancement could be explained in terms of an entrainer effect. For S-L-V equilibrium, the solubility enhancement depends heavily on which species is present as an excess solid phase.

1.16 SOLUBILITY OF INORGANIC MATERIAL IN—SUPERCRITICAL CARBON DIOXIDE

Most of the investigations on solubility have been concerned with organic systems. Solubility data for inorganic systems have been reported less frequently. Tolley and Tester used supercritical carbon dioxide in extractive metallurgy. They determined the solubility of titanium tetrachloride ($TiCl_4$) in supercritical carbon dioxide, as shown in Figure 10. Titanium tetrachloride is highly soluble in supercritical carbon dioxide. Solubility initially decreases as the pressure rises from ambient pressure to near the supercritical pressure, and then it increases dramatically as the pressure rises around the supercritical point. tetrachloride and carbon dioxide were found to be completely miscible at any combination of temperature and pressure.

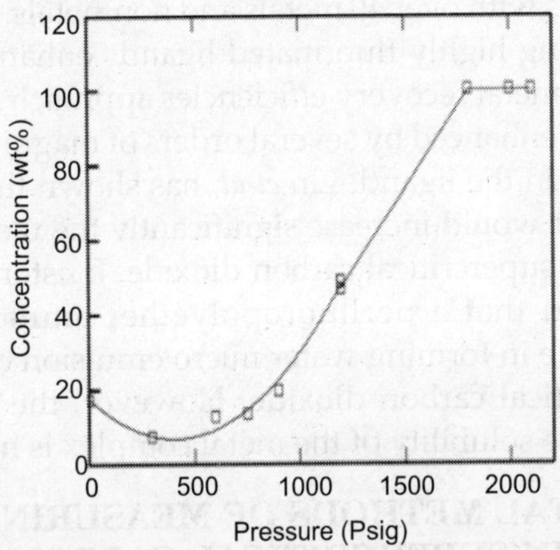

Fig. 10 : $TiCl_4$ Solubility in supercritical carbon dioxide at 56°C

In some cases, however, direct extraction of metal ions by supercritical carbon dioxide is known to be highly inefficient because of the charge neutralization requirement and the weak solute-soluble in pure supercritical carbon dioxide. The metal ions must be present as electrically neutral complexes to be extracted by supercritical carbon dioxide. Laintz *et al.* first reported the use supercritical fluids modified by the addition of complex agents in extraction of metal ions from liquid and solid materials.

This has opened up a new area of research for the use of supercritical fluids as solvents. The currently modification of supercritical fluids focuses on three potential applications including environmental treatment, metallurgical processing, and electronic materials/ceramics production. The solubility of the metal-chelate complex in the supercritical fluid is the most important property. It needs to be determined to develop As the pressure was increased above 1500 psig, titanium any of extraction technologies. Metal complex solubility and metal extraction using chelating agents have recently been widely investigated.

Solubility is a function of pressure and temperature. It indicates the relative extractability of a substance and sets the limit of extractability. Therefore, solubility is one of the keys to achieve quantitative extraction in a reasonable time using a minimum amount of fluid. An accurate metal-chelate complex solubility database has become more and more important. In recent studies, the solubility is focused on the metal-chelate complex solubility rather than the solubility of the chelating agent itself. The metal-chelate complex solubility rather than the solubility of the chelating agent itself would be the limiting factor. The chelate is more soluble in supercritical fluid because the chelate is organic.

A widely used chelating agent is diethyl dithiocarbamate (DDC), which forms stable complexes with over 40 metals and nonmetals. Yazdi and Beckman have shown that adding highly fluorinated ligands enhances the solubility of metal complexes. The metal recovery efficiencies approach 87%. Laintz showed that the solubility was enhanced by several orders of magnitude by substituting fluorine for hydrogen in the ligand. Lin *et al.* has shown that the presence of a small amount of water would increase significantly the metal-chelate complex solubility in modified supercritical carbon dioxide. Jonston *et al.* and Eastoe *et al.* first demonstrated that a perlluoropolyether ammonium carboxylate surfactant was effective in forming water micro emulsion droplets (< 10 nm in diameter) in supercritical carbon dioxide. However, the affect of this small amount of water on the solubility of the metal complex is not well understood.

1.17 EXPERIMENTAL METHODS OF MEASURING THE SOLUBILITY IN SUPERCRITICAL CARBON DIOXIDE

There are many ways to measure the solubility in supercritical fluids. All these methods can be divided into two classifications depending on how the compositions are determined. One is the analytical method or direct sampling method, and the other is the synthetic method or indirect method. The analytical method requires chemical analysis to determine the composition of the coexisting phases at equilibrium. The synthetic method or indirect method involves an indirect determination of equilibrium composition without sampling. The idea of this method is to prepare a mixture of known composition and then investigate the phase behavior in an equilibrium cell. Most techniques used for measuring solubility of solid components in supercritical fluids are analytical methods. These methods can be classified into four different categories depending on the analysis methods: a) gravimetric methods, b) chromatographic methods, ç) spectroscopic methods, d) miscellaneous methods.

A gravimetric method is most widely used for investigation of solubility in supercritical fluids. The basic idea is to reach a coexisting equilibrium phase in an extraction cell. The procedure includes passing the supercritical fluid through the sample dropping the pressure to precipitate the solute, and weighing the sample. A schematic diagram of a basic system is shown in Figure 11. A typical experiment involved setting the flow and allowing the system to reach a steady state. A pre weighted trap or cell is introduced to the system while the rate of flow of carbon dioxide is monitored. The cell was reweighted and the total mass of carbon dioxide passed the cell in the period was calculated. The solubility can be obtained in terms of mole fraction. Experimental errors are quoted in the range of 3-5% for solubility data.

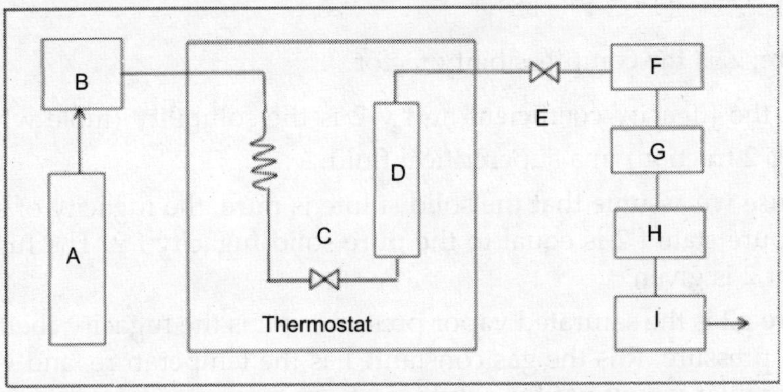

Fig. 11 : Schematic diagram of the gravimetric method (A: CO_2 cylinders; B: CO_2 pump; C: supply valve; D: extraction cell; E: vent valve; F: analyte valve; G: restrictor and restrictor fitting; H: collection vessel; I: flow meter).

1.18 THERMODYNAMIC THEORY OF SUPERCRITICAL EXTRACTION

1.18.1 Thermodynamic Basis

For solid-supercritical fluid equilibrium, we have the following equilibrium relations for component i: where f iF is the fugacity of component i in the supercritical fluid phase and f iS is that in the solid phase. For the binary system, the supercritical fluid phase fugacity, recalling its definition is:

$$f_i^F = f_i^S ; T_i^F = T_i^S ; P_i^F = P_i^S \quad 1$$

$$f_2^F = f_2^{puneS} = p_2^{Sat}\phi_2^S\left(\int_{p_2}^{p} Sat \frac{V_2^S}{RT}dp\right) \quad 2$$

$$y_2 = \frac{f_2^F}{p\phi_2^F} = \frac{f_2^G}{p\phi_2^F} = \frac{p_2^{Sat}\phi_2^S}{p\phi_2^F}\exp\left(\int_{p_2^{Sat}}^{F} \frac{v_2^S}{RT}dp\right) = \frac{p_2^{Sat}}{p}\frac{1}{\phi^F}\left[\frac{v_2^S(p-p_2^{Sat})}{RT}\right] \quad 3$$

$$E = \frac{1}{\phi_2^F}\left[\frac{v_2^S\left(p-p_2^{Sat}\right)}{RT}\right] \quad 4$$

$$y_2 = \frac{p_2^{Set}}{p} E \quad 5$$

$$\text{In}\, \phi_2^F = \frac{1}{RT} \int_v^{\infty} \left[\left(\frac{\partial p}{\partial n_i} \right)_{T.V.n_{\neq j}} - \frac{RT}{V} \right] dv - \text{In Z} \quad 6$$

Where, Z is the compressibility factor.

ϕ_2^S is the fugacity coefficient and y 2 is the solubility (mole where P is pressure, φ 2 fraction) in a supercritical fluid.

Because we assume that the solid solute is pure, the fugacity of solute in the solid pure state f 2 is equal to the pure solid fugacity f 2. The fugacity of component 2 is given

Where p2 is the saturated vapor pressure, φ 2 is the fugacity coefficient at saturation pressure, R is the gas constant, T is the temperature, and v 2 is the solid-state molar volume of the solute.

Assuming that the molar volume of solid-state solute is constant over the pressure range, and the saturated vapor of the solid solute vapor system behaves are ideal gases, we can derive as:where the supercritical fluid phase fugacity coefficient at saturation pressure has been set equal to unity and P, T are the system pressure and temperature.

The saturated vapor pressure and solid molar volume are physical properties of the pure solid phase. Therefore, the solid solubility in supercritical fluid is primarily a function of system pressure, temperature, solid compound physical properties, and the fugacity coefficient of the solid phase in the supercritical fluid. Finally we define an enhancement factor E as follows:

The enhancement factor, E, is nearly always greater than unity and E → 1 as

Sat

p → p2 . 7

1.18.1 Equation of state

Fugacity coefficients can be calculated by the following equation:

$$\text{In}\, \phi_2^F = \frac{1}{RT} \int_v^{\infty} \left[\left(\frac{\partial p}{\partial n_i} \right)_{T.V.n_{\neq j}} - \frac{RT}{V} \right] dv - \text{In Z} \quad 8$$

The empirical equations of state methods provide one of the most useful techniques in the high-pressure phase equilibrium calculation. The cubic equations of state such as the Soave-Redlick-Kwong (SRK) equation or the Peng-Robinson (PR) equation are widely used to evaluate the fugacity coefficient.

There are more than one hundred empirical equations of state that have been published. All these empirical equation can be divided into two classes: cubic equations of state and multiple parameter equations of state. Cubic equations usually have two or three parameters and are derived from the Van der Waal equation. Some multiple parameter equations have more than 20 parameters. The evolution of cubic equation of state is: Van der Waal (1873) — Redlick-Kwong (1949) — Wilson (1965) — Soave (1972) — Peng-Robinson (1976). The evolution of multiple parameter equation of state is: Beattie-Bridgeman (1928) — Benedice-Webb-Rubin (1940-1942) — Starling (1971) — Starling-Han (1972).

In 1873, Van der Waal developed an equation that can describe the volumetric properties of a fluid:

$$p = \frac{RT}{v-b} - \frac{a}{v^2} \tag{9}$$

$$a = \frac{27}{64}\left(\frac{RT_C}{P_C}\right)^2 \tag{10}$$

$$b = \frac{1}{8}\frac{RT_C}{P_C} \tag{11}$$

Where, v is the molar volume of the mixture, a and b are constants that depend on composition, Tc is critical temperature and Pc is critical pressure. The equation of Van der Waal gives only an approximate description of gas-phase properties, but it was a major contribution for the comparison of later cubic equations of state.

The Redlich-Kwong EOS (1949) is a modification of the Van der Waal EOS. Like many early investigations, Redlick-Kwong modified the pressure, and developed a new equation of state in 1949:

$$p = \frac{RT}{v-b} - \frac{a}{T^{0.5}v(v+b)} \tag{12}$$

$$a = 0.42748\frac{R^2T_c^{2.5}}{Pc} \tag{13}$$

$$b = 0.08664\frac{RT_C}{Pc} \tag{14}$$

The Soave-Redlich-Kwong EOS was the first modification of the simple Redlich-Kwong EOS. Soave modified the Redlick-Kwong equation by defining the parameter, a, was a function of Tr and ω. The pressure curve could be well reproduced after this modification. The EOS requires three input parameters per pure compound Tc, Pc and ω.

$$p = \frac{RT}{v-b} - \frac{a(T)}{v(T_c)\alpha(T)} \qquad 15$$

$$\alpha(T) = \alpha(T_c)\alpha(T) \qquad 16$$

$$\alpha(T_c) = 0.42748\frac{(RT_c)^2}{Pc} \qquad 17$$

$$\alpha(T) = \left[1 + \left(0.480 + 1.574\omega - 0.176\omega^2\right)\left(1 - \sqrt{T/Tc}\right)^2\right] \qquad 18$$

$$b = 0.08664\frac{RT_c}{P_c} \qquad 19$$

The disadvantage of Redlick-Kwong and Soave-Redlick-Kwong equations of state is that the equations cannot predict the density of liquid accurately. Peng and Robinson developed the Peng-Robinson EOS to overcome this disadvantage in 1976 by a modified Redlick-Kwong equation. The Peng-Robinson EOS is the EOS most widely used in chemical engineering thermodynamics. It gives slightly better predications of liquid densities than the Soave-Redlich-Kwong EOS.

$$p = \frac{RT}{v-b} - \frac{a(T)}{v(v+b) + b(v-b)} \qquad 20$$

$$\alpha(T) = \alpha(T_c)\alpha(T) \qquad 21$$

$$\alpha(T_c) = 0.45724\frac{(RT_c)^2}{Pc} \qquad 22$$

$$\alpha(T) = \left[1 + b\left(1 - \sqrt{T/T_c}\right)\right]^2 \qquad 23$$

$$\beta = 0.37464 + 1.54226\omega - 0.26992\ \omega 2 \qquad 0 \le w \le 0.5 \qquad 24$$

$$b = 0.07780\frac{RT_c}{P_c} \qquad 25$$

1.18.3 Solubility calculation

The solubility of a material in supercritical fluid is essential for evaluating the viability of a minerals extraction recovery process. The cubic equations of state, Soave- Redlick-Kwong equation or Peng-Robinson equation, have most widely used in predictions of solubility in supercritical fluid. However, the interaction parameters have been determined mostly by fitting the experimental solubility data. It gives better predictions only after proper use of mixing rules and the assignment of the interaction parameters. Carleson et al have recently developed a group contribution method to predict interaction parameters in the absence of experimental data. Brennecke and Eckert reviewed the various equations of state and concluded that the Peng-Robinson EOS may be as good as more complicated equations.

The mixture parameters, a and b, are related to the pure component terms ai and bi

$$a=\sum_{i=1}^{n}\sum_{j=1}^{n}x_i x_j a_{ij} \qquad 26$$

$$a_{ij}=\left(1-k_{ij}\right)\left(a_i a_j\right)^{1/2}, i\neq j \qquad 27$$

$$b=\sum_{i=1}^{n}x_i b_i \qquad 28$$

$$a_n = a_i \qquad 29$$

Using mixing rules and the Peng-Robinson EOS for a binary system, the fugacity coefficient for component in a mixture can be related by

$$\text{In}\,\varphi_2=\frac{b_2}{b}\left(\frac{Pv}{RT}-1\right)-\text{In}\frac{P(v-b)}{RT}-\frac{a}{2\sqrt{2}RT}\left[\frac{2(y_1a_{12}+y_2a_{22})}{a}-\frac{b_2}{b}\right]\text{In}\frac{v+\left(1+\sqrt{2}\right)b}{v+\left(1-\sqrt{2}\right)b} \qquad 30$$

Recalling equation 2-4, the solid solubility, y2, in supercritical fluid is primarily a function of system pressure, temperature, solid compound physical properties, and the fugacity coefficient of the solid phase in the supercritical fluid:

$$y_2=\frac{p_2^{Set}}{p}\frac{1}{\phi_2^F}\left[\frac{v_2^S\left(p-p_2^{Set}\right)}{RT}\right] \qquad 31$$

1.19 SUPERCRITICAL FLUID CHROMATOGRAPHY ANALYSIS AND EXTRACTION

Chromatography and extraction are two closely related analytical processes used extensively for chemical separation and isolation. Both rely on the distribution of an analyte between two phases, a separating phase and stationary phase. In extraction, the separating phase is commonly referred to as the extracting phase and the sample as the stationary phase. In chromatography, the separating phase is called the mobile phase and the stationary phase is an immobilized liquid or solid phase over which the mobile phase passes. Quantitatively the distribution of an analyte between two phases can be expressed as where K is called the partition coefficient, C, represents the concentration of the analyte in the mobile (or extracting) phase, and C; represents the concentration of the analyte in the stationary phase. In extraction, this distribution is used to separate the analyte from the sample. In chromatography, compounds with different K values can be isolated from each other through repetitive distributions between a separating (mobile) phase passing over a stationary phase.

1.20 ANALYTICAL SUPERCRITICAL FLUID CHROMATOGRAPHY AND EXTRACTION

The most common separating phases have been liquids and gases. Liquid extraction and liquid chromatography (LC) are methods in which the separating phase is liquid, while in distillation and gas chromatography (GC) the separating phase is a gas. When supercritical fluids are used as the separating phase rather than gases or liquids, the separation processes are called supercritical fluid extraction (SFE) and supercritical fluid chromatography (SFC).

The definition of a supercritical fluid is best described by using a typical pressure-temperature phase diagram as shown in Figure 2. Above the critical pressure of a substance, a phase transition to a gaseous state is no longer observed as the liquid form of the substance is heated. Similarly, above the critical temperature of a substance, a phase transition to a liquid state is no longer observed as the gaseous form of the substance is pressurized. In the region above the critical temperature and pressure, a substance can no longer be classified as either a gas or a liquid since it has properties of both. In this region above the critical temperature and pressure, a substance is said to be a supercritical fluid. From a practical point of view, supercritical fluids can be thought of as gases that have been compressed to densities at which they can exhibit liquid-like interactions.

1.20.1 Characteristics

It is both the liquid-like and gas-like characteristics of densities, diffusivities, and viscosities fall into ranges between those of liquids and gases. Under practical analytical operating conditions, pressures from 50- 500 atm. and temperatures from ambient to 30°C, densities of supercritical fluids range from one to eight-tenths of their liquid densities. Diffusivities of analytes in supercritical fluids throughout this operating range vary between 10T3 and lop4 cm^2/s compared to values of less than 10m^5 cm^2/s for liquids.

Viscosities of supercritical fluids are typically l0-100 times less than those of liquids. On the other hand, viscosities of supercritical fluids are considerably higher and diffusivities considerably lower than in gases. Moreover, densities of supercritical fluids can be 100-1000 times greater than those of gases.

Advantages of supercritical fluids over liquid phases rest with improved mass transfer processes due to lower fluid viscosities and higher analyte diffusivities, while advantages over gas phases rest with increased molecular interactions due to higher densities.

Other characteristics of supercritical fluids that are important to consider include the operational temperature and pressure range. Table 6 provides a list of nine of the most common supercritical fluids used in extraction and chromatography along with temperature, pressure, density, and dipole moment information. These nine are chosen primarily because of the convenience of their critical temperatures and critical pressures. These temperatures and pressures low enough for use with commercial instrumentation. The polarity of the supercritical fluid, as reflected in its dipole moment and polarizability, is also of considerable importance.

1.20.2 Relationship of Supercritical Fluid Chromatography to Liquid and Gas Chromatography

Because the characteristics of supercritical fluids fall between those of gases and liquids, supercritical fluid chromatography is a separation method with applications intermediate between those of gas and liquid chromatography. It serves as a bridge between the two techniques. Yet, fundamental chromatographic theory applies to SFC in the same manner as to GC and LC. To compare SFC with GC and LC, it is informative to evaluate practical chromatographic parameters such as efficiency, speed of analysis, migration, and selectivity. Although chromatography is a non equilibrium process, efficiencies of chromatographic columns are typically reported as the number of theoretical equilibration steps that occur during a chromatographic separation. This number is called the number of theoretical plates (n); the more plates a column has the more efficient is the separation. Often the generation of high efficiencies in chromatography requires considerable time; thus, the speed of analysis is also an important consideration when comparing techniques.

Table 5 : Compares the Tube efficiency and analysis time ranges for various chromatographic techniques. (J. W. King *et al.*)

Technique[b]	Velocity Range (cm/s)	Efficiency Range (n)	Efficiency Time Range (n/s)	Elution Time Range[c] (min)	Practical Analysis Time Range[d] (min)
LC (packed)	0.1-0.4	5,300-8,500	14-35	2.5-10	0.5-60
SFC (packed)					
Low density	0.5-1.5	3,300-3,700	31-79	0.7-2	03-30
High density	05-1.5	3,500-5,100	42-83	0.7-2	0.3-30
SFC (open tubular)					
Low density	0.5-4	50,000-221.000	18-33	25-200	5-90
High density	0.5-4	20,000-137.000	11-13	25-200	5-90
GC (open tubular)	15-50	64,000- 112,000	93-180	6-20	1.5-60

LC (packed) 10-cm column length with 5-μm packing, SFC (packed): 10-cm column length with 5-μm packing. SFC (open tubular): 10-m column length with 50-μm i.d. GC (open tubular): 30-m column length with 300-μm i.d. All except the last column are calculated for nonprogrammed elution with k = 5.

Nonprogrammed conditions, for a solute with k = 5.

Typical programmed conditions.

While efficiency and analysis time are primarily a function of the viscosity of the mobile phase and the diffusivity of the analyte in the mobile phase, migration and selectivity are more a function of the volatility and solubility of the analyte.

The more time the analyte spends in the stationary phase, the longer it will take to migrate through the column. Selectivity is a relative measure of the times two analytes spend in the stationary phase. Thus, in all forms of chromatography the affinity of the stationary phase for the analyte is a critical parameter in separation and selectivity. In addition, analytes that are more volatile (in GC) or more soluble in the mobile phase (in LC) will spend less time in the stationary phase and will migrate through the column faster. In SFC, both volatility and solubility in the mobile phase are important parameters. Thus, temperature, mobile phase density, and mobile phase composition are important parameters for controlling migration in SFC.

1.20.3 Columns

The column is the heart of SFC, as it is in all forms of column chromatography. Both packed and open tubular columns can be used with their respective advantages and disadvantages. The following sections describe both theoretical and practical column considerations.

1.20.4 Column Efficiency

The expanded form of the Golay equation for open tubular columns is given by

$$h = \frac{2D_m}{u} + \frac{d_c^2\left(1+6k+11k^2\right)u}{96(1+k)^2 D_m} + \frac{2kd_r^2 u}{3(1+k)^2 D_s}$$

where h is the plate height, u is the average mobile phase linear velocity along the column, d, is the column internal diameter, k is the capacity factor, df is the stationary phase film thickness, and D, and D, are the solute diffusion coefficients in the mobile and stationary phases, respectively.

Figure 12 shows calculated van Demeter curves for open tubular columns with internal diameters from 25 to 100μm L-23. Since both pressure and stationary phase dimensions were held constant, the k values increased in Figure 12 with decreasing column diameter. The D_m, (CO_2 mobile phase at 40°C and 72 atm) and D_s, values were assumed to be 2 x 10^{-4}cm²/s and 1 x 10^{-6} cm²/s, respectively. These conditions give a mobile phase density of 0.22g/mL.

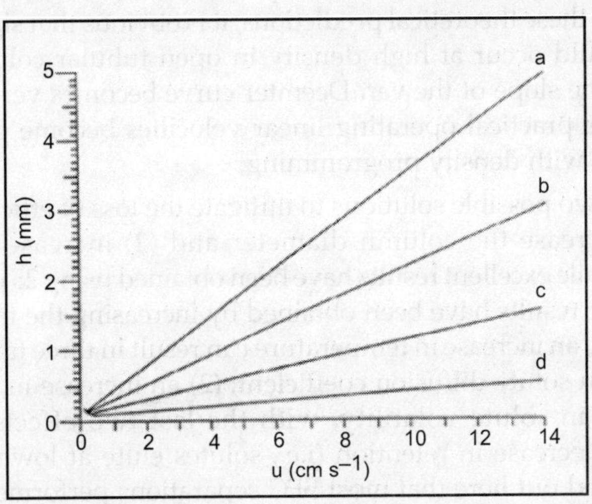

Fig. 12 : The SFC Van Deemeter plots for n-C12 on (a) 100-μm id (k=224), (b) 75-μm id (k=272), (c) 50-μm id (k=390) and (d) 25μm id (k=11.36) open tubular columns Conditions; CO_2; 40 °C; 72 atm. (J. W. King *et al.*)

Table 6 : Practical Open Tubular Column Efficiencies at $10_{\mu\ opt}$ for Different Column Diameters at k=3[a] (J. W. King *et al.*)

d_s (μm)	L(m)	$10u_{opt}$ (cm/s)	h (mm)	n	n/m	$44t_g$ (min)	n/min
100	24	1.1	0.44	5×10^4	2300	145	370
75	24	1.4	0.30	8×10^4	3300	114	700
50	23	2.0	0.22	1×10^5	4400	77	1300
25	7_b	4.3	0.18	4×10^4	5600	11	3500

* Length was shorter because of pressure drop

So far, the discussion of column efficiency has been limited to low density supercritical fluid conditions, where diffusion coefficients are, largest and efficiencies are highest. At higher densities, the results are not as favorable. Two factors must be considered when evaluating column efficiencies at increasing densities. The first is the effect of density alone; as the density increases, D, decreases and h increases at u larger than u_{opt}. The second factor is the inherently lower D_m, values characteristic of larger solute molecules that are eluted at the higher densities. Both factors were considered in the calculation of the van Deemter curves shown in Figure 12.

If one were to control the linear velocity at cm^2/s during density programming, efficiencies would decrease by nearly 75% from low-to-high density. For very large compounds, diffusivities would be even lower; for a D_m, of 3×10^{-5} cm^2/s, the column efficiency would drop to about 700-800 plates per meter. From these theoretical predictions, it is obvious that significant losses in efficiency could occur at high density in open tubular column SFC. This arises because the slope of the van Deemter curve becomes very steep at high density, and the practical operating linear velocities become greater than or equal to 10 u_{opt}, with density programming.

There are two possible solutions to mitigate the loss of efficiency at higher density: (1) decrease the column diameter and (2) increase the operating temperature. While excellent results have been obtained using 25 pm id columns, more immediate results have been obtained by increasing the temperature. At constant density, an increase in temperature can result in three favorable effects: (1) an increase in solute diffusion coefficient; (2) an increase in solubility; and (3) an increase in solute volatility, with the last two effects leading to a corresponding decrease in retention (i.e., solutes elute at lower densities). It should be pointed out here that most SFC separations performed today using CO_2 are carried out at temperatures near or at 100°C.

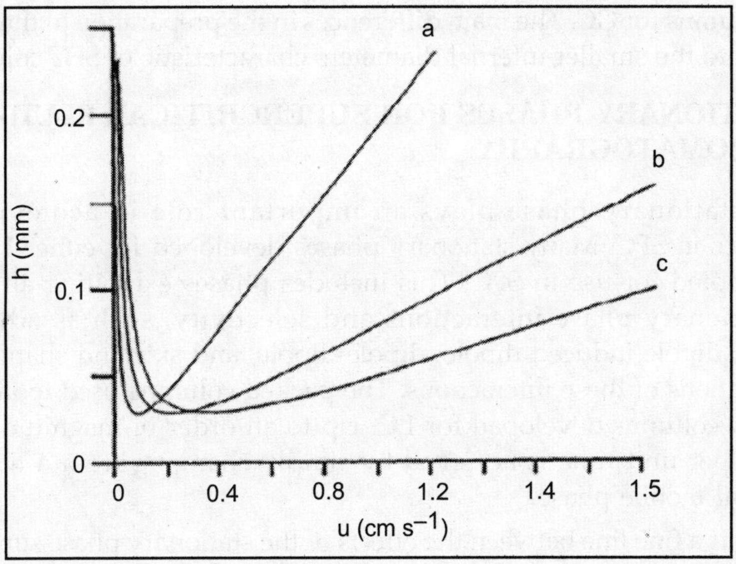

Fig. 13 : The SCE Van Deemetr plots for three compounds with D_m values of (a) 0.79 g/ml, (b) 0.45 g/ml, (c) 0.28 g/ml. conditions 50μm id open tubular column; CO_2; 40 °C (J. W. King *et al.*)

1.20.5 Packed Column Technology

Since the early days of SFC, packed column SFC technology has depended on materials available from the current state-of-the-art LC technology. It is not surprising that LC packing materials perform well under SFC conditions, since both techniques depend on the ability of the mobile phase to solvate analyte molecules.

Particle sizes referred to in publications normally vary from 3 to 10pm in diameter with pore sizes ranging from 100 to 300 8, (corresponding to a surface area of ca. 100-300m^2/g). Of these, the most commonly used particle size is 5- pm diameter. This particular size is popular because it is small enough to give relatively small plate heights, while being commercially available in sufficient uniformity and narrow distribution to allow efficient packing to be accomplished.

Smaller particles provide smaller plate heights; however, they also reduce permeability and increase the pressure drop across the column. The feasibility of working with small diameter particles in SFC has been discussed by several groups.

1.20.6 Open Tubular Column Technology

Open tubular columns for SFC must possess the usual qualities of high efficiency, inertness, and lasting stability, which .are characteristic of open tubular columns for GC. The main differences in the preparation of the columns are related to the smaller internal diameters characteristic of SFC columns.

1.21 STATIONARY PHASES FOR SUPERCRITICAL FLUID CHROMATOGRAPHY

The stationary phase plays an important role in achieving high performance in SFC. Many stationary phases developed for either LC or GC can be adopted for use in SFC. This includes phases exhibiting all types of solute-stationary phase interactions and selectivity, such as adsorption, dispersion, dipole-induced dipole, dipole-dipole, and size and shape, as well as combinations of these interactions. The packed columns used today in SFC are usually columns developed for LC. Up to an order of magnitude greater resolution per unit time is achieved by simply changing from a liquid to a supercritical mobile phase.

There is a fine line between the effects of the stationary phase support and the stationary phase in packed columns, since they both usually contribute to the retention mechanism. Furthermore, the mobile phase and/or mobile phase modifiers interact with the stationary phase to form a modified surface. This final surface should be considered as the real stationary phase. Adsorbents, such as silica and alumina, have been used extensively as stationary phases in the past. These phases are useful for non polar compounds; however, they lead to both reversible and irreversible adsorption of polar solutes in SFC, especially when neat CO_2 is used as the mobile phase. The limited success experienced to date in achieving a high level of deactivation of these materials suggests their rather limited future potential.

Modification of the typical small particle size silicas and aluminas with bonded stationary phases such as octyl, octadecyl, cyanoalkyl, aminoalkyl, and diolalkyl provide less adsorptive packing materials and a wide range of polarities for dipole-dipole and dipole-induced dipole interactions. In most cases, except for the most nonpolar molecules, polar organic modifiers are required for elution of analytes from these materials. Most commercial phases are monomeric in nature because they produce a monolayer coverage of phase on the solid support. Excess silanol groups in this monolayer may be either end-capped, used to induce polymerization within this monolayer, or they may be left to take part in selective interactions as part of the stationary phase.

Polysiloxanes are extensively used as polymeric backbones in stationary phases for open tubular columns. The chemical and physical stabilities of the poly siloxanes, along with the desirable flexibility of the Si-0 bond, which leads to good diffusion of sample analytes, make them ideal as stationary phases. Poly siloxanes have been substituted with a wide range of chemical groups for elective interactions with different types of samples. Dispersion interactions are commonly used in open tubular column SFC. The great inertness and efficiency of columns coated with poly methylsiloxanes are utilized in SFC, but enhanced partitioning was 'demonstrated using n-octyl substituted poly siloxanes compared to methyl substituted phases. This noctyl phase also has a sufficient density of C-C bonds such that these columns could be used for a limited time with neat NH_3 as the mobile phase.

The biphenyl phase with 30mol% substitution is usually preferred over the 50% phenyl phase because the larger, more polarizable biphenyl group provides greater interaction with the analytes. In addition, the biphenyl phase contains a higher percentage of methyl groups than the corresponding 50% phenyl phase and is therefore easier to immobilize on the column wall. Analytes containing either electron-donating or electron-withdrawing groups can induce polarity in the biphenyl stationary phase. The lack of polar interactions makes this phase ideal for the separation of closely related polar solutes without excessive retention.

The most widely used polar stationary phases in open tubular column SFC are the cyanopropyl poly siloxanes. With CO_2 as the mobile phase, these stationary phases have been particularly useful for the analysis of compounds containing carboxylic acid functional groups.

A highly ordered liquid crystalline poly siloxane stationary phase was reported by Chang and co-workers for use in SFC. A dramatic enhancement in resolution over GC was demonstrated for selected geometrical isomers. The SFC elution was performed at 12O"C, where the stationary phase was more ordered than at the 230°C elution temperature in GC. Chiral separations in SFC to date have been primarily explored using packed column technology developed for LC analysis. A thermally stable chiral amide phase developed for GC was found to give higher resolution in SFC than in GC for some derivatives of amino acids. The gain in selectivity at the lower elution temperature more than compensated for the loss in efficiency from the lower diffusion in the supercritical fluid.

1.22 MOBILE PHASES

The mobile phase in SFC is the most influential parameter governing solute retention on the column. Unlike in GC, where the mobile phase is relatively inert, SFC mobile phases play an active- role in altering the distribution coefficient of the solute between the stationary phase and a compressed carrier fluid phase. The mobile phase chosen in SFC is often selected with respect to its departure from ideal gas behavior, a characteristic that allows its densification through the application of external pressure. Supercritical fluid chromatography also differs from LC where solute retention is usually adjusted by changing either the chemical nature of the mobile or stationary phase within the column. Only at very high applied pressures does one observe significant changes in LC retention parameters.

1.22.1 General Characteristics

Fluid density is the key parameter for understanding the behavior of supercritical fluids. Since density is a function of both pressure and temperature, the effects of these two variables can best be understood by using a corresponding states plot, in which the reduced density is expressed as a function of reduced temperature and pressure. The critical point of a fluid occurs when the above physical properties (pressure, temperature, and density) are all equal to their critical values', hence; the reduced pressure, temperature, and density will all be equal to unity. This corresponds to the apex of the gas-liquid region as shown on the plot of reduced state in Figure 2.

Supercritical fluid chromatography is performed above the critical temperature of the fluid, that is, above the isotherm equal to unity. Reduced pressures ranging from 0.6 to values in excess of 20 have been reported for SFC. This range of pressure and temperature results in reduced fluid densities ranging from 0.3 to values in excess of 2.0. Inspection of Figure 1.4 reveals that supercritical fluids under high pressures will approach reduced densities that are similar to those exhibited by the liquid state (2.5-3.0). The shaded regions in Figure 14 are typical operating conditions that have been reported for SFC. The choice of these conditions is largely mandated by the desire to affect the largest change in fluid density commensurate with performing SFC at a low temperature. This is accomplished by operating close to the critical temperature (T,) of the fluid and in the region of the eluent's critical pressure (P,).

It is obvious from this discussion that the mobile phase in SFC's can take on a range of densities intermediate between those encountered in gas or liquid chromatography. Of equal importance to the chromatographer are the superior mass transfer characteristics exhibited by supercritical fluids. For example, the diffusivity of supercritical CO_2 is approximately two orders of magnitude greater than those exhibited by liquid solvents. Similarly, the viscosity of supercritical CO_2 is at least 20 times larger than the viscosities associated with liquid media. These physical properties influence the theoretical plate heights that are obtainable with SFC and result in a smaller non equilibrium contribution to peak broadening in SFC relative to that found for LC methods.

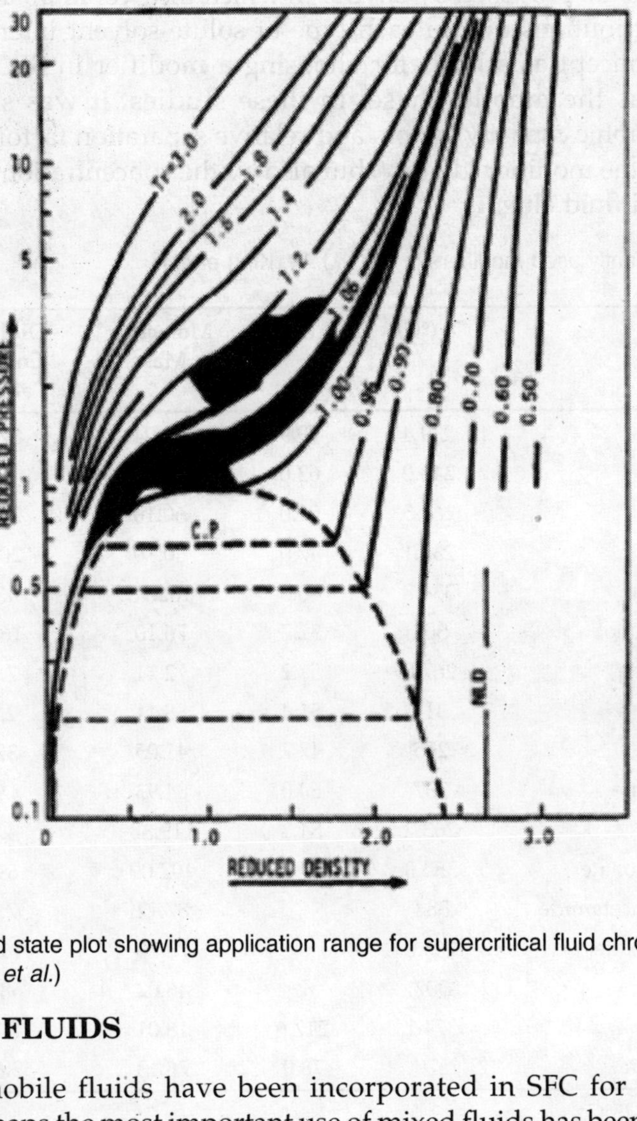

Fig. 14 : Reduced state plot showing application range for supercritical fluid chromatography (J. W. King *et al.*)

1.23 MIXED FLUIDS

Mixed mobile fluids have been incorporated in SFC for a number of purposes. Perhaps the most important use of mixed fluids has been the addition of a polar organic modifier to the supercritical fluid to enhance the solvent power of the eluent. This step is generally taken to enhance the solubilization of polar solutes in dense fluids or to reduce the retention volume of the analyte in the column.

Table 7 lists several useful modifiers that have been utilized in SFC. Note that the addition of these solvents into a supercritical fluid phase will modify the polarity of the eluent due to the high dielectric constants or polarity indexes associated with the organic modifiers. The polarity indexes in Table 8 are derived from the scheme proposed by Snyder in which the overall polarity index is the sum of contributions due to each type of solute-solvent interaction. Randall used this concept as a basis for choosing a modifier in SFC where CO_2 is employed as the mobile phase. In these studies, it was shown that the chromatographic capacity factors and relative separation factors were affected not only by the modifier identity, but also by the concentration of the modifier in the mixed fluid eluent.

Table 7 : frequently used modifiers in SFC (J. W. King *et al.*)

Modifier	T_c(°C)	P_c(atm)	Molecular Mass	Dielectric Constant' at 20°C	Polarity Index
Methanol	239.4	79.9	32.04	32.70	5.1
Ethanol	243.0	63.0	46.07	24.3	4.3
1-Propanol	263.5	51.0	60.10	20.33	4.0
2-Propanol	235.1	47.0	60.10	20.33	4.0
1-Hexanol	336.8	40.0	102.18	13.3	3.5
2-Methoxy ethanol	302	52.2	76.10	16.93	5.5
Tetrahydrofuran	267.0	51.2	72.11	7.58	4.0
1,4-Dioxane	314	51.4	88.11	2.25	4.8
Acetonitrile	275	47.7	41.05	37.5	5.8
Dichloromethane	237	60.0	84.93	8.93[b]	
Chloroform	263.2	54.2	119.38	4.81	4.1
Propylene carbonate	352.0		102.09	69.0	6.1
N,N-Dimethylacetamide	384		87.12	37.78[b]	6.5
Dimethyl sulfoxide	465.0		78.13	46.68	7.2
Formic acid	307		46.02	58.5[c]	
Water	374.1	217.6	18.01	80.1	10.2
Carbon disulfide	279	78.0	76.13	2.64'	

•Data taken at 25°C.

The modifiers listed in Table 7 have quite different critical temperatures and pressures. These data suggest that caution must be taken when using mixed fluids to assure that the components are miscible over the range of temperatures and pressures that are used. These conditions can be established by using thermodynamic data or by making precise phase equilibrium measurements.

The Calculation of pseudo critical constants for mixed mobile phases has been approximated by the method of Kay. Alternatively, useful compendiums of actual vapor-liquid equilibrium at high pressure exist, which define conditions for the existence of the one phase region for such systems as CO_2, and organic co solvents. Recently, a laser light scattering method has been utilized to determine phase transitions of mixed mobile phases in the critical region.

Frequently, modifiers are added to the supercritical fluid eluent to eliminate adsorptive effects exhibited by solutes in packed column SFC. In this case, the modifier eliminates the strong interaction between adsorptive siters and the polar solute resulting in symmetrical peak profiles. The dramatic results that can be produced by the inclusion of such modifiers in SFC are shown in Figure 1.6 for the separation azo-dyes on a column packed with diol-modified silica [SS]. In this case, the peak shape is improved and both the order of elution and resolution between the component peaks are affected by the choice of modifier.

Similarly, water has been used as modifier in CO_2, to improve the symmetry of fatty acid peaks eluting from columns packed with bonded silica stationary phases.

Mixed fluids may also incorporate special additives that can affect both the solubilization of the solute in the fluid phase or enhance solute elution through the chromatographic column. Such additives, because of their extremely polar nature, may have limited solubility in common SFC mobile phases. These compounds can be solubilized in the supercritical fluid eluent by dissolving them in a suitable modifier, thereby making the mobile phase a ternary system. An excellent example of this principle is the use of citric and trifluoroacetic acids in methanol-carbon dioxide mobile phases to affect the capacity factors and peak shapes of polar aromatic acids eluting from packed silica SFC columns. Similarly, polar ionic solutes can be chromatographed using non polar supercritical fluid eluents, such as ethane, by incorporating reverse micelles in the mobile phase.

Figure provides a schematic diagram of a typical syringe pump (figure 15) used in SFC. When the piston is withdrawn, mobile phase from the supply tank fills the cylinder. The cylinder head is cooled to keep the mobile phase in the liquid state.

Liquids are preferable for pumping, since they are denser and less compressible than supercritical fluids or gases. The pumping rate is controlled with a drive screw that is connected to the motor either directly or through a gear train assembly. Computer control of the drive screw offers several advantages for SFC: pulse less flow, pressure or density programming, micro flow rate control, and rapid pressure ramp operation. Dual syringe pumps can be used for composition gradient elution, but difficulties in correcting for mismatched solvent compressibility can affect composition reproducibility, cross contamination, and accuracy of the gradient. (Figure 15)

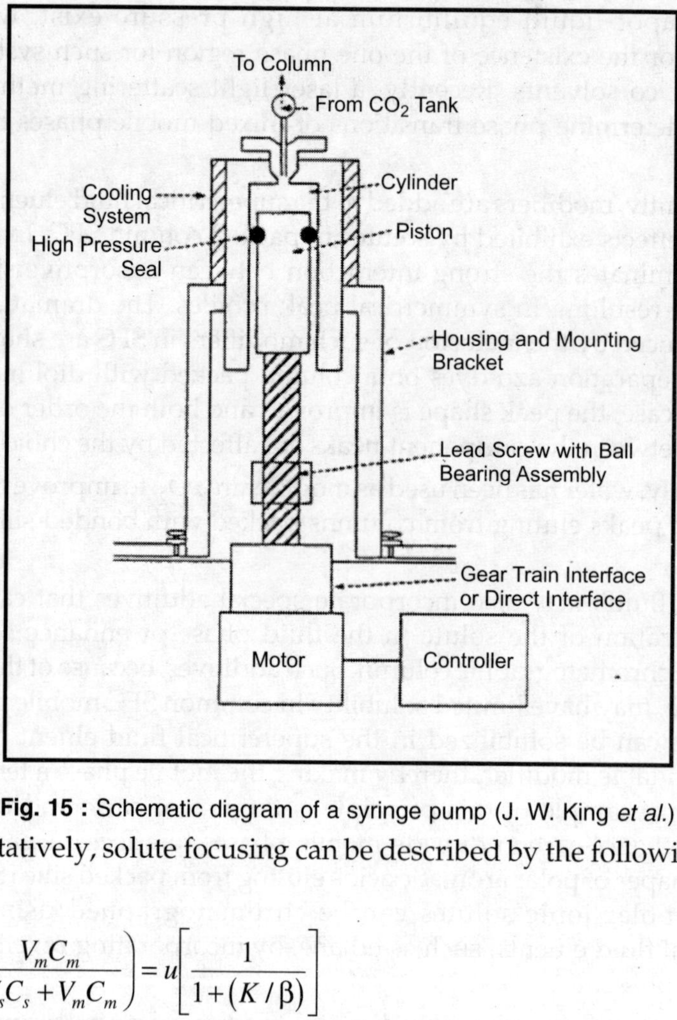

Fig. 15 : Schematic diagram of a syringe pump (J. W. King *et al.*)

Quantitatively, solute focusing can be described by the following equation where

$$v = u\left(\frac{V_m C_m}{V_s C_s + V_m C_m}\right) = u\left[\frac{1}{1+(K/\beta)}\right] \qquad 32$$

v is the velocity of the solute band, u is the mobile phase velocity, V, and V, are the respective stationary and mobile phase volumes, C, and Cm are the respective concentrations of the solute in the stationary and mobile phase, K is the partition coefficient described in equation 32, and b is called the phase ratio (V,/V,).

Thus, if the partition coefficient of the solute decreases or the phase ratio of the column increases as the solute enters the column, its zone velocity will decrease and it will become focused at the head of the column. Temperature gradients retention gaps and varying stationary phase thicknesses have been used to focus solutes.

One approach for reducing peak splitting and focusing the solute is to place a mixing chamber between the injection valve and the column. This provides time for the solvent to become diluted by the mobile phase, decreasing the solvent strength and increasing the partition coefficient. When the solute reaches the column, the phase ratio is decreased and the solute is focused at the head of the column.

While developments in direct injection continue, the most common method used for injection in SFC, especially with respect to open tubular columns, is split injection. Splitting the injection decreases the volume introduced onto the column and eliminates many of the problems associated with direct injection.

Several split injection methods are employed. Dynamic split is the simplest and most popular. This split assembly consists of a stainless steel tube connected directly to the injection valve. The other end of the stainless steel tube is connected to a tee. An open tubular column or transfer line is inserted concentrically through the tee and into the stainless steel tube. On the outlet of the tee is a restriction device, usually a fused silica restrictor, to control the flow split. The sample split occurs as part of the sample enters the open tubular column and part of the sample passes around the column and exits through the tee and split restrictor.

Advantages of the dynamic split are good resolution for complex mixtures and narrow solvent peaks. Disadvantages include nonlinearity, sample discrimination, and small volume injections. A timed-split method is commonly used to enhance linearity and decrease discrimination from split injections. In timed-split injection, fast valve switching is used to permit only a fraction of the contents of the sample loop to be injected directly onto the column.

Various procedures for solvent elimination have been used in attempts to inject large sample volumes into the column. In one method, the sample is injected onto a pre column where the solutes are selectively retained while the solvent is vented from the instrument through a restrictor. This venting process can be enhanced by purging with a gas until the solvent is evaporated and the solutes are precipitated on the walls of the pre column.

Complete elimination of the sample solvent can be achieved with the back flush technique. With this approach, the split restrictor of a dynamic split injector described above is closed until the entire sample has entered the column. Then, the split is opened simultaneously with a rapid negative pressure ramp. This depressurization at the injector causes a reversal in flow at the head of the column and sweeps the solvent out of the split restrictor.

All solvent elimination methods suffer from this weakness. Volatile components can be partially eliminated with the solvent. Fortunately, most components of interest in SFC have relatively low volatility.

Analytical supercritical fluid extraction (SFE) involves the use of compressed gases, held above their critical temperature (T °C,), for the extraction of analytes from a variety of sample matrices. The technique offers some unique advantages over conventional sample preparation techniques, particularly when CO_2, is used as the extraction fluid. As noted in previous sections, the same properties that make supercritical fluids unique mobile phases for SFC, are also responsible for their performance when they are used in the extraction mode. For example, adjustment of the fluid pressure permits, to a degree, the selective extraction of specific analytes for subsequent analysis. Improvements, in the kinetics of extraction are also realized by using supercritical fluids, due to the higher diffusion coefficients exhibited by solutes in the dense fluid media compared to their diffusivities in liquid-liquid extraction solvents. Recently, supercritical fluids have been cited as excellent extraction solvents, since their use avoids the problem of solvent waste disposal as well as exposure of laboratory personnel to toxic solvents. Analytical SFE developed somewhat later than SFC, although Stahl reported on the coupling of SFE with thin-layer chromatography (TLC) as early as 1976. Supercritical fluid extraction has also been utilized by chemical engineers since the 1970s and the literature in this field contains valuable information for the analytical chemist. Today, analytical SFE is practiced ranging from the sub milligram to the 100-g level. Analytical SFE can be performed as an independent sample preparation technique or be coupled "on-line" to such chromatographic methods as GC and SFC. In this section we discuss the fundamental concepts governing this technique, its practice, and a sampling of the applications in which it has been used.

1.24 APPLICATIONS OF SUPERCRITICAL FLUID EXTRACTION

Analytical SFE has produced a plethora of applications over the short time that it has existed. Representative applications abound in such diverse areas as polymer characterization, food analysis, flavor and fragrance chemistry, and the environmental sciences. Several useful references are available that cite numerous applications of both on- and off-line SFE. For this reason, this section avoids citing numerous applications of SFE and focuses instead on selected applications that illustrate concurrently the technique and breathe of SFE.

It was noted earlier that CO_2 could be compressed to densities that yielded equivalent solvent strengths to those exhibited by liquid solvents, such as n hexane and methylene chloride. Authors shown a GC comparison of a cardamom oil extract obtained from an n-hexane extraction versus an off-line CO_2 extraction. The resultant chromatograms are remarkably similar, verifying the equivalent solvent power of CO_2 to n-hexane. However, the CO_2 extract GC profile contains some additional flavor notes, particularly at the beginning of the programmed temperature GC run, which are absent in the liquid-derived extract. This result is not unexpected, since SFE has been shown to yield natural product extracts, free of processing artifacts.

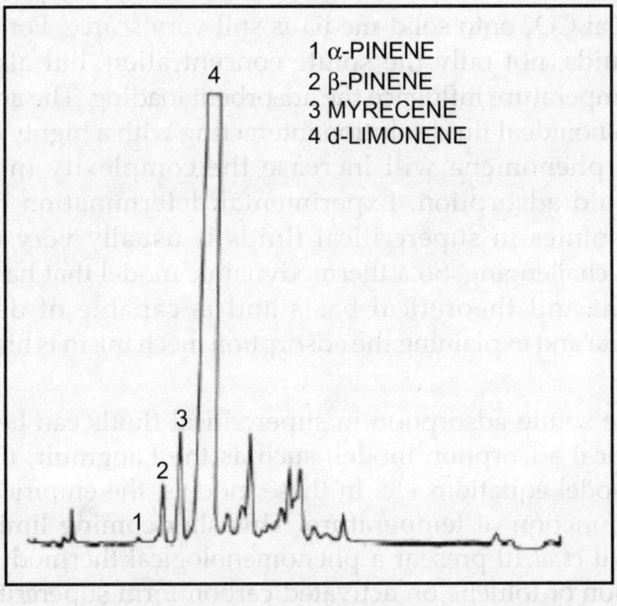

Fig. 16 : Orange peel oil analyses by gas chromatography (Nautiyal & Tiwari, Science & Technology, 1(1):29-33, 2011.

The compositions of the constituents at the conditions of subcritical CO_2 were α-pinene (0.99%), myrecene (2.65%), d-limonene (88.68%), terpinolene (0.55%), C8-aldehyde (0.33%), citronellol (0.11%) and linalool (0.13%) (figure 16). The decrease in the extraction of orange oil may be attributed to the fact that above 55 some degradation products start forming, thus reducing the yield. It was observed that d-limonene was the major constituents (about 90%) of the oil and the other components were α-pinene, myrecene, terpinolene, C8-aldehyde, citronellol and linalool. Out of these except myrecene that is 2.5-3%, the rest of the constituents were less than 1% each.

1.24.1 Theoretical Study of Adsorption on Activated Carbon from Supercritical Fluid by SLD-ESD Approach

The supercritical carbon dioxide processes in conjunction with solid media or materials have increased attention in recent years due to the unique solvent characteristics These processes involve solute extraction from solid matrices solid adsorbent regeneration and decontamination and supercritical fluid chromatography etc. To develop and design these processes, it is very important to study and understand the adsorption equilibrium between the solid and fluid phase. The adsorption isotherm for solutes in the supercritical fluid determines the thermodynamic partitioning between phases. Presently, although some experimental adsorption isotherm data can be found in relevant supercritical literatures, the experimental data for solute adsorption equilibrium from supercritical CO_2 onto solid media is still very scarce. For adsorption in supercritical fluids, not only the solute concentration, but also the system pressure and temperature influence the adsorbent loading. The adsorbed phase often involves a nonideal fluid solution interacting with a highly complex solid surface. These phenomena will increase the complexity in the study of supercritical fluid adsorption. Experimental determination of adsorption isotherms for solutes in supercritical fluids is usually very tedious, time consuming and challenging. So a thermodynamic model that has a reasonable physical insight and theoretical basis and is capable of describing the experimental data and explaining the adsorption mechanism is highly attractive and significant.

Usually the solute adsorption in supercritical fluids can be fitted by the common empirical adsorption model, such as the Langmuir, the Freundlich and the Toth model equations etc. In these models, the empirical parameters will vary as a function of temperature. This shortcoming limits their wide applicability. Wu *et al.*10 present a phenomenological thermodynamic model for the adsorption of toluene on activated carbon form supercritical CO_2. The P-R equation of state and the real adsorption solution theory are applied to the bulk and adsorbed phase, respectively. However, in their model, all parameters are temperature dependent. And each temperature dependence, there are 8 parameters required in order to correlate the adsorption isotherm. Akman and Sunol use the Toth isotherm and the P-R equation of state to model the phenol adsorption on activated carbon. In their model they need the adsorption isotherm of phenol onto activated carbon in aqueous solution as input data. Afrane and Chimowitz develop a statistical mechanical model that applies the lattice-solution model to represent the adsorbed phase. With the additionally known information on heats of adsorption of supercritical fluids on adsorbent, they use this model to correlate the solute distribution coefficients in supercritical fluids between adsorbed and bulk phase at infinite dilution.

However, this model is incapable of representing the adsorption isotherm at finite dilute conditions in supercritical fluids. Most these models above, except the one by Wu *et al.* don't consider the solvent competition effect on adsorption, which may play a very important role in adsorptive processes. Also they don't reflect the effect of adsorbent structure on the adsorption loading. Over the past decades, there has been rapid development in the application of molecular simulation and density functional theory for the study of adsorption. These theoretical approaches consider the adsorbent structure, but are computationally intensive for practical application in the present stage, especially for supercritical fluid adsorption.

Recently, a complete theoretical analysis has been conducted using Monte Carlo simulation methods to study the adsorption characteristics of benzene onto activated carbon in supercritical carbon dioxide. However, the molecular simulation results are not compared with the experimental data.

Practical process design often requires rapid methods for obtaining good correlation and approximation of adsorption behavior over a wide range of pressures and temperatures. Also the methods should have a clear physical insight for adsorption phenomena with parameters as few as possible. The simplified local density (SLD) approach 15, 16 is a method that can be used with any equation of state and can offer some predictive capability with only two temperature-independent adjustable parameters for adsorption modeling of pure fluids in slit-shaped pores. Recently the SLD theoretical approach was used to successfully model a variant of fluid adsorption17 by incorporating with the Elliott, Suresh, Donohue (ESD) equation of state 18. This paper focuses on the SLD approach with the ESD equation to study the adsorption of solutes onto activated carbon from supercritical carbon dioxide. Toluene is selected as a model solute in this study. The adsorption characteristics of toluene are investigated both at infinite dilution and finite concentrations.

1.25 THEORETICAL MODEL

The ESD equation of state proposed by Elliott *et al.* 18 is

$$\frac{PV}{RT}=1+\frac{4\langle c\eta\rangle}{1-1.9\eta}-\frac{9.5\langle qY\eta\rangle}{1+1.7745\langle Y\eta\rangle} \tag{33}$$

Where, V is the molar volume, T is temperature, and R is the ideal gas constant. η is the reduced density (η=$b\rho$). $b=\sum_i x_i b_i$, xi is the fluid mole fraction and bi is the component's size parameter. q is a shape factor for the repulsive term ($c=\sum_i x_i c_i$). q is a shape factor for the attractive term (q = 1 1.90467(c-1)= $\sum_i x_i q_i$). ρ is the molar density, and

$$\langle c\eta\rangle=\rho\sum_i\sum_j x_i x_i (cb)_y \tag{34}$$

$$\langle qY\eta\rangle=\rho\langle qYb\rangle=\rho\sum_i\sum_i x_i x_j (cq)_{ij} Y_{ij} \tag{35}$$

$$\langle Y\eta\rangle=\rho\langle Yb\rangle=\frac{\langle q\eta Y\rangle}{\sum_i x_i q_i} \tag{36}$$

$$\langle bq\rangle_{ij}=\frac{1}{2}\left(b_iq_j+b_jq_i\right),\ \langle cb\rangle_{ij}=\frac{1}{2}\left(c_ib_j+c_jb_i\right) \quad 37$$

Yij is a temperature-dependent attractive energy parameter $\left(Y_{ij}=\exp\left(\varepsilon_{ij}/kT\right).1.0617\right).\varepsilon_{ij}=\left(1.k_{ij}\right)\sqrt{\varepsilon_n\varepsilon_{ij}}$ is the parameter for dispersion forces and *kij* is the binary interaction coefficient. The equation can also be represented in terms of fugacity. Details of the explanation for the equation and parameters are in the references 18,19 cited above. Although the ESD equation also can represent associating fluids, none of the components presented in this paper have associative characteristics, so the associating term is omitted.

Here it is just extenuation of this theory to binary mixture. In the following section we use component A to represent solute and component B for solvent. For the slit-shape pore system in the modeling, the fluid-solid interaction potential with one wall for one component I (I=A, B) is represented by 10-4 potential:

$$\Psi_{1I}(z)=4\pi\rho_{atoms}\sigma_{fsI}^2\varepsilon_{fsI}\left\{\begin{array}{l}\frac{0.2}{EtaI^{10}}-\frac{0.5}{EtaI^4}-\frac{0.5}{(EtaI+\alpha I)^4}\\ -\frac{0.5}{(EtaI+2\alpha I)^4}-\frac{0.5}{(EtaI+3\alpha I)^4}-\frac{0.5}{(EtaI+4\alpha I)^4}\end{array}\right\} \quad 38$$

Where, $\alpha I=3.35/\sigma fsI$ (I=A, B). αfsI (Å) is the average value of the fluid molecule I and solid molecular diameters $\left|\sigma_{fiI}=\left(\sigma_{ffI}+\sigma_{ss}\right)/2\right|.EtaI=\left(z+0.5\sigma_{ss}\right)/\sigma_{fiI}$ is the dimensionless distance from the carbon centers in the first plane, and z is the particle position in the slit relative to the carbon surface, as seen in the schematic diagram of the pore model in Fig 1, where H is the slit width. ñ *atoms* represents the number of carbon plane atoms per square Angstrom 20 (0.382 atoms/Å^2). The fluid-solid potential in relation to the second wall, $_{\o 2T}$ (z) can be calculated by replacing *EtaI* in eq 3 with *XiI*, which is the distance from the second wall divided by the fluid-solid diameter. The total fluid-solid potential for component I is expressed as

$$\psi_{TI}[z]=\psi_{1I}[z]+\psi_{2I}[z] \quad 39$$

The chemical potential of fluid inside a porous medium can be described by two contributions, that is, fluid-fluid contribution and fluid-solid contribution. At adsorption equilibrium, the chemical potential in pore is equal to that in the bulk phase. For component I in slit pore, we have,

$$\mu_{bulk,I}[T,\rho_{bulk},y_I]=\mu_{ff,I}[T,\rho(z),x_I(z)]+\mu_{fs,I}[z] \qquad 40$$

$$\mu_{ff,I}[T,\rho(z),x_I]=\mu_I^{\circ}[T]+RT\ln\left\{\frac{f_{ff,I}[T,\rho(z),x_I(z)]}{f_I^0[T]}\right\} \qquad 41$$

$$\mu_{bulk,I}[T,\rho_{bulk},y_I]=\mu_I^{\circ}[T]+RT\ln\left\{\frac{f_{bulk,I}[T,\rho_{bulk},y_I(z)]}{f_I^0[T]}\right\} \qquad 42$$

In these equations ì *bulk, I* is the bulk chemical potential of component I at bulk composition *yI*, µ*ff, I* is the fluid-fluid contribution to the chemical potential of component I. *I f°* and µ ^{0} *I* are the standard state fugacity and chemical potential respectively, and µ*fs,I* is the fluid-solid contribution to the chemical potential $\mu_{fs\ I= NA\Psi TI[Z]}$, where *NA* is Avogadro's number. The local chemical potential due to fluid-fluid interactions is designated by µ*ff,, I* and dependent on *T* and local density $y_1(z)$ and local composition *xI(z)*. Note that µ*ff, I*, µ*fs, I* and *fff, I* are functions of *z* (position), but µ *bulk, I, If°* and µ ^{0} *I* are not. Based on the above equations, an expression for *fff, I* can be derived,

$$f_{ff,I}[T,\rho(z),x_I(z)]=f_{bulk,I}[T,\rho_{bulk},y_I]\exp\left[\frac{-\Psi_{TI}(z)}{kT}\right] \qquad 43$$

The fugacity of bulk fluid can be obtained through the ESD equation of state 18. Since *fbulk,I* is independent of position in the pore and $_p$*TI* is dependent on position only, the local fugacity *fff,I* can be calculated from eq (8). For a binary mixture, three equations will be solved simultaneously for local composition (*xA (z)* and *xB(z)*)and local density $y_1(z)$.

$$f_{ff,A}[T,\rho(z),x_A(z)]=f_{bulk,A}[T,\rho_{bulk},y_A]\exp\left[-\frac{\Psi_{TA}(z)}{kT}\right] \qquad 44$$

$$f_{ff,B}[T,\rho(z),x_B(z)]=f_{bulk,B}[T,\rho_{bulk},y_A]\exp\left[\frac{-\Psi_{TB}(z)}{kT}\right] \qquad 45$$

$$x_A(z)+x_B(z)=1 \qquad 46$$

Within the slit pore, the local fugacity *f,ff ,I* , can be calculated through the following equation 17,18,

$$\ln(f_{gI}) = -\frac{4}{1.9}c_I \ln[1 - 1.9\eta(z)] + \frac{4cb_I\rho(z)}{1-1.9\eta(z)} \qquad 47$$

$$-\frac{9.5}{1.7745}\frac{\ln(1+1.7745\langle Y(z)\eta(z)\rangle)}{\langle Y(z)b\rangle}\left(\sum_J x_J Y_{IJ}(b_I q_J + b_J q_I) - \frac{\langle qY(z)b\rangle}{\langle Y(z)b\rangle}Y_{II}b_I\right) \qquad 48$$

$$-\frac{9.5\langle qY(z)b\rangle}{\langle Y(z)b\rangle}\frac{Y_{II}b_I\rho(z)}{1+1.7745\langle Y(z)\eta(z)\rangle} + \ln[x_I\rho(z)RT] \qquad 49$$

Where, $Y(z)$, $\rho(z)$, and $\eta(z)(=b\tilde{n}z)$ are the local variables within the silt pore. The position dependence of attractive energy parameter *Yij* has been given elsewhere 17. The cross parameter *Yij* used to calculate *Yij* uses the same *Kij* as the bulk phase. The local density and local composition can be obtained by solving the above equations. Thus, total adsorption per unit weight adsorbent is calculated by the following expression.

$$n_A^{total} = \frac{Area}{2}\int_{z=0}^{z\text{ at for wall}}[r(z)x_A(z)]dz \qquad 50$$

Where, *Area* is the surface area per unit weight of the adsorbent. In the case of adsorption in a slit with homogeneous parallel walls, the integration over the entire slit width is divided by two since two walls contribute to the surface area of a slit.

In this study, the value of *Area* was taken as input data from the original publication of the experimental data. Table 1 lists the pure component ESD parameters19 used in this model, all of which are obtained from bulk fluid properties and were not adjusted parameters in this study. The binary interaction coefficients for the mixtures were obtained by fitting their VLE data 21, 22 using the ESD equation of state, and they are also given in Table 1. The values of f_{ff} for benzene and carbon dioxide are tabulated Lenard-Jones diameters of each fluid, 23 and f_{ss} = 3.4 Angstroms is the reported diameter of carbon 20. For toluene the Lenard-Jones parameters are approximated by the critical

$$n_B^{total} = \frac{Area}{2}\int_{z=0}^{z\text{ at for wall}}[r(z)x_B(z)]dz \qquad 51$$

The value of *Area* was taken as input data from the original publication of the experimental data. Table 1 lists the pure component ESD parameters19 used in this model, all of which are obtained from bulk fluid properties and were not adjusted parameters in this study. The binary interaction coefficients for the mixtures were obtained by fitting their VLE data using the ESD equation of state, and they are also given in Table 1. The values of f_{ff} for benzene and carbon dioxide are tabulated Lenard-Jones diameters of each fluid, and f_{ss} = 3.4 Angstroms is the reported diameter of carbon 20. For toluene the Lenard-Jones parameters are approximated by the critical volume, $\frac{\sigma_i}{\sigma_{CO_2}} = \left(\frac{Vc_i}{Vc_{CO_2}}\right)^{1/3}$ and critical temperature $e^{IJ}/k = 0.77T_c$.

CONCLUSIONS

This chapter specifically deals with various features of supercritical carbon dioxide extraction technology with its thermo dynamical properties, mobile properties, processing of Organic and Inorganic chemicals and their phase transfers. Theoretical models that helps in understandings of processing stream lining, feasibility, safety and economy. Various useful extractions of natural products have also been described to prove its future sustainability with regards to conversion, utilization, energy involvement, adsorption and chemical processing. As far as extraction of essential oil is concerned so the studied Dill seed oil extraction by SC-CO_2 and its chromatogram explains that how neat the technology is with reference to products purity, quality, yield and their ingredient composition. In the commerce all these factors are demanded by the customers and indeed required for formulating the foods, flavors, beverages and drug products. Environmental problems and threat due to emissions of pollutants from combustion of solid, liquid and gaseous fuels in various stationary and mobile energy systems as well as the emissions from manufacturing plants have also become major global problems involving not only the pollutants such as NOx, SOx, and suspending particulate matter, but also the greenhouse gases (GHG) such as carbon dioxide (CO_2) and methane (CH_4). There are increasing concerns for global climate change and thus heightened interest worldwide for reducing the emissions of GHG, particularly CO_2. This will facilitate the researches globally in the field of Synthetic Organic chemistry, CO_2 conversion over heterogeneous catalysis, synthesis gas production from CO_2, processing of polymer synthesis employing SC-CO_2, thermodynamics of chemical reactions and on entire chemical processing and eco friendly processing

ACKNOWLEDGEMENT

I wish to dedicate this chapter to my research mentor Prof. K. K. Tiwari, Ret. Professor & Head of Chemical Engineering, Institute of Chemical Technology (UDCT) and to my beloved parents. Who has untiringly supported, trained and guided me for employing this technology in the areas of Chemical Engineering, Foods & Flavours, Medicinal herbs and Essential oils, in which I obtained my PhD in the year 1995. I am also indebted to my working research colleagues for their morale support. I have employed this technology for extracting the various commercial essential oils, viz. Dill seed oil, Sandalwood oil (industry project), Squalene from Rajgeera seed and Orange peel oil for my doctoral degree. These all products were also compared with the conventional techniques so as to prove the advantages and disadvantages of the supercritical carbon dioxide extraction over the conventional techniques. Undoubtedly in all the researched aspects the technology was found to be fullproof technology for meeting the entire specifications of finished products.

REFERENCES

Can Erkey. Supercritical Carbon Dioxide Extraction of Metals Fro-aqueous Solutions: a Review. Journal of Supercritical Fluids, 2000, 17, 259-287.

Chunsan, S., Global challenges and strategies for control, conversion and utilization of CO2, for sustainable development involvoing energy, catalysis, adsorption and chemical processing, Catalysis Today, 115, 2-32, 2006.

David Filmore "The Greening of Catalysis", Today's Chemist at Work (November 2002) 29.

Ekhtera, M.R., Mansoori, G.A., Mensinger, M.C., Rehmat, A. and Deville, B. "Supercritical Fluid Extraction for Remediation of Contaminated Soil" in "Supercritical Fluids: Extraction and Pollution Prevention" M. Abraham and A. Sunol (Editors), ACSSS Vol. 670, pp. 280-298, American Chemical Society, Washington, D.C., 1997.

Eric J. Beckman "Using CO_2 to Produce Chemical products Sustainably", Environmental Science & Technology (1 September 2002) 347A.

Fornari, R. E., Alessi, P., & Kikic, I.. High-pressure Fluid Phase Equilibria: Experimental Methods and Systems Investigated (1978-1987), Fluid phase Equilibria, 1990, 57, 1-33.

Frank V. Bright and Mary Ellen P. McNally. Supercritical Fluid Technology Theoretical and Applied Approaches to Analytical Chemistry. ACS Symposium Series, 1992.

Frank, P. Lucien, Neil R. Foster. Solubilites of Solid Mixtures in Supercritical Carbon Dioxide: a Review. Journal of Supercritical Fluids, 2000, 17, 111-134.

Hartono, R., Mansoori,G.A. and Suwono, A. "Prediction of Molar Volumes, Vapor Pressures and Supercritical Solubilities of Alkanes by Equations of State" Chemical Engineering Communications, Vol. 173, pp. 23-42, 1999.

J. Calvin Giddings "High Pressure Gas Chromatography of Nonvolatile Species", Science 162 (4 October 1968) 67. 3. A.I. Cooper, et. al. "Extraction of a hydrophilic compound from water into liquid CO2 using dendritic surfactants", Nature 389 (25 September 1997) 368.

J. R. Williams and A. A. Clifford, Supercritical Fluid Methods and Protocols. Human Press, Totowa. New jersey, 1997.

J.B. McClain, et. al. "Design of Nonionic Surfactants for Supercritical Carbon Dioxide", Science 274 (20 December 1996) 2049.

J.M. DeSimone, et. al. "Synthesis of Fluoropolymers in Superdcritical Carbon Dioxide", Science 257 (14 August 1992) 945.

Jawwad A. Darr and Martyn Poliakoff. New Directions in Inorganic and Metal-organic Coordination Chemistry in Supercritical Fluids. Chemical Review, 1999, 99: 495-541.

Jerry W. King, Herbert H. Hill, Jr., Milton, L. L., Analytical supercritical fluid chromatography and extraction, US Dept. of Agric.., National Centre for Agriculture Utilization Research, Peoria, IL. Pp 7069-7086.

John M. Prausnitz, Rudiger N. Lichtenthaler, Edmundo Gomes Azevedo, Molecular Thermodynamics of Fluid-phase Equlibria. Prentice Hall PTR.P845, 1999.

K. D. Bartle, A. A. Clifford, S. A. Jafar, and G. F., Shilstone, Solubilities of Solids and Liquids of Low Volatility in Supercritical Carbon Dioxide. J. Phys. Chem. Ref. Data, 1991, 20(4), 713-756.

Keith W. Hutchenson, Neil R. Foster, Innovations in Supercritical Fluids: Science and Technology. American Chemical Society. Washington, DC, 1995.

Knapp, H., Doring, R. Oellrich, L., Plocker, U. and Prausnitz, J. M.. Vapor-Liquid Equilibria for Low Boiling Substances. DECHEMA Chemistry Data Series, Frankfurt, 1982.

Kwak, T.Y. and Mansoori, G.A. "Van der Waals Mixing Rules for Cubic Equations of State - Applications for Supercritical Fluid Extraction Modelling", Chemical Eng. Science, 41, 5, pp.1303-1309, 1986.

Kwak, T.Y., Benmekki, E.H. and Mansoori, G.A. "Van der Waals Mixing Rules for Cubic Equations of State (Applications for Supercritical Fluid Extraction Modeling and Phase Equilibria Calculations)", ACS Symposium Series 329, pp.101-114, American Chemical Society, Washington, D.C., 1987.

Kwon, Y.J. and. Mansoori, G.A. "Solubility modeling of solids in supercritical fluids using the Kirkwood-Buff fluctuation integral with the hard-sphere expansion (HSE) theory", The Journal of Supercritical Fluids, Vol. 6, pp. 173-180, 1993.

L. Padrela, M.A. Rodrigues, S.P. Velaga, H.A. Matos and E.G. Azevedo (2009). "Formation of indomethacin–saccharin cocrystals using supercritical fluid technology". European Journal of Pharmaceutical Sciences. 38, pp. 9–17. doi:10.1016/j.ejps.2009.05.010

L. Padrela, M.A. Rodrigues, S.P. Velaga, H.A. Matos and E.G. Azevedo (2009). "Screening for pharmaceutical cocrystals using the supercritical fluid enhanced atomization process". *Journal of Supercritical Fluids*. article in press, corrected proof. doi:10.1016/j.supflu.2010.01.010

Laintz, K. E., Wai, C. M., Yonker, C. R., Smith, R. D. Extraction of Metal Ions from Liquid and Solid Materials by Supercritical Carbon Dioxide. Anal. Chem. 1992, 64, 2875-2878.

Laintz, K. E., Yu, J., Wai, C. M., Smith, R. D. Separation of Metal Ions with Sodium Bis(trifluoroethyl)dithiocarbamate Chelation and Supercritical Fluid Chromatography. Anal. Chem., 1992, 64, 311-315.

Lin, Y., Brauer, R. D., Laintz, K. E., Wai, C. M., Supercritical Fluid Extraction of Lanthanides and Actinides from Solid Materials with Fluorinated Diketone. Anal. Chem, 1993, 65, 2549-2551.

Lin, Y., Wai, C. M., Jean, F. M., Brauer, R. D., Supercritical Fluid Extraction of Thorium and Uranium Ions from Solid and Liquid Materials with Fluorinated Diketone and Tributyl Phospate. Environ. Sci. Technol, 1994, 28, 1190-1193.

Lotfollahi, M., Modarress. H. and Mansoori, G.A. "Themodynamic Modeling for Solubility Calculation of 2-Naphtol, Acridine, 1,4-Naphthoquinone and Benzoic Acid in Supercritical Flouroform" AKUT Journal of Science & Technology, Vol.11, No.42, pp.148-157, 2000.

Mansoori, G.A. "Phase Equilibrium of Mixtures Consisting of Molecules with Large Size and Shape Differences (Thermodynamic Modeling of Supercritical Fluid Extraction and Retrograde Condensation, SFE/RC)", GRI Document Number: GRI- 88/0360 , 88p, Gas Research Institute, Chicago, IL USA, August 1988.

Mansoori, G.A. and Ely, J.F. "Density Expansion (DEX) Mixing Rules (Thermodynamic Modeling of Supercritical Extraction)", J. Chem. Phys., 82, 406, 1985.

Mansoori, G.A., "Phase Equilibria of Mixtures Consisting of Molecules with Large Size and Shape Differences. (Thermodynamic Modeling of Supercritical Fluid Extraction and Retrograde Condensation, SFE/RC), GRI Document Number: GRI- 90/0131, 101p, Gas Research Institute, Chicago, IL, USA, May 1990.

Mansoori, G.A., "Phase Equilibrium of Mixtures Consisting of Molecules with Large Size and Shape Differences (Thermodynamic Modeling of Supercritical Fluid Extraction and Retrograde Condensation, SFE/RC)", GRI Document Number: GRI- 89/0159 , 121p, Gas Research Institute, Chicago, IL USA, June 1989.

Mansoori, G.A., Schulz, K. and Martinelli, E. "Bioseparation Using Supercritical Fluid Extraction / Retrograde Condensation", (Feature Article) BIO/TECHNOLOGY, Vol. 6, pp.393-396, 1988.

Mansoori, G.A., Suwono, A., Sitompul, J.P. and Samudro, H.M. "Fractionation of wax by supercritical extraction: Solubility correlation" Ratnawati, Proceedings of the International Conference on Fluid and Thermal Energy Conversion '97, ISSN 0854- 9346, pp. 573-580, 1997.

Martinelli, E., Schulz, K. and Mansoori, G.A. "Supercritical Fluid Extraction / Retrograde Condensation (SFE/RC) with Applications in Biotechnology", pp. 451- 478, in "Supercritical Fluid Technology", Edited by T.J. Bruno and J.F. Ely, CRC Press, Boca Raton, FL, 1991.

McHugh M.A. and V. Krukonis, Supercritical Fluid Extraction. Principles and Practice. Butterworths, Boston, 1986.

Michael E. Paulaitis, Johan M. L. Penninger, Ralph D. Gray. Chemical Engineering at Supercritical Fluid Conditions, Ann Arbor Science Publishers, 1983.

Neil G. Smart, Carleson T., Kast T., *et al.*, Solubility of Chelating Agents and Metal-containing Compound in Supercritical Fluid Carbon Dioxide. Talanta, 1997, 44, 137-150.

O.H. Nautiyal & K.K. Tiwari, Supercritical Carbon Dioxide Extraction of Indian Orange real Its end Hydrodistribution Comparison on there. Composition, Sci & Technol; 2011, 1(1), 29-33.

Park, S.J., Kwak, T.Y. and Mansoori, G.A. "Statistical Mechanical Description of Supercritical Fluid Extraction and Retrograde Condensation.", International J. Thermophysics, 8, pp. 449-471, 1987.

R. Scott Oakes, Anthony A. Clifford, Keith D. Bartle, Mark Thornton Pett and Christopher M. Rayner (1999). "Sulfur oxidation in supercritical carbon dioxide: dramatic pressure dependent enhancement of diastereoselectivity for sulphoxidation of cysteine derivatives". *Chemical Communications* (3): 247–248. DOI:10.1039/a809434i.

Ralf Dohrn, Gerd Brunner, High-Pressure Fluid-phase Equilibrium: Experimental Methods and Systems Investigated (1988-1993). Fluid Phase Equilibrium, 1995, 106, 213-282.

Ratnawati and Mansoori, G.A. "Prediction of Thermodynamic Properties and Supercritical Solubilities of Wax Components Using Equations of State", Proceedings of the 3rd international symposium on advanced and aerospace science and technology in Indonesia (ISASTI 98), Jakarta August 31-September 3, 1998, Vol. 2, ISASTI-98-2.6.3, pp.469-478, 1998.

Sang-Do Yeob and Erdogan Kirana (2005). "Formation of polymer particles with supercritical fluids: A review". *The Journal of Supercritical Fluids* **34** (3): 287–308. DOI:10.1016/j.supflu.2004.10.006.

Stephen K. Ritter "Microchips' Heavy Burden", Chemical & Engineering News (23 December 2002) 25.

Tolley W. K, Tester L. S., Supercritical CO2 Solubility of TiCl4. Report of Investigations, 1989.

Touba, H. and Mansoori, G.A. "Structure and Property Prediction of Sub- and Supercritical-Water", Fluid Phase Equilibria, Vol. 151, pp. 459-468, 1998.

Touba, H., Mansoori, G.A. and Matteoli, E. "Subcritical and Supercritical Water Radial Distribution Function", International Journal of Thermophysics, Vol. 19, No. 5, pp. 1447- 1471, 1998.

U. K. Deiters, G. M. Schnelder. High-pressure Phase Equilibria: Experimental Methods. Fluid Phase Equilibria, 1986, 29, 145-160.

Zosel, K. Angew. Separation with Supercritical Gases: Practical Applications. Chem. Int. Ed., Engl, 1978, 17, 701.

❑❑❑

CHAPTER - 22

BOD Biosensor: A Quick and Robust Technology In 21st Century For Biochemical Oxygen Demand Estimation

Purnima Dhall[1], Anil Kumar[2], Tushya Kumar Saxena[3], T. O. Siddiqi[5], Altaf Ahmed[5], Rita Kumar[4]

[1]*Institute of Genomics and Integrative Biology, Mall Road, Delhi-110007, India*
[2]*National Institute of Immunology, Aruna Asaf Ali Marg, New Delhi-110067, India*
[3]*National Physical Laboratory, Dr. K.S. Krishnan Marg, New Delhi - 110012, India*
[5]*Jamia Hamdard University, Hamdard Nagar, New Delhi-110062, India*
[1]*purnimadh@igib.in (Research Scholar),* [2]*anilk@nii.ac.in (Staff Scientist),*
[3]*tushyaks@gmail.com (Scientist G),* [4]*tariq117@rediffmail.com*
[5]*aahmed@jamiahamdard.ac.in,* [4]*rita@igib.res.in(Chief Scientist)*

1. INTRODUCTION

Water is the source that upholds every part of life on earth and is a key element of sustainable development. It is essential to the survival of healthy and safe lives of mankind. Ecosystems are inevitably linked with water. Lack of access to ample and safe drinking water is a serious setback among human population. Noxious substances from industries when enter into lakes, streams, rivers, oceans, and other water bodies, they get dissolved or lie suspended in water or get deposited on the bed. This results in the pollution of water whereby the quality of the water deteriorates, affecting aquatic ecosystems.

The strain of escalating population, growth of industries, urbanization, energy intensive life style, loss of forest cover, lack of environmental awareness and implementation of environmental rules and regulations, environment improvement plans, untreated effluent discharge from industries and municipalities, use of non-biodegradable pesticides/fungicides/herbicides/insecticides, use of chemical fertilizers instead of organic manures, etc are basis of water pollution. The pollutants from industrial discharge and sewage, besides finding their way to surface water reservoirs and rivers are also percolating into ground to pollute ground water sources, threatening food security, access to safe drinking and bathing water and providing a major health and environmental management challenge. Contaminated water from inadequate waste water management provides one of the greatest health challenges restricting development and increasing poverty through costs to health care.

Water pollution is a sensitive problem all over the world. In the wake of increasing urbanization and industrialization, the pollution potential is gaining thrust day by day. Monitoring of waste water quality parameters is currently a subject of growing concern globally.. Oxygen, although poorly soluble in water, is fundamental to aquatic life. In the absence of free dissolved oxygen, aquatic systems become inhabitable to most aquatic flora and fauna. Because the solubility of oxygen in water is so low, even little decrease in dissolved oxygen levels can compromise the health of natural water systems. Organic pollutants requiring oxygen for their decomposition exert a rapid and direct influence on the ecology of these environments. Therefore it is required to monitor the load of organic pollutants in the waste water.

Biochemical oxygen demand (BOD) is extensively used as an indicator of biochemically degradable organic pollutants present in natural waters and waste water effluents. The five-day BOD test was developed over a hundred years ago in England and length of the test period was chosen based on the maximum time required for any British river to flow from its source to the sea. American Public Health Association described the current standard method for determination of BOD in 1936. The Internationally approved assay quantifies the amount of dissolved oxygen (DO) required for heterotrophic microorganisms present in a water system to oxidize organic pollutants to a stable inorganic form. The amount of oxygen consumed during this 5 day period is dependent upon the concentration of organic matter, temperature, microorganism population, presence of toxins, nature of organic matter and type of microorganisms present. The decrease in dissolved oxygen is determined by means of chemical procedures.

Although the five day BOD assay is the best known and most fundamental test in the field of water pollution, there are many problems with the test, particularly in terms of long duration, accuracy, precision and the interpretation of results. As this test requires five days in order to know the organic load of waste water sample, it is not suitable in cases where rapid real time feedback for process control or environmental monitoring is required. One of the practical limitations is the limited solubility of oxygen and for this the dilution of the waste water sample is typically required to bring the oxygen demand within the limited linear range of BOD_5 method i.e., 1-8 mg/l. A poor choice of dilution can produce lack of a part of the BOD data thus causing the test to be imprecise. Secondly, it is also necessary to have a requisite population of microorganisms capable of oxidizing the organic material in the sample. When insufficient numbers of microorganisms are present in the sample, the dilution water is seeded. Common source of seed material is sewage which is inconsistent in number and types of microorganisms and therefore may not give reproducible results. Finally, the presence of toxic substances in the sample may also affect (or even kill) the survival of microorganisms, even at low concentrations, leading to a reduction in the measured BOD of the sample.

In the present study, a novel rapid method for determination of biochemical oxygen demand (BOD) has been developed. Using the developed method, BOD of a sample can be determined within 2 hours as compared to 3-5 days with the standard $BOD_{3\text{-}5day}$ assay. Moreover the test is based on specified consortia instead of undefined seeding material, therefore it minimizes the variability among the results. The device is coupled to software which automatically calculates the dilution required, so, the prior dilution of the sample is not required before BOD estimation. The developed method is expected to be convenient for rapid online monitoring of different industrial discharges and therefore, will indirectly help in improvising the efficiency of treatment plants.

Two million tons of sewage, industrial and agricultural waste is discharged into the world's waterways globally and approximately 1.8 million children under five years-old die every year from water related disease. By 2050 the global polulation will exceed nine billion it is expected wheras the urban population was nearly double from current 3.4 billion to 6.4 billion (Corcoran *et al.*, 2010; Pedersen, 2012; Matiasi, 2013). The demand of fresh water also increased in the similar manner. With increase in global urbanization and industralization the utilization of water and discharge of wastewater increased to heights. Worldwide, almost 900 million people still do not have access to safe water. Inadequate infrastructure and management systems for the increasing volume of wastewater that we produce are at the heart of the wastewater crisis. Due to fresh water contamination by untreated wastewater worldwide some 2.2 million people die each year from diarrhoeal disease (Corcoran *et al.*, 2010).

These deleterious consequences necessitate monitoring of wastewater, which is also an essential part of wastewater management. Continuous monitoring and control of effluent directly results into saving of water, energy and money. Effective environmental monitoring improves natural resource management, directly impacting our ability to maintain sustainable ecosystem, protect public health and support a healthy economy (Kumar and Kumar, 2006). Amongst the several enlisted, Biochemical Oxygen Demand (BOD) is one of the most important and widely used parameter used to assess the strength of water pollution. BOD, sometimes referred to as biological oxygen demand is a quantitative expression of microbes' ability to deplete oxygen content of a wastewater.

But the conventional technology has several drawbacks mentioned above. In order to get rapid results, the biosensors plays crucial role. A strategic approach can lead to the development of an ideal BOD biosensor provided all the lacuane are kept in mind.

2. LITERATURE REVIEW

Waste-water generation and its subsequent treatment is a major problem for every industry and for the society as well. Prior to treatment, the waste-water needs to be monitored so as to permit the waste-water to be discharged into the local water resources or to design efficient treatment facilities. BOD is one of the most important and widely used parameter for indicating the strength of water pollution. Conventional BOD analysis is being carried out by the method described in Standard Method of Analysis of Water and Waste-waters (APHA, 1998). This test requires 5 day incubation, which has further been modified by Central Pollution Control Board, Delhi. They have reduced the incubation time for BOD test from 5 days at 20°C to 3 days at 27°C, which is more suitable for Indian environmental conditions (Laboratory Analytical Techniques Series LATS/4/87-88, CPCB Publication). Three days BOD test has been included in their technical bulletin (BIS, 1993).

Since currently used BOD test measurement requires fairly long incubation period (3-5 days), rapid and sensitive on-line monitoring of the Biochemical Oxygen Demand (BOD) calls for a method that must have theoretical validity should be simple and inexpensive, the determination time must be short and the results must be precise and reproducible.

In this context, efforts have been made for design and development of BOD biosensor where microbes have been exploited to serve the purpose of biochemical component of the biosensor. Microbial biosensors can fulfill all of these criteria. Microbial biosensors consist of microorganisms immobilized in a membrane and coupled with electrochemical transducer that converts a biochemically generated signal into an electronic signal that can be processed and quantified (Richardson *et al.*, 1991). Earlier, BOD biosensors have been tried for various synthetic substrates (Paret, *et al.*, 1995; Jia, *et al.*, 2003; Tan, *et al.*, 1993; Riedel, *et al.*, 1990; Qian and Tan 1998; Kim and Park 2001). First microbial BOD biosensor was described by Karube, *et al.* (1977). *Trichosporon cutaneum* has been mainly used by many workers for the fabrication of BOD biosensor (Riedel, *et al.*,1990; Karube, *et al.* 1990). The major difficulty experienced by these workers was the application of BOD biosensor in limited types of waste-waters. A flow through BOD sensor using immobilized yeast cells has been described by Kulys and Kadziauskiene in 1980. Pure cultures used for fabrication of BOD biosensor include *Hanseneula anamola* (Kulys and Kadziauskiene, 1980), *Bacillus subtilis* (Riedel, *et al.*, 1988), *Gluconobacter oxydans* (Rashetilov, *et al.*,

1998), *Serratia marcescens* LSY4 (Kim and Kwon,1999) and thermophilic organisms (Kubo, *et al.*, 1991). These types of BOD biosensors were able to reduce the time of BOD test from 3-5 days to within an hour. The sensitivity of the microbial biosensor has been further increased remarkably and it has been reported that BOD analysis can be performed within few minutes by use of BOD biosensor (Riedel, *et al.*, 1988, 1990).

Such BOD biosensors are unable to exhibit reproducible and comparable results to conventional BOD methods as the immobilized single microbe may not be able to assimilate all the organic compounds present in the test samples. Reports have been published, where a random mixture of two to three microbes have been selected for the construction of mixed culture based BOD biosensor (Galindo, *et al.*, 1992; Riedel, *et al.*, 1988; Li, *et al.*, 1994; Heim, *et al.*, 1999; Raud , *et al.*, 2011; Verma and Singh 2013). Konig, *et al.* (1999) has recently developed a disposable sensor based on the respiration activity of nitrifying bacteria for inhibition of nitrification in waste-water.

Various biological recognition elements, including cofactors, enzymes, antibodies, microorganisms, organelles, tissues, and cells from higher organisms, have been used in the fabrication of biosensors.

A microbial BOD sensor based on the salt tolerent yeast *Arxula adeninivorans* has been developed for rapid monitoring (Lehmann, *et al.*, 1999) . The sensor reported by Sakai, *et al.*, 1995 based on magnetic activated sludge. Another researcher Jing, *et al.*, 2000 reported a sensor based on an induced microbial consortium obtained from activated sludge. Tan and Qian, 1997 use thermally killed vaccum dried cells of Bacillus subtilis for sensing BOD of wastewater. An automated whole cell biosensor system was developed by Heim, *et al.*, 1999 through the integration of immobilized cells of *Rhodococuus erythropolis* and *Issatchenkia orientalis.*

However, their application, with respect to accuracy and reproducibility seems to be limited to a few selected waste-waters and cannot be utilized as an ideal device for all types of effluents. This may be due to a random selection of microorganisms used for the construction of BOD biosensor, whereas, pre-testing of selected microbes in BOD analysis is necessary for the construction of a suitable and reliable BOD biosensor. Some of the systems have already been commercialized (Oxi direct, Quick BOD-1, BOD 2000, ARAS, DKKTM BODsensor, BOD Bart, BSBmodul), but it seems that the performance of these sensors is not fully satisfactory, due to the current state of technological development/ their limitations, such as the limited detection capacity for a wide substrate spectrum, have not been solved .

Table 1 :

Instrument	Company	Biological Element	Estimation Time	Shelf Life In days	References Where these products are used
Oxi Direct	Tintometer GmbH, Lovi bond Water Testing	-	1-28 days (user selectable)	-	Teo-Ming and Khairul, 2011
BOD Bart	Droycon Bioconcepts Inc. 315 Dewdney Avenue Regina, Saskatchewan, Canada	Heterotrophic aerobic bacteria.	20 hours	-	Mayur and Indu, 2009
BOD-2000 BOD-3000	Nisshin Denki & Central Kagaku Co. Ltd. Tokyo, Japan	T.Cutaneum	20 - 40 min	30	Jing and Mattiasson, 2002
ARAS	Dr. Lange FmbH, Berlin, Germany	R. Erythoplis + I. Orientalis	1 - 3 min	30	Kristina, *et al.*, 2000
DKKTM BODsensor	DKK corporation Japan	T.Cutaneum	5 min	-	Jing and Mattiasson , 2002
BSBmodul	Prufgeratewerk Medingen GmbH, Dresden, Germany	T.Cutaneum, C.Parapsilosis	3 <1	30	(Gabriele, *et al.*, 1996)
RACODTM meter	USFilter, Vineland NJ, USA	Activated Sludge	10 min for high range and 30 min for low range	-	http:// www.usfilter. com/
QBOD meter & EZ-BODe meter	Bioscience Inc., Bethlehem USA	Activated Sludge	20 min 15-60 min	60 - 90	http://www. bioscienceinc. com,
BOD BioMonitor	LAR Analytik & Umweltmes-stechnik GmbH, Berlin, Germany	Activated Sludge	-	-	Iranpour, *et al.*, 1997
RODTOX 2000	Kelma, Belgium	Activated Sludge	20-40min	14	Vanrolleghem, et al. 1994

Unlike other biosensor applications that require high sensitivity, selectivity and specificity, the BOD sensor is aimed at being highly capable of analyzing a sample of complex constituents with relatively low selectivity. Thus the sensor can respond to all kinds of biodegradable organic solutes in the sample. It is also important that sensor should give results comparable to those obtained using the conventional BOD methods.

The performance of BOD biosensors such as response time, linearity of the calibration curve, operational stability, and agreement with BOD5 varies depending upon the species of microorganisms used, phase of cell growth, cell loading, the calibration solution, the measuring techniques and operational conditions.

A literature survey on the development of BOD biosensors reveals that there is a lack of information regarding the optimization of microbial membrane for the construction of the sensor.

3. MATERIALS AND METHODS

3.1 Isolation of Bacteria form Different Samples

Collection of samples: Soil sample and effluent samples were collected from industrial premises

Preparation of soil extract: Soil samples were dried at 60°C for 4hrs in the oven and dissolved in 1 liter of triple distilled water, autoclaved at 15psi for 1hour. The mixture was centrifuged at 4000rpm for 20min and the supernatant will be collected in autoclaved bottles.

Preparation of enrichment media: Soil extract was inoculated by different soil samples and incubated in shaker at 37°C and 150rpm.

Serial dilutions and plating for isolation of pure cultures: Plates were prepared from different media and will be plated with different dilutions (10^{-3}, 10^{-5}, 10^{-7}, 10^{-8}, 10^{-9}, 10^{-10}, 10^{-11}) of enriched media and incubated at 37°C overnight. Colonies obtained were chosen on the basis of their growth characteristics for isolation and streaked on the plates of respective media.

3.2. Screening of Isolated Colonies

Isolated bacterial strains were screened by using conventional estimation procedure

Chemical Oxygen Demand (COD) Analysis: Chemical oxygen demand is defined as the amount of specified oxidants reacts with the sample under controlled conditions. The quantity of oxygen consumed is expressed in terms of its oxygen equivalence. Both organic and inorganic components of a sample are subjected to oxidation, but in most cases the organic component predominates and is of the greater interest. COD often are used as a measurement of pollutants in wastewater and natural waters.

Principal: Most of the organic matters are destroyed when boiled with a mix of $K_2Cr_2O_7$ and H_2SO_4 producing CO_2 and water. A sample is refluxed with a known amount of $K_2Cr_2O_7$ in H_2SO_4 medium and excess of dichromate is titrated against ferrous ammonium sulphate. The amount of dichromate consumed is proportional to the oxygen required to oxidize organic matter.

In our course of study the COD of the waste was determined by using the Winkler's titration method.

The principal reaction using dichromate as the oxidizing agent may be represented in a general way by the following unbalanced equation

$$\text{Organic matter } (C_aH_bO_c) + Cr_2O_7^{-2} + H^+ \xrightarrow[\text{Heat}]{\text{Catalyst}} Cr^{+3} + CO_2 + H_2O$$

Biochemical Oxygen Demand (BOD) Analysis: The determination of biochemical oxygen demand (BOD) is an empirical test in which standardized laboratory procedures are used to determine the relative oxygen requirements of wastewater, effluents and polluted waters. The BOD test has its widest application in measuring waste loading to treatment plants and in evaluating the BOD removal efficiency of such treatment systems.

Principal: It is one of the most important tests used for regulation of discharge via limits on BOD_5 of the effluent. It also evaluates the efficiency of wastewater treatment system by comparison of the BOD_5 of effluent with BOD_5 of the influent. BOD has been determined conventionally by taking a sample of water, aerating it well, placing it in a sealed bottle, incubating for a standard period of time at $20 \pm 1\ ^0C$ in the dark, and determining the oxygen consumption in the water at the end of incubation.

The most widely used parameter of organic pollution applied to both wastewater and surface water is the 5-day BOD. This determination involves the measurement of the dissolved oxygen used by microorganisms in the biochemical oxidation of the organic matter. The method consists of filling with sample in an airtight bottle of specified size and incubating it at the specified temperature for 3days. Dissolved oxygen is measured initially and after incubation, and the BOD (biochemical oxygen demand) is computed from the difference between initial and final DO (dissolve oxygen).

3.3 Immobilization

A biosensor is a self-contained integrated device, which is capable of providing specific quantitative or semi-quantitative analytical information using a biological recognition element (biochemical receptor) which is retained in direct spatial contact with a transduction element. The adsorption method was used for the immobilization of microbial consortium on nylon membrane (Rawson, 1995). The microbial consortium were harvested in their log phase of growth, cells were washed three times with sodium phosphate buffer pH6.8 by centrifugation. Nylon membrane was placed on membrane filter and 500µl of the cells were filtered through the membrane and then membrane was left to dry for 18–20 h at room temperature.

3.4. Conditioning, Storage and Shelf Life

After the preparation of membrane, before use, pre-conditioning was required. Different parameters (conditions and different GGA concentration) were considered for pre-conditioning of the membranes (Figure1). For studying the first parameter conditions, stirring, non stirring and shaking was considered. Simultaneously, different concentrations of GGA, low moderate and high concentration were taken in to account. The microbial membranes were activated by immersing the membranes in sodium phosphate buffer containing different concentrations of glucose - glutamic acid (GGA 1920 - 12,000 mg/l) and studied by keeping the membrane for stirring, non stirring and under shaking conditions.

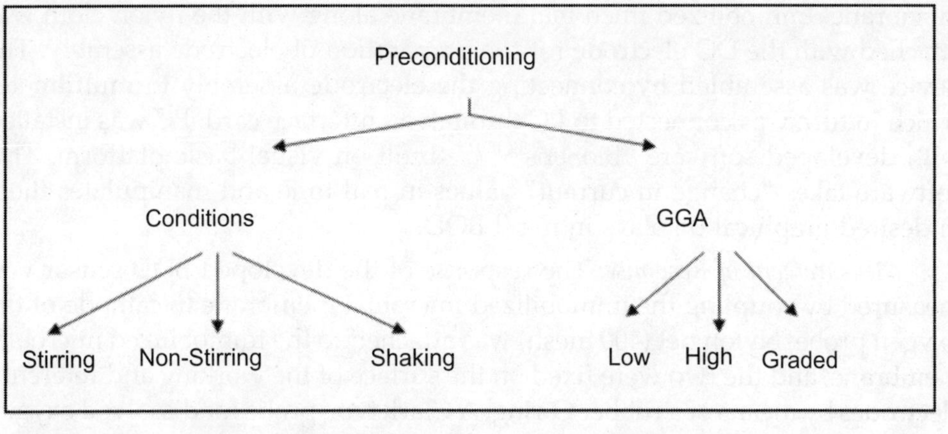

Fig. 1 : Different parameters for pre-conditioning of immobilized microbial membrane

3.5. Factors Important for Sustained use of Membrane (Stability Viability, Leaching and Storage Conditions)

Stability study of the immobilized microbial membrane: The prepared immobilized microbial membranes were assessed for their stability during storage at different temperatures and pH. Stability of the prepared immobilized microbial membranes was assessed at intermittent time intervals, in terms of their response. The stability study was carried out while storing the prepared membranes at different temperatures viz., 4°C, 15°C, 25°C and 37°C and at different pH ranging from 6.0-8.0.

Viability study of the immobilized microbial membrane: the viability of the prepared membranes was assessed at regular time intervals during storage at different temperatures ranging from 4°C to 37°C and different pH varying between 6.0 - 8.0 for checking the viability of the bacterial strains immobilized on the membrane, the membrane was placed on an agar plate in an inverted position and incubated at 37C for 16-20 hrs. The colonies were observed for growth on the agar plates.

Leaching studies of the immobilized microbial membrane: In order to check the leaching of the bacterial cells during storage, a loopful of buffer in which the membrane was stored, was streaked on nutrient agar plates. The plates were incubated at 37°C for 16-20 hrs and observed for growth. Simultaneously, the leaching rate of the bacterial strains from the membranes was assessed by observing the optical density of the storage buffer at regular time intervals.

3.6. Assembly of the Microbial Sensor and Measurement of Response

Assembly: The microorganisms were grown and immobilized on the nylon membrane. Immobilized microbial membrane along with the nylon cloth was attached with the DO electrode for the preparation of electrode assembly. The device was assembled by connecting the electrode assembly to multiimeter which in turn was connected to PC through an interface card. PC was installed with developed software "BioSens^{BOD}" built on visual basic platform. This software takes "change in current" values in real time and manipulates them in desired graphical displays in mg/l BOD.

Measurement of Response: The response of the developed BOD sensor was measured by coupling the immobilized microbial membrane to cathode of the oxygen probe. Nylon net (400 mesh) was attached to the immobilized microbial membrane, and the two were fixed on the surface of the working and reference electrodes by means of a rubber O-ring. A Clark type probe for dissolved oxygen was used as a physical transducer, which consisted of a platinum cathode as the working electrode and a silver anode as the reference electrode. In order to stabilize the BOD sensor system, the sensor was immersed in 100 ml of the potassium phosphate buffer system under constant and moderate stirring. The working and reference electrodes of the BOD sensor were connected to a potentiostat and the output current was recorded through a multimeter, which amplified the response to nA. An applied potential of –0.650 mV versus Ag/AgCl was delivered to the Pt-working electrode throughout all the measurements. The BOD sensor measurements were made using steady state method. The steady state indicates the consumption of oxygen by microorganisms which diffuse from a sample solution to the membrane at equilibrium. In steady state method, the difference of current between the two steady states reflects the respiration rate of substrate and was used for BOD estimation. The measuring time was 10-15 min followed by 15-16 min recovery time. In order to stabilize the BOD sensor system and measure the response of the immobilized microbial membrane, 100 ml of phosphate buffer (50 mM) pH 6.8 was placed in a thermo stated cell at 35 ± 2°C under constant and moderate stirring. Aliquots of stock synthetic (GGA) were added after a stable current was attained for 30 min (initial steady state current). The current change (decrease) was observed after addition of the samples until a final steady state was reached. The response was calculated on the basis of current difference between the initial steady state current and the final steady state current (Dhall *et al.*, 2008).

3.7. Preparation of Response, linearity & Calibration curve for the immobilized microbial membrane

Response Curve: Different concentrations 15 mg/l - 90 mg/l of GGA were checked for the response over a period of 20min. the depletion of total oxygen was observed.

Linearity Curve: Linearity in response time over a certain concentration range is a measure of the detection capacity to analyze waste water with varying concentrations. The BOD values of different concentrations of GGA as were determined by the developed sensor. The results were plotted and linearity observed.

Calibration Curve: Stock solution of GGA having a concentration of 12,000 mg/l was prepared. Different aliquots from the stock solution of GGA were added in the measuring cell of the BOD sensor system, to achieve the desired GGA concentrations of 15 - 300 mg/l (having a BOD of 11 - 220 mg/l). The response of the sensor with different GGA concentrations was observed and recorded. The readings were plotted and on the same graph, a second mantissa was drawn showing the conventional BOD (BOD_5) values against the same GGA concentrations as used with the developed BOD sensor.

3.8. BOD estimation of waste water from different industries by using developed BOD biosensor

The BOD biosensor was assembled by connecting the immobilized electrode to developed highly stable constant volt source and multimeter which in turn is connected to a mobile PC through RS232C interface. Mobile PC was installed with developed software "BioSensBOD" build on visual basic platform. This software acquires the real time current data from the multimeter and plots the same in the form of desired graphical display as well as save the same in the user defined file along with the time in seconds. Initially the, electrode was dipped in sodium phosphate buffer placed on the magnetic stirrer and external polarization voltage was applied through the highly stable developed voltage source. Current through the electrode was measured by the multimeter. Then stability of the immobilized microbial membrane was observed as displayed by developed software installed in a mobile PC which in turn is connected to a multimeter through RS232C interface. Change in current (i.e. ÄI = I max – I min) was calibrated for different concentrations of GGA. Sample solution was replaced now with fresh sodium phosphate buffer and assembly was stabilized. In order to calculate the BOD, the percentage of the waste water as determined by the software was added in sodium phosphate buffer. Finally, BOD value of waste water was calculated with the help of BOD calculator as mentioned above. This BOD value was compared to BOD_5 as determined by titration-based method.

4. THEME AREA OF TARGET TECHNOLOGY AND OUTCOME OF THE STUDY

Water pollution requires more attention, and monitoring of water quality is an important aspect of wastewater management. Water quality is evaluated in terms of organic matter present in it which is usually calculated before the discharge of waste water in to river water stream. Regular monitoring of BOD discharge is required at all publicly owned industrial wastewater treatment plants. Biochemical oxygen demand is most widely used parameter for such estimation and requires minimum of 3–5 days and it's a universal method for measuring organic load. Results of BOD tests cannot be obtained immediately, so they can be hardly used as feedback data for process control of waste water treatment or as the data proving legal observance of effluent water quality. Many studies aiming at shortening the measuring period of BOD were conducted for a long time until microbial BOD sensors were developed to meet such shortcomings. Determination of BOD load in short time is now possible with the help of microbial BOD sensors. Many research reports have been published with modifications occurring at every step to circumvent the lacunae faced by the previous authors. Lots of efforts have been put henceforth for the development of BOD biosensors which of late include the determination of BOD load in real wastewaters but still there remains a number of lacunae viz, determination of BOD load of all types of waste water, the capability of sensor to meet the varying BOD load of wastewater being emanated from any industry and practical feasibility of the BOD biosensor to determine the BOD load of wastewater as and when it comes to the laboratory (off-line) or online. This is possibly due to the fact that BOD determination is multi-factorial and until and unless all the parameters are taken into account, it will not be possible to reach the desired goal. Biosensors have passed the point of mere combinations of biological components with transuding elements and now practical applications must be realized. Though few BOD biosensors are in the market for the purposes but as of now there does not seem to be any ideal biosensor which has real reproducibility for varying loads of pollution in different industrial wastewaters and which is capable of determining the BOD load instantly. In the present scenario, based on existing lacunae, an attempt was made to develop an ideal device (BOD biosensor) having a computer-aided software capable of determining the varying BOD load of industrial waste waters which facilitated the instant monitoring.

In the present study, a synergistic microbial consortium pretested as a reference seeding material in BOD analysis was used as a bio-receptor. The microbial consortium was immobilized on the nylon membrane and was preconditioned in order to be able to cater to all types of industrial waste water. The immobilized microbial membranes was tested for stability, viability and leaching. It was observed that the membranes were viable at 4°C and 6.8 pH. The membranes could be stored up-to 400 days. The subsequent step in the study was to estimate the leaching rate of the microorganisms from the immobilized support i.e., nylon membrane and the leaching was found to be negligible. The shelf life of the immobilized microbial membrane to be used for determining BOD load was increased to 400 days. It is pertinent to note here that the available biosensors besides having other drawbacks had a shelf life of up-to 60 days only.

The sensor response was measured by coupling the immobilized membrane to the cathode of the oxygen probe. A Clark type probe for dissolved oxygen was used as the physical transducer, which consisted of a platinum cathode as the working electrode and a silver anode as the reference electrode. The working and reference electrodes of the BOD sensor were connected to a potentiostat and the output current was recorded through a multimeter, which amplified the response to nA. An applied potential of "0.650 mV versus Ag/AgCl was delivered to the Pt-working electrode throughout all the measurements.

The BOD sensor measurements were made using steady state method. The steady state indicates the consumption of oxygen by microorganisms which diffuse from a sample solution to the membrane at equilibrium. In steady state method, the difference of current between the two steady states reflects the respiration rate of substrate and was used for BOD sensor estimation. The measuring time was 10–15min followed by 15–16 min recovery time. In order to stabilize the BOD sensor system and measure the response of the immobilized microbial membrane, 100ml of phosphate buffer (50mM) pH 6.8 was placed in a thermo stated cell at 35 ± 2°C under constant and moderate stirring. Aliquots of stock synthetic/industrial samples were added after a stable current was attained for 30 min (initial steady state current). The current change (decrease) was observed after addition of the samples until a steady state was reached. The response was calculated on the basis of current difference between the initial steady state current and final steady state current.

Further, the calibration curve was plotted in order to get the BOD values in mg/l. Since GGA is used as a reference standard in conventional BOD_5 measurement, all the BOD measurements with the sensor in this study were also carried out using GGA solution. A stock solution containing equal volume of 150 mg/l of GGA was used with an assigned 5 day BOD value of 220 mg/l. Different concentrations of GGA ranging from 15 – 120 mg/l were used for the calibration of the BOD by conventional method.

The developed BOD biosensor was used to estimate the BOD load of large number of industrial wastewater samples. The software is meant for graphical displays, BOD calculation, online data acquisition and other calculations. The software acquires the real time current data from the electronic measurement unit and plots the same in the form of desired graphical display as well as saves the same in the user defined file along with the time in seconds. The correction factor was also taken into consideration while integrating software with the device.

Initially beverage industry was chosen and several inlet and outlet samples were collected over different periods of time and analyzed for the determination of BOD by the conventional method as well as by the developed BOD biosensor.

The BOD values of inlet and outlet samples of beverage effluent as determined by developed software aided BOD biosensor were compared with the BOD values as determined by the conventional method. The percentage variation in the BOD results was limited to ±8% in case of inlet samples and ±10% in case of outlet samples. Conventionally, a percentage variation of ±18% is observed. The ratio of BOD_5/Biosensor varied from 0.92 – 1.06 in case of inlet samples and for outlet samples, BOD_5/Biosensor values varied from 0.91 – 1.10.

The characteristics of waste water vary from industry to industry depending on the manufacturing process and the raw material used. In order to check the authenticity of the developed BOD biosensor, different industries were selected viz., pulp and paper, distillery, sugar, tannery, dairy, pharmaceutical and paint. Samples (inlet and outlet) were collected over a period of one year from each industry. The BOD load was determined by using both the methods i.e., conventional BOD and BOD biosensor. The BOD values obtained showed good correlation with the conventionally analyzed BOD values.

Table 2: The following table depicts correlation in the range of BOD values as determined by the two methods and also percentage deviation when viewed in case of individual samples.

Industry	Range of BOD load				Percentage deviation	
	Conventional BOD_5 (mg/l)		BOD Biosensor (mg/l)		In case of individual samples	
	Inlet	Outlet	Inlet	Outlet	Inlet	Outlet
Pulp and Paper	900-2000	175-298	840-2048	180-300	± 10.5%	± 10%
Distillery	30070-70,000	1740.4- 2170.4	35314.9- 78193	1501-2234	± 9.8%	± 9.6%
Sugar	859-1365	111-329	917-1485.3	100-300	± 10.4%	± 9.2%
Tannery	1440.8- 2872.6	168-204	1532-3051	169-219	± 10.3%	± 9.7%
Dairy	923-3670	10-52	952-3605	11-52	± 7.9%	± 9.0%
Pharmaceutical	1039-1526	10-18	1012-1122	9.5-19	± 9.5%	± 9.0%
Paint	1262-1589	30-59	1310-1655	31-57	± 6.2%	±

Developed BOD Biosensor

Advantages of Developed BOD Biosensor

- Determines the water pollution quickly 2 hours of time
- Determines the water pollution of all types of wastewater
- Has prolonged shelf life of more than 400 days
- Enhanced repeatability and reproducibility values
- Elimination of COD estimation

Distinctiveness of Innovation

- **Bio-component:** can determine BOD load of all types of waste water
- **Immobilization:** increased shelf life > 400 days, extended stability and viability
- **Software:** Reduces manual errors, reduction in estimation time

CONCLUSION

The present study was undertaken to develop rapid and reproducible methods for BOD analysis. The determination of BOD by means of biosensors is a rather advanced trend of biotechnology. The developed BOD Biosensor is robust, simple and cheap analytical tool that can be successfully used for monitoring the wastewater load within time period thereby increasing the efficency of the treatment plant.

The chapter begins with the Introduction of the subject, describing in detail the need for wastewater management, the first step to initiate the same i.e., surveillance, the conventional methods used to monitor BOD and the need for rapid pollution monitoring devices. Besides, an exhaustive Review of Literature is presented. The shortcomings of the devices developed so far has also been discussed.The next section is methodology involved in the developed technology and finally the results and theme area of the target technology. Till date no such BOD biosensor is available which is applicable to all types of wastewater i.e., wastewater with low, moderate and high organic load. The developed technology 'BOD Biosensor' is rapid tool to monitor all types of wastewater.

ACKNOWLEDGEMENT

We acknowledge the Central Pollution Control Board, New Delhi, for financial assistance. We are also thankful to Prof. S.K. Brahmachari 'DG' CSIR and Dr. Rajesh S.Gokhale, Director CSIR-IGIB for providing necessary facilities.

REFERENCES

APHA, (1998).Standard methods for the examination of waters and waste-water. 20th edition, American Public Health Association, Washington, D.C.

B I S. (1993). Indian Standard, Methods of Sampling and Test (Physical and chemical) for water and waste-water. Part 44 Biochemical Oxygen Demand (BOD), First revision, Bureau of Indian Standard IS 3025 (part 44).

Corcoran, E., Nellemann, C., Baker, E., Bos, R., Osborn, D., & Savelli, H. (eds). (2010). Sick Water? The central role of wastewater management in sustainable development. A Rapid Response Assessment. United Nations Environment Programme, UN-HABITAT, GRID-Arendal.

Dhall, P., Kumar, A., Joshi, A ., Saxsena, T.K., Manoharan, A., Makhijani, S.D., *et al.* (2008). Quick and reliable estimation of BOD load of beverage industrial wastewater by developing BOD biosensor. Sensors and Actuators B, 133, 478–483.

F, Li., Tan, T.C., & Lee, Y.K. (1994). Effects of pre-conditioning and microbial composition on the sensing efficacy of a BOD biosensor. Biosensor and Bioelectronics , 9, 197-205.

Gabriele, C., Markus, M., Christiane, Z., Meinhard, K., Friedrich, S., & Karl, C. (1996). Highly sensitive electrochemical biosensors for water monitoring. Food Technology and Biotechnology, 34(1), 23-29.

Galindo, E., Garcia, J.L., Torres, L.G., & Quintero, R. (1992). Characterization of microbial membranes used for the estimation of biochemical oxygen demand with a biosensor. Biotechnology Techniques, 6, 399-404.

Heim, S., Schnieder, I., Binz, D., Vogel, A., & Bilitewski, U. (1999). Development of an automated microbial sensor system. Biosensor and Bioelectronics, 14, 187-193.

Iranpour, R., Straub, B., & Jugo, T. (1997). Real Time BOD Monitoring for Wastewater Process Control. Journal of Environmental Engineering, 123(2),154–9.

Jia, J., Mingyu, T., Chen, X., Qi, L., & Dong, S. (2003). Co-immobilized microbial biosensor for BOD estimation based on sol–gel derived composite material. Biosensors and Bioelectronics, 18, 1023-1029.

Jing, L., & Mattiasson, B. (2002). Microbial BOD Sensors for Wastewater Analysis. Water Research, 36 , 3786–3802

Jing, L., Lovisa, B., & Mattiason, B. (2000). Immobilised activated sludge based biosensor for biochemical oxygen demand measurement. Biosensor and Bioelectronics, 14, 883-893.

Karube, I., Matsunaga, T., Mitsuda, S., & Suzuki, S. (1977). Microbial electrode BOD sensors. Biotechnology and Bioengineering, 19, 1535-1547.

Kim, M.N., & Park, K.H. (2001). Klebsiella BOD sensor. Sensors and Actuators B, 80, 9-14.

Kim, M.N., & Kwon, H.S. (1998). Biochemical oxygen demand sensor using *Serratia marcescens* LSY 4. Biosensor and Bioelectronics, 14,1-7.

Konig, A., Bachmann, T.T., Metzer, J.W., & Schmid, R.D. (1999). Disposable sensor for measuring the BOD for nitrification and inhibition of nitrification in wastewater. Applied Microbiology and Biotechnology, 51, 112-117.

Kristina, T., Matthias, L., Chiyui, C., Reinhard, R., Klaus, R. , & Gotthard, K. (2000). Measurement of biodegradable substances with a mycelia-sensor based on the salt tolerant yeast Arxula adeninivorans LS3. Sensors and Actuators B: Chemical, 67 (1–2), 142–148.

Kubo, I., Sode, K., & Karube, I. (1991). In Advance in biosensor edited by Turner, A.P.F.1; 1-32. JAI Press Ltd.

Kulys, J., & Kadziauskiene, K. (1980). Yeast BOD sensor. Biotechnology and Bioengineering , 22, 221-226.

Laboratory Analytical Techniques Series (*LATS/4/87-88*) Validity of BOD determinations at higher temperature as against standard condition of 20^{0}C for 5 days. Published by Central Pollution Control Board, Delhi.

Lehmann, M., Chan, C., Lo, A., Lung, M., Tag, K., Kumze, G., *et al.* (1999). Measurement of biodegradable substances using the salt tolerant yeast Arxula adeninivorans for a microbial sensor immobilized with poly(carbamoyl) sulfonate (PCS). Part II : Application of the novel biosensor to real samples from coastal and island regions. Biosensor and Bioelectronics, 14, 295- 302.

Matiasi, TM. (2013). Wastewater Management and reuse for sustainable development. Scholarly Journal of Agricultural Science, 3(7), p249-256.

Mayur, M.K., & Indu, M. (2009). Rapid determination of biological oxygen demand. Journal of Civil and Environmental Engineering, 1(1),15-22.

Paret, E., Reuter, V., Gaaillard, T., & Vasel, J.L. (1995). Bioreactors and biomembrances for biochemical oxygen demand estimation. Trends in Analytical Chemistry, 14, 371-378.

Pedersen, T. A. (2012). Water infrastructure and sustainbility. Infrastructure sustainability and design Ed. Spiro Pollalis, Andreas Georgoulias, Stephan Ramos, Daniel Schodek.

Qian, Z., & Tan, T.C. (1998). A model for multicomponent biosensing and its application to a dead cell-based bod biosensor. Chemical Engineering Science, 53(18), 3281-3294.

Raud, M., Tutt, M., Jõgi, E., & Kikas, T. (2011). BOD biosensors for pulp and paper industry wastewater analysis. Environmental Science and Pollution Research , 19(7), 3039-45.

Rawson, D.M. (1995). in "Encyclopedia of Analytical Science" (A Townshend, Ed.) 4614-4621. Academic Press, London, UK,.

Reshetilov, A.N., Efremov, D.A., Iliasov, P.V., Boronin, A,M., Kukushkim, N.I., & Greene, R.V. (1998). Effects of high oxygen concentration on microbial biosensor signals : hyperoxygenation by means of perflourodecalin. Biosensor and Bioelectronics, 13, 795-799.

Richardson, N.J.,Gardner, S., & Rawson, D.M. (1991). A chemically mediated amperometric biosensor for monitoring eubacterial respiration. Journal of Apllied Microbiology, 70, 422-426.

Riedel, K., Lange, K.P., Stein, H.J., Kuhn, M., Ott, P., & Scheller, F. (1990). 1990. A microbial sensor for BOD . Water Research, 24(7), 883-887.

Riedel, K., Lehman, M., Tag, K., Renneberg, R., & Kumze, G. (1998). Arxula adeninivorans based sensor for the estimation of BOD. Analytical Letter, 31(1), 1-12.

Riedel, K., Renneberg, R., Kuehn, M., & Scheller, F. (1988). A fast estimation of biochemical oxygen demand using microbial sensors. Applied Microbiology and Biotechnology, 28, 316-318.

Sakai, Y., Abe, N., Takeuchi, S., & Takahashi, F.J. (1995). BOD sensor using magnetic activated sludge. Journal of Fermentation and Bioengineering, 80(3). 300-303.

Tan, T.C., & Qian, Z. (1997). Dead Bacillus subtilis cells for sensing biochemical oxygen demand of wastes and wastewaters. Sensors and Actuators B, 40, 65-70.

Tan, T.C., Li, F., & Neoh, K.G. (1993). Measurement of BOD by initial rate of response of a microbial sensor. Sensors and Actuators B, 10, 137-142.

Teo-Ming, T., & Khairul, Z.M.D. (2011). Electron Beam Decomposition Of Pollutant Model Compounds In Aqueous Systems. NUKLEONIKA, 56(4),349"355.

Vanrolleghem, P.A., Kong, Z., Rombouts, G., & Verstraete, W. (1994). An on-line respirographic biosensor for the characterization of load and toxicity of wastewater. Journal of Chemcial technology and Biotechnology, 59, 321–33.

Verma, N., & Singh, A. K. (2013). Development of Biological Oxygen Demand Biosensor for Monitoring the Fermentation Industry Effluent. ISRN Biotechnology , Article ID 236062: 6 pages

❑❑❑

CHAPTER - 23

Use of Geo-spatial Technology as an Evolving Technology of 21st Century for Natural Resource Management in Different Regions of India

J. P. Singh[1], D. Deb[2] and R. S. Chaurasia[3]
Indian Grassland and Fodder Research Institute, Jhansi (Up), India
[1]Principal Scientist, e-mail: jpsingh.igfri@gmail.com,
[2]Scientist, e-mail: debiasri@gmail.com
[3]Senior Research Fellow (GIS & RS), E-mail: sharan25.jhs@gmail.com

INTRODUCTION

The evolution of National Natural Resource Management System (NNRMS) towards fully harnessing the potentials of space remote sensing and the development of the series of Indian Remote Sensing Satellites, besides establishment of necessary ground based data establishment of necessary ground based data reception processing and dissemination systems as well as remote sensing facilities at National Remote Sensing Centre (NRSC), Space Applications Centre (SAC) and Regional Remote Sensing Service Centers (RRSSCs) for efficient and effective analysis of remotely sensed data are the major steps accomplished in pursuit of this goal. With the establishment of Remote Sensing Applications Centers in several States under many Governmental organizations, remote sensing today has come to stay as an integral part of the national development efforts in the vital sectors of agriculture, hydrology, geology, forestry, oceanography, mineral resources and disaster management like drought, flood, cyclone, earthquake, landslides crop pests, forest fires etc., thus touching every facet of national development. Today, India has acquired a strong self-reliant base to harness the full potential of this technology and as a result, the national objective of achieving sustainable development at micro level is being addressed through the integration of remotely sensed data with other relevant collateral information to arrive at locale specific, environment friendly, economically viable and culturally acceptable treatment packages (Rao, 1991 and Jayaraman, *el at.* 1993).

The remarkable developments in space technology during the past three decades have established their immense potential for the optimum utilization of this technology especially in the field of agriculture for taking up many application project in various sectors. Indian remote Sensing Satellites, IRS-IA launched in March 1988 and IRS IB launched in August 1991 are provided good quality data with a combined repetitively of 11 days. Full-fledged operation remote sensing programme, which only a few nations could achieve around the generation, Indian Remote Sensing programme is now well poised to reach even greater heights through the development of second generation of Remote Sensing Satellite series, viz., IRS-IC and IRS-ID with better capabilities. Krishna Rao *et al.* (1997) estimated the chilli crop acreage by digital analysis of IRS IC LISS III data covering five mandals of Guntur district of Andhra Pradesh. Presently IRS P6, Cartosat I and Cartosat II provide high resolution information. Under the umbrella of National Natural Resources Management System (NNRMS), several new application areas were achieved with the active involvement of user agencies. IRS data is being used on an operational basis for several applications such as agriculture crop acreage and yield estimation, draught monitoring and assessment flood mapping, landuse and land cover mapping, wasteland management, urban planning, mineral prospecting, forest resources survey and management, soil mapping, water resources management, fisheries potential forecasting, coastal zone management environment impact assessment etc.

Remote Sensing Technique

Remote Sensing is an extensive science, drawing from many areas for support and development. Remote sensing is an interesting and exploratory science, as it provides images of areas in a fast and cost-efficient manner, and attempts to demonstrate the "what is happening right now" in a study area. While air photos and fieldwork remain critical as sources of information, the cost and time to carry out these methods sometimes may not be feasible for the study. Satellite and digital imagery acquired recently, provide more overall detail to assist the researcher in the classification process. Literature reviews and map interpretation are methods that can also be used for interpretation processes. The benefits of remote sensing continue to arise. It can be used to access hard to reach areas for fieldwork, and provides a more detailed, permanent and objective survey that offers a different perspective. Air photos are still favored and easily accessible sources of information for classification. It depends greatly on the support of governments and private industries worldwide. Satellite and digital imagery play an important role in remote sensing; providing information about the land studied.

Remote Sensing Systems offer four basic components to measure and record data about an area from a distance. These components include the energy source, the transmission path, the target and the satellite sensor(Fig.1). The energy source, electromagnetic energy, is the crucial medium required to transmit information from the target to the sensor. Remote sensing provides important coverage, mapping and classification of land use/ land cover features, such as vegetation, soil, water, forests and manmade activities etc.

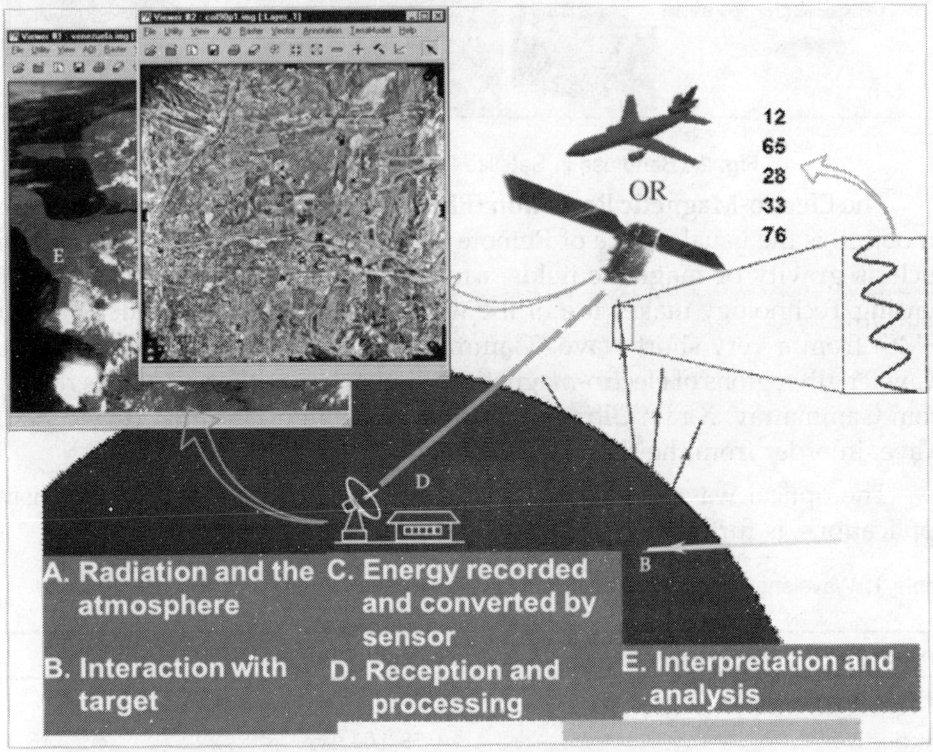

Fig. 1 : Mechanism of Remote Sensing

Bands Used in Remote Sensing: Emission of EMR (Electo-Magnetic Radiation) from gases is due to atoms and molecules in the gas. Atoms consist of a positively charged nucleus surrounded by orbiting electrons, which have discrete energy states. Transition of electrons from one energy state to the other leads to emission of radiation at discrete wavelengths. The resulting spectrum is called line spectrum. Molecules possess rotational and vibrational energy states. Transition between which leads to emission of radiation in a band spectrum. The wavelengths, which are emitted by atoms/molecules, are also the ones, which are absorbed by them. Emission from solids and liquids occurs when they are heated and results in a continuous spectrum. This is called thermal emission and it is an important source of EMR from the viewpoint of remote sensing (Fig. 2).

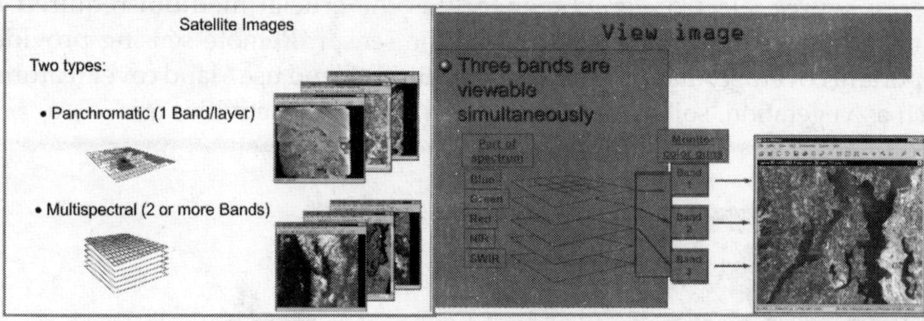

Fig. 2 : Band use in Satellite Remote Sensing technology

The **Electro-Magnetic Radiation (EMR)**, which is reflected or emitted from an object, is the usual source of Remote Sensing data. However, any medium, such as gravity or magnetic fields, can be used in remote sensing. Remote Sensing Technology makes use of the wide range Electro-Magnetic Spectrum (EMS) from a very short wave "Gamma Ray" to a very long 'Radio Wave'. Wavelength regions of electro-magnetic radiation have different names ranging from Gamma ray, X-ray, Ultraviolet (UV), visible light, Infrared (IR) to Radio Wave, in order from the shorter wavelengths.

The optical wavelength region, an important region for remote sensing applications, is further subdivided as follows:

Table 1: Wavelength regions of electro-magnetic radiation

Name	Wavelength (mm)
Optical wavelength	0.30-15.0
Reflective	0.38-3.00
1. Visible	1. 0.38-0.72
2. Near IR	2. 0.72-1.30
3. Middle IR	3. 1.30-3.00
Far IR (Thermal, Emissive)	7.00-15.0

Microwave region (1mm to 1m) is another portion of EM spectrum that is frequently used to gather valuable remote sensing information. The sunlight transmission through the atmosphere is effected by absorption and scattering of atmospheric molecules and aerosols. This reduction of the sunlight's intensity called extinction.

Energy Interactions, Spectral Reflectance and Color Readability in Satellite Imagery: All matter is composed of atoms and molecules with particular compositions. Therefore, matter will emit or absorb electro-magnetic radiation on a particular wavelength with respect to the inner state. All matter reflects, absorbs, penetrates and emits Electro-magnetic radiation in a unique way. Electro-magnetic radiation through the atmosphere to and from matters on the earth's surface are reflected, scattered, diffracted, refracted, absorbed, transmitted and dispersed. For example, the reason why a leaf looks green is that the chlorophyll absorbs blue and red spectra and reflects the green. The unique characteristics of matter are called spectral characteristics (Fig. 3).

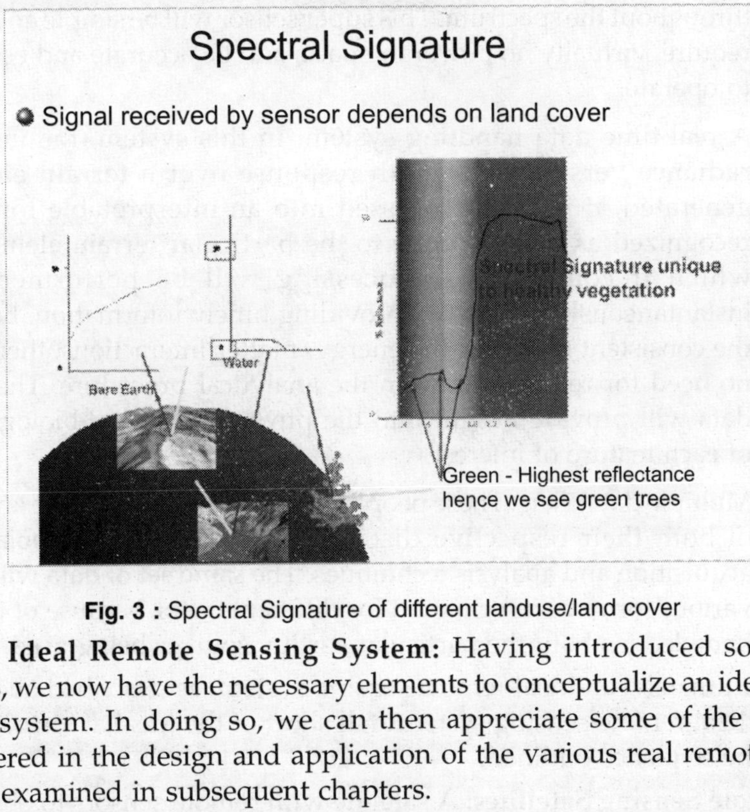

Fig. 3 : Spectral Signature of different landuse/land cover

An Ideal Remote Sensing System: Having introduced some basic concepts, we now have the necessary elements to conceptualize an ideal remote sensing system. In doing so, we can then appreciate some of the problems encountered in the design and application of the various real remote-sensing systems examined in subsequent chapters.

The basic components of an ideal remote-sensing system are as follows.

- A uniform energy source. This source will provide energy over all wavelengths, at a constant, known, high level of output, irrespective of time and place.
- A non-interfering atmosphere. This will be an atmosphere that will not modify the energy from the source in any manner, whether that energy is on its way to earth's surface or coming from it. Again, ideally

this will hold irrespective of wavelength, time, place, and sensing altitude involved.

- A series of unique energy/matter interaction at the earth's surface. These interactions will generate reflected and/or emitted signals that are not only selective in respect to wavelengths, but also are known, invariant, and unique to each and every earth surface feature type and subtype of interest.
- A super sensor. This will be a sensor, highly sensitive to all wavelengths, yielding spatially detailed data on the absolute brightness (or radiance) from a scene (a function of wavelength), throughout the spectrum. This super sensor will be simple and reliable, require, virtually no power or space, and be accurate and economical to operate.
- A real-time data handling system. In this system, the instant the radiance versus wavelength response over a terrain element is generated, it will be processed into an interpretable format and recognized as being unique to the particular terrain element from which it comes. This processing will be performed nearly instantaneously (real time), providing timely information. Because of the consistent nature of the energy/matter interactions, there will be no need for reference data in the analytical procedure. The derived data will provide insight into the physical-chemical-biological state of each feature of interest.
- Multiple data users. These people will have comprehensive knowledge of both their respective disciplines and of remote-sensing data acquisition and analysis techniques. The same set of data will become various forms of information for different users, because of their vast knowledge about the particular earth resources being used.

Unfortunately, an ideal remote-sensing system, as described above, does not exist. Real remote-sensing systems fall short of the ideal at virtually every point in the sequence outlined.

Remote Sensing Satellites: A satellite with remote sensors to observe the earth is called a remote-sensing satellite, or earth observation satellite. Remote Sensing Satellites are characterized by their altitude, orbit and sensor.

TRIOS Series (1960-1965): The Television and Infrared Observation Satellites.

NOAA It is the first generation of National Oceanic and Atmospheric Administration satellites and was as the first operation operational remote sensing satellite system. The third generation NOAA satellites are also successfully used for vegetation monitoring, apart from meteorological monitoring. It is equipped with Advanced Very High Resolution Radiometer (AVHRR) sensors, and is established at an altitude of 850 km.

GMS(Geo-synchronous meteorological satellite): It is established at an altitude of 36,000 km, and its main purpose is meteorological observations.

Landsat is established at an altitude of 700 km is a polar orbit and is used mainly for land area observation.

Other remote sensing satellite series in operations are: SPOT, MOS, JERS, ESR, RADARSAT, IRS etc.

Indian Remote Sensing Programme

The Indian Remote Sensing Satellite (IRS-A), the first in the operational series of Indian Remote Sensing Satellites has been functioning satisfactorily for more than 20 years but still continues to provide quality data. The second satellite in the IRS series, IRS-IB, launched is performing very well. These two satellites have become the mainstay of the National Natural Resources Management System (NNRMS) IRS-1A/1B provides imagery from the two cameras, linear Imaging Self Scanners, LISS-I with both the resolution 72.5m and LISS-IIA and LISS-IIB both with a resolution of 36.25m. IRS-1A and 1B together provide imagery with a combined repetivity of 11 days. While IRS-IA has so far provided more than 5, 00,000 scenes, IRS-1B has provided more than 2,00,000 scenes. The successful implementation of the operational IRS-IA 1B system in the country. The second generation remote sensing satellites IRS-IC and ID taking in to account the technology development scenario and user requirements during the nineties. The Indian Remote Sensing (IRS) Satellites viz., IRS 1A, 1B, 1C, 1D, P4, P6, Cartosat I and Cartosat II etc. is being widely used.

Scope of IRS Mission

Sustainable development of natural resources relies on maintaining the fragile balance between productivity functions and conservation practices through precise identification and systematic monitoring of problem area in various resources and developmental sectors. The process of sustainable development packages evolving from such an integrated effort will be economically acceptable and environmentally friendly. Towards this, Department of space had initiated pilot studies in 21 perennially drought affected districts of the country to generate locale specific action plans. These pilot studies carried out has demonstrated the efficacy of using remote sensing based approach for optimal utilization of land and water resources towards combating drought on a long term basis. Based on the results obtained form these pilot studies, Department of Space has launched a major, unique programme on Integrated Mission for Sustainable Development. This mission, as of now, covers a total of 157 problem districts of the country, covering nearly 45% of India's geographical area which are perennially affected and tribal areas. Nationwide crop yield forecast is now possible and is being regularly practiced since last decade.

The integration of the various thematic maps and attributes data, and further analysis for identified alternatives for development are carried out using geographic information system to identify set of coherent micro-level land units which are unique in terms of their resources potential and problems. Specific developmental plans for these units are arrived at in consultation with and close coordination between space scientists, experts from various central/state developmental departments, agricultural universities/research institutions, district level officials and local farmers, so as to ensure the technical feasibility and cultural acceptability of such action plans. Further, methodology has been developed to overlay the land capability map over the cadastral maps to provide information at the field levels. Various elements of such action plans are prioritized and categorized as those relating to land and water resources and others. Sensitivity of each element of the action plan would also be studied to see visible regress over the coming years, once they are implemented. The parameters such as, vegetation index, forest cover, land use, agricultural production, ground water table, soil erosion, etc., would be identified for bench marking the impact of such an implementation. The action plans are being implemented by the district authorities for these watersheds. The initial feedback on the implementation of action plans in the watersheds of Anantapur has been encouraging as shown by increased ground water levels through water harvesting structures and related activities. The supports for implementation is derived from ongoing developmental programmes such as Drought Prone Area Development Programme (DPAP), Desert Development Programme (DDP), Integrated Wasteland Development Programme (IWDP), National Watersheds Development Project for Rain-fed Areas (NWDPRA), Hill Area Development Programme (HADP), etc. It is also proposed to use satellite data for monitoring of the impact of these action plans.

Further, in view of the advantages of the integrated approach wherein local specific action plans will be generated with cadastral overlays, Ministry of Rural Development has suggested taking up of 92 selected blocks from among the IMSD districts, on an urgent basis in a time frame of 18 months. Ministry of Rural Development provided funds for implementation of these action plans through pooling of resources from the various ongoing schemes for rural development.

National (Natural) Resources Information System (NRIS)

A National Natural Resources Information System (NRIS) for the country has been evolved to aid decision makers at various levels. A number of pilot scale studies on various themes viz., wasteland development, land capability classes, district level planning, regional mineral targeting, etc., were carried out towards implementation of NRIS. Several geographic information packages have also been developed indigenously to cater to computer based decision support systems. More particularly crop wise forecast of production at regional to national level.

Training and Education in Remote Sensing

With the increased awareness and utilization of remote sensing in India, need for adequate number of trained manpower for harnessing the benefits of remote sensing technology has steeply gone up. Adequate efforts are being made to increase the present throughput of trained manpower in various themes in collaboration with central/state/academic institution by way of augmenting the existing training infrastructure. Regular training courses are being conducted by several training institutions such as Indian Institute of Remote Sensing (IIRS, Dehradun), Centre of Studies for Resources Engineering (IIT, Bombay), Institute of Remote Sensing (Anna University, Madras), Survey of India, ecological Survey of India Training Institute, Forest Survey of India and Indian Agricultural Research Institute (IARI, Delhi). Besides these regular courses, on the job training is being provided by National Remote Sensing centre (NRSC, Hyderabad) and Space Applications Centre (SAC, Ahmedabad) for specific themes and training in digital analysis and GIS by RRSSCs. Efforts are also on to introduce remote sensing evening school and college curriculum. Many universities have introduced remote sensing in their post-graduate courses as a full-fledged degree course or a part of a core subject.

International Collaboration

India has many collaborative programme with several countries in promoting active cooperation in remote sensing. For example, the ESCAP/ UNDP Regional Remote Sensing Programme (RRSP), under the execution of the ESCAP, is playing a crucial role in promoting active cooperation in remote sensing among member counties of Asia-Pacific region, by bringing together experts from different areas who can share their experiences, disseminating information on available experts where needed. The Shares (Sharing of Experience) program initiated by India is also continuing to provide assistance to candidates from developing countries for participation in remote sensing training courses in India. The data reception/processing courses in India. The data reception/processing facility at Norman, USA has been recently established, to receive data from India Remote Sensing Satellite (IRS) as part of arrangements between EOSAT, USA and Department of Space/Antrix/NRSC, India, IRS-P6, Cartosat I & II data are also being acquired at this station.

Geographic Information System (GIS)

The year 1962 saw the development of the world's first true operational GIS in Ottawa, Ontario, Canada by the federal Department of Forestry and Rural Development. Developed by Dr. Roger Tomlinson, it was called the "Canada Geographic Information System" (CGIS) and was used to store, analyze, and manipulate data collected for the Canada Land Inventory (CLI). CGIS was the world's first "system" and was an improvement over "mapping" applications as it provided capabilities for overlay, measurement, and digitizing/scanning. It supported a national coordinate system that spanned the continent, coded lines as "arcs" having a true embedded topology, and it stored the attribute and locational information in separate files. As a result of this, Tomlinson has become known as the "father of GIS," particularly for his use of overlays in promoting the spatial analysis of convergent geographic data. CGIS lasted into the 1990s and built the largest digital land resource database in Canada. It was developed as a mainframe based system in support of federal and provincial resource planning and management. Its strength was continent-wide analysis of complex data sets. The CGIS was never available in a commercial form. By the early 1980s, M&S Computing (later Intergraph), Environmental Systems Research Institute (ESRI) and CARIS emerged as commercial vendors of GIS software, successfully incorporating many of the CGIS features, combining the first generation approach to separation of spatial and attribute information with a second generation approach to organizing attribute data into database structures. By the end of the 20th century, the rapid growth in various systems had been consolidated and standardized on relatively few platforms and users were beginning to export the concept of viewing GIS data over the Internet, requiring data format and transfer standards. More recently, there is a growing number of free, open source GIS packages which run on a range of operating systems and can be customized to perform specific tasks.

GIS can be defined as a data management system designed to input, store, retrieve, manipulate, analyze, and display spatial data for the purposes of research and decision-making (De Mers, 1997). Use of geographic information systems (GIS), a collection of computer hardware and software used to analyze and display geographically referenced information (Table 2), can facilitate this planning process. Spatial data layers like soil type, slope, and land cover can be used to develop suitability assessments that can identify optimal locations for agroforestry practices to solve landowner and community concerns. By selecting data with the appropriate spatial resolution, this assessment process can be used at any scale for planning agroforestry practices. The most significant benefit of using GIS-guided suitability assessments is the ability to combine different assessments to determine locations where multiple objectives can be achieved.

In a GIS, a database is associated with map features, and data values are geographically referenced, so resource managers can spatially represent information such as soil types or plant communities. Since land use and a diversity of related disciplines (i.e., agriculture, forestry, rural planning, and conservation) all deal with spatial characteristics of landscapes (Lacher 1998), GIS has gained considerable use in land use planning and natural-resource management, providing a spatial framework to aid in the decision-making process (Zeiler 1999).

Table 2: Major categories of computer-based spatial information technologies.

Category	Description
Databases	Organizes and facilitates the management and querying of large quantities of data and information
Geographical Information Systems (GIS)	Brings in a geographic or spatial component to a database; manages, manipulates and analyzes spatial data
Computer-Based Models	Mathematical computer models that represent real world processes and predict outcomes based on input scenarios
Knowledge-Based or Expert Systems	Adopts 'Artificial Intelligence' in the form of organizing, manipulating and obtaining solutions using knowledge in the form qualitative statements, expert rules (i.e. rules of thumb) and a computer language representation system for storing and manipulating knowledge.
Hybrid Systems	Integrates two or more of the above computer-based technologies (e.g. (GIS, KBS and Models) for more versatile, efficient and comprehensive DSTs.

Geo-databases

A database with extensions for storing, querying, and manipulating geographic information and spatial data.

GIS software

GIS Software can be accessed, transferred, transformed, overlaid, processed and displayed using numerous software applications. Within industry commercial offerings from companies such as ESRI and Map-info dominate, offering an entire suite of tools. Government and military departments often use custom software, open source products, such as GRASS, or more specialized products that meet a well-defined need. Although free tools exist to view GIS datasets, public access to geographic information is dominated by online resources such as Google Earth and interactive web mapping.

Basics of ArcGIS/ ArcInfo Workstation

ArcGIS is a desktop mapping program produced by ESRI (Environmental Systems Research Institute, Inc.) that allows you to create your own maps from scratch starting with geographic data in electronic form. There are several interrelated component programs, the basic ones being *ArcCatalog, ArcMap*, and *ArcToolbox*. These three components comprise what is now known as ArcGIS Desktop, or ArcView. When other advanced components are added, it comprises ArcGIS Workstation, or ArcInfo. It is a complex program. Users need to be familiar with Microsoft Windows and must be willing to spend time to learn how to use ArcGIS.

ArcCatalog

ArcCatalog allows the user to easily access and manage geographic data that is stored in folders on local disks or relational databases that are available on the user's network. Data can be copied, moved, deleted, and quickly viewed before it is added to a map. In addition, metadata can be either read or created using this ArcGIS application.

ArcMap

ArcMap allows the user to display and query maps, create quality hardcopy maps and perform many spatial analysis tasks. ArcMap provides an easy transition from viewing a map to editing its spatial features.

ArcToolbox

ArcToolbox provides an environment for performing geo-processing operations (i.e., operations that involve alteration or information extraction). Tools step the user through the many geo-processing tasks. ArcToolbox is embedded in both ArcCatalog and ArcMap.

Data Retrieval

Data collection and preparation is one of the most expensive and time-consuming aspects of creating a GIS facility. There are many governmental and commercial data sources that provide digital and tabular data sets as well as analogue data including maps, aerial photographs, and satellite imagery.

ArcGIS Supported Data Formats

ArcGIS allows the user to work with an extensive array of data sources. These are ArcIMS feature services, ArcIMS map services, ArcInfocoverages, DGN (through v8). DWG (through v2004), DXF, Geodatabases, Geography Network connections, OLE DB Tables, PC ARC/INFO coverage.

Raster Formats

ARC Digitized Raster Graphics (ADRG) (*.img or *.ovr and *.lgg), ArcSDERasters, Band Interleaved by Line (ESRI BIL) (*.bil and *.hdr, *.clr, *.stx), Band Interleaved by Pixel (ESRI BIP) (*.bip and *.hdr, *.clr, *.stx), Band Sequential (ESRI BSQ) (*.bsq and *.hdr, *.clr, *.stx), Bitmap (BMP), Device Independent Bitmap (DIB) format, or MicrosoftWindows Bitmap (*.bmp) ,Compressed ARC Digitized Raster Graphics (CADRG) ,Controlled Image Base (CIB),Digital Geographic Information Exchange Standard (DIGEST) Arc Standard Raster Product (ASRP), UTM/UPS Standard Raster Product (USRP) (*.img and *.gen, *.ger, *.sou, *.qal, *.thf), Digital Terrain Elevation Data (DTED) Level 0, 1 and 2 (*.dt0, *.dt1, *.dt2),ER Mapper (*.ers) ,ERDAS 7.5 GIS (*.gis and *.trl) ,ERDAS 7.5 LAN (*.lan and *.trl) ,ERDAS IMAGINE (*.img),ERDAS RAW (*.raw), ESRI GRID (*.clr),ESRI GRID Stack ,ESRI GRID Stack File (*.stk), ESRI SDE Raster, Graphics Interchange Format (GIF) (*.gif) , Intergraph Raster Files (*.cit and *.cot), JPEG File interchange Format, JIFF (*.jpg, *.jpeg, *jpe), JPEG 2000 (.jp2), Multiresolution Seamless Image Database (MrSID) (*.sid; generations 2 and 3; Note that the export command Raster to MrSID outputs in MrSID generation 2 format), National Image Transfer Format (NITF) (*.ntf), Portable Network Graphics (*.png). Tagged Image File Format (TIFF) (*.tif, *.tiff, *.tff) , SDC (Smart Data Compression), SDE layers, Shapefiles, Text Files (.TXT), and VPF. Additional Data Types Supported via Importers in ArcInfo are ADS, DFAD, DIME, DLG, ETAK, GIRAS, IGDS, IGES, MOSS, S-57, SDTS (Point, Raster, and Vector), SLF, TIGER (through v2000) and Sun Raster.

Data Sources

A data source is any geographic data that may be used as input to or output from a geo-processing tool. Supported data sources include:

1. Geo-database feature datasets
2. Geo-database feature classes
3. Shapefile datasets
4. Coverage datasets
5. Coverage feature classes
6. CAD feature datasets
7. CAD feature classes
8. SDC datasets
9. SDC feature classes
10. VPF datasets
11. VPF feature classes
12. Raster datasets
13. Raster dataset bands
14. Raster catalogs
15. TIN datasets
16. Layers
17. Layer files
18. Tables
19. Table views

Viewing Data in ArcCatalog

Once the user has successfully acquired GIS data in one of the aforementioned supported formats, it can be previewed using the ArcCatalog application. If the data format is listed under the above heading "ArcGIS Supported Data Types," it can be simply viewed without the need to actually import using an import utility. If the data format is listed under any of the other headings (above), the data will first need to be imported. The ArcCatalog application window includes the catalog display that allows you to preview data, either spatially or tabularly, a catalog tree for browsing the data, and several toolbars (Fig.4).

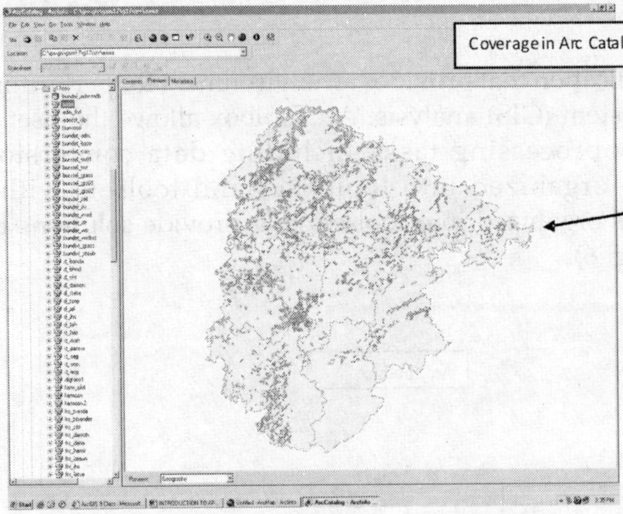

Fig. 4 : Screenshot of ArcCatelog

Viewing Data in ArcMap

The ArcMap application window consists of a map display for viewing spatial data, a table of contents for listing the layers shown in the display and a variety of toolbars for working with data. When ArcMap opens, the ArcMap dialog appears on top of the application window. To open a data layer, the user can specify, whether or not they want to start using ArcMap with a new empty map, a template, or an existing map (Fig. 5).

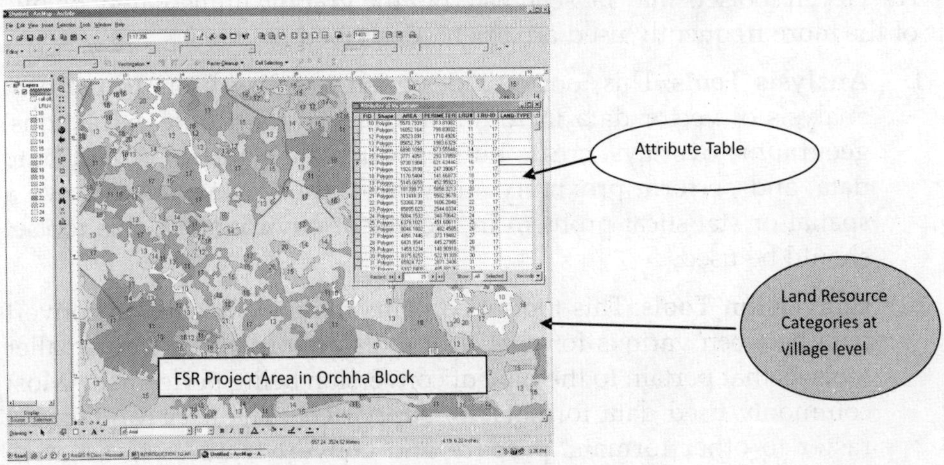

Fig. 5 : Screenshot of ArcMap

Using ArcToolbox

ArcToolbox is the application that provides an environment for performing geographic information system (GIS) analysis. ArcToolbox allows the user to perform a variety of geoprocessing tasks including data conversion. Geoprocessing tools are organized into toolboxes and toolsets within ArcToolbox. The toolbox is organized into toolsets that provide solutions for different types of tasks (Fig. 6).

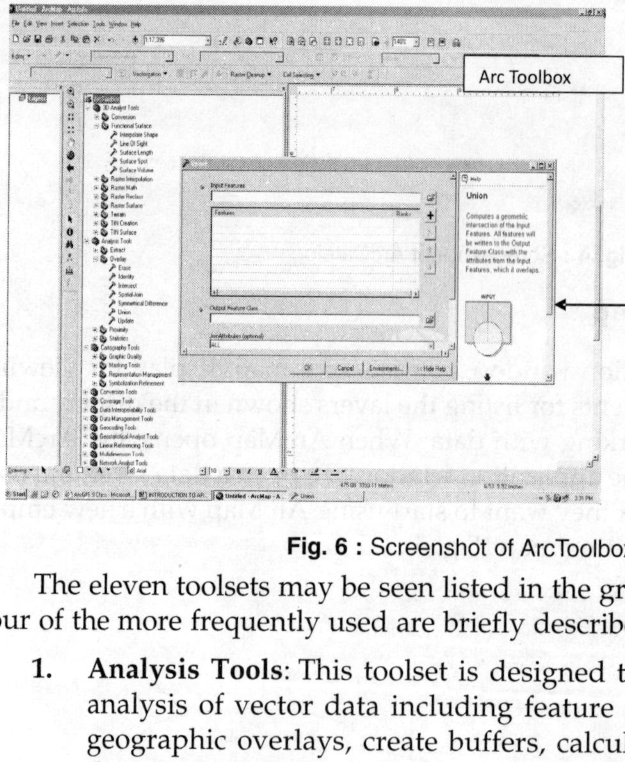

Fig. 6 : Screenshot of ArcToolbox

The eleven toolsets may be seen listed in the graphic immediately below. Four of the more frequently used are briefly described.

1. **Analysis Tools**: This toolset is designed to allow users to perform analysis of vector data including feature and attribute extractions, geographic overlays, create buffers, calculate statistics on attribute data, and perform proximity analysis. If the user wants to solve a spatial or statistical problem in the vector environment, this toolset should be used.

2. **Conversion Tools**: This toolset contains the tools needed to convert data between various formats. The tools are organized into smaller toolsets that pertain to the type of conversion being performed. Most commonly used data formats are supported. The user can convert raster to other formats, prepare and convert features to a native computer-aided design (CAD) format, convert: feature classes to coverage format; tables to dBase format; features and CAD files to geo-database feature classes; data to raster; and convert features to

shapefiles. This toolset should be used whenever a user needs to change from one type of dataset to another.

3. **Data Management Tools:** This toolset allows the user to manage and maintain feature classes, datasets, layers, and raster data structures. Database join operations, topology building, projections and transformations operations, workspace management, and much more. If the user needs to modify the characteristics of a particular dataset they can do so using this toolset.

4. **Spatial Analyst Tools**: This toolset is designed to allow users to perform cell-based (raster) analysis including a variety of neighborhood, overlay, reclass, map algebra, extractions, density, distance, cost surface functions, and more. If the user wants to solve a spatial or statistical problem in the raster environment, this toolset should be used.

Global Positioning Systems (GPS)

GPS is a means for inputting spatial data with real world coordinates into a GIS and has become an important tool for researchers locating and recording information in the field. Remote sensing involves using spatial data from photographic and satellite images, and software tools to analyze and interpret these data.

GPS based ground survey /route line mapping: Intensive ground-truthing and field observation were carried out to generate the geo-spatial information and route mapping (Fig.7).

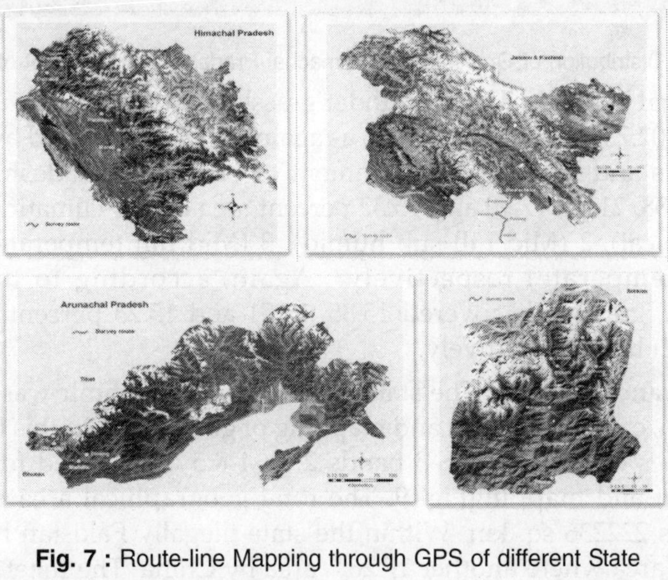

Fig. 7 : Route-line Mapping through GPS of different State

Application of Geo-spatial technologyin Grassland Management

Vast areas mostly under natural vegetation dominated by grasses, which are unfenced, unfertilized and non-irrigated, where animals (wild and domestic) grazed are called grassland/rangeland. The grassland vegetation consists of a number of perennial and annual grasses mixed with legumes and forbs. The availability of grasslands area can be assessed more precisely with the help of satellite remote sensing and GIS tools(Fig.8).

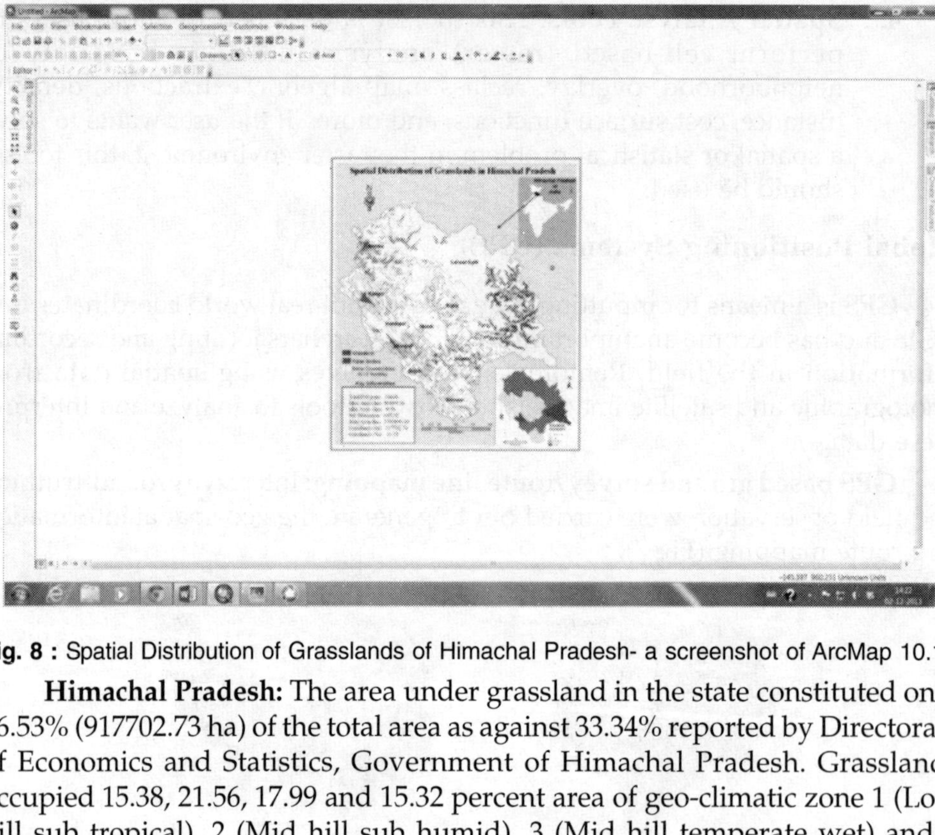

Fig. 8 : Spatial Distribution of Grasslands of Himachal Pradesh- a screenshot of ArcMap 10.1

Himachal Pradesh: The area under grassland in the state constituted only 16.53% (917702.73 ha) of the total area as against 33.34% reported by Directorate of Economics and Statistics, Government of Himachal Pradesh. Grasslands occupied 15.38, 21.56, 17.99 and 15.32 percent area of geo-climatic zone 1 (Low hill sub tropical), 2 (Mid hill sub humid), 3 (Mid hill temperate wet) and 4 (High hill temperate) respectively. Again, according to the hill zone classification, grasslands covered 15.35, 19.51 and 15.23 percent area of low, mid and high hills, respectively.

Jammu and Kashmir: The state of Jammu and Kashmir was targeted for identification, characterization and mapping of grasslands. In this investigation total 21 scenes of IRS P6 LISS-3 bands 2, 3, 4 &5 were used for grasslands identification and mappingFig. 9. The total geographical area of Jammu & Kashmir was 222236 sq. km. Within the state illegally Pakistan has occupied about 34.8% area where another 17.26% area by China. The relief ranges from

500 m. in Jammu to >6000 m. in Ladakh region. The study reveals that about 9595 sq. km(4.32%) area is under productive grasslands and where as other grazinglands including scrubs and other unpalatable grasslands were 10455 sq. km(9.81%) of the total geographical area. The area under grasslands in Jammu, Kashmir and Ladakh were 3.53, 13.22 and 5.76 percent respectively together contributing about 6756.5 sq. kmor 6.34%. Where as in POK it was 2.16% and in China occupied area it was 3.04 percent.

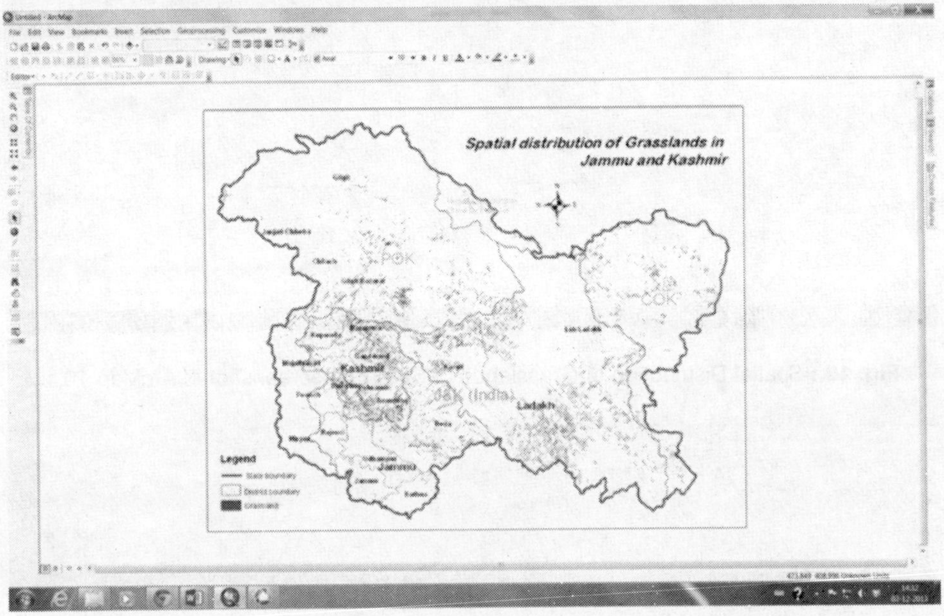

Fig. 9 : Spatial Distribution of Grasslands of J & K- a screenshot of ArcMap 10.1

Sikkim: In this investigation IRS P6 LISS-3 bands 2, 3, 4 &5 were used for grasslands identification and mapping(Fig. 10). The study reveals that about 14.13 % area is under pasture lands of total geographical area of Sikkim.

Bundelkhand: Based on the intensive field survey, study of IRSP6 imagery and geo-spatial analysis geo-referenced information on grassland have been generated at district level.IRSP6 data was used for the identification and analysis of grasslands using ERDAS Imagine software. ArcGIS- ArcInfo workstation was used for the geo-spatial analysis (Fig.11). And Geographical Information System (GPS) was used for intensive ground truthing and sample survey. The study reveals that the area under grasslands was estimated as 3.54% of the total geographical area of Bundelkhand region (about 7160250 ha).

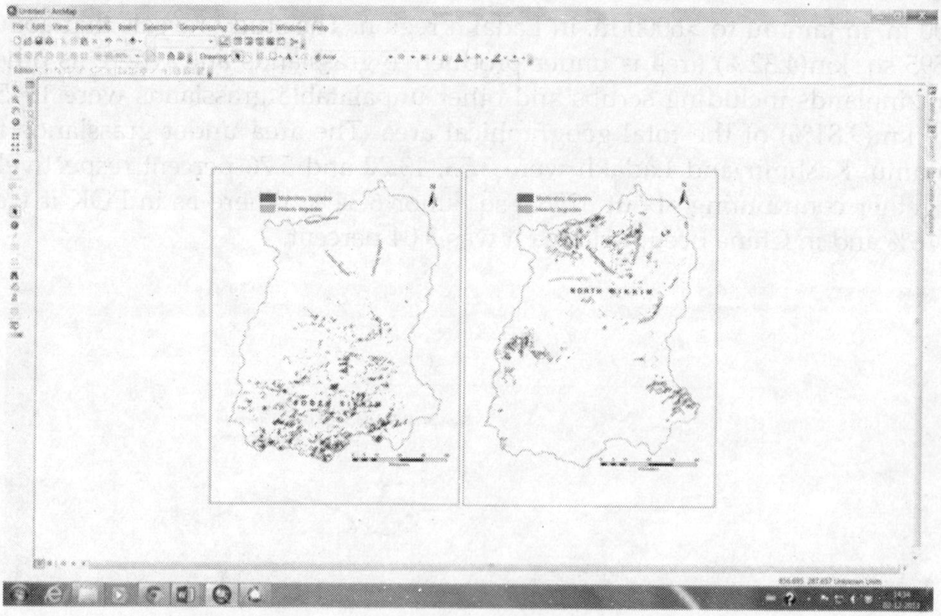

Fig. 10 : Spatial Distribution of Grasslands of Sikkim- a screenshot of ArcMap 10.1

Fig. 11 : Spatial distribution of Grasslands of Bundelkhand Region - a screenshot of ArcMap 10.1

Application of Geo-spatial Technology in Forage Resource Study

The availability of forage from rangelands can be assessed more precisely with the help of satellite remote sensing and GIS tools. The present study reveals that forage production from the rangelands of the Bundelkhand region was approximately 2.57 m t DM/ year. Based on the intensive field survey, study of IRSP6 imagery and geo-spatial analysis geo-referenced information on range forages have been generated at district level. It covers 7160250 haarea located between $23^{0}8'$-$26^{0}31'$N latitude and $78^{0}11'$-$81^{0}31'$E longitude. SOI toposheets number 54K, L, J, P, O; 63 A, B, C, D, H, G; 55I and 65M were used for the generation of base map. IRSP6 data dated October 2004 was used for the identification and analysis of grazinglands using ERDAS Imagine (ver. 9.3) software. ArcGIS- ArcInfo workstation (ver.10.1) was used for the geo-spatial analysis. The study reveals that about 1.99 m ha land (27.88%) classified as grazinglands including the forest lands. It was found maximum (55.62%) in Panna district where as minimum (4.55%) in Banda district.

Application of Geo-spatial Technology in Crop Yield Estimation

In many countries Crop yield estimation are based on conventional techniques of data collection for crop and yield estimation based on ground-based field visits and report. Such reports are costly, time consuming and large errors due to incomplete ground observation which leading to poor crop yield assessment and crop area estimation (Reynolds *et al*, 2000). Many empirical models have been developed to try and estimate yield before harvesting. With the development of satellites, remote sensing images provide access to spatial information at global scale; of features and phenomena on earth on an almost real-time basis. They have the potential not only in identifying crop classes but also estimating crop yield and can identify and provide information on spatial variability as well as permit more efficiency in field scouting (Schuler, 2002). Remote sensing could be used for crop growth monitoring and yield estimation. For example, the traditional approach of crop estimation in India involves complete enumeration for estimating crop acreage and sample surveys based on crop cutting experiments for estimating crop yield. Remote sensing technology application for agriculture (Agro-RS) was introduced to China in the late 1970s. Twenty years on, there more than 200 scientists and technicians throughout China works on resources survey, agro-ecological assessment, sown areas, crop condition and disaster monitoring, and yield estimation using remote sensing by Ministry of Agriculture. They have participated in national key projects of Agro-RS, international exchanges, resources and crop monitoring. In 1999, The Center for Remote sensing application of the Ministry of Agriculture organized sub-centers all over China to monitor sown area and production of winter wheat, corn and cotton using satellite remote sensing at national scale. The monitoring results are now a part of the official resources of agricultural information system of the Ministry.

The crop acreage and corresponding yield estimate data are used to obtain production estimates (Singh *et al*, 2002). Final production estimates based on the sampling method become available after the crops are actually harvested. Although the approach is fairly comprehensive and reliable, there is a need to reduce the cost and also to improve upon the accuracy and timeless of crop production statistics. To achieve timely and accurate information on the status of crops and crop yield, there is need to have an up-to-date crop monitoring system that provides accurate information on yield estimates way before the harvesting period. The earlier and more reliable information are the greater the value (Reynolds *et al*, 2000). Remote sensing data has the potential and the capacity to achieve this.

In the present study IRS P6 LISS III (Row 98, Path 53) data dated February 2008 was selected. After the geometric and radiometric correction and histogram enhancement the image was classified using Erdas Imagine Professional s/w ver. 9.3. It was modified on the basis of the information gathered during the ground truthing and field data verification. Finally information on wheat yield production was generated in ArcGIS ArcInfo Workstation ver10.1 and presented in Fig.12. The study reveals that the total area under a single crop (Wheat) is

Fig. 12 : Estimation of Seed Yield Production - a screenshot of ArcMap 10.1

about 43% (ha) of the total geographical area. Based on crop health (plant vigor) it was classed as high yielding crop (34.67ha), medium yielding crop (23.97ha) and low yielding crop (9.80 ha). Again based on ground sample data the seed yield was estimated under Arc GIS environment. The total seed yield was estimated as 202.89 ton. This technique can be applied for the estimation of seed production for any crop at regional to nation level with suitable modification.

Application of Geo-Spatial Technology for Biomass Estimation

Biomass is an important element in the carbon cycle, specifically in carbon sequestration which is useful to help in quantifying the pools and fluxes of greenhouse gasses (GHG) from the terrestrial biosphere to the atmosphere associated with land-use and land cover changes. Development and applications of appropriate biomass estimation methods for precise assessment of above ground biomass is important for national development planning as well as for scientific studies of ecosystem productivity, carbon budgets etc. Mathematical modeling to forecast growth/production of different components of forage and fodder crops is an essential tool to predict the performance of the system. Prominent among the methods of forecasting are based on models that utilize data on crop biometrical characters, weather parameters, farmer's eye estimates, agro meteorological conditions and remotely sensed crop reflectance observations etc. has modeled the performance of *Acacia tortilis* – *Cenchrus ciliaris* silvopastoral system spread over three sites. Modeling growth and yield of multipurpose tree species have been tried in F/FRED project of Winrock International. But developing a biomass equation requires harvesting of trees and measurement of sample trees for their biomass which is quite a tedious, time consuming task and normally tree felling is not permitted. To overcome this problem an alternative is Geomatics (GIS/RS/GPS) based biomass assessment technique which does not require harvesting of trees. Locally developed biomass equations give better estimation compare to existing regional or global biomass equations. Vegetation Indices developed using RS parameters can be used to build above-ground biomass and further can be a useful tool to asses carbon sequestration. On the basis of RS parameters biomass equations can be developed and validated through the use of geo-spatial tools (Fig. 13). The sampled information can be precisely and accurately up-scaled to regional or national level.

Similar type of work of estimating tree above ground biomass through statistical modelling using Remotely sensed parameters captured by Geomatic tools was undertaken at Indian Grassland and Fodder Research Institute in which project predictive equations for biomass production from some shrub and multipurpose trees were developed on the basis of several species available at IGFRI, Jhansi Central Research Farm which will be able to provide objective crop forecasts with reasonable precisions well in advance before harvests for taking timely decisions.

Research Approach

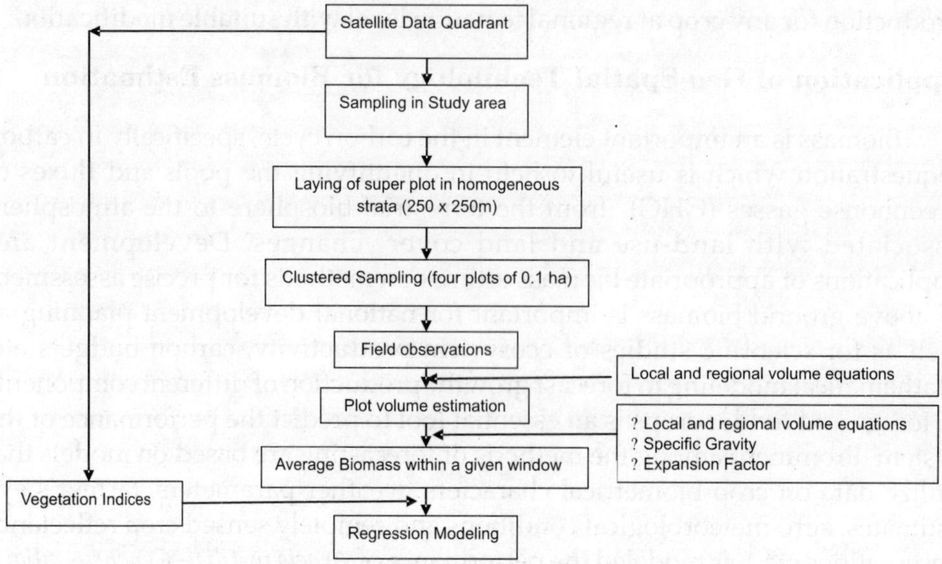

Fig. 13 : Broad steps of biomass estimation

The database used for this study purpose contains information on Altitude, Soil type, Crown density, Stand ht., CBH, Dia, Tree-Height , Ht-1st-forking, dbh, Radius, and Basal area of all these species along with remotely sensed parameters like Normalized Difference Vegetative Index (NDVI). Based on these biometric values total wood biomass of particular tree species can be calculated using the volume equations given in the State of Forest Report 2005, forest survey of India , Ministry of Environment & Forests, Dehradun. The sampling of tree data was done by selecting total 20 zonal sites i.e. quadrants, then 100 sites per quadrant i.e. total 2500 plots (each of 250m x 25m size) selected and finally 4 sample plots from each sites cumulating 10000 permanent sample plots were used. The dbh range of sample trees was 3.00 cm to 35.00 cm which constitutes the predominant diameter range of the region.

Study sites and data collection: In the present study Data was collected on different biometric or physiological characters of several tree and shrub species, grown at different sample sites representing the Central Highland physiographic zone of Madhya Pradesh and Uttar Pradesh, which are identified inNational Carbon Project (NCP) for Vegetation Carbon Pool Assessment (VCP) under ISRO Geosphere Biosphere Program (IGBP) as one of the 20 Zonal sites of 350 x 350km more or less equivalent to one quadrant of AWiFS scene.

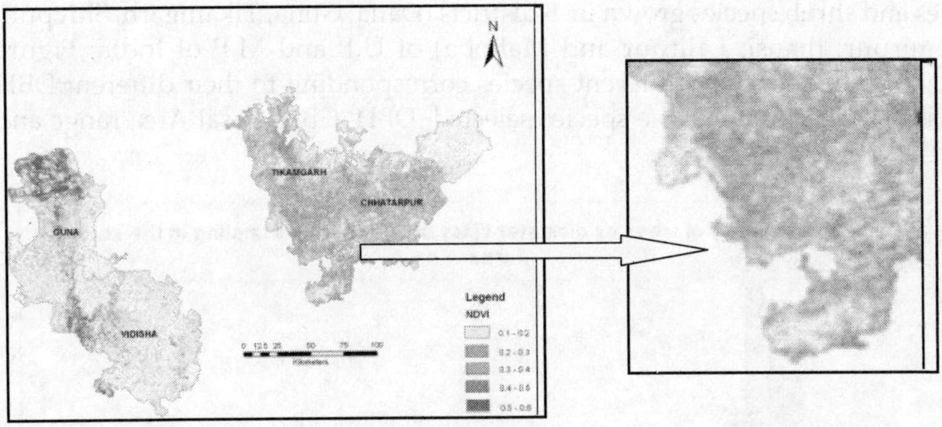

Fig. 14 : Data collection from different District of MP part of Bundelkhand Region

Sample tree selection:For collection of tree data in total 20 zonal sites i.e. quadrants were first selected then 100 sites per quadrant i.e. total 2500 plots (each of 250m x 250m size) selected and finally 4 sample plots from each sites cumulating 10000 permanent sample plots were used. The following diagram shows the final sample plot (Fig. 15).

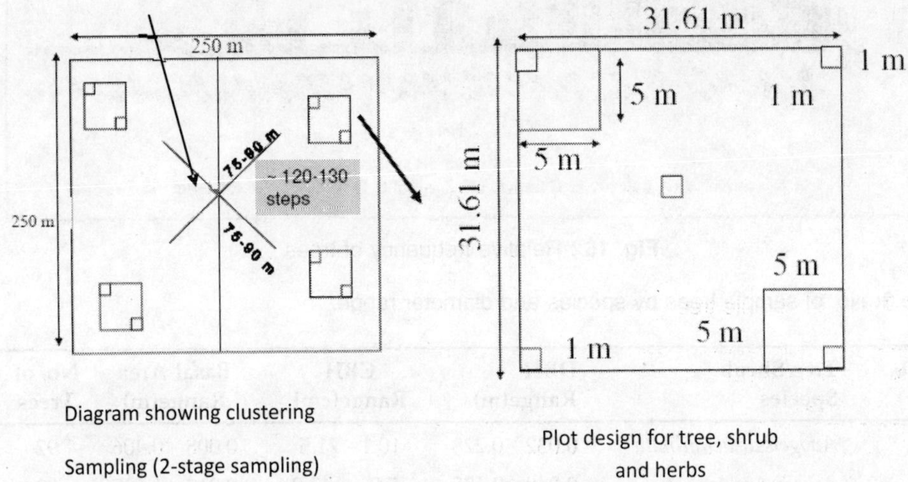

Fig. 15 : Sample of tree selection each of 250m x 250m in size

First of all the data that was collected, arranged and classified to study different descriptive statistics, distribution of the data for its suitability to build biomass models. The database consists of data on different physiological parameters like CBH (Collar Dia. At Breast Height), Diameter, Tree Height, Height at First Forking, DBH (Diameter at Breast Height), Basal Area etc. of 7 trees and shrub species grown in 8 districts (Datia, Guna, Tikamgarh, Shivpuri, Hamirpur, Jhansi, Lalitpur and Mahoba) of U.P and M.P of India. Figure 16.shows frequency of different species corresponding to their different DBH classes.Table 3.contains the species selected, DBH, CBH, Basal Area range and No. of trees.

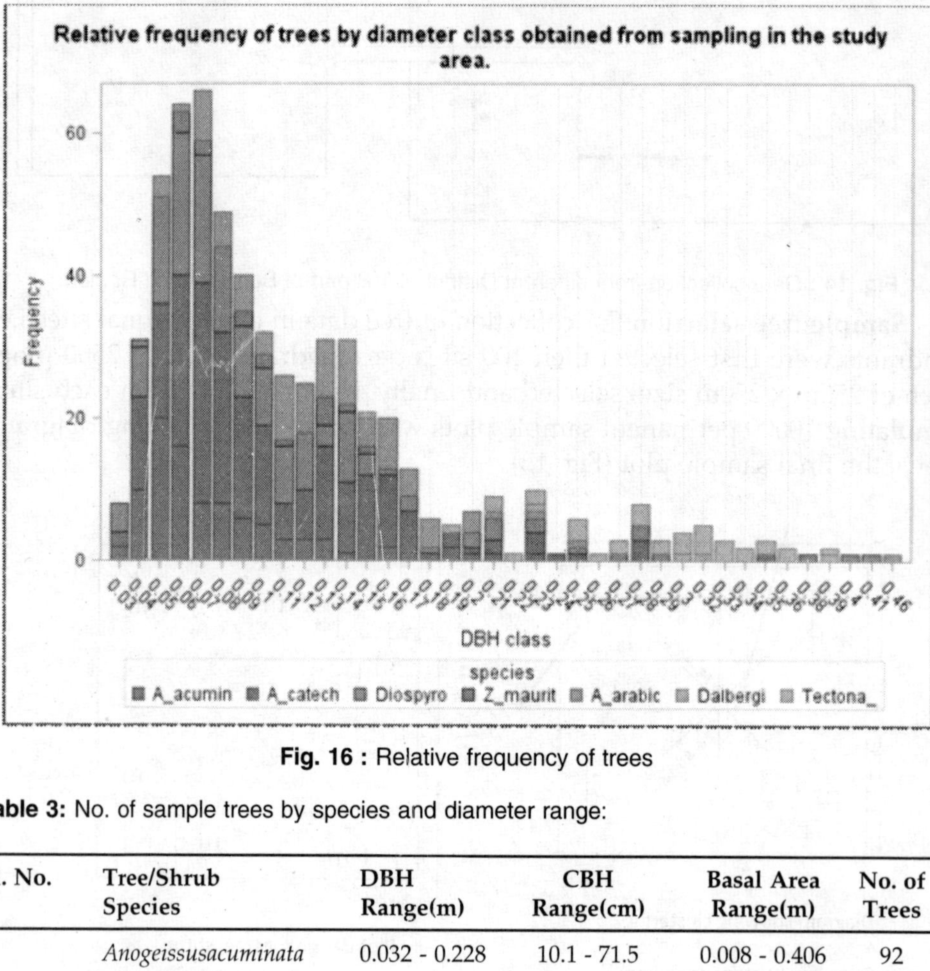

Fig. 16 : Relative frequency of trees

Table 3: No. of sample trees by species and diameter range:

Sl. No.	Tree/Shrub Species	DBH Range(m)	CBH Range(cm)	Basal Area Range(m)	No. of Trees
1	*Anogeissusacuminata*	0.032 - 0.228	10.1 - 71.5	0.008 - 0.406	92
2	*Acacia Arabica*	0.049 - 0.455	15.7 – 143.0	0.019 - 1.627	83
3	*Acacia Catechu*	0.033 - 0.345	10.6 - 108.5	0.008 - 0.936	220
4	*Dalbergiasissoo*	0.154 - 0.386	48.5 - 121.5	0.187 - 1.174	9
5	*Diospyrosmelanoxylon*	0.032 - 0.409	10.2 - 128.6	0.008 - 1.316	145
6	*Tectonagrandis*	0.229 - 0.387	—	0.414 - 1.176	30
7	*Zizyphusmauritiana*	0.040 - 0.145	12.6 - 45.7	0.012 - 0.166	17

The descriptive statistics of the data were calculated as follows:

Table 4: Tree sample analysis of different tree spacies

Botanical Name	N Obs	Variable	Mean	Std. Dev.	Minimum	Maximum	Coeff. of Variation
A. acuminata	92	CBH(cm)	24.56543	13.04545	10.1	71.5	53.1049
		Dia(cm)	7.819427	4.152499	3.214933	22.759176	53.1049
		Tree-Height (mts)	2.810652	1.441602	0	7.23	51.29067
		dbh(D) m	0.078194	0.041525	0.032149	0.2275918	53.1049
		Basal area	0.061418	0.075788	0.008118	0.4068203	123.3982
		Frequency	411.5	26.70206	366	457	6.488957
A. arabica	83	CBH(cm)	41.25783	17.42643	15.7	143	42.23788
		Dia(cm)	13.13279	5.54701	4.997469	45.518352	42.23788
		Tree-Height (mts)	3.39759	1.089302	1.7	6.7	32.06103
		dbh(D) m	0.131328	0.05547	0.049975	0.4551835	42.23788
		Basal area	0.159333	0.187097	0.019615	1.6272811	117.4253
		Frequency	499	24.10394	458	540	4.830449
A. catechu	220	CBH(cm)	31.68636	16.4838	10.6	108.5	52.02173
		Dia(cm)	10.22788	5.287854	3.374088	34.536652	51.70037
		Tree-Height (mts)	3.455455	0.798753	1.5	5.5	23.11572
		dbh(D) m	0.102279	0.052879	0.033741	0.3453665	51.70037
		Basal area	0.104021	0.121675	0.008941	0.9368067	116.9714
		Frequency	110.5	63.6527	1	220	57.60426
Dalbergiasissoo	9	CBH(cm)	77.62889	23.31788	48.5	121.5	30.03763
		Dia(cm)	24.71006	7.422318	15.43804	38.674684	30.03763
		Tree-Height (mts)	9.844444	2.932197	7.5	16.5	29.78529

Contd.

		dbh(D) m	0.247101	0.074223	0.15438	0.3867468	30.03763
		Basal area	0.518014	0.319457	0.187186	1.1747435	61.66955
		Frequency	545	2.738613	541	549	0.502498
Diospyrosme lanoxylon Tectonagrandis	14530	CBH(cm)	32.16966	20.96043	10.2	128.6	65.15591
		Dia(cm)	10.42082	6.903927	3.246764	40.934686	66.25131
		Tree-Height (mts)	5.388966	3.813538	0	14.6	70.76568
		dbh(D) m	0.104208	0.069039	0.032468	0.4093469	66.25131
		Basal area	0.122466	0.204563	0.008279	1.3160502	167.0367
		Frequency	293	42.00198	221	365	14.33515
		Tree-Height (mts)	10.40033	1.643651	4.9	12.7	15.80383
		dbh(D) m	0.301906	0.04155	0.229852	0.3870015	13.76262
		Basal area	0.728973	0.197799	0.41494	1.176291	27.13398
		Frequency	581.5	8.803408	567	596	1.513914
Z. mauritiana	17	CBH(cm)	30.77647	10.55619	12.6	45.7	34.29955
		Dia(cm)	9.796463	3.360143	4.010708	14.546774	34.29955
		Tree-Height (mts)	4.752941	1.305813	2.5	7.5	27.47378
		dbh(D) m	0.097965	0.033601	0.040107	0.1454677	34.29955
		Basal area	0.083721	0.05147	0.012634	0.1661969	61.47764
		Frequency	558	5.049753	550	566	0.904974

The scatter plot of sample tree wood volume against DBH (Figure 17) demonstrated a good association between these two variables.

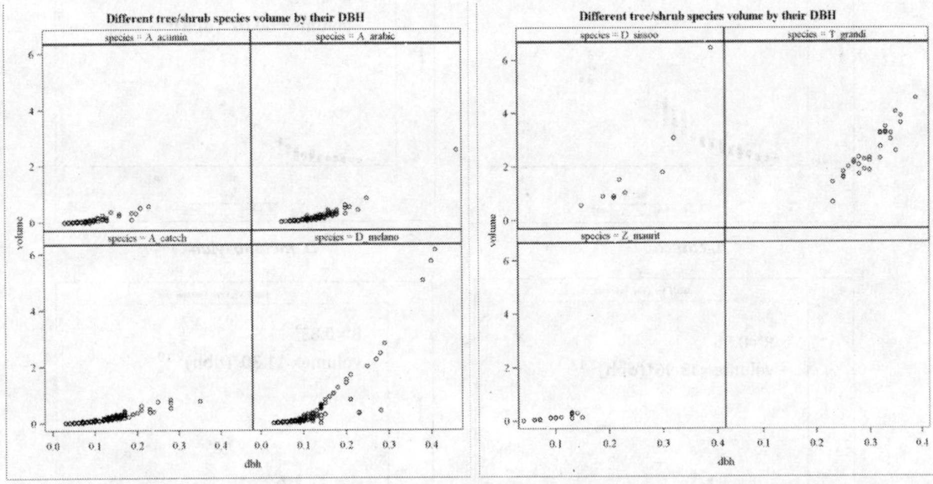

Fig. 17 : The scatter plot of sample tree wood volume against DBH

Most commonly used non linear functions for fitting relationship between wood volume and dbhwere tried for all the species and the best fitted one was of the type

$$\text{wood volume} = a^* (\text{dbh})^b$$

In the present analysis the modified Gauss-Newton method has been used. The following Figure 3 demonstrates the samples of all the 7 tree and shrub species with a good list square fit by the power modelbetween wood volume and DBH. The best fit can be observed from a good R^2 (coefficient of determination)value obtained from the power model. As, for non linear models the R^2 alone is not enough to judge the fit of the model, so The residual diagnostics was also performed to assess the goodness of fitof the model. The predicted volume against dbh, it closely matches the observed ones. Observed Vs predicted value plot and autocorrelation plot of residuals also shows the close association. Autoregressive procedure is performed here also to identify the presence of autocorrelation. The first order Durbin-Watson test is not significant which signifies that the error terms are independent.

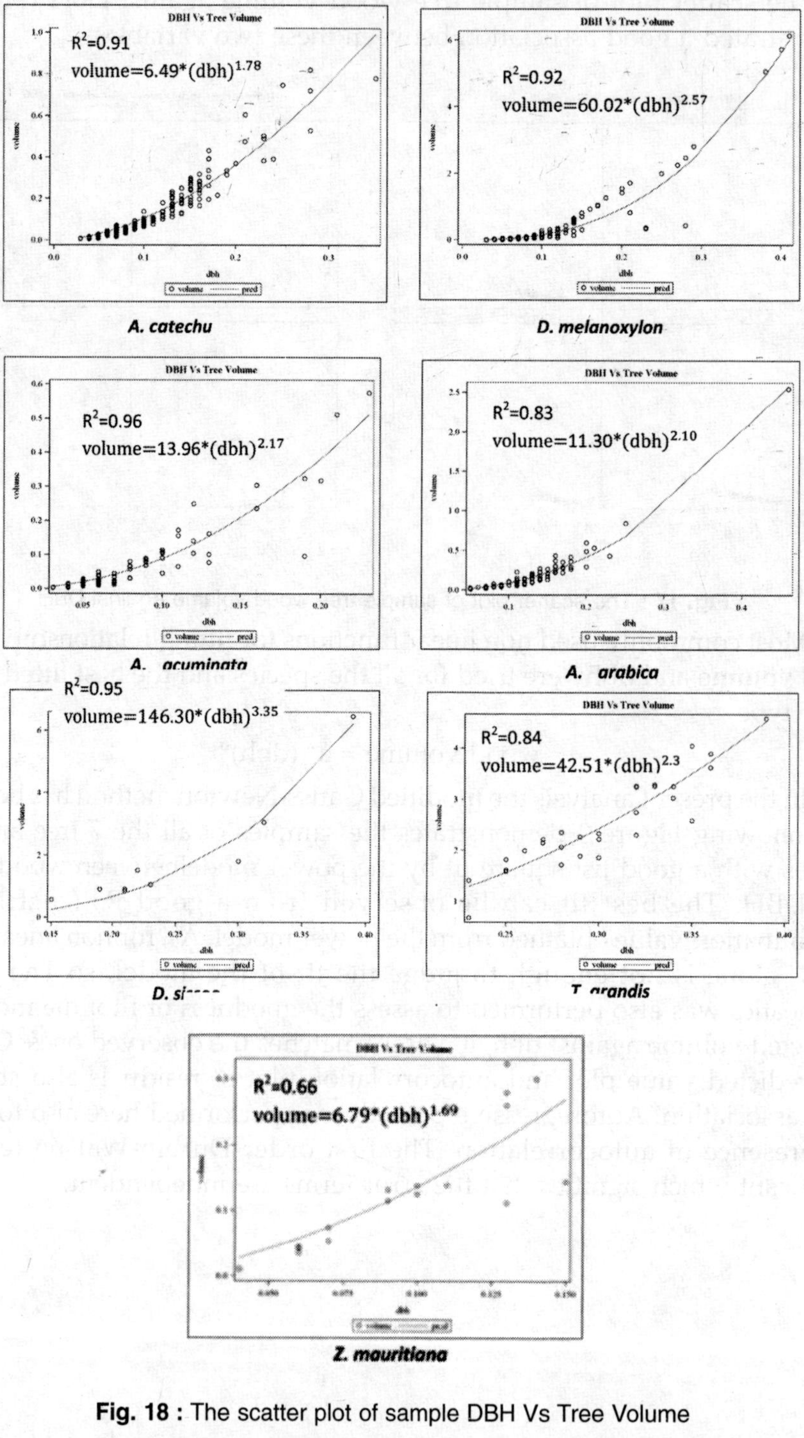

Fig. 18 : The scatter plot of sample DBH Vs Tree Volume

REFERENCES

De Mers, M. N. 1997. Fundamental of Geographic Information Systems. Wiley, New York, 486p.

Jayaraman, V., Chandrasekhar, M.G., and Rao, U.R., 1993. Remote Sensing for National Development : Implementing results achieved is 4th National Indian Satellite Programme. Presented at the UN/IAF Workshop on "Organising Space Activities in Develping Countries: Resources and Mechanics" on 16/3/193 during 44th IAF Congress at Graz, Austria.

Krishna Rao M. V., Hebbar K. R. and Venkataratnam L., 1997 Chilli crop inventory using IRS-1C LISS-III data. Scientific Note, NRSA, Hyderabad.

Lacher, T.E. 1998. The spatial nature of conservation and development. In: Savitsky B.G. and Lacher T.E. (eds), GIS Methodologies for Developing Conservation Strategies: Tropical Forest Recovery and Wildlife Management in Costa Rica. Columbia University Press, New York, NY. pp. 3–12.

Rao, U.R., 1991. Remote Sensing for National Development, Current Science, 61 (3&4): pp. 121-128.

Reynolds, C.A., M.Yitayew, D.C. Slack, C.F. Hutchison, A. Huete and M.S. Petersen. 2000. Estimating Crop Yields and Production by Integration the FAO Crop Specific Water-Balance Model with Real-time Satellite and Data and Ground Based Ancillary Data. International Journal of Remote Sensing. 21 (18): pp. 3487-3508.

Schuler, R.T. 2002. Remote Sensing Experiences in Production Fields. Retrieved on May 2007.

Singh, R., Semwali, D.P., Rai, A. and Chhikara, R.S., 2002. Small Area Estimation of Crop Yield Using Remote Sensing Satellite Data. International Journal of Remote Sensing.23 (1): pp. 49-56.

Zeiler, M. 1999. Modeling our world: the ESRI guide to geodatabase design. ESRI Press. Redlands, CA. 199p.

❑❑❑

CHAPTER - 24

Solar Energy and Its Future Prospect

Amitava Pradhan
BE, Electrical (Jadavpur University)
1/2D/1 R K Naskan Lane, Kolkata-700010

I'd put my money on the sun and solar energy. What a source of power! I hope we don't have to wait until oil and coal run out before we tackle that.
– Thomas Alva Edison, 1931

Energy is vital for the whole universe. Since the formation of the universe, energy acts a specific role. Steven Hawkins, George Ellis and Roger explained "The Theory of Relativity "Time and space had a finite beginning than corresponded to the origin of matter and energy from the time of BIG BANG.". Before invention of fire, energy hovers everywhere but people did not have any knowledge about that. Living being requires energy for every day work which cells of the body provide them. Energy is also a basic requirement for the existence and development of human life. Energy plays an important role in the entire process of evolution, growth and survival of all living being and also in the social –economic development and human welfare of country. Energy is defined as the ability to work. Then we run or walk or do any type of work, we burn the energy in our body produced in cells by transforming food. Cars,planes,trolleys,ships, aeroplanes etc and all kind of machineries require energy to run. There are many sources to get energy as coal, natural oil, natural gas, wind, water, wave, sun and nuclear etc. The commercial sources of energy as fossil fuels (coal, oil, and natural gas) hydro-power and then nuclear power provide the need of energy now of the world. The demand of energy is growing an alarming rate. As for example, according to International Energy Agency the Global consumption of energy has increased from 4606 Mtoe (Million Ton Oil equivalent) in 1973 to 7287 Mtoe in 2003.

The discovery of fire led to use the energy for cooking food and heating. For several thousands of years, the demand of energy was met by the sun, biomass (wood, leaves and twigs) and wind. As early as 4000 BC, the first sailing ship and wind mill were run by wind but wood, leaves dung cakes and twigs were the major source of energy of village areas. With advent of industrial revolution, the use of energy has been soaring day by day. Since the invention of the fire, man discovered new and developed source of energy gradually. Comparing the different kinds of energies invented till, solar energy is the best as it inexhaustible, pollutionless and cheap. In the first stage, coal was the main source of energy then came oil and nature gas. Electricity is being generated by from these fossil fuels. Man has now known the adverse affect of the use of fossil fuels as high quantity of harmful gases emits in the atmosphere thus is creating pollution and ozone depletion which in dangerous to living being and the existence of the earth. In the other hand the stock of fossil fuels are decreasing rapidly day by day. Due to the problems associated with fossil fuels, alternative sources of energy have become necessary and relevant to the world at present. The sun and wind can never be exhausted and remain constant source of energy therefore they are called renewable. It is the source of energy which can reduce significantly chemical, radioactive and thermal pollution. So the energy is considered clean and non-polluting. As it is searing question to the world now how constant and pollutionless energy can be got needed for transport, industries and households requirement, the answer is solar.

Solar energy is the most readily available source of energy. It does not belong to anybody and is, therefore, free. It is also the most important of the non-conventional sources of energy because it is non-polluting and, therefore, helps in lessening the greenhouse effect. Solar energy has been used since prehistoric times, but in a most primitive manner. French physicist Edund Bequerel discovered that sunlight could also produce electricity. The knowledge of the sun's ability to produce both heat and energy has led to the invention of numerous technologies for capturing energy of the sun. At recent tine many technologies as photovoltaic, solar thermal electric system, solar hot water system and passive solar building design are being used to get energy form the sun. In the modern age, solar power technology arrived in 1954 when Bell Laboratories, experimenting with semiconductors, accidentally found that silicon doped with certain impurities was very sensitive to light. This resulted in the production of the first practical solar cells with a sunlight energy conversion efficiency of around 6 percent. [The first spacecraft to use solar panels was the US satellite Vanguard 1, launched in March 1958 with solar cells made by Hoffman Electronics. This milestone created interest in producing and launching a geostationary communications satellite, in which solar energy would provide a viable power supply.] This was a crucial development which stimulated funding from several governments into research for improved solar cells. In 1970 the first highly effective Ga As heterostructure solar cells were created by Zhores Alferov and his team in the USSR. Metal Organic Chemical Vapor Deposition (MOCVD, or OMCVD) production equipment was not developed until the early 1980s, limiting the ability of companies to manufacture the GaAs solar cell. In the United States, the first 17 percent efficient air mass zero (AM0) single-junction GaAs solar cells were manufactured in production quantities in 1988 by Applied Solar Energy Corporation (ASEC). The "dual junction" cell was accidentally produced in quantity by ASEC in 1989 as a result of the change from GaAs on GaAs substrates to GaAs on Germanium (Ge) substrates. The accidental doping of Ge with the GaAs buffer layer created higher open circuit voltages, demonstrating the potential of using the Ge substrate as another cell. As GaAs single-junction cells topped 19 percent AM0 production efficiency in 1993, ASEC developed the first dual junction cells for spacecraft use in the United States, with a starting efficiency of approximately 20 percent. These cells did not utilize the Ge as a second cell, but used another GaAs-based cell with different doping. Eventually GaAs dual junction cells reached production efficiencies of about 22 percent. Triple Junction solar cells began with AM0 efficiencies of approximately 24 percent in 2000, 26 percent in 2002, 28 percent in 2005, and in 2007 have evolved to 30 percent AM0 production efficiency currently. Recent world record claims of efficiency for multiple junction solar cells.

Photovoltaic cell (solar cell) is method of generating electric power by converting solar radiation into direct electricity using semiconductors that exhibit the photovoltaic effect.

A **solar cell** or **photovoltaic cell** is a device that converts solar energy into electricity by the photovoltaic effect. Sometimes, the term solar cell is reserved for devices intended specifically to capture energy from sunlight, while the term photovoltaic cell is used when the source is unspecified. Assemblies of cells are used to make solar panel, solar modules, or photovoltaic arrays. Photovoltaic is the field of technology and research related to the application of solar cells for solar energy. The term "photovoltaic" comes from the Greek ward (phos) meaning "light," and "voltaic," meaning electric, from the name of the Italian physicist Volta, after whom a unit of electrical potential, the volt, is named. The term "photo-voltaic" has been in use in English since 1849.

The photovoltaic effect was first recognized in 1839 by French physicist A. E. Becquerel. However, it was not until 1883 that the first solar cell was built, by Charles Fritts, who coated the semiconductor selenium with an extremely thin layer of glod to form the junctions. The device was only around 1 percent efficient. Sven Ason Berglund had a number of patents concerning methods of increasing the capacity of these cells. Russell Ohl patented the modern junction semiconductor solar cell in 1946 (U.S. Patent 2402662 (PDF), "Light sensitive device"), which was discovered while working on the series of advances that would lead to the transistor.

THREE GENERATIONS OF SOLAR CELLS

Solar Cells are classified into three generations which indicates the order of which each became important. At present there is concurrent research into all three generations while the first generation technologies are most highly represented in commercial production, accounting for 89.6 percent of 2007 production.

First Generation

First generation cells consist of large-area, high quality and single junction devices. First Generation technologies involve high energy and labor inputs which prevent any significant progress in reducing production costs. Single junction silicon devices are approaching the theoretical limiting efficiency of 33 percent and achieve cost parity with fossil fuel energy generation after a payback period of 5-7 years. They are not likely to get lower than US$1/W.

Second Generation

Second generation materials have been developed to address energy requirements and production costs of solar cells. Alternative manufacturing techniques such as vapor deposition, electroplating, and use of Ultrasonic Nozzles are advantageous as they reduce high temperature processing significantly. It is commonly accepted that as manufacturing techniques evolve production costs will be dominated by constituent material requirements, whether this be a silicon substrate, or glass cover. Second generation technologies are expected to gain market share in 2008.

Such processes can bring costs down to a little under US$0.50/W but because of the defects inherent in the lower quality processing methods, have much reduced efficiencies compared to First Generation.

The most successful second generation materials have been cadmium telluride (CdTe), copper indium gallium solenoid, amorphous silicon and micromorphous silicon. These materials are applied in a thin film to a supporting substrate such as glass or ceramics reducing material mass and therefore costs. These technologies do hold promise of higher conversion efficiencies, particularly CIGS-CIS, DSC and CdTe offers significantly cheaper production costs.

Among major manufacturers there is certainly a trend toward second generation technologies however commercialization of these technologies has proven difficult. In 2007, First Solar produced 200 MW of CdTe solar cells making it the fifth largest producer of solar cells in 2007 and the first ever to reach the top ten from production of second generation technologies alone. Wurth Solar commercialized its CIS technology in 2007 producing 15 MW. Nanosolar commercialized its CIGS technology in 2007 with a production capacity of 430 MW for 2008 in the USA and Germany. Honda Soltec Co., Ltd., a Honda company, also began to commercialize their CIGS base solar panel in 2008.

In 2007, CdTe production represented 4.7 percent of total market share, thin-film silicon 5.2 percent and CIGS 0.5 percent

Third Generation

Third generation technologies aim to enhance poor electrical performance of second generation (thin-film technologies) while maintaining very low production costs.Current research is targeting conversion efficiencies of 30-60 percent while retaining low cost materials and manufacturing techniques. They can exceed the theoretical solar conversion efficiency limit for a single energy threshold material that was calculated in 1961 by Shockley and Queisser as 31 percent under 1 sun illumination and 40.8 percent under maximal concentration of sunlight (46,200 suns, which makes the latter limit more difficult to approach than the former).

There are a few approaches to achieving these high efficiencies:

Multifunction photovoltaic cell (multiple energy threshold devices).

Modifying incident spectrum (concentration).

Use of excess thermal generation (caused by UV light) to enhance voltages or carrier collection.

Use of infrared spectrum to produce electricity at night.

Technologies includes:

- Silicon nanostructures
- Up/Down converters
- Hot-carrier cells
- Thermoelectric cells

High Efficiency Cells

High efficiency solar cells are a class of **solar cells** that can generate electricity at higher efficiencies than conventional solar cells. While high efficiency solar cells are more efficient in terms of electrical output per incident energy (watt/watt), much of the industry is focused on the most cost efficient technologies (cost-per-watt or $/watt). Still, many businesses and academics are focused on increasing the electrical efficiency of cells, and much development is focused on high efficiency solar cells.

First Industry Partner to Develop Next Generation Solar Inverters

As the first industry partner to use ESIF, Advanced Energy Industries is testing its new solar photovoltaic (PV) inverter technology with the facility's utility-scale grid simulators and hardware-in-the-loop systems. Solar inverters are responsible for a number of critical functions within a solar PV system, including converting the direct current output into alternating current for the grid. Advanced Energy's inverter will help support a smarter grid that can handle two-way flows of power and communication while reducing hardware costs.

In the last four years, solar generation in the U.S. has more than doubled, while at the same time the costs of photovoltaic systems have dropped 80%. As more and more solar power contributes to the U.S. energy mix, lower cost advanced solar inverters will help usher in an increasingly diverse electricity portfolio, while providing American consumers and businesses with reliable and affordable energy options.

Congress provided $135 million to construct and equip the user facility. The President's FY 2014 budget request includes an additional $20 million for facility operations. The Department encourages utilities, manufacturers, universities and other national labs to fully utilize ESIF's unique capabilities and resources. Find more information on the Energy Systems Integration Facility.

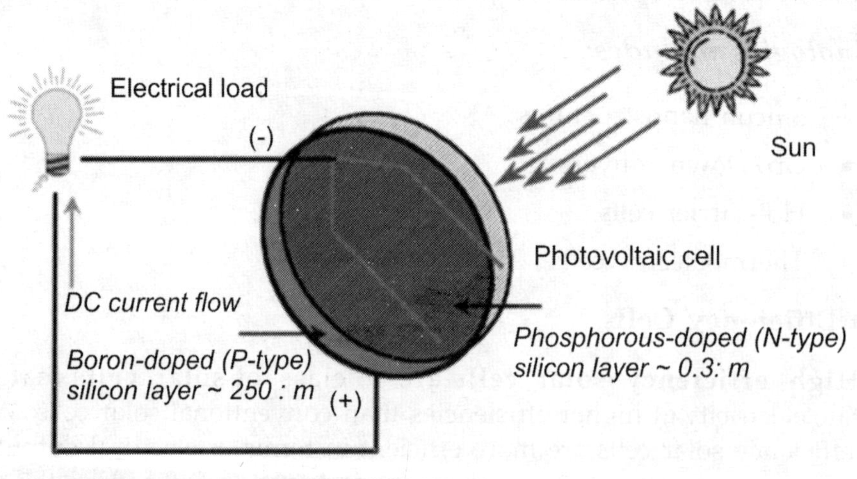

Semiconductor is a poor electric conductor as a consequence of having just the right number of electrons to completely fill its valance bond.

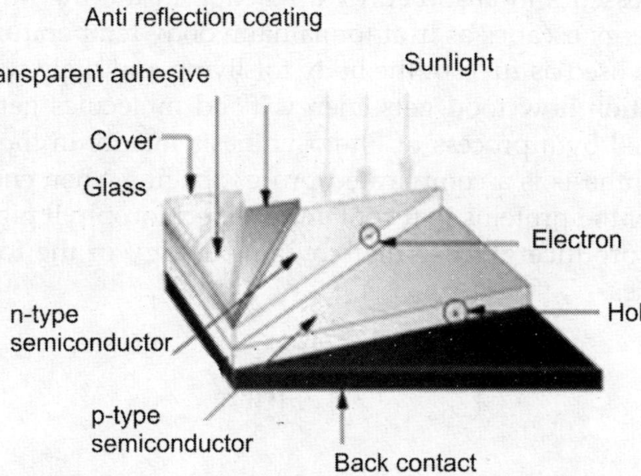

Some research and development was carried out in a few countries to exploit solar energy more efficiently, but most of this work remained mainly academic. After the dramatic rise in oil prices in the 1970s, several countries began to formulate extensive research and development programmes to exploit solar energy. When we hang out our clothes to dry in the sun, we use the energy of the sun. In the same way, solar panels absorb the energy of the sun to provide heat for cooking and for heating water. Such systems are available in the market and are being used in homes and factories. In the next few years it is expected that millions of households in the world will be using solar energy as the trends in USA and Japan. In India too, the Indian Renewable Energy Development Agency and the Ministry of Non-Conventional Energy Sources are formulating a programme to have solar energy in more than a million households in the next few years. However, the people's initiative is essential if the programme is to be successful. Solar photovoltaic is now, after hydro and wind power, the third most important renewable energy source in terms of globally installed capacity.

It is said that we float in the ocean of energy. The space is filled with an energy called "Dark Energy/vacuum energy "that permeates all of space and tends to accelerate the expansion of the universe. In 1998, "Observations of Type La Supernovae by High-Z-supernovae search team followed by "Supernovae Cosmology Project" in 1999 suggested that the universe is accelerating and "Nobel Prize" was awarded for this work in 2011. Recently observations estimated that space consists of 68.3% Dark Energy a combination of 26.8% dark matter 4.9% of baryonic matter.

Living being also needs energy to remain alive and do daily activities. Large food molecules contain energy comes from sun in the form of chemical bonds but it requires good deal of complex chemical reaction to liberate the energy. The process of liberation happens in the cells of the body of living being. The energy is produced in the cytosol of cells. Large food molecules which are processed and absorbed by a reaction inside the Mitochondria of the cell. The energy escapes as heat to maintain body temperature and supply energy which is used as fuels of the body for living and daily work. Now it is important question how food gets energy .Food molecules get energy from the sun produced by a process of Photosynthesis mainly in the leaves of the plants. Photosynthesis is a complicated process begins when energy from the sun absorbed by the proteins that contains green chlorophyll pigment. By this process plants produce glucose that contains energy in the food, the other living being takes.

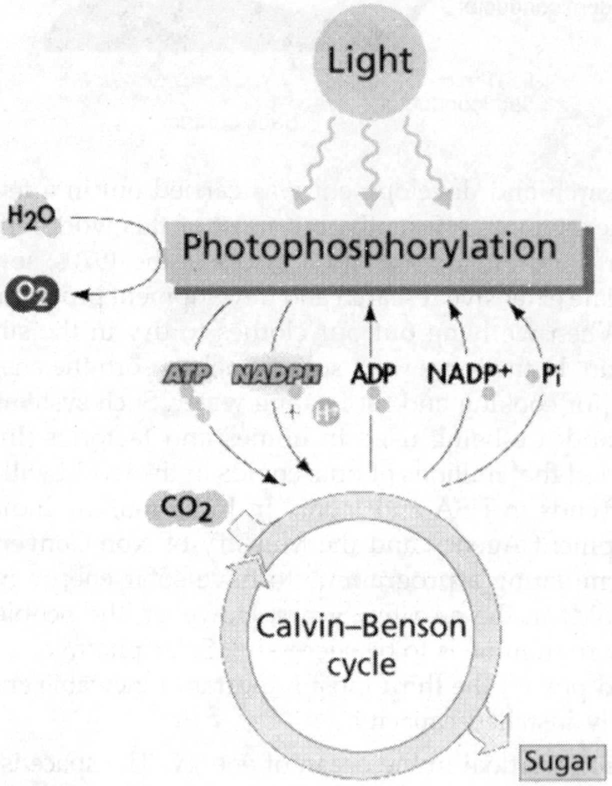

At present energy is being obtained also from nuclear. Nuclear energy is the energy that is trapped inside each atom. The ancient Greeks believed that the smallest part of nature is an atom. But they did not know 2000 years ago that atoms are made up of further smaller particles—a nucleus of protons and neutrons, surrounded by electrons, which swirl around the nucleus much like the earth revolves around the sun.

One of the laws of the universe is that matter and energy can neither be created nor destroyed. But they can be changed in form. Matter can be changed into energy. Albert Einstein's famous mathematical formula $E = mc^2$ explains this. The equation says: E [energy] equals m [mass] times c^2 [c stands for the speed or velocity of light]. This means that it is mass multiplied by the square of the velocity of light. Scientists used Einstein's equation as the key to unlock atomic energy and to create atomic bombs. An atom's nucleus can be split apart. This is known as fission. When this is done, a tremendous amount of energy in the form of both heat and light is released by the initiation of a chain reaction. This energy, when slowly released, can be harnessed to generate electricity. When it is released all at once, it results in a tremendous explosion as in an atomic bomb.

Nuclear energy can also be harnessed by fusion. A fusion reaction occurs when two hydrogen atoms combine to produce one helium atom. This reaction takes place at all times in the sun, which provides us with the solar energy. This technology is still at the experimental stage and may become viable in future. Uranium is the main element required to run a nuclear reactor where energy is extracted. Uranium is mined from many places around the world. It is processed (to get enriched uranium, i.e. the radioactive isotope) into tiny pellets. These pellets are loaded into long rods that are put into the power plant's reactor. Inside the reactor of an atomic power plant, uranium atoms are split apart in controlled chain reaction. Other fossile material includes plutonium and thorium. In a chain reaction, particles released by the splitting of the atom strike other uranium atoms and split them. The particles released by this further split other atoms in a chain process. In nuclear power plants, control rods are used to keep the splitting regulated, so that it does not occur too fast. These are called moderators. The chain reaction gives off heat energy. This heat energy is used to boil heavy water in the core of the reactor. So, instead of burning a fuel, nuclear power plants use the energy released by the chain reaction to change the energy of atoms into heat energy. The heavy water from around the nuclear core is sent to another section of the power plant. Here it heats another set of pipes filled with water to make steam. The steam in this second set of pipes rotates a turbine to generate electricity. If the reaction is not controlled, you could have an atomic bomb. But in atomic bombs, almost pure pieces of uranium-235 or plutonium, of a precise mass and shape, must be brought together and held together with great force. These conditions are not present in a nuclear reactor. The reaction also creates radioactive material. This material could hurt people if released, so it is kept in a solid form. A strong concrete dome is built around the reactor to prevent this material from escaping in case of an accident. Experiences with nuclear programmes differ and the future of nuclear power remains uncertain because of public reaction. But in the past few years the capacity of operating nuclear plants has increased more than twentyfold. There are more than 400 nuclear power plants providing about 7% of the world's primary energy and about 25% of the electric power in industrialized nations. The growth of nuclear power combined with the shift from carbon-heavy fuels such as coal and oil to carbon-light gas contribute to the gradual 'de-carbonization' of the world energy system. Chernobyl, Three Mile Island, Fukushima Nuclear power Plant in Japan accident due to tsunami on 11th march'2011 and other nuclear accidents have increased the fear harnessing nuclear energy. Another issue with international and local implications is the storage and disposal of radioactive wastes: both from nuclear reactors making electricity and from the production of military weapons. Earlier disposal practices, such as dumping of nuclear waste at sea, have been completely stopped by formal treaty because of environmental concerns (and by cessation of furtive scuttling of nuclear submarines). Regimes for transport and temporary storage of civil and defense nuclear wastes now function, although sites and designs for permanent disposal have yet to be accepted. People are concerned about both low- and high-level radioactive wastes; the latter, though smaller in volume is more technically problematic. With the rise of nuclear electrification, the volume of spent fuel and other wastes has risen substantially; but is still small in some countries such as the US, the volume of high-level waste from commercial power plants has now reached hundreds of millions tones.

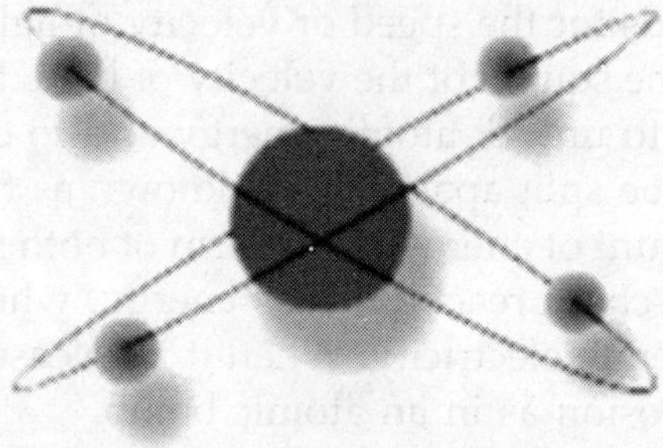

Actual Power Supply Position

The country has been facing growing shortages over the past five years. During the year 2007-08 (1st year of 11th Plan), the peak deficit was about 18,000 MW (16.5%) and the average Energy Shortage in the country was about 73 Billion kWh (10%). During the year 2008-09 (2nd year of 11th Plan), the peak deficit was about 13,000 MW (12%) and the average energy shortage in the country was about 86 Billion kWh (11%). During the year 2009-10 (3rd year of 11th Plan), the peak deficit wasabout 15,157 MW (12.7%) and the average energy shortage in the country was about 84 Billion kWh(10.1%).[4]

Solar Energy

Solar energy has the greatest potential of all the sources of renewable energy. If only a small amount of this form of energy could be used, it will be one of the most important supplies of energy specially when other sources in the country have depleted energy comes to the earth from the sun. This energy keeps the temperature of the earth above than in colder space, causes current in the atmosphere and in ocean. It causes the water cycle and generates photosynthesis in plants. The solar power where sun hits atmosphere is 101W. The solar power on the surface of earth is 1016W. The total worldwide power demand of all needs of civilization is 113W. Therefore, the sun gives us 1000 times more power than we need. If we can use 5% of this energy, it will be 50 times what the world will require electrical energy that can be produced from the solar energy by photovoltaic solar cells. SPV cell converts the solar energy directly to electrical energy. The most significant applications of SPV cells in India are the energization of pump sets for irrigation, drinking water supply and rural electrification covering street lights, community TV sets, medical refrigerators and other small power loads. Sunshine available in India is for nearly 300 days in a year.

Solar Map of India

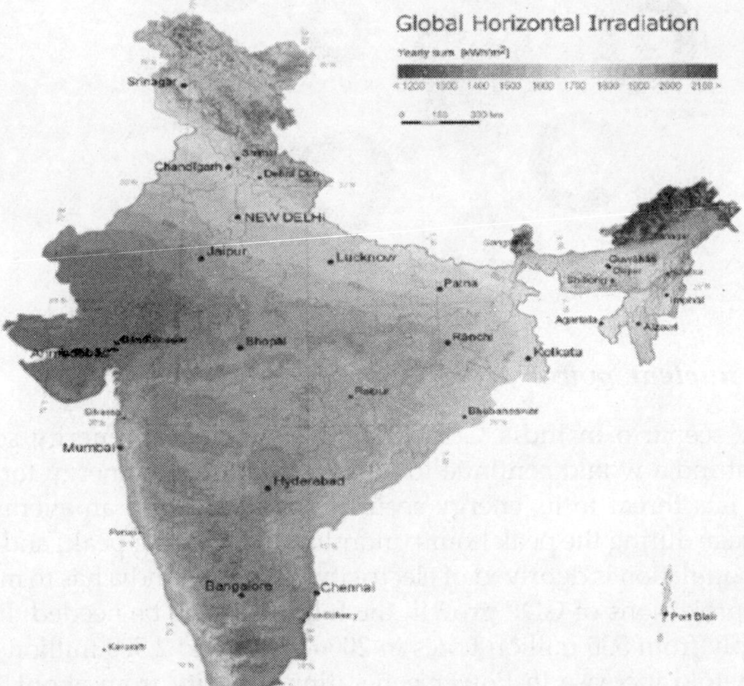

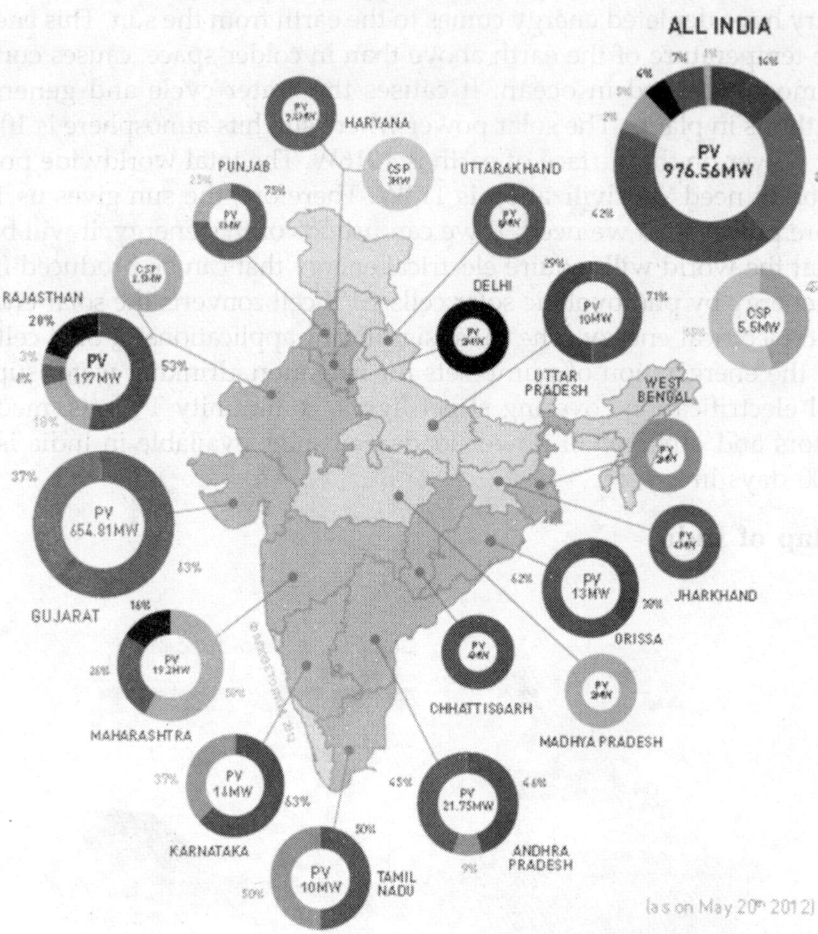

India has nuclear power projects as given below

Energy scenario in India Critical analysis of Indian energy scenario suggests that India would continue to be a net importer of energy for a long time which is a threat to its energy security. India faces on an average 17% power shortage during the peak hours (morning and evening peak) and almost 40% of our population is deprived of electricity till date. If India has to maintain the present projections of GDP growth the following will be needed: Increase in Coal supply from 500 million tones in 2006-07 to over 2,500 million tons in 2031-32 . Six-fold increase in Power generating capacity from about 150,000 MW to 900,000 MW in 2032.This will enhance GHG (Green House Gases) emission level by manifold. Therefore, energy efficiency and application of renewable energy in domestic, commercial & industrial sectors is imperative for India to meet the goals of economic development as well as achieve the target towards emission reduction. To achieve energy security, Government of India has initiated number of programmes targeting energy conservation, improving energy use efficiency and promoting optimal energy.

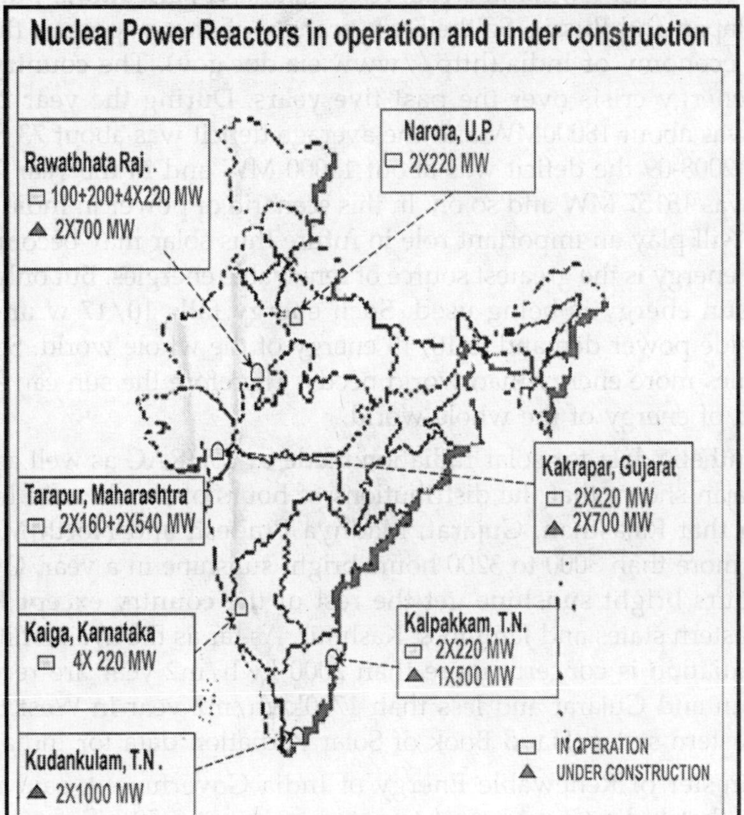

The long term potential of various renewable energy sources in the country and status of utilization (as on 31.12.2010) are as follows.

Energy Source	Potential(MW)	Achievement(MW)
Biomas	16880	997
Biogas	5000	1562
Wind	45000	13065
Small Hydro	15000	2939
Urban & Industrial Waste	2700	72
Solar	900,000@ 1% land use	17

(*Source:* MNRE website)

India is now the 11th largest economy and 4th largest purchasing power in the world. India has emerged as one of the leading destination for investors from developed countries due to lower cost of manpower and good quality of production. In spite of global financial crisis, energy demand in India increases rapidly for industrial, commercial, residential and agricultural purposes than China, Japan and Russia. So the acute scarcity of energy poses a threat on the overall economy of India.(http//www.eia.doc.gov). The country has been facing energy crisis over the past five years. During the year 2007-08 the deficit was about 18000MW and the average deficit was about 73 Billion KW. During 2008-09 the deficit was about 13000 MW and in the year 2009-10 the deficit was 15157 MW and so on. In this scenario of power in India alternative energy will play an important role in future thus solar may become as savior as solar energy is the greatest source of renewable energies. But only negligible of the sun energy is being used. Such energy falls 10/17 w and the total worldwide power demand is 10/13 energy of the whole world. So sun gives 1000 times more energy than world needs. Therefore the sun can solely meet demand of energy of the whole world.

Synthetic data for solar radiation made by ISHRAC as well as Mani and Rangarajan shows that the distributions of hours of sunshine in India. It can be seen that Rajasthan, Gujarat, Madhya Pradesh and North Maharashtra receive more than 3000 to 3200 hours bright sunshine in a year. Over 2600 to 2800 hours bright sunshine get the rest of the country except Kerala, the north eastern states and Jammu & Kashmir. As far as the availability of global solar radiation is concern, more than 2000 kwh/m2 year are received over Rajasthan and Gujarat and less than 1700kwh/m2 year in West Bengal and north-eastern states.(Hand Book of Solar Radiation data for India By Moni).

Minister of Renewable Energy of India Government, said recently in London that India Government targeted to invest $ 50 billion in renewable sector in India in the next five years. India has seen an impressive increase in installed power capacity from 1350 MW at the time of independence, 65 years ago to about 2, 00,000 MW at present. Still now the average per capita consumption of energy in India quite low at around 800 units per annum and stands 5th position in terms of renewable energy capacity after US,China,Germany and Spain. India Government has decided to increase the share of renewable energy in power production during 12th plan period by enhancing the installed capacity about 30,000MW. The Ministry has started the ambitious "Jaharlal Nehru National Solar Mission" which aims to harness 22,000Mw of solar by 2022.The challenge not only before India but before whole world in the solar energy sector to reduce the cost of generation by inventing new technologies. Therefore India has started encouraging easy cost friendly technology, indigenous research and development. In spite of growing the supply of energy, the price of energy has been rising day by day thus it is not keeping pace with the demand. So solar power despite initial challenges is becoming an important. For this reason India has turned the focus on solar power led by **Jawaharlal Nehru National Solar Mission** (JNNSM). Solar will become a crucial component of India's energy portfolio in the next decade. The research and survey in this regard have given three major conclusions.

a) India's solar market could be worth billions of dollars over next decade.

b) Project execution, financing and localization are crucial.

c) Local players will dominate the solar industry.

The JNNSM has targeted to reach 20 gigawatts by 2022.but based on electricity demand growth and rising cost of fossil fuel , it is estimated that the solar power capacity will reach more than [50 gigawatts] by 2022.The solar industries will rapidly evolve as solar reaches grid parity with conventional power between 2016 and 2018.The newer inventions will lead the solar power cheap prices will continue falling over next year and it will become as much as 15% lower than that of the most expensive grid connected conventional energy. JNNSM has started programme in Gujarat and Rajasthan which will add 12 to 14 gigawatts to the grid connected utilities. The market will see a dramatic change in the last part of the decade in solar scenario as domestic business of solar power potential is huge in India for its typical size, available infrastructure and negligible security issue.

ENERGY USING IN INDIA [Figure 3 : All India Installed Capacity (as on 31st December, 2011)]

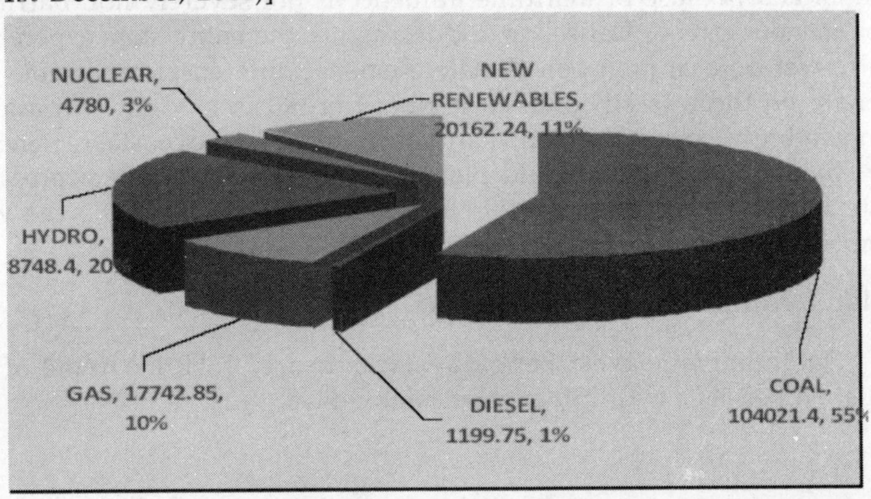

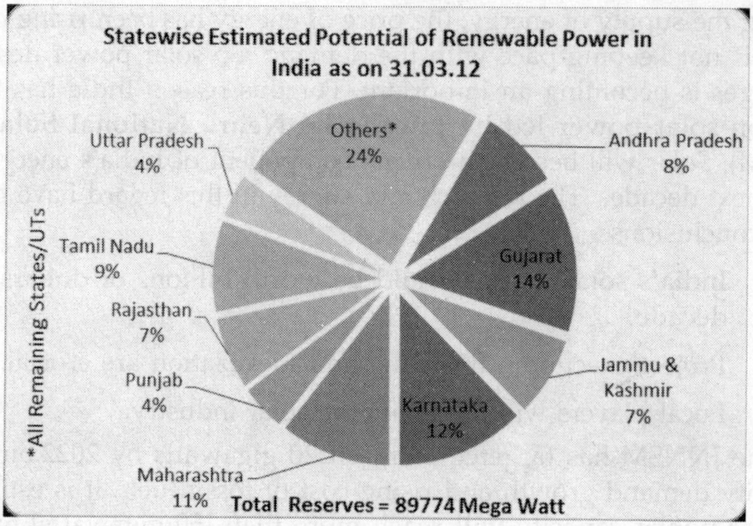

West Bengal Solar Scenario

West Bengal located in the eastern part of the country with population (2011) of 91,347,736 which is the 4th largest and density of 1,029.2/km2 (2,665.7/sq mi).

The annual rainfall varies in the different parts of the state. North Bengal receives the highest rainfall, 200 to 400 cm.

The Tropic of Cancer passes 6 km north of Nabadwip, so, according to latitude, the northern part of the state falls in the temperate belt and the southern part fall in the tropical belt. But the southern part receives adequate rainfall and because of maritime influence is not severely hot. Barring the mountainous pats of Darjeeling and Jalpaiguri, the entire state experiences a warm wet tropical monsoon climate. Regional differences are visible in the climate. In the western plateau region, rainfall is low and variations in temperature are more common; maritime influence in the coastal region makes the climate here moderate and pleasant. The summer temperatures in the state ranges between 26 °C (79 °F) and 40 °C (104 °F) while the winter temperatures range from 13 °C (55 °F) to 19 °C (66 °F).

Solar Irradiation in West Bengal

On an average West Bengal receives nearly 1600 kWh/m2 of solar radiation per year with 250 average sunny days.

Solar irradiation data of West Bengal cities monthwise

City	Jan	Feb	Mar	Apr	May	Jun	July	Aug	Sep	Oct	Nov	Dec	Avg
Asansol	4.1	4.97	5.7	6.11	6.09	4.96	4.33	4.13	4.08	4.39	4.26	4	4.76
Baranagar	4.13	4.89	5.59	5.99	5.79	4.49	4.09	3.9	3.88	4.32	4.21	4.02	4.61
Barasat	4.13	4.89	5.59	5.99	5.79	4.49	4.09	3.9	3.88	4.32	4.21	4.02	4.61
Barddhaman	4.1	4.97	5.7	6.11	6.09	4.96	4.33	4.13	4.08	4.39	4.26	4	4.76
Haora	4.13	4.89	5.59	5.99	5.79	4.49	4.09	3.9	3.88	4.32	4.21	4.02	4.61
Kamarhati	4.13	4.89	5.59	5.99	5.79	4.49	4.09	3.9	3.88	4.32	4.21	4.02	4.61
Kulti	4.19	5.01	5.59	6.01	6.11	4.85	4.24	4.05	4.06	4.45	4.21	4	4.73
Naihati	4.13	4.89	5.59	5.99	5.79	4.49	4.09	3.9	3.88	4.32	4.21	4.02	4.61
Nangi	4.13	4.89	5.59	5.99	5.79	4.49	4.09	3.9	3.88	4.32	4.21	4.02	4.61
Panihati	4.13	4.89	5.59	5.99	5.79	4.49	4.09	3.9	3.88	4.32	4.21	4.02	4.61
Siliguri	4.03	4.95	5.82	6.14	5.97	4.95	4.19	4.24	3.96	4.76	4.47	4	4.79

Solar irradiation measured in kwh/m2/day onto a horizontal surface

2MW Solar Plant in West Bengal by Jamuria

West Bengal has commissioned the 2MW India's largest grid connected solar power plant in India at Jamuria, near Asansol. The project had been set up under West Bengal Green Energy Development Corporation Ltd and the power purchase agreement had been signed with DPSC Ltd at a price of Rs.5/ per unit. The project had entailed an investment of Rs.360 million and is funded by Power Finance Corp with a debt: equity ratio of 70:30.

5MW Solar Plant in West Bengal by Astonfield Renewable Sources

Astonfield Renewable Sources Ltd is setting up a 5MW solar photo-voltaic plant in Bankura district of West Bengal with an investment of $20 million. Astonfield Renewable Sources Ltd signed a power purchase agreement with WBSEB.

ONGC Solar Project

ONGC, Kolkata based solar EPC company Vikram Solar and an US based player have taken initial interest in developing solar project at Purulia district in West Bengal.

WBGECL is Looking for Nano Solar Cell Technology Projects

West Bengal Green Energy Corp Ltd (WBGECL) is keen to set up projects with nano technology photovoltaic – cell projects and related R&D into the state. The nano PV cells are most efficient and reduce overall cost of power production. WBGECL has signed an agreement with universities to understand technology by training up scientist at lab level.

World's Largest Solar Complex

In 2008, Bhaskar Silicon Ltd launched the largest integrated solar power complex in the world for an investment of Rs.55 billion in Haldia. The plant would generate 250MW of solar power annually.

Government Initiatives for Solar Energy in West Bengal

Solar energy is being utilized in West Bengal, mainly for village electrification programme. However, there are some applications in respect of Solar Thermal energy programme also. The State of West Bengal has made significant progress in respect of village electrification through Solar PV route. There are about 2,000 villages in west Bengal where conventional electric line cannot be extended due to prohibitive cost. 400 villages out of these 2000 villages have already been electrified by Solar PV route.

Two Types of PV systems are being utilized for village electrification

- Solar Home Lighting system with 40 WP/50 WP/70 WP SPV Module.
- Centralised Solar PV Power Plants of capacity 25-50 kW range and setting up of mini grids in the villages from where people get grid quality electricity.

The total Solar PV installed capacity in the State of West Bengal has exceeded 1 MW recently.

There are more than 15 Stand Alone type Power Plants in Sundarabans area of west Bengal operating for about last 5 years in revenue-oriented mode. Micro level entrepreneurs are maintaining the Solar Home Lighting Systems.

The number of which has crossed eighty thousand. Every year about Ten thousand solar consumers are being added in the state. West Bengal Renewable Energy Development Agency in association with MNES, Govt. of India is formulating a major scheme to set up about 200 nos. of SPV Power Plants of capacity 25 kW to 100 kW for electrification of entire Sundarabans Islands, which has unique eco-system in the whole world.

WBREDA has also installed a large number of Solar Street lights in different remote areas of West Bengal, particularly in Jetties and Forest areas. The total number of Solar PV Street Lights working in the State has exceeded 2,000. Recently WBREDA has installed some solar street lights in the city of Kolkata.

In order to make available the Solar PV system at doorsteps WBREDA has set up a large number of Aditya Solar Shops and Rural Aditya in different parts of West Bengal. The main Aditya solar shops are being looked after by WBREDA and Rural Aditya Solar Shops are being looked after by private entrepreneurs.

In the area of Solar Thermal, WBREDA has so far installed more than 5 lacs liters/day Solar Water Heating Systems and sold more than 10,000 Solar Cookers in the State. WBREDA has a plan to install 50,000 Solar Home Lighting Systems in the State during the next five years. A large number of families in the city of Kolkata is now using Solar Water Heating system.

For Street Lighting System, WBREDA will maintain the system, initially for 05 years at free of cost. However, necessary up keeping measures like regular cleaning of module, cutting of tree branches(if required), periodic top up of battery with distilled water (distilled water will be supplied by WBREDA) are to be ensured by users for sustenance of systems. Systems are to be installed at shadow free areas and security of systems will be the responsibility of users.

No commercial organization is entitled to avail capital subsidy for solar PV street lighting programme. Govt. organization/ Govt. aided organization/ registered NGOs may apply to obtain capital subsidy in respect of Solar PV street lighting system.

The application is to be written to the Director, WBREDA in their respective letter head of the applicant mentioning the quantity required, specific location of installation, utility of the system. The application must be vetted through the local Panchayet Samity/ Chairman of Municipal Authority.

After due scrutiny of the application, WBREDA may issue subsidy sanction order and may intimate the applicant to place their contribution to WBREDA. After availability of the users' contribution at WBREDA; WBREDA will do the work through its selected agencies (through tendering process) as per govt. norms. WBREDA may reject the application also.

No subsidy will be granted for SPV-SLS which are not used for community purpose. It may be noted that Hon'ble Member of the Parliament/Hon'ble Member of the Legislative Assembly/Panchayet Samity/Zilla Parishad may provide the user contribution from their respective head of fund for installation of Solar PV SLS.

For MP LADS / BEUP the norms are as follows

- The Hon'ble MP/ MLA may write to WBREDA mentioning the quantity of requirement, area of installation and utility of systems
- WBREDA will then send a reply mentioning availability of subsidy

and detailed description, specifications of system

- The Hon'ble Member may then forward the proposal of WBREDA to the respective District Magistrate (D.M.) for sanctioning the project
- After due scrutiny, as per guidelines; the D.M. office, then may sanction the project and issue a sanction letter
- WBREDA will then collect the fund from the D.M. office
- WBREDA will then physically implement the project at site.

Normally it takes 45 to 60 days to install such system at a particular location in and around Kolkata after receipt of user contribution by WBREDA.

It may take 65 to 80 days for balance districts of West Bengal – after availability of user contribution by WBREDA. At present per system user contribution is Rs. 5,500/-.

The subsidy pattern may change time to time as per prevailing scheme of the Govt. of India and Govt. of West Bengal.

From a 1 sq. meter SWHS, 50 liters hot water is available per day. From this system, hot water is available almost for 365 days in a year with average temperature in the tune of 400 to 950 C. The life of the system is 20 years. The way to avail subsidy for the SWHS is same as Solar PV Street Lighting System. First, the user has to place application. Then WBREDA will sanction the application and will issue subsidy sanction letter for eligible application (or will communicate the reason for its not sanction). After receipt of sanction; the applicant will have to place their user contribution portion to WBREDA. After receipt of fund, WBREDA will install the system within 60 days from the date receipt of fund. The subsidy pattern may change time to time as per prevailing scheme of the Govt. of India and Govt. of West Bengal.

Solar Cookers

For midday meal preparation, Solar Cooker may be installed. If sunlight is available, any item (except fry) can be cooked tentatively within one hour. Each cooker (tentative cost with container is Rs.20,000/-) can prepare meal for 15 people at a time. The Zilla Parishad/Interested School Authority may send a list of schools with commitment for at least 50% contribution from their end. WBREDA may arrange for balance fund. In West Bengal, Solar Cooker can be used for cooking approximately for 320 days in a year. This will function for a long time, until and unless it is broken by any external reason. This will reduce the quantity of fire wood consumption and also reduce the pollution level. Govt. subsidy is available. Family size solar cooker are also available in the market of domestic use.

Solar Passive Architecture

WBREDA has constructed its four-storied Administrative Building with Solar Passive Architecture Concept. In addition, the Administrative Building of WBREDA has a 25 kW Grid Interactive Roof Top Solar PV Power Plant. In the building, net-metering concept has been adopted and a MOU has been signed with State Electricity Board in this respect. One 25 kW Roof Top SPV Power Plant is already operating since 1998 at Bidyut Bhavan, Kolkata.

WBREDA has taken up a programme to establish one Eco-friendly Housing Complex at New Town, Kolkata where 25 Nos. of homes are being built up with solar passive and active concept. The integrated solar building are being constructed under this programme. In addition, the sewerage system of the building will be connected with a Community Biogas Plant from where gas will be supplied to a community Center being constructed in the Housing Complex. The land development work and system engineering works are in progress. This will be the first Solar Housing Complex of he country.

Contact us today for a free solar evaluation of your home and business to get started

Solar radiation is abundantly available in West Bengal. The best solar insulation is available at western part of state (Bankura, Purulia & West Medinipur Districts). For the balance portion of the state, 320 sunny days in a year is available.

Bengal Renewable Energy Development Agency (WBREDA) is working with Renewable Energy & energy Efficiency in the state of West Bengal. The main objectives of such works are :-

- To provide electricity in un-electrified areas
- Chopping the peak demand of electricity from conventional sources
- To mitigate climate change problems
- To ensure energy security of the country

Potential of Renewable Power in the State of West Bengal

1.	Wind Power Potential	-	450 MW
2.	Biomass Potential	-	350 MW
3.	Small Hydro	-	300 MW(including canal drop)
4.	Solar PV (assuming 1% of the state)	-	16000 MW
5.	Solar Roof Top	-	300 MW
6.	Solar Thermal	-	400 MW (Electricity equivalent)
7.	Waste to Energy	-	150 MW

Total: 17,900 MW

Solar Photovoltaic Programmes:- [Here electricity is produced from Sun Light]: Solar Lantern, Home Lighting System, Street Lighting System, Solar Inverter, Solar Power Plant, Solar Generator, Remote Village Electrification, Solar Powered Signboard, Solar Powered Mobile Tower, Solar Pump, Solar PV Electrification at School, College, Institutions.

Solar Thermal Programme:- [Here heat energy of the sun is utilized]: Solar Water Heating Systems for domestic premises, institution & commercial establishments. Solar Cooker for individual, community and commercial use; Solar Drier, Solar Air-conditioning System.

Battery operated vehicle:- Battery operated Two Wheeler, Three Wheeler; Four Wheelers are being promoted by WBREDA. So far, more than 10 thousands battery operated two wheelers have been sold in West Bengal. Remote Village Electrification (RVE) :- Providing electricity at remote & isolated locations through solar photovoltaic Systems. More than 100 such villages have been electrified so far.

Remote Village Electrification (RVE) :- Providing electricity at remote & isolated locations through solar photovoltaic Systems. More than 100 such villages have been electrified so far

- Rabirashmi Abasan:-: The first Solar Housing complexion the country at New Town, Kolkata.
- Small Hydro project:- Small Hydro Projects for rural electrification, institutional electrification, supply of electricity to the grid etc.
- Tidal Power:- A scheme for production of electricity from the tides is being conceived at Durgadowani, Gosaba.
- Energy from Municipal Solid Waste:- Some technology demonstration projects at Howrah Municipal Corporation, Baruipur Municipality, South Dum Dum Municipality, English Bazaar Municipality have been initiated.
- Geothermal Energy:- Investigation is being taken up.
- Information & Public Awareness:- Different programmes for creating large scale public awareness among the people: Participation in Fairs & Exhibitions, Display Boards, Demonstration Programmes, Publications, Aditya Solar Shop (Alipore, Durgapur, Siliguri), Renewable Energy Clubs etc.
- Capacity Building:- Training programmes at technician level, engineers level etc. for capacity building. WBREDA provides support for research works in Renewable Energy & climate change.

- Energy Efficiency Programme:- Through different measures (procurement of energy efficient appliances and use of appliances in efficient manner); conservation of electricity can be done and this saved electricity can be supplied to unelectrified areas. WBREDA works for Energy efficiency by large scale public awareness through publication, exhibition, display, demonstration, training programmes etc.
- Only one grid connceted solar PV project has been installed so far in West Bengal,having capacity- 1MW at Jamuria near Asansol . One project has been installed at a school near Tollygunj, Kolkata, where from excess power is being pushed to the CESC grid. Similar some other projects are in the pipeline. 13 nos. of Solar PV Power Plants have been installed so far since February, 1996 with aggregated capacity of 624 KWp. Solar PV home lighting system plants are providing electricity to the local people through local mini grid Nearly 2 lacs of such systems have been installed so far across the state. These type of systems have module (18Wp, 37 Wp, 50 Wp, 74 Wp, 100 Wp), battery with matching capacity, cables and switches, matching load (light, fan, TV, Music System etc .

Proposed Climate Action Plan of the State

- Solar Power is the main renewable energy source of the state and without considering Solar Energy the total potential of the state is only 1250 MW.
- In order to reduce power sector emission by about 20% the state needs to produce 2,000 MW of renewable power by the year 2020-21 . Share of Solar in this will be 1600 MW.
- To reduce the same by 30% it needs to produce 3,000 MW of renewable power by the year 2030-31 out of which 2400 MW needs to be from solar energy.
- Alternatively, the state can buy a portion of renewable power from other states to reduce its emission intensity.

Projection and plans for generation

- As per plans and projections under the State Climate Action Plan the state of West Bengal may be able to generate 250 MW of Solar power till 2015 and 750 MW till 2020.
- During next decade the state of West Bengal may plan for 1500 MW of Solar power installation.

- The State will generate additional 100 MW power Solar Roof Top by the year 2020 and 300 MW from Solar Roof Top by the year 2030-31.
- The grid parity of Solar power is expected to come only in the year 2015. As such, till such time Solar Power Plant will run on subsidy. The Solar Water Heating programme will also play a significant role in reducing demand.

Table below shows the Installation programmes of RE technologies in the state upto 2020-21 and 2030-31.

Sl.No.	Source	2020-21	2030-31
1.	Wind Farm and other Small Wind system.	150 MW	250 MW
2.	Biomass	150 MW	200 MW
3.	Small Hydro	200 MW	100 MW
4.	Waste to Energy	50 MW	100 MW
5.	Roof Top Solar PV	100 MW	200 MW
6.	Solar Farm	1000 MW	1500 MW
7.	Solar Water Heating system	150MW (Electrical equivalent)	250 MW (Electrical equivalent)
8.	Other Solar Energy programme like Solar Street lights, Replacement of Bill Board, Community lights, etc. andOff grid system.	200 MW	400 MW
	Total	2000 MW	3000 MW

The following infrastructure has to be created in the state for achieving the target.

- 1 MW Solar power plant needs 4 acres of land (in case of crystalline silicon) and 8 acres of land (in case of thin film Solar cells). It is presumed that the efficiency of Solar cells shall be almost double by the year 2030-31 from the present level.
- The state will need 6,000 acres of land (non-agricultural) by the year 2020-21 for Solar farm projects and additional 6,000 acres of land by the year 2030-31.
- The state has good Solar Radiation in Purulia & Bankura and it is expected most of Solar power plants will be set up in these two districts.

- Additionally the Western part of Burdwan and Birbhum districts also have encouraging potential for solar power.

Solar projects in West Bengal are given in chart below.

S.No.	Type of project	Remarks
1.	Grid connected SolarPV Project	Only one such project has been installed so far in West Bengal, capacity- 1MW at Jamuria near Asansol
2.	Do	One project has been installed at a school near Tollygunj, Kolkata, Where from excess power is being pushed to the CESC grid. Similar some other projects are in the pipeline.
3.	Off grid power plant	13 nos. of Solar PV Power Plants have been installed so far since February, 1996 with aggregated capacity of 624 KWp. These plants are providing electricity to the local people through local mini grid.
4.	Solar PV HomeLighting System	Nearly 2 lacks of such systems have been installed so far across the state. These type of systems have module (18Wp, 37 Wp, 50 Wp, 74 Wp, 100 Wp), battery with matching capacity, cables and switches, matching load (light, fan, TV, Music System etc.)
5.	Solar PV Lantern	It is being used both at electrified (as single source of light) and unelectrified (as emergency charger) areas.
6.	Solar PV Pump	Some technology demonstration projects have been completed so far for irrigation and drinking water purposes.
7.	Solar PVStreet Lighting System	Nearly 10 thousands of such systems have been installed so far across the state. These type of systems have module (74 Wp, 100 Wp), battery with matching capacity, cables and control systems matching load (11/ 18W CF Lamp).
8.	Solar PV Power Plant	More than 100 institutions which includes schools, students hostels, hospitals, Health centers, offices etc. have been given electricity through Solar PV Power Plants. (Capacity in the range of 1KWp to 100 KWp).

The National Solar Mission is one of the most important policies that seeks to create policy conditions necessary to promote the diffusion of solar energy use all over the country.

The following are some of the fiscal and policy incentives available now for production and use of solar energy systems:

- 100% foreign direct investment allowed in manufacturing and power projects.
- Zero customs and excise duties on wafers, solar cells, modules and some raw materials.
- 5% customs and excise duty on other raw materials and components.
- Tax holiday for manufacturing units in backward and specified areas, and for power projects.
- 80% depreciation in the first year for capital investments on solar projects. Support for R&D and technology validation projects.

Infrastructure Requirement for Solar Power Plant

- 1 MW Solar power plant needs 4 acres of land (in case of crystalline silicon) and 8 acres of land (in case of thin film Solar cells). It is presumed that the efficiency of Solar cells shall be almost double by the year 2030-31 from the present level.
- The state will need 6,000 acres of land (non-agricultural) by the year 2020-21 for Solar farm projects and additional 6,000 acres of land by the year 2030-31.

- The state has good Solar Radiation in Purulia & Bankura and it is expected most of Solar power plants will be set up in these two districts.Additionally the Western part of Burdwan and Birbhum districts also have encouraging potential for solar power.

The Techniques to Generate Electricity from the Sun

On a much larger scale, solar thermal power plants employ various techniques to concentrate the sun's energy as a heat source. The heat is then used to boil water to drive a steam turbine that generates electricity in much the same fashion as coal and nuclear power plants, supplying electricity for thousands of people.

In one technique, long troughs of U-shaped mirrors focus sunlight on a pipe of oil that runs through the middle. The hot oil then boils water for electricity generation. Another technique uses moveable mirrors to focus the sun's rays on a collector tower, where a receiver sits. Molten salt flowing through the receiver is heated to run a generator.

Other solar technologies are passive. For example, big windows placed on the sunny side of a building allow sunlight to heat-absorbent materials on the floor and walls. These surfaces then release the heat at night to keep the building warm. Similarly, absorbent plates on a roof can heat liquid in tubes that supply a house with hot water.

Solar energy is lauded as an inexhaustible fuel source that is pollution and often noise free. The technology is also versatile. For example, solar cells generate energy for far-out places like satellites in Earth orbit and cabins deep in the Rocky Mountains as easily as they can power downtown buildings and futuristic cars.

But solar energy doesn't work at night without a storage device such as a battery, and cloudy weather can make the technology unreliable during the day. Solar technologies are also very expensive and require a lot of land area to collect the sun's energy at rates useful to lots of people.

Despite the drawbacks, solar energy use has surged at about 20 percent a year over the past 15 years, thanks to rapidly falling prices and gains in efficiency. Japan, Germany, and the United States are major markets for solar cells. With tax incentives, solar electricity can often pay for itself in five to ten years.

The Solar Appliances Available in the Market

Solaer A.C

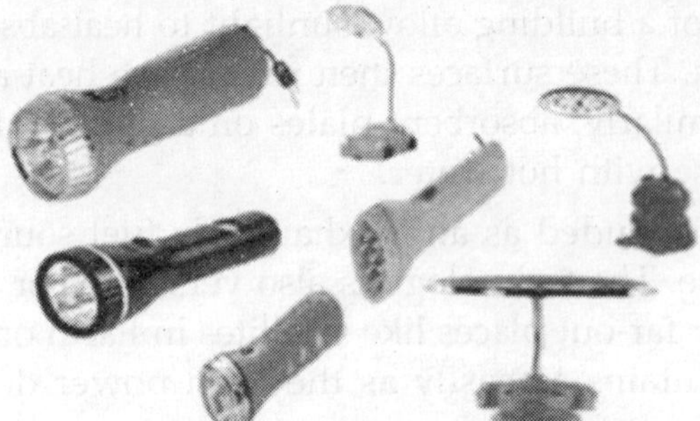

Solar LED Torch lamps

Solar torches & table lamps.

Solar powered car

Solar coffee maker

solar fridge

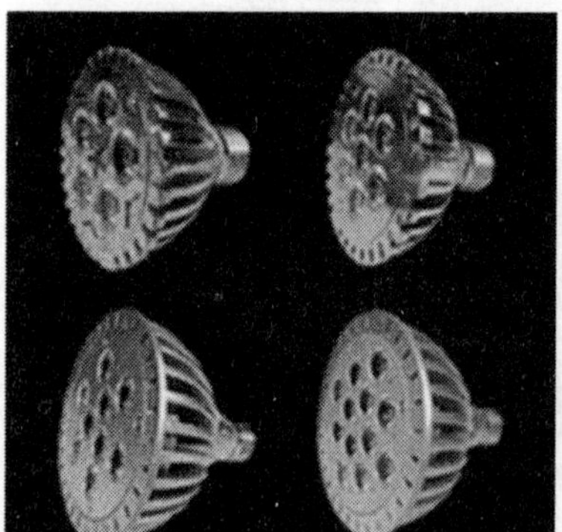

Solar Led Bulb Solar watch

Multi hue solar ball light

Solar lighted house.

Solar ceiling fan with panel

Solar energy is lauded as an inexhaustible fuel source that is pollution and often noise free. The technology is also versatile. For example, solar cells generate energy for far-out places like satellites in Earth orbit and cabins deep in the Rocky Mountains as easily as they can power downtown buildings and futuristic cars.

But solar energy doesn't work at night without a storage device such as a battery, and cloudy weather can make the technology unreliable during the day. Solar technologies are also very expensive and require a lot of land area to collect the sun's energy at rates useful to lots of people.

Despite the drawbacks, solar energy use has surged at about 20 percent a year over the past 15 years, thanks to rapidly falling prices and gains in efficiency. Japan, Germany, and the United States are major markets for solar cells. With tax incentives, solar electricity can often pay for itself in five to ten years.

CONCLUSIONS

There is an urgent need for transition from petroleum-based energy systems to one based on renewable resources to decrease reliance on depleting reserves of fossil fuels and to mitigate climate change. Renewable energy has the potential to create many employment opportunities at all levels, especially in rural areas.

Therefore, attention is needed in the following areas :

1. Innovative financing
2. Mainstreaming of renewables is very essential.
3. Energy security, economic growth and environment protection are the national energy policy drivers of any country of the world.
4. There is a need to boost the efforts for further development and promotion of renewable energy sources.
5. Promoting renewable energy technologies as a way to address concerns about energy security and economic growth.
6. Specific action included promoting deployment, innovation and basic research in renewable energy Technologies.

REFERENCES

Agrafiotis, C.; Roeb, M.; Konstandopoulos, A.G.; Nalbandian, L.; Zaspalis, V.T.; Sattler, C.; Stobbe, P.; Steele, A.M. (2005). "Solar water splitting for hydrogen production with monolithic reactors". Solar Energy 79 (4): 409–421.

Balcomb, J. Douglas (1992). Passive Solar Buildings. Massachusetts Institute of Technology. ISBN 0-262-02341-5

Bolton, James (1977). Solar Power and Fuels. Academic Press, Inc. ISBN

Butti, Ken; Perlin, John (1981). A Golden Thread (2500 Years of Solar Architecture and Technology). Van Nostrand Reinhold. ISBN 0-442-24005-8.

Carr, Donald E. (1976). Energy & the Earth Machine. W. W. Norton & Company. ISBN 0 393 06407 7.

Daniels, Farrington (1964). Direct Use of the Sun's Energy. Ballantine Books. ISBN 0-345-25938 6.

Hand Book of Solar Radiation data for India By Moni.

Hunt, V. Daniel (1979). Energy Dictionary. Van Nostrand Reinhold Company. ISBN 0 442 27395 9.

Indian Journal of Electrical and Biomedical Engineering Volume.1 Number.1 January-June 2013, pp.10-16@ Academic Research Journals, India

Karan, Kaul; Greer, Edith; Kasperbauer, Michael; Mahl, Catherine (2001). "Row Orientation Affects Fruit Yield in Field-Grown Okra". Journal of Sustainable Agriculture 17 (2/3): 169 174.

Leon, M.; Kumar, S. (2007). "Mathematical modeling and thermal performance analysis of unglazed transpired solar collectors". Solar Energy 81 (1): 62–75.

Tiwari, G. N.; Singh, H. N.; Tripathi, R. (2003). "Present status of solar distillation". Solar Energy 75 (5): 367–373. doi:10.1016/j.solener.2003.07.005.

Tritt, T.; Böttner, H.; Chen, L. (2008). "Thermoelectrics: Direct Solar Thermal Energy Conversion". MRS Bulletin 33 (4): 355–372.

Tzempelikos, Athanassios; Athienitis, Andreas K. (2007). "The impact of shading design and control on building cooling and lighting demand". Solar Energy 81 (3): 369–382

Vecchia, A.; Formisano, W.; Rosselli, V; Ruggi, D. (1981). "Possibilities for the Application of Solar Energy in the European Community Agriculture". Solar Energy 26 (6): 479–489.

Zedtwitz, P.v.; Petrasch, J.; Trommer, D.; Steinfeld, A. (2006). "Hydrogen production via the solar thermal decarbonization of fossil fuels". Solar Energy 80 (10): 1333–1337.

□□□

Section 5

Database, Modeling, Analytics and Business Intelligence Software

CHAPTER - 25

Future Challenges in Application of Algorithms and Tools for Clustering of Gene Expression Data

Sanchita[1] and Ashok Sharma[2]
Biotechnology Division, CSIR-Central Institute of Medicinal and Aromatic Plants, Lucknow- 226015, India
[1]0804sanchita@gmail.com
[2]ashoksharma@cimap.res.in

INTRODUCTION

Functional genomics is the science where genes are employed to determine their function. The gene expression is an approach to analyze the functional changes in the genes. The expression level for a gene across different experimental conditions are cumulatively called the gene expression profile and the expression levels for all the genes under an experimental condition are cumulatively called the sample expression profile. Different techniques for gene expression analysis have been used so far. cDNA-AFLP (Bachem *et al.*, 1996), SAGE (Serial Analysis of Gene Expression) (Neto, Neto & Costa, 2012) and MPSS (Massive Parallel Signature Sequencing) (Brenner *et al.*, 2000) are the techniques for expression analysis where the genomic or transcriptome sequence of the organism is not needed. Some advanced and largely used techniques are Microarrays (Schena *et al.*, 1995) and Real-time PCR (Higuchi *et al.*, 1993) where the previous knowledge of the sequence is required. These two techniques are most frequently used for gene expression analysis (Perez-Torres *et al.*, 2009). DNA microarray technology has made it possible to simultaneously monitor the expression levels of thousands of genes during important biological processes and across collections of related samples (Jiang, Tang & Zhang, 2004). Microarray data are usually presented in an expression matrix in which each column represents all the gene expression levels from a single experiment and each row represents the expression of a gene across all experiments. Each element in the matrix is a log ratio, which is defined as logarithmic value of the ratio of the gene expression level in the testing sample to the gene expression level in the reference sample. The first objective in microarray data analysis is to identify genes for which the expression level is significantly changed under different experimental conditions. One of the goals of microarray data analysis is to cluster the expressed genes or samples having similar expression profiles to make a meaningful biological inference from the set of genes or samples. The similarity in expression or coexpression implies some kind of regulatory or functional similarity of the genes or it can be said that the functionally similar genes are found to be coexpressed. Thus, finding genes that might be involved in the same biological process requires clustering of genes into groups based on their similarity in expression profiles. Elucidation of the patterns hidden in gene expression data enhances the understanding of functional genomics. However, the large number of genes and the complexity of biological networks make it difficult to interpret the resulting mass of data, which often consists of millions of measurements. A first step towards the solution to this problem is the use of clustering techniques, which is essential in the data mining process to reveal natural structures and identify interesting patterns in the underlying data (Jiang, 2004). Clustering is one of the unsupervised approach to classify data into groups of genes or samples with similar patterns that might be characteristic of the group. It is the task of assigning a set of objects into groups (called clusters) so that the objects in the same cluster are more similar to each other than to those in other clusters. Many clustering algorithms have been applied to gene expression data but the most popular among them are Hierarchical Clustering (HCL), K-Means Clustering (KMC), Self Organizing Maps (SOMs), Support Vector Machine (SVM) and Principal Component Analysis (PCA). These clustering algorithms have been proven useful for identifying biologically relevant groups of genes and samples. To select the most appropriate algorithm for clustering is one of the problems faced by the biologists. A solution to this problem is to apply more than one clustering algorithms upon the same data set and to compare the results obtained from them. As all algorithms have their own merits and demerits. This chapter presents the analysis and comparison among the performance of each of the five above mentioned algorithms. The comparison is based upon the implementation of gene expression data to different algorithms available in earlier reports. The application of more than one clustering algorithms may facilitate the generation of more accurate and reliable results. Most common cluster analysis technique is hierarchical, resulting into a classification, having an increasing number of nested classes and the result resembles a phylogenetic classification (Quackenbush, 2001). Non-hierarchical clustering techniques also exist, such as k-means clustering, which simply partition objects into different clusters without specifying the relationship between individual elements. Clustering techniques can further be classified as divisive or agglomerative. A divisive method begins with all elements in one cluster that is gradually broken down into smaller and smaller clusters. Agglomerative techniques start with usually single-member clusters and gradually fuse them together. Finally, clustering can be either supervised or unsupervised. Unsupervised clustering is appropriate when there is no information about which data objects should be grouped together, while supervised clustering is applicable when cluster information is available for a subset of the data objects and this information is used in determining the needed criteria or training to subsequently group data objects for which no cluster information is known (Tjaden, 2006). Supervised methods use existing biological information about specific genes that are functionally related to 'guide' the clustering algorithm. Many clustering techniques are available to analyse gene expression data such as Hierarchical Clustering, K-Means Clustering, Self Organizing Maps (SOMs), Support Vector Machine (SVM), Principal Component Analysis (PCA), CLICK (CLuster Identification via Connectivity Kernels), DHC (a Density-based Hierarchical Clustering method), CAST (Cluster Affinity Search Technique), Self Organizing Tree Algorithm (SOTA), Partitioning Around Medoids (PAM), Diana, Fanny, Model Based Clustering, Expectation Maximization Algorithm, FLDA (Fisher's Linear Discriminant Analysis), CART (Classification And Regression Trees), FLAME (Fuzzy Clustering by Local Approximations of Memberships), etc. Among all the available algorithms, hierarchical clustering, PCA, k-means, SOMs and SVMs are the most widely used algorithms. These algorithms have been proven useful for identifying biologically relevant groups of genes and samples. The performance of different clustering algorithms is strongly dependent on data distribution. It has been generally accepted that the application of more than one clustering technique may facilitate the generation of accurate and reliable results (Azuaje, 2003b). In the present era of high throughput technologies, the ever increasing amount of biological data needs to be quickly analyzed and interpreted. Amongst the various approaches available, clustering is one of the method used to gain insight into biological processes (Pirim *et al.*, 2012). Clustering analysis is presently being widely used as an important tool in studying gene expression data (Sirinukunwattana *et al.*, 2013; Verbanck, Le & Pages, 2013). It is being used to study genomic data such as gene expression profiles for inferring their biological function and regulation of genes. It is also being used for the identification of diseases based on genetic variation and identification of prognostic markers for known diseases (Sirinukunwattana *et al.*, 2013).

Hierarchical Clustering

Hierarchical clustering is the most popular method for microarray data analysis. The basic process of hierarchical clustering was given by S.C. Johnson in 1967 (Johnson, 1967). In this algorithm, genes with similar expression patterns are grouped together and are connected by a series of branches to form a dendrogram. Firstly, it considers each gene as an individual cluster and genes that are similar to each other form nested clusters based on the pairwise distances. Hierarchical clustering is broadly classified into two methods: agglomerative and divisive. The agglomerative clustering starts with usually single-member clusters and gradually fuses them together whereas divisive method begins with all elements in one cluster that is gradually broken down into smaller clusters. The hierarchical clustering includes different algorithms based on the pair wise distances calculated between the growing clusters (Quackenbush, 2001). Single-linkage clustering, the distance between two clusters is calculated as the minimum distance between members of each cluster. Complete-linkage clustering, the distance between two clusters is calculated as the maximum distance between members of the relevant clusters and Average-linkage clustering, the distance between clusters is calculated using average values of all the members of each cluster. Among the three approaches for hierarchical clustering the average linkage algorithm generally works well with standardized microarray data and single linkage generally performs poorly (Shannon, Culverhouse & Duncan, 2003). The hierarchical clustering has particularly been used to establish taxonomies of plants and animals with respect to genetic background, in organizing and cataloging materials, e.g., library documents, to facilitate the storage and retrieval of information (Ward, 1963). The use of hierarchical clustering is not restricted to classification only, it has been successfully applied in information retrieval (Jardine & Van Rijsbergen, 1971; Van Rijsbergen, 1974; Voorhees, 1986). The hierarchical agglomerative clustering methods can also be used for document retrieval by clustering the documents based on the terms that they had in common. It was suggested that the complete linkage method is probably the most effective method in terms of retrieval performance (Willett, 1988). Hierarchical clustering has been applied to gene expression data for the first time in 1998 (Eisen *et al.*, 1998). They applied average linkage hierarchical clustering to gene expression data of budding yeast *Saccharomyces cerevisiae* and primary human fibroblasts stimulated with serum following serum starvation. They found that hierarchical clustering illustrates relationship among genes, represented by a tree whose branch lengths reflect the degree of similarity between the genes. They also found that clustering of gene expression data makes group of genes having similar function. This can help to assign functions to the genes having no prior information. Hierarchical clustering has been previously used for finding subtypes of cells using 96 samples of normal and malignant lymphocytes. Applying a hierarchical clustering algorithm to these samples, the diversity was occurred in gene expression data among the tumors of DLBCL patients. They identified two molecularly distinct forms of DLBCL, which had gene expression patterns indicative of different stages of B-cell differentiation. These two groups correlated well with patient survival rates, thus confirming that the clusters were meaningful (Alizadeh *et al.*, 2000).

K-means Clustering

K-means is one of the simplest unsupervised clustering algorithms. It follows a simple and easy way to classify a given data set through a given number of clusters. The main idea for k-means clustering is to define k centroids, one for each cluster. It is a well-known partitioning method. It is a simple and fast method, commonly used due to its straightforward implementation and small number of iterations (Tavazoie *et al.*, 1999). This algorithm divides the data set into k disjoint subsets. The number of clusters (k) is chosen by the user and is given as an input where the computer randomly assigns each gene to one of the k clusters. The distance between each gene and the center of each cluster is calculated. The grouping of genes into clusters is being done in such a way that the genes inside every cluster are as close to the center of the cluster as possible while at the same time there is maximal distance between genes of different clusters. It has been applied to obtain gene expression matrices, groups of functionally related and co-regulated genes. K-mean clustering was used to analyze gene expression data for the first time (Tavazoie *et al.*, 1999). They used k-means clustering to cluster expression profiles of 3000 most variable yeast genes during the cell cycle into 30 clusters. It was found that for half of these clusters, strong sequence patterns were present in the gene upstream sequences. K-means algorithm combined with Genetic Algorithms (GAs) have been proposed for improving the efficiency of the K-means algorithm (Zhang, Ho & Lin, 2004). This was used to rearrange the clusters in crossover operation based on the distance of clustering centres to avoid generating meaningless offspring. Experiments were performed on four publicly available time series data sets which demonstrated the effectiveness and efficiency of the proposed algorithm. The approach took the advantage of the global search capacity of GAs and used K-means for local fine tuning. This algorithm outperformed other algorithms on clustering quality and converged faster than other GAs-based clustering algorithms. K-means clustering algorithm has been extensively studied for gene expression analysis (Zhang & Fenstermacher, 2005). Katara *et al.*, (2010) used k-means clustering method for the analysis of microarray gene expression data of *Toxoplasma gondii* (Gautam, 2010). On the basis, of co-expression, some probable gene targets in *Toxoplasma gondii* were found (IL-16 and Inhibitor of kappa light chain Epsilon etc.). Their main aim in the study was to analyse the expression pattern of microarray data of *Toxoplasma gondii* to find out new probable drug targets with the help of Hierarchical and k-means Clustering methods and to do comparison of the results of both methods to confirm the expression pattern. The clusters of k-means were found to be very similar to the clusters found with hierarchical clustering. There was a little difference found in the cluster sizes and gene distribution, but both algorithms have the same basic patterns as the means of the clusters were very similar to each other. A novel Metric Matrics k-means (MMk-means) clustering algorithm have been developed recently to cluster genes to their functional roles to obtain further knowledge on many *Plasmodium falciparum* genes (Osamor, 2010). To pursue this aim, the results of three different k-mean algorithms were compared. Robust k-means clustering algorithm, Traditional k-means clustering algorithm, Metric Matrices k-means (MMk-means) clustering algorithm from an *in-vitro* microarray data (Le Roch *et al.*, 2003) with the classification from an *in-vivo* microarray data (Daily *et al.*, 2007) in order to perform a comparative functional classification of *P. falciparum* genes. They further validated the effectiveness of their MMk-means algorithm. The new algorithm (MMk-means) was based on the recently established relationship between principal component analysis and the k-means clustering. The results from this study indicated that the resulting distribution of the comparison of the three algorithms' *in vitro* clusters against the *in vivo* clusters were similar. This confirmed the effectiveness of MMk-means method.

Support Vector Machine

The Support Vector Machine (SVM) is a pattern recognition algorithm that has been used to analyze an increasing variety of complex biological data sets, including microarray expression profiles, DNA and protein sequences, protein-protein interaction networks etc. It is a sophisticated supervised classification method (Brown *et al.*, 2000). In order to apply the SVM, it must be trained by using the same members of each class that have to be identified. The goal for SVM is to find a plane in a high-dimensional space that perfectly splits into two or more sets of biological samples (Butte, 2002). All examples on the one side of the hyperplane are labeled positive and all the examples on the other side are labeled negative. In sufficiently high dimensional data, many hyper planes can be found that can separate the examples. Thus, such a hyper plane should be found that are as far away as possible from all the examples. More precisely, a hyper plane should separate the positive examples from the negative ones and maximize the minimum distance of the closest points to the hyperplane. This hyper plane distinguishes the data into different classes and based upon this differentiation the SVMs are provided with similar data that they recognize and assign them for particular class (Ben-Dor *et al.*, 2000). SVMs have been successfully applied to a wide range of pattern recognition problems, including handwriting recognition (Adankon & Cheriet, 2009), object recognition (Pontil & Verri, 1998), speaker identification (Campbell *et al.*, 2006), face detection in images (Heisele, Ho & Poggio, 2001) and text categorization (Kwok, 1998). SVMs was applied to analyze gene expression data for the first time (Brown *et al.*, 2000). They applied this algorithm to six functional classes of yeast genes using gene expression matrices from 79 samples. Genes from some of the classes, such as ribosomal proteins and histones were expected to be coexpressed. A good classification accuracy was achieved for these classes. Some other functional classes, such as protein kinases, were not expected to have distinct gene expression profiles. It was shown that SVM provided the best prediction accuracy for the functional classes that were expected to be co-regulated. The SVM method have been used for cancer classification with microarray data (Chu & Wang, 2005). They have applied a powerful classifier i.e. the support vector machine (SVM) and four effective feature reduction methods i.e. principal components analysis (PCA), class-separability measure, Fisher ratio and *t*-test to the problem of cancer classification based on gene expression data. The results proved the effectiveness of the SVMs as the SVMs obtained very high classification accuracies with much fewer genes compared with previously published methods. The capability of microarray data to discriminate between closely related DNA samples have been demonstrated by applying SVMs upon a set of *Bacillus anthracis* strains (Doran *et al.*, 2007). The genomes of *B. anthracis* strains are monomorphic and therefore, typically difficult to distinguish using conventional molecular biology tools or microarray data clustering techniques. Using SVMs as a supervised learning technique, they showed that a low-density fingerprint microarray contained enough information to discriminate between *B. anthracis* strains with 90% sensitivity. They proposed SVM for classification of microarray based DNA fingerprints, utilizing closely related *B. anthracis* strains as the model system and test set for SVM development. Thus, they concluded that the low-density, genome independent fingerprint microarray contains enough information to distinguish between very closely related isolates of *B. anthracis* when combined with a SVM classifier method.

Self Organizing Map

A self-organizing map (SOM, Kohonen's Map) or self-organizing feature map (SOFM) is a type of artificial neural network that is trained using unsupervised learning to produce a two dimensional representation of the input space of the training samples, called a map. The algorithm for SOM was introduced by Kohonen in 1981. A SOM consists of components called nodes or neurons. Each node has its associated weight vector which is initialized with random values ranging from 0 to 1. Usually the arrangement of nodes is a regular spacing in a hexagonal or rectangular grid. The SOM describes a mapping from a higher dimensional input space to a lower dimensional map space. The procedure for placing a vector from data space onto the map is to first find the node with the closest weight vector to the vector taken from data space. Once the closest node is located, it is assigned the values from the vector taken from the data space. This Kohonen technique creates a network that stores information in such a way that any topological relationships within the training set are maintained. SOMs operate in two modes: training and mapping. Training builds the map using input examples. Mapping automatically classifies a new input vector. Once the SOM has been trained so that the weight vectors of the neurons are updated, clustering is done for all the remaining input vectors. SOMs have been successfully applied for the analysis and organization of large data. The SOM algorithm has been applied to several pattern analysis tasks viz. to analyze voice quality by providing the visualization of certain deviations and in speech recognition (Kangas, 1994). The algorithm has also been used to explore the structures in the large datasets (Kaski, 1994). The implementation of SOMs upon gene expression data was firstly done by Tamayo *et al.*, (1999) (Tamayo *et al.*, 1999). They have reported, whether the SOM approach could be applied to complex data sets involving multiple cell lines HL-60, U937, Jurkat and NB4 cells. They generated a total of 17 RNA samples, yielding 6,416 data points in 17-dimensional space. Of these, 1,036 genes passed the variation filter. The genes were classified, thereby grouping 1,036 genes into 24 categories. This proved that SOMs can be successfully applied to complex dataset. Toronen *et al.*, (1999) analyzed a publicly available data on the changes in gene expression during a diauxic shift (shift from anaerobic to aerobic metabolism) in yeast (Toronen *et al.*, 1999). Their results showed that SOM rapidly and reliably clustered the gene expression data into groups, which not only showed similar gene expression profiles but also contained functionally relatedness. SOM have been applied to the fibroblast dataset taken from an experiment showing the response of human fibroblasts to serum (Suresh, 2008). They found the group of genes shared similar expression patterns over multiple conditions. For large groups of clustered genes, they observed the strong tendency to share common characters in cellular processes. They concluded that clustering of similar genes helps biologists to find the function of unknown genes and the SOM approach presented by them makes the analysis easy. They also concluded that SOM solved the problem related to data dimensionality and therefore well suited for DNA microarray data analysis.

Principal Component Analysis

Principal component analysis (PCA) was invented by Karl Pearson in 1901 (Pearson, 1901). It is now used in exploratory data analysis. PCA has been widely used in analyzing gene expression data specifically for reducing the dimensionality of the large data sets. Its application to gene expression data for the first time showed that PCA allow to summarize the ways in which gene responses to different conditions (Raychaudhuri, Stuart & Altman, 2000). It is a statistical technique for determining the key variables in a multidimensional data set that explain the differences in the observations and can be used to simplify the analysis and visualization of multidimensional data sets. PCA is often used as a pre-processing step to clustering (Everitt, 1993). If m observations on n variables are given, then the goal of PCA is to reduce the dimensionality of the data matrix by finding r new variables, where r is less than n. These new variables (r) termed as principal components (PCs) are uncorrelated and consist most of the variation in the original data. A PCA analysis of DNA microarray data can consider the genes or experiments as variables (Raychaudhuri *et al.*, 2000). When genes are variables, the analysis creates a set of "principal gene components" that indicate the feature of genes that best explain the experimental responses they produce. When experiments are the variables, the analysis creates a set of "principal experiment components" that indicate the features of the experimental conditions that best explain the gene behaviors they elicit. PCA is used prior to cluster analysis as the Principal Components (PCs) may "extract" the cluster structure in the data set. Since PCs are uncorrelated and ordered, the first few PCs contain most of the variations in the data are usually used in cluster analysis. The data typically consists of a set of objects described by a number of characters. In microarray data, an object could be a gene and a character could be the level of expression of that gene under a particular condition. Principal components reduce the number of characters by forming new characters that are combinations of the old ones (Ooyen, 2001). PCA has been successfully applied to data compression, image processing, visualization, exploratory data analysis, pattern recognition and time series prediction (Vemuri, 2004). Examination of the components also provided insight into the underlying factors that have been measured in the experiments. The PCA analysis have been applied to sporulation data set (Chu *et al.*, 1998). In this work, 7 different measurements of gene expression were made over time. PCA on the time-points suggested that most of the observed variability in the experiment could be summarized in 2 components i.e. 2 variables captured most of the information. The result confirmed that the PCA could find a reduced set of variables that were useful for understanding the experiments. The effectiveness of principal components (PCs) in capturing cluster structure have been studied (Yeung & Ruzzo, 2001). They compared the quality of clusters obtained from the original data to the quality of clusters obtained after projecting onto subsets of the principal component axes. Their empirical study showed that clustering with the PCs instead of the original variables does not necessarily improve and often degrade the cluster quality. They observed that the first few PCs (which contain most of the variation in the data) do not necessarily capture most of the cluster structure. They also showed that clustering with PCs has different impact on different algorithms and different similarity matrices. Thus, they didn't consider PCA to be recommended before clustering except in special circumstances. Song *et al.*, (2007) proposed a unified approach for gene clustering and dimension reduction based on functional data analysis (FNDA) to group time-course gene expression profiles with respect to their shapes or patterns (Song *et al.*, 2007). They applied this method to a time course microarray data set on the yeast cell cycle and demonstrated that the method was able to identify clusters of genes with expression profiles focused on particular phase of the cell cycle. They used FPCA before clustering as a tool to reduce the dimensionality of the data. They found that a model based clustering provides a solution to determine the number of clusters and in combination with FPCA before clustering, it can improve the quality of clustering through reducing dimensionality of data. Development of high-throughput technology makes it possible to measure expressions of thousands of genes simultaneously. Genes have the inherent pathway structure, where pathways are composed of multiple genes with coordinated biological functions. It is of great interest to identify differential gene pathways that are associated with the variations of phenotypes. Zhu and Li (2011) proposed a 2-step statistical method for analyzing high-throughput biological data while utilizing pathway information (Zhu & Li, 2011). An important intermediate step was nonlinear dimension reduction, which would turn high-dimensional data into a much lower dimensional data and could permit flexible predictor interactions within the groups as well as flexible pathway effects on the phenotype response. Due to incredible growth of high dimensional dataset, conventional data base querying methods are inadequate to extract useful information, so researchers are forced to develop new techniques to meet the raised requirements. Hence, to improve the efficiency and accuracy of mining task on high dimensional data, the data must be pre-processed by an efficient dimensionality reduction method. K-means is a well known partitioning based clustering technique that attempts to find a user specified number of clusters represented by their centroids. As original K-means clustering algorithm often does not work well for high dimensional data. PCA method have been used as a first phase for K-means clustering to obtain a reduced dataset containing possibly uncorrelated variables which would simplify the analysis and visualization of multi dimensional data set (Dash, 2010). The experimental results showed that the proposed algorithm provided better efficiency and accuracy in comparison to original k-means algorithm with reduced time. To reduce the high dimensionality of the microarray data remains to be a unique challenge in bioinformatics data analysis. PCA is a classic dimension reduction approach and to be powerful for analyzing the data having highest variation (Ma & Dai, 2011).

Comparative Evaluation of Clustering Algorithms

Several studies have been done to compare the different clustering algorithms for their performance in clustering the expression data. Clustering techniques have proven to be helpful to understand gene function, gene regulation, cellular processes, and subtypes of cells. Genes with similar expression patterns (coexpressed genes) can be clustered together. This approach may further help in understanding the functions of many genes for which information has not been previously available. The biological functions of several genes, as well as their interaction in certain pathways governing the ES cell pluripotency have been identified by using different clustering algorithms (Chen *et al.*, 2002). The *Pou5f1* (*Oct*-3/4) gene, which encoded the transcription factor Oct-3/4 and expressed specifically in totipotent embryonic cells and germ cells, has been widely accepted as a marker that measures the pluripotency of ES cells. They observed that Oct-3/4 showed down regulation immediately in response to the withdrawal of LIF and the conditioned media. The down regulation of other genes, of which many were unknown, at both 4 hours and 8 hours post-LIF withdrawal suggested these genes might carry a similar function to Oct-3/4, or that they might be used as alternative markers for ES cell pluripotency. The clustering results appeared to reflect certain biological relations among the genes. Different algorithms displayed different properties: *k*-means generated clusters with slightly better structural quality; *k*-means and SOM appeared more consistent with the biological information implicated in the redundant clones and the several known genes involved in the same pathways. Average linkage hierarchical clustering was the worst among the four algorithms in this particular test situation. The SOM network have been compared with hierarchical clustering methods on 252 data sets (Mangiameli, Chen & West, 1996). These data sets were designed to include data imperfections such as dispersion, outliers, irrelevant information and nonuniform cluster densities. They found that SOM outperformed hierarchical clustering methods for 191 of the 252 data sets. It was more robust and had higher accuracy. However, when the dispersion of the data set was low or cluster densities varied greatly, SOM was inferior to hierarchical clustering methods. The SOM network did better than the best of the seven popular hierarchical clustering algorithms in about 76% of the case tested and even better with high-dispersion data sets. The six clustering algorithms have been compared and evaluated their performances on a well-known publicly available microarray data set on sporulation of budding yeast and on two simulated data sets (Datta, 2003). They also formulated three reasonable validation strategies that can be used with any clustering algorithm. They evaluated each of those six clustering methods with these validation measures. It was found that the 'best' method depends on the exact validation strategy and the number of clusters to be used, but overall Diana appeared to be a efficient performer. It was shown that the group means produced by Diana were the closest and those produced by UPGMA were the farthest from a model profile based on a set of hand-picked genes. They found that while the standard hierarchical clustering (UPGMA) seems to be the most commonly employed clustering technique in microarray data analysis, its optimality or superiority over other methods have not been demonstrated in microarray literature. The three major Clustering algorithms: Hierarchical Clustering (HC), Self-Organizing Map (SOM), and Self Organizing Tree Algorithm (SOTA) using Yeast *Saccharomyces cerevisiae* gene expression data have been studied and compared their performance (Yin, Huang & Ni, 2006). They then introduced Cluster Diff, a new data mining tool, to conduct the similarity analysis of clusters generated by different algorithms. The performance study showed that SOTA is more efficient than SOM while HC is the least efficient. They concluded that HC methods allow a visual, convenient representation of genes. They can also generate an order of the genes, though the order is not unique. However, they are neither robust nor efficient.

Tools

These algorithms have been used to analyze the clustering of gene expression data through different tools. The tools have been developed for making the better utilization of these algorithms. Major tools which utilize these algorithms are genesis, MultiExperiment Viewer (MeV), Expression Profiler, Gene Cluster, Gene Spring, Spotfire, Gene Pattern and J express. Bioconductor packages are also available dealing with different clustering algorithms. Genesis (http://genome.tugraz.at/) has incorporated all the algorithms (Sturn, Quackenbush & Trajanoski, 2002). The results of the clustering analysis can be seen across all implemented methods and it enables analysis of the outcome of different algorithms. MeV (http://www.tm4.org/mev.html) is a data visualization and analysis tool developed from TIGR. The display elements are active, providing users with a direct link to annotation and other information associated with the underlying genes. Gene Spring and Spotfire are commercial tool applied for clustering of microarray data.

CONCLUSION

The clustering techniques are undoubtedly helpful to understand gene function, gene regulation, cellular processes, and subtypes of cells. Clustering the genes with similar expression patterns (co expressed genes) having similar cellular functions, may further help in understanding of the functions of many genes for which information has not been previously available. Hierarchical clustering efficiently illustrates relationship among genes. But, the membership of a gene in one cluster cannot be changed to another cluster, once the cluster to which it belongs is formed during the hierarchical clustering process. Similarly, k-means clustering has been found to be successful in revealing functionally related and co-regulated genes; it is a fast method for clustering of expression data, but has the limitation of requiring prior knowledge of the number of clusters, *k*. The performance of k-means clustering is better than hierarchical clustering algorithm as the membership of the genes can be changed from one cluster to another during k-means clustering process. In general k-means clustering is recommended for huge dataset while hierarchical clustering algorithms are recommended for small dataset. But as hierarchical clustering is simple and fast and produces a final clustering result in the form of a hierarchical tree that is easy to visualize, it is the most popular clustering technique. SOM also rapidly and reliably clusters gene expression data set into groups having similar gene expression profiles and also containing functionally related genes. The SOM algorithm places genes with similar, but not identical profiles in neighbouring groups. One of the main drawbacks of utilizing SOMs for clustering is that they require the user to specify the number of clusters. The SOM algorithm is the same as the k-means algorithm in the final stages of its training procedure. Thus, SOMs can be used as possible substitutes for the more classical k-means clustering algorithm. It has been proved that SOMs can be successfully applied to complex dataset. PCA is used prior to cluster analysis as the Principal Components (PCs) may "extract" the cluster structure in the data set. PCA has proved to be a classic dimension reduction approach and is powerful for analyzing the data having highest variation. However, reducing the dimensionality of the data by summarizing the microarray experiments may make the expression data less biologically interpretable by researchers. SVMs provide the best prediction accuracy for the functional classes that are expected to be co-regulated. They can not only classify new samples but also help in the identification of those which have been wrongly classified by the experts. The SVMs are capable to discriminate between closely related DNA samples which are typically difficult to distinguish using conventional molecular biology tools or microarray data clustering techniques. The application of more than one clustering technique may facilitate the generation of accurate and reliable results (Azuaje, 2003a). These tools and techniques will be playing a very important role in future for the analysis and interpretation of ever increasing data obtained from high throughput technologies. More robust, efficient and fast algorithms are expected to be developed to take care of limitations of currently available tools.

ACKNOWLEDGEMENT

This work was supported by senior research fellowship award to one of the authors, Sanchita from CSIR, New Delhi.

REFERENCES

Adankon, M. M. & Cheriet, M. (2009). Model selection for the LS-SVM. Application to handwriting recognition. Pattern Recognition 42, 3264-3270.

Alizadeh, A. A., Eisen, M. B., Davis, R. E., Ma, C., Lossos, I. S., Rosenwald, A., Boldrick, J. C., Sabet, H., Tran, T., Yu, X., Powell, J. I., Yang, L., Marti, G. E., Moore, T., Hudson, J., Jr., Lu, L., Lewis, D. B., Tibshirani, R., Sherlock, G., Chan, W. C., Greiner, T. C., Weisenburger, D. D., Armitage, J. O., Warnke, R., Levy, R., Wilson, W., Grever, M. R., Byrd, J. C., Botstein, D., Brown, P. O. & Staudt, L. M. (2000). Distinct types of diffuse large B-cell lymphoma identified by gene expression profiling. Nature 403, 503-11.

Azuaje, F. (2003a). Clustering-based approaches to discovering and visualising microarray data patterns. Briefings in Bioinformatics 4, 31-42.

Azuaje, F. (2003b). Clustering-based approaches to discovering and visualising microarray data patterns. Briefings Bioinformatics 4, 31-42.

Bachem, C. W. B., vanderHoeven, R. S., deBruijn, S. M., Vreugdenhil, D., Zabeau, M. & Visser, R. G. F. (1996). Visualization of differential gene expression using a novel method of RNA fingerprinting based on AFLP: Analysis of gene expression during potato tuber development. Plant Journal 9, 745-753.

Ben-Dor, A., Bruhn, L., Friedman, N., Nachman, I., Schummer, M. & Yakhini, Z. (2000). Tissue classification with gene expression profiles. Journal of Computational Biology 7, 559-583.

Brenner, S., Johnson, M., Bridgham, J., Golda, G., Lloyd, D. H., Johnson, D., Luo, S. J., McCurdy, S., Foy, M., Ewan, M., Roth, R., George, D., Eletr, S., Albrecht, G., Vermaas, E., Williams, S. R., Moon, K., Burcham, T., Pallas, M., DuBridge, R. B., Kirchner, J., Fearon, K., Mao, J. & Corcoran, K. (2000). Gene expression analysis by massively parallel signature sequencing (MPSS) on microbead arrays. Nature Biotechnology 18, 630-634.

Brown, M. P. S., Grundy, W. N., Lin, D., Cristianini, N., Sugnet, C. W., Furey, T. S., Ares, M. & Haussler, D. (2000). Knowledge-based analysis of microarray gene expression data by using support vector machines. Proceedings of the National Academy of Sciences of the United States of America 97, 262-267.

Butte, A. (2002). The use and analysis of microarray data. Nature Reviews Drug Discovery 1, 951-960.

Campbell, W. M., Campbell, J. P., Reynolds, D. A., Singer, E. & Torres-Carrasquillo, P. A. (2006). Support vector machines for speaker and language recognition. Computer Speech and Language 20, 210-229.

Chen, G. X., Jaradat, S. A., Banerjee, N., Tanaka, T. S., Ko, M. S. H. & Zhang, M. Q. (2002). Evaluation and comparison of clustering algorithms in analyzing es cell gene expression data. Statistica Sinica 12, 241-262.

Chu, F. & Wang, L. P. (2005). Applications of support vector machines to cancer classification with microarray data. International Journal of Neural Systems 15, 475-484.

Chu, S., DeRisi, J., Eisen, M., Mulholland, J., Botstein, D., Brown, P. O. & Herskowitz, I. (1998). The transcriptional program of sporulation in budding yeast. Science 282, 699-705.

Daily, J. P., Scanfeld, D., Pochet, N., Le Roch, K., Plouffe, D., Kamal, M., Sarr, O., Mboup, S., Ndir, O., Wypij, D., Levasseur, K., Thomas, E., Tamayo, P., Dong, C., Zhou, Y., Lander, E. S., Ndiaye, D., Wirth, D., Winzeler, E. A., Mesirov, J. P. & Regev, A. (2007). Distinct physiological states of Plasmodium falciparum in malaria-infected patients. Nature 450, 1091-U15.

Dash, R., Mishra, D., Rath, A.K., Acharya, M. (2010). A hybridized K-means clustering approach for high dimensional dataset. International Journal of Engineering, Science and Technology 2, 59-66.

Datta, S. (2003). Comparisons and validation of statistical clustering techniques for microarray gene expression data. Bioinformatics 19, 459-66.

Doran, M., Raicu, D. S., Furst, J. D., Settimi, R., Schipma, M. & Chandler, D. P. (2007). Oligonucleotide microarray identification of Bacillus anthracis strains using support vector machines. Bioinformatics 23, 487-492.

Eisen, M. B., Spellman, P. T., Brown, P. O. & Botstein, D. (1998). Cluster analysis and display of genome-wide expression patterns. Proc Natl Acad Sci U S A 95, 14863-8.

Everitt, B. S. (1993). Cluster Analysis. John Wiley & Sons, New York, NY.

Gautam, B., Katara, P., Singh, S., Farmer, R. (2010). Drug target identification using gene expression microarray data of Toxoplasma gondii. International Journal of Biometrics and Bioinformatics 4, 113-124.

Heisele, B., Ho, P. & Poggio, T. (2001). Face recognition with support vector machines: Global versus component-based approach. Eighth IEEE International Conference on Computer Vision, Vol Ii, Proceedings, 688-694.

Higuchi, R., Fockler, C., Dollinger, G. & Watson, R. (1993). Kinetic Pcr Analysis - Real-Time Monitoring of DNA Amplification Reactions. Bio-Technology 11, 1026-1030.

Jardine, N. & Van Rijsbergen, C. J. (1971). The use of hierarchic clustering in information retrieval. Information Storage & Retrieval 7, 217-240.

Jiang, D., Tang, C. and Zhang, A. (2004). Cluster Analysis for Gene Expression Data: A Survey. IEEE Transactions on Knowledge and Data Engineering 16, 1370-1386.

Johnson, S. C. (1967). Hierarchical clustering schemes. Psychometrika 32, 241-54.

Kangas, J. (1994). On the analysis of pattern sequences by self-organizing maps.

Kaski, S. (1994). Data exploration using self-organizing maps. In Acta Polytechnica Scandinavica. Mathematics.

Kwok, J. T. Y. (1998). Automated text categorization using support vector machine. Iconip'98: The Fifth International Conference on Neural Information Processing Jointly with Jnns'98: The 1998 Annual Conference of the Japanese Neural Network Society - Proceedings, Vols 1-3, 347-351.

Le Roch, K. G., Zhou, Y. Y., Blair, P. L., Grainger, M., Moch, J. K., Haynes, J. D., De la Vega, P., Holder, A. A., Batalov, S., Carucci, D. J. & Winzeler, E. A. (2003). Discovery of gene function by expression profiling of the malaria parasite life cycle. Science 301, 1503-1508.

Ma, S. G. & Dai, Y. (2011). Principal component analysis based methods in bioinformatics studies. Briefings in Bioinformatics 12, 714-722.

Mangiameli, P., Chen, S. K. & West, D. (1996). A comparison of SOM neural network and hierarchical clustering methods. European Journal of Operational Research 93, 402-417.

Neto, A. S. L., Neto, O. P. D. & Costa, C. H. N. (2012). Application of serial analysis of gene expression to the study of the gene expression profile of Leishmania infantum chagasi Promastigote. Journal of Biomedicine and Biotechnology, 2012, 1-7.

Ooyen, A. V. (2001). Theoretical aspects of pattern analysis. In New Approaches for the Generation and Analysis of Microbial Fingerprints (ed. l. Dijkshoorn, Tower, K.J., Struelens, M.), pp. 31-45. Elsevier, Amsterdam.

Osamor, V. C., Adebiyi, E.F., Doumbia, S. (2010). Clustering Plasmodium falciparum genes to their functional roles using k-means. International Journal of Engineering and Technology 2, 215-225.

Pearson, K. (1901). On lines and planes of closest fit to systems of points in space" (PDF). Philosophical Magazine, vol. 2, pp. 559–572.

Perez-Torres, E., Paredes, M., Polanco, V. & Becerra, V. (2009). Gene expression analysis: A way to study yolerance to abiotic stresses in crops species. Chilean Journal of Agricultural Research 69, 260-269.

Pirim, H., Eksioglu, B., Perkins, A. & Yuceer, C. (2012). Clustering of high throughput gene expression data. Comput Oper Res 39, 3046-3061.

Pontil, M. & Verri, A. (1998). Support vector machines for 3D object recognition. IEEE Transactions on Pattern Analysis and Machine Intelligence 20, 637-646.

Quackenbush, J. (2001). Computational analysis of microarray data. Nat Rev Genet 2, 418-27.

Raychaudhuri, S., Stuart, J. M. & Altman, R. B. (2000). Principal components analysis to summarize microarray experiments: application to sporulation time series. Pac Symp Biocomput, 455-66.

Schena, M., Shalon, D., Davis, R. W. & Brown, P. O. (1995). Quantitative monitoring of gene-expression patterns with a complementary-DNA microarray. Science 270, 467-470.

Shannon, W., Culverhouse, R. & Duncan, J. (2003). Analyzing microarray data using cluster analysis. Pharmacogenomics 4, 41-52.

Sirinukunwattana, K., Savage, R. S., Bari, M. F., Snead, D. R. & Rajpoot, N. M. (2013). Bayesian hierarchical clustering for studying cancer gene expression data with unknown statistics. PLoS One 8, e75748.

Song, J. J., Lee, H. J., Morris, J. S. & Kang, S. H. (2007). Clustering of time-course gene expression data using functional data analysis. Computational Biology and Chemistry 31, 265-274.

Sturn, A., Quackenbush, J. & Trajanoski, Z. (2002). Genesis: cluster analysis of microarray data. Bioinformatics 18, 207-8.

Suresh, R. M., Dinakaran, K., Valarmathie, P. . (2008). Clustering gene expression data using self-organizing maps Journal of Computer Applications 1, 6-7.

Tamayo, P., Slonim, D., Mesirov, J., Zhu, Q., Kitareewan, S., Dmitrovsky, E., Lander, E. S. & Golub, T. R. (1999). Interpreting patterns of gene expression with self-organizing maps: methods and application to hematopoietic differentiation. Proc Natl Acad Sci U S A 96, 2907-12.

Tavazoie, S., Hughes, J. D., Campbell, M. J., Cho, R. J. & Church, G. M. (1999). Systematic determination of genetic network architecture. Nature Genetics 22, 281-285.

Tjaden, B. a. C., J. (2006). A survey of computational methods used in microarray data interpretation. Applied Mycology and Biotechnology 6.

Toronen, P., Kolehmainen, M., Wong, C. & Castren, E. (1999). Analysis of gene expression data using self-organizing maps. FEBS Letters 451, 142-146.

Van Rijsbergen, C. J. (1974). Further experiments with hierarchic clustering in document retrieval. Information Storage & Retrieval 10, 1-14.

Vemuri, V., Tang, N. (2004). Solving inverse problems via machine learning and knowledge discovery. In Knowledge-Based Intelligent Systems for Healthcare (ed. T. Ichimura, Yoshida, K.). CRC Press.

Verbanck, M., Le, S. & Pages, J. (2013). A new unsupervised gene clustering algorithm based on the integration of biological knowledge into expression data. BMC Bioinformatics 14.

Voorhees, E. M. (1986). Implementing agglomerative hierarchic clustering algorithms for use in document retrieval. Information Processing & Management 22, 465-476.

Ward, J. H. (1963). Hierarchical grouping to optimize an objective function. Journal of the American Statistical Association 58, 236-244.

Willett, P. (1988). Recent trends in hierarchic document clustering; a critical review. Information Processing & Management 24, 577-597.

Yeung, K. Y. & Ruzzo, W. L. (2001). Principal component analysis for clustering gene expression data. Bioinformatics 17, 763-74.

Yin, L., Huang, C. H. & Ni, J. (2006). Clustering of gene expression data: performance and similarity analysis. BMC Bioinformatics 7 Suppl 4, S19.

Zhang, H., Ho, T. B. & Lin, M. S. (2004). An evolutionary K-means algorithm for clustering time series data. Proceedings of the 2004 International Conference on Machine Learning and Cybernetics, 1282-1287.

Zhang, Z. & Fenstermacher, D. (2005). An introduction to MAMA (Meta-Analysis of MicroArray data) System. Conf Proc IEEE Eng Med Biol Soc 7, 7730-7733.

Zhu, H. J. & Li, L. X. (2011). Biological pathway selection through nonlinear dimension reduction. Biostatistics 12, 429-444.

❑❑❑

CHAPTER - 26

Relevance of Biological Databases in Post Genomic Era

Anil Kumar* and Nikita Chordia
School of Biotechnology, Devi Ahilya University, Khandwa Rd., Indore-452001, India
E mail: ak_sbt@yahoo.com

SUMMARY

The vast amounts of biological data generated from various studies have become the cornerstone of bioinformatics. The very first challenge of this enormous data is to store and handle this large volume of information through the establishment and use of computer databases. These data describe a unique array of information on biological entities such as DNA, protein and other molecules. However, still a large amount of data remains hidden which needs to be explored by accessing these data from databases.

Biological databases play a vital role in the biological research from the fundamental molecular biology to the applied areas of biology viz. medicine, agriculture, biochemical industries etc. This chapter introduces some basic concepts related to databases such as features, construction and classification of biological databases, submission and retrieving of data from biological databases.

1. INTRODUCTION

As amount of biological data from all over the world has heavily increased, and therefore, the need for storing and communicating large datasets has grown tremendously. Databases are required to keep research efficient and to get optimal information of the data obtained in the laboratory (Kohler, 2004). The most common data available in databases include nucleotide sequences, amino acid sequences and the 3D structural data produced by X-ray crystallography and NMR spectroscopy. Other types of data include metabolic pathways, gene expression data, molecular interaction, physico-chemical data and other data related to biological function and processes (Stein, 2003).

Databases are available related to different fields viz. genomes, nucleotides, proteins and taxonomy. Within each field several databases present their contents in different ways, different file formats and with different purposes (Nelson *et al.*, 2003). The format of database and information therein does not change significantly and therefore it becomes useless within a few years for the users. Some databases maintained by the responsible organizations contain global data collection, while others have limited data and are maintained only for a limited time. The main functions of biological databases include (Kohler, 2004):

Availability of Biological databases to scientists: Published data may be difficult and time consuming to find and collect from literature. Availability of data as much as possible at one place helps the scientist in more efficient research.

Availability of data in computer readable form: Availability of data in computer readable form than on the printed paper helps in involving computers in research and analysis.

Databases are fundamental to modern biology research. It is now unthinkable to design research projects or experiments without a prior query or consultation of a few bioinformatics database. Database technologies are improved to facilitate the integration and visualization of different data types viz. information about pathways, protein structure, gene variation, chemical inhibition and clinical information. However, the complexity of biological data represents major challenges in molecular biology database integration. Therefore, it requires high-level expert interpretation to meet the requirements of the biological research and development (Toby, 2012).

Biological database may be considered as a pool of knowledge containing data on variety of biological molecules. These powerful databases allow scientists to quickly find answers to questions relevant to their research without reading long lists of publications. For example, information regarding a disease, associated diseases, targeted drugs, pathways and networks they act within may be searched using one database. The powerful search query system of database allows scientists to quickly find answers to questions.

For the advancement of biological discovery, there is requirement of continuing development of currently existing databases as well as the conceptualization and creation of new types of databases. Keeping database up to date and accurate is a future task that requires active involvement of the entire biological community. There is much relevance of these databases in post genomic era of 21st century.

2. HISTORY

Probably one of the first biological sequence database was the book "Atlas of Protein Sequences and Structures" by Margaret Dayhoff and co-workers in 1965. It contained the 65 protein sequences determined at that time and the new editions of the book were published in 1970. Thereafter, computer became the storage medium of choice and became accessible to scientists. At that time, tapes and various kinds of disks were used for the distribution of databases. On requests, universities and academic institutes were getting databases on disks. Since 1990s, world wide web (www) is used for sharing the biological databases.

The first protein sequenced was of insulin which consisted of just 51 residues in two chains. It was made available as database in 1956. Around mid nineteen sixties, the first nucleic acid sequence of yeast tRNA was determined. Thereafter, the structure database called PDB (Protein Data Bank) was created with 10 entries in 1972. Now, this PDB has grown into large database with more than 38,000 entries (Berman *et al.*, 2007). Initial databases of protein sequence were maintained at the individual laboratories. However, in 1986, the large protein sequence database was developed called SWISS-PROT protein sequence database. Now it has more than 70,000 protein sequences from more than 5000 model organisms (Apweiler *et al.*, 2011).

These databases are available for study and research to academic institutes and industries. These huge varieties of divergent data are available as public domain information in the larger interest of research community through internet. Even on request to the database manager, data can be available in the CD-ROMs. These databases are constantly updated with additional entries.

3. FEATURES OF BIOLOGICAL DATA

The various features of biological databases are as follows:

1. Heterogeneous data: Biological databases deal with the diversified data types (Diederich, 1997). Some of the biological data types are as follows:

   a. Sequences: Sequence data type includes DNA, RNA and amino acid (protein) sequences. Due to availability of automated sequencers and large scale genome sequencing projects, sequence data have grown tremendously.

   b. Shapes: Data shapes include the 3D molecular structural data. For example the interaction of two molecules, behavior of molecule at potential binding site.

c. Patterns: This feature includes characterization of the biological unit. For example the regulatory sequences (promoters, transcription factors, etc), motifs, domains are the biological patterns.

d. Graphs/Network: The relationships between biological data are indicated using graphs or networks. Examples of these include pathways (signalling pathway, metabolic pathways, gene regulatory networks), genetic maps etc.

e. High Dimensional Data: Data generated from microarray experiments that involve thousands of genes, hundreds of experimental conditions, clustering studies on gene etc. All these data are high dimensional data that are used to compare the behavior of various biological units in different conditions.

f. Temporal Data: The data used for studying the dynamics of biological system like electrophysiology recording, protein structure dynamics, cellular structure dynamics etc.

g. Model Data: The biological phenomena are represented as computational mathematical and statistical model that are used for parameter testing, estimation etc.

2. High Volume Data: In addition to data heterogeneity, biological data are in large quantity. The large amount of data is required to support comprehensive investigations in various fields.

3. Large scale data integration: Research is in progress worldwide from many years. Therefore, data need to be collected from various laboratories across various structural and functional scales. All these data are integrated in databases and made available to use.

4. Uncertainty: In addition to observed results from experiments, some assumed data based on evidence are also available. These assumed data must be modelled and recorded as a part of data.

5. Data Curation: There are many inconsistencies in the biological data as these are collected from various sources. Therefore, there is always a chance of missing links. Some inconsistencies may be because of lack of knowledge in the concerned field. To improve data inconsistencies, data analysis is essential which can be done using automatic data curation that helps in understanding the missing links in biological databases.

6. Continual Change: Daily new data are generated in the laboratories that may contradict the old data. Therefore, there is always a necessity for developing databases schemas to incorporate any new data.

7. Data sharing: There is a practice of generating data which may be used by other investigators. There is a requirement of checking the data for reproducibility either by other scientists or the same scientist. Therefore data must be shared via databases for scientific community examination (Karp, 1996).

4. CONSTRUCTION OF BIOLOGICAL DATABASE

A biological database is the collection of data that is organized in such a manner that its contents can be easily accessed, managed and updated. The first step requires the collection of information from the experiments conducted in the laboratories. It is followed by the organization of information as data. The organized data is stored in EDS (Electronic data storage) at the server which is connected to the network (internet). By this process, the databases are accessible to all the users (online available). The users can access the database online. Fig. 1 shows the construction and accession of a database.

Fig. 1 : Construction and accession of a database

5. CLASSIFICATION OF DATABASES

5.1 Classification Based on Data source

Databases are generally classified into primary, secondary and composite databases.

Primary database consists of original biological data. Primary database is also called as Derived database because it contains data derived experimentally. This database contains information of the bimolecular (nucleic acid and protein) sequences and structure of alone and associated annotation information of the organisms, species, functions, bibliographic information etc. The primary databases are archives of raw sequences or structural data submitted by the scientific community. The three major publicly available nucleic acid raw sequence data submitted by researchers are GenBank (Benson *et al.*, 2010), EMBL (European Molecular Biology Laboratory)(Kulikova *et al.*, 2007) and DDBJ (DNA Databank of Japan) (Miyazaki *et al.*, 2003) . In these databases, most of the data are directly submitted by the authors with minimal annotation. SWISS-PROT (Apweiler *et al.*, 2011) and PIR (Protein Information Resource) (Wu *et al.*, 2003) contains protein sequences with annotation. For the three dimensional structure of macromolecules (nucleic acid and protein), there is one centralized database, the PDB (Protein Data Bank) (Berman *et al.*, 2007). This database archives atomic coordinates of macromolecules determined by x-ray crystallography and NMR.

Secondary Database contains derived information from the primary database. Sequence and structure annotation information in the primary database is often minimal. For more sophisticated biological knowledge, there is requirement of much more processing of primary data. For that, primary sequences are computationally processed, the amount of computation processing greatly varies for secondary database. Some databases contain the simple annotation like simple archives of translated sequence data from identified open reading frames in DNA, whereas others provide higher level of additional annotation and information related to structure and functions. The annotation of each entry is manually curated by the human experts. The annotation of raw sequence includes information about function, classification, domain structure, catalytic sites, cofactor binding, posttranslational modification(s), metabolic pathway information, disease association and similarity with other sequences. Examples of secondary databases are PROSITE (Sigrist *et al.*, 2010) and Pfam (Finn *et al.*, 2008) for sequence related information, CATH (Orengo *et al.*, 2007) and SCOP (Structural classification of Proteins) (Andreeva *et al.*, 2004) for classification of proteins, DSSP(Dictionary of protein secondary structure) (Kabsch and Sander, 1983) and DALI (Holm and Rosenström, 2010) for structure related information.

Composite databases are combination of variety of different primary databases and therefore, these databases avoid the need to search the multiple databases. It has been generally observed that information available in a single primary database is insufficient to complete a specific task. In composite database, data are compiled from the primary databases and are filtered to retain only the non-redundant data. Various options for search are incorporated in the composite database. The examples include NCBI (National Centre for biotechnology Information) which hosts the nucleotide and protein databases from variety of servers like GenBank (Benson *et al.*, 2010), RefSeq (Pruitt et al, 2007), and PDB (Wheeler *et al.*, 2007). It also has link to OMIM (Online Mendelian Inheritance in Man) which contains information about the protein involved in genetic disease (Hamosh *et al.*, 2005). It provides free access to various persons involved in research. Another composite database is NRDB (non-redundant database) which combines sequences from GenBank (CDS translations), PDB, Swiss-Prot, PIR (Protein information Resource), and PRF (Protein Research Foundation). The INSD (International Nucleotide Sequence Database) is an amalgam of nucleotide sequences in EMBL(The European Molecular Biology Laboratory), GenBank, DDBJ (DNA DataBank of Japan) and UniProtKB; UniProt (universal protein sequence database) (Bairoch *et al.*, 2005) is a collection of protein sequences from PIR (Protein information Resource), Swiss-Prot, and TrEMBL (Translated EMBL).

5.2 Classification Based on Data Type

Biological databases can be broadly classified into ten categories based on the composition of their data types.

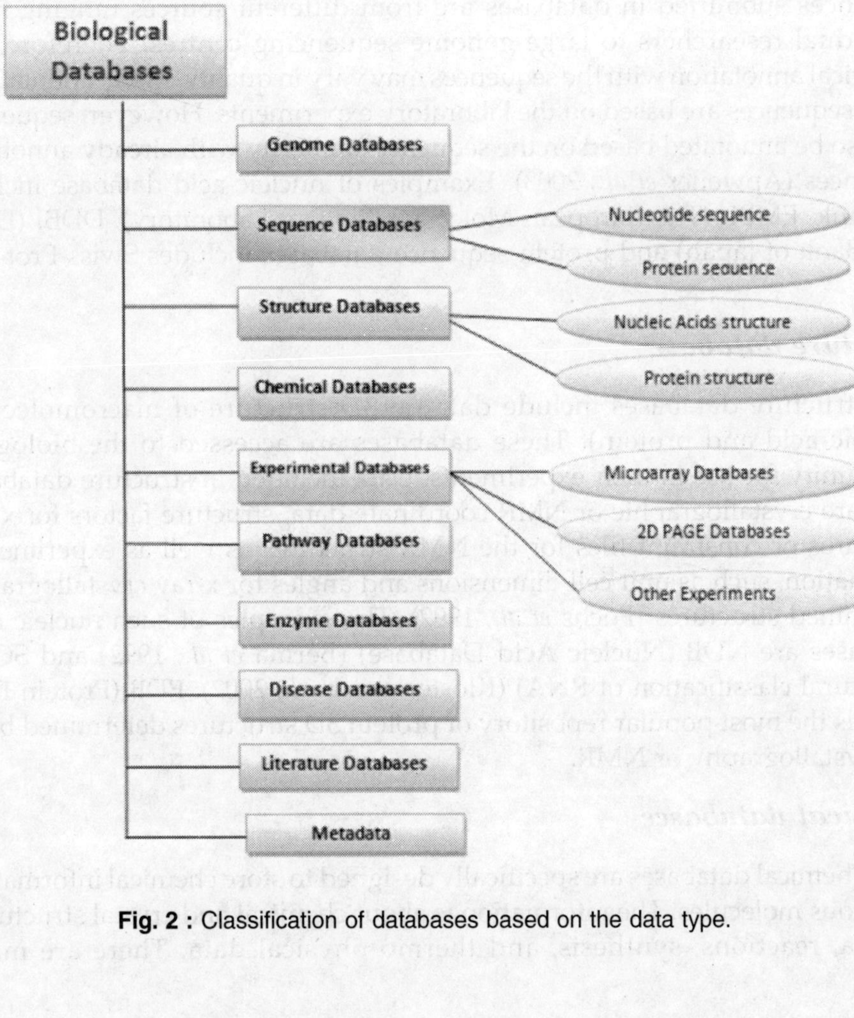

Fig. 2 : Classification of databases based on the data type.

Genome databases

Genome databases are whole genome repository of whole genome nucleotide sequences with annotation of various organisms. These databases are available for all three main domains of life - prokaryotes, eukaryotes and viruses as well as many phages, viroids and plasmids. These databases also provide sequence map with contigs and integrated genetic and physical maps along with annotated gene information (Baker and Brass, 1998). Examples of Genome Database are HGD (Human Genome Database), MGD (Mouse Genome Database), MBGD (Microbial Genome Database), GIB (Genome Information Broker).

Sequence database

Sequence databases include both nucleic acid and protein sequences. Sequences submitted in databases are from different sources ranging from individual researchers to large genome sequencing centres. Therefore, the biological annotation with the sequences may vary in quality. Many annotations of the sequences are based on the laboratory experiments. However, sequences can also be annotated based on the sequence similarity with already annotated sequences (Apweiler *et al.*, 2003). Examples of nucleic acid database include GenBank, EMBL (The European Molecular Biology Laboratory), DDBJ (DNA Data Bank of Japan) and protein sequence databases includes Swiss-Prot and PIR.

Structure database

Structure databases include data on 3D structure of macromolecules (nucleic acid and protein). These databases are accessed to the biological community for use in their experiments. Data included in structure databases often are crystallographic or NMR coordinate data, structure factors for x-ray structures or constraint files for the NMR structures as well as experimental information, such as unit cell dimensions and angles for x-ray crystallography determined structures (Fuchs *et al.*, 1992). The examples of such nucleic acid databases are NDB (Nucleic Acid Database) (Berma *et al.*, 1992) and SCOR (Structural classification of RNA) (Klosterman *et al.*, 2002). PDB (Protein Data Bank) is the most popular repository of protein 3D structures determined by x-ray crystallography or NMR.

Chemical databases

Chemical databases are specifically designed to store chemical information of various molecules. The information is about chemical and crystal structures, spectra, reactions, synthesis, and thermo-physical data. There are many techniques for storing chemical data in digital form like Molfile and SMILE Notation. PubChem (Bolton *et al.*, 2008), ChemSpider (Pence and Williams, 2010) and ChemBank (Seiler, 2008) are few examples of chemical databases.

Experiment databases

These databases contain data obtained from experiments viz. Microarray, SAGE (Serial Analysis of Gene Expression), mass spectrometry and other experiments performed in the laboratory. These databases contain information viz. gene expression, protein profiling, abundance of mRNA and cancer gene expression. Some of the examples are GEO (Gene Expression Omnibus) (Edgar, 2002), ArrayExpress(Parkinson *et al.*, 2007), CGED (Cancer Gene Expression Database) (Kato *et al.*, 2005).

Pathway databases

These are the databases with various data on metabolic pathways as well as signalling pathways. KEGG (Kyoto Encyclopedia of Genes and Genomes) (Kanehisa and Goto, 2000) and MetaCyc (Krieger *et al.*, 2004) are noteworthy pathway databases. These databases contain data about genomics, transcriptomics, proteomics, and metabolomics, pathway maps for biological interpretaion of higher-level systemic functions. Organism specific databases are also there such as EcoCyc for *Escherichia coli* and Flybase for *Drosophilla*.

Enzyme database

These databases provide information about various enzymes, their nomenclature, structure, function etc. The database also provides the pathway information where a specific enzyme is involved. The examples of enzyme databases are The Enzyme Database (Bairoch, 2000), REBASE (Roberts *et al.*, 2010), BRENDA (Schomburg *et al.*, 2004) etc.

Disease database

These are the exclusive sources for disease related information. These databases contain information on a disease, symptom, physical sign, drugs and common laboratory abnormality. These databases are helpful in rapid identification of medically relevant polymorphism from the large volume of data. The KEGG (Kyoto Encyclopedia of Genes and Genomes) DISEASE database is a collection of disease entries capturing knowledge on genetic and environmental perturbations (Kanehisa and Goto, 2000). OMIM (Online Mendelian Inheritance in Man) is an example of disease databases that provides data about human gene and genetic disorders (Hamosh *et al.*, 2005).

Literature databases

Literature or bibliographic databases are scientific databases consisting of numerous research papers and articles from various journals. Literature databases are searchable collections of up-to-date and accurate information from trusted sources such as encyclopedias, journals, reference books and other authoritative resources. PubMed (Roberts, 2001) available at NCBI is widely used bibliographic database. It is maintained by NLM (National laboratory of Medicine) and helps to stay current with the literature of various subjects. MEDLINE (Medical Literature Analysis and Retrieval System Online) is the NLM's premier bibliographic database covering the fields of medicine, nursing, pharmacy, dentistry, veterinary medicine and health care. MEDLINE is freely available on the Internet and searchable via PubMed and NCBI's Entrez system.

Metadata

Metadata database includes the information about the existing databases. Metadata is a structured information that locates a database and makes it easier to retrieve, use and manage the information. Database metadata can also include information like resource ownership, location, documentation, author, creation date, version, etc (Eccles *et al.*, 1990). Some examples of metadata are MetaBasis, BioRegistry, RASHdb.

6. SUBMISSION OF SEQUENCES TO DATABASES

Researchers are encouraged to submit their new sequences directly to any of the International sequence database such as NCBI (National Centre for Biotechnology Information) which manages GenBank, EMBL/EBI (European Molecular Biology Laboratory) or DDBJ (DNA Database of Japan). New sequences are exchanged daily by the NCBI, DDBJ and EMBL. NCBI reviews new entries and update the existing ones. A database accession number is provided on submission of sequences that is required for publishing the sequence.

The simplest way of submitting the sequence is through the NCBI's tool called BankIt and Sequin. BankIt is used with a single sequence, a simple set of sequences or a small batch of different sequences. It is used when a web-based submission tool is preferred and the feature annotation for sequences is not complicated and advanced sequence analysis tools are not required. Sequin is used when off line submission is preferred, sequence or sequences are complex and graphical viewing and editing options including an alignment editor are required. Another program called tbl2asn is also available which is a command line program with same functions as Sequin. It is used primarily for submission of complete genomes and large batches of sequences. Another program called

Barcode Submission Tool is a WWW-based tool for the submission of sequences and trace read data for Barcode of Life projects based on the COI gene (Kans and Ouellette, 2001).

7. SUBMISSION OF STRUCTURE TO DATABASES

PDB is the largest worldwide repository of the structures of macromolecules. An investigators can submit the newly discovered experimental structure of a macromolecule (protein or nucleic acid) to PDB using the web based tool ADIT (Auto Deposition Input Tool). To deposit a structure, the user uploads the relevant coordinate and experimental data files and adds additional information using the ADIT editor. Data can be easily submitted either in PDB or in mmCIF format. AutoDep then calls a suite of validation programs, whose output is returned via the WWW to the depositor within minutes of sending the data to the PDB. The entry and the output of the validation suite are then evaluated by a PDB scientific staff member, who completes the annotations and returns the entry to the author for comment and approval. Thereafter, the entry is released with ID (Yang *et al.*, 2004).

8. RETRIEVING BIOLOGICAL DATABASES

Databases are developed to provide efficient and user friendly access of stored data. There are ways to retrieve any kind of biological data. These are termed as biological database retrieval systems. These systems allow text searching of multiple databases and provide relevant links that match the search criteria. There are two widely used powerful data retrieval systems viz., SRS (Sequence Retrieval System) (Etzold *et al.*, 1996) and Entrez (Geer and Sayers, 2003) that provide access to multiple databases for retrieval of integrated search results (Blaschke *et al.*, 2003).

For complex queries in a database, Boolean operators are used. This database is used to join a series of keywords using logical terms such as AND, OR and NOT. They indicate the relationship between the keywords in a search. They are used as follows:

- AND: It is used when search result contains both words.
- OR: It means to search for results containing either word or both
- NOT: It excludes results containing either one of the words.

In addition to Boolean operators, parentheses () can also be used so that the computer knows which part of the search is to be executed first. Items contained within parentheses are executed first. Most search engines of public biological databases use some form of this Boolean logic.

SRS

SRS (http://srs.ebi.ac.uk) is a homogeneous interface to over 80 biological databases viz. databases of sequences, metabolic pathways, transcription factors etc. It was developed at the European Bioinformatics Institute (EBI) at Hinxton, UK. It is a database system that works with the flat files. In addition many bioinformatics tools are incorporated and combined with databases searches like BLAST, SSEARCH, FASTA, CLUSTALW, PHYLIP and many more. The SRS helps the researchers in various ways like fast access to diverse data, integration of data, ability to perform cross database queries and seamless integration of data and analysis tools (Etzold *et al.*, 1996).

Entrez

Entrez (http://www.ncbi.nlm.nih.gov/Entrez) has been developed and maintained at NCBI (National Centre for Biotechnology Information). The key feature of Entrez is its ability to integrate information, which comes from cross-referencing between NCBI databases based on pre-existing and logical relationships between individual entries. There are many databases that are accessible through the Entrez such as databases for genomes, genes, nucleotides, proteins, pathways, chemical, literature etc. Entrez is highly convenient and users do not have to visit multiple databases located at distances (Geer and Sayers, 2003).

9. PITFALLS OF BIOLOGICAL DATABASES

Redundancy is the major problem that is affecting the primary databases. The same gene is found under multiple names resulting in multiple entries and creates confusion about the data. There are many reasons for duplication of data in the database. These reasons include the repeated submission of identical or overlap sequence by the same or different authors, revising annotations and the poor database management that fails to detect the redundancy. This phenomena makes some primary databases excessively large.

Steps have been taken to reduce the redundancy from the databases. NCBI (National Centre for biotechnology Information) has created a database called RefSeq (Pruitt *et al*, 2007) which is nonredundant database. In this database, the sequences from the same organism and associate sequence fragments are merged into a single entry. Protein sequences derived from the same DNS sequence are linked as explicitly related entries. The SWISS-PROT database has the minimal redundancy of protein sequences as compared to other databases (Apweiler *et al.*, 2011).

Another major problem of biological databases is the dependency on the sequence information and annotation without knowing the accuracy of data.

There are many errors in the nucleotide sequences due to sequencing errors. This error causes change in the frameshift that makes protein translation impossible. The sequencing error can be due to contamination of gene sequences with the cloning vectors or may be because of other reason(s). These problems were more common before 1990s .Now a days, the sequence quality has been really improved. So more care should be taken while using dated sequences. These errors are also passed to the other databases causing propagation of errors.

Erroneous or inconsistency in annotation is also a problem caused by the genuine disagreement between researchers in the field. Besides, it may result from imprudent assignment of protein functions by sequence submitters. There are also some errors that are simply caused by omissions or mistakes in typing. Errors in annotation is damaging as large number of new sequences are assigned function(s) based on the already annotated sequences. Therefore a wrong annotation can be passed to all the related genes in the entire database. Some of the errors can be corrected by studying the protein domains and families or by the experimental work.

ACKNOWLEDGEMENTS

The authors acknowledge the facilities of the Department of Biotechnology, Ministry of Science and Technology, Government of India, New Delhi (DBT) under the Bioinformatics sub centre in the preparation of this manuscript.

REFERENCES

Andreeva, A., Howorth, D., Brenner, S. E., Hubbard, T. J., Chothia, C., *et al.* (2004). SCOP database in 2004: refinements integrate structure and sequence family data. Nucleic acids research, 32(suppl 1), D226-D229.

Apweiler, R., Martin, M. J., O'Donovan, C., Magrane, M., Alam-Faruque, Y., *et al.* (2011). Ongoing and future developments at the Universal Protein Resource. Nucleic acids research, 39(Database issue), D214-9.

Bairoch, A., Apweiler, R., Wu, C. H., Barker, W. C., Boeckmann, B., *et al.* (2005). The universal protein resource (UniProt). Nucleic acids research, 33(suppl 1), D154-D159.

Bairoch, A. (2000). The ENZYME database in 2000. Nucleic acids research,28(1), 304-305.

Baker, P. G., & Brass, A. (1998). Recent developments in biological sequence databases. Current Opinion in Biotechnology, 9(1), 54-58.

Benson, D. A., Karsch-Mizrachi, I., Lipman, D. J., Ostell, J., & Sayers, E. W. (2010). GenBank. Nucleic acids research, 38(suppl 1), D46-D51.

Berman, H., Henrick, K., Nakamura, H., & Markley, J. L. (2007). The worldwide Protein Data Bank (wwPDB): ensuring a single, uniform archive of PDB data. Nucleic acids research, 35(suppl 1), D301-D303.

Berman, H. M., Olson, W. K., Beveridge, D. L., Westbrook, J., Gelbin, A., *et al.* (1992). The nucleic acid database. A comprehensive relational database of three-dimensional structures of nucleic acids. Biophysical Journal, 63(3), 751.

Blaschke, C., Hirschman, L., and Valencia, A. (2002). Information extraction in molecular biology. Briefings in Bioinformatics, 3(2), 154-165.

Bolton, E. E., Wang, Y., Thiessen, P. A., & Bryant, S. H. (2008). PubChem: integrated platform of small molecules and biological activities. Annual reports in computational chemistry, 4, 217-241.

Diederich, J. (1997). Basic properties for biological databases: character development and support. Mathematical and Computer Modelling, 25(10), 109-127.

Eccles, J. R., & Saldanha, J. (1990). Metadata-based generation and management of knowledgebases from molecular biological databases.Computer methods and programs in biomedicine, 32(2), 115-123.

Edgar, R., Domrachev, M., & Lash, A. E. (2002). Gene Expression Omnibus: NCBI gene expression and hybridization array data repository. Nucleic acids research, 30(1), 207-210.

Etzold, T., Ulyanov, A., & Argos, P. (1996). [8] SRS: Information retrieval system for molecular biology data banks. Methods in enzymology, 266, 114-128.

Finn, R. D., Tate, J., Mistry, J., Coggill, P. C., Sammut, S. J., *et al.* (2008). The Pfam protein families database. Nucleic acids research, 36(suppl 1), D281-D288.

Fuchs, R., Rice, P., & Cameron, G. N. (1992). Molecular biological databases—present and future. Trends in biotechnology, 10, 61-65.

Geer, R. C., & Sayers, E. W. (2003). Entrez: making use of its power. Briefings in Bioinformatics, 4(2), 179-184.

Hamosh, A., Scott, A. F., Amberger, J. S., Bocchini, C. A., & McKusick, V. A. (2005). Online Mendelian Inheritance in Man (OMIM), a knowledgebase of human genes and genetic disorders. Nucleic acids research, 33(suppl 1), D514-D517

Holm, L., & Rosenström, P. (2010). Dali server: conservation mapping in 3D.Nucleic acids research, 38(suppl 2), W545-W549.

Kabsch, W., & Sander, C. (1983). Dictionary of protein secondary structure: pattern recognition of hydrogen bonded and geometrical features. Biopolymers,22(12), 2577-2637.

Kanehisa, M., & Goto, S. (2000). KEGG: kyoto encyclopedia of genes and genomes. Nucleic acids research, 28(1), 27-30.

Kans, J. A., & Ouellette, B. F. (2001). Submitting DNA sequences to the databases. Bioinformatics: A Practical Guide to the Analysis of Genes and Proteins, 65-81.

Karp, P. D. (1996). Database links are a foundation for interoperability. Trends in Biotechnology, 14(8), 273-279.

Kato, K., Yamashita, R., Matoba, R., Monden, M., Noguchi, S., *et al.* (2005). Cancer gene expression database (CGED): a database for gene expression profiling with accompanying clinical information of human cancer tissues. Nucleic acids research, 33(suppl 1), D533-D536.

Krieger, C. J., Zhang, P., Mueller, L. A., Wang, A., Paley, S.,*et al.*(2004). MetaCyc: a multiorganism database of metabolic pathways and enzymes. Nucleic acids research, 32(suppl 1), D438-D442.

Klosterman, P. S., Tamura, M., Holbrook, S. R., & Brenner, S. E. (2002). SCOR: a structural classification of RNA database. Nucleic acids research,30(1), 392-394.

Kohler, J. (2004). Integration of life science databases. Drug Discovery Today: BIOSILICO, 2(2), 61-69.

Kulikova, T., Akhtar, R., Aldebert, P., Althorpe, N., Andersson, M., *et al.* (2007). EMBL nucleotide sequence database in 2006. Nucleic acids research, 35(suppl 1), D16-D20.

Margaret O. Dayhoff, Richard V. Eck. Atlas of Protein Sequence and Structure: 1967-68; National Biomedical Research Foundation, 1969.

Miyazaki, S., Sugawara, H., Gojobori, T., & Tateno, Y. (2003). DNA data bank of Japan (DDBJ) in XML. Nucleic Acids Research, 31(1), 13-16.

Nelson, M. R., Reisinger, S. J., & Henry, S. G. (2003). Designing databases to store biological information. Biosilico, 1(4), 134-142.

Orengo, C. A., Michie, A. D., Jones, S., Jones, D. T., Swindells, M. B., *et al.* (1997). CATH–a hierarchic classification of protein domain structures. Structure, 5(8), 1093-1109.

Parkinson, H., Kapushesky, M., Shojatalab, M., Abeygunawardena, N., Coulson, R., *et al.*. (2007). ArrayExpress—a public database of microarray experiments and gene expression profiles. Nucleic acids research, 35(suppl 1), D747-D750.

Pence, H. E., & Williams, A. (2010). ChemSpider: an online chemical information resource. Journal of Chemical Education, 87(11), 1123-1124.

Pruitt, K. D., Tatusova, T., & Maglott, D. R. (2007). NCBI reference sequences (RefSeq): a curated non-redundant sequence database of genomes, transcripts and proteins. Nucleic acids research, 35(suppl 1), D61-D65.

Roberts, R. J., Vincze, T., Posfai, J., & Macelis, D. (2010). REBASE—a database for DNA restriction and modification: enzymes, genes and genomes.Nucleic acids research, 38(suppl 1), D234-D236.

Roberts, R. J. (2001). PubMed Central: The GenBank of the published literature. Proceedings of the National Academy of Sciences, 98(2), 381-382.

Schomburg, I., Chang, A., Ebeling, C., Gremse, M., Heldt, C., *et al.* (2004). BRENDA, the enzyme database: updates and major new developments. Nucleic acids research, 32(suppl 1), D431-D433.

Seiler, K. P., George, G. A., Happ, M. P., Bodycombe, N. E., Carrinski, H. A., *et al.* (2008). ChemBank: a small-molecule screening and cheminformatics resource database. Nucleic acids research,36(suppl 1), D351-D359.

Sigrist, C. J., Cerutti, L., De Castro, E., Langendijk-Genevaux, P. S., Bulliard, V., *et al.* (2010). PROSITE, a protein domain database for functional characterization and annotation. Nucleic acids research, 38(suppl 1), D161-D166.

Stein, L. D. (2003). Integrating biological databases. Nature Reviews Genetics,4(5), 337-345.

Toby, I. (2012). Biological databases as research tools in the post-genomic era.Aviation, space, and environmental medicine, 83(4), 452.

Wheeler, D. L., Barrett, T., Benson, D. A., Bryant, S. H., Canese, K.,*et al.* (2007). Database resources of the national center for biotechnology information. Nucleic acids research, 35(suppl 1), D5-D12.

Wu, C. H., Yeh, L. S. L., Huang, H., Arminski, L., Castro-Alvear, J., *et al.* (2003). The protein information resource. Nucleic acids research, 31(1), 345-347.

Yang, H., Guranovic, V., Dutta, S., Feng, Z., Berman, H. M., *et al.* (2004). Automated and accurate deposition of structures solved by X-ray diffraction to the Protein Data Bank. Acta Crystallographica Section D: Biological Crystallography, 60(10), 1833-1839.

□□□

CHAPTER - 27

Distributed Databases in Automating Processes with Some Applications

V.V.Sumanth Kumar[1], N.Showri Raju[2], R.Nagarjuna Kumar[2], N.Ravi Kumar[2] and G.R.Maruthi Sankar[2]

[1]National Academy of Agricultural Research Management, Rajendranagar, Hyderabad.
[2]Central Research Institute for Dryland Agriculture, Santoshnagar, Hyderabad.
Email: nsraju@crida.in

ABSTRACT

A Distributed Database is a database that is under the control of a central database management system (DBMS) in which storage devices are not all attached to a common CPU and may be dispersed over a network of computers interconnected through internet. To ensure that the Distributive databases are up to date and current, there are two processes: replication and duplication. Replication involves using specialized software that looks for changes in the distributive database. Once the changes have been identified, the replication process makes all the databases look alike. The replication process can be very complex and time consuming depending on the size and number of the distributive databases. Duplication on the other hand is not as complicated. It would basically identify one database as a master and then duplicates that database. This is to ensure that each distributed location has the same data. In the duplication process, changes to the master database only are allowed. This is to ensure that local data will not be overwritten. Both of the processes can keep the data current in all distributive locations. The most commonly used databases are DB2, MySQL, Oracle, MS-Access, Ingres, Firebird, MS SQL Server, Teradata, Sybase, Informix and Postgre SQL. Use of single or combination of databases depending on the requirement is key to success. This distributed data management with different levels of transparency like network transparency, fragmentation transparency, replication transparency, etc. Increase reliability and availability of data to the users as well as reduces the database downtime and increase the database performance, reduces network failure due to reduction of network traffic.

INTRODUCTION

A Distributed Database that consists of two or more data files located at different sites on a computer network. Because the database is distributed, different users can access it without interfering with one another. However, the *DBMS* must periodically synchronize the scattered databases to make sure that they all have consistent data. Another definition is a distributed database is a network of databases managed by multiple database servers that appears to a user as single logical database. The data of all databases in the distributed database can be simultaneously accessed and modified.

Distributed Database Architecture

A distributed database system allows applications to access data from local and remote databases. In a homogenous distributed database system, each database is an Oracle Database. In a heterogeneous distributed database system, at least one of the databases is not an Oracle Database. Distributed databases use a client/server architecture to process information requests.

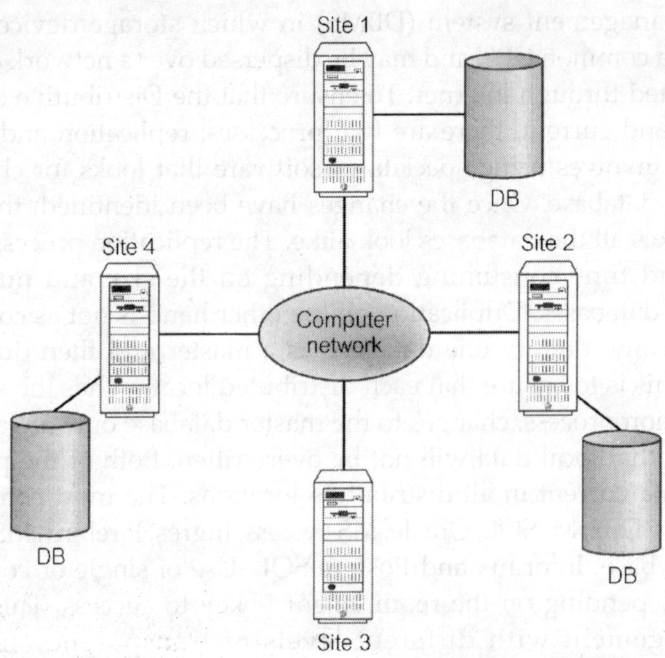

Distributed Database Architecture

Homogenous Distributed Database

A homogenous distributed database system is a network of two or more Oracle Databases that reside on one or more machines. An application can simultaneously access or modify the data in several databases in a single distributed environment. For a client application, the location and platform of the databases are transparent. You can also create synonyms for remote objects in the distributed system so that users can access them with the same syntax as local objects. In this way, a distributed system gives the appearance of native data. An Oracle Database distributed database system can incorporate Oracle Databases of different versions. All supported releases of Oracle Database can participate in a distributed database system. Nevertheless, the applications that work with the distributed database must understand the functionality that is available at each node in the system. A distributed database application cannot expect an Oracle7 database to understand the SQL extensions that are only available with Oracle Database access. Users on mfg do not have to know that the data they access resides on remote databases.

Distributed Databases Versus Distributed Processing

The terms **distributed database** and **distributed processing** are closely related, yet have distinct meanings. There definitions are as follows:

- **Distributed database:** A set of databases in a distributed system that can appear to applications as a single data source.
- **Distributed processing:** The operations that occurs when an application distributes its tasks among different computers in a network. For example, a database application typically distributes front-end presentation tasks to client computers and allows a back-end database server to manage shared access to a database. Consequently, a distributed database application processing system is more commonly referred to as a client/server database application system. Distributed database systems employ a distributed processing architecture. For example, an Oracle Database server acts as a client when it requests data that another Oracle Database server manages.

Distributed Databases Versus Replicated Databases

The terms distributed database system and database replication are related, yet distinct. In a pure (that is, not replicated) distributed database, the system manages a single copy of all data and supporting database objects. Typically, distributed database applications use distributed transactions to access both local and remote data and modify the global database in real-time.

The term replication refers to the operation of copying and maintaining database objects in multiple databases belonging to a distributed system. While replication relies on distributed database technology, database replication offers applications benefits that are not possible within a pure distributed database environment.

Most commonly, replication is used to improve local database performance and protect the availability of applications because alternate data access options exist. For example, an application may normally access a local database rather than a remote server to minimize network traffic and achieve maximum performance. Furthermore, the application can continue to function if the local server experiences a failure, but other servers with replicated data remain accessible.

Heterogeneous Distributed Database Systems

In a heterogeneous Distributed Database System, at least one of the databases is a non-Oracle Database system. To the application, the heterogeneous distributed database system appears as a single, local, Oracle Database. The local Oracle Database server hides the distribution and heterogeneity of the data.

The Oracle Database server accesses the non-Oracle Database system using Oracle Heterogeneous Services in conjunction with an agent. If you access the non-Oracle Database data store using an Oracle Transparent Gateway, then the agent is a system-specific application. For example, if you include a Sybase database in an Oracle Database distributed system, then you need to obtain a Sybase specific transparent gateway so that the Oracle Database in the system can communicate with it.

Alternatively, you can use generic connectivity to access non-Oracle Database data stores so long as the non-Oracle Database system supports the ODBC or OLE DB protocols.

Heterogeneous Services

Heterogeneous Services (HS) is an integrated component within the Oracle Database server and the enabling technology for the current suite of Oracle Transparent Gateway products. HS provides the common architecture and administration mechanisms for Oracle Database gateway products and other heterogeneous access facilities. Also, it provides upwardly compatible functionality for users of most of the earlier Oracle Transparent Gateway releases.

Transparent Gateway Agents

For each non-Oracle Database system that you access, heterogeneous services can use a transparent gateway agent to interface with the specified non-Oracle Database system. The agent is specific to the non-Oracle Database system, so each type of system requires a different agent.

The transparent gateway agent facilitates communication between Oracle Database and non-Oracle Database systems and uses the heterogeneous services component in the Oracle Database server. The agent executes SQL and transactional requests at the non-Oracle Database system on behalf of the Oracle Database server.

Generic Connectivity

Generic connectivity enables you to connect to non-Oracle Database data stores by using either a heterogeneous services ODBC agent or a heterogeneous services OLE DB agent. Both are included with your Oracle product as a standard feature. Any data source compatible with the ODBC or OLE DB standards can be accessed using a generic connectivity agent.

The advantage to generic connectivity is that it may not be required for you to purchase and configure a separate system-specific agent. You use an ODBC or OLE DB driver that can interface with the agent. However, some data access features are only available with transparent gateway agents.

Some Applications

Deliverables may include "The critical food crop zones identified for strengthening online data collection and equipments installed". We believe, automation is essential in data collection especially where data need to be collected from a large number collection centres across geographical regions. The process now in NARS is data used to send from centres to the concerned institutes in Excel sheets by e-mail. The main issue with this system is, centres used to send the data in different formats irrespective of standard formats provided to them. Many a times excel sheets used to carry viruses which are detrimental to the main system. In some places they used to send them as hardcopies by post. We can avoid all these problems by automating the entire data flow from entry to data analysis.

For implementation of this distributed architecture, we need to have a PC with MySQL Database server installed (Community edition comes for free) and a high end clustered server at a central location with Oracle Database server running. The data generated at a research station will be fed into MySQL which will get replicated into Oracle database with the help of tools like golden gate.

As the data movement is bi-directional, a small data change in a single database will get replicated in other databases. In this architecture we need to purchase only one database license.

Another application of the above technology lies in developing a central database for long-term data generated based on agricultural experiments including performance on farmers fields, technological gaps and implementation issues, village/farm level constraints in adoption of best bet practices, research gaps etc. Once the data is loaded in to the Primary data warehouse, we can send the data as input to the SAS System. We have to create db link in the database for enabling SAS to access the data.

We propose a SAT Streaming Server in the lines of YOUTUBE. We need to develop the videos & audios of climate-resilient technologies which can be classifying them based on crop/variety. In this the Production video server would be installed in an organization and standby databases have to be installed at respective research and extension locations. The video can be stored in Oracle database itself and associated language audio also can be stored in the different column of the same of record. This architecture can be implemented by using Oracle 11g Active DataGuard technology to allow same copies of databases. The research stations will have read only access to all the video and multimedia fed into the master database at a central location. Whenever master database gets modified, that modification gets reflected in all the copies databases. The advantage is to have a quick response as video are loaded in the every PC. With one can add a new language audio to the existing video and the entire video need not to be developed again. This can be developed in Hindi, English and other 10+ regional languages.

Oracle 11g can easily host enormous number of huge videos. Going forward, as the number of videos increases (with various local language videos), we can go for Oracle Real Application Clusters. Once the proposed streaming system is in place, the videos can be viewed 'n' number of times by millions of farmers in the country.

Now a days many of farmers are having mobiles. So this application can be used by farmers who got 3G complied mobiles. It won't take much time for 3G mobiles to reach farmers as it is provided by BSNL. We need a cluster of dedicated servers/ databases to ensure proper response time. Oracle is robust enough to host the Tera Bytes of metrological data. The World's largest commercial database is running on Oracle 10g with a size of 29.2 Tera Bytes.

CONCLUSION

In this paper, details of distributed data management with different levels of transparency like network transparency, fragmentation transparency, replication transparency, etc are discussed. Increase in reliability and availability of data to the users will reduce the database downtime and increase the database performance, reduces network failure due to reduction of network traffic.

REFERENCES

Elmasri and Navathe. Fundamentals of database systems (3rd Edition), Addison-Wesley Longman, ISBN 0-201-54263-3.

Özsu, M.T. and Valduriez, P. (2011). Principles of Distributed Databases (3rd Edition). Springer, ISBN 978-1-4419-8833-1.

Oracle Database Administrator's Guide 10g (Release 1), http://docs.oracle.com/cd/B14117_01/server.101/b10739/ds_concepts.htm

Principles of Distributed Database Systems. www.pcbookenus.co.uk/ cat801207.html. *pp 562. (1991). ISBN: 0-13-691643-0.*

❑❑❑

CHAPTER - 28

Framework for Development of Meteorological Data Warehouse

N.Showri Raju, G.R.Maruthi Sankar and R.Nagarjuna Kumar
Central Research Institute for Dryland Agriculture, ICAR, Santoshnagar, Hyderabad-500059, Andhra Pradesh.
Scientist (Computer Applications in Agriculture); Principal Scientist (Agricultural Statistics)
E-mail address : nsraju@crida.in

ABSTRACT

The details of a frame work for development of data warehouse are discussed in this paper. The concepts of data ware housing, its data ware house process, its architecture, components, data sources, data transformation, apart from free and shareware and commercial software available are described. The details of power of Data Warehouse are also described with a procedure for a better reporting of data and analysed results. The data Warehouse should be made to deliver clear indications on how the research or business enterprise is performing. There is a need to plot out the expected users for the Data Warehouse in the enterprise so that they will have the appropriate reports in a format which is quickly understandable.

INTRODUCTION

The concept of data warehousing is not hard to understand. The notion is to create a permanent storage space for the tera and pita bytes of data needed to support weather reporting, analysis, and other Business intelligence functions. This paper designs and implements the meteorological data warehouse as well as the meteorological data report based on Business intelligence tools. The purpose is to apply data warehouse technology in the meteorological research area. Using On-Line Analytical Processing (OLAP) and the multidimensional report, we could get the beneficial data. The system generates meteorological data report, which can publish the report to the browser. This research is beneficial for meteorological phenomenal studies. On the surface, it may seem not effective to store data in more than one place. The advantages, however more than justify the effort and cost of doing this exercise. Based on the meteorological information on different weather parameters, background and ideology of data warehouse construction, this article analyzes multiple meteorological data sources, designs the meteorological data warehouse architecture, target data model and ETL process. We have applied this architecture to provide a dynamic and flexible weather data warehouse that provides a wide variety of weather data from different sources to different weather-based applications. The weather data warehouse is very much required to take effective climate change mitigation strategies, weather aberrations and also Produce Reports for Long Term Trend Analysis, aggregations of weather changes and other aspects.

What is Data Warehousing?

A data warehouse is a collection of data in support of management decision-making process that is subject-oriented, integrated, time-variant, and nonvolatile. The data warehouse is focused on the concept (for example, sales) rather than the process (for example, issuing invoices). It contains all the relevant information on a concept gathered from multiple processing systems. This information is collected and stored at regular intervals and is relatively stable.

A data warehouse is an integrated store of information collected from other systems that becomes the foundation for decision support and data analysis. Although there are many types of data warehouses, based on different design methodologies and philosophical approaches, they all have these common traits.

- Information is organized around the major subjects of the enterprise reflecting a data-driven design.
- Raw data is gathered from the nonintegrated operational and legacy applications, cleansed, and then summarized and presented in a way that makes sense to end users.
- Based on the feedback from end users and discoveries in the data warehouse, the data warehouse architecture will change over time, reflecting the iterative nature of the process.

The data warehousing process is inherently complex and, as a result, is costly and time-consuming. Over the past several years, Microsoft company has been working within the software industry to create a data warehousing platform that consists of both component technology and leading products that can be used to lower the costs and improve the effectiveness of data warehouse creation, administration, and usage. Microsoft also has been developing a number of products and facilities, such as Microsoft SQL Server version 7.0, that are well suited to the data warehousing process. Coupled with third-party products, that can be integrated using the Microsoft Data Warehousing Framework, customers have a large selection of interoperable, best-of-breed products from which to choose for their data warehousing needs.

The SQL Server 7.0 offers broad functionality in support of the data warehousing process. In conjunction with the Data Warehousing Framework, Microsoft plans to deliver a platform for data warehousing that helps reduce costs and complexity, and improves effectiveness of data warehousing efforts.

Data Warehousing Process

From the information technology perspective, data warehousing is aimed at the timely delivery of the right information to the right individuals in an organization. This is an ongoing process, not a one-time solution, and requires an approach different from that required in the development of transaction-oriented systems.

A data warehouse integrates the operational data by using consistent naming conventions, measurements, physical attributes, and semantics. The first step in the physical design of the data warehouse are determining which subject areas should be included and developing a set of agreed-upon definitions. This requires interviewing end users, analysts, and executives to understand and document the scope of the information requirements. The issues must be thoroughly understood before the logical process can be translated into a physical data warehouse.

Following the physical design, operational systems are put in place to populate the data warehouse. Because the operational systems and the data warehouse contain different representations of the data, populating the data warehouse requires transformations of the data: summarizing, translating, decoding, eliminating invalid data, and so on. These processes need to be automated so that they can be performed on an ongoing basis: extracting, transforming, and moving the source data as often as needed to meet the business requirements of the data warehouse.

Finally, the information is made available for browsing, analyzing, and reporting. Many tools assist in analysis, from simple report writers to advanced data miners. Ultimately, the analysis drives the final iterations of the data warehousing process, causing revisions in the design of the data warehouse to accommodate new information, improve system performance, or allow new types of analysis. With these changes, the process restarts and continues throughout the life of the data warehouse.

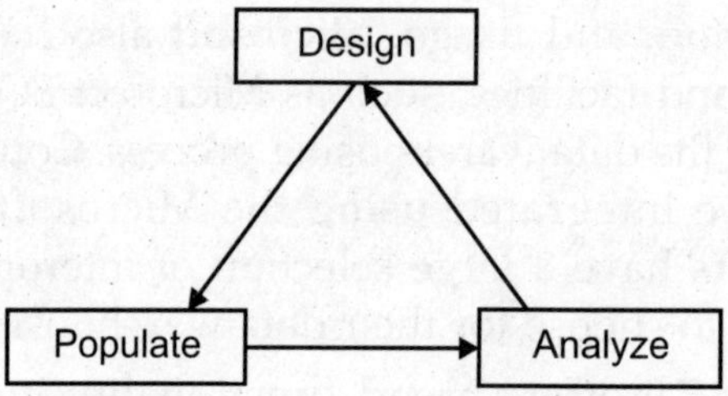

Data Warehousing Architecture

Many methodologies have been proposed to simplify the information technology efforts required to support the data warehousing process on an ongoing basis. This has led to debates about the best architecture for delivering data warehouses in organizations. Two basic types of data warehouse architecture exist: *enterprise* data warehouses and *data marts*.

Enterprise Architecture

The enterprise data warehouse contains enterprise-wide information integrated from multiple operational data sources for consolidated data analysis. Typically, it is composed of several subject areas, such as customers, products, and sales, and is used for both tactical and strategic decision making. The enterprise data warehouse contains both detailed point-in-time data and summarized information, and can range in size from 50 gigabytes (GB) to more than 1 terabyte (TB). The Enterprise data warehouses can be very expensive and time-consuming to build and manage. They are usually created from the top down by centralized information services organizations.

Data Mart Architecture

The data mart contains a subset of enterprise-wide data that is built for use by an individual department or division in an organization. Unlike the enterprise data warehouse, the data mart is usually built from the bottom up by departmental resources for a specific decision-support application or group of users. The data marts contain summarized and often detailed data about a subject area. The information in the data mart can be a subset of an enterprise data warehouse (dependent data mart) or can come directly from the operational data sources (independent data mart). The enterprise data warehouses and data marts are constructed and maintained through the same iterative process described earlier. Furthermore, both approaches share a similar set of technological components.

Data Warehousing Components

A data warehouse always consists of a number of components, including:

- Operational data sources.
- Design/development tools.
- Data extraction and transformation tools.
- Database management system (DBMS).
- Data access and analysis tools.
- System management tools.

Several years ago, Microsoft recognized the need for a set of technologies that would integrate these components. This led to the creation of the Microsoft Data Warehousing Framework, a roadmap not only for the development of Microsoft products such as SQL Server 7.0, but also for the technologies necessary to integrate products from other vendors.

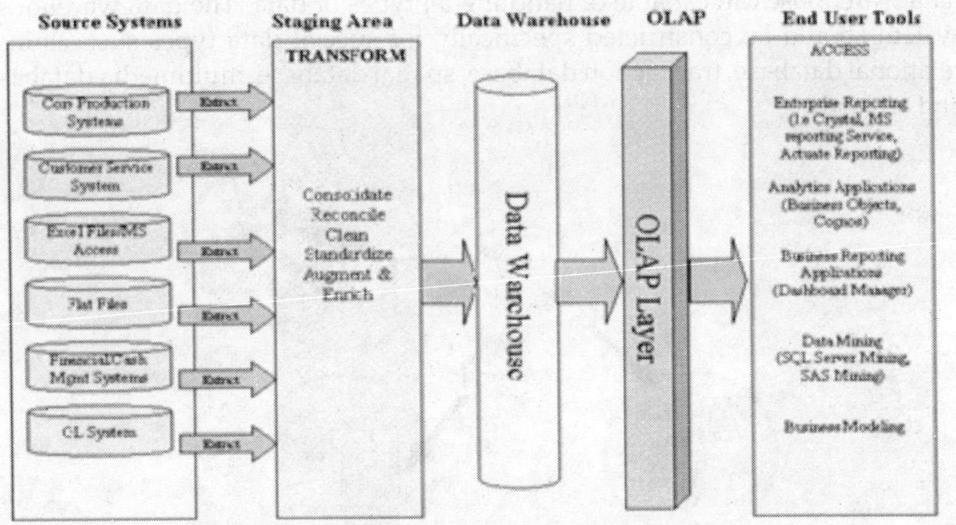

Many companies would build data warehouses to predict developments in a particular field so that based on the data warehouse can be obtained by new policies that benefit. In building a data warehouse, there are four steps that must be considered, the fourth thing is the identification of sources of data, extraction, transformation, and loading data into the database.

1. Identify data sources

The first step before developing data warehouses, things to note is to identify existing data sources, for example in building a library data warehouse, there are two types of data sources that need to be considered, namely internal and external data. The internal data is data that already exists in the library, for example a database collection of books, while the external data source is data that does not exist in library databases, external data can be combined to create the appropriate variable.

The data clustering is one technique used in the identification of data sources. Basically clustering of data is a process for classifying a set of data without a class attribute that has been defined previously, based on the principle of conceptual clustering is to maximize and minimize intra-class similarity. For example, a set of objects can be a set with clustering to make classes and then became a set of rules that can be derived based on a certain classification.

The analysis with clustering, it is helpful to build partitions of a large number of objects with based on the principle of "divide and conquer" which decomposition of a large-scale system, into smaller components, to simplify the design process and implementation. Because of the variety of data types and different purposes of the data warehouse, it is unrealistic to expect that data warehouse can capable of handling all types of data. The data warehouse system should be constructed specifically for special data types such as in a relational database, transaction database, spatial database, multimedia database and so forth.

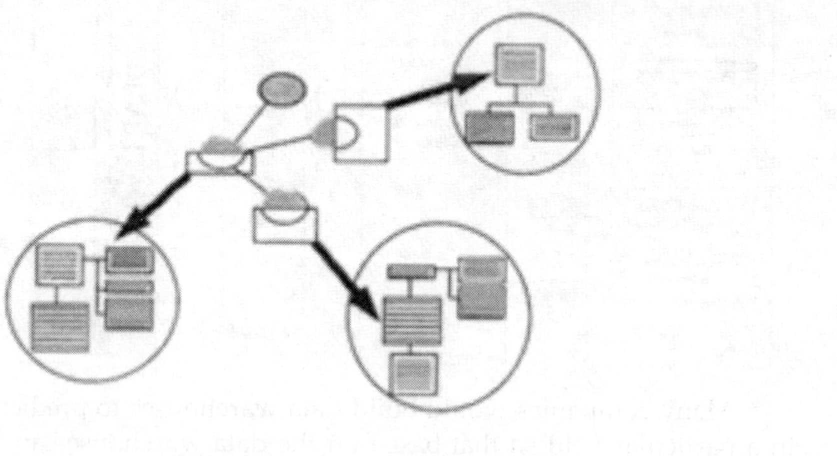

Fig. 1 : Identifying data from various data sources

2. Data Extraction

At this stage takes the longest time because this step is a step we want to retrieve data from various sources. The issues of interest in this phase is duplication data and inconsistencies data. The data collected in the transaction process is often placed at different locations. So it takes the ability of the system to collect data quickly. If the data is stored in the regional branch, the data must be uploaded to a centralized server. This can be done daily, weekly, or monthly depending on the amount of data, security and cost. Data can be summarized first before sending them to a central storage place. For example, a hardware store may send data which showed that 10 rolls of cable have been sold on this day by employee number 10 compared to the transaction detail data transmission.

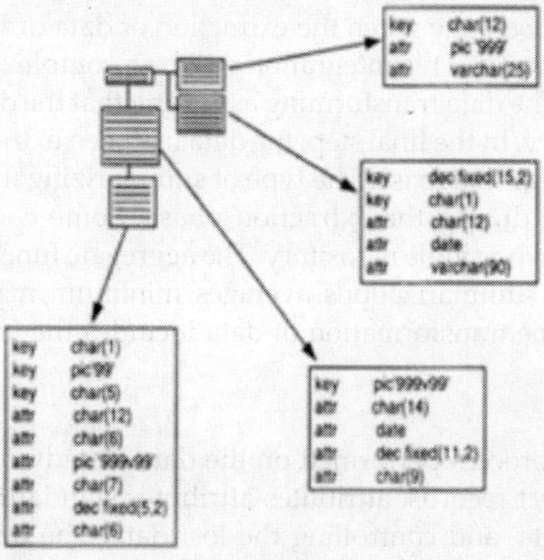

Figu. 2 : Add the Attribute

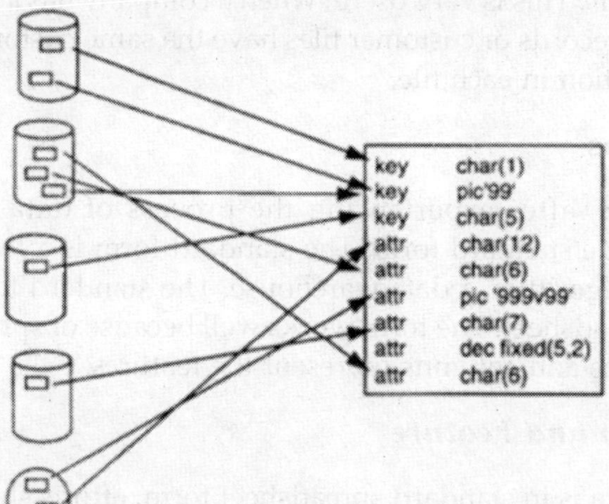

Fig. 3 : Defining System Record

3. Data Transformation

The next stage after extracting data from various sources is a transformation. Transformation of data associated with the conversion process from data source to data destination. This process consists of 2 steps: mapping data from all data elements by using transformation rule 1-to-many and many-to-1 generation of code that creates a real transformation program.

Transformation is needed to ensure consistency of data, data transformation can be done when the extraction of data or when entering data into the data warehouse. This integration will be a complex problem when the data is very large. The data transforming assuming that the data has been stored in a single repository. In the final step, the data has been extracted from multiple databases into a single database. The type of summarizing in this step is similar with summarizing during the extraction phase. Some companies choose to summarize the data in a single repository. The aggregate functions are frequently used, among others summarizations, averages, minimum, maximum, and count. The important in the transformation of data includes the following.

Data Cleansing

The cleaning process performed on the data already collected in order to remove the incorrect records, attributes-attributes standardize, rationalize the structure of the data, and controlling the lost data. The data are inconsistent and many errors make the results inaccurate data warehouse. It is very important to make the data consistent. Data cleansing can also help companies to consolidate records. This is very useful when a company has a lot of records for a customer. Any records or customer files have the same customer number, but different information in each file.

Standard Forms

Furthermore, after experiencing the process of data cleansing, data transferred into the standard form. The standard form is a form of data to be accessed by the algorithm, a data warehouse. The standard form is usually in the form of a spreadsheet. The form works well because of spreadsheet rows is represent the cases and columns represent the features.

Data Reduction and Feature

After the data is in standard spreadsheet form, efforts should be made to reduce the number of features. There are several reasons to reduce the number of features in a spreadsheet. A bank may have hundreds of features when they wanted to predict credit risk. This means that companies have data in very large quantities. Working with a large of data can make prediction algorithm decreases performance.

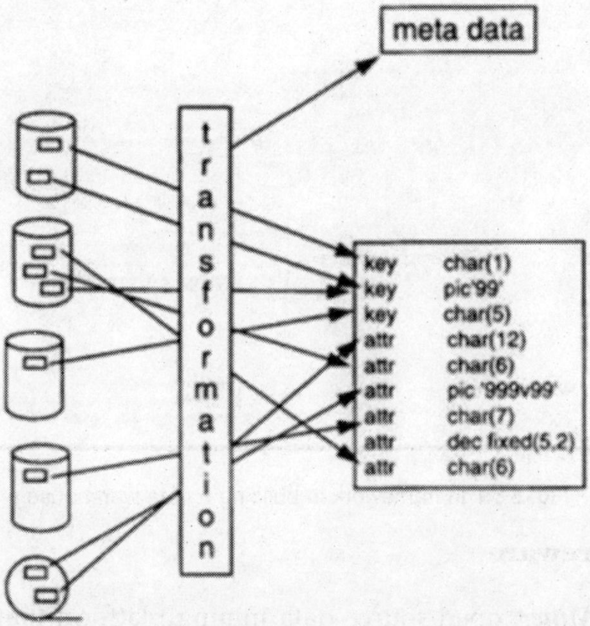

Fig. 4 : The process of transformation

Loading data into the data warehouse

After the extraction, transformation and data cleansing performed, the data loaded into the data warehouse. The categorized two types of loading data is loading data containing the operational database and loading data into the data warehouse from changes that occur of the operational database.

Some types of information can be produced from the formation of a data warehouse, the information may be based on association rules, characteristic rules, classification rules, discriminate rules, clustering, sequential pattern, and deviation analysis. Furthermore, there is another classification according to level of abstraction of the information obtained, among others, generalized knowledge, primitive-level knowledge and multiple levels of knowledge. A flexible data warehouse system can gather information at various levels of abstraction. Various Free and Shareware and commercial data warehousing tools are as follows.

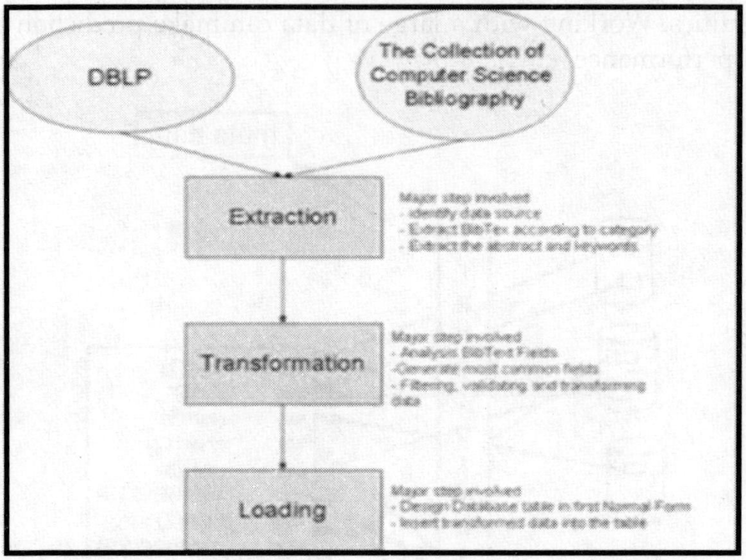

Fig. 5 : The framework in building a data warehouse

Free and Shareware

- *AlphaMiner,* open source data mining platform that offers various data mining model building and data cleansing functionality.
- *Gnome Data Mining Tools,* including apriori, decision trees, and Bayes classifiers.
- *IBM Intelligent Miner,* University scholars can now receive free copies of DB2 UDB and Intelligent Miner for educational or research purposes.
- *KNIME,* extensible open source data mining platform implementing the data pipelining paradigm (based on eclipse).
- *Machine Learning in Java (MLJ),* an open-source suite of Java tools for research in machine learning.
- *Orange,* C++ components for data mining, includes pre-processing, modelling and data exploration techniques.
- *RapidMiner,* a leading open-source system for knowledge discovery and data mining.
- *Weka,* collection of machine learning algorithms for solving real-world data mining problems. It is written in Java and runs on almost any platform.

Commercial

- *Clementine from SPSS,* leading visual rapid modeling environment for data mining. Now includes Clementine Server.
- *Data Applied,* offers a comprehensive suite of web-based data mining techniques, an XML web API, and rich data visualizations.
- *IBM Intelligent Miner Data Mining Suite,* now fully integrated into the IBM InfoSphere Warehouse software; includes Data and Text mining tools (based on UIMA).
- *KXEN (Knowledge eXtraction ENgines),* providing Vapnik SVM (Support Vector Machines) tools, including data preparation, segmentation, time series, and SVM classifiers.
- *Microsoft SQL Server 2008,* empowers informed decisions with predictive analysis through intuitive data mining, seamlessly integrated within the Microsoft BI platform, and extensible into any application.
- *Oracle Data Mining (ODM),* provides GUI, PL/SQL-interface, and Java-interface to Attribute Importance, Bayes Classification, Association Rules, Clustering, SVM, and more.
- *Salford Systems Data Mining Suite,* CART Decision Trees, MARS predictive modeling, automated regression, TreeNet classification and regression, data access, preparation, cleaning and reporting modules, RandomForests predictive modeling, clustering and anomaly detection.
- *SAS Enterprise Miner,* an integrated suite which provides a user-friendly GUI front-end to the SEMMA (Sample, Explore, Modify, Model, Assess) process.
- *SPSS* featuring Clementine, SPSS and other data mining tools.
- *Statistica Data Miner,* a comprehensive, integrated statistical data analysis, graphics, data base management, and application development system.
- *Teradata Warehouse Miner and Teradata Analytics*, providing analytic services for in-place mining on a Teradata DBMS.
- *XLMiner,* Data Mining Add-In For Excel.

CONCLUSION

The power Data Warehouse consumers are business analysts and managers. Data Warehouses are meant to deliver clear indications on how the business is performing. Plot out the expected users for the Data Warehouse in the enterprise so that they will have the appropriate reports in a format which is quickly understandable. Always remember that data has to be presented attractively and in a format business managers will feel comfortable. Text files with lines of numbers will not suffice.

REFERENCES

Boehnlein Michael and Ulbrich-vom Ende Achim (1999). Deriving Initial Data Warehouse Structures from the Conceptual Data Models of the Underlying Operational Information Systems: DOLAP 99 Kansas City Mo USA.

Inmon., and William, H. (2000). Building the Data Warehouse: Getting Started.

Jarke, M., Jeusfeld, M., Quix, C., and Vassiliadis, P. (1999). Architecture and quality in data warehouses: An extended repository approach.

Rizzi Stefano., Lechtenborger Jens., Abell Alberto., and Trujillo Juan. (2006). Research in Data Warehouse Modeling and Design: Dead or Alive?: Conference held on 10th November, Arlington, Virginia, USA.

Rawat Laxmi (1998). Changing facets of weather and climate in Doon Valley, FRI.

Sharma Gajendra (2008). Data mining, data warehousing and OLAP (Second Edition), Katson Books.

Wah., and Teh Ying. (2007). Building Data Warehouse. Malaysia: Department of Information Science University Malaya.

❑❑❑

CHAPTER - 29

Highlights on Big Data, Predictive Analytics and Business Intelligence Software

Ajit Kumar Roy
National Consultant (Impact Assessment) for East and North East Region
NAIP Project (World Bank Funded)
Address: 4th floor, 1/2D/4 Ramakrishna Naskar Lane, Kolkata 700010
Email:akroy1946@yahoo.co.in/akroy1946@rediffmail.com

INTRODUCTION

According to analyst firm Gartner, Big Data is at the portion of the hype cycle called the "peak of inflated expectations." The business world is awash with all sorts of claims about the magic of Big Data and how it will transform industries by increasing productivity and profits and opening up opportunities that nobody even knew existed. But this will only happen if companies are able to hire enough people who actually understand what Big Data is, how to collect it, and preserve it. Computing and analytical skills are also required to get Big Data to reveal its hidden secrets and visualise it in novel ways. And there unfortunately, is the rub. There are just not enough data scientists, people with the required skills to satisfy this unmet demand. The shortfall in Big Data experts is set to rise and in the UK alone, one digital industries employer body has predicted there will be a need for 69,000 of these experts in the next five years. This claim is not original. Back in 2011, McKinsey & Co was claiming a US shortfall in Big Data experts of 140,000 - 190,000 by 2018.The shortfall in Big Data experts is being manifested in a number of ways. The first and most obvious is through recruiters casting an ever-widening net in their search for appropriate talent. There is some agreement that Big Data analysis and data visualisation requires skills in computing as well as statistics and mathematics. This has meant that university graduates with statistics, computer science and engineering have been the main source of potential employees. Lately this has widened to include subject areas such as astrophysics and computational chemistry. The demand for Big Data experts has driven a more direct approach to tackling the shortfall problem with industry partnering with universities to create courses, majors and degrees that focus on these specific skills. In the midst of the Big Data hype, some clear notes of sanity have come from an unexpected quarter. UK supermarket giant Tesco has claimed it has no problems hiring graduates with the right skills. Basically its strategy is to look for smart people who may be mathematicians, scientists or engineers. Surprisingly enough, this vindicates the long-held belief that universities should first and foremost produce graduates who are equipped with the ability to think, apply those thoughts and solve problems. Although over-emphasised by some in industry, product or technology specific skills are largely useless. By the time universities mobilise to refactor their courses to the latest hyped technology and graduate students with those skills, the world will have moved on to the next "Big" thing. Big Data is real and some of the challenges it poses will need to be solved by scientists and engineers and mathematicians in the coming years. Setting aside truly massive data being generated by radio astronomy and some other fields of science, we are actually mostly there in terms of having techniques and technology that allows us to process and make sense of Big Data. Underlying this all however are the general skills required to handle and make sense of all data, big and small. These skills still rely on knowledge of basic mathematics, statistics, science and computing. What the interest in Big Data has done is to highlight to companies the importance of data generally. It's not as though companies have never looked at data analytics before, they simply may not have recognised its central importance to the business, nor understood what the data has been trying to say for years. The chapter attempts to highlight the concept and need for business software dealing with bigdata in the global competitive market.

WHAT IS BIG DATA?

What is Predictive Analytics?

Predictive Analytics as a discipline has become vital in today's data centric world. Predictive analytics is a branch of data mining used for forecasting and modelling using historical data. In simple terms predictive analytics means using quantitative methods and data mining to derive insights from historical data, and then drawing on those insights to shape business decisions and improve business performance. In this tough global economy, sloppy decision making can get one punished. So, leading organizations are turning to predictive analytics to compete and thrive. It is widely used in industries like insurance, medical, credit industries, online shopping and retail industry. Predictive analytics can narrow your target audience and allow you to tailor your ads to each online customer. Your marketing team will have the opportunity to target most potential customer

Predictive Analytics & Big Data

Predictive analytics has been used for many years to learn patterns from historical data to literally predict the future. Well known techniques include neural networks, decision trees, and regression models. Although these techniques have been applied to a myriad of problems, the advent of big data, cost-efficient processing power, and open standards have propelled predictive analytics to new heights. Creating predictive analytic solutions is just part of the equation to tame big data. Once built, these solutions need to be transitioned to the operational environment where they create substantial business value. In the agile world we live today, the PMML standard delivers the necessary representational power for solutions to be quickly and easily exchanged between systems, allowing for predictions to move at the speed of business. Predictive Analytics World focuses on concrete examples of deployed predictive analytics. Hear from the horse's mouth precisely how Fortune 500 analytics competitors and other top practitioners deploy predictive modelling, and what kind of business impact it delivers.

Forecasting and Predictive Analytics

Much like visual analytics, forecasting used to be seen as the domain of the scientist. But everyone wants to know the future. Forecasting tools are maturing to help businesses identify emerging trends and make better plans. We expect forecasting and predictive analyses to become much more common as people use them to get more value from their data.

Mobile BI's growth

It is predicted that Mobile BI (Business Intelligence) would go mainstream and it did. Now everyone from salespeople to insurance adjusters to shop floor managers use tablets to get data about their work right in the moment. To date mobile BI has been lightweight involving the consumption of reports, with a bit of interactivity. But the tremendous value that people have seen in mobile BI is driving a trend for more ability to ask and answer questions.

Pervasive analytics

It is talked for years about terms like "pervasive BI" or "BI for the masses". There's a whole market for data that is outside of the market for "business intelligence." When we talk more about data, and less about software categories like BI, we get to the crux of maximizing business value and fast, easy-to-use visual analytics is the key that opens the door to organisation wide analytics adoption and collaboration.

Business Analytics and Data Scientist

Data Scientists need advanced analytics skills and thus they need formal education in statistics, computational mathematics or predictive analytics. Data scientists spend more time on computer algorithms than they do working with people. If one love working on data, software and systems, this is a good fit. Education options depend on situation:

- For full-time or part-time courses in analytics with core topics in statistics, algorithms, quantitative methods, data mining and predictive analytics - along with tools training in SAS, R, etc.Training on software tools is widely available through vendors such as SAS, SPSS and Angoss.
- Short, hands-on courses in advanced topics such as logistic regression, decision trees and data mining are offered by analytics consulting companies.

A business analytics professional manager will need a basic understanding of analytical techniques that most data professionals can learn quickly. Analysts/managers spend more time interfacing with people than computers and are often working with broader business questions that can be solved using simpler analytics techniques. This track requires less time for transitioning, especially if you already have experience working with data. Data professionals already equipped with SQL skills to manipulate data will need training in data analysis and people skills to start tackling business analytics challenges. Although 80 percent of business problems can be solved via business analytics techniques and don't require advanced data analysis, historically there has not been formal business analytics training offered, and most people have learned it on the job. Even today there isn't much in the marketplace.

Business Intelligence

Maintaining a competitive edge is not as easy as it used to be. In the past, companies simply had to offer superior products and services, and treat customers courteously in order to create sustained profitability and growth. Today, organizations must be able to think on their feet, leveraging their most important asset - their enterprise data - to understand the status of their mission-critical activities, detect vital operational patterns, anticipate industry trends, and achieve the agility that will enable them to conduct business more dynamically. However, as companies deploy more and more business applications, and information architectures become increasingly complex, obtaining that type of actionable insight can become a tremendous challenge.

What is Business Intelligence Software?

Business intelligence software enables companies to perform reporting and in-depth analysis of detailed information from across their entire organization. Data from various systems, applications, and databases is accessed, gathered, compiled, formatted, and presented to end users, facilitating faster, more effective decision support by providing them with timely and vital insight about key operations and activities.

Key Benefits for the Company

Dramatic benefits can be achieved through the purchase and implementation of a business intelligence software package. The primary advantages include:

- Improved access to and integration of business data from disparate sources.
- Complete 360-degree visibility into corporate activities.
- More rapid information sharing across the enterprise.
- Faster and more accurate detection of the positive and negative trends that impact the business.
- Real-time tracking of key performance indicators and critical metrics.
- Improved collaboration and communication with customers, suppliers, vendors, and other business partners.
- Enhanced strategic planning.

Need for Business Intelligence Software

Every company, of every size, in every industry can derive tremendous value from a business intelligence solution. In most organizations today, critical business information is scattered across disparate systems and applications that exist among various departments and business units. Without a business intelligence solution in place, retrieving, consolidating, and formatting that data then harnessing it to support planning and decision making at both the strategic and operational level would require extensive time and effort from IT staff, and delay the delivery of vital intelligence needed to support mission-critical business activities.

Common Business Intelligence Software Features

The business intelligence software packages on the market today typically provide the following features to enable better, faster, more informed decision-making across the enterprise:

Web-based access

The traditional client/server reporting tools of the past made actionable business intelligence available to only a small percentage of an organization's information consumers. So, over the past several years, the majority of business intelligence vendors have incorporated Web-based access into their offerings, making reporting and analysis capabilities readily available to a broader base of users and user types.

Ad hoc reporting

To minimize burden on IT resources, and ensure that front line workers have immediate access to the insight they need to perform their jobs on a day-to-day basis, most business intelligence tools offer the ability for functional end users to easily build and run their own reports, while shielding them from the technical complexities of the underlying data.

Flexible output formats

Most of today's popular business intelligence systems enable users to present report output in a variety of formats, including spreadsheets, word processing documents, HTML, and other mediums.

Dynamic scheduling and delivery

This capability allows users to schedule reports to run and/or refresh at pre-determined intervals, and to have completed reports automatically "pushed" to relevant users via email, mobile devices, and other communication vehicles.

Financial reporting

As legislation becomes increasingly stringent, and the penalties for non-compliance become greater, more and more business intelligence solutions are incorporating financial reporting capabilities into their offerings. Examples include templates for balance sheets and profit and loss statements, the ability to process and calculate financially of oriented data, and dynamic conversion of foreign currencies.

What to Look for When Choosing a Business Intelligence Solution?

While most business intelligence solutions will provide a broad array of reporting and analysis capabilities, there are some more advanced features that will set some systems apart from the pack. These include:

Scalability

As the value of a business intelligence environment becomes clear, more and more users will want to leverage it. Additionally, as an organization thrives, the number of reports needed, and the number of data sources to be accessed, will grow. Not all business intelligence solutions are fully scalable, so be sure to choose one that can address expanding capacity needs and support broader access and reporting requirements as they emerge.

Unlimited data access

Finding a business intelligence solution that accesses common or widely-used systems is easy. But, if your organization maintains data sources that are proprietary, antiquated, or obscure, you may be challenged to find a vendor that can easily access and report on the information contained within them. However, there are some vendors that have either developed a portfolio of data adapters or partnered with an application integration company to address this very requirement.

Visualization

Enterprise data can be highly complex, making it difficult for functional users to understand and interpret it. While most business intelligence software packages offer some basic visualization capabilities such as simple charts and graphs, more advanced visualization techniques such as matrixes, scatter plots, histograms, and maps may be needed if your information is scientific or mathematical in nature.

Predictive analytics

Are forecasting and advance planning part of your business intelligence needs? Then you may want to look for a solution that offers predictive analytics, sophisticated algorithms and formulas that mine historical data for patterns and trends, and use it to make weighted anticipations regarding future events and activities. (*Source:www.tableausoftware.com/desktop*)

TOP 10 BUSINESS INTELLIGENCE SOLUTIONS

These are many options when selecting a business intelligence solution. To make search a bit easier, we've featured some of the leading business intelligence vendors in this chapter. Review these companies, and one be well on the way to finding the right business intelligence solution for one's company.

SAP

SAP Americas is a subsidiary of SAP AG, one of the world's largest business software companies and the third-largest software supplier overall. SAP Americas' corporate headquarters are located in Newtown Square, PA, a suburb of Philadelphia.

Founded in 1972 as Systems Applications and Products in Data Processing, SAP has a rich history of innovation and growth that has made them a leader in providing collaborative business solutions for all types of industries in every major market. The company, headquartered in Walldorf, Germany, employs more than 52,000 people in more than 50 countries, and serves more than 76,000 customers in more than 120 countries. SAP has leveraged their extensive experience to deliver a comprehensive range of solutions to empower every aspect of business operations. Organizations of all sizes can use SAP solutions including small business solutions and solutions for midsize companies to reduce costs, improve performance, and gain the agility to respond to changing business needs. By deploying top-of-the-line technology, services, and development resources, SAP has delivered a business platform that unlocks valuable information resources, enabling organizations to make collaborative, efficient, and action-oriented decision making. Business intelligence solutions from SAP deliver fact-based, quality information to empower companies to act decisively, from anywhere at any time, to help their business run better. SAP also provides comprehensive support through the Global Solution Centre, which identifies customer needs and develops solutions to meet those needs.

Highlights

- As one of the largest business software companies, SAP can integrate BI throughout SAP applications.
- Strong data scalability and performance, thanks to in-memory analytics and Column-based vectoring.
- Gartner listed SAP as a Leader in its Magic Quadrant for Business Intelligence.

- SAP HANA, the real-time in-memory computing platform.
- SAP's move into Big Data analysis.

Technology

SAP's Enterprise Services Architecture outlines a framework for delivering a true software-as-a-service infrastructure on top of existing business systems. The framework includes components like NetWeaver Portal, Visual Composer, Exchange Infrastructure and Master Data Management each of which plays a role in building business applications on top of existing applications and business data. The platform also includes an extensive library of connectors for seamless integration into a wide variety of data sources.

Software Highlights

SAP Business Objects is built with comprehensive functionality to allow companies to access and analyse quality information, regardless of where the data resides. The solution uses a single platform with a common semantic layer, security, and delivery mechanism to deliver business insight. SAP Business Objects also integrates with other enterprise applications for improved decision making.

SAP Business Objects Includes

SAP Crystal Reports : Connect to virtually any data source, design and format interactive reports, and share them both internally and externally

- *SAP Business Objects Web Intelligence*: perform ad hoc queries and intuitive analysis across heterogeneous data sources online or offline.
- *SAP Business Objects Analysis Edition for OLAP*: companies can perform analysis of multi-dimensional data sets using the OLAP tool designed for financial and business analysts.
- *SAP Business Objects Analysis Edition for Microsoft Office*: helps companies perform advanced analysis of data that resides in business warehouse by using an intuitive UI within the Microsoft Office environment.
- *SAP Business Objects Predictive Analysis*: mine your information assets to predict future trends
- *SAP Business Objects Dashboards*: create interactive dashboards to visualize complex data quickly

- *SAP Business Objects Explorer*: search and explore business data for instant insight.
- *SAP Business Objects Explorer Mobile App*: access reports, metrics, and data from your mobile device.
- *SAP Business Objects Visual Intelligence*: visualizes your data reporting.
- *SAP Business Objects Mobile*: access reports, metrics, and data from your mobile device.
- *SAP Business Objects BI Platform*: uses a single platform with a common semantic layer, security and delivery mechanism to provide business insight.
- *SAP Business Objects Integration*: connects BI with enterprise applications to improve decision making.
- *SAP Business Objects Live Office*: integrates BI with Microsoft Office to incorporate data in Power Point, Excel and Word.
- *SAP Business Objects Event Insight*: alerts can be sent to mobile devices to let people know of events that are happening in real-time.
- *SAP Stream work*: brings together people and data for collective decision making.
- *SAP Business Objects BI on Demand*: a powerful, on-demand version of the SAP Business Objects solution.

DOMO

Domo is a cloud-based executive management platform that is redefining the business intelligence (BI) market and transforming the way business is managed. Domo gives users direct, real-time access to all the business information they care about, all in one place. Domo solves universal pain points felt by CEOs, other managers and IT professionals for whom traditional BI reporting is often too cumbersome, too complex and too slow. The company was started by Josh James, co-founder and long-time CEO of web analytics powerhouse, Omniture. With $63 million in funding, Domo is backed by an all-star list of angels and investors including Benchmark, IVP, Andreessen Horowitz, Ron Conway and David Lee of SV Angel, Hummer Winblad, plus the who's who of SaaS and Internet technology.Domo's founding team consists of some of the most sought after talent in the industry with experience that includes Amazon, American Express, Ancestry.com, eBay, Endeca, Face book, Google, LinkedIn, MLB.com, Omniture, salesforce.com and SAP.

Highlights

Domo is a cloud-based executive management platform delivered as a Service. Designed for the end user, Domo gives executives direct access to all the business information they care about, all in one place.

Technology Model

Domo is a cloud-based business intelligence solution that delivers all the information you need in a single dashboard view. Domo is designed to provide direct access to your business data via any device without having to depend upon IT to generate information and reports for you.

Domo Key Features

CEO/C-Suite

Definitive CXO dashboard

Real-time data on a single dashboard

Accessible from any device

Finance

Connect to all sources of financial data

See information in a single dashboard

Let decision makers view real-time data

Reduce ad-hoc report requests

IT/BI

Deliver real, self-service BI

Avoid expensive data warehousing projects

Eliminate hours of ad-hoc reporting

Spend more time doing what you do best

Marketing

See all your online and offline marketing data in real-time

Get a single view of all your key metrics

Adapt with greater efficiency

Track your successes to revenue

Operations

See all your critical data
Quickly identify opportunities and risks
Get updates in real-time
Make better decisions, faster

Sales

People metrics
Pipeline metrics
Performances metrics
Single dashboard

ORACLE

After 30 years of providing leading-edge solutions to a vast and growing base of customers, Oracle remains the gold standard for database technology and applications in enterprises throughout the world. The Company is the world's leading supplier of software for information management, and the world's second largest independent software company. Oracle technology can be found in nearly every industry, and in the data centres of 98 of the Fortune 100 companies. Oracle is the first software company to develop and deploy 100 percent internet-enabled enterprise software across its entire product line: database, business applications, and application development and decision support tools. It is innovation that drives Oracle's success. Oracle was one of the first companies to make its business applications available through the internet-an idea that is now pervasive. With the release of Oracle Fusion Middleware, Oracle has begun debuting new products and functionality that reflect the company's goal: connecting all levels of enterprise technology to help customers access the knowledge they need to respond to market conditions with speed and agility. Today, Oracle Real Application Clusters, Oracle E-Business Suite, Oracle Grid Computing, support for enterprise Linux, and Oracle Fusion all fuel a commitment to innovation and results that has defined Oracle for thirty years. The company's success speaks for itself. Oracle applications are now running in over 1,500 public sector organizations, all 10 of the world's top 10 banks, all 20 of the world's top 20 telecom companies, and all 10 of the top 10 academic universities worldwide.

Highlights

- Widely established and respected vendor of business intelligence solutions.

- Market leader for data warehousing tools.
- Gartner recognized Oracle as a Leader in the Magic Quadrant for Business Intelligence.
- IDC recognized Oracle as the #1 vendor in business analytics.
- Oracle solutions are designed to integrate seamlessly with any existing database systems.
- Hosted and on-premise B.I. solutions available.

Key strengths

- Comprehensive BI functionality built on a unified infrastructure: includes interactive dashboards, full ad hoc queries and analysis, proactive intelligence delivery and alerts, enterprise and financial reporting, online analytical processing (OLAP) analysis and presentation, high-volume production reporting, real-time predictive intelligence, disconnected analytics, as well as integration with Microsoft Office.
- Pervasive insight to everyone, everywhere: provides relevant insight to everyone, not just analysts. All levels of the organization can see information optimized for their role.
- Unified business model: built on an enterprise information model that unifies meta-data across the Oracle BI tools and analytical applications for the lowest TCO.
- Hot-Pluggable BI infrastructure: integrates with any data source, extraction, transformation and load (ETL) tool, major business application, application server, security infrastructure, portal technology, other front-end and analytical tools, and databases including IBM DB/2, Teradata, Microsoft SQL Server; SAP Business Information Warehouse (BW), Microsoft Analysis Services; flat files; XML data; and unstructured data.

Technology

Hosted: Oracle On-Demand delivers business solutions online.

On-Premise : Complete web-service oriented architecture allows BI functionality to be added to any data source, warehouse or ETL tool, and any data source including relational databases like Oracle Database, IBM DB/2, Teradata, Microsoft SQL Server; multidimensional sources such as Oracle Essbase, SAP NetWeaver BI, Microsoft Analysis Services; flat files; XML data; and unstructured data.

Oracle Business Intelligence Key Features

- Oracle Business Intelligence Foundation Suite
  - Rich end-user experience
  - Integrated OLAP analysis and modelling
  - Integrated scorecard application
  - Translate insight to action
  - Universal data access
- Oracle Business Intelligence Suite, Enterprise Edition 11g (OBIEE+)
  - Comprehensive BI functionality built on a unified infrastructure
  - Powerful user experience
  - Unified business model
  - Hot-Pluggable
  - Best-in-class scalability, reliability and performance
- Oracle Business Intelligence Publisher
  - Reduce complexity and lower costs
  - Uses data from anywhere
  - Uses the tools you know
  - Hot-Pluggable
  - Pre-integrated with Oracle
- Oracle Essbase
  - Rich business user experience
  - Highly advanced calculation engine
  - Custom analytic environment
- Oracle Scorecard and Strategy Management
  - Strategic financial planning in a single, centralized model
  - Built-in performance management frameworks
  - View/manage by organizational structures
  - Organize KPIs, analytics, and workflows
  - Extensive collaborative features
  - Portal-style dashboards showing integration into Oracle Essbase and other Oracle BI solutions

- Oracle Business Intelligence Standard Edition One (OBIE)
    - Based on Oracle BI Enterprise Edition technology
    - Flexible upgrades and deployment
    - Report-building functionality for end-users
- Oracle Real-Time Decisions
    - Personalized, optimized, and context-centric decisions
    - Cross-channel learning and decisions
    - Single solution for multiple management use cases
    - Complete decision framework leveraging data, rules, and predictive models. Closed loop BI and insight discovery
    - Business controls supporting collaboration over end-to-end decision lifecycles. Adaptive targeting automation with self-learning
    - Decision services for business process optimization
    - Scalable and flexible enterprise infrastructure
- Oracle Essbase Analytics Link
    - Management and financial analytic reporting through real-time or on-demand transfer of data from Oracle Hyperion Financial Management to Oracle Essbase
- Oracle Endeca Information Discovery
    - Oracle Endeca database server
    - Studio for configuring analytical applications
    - Integration Suite for integrating different data sources into a single view
    - Extensible Value-Added Modules for quick value through configuration instead of coding Oracle Business Indicators

Birst

Highlights

- Unified solution for Business Intelligence and Analytics with pixel-perfect reporting, ad hoc query, data discovery and in-memory analytics from a single multi-tenant platform.

- Automation of complex data management and warehousing tasks.
- Typically requires the cost, time, and resources of larger BI vendors.
- Deployed either in the Cloud or as an on-premise virtual appliance.
- Birst has been listed in CIO Magazine's Top 20 companies to watch in 2012 and is the winner of Red Herring Award, 2012, Cloud Awards for Data Innovation and 2011 JMP Hot 100 Software Companies award.

Key strengths

- 1/3 the Cost, Time and Resources of Big BI Vendors
- Birst's ease-of-use and self-service capabilities allow even the largest implementations to be managed by a single administrator. When compared to Micro Strategy, SAP Business Objects, and Oracle OBIEE, Birst typically requires 1/3 the cost, time and resources.
- End to End BI from a Single Solution with ETL and Data Warehouse Automation
- Includes a variety of pre-built connectors for both cloud and on-premise data sources. A data streaming engine enables BI developers to write and execute sophisticated scripts for joining and transforming data from multiple heterogeneous sources.
- *Seamless Upgrade Path*
- Birst provides a seamless upgrade path from Birst Visualization Edition and the ability add on features such a mobile BI, Bing maps, operational reporting and data warehouse automation.
- *High capacity*
- Large or small, Birst can handle any amount of data and any type of columnar data, whether its csv files or relational databases.
- *Flexibility*
- Combine and analyse multiple systems data to see across the entirety of your business, such as finance and operations or marketing and website, all within the Birst platform.
- *Speed*
- Birst automates the whole full-function analytical environment creation process, allowing you to go from your data to your dashboards faster than other traditional solutions. A customized Birst

solution can be deployed in weeks and subsequent features added iteratively

- *Analysis and Reporting*
- With sophisticated analysis and reporting capabilities, Birst's ad-hoc reporting provides organizations with the ability to create reports and share data in a wide range of formats.
- *State-of-the-art Security*
- Birst provides multiple layers of physical, database, operational, and encryption security. Even control user access through role-based visibility, which can include both row-level data as well as feature visibility. ISO 27001-based procedures and policies are included in operational security provisions and reviewed regularly as part of the SOC 2 Type II audit process. Data and application security measures include Secure Socket Layer (SSL) connections for all data storage and communications in separate database schemas.

Technology

Birst delivers its platform as a fully integrated BI solution that's designed for either SaaS (software-as-a-service). Cloud delivery or on-premise deployment via a software appliance. The Birst platform pools all the necessary components that a business might need in order to develop, deploy, and maintain enterprise-class dash boarding, reporting, and data discovery. All components of the Birst platform share a single, unified metadata layer, as well as a consistent end user experience. Birst's in-memory database is designed specifically for analytics, making it unique in that it's SQL-compliant and able to handle multi-pass data aggregations. Designed for efficient data bulk-loading, Birst builds indexes based upon context, thus maximizing your performance while also reducing your memory footprint.

Additionally, Birst's relational ROLAP engine executes connections across heterogeneous sources, mapping the data to a virtual logical cube of all data. The ROLAP engine also provides support for cell-based calculations, positional references, and differentiation between filters and slicers. Birst's platform supports both ROLAP and MOLAP data sources via MDX and SQL generation.

Birst Agile Business Intelligence Key Features

Reporting

- Drag-and-drop functionality enables pixel perfect banded reporting and ad hoc query with pivot table creation, data visualizations, and interactive drill down for any user, regardless of technical know-how.

- Intuitive Data Visualization: Bar, Column, Pyramid, Pie, Line, Bar/Line, Area, Stacked, Meter, Bubble, Tree Maps, Heat Maps, Funnel and Geo Maps.
- Logic-based query language performs Excel-style calculations, offering drill through and drill across OLAP-style execution.
- Reusable templates and editable reports make ongoing analysis easy.
- Maximized consistency with highly precise layout across print, PDF, browsers and mobile devices.
- Expand any report with Birst's open APIs.
- Export to PDF, Excel, PowerPoint, CSV, etc.
- Caching for improved speed.
- *Alerts and notifications in real-time.*

Analytics

- Relational OLAP (ROLAP) with filters, slicers, aggregators and cell-level calculators.
- Point-and-click multi-pass calculations, inheritance, business rules, virtual measures, etc.
- Time-series analysis, forecasts and financial models powered by rich data visualizations.
- Role-based report generation and sharing functions.
- High performance ROLAP engine: handles large volumes of data and concurrent user; dynamic cubing, query reuse, and partitioning for scalability.

Dashboards

- Aggregate data from across departments and other sources.
- Click-based drill down for deep analysis.
- Non-executive and/or tech-wary users can utilize drag-and-drop tools and drop down menus for simple dash creation.
- Point-and-click data integration from the data warehouse or Birst Live Access frees IT staff to focus on higher priorities.

Mobile

- Tap, swipe, and pinch data visualizations on the iPad.
- Birst Mobile SDK offer iOS developers an API free of data integration, quality and consolidation concerns.

Solution accelerators

- Solution accelerators feature pre-built metadata, data transformations and metrics.
- Sales analytics: out-of-the-box sales-specific reports offer insight into sales productivity; integration with CRMs like Microsoft Dynamics, Sales force, Oracle, etc.
- Wealth management: quickly match resources to customer needs with insights from customized dashboards for execs, managers, and support personnel and ad hoc reporting for custom queries.
- Insurance: regional, agency and agent-level insights identify performance indicators for improved customer relationships and sales opportunities; industry-specific templates map policies, premiums, and even claims for easy, visuals-based comprehension.

Platform technology

- Data streaming engine, with Visual Basic-like scripts, pre-built connectors, and integrated ETL capabilities make for highly functional data extraction, transformation and loading.
- Kimball-style star schema data warehouses with native change data capture and history management; Type 1 and 2 slowly changing dimensions and automatic snapshot management.
- Unique, SQL-compliant in-memory database for multi-pass data collection and more efficient bulk-loading and reduced memory footprint.
- Functionality for both MOLAP and ROLAP data sources via MDX generation and SQL.

Security

- User and user group access and viewing permissions.
- Forms-based authentication or OpenID for logging on.
- SHA-hashed passwords with a random salt.

- Physical safeguards: biometric scans, camera surveillance monitoring, etc.
- Regularly reviewed SOC 2 Type II audit process for ISO 27001-based policies; Secure Socket Layer (SSL) connections.

COGNOS

Cognos, an IBM company, is a world leader in business intelligence and corporate performance management (CPM) software for the enterprise. IBM Cognos solutions let companies improve and direct corporate performance by enabling all of the key steps in the management cycle, including planning and budgeting; measuring and monitoring performance; and reporting and analysis. Whether customers choose to apply Cognos software strategically on an enterprise scale, or leverage it as a point solution to address key operational requirements. Cognos allows customers to better monitor, understand, and drive the successful performance of their business.Cognos customers are involved in every industry sector including all industries within manufacturing such as automotive, energy, natural resources, consumer packaged goods, and high tech. Cognos solutions are sold directly and are also available from more than 3,000 worldwide partners and resellers. These solutions are supported by an experienced and award-winning field force of more than 1,800 customer-facing personnel. Founded in 1969, Cognos employs over 3,400 people and serves more than 23,000 customers in over 135 countries. Cognos was acquired by IBM in January 2008

Highlights

- The IBM Cognos BI suite serves more than 23,000 customers in more than 135 countries.
- Complete corporate performance management solution. Supports enterprise planning, score carding, and business intelligence.
- Limitless BI workspace with capabilities for planning, collaboration, real-time Monitoring, predictive analytics, scenario modelling, and more.
- Continuously ranked in the "Leaders" Quadrant in Gartner's Magic Quadrant for Business Intelligence

Key strengths

IBM Cognos Business Intelligence offers a complete range of BI capabilities, including query and reporting, dashboards, scorecards, analysis, and more. By leveraging the features and capabilities built into IBM Cognos

Business Intelligence, every individual within an organization can access and explore data, analyze key information, collaborate with key stakeholders and make smarter business decisions that yield better results.

- IBM Cognos Business Intelligence delivers the complete range of BI capabilities on a single, service-oriented architecture (SOA). Customers can author, share, and use reports that draw on data across all enterprise sources.
- IBM Cognos Business Intelligence enables the guided exploration of information that pertains to all dimensions of a business, regardless of where the data is stored. The solution gives businesses the power to analyze and report against online analytical processing (OLAP) and dimensionally aware relational sources.
- IBM Cognos Business Intelligence enables customers to perform complex analyses quickly and easily to get to the "why" behind an event or action to improve business performance.

Technology

The IBM Cognos Business Intelligence solution resides on an IBM DB2 balanced data warehouse running on an IBM System platform, which provides a flexible and scalable business intelligence infrastructure to support the delivery of information as a service. Built with modern, service-oriented architecture, IBM Cognos Business Intelligence integrates with technology standards today, and can adapt as companies evolve.

IBM Cognos Business Intelligence Key Features

Reports

- Author, view, and modify reports and queries to meet the needs of all users.
- Leverage proven scalability with an N-tiered, multi-server, multithreaded architecture.
- Access a broad range of heterogeneous data sources to gain a complete and consistent view of the organization.
- Get a single view of all data sources thanks to a single metadata layer that manages data translation.

Analysis

- View, assemble, and analyse all information needed to make better business decisions.

- Use sophisticated tools to validate key information, build "what if" scenarios, and leverage predictive analytics.
- Provide self-service access to information.
- Easily conduct complex analyses and tasks.

Scorecards

- Use key performance indicators (KPIs) to track performance.
- Visually capture organization strategy to enable departments and employees to set priorities.
- View scorecards to identify problem areas and high-priority objectives.
- Easily share and track metrics.

Dashboards

- View, interact with, and personalize dashboards to analyse information and share results.
- Assemble and format data with features such as drag-and-drop, filtering, widgets and more.
- Distribute and integrate dashboards to improve collaboration and alignment.
- Schedule and burst dashboards to a broad range of key holders.

Mobile

- Interact with reports, dashboards, analysis and more on tablets, smart phones, and notebook computers.
- Quickly and easily access business insight from wherever.
- Easily deploy business intelligence to any device.

Real-time Monitoring

- View up-to-the-minute information in context.
- Respond to changing business conditions with real-time analytics and notifications
- Set business-defined alerts.
- Leverage drill-down capabilities to determine the root cause of an issue.

Collaboration

- Use a broad range of social networking capabilities to share insights and ideas.
- Capture insight and improve transparency with report-level features that clearly describe data.
- Connect people and coordinate decisions with workflow and task management functionality.

Statistics

- Facilitate fact-based decision-making by including statistics in business reporting.
- Add statistical evidence to validate business information.

Planning and budgets

- Conduct high-performance, on-demand customer and profitability analyses.
- Create, compare, and assess budgets, plans, business scenarios and more.
- Evaluate what-if scenarios to create business forecasts for the future.

SAS

SAS is a leader in business intelligence and analytical software and services. Customers at 55,000 sites use SAS software to improve performance through insight from data, resulting in faster, more accurate business decisions; more profitable relationships with customers and suppliers; compliance with governmental regulations; research breakthroughs; and better products and processes. Founded in 1976, SAS is based Cary, North Carolina and employs about 12,000 people. SAS has been among FORTUNE magazine's "100 Best Companies to Work For" in the United States every year since 1998, and was also named #1 on that list in 2010 and 2011. It also offers industry-specific integrated software and support packages. Its clients span the commercial, private, and government sectors.

Highlights

Exceptionally strong in advanced analytic analysis. Full analysis power revealed in the hands of uses with knowledge of SAS programming. Subscription-based pricing model.

Key strengths

- SAS business intelligence offers decision-makers fast, simple access to reports and analysis. Self-service reporting and familiar interfaces are tailored to the different skills and needs of individuals, enabling everyone to generate reports on their own.
- The SAS Business Intelligence solution suite gives companies the information when they need it, in the format they need. By integrating data from across the enterprise and delivering self-service reporting and analysis, IT spends less time responding to requests, and business users spend less time looking for information, so more time is spent on making better, more informed decisions.
- SAS ensures that customers have the breadth of BI capabilities to meet the needs of every type of user: managers looking for dashboards; groups who want to view or build reports on the Web; analysts or power users; and IT staff who need to deploy, manage, control and maintain the entire solution.

Technology

SAS's on-demand, hosted solution delivers end-to-end linked technologies, including data access, data quality and a common metadata layer, that increase consistency of data and business rules. This ensures that large volumes of raw data are converted into accurate information for reporting and analysis. A point-and-click interface allows users to exploit the power of SAS and publish dynamic results throughout the organization. Interactive dialog boxes guide users through analytic and reporting tasks that range from simple to complex, and can export the results to other Windows and server-based applications. By leveraging existing data and system assets and bringing Business Intelligence to everyone through familiar and intuitive interfaces, SAS helps organizations leverage existing skill sets, serve all user types, lower total cost of ownership and deliver critical business intelligence to more people faster than ever.

SAS Business Intelligence Key Features

- SAS Enterprise Business Intelligence.
- Portal and customizable dashboards.
- Business visualization.
- Web and desktop reporting.

- Mobile analytics.
- Microsoft Office and SharePoint integration.
- Query and analysis.
- OLAP storage and OLAP data exploration interface.
- Business metadata management.
- Flexible deployment options.
- Guided analysis and model development.
- Applications development.

SAS Office Analytics

- Makes consistent data from multiple sources easily available.
- Provides business users with self-sufficient access to SAS Analytics from within Microsoft Office.
- Surfaces results directly in Outlook.
- Encourages collaborative decision support.
- Helps satisfy corporate and governmental compliance regulations.
- Data access and management.
- Graphics and reporting.
- Guided analysis and model development for power users.
- Business metadata management for IT.

SAS Visual Analytics

- Empower users with big data exploration to drive improved decision making.
- Answer complex questions faster, enhancing contributions from your analytic talent.
- Improve information sharing and collaboration.
- Provide room to grow at a self-determined pace.
- High-performance SAS LASR Analytic Server.
- Visual data exploration.
- Self-service approachable analytics.
- Web-based report building and distribution.

- Report viewing.
- Mobile intelligence.
- Centralized user hub.
- Environment and data administration for IT.

SAS Visual BI

- Visually query data.
- Overcome data limitations.
- Interact with data to gain insights into relationships and patterns.
- See long-term trends instead of year-to-date views.
- Make better, faster decisions and share results throughout your organization.
- Highly interactive business graphics.
- Visual querying and data filtering.
- Visual analytics.
- Leverage core SAS capabilities.

Micro Stategy

Micro Strategy Incorporated is a worldwide provider of business intelligence software that enables companies to report, analyse and monitor the data stored across their enterprise. Micro Strategy provides sophisticated analytical performance to every business user in the format that suits them best, from high-level dashboards to custom reports and advanced analysis via iPad, iPhone, Android, BlackBerry, and the Web. The company provides integrated reporting, analysis, and monitoring software that helps leading organizations make better business decisions every day. Micro Strategy's flagship BI solution, Micro Strategy 9, is an integrated business intelligence platform that's designed to enable organizations to consolidate business intelligence applications onto a single platform for smarter, faster, and more comprehensive reporting, analysis and monitoring of real-time business information that drives greater performance and greater bottom-line growth.

Highlights

Named by Retail Info Systems (RIS) News to its 2010 Software Leader Board.

Strong, comprehensive and unified BI functionality - reporting, real-time business monitoring, integration, and analysis.

On-demand BI solution was built from the ground-up by Micro Strategy.

Key strengths

- Micro Strategy Business Intelligence Solutions enable improved and more predictable business performance by putting actionable information into the hands of every business person in the enterprise. The company's technology offers an unprecedented range of monitoring, reporting, and analysing capabilities within a single architecture to allow every-one to make better business decisions every day, and drive business performance goals.
- The company's solution product, Micro Strategy 9, unifies reporting, analysis, and real-time business monitoring into one seamless experience for the business user, into one efficient and scalable architecture for the IT professional, and into one economical and extensible utility for the CIO.
- The Micro Strategy 9 platform consists of product components, such as Intelligence Server, a foundation for the BI platform; Report Services, the enterprise reporting engine that delivers a range of enterprise reports, including production and operational reports, managed metrics reports, and scorecards; OLAP Services, an extension of Intelligence Server that allows Web and desktop users to manipulate Intelligent Cubes databases.
- Micro Strategy provides a robust, holistic business view of enterprise data. Users do not need to understand databases, table structures, or query languages -- just how to point and click. Micro Strategy's workflow guides help users "drill" into detail as represented by their business model, not their database model. With drill anywhere capabilities, users can view summary- to detail-level data, with access to the entire breadth and depth of data contained in a database.

Technology

Micro Strategy's enterprise BI solution is built and delivered from Micro Strategy Intelligence Server, the industry's most advanced, scalable secure and robust business intelligence server. Micro Strategy Intelligence Server provides the core analytical processing and job management for all reporting, analysis and monitoring applications. Employing a Services-Oriented Architecture (SOA), Micro Strategy Intelligence Server makes it easy to standardize on a single, open platform for all an enterprise's reporting and analysis needs through a number of access channels: Web browsers, Microsoft Office, Desktop clients, and emails. It is the first and only BI server to provide the full range of BI applications through a unified metadata and a single integrated server running on Windows®, UNIX, or Linux.

Micro Strategy Business Intelligence Platform Key Features

Scorecards and dashboards

- With easily configurable dashboards, scorecards, and portals, Micro Strategy 9 provides the ability to deliver detailed data on current and historical operational performance so people can see what is happening across the enterprise, and how well the business is operating.
- Scorecards and dashboards provide "at-a-glance" information about business performance across the enterprise. They are typically generated for managers and executives who need an overall view of business performance and find tremendous value in viewing timely, visually intuitive snapshots of strategic financial and operational data.

Enterprise reporting

- Provides advanced reporting technology with a more intuitive user experience and delivery via the Web, giving more users access to report information.
- Delivers the detailed information that impacts decision-makers throughout the enterprise. Individuals at all organizational levels and job functions, as well as supply chain partners and customers, rely on powerful, flexible enterprise reporting systems that present targeted data in the most consumable format for day-to-day operations.

Advanced and predictive analytics

- Presents views of the business from many different angles so that managers can uncover the causes of performance problems, uncover opportunities that the business should exploit, or predict business results.
- Supports advanced and predictive analysis capabilities, enabling users for the first time to perform analyses such as hypothesis testing, churn prediction and customer scoring models within a single unified web interface.

- With built-in support for over 270 statistical, mathematical and financial functions, Micro Strategy lets users create reporting applications that combine ease-of-use with unparalleled backend sophistication.

SISENSE

Highlights

- One of the Fastest Growing BI Companies in the market.
- Customers in all industries from global leaders like Target to Start Ups like Wix.
- Fully functional Free Trial & One-on-One Demo available.
- SiSense delivers an End-to-End Business Intelligence suite that allows teams to turn mountains of Data into Actionable Intelligence in hours, not days. Leaders of all sizes use SiSense's modern In-Memory technology to access large amounts and interact with rich Web-based Visualizations & Dashboards without scripting, programming or even setting up Enterprise Data Warehouse systems (EDW) or OLAP cubes.

Key strengths

- Mind-Blowing Insights for the Business, without giving IT a Headache.
- Interactive Dashboards & Reports for executives, employees, customers & partners
- Intuitive & Rich Web-based Visualizations for Ad-hoc analysis & data exploration
- Dynamic Drilling, Filtering & Sorting in the Browser
- Share via the Web, Export to Excel, PowerPoint, PDF & others
- Centralized Data Store & Management without having to build an Enterprise Data warehouse (EDW)
- Enterprise-Grade Security & Data Quality. Natively integrates with Active Directory.
- Works on any Browser: deployed as HTML 5/Javascript (no plugins required, not even Flash!)

Working with data has never been so simple

- Intuitive Interface for Easy Data Mash-ups from disparate systems & sources
- Connect natively to on-premises & Cloud data (including ODBC databases, Spreadsheets, CSVs, Google Adwords, Google Analytics & More)
- Clean, transform & extend Data without compromising its source
- Add any data without having to rebuild your entire data model
- Automatically discover database schemas to avoid errors & lost time
- Scales to 100s of millions of rows & thousands of users - out of the box
- Incredibly fast import & query response - up to 20 times faster than existing solutions
- Analyse machine-generated data such as website logs without breaking a sweat

More bang for your buck. No Hidden Costs

- Risk-Free subscription model (pay for what you need with minimal upfront investment)
- Requires less hardware than any other solution
- Implemented in days, not months, not years
- 30-day fully functional trial & FREE Proof-of-Concepts available
- Can be deployed quickly without 3rd party consultants or system integrators
- All components are purchased & deployed as One Suite. No need to stitch multiple software components together

Technology built for the future, today

- Unique Elastic-IQ Engine turns commodity machines into high-performance hardware, optimizing CPU, RAM & Disk use
- Columnar Database Technology provides best-in-class Query & Data processing performance
- Scales far beyond the physical barriers imposed by traditional In-Memory technologies

- Built to run seamlessly On-premises or in your Cloud
- Designed for modern CPU architecture, taking advantage of in-core, multi-core & CPU cache hierarchies (L1,L2 & L3)
- Native support for modern Compression & Decompression algorithms
- Multi-dimensional without OLAP

Standard, open and extensible

- Complies with SQL-92 standard - no proprietary scripting
- Easily Integrates with Websites & Portals using standard web protocols. Supports Single-Sign-On (SSO)
- Create Custom Visualizations Using JavaScript
- Connect to non-standard or proprietary data sources via a simple API
- Does not require proprietary hardware appliances

Technology

Perpetual Licenses and/or Subscription. Procured over the web.

Software Highlights

Prism elasticube

- Intuitive Interface for Easy Data Mash-ups from disparate systems and sources
- Connect natively to on-premises and Cloud data [including ODBC databases, Spreadsheets, CSVs, Google Adwords, Google Analytics and More]
- Scales to 100s of millions of rows and thousands of users - out of the box
- Incredibly fast import and query response - up to 20 times faster than existing solutions

Prism BI studio and web

- Interactive Dashboards & Reports for executives, employees, customers and partners

- Intuitive and Rich Visualizations for Ad-hoc analysis and data exploration
- Dynamic Drilling, Filtering and Sorting in the Browser
- Share via the Web. Export to Excel, PowerPoint, PDF and others
- Centralized Data Store and Management without having to build an Enterprise Data Warehouse (EDW)
- Enterprise-Grade Security and Data Quality. Natively integrates with Active Directory
- Works on any Browser: deployed as HTML 5/Javascript (no plugins required, not even Flash)

ACTUATE

Highlights

- High scalability to support extranet deployments.
- Strong reporting and Business Performance Management (BPM) dashboards.
- Platform is backed by the open source information application developer community, grounded in BIRT.
- Actuate Corporation provides software and services for business intelligence, performance management, and reporting applications in the United States and internationally.
- Actuate products and services are used in the development and deployment of Internet applications in a range of business functions, including financial management, sales management, account management, and customer self-service. The company also provides performance management solutions software and services, including the flagship Actuate Performance soft Suite.
- Actuate is headquartered in San Mateo, California and employs 580 people in the U.S. and abroad.

Key strengths

- Actuate's Information Application Platform is the foundation on which Global 9000 organizations (companies with annual revenues greater than $1 billion) and packaged application software vendors create reporting and analytics applications that scale to empower 100 percent of their user community inside and outside the firewall.

- Actuate offers a wide variety of business intelligence products, and analytics and reporting capabilities for any size project. From tapping data warehouses to implementing operational reporting within a department or across the business. Actuate's comprehensive business intelligence reporting platform offers organizations a cost-effective report authoring, deployment and delivery environment that meets the needs of every user, regardless of skill or experience.
- Actuate's Information Applications include Business Performance Management (BPM) dashboards, Information Portals as well as business analytic, enterprise reporting and spreadsheet reporting applications. Information Applications built with Actuate enable companies to increase their business agility, improve customer and partner relationships, adhere to corporate governance policies, and increase revenues while leveraging existing technology assets.
- When tested against other business intelligence products, Actuate's Information Application Platform has been proven to offer industry-leading scalability, the best performance, lowest total cost of ownership.

Technology

Actuate provides business intelligence users with a robust platform that supports all BI applications in an environment capable of unlimited scalability and 24/7 service. Several tiers are available within each product group, with applications and services developed to meet the needs of every user in the organization, from novice to expert and beyond. As a business intelligence solution, the Actuate enterprise reporting platform centers on the Actuate iServer. Actuate's on-demand solution delivers Rich Internet Applications (RIA)-ready information platform for both customer and employee-facing applications. Its platform is backed by the open source information application developer community, grounded in BIRT, the Eclipse Foundation's only top level Business Intelligence and reporting project. Two of the unique strengths of the Actuate Information Application Platform are its ability to access multiple data sources simultaneously and access relational and non-relational data sources.

Actuate Key Features

Eclipse BIRT

Actuate Corporation started the Eclipse BIRT Project in 2004 along with the Eclipse Foundation. There are over 750,000 developers using BIRT (Business

Intelligence Reporting Tools), and downloads number in the millions. An open source project, BIRT is at the top of the BI market due to its ease of use and flexibility. BIRT runs on the Eclipse IDE and provides data visualization and reporting tools and technologies in order to build information applications. Eclipse BIRT gives developers everything they need in order to transform data, access data sources, apply business logic to data, and present the results to users.

Actuate One

Charting and graphing with new HTML5 charting library that augments Adobe Flash objects for rich visualizations.

Impact analysis to preview effect of changes in advance of permanently altering a report.

- Big data support with Hadoop data access connector (via Hive environment) and support for SFDC and DBDC connectors.
- Cloud support for SaaS implementations with multi-account, multi-tenancy.
- Database support for standard RDBMS, adding to previous Postgres support Microsoft SQL Server, Oracle, and DB2.
- Support for Interactive Viewer features on mobile devices.
- Encyclopedia metadata support for IBM DB2 v9.7 and Microsoft SQL Server 2008.
- Enhanced BIRT engine for integrated, 64-bit, in-memory analysis.
- Fully functional, live Excel export.
- e.Reports data connector that leverages e.Report documents as data sources.
- Support for radar charts that enable multiple series to be rendered, allowing for easy comparison of related data.
- Enhanced administration of BIRT iServer with encyclopedia tools that help migrate encyclopedia metadata from the standard PostgreSQL database to another PostgreSQL database or supported third-party relational database management system.
- Support for new third party products includes the latest editions of Adobe Acrobat, Google Chrome and Safari.
- Advanced Function Print (AFP) export allows export from BIRT documents to the compact AFP file format, facilitating storing and printing BIRT-based documents.

- BIRT 360 dashboard print support enables business users to print snapshots of their dashboards and collaborate with other users.
- Cloud ready, with elastic clustering and provisioning for uninterrupted service

BIRT i Server

- Big data support with Hadoop data access connector (via Hive environment) and support for SFDC and DBDC connectors
- Database support for standard RDBMS, adding to previous Postgres support Microsoft SQL Server, Oracle, and DB2
- Encyclopaedia metadata support for IBM DB2 v9.7 and Microsoft SQL Server 2008.
- New administration scripts that make it easier for users to run the various server administration tools, including Squirrel Data Exporter, an Encyclopaedia Data Store Administrator, a System Data Store Administrator, and an Encyclopaedia Data Store Upgrader.
- Support for a large number of volumes.
- Control over user and role based access to content.
- Integrated or stand-alone access to content creation applications and services.
- Data drivers for popular data source types and tools to develop access to custom data sources.

BIRT on Demand

- Publish interactive, analytical dashboards securely to all users
- Add enhanced BI & Analytic capabilities to existing SaaS/Web applications
- Deliver information to mobile devices effortlessly with built in support for Apple and Android.
- Add instant interactivity to existing BIRT content.
- Provide the uptime and data security assurance enjoyed by millions of Amazon Web Services customers.

e.Report

- Personalized reports that are easy to read, use, and understand.

- Deliver reports as visual dashboards with the functionality to drill to detail, as brochures, or even as forms.
- Users can choose to save full or partial reports in PDF, PowerPoint, Word, Rich Text, Excel or plain text without re-running the report.
- Page Level Security personalizes content for every user, sending the right pages and data to each individual on request without re-running the main report on the server.
- Users receive actionable content with every e.Report. Choose from simple hyperlink drill-through, to isolating data through Smart Search and visualizing it.
- Manage report scalability with Page Level Security. Page Level Security generates one document that includes security rules for each recipient and offers significant performance and maintenance advantages over report bursting techniques.

QLIKVIEW

QlikTech is the company behind QlikView, the leading Business Discovery platform that delivers user-driven business intelligence (BI). Their mission, "Simplifying decisions for everyone, everywhere," is about harnessing the real potential of data and unleashing its power to change the world.QlikTech was founded in Sweden in 1993 with the aim of solving critical problems for organizations of all sizes, including the largest global enterprises. More than 28,000 customers in 100 countries depend on QlikTech to support their most important decisions. QlikTech's success has placed them in the top three of Forbes' 2012 list of America's 25 fastest-growing tech companies, alongside Apple and LinkedIn.

Highlights

- Empower business users: QlikView's associative experience provides answers as fast as you can think up questions. It lets you interact with data without limitations to generate insight in ways you never imagined.
- QlikView lets IT deliver a complete self-service BI experience, serving the business like never before all while assuring strict data security, quality, and governance.
- QlikView makes it easy for business analysts and BI developers to create Cutting-edge BI application that users can enhance and extend as business needs change.

- Network Product Guide's 2013 Hot Companies and Best Products Awards named QlikTech Corporate Social Responsibility and Philanthropy Company of the Year.
- QlikTech received the 'CSR on a Shoestring' award at the 2013 PR News CSR Awards.

QlikView Key Strengths

- Collaborative decision-making with colleagues via Social Business Discovery Analytics based on ERP, CRM, data warehouse, SQL database, Excel data, and more.
- Real-world, real-time information from the field via Mobile Business Discovery.
- Consolidate relevant data from multiple sources into a single application.
- Explore the associations in your data.
- Enable social decision-making through secure, real-time collaboration.
- Visualize data with engaging, state-of-the-art graphics.
- Search across all data - directly and indirectly.
- Interact with dynamic apps, dashboards, and analytics.
- Access, analyse, and capture data from mobile devices.

QlikView Technology

QlikView is an In-memory BI Pioneer : In-memory is important for performance, but it takes a lot more to deliver a Business Discovery platform. Traditional BI based on queries and cubes may run in memory for faster response time, but they still require IT to manually maintain the data associations users depend on.

Analytics & Big Data Professionals

Well known techniques include neural networks, decision trees, and regression models. Although these techniques have been applied to a myriad of problems, the advent of big data, cost-efficient processing power, and open standards have propelled predictive analytics to new heights.

Creating predictive analytic solutions is just part of the equation to tame big data. Once built, these solutions need to be transitioned to the operational environment where they create substantial business value. In the agile world we live today, the PMML standard delivers the necessary representational power for solutions to be quickly and easily exchanged between systems, allowing for predictions to move at the speed of business.

Many people think analytics is about gathering data using software tools and creating dashboards and reports. However, analytics is much more. Analytics goes beyond data; its primary goal is to enable business decisions based on that data. This involves working with stakeholders to understand the gaps in the business and using this knowledge as a guide to manipulate data, derive useful insights, and make recommendations - all key actions to increase revenue and lower costs. Wherever you sit in your organization, what's most important is the bottom line. And so whether you lead business or IT units or are in the trenches, the analytics profession has likely crossed your mind. What does it entail? Who are true analysts? How does one become an analyst? Those of you specifically in a data management, data warehousing or business intelligence role may wonder how to further develop your analytics career. On the surface, an "analytics career" can be quite broadly defined, and the transition to it can seem very confusing. Analytics may be data-driven, but in any team, strong leadership is critical for making sure that the project fulfils an organization's needs.

Analytics Professional : An analytics professional can use analytics tools and technologies to build the advanced analytical solutions. The analytics professional may have a focus in one or more areas like statistical, text, machine learning, optimization, simulation, graph theory and forecasting but it is unlikely that this person has deep enough knowledge to develop advanced analytic solutions across the board.

Today it seems that analytical jobs require deep knowledge in R and Hadoop. It is found the best analytics professionals can use COTS analytic tools to derive deployable, repeatable analytic solutions. While there are no universal certification processes for analytics professionals, it is process in the making. There are academic programs designed to create these professionals, such as North Carolina State University's Master of Science in Analytics. In 2012, INFORMS announced an analytics certification. Without a professional standard, many organizations have difficulty distinguishing between a person that knows how to use a software tool or a programming language and a person that knows analytics.

Senior Analytics Professional : A senior analytics professional must have inferential logic and the ability to scrutinize the work of other analytics professionals in the organization, making sure that the analytics that are developed are sound. This person should advise on the modelling approach, make sure that there aren't any "leakers" that have been included in the model, make sure that segment of the population that has been included is correct, and even make sure that the top variables in the model aren't an artifact of a poorly designed data preparation process.

Analytic Thought Leader : "Thought leadership" is such a buzzword that it's often hard to determine what it really means. From an analytics perspective, a thought leader helps the organization design and map analytic problems. Well, that level of knowledge comes from a strong background in different analytic routines and research methods. It's essential that the thought leader has significant practical experience using a mix of analytic routines and also a research-methods background so that he can apply the most appropriate methodology to the problem.

Generally, advanced degrees in the social sciences, applied mathematics, statistics or economics are good indications that the individual will have sufficient design of experiments skills to be a thought leader. Think about the problems that you are solving; most of the time these are "people problems" - they come down to social science research studies. Without a broad base of knowledge, experience and education, the analytics thought leader may apply the same algorithm to every problem that he approaches. Or, he may apply an overly complex solution because it is the one that he is most familiar with, instead of focusing on determining the right problem to solve. Communication skills for the analytic thought leader are a must. This person needs to be able to explain to the analytics professionals what analysis needs to be done, but also be able to talk to the business owners, interpreting the results of the analytics in a business context.

The Champion: Every team needs someone with the skills of a champion, someone who has enough clout to enforce changes and the initiative to not only find but resolve problems. In order to accomplish great things for the team, this person must have the power necessary to enforce process change. Without a champion, the true value of your analytics will likely be only partially realized.

CONCLUSION

The effective use of big data has the potential to transform economies. delivering a new wave of productivity growth and consumer surplus. Using big data will become a key basis of competition for existing companies, and will create new competitors who are able to attract employees that have the critical skills for a big data world.

Policy makers need to recognize the potential of harnessing big data to unleash the next wave of growth in their economies. They need to provide the institutional framework to allow companies to easily create value out of data while protecting the privacy of citizens and providing data security. They also have a significant role to play in helping to mitigate the shortage of talent through education and immigration policy and putting in place technology enablers including infrastructure such as communication networks; accelerating research in selected areas including advanced analytics; and creating an intellectual property framework that encourages innovation. Creative solutions to align incentives may also be necessary, including, for instance, requirements to share certain data to promote the public welfare.

The compliation on big data, predictive analysies and business analystics reference is expected to provide readymade reading material to have an idea and apply the modern tool for practical solutions.

Acknowledgements : The chapter is a compilation of information from various secondary sources for educational purpose. Thanks are due to those who have originally developed these.

REFERENCES

A. Brady and T. Menzies, "Case-Based Reasoning vs. Parametric Models for Software Quality Optimization," Proc. 6th Int'l Conf. Predictive Models in Software Eng. (PROMISE 10), ACM, 2010.

K. Dejaeger *et al.*, "Data Mining Techniques for Software Effort Estimation: A Comparative Study," IEEE Trans. Software Eng., vol. 28, no. 2, pp. 375-397.

T. Hall *et al.*, "A Systematic Review of Fault Prediction Performance in Software Engineering,"IEEE Trans. Software Eng., vol. 38, no. 6, pp. 1276-1304.

T. Menzies and T. Zimmermann, "Goldfish Bowl Panel: Software Development Analytics," Proc. 2012 Int'l Conf. Software Eng. (ICSE 2012), IEEE, 2012, pp. 1032-1033.

T. Menzies *et al.*, "Local vs. Global Lessons for Defect Prediction and Effort Estimation,"IEEE Trans. Software Eng., preprint, published online Dec. 2012;

□□□

CHAPTER - 30

Wavelet Analysis – An Emerging Tool for Modelling Complex Data from Diverse Disciplines

Subhabaha Pal
SAP Technical Manager, Manipal Global Education, Manipal Towers, Old Airport Road, Bangalore, India
E-mail: subhabaha.pal@manipalglobal.com
Satyabrata Pal
Formerly, Dean, Post Graduate Studies, Bidhan Chandra Krishi Viswavidyalaya, Nadia, W.B., India
E-mail: satyabrata.pal@hotmail.com
and
Arunava Ghosh
Assistant Professor (Sr. Scale), Uttar Banga Krishi Viswavidyalaya, Pundibari, Coochbehar, West Bengal, Pin-736165, India,
E-mail: arunava_ubkv@yahoo.co.in

ABSTRACT

Wavelet analysis is a technique possessing mathematical properties and it has been used by the scientific research community for its power to analyse rapidly changing transient signals used to represent data or functions - the wavelets used in the analysis are, however, functions that break the data down into different scales or resolutions. Wavelets possess the competence to handle spikes and discontinuities than traditional Fourier analysis and make the noisy data to de-noisy. Though traditional applications of wavelets have focused on image compression and analysis, wave propagation but they are also being used to analyse time series, biological processes, spectroscopic data of chemical compounds, seismic signals for earthquake prediction, atmospheric data for weather prediction, computer graphics, medical image technology, detection of aircraft and submarines, non-parametric regression, density estimation, and long memory wavelet models. Indeed, wavelets permit complex information such as music, speech, images and patterns to be decomposed into elementary forms at different positions and scales and subsequently being reconstructed with high precision. Signal transmission is based on the transmission of a series of numbers, indeed, the series representation of a function is important in all types of signal transmission.Wavelet transform of function is the improved version of Fourier transform. Fourier transform is a powerful tool for analysing the components of a stationary signal. But the Fourier transform fails to analyse the non-stationary signal where as a wavelet transform allows the components of a non-stationary signal to be analysed.

Keywords : Wavelet transform, Fourier transform, Signal transmission, Wavelet, Density estimation, Non-parametric regression, Wavelet analysis

1. INTRODUCTION

Signal data refer to data embodying some type of time or spatial relationship. The majority of signal data encountered in practical situations are a combination of low and high frequency components, the low frequency component being somewhat Stationary over the length of the signal data (example of a low frequencycomponent, a moving average in a time series,or a constant background colour in a photograph). High frequency components are jump discontinuities or noisy pieces of the signal, such as outliers in a time series or a shift from the background to a person's face in the photograph.The concept of 'wavelet' was first introduced by Jean Morlet, a French geophysicist in 1982. In fact, Morlet, et al (1982) presented an account of the theory of wave propagation. The wavelet means small wave and the study of wavelet transform is an essential tool for seismic signal analysis. Alex Grossmann studies inverse formula for the wavelet transform. Grossmann and Morlet did a detailed mathematical study on the continuous wavelet transforms and their various applications, and in Grossmann and Morlet (1984) an account of the above detailed study was presented. Deubechies (1990) and Mallat (1999) introduced wavelet analysis to improve representation of seismic signal analysis by changing from short time Fourier analysis (Fourier transform of a signal do not contain any local information) to a wavelet analysis in order to detect and analyse abrupt changes in signals. In time-frequency analysis of a signal, the classical Fourier transform analysis was inadequate To overcome the drawback, Dennis Gabor (1946)first introduced the windowed-Fourier transform, i.e., short-time Fourier transform known later as Gabor transform. Later many mathematicians, like, I. Daubechies (1990), A. Grossmann (1984), S. Mallat (1989, 1999), Y. Meyer (1993), R. A. Devore (1992) made remarkable contribution to wavelet theory. The modern applications of wavelet theory include diverse fields, like wave propagation, data compression, signal processing, image processing, pattern recognition, computer graphics, etc.

Wavelet analysis employs two functions, often referred to as the father and mother wavelets, to generate a family of functions that break up and reconstruct a signal. The father wavelet is similar in concept to a moving average function, while the mother wavelet quantifies the differences between the original signal and the average generated by the father wavelet. The combinationof the two functions allows wavelet analysis to analyse both the low and high frequency components in a signal simultaneously. The wavelet transform is a synthesis of ideas emerging over many years from different fields, notably mathematics, physics and engineering and very recently statistics.To be broad, the wavelet transform can provide economical and informative mathematical representations of many different objects of interest (e.g. functions, signals or images) quickly and easily through fast algorithms readily available in a variety of computer packages. As a sequel, wavelets are used widely in areas, like, functional and numerical analysis in mathematics, computer science, engineering, econometrics, statistics and also in the context of real-life problems encountered by researchers in the areas, like, physics, chemistry, biology, environment, seismology, signal processing, imaging (image analysis), data compression, and in life sciences (including medical science), in applied field of multidisciplinary interest; nay, in the areas, like, non-parametric regression and density estimation in statistics, in the area of forecasting of exchange rates in econometrics.

This book chapter is devoted to a presentation of a brief overview on the wavelets focusing their applications in problems appearing in varied disciplines, specially, in the area of statistics. A variety of wavelet and wavelet-related methods have emerged in recent years with potential applications to an increasing range of statistical problems. This paper restricts itselfto that subset of wavelet methods and their applications in statistics which is believed to be both relatively accessible and be of real practical value.

2. INTRODUCING WAVELETS

The mathematical effort on approximating signal data with functions is not a new concept, and in fact, Joseph Fourier developed a method using sines and cosines torepresent other functions in the early 1800's. Fourier analysis generates a set of base functions comprised of sine functions and cosine functions with different amplitudes and frequencies to approximate a signal, and because of the smooth and periodic behaviour of sine and cosine functions,Fourier series offers a very good representation for analysing signal data that does not change with time or involve jump discontinuities. As an example, a well behaved signal is received when we hear the sound from a musical instrument. Fourier analysis can't approximate any signal which is of much more complex type including many jump discontinuities and also possesses the attribute that the signal appears to be dampening with time.

As mentioned in the Introduction that with the joint effort by Jean Morletand Alex Grossman in 1984, the wavelet theory began to synthesize and wavelets took shape for the first time. Morlet was a petrol eumengineer working on developing methods for analysing seismic signals to help geologists locate underground oil deposits. Geologists use sound waves to determine what type of material lies underneath the surface at different depths. If the waves move very fast through one rock layer, then it may be a salt dome which traps a layer of oil underneath. The seismic signals containmany jump discontinuities as the waves pass from one rock layer to the next, resulting in more complex patterns. Morlet developed his own method of analysing the seismic signals by creating functionsthat were localized in space, and asked Alex Grossman, a physicist, to confirm that the use of "wavelets" of constantshape was mathematically sound. Mackenzie (2001) contains a very low level introduction to wavelets, their applications, andmore on the history including work by Morlet *et al.* (1982), Grossman *et al.* (1984), Mallat (1989, 1999), and Daubechies (1990).

Image analysis has been the application of choice for wavelets. In 1995 the FBI had roughly 200 million fingerprint records stored as inked impressions on paper cards, which they wanted to convert to digital form. Each card required 10 MB of storage space based on a resolution of 500 pixels per inch with 256 levels of gray-scale, which meant that the FBI needed 2,000,000,000 MB or 2,000,000 gigabytes worth of storage space. An algorithm based on wavelets was chosen as the FBI standard for fingerprint image compression, because it yielded compression ratios between 15:1 and 20:1 with minimal loss of image quality. A compression ratio of 20:1 meant that only 100,000 gigabytes of space was needed, and while this was still alarge amount of memory it was a substantial savings. The new JPEG-2000 image compression standard is also based on analgorithm that uses wavelets, and has a compression ratio of 20:1.

Image analysis is not the only area of application for wavelet analysis. Wavelets can be used in the analysis and modeling of other types of signal data. Chemists are using wavelets to help reduce the number of potential predictors and improve the modeling of spectroscopic signals, Cocchi, *et al.* (2003), Statisticians and mathematicians are using wavelets to analyze time series, Bilen, and Huzurbazar, (2002), Percival and Walden (2000), and scientists are using wavelets to study the breathing patterns of new-born babies Addison, P. (2004).

It is mentioned in the Introduction that wavelet analysis employs two functions, often referred to as the father and mother wavelets. The father wavelet is usually referred to as the scaling function, φ, while the mother wavelet is simply the wavelet and is represented by the function, φ. The wavelet may be seen as a complement to the classical Fourier decomposition method. Suppose, a certain class of functions, f(x) is given and we want to find 'simple functions' $f_0, f_1, f_2,$ ....such that,

$$f(x) = \sum_{n=0}^{\infty} a_n f_n(x), \text{ for some coefficient } a_n, \; n = 0, 1, 2, \ldots\ldots\ldots \qquad 1$$

Wavelet is a mathematical tool leading to representations of the type (1) for a large class of functions f.

A wavelet means a small wave (the sinusoids used in Fourier analysis are waves) and in brief, a wavelet is an oscillation that decays quickly. Following the definition of wavelet, equivalent mathematical conditions for wavelet are:

$$\int_{-\infty}^{\infty} |\psi(t)|^2 dt < \infty \qquad 2$$

$$\int_{-\infty}^{\infty} |\psi(t)| dt < \infty, \qquad 3$$

$$\int_{-\infty}^{\infty} \frac{|\hat{\psi}(\omega)|}{|\omega|} d\omega < \infty \qquad 4$$

Where $\hat{\psi}(\omega)$ is the Fourier Transform of $\psi(t)$. Equation (4) is called the admissibility condition.

Wavelet Transform– Recalling that the concept of wavelet transform was first introduced by Jean Morlet as a mathematical tool for seismic wave analysis, he first considered wavelets as a family of functions constricted by translations and dilations of a single function called the "Mother Wavelet" $\psi(t)$. These are defined as follows:

$$\psi_{a,b}(t) = \frac{1}{\sqrt{|a|}} \psi\left(\frac{t-b}{a}\right), \quad a, b \in R, \; a \neq 0 \qquad 5$$

The parameter a, is the scaling parameter or scale, and it measures the degree of compression. The parameter b is the translation parameter which represents the time location of the wavelet. If $|a| < 1$, then the wavelet in (5) represents a compressed version (smaller support in time-domain) of the mother wavelet and corresponds mainly to higher frequencies. On the other hand, if $|a| > 1$, then $\psi_{a,b}(t)$ has a larger time-width than $\psi(t)$ and corresponds to lower frequencies. Thus, wavelets possess time-widths adapted to their frequencies. Due to the adaptability property, Morlet wavelets have been successfully employed in signal processing and time-frequency signal analysis.

3. WAVELET SERIES AND WAVELET COEFFICIENTS

If a function, f $L_2(R)$, the series

$$\sum_{j\in z}\sum_{j\in Z}(f,\psi_{j,k})\psi_{j,k}(t) \quad \ldots\ldots \qquad 6$$

Is called the wavelet series of f and is defined as under:

$$(f,\psi_{j,k}) = d_{j,k} = \int_{-\infty}^{\infty} f(t)\psi_{j,k}(t)dt \qquad 7$$

$(f, \psi_{j,k})$ is called the wavelet coefficients of the function, f.

It is mentioned earlier that a signal is represented as a function, $f(x)$ which has a series representation given below:

$$f(x) = \sum_{n=0}^{\infty} a_n x^n$$

It is evident from the above representation that all information about the function $f(x)$ is stored in the coefficients, $\{a_n\}_{n=0}^{\infty}$

Signals can be classified into two classes –

- Continuous Signals
- Discrete Signals

4. CONTINUOUS SIGNALS

The signal which is described by a continuous function (for example, a recording of a speech signal or music signal, which measures the current in the cable to the loudspeaker as function of time) is called continuous signals.

Wavelets are frequently used to remove noise from music recordings. In fact, often a music signal consists of the music itself embedded with some noise. The music signal itself describes the change of music over time. The signal can be regarded as the current through the loudspeaker when we play arecording. The process of representing the music piece via wavelets implies actually the representation of this signal via the coefficients, $\{d_{j,k}\}$ in (7), indeed, these coefficients indicate the presence some odd elements (noise) in the music. The noise contribution is usually small compared to the music, but it causes irritation for the ears; it also contributes to the coefficients $\{d_{j,k}\}$ but usually less than the music itself. The idea is now to remove the coefficients in (7) which are smaller than a certain threshold value (more specifically, this procedure is not applied on the signal itself, but on it's so called wavelet transform). Here, as a working rule these coefficients are replaced by zeroes; thus, the remaining coefficients represent the music. The motto is to remove the part of the signal which has no relationship with the music; unfortunately, though the above procedure also might cancel smaller parts of the music itself, but still the signal (music) is usually considered by the ears as an improvement (Christensen (2004), Mallat (1989, 1999)).

5. DISCRETE SIGNALS

The signal which is described by a sequence of numbers or pairs of numbers, is called discrete signals.

A digital black-white photo consists of a split of its picture into a large number of small squares, called pixels; to each pixel, the camera associates a light intensity, measured on a scale from, say, 0 (completely white) to 256 (completely black). Collectively, this information constitutes the picture. Thus, mathematically a photo consists of a sequence of pairs of numbers, namely, a number of the pixelstogether with the associated light intensity,(Christensen (2004), Mallat (1989, 1999)).

6. SOME APPLICATIONS OF WAVELETS

Wavelets are a powerful statistical tool which can be used for a wide range of applications presented below:

- Signal processing
- Data compression
- Smoothing and image de-noising
- Fingerprint verification
- Biology for cell membrane recognition, to distinguish the normal from the pathological membranes
- DNA analysis, protein analysis
- Blood-pressure, heart-rate and ECG analyses
- Finance (which is more surprising), for detecting the properties of quick variation of values
- In Internet traffic description, for designing the services size
- Industrial supervision of gear-wheel

- Speech recognition
- Computer graphics and multi-fractal analysis
- Many areas of physics including molecular dynamics, astrophysics, optics, turbulence and quantum mechanics.

8. STATISTICAL APPLICATIONS

Some relatively well-established applications of wavelet methods in statistical problems have been reviewed in this section. These methods include nonparametric regression, density estimation, inverse problems, change-point problems and some specialized aspects of time series analysis.

8.1. Non-parametric Regression

The standard univariate nonparametric regression setting is as follows:

$$y_i = g(t_i) + \varepsilon_i, \qquad 8$$

where, ε_i are independent $N(0,\sigma^2)$ random variables. The main objective is to recover the underlying function, g from the noisy data y_i without assuming any particular parametric structure for the function, g.

One of the basic approaches to the nonparametric regression is to expand the unknown function, g in the form of a generalized Fourier series and then to estimate the generalized Fourier coefficients from the data. The original nonparametric problem is thus transformed to a parametric problem, although the potential number of parameters is infinite. An appropriate choice of the basis for the expansion is therefore a key point in relation to the efficiency of such an approach. A 'good' basis should be parsimonious in the sense that a large set of possible response functions can be approximated well with only a few terms of the employed generalized Fourier expansion As has been mentioned that wavelet series allows a parsimonious expansion for a wide variety of functions including functions applied in inhomogeneous cases also, it is, therefore, natural to apply the generalized Fourier series approach by using a wavelet series.

Let us suppose, without loss of generality, that t_i's are within the unit interval [0,1]. For simplicity, it is assumed that the sample points are equally spaced, i.e., $t_i = i/n$, and that the sample size n is a power of 2 ($n=2^J$), for some positive integer, j. These assumptions allow performance of both the Discrete Wavelet Transform (DWT) and Inverse Discrete Wavelet Transform (IDWT) using Mallat (1989) fast algorithm. For non-equispaced or random designs, or sample sizes which are not a power of 2 or data contaminated with correlated noise, modifications are needed to the standard wavelet-based estimation procedures.

8.2. Linear Estimation

Firstly linear wavelet estimators of the function, g are considered here. Suppose that the function, g is expanded as a wavelet series on the interval [0,1] as described in equation (3) with $j_0 = 0$:

$$j,\ g(t) = c_0\phi(t) + \sum_{j=0}^{\infty}\sum_{k=0}^{2^J-1} w_{jk}\psi_{jk}(t), \qquad 9$$

where, $c_0=(g, \phi)$ and $w_{jk} = (g, \psi_{jk})$.

It is not possible to estimate an infinite set of w_{jk} from the finite sample, so it is usually assumed that the function, g belongs to a class of functions with a certain regularity. The corresponding norm of the sequence of w_{jk} is therefore finite and w_{jk} must decay to zero. Then, following standard generalized Fourier methodology, it is assumed that ,

$$g(t) = c_0\phi(t) + \sum_{j=0}^{M}\sum_{k=0}^{2^J-1} w_{jk}\psi_{jk}(t) \qquad 10$$

For some M < J and a corresponding truncated wavelet estimator, is of the form:

$$\widehat{g}_M(t) = \widehat{c}_0 f(t) + \sum_{j=0}^{M}\sum_{k=0}^{2^J-1} w_{jk}\psi_{jk}(t), \qquad 11$$

In such a setting, the original nonparametric problem essentially transforms to linear regression and the sample estimates of the scaling coefficient and the wavelet coefficients are given as follows:

$$\hat{c} = \frac{1}{n}\sum_{i=1}^{n}\phi(t_i)y_i,\ \hat{w}_{jk} = \frac{1}{n}\sum_{i=1}^{n}\psi_{jk}(t_i)y_i\,. \qquad 12$$

The performance of the truncated wavelet estimator depends on an appropriate choice of M. Intuitively it is clear that the 'optimal' choice of M should depend on the regularity of the unknown response function. Too small a value of M will result in an over-smoothed estimator, whereas setting M = J-1 simply reproduces the data. The problem of choosing M has much in common with model selection, and the associated models can judged by applying model selection criteria, like, Akaike's Information Criterion. The problem is also similar to the selection of a bandwidth in kernel estimation or the smoothing parameter in spline fitting.

8.3. Non-linear Estimation

Dohono *et al.* (1994, 1995, 1998) proposed a non-linear wavelet estimator of the function, g based on a reconstruction from a more judicious selection of the empirical wavelet coefficients. This approach is now widely used in statistics, particularly in signal processing and image analysis.

Owing to the orthogonality of the matrix W, the DWT (Discrete Wavelet Transform) of white noise is also an array of the independent $N(0,\sigma^2)$ random variables, so from equation (8), it follows that –

$$\hat{w}_{jk} = w_{jk} + e_{jk},\ j = 0, 1, 2, \ldots\ldots, J\text{-}1, k = 0, 1, \ldots., 2^J\text{-}1, \qquad 13$$

Where are independent $N(0, \sigma^2/n)$ random variables. The sparseness of the wavelet expansion makes it reasonable to assume that essentially only a few large contain information about underlying function g, whereas small can be attributed to the noise which uniformly contaminates all wavelet coefficients.

To obtainan approximate wavelet representation of the underlying function g, it is decided that the significantly large wavelet coefficients can be retained, and the set containing all other coefficients is made equal to 0.

8.4. Density Estimation

The ideas in relation to non-parametric regression can also be applied to other related statistical problems like density estimation.

Let $x_1, x_2, x_3, \ldots\ldots, x_n$ be observations of an unknown density, f supported on the unit interval [0,1]. An wavelet expansion series representation of f is:

$$f(x) = c_0\phi(x) + \sum_{j=0}^{\infty}\sum_{k=0}^{2^J-1} w_{jk}\psi_{jk}(x) \qquad 14$$

where $c_0=(f, \phi)$ and $w_{jk} = (f, \Psi_{jk})$. $j_0 = 0$ is chosen here for convenience.

In practice, the above choices may not necessarily be optimal, but modifications for the more general case are straightforward.

For an unknown density f, sample estimates of the scaling and wavelet coefficients are obtained from the method-of-moments estimates:

$$c = \frac{1}{n}\sum_{i=1}^{n}\phi(x_i),\ \hat{w}_{jk} = \frac{1}{n}\sum_{i=1}^{n}\psi_{jk}(x_i)y_i\,. \qquad 15$$

By analogy, the method discussed in relation to non-parametric regression, a linear wavelet estimator for the density f is obtained by truncating the infinite series in equation (14) for some positive M:

$$\hat{f}_M(x) = \hat{c}_0 \phi(x) + \sum_{j=0}^{M} \sum_{k=0}^{2^j - 1} \hat{w}_{jk} \psi_{jk}(x) \qquad 16$$

Again the choice of M is a key point and may be arrived at by the use of one of the several model selection procedures.

For further studies on the topic of Wavelet Analysis, the readers may visit the following papers, Abramovich *et al.* (2000), Delyon *et al.* (1995), Neumann and Spokoiny, (1995), Wang (1995), Hall *et al.* (1997), Johnstone and Silverman (1990),

9. CONCLUSION

Though it is now an admitted fact that wavelet analysis has already instituted itself as a valuable tool for image analysis and compression, yet its applications too ther types of signal data are being continuously explored and with the advancement of time novel applications of wavelet analysis are emerging almost often encompassing different disciplines and varied problems, a glimpse of which has been presented above. For statisticians and other data analysts wavelets offer potentially powerful tools to aid in the analysis and pre-processing of data. Wavelet analysis is well suited for signals that are intermittent, non-stationary, or noisy, and wavelet coefficients effectively reveal characteristics of the data that other techniques might miss.

REFERENCES

Abramovich, Felix, Bailey, Trevor C., Sapatinas, Theofanis, 2000, The Statistician, Royal Statistical Society, 49, Part 1, pp. 1-29.

Addison, P., 2004, "The little wave with the big future", Physics World, 17 (3): 35-39.

Antoniasdis, A., Pham, D.T.,1998,"Wavelet Regression for Random or Irregular Design", Comput.Statist. Data Anal., 28 : 353-369.

Bilen, C., Huzurbazar, S. (2002), "Wavelet-Based Detection of Outliers in Time Series", Journal of Computational and Graphical Statistics, 11 (2): 311-327.

Cai, T.T., 1999, "Adaptive Wavelet Estimation: A Block Thresholding and Oracle Inequality Approach", Ann. Statist., 27 : 898-924.

Cai, T.T., Silverman, B.W., 1998, "Incorporating Information on Neighbouring Coefficients into Wavelet Estimation", Technical Report, 98-13, Department of Statistics, Purdue University, West Lafayette.

Christensen, O, 2004,"Approximation Theory-From Taylor Polynomials to Wavelets", Birkhauser, Boston.

Cocchi, M., Seeber, R., Ulrici, A., 2003, "Multivariate calibration of analytical signals by WILMA (wavelet interface to linearmodeling analysis)", Journal of Chemometrics, 17: 512-527.

Daubechies, I., 1990, "The Wavelet Transform, Time-Frequency Localization and Signal Analysis", IEEE Transformation and Information Theory, 36: 961-1005.

Daubechies, I., 1990, "Ten Lectures on Wavelets" SIAM, Philadelphia, PA, 1992.

Debnath, L., 2002,"Wavelet Transformation and Their Applications", Birkhauser Boston.

Delyon, B., Juditsky, A.,1995,"Estimating Wavelet Co-efficients", Lecture Notes Statistics, 103: 151-168.

DeVore, R.A., 1992, "Image Compression through Wavelet Transform Coding", Information Theory, IEEE Transactions on Information Theory, 38 (2): 719-746, ISSN 0018-9448.

Gabor, Dennis, 1946, "Theory of communication. Part 1: The analysis of information", Electrical Engineers – Part III, Radio and Communication Engineering, Journal of the Institution of Engineers. 93 (26) : 429-441.

Grossman, A., Morlet, J., 1984, "Decomposition of Hardy Functions into Square Integrable Wavelets of Constant Shape", SIAM Journal of Analysis, 15: 723-736.

Hall, P., Turlach, B.A., 1997, "Interpolation Methods for Nonlinear Wavelet Regression with Irregularly Spaced Design", Ann. Statist., 25: 1912-1925.

Johnstone, I.M., Silverman, B.W., 1990, "Wavelet Threshold Estimators for Data With Correlated Noise", J.R.Statist. Soc., B, 59: 319-351.

Kovac, A., Silverman, B.W., 2000, "Extending the Scope of Wavelet Regression Methods by Coefficient-dependent Thresholding", J.Am.Statist.Ass., 95.

Mackenzie, D., 2001, "Wavelets: Seeing the Forest and the Trees".The National Academy of Sciences, Washington, DC.

Mallat, S, 1989, "A Theory of Multi resolution Signal Decomposition: The Wavelet Representation", IEEE Trans. Inf. Theory, 38: 617-643.

Mallat, S.,1999, "A Wavelet Tour of Signal Processing", Academic Press, New York.

Meyer, Y., 1993, "Wavelets: Their Past and Their Future, Progress in Wavelet Analysis and Its Applications", Gif-sur-Yvette, pp 9-18, 1993.

Morlet, J.; Arens, G.; Fourgeau, E. and Giard, D., 1982, "Wave propagation and sampling theory, Part1: Complex signal land scattering in multilayer media" Journal of Geophysics, 47: 203-221.

Neumann,M.H.,Spokoiny, V., (1995),"On the Efficiency of Wavelet Estimators under Arbitary Error Distributions", Math. Meth. Statist., 4: 137-166.

Percival, D., Walden, A. (2000), Wavelet Methods for Time Series Analysis.Cambridge University Press.

Strang, G., 1989, "Wavelets and Dilation Equations: A brief introduction", SIAM Review, 31: 614-627.

Wang, Y., 1995, "Jump and Sharp Cusp Detection by Wavelets", Biometrika, 82, 385-397.

Walnut, D.F., 2001,"AnIntroduction to Wavelet Analysis", Birkhäuser, Boston, 2001.

Wells, R.O., 1993, "Parametrizing Smooth Compactly Supported Wavelets", Transform American Mathematical Society, 338(2): 919-931.

Wojtaszczyk, P., 1997,"A Mathematical Introduction to Wavelets", Cambridge University press, Cambridge, U.K, 1997.

❑❑❑

CHAPTER - 31

Conjoint Analysis: An Emerging Tool in Market Research

Prasenjit Pal
Assistant Professor, Dept-Fisheries Extension, College of Fisheries, Central Agricultural University (CAU), Lembucherra, Tripura 799210
Email: prasenjit3agstat@gmail.com

1. INTRODUCTION

The concept of product management in market research is all about trade-offs. Whether the objective is to increase market share, profit margin or revenue, every product manager makes trade-offs—quality vs. cost, time to market vs. breadth of features, richness of the offering vs. ease of use, etc. So, how does anybody know what the market wants? What market segments exist? What those segments prefer? What will they pay? or what trade-offs to make? The answer is to get the market to make the trade-offs. The conjoint analysis is the tool to measure the trade-off i.e. to understand customer preferences, values and choices. Conjoint analysis is used for many marketing decisions, including new product development process, selecting among alternative product designs, targeting, and pricing. It is also used to predict their choices for future products and services. Conjoint Analysis assumes that a product can be "broken down" into its component attributes. For example, a car has attributes such as colour, price, size, miles-per-gallon, and model style. Using Conjoint Analysis, the value that individuals place on any product is equivalent to the sum of the utility they derive from all the attributes making up a product. Further, it assumes that the preference for a product and the likelihood to purchase it are in proportion to the utility an individual gains from the product. It is generally inappropriate for products which are evaluated by consumers on the basis of their "image", such as beer or cigarettes, rather than on the basis of their constituent attributes. It is so widely used in market research that helps to understand the market's preferences including product development, competitive positioning, pricing, product line analysis, segmentation and resource allocation.That gives the better insight to the market revenue, share, profit which in turn helps to provide the better market intelligence. The present chapter deals with the genesis, usefulness and analysis procedure of conjoint analysis in different software with example.

2.THE GENESIS OF CONJOINT ANALYSIS

Conjoint analysis has received considerable academic and industry attention as a major set of techniques for measuring buyers' tradeoffs among multiattributed products and services (Green and Rao 1971; Johnson 1974; Srinivasan and Shocker 1973b), a state-ofthe-art review of conjoint analysis in 1978 (Green and Srinivasan 1978). Just prior to 1970, marketing professor Paul Green recognized that Luce and Tukey's (1964) article on conjoint measurement, might be applied to marketing problems: to understand how buyers made complex purchase decisions, to estimate preferences and importances for product features, and to predict buyer behavior. Green could not have envisioned the profound impact his work on full-profile card-sort conjoint analysis would eventually achieve when he and coauthor Rao published their historic article "Conjoint Measurement for Quantifying Judgmental Data" in the Journal of Marketing Research (JMR) (Green and Rao 1971). Near the end of the 1970s, academics Paul Green and Seenu Srinivasan published an influential paper in the Journal of Consumer Research summarizing the use of conjoint analysis in industry, outlining new developments, and giving advice regarding best practices (Green and Srinivasan 1978).

By the early 1980s, when commercial software became available in 1985, the floodgates were opened. Based on Green's work with full-profile conjoint analysis, Steve Herman and Bretton-Clark Software released a software system for IBM personal computers. Also in 1985, Johnson and his new company, Sawtooth Software, released a software system (also for the IBM personal computer) called Adaptive Conjoint Analysis (ACA). Based on industry usage studies conducted by leading academics (Vriens, Huber, and Wittink 1997), ACA was the most widely used conjoint technique and software system worldwide. By the end of the decade, ACA would yield that position to discrete choice analysis. Two main factors were responsible for discrete choice analysis overtaking ACA and other ratings-based conjoint methods by the turn of the century: (1) the release of commercial software for discrete choice modeling (CBC for choice-based conjoint) by Sawtooth Software in 1993 and (2) the application of hierarchical Bayes (HB) methods to estimate individual-level models from discrete choice data. The 1990s represented a decade of strong growth for conjoint analysis and its application in a fascinating variety of areas viz. design of Web sites, litigation and damages assessment, human resources and employee research, and Web-based sales agents for helping buyers search and make decisions about complex products and services. By the end of the decade, analysts had become so trusting of the technique that some used conjoint analysis to help them personally decide among cars to buy or members of the opposite sex to date.

Since 2000, academics have been using HB-related methods to develop more complex models of consumer preference, relaxing the assumptions of additivity by incorporating noncompensatory effects, incorporating descriptive and motivational variables, modeling the interlinking web of multiple influencers and decision makers, and linking survey-based discrete choice data with sales data. Since the development of the web the lead user method and conjoint analysis are facing new challenges in an online world (Lüthje, Herstatt 2004; Netzer *et al.*, 2008; Belz, Baumbach 2010). The new approach of the separation of lead users and non-lead users within conjoint analysis can lead to breakthrough innovations will extend traditional conjoint analysis and adaptive conjoint analysis by a lead user identification technique based on a former approach by Lüthje, Herstatt and von Hippel in 2005. According to the separation of user groups, the resulting overall conjoint measurement is influenced by the high amount of non-lead users, who tend to prefer general innovations more often. New research has shown that staging the interview as a screening task (to select a consideration set) followed by focused trade-offs among considered products may lead to more accurate market simulation models, especially for high-involvement products and services described by many attributes (Gaskin, Evgeniou, Bailiff,and Hauser 2007; Johnson and Orme 2007).Software developers continue to make conjoint analysis more flexible, as well as faster and less expensive to carry out. Software systems often support multiple formats, including paper-based, PC-based, Web-based, and hand-held-device interviewing. In retrospect, very few would disagree that conjoint analysis represents one of the great success stories in quantitative marketing research.

3. BENEFITS OF CONJOINT ANALYSIS

Conjoint analysis has been successfully applied in many industries, such as Air Travel, Smart Phones, Computers, Financial Services, Health Care, Real Estate, and Electronics. There are various benefits of using a conjoint analysis in market research or business analytics. Most importantly, the consumer himself does a trade-off analysis between the desirability of various features in a comparable scenario. Secondly, it may reveal hidden factors that are not even considering in the study. Thirdly, it uses realistically possible choices and considers preferences at an individual level. Further, it can also help in segmentation based on different desired features in different consumer groups. Conjoint analysis not only helps us in deciding the features of planned products but may also reveal which of the existing products consumers prefer most and why. On the other hand, conjoint analysis may sometimes be too complex and may confuse the respondents who might provide overly simplistic answers instead of doing a real comparison.

4. ANALYSIS OF COJOINT DATA

There are three phases in the analysis of conjoint data: collection of trade-off data through a questionnaire, statistical analysis of the data, and market simulation.

i) **Questionnaire:** In the interactive, conjoint portion of the questionnaire, respondents are given various tasks which allow for the measurement of their perceptions of market research companies. Attributes for this project include Company Size, Location, Price, and Gestalt. Each attribute can contain different "levels" comprising different aspects of the attribute. In order to understand respondents' perceptions of market research companies on the basis of these various combinations of attribute levels, the participants are first asked to rank order their preference for the various levels within each attribute. This is especially important when the preference for various levels may not be "linear"—rising steadily from the lowest to the highest level within an attribute. Next, they are presented with different levels within the same attribute and asked how important the difference between the levels is to them. This task provides the research program with preliminary information on the distance—in terms of preference—between levels of an attribute.

In the next step of the questionnaire, survey participants are presented with pairs of market research company profiles (conjoint tasks). Each description contains between two and four attributes. Respondents are asked which of the two company descriptions they would be more likely to prefer. Decision tasks such as these are repeated 20 times to provide information on each respondent's preference for the attributes and levels. Finally, participants are presented with five composite market research companies containing all four attributes and they are asked to express the likelihood they would hire such a company on a 100-point scale. The conjoint/decision tasks and the final selection exercises are wholly interactive. The computer program generates an optimal set of trade-off tasks for each individual. These tasks are generated by the information respondents provide on the attributes they value or find important.

ii) **Statistical analysis of the data:** Conjoint analysis applies a complex form of analysis of variance to a respondent's choice task data to calculate a utility for each level of each attribute. These are basically index numbers which measure how valuable or desirable a particular feature is to the respondent. The idea is each respondent's choice tasks reveal something about the relative utility that he or she has for each feature. Features which a respondent is reluctant to give up from one choice task to another are judged to be of higher utility to that respondent than features which are quickly given up. A respondent's "utility" is a measurement of his or her relative strength of preference for each level of each attribute of the research company. The respondent's utilities are estimated using a "least squares updating" algorithm. Initial estimates of utilities are based on the respondent's rank orders of preference and his or her ratings of attribute importance. Estimates are updated following each trade-off task, and the initial estimates have decreasing influence as the interview progresses.

The final estimates are true least squares, with the same weight being applied to each of the respondent's answers. For the purposes of modeling, the final estimates are scaled so that the sums of each individual's utilities predict most accurately that person's likelihood of hiring a particular company. Utilities scaled in this way are ideal for predicting the likelihood of acceptance; they can be very misleading when reported in the aggregate or for comparing segments. For these purposes, utilities are re-scaled in such a way that the sum of the *differences* between the maximum and minimum level of each attribute equals the number of attributes times 100. This method assures that all survey respondents' utilities are equally rated in reports and analyses. The best way to interpret utilities involves analysis of the gaps between utility levels within an attribute. This "gap" or range between utility levels within an attribute indicates that the survey participants see greater importance between certain attribute levels than between other attribute levels. As a result, these attributes with greater ranges are used to differentiate or discriminate between different market research companies.

iii) **Market simulation:** Market simulation consists of describing each market research company profile in terms of its attributes, adding up the respondent's value for all of a company's attributes and using this information to determine the relative value of each company to each respondent. Acceptance likelihood is calculated by adding up the sums of the attribute level utilities contained in the company profile. Through market simulation, a "base case" is specified which contains selected attribute levels across all company attributes. Simulations can be run to determine the sensitivity of a respondent's likelihood of acceptance to modifications on each attribute.

Number of profiles to evaluate in conjoint analysis: In the case of having *N* attributes with *k* levels each, the number of profiles or stimuli that must be evaluated is: k^N.For example, if we have 6 attributes with 3 levels each, the number of profiles to be evaluated are $3^6=729$. If there are two more attributes with the same number of levels, in other words, 8 attributes with 3 levels each, the number of stimuli will increase significantly, since the number of profiles to be evaluated becomes 6,561. If the number of levels varies between the attributes, for example N attributes with k levels and M attributes with l levels, then the number of stimuli to be evaluated is: $k^N l^M$. For example, if we have 2 attributes with 3 levels and 3 attributes with 2 levels, the total number of profiles to be evaluated will be $3^2 2^3$.

The number of profiles established is determined by a full factorial design. This design uses all the possible combinations of attribute levels or factors. These factors are studied because they are believed to have a conjoint effect over a variable answer. The factor effect is defined as the variation experienced by the variable answer when a change is produced in the factor level. Frequently, this is known as the main effect because it refers to the fundamental interest factors of the experiment (Louviere, 1988). A full factorial design allows estimates to be obtained of the parameters corresponding to the main effects and to all the interaction effects. Evidently, this provides excessive information; therefore the person interviewed is unable to make a proper evaluation. The person would lose interest and their evaluation would negatively influence the quality of the answers obtained (Vázquez, 1990).

The fractional factorial designs have been created in order to solve this problem. The fractional factorial design is the most commonly used design in Conjoint Analysis (Martín, 1987). It reduces the information load to be evaluated by the interviewed person by means of partially or fully disregarding the interactions of the model. Although fractional factorial designs greatly reduce the difficulties present in a full factorial design, when the number of attributes and levels is elevated, the fractional factorial design is also configured by a high number of profiles and consequently there is still some information overloads which impede the required quality of the answers. Therefore, when there are many attributes, experiments with conjoint analysis include problems of information overload that affect the validity of such experiments. These problems can be avoided or reduced by using integrated conjoint experiments.

5. DETAILS PROCEDURE OF CONJOINT ANALYSIS IN SPSS

To obtain a conjoint analysis, enter command syntax for a CONJOINT command into a syntax window, and then run it.For an example of command syntax for a CONJOINT command in the context of a complete conjoint analysis—including generating and displaying an orthogonal design—see

"Using Conjoint Analysis to Model Carpet-Cleaner Preference".For complete command syntax information about the CONJOINT command, see the *SPSS Command Syntax Reference*.

i) **To run a command from a syntax window:** From the menus choose:

File

New

SPSS Syntax...

This opens an SPSS syntax window. Enter the command syntax for the CONJOINT command.

ii) **Requirements:** The Conjoint procedure requires two files—a data file and a plan file—and the specification of how data were recorded (for example, each data point is a preference score from 1 to 100). The plan file consists of the set of product profiles to be rated by the subjects and should be generated using the Generate Orthogonal Design procedure. The data file contains the preference scores or rankings of those profiles collected from the subjects. The plan and data files are specified with the PLAN and DATA subcommands, respectively. The method of data recording is specified with the SEQUENCE, RANK, or SCORE subcommands. The following command syntax shows a minimal specification:

```
CONJOINT PLAN='CPLAN.SAV' /DATA='RUGRANKS.SAV'
/SEQUENCE=PREF1 TO PREF22.
```

iii) **Specifying how data were recorded:** Data can be recorded in one of three ways: sequentially, as rankings, or as preference scores. These three methods are indicated by the SEQUENCE, RANK, and SCORE subcommands as part of a CONJOINT command.

SEQUENCE Subcommand indicates that data were recorded sequentially so that each data point in the data file is a profile number, starting with the most preferred profile and ending with the least preferred profile. This is how data are recorded if the subject is asked to order the profiles from the most to the least preferred. The researcher records which profile number was first, which profile number was second, and so on.

```
CONJOINT PLAN=* /DATA='RUGRANKS.SAV'
/SEQUENCE=PREF1 TO PREF22.
```

The variable *PREF1* contains the profile number for the most preferred profile out of 22 profiles in the orthogonal plan. The variable *PREF22* contains the profile number for the least preferred profile in the plan.

RANK Subcommand indicates that each data point is a ranking, starting with the ranking of profile 1, then the ranking of profile 2, and so on. This is how the data are recorded if the subject is asked to assign a rank to each profile, ranging from 1 to *n*, where *n* is the number of profiles. A lower rank implies greater preference.

CONJOINT PLAN=* /DATA='RUGRANKS.SAV'

/RANK=RANK1 TO RANK22.

The variable *RANK1* contains the ranking of profile 1, out of a total of 22 profiles in the orthogonal plan. The variable *RANK22* contains the ranking of profile 22.

SCORE Subcommand indicates that each data point is a preference score assigned to the profiles, starting with the score of profile 1, then the score of profile 2, and so on. This type of data might be generated, for example, by asking subjects to assign a number from 1 to 100 to show how much they liked the profile. A higher score implies greater preference.

CONJOINT PLAN=* /DATA='RUGRANKS.SAV'

/SCORE=SCORE1 TO SCORE22.

iv) Optional subcommands: The CONJOINT command offers a number of optional subcommands that provide additional control and functionality beyond what is required.

SUBJECT Subcommand allows to specify a variable from the data file to be used as an identifier for the subjects. If a subject variable is not specified, the CONJOINT command assumes that all of the cases in the data file come from one subject. The following example specifies that the variable *ID*, from the file *rugranks.sav*, is to be used as a subject identifier.

CONJOINT PLAN=* /DATA='RUGRANKS.SAV'

/SCORE=SCORE1 TO SCORE22 /SUBJECT=ID.

FACTORS Subcommand allows specifying the model describing the expected relationship between factors and the rankings or scores. For not specifying a model for a factor, CONJOINT assumes a discrete model.

DISCRETE Model indicates that the factor levels are categorical and that no assumption is made about the relationship between the factor and the scores or ranks. This is the default.

LINEAR model indicates an expected linear relationship between the factor and the scores or ranks. MORE indicates that higher levels of a factor are expected to be preferred, while LESS indicates that lower levels of a factor are expected to be preferred. Specifying MORE or LESS will *not* affect estimates of utilities. They are used simply to identify subjects whose estimates do not match the expected direction.

IDEAL model indicates an expected quadratic relationship between the scores or ranks and the factor. It is assumed that there is an ideal level for the factor, and distance from this ideal point (in either direction) is associated with decreasing preference. Factors described with this model should have at least three levels.

ANTIIDEAL model indicates an expected quadratic relationship between the scores or ranks and the factor. It is assumed that there is a worst level for the factor, and distance from this point (in either direction) is associated with increasing preference. Factors described with this model should have at least three levels. The following command syntax provides an example using the FACTORS subcommand:

```
CONJOINT PLAN=* /DATA='RUGRANKS.SAV'
/RANK=RANK1 TO RANK22 /SUBJECT=ID
/FACTORS=PACKAGE BRAND (DISCRETE) PRICE (LINEAR LESS)
SEAL (LINEAR MORE) MONEY (LINEAR MORE).
```

PRINT subcommand allows controlling the content of the tabular output. For example, for a large number of subjects, choose to limit the output to summary results only, omitting detailed output for each subject, as shown in the following example:

```
CONJOINT PLAN=* /DATA='RUGRANKS.SAV'
/RANK=RANK1 TO RANK22 /SUBJECT=ID
/PRINT=SUMMARYONLY.
```

The Conjoint procedure uses the analysis of the experimental data to make predictions about the relative preference for each of the simulation profiles. In the following example, detailed output for each subject is suppressed, and the output is limited to results of the simulations:

```
CONJOINT PLAN=* /DATA='RUGRANKS.SAV'
/RANK=RANK1 TO RANK22 /SUBJECT=ID
/PRINT=SIMULATION SUMMARYONLY.
```

PLOT subcommand controls whether plots are included in the output. Like tabular output (PRINT subcommand), it can be controlled whether the output is limited to summary results or includes results for each subject. By default, no plots are produced. In the following example, output includes all available plots:

```
CONJOINT PLAN=* /DATA='RUGRANKS.SAV'
/RANK=RANK1 TO RANK22 /SUBJECT=ID
/PLOT=ALL.
```

UTILITY subcommand writes an SPSS data file containing detailed information for each subject. It includes the utilities for DISCRETE factors, the slope and quadratic functions for LINEAR, IDEAL, and ANTIIDEAL factors, the regression constant, and the estimated preference scores. These values can then be used in further analyses or for making additional plots with other procedures.

The following example creates a utility file named rugutil.sav:

CONJOINT PLAN=* /DATA='RUGRANKS.SAV'
/RANK=RANK1 TO RANK22 /SUBJECT=ID
/UTILITY='RUGUTIL.SAV'.

Preference data for the carpet-cleaner example

	ID	PREF1	PREF2	PREF3	PREF4	PREF5	PREF6	PREF7
1	1	13	15	1	20	14	7	11
2	2	15	7	18	2	12	3	11
3	3	2	18	14	16	22	13	20
4	4	13	10	20	14	2	18	16
5	5	13	18	2	10	20	15	9
6	6	15	2	3	12	18	7	20
7	7	13	7	15	18	2	3	10
8	8	15	7	13	4	6	16	8
9	9	20	9	10	11	4	5	13
10	10	8	21	19	17	4	11	12

The preference data collected from the subjects is stored in *carpet_prefs.sav*. The data consist of responses from 10 subjects, each identified by a unique value of the variable *ID*. Subjects were asked to rank the 22 product profiles from the most to the least preferred. The variables *PREF1* through *PREF22* contain the IDs of the associated product profiles, that is, the card IDs from *carpet_plan.sav*. Subject 1, for example, liked profile 13 most of all, so *PREF1* has the value 13. Analysis of the data is a task that requires the use of command syntax—specifically, the CONJOINT command. The necessary command syntax has been provided in the file *conjoint.sps*.

CONJOINT PLAN='file specification'
/DATA='file specification'
/SEQUENCE=PREF1 TO PREF22
/SUBJECT=ID
/FACTORS=PACKAGE BRAND (DISCRETE)
PRICE (LINEAR LESS)

SEAL (LINEAR MORE) MONEY (LINEAR MORE)
/PRINT=SUMMARYONLY.

The PLAN subcommand specifies the file containing the orthogonal design—in this example, *carpet_plan.sav*.

The DATA subcommand specifies the file containing the preference data—in this example, *carpet_prefs.sav*. If the preference data is chosen as the active dataset, replace the file specification with an asterisk (*), without the quotation marks.

The SEQUENCE subcommand specifies that each data point in the preference data is a profile number, starting with the most-preferred profile and ending with the least-preferred profile.

The SUBJECT subcommand specifies that the variable *ID* identifies the subjects.

The FACTORS subcommand specifies a model describing the expected relationship between the preference data and the factor levels. The specified factors refer to variables defined in the plan file named on the PLAN subcommand.

The keyword DISCRETE is used when the factor levels are categorical and no assumption is made about the relationship between the levels and the data. This is the case for the factors *package* and *brand* that represent package design and brand name, respectively. DISCRETE is assumed if a factor is not labelled with one of the four alternatives (DISCRETE, LINEAR, IDEAL, ANTIIDEAL), or is not included on the FACTORS subcommand.

The keyword LINEAR, used for the remaining factors, indicates that the data are expected to be linearly related to the factor. For example, preference is usually expected to be linearly related to price. The quadratic models can be specified (not used in this example) with the keywords IDEAL and ANTIIDEAL.

The keywords MORE and LESS, following LINEAR, indicate an expected direction for the relationship. Since we expect higher preference for lower prices, the keyword LESS is used for *price*. However, we expect higher preference for either a *Good Housekeeping* seal of approval or a money-back guarantee, so the keyword MORE is used for *seal* and *money* (recall that the levels for both of these factors were set to 1 for *no* and 2 for *yes*).Specifying MORE or LESS does not change the signs of the coefficients or affect estimates of the utilities. These keywords are used simply to identify subjects whose estimates do not match the expected direction. Similarly, choosing IDEAL instead of ANTIIDEAL, or vice versa, does not affect coefficients or utilities.

The PRINT subcommand specifies that the output contains information for the group of subjects only as a whole (SUMMARYONLY keyword).

Information for each subject, separately, is suppressed. Try running this command syntax. Make sure that it has included valid paths to *carpet_prefs.sav* and *carpet_plan.sav*. For a complete description of all options, see the CONJOINT command in the *SPSS Command Syntax Reference*.

Utility scores

		Utility Estimate	Std. Error
package	A*	-2.233	.192
	B*	1.867	.192
	C*	.367	.192
brand	K2R	.367	.192
	Glory	-.350	.192
	Bissell	-.017	.192
price	$1.19	-6.595	.988
	$1.39	-7.703	1.154
	$1.59	-8.811	1.320
seal	no	2.000	.287
	yes	4.000	.575
money	no	1.250	.287
	yes	2.500	.575
(Constant)		12.870	1.282

This table shows the utility (part-worth) scores and their standard errors for each factor level. Higher utility values indicate greater preference. As expected, there is an inverse relationship between price and utility, with higher prices corresponding to lower utility (larger negative values mean lower utility). The presence of a seal of approval or money-back guarantee corresponds to a higher utility, as anticipated. Since the utilities are all expressed in a common unit, they can be added together to give the total utility of any combination. For example, the total utility of a cleaner with package design *B**, brand *K2R*, price *$1.19*, and no seal of approval or money-back guarantee is:

utility (package B*) + utility (K2R) + utility ($1.19)

+ utility (no seal) + utility (no money-back) + constant

or

$$1.867 + 0.367 + (-6.595) + 2.000 + 1.250 + 12.870 = 11.759$$

Coefficients

	B Estimate
price	-5.542
seal	2.000
money	1.250

This table shows the linear regression coefficients for those factors specified as LINEAR (for IDEAL and ANTIIDEAL models, there would also be a quadratic term).The utility for a particular factor level is determined by multiplying the level by the coefficient. For example, the predicted utility for a price of $1.19 was listed as –6.595 in the utilities table. This is simply the value of the price level, 1.19, multiplied by the price coefficient, –5.542.

Importance values

package	35.635
brand	14.911
price	29.410
seal	11.172
money	8.872

Averaged Importance Score

This table provides a measure of the relative importance of each factor known as an importance score or value. The values are computed by taking the utility range for each factor separately and dividing by the sum of the utility ranges for all factors. The values thus represent percentages and have the property that they sum to 100. The calculations, it should be noted, are done separately for each subject, and the results are then averaged over all of the subjects. The results also show that a money-back guarantee plays the least important role in determining overall preference. Price plays a significant role but not as significant as package design. Perhaps this is because the range of prices is not that large.

Correlation coefficients

	Value	Sig.
Pearson's R	.982	.000
Kendall's tau	.892	.000
Kendall's tau for Holdouts	.667	.087

This table displays two statistics, Pearson's *R* and Kendall's tau, which provide measures of the correlation between the observed and estimated preferences. The table also displays Kendall's tau for just the holdout profiles. Remember that the holdout profiles (4 in the present example) were rated by the subjects but not used by the Conjoint procedure for estimating utilities. Instead, the Conjoint procedure computes correlations between the observed and predicted rank orders for these profiles as a check on the validity of the utilities.

Reversals

When specifying LINEAR models for *price, seal,* and *money*, we chose an expected direction (LESS or MORE) for the linear relationship between the value of the variable and the preference for that value. The Conjoint procedure keeps track of the number of subjects whose preference showed the opposite of the expected relationship—for example, a greater preference for higher prices, or a lower preference for a money-back guarantee. These cases are referred to as reversals.

Number of reversals by factor and subject

Factor	price		3
	money		2
	seal		2
	brand		0
	package		0
Subject	1	Subject 1	1
	2	Subject 2	2
	3	Subject 3	0
	4	Subject 4	0
	5	Subject 5	0
	6	Subject 6	1
	7	Subject 7	0
	8	Subject 8	0
	9	Subject 9	1
	10	Subject 10	2

This table displays the number of reversals for each factor and for each subject. For example, three subjects showed a reversal for *price*. That is, they preferred product profiles with higher prices.

To enter a simulation case in the plan file

On a new row in the Data Editor window, select a cell and select the desired value from the list (value labels can be displayed by choosing Value Labels from the View menu). Repeat for all of the variables (factors). Select Simulation for the value of the *STATUS_* variable. Enter an integer value, to be used as an identifier, for the *CARD_* variable. Simulation cases should be numbered separately from the other cases. Run simulations at any later point simply by including simulation cases in plan file and rerunning CONJOINT.

Package	Brand	Price	Seal	Money	STATUS_	CARD_
A*	Bissell	J1 59	no	yes	Design	17
B*	Bissell	$1 19	no	no	Design	18
A*	Bissell	$1 59	yes	no	Holdoul	19
C*	K2R	$1.19	yes	no	Holdout	20
A*	Glory	$1 59	no	no	Holdoul	21
A*	Bissell	$1 19	no	no	Holdout	22
C*	K2R	J1 19	no	no	Simulation	1
B*	Glory	$1 19	yes	yes	Simulation	2

Simulation results

Card Number	ID	Maximum Utility[a]	Bradley-Terry-Luce	Logit
1	1	30.0%	43.1%	30.9%
2	2	70.0%	56.9%	69.1%

This table gives the predicted probabilities of choosing each of the simulation cases as the most preferred one, under three different probability-of-choice models. The maximum utility model determines the probability as the number of respondents predicted to choose the profile divided by the total number of respondents. For each respondent, the predicted choice is simply the profile with the largest total utility. The BTL (Bradley-Terry-Luce) model determines the probability as the ratio of a profile's utility to that for all simulation profiles, averaged across all respondents. The logit model is similar to BTL but uses the natural log of the utilities instead of the utilities. Across the 10 subjects in this study, all three models indicated that simulation profile 2 would be preferred.

6. THE CONJOINT FUNCTIONS IN R PACKAGE

The conjoint package is an implementation of traditional conjoint analysis method for R program. To use the package it is necessary to install base R computer program and two other packages: clusterSim for segmentation and

AlgDesign for generating fractional factorial designs .Current version of the conjoint package (1.33) has twelve following functions (in alphabetical order): caBTL(), caImportance(), caLogit(), caMaxUtility(), caModel(), caPartUtilities(), caSegmentation(), caTotalUtilities(), ca-Utilities(), Conjoint(), Show All Simulations(), ShowAllUtilities().

Required arguments of these functions with short characteristic are presented below (in order of typical conjoint analysis procedure). First two functions are used to estimate part-worth utilities of attributes levels and theoretical total profiles utilities. The conjoint is an easy to use R package for traditional conjoint analysis based on full-profile collection method and multiple linear regression model with dummy variables. The conjoint model is estimated by least squares method based on lm () function from stats package.

Function's Characteristic

caPartUtilities (y, x, z) {function calculates matrix of individual levels utilities for respondents (with intercept on first place)

caTotalUtilities (y, x) {function calculates matrix of theoretical total utilities for respondents (for *n* profiles and all respondents)

caImportance (y, x) {function calculates importance of all attributes. The sum of importance should be 100%

caUtilities (y, x, z) { function calculates utilities of attribute's levels

Conjoint (y, x, z) {function returns part-worth utilities of levels (model parameters for whole sample), vector of percentage attributes' importance, sum of them and corresponding charts (barplots). The sum of importance should be 100%

ShowAllUtilities (y, x, z) {function returns basic matrix of part-worth utilities (with the in-

tercept), matrix of total utilities (for *n* profiles and all respondents) and vector of percentage attributes' importance, with sum of them. The sum of importance should be 100%

caBTL (sym, y, x) {function estimates participation of simulation pro_les using probabilistic model BTL (Bradley-Terry-Luce). The sum of participation should be 100%

caLogit (sym, y, x) { function estimates participation of simulation pro_les using logit model. Thesum of participation should be 100%

caMaxUtility (sym, y, x) { function estimates participation of simulation pro_les using model of maximum utility (first position"). The sum of participation should be 100%

ShowAllSimulations (sym, y, x) {function returns 3 vectors of percentage participations using maximum utility, BTL and logit models. The sum of importance for every vector should be 100%

caModel (y, x) { function estimates parameters of conjoint analysis model

caSegmentation (y, x, c=3) { function divides respondents into three or *n* clusters using *k*-means method { function kmeans() from package stats

Function's Arguments

Y matrix (vector) of empirical preferences

x matrix of profiles

z vector with level names sym matrix of simulation profiles

c number of clusters (optional), default value: c=3

7. CONCLUSION

On the whole, conjoint analysis is an extremely useful tool that can be used effectively to decide among various available options. Its popularity as a tool is because it is based on the assumption that every consumer purchase decision is taken after simultaneous consideration of multiple attributes. Conjoint analysis often offers the best way to decide what to choose in difficult trade-off situations like quality vs. cost, quantity vs. quality, brand vs. price, richness of features vs. time to market and so on. The many forms of conjoint analysis have been used in numerous industries over the years in the area of product development with great success. With each advance made in this area of research, the opportunities to use this unique method continue to grow.

ACKNOWLEDGEMENT

Thankful to the University Authority for providing the necessary help and infrastructure for pursuing the research activities.

REFERENCES

Akaah, I. P., and P. K. Korgaonkar. 1988. A conjoint investigation of the relative importance of risk relievers in direct marketing. Journal of Advertising Research, 28:4, 38–44.

Cattin, P., and D. R. Wittink. 1982. Commercial use of conjoint analysis: A survey. Journal of Marketing, 46:3, 44–53.

Cattin, Philippe and Dick Wittink (1982), 'Commercial use of conjoint analysis: A survey', Journal of Marketing 46(Summer), 44–53.

Chakraborty, Goutam, Richard Ettenson and Gary Gaeth (1994), 'How consumers choose health insurance', Journal of Health Care Marketing 14(1), 21–33.

Dahan, Ely and V. Srinivasan (2000), 'The predictive power of internet-based product concept testing using visual depiction and animation', Journal of Product Innovation Management **17**, 99–109.

Garcia, Rosanna, Paul Rummel, and John R. Hauser (2007), "Validating Agent-Based Marketing Models Using Conjoint-Analysis," Journal of Business Research, 60, 8, (August), 848-857.

Green, P. E., and Y.Wind. 1973. Multiattribute decisions in marketing: A measurement approach. Hinsdale, Ill.: Dryden Press.

Green, Paul and V. Srinivasan (1978), 'Conjoint analysis in consumer research: Issue and outlook',Journal of Consumer Research 5 (September), 103–123.

Green, Paul and Yoram Wind (1975), 'New way to measure consumers' judgments', Harvard Business Review 53, 107–117.

Gustafsson, Anders, Fredrik Ekdhl and Bo Bergman (1999), 'Conjoint analysis: a useful tool in the design process', Total Quality Management 10(3), 327–43.

Hauser, John R., Songting Dong, and Min Ding (2012), "Self-Reflection and Articulated Consumer Preferences," Forthcoming Journal of Product Innovation Management.

Jain, Dipak C., Eitan Muller and Naufel J. Vilcassim (1999), 'Pricing patterns of cellur phones and phonecalls: A segment-level analysis', Management Science 45(2), 131–41.

Johnson, Richard (1974), 'Trade-off analysis of consumer values', Journal of Marketing Research 11 (May), 121–27.

Liberali, Guilherme, Glen L. Urban, and John R. Hauser (2013), " Competitive Information, Trust, Brand Consideration, and Sales: Two Field Experiments " International Journal for Research in Marketing, 30, 2, (June), 101-113

Moore, William L., Jordan J. Louviere and Rohit Verma (1999), 'Using conjoint analysis to help design product platforms', Journal of Product Innovation and Management 16, 27–39.

Netzer O., Toubia O., Bradlow E. T., Dahan E., Evgeniou T., Feinberg F. M., Feit E. M., *et al.*, Beyond conjoint analysis: Advances in preference measurement. Marketing Lett. (2008) 19(3–4):337–354.

Parker, Barnett and V. Srinivasan (1976), 'A consumer preference approach to the planning of rural primary health-care facilities', Operations Research 24(5), 991–1025.

Reutterer, Thomas and Herbert W. Kotzab (2000), 'The use of conjoint analysis for measuring preferences in supply chain design', Industrial Marketing Management 29, 27–35.

Seaton, F. B. and H. A. Laskey (1999), 'Effects of production location on perceived automobile values', Journal of Global Marketing 13(1), 71–85.

Selove, Matthew and John R. Hauser (2011), "The Strategic Importance of Accuracy in Conjoint Design," (Cambridge, MA: MIT Sloan School of Management).

Shepherd, Dean A., Richard Ettenson and Andrew Crouch (2000), 'New venture strategy and profitability: A venture capitalist's assessment', Journal of Business Venturing 15, 449–467.

Toubia, Olivier, John R. Hauser and Rosanna Garcia (2007), "Probabilistic Polyhedral Methods for Adaptive Choice-Based Conjoint Analysis: Theory and Application," Marketing Science, 26, 5, (September-October), 596-610.

Vavra, Terry G., Paul Green and Abba M. Krieger (1999), 'Evaluating ezpass: Using conjoint analysis to assess consumer response to a new tollway technology', Marketing Research 11(2), 5–18.

Vriens, Marco, Gerard H. Loosschilder, Edward Rosbergen and Dick R. Wittink (1998), 'Verbal versus realistic pictorial representations in conjoint analysis with design attributes', Journal of Product Innovation Management 15, 455–67.

Wind, Jerry, John Grashof and Joel Goldhar (1978), 'Market-based guidelines for design of industrial products', Journal of Marketing pp. 27–37.

Wittink, Dick and Philippe Cattin (1989), 'Commercial use of conjoint analysis: An update', Journal of Marketing 53 (July), 91–96.

Yee, Michael, Ely Dahan, John Hauser, and James Orlin (2007), "Greedoid-Based Non-compensatory Two-Stage Consideration-then-Choice Inference," Marketing Science, 26, 4, (July-August), 532-549. Appendices.

❑❑❑

CHAPTER - 32

Nonlinear Growth Models under Heteroscedastic and Autocorelated Error Structure

Amrit Kumar Paul* and Ranjit Kumar Paul
Indian Agricultural Statistics Research Institute, New Delhi-12
Email: apaul_66@yahoo.com

1. INTRODUCTION

Growth is a complex biological process that must be evaluated carefully if a profitable combination of growth and efficiency is to be realized. Knowledge relating to birth weight, mature weight, maturity rate and the point of infection of the growth curve in various breeds and crosses is very useful in selecting breed combinations that can produce the most efficient growth pattern. The effect of cow size on economy of production has been a discussing subject among cattlemen and animal scientists. Growth models are used to predict rates and change in the shape of the organism. They can be applied to determine the food requirements so as to get a desired growth. The estimated parameters of growth function can evaluate various growth characteristics of animal like rate of maturing, rate of gain, mature size and related characters. However a series of weight age data points is analytically unwieldy and difficult to interpret. One method of condensing the information contained in such a data series in a few biological interpretable parameters is the use of nonlinear models. A number of such nonlinear models are available in the literature. The growth pattern of cows has been studied under homoscedastic error structure in the literature. However comparison of such models is needed to find most appropriate model. Such comparison of nonlinear models for weight age data in cattle has been done under homoscedastic error structure, Brown *et al.* (1976). Non-linear functions are particularly suited to model growth data, because predictions outside the data range can be made more reliably than by linear models, and the entire growth process can be described by few parameters. For example, growth data models commonly apply the Gompertz function, where the estimated parameters can have biological meaning. Non-linear models are, however, more complicated to solve than linear models, and several algorithms have been proposed to estimate the parameters and variance components of non-linear mixed effects models. However, generally growth data do not follow homoscedastic error structure. Errors of growth model generally have heteroscedastic error structure. Kolluru (2000) studied only Logistic model under heteroscedastic error condition for cattle growth. Therefore, there is a need to study other models also under heteroscedastic error structure and this study should be extended to other breeds of cattle also. Keeping these things in mind the present study has been taken up to study growth pattern of Friesian × Sahiwal and Friesian × Sahiwal × Hariana breed using nonlinear models. The models taken are Logistic and Gompertz.

2. MATERIALS AND METHODS

Data used in the study were collected from history sheets of cattle birth to 36 months of age from military dairy farms at Agra, India for Friesian × Sahiwal breed and for Friesian × Sahiwal × Hariana breed. Logistic and Gompertz Models are fitted. Performance of the breeds is studied by these nonlinear models. The functional forms of these models are as follows.

i. Logistic model

$$Y_t = \frac{\beta_1}{1+\beta_2 \exp(-\beta_3 \mathbf{t})}$$

ii. Gompertz model

$$Y_t = \beta_1 \exp(-\beta_2 \mathbf{e}^{-\beta_3 \mathbf{t}}).$$

Where Y_t denotes the weight at t^{th} month, β_1, β_2 and β_3 are the parameters of the model, β_1 denotes asymptotic weight, β_2 is a scaling parameter and β_3 denotes rate of maturity.

2.1 Measures of Model Adequacy

The empirical comparison of models can be done with goodness of fit statistics R^2, MSE and RMSE. Higher the value of R^2 and lower the values of other measures of statistics, better are the models. It is concluded that the model which has minimum RMSE and maximum R^2, will be the best fitted model.

R^2 = 1—(Residual sum of squares / Total sum of squares), where Residual sum of squares $= \sum_{i=1}^{n}(Y_i - \hat{Y}_i)^2$, Total sum of squares $= \sum_{i=1}^{n}(Y_i - \overline{Y})^2$, $\hat{Y}_i$ is predicted values or estimated value and $\overline{Y}$ is mean of dependent variables.

$$\text{Mean Square Error (MSE)} = \frac{\sum_{i=1}^{n}(Y_i - \hat{Y}_i)^2}{n-p}$$

$$\text{Root mean squared error (RMSE)} = \left[\sum_{i=1}^{n}\frac{\left(Y_i - \hat{Y}_i\right)^2}{n-p}\right]^{1/2}$$

As in case of the animal growth data, many a times, the above assumption is violated. In the present study data revealed heteroscedasticity. This is tested by using the Rank correlation test. It can be observed that the rank correlation is high, which reveals the heteroscedasticity of error variance is present in the growth data in the above mentioned breeds.

As the data is found to be heteroscedastic in nature, OLS is not to be used any more. So to estimate the parameters we go for using the procedure explained in Model with heteroscedastic error structure. Logistic and Gompertz models are modified incorporating heteroscedasticity of variance. For the procedure discussed a computer program has been developed in IML (Interactive Matrix Language) a module of SAS and the parameters under heteroscedastic error structure are estimated. Parameters are estimated and weights are predicted, using homoscedastic error structure, heteroscedastic error structures. Results are given in Table 1 and Table 2.

2.2 Test for Heteroscedasticity of Variance

Various tests are available in literature for testing heteroscedasticity in data. We will consider here Rank Correlation Test which is easy to use both computationally and conceptually. It is the simplest test and is used for both small and large samples. Technique involved has following steps;

Let us consider the following model,

$$Y_t = f(\mathbf{X}_t, \boldsymbol{\beta}) + e_t \qquad 1$$

Where Y_t is the weight at tth month, X_t is covariate vector for tth month, â is a parameter vector, f is a non-linear function; it is either Logistic or Gomperz model function and e_t is the error term.

(i) Regress **Y** on **X** and obtain residuals.

(ii) Order the residuals (ignoring their sign) and X values in ascending or descending order and compute the rank correlation coefficient by following formula

$$R_{e,x} = 1 - \{6 \Sigma d_i^2 / (n(n^2 - 1))\} \qquad 2$$

d_i = difference between the ranks of corresponding pairs of x_i and e_i.

n = Number of observations in the sample.

A high rank correlation suggests the presence of heteroscedasticity.

2.3 Models with Hetroscedastic Error Structure

Logistic and Gompertz model are used for developing appropriate models under heteroscedastic error structure for growth of cattle, as it is well known that in most of the cases growth data follows logistic and Gompertz model. However, as far as cattle growth is concerned, it is assumed that the errors are independently distributed with constant variance. However, this assumption rarely meets in the reality, particularly for growth models.

Consider the model (1) again, i.e,

$$Y_t = f(X_t, \beta) + e_t$$

Usually, it is assumed that the errors e_t have zero means and uncorrelated and have common variance σ^2 (say).

Though the first assumption ensures that the model f for mean response is correctly specified. This assumption is rarely called into question. The remaining assumptions are fairly restrictive and may not hold in some applications. For the present data, which are observed over time, the specification of uncorrelated errors may be unrealistic. Assumption of constant intra-individual response variance is violated frequently in practice. For example growth data often exhibit constant coefficient of variation rather than constant variance (Davidian and Giltinan, 1995); that is, variance proportional to the squares of the mean response. In this case, a more appropriate assumption would be:

$$E(Y_t) = f(X_t, \beta),\ V(Y_t) = (CV)^2 [f(X_t, \beta)]^2 \qquad 3$$

where, CV, the scale parameter, is the coefficient of variation.

Since the heterogeneity of variance is evident as tested by the method given in 1.1, hence ordinary least squares estimation may be inefficient relative to methods that consider heteroscedasticity. Since the variance of Y_t is proportional to its expected value, it can be written as

$$V(Y_t) = \sigma^2 / w_t \qquad 4$$

for some constants w_t, t = 1, …., n

Under this setting with the assumption of independent, normal errors, it is straightforward to show that the maximum likelihood estimator β of parameter is the value $\hat{\beta}_{WLS}$ that minimizes

$$\sum_{t=1}^{n} w_t\{Y_t - f(X_t,\beta)\}^2 . \quad 5$$

Estimating equivalently $\hat{\boldsymbol{\beta}}_{\mathbf{wls}}$ by the normal equations

$$\sum_{t=1}^{n} w_t(Y_t - (f(\mathbf{X}_t,\boldsymbol{\beta}))\mathbf{f}_{\boldsymbol{\beta}}(\mathbf{X}_t,\boldsymbol{\beta}) = 0 . \quad 6$$

As the ordinary least squares, the maximum likelihood estimation for σ^2 is usually replaced by

$$\hat{\sigma}_{WLS}{}^2 = \frac{1}{n-p}\sum_{t=1}^{n} w_t\{Y_t - f(X_t,\hat{\beta}_{WLS})\}^2 \quad 7$$

where p is the number of parameters to be estimated.

For definiteness, consider the constant coefficient of variation, except for the multiplicative constant σ^2 variance is known up to the value of the regression parameter β, which appears through the mean response. An obvious approach is thus to take advantage of the functional form for a variance to construct estimated weights, replacing β by a suitable estimate, and to apply the weighted least squares idea. The OLS estimator $\hat{\beta}_{OLS}$ is a natural choice to use for construction of estimated weights. Formally, an estimator for β that takes into account the assumed mean-variance relationship may be obtained by forming estimated weights.

$$\hat{w}_t = \frac{1}{f^2(X_t,\hat{\beta}_{OLS})} \quad 8$$

And then solving (6), using the in place of w_t, we recompute the parameter estimates. Now using these new parameter estimates, weights are again computed and the process is continued till the convergence criterion is met.

This is a special case of a very general class of methods for estimation of β known in the context of nonlinear regression as generalized least squares (GLS). GLS method can be characterized by the following scheme.

Step1. Estimate β by a preliminary estimator $\hat{\beta}_{PRL}$ e.g. the OLS estimator

Step 2. Form estimated weights $\hat{w}_t = \dfrac{1}{f^2(X_t,\hat{\beta}_{OLS})}$

Step3. Using the weights from step 2, re-estimate β by the weighted least squares. Treating the resulting estimator as a new preliminary estimator, return to step 2. Denote the final estimate by $\hat{\beta}_{GLS}$ and calculate variance by formula given above in (7). The process is continued till the convergence criterion is met.

Computational Aspects

For implementation of above explained procedure we will consider functional form of mean response as

$$f(\mathbf{X}_t, \boldsymbol{\beta}) = \frac{\beta_1}{1+\beta_2 \exp(-\beta_3 t)} \text{ for Logistic function and}$$

$$f(\mathbf{X}_t, \boldsymbol{\beta}) = \beta_1 \exp(-\beta_2 e^{-\beta_3 t}) \text{ for Gompertz function.}$$

Where $\beta = \begin{pmatrix} \beta_1 \\ \beta_2 \\ \beta_3 \end{pmatrix}$

Logistic and Gompertz model fitted for all sets of data estimated parameters denoted by β_{OLS} by using SAS software.

A program written in SAS/IML is used to obtain parameter estimate under heteroscedastic error variance models. Steps are given as follows:

Step1

The preliminary estimates of β are calculated by Gauss-Newton procedure. This procedure has been discussed with full detail SAS USER's guide. After calculating preliminary estimates of β we go for step 2.

Step2

In step 2, the motive is to form weights to use them for weighted least square procedure. Since functional form of mean response is known, we estimate the value of mean response. After calculating estimated values, are formed by using equation (8) for functions of Logistic and Gomperz models. Once weights have been calculated we go for step 3.

Step3

Third step consists of applying Weighted Least Squares (WLS) to obtain estimates by using weights obtained from previous step. Now from (5) objective function to be minimized can be written in matrix notation as

$$O(\boldsymbol{\beta}) = [\mathbf{Y} - f(\mathbf{X}, \boldsymbol{\beta})]' \mathbf{W}^{-1} [\mathbf{Y} - f(\mathbf{X}, \boldsymbol{\beta})] \qquad 9$$

where $O(\beta)$ is objective function to be minimized, W is a diagonal matrix, whose diagonal elements are the weights, Y is vector of observations and f is the function.

To get estimate of β we minimize objective function i.e. equation (9). Because closed form solution of the generalized least squares estimating equations are rarely available, computation of nonlinear least squares estimates required the use of iterative numerical Newton-Raphson technique for Quadratic Taylor Series expansion, which is given by

$$\beta = \beta^* - J^{-1}(\beta^*) S(\beta^*) \qquad 10$$

Where β^* is a given approximation of β, $J(\beta^*)$ is known as Hessian Matrix, whose elements are second order partial derivatives of the objective function with respect to parameters, that is

$$J_{k_1,k_2} = \left(\frac{\partial^2}{\partial \beta_{k_1} \partial \beta_{k_2}} \right) O(\boldsymbol{\beta}^*) \qquad 11$$

$S(\beta^*)$ is a px1 vector of partial derivatives matrix of objective function at approximate value of β, that is

$$S_i = \left(\frac{\partial}{\partial \beta_i} \right) O(\boldsymbol{\beta}^*) \qquad 12$$

Computation of the Hessian matrix may be quite burdensome. Actually J (β^*) is replaced by its expectation. In general, the expectation matrix will be easier to calculate than J (β^*). The expectation of $J(\beta^*)$ can be written as

$$2\mathbf{Z}(\boldsymbol{\beta}^*)' \mathbf{W}^{-1} \mathbf{Z}(\boldsymbol{\beta}^*) \qquad 13$$

where Z_{nXp} is matrix of first order partial derivatives of mean response with respect to parameters such that

$$Z_{ij} = \left(\frac{\partial}{\partial \beta_j} \right) f(\mathbf{X}_j, \boldsymbol{\beta}^*), \quad i = 1,2 \ldots\ldots n.\ j = 1,2 \ldots\ldots p \qquad 14$$

Vector S can be computed by the formula given below,

$$S(\beta) = 2\, Z(\beta^*)' W^{-1} [Y - f(\beta^*)] \qquad 15$$

Since it is an iterative process so first we will estimate value of S and J by preliminary estimates of $\beta^* = \beta_{PRL}$, i.e., β_{OLS} and will use them in equation (10). After getting new estimates of β (say β^1) and use again in equations (13) and (14), and finally from equation (10) we estimate the parameters again. This process is continued till the values of β converges. Final value of estimates of β is represented as β_{GLS}.

3. RESULTS AND DISCUSSION

It can be seen from table1 that for Friesian ×Sahiwal breed at Agra station RMSE (9.3217) is less for Gompertz model than RMSE (15.0360) by Logistic model and R^2 is also more for Gompertz model than Logistic model, predicted values can be seen from Fig 4 & Fig 8 for logistic model and from Fig1 & Fig5 for Gompertz model under homoscedastic error structure, so it is concluded that results of Gompertz model better than Logistic model under homoscedastic error structure, growth rate is better for Logistic model. For Friesian ×Sahiwal ×Hariana breed RMSE (10.4996) is less by Gompertz model than RMSE (16.1711) of Logistic model, it can be seen from Table 2. Thus results for Gompertz model are better than Logistic model. Growth rate by Logistic model is better than Gompertz model.

As data having heteroscedasticity of variance which can be seen from rank correlation test, rank correlation coefficient for F×S breed is 0.6201 and F×S×H breeds is 0.5808. So modified models, incorporating heteroscedasticity of variance RMSE (0.0851) is less by Gompertz model than RMSE (0.1534) by logistic model for Friesian ×Sahiwal breed, thus results of Gompertz model are better than logistic model. Similarly results of Gompertz model are better than Logistic model for Friesian ×Sahiwal ×Hariana breed. When results are compared under homoscedastic error condition and heteroscedastic error condition, RMSE is found less for heteroscedastic error condition .This shows that when model fitted under heteroscedastic error condition, it gives better results than homoscedastic error condition for both models and breeds.

It has been observed from Table1 and Table2 that growth rate of Friesian ×Sahiwal ×Hariana breed is found better than growth rate of Friesian ×Sahiwal breed, this shows that tripple cross have a good impact on growth rate. Asymptotic weight is found more for Friesian ×Sahiwal breed than Friesian ×Sahiwal ×Hariana breed.

Table 1 : Parameter estimates of logistic and Gompertz models under homoscedastic and heteroscedastic error structure for F×S breed

Parameter	Logistic	Gompertz	Heteroscedasticity of error variance (logistic model)	Heteroscedasticity of error variance (Gompertz model)
β_1	410.5000(13.6002)	446.1000(12.8978)	343.9066(4.0048)	315.6594(1.4062)
β_2	8.0829(0.8657	2.5350(0.0807)	10.4364(0.1656)	2.5214(0.0051)
β_3	0.1623(0.0114)	0.0951(0.0051)	0.2531(0.0034)	0.1354(0.0008)
Goodness of fit statistics				
R^2	0.9887	.9956	0.9999	0.9999
MSE	226.0819	85.8952	0.0235	0.0072
RMSE	15.0360	9.3217	0.1534	0.0851

Table 2 : Parameter estimates of logistic and Gompertz models under homoscedastic and heteroscedastic error structure for F×S×H breed

Parameter	Logistic	Gompertz	Heteroscedasticity of error variance (logistic model)	Heteroscedasticity of error variance (Gompertz model)
β1	339.5000 (14.1131)	367.3000 (13.6603)	285.6676 (2.7842)	315.6594 (1.4062)
β2	6.9597 (0.9061)	2.3697 (0.0978)	9.2417 (0.1272)	2.5214 (0.0051)
β3	0.1614 (0.0147)	0.0967 (0.0070)	0.2618 (0.0032)	0.1354 (0.0008)
Goodness of fit statistics				
R2	0.9810	0.9920	0.9999	0.9999
MSE	261.5043	110.2422	0.0203	0.0072
RMSE	16.1711	10.4996	0.1427	0.0851

Rank correlation coefficient for Friesian × Sahiwal breed at Agra Station is 0.6201

Rank correlation coefficient for Friesian × Sahiwal × Hariana breed is 0.5808

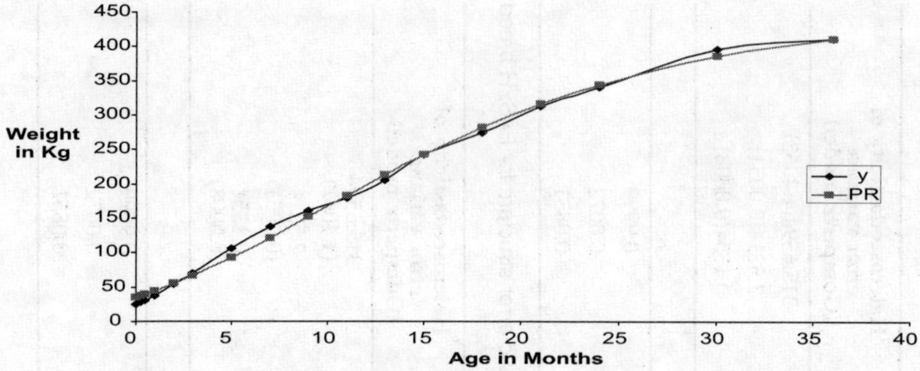

Fig. 1 : Graph for F×S breed by Gompertz model under homo

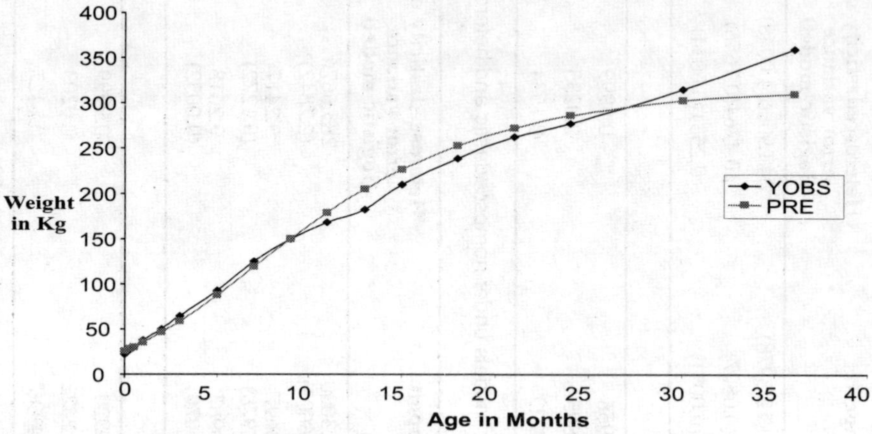

Fig. 2 : Graph for F×S breed by Gompertz model under het

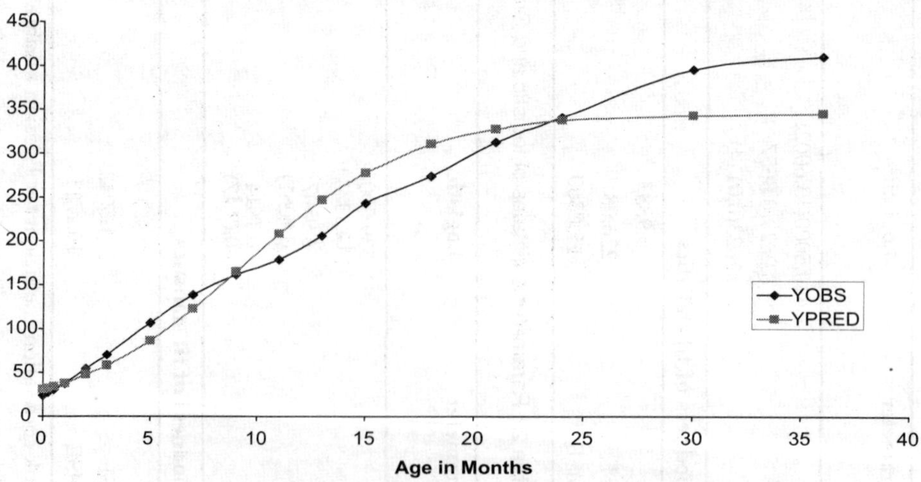

Fig. 3 : Graph for F×S breed By Logistic model Under Het

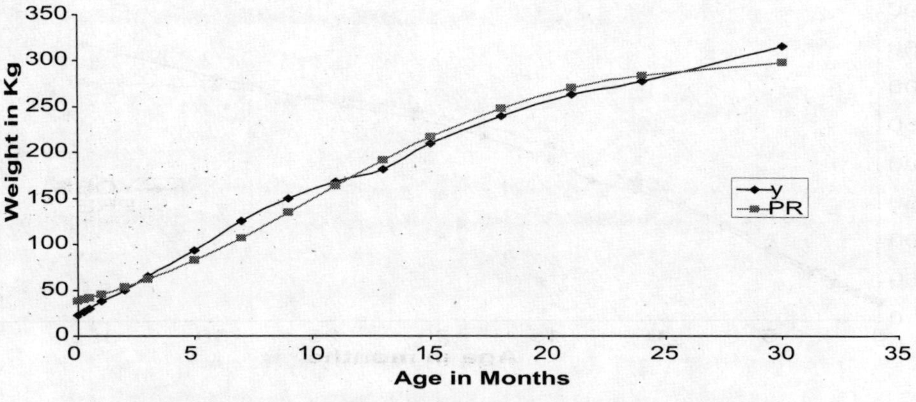

Fig. 4 : Graph for F×S×H breed by Logistic model under homo

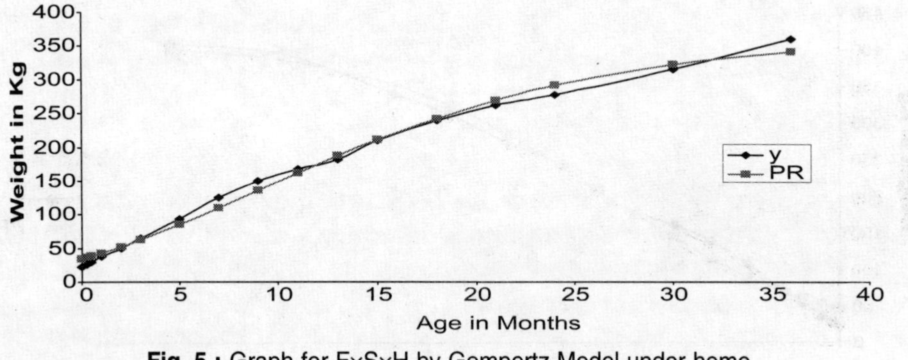

Fig. 5 : Graph for F×S×H by Gompertz Model under homo

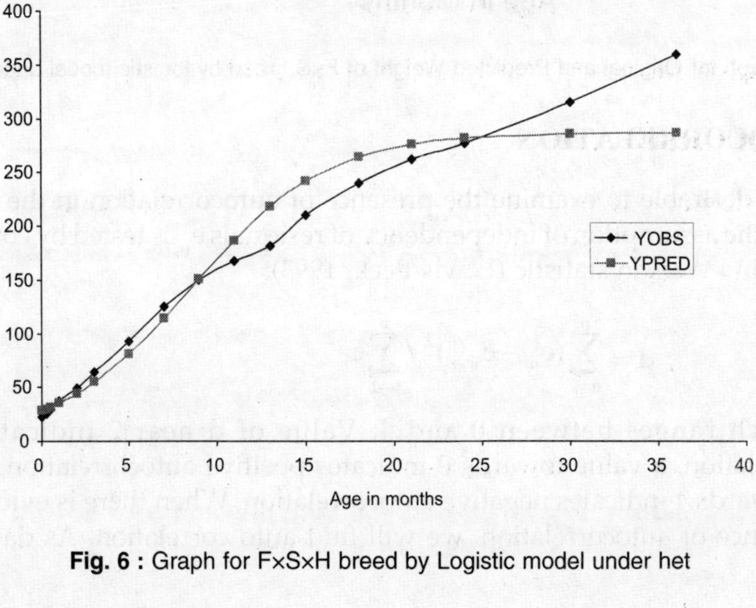

Fig. 6 : Graph for F×S×H breed by Logistic model under het

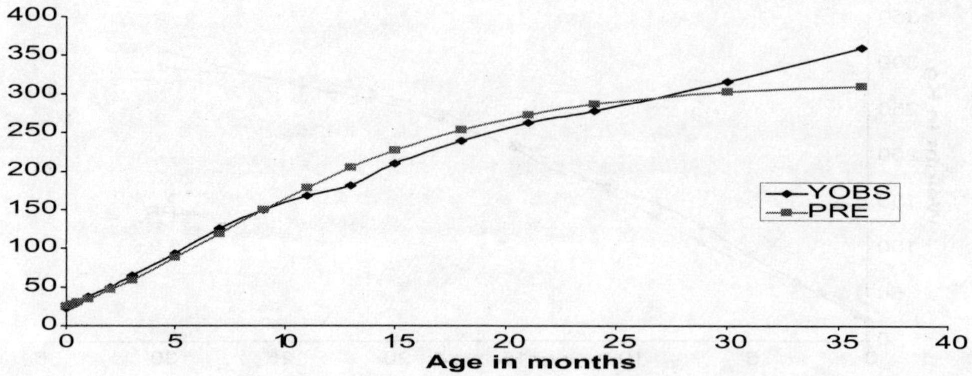

Fig. 7 : Graph for F×S×H breed by Gom model under het

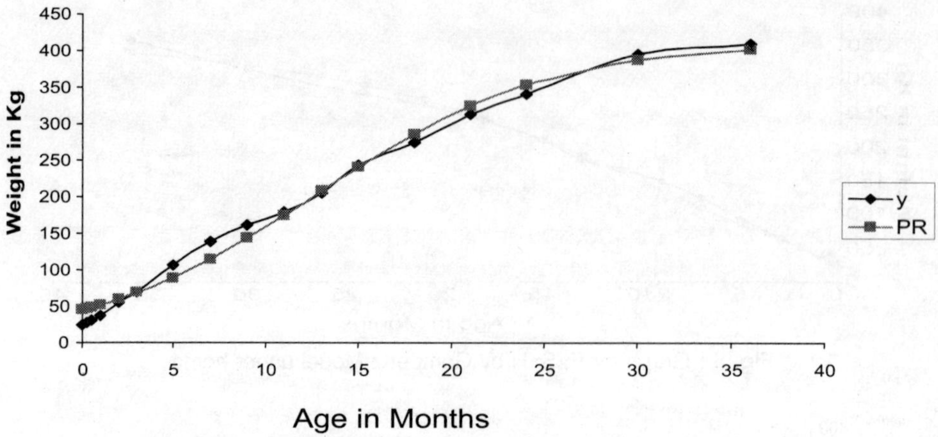

Fig. 8 : Graph for Original and Predicted Weight of F×S breed by logistic model under homo

4. AUTOCORRELATION

It is desirable to examine the presence of autocorrelation in the data. To this end, the assumption of independency of residuals $e_{u,}$ is tested by computing the Durbin –Watson statistic (Lewis-Beck, 1993):

$$d = \sum_{u=2}^{n}(e_u - e_{u-1})^2 / \sum_{u=1}^{n} e_u{}^2$$

which ranges between 0 and 4. Value of d near 2 indicates little autocorrelation, a value towards 0 indicates positive autocorrelation, while a value towards 4 indicates negative autocorrelation. When there is evidence for the presence of autocorrelation, we will find auto correlation. As data in the present study are unequal spaced, so a method has been developed to find autocorrelation in unequal spaced data.

4.1 Autocorrelation for Unequally Spaced Observations

When observations are taken on subjects at arbitrary time points, there..must be an underlying continuous time process (Jones, 1981, 1985; Diggle, 1988, 1990; Chi and Reinsel, 1989). For equally spaced observations, there may or may not be an underlying continuous time process. Unequally spaced observations differ from equally spaced observations with some missing observations, in that there is no basic sampling interval. Sometimes there is a basic sampling interval, but it is so small that almost all of the observations would be missing. The mathematical model for a continuous time AR (1) process, denoted CAR (1), is (Jones and Boateng, 1991),

$$\frac{d}{dt}\varepsilon(t) + \alpha\,\varepsilon(t) = G\eta(t) \qquad 16$$

where G is a constant, G^2 is variance per unit time, $\eta(t)$ is continuous time 'white noise', white noise is a term used in time series analysis for a square of independent random variables, ε (t) is error at t^{th} time. A model for a.continuous time process is a differential equation driven by white noise. i.e,

$$\eta(t) = \frac{d}{dt}\omega(t), \qquad 17$$

the derivative of a Wiener process. Since this derivative does not exit, the proper way to write the model is in differential form,

$$d\varepsilon(t) + \alpha\,\varepsilon(t)dt = Gd\omega(t) \qquad 18$$

Although $d\omega(t)$ has the same existence problem, when (18) is solved .by integration, a proper solution is obtained. The Wiener process is assumed to .have unit variance per unit time, the constant G in front of scales the input so that it has variance G^2 per unit time.

Consider the solution of (1.13) with the random input removed

$$\frac{d}{dt}\varepsilon(t) + \alpha\varepsilon(t) = 0 \qquad 19$$

If (19) is integrated from time t_1 to time t_2, the solution is a prediction,

$$\boldsymbol{\varepsilon}(t_2) = \exp\{-\alpha(t_2 - t_1)\}\,\boldsymbol{\varepsilon}(t_1) \qquad 20$$

The solution, (20) is now in the form of a discrete time AR (1) process with.an auto regression coefficient.

The equation (20) can be generalized as

$$\varepsilon (t_n) = \exp \{-\alpha (t_n - t_{n-1})\} \varepsilon (t_{n-1}) \qquad 21$$

fitting equation (21) by nonlinear modeling technique we estimate á (autocorrelation).

To obtain the value of α (autocorrelation) a computer program using SAS 11.NLIN has been developed, estimated the values of autocorrelation of different 12.breed which is given below.

Station	Name of Breed	Model	Auto-correlation
Dehradun	F×S	Logistic	0.1254
Dehradun	F×S	Gompertz	0.1330
Dehradun	F×S×H	Logistic	0.4448
Dehradun	F×S×H	Gompertz	0.4319

As the data is found heteroscedastic in nature, OLS is not to be used any more. So to estimate the parameters we go for using the procedure explained in

Model with heteroscedastic error structure along with autocorrelation. Logistic and Gompertz models are modified incorporating heteroscedasticity of variance along with autocorrelation. For the procedure discussed a computer program has been developed in IML (Interactive Matrix Language) a module of SAS and the parameters under heteroscedastic error structure along with autocorrelation are estimated.

4.2 Models with Heteroscedastic Error Structure along with Autocorrelation

Correlation among observations on a given individual (cattle) is especially likely in the repeated measurement (weight) context. In many cases, a systematic pattern of correlation is evident, which may be characterized accurately by a relatively simple model. To accommodate intra-individual correlation, assumption (ii) is replaced by a description of the assumed correlation pattern among the elements of e (residuals). As data used in the study is unequally spaced, so a method to estimate α (autocorrelation) is given in section 1.1 in detail. Estimated α is used for further analysis.

Let us consider the following model,

$$Y_j = f(X_j, \beta) + e_j$$

X_j is covariate vector and β is parameter vector and f is a non-linear function.

Formally, suppose that

$$\text{corr (e)} = \Gamma(\alpha), \qquad 22$$

where the correlation matrix $\Gamma(\alpha)$ is a function of a vector of correlation parameters α. The choice of a suitable correlation matrix depends on the nature of the repeated measurement factor. Some common correlation structures are described as follows. When variance is constant across the response range and equal to some value α^2, as in assumption (iii),

$$\text{cov (e)} = \sigma^2 \Gamma(\alpha). \qquad 23$$

For the important special case where the repeated observations are taken over time, standard models for serial correlation patterns are available, i.e, the autoregressive (AR) model of order one.

For definiteness, we will assume that the observations are indexed in the order in which they were collected. In the simplest case where the n repeated measurements are equally spaced in time, if the correlation between two adjacent observation is á, then the correlation between any two measurements j_1 and j_2 is given by

$$\text{corr}(e_{j1}, e_{j2}) = \alpha^{|j_1 - j_2|} \qquad 24$$

This may be expressed by the correlation matrix

$$\Gamma(\alpha) = \begin{bmatrix} 1 & \alpha^{(t_2-t_1)} & \alpha^{(t_3-t_1)} & . & . & . & \alpha^{(t_n-t_1)} \\ & 1 & \alpha^{(t_3-t_2)} & . & . & . & \alpha^{(t_n-t_2)} \\ & & & . & . & & . \\ & & & & . & . & . \\ & & & & & . & . \\ & & & & & . & \alpha^{(t_n-t_{n-1})} \\ & & & & & & 1 \end{bmatrix} \qquad 25$$

here $t_1, t_2, \ldots, t_n$ are time at which measurements are taken.

The AR (1) correlation matrix may be generalized to accommodate situations where the observations are not equally spaced. If the and the measurements are taken at times , respectively $j_1 \ldots j_2$ then (j_1, j_2) and (j_2, j_1) elements of (25) correlation matrix would be replaced by $\alpha^{|t_{j1}-t_{j2}|}$ Liang and Zeger (1986) and Chi and Reinsel (1989).

The OLS estimator $\hat{\beta}_{OLA}$ is a natural choice to use for construction of estimated weights. Formally, an estimator for β that takes into account the assumed

mean-10.variance relationship may be obtained by forming estimated weights.

$$\hat{W}_j = \frac{1}{f^2\left(X_j, \hat{\beta}_{OLS}\right)} \quad 26$$

After getting correlation matrix we construct general variance covariance matrix W_1 as follows

$$W_1 = W^{½}\,\Gamma(\alpha).\,W^{1/2} \quad 27$$

W is the diagonal matrix whose diagonal elements are the weights estimated in (26) and Γ (α) is defined in (25), objective function O (β) is

$$O(\beta) = (Y - f(X, \beta))'W_1^{-1}(Y - f(X, \beta)) \quad 28$$

Y is vector of observations and f is mean response.

To get estimates of β we will minimize objective function i.e. equation (28). Because closed form solution of the generalized least squares estimating equations are rarely available, computation of nonlinear least squares estimates required the use of iterative numerical Newton-Raphson technique for Quadratic Taylor Series expansion, which is given by

$$\beta = \beta^* - J^{-1}(\beta^*)S(\beta^*) \quad 29$$

where J_{pxp} is known as Hessian Matrix, whose elements are second order partial derivatives of the objective function with respect to parameters, such that

$$J_{k1,\,k2} = \left(\frac{\partial^2}{\partial\beta_{k1}\partial\beta_{k2}}\right)O(\beta) \quad 30$$

where O (β) is objective function to be minimized.

And S_{px1} is a vector of partial derivative of objective function with respect to parameter vector such that

$$S_i = \left(\frac{\partial}{\partial\beta_i}\right)O(\beta) \quad 31$$

where O (β) is objective function to be minimized.

Computation of the Hessian matrix may be quite difficult. Actually J (β) is replaced by its expectation. In general, the expectation matrix will be easier to calculate than J (β).

The expectation of J (β) can be written as

$$2Z'W_1^{-1}Z(\beta) \qquad 32$$

where Z_{nxp} is matrix of first order partial derivatives of mean response with respect to parameters such that

$$Z_{ij} = \left(\frac{\delta}{\partial \beta_j}\right) f(X_j, \beta),\ i = 1, 2 \ldots\ldots n.,\ j = 1, 2 \ldots\ldots p \qquad 33$$

where

n=number of observations and,

p= number of parameters to be estimated.

Vector S can be computed by the formula given below,

$$S(\beta) = 2\,Z'\,W_1^{-1}\,[Y - f(\beta)] \qquad 34$$

It is an iterative process so first we will estimate value of S and J by preliminary estimates of $\beta = \beta_{OLS}$ and will use them in equation (29). After getting new estimates of β say β* and use again in equation (29), till the values of β converges. Final value of estimates of β will be represented as β_{GLS}.

For obtaining numerical values of the parameters a computer program is developed in SAS/IML.

4.3 RESULTS AND DISCUSSION

It can be observed from Table 3 that for F×S breed at Dehradun farm RMSE (11.3109) is less for Gompertz model than RMSE (16.7320) by logistic model, this shows that results of Gompertz model are better than logistic model under homoscedastic error condition. As data of the breed having heteroscedasticity of variance and have autocorrelation which is tested by Durbin Watson test, data in the present study is unequal spaced so method developed to find autocorrelation of unequal spaced data. Auto correlation is 8.found 0.1254 when residuals by logistic model are used and it is found 0.1330 when Gompertz model is used.

From Table 4, it is observed that for F×S×H breed RMSE (23.9571) by Gompertz model is less than RMSE (24.3640) by logistic model under homoscedastic error structure, so results of Gompertz model are better than logistic model under homoscedastic error structure. RMSE (0.2942) of logistic model and RMSE (0.2975) by Gompertz model under heteroscedastic error structure along with auto correlation are less than RMSE under homoscedastic error structure and R^2 found more for both models under heteroscedastic error structure this shows that results under heteroscedastic error structure are better than homoscedastic error structure. Mature weight found more for F×S breed

.than mature weight of F×S×H breed under homoscedastic error structure where .as mature weight found more for F×S×H breed than F×S breed. Growth rate is also found to be better for F×S×H than F×S breed.

Table 3 : Parameter estimate of models under homoscedastic error variance and heteroscedastic error variance along with auto-correlation of Friesian × Sahiwal breed at Dehradun station

Parameter	Logistic model under Homoscedastic error variance	Gompertz model under Homoscedastic error variance	Logistic model under heteroscedastic error variance along with autocorrelation	Gompertz model under heteroscedastic error variance along with autocorrelation
β_1	354.4000 (15.6193)	382.5000 (15.7104)	299.9152 (3.3298)	328.5822 (1.7363)
β_2	6.6555 (0.8399)	2.3190 (0.0966)	9.4134 (0.1504)	2.5333 (0.0064)
β_3	0.1534 (0.0142)	0.0927 (0.0072)	0.2643 (0.0035)	0.1377 (0.0009)
		Goodness of fit statistics		
R^2	0.9803	0.9910	0.9999	0.9999
MSE	279.9608	127.9378	0.0146	0.0057
RMSE	16.7320	11.3109	0.1210	0.0965
Autocorrelation			0.1254	0.1330

Figures in the brackets indicate standard errors.

Table 4 : Parameter estimate of different models under homoscedastic error variance and heteroscedastic error variance along with auto-correlation of Friesian × Sahiwal × Hariana breed at Dehradun station

Parameter	Logistic model under Homoscedastic error variance	Gompertz model under Homoscedastic error variance	Logistic model under heteroscedastic error variance along with autocorrelation	Gompertz model under heteroscedastic error variance along with autocorrelation
β_1	327.8000 (17.2990)	349.2000 (23.9764)	362.7186 (28.6022)	475.8925 (52.2318)
β_2	8.5121 (1.9712)	2.5636 (0.2814)	13.3927 (1.4666)	2.9731 (0.1243)
β_3	0.1949 (0.0262)	0.1156 (0.0176)	0.2429 (0.0179)	0.0941 (0.0100)

Contd.

Goodness of fit statistics				
R_2	0.9606	0.9619	0.9999	0.9999
MSE	593.6078	573.9470	0.0865	0.0885
RMSE	24.3640	23.9571	0.2942	0.2975
Autocorrelation			0.4448	0.4319

Figures in the brackets indicate standard errors.

CONCLUSION

As in linear regression, leaving correlation of errors out of account leads to an underestimation of the standard deviations of parameter estimates. On the other hand, the use of models that accommodate correlated errors requires more care and more computation. A comparative study under homoscedastic error structure and heteroscedastic error structure along with autocorrelation is carried out and it is found that results under heteroscedastic error structure are better than results under homoscedastic error structure for both Gompertz and Logistic models.

ACKNOWLEDGEMENT

The authors are grateful to Dr. S. D. Wahi, Head (A), Division of Statistical Genetics, IASRI for his encouragement and valuable suggestions. The authors are thankful to the Director, IASRI for providing facilities to carry out the analysis.

REFERENCES

Brown, J.E., Fitzhugh, H.A. and Cartwright, T.C. (1976). A comparison of Nonlinear Models for Describing Weight-Age Relationships in Cattle, Journal of Animal Science 43, 810-818

Chi, E.M. and Reinsel, G.C. (1989). Models for longitudinal data with random 8.effects and AR(1) errors. J.Am.Statist, Assoc, 84, 452-9.

Davidian, D. and Giltinan, M. (1995). Non linear models for repeated measurement data. Chapman Hall, London.

Jones, R.H. and Boadi-Boateng, F. (1991). Unequally spaced longitudinal data with AR(1) serial correlation. Biometrics, 47, 161-75.

Kolluru, R. (2000). On Some Aspect of Growth Patterns of Crossbred Cattle, Unpublished M.Sc. Thesis, Indian Agricultural Research Institute, New Delhi.

Kolluru, R., Rana P S and Paul A K (2003).Modelling for growth pattern in crossbred cattle, Journal of Animal Science 73(10), 1174-1179

Liang, K.Y. and Zeger, S.L. (1986). Longitudinal data analysis using generalized linear models. Biometrika, 73, 13-22.

Marquardt, D.L. (1963). An algorithm for least squares estimation of non-linear parameters. J. Soc. Ind. App. Math. 2, 431.

SAS. (2012). SAS Users' Guide Version 9. SAS Institute Incorporation. Cary, NC. U.S.A.

❑❑❑

CHAPTER - 33

Nonlinear Time-Series Analysis: An Application of GARCH and EGARCH Models in Agriculture

Ranjit Kumar Paul* and Amrit Kumar Paul
Indian Agricultural Statistics Research Institute, New Delhi
Email: ranjitstat@gmail.com

1. INTRODUCTION

Agriculture plays a crucial role in addressing the needs of a growing global population, and is inextricably linked to poverty eradication, especially in developing countries. Sustainable agriculture and rural development are essential to the implementation of an integrated approach to increasing food production and enhancing food security and food safety in an environmentally sustainable way. Attaining food security has been our major concern since independence. Appropriate policy measures in agriculture made it possible to achieve food security as well as required national confidence to meet the growing food demands, despite a growing population. The increased agricultural production has been achieved largely through an increase in the yield of grain per hectare, rather than from an increased cultivated area. The increase in production has been the result of widespread cultivation of new high-yielding varieties coupled with a package of agricultural inputs that permit the genetic expression of their high yield potential. India is now even in a position to export agricultural commodities, fish products, milk products and earns a lot of foreign exchange. The present share of the agricultural sector in total exports is 15 to 17 percent. However, the export of many agricultural commodities show a high degree of fluctuations, caused by time lags between production decisions and delivery to the market. For the Government, unforeseen variations in export can complicate budgetary planning and increase risks for attainment of debt targets. For exporters, price volatility increases cash flow variability and reduces collateral value in the market. There is a need for an aggressive export growth-oriented policy to raise the share of agricultural sector in total exports to 25%. This should come through diversification of agriculture. In our country, the exports have been allowed only after domestic requirements are met, which is the major cause of fluctuations in exports from year to year. Modelling and forecasting such fluctuating data of commodities is crucial for the sake of Government as well as for the exporters.

A fundamental problem in statistics is to develop models based on a sample of observations and inferences using the model so developed. In agricultural research, data are usually collected over time. One characteristic of such data is that the successive observations are dependent. Each observation of the observed data series, Y_t, may be considered as a realization of a stochastic process $\{Y_t\}$, which is a family of random variables $\{Y_t, t \in T\}$, where $T = \{0, \pm 1, \pm 2, \ldots\}$, and apply standard time-series approach to develop an ideal model which will adequately represent the set of realizations and also their statistical relationships in a satisfactory manner.

The most widely used technique for analysis of time-series data is; undoubtedly, the Box Jenkins' Autoregressive integrated moving average (ARIMA) methodology (Box *et al.*, 2007). There are a lot of applications of ARIMA model in the context of agriculture viz. Paul and Das (2010, 2013 a), Paul *et al.* (2013 b, 2013c). However, it is based on some crucial assumptions, like linearity and homoscedastic prediction error variances. Further, time series data often exhibit features which cannot be explained by ARIMA model, which is linear. As an example, the famous time series of average monthly sunspot numbers exhibits a cyclical behavior in such a way that the series generally increases at a faster rate than it decreases. Similarly, asymmetric phenomenon arises with economic series, which tend to behave differently when the economy is moving into recession rather than when coming out of it. Many financial time series show periods of stability, followed by unstable periods with high volatility. The loss in continuing to use the age-old ARIMA methodology is that this type of behavior cannot be explained satisfactorily, and so nonlinear time series models are usually needed to describe data sets in which variance changes through time. The search for an appropriate model of this type would lead to a greater insight into the underlying mechanism. An excellent description of these and other related issues is given in Chatfield (2001). In reality, underlying relationships among variables are highly complex and cannot be described satisfactorily through a linear modelling approach. There are many features, like existence of threshold value, which can be described only through a nonlinear approach. During the last few decades a new area of "Nonlinear time-series modelling" is fast coming up. Here, there are basically two approaches, viz. Parametric or Nonparametric. Evidently, if in a particular situation, we are quite sure about the functional form, we should use the former; otherwise the latter may be employed.

The most promising parametric nonlinear time series models are Autoregressive conditional heteroscedastic (ARCH), Generalized ARCH (GARCH) and Exponential GARCH (EGARCH) models. In the coming years, there is a need to explore the application of these models along with other extensions of GARCH model in agriculture to capture volatility in commodity prices or export prices or volatile yield of a crop. In this chapter, application of GARCH and EGARCH models are discussed.

2. AUTOREGRESSIVE CONDITIONAL HETEROSCEDASTIC (ARCH) MODEL

The most promising parametric nonlinear time-series model has been the Autoregressive conditional heteroscedastic (ARCH) model, which was introduced by Engle (1982). It allows the conditional variance to change over time as a function of squared past errors leaving the unconditional variance constant. The presence of ARCH type effects in financial and macro-economic time-series is a well established fact. The combination of ARCH specification for conditional variance and the Autoregressive (AR) specification for conditional mean has many appealing features, including a better specification of the forecast error variance. The AR-ARCH model has also been used as the basic "building blocks" for Markov switching and mixture models (See e.g. Lanne and Saikkonen 2003). Ghosh *et al.* (2010 a) applied Periodic and ARCH models for describing rainfall data.

The ARCH (q) model for series $\{\varepsilon_t\}$ is defined by specifying the conditional distribution of ε_t given information available up to time $t-1$. Let ψ_{t-1} denote this information. It consists of the knowledge of all available values of the series, and anything which can be computed from these values, *e.g.* innovations, and squared observations. In principle, it may even include knowledge of the values of other related time-series, and anything else which might be useful for forecasting and is available by time $t-1$.

We say that the process $\{e_t\}$ is ARCH (q), if the conditional distribution of $\{e_t\}$ given available information $\{Y_{t-1}\}$ is

$$\varepsilon_t \mid \psi_{t-1} \sim N(0, h_t) \text{ and } h_t = a_0 + \sum_{i=1}^{q} a_i \varepsilon_{t-i}^2 \qquad 1$$

where $a_0 > 0$, ai ≥ for all i and $\sum_{i=1}^{q} a_i < 1$

2.1 Properties of the ARCH Model (Tsay, 2005)

To study the properties of ARCH model, consider the simple ARCH (1) model. The conditional variance equation of the this model is defined as

$$\varepsilon_t = \eta_t h_t^{1/2}$$

η_t is white noise and conditional variance h_t satisfies

$$h_t = a_0 + a_1\varepsilon_{t-1}^2$$

where $a_0>0$, $a1\geq 0$. The important properties of ARCH models are mentioned below:

(i) The unconditional mean of ε_t remains zero because,

$$E(\varepsilon_t) = E[E(\varepsilon_t | \Psi_{t-1})] = E\left[\sqrt{h_t}\, E(\varepsilon_t)\right] = 0$$

(ii) The unconditional variance of ε_t can be defined as

$$\text{var}(\varepsilon_t) = E(\varepsilon_t^2) = E\left[E(\varepsilon_t^2 \mid \psi_{t-1})\right] = E(a_0 + a_1\varepsilon_{t-1}^2) = a_0 + a_1 E(\varepsilon_{t-1}^2)$$

If ε_t is a stationary process with $E(\varepsilon_t) = 0$, $\text{var}(\varepsilon_t) = \text{var}(\varepsilon_{t-1}) = \text{var}(\varepsilon_{t-1}) = E(\varepsilon_{t-1}^2)$. Therefore, var $(\varepsilon_t) = a_0 + a_1$ $\text{var}(\varepsilon_t)$ and and so $\text{var}(\varepsilon_t) = a_0 / (1 - a_1)$. Since variance of ε_t must be positive, therefore $0 \leq a_1 < 1$.

(iii) In some applications, higher order moments of ε_t are required to exist and, hence, a_1 must satisfy some additional constraints. For instance, to study its tail behavior, we require that the fourth moment of ε_t is finite.

2.2 Forecasting

Forecasts of the ARCH model can be obtained recursively as those of an AR model. Consider an ARCH (q) model. At the forecast origin t, the one-step ahead forecast is

$$h_t(1) = a_0 + a_1\varepsilon_t^2 + \ldots + a_q\varepsilon_{t+1-q}^2 \qquad 2$$

The two-step ahead forecast is $h_t(2) = a0 + a_1 h_t(1) + a_2\varepsilon_{t+2-q}^2$, and l- step ahead forecast is $h_t(l) = a_0 + \sum_{i=1}^{q} a_i h_i(l-i)$ where $h_t(l-i) = \varepsilon_{t+l-i}^2$ if $l-i \leq 0$.

However, ARCH model has some drawbacks. Firstly, when the order of ARCH model is very large, estimation of a large number of parameters is required. Secondly, conditional variance of ARCH(q) model has the property that unconditional autocorrelation function (Acf) of squared residuals; if it exists, decays very rapidly compared to what is typically observed, unless maximum lag q is large. To overcome these difficulties, Bollerslev (1986) proposed the Generalized ARCH (GARCH) model in which conditional variance is also a linear function of its own lags. This model is also a weighted average of past squared residuals, but it has declining weights that never go completely to zero. It gives parsimonious models that are easy to estimate and, even in its simplest form, has proven surprisingly successful in predicting conditional variances. Angelidis *et al.* (2004) evaluated the performance of GARCH models in modelling the daily Value-at-Risk (VaR) of perfectly distributed portfolios in five stock indices, using a number of distributional assumptions and sample sizes.

3. GENERALIZED ARCH (GARCH) MODEL

To overcome the weaknesses of ARCH model, Bollerslev (1986) proposed the Generalized ARCH (GARCH) model independently of each other, in which conditional variance is also a linear function of its own lags and has the following form

$$\varepsilon_t = \xi_t h_t^{1/2} \quad h_t = a_0 + \sum_{i=1}^{q} a_i \varepsilon_{t-i}^2 + \sum_{j=1}^{p} b_j h_{t-j} \qquad 3$$

where $\xi_t \sim$ IID$(0,1)$. A sufficient condition for the conditional variance to be positive is

$a_0 > 0$, $a_i \geq 0$, i = 1, 2, ...q. bj ≥ 0, j = 1,2,.......,p

The GARCH (p, q) process is weakly stationary if and only if

$$\sum_{i=1}^{q} a_i + \sum_{j=1}^{p} b_j < 1$$

The conditional variance defined by (3) has the property that the unconditional autocorrelation function of ε_t^2; if it exists, can decay slowly. For the ARCH family, the decay rate is too rapid compared to what is typically observed in financial time-series, unless the maximum lag q is long. As (3) is a more parsimonious model of the conditional variance than a high-order ARCH model, most users prefer it to the simpler ARCH alternative.

The most popular GARCH model in applications is the GARCH$(1,1)$ model. To express GARCH model in terms of ARMA model, denote $\eta_t = \varepsilon_t^2 - h_t$. Then from equation (3)

$$\varepsilon_t^2 = a_0 + \sum_{i=1}^{Max(p,q)} (a_i + b_i)\varepsilon_{t-i}^2 + \eta_t \sum_{j=1}^{p} b_j \eta_{t-j} \quad 4$$

Thus a GARCH model can be regarded as an extension of the ARMA approach to squared series $\{\varepsilon_t^2\}$. Using the unconditional mean of an ARMA model, we have

$$E(\varepsilon_t^2) = \frac{a_0}{1 - \sum_{i=1}^{Max(p,q)} (a_i + b_i)} \quad 5$$

provided that the denominator of the prior fraction is positive.

Paul *et al.* (2009) compared the efficiency of GARCH model and ARIMA model as far as modelling and forecasting of India's volatile spices export data. Paul *et al.* (2013 c, 2013 d) studied the ARIMA with exogenous variables (ARIMAX) model. They have developed the formulae for more than one-step ahead out-of-sample forecasts along with forecast error variances for the fitted ARIMAX-GARCH model by recursive use of conditional expectation.

3.1 Properties of GARCH Model

The most widely used GARCH specification asserts that the best predictor of the variance in the next period is a weighted average of the long-run average variance, the variance predicted for this period, and the new information in this period that is captured by the most recent squared residual. Such an updating rule is a simple description of adaptive or learning behavior and can be thought of as Bayesian updating.

The properties of GARCH models can easily be studied by focusing on the simplest GARCH(*1,1*) model with

$$\varepsilon_t = \xi_t h_t^{1/2} h_t = a_0 + a_1 \varepsilon_{t-1}^2 + b_1 h_{t-1}, \quad 6$$

where $\xi_t \sim IID(0,1)$ and $0 \le a_1, b_1 \le 1, (a_1 + b_1) < 1$.

The GARCH model that has been described is typically called the GARCH(*1,1*) model. The (*1,1*) in parentheses is a standard notation in which the first number refers to how many autoregressive lags, or ARCH terms, appear in the equation, while the second number refers to how many moving average lags are specified, which here is often called the number of GARCH terms. Sometimes models with more than one lag are needed to find good variance forecasts.

First a large ε_{t-1}^2 or h_{t-1} gives rise to a large h_t. This means that a large ε_{t-1}^2 tends to followed by another large ε_t^2, generating again the well known behavior of volatility clustering in financial time-series.

Second it can be seen that if $1-2a_1^2-(a_1+b_1)^2>0$, then

$$\frac{E(\varepsilon_t^4)}{E(\varepsilon_t)^2}=\frac{3\,1-(a_1+b_1)^2}{1-(a_1+b_1)^2-2a_1^2}>3$$

Consequently, similar to ARCH models, the tail distribution of a GARCH(*1,1*) process is heavier than that of a normal distribution.

Third, the model provides a simple parametric function that can be used to describe the volatility evolution.

3.2 Forecasting Volatility by GARCH Model

Forecasts of a GARCH model can be obtained using methods similar to those of an ARMA model. Although this model is directly set up to forecast for just one period, it turns out that based on the one-period forecast, a two-period forecast can be made. Ultimately, by repeating this step, long-horizon forecasts can be constructed. For the GARCH(*1,1*), the two-step forecast is a little closer to the long-run average variance than is the one-step forecast, and, ultimately, the distant-horizon forecast is the same for all time periods as long as $(a_1+b_1)<1$. This is just the unconditional variance. Thus, the GARCH models are mean reverting and conditionally heteroscedastic, but have a constant unconditional variance.

Consider the GARCH(*1,1*) model in (6) and assume that the forecast origin is *t*, the one-step ahead forecast is $h_t(1)=a_0+a_1\varepsilon_t^2+b_1h_t$

For multi-step ahead forecasts, use $\varepsilon_t^2=\xi_t^2h_t$ and rewrite the volatility equation in (6) as

$$h_{t+1}=a_0+(a_1+b_1)h_t+a_1h_t(\varepsilon_t^2-1)$$

For two-step ahead forecasts $h_{t+2}=a_0+(a_1+b_1)h_{t+1}+a_1h_{t+1}(\varepsilon_{t+1}^2-1)$

Since $E\left((\varepsilon_{t+1}^2-1)/\psi_t\right)=0$

The two-step ahead volatility forecast at the forecast origin *t* satisfies the equation

$h_t(2) = a_0 + (a_1 + b_1)h_t(1)$

In general we have $h_t\ l = a_0 + (a_1 + b_1)h_t(l-1), l > 1$

Fan and Yao (2003) and Straumann (2005) have given a good description of various estimation procedures for conditionally heteroscedastic time- series models.

The Akaike information criterion (AIC) and Bayesian information criterion (BIC) values for GARCH model with Gaussian distributed errors are computed by:

$$AIC = \sum_{t=1}^{T}\left(\log\tilde{h}_t + \varepsilon_t^2\tilde{h}_t^{-1}\right) + 2(p+q+1) \quad 7$$

and

$$BIC = \sum_{t=1}^{T}\left(\log\tilde{h}_t + \varepsilon_t^2\tilde{h}_t^{-1}\right) + 2(p+q+1)\log(T-v+1) \quad 8$$

where T is the total number of observations.

Evidently, the likelihood equations are extremely complicated. Fortunately, the estimates can be obtained by using a software package, like EViews, SAS, SPLUS GARCH, GAUSS, TSP, MATLAB, and RATS.

4. EXPONENTIAL GARCH (EGARCH) MODEL

The EGARCH model was proposed by Nelson (1991) to allow for asymmetric effects between positive and negative shocks on the conditional variance of future observations. Another advantage is that there are no restrictions on the parameters. In the EGARCH model, the conditional variance, h_t, is an asymmetric function of lagged disturbances. The model is given by

$$\varepsilon_t = \xi_t h_t^{1/2}, \quad \ln(h_t) = a_0 + \frac{1 + b_1 B + \ldots + b_{q-1}B^{q-1}}{1 - a_1 B + \ldots + a_p B^p}\, g(\varepsilon_{t-1}) \quad 9$$

where

$$g(\varepsilon_\tau) = (\theta + \gamma)\varepsilon_\tau - \gamma E(|\varepsilon_\tau|), \text{ if } \varepsilon_t \geq 0$$

$$(\theta - \gamma)\varepsilon_\tau - \gamma E(|\varepsilon_\tau|), \text{ if } \varepsilon_t < 0$$

B is the backshift (or lag) operator such that

$$Bg(\varepsilon_t) = g(\varepsilon_{t-1})$$

The EGARCH model can also be represented in another way by specifying the logarithm of conditional variance as

$$\ln(h_t) = a_0 + \beta \ln(h_{t-1}) + \alpha\left|\frac{\varepsilon_{t-1}}{\sqrt{h_{t-1}}}\right| + \gamma\frac{\varepsilon_{t-1}}{\sqrt{h_{t-1}}} \qquad 10$$

This implies that the leverage effect is exponential, rather than quadratic, and that forecasts of the conditional variance are guaranteed to be nonnegative.

The EGARCH model in (9) shows some differences from the standard GARCH model:

- Volatility of the EGARCH model, which is measured by the conditional variance h_t, is an explicit multiplicative function of lagged innovations. On the contrary, volatility of the standard GARCH model is an additive function of the lagged error terms, which causes a complicated functional dependency on the innovations.
- Volatility can react asymmetrically to the good and bad news.
- For the general distributions of ε_t the parameter restrictions for strong and covariance-stationarity coincide.
- The parameters in EGARCH model are not restricted to positive values.

The function $g(.)$ in (9) is piecewise linear. It contains two parameters which define the 'size effect' and the 'sign effect' of the shocks on volatility. The first is a typical ARCH effect while the second is an asymmetrical effect, for example, the leverage effect. The term $\gamma(|\varepsilon_t| - E|\varepsilon_t|)$ determines the size effect and the term $\theta\varepsilon_t$ determines the sign effect. The parameter γ is thus typically positive and θ is negative.

Ghosh *et al.* (2010 b) employed GARCH and EGARCH nonlinear time-series models for volatile fruits and vegetables seeds export data from India.

4.1 Properties of EGARCH Model

The properties of the EGARCH model may be summarized as follows:

- The function $g(\varepsilon_t)$ is linear in with slope coefficient $\theta + 1$ if ε_t is positive while $g(\varepsilon_t)$ is linear in with slope coefficient θ - 1 if is negative
- Suppose that $\theta = 0$. Large innovations increase the conditional variance if $(|\varepsilon_t| - E|\varepsilon_t|)>0$ and decrease the conditional variance if $(|\varepsilon_t| - E|\varepsilon_t|)<0$.
- Suppose that $\theta > 1$. The innovation in variance, $g(\varepsilon_t)$, is positive if the innovations are less than $(2\pi)^{1/2}/(\theta-1)$. Therefore, the negative innovations in returns, cause the innovation to the conditional variance to be positive if θ is much less than 1.

Nelson gives complicated formulas of the unconditional moments. One problem is that under other leptokurtic distributions such as the Student-*t*, the unconditional variance does not exist. The reason is that exponential growth of the conditional variance changes with the level of the shocks, which leads to the explosion of the unconditional variance when the probability for extreme shocks is sufficiently large. Therefore the existence of the unconditional moments depends on the choice of the distribution of the innovations, which is an undesirable property of the EGARCH models. In empirical studies it has been found that EGARCH often overweighs the effects of larger shocks on volatility and thus results in poorer fits than standard GARCH models.

4.2 Estimation of Parameters for GARCH and EGARCH Models

For volatility estimation with GARCH models, Salih *et al*. (2003) proposed an approach based on constrained nonlinear programming formulation. For estimating parameters of GARCH model, most widely used method is the Gaussian maximum likelihood estimation (GMLE) method. For heavy tailed error distribution, Peng and Yao (2003) proposed the Least absolute deviations estimation (LADE) method. For estimation of conditionally heteroscedastic time-series models from a mathematically rigorous perspective, Straumann (2005) may be referred. Huang *et al*. (2008) discussed situations under which a particular estimation procedure should be used. However, no method can be called as the "Best". We now discuss GMLE and LADE methods in some detail.

In respect of the GMLE, the loglikelihood function of a sample of T observations, apart from constant, is

$$L_T(\theta) = T^{-1}\sum_{t=v}^{T}\left(\log h_t + \varepsilon_t^2 h_t^{-1}\right) \qquad 11$$

where $v > p$. However, generally, maximum likelihood estimators are derived by minimizing

$$L_T(\theta) = T^{-1}\sum_{t=v}^{T}\left(\log\sqrt{\tilde{h}_t} - \log f\left(\frac{\varepsilon_t}{\sqrt{\tilde{h}_t}}\right)\right) \qquad 12$$

where $\tilde{h}_t$ is the truncated version of h_t (Fan and Yao, 2003). Besides normal distribution, the function *f*(.) can also take the following forms:

(i) *t*-distribution with v degrees (v>2) of freedom:

$$f(x) = \frac{\Gamma((\nu+1)/2)}{(\pi\nu)^{1/2}\,\Gamma(\nu/2)}\left(\frac{\nu}{\nu-2}\right)^{1/2}\left(1+\frac{x^2}{\nu-2}\right)^{-(\nu+1)/2}$$

(ii) Generalized Gaussian distribution:

$$f(x)=\frac{v\exp\left(-\frac{1}{2}|x/\lambda|^{v}\right)}{2^{(1+1/v)}\lambda\Gamma(1/v)}$$

where

$$\lambda=\left[2^{(-2/v)}\Gamma(1/v)/\Gamma(3/v)\right]^{1/2}\text{and } 0<v<2.$$

For heavy tailed error distributions, LADE method may be employed, which minimizes

$$\sum_{t=v}^{T}\left|\log\varepsilon_t^2-\log(h_t)\right|,$$

where $v = p+1$ if $q = 0$ and $v > p+1$ if $q > 0$. The Akaike information criterion (AIC) and Bayesian information criterion (BIC) values for GARCH model with t- distributed errors are computed by:

$$AIC=\sum_{t=v}^{T}\left(\log\sqrt{\tilde{h}_t}-\log f\left(\frac{\varepsilon_t}{\sqrt{\tilde{h}_t}}\right)\right)+2(p+q+1) \qquad 13$$

and

$$BIC=\sum_{t=v}^{T}\left(\log\sqrt{\tilde{h}_t}-\log f\left(\frac{\varepsilon_t}{\sqrt{\tilde{h}_t}}\right)\right)+2(p+q+1)log(T-v+1) \qquad 14$$

where T is the total number of observations.

The estimation procedures for fitting of EGARCH model is along the same lines as above with the form of h_t replaced by the form given in Equation (10). The AIC and BIC values for EGARCH model with Gaussian distributed errors are computed by:

$$AIC=\sum_{t=1}^{T}\left(\log\tilde{h}_t+\varepsilon_t^2\tilde{h}_t^{-1}\right)+2(p+q+1) \qquad 15$$

and

$$BIC=\sum_{t=1}^{T}\left(\log\tilde{h}_t+\varepsilon_t^2\tilde{h}_t^{-1}\right)+2(p+q+1)\,log(T-v+1) \qquad 16$$

Evidently, the above procedures are computationally very cumbersome. Fortunately, several software packages are available to accomplish the task, like EViews, Statistical Analysis System (SAS), and SPLUS GARCH toolkit.

5. TESTING FOR ARCH EFFECTS

Let $e_t = y_t - fy_{t-1}$ be the residual series. The squared series $\{\varepsilon_t^2\}$ is then used to check for conditional heteroscedasticity, which is also known as the ARCH effects. To this end, two tests, briefly discussed below, are available. The first one is to apply the usual Ljung-Box statistic $Q(m)$ to the $\{\varepsilon_t^2\}$ series. The null hypothesis is that the first m lags of autocorrelation functions of the $\{\varepsilon_t^2\}$ series are zero. The second test for conditional heteroscedasticity is the Lagrange multiplier test of Engle (1982). This test is equivalent to usual F-statistic for testing, $i = 1, 2, \ldots, q$ in the linear regression

$$\varepsilon_t^2 = a_0 + a_1 \varepsilon_{t-1}^2 + \ldots + a_q \varepsilon_{t-q}^2 + e_t, \; t = q+1, \ldots, T \qquad 17$$

where e_t denotes the error term, q is the prespecified positive integer, and T is the sample size.

Let $SSR_0 = \sum_{t=q+1}^{T} (\varepsilon_1^2 - \varpi)^2$, where $\varpi = \sum_{t=q+1}^{T} \varepsilon_1^2 / T$ is the sample mean of $\{\varepsilon_t^2\}$,

and $SSR_1 = \sum_{t=q+1}^{T} \hat{e}_t^2$, where $\hat{e}_t$ is the least squares residual of (17). Then, under H_0,

$$F = \frac{(SSR_0 - SSR_1)/q}{SSR_1(T-q-1)} \qquad 18$$

is asymptotically distributed as chi-squared distribution with q degrees of freedom. The decision rule is to reject H_0 if $F > \chi_q^2(\alpha)$, where $\chi_q^2(\alpha)$ is the upper $100(1-\alpha)^{th}$ percentile of χ_q^2 or, alternatively, the p-value of F is less than α.

6. ILLUSTRATION-1 (PAUL *ET AL.*, 2009)

Paul *et al.* (2009) found that AR(*1*)-GARCH (*1,1*) model was better than ARIMA model for modeling and forecasting of all-India data of monthly export of spices during the period April, 2000 to November, 2006. First of all they fitted ARIMA model. The appropriate model was chosen on the. ARIMA(*1,1,1*) model is selected for modelling and forecasting of the export of spices based on minimum Akaike information criterion (AIC) and Bayesian information criterion (BIC) values. The estimates of parameters of above model are reported in Table 1. The graph of fitted model along with data points is exhibited in Fig. 1. Evidently, the fitted ARIMA(*1,1,1*) model is not able to capture successfully the volatility present at various time-epochs, like October, 2001; May, 2002; March, 2004; and March, 2006.

Table 1 : Estimates of parameters along with their standard errors for fitted ARIMA(*1,1,1)* model

Parameter	Estimate	Standard error
AR1	-0.100	0.159
MA1	0.696	0.119
Constant	1.468	0.966

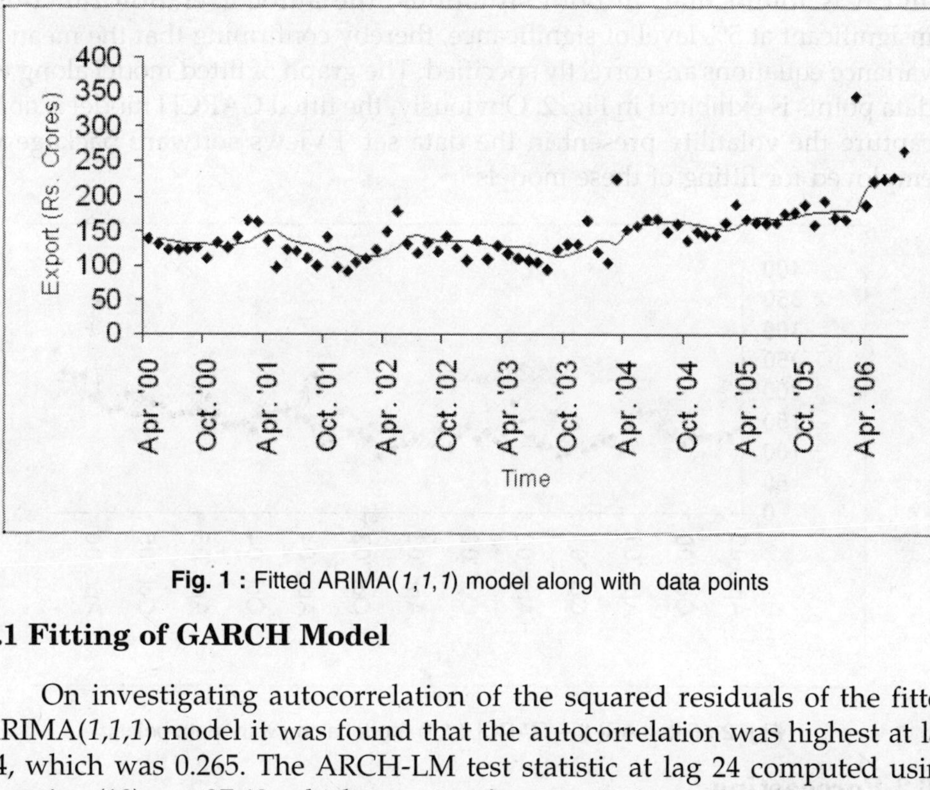

Fig. 1 : Fitted ARIMA(*1,1,1*) model along with data points

6.1 Fitting of GARCH Model

On investigating autocorrelation of the squared residuals of the fitted ARIMA(*1,1,1*) model it was found that the autocorrelation was highest at lag 24, which was 0.265. The ARCH-LM test statistic at lag 24 computed using equation (10) was 37.48, which was significant at 5% level of significance. But it is not reasonable to apply ARCH model of order 24 in view of the enormously large number of parameters. Therefore, the parsimonious GARCH model is applied. The AR(*1*)-GARCH(*1,1*) model is selected on the basis of minimum AIC and BIC values. The estimates of parameters of the above model along with their corresponding standard errors in brackets ( ) are

$$y_t = 157.99 + 0.829\, y_{t-1} + \varepsilon_t$$
$$(33.692) \quad (0.087)$$

where $\varepsilon_1 = h_t^{1/2}\xi_t$, and h_t satisfies the variance equation

$$h_t = 1427.855 + 0.354\ \varepsilon_{t-1}^2 + 0.509\ h_{t-1}$$
$$(237.058)\quad (0.277)\qquad (0.206)$$

Using eqs. (7) and (8), the AIC and BIC values for fitted AR(*1*) – GARCH(*1,1*) model, are respectively computed as 479.77 and 521.97. To study the appropriateness of the fitted GARCH model, the autocorrelation function of the standardized residuals and squared standardized residuals are computed and it is found that, in both situations, the autocorrelation function is insignificant at 5% level of significance, thereby confirming that the mean and variance equations are correctly specified. The graph of fitted model along with data points is exhibited in Fig. 2. Obviously, the fitted GARCH model is able to capture the volatility present in the data set. EViews software package was employed for fitting of these models.

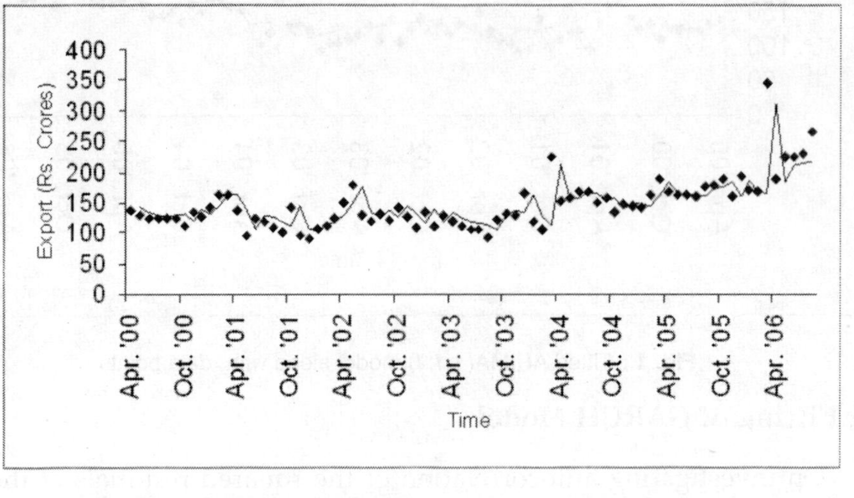

Fig. 2 : Fitted AR(*1*) – GARCH(*1, 1*) model along with data points

6.2 Forecasting

One-step ahead forecasts of export of spices along with their corresponding standard errors inside the brackets ( ) for the months of September, 2006 to November, 2006 in respect of above fitted models are reported in Table 2. A perusal indicates that, for fitted GARCH model, all the forecast values lie within one standard error of forecasts. However, this attractive feature does not hold for fitted ARIMA model.

The Mean square prediction error (MSPE) values and Mean absolute prediction error (MAPE) values for fitted GARCH model are respectively computed as 18.14 and 15.00, which are found to be lower than the corresponding ones for fitted ARIMA model, viz. 33.17 and 29.02 respectively.

Table 2 : One-step ahead forecasts of export of spices (Rs. Crores) for fitted models

Months	Actual Price	Forecasts by	
		ARIMA(*1,1,1*)	AR(*1*)-GARCH(*1,1*)
Sep. '06	270.91	235.67(29.58)	247.14 (40.93)
Oct. '06	232.59	240.27 (30.12)	231.89 (48.17)
Nov. '06	286.21	241.50 (31.16)	265.68 (53.31)

To sum up, it may be concluded that the AR(*1*)-GARCH(*1,1*) model has performed better than the ARIMA(*1,1,1*) model for present data for both modelling as well as forecasting purposes.

7. ILLUSTRATION-2 (GHOSH *ET AL*., 2010 B)

All-India data of monthly export of fruits and vegetables seeds during the period April, 2000 to January, 2007 comprising 82 data points are obtained from Indiastat website (www.indiastat.com) available at the Indian Agricultural Statistics Research Institute, New Delhi and the same are exhibited in Fig. 3. The first 76 data points, i.e. the data during the period April, 2000 to July, 2006 are employed for building the models while the data for the remaining 6 months, i.e. from August, 2006 to January, 2007, are used for validation purpose. The data vary from a minimum of Rs.1.93 crores in November, 2003 to a maximum of Rs.42.44 crores in September, 2002.

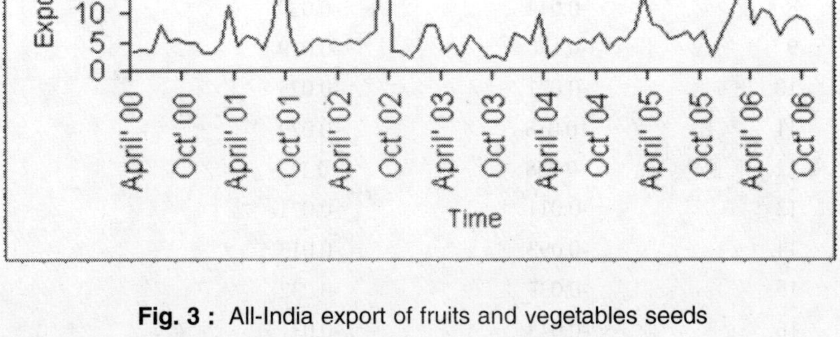

Fig. 3 : All-India export of fruits and vegetables seeds

Evidently, ARIMA methodology is not capable of handling data sets when the ratio of maximum value to minimum value is as high as 22. A perusal of Fig. 1 indicates presence of volatility at several time-epochs. Maximum volatility was noticed in September, 2002 followed by the one in September, 2001, when the export jumped to the level of Rs.19.60 crores. Then again volatility was seen in March, 2006, when export rose to Rs.15.30 crores, and so on.

In the present investigation, the GMLE procedure available in EViews software package, Ver. 4 is used for data analysis. Further, AIC and BIC values for *t*-distributed errors in GARCH model are computed separately by writing computer programs in C.

7.1 Fitting of the GARCH model

The sample autocorrelation functions $(\hat{\rho}_j)$ up to the first sixteen lags of the data are computed and reported in Table 3. A perusal indicates that $\hat{\rho}_1$ is largest up to lags of as high order as 8, and then significant at lag 12. The same situation holds for the case of partial autocorrelation function (pacf). It is well-known that efficiency of the estimates decreases as the number of parameters increases, therefore AR(*1*) model may be suitable in the present situation.

Table 3 : Sample Autocorrelation function (Acf) and Partial autocorrelation function (Pacf) for the series

Lag	Acf of the series	Pacf of the series
1	0.092	0.002
2	-0.023	-0.022
3	-0.078	-0.015
4	-0.034	-0.028
5	0.053	-0.027
6	0.083	-0.026
7	-0.029	-0.022
8	-0.044	-0.030
9	-0.130	-0.019
10	-0.021	-0.025
11	0.018	-0.029
12	0.258	0.112
13	-0.011	-0.021
14	-0.093	-0.013
15	-0.037	-0.032
16	-0.043	-0.031

Also, the AIC and BIC values for fitted GARCH and EGARCH models has been found to be minimum when the mean equation depends on recent past only. Investigating the autocorrelation function (Acf) of squared residuals of AR(*1*) model, reported in Table 2, it is found that the Acf and Pacf are maximum at lag *12*, which is *0.259* and 0.247 respectively. But if we go for AR(*1*)-ARCH(*12*) model, a very large number of parameters are needed to be estimated. So, to get a parsimonious model, the AR(*1*)-GARCH(*1,1*) model is selected.

From the summary statistics of the data set, it is observed that the kurtosis is as high as 33.96, which reflects a "leptokurtic" behaviour. Therefore, instead of Gaussian, error distribution is assumed as Student's *t*-distribution.

The mean and conditional variance for fitted AR(*1*)-GARCH(*1,1*) model are computed as follows:

$$\underset{(1.351)}{y_t = 6.108} - \underset{(0.322)}{0.053}\, y_{t-1} + \varepsilon_t$$

where

$$\varepsilon_t = h_1^{1/2}\xi_t,$$

and h_t satisfies the variance equation

$$h_t = \underset{(1.970)}{8.470} + \underset{(0.191)}{0.208}\varepsilon_{t-1}^2 + \underset{(0.160)}{0.215}\, h_{t-1}$$

The values within brackets denote corresponding standard errors of the estimates. The AIC and BIC values, for fitted GARCH model, computed from Equations (13) and (14) are respectively 136.59 and 168.64.

To study the appropriateness of the fitted GARCH model, the autocorrelation function of the standardized residuals and squared standardized residuals are computed and reported in Table 5 and Table 6. It is found that, in both situations, the autocorrelation function is insignificant at 5% level of significance, thereby confirming that the mean and variance equations are correctly specified. The conditional standard deviation for fitted model is plotted in Fig. 4 and the fitted AR(*1*)-GARCH(*1, 1*) model is exhibited in Fig. 5. A visual inspection shows that the fitted model is not able to properly capture the volatility present at various time epochs in the data set, perhaps due to the fact that positive and negative shocks are not symmetric.

Table 4 : Sample Autocorrelation function (Acf) and Partial autocorrelation function (Pacf) for the squared residual series

Lag	Acf of squared residuals	Pacf of squared residuals
1	0.092	0.092
2	-0.022	-0.031
3	-0.074	-0.070
4	-0.030	-0.017
5	0.055	0.057
6	0.084	0.068
7	-0.023	-0.039
8	-0.038	-0.024
9	-0.123	-0.108
10	-0.008	0.009
11	0.026	0.009
12	0.259	0.247
13	-0.014	-0.061
14	-0.097	-0.073
15	-0.037	0.017
16	-0.044	-0.049

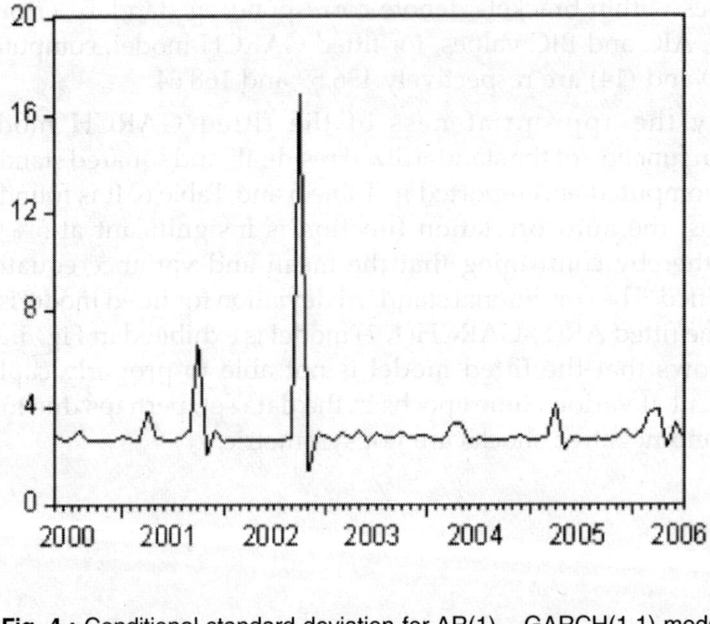

Fig. 4 : Conditional standard deviation for AR(1) – GARCH(1,1) model

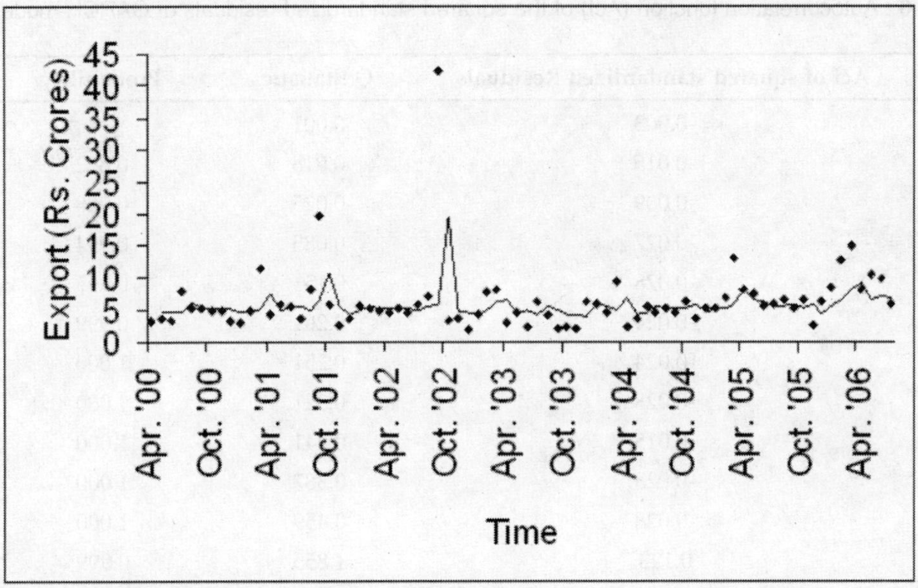

Fig. 5 : Fitted AR(*1*) – GARCH(*1,1*) model along with the data points.

Table 5 : Autocorrelation function (Acf) of the standardized residuals of GARCH model

Lag	Acf of standardized Residuals	Q Statistic	Probability
1	0.067	0.348	—
2	-0.044	0.498	0.480
3	-0.095	1.219	0.543
4	-0.052	1.435	0.697
5	0.042	1.580	0.812
6	0.075	2.048	0.842
7	-0.038	2.174	0.903
8	-0.050	2.390	0.935
9	-0.128	3.820	0.873
10	-0.008	3.826	0.922
11	0.070	4.264	0.935
12	0.265	10.688	0.470
13	-0.019	10.723	0.553
14	-0.104	11.739	0.549
15	-0.050	11.984	0.608
16	-0.050	12.228	0.662

Table 6 : Autocorrelation function (Acf) of the squared standardized residuals of GARCH model

Lag	Acf of squared standardized Residuals	Q Statistic	Probability
1	-0.003	0.001	—
2	-0.015	0.018	0.892
3	-0.009	0.025	0.988
4	-0.027	0.085	0.994
5	-0.028	0.151	0.997
6	-0.024	0.201	0.999
7	-0.024	0.251	1.000
8	-0.028	0.321	1.000
9	-0.015	0.341	1.000
10	-0.023	0.387	1.000
11	-0.028	0.459	1.000
12	0.123	1.855	0.999
13	-0.016	1.879	1.000
14	-0.013	1.895	1.000
15	-0.031	1.985	1.000
16	-0.033	2.089	1.000

7.2 Fitting of the EGARCH Model

To capture the asymmetric nature of volatility in the data, EGARCH model is now employed. The mean equation of fitted model is

$$y_t = 40.365 + 0.972\, y_{t-1} + \varepsilon_t$$
$$(52.370) \quad (0.040)$$

where $\varepsilon_t = h_t^{1/2}\eta_t$

and h_t satisfies variance equation

$$h_t = 2.132 - 1.026\, ln(h_{t-1}) + 1.484 \left|\varepsilon_{t-1} / \sqrt{h_{t-1}}\right| + 0.469 \left|\varepsilon_{t-1} / \sqrt{h_{t-1}}\right|$$
$$(0.543) \quad (0.129) \qquad (0.289) \qquad (0.179)$$

To study the appropriateness of the fitted EGARCH model, the autocorrelation function of the standardized residuals and squared standardized residuals are computed and reported in Table 7 and Table 8. It is found that, in both situations, the autocorrelation function is insignificant at 5% level of significance, thereby confirming that the mean and variance equations are correctly specified.

Table 7 : Autocorrelation function of the standardized residuals of EGARCH model

Lag	Acf of standardized residuals	Q Statistic	Probability
1	-0.135	1.419	
2	-0.173	3.796	0.071
3	-0.181	6.422	0.06
4	0.038	6.54	0.088
5	0.146	8.289	0.082
6	-0.036	8.395	0.136
7	-0.074	8.863	0.181
8	0.006	8.867	0.262
9	-0.177	11.616	0.169
10	0.008	11.621	0.236
11	-0.029	11.697	0.306
12	0.14	13.492	0.262
13	0.08	14.094	0.295
14	-0.102	15.087	0.302
15	0.029	15.166	0.367
16	-0.045	15.367	0.425

Table 8 : Autocorrelation function of the squared standardized residuals of EGARCH model

Lag	Acf of squared standardized residuals	Q Statistic	Probability
1	0.016	0.02	
2	-0.031	0.098	0.753
3	0.005	0.101	0.951
4	-0.016	0.122	0.989
5	-0.053	0.351	0.986
6	-0.073	0.799	0.977
7	-0.041	0.941	0.988
8	-0.017	0.967	0.995
9	-0.061	1.297	0.996
10	0.271	7.799	0.554
11	0.011	7.81	0.647
12	0.039	7.948	0.718
13	0.011	7.959	0.788
14	-0.019	7.995	0.844
15	0.097	8.891	0.838
16	-0.065	9.303	0.861

The AIC and BIC values for fitted EGARCH model, computed from Equations (15) and (16), are respectively found as 86.26 and 124.72, which are much less than the corresponding values, viz. 136.59 and 168.64 for the fitted GARCH model. All this clearly shows the superiority of EGARCH model over GARCH model for the data under consideration for modelling purposes.

As visual inspection, the conditional standard deviation for fitted model is plotted in Fig. 6 and fitted EGARCH model along with data is exhibited in Fig. 7. Evidently, the fitted model is able to capture quite well the volatility present at various time-epochs.

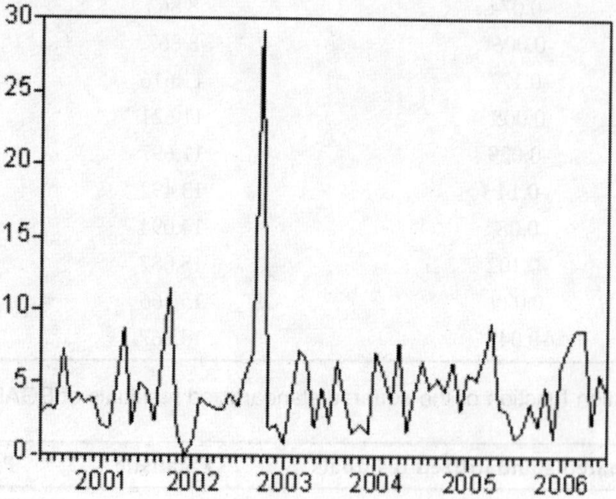

Fig. 6 : Conditional standard deviation for AR(1) – EGARCH(1,1) model

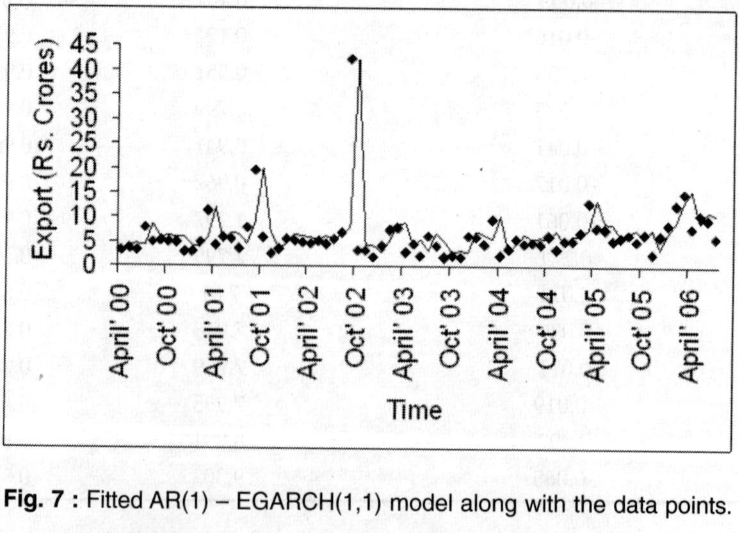

Fig. 7 : Fitted AR(1) – EGARCH(1,1) model along with the data points.

8. FORECASTING

One-step ahead forecasts for monthly export of fruits and vegetables seeds data (in Rs. Crores) for the period August, 2006 to January, 2007 along with the corresponding forecast standard errors in brackets ( ) are reported in Table 9.

Table 9 : One-step ahead forecasts of export data (in Rs. Crores)

Months	Actual value	Forecast by AR(*1*)-GARCH(*1,1*)	Forecast by AR(*1*)-EGARCH(*1,1*)
August, '06	8.31	5.58 (2.699)	6.81 (1.751)
September, '06	9.52	5.45 (3.010)	7.64 (2.998)
October, '06	8.76	5.40 (3.152)	8.40 (4.088)
November, '06	6.06	5.38 (3.160)	9.11 (4.998)
December, '06	7.53	5.38 (3.161)	9.77 (5.747)
January, '07	8.62	5.37 (3.161)	10.39 (6.360)

The Mean square prediction error (MSPE) and Mean absolute prediction error (MAPE) values for fitted EGARCH model are respectively computed as 1.98 and 1.80, which are found to be lower than the corresponding ones for fitted GARCH model, viz. 2.91 and 2.08 respectively. Also, the performance of fitted GARCH and EGARCH models is evaluated through the Relative mean absolute prediction error (RMAPE), defined as

$$\text{RMAPE} = 1/6\sum_{i=1}^{6}\{|y_{t+i} - \hat{y}_{t+i}| / y_{t+1}\}\times 100$$

The RMAPE values for fitted GARCH and EGARCH models are respectively computed as 31.895 and. 23.780, indicating thereby the superiority of latter over the former for forecasting purposes. Further, it is observed that, under the situation of moderate forecast standard errors during August, 2006 to October, 2006, the EGARCH model has performed better than the GARCH model from the viewpoint of point forecasts. The increase in volatility during November, 2006 is also reflected in increased standard error of forecast during December, 2006 but ultimately the EGARCH model quite successfully forecasts the value in January, 2007. Finally, from the viewpoint of interval prediction, it may be noted from Table 4 that, for fitted EGARCH model, the actual values during August, 2006 to January, 2007 lie in the 95% prediction-interval, which is the interval containing point forecasts plus/minus two times standard errors of forecasts.

CONCLUSION

For India's spice export data, the usual assumption of homoscedastic error variance is not satisfied. For modeling and forecasting of such data set, GARCH nonlinear time series model has performed better than the well known Box-Jenkins ARIMA model. It implies that for data sets exhibiting volatility, ARIMA approach should be abandoned in favour of GARCH methodology in order to obtain more accurate forecasts and changing forecast interval lengths. To this end, modelling and forecasting of volatility is carried out through GARCH and EGARCH approaches. As an illustration, monthly export of fruits and vegetables seeds time-series data at all-India level is considered. It is shown that AR-EGARCH model performs satisfactorily for the given data set. In future, other extensions of GARCH model may be explored to capture the volatility in agriculture.

ACKNOWLEDGEMENT

The authors are grateful to Dr. Prajneshu, Emeritus Scientist, ICAR and Dr. S. D. Wahi, Head (A), Division of Statistical Genetics, IASRI for their encouragement and valuable suggestions. The authors are thankful to the Director, IASRI for providing facilities to carry out the analysis.

REFERENCES

Angelidis, T., Benos, A. and Degiannakis, S. (2004). The use of GARCH models in VaR estimation. Stat. Meth., 1, 105-128.

Bollerslev, T. (1986). Generalized autoregressive conditional heteroscedasticity. J. Econ., 31 307-327.

Box, G. E. P., Jenkins, G. M. and Reinsel, G. C. (2007). Time-Series Analysis: Forecasting and Control. 3rd edition. Pearson Education, India.

Campbell, J. Y., Lo, A. W., and MacKinlay, A. C. (1997). The Econometrics of Financial Markets, Princeton, New Jersey: Princeton University Press.

Chatfield, C. (2001). Time series forecasting, Chapman and Hall, U.S.A.

Engle, R. F. (1982). Autoregressive conditional heteroscedasticity with estimates of the variance of U.K. inflation. Econometrica, 50, 987-1008.

Fan, J. and Yao, Q. (2003). Nonlinear Time Series: Nonparametric and Parametric Methods, Springer, U.S.A.

Ghosh, H., Paul, R. K. and Prajneshu, (2010 a). Nonlinear Time Series Modeling and Forecasting for Periodic and ARCH Effects. Journal of Statistical Theory and Practice, 4 (1), 27-44.

Ghosh, H., Paul, R. K. and Prajneshu, (2010 b). The GARCH and EGARCH Nonlinear Time-Series Models for Volatile Data: An Application. Journal of Statistics and Applications, 5 (2), 177-193.

Huang, D. Wang, H. and Yao, Q. (2008). Estimating GARCH models: When to use what? Econometrics J., 11, 27-38.

Lanne, M. and Saikkonen, P. (2003). Modeling the U.S. short-term interest rate by mixture autoregressive processes. J. Fin. Econ., 1, 96 – 125.

Nelson, D. (1991). Conditional heteroskedasticity in asset returns: A new approach. Econometrica, 59, 347-370.

Paul, R. K., Ghosh, H., and Prajneshu (2009). GARCH Nonlinear Time Series Analysis for Modelling and Forecasting of India s Volatile Spices Export Data. *J. Ind. Soc. Agri. Stat.* 62 (2) 123-132

Paul, R. K. and Das, M. K. (2010). Statistical modelling of inland fish production in India. Journal of the Inland Fisheries Society of India, 42(2), 1-7.

Paul, R. K. and Das, M. K. (2013 a). Forecasting of average annual fish landing in Ganga Basin. Fishing chimes, 33 (3), 51-54

Paul, R. K., Prajneshu, and Ghosh, H. (2013 b). Modelling and forecasting of wheat yield data based on weather variables. Indian Journal of Agricultural Science, 83 (2), 180-183

Paul, R. K., Panwar, S., Sarkar, S. K., Kumar, A. Singh, K. N., Farooqi, S. and Chaudhary, V. K. (2013 c). Modelling and Forecasting of Meat Exports from India. Agricultural Economics Research Review, 26 (2), 249-256.

Paul, R. K., Ghosh, H. and Prajneshu (2013 d). Development of out-of-sample forecast formulae for ARIMAX-GARCH model and their application. Journal of the Indian Society of Agricultural Statistics, 68(1), 85-92.

Peng, L. and Yao, Q. (2003). Least absolute deviations estimation for ARCH and GARCH models. Biometrika, 90, 967-975.

Straumann, D. (2005). Estimation in conditionally heteroscedastic time series models. Springer, Germany.

Tsay, R. S. (2005). Analysis of financial time series. 2nd Ed. John Wiley, U.S.A.

❑❑❑

CHAPTER - 34

Use of Modelling in Agriculture

Amitava Rakshit , Sumit Rai, and Avinash Rai
Department of Soil Science and Agricultural Chemistry, Institute of Agricultural Science, Banaras Hindu University, UP-221005, India
Email: amitavar@bhu.ac.in

INTRODUCTION

Agricultural systems and the environment in which it operates have become increasingly complex which encompass both agricultural production and marketing systems. Both of them are rich in complexity and diversity (Spedding, 1975) and to understand the complexity and structure of such systems and their functions require the use of mathematical modelling frameworks that represent their key features. Disciplines that are required to develop and solve such models include: biology, computer programming, statistics, mathematics, economics, and social science. Models are being developed to investigate specific issues such as weed infestation, soil health, nitrogen cycling, the effects of climate change, climate variability, and to assist developing countries to improve their production at their farm gate. During the first half of 20th Century, most agricultural products were produced by means of labour and the majority of the produce was used for own consumption. However, as time progressed labour was substituted for machines, production became more market-oriented and consequently the practice of farming also transformed from "a way of living" to business enterprises run on business principles. At present, evidence of these changes can clearly be seen in everyday life: biotechnological products are produced, the world economy has become highly competitive and sensitive because of globalisation, precision farming is done by means of satellites and computers and specifically designed computer software is used to assist agribusiness managers in management decisions. Agricultural systems had their beginnings in the late 1950s. The concepts of system dynamics emerged in the 1960s and further developments emerged during the 1970 and 1980s with computer programming techniques (Barrett and Nearing, 1998). In the late 1980s the trend was beginning to appear of farmers purchasing computers to solve management problems (McPhee ,2009). In the 1990s the portable computer (PC) revolution decreased the price of PCs increasing the access-ability of PCs into every household. The internet came into wide spread use in the late 1990s and has made information more readily available. The current decade has evaluated the uptake and use of Agricultural Systems (McCown 2002; Carberry *et al.*, 2002) and the techniques of evaluating systems have been discussed (Mitchell and Sheehy, 1997; Mitchell, 1997; Tedeschi *et al.*, 2006). Agricultural systems have been developed for research and industry applications with an aim to address and answer specific questions or problems not only for pest control, irrigation, environmental, and rural innovation but also for precision management, climate change and variability, food security, feed stock for bio-fuel, soil carbon sequestration, environmental impact, sustainability and ecosystem services. Specific systems have been developed to investigate weed infestation, soil health, and nitrogen cycling. Dynamic crop growth simulation is a relatively recent technique that facilitates quantitative understanding of the effects of these factors, and agronomic management factors on crop growth and productivity. Generally, the models are quantitative description of the mechanisms and processes that result in growth of the crop (Rakshit *et al.*,2008). The processes could be crop physiological, meteorological, physical and chemical processes The results obtained by these approaches and methods forced us to analyse and describe agricultural systems and their functioning in order to facilitate better decision-making. Consequently, the systems approach as well as the methodology and methods of constructing models and developing simulation techniques is being widely adopted and further developed to be utilised in an agricultural context. The objectives of this paper is to include model evaluation, parameter estimation, and application of biological models, including crops, disease and soils.

Scope of Simulation Modelling for Biological and Agricultural Systems

Clmatic variability and characterization*:* Crop models together with GIS can greatly facilitate demarcation of homologous zones at mega-, macro-, meso- as well as micro level depending upon the availability of data and objectives. These tools have been used to determine potential and attainable yields for a given level of inputs for various crops. Potential yield of cultivars varies with season/year and location. Estimates of such yields for different varieties can establish a reference point for site quality and remove the confounding effects associated with large climatic variation.

Precision crop management: Once potential yields have been quantified, these can be converted to attainable yields to determine magnitudes of yield gap. Crop growth modelling can be used to in matching agro-technology with the farmers resources and in analysing the precise reasons for yield gap. Recent studies have shown that simulation models can help fine tune the N fertiliser application recommendations in irrigated rice (Berge *et al.*, 1996). Studies done in China, India, Indonesia and Philippines showed that simulation model recommendations helped in increasing the fertiliser use efficiency by 15-20 %.

Crop protection and disease surveillance: At a regional level, GIS, requisite environmental data coupled with epidemic simulation models further provide geographic delineation of disease and insect pest risk zones. These zones can also help us in making strategic decisions on deployment strategies for varieties and to determine how long host plant resistance would be expected to last. Historical climate data from sites have been shown to be useful for characterizing the conduciveness of a site to specific diseases. Attempts are also being made to integrate disease predictive systems with online weather and weather-interpolation systems. Yield loss studies have conventionally quantified the relations between nitrogen application rate, disease severity, season and grain yield. This has resulted in a qualitative understanding of the host-pathogen-environment interactions and in disease management recommendations. However, validity of such recommendations is limited, as they are strongly influenced by disease onset, disease spreading rate, farm management practices, environmental conditions and their interactions. Physiologically based simulation models can be applied to understand the damage mechanisms and analyse their effects on crop growth and yield of rice.

Climate Change and Yield Forecasting: Crop models are being used to estimate the impact of increased carbon dioxide and temperature on crop production (Matthews *et al.*, 1995). It was assumed that the trends in potential yields would also be shown in actual yield. These models can utilize the input from Global Circulation Models (GCM) to quantify the impact of climate changes. Reasonably precise estimates of acreage and yield before the actual harvest are of immense value in policy planning. The relatively small cost and speed of assessment makes crop growth simulation models promising for areas where significant daily weather data are readily available. In this approach, the model is run using actual weather data during the cropping season for the geographical region of interest. Weather data for typical years are used to continue simulations until harvest. Horie *et al.* (1992) showed an example where crop models, regional weather databases and historical yield data is used to forecast rice yields for different regions of Japan. There is an urgent need to develop such models for Indian situation. Optimal Sowing Dates for Hybrid Seed Production: A major constraint to utilizing hybrid seed technology is the need to buy fresh seeds every planting season and the high cost of seed production. This limited seed production is largely due to poor out-crossing and asynchronous flowering of male and female parents. Environmental factors such as temperature, humidity, and wind speed as the time of pollination and fertilization play a great role in regulating outcrossing percentage. To synchronise these at several locations to determine the optimal planting dates, crop simulation modelling is a more efficient tool in making decisions about the planting calender of parents in different environments (Xu, 1995).

Increased Efficiency of Multi-environment Evaluation: Development and release of a variety is a complex process that may extend over a period of 10-15 years. Once the breeding lines have become homozygous, they are bulked and then tested in observational, replicated and multilocation yield trials. These multi-site trials are expensive and need several crop seasons/locations to understand genotype by environment (G x E) interactions.

Owing to the inherent complexity of agriculture, modelling studies started only in the early 1970s. Rapid accumulation of knowledge in the agricultural field and the increased accessibility to information technology have contributed to the development of a wide number of agricultural models over the last three decades (Table 1).

VALIDATION

Once the analysts believe that the simulation model is programmed correctly, they must face the next question: is the conceptual simulation an accurate representation of the system under study. This section discusses the validation part taking some examples which have been presented in Table 2. The model validation stage involves the confirmation that the calibrated model closely represents the real situation. The procedure consists of a comparison of simulated output and observed data that have not been previously used in the calibration stage. Ideally, all mechanistic models should be validated both at the level of overall system output and at the level of internal components and processes.

Models Can Make Farmers More Efficient

Mathematical modeling can also be used as an aid for long-term planning in agricultural enterprise. Many of the problems faced by farmers in different parts of the world can be solved analytically. Mathematics modeling, mathematical theory, operations research, and practical applications are useful tools for predicting crop yield or for planning how much land should be cultivated. Some of these methods could be included as practical examples in mathematics curricula, allowing students to gain an interest in these topics as well.

Table1: Different models in agriculture system

S.No.	Model	Parameters	Approaches in Biological System	Reference
1.	Rhizosphere Simulation Model	Root length, Root radius, Root exudation rate per unit root surface, Volume of water entering the root, Absolute diffusion coefficient in water, Slope of the adsorption isotherm, Decay rate of solute, Soil cylinder radius, Number of soil sub-cylinders, Soil water content, Soil water content threshold, Soil bulk density	CC, ND, CP and CY	Kirk *et al.* (1999a), Kirk *et al.* (1999b), Olesen *et al.* (2001), Lide (2003), Walczak *et al.* (2006), Williams and Yanai (1996), Zhou and Li (2001)
2.	Free ion activity model (FIAM), Terrestrial biotic ligand model (TBLM) and diffusive gradients in thin films (DGT) technique	R_{max}* is the concentration (mg kg^{-1}) of M^+ (metal) and H^+ binding sites in root apoplasm, K_{HApo} the thermodynamic constant (M^{-1}) of Hþ binding in root apoplasm and $\{H^+\}$ the H^+ activity (M) in soil solution as deduced from pH measurements in $CaCl_2$ soil extracts. The estimation of M^+ concentration in the whole roots (R_{MTot}) using TBLM The parameters Rmax* and K_{HApo} are computed as fitting parameters during TBLM implementation	CC, ND, CP and CY	Bravin *et al.*, 2010
3.	New compensated root water and nutrient uptake model, implemented in HYDRUS	Volumetric water content, soil water potential, unsaturated hydraulic conductivity, time, spatial coordinates, sink/source	CC, ND, CP and CY	Simunek and Hopmans 2009; Simunek *et al.*, 2006, Richards 1931;

Contd.

		term, root water uptake (transpiration); Tp, Ta, Tac for potential, actual non-compensated, and actual compensated root water uptake rate, respectively; α– water stress response function; ω_c – water stress index; Rp – potential root nutrient uptake rate; Pa – passive root nutrient uptake rate; Ap, Aa, Aac for potential, actual non-compensated, and actual compensated root nutrient uptake rate, respectively; α_{MM} – nutrient stress response (Michaelis–Menten) function; π_c – nutrient stress index).		
4.	Dynamic Interaction between Heavy metals (M) and soil acidity model	T is the biomass (kgm^{-2}), S is the concentration of M+ in biomass ($mg\ kg^{-1}$), A and H are the concentrations of M+ ($mg\ l^{-1}$) and H+ ($mg\ l^{-1}$) in the soil solution, respectively. t is the time, W is the flux of protons to the soil during rainfall ($mgm^{-2}\ year^{-1}$), p is the available water for roots (mm) and α, β and ϕ are coefficients of absorption ($l\ kg^{-1}year^{-1}$), leaching ($year^{-1}$), reaction ($year^{-1}$), respectively. h (T) is the function of biomass net growth and μ(S) is the function of mortality or metabolic inefficiency.	CC, ND, CP and CY	Guala *et al.* 2010, 2009; De Leo *et al.*, 1993
5.	Quantitative Evaluation of the Fertility of Tropical Soils (QUEFTS) Model	y is yield target ($Mg\ ha^{-1}$), x is nutrient uptake for a given yield target ($kg\ ha^{-1}$), b is yield potential	CC, ND, CP and CY	Setiyono *et al.*, 2010 and Dobberman *et al.*, 2006

Contd.

	(Mg ha^{-1}), and c is uptake at yield approaching the maximum yield (kg ha^{-1})		
Explicit three-dimensional simulation model and L-System root growth model	buffer power *b*, volumetric water content θ, impedance factor *f*, and initial concentration *c*, the diffusion coefficient *Dl*; Michaelis–Menten parameter is maximal influx *Fm* and Michaelis–Menten constant is *K*m.Root system parameters as initial growth rate *r0 and r1*, maximal root length *k*0 and *k*1, length of basal zone *lb*0, apical zone *la* and inter-branch distance *l*0*n*.	CC, ND, CP and CY	(Leitner, Klepsch, Bodner, *et al.*, 2010; Roose *et al.*, 2001
Decision support system for agrotechnology transfer (DSSAT) cropping system model	Relative cloudiness factor (0 _/1), Average annual air temperature (8C), Atmospheric carbon dioxide concentration (mmol[CO2]/mol [air]), Dew point temperature, Day length on day of simulation (from sunrise to sunset) (h), Hourly air temperature, Daily photosynthetically active radiation or photon flux density (moles[quanta]/(m^2d)), Daily total precipitation, Daily total solar radiation Amplitude of annual air temperature (used to calculate soil temperature), Maximum daily temperature, Minimum daily temperature, Wind speed (km/d), Latitude, Bulk density, soil layer L (g[soil]/cm^3[soil]), Thickness of soil layer L (cm), Soil water content at drained upper limit in soil layer	SA, CC, ND, CP and CY	Jones *et al.*, 2003

Contd.

	L (cm3[water]/cm^3[soil]), Soil water content in soil layer L at lower limit of plant extractable soil water (cm3[water]/cm^3[soil]), Ammonium N in soil layer L (mg[N]/g[soil]), Actual number of soil layers, Nitrate in soil layer L (mg[N]/g[soil]), pH in soil layer L, Soil water content in layer L at saturation (cm^3[water]/cm^3[soil]), Temperature of soil surface litter, Soil temperature in soil layer L, Soil water content in layer L (cm^3[water]/cm^3[soil]), Change in soil water content due to drainage in layer L (cm^3[water]/cm^3[soil]), Water available for infiltration-rainfall plus net irrigation minus runoff (mm/d), Nitrogen stress factor (1_/no stress, 0_/max stress), Root length density for soil layer L (cm[root]/cm^3[soil]), Daily senesced plant matter. I_/0 for surface, 1 for soil; J_/1 for C, 2 for lignin, 3 for N (g[C,N,or lignin]/(m^{2}d)), Day when plant stage I occurred, Rate of root uptake of NH4 (kg[N]/(ha d)), Rate of root uptake of NO3 (kg[N]/(ha d), Healthy LAI, LAI (m2[leaf]/m2[ground]), Potential ET rate (mm/d), Potential plant transpiration rate (mm/d), Light interception by leaves, Unsaturated soil water flow: + = upward, - = downward (cm/d), Day of emergence, Harvest maturity date, Change in soil	

Contd.

		water content due to root water uptake in layer L (cm^3[water]/ cm^3[soil]), Actual daily root water uptake over soil profile (cm/d), Potential daily root water uptake over soil profile (cm/d), Fertilizer type for current application, Fertilizer incorporation depth on current day of simulation (cm), Residue left on surface of soil (kg[residue]/ ha), N concentration of the residue for current application (%), Amount of nitrogen in fertilizer applied on current day of simulation (kg[N]/ ha), End of season or harvest date, Irrigation amount for today (mm/ d), Amount of residue applied to the soil (kg[dry matter]/ha), Incorporation depth of newly added residues (cm), Residue type for current application and Planting date		
8.	Goidanich, Rule of 3 10, DM CAST, EPI Winter, EPI Summer, POM, PCOP, Dyonis, MILVIT, PERO, VINEMILD, PRO, Freiburg, PLASMO and Dm simulator	Temperature, precipitation, relative humidity, leaf wetness duration, daily time step, hourly time step, monthly time step, number of minutes of interval in night and day.	CP , ND and CY	Friesland and Orlandini 2011
9.	A dual porosity model	Macroscopic space variable, Microscopic space variable, Radial distance inside soil particle (cm), Length of unit cell containing a soil particle, associated extra-particle solution and gas, and root hairs (cm), Length of root with root hairs (cm), Length of root hairs (cm),	SA, CC, ND, CP and CY	Zygalakis *et al.*,2011

Contd.

	Length of zone of root influence (cm), Radius of soil particle (cm), Radius of the main root (cm), Radius of root hair (cm), Concentration of nutrient in extra- and intra-particle solutions, Concentration of nutrient on extra- and intra-particle surfaces per unit solid mass, Rate constants for backward and forward sorption reactions on extra-particle surfaces, Rate constants for backward and forward sorption reactions on intra-particle surfaces, Coefficient in equilibrium sorption equation, Water content of whole soil per unit soil volume, Water content of extra- and intra-particle space per unit space volume, Soil solid mass per unit whole soil, particle and solid volume, Porosity of extra- and intra-particle space per unit whole soil volume, Soil mass per unit external and internal surface area of particle, Nutrient diffusion coefficient in intra-particle pores, Nutrient diffusion coefficient in free solution, Nutrient diffusion impedance factor for extra- and intra-particle pores, Nutrient efflux parameter for root hair and root, Maximal nutrient influx into root hair and root and Michaelis–Menten constant for root hair and root nutrient uptake		

* Crop Yield, Climate change, Nutrient dynamics, Crop Protection, Disease surveillance and System approach

Table 2 : Validation of different models used in agricultural system

S.No.	Crop simulation models	Crop	Experimental set-up/ parameters used	Validation	Reference
1.	CROPGRO- v3.5	Soybean	Using a new procedure for spatial validation of management zones across the field delineated using a NDVI classification technique	The variability in soy bean populations with in the field provided validation of the plant population and soil type effects on soybean yields closely predicted by the model	Basso *et al.*, 2001
2.	Environmental Policy Integrated Climate (EPIC) crop model	Winter wheat, maize, spring barley and winter rye	Six daily meteorological variables from the CGMS database were used to run EPIC from 1996 until 2007: minimum and maximum temperature (^{0}C), precipitation (mm), global radiation (MJ m^{-2}), mean vapour pressure (hPa), and mean wind speed at 10 m (m s^{-1}) along with a set of 13 soil properties, including soil organic carbon (%), sand, silt and clay (%), bulk density (g cm^{-3}), base saturation (%), cation exchange capacity and sum of base cations (cmol+ kg^{-1}), pH, stoniness (vol.%), saturated hydraulic conductivity (mm h^{-1}), and wilting point and field water capacity (cm^3 cm^{-3}).	EPIC was a better predictor for winter wheat, winter rye and spring barley than for maize. The variability showed that our regional model implementation necessarily simplifies effects of crop management options, causing a flatter yield reproduction across European regions. The results substantially altered when we used different PET methods, N-fertilizer distribution, irrigation strategy, or crop cultivars and the results obtained demonstrated a comprehensive and spatially extensive validation of a spatial Pan-European EPIC implementation.	Balkovic *et al.*, 2013

Contd.

3.	ISAREG	Maize and wheat	To simulate and evaluate the irrigation scheduling in the test crop variables include effective precipitation, P_e (mm), reference evapotranspiration, ET_0 (mm), dates of the crop development stages and correspondent crop coefficients, root depths, the fraction of available soil water permitting unrestricted evapo transpiration, for each layer the respective depth, the available soil water and the potential ground water contribution	The crop coefficients were derived from field data using the model ISAREG, which constitutes the essential part of the calibration process. For each crop, 10 data sets were selected to calculate the crop coefficients, and 10 other data sets were later utilized to validate those values.	
4.	CropSyst	Direct seeded rice–wheat cropping system	To quantify the interactive effect of different water and nitrogen treatments on the productivity of DSRWCS five input data files which is structured in the following sections: phenology, morphology, growth, residue, nitrogen, harvest index, salinity tolerance and CO_2- elevation response are required to run CropSyst – (simulation control), (location), (soil), (crop) and (management) files.	The CropSyst model simulated the biomass and grain yield reasonably well for DS rice and wheat in DSRWCS. The model underestimatedthe biomass and grain yield at higher levels of N (150 kg ha–1) for DS rice, but simulated well at all levels of N in the case of wheat.	Singh *et al.*, 2013

CONCLUSIONS

In conclusion, the above discussion suggests that we should develop decision support systems which properly take into account the complexity and dynamics of the systems environment which comprise subject matter, as well as economic components in other words knowledge-based and bio-economic models which will contain appropriate input-output-relationships as generalized production functions. Further this will take into account space and time variability by incorporating the relevant, non-controllable yield factors, preferably with their direct values or at least with their probability distributions, and will contain biological and technological, as well as economic components, in order to provide effective decision support for the agricultural land users. Obviously, such models will have to be developed by multi-disciplinary teams, comprising subject matter experts from the fields of agriculture and business management, as well as computer scientists and statisticians. In order to guarantee practical relevance and user friendliness, extension specialists and selected professional farmers should be involved in the model building process as early as possible. Judicious use of such models is possible only if the user has a sound understanding of model structure, scope and limitations. Within the local agricultural context, crop modelling is a new discipline and having a tremendous potential in times to come.

REFERENCE

Balkovic, J., Velde, M., Schmid, E., Skalsky, R., Khabarov, N., Obersteiner, M., Sturmer, B. and Xiong, W. (2013) Pan-European crop modelling with EPIC: Implementation, up-scaling and regional crop yield validation. Agricultural Systems 120, 61–75

Barrett, J.R., and Nearing, M.A. (1998) Humanization of decision support using information from simulations, In: R.M. Peart & R.B. Curry (eds.), Agricultural Systems Modeling and Simulation. Marcel Dekker, Inc., pp. 1-17, New York.

Basso, B., Ritchie, J.T., Pierce, F.J., Braga, R.P. and Jones, J.W. (2001) Spatial validation of crop models for precision agriculture. Agricultural Systems, 97-112.

Berge, H.F.M., Aggarwal, P.K. and Kropyy. M.J. (eds.) (1996) Systems modelling in rice Research. Elsevier. Pub., Netherlands.

Bravin, M.N., Michaud, A.M., Larabi, B. and Hinsinger, P. (2010) RHIZOtest: A plant-based biotest to account for rhizosphere processes when assessing copper bioavailability. Environmental Pollution 158, 3330-3337.

Carberry, P.S., Hochman, Z. and McCown, R.L. (2002) The FARMSCAPE approach to decision support: Farmers, Advisers, Researchers Monitoring, Simulation, Communication, And Performance Evaluation. Agricultural Systems, 74, 179-220.

De Leo, G., Del Furia, L. and Gatto, M. (1993) The interaction between soil acidity and forest dynamics: a simple model exhibiting catastrofic behavior. Theor. Popul. Biol. 43 (11), 31–51.

Dobermann, A., Ferguson, R.B., Hergert, G.W., Shapiro, C.A., Tarkalson, D., Walters, D.T. and Wortmann, C.S. (2006) Nitrogen response in high-yielding corn systems of Nebraska. In: Schlegel, A.J. (Ed.), Proceedings of the Great Plains Soil Fertility Conference. Denver, CO, March 7–8, 2006. Kansas State University, Manhattan, KS, pp. 50–59.

Friesland, H. and Orlandini, S. (2011) Simulation models of plant pests and diseases. In: COST Action 718 – Meteorological Applications for Agriculture Final report, European Commission, pp 1-19.

Guala, S.D., Vega, F.A. and Covelo, E.F. (2009) Modification of a soil–vegetation nonlinear interaction model with acid deposition for simplified experimental applicability. Ecol. Model. 220 (18), 2137–2141.

Guala, S.D., Vega, F.A. and Covelo, E.F. (2010) The dynamics of heavy metals in plant–soil interactions. Ecological Modelling 221, 1148–1152.

Horie, T., Yajima, M. and Nakagawa, H. (1992) Yield forecasting. 211-236. In: Teng P.S., Penning de Vries FWT Systems approaches for agricultural development. Elsevier Applied Sciences, London. pp. 309.

Jones, J.W., Hoogenboom, G. Boote, K.J., Batchelor, W.D., Hunt, L.A., Wilkens, P.W., Singh, U., Gijsman, A.J. and Ritchie, J.T. (2003) The DSSAT cropping system model. *Europ. J. Agronomy* 18, 235-265.

Kirk, G.J.D., Santos, E.E. and Santos, M.B. (1999b) Phosphate solubilization by organic anion excretion from rice growing in aerobic soil: rates of excretion and decomposition, effects on rhizosphere pH and effects on phosphate availability and uptake. New Phytologist 142, 185-200.

Kirk, G.J.D., Santos, E.E., Findenegg, G.R. (1999a) Phosphate solubilization by organic anion excretion from rice (*Oryza sativa L.*) growing in aerobic soil. *Plant Soil* 211, 11-18.

Leitner, D., Schnepf, A., Klepsch, S. and Roose, T. (2010) Comparison of nutrient uptake between three dimensional simulation and an averaged root system model. Plant Biosystems - An International Journal Dealing with all Aspects of Plant Biology: Official Journal of the Societa Botanica Italiana, 144(2), 443-447.

Lide, D.R. (2003) CRC Handbook of Chemistry and Physics. CRC Press.

Matthews, R.B., Kropff, M.J., Bachelet, D., Van Laar, H.H. (1995) Modeling the Impact of Climate Change on Rice Production in Asia. CABI, Los Banos, Philippines.

McCown, R.L. (2002) Changing systems for supporting farmer's decisions: problems, paradigms, and prospects. Agricultural Systems 74, 179–220.

McPhee, M.J. (2009) Mathematical modelling in agricultural systems: A case study of modelling fat deposition in beef cattle for research and industry. In: 18th World IMACS / MODSIM Congress, Cairns, Australia 13-17 July 2009, pp 59-71.

Mitchell, P.L. (1997) Misuse of regression for empirical validation of models, *Agricultural Systems*, 54(3), 313-326.

Mitchell, P.L., and Sheehy, J.E. (1997) Comparison of predictions and observations to assess model performance: a method of empirical validation, In: M.J. Kropff, P.S. Teng, P.K. aggarwal, J. Bouma, B.A.M. Bouman, J. J.W. & H.H. Van Laar (eds.), Applications of systems approaches at the field level. Kluwer Academic Publishers, pp. 437-451, Great Britain.

Olesen, T., Moldrup, P., Yamaguchi, T. and Rolston, D.E. (2001) Constant slope impedance factor model for predicting the solute diffusion coefficient in unsaturated soil. *Soil Science* 166, 89-96.

Rakshit, A.,D. Sen, N. C. Sarkar, and R. K. Maity(2008) Evaluating different model based decision support systems(DSS) in Agriculture. International Journal of Agriculture Environment & Biotechnology 1(3):64-67.

Richards, L.A. (1931) Capillary conduction of fluid through porous mediums. Physics 1, 318–333.

Roose, T., Fowler, A.C. and Darrah, P.R. (2001) A mathematical model of plant nutrient uptake. J Math Biol 42(4), 347–360.

Setiyono, T.D., Waltersa, D.T., Cassmana, K.G., Witt, C. and Dobermann A. (2010) Estimating maize nutrient uptake requirements. Field Crops Research 118,158–168.

Simunek, J. and Hopmans, J.W. (2009) Modelling compensated root water and nutrient uptake ecological modelling 220, 505–521.

Simunek, J., van Genuchten, M.Th., Sejna, M. (2006) The HYDRUS Software Package for Simulating Two- and Three-dimensional Movement of Water, Heat, and Multiple Solutes in Variably-saturated Media, Technical Manual, Version 1.0, PC Progress, Prague, Czech Republic, p. 241.

Singh, A.K., Goyal, V., Mishra, A.K. and Parihar, S.S. (2013) Validation of CropSyst simulation model for direct seeded rice–wheat cropping system. Current Science, 104(10), 1324-1331.

Spedding, C.R.W (1975) The Biology of Agricultural Systems. Chapter 5, The Principles of Animal Production. Academic Press, London. pp. 101-147.

Tedeschi, L.O., Fox, D.G., Baker, M.J. and Kirschten, D.P. (2006) Identifying differences in feed efficiency among group-fed cattle, Journal of Animal Science, 84(3), 767-776.

Walczak, R.T., Moreno, F., Slawinski, C., Fernandez, E. and Arrue, J.L. (2006) Modeling of soil water retention curve using soil solid phase parameters. Journal of Hydrology 329.

Williams, M. and Yanai, R.D. (1996) Multi-dimensional sensitivity analysis and ecological implication of a nutrient uptake model. Plant Soil 180, 311-324.

Xu, Q. (1995) A model for simulating hybrid rice seed production. p. 97-108. In: P.K. Aggarwal, R.B. Matthews, M.J. Kropff, H.H. van Laar (eds). Applications of systems approach in plant breeding. SARP Research Proceedings, AB-DLO, Wageningen and IRRI, Philippines. pp. 144.

Zhou, M. and Li, Y. (2001) Phosphorus-sorption characteristics of calcareous soils and limestone from the Southern Everglades and adjacent farmlands. Soil Science Society of America Journal 65, 1404-1412.

Zygalakis, K.C., Kirk, G.J.D., Jones, D.L., Wissuwa, M. and Roose, T. (2011) A dual porosity model of nutrient uptake by root hairs. New Phytologist 192, 676–688.

❑❑❑

CHAPTER - 35

Computational Economics: Advances and Application of IT Tools

Anil Datt Upadhyay
Assistant Professor
College of Fisheries, Lembucherra, Tripura-799210

INTRODUCTION

The role for economic theory is no longer simply to explain how the existing system works, but also to explore how the economic system can be changed to become more adaptive and resilient in the face of the challenges of the 21st century, and how it can be more directly designed to support human well-being, in the present and the future. Simultaneous changes are needed, in both the actual economy and also in theoretical approaches of economics. The economic theory that was accepted as standard in the non-communist world during the second half of the twentieth century erects serious impediments to meeting the challenges of the twenty-first century. In order to redirect economics to be more useful, and more truly reflect the world we now face, a good starting point is to go back to the goals that are embedded in economic thinking. Here it is useful to make the distinction between intermediate and final goals. Final goals are ends that are worth achieving in themselves, while intermediate goals are pursued because they are expected to contribute to the final goals. As final goals for any economy are *'well-being and equity in the present' and* second is *'productive capital for the future'*. Productive capital needed to maintain well-being also necessarily includes natural resources, as well as human health and education, and cohesive social systems. Increasing production and consumption are important intermediate goals for humankind in some times and places. Other obviously critical intermediate goals include climate mitigation, and promoting resilience and adaptation within both human society and ecological systems. Responding to global inequity as well as global climate change requires coordinated public policy to fundamentally redirect existing economic systems. In addition to a much greater emphasis on equity, economic theory that is appropriate to the needs of the twenty-first century will need to be more concerned with the meta-externalities of the economic system. The business sphere is currently creating meta-externalities of culture and politics that place great burdens on the core sphere, and that tie the hands of governments. This does not necessarily imply that the for-profit sphere is "bad" and the others "good"—rather that institutional changes must be made to bring the purposes and functions of all three spheres into better harmony. To address such a complex issues, economic theories and models that developed in the past should embedded with new advent in computational technologies. In venturing a vision of technological possibilities rather than simply projecting linear or exponential changes in performance, it is crucial to think not only of how technical improvements lead to the substitution of a new generation of tools for existing ones, but also of how entirely new uses, and indeed new needs, might emerge.

Neo Classical Vs Evolutionary Economics

The current frontiers of development economics are too many and in recent years, the subject has made excellent use of economic theory, econometric methods, sociology, anthropology, political science and demography and has burgeoned into one of the liveliest areas of research in all the social sciences.

Neo-classical and Evolutionary Economics - a Brief Comparison

Neo-Classical Theory	Evolutionary Theory
Use of physical metaphors	use of biological metaphors
Equilibrium as a central concept	emphasis on factors causingdisequilibrium
Static/comparative statics	dynamic
High degree of precision	less precise open for nonquantifiablefactors
Assumes perfect information	system operates underuncertainty
Time not an issue	time as important factor'history matters'
Entrepreneurship unimportant	entrepreneurship central factor
All economic activities are Equal' (potato chips, wood different Because innochipsand computer Chips)	economic activities are different because innovation 'focuses' at any point in time
Postulates 'the 'the representative Firm'	representative firm' does not exist
The market as price setter	the market also asselection mechanism among firms
Technology as a free good'manna From heaven'	technology as an important factor in wealth creationand distribution
'The market is always right'/ Laissez-faire	opens for a more activeeconomic policy

Computational Economics

Research at the interface of economics and computation has flourished in the past twenty years, largely in response to the internet's emergence as the world's first large-scale computational artifact created not by a single entity, but by the strategic interactions of many. Economics studies systems governed by the conflicting interests of multiple parties, whereas computer science analyzes systems that operate under constraints on computational resources such as processing time, memory, and communication. Overlaying these two perspectives leads to a rich set of mathematical problems that encompass the design of markets under limitations on computation and communication, algorithms for identifying the equilibria of those markets, theorems bounding the inefficiency of said equilibria compared to a centrally regulated system, and the analysis of how all of these aspects of a system are influenced by the structure of the network of interactions among its participants. Recent research in the area has moved beyond analyzing equilibria to study the dynamics of the processes of learning and adaptation by which many interconnected algorithms may update their behavior in response to the observed behavior of other agents with whom they interact.

The scope of computational economics encompasses modeling of economic systems, whether agent-based, general equilibrium, macroeconomic, rational expectations, computational econometrics and statistics, computational finance, computational tools for the design of automated internet markets, programming tools specifically designed for computational economics, and pedagogical tools for the teaching of computational economics. Some of these areas are unique to computational economics, while others extend traditional areas of economics by solving problems that are difficult to study without the use of computers and associated numerical methods. It is rightly pointed out that computer technology presents economists with new tools, but also raises novel methodological issues (Kenneth *etal* 2005).

Agent-based computational economics: Agent-based computational economics (ACE) is the computational study of economic processes, including whole economies, as dynamic systems of interacting agents. As such, it is an economic adaptation of the complex adaptive systems paradigm. Agents can represent social, biological, and/or physical entities. The theoretical assumption of mathematical optimization by agents in equilibrium is replaced by the less restrictive postulate of agents with bounded rationality *adapting* to market forces, including game-theoretical contexts. Starting from initial conditions determined by the modeler, an ACE model develops forward through time driven solely by agent interactions. Starting from specified initial conditions, the computational economic system is modeled as evolving over time as its constituent agents repeatedly interact with each other. In these respects, ACE has been characterized as a bottom-up culture-dish approach to the study of the economy. In contrast to other standard modeling methods, ACE events are driven solely by initial conditions, whether or not equilibria exist or computationally tractable. ACE modeling, however, includes agent adaptation, autonomy, and learning. It has a similarity to, and overlap with, game theory as an agent-based method for modeling social interactions. Other dimensions of the approach include such standard economic subjects as competition and collaboration, market structure and industrial organization, transaction costs, welfare economics and mechanism design, information and uncertainty, and macroeconomics. Computational economics uses computer-based economic modeling for solution of analytically and statistically formulated economic problems.

Computational Modeling in Economics

In economics, a model is a theoretical construct representing economic processes by a set of variables and a set of logical and/or quantitative relationships between them. Frequently, economic models posit structural parameters. A model may have various parameters and those parameters may change to create various properties. Methodological uses of models include investigation, theorizing, fitting theories to the world. In general terms, economic models have two functions: first as a simplification of and abstraction from observed data, and second as a means of selection of data based on a paradigm of econometric study.

Econometric models are statistical models used in econometrics. An econometric model specifies the statistical relationship that is believed to hold between the various economic quantities pertaining to a particular economic phenomenon under study. An econometric model can be derived from a deterministic economic model by allowing for uncertainty, or from an economic model which itself is stochastic. However, it is also possible to use econometric models that are not tied to any specific economic theory. A simple example of an econometric model is one that assumes that monthly spending by consumers is linearly dependent on consumers' income in the previous month. Then the model will consist of the equation

$$C_t = a + bY_{t-1} + e_t,$$

where C_t is consumer spending in month t, Y_{t-1} is income during the previous month, and e_t is an error term measuring the extent to which the model cannot fully explain consumption.

Then one objective of the econometrician is to obtain estimates of the parameters a and b; these estimated parameter values, when used in the model's equation, enable predictions for future values of consumption to be made contingent on the prior month's income. The common econometric models are Linear regression model, Generalized linear models, Probit model, Logit model, Tobit model, ARIMA, Vector Autoregression, Cointegration, Hazard etc.

Economic Models : According to whether all the model variables are deterministic, economic models can be classified as stochastic or non-stochastic models; according to whether all the variables are quantitative, economic models are classified as discrete or continuous choice model; according to the model's intended purpose/function, it can be classified as quantitative or qualitative; according to the model's ambit, it can be classified as a general equilibrium model, a partial equilibrium model, or even a non-equilibrium model; according to the economic agent's characteristics, models can be classified as rational agent models, representative agent models etc.

1. **Stochastic models**: These models are formulated using stochastic processes. Most of econometrics is based on statistics to formulate and test hypotheses about these processes or estimate parameters for them. A widely used bargaining class of simple econometric models popularized by Tinbergen and later Wold arc autoregressive models, in which the stochastic process satisfies some relation between current and past values. Examples of autoregressive models are autoregressive moving average models(ARIMA), autoregressive conditional heteroskedasticity (ARCH) and Generalized Autoregressive Conditional Heteroskedasticity GARCH models.
2. **Non-stochastic models** : Non stochastic models may be purely qualitative, such models involved in some aspect economics is undoubtedly of social choice theory or quantitative involving rationalization of financial variables. In some cases economic predictions in a coincidence of a model merely assert the direction of movement of economic variables, and so the functional relationships are used only stoical in a qualitative sense.
3. **Qualitative models** : Although almost all economic models involve some form of quantitative analysis, qualitative models are occasionally used. The qualitative model like scenario planning in which possible future numbered events is played out. Another example is non-numerical decision tree analysis. Qualitative models often suffer from lack of precision.

Computational Software in Economic Analysis

A. Stochastic Frontier Production and Cost Function Estimation: The level of technical efficiency of a particular production system (firm) is characterized by the relationship between observed production and some ideal or potential production (Greene 1993). Farrell's (1957) definition of technical efficiency led to the development of methods for estimating the relative technical efficiencies of firms. The common feature of these estimation techniques is that information is extracted from extreme observations from a body of data to determine the best practice production frontier (Lewin and Lovell 1990).

Stochastic estimations incorporate a measure of random error. This involves the estimation of a stochastic production frontier, where the output of a firm is a function of a set of inputs, inefficiency and random error. An often quoted disadvantage of the technique, however, is that they impose an explicit functional form and distribution assumption on the data. In contrast, the linear programming technique of data envelopment analysis (DEA) does not impose any assumptions about functional form, hence it is less prone to misspecification. Further, DEA is a non-parametric approach so does not take into account random error. Hence, it is not subsequently subject to the problems of assuming an underlying distribution about the error term. However, since DEA cannot take account of such statistical noise, the efficiency estimates may be biased if the production process is largely characterized by stochastic elements.

Economic, Allocative And Technical Efficiency: Technical efficiency is just one component of overall economic efficiency. However, in order to be economically efficient, a firm must first be technically efficient. Profit maximization requires a firm to produce the maximum output given the level of inputs employed (i.e. be technically efficient), use the right mix of inputs in light of the relative price of each input (i.e. be input allocative efficient) and produce the right mix of outputs given the set of prices (i.e. be output allocative efficient) (Kumbhaker and Lovell 2000).

FRONTIER 4.1

The most commonly used package for estimation of stochastic production frontiers in the literature is FRONTIER 4.1 (Coelli, 1996a). This incorporates the maximum likelihood estimation of the parameters. The estimation process consists on three main steps. At the first step OLS is applied to estimate the production function. This provides unbiased estimators for the b''s (except for the intercept term and the variance estimate). The OLS estimates are used as starting values to estimate the final maximum likelihood model. First, the value of the likelihood function is estimated for different values of g between 0 and 1 given the values for the b's derived in the OLS. Finally an interactive Davidon-

Fletcher-Powell algorithm calculates the final parameter estimates, using the values of the b″s from the OLS and the value of g from the intermediate step as starting values. FRONTIER 4.1 has been created specifically for the estimation of production frontiers. Advantages of FRONTIER 4.1 are-

1. It is a single purpose package specifically designed for the estimation of stochastic production frontiers.
2. An advantage of the former model (FRONTIER) is that estimates of efficiency are produced as a direct output from the package.
3. The user is able to specify the distributional assumptions for the estimation of the inefficiency term in a program control file.
4. FRONTIER is able to accommodate a wider range of assumptions about the error distribution term than LIMDEP.
5. Neither package can include gamma distributions. Only FRONTIER is able to estimate an inefficiency model as a one-step process.

LIMDEP 10

LIMDEP 10 is an integrated statistical package for estimation and analysis of linear and nonlinear models, with cross section, time series and panel data. This software has long been a leader in the field of econometric and statistical analysis and has provided many recent innovations including cutting edge techniques in panel data analysis, frontier and efficiency estimation and discrete choice modeling. The collection of techniques and procedures for analyzing panel data is without parallel in any other statistical software. The main feature of the LIMDEP 10 package is a suite of more than 100 built-in estimators for all forms of the linear regression model, and stochastic frontier, discrete choice and limited dependent variable models, including models for binary, censored, truncated, survival, count, discrete and continuous variables and a variety of sample selection models. In addition to the estimation programs, LIMDEP provides:

i. Data management, including input from all standard sources (such as Excel), all manner of transformations and sample controls
ii. Built-in estimation programs plus a programming language, matrix algebra package and scientific calculator that allow you to write your own estimators, test statistics and simulation and analysis programs
iii. Model specification and post estimation tools for simulation, hypothesis testing and partial effects for all models
iv. Random number, vector and matrix capabilities for bootstrapping, Gibbs sampling and Monte Carlo simulation

v. A wide range of graphical and numeric descriptive statistics capabilities

vi. Optimization tools that allow you to construct your own likelihood, GMM, or maximum simulated likelihood estimators

vii. Analysis tools including graphics, numerical analysis and post estimation tools for specification and hypothesis testing

viii. An extensive PDF documentation set, with over 2,500 pages, containing full reference guides for the programs, background econometrics, and sample applications

Data Envelop Analysis (DEA)

Building on the ideas of Farrell (1957), the seminal work "Measuring the efficiency of decision making units" by Charnes, Cooper & Rhodes (1978) applies linear programming to estimate an empirical production technology frontier for the first time. In Germany, the procedure was used earlier to estimate the marginal productivity of R&D and other factors of production (Brockhoff 1970). Other than comparing efficiency across DMUs within an organization, DEA has also been used to compare efficiency across firms. There are several types of DEA with the most basic being CCR based on Charnes, Cooper & Rhodes, however there are also DEA which address varying returns to scale, either CRS (constant returns to scale) or VRS (variable). The main developments of DEA in the 1970s and 1980s are documented by Seiford & Thrall (1990).

DEA has been used for both production and cost data. Utilizing the selected variables, such as unit cost and output, DEA software searches for the points with the lowest unit cost for any given output, connecting those points to form the efficiency frontier. Any firm not on the frontier is considered inefficient. A numerical coefficient is given to each firm, defining its relative efficiency. Different variables that could be used to establish the efficiency frontier are: number of employees, service quality, environmental safety, and fuel consumption.

Some of the advantages of DEA are:

i. No need to explicitly specify a mathematical form for the production function

ii. Proven to be useful in uncovering relationships that remain hidden for other methodologies

iii. Capable of handling multiple inputs and outputs

iv. Capable of being used with any input-output measurement

v. The sources of inefficiency can be analysed and quantified for every evaluated unit

Some of the disadvantages of DEA are:

i. The results are sensitive to the selection of inputs and outputs (Berg 2010).

ii. You cannot test for the best specification (Berg 2010).

iii. The number of efficient firms on the frontier tends to increase with the number of inputs and output variables (Berg 2010).

KonSi Data Envelopment Analysis : KonSi Data Envelopment Analysis for Benchmarking Software provides performance measurement using Data Envelopment Analysis (DEA). It is widely adopted in different business-unit based enterprises. KonSi Data Envelopment Analysis for Benchmarking is easy to apply to various practical tasks, when the analyst has to evaluate the efficiency of many units under benchmarking research. KonSi Data Envelopment Analysis for Benchmarking is applied to marketing research of shops, retail chains, banks, insurance companies etc. It is used as analytical tool for benchmarking and competitive intelligence. KonSi Data Envelopment Analysis for Benchmarking will allow you to use following methods and terms of Data Envelopment Analysis DEA models, Controlled Uncontrolled inputs/outputs, Input minimization Output maximization models, reference contribution, you can get various reports on results of performance measurement as graphics, MS Word documents and MS Excel spreadsheets.

Economic Models for Forecasts: The forecast of evolution of economic phenomena represent on the most the final objective of econometrics. It represent a real attempt of validity elaborate model. Unlike the forecasts based on the study of temporal series which have an recognizable inertial character the forecasts generated by econometric model with simultaneous equations are after to contour the future of ones of important economic variables toward the direct and indirect influences bring the bear on their about exogenous variables. For the relief of the calculus who the realization of the forecasts based on the econometric models its suppose is indicate the use of the specialized informatics programs.

EViews Econometric Modeling Software: EViews which is applied because it reduces significant the time who is destined of the econometric analysis and it assure a high accuracy of calculus and of the interpretation of results. EViews is user-friendly interface that quickly and efficiently develop statistical and forecasting models and simulations. As a widely used Windows-based econometric software program, EViews 8 offers more of the power and ease-of-use. EViews allows to:

i. Easily find, move, and manage data from many sources

ii. Efficiently perform econometric and statistical analysis, generate forecasts and perform model simulations.

iii. Quickly produce high quality graphs and tables for reports and publications, and inclusion in other applications.

Time Series Statistics and Tools in EViews: It explore the time series properties of data with tools ranging from simple autocorrelation plots to frequency filters, from Q-statistics to unit root tests. EViews provides autocorrelation and partial autocorrelation functions, Q-statistics, and cross-correlation functions, as well as unit root tests (ADF, Phillips-Perron, KPSS, DFGLS, ERS, or Ng-Perron for single time series and Levin-Lin-Chu, Breitung, Im-Pesaran-Shin, Fisher, or Hadri for panel data), cointegration tests (Johansen for with MacKinnon-Haug-Michelis critical values and p-values ordinary data, and Pedroni, Kao, or Fisher for panel data), causality, and independence tests.

Panel and Pooled Data Statistics and Tools in EViews: EViews facilitate working with both panel or pooled/time series-cross section data. Define panel structures with virtually no limit on the number of cross-sections or groups, or on the number of periods or observations in a group. Dated or undated, balanced or unbalanced, and regular or irregular frequency panel data sets are all handled naturally within the EViews framework.

Single Equation Estimation: EViews allows you to choose from a full set of basic single equation estimators including: ordinary and nonlinear least squares (multiple regression), weighted least squares, two-stage least squares (instrumental variables), quantile regression (including least absolute deviations estimation), and stepwise linear regression. Weighted estimation is available for all of these techniques. Specifications may include polynomial lag structures on any number of independent variables.

Generalized Method of Moments (GMM): EViews supports GMM estimation for both cross-section and time series data (single and multiple equation).

ARCH: If the variance of series fluctuates over time, EViews can estimate the path of the variance using a wide variety of Autoregressive Conditional Heteroskedasticity (ARCH) models. EViews handles GARCH(p,q), EGARCH(p,q), TARCH(p,q), PARCH(p,q), and Component GARCH specifications and provides maximum likelihood estimation for errors following a normal, Student's t or Generalized Error Distribution. The mean equation of ARCH models may include ARCH and ARMA terms, and both the mean and variance equations allow for exogenous variables.

System Estimation: EViews also offers powerful tools for analyzing systems of equations.

User-Specified Maximum Likelihood: For custom analysis, EViews' easy-to-use likelihood object permits estimation of user-specified maximum likelihood models. You simply provide standard EViews expressions to describe the log likelihood contributions for each observation in your sample, set coefficient starting values, and EViews will do the rest.

CONCLUSIONS

In the past century, people have looked to the physical and biological sciences to solve important problems. The social sciences offer equal promise for improving human welfare; our lives can be greatly improved through a deeper understanding of individual and collective behavior. But to realize this promise, the social sciences, like the natural sciences, need to match their institutional structures to today's intellectual challenges.

The Agent-Based Approach is one of the most productive and promising areas of current research at the frontiers of economic research. A major thrust of many agent-based models has been to study learning dynamics. This is an area where the agent-based complexity approach has intersected with the experimental behavioral approach, with experiments increasingly involving subjects interacting with computerized systems in repeated games or market interactions in which learning takes place.

ACKNOWLEDGEMENT

The encouragement, suggestions and other supports that I received by the Dean, College of Fisheries Central Agricultural University, Lembucherra, Agartala is duly acknowledged.

REFERENCES

Alvin E. Roth(2002)The Economist As Engineer: Game Theory, Experimentation, And Computation as Tools For Design Economics1Econometrica, Vol. 70, No. 4 (July, 2002), 1341–1378

Berg, S. (2010) Water Utility Benchmarking: Measurement, Methodology, and Performance Incentives. London, UK: IWA Publishing, 2010. 172 p. ISBN: 9781843392729.

Brockhoff, K. (1970). "On the Quatification of the Marginal Productivity of Industrial Research by Estimating a Production Function for a Single Firm", German Economic Review vol. 8, pp. 202–229.

C.G. Renfro (2004). The Early Development of Econometric Modeling Languages, in C.G. Renfro (ed) Computational Econometrics: Its Impact on the Development of Quantitative Economics, Amsterdam: IOS Press.

C.G. Renfro (2009). The Practice of Econometric Theory. An Examination of the Characteristics of Econometric ComputationHeidelburg, London, and New York: Springer. Pp 311.

Charnes, A., W. Cooper, & E., Rhodes (1978) "Measuring the efficiency of decision-making units," European Journal of Operational Research vol. 2, pp. 429–444.

Coelli, T. (1996a). A guide to FRONTIER version 4.1: a computer program for frontier production function estimation. CEPA Working Paper 96/07, Department of Econometrics, University of New England, Armidale, Australia.

Guido M. Imbens Jeffrey M. Wooldridge (2008) Recent Developments In The Econometrics Of Program Evaluation

Greene, W. H. (1993). "Frontier Production Functions", EC-93-20. Stern School of Business, New York University.

Greene, W. (1995). LIMDEP (Version 7): User's Manual and Reference Guide, Econometric Software Inc., New York.

Jean-Louis Brillet (2012) Structural Econometric Modeling: Methodology And Tools With Applications Under EVIEWS. Pp 493.

Kenneth L. Judd(2005)Computationally Intensive Analyses in Economics. In The Handbook of Computational Economics, vol. II, edited by K. L. Judd and L. Tesfatsion. Hoover Institution, 434 Galvez Mall, Stanford, CA, 94305. Pp 1-13.

Kevin Sheppard (2013)Introduction to Python for Econometrics, Statistics and Data Analysis. University of Oxford. Pp 351.

Kumbhaker, S. C. and Lovell C. A. K. (2000). Stochastic Frontier Analysis. Cambridge: Cambridge University Press.

Leigh Tesfatsion(2005)Agent-Based Computational Economics: A Constructive Approach To Economic Theory. A report of Economics Department, Iowa State University, Ames, IA 50011-1070.pp 50.

Lewin, A. Y. and C. A. K. Lovell (1990). Editors Introduction, Journal of Econometrics, 46, 3-5.

Ramanathan, R. (2003) An Introduction to Data Envelopment Analysis: A tool for Performance Measurement, Sage Publishing.

Raymond J. G. M. Florax And Arno J. Van Der Vlist (2003)Spatial Econometric Data Analysis: Moving Beyond Traditional Models. International regional Science review 26, 3: 223–243 (July 2003)

Seiford, L.M., & R.M. Thrall (1990) "Recent Developments in DEA: The Mathematical Programming Approach to Frontier Analysis," Journal of Econometrics vol. 46: pp. 7–38.

Thomas Sargent and John Stachurski(2013) Quantitative Conomics. http://quant-econ.net. Pp 385.

Tofallis, C. (2001) "Combining two approaches to efficiency assessment." Journal of the Operational Research Society 52 (11), 1225–1231.

❑❑❑

CHAPTER - 36

Application of Testing Metrics Model in Modern Software Testing Project Management

Arnab Roy
CTAL-TTA, Test Lead, Wipro Limited
1620 Worcester Rd, Apt #B346,
Framingham, MA 01702, USA
Email: aroy83in@gmail.com

In today's technology driven 21st century, software has become an integral part of our day to day work. Starting from checking day's schedule in tablet after waking up in the morning till setting up alarm before going to bed at night, we are using numerous software applications in a day without even realizing the efforts spent to make those applications work perfectly every time we use it. If we look deeply, each software application in computer or in any electronic/computer controlled device go through multiple rigorous cycles of testing to ensure that it is working as intended after it was built by developers and before it was launched in market for public use. In software industry, this process is termed as software quality assurance (QA) or software testing which is being considered as one of the most flourishing verticals of IT software services sectors in 21st century.

Software testing is one of the most important phases of software development life cycle and it consumes anything between 10% to 45% of project budget depending on the type of the software and methodology followed in the development and testing life cycle. There are different types testing e.g. unit testing, integration testing, system testing, user acceptance testing, alpha, beta testing which are exercised during the testing phase and QA team needs to provide the sign off before any product is released and implemented in production or in consumer market. With the ever increasing complexity of today's software products along with the competitive market due to easy availability of multiple product options/vendors, the importance and awareness of software quality assurance has increased over years. Consequently, various software testing methodologies have been evolved in last two decades in order to perform testing in more structured and controlled manner. In addition, there is a continuous urge for improving the operational efficiency of the testing process in the organizations in order to produce better quality software at less cost.

One of the most effective ways to monitor the software testing process is the usage of testing metrics. Metrics are defined as "standards of measurement" and have long been used in the IT industry to indicate a method of gauging the effectiveness and efficiency of a particular activity within a project. Although test metrics are gathered during the test effort, they can provide measurements of different activities performed throughout a project.Analysis of the defined metrics helps to identify the areas of improvement and the actions to be taken to mitigate them. Usage of testing metrics is not limited to any single cycle of the software testing; rather it is a continuous process and helps teams to improve the overall quality of the software product.

This article illustrates some of the most effective and popular testing metrics generally used in the modern testing organizations which can be adopted to instill a culture of continuous improvement in overall software testing life cycle.

WHAT IS SOFTWARE QUALITY?

The literal meaning of quality signifies that it can be discussed, felt or judged but it is not something which can be measured or quantified. Another popular notion is to link quality with something which is expensive, well built or luxurious. In short, quality is not a single idea, but rather a multidimensional concept. There is always a level of abstraction when we define quality as someone may refer to in a broader sense and someone may be referring it in details. In software testing, the term 'quality' is quite different from its literal meaning. Software quality is a set of measureable attributes against some predefined parameters. In software, the simplest and most understandable way of sensing product quality is measured as the lack of "bugs" in the system. It also ensures that the software is working as per the requirement outlined by the business. The different dimensions of software quality are measured using different parameters like number of bugs found in system, customer satisfaction, reliability etc.

Importance of Metrics in Software Testing Cycles

It is often said that if something cannot be measured, it cannot be monitored or improved. If we are able to measure something through some attributes, we can visualize and comprehend it more. The more we comprehend; we are in a better position to improve it.

Metrics help us to visualize the progress, health and current status of the software testing project. As metrics are completely data driven, we can leverage the current data to compare with historic data to evaluate past performance, status and analyze future trends. Such analysis actually helps us to take crucial decisions of future project activities and make calculative risks based on the project trend. When properly used, metrics can figure out the problem areas of the testing project and can help us to incorporate pragmatic, result oriented process change initiatives.

Which Metrics to Use?

By now, we have a generic idea of the importance and benefits of using metrics in projects. It is also very important to choose the appropriate metrics based on the project type, condition and methodology. There is no 'absolute set of metrics' which are beneficial to all projects and to improve project health.To identify the correct metrics for a project and make sure that we get some value out of it, we should answer the following questions:

- What is the purpose behind using the metrics?
- What data items to be collected and how to analyze and report the data?
- What is the correlation between the data and conclusion?

Based on the answers received for the above mentioned questions, we can figure out the most useful metrics of the project. Based on the analysis of the metrics, appropriate actions can be taken and if necessary metrics can be refined and measurement goals can be adjusted for the better. For example, the project which is running on tight budget, should focus more on collecting data related to testing efforts in various phases of testing in order to optimize the cost of quality whereas the project which is running out of time, should concentrate more on testing progress and defects identified/fixed with respect to time in order to estimate whether the high quality product can be delivered within schedule.

How to Analyze Testing Metrics?

It is worth noting that most of the organizations invest considerable amount of resource and time to collect data and analyze the metrics. Sometimes dedicated resources are allocated for the task. A good amount of time is spent to gather the metrics data and to compile it and most importantly, equal or even more time should be utilized to analyze and monitor the metrics throughout the testing life cycle. In most cases, testing project teams refer and analyze multiple metrics to get an accurate picture of the project.Many of the market leading tools (both commercial and open-source) provide enhanced reporting features to generate canned reports and graphs from the data collected for the metrics identified for the project. These reports and graphs are quite helpful while publishing the testing status on regular basis and make the reports more readable to the stakeholders.

Categories of Testing Metrics

Testing metrics can be classified into three categories:product metrics, process metrics, and project metrics.Product metrics describe the characteristics of the product such as size, complexity, design attributes, performance and quality. Process metrics are generally used to measure, monitor and enhance processes of software development, testing and maintenance. Examples include the defect removal efficiency during development, defect arrival pattern during testing and defect fix response time for maintenance process. Project metrics illustrates different project characteristics and its execution. Examples include number of software engineers, staffing pattern over testing life cycle, cost, schedule and productivity. Some metrics can be classified under multiple categories. For example, in-process quality metrics of a project can be categorized under both project and process metrics.

Software quality metrics are the subset of the software metrics that focus on the quality characteristics of the process and product.Software quality metrics can be further classified under end-product quality metrics and in-process quality metrics. The testing team should realize the benefits of monitoring the correlation between different in-process metrics, project characteristics and product quality. Also, based on the findings, testing process and product quality can be improved significantly.

In this article, we will be discussing about the most useful and widely used metrics which falls under two sets of software quality metrics: process quality and product quality metrics. For each type of metrics, we will be discussing the parameters of the metrics, interpretation and usage in real world project scenarios mainly encountered in manual testing projects.

Test Progress S curve

One of the most important tasks of software testing management is to track the test progress during test execution window. Test progress S curve over time is a highly recommended metric for such tracking activity. This curve depicts the testing progress in terms of attempted test cases and successful test cases over time against test plan (amount of testing done per week). 'S' curve signifies data are cumulative over time and resemble an 'S' shape as a result of the period of intense test activity, causing a steep planned test ramp up.

The goal of the metric is to compare the test progress along with test plan during test execution and to identify any deviation of progress from the plan. Any slippage in schedule can be tracked immediately using this metric which enables the teams to take proactive measure at the earliest. This metric is very useful to gauge whether any resource ramp up is required in team in near future in order to complete testing on schedule. Adjoining *Figure 1* illustrates the test progress 'S' curve drawn in the middle of test execution cycle for a major release.

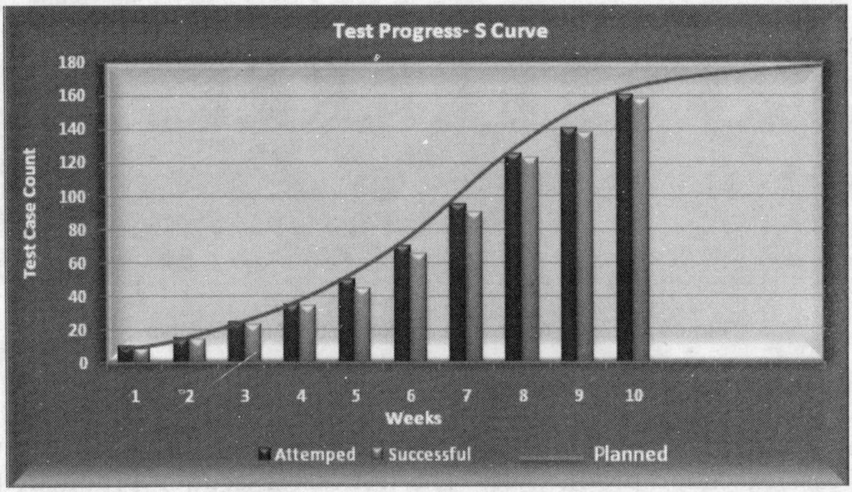

Figure 1: Test Progress- S Curve

Test Progress Curve for Test Scores- S curve

Test cases are written to cover different modules of the system and all modules might not have the same level of criticality or business importance. Hence, to plan and track execution in more precise way, test cases should be assigned with a point/score based on its priority/criticality. The test score assignment should be done during the test planning phase and should remain unchanged across next phases of testing.

To track test scores using the S curve, the teams need to express the test plan (amount of testing done every week) and track the week-by-week progress in terms of test points. This metric provides an accurate picture of the test progress against the test plan and any slippage in schedule beyond a predefined limit can be identified on weekly/monthly basis. Tracking test progress in a normalized way based on the weightage of the test cases proves to be very useful particularly for large testing efforts, where the number of test cases is in the hundreds of thousands. *Figure 2* illustrates the test progress 'S' curve using test score drawn in the middle of test execution cycle of a testing project.

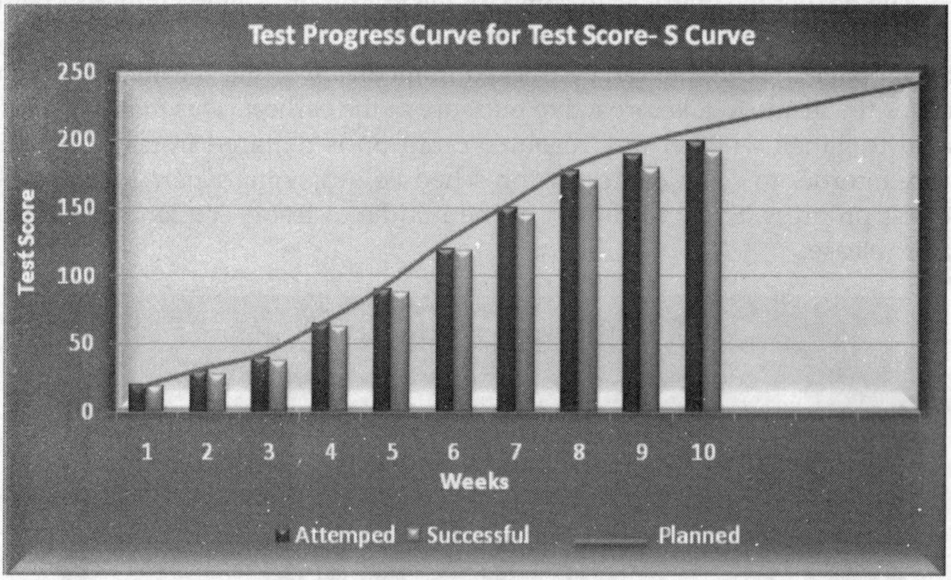

Figure 2 : Test Progress Curve for Test Scores- S curve

Test Case Execution Productivity Trend

An effective metric to measure the efficiency of team during test execution is test case execution productivity. The test case execution productivity is calculated as number of test case executed by single resource per unit amount of time where the unit may be per hour, day or week or even quarter, but genrally hour or day is used. This metric depicts the trend of execution productivity of the team over a period of time (month, quarter, release) when calcualted productivity figures are consolidated in a graph against time.

The purpose of this metric is to monitor the productivity of the team over months or quarters or releases and identify the problem areas in the team if the variance in productivity from the baselined limit is significantly high and to take remedial action to bring the productivity back on track. Based on the historcial data from past releases, an upper and lower limit of productivity can be set and corrective actions can be taken when the current productivity crosses any of the limits. There are other factors like complexity of the project, experience of the team, number of defects found/retested which might impact the execution productivity of the team and such factors should be considered properly while analyzing the execution productivity trend.*Figure 3* illustrates the test case execution productivity of the team over a period of four months.

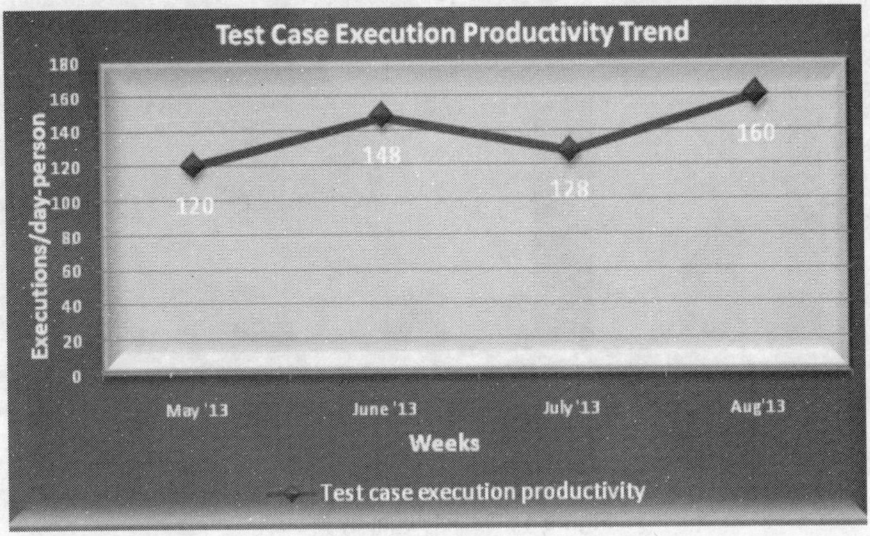

Figure 3 : Test Case Execution Productivity Trend

Defect count by State/Priority/Severity

A Software Test Defect is one of the most important QA artifacts of the testing process. Software testers routinely log defects as soon as they notice any deviations in the system's behavior. Every defect is reported with a set of attributes that give the information that lets a programmer or another tester reproduce it. Defect state, priority, severity, root cause are few of the important attributes of a defect. One of the most important aspect of analyzing the testing team's progress and effectiveness is to analyze the defects found by team during test execution window on a regular basis. The widely used defect based metrics for this purpose are defect count by state, priority and severity.

Once a defect is found and logged by testing team in defect management tool, it goes through different phases (submitted, open, Pending QA testing, Closed, Reopened, Deferred) before it is being closed or deferred for that release. Defect count by state metric (*Figure 4*) is usually prepared based on the defects found by team till that week of execution and provides a clear picture of the team's progress at that moment. Based on the analysis of this metric, leads can gauge the performance of the team. For example, if the count of rejected defects is high, then leads should evaluate the problem areas (example : ambiguous requirement, bad test data, unstable test environment) and should work to mitigate them. This metric serves as useful reference during defect triage/status meetings where members from different teams (developers, testers, business) participate and take joint decision on whether opened defects should be fixed or deferred or rejected.

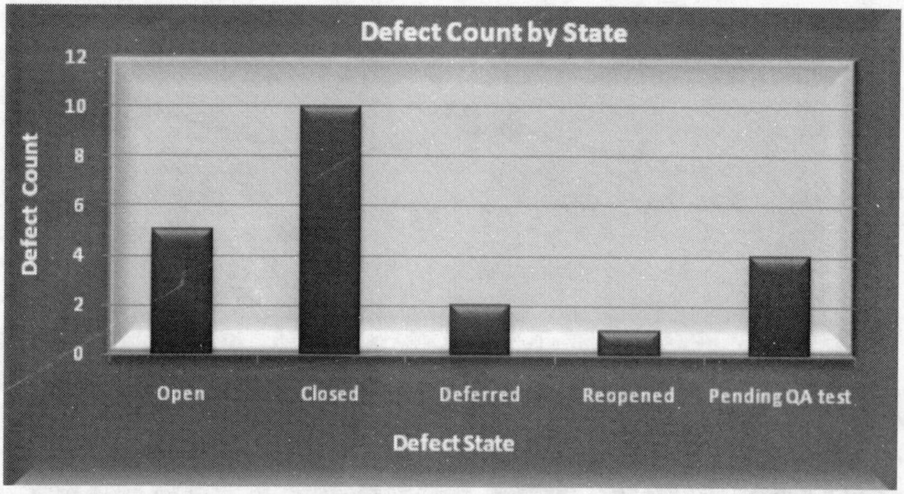

Figure 4 : Defect count by State

Defect Priority signifies how important it is to fix this defect. If the defect is impacting the system functionality completely or significantly, that defect is considered as show stopper and further testing cannot be started unless the defect is fixed. Hence the defect is tagged as high priority one.Defect count by priority metric (*Figure 5*) shows the defects which need immediate action from the developers and test leads should follow up with them to fix those defects. This metric also helps the management to decide on release readiness and to take 'go-no go' decision while analyzing exit criteria just before the production implementation of the project.

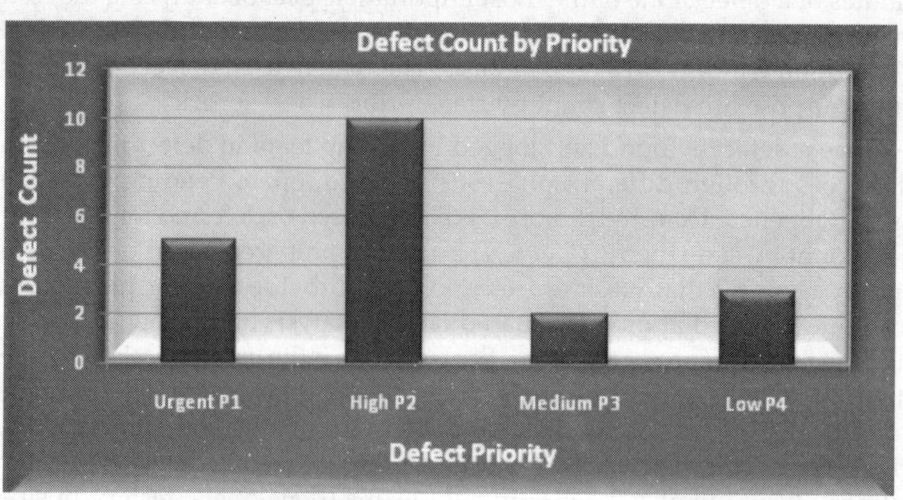

Figure 5 : Defect count by Priority

Defect Severity signifies the criticality of the defect. It signifies the impact the defect is having on the functioning of the system as a whole. The more catastrophic the failure and greater the impact to the test case, the greater is the severity of the defect. Defect count by severity metric shows the different levels of severity of the defects logged till date or for that week. It provides an accurate and quick insight to the product health and enables team to focus on areas which need more attention. This metric helps to prioritize the defects which need to be retested by testing team in upcoming weeks.

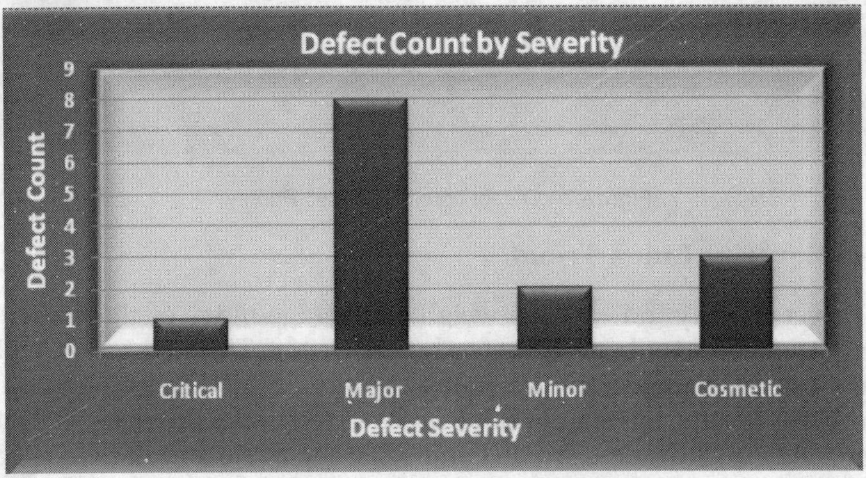

Figure 6 : Defect count by Severity

Defect Count : State vs. Priority

Defect count : State vs. Priority provides an idea of the current status of the defects in more detailed and sophisticated manner. Defects which are open with high priority are the most important ones and test lead should publish the list to the developers for their immediate action. Similarly, testing team should prioritize the retesting of defects which are in 'pending QA test' with higher priority.

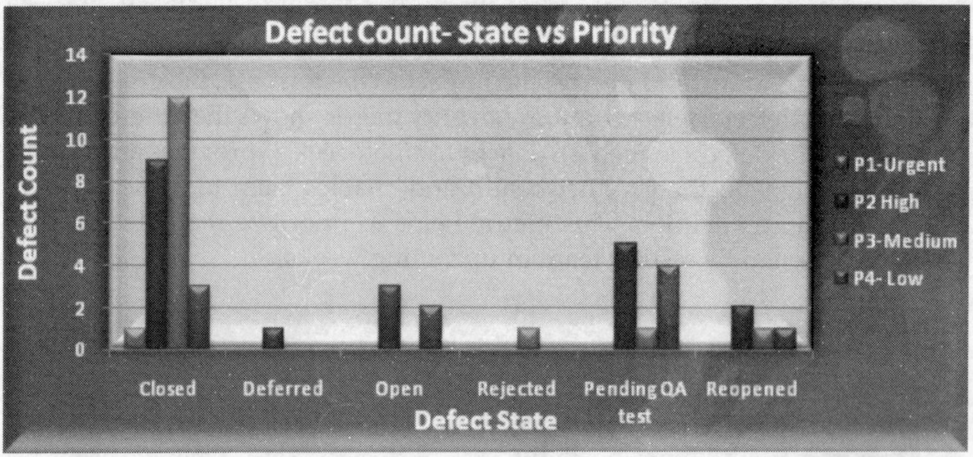

Figure 7 : Defect count : State vs Priority

Defect Severity Index Trend

Defect severity index is the weighted average index of the Severity of defects. A higher severity defect gets a higher weight. This index is a weighted average value to provide an idea of the severity of the defects found during testing cycle. Ideally, this should slope down as test cycles progress.This metric determine the quality of the product under test and at the time of release, based on which one can take decision for the release of the product. The formula to calculate Defect Severity Index is:

$$\textit{Defect Severity Index} = \left(\frac{\Sigma(\text{Severity Index} * \text{No of Valid Defects of that severity})}{\text{Total number of Valid Defects}} \right)$$

Defect severity Index can be further calculated separately for open defects or for all defects for the release using the same above mentioned formula.

Defect Severity Index Trendis derived by plotting the Defect Severity Index against the corresponding cycle/month/quarter. This metric provides an overall feel of the quality of the product across multiple test cycles or releases. In the graph illustrated below (*Figure 8*), the defect severity index is sloping down consistently from cycle 1 to cycle 10. This indicates an increasingly favorable trend. As the test cycle progresses, the severity index is sloping down which suggests increasing quality of the application as lesser number of critical and high severity defects are being reported during the final phases of testing.

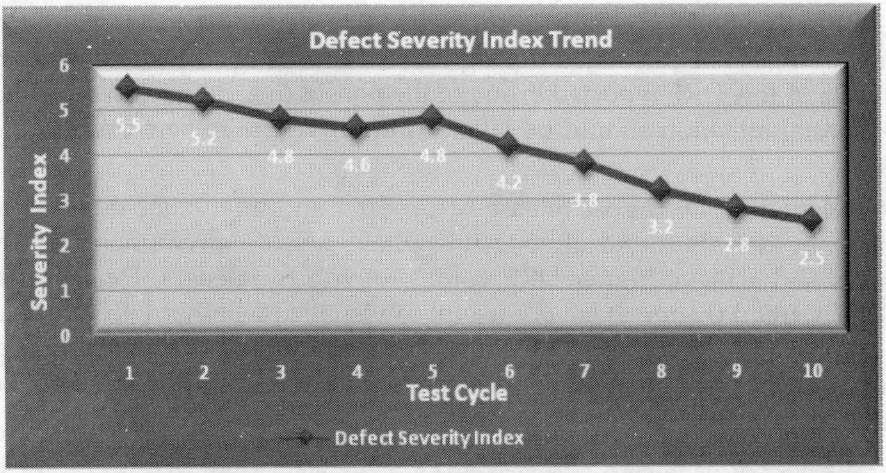

Figure 8 : Defect Severity Index Trend

Defect Removal Efficiency (DRE) trend

One of the most popular and effective metrics to measure the efficiency of the testing team is Defect removal efficiency or DRE. Apart from measuring how efficiently the team has identified and removed defects from the software under test during testing cycle, DRE also points out the defects missed out in testing phase which have been carried out to next phase. It also serves as indirect measure of quality of the software product.

DRE is calculated as percentage of defect detected by the team during testing phase against the total number of the defects detected across the complete life cycle of the product including the post-delivery to end users. A higher value of DRE confirms the higher product quality because it indicates the ability of the testing team to catch product defects prior to production implementation.

The formula for calculating DRE is as following:

$$DRE\ (\%) = \left(\frac{\text{DT}}{\text{DT} + \text{UD}} \times 100 \right) \%$$

DT=Number of valid defects found during testing

UD= Number of defects found by user after release of software in production.

The value of DRE ranges between 0-100. The value of DRE is also dependent on multiple factors like the complexity of the project, experience of the team, testing methodology adopted, quality of the requirement etc. In general, any DRE value more than 90% is considered to be good as per industry standard and historical records.

Even though DRE is a powerful metric for efficiency calculation for testing team, it can also be calculated during various phases of software development life cycle. A low DRE reported in any of the phases (e.g. design phase) indicates that special attention should be taken to improve the review process of that phase.

Calculating DRE post release of product and analyzing the root cause behind the defects found after testing phase help to strengthen the testing process and achieve higher DRE values for future releases. Defect removal efficiency trend (*Figure 9*) is very useful to visualize whether DRE of the team has improved over releases. A falling DRE trend indicates that team needs to analyze further and should take corrective measure to improve the efficiency of testing process.

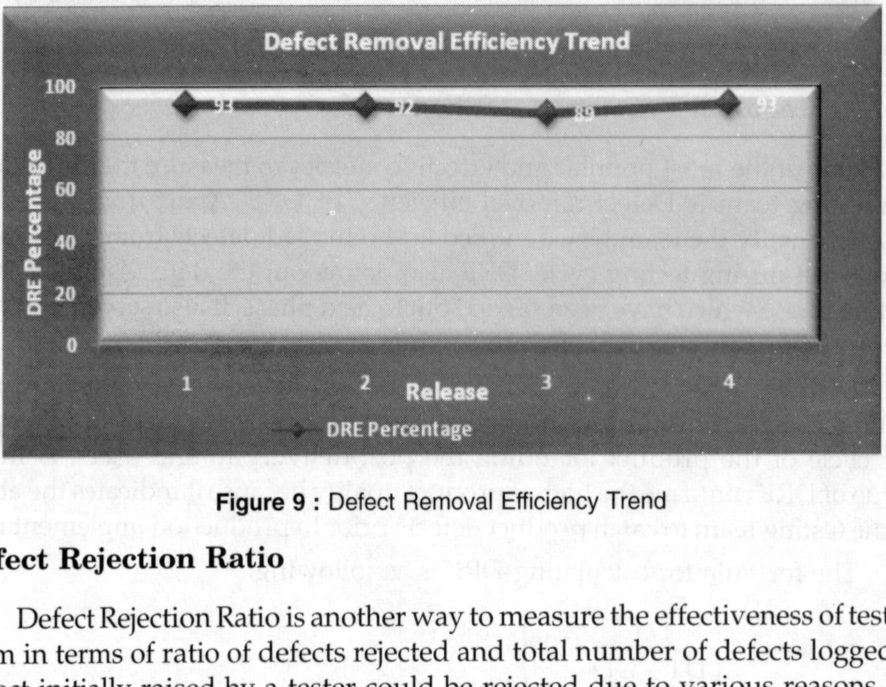

Figure 9 : Defect Removal Efficiency Trend

Defect Rejection Ratio

Defect Rejection Ratio is another way to measure the effectiveness of testing team in terms of ratio of defects rejected and total number of defects logged. A defect initially raised by a tester could be rejected due to various reasons like incomplete understanding of requirement, invalid test data setup, unstable test environment etc. This metric is also a measure of quality of work of the team. The less the count of rejected defects, the better is the quality of the test plan, scripts and data.Too many defects being rejected results in inefficiency due to time and effort spent on something that wasn't a problem. Defect rejection ratio can be calculated using the following formula:

$$\textit{Defect Rejection Ratio} = \frac{\text{\# of defects rejected as invalic}}{\text{Total \# of defects logged}}$$

If the defect rejection ratio is high in the team, there might be multiple factors which need attention and rework. For example, the requirement document might be ambiguous or the test data setup strategy might not be in line with test scenarios. In such cases, test lead/managers should organize brainstorming session with the team to find the root cause of the issue and devise an improvement plan.

There are few other factors which indirectly impact the defect rejection ratio of team. One of the most common factors is defect logging culture in team. Some teams log defect only after confirming the test data and scenario with development team which in fact reduces the chance of a defect being rejected. Some team log nearly log all observations as defects in fear of defect slippage which might lead to high defect rejection ratio. The other factor worth mentioning is stability of test environment. If a test environment undergoes changes which are not in control of testing team, there is a fair chance of a defect scenario becomes non producible at some later point of time causing the defect to be rejected.*Figure 10* displays the defect rejection ratio calculated in percentage plotted against several releases. It provides a high level overview of the trend of team's effectiveness and quality of work.

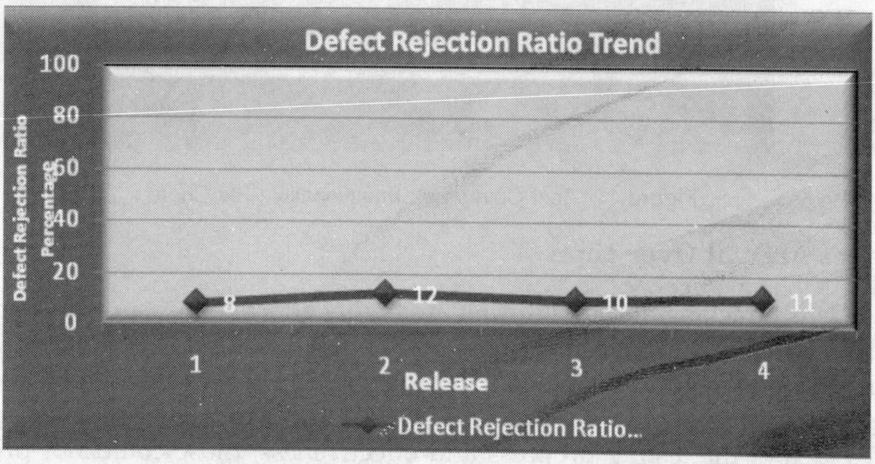

Figure 10 : Defect Rejection Ratio Trend

Test Coverage

Test coverage defines the extent to which the test suite (test case set) covers the software's functionality. Considering the increasing complexity and huge number of functionalities incorporated in modern software, it is not practical to develop test suite which covers all possible combination of inputs for all functionalities. Rather test managers and leads need to smartly strategize the test plan which ensures optimum coverage of the software components based on its business and functional importance. In such situation, test coverage metric provides the accurate picture of functionalities/components covered under test plan and the ones which are not covered. It also serves as an important measure of the effectiveness of testing process.

The metric measures the coverage as amount or percentage of functionalities/ components/ use cases actually planned and tested successfully against the total number of functionalities/ components/ use cases for that software product. This metric is an indication of completeness of testing. High level of test coverage is considered as one of the exit criteria for testing process in most of the organizations. *Figure 11* depicts the overall test coverage of a testing team with respect to complete functionalities.

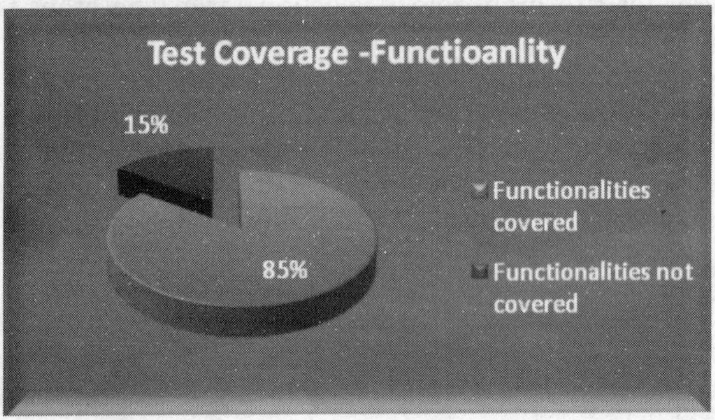

Figure 11 : Test Coverage : Functionality : Pie Chart

Defect Arrival Over time

Defect tracking and monitoring are highly effective measures to track the software quality during testing phase of software development life cycle. Defect arrival rate over time is one of the widely used metrics developed for this purpose. Even though other defect related metrics we have discussed earlier, gives idea of the testing progress and effectiveness, those could not provide the overall picture of the software quality while a release is nearing. Distinct pattern of defect arrival rates may imply different states of software quality at the end of testing cycle.

The defect arrival rate metric is compiled by plotting the defects detected during each week/month of testing cycle against time. While compiling the chart, it is always advisable to include data for comparable baseline (past release, similar project, and model curve) from the available historical records. In case of unavailability of historical records, an expected defect arrival pattern should be predicted for specific points of the project schedule (e.g. after 1st week of testing, midway, 2 weeks before end of testing etc.). It will help the managers to visualize the variation of actual defect arrival from the expected rate and will trigger the investigation to find the root cause.

A defect arrival pattern is considered to be positive which has higher arrivals earlier, an earlier peak (relative to the baseline), and a decline to a lower level earlier before the release date. A defect arrival pattern which has no or little variance from the baseline trend across the different phases of testing cycle is also considered as positive trend. The rear end of the defect arrival curve is very important as it is a direct indication of software quality before its release. Spikes at the end of the curve indicate high defect activity just before the product release which might disclose quality issues. Also, logging high severity defects at the end of the cycle might be a sign of lack of readiness of some of the components of the software which might hamper the release schedule.

Based on the analysis of the defect arrival pattern with the baseline, brainstorming sessions should be conducted to figure out the root cause of the deviation and necessary corrective actions should be initiated. Sometimes, good practice in the team can help in developing a healthy defect arrival trend. For example if the testers log the defect immediately after it was detected, it will contribute in building a positive defect arrival rate trend. *Figure 12* illustrates the defect arrival pattern curves of different releases of a software product.

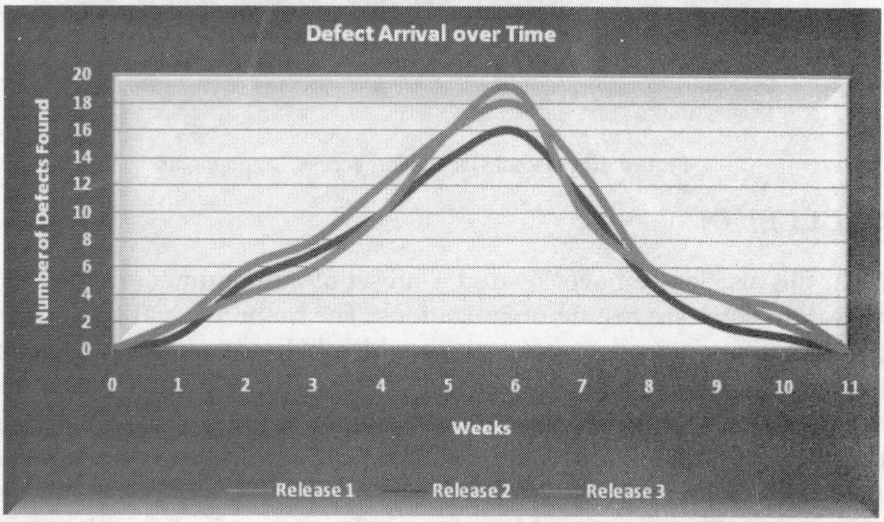

Figure 12 : Defect Arrival over Time

Defect Distribution Across Components

Today's complex software systems consist of several components and all the components do not have same functional complexity. Consequently, during testing phase, all the software components do not yield same number of defects. Defect distribution across components is a useful metric to analyze and compare how the defects are distributed across various components of the system. This metric also helps the test team to reveal the components which are more prone to failures and the functionalities which are more complicated to validate compared to what were anticipated during planning phase. Test teams should analyze these details and pay special attention to those failure prone components during future releases of the same software. This metric also gives an idea of how reliable and stablethe various components of the software will be after the release to end users.*Figure 13* illustrates the distribution of defects found in a test cycle across components of a software product calculated in percentage value.

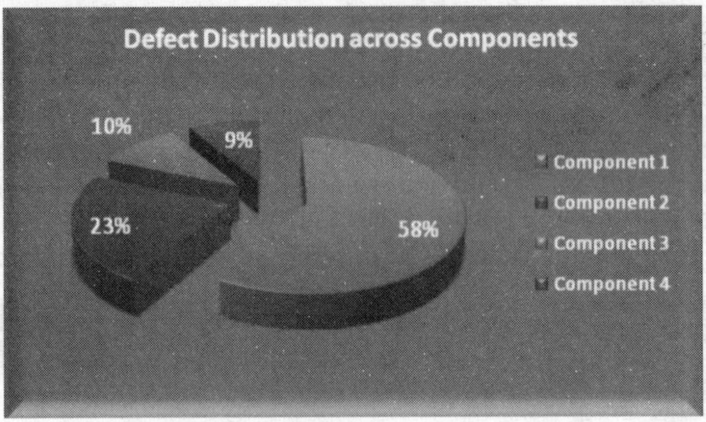

Figure 13 : Defect Distribution across Components

CONCLUSION

In this article, we have covered a subset of large number of metrics used across most software testing organizations. The main focus of this article was to discuss different varieties of metrics which help the teams to visualize the vital project attributes and the benefits of using those metrics effectively. As mentioned earlier, it is very important to choose the appropriate metrics based on the type and methodology being used for the project as there is no 'absolute set' of metrics that can be used in every project. For example, all metrics mentioned in this article, might not be viable for a particular software testing process.

Project managers and leads should educate their team members about the true intend behind deploying the metrics so that they can also contribute in choosing the right metrics and post deployment, analyze the metrics to determine the project health and quality of the software product under test. The effectiveness of the metrics culture can be utilized further by analyzing the trend of data over time as any single data instance might not project the actual pattern of the project parameter. It should be also noted that after deriving all the metrics and data points, teams should use them judiciously during analysis and decision making process as depending more on the metrics data and not paying attention to other project factors might lead to incorrect analysis.

Finally, we can conclude this article by saying that metrics are excellent tools for performance and quality improvement and help management and team to focus on improvement areas. And it is not only important to deploy the metrics model, it is equally important to continuously enhance the metrics model in order to maintain the ever rising trend of continuous improvement in an industry where being competitive and adaptiveare key to success.

REFERENCES

Kan S.H. (2002), Metrics and Models in Software Quality Engineering, Second Edition, Addison Wesley

Walia M,Realizing Efficiency and Effectiveness in Software Testing through a Comprehensive Metric Model:Retrieved from http://www.infosys.com/engineering-services/white-papers/Documents/comprehensive-metrics-model.pdf

Mindlance, Testing Metrics:Retrieved from http://www.mindlance.com/documents/test_management/testing_metrics.pdf

❑❑❑

CHAPTER - 37

Emergence of Corporate Governance in 21st Century: A Case Study of Air India

Ruchi Goyal[1] and Poonam Sethi[2]

[1]*Department of Commerce, D.D.U. College, University of Delhi. New Delhi-110015*

[2]*Department of Commerce, Hindu College, University of Delhi, Delhi-110007*

1. INTRODUCTION

Until the 1990s, the phrase Corporate Governance (CG) was relatively unknown but since then it has gained a huge importance when the corporate sector was surrounded with problems of unethical practicesand flagrant violations of rules and regulations in a number of countries. CG has received increased attention as multiple cases of risk of corporate failures both for public and private sectors. Multiple corporate failures worldwide, such as those of Maxwell, Enron, Global crossing, and Sunbeam forced the regulatory authorities to set up codes and standards on CG.The Indian market has also faced a number of scams since early nineties.Harshad Mehta Stock Scam in 1992 is one of the corporate frauds in the country which finally resulted in setting up of Kumar Mangalam Birla Committee in 1999. Based on their recommendations in 2000, Clause 49 on CG was inserted in the listing agreement of every stock exchange in India. The purpose was to promote and raise standards of CG of listed companies. CG has now become most common phrase in the business world of 21st century. It is important for financial health of the corporations and relationshipwith the public at large; may it be an individual or community especially after the collapse of Satyam Software Services Ltd. in 2008.It has been made mandatory for the Indian companies to comply with CG norms, to give reports and disclosures as per the listing agreement and various provisions of the Companies Act in their annual reports. The importance ofCG in the 21st century keeps on increasing as the economy is growing.

2. DEFINITION OF CORPORATE GOVERNANCE

Different persons in different situations and circumstances have defined CG in their own words in which the most well-known definition of CG has been given by Sir Adrian Cadbury in 1992, father of CG as "Corporate Governance is the system by which the companies are directed and controlled". In the words of James McRitchie, "Corporate Governance is most often viewed as both the structure and the relationships which determine corporate direction and performance. The board of directors is typically central to Corporate Governance. Its relationship to the other primary participants, typically shareholders and management, is critical. Additional participants include employees, customers, suppliers, and creditors. The Corporate Governance framework also depends on the legal, regulatory, institutional and ethical environment of the community. Whereas the 20th century might be viewed as the age of management, the early 21st century is predicted to be more focused on governance. Both terms address control of corporations but governance has always required an examination of underlying purpose and legitimacy". CG is about the whole set of legal, cultural, and institutional arrangements that determine what public corporations can do, who controls them, how that control is exercised, and how risks and return from activities they undertake are allocated. According to American Management Association, "Corporate Governance is about how suppliers of capital get managers to return profits, make sure managers do not misuse the capital by investing in bad projects and how shareholders and creditors monitor managers". According to Organization for Economic Cooperation and Development in April 1999, "Corporate Governance is the system by which organizations are controlled. The Corporate Governance structure specifies the distribution of rights and responsibilities among different participants in the corporation, such as board, managers, shareholders and other stakeholders, and spells out the rules and procedures for making decisions on corporate affairs. By doing this, it also provides the structure through which the company objectives are set and the means of attaining those objectives and monitoring performance". Wolfensohn defined "Corporate Governance is about promoting corporate fairness, transparency and accountability".

Therefore, CG is a multi-faceted subject. An important theme of CG deals with issues of accountability and fiduciary duty, essentially advocating implementation of guidelines and mechanisms to ensure good behaviour and protect shareholders. Another key focus is the economic efficiency view, through which CG system should aim to optimize economic results with a strong emphasis on shareholders' welfare. There are yet other sides to the CG subject, such as the stakeholder view, which calls for more attention and accountability to players other than the shareholders, for example employees, and customers.

3. IMPORTANCE OF CORPORATE GOVERNANCE

There have been largest insolvencies, scams, scandals and frauds in various companies due to CG failures in the world. The stability of global financial system is endangered if there are deficiencies in CG. It is now recognized as a continuous process in most of the countries. However, beyond such crises, there exist several structural reasons that explain importance of CG for economic development and well-being. Various structural reforms in the form of price deregulation and increased competition have increased companies' exposure to risk from market forces. These developments have forced the entities to use capital in more complex ways, enhancing need for good CG in 21st century.

Investor relations is an essential part of good CG where executive managers must strive to communicate with the stakeholders and endeavour to create and maintain a relationship of trust and disclosing all relevant information to the stock market. Good CG creates the environment where board of directors becomes accountable to the stakeholders. It helps to increase revenue and profitability and provides stability and growth to the company which builds brand image and confidence among stakeholders, viz. shareholders, customers, investors, suppliers, and government. CG has succeeded in attracting a good deal of public interest because of its apparent importance for economic health of corporations and society in general. It is the set of processes, customs, policies, laws and institutions affecting the way a corporation is directed, administered or controlled.

4. LITERATURE REVIEW

While there ourselves to some salient works. Reed (2002b)highlighted that CG changes have have been a large number of studies that have examined various aspects of CG in a number of sectors, we confine been directed towards Anglo-American model of CG in developing countries since it is a more logical counterpart of macro level changes in the international economy and has tried to provide a framework for analysis of nature of governance responsibilities within the Anglo-American model and the desirability of one model over other which takes into account a variety of concerns, such as growth, employment, risk and normative values. What is more important is the manner and conditions under which choices about governance are made rather than nature of responsibilities with a model of governance and choice of governance models. So, legitimacy of CG reforms in developing countries can only be forecast upon governance reforms occurring in the larger global economy.

Reed (2002a) tried to evaluate new Anglo-American model from the perspective of its potential development impact and focused on three key variables, viz. growth, shareholder concerns, and employment. This model has introduced volatility into the economy, both in terms of growth and employment and this volatility exists because of the role played by financial markets but the author is doubtful regarding sustainability of potential development impact of the new model. Furthermore, in order to improve performance of the model,the author provided various policy measures, like increasing stringency in application of corporate law, increasing investment in protection and education of small investors, restructuring existing system of institutional investing, developing feasible and enforceable requirements of accountability and transparency, systematic consultation with civil society groups that are engaged in assessment and evaluation of corporate behaviour. The author suggested that implementation of these policy measures is far more important than just only proposing them and governance reforms must take place in a larger context of political and legal reform that can enable society to exercise effective control over corporations in India.

Vera-Munoz(2005) specified audit committee roles and responsibilities in the wake of CG reforms asultimate monitor and effective overseer of financial reporting process and must have a general understanding of company's major economic, operating and financial risks, broad awareness of interrelationship of company's operations and its financial reporting, ability to ask probing questions about company's financial reporting process and independence shouldexist in terms of decision making. Furthermore, author highlighted various key challenges of audit committee, such as balancing practicality and priorities with new governance mechanisms, dramatic increase in board member turnover due to perceived risks of being a director of a public company, to identify mediating mechanisms behind cause-and-effect relationships and to examine what types of coalitions might develop as a result ofoversight structure, and how coalition behaviour affects audit committee effectiveness, links experience with bias, understanding how the "tone at the top" gets established and how it is assessed.The audit committee diligence studies have established that greater meeting frequency is associated with reduced incidence of financial reporting problems and with greater external audit quality, merger and acquisition activities. Finally, whistle blower provisions, shortcomings and suggestions for future research have been given.

Khanna *et al.* (2004a) argued that globalization of product and talent markets have affected CG of firms in the Indian software industry. The authors have cited that how Infosys has come out with good CG in India. The firm has adopted shareholder style CG as a signal of its high quality, to benefit indirectly from positive externalities or as a consequence of its Chief Executive Officer's (CEO) ideological bent. The authors have not found much of a role for capital markets as drivers of this process and analyzed, in general, manner in which the company has attempted to shape CG. Furthermore, the authors have discussed how the company's CEO's ideological bent results in a pro-active role taken by coalition of firms to educate regulators in adoption of good CG and finally the authors have explored various reasons of limited effects of globalization on CG convergence. In the ongoing work, the authors are collecting large sample data to throw some light on quantification of various barriers to the diffusion of US style CG and extent to which such practices should diffuse in the emerging market context of India.

Siddiqui(2010) tried to investigate development of CG regulations in emerging economies by taking the case of Bangladesh and considered three issues in particular, type of CG model suited to the country, type of model that it has adopted in reality and what has prompted for such adoption. The author has found that the country has adopted the Anglo-American shareholder model of CG. It was suggested that such model is not suitable for the country; rather adoption of stakeholder model will be more appropriate in the ongoing financial crisis. Presence of representatives of banks and workers on the board would protect the interests of employees and banks, thereby contributing to better loan recovery and improvement of working conditions. The findings suggest that in Bangladesh, organizations have lack of motivation to act in a socially responsible manner unless such action has direct relation with organizational resources. Furthermore, the author analyzed behaviours of principal actors in the country's CG scenario by using new institutionalism as a theoretical foundation which has revealed that such adoption has been prompted by exposure to legitimacy threats rather than efficiency reasons. Finally, the author suggested that Securities and Exchange Commission, being a government-funded regulatory body, has to promote government agenda to legitimize its actions to the donor agencies and ensure continued flow of support towards the Bangladesh government.

Claessens(2006) has shown that good CG is associated with a lower cost of capital, higher returns on equity, greater efficiency and more favourable treatment of all stakeholders. The author used firm-level data through which it can be seen that there exist relationships between countries' CG frameworks on one hand and performance, valuation, cost of capital and access to external financing on the other. The author has further discussed that the general importance of CG has been established but still, it lacks knowledge in CG of banks, role of institutional investors, enforcement, state-owned firms, family-owned firms, best practice in relation to other stakeholders, impact on poverty alleviation and dynamic aspects of institutional change. Finally, it was concluded that in reality, owners and managers at firm-level and political and economic factors at market and country-level, are resistant in making good CG reforms but firms and countries should recognize benefits of good CG and voluntarily bring in more reforms. Moreover, these findings are not applicable to every country or situation. CG reform depends on local capacity in terms of data, people and other resources.

Khanna *et al.*(2006b) examined debates about role of global competition and based on cross-sectional data, tested the hypothesis that similarity in CG between two countries is correlated with economic integration between those countries. Based on the evidence, the authors found that economically independent countries have similar CG laws protecting stakeholders and there was no relationship between CG practices and globalization at all levels. Globalization may have induced adoption of some CG standards but these may not have been implemented.

Som (2006)tried to provide CG codes to resolve specific governance issues plaguing Indian firms. This paper highlights those areas where CG codes have been diverged from international best practices and how these areas are proving to be challenges in promoting good governance culture. The author found that ownership concentration, prevalence of principal promoters, lack of protection for minority shareholders, lack of strict enforcement rights of regulatory authorities, disregard for disclosure norms and transparency are some of the factors which have restricted Indian corporate sector's progress on the path of good governance principles. It was concluded that adoption and implementation of international best practices in India remains inadequate due to reasons of path dependency. The task of adapting, refining and adjusting CG practices is an ongoing process and should be reviewed systematically and periodically.

5. METHODOLOGY OF THE STUDY

This study is based on secondary data which was obtained from published sources in the form of books, journals, official websites, relevant Acts, newspapers, magazines, reports of various committees set up for the growth and development of CG, review of annual reports and articles available through electronic media and press media.

6. WHAT CONSTITUTES GOOD CORPORATE GOVERNANCE?

Good CG helps an organization to achieve several objectives, like developing appropriate strategies that result in achievement of stakeholder objectives, attracting, motivating and retaining talent, creating a secure and prosperous operating environment and improving performance, managing and mitigating risk and protecting and enhancing the company's reputation. Firm commitment and adoption of ethical practices by an organization across its entire value chain and in all of its dealings with a wide range of stakeholders encompassing employees, customers, vendors, regulators and shareholders in both good and bad times are true characteristics of good CG.

7. PRINCIPLES OF CORPORATE GOVERNANCE

The framework of CGdepends on economic, legal, regulatory and institutional environment and factors, such as business ethics and corporate awareness of environmental and societal interests of the communities; these also have an impact on reputation and long-term success of the company.The principles of CG focus on governance problems that arise from separation of ownership and control. CG is affected by relationships among participants in the governance system. It is essential to bring in voluntary codes along with written down legislation and regulations so as to introduce a framework of good CG practices in the corporate world. Thus, it is necessary to comply with codes of governance, stipulated by the regulator for sound governance. The essence of CG lies in three inter-related elements which are depicted in Fig. 1.

Transparency of Operations: Companies should voluntary disseminate adequate and timely information of its operations to its stakeholders. They should give full disclosures of material information and publicize the roles and responsibilities of board and management to ensure that all investors have access to clear and factual information.

Accountability towards stakeholders: It is necessary that companies should take care of interests of each class of stakeholders for good CG to happen.So, accountabilityof companies lies in helping shareholders in exercising their rights through communicating understandable information and making them to participate in general meetings.

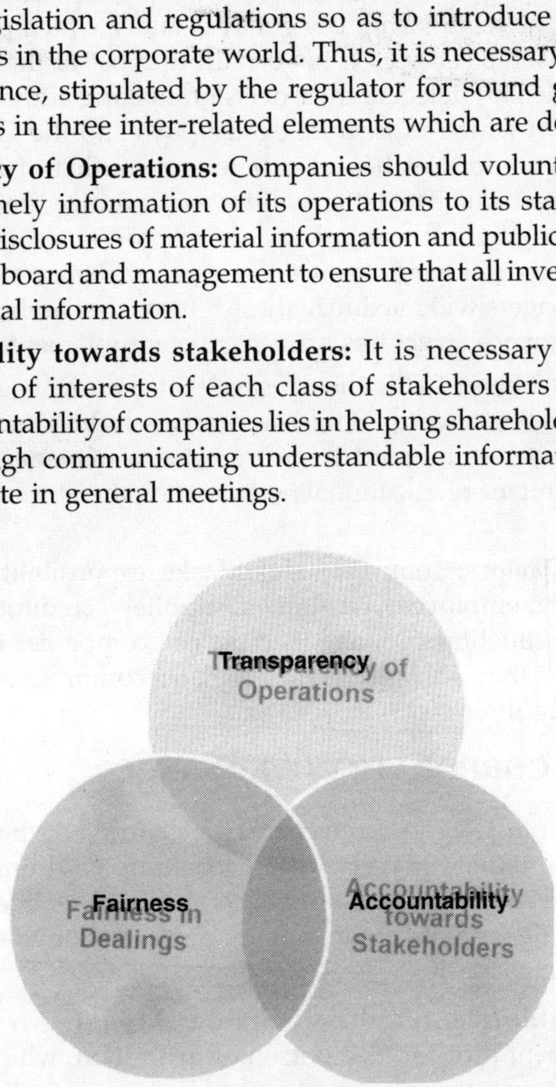

Fig. 1 : Principles of Corporate Governance

Fairness in Dealings: Companies should have a value system which must be reflected in their ethical and responsible decision-making. Therefore, Boards should develop a code of conduct for their directors and executives that promote ethical behaviour and responsible decision-making.

8. THEORIES OF CORPORATE GOVERNANCE

CG has been defined in many ways. Some of them are discussed below.

Agency Theory: This focuses on relationship between the company and its shareholders. The relationship is a contract under which principal engages agent to perform some service on his behalf. In most of the companies also, shareholders (principal) delegate their decision-making authority to the Board of directors (agent) which in turn delegates power to the CEO. The agency problems arise in companies because there is a conflict of interest between owners and management. The latter will try to maximize their interests at the cost of owners, thereby not maximizing shareholders' wealth which in turn negates overall corporate performance. So, Agency theory says that, in large corporations, managers will maximize these returns to shareholders only when appropriate governance structures are effectively implemented.

Stewardship Theory: This theory says that the managers will, on their own, act as responsible stewards of the corporations and his interests are aligned with that of the corporation and its owners. So, a manager as a steward is motivated to maximize organizational performance, thereby satisfying interests of shareholders.

Stakeholder Theory: Companies should take responsibility of wider group of stakeholders, viz. employees, customers, suppliers, creditors and the wider community and competitors. Managers must run companies in the interest of stakeholders. Since, they are large in number, so a compromise must be found between conflicting interests.

9. MODELS OF CORPORATE GOVERNANCE

The structure of CG varies from country to country. Each model takes into consideration various key players in the corporate environment, the share ownership pattern in the given country, composition of Board of directors, regulatory framework and disclosure requirements for companies. Two models are discussed here.

(a) **Shareholder-centered or Outsider Model:** An "outsider" (or independent director) is a person or institution, which is not directly related to any corporation. An "insider" (or executive director) is a person who is employed or having direct relationship with the corporation. Most corporations follow Anglo-US model that includes both "outsiders" and "insiders" whereas in countries with Anglo-Saxon legal tradition, such as United States, United Kingdom, Australia, CG usually focuses on firm's outside investors, mainly shareholders. This model is embedded with a legal framework that clearly defines rights and responsibilities of management, directors and shareholders and where interaction among these can take place during or outside annual general meeting.

(b) **Stakeholder-centered or Insider Model:**In this model, interactions are defined by formal and informal rules developed over the relationship's history. The model possesses higher debt-equity ratio, lower levels of turnover and layoffs, higher internal knowledge sharing, higher employee-firm fit, higher levels of firm-specific training for employees in comparison with the outsider model.

10. REGULATORY FRAMEWORK OF GOVERNANCE SYSTEM IN INDIA

Bombay Stock Exchange has largest number of listed companies in the World but ownership remains concentrated in families and an insider-dominated structure seems to persist. Indian System of CGis a 'hybrid' of the outsider and insider model. India is following global trend in reforming its CG System. Securities Exchange Board of India (SEBI) Act, 1992 established an independent capital market authority, SEBI with a view to protect the interests of investors in securities and to promote and regulate the securities market. Confederation of Indian Industry (CII) in 1998 produced a desirable code on CG which aimed at reforming it. Kumar Mangalam Birla Committee was set up by SEBI on May 7, 1999 to promote and raise the concept of CG in respect of listed companies in India. It gave two sets of recommendations: mandatory and non-mandatory. Some of the mandatory recommendations were focused on composition of Board, strengthening responsibilities of audit committee, improving quality of financial disclosures, etc. In January 2000, Clause 49 on CG was inserted in the Listing Agreement by SEBI for effective implementation of recommendations of Kumar Mangalam Birla Committee.

11. CORPORATE GOVERNANCE: A CASE STUDY OF AIR INDIA

(a) **Relevance of the Study:** Liberalization and deregulation have increased pressure on the indigenous entities to perform when pitched against global giants entering the market.With greater degree of privatization, Aviation Sector has gained huge potential for growth in a developing economy, like India. The Indian market is growing at about twice the global average; about 12% domestically and 8-9%

internationally. There is no doubt that India is a market with big potential and that aviation could be a much more significant contributor to the Indian economy. But this requires well-coordinated policy measures which will enable competitiveness. Today, the Indian Aviation Industry is facing major hurdles. For example, Air India, the national carrier is being sustained on life support of State and the failure of Kingfisher is very well-known. Further, the sector is not generating sustainable profits that one would expect from such a large high-growth market. Considering the stage of growth and investment potential in the sector, this study intends to bring out various implications with the implementation of sound CG which is not only relevant at the level of individual company, but is also a critical ingredient at the system level.

(b) **About Air India (AI):** It is the national carrier, popularly known as "Maharaja", which was founded by JRD Tata in July 1932 under the aegis of Tata Airlines. Timeline of AI, in brief, is reported in Table 1.

Table 1: Timeline of Air India

Year	Events
1932	The first scheduled service founded as Tata Airlines by JRD Tata, owned by the Indian government.
1946	Post World War II, Tata Airlines got converted into a public company and renamed as Air India Ltd.
1948	Started its international operations connecting its flights from Bombay to London
1953	Government nationalized the air transportation industry under Air Corporation Act 1953.
1954	Expanded its operations to a number of international destinations
1960	Introduction of first Boeing aircraft and started using jets
1962	Became world's first all-jet airline
1986	Took delivery of Airbus and became largest operator of this type in passenger service
1988	Started using two Boeings in a mixed passenger-cargo configuration
1993	AI Boeing operated first non-stop flight between New York and Delhi
1997	Launched official website andbecame a major global alliance by tying with Air France
2003	Started operating flights to Shanghai through Bangkok
2004	A strategic alliance signed with Lufthansa
2005	Launch of Air India Express; low cost airline
2007	Initiated its cargo service; Invited to join Star Alliance; Merger with Indian Airlines to form National Aviation Company of India (NACIL)
2012	Year of significant economic losses which affected market standing and pushed to fourth place in the Indian aviation market

AI could not see a single year of profit since it got merged with Indian Airlines in 2007. Key facts about AI are reported in Table 2. Currently, it is on the verge of privatization and has been facing enormous financial losses and escalating labour disputes since 2007. The airline has been seeking financial support from the government for many years to save it. There have been financial constraints on operating the airline and domestic market share has gone down to 19.1% due to stiff competition from the Indian private carriers.

Table 2 : Key Facts about Air India

Founded:	July 1932(as Tata Airlines)
Headquarters:	New Delhi, India
Parent Company:	Air India Limited
Subsidiaries:	Air India Express, Air India Regional
Merger:	Air India and Indian Airlines in 2007
Employee Strength:	12,654 employees during 2010-11
Financial Summary:	Cash Inflows in 2012: Rs. 1,348 crores,Cash Outflows in 2012: Rs. 1,752 crores.

Source: www.airindia.com

AI has been incurring huge losses of about Rs. 28,000 crores(Table 3). Further, current debts of AI have mounted to around Rs. 43,000 crores since its merger with Indian Airlines in 2007.Ninetyfive of its daily flights do not even meet cash cost of operations.

Table 3 : Profit/Loss Scorecard (in Rs. Crores)

Year	Profit/Loss
2007-08	-2,226
2008-09	-5,548
2009-10	-5,552
2010-11	-6,865
2011-12	-7,559

Source:HT Business, 4th April, 2013

(c) **What Went Wrong?** The national carrier delivered a significant improvement in its performance in the financial year 2013 but still soaking up over a billion dollars of India's precious budget every year. AI has a negative overall brand image and reputation of poor customer service and rude staff, frequent delays and cancellations.Comptroller and Auditor General had blamed the decision to buy new aircrafts and ill-timed merger with Indian Airlines in 2007 as major causes of debt troubles in AI. There has been a financial distress faced by AI since its merger with Indian Airlines due to poor management and discontent among employees. They were not paid salaries for months which resulted in strikes and took out the airline from business.Combined losses at the time of merger of both AI and Indian Airlines were Rs. 770 crores and after the merger, it went up to Rs. 7,200 crores in 2009. The merger was logical but its execution was shoddy. Furthermore, stringent policies and numerous procedural delays of the government have made it difficult for the airline to survive in the aviation industry. Recently, government has allowed foreign airlines to buy up to 49% in Indian carriers which has become a challenge for AI. It is currently the largest international operator from India but is facing stiff competition from private carriers on international routes. The airline is poorly equipped to meet this challenge in terms of its fleet composition which has added to its complexity and cost. Grounding of dreamliners has also impacted the financial performance of the airline and might decline profits further in future. Pilots who were exclusively trained for running dreamliners remain sitting idle and the airline may be forced to incur re-training costs on other types if the grounding is extended. AI pilots are best paid in the industry (Table 4)and a pay cut to match industry average is essential especially for AI which has been incurring huge losses and sustaining on taxpayers' money.

Table 4: Salaries (in Rs. Lakh/month) of Captain and Co-pilot

Airlines	Captain	Co-pilot
Ex-Air India*	5.95-8.72	2.1-4.55
Ex-Indian Airlines*	3.95-5.67	2.63-4.17
Jet Air (narrow body)	4.49	2.29
Jet Air (wide body)	5.09	2.9
IndiGo airlines	4.25	2.8

*Does not include several allowances and reimbursement on international flights, etc.

Source: HT Business, 15th January, 2013

Furthermore, the value of a barrel of oil has a direct impact on the airline. It is very difficult for it to raise ticket prices as it would scare the passengers away. Increase in fuel prices has an adverse impact on the cost of operation of the airline and it may lead to economic recession which will substantially decline the demand for air travel and air cargo.

It can be quoted that poor governance and political interference can be the factors responsible behind AI's poor performance. The former chairman and managing director of AI failed on all parameters and his lackluster performance sunk it into huge financial losses. He lacked clear-cut mission and vision of the airline and never focused on the airline's turnaround and cutting of financial losses. He never bothered to raise employees' morale at all levels and failed to upgrade service quality to match up to the expectations of travelling public.

(d) **How IndiGo managed to flourish while Air India did not in the same industry?** IndiGo today has become a market leader with a market share of 29.5% while AI has a market share of 19.1%. IndiGo is best known for its on-time performance while AI has an image of frequent flight cancellations and delays. Moreover, AI expanded its operations on non-profitable routes. Things were not in control since AI never had a professional airline management in place. Unlike AI, IndiGo had an experienced and professional team and had more rational and professional approach and its first CEO was appointed eighteen months before its launch. So, an experienced and professional team, on-time performance, low fares, consistent on-board and ground service has been the reasons behind IndiGo's success. Further, unlike AI, it continued its gradual expansion, waited for five years to launch its international operations and not expanded aggressively in a rapidly growing market.

(e) **Prospects forAir India**

AI has shown an 8.3% increase in revenue from passengers during 2012-13 and the load factor, which is number of occupied seats on an aircraft, has increased from 68.5% to 71.8%. Revenue per passenger per km, i.e. yield of the airline has also gone up 19.2% and number of passengers carried stood higher by 3.4%. It is expected that the state-owned AI is likely to post an operating profit in 2012-13 and if it is able to earn, then this would be the first time since its merger with Indian Airlines in 2007. There is a need to cut redundant costs and optimally utilizing resources to meet annual financial projections envisaged in the financial restructuring plan. Several steps have been taken for network expansion.Recovery of the airline would be dependent on successful implementation of the turnaround plan in 2013. On the international front too, AI has offered better timings and better onward connectivity to passengers. The airline has attained nearly 80% of on-time performance (Table 5) in 2013 and has been successful in getting confidence of corporate customers. Performance of the airline has to be consistent and it can do better if more capacity is added on domestic routes. The airline has reconfigured 10 of its Airbus A320s to all economy class which has given a big opportunity for budget travellers in terms of offering capacity. It has also brought down the number of business class seats from 20 to 12.Recently, pilots who had resigned from the airline are now looking to join back since the airline is in a better position now with its improved performance and better working conditions. This shows that the airline has better prospects. Industries experts say that while salary and perks may be better in some foreign carriers, AI pilots will find it difficult to adapt to working conditions of other professionally run carriers.

Table 5 : On-Time Performance of Scheduled Domestic Airlines

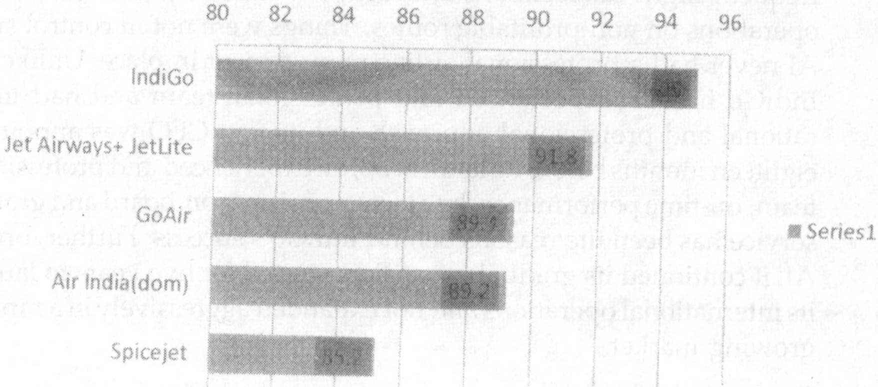

Source: www.dgca.nic.in

According to a retired AI pilot, "AI pilots are pampered a lot and they will find it very claustrophobic to work in any professionally run airline."

CONCLUSION

It can be said that despite huge losses, a two-month pilot strike, grounding of Dreamliner fleet in AI, things are finally looking up for it for the first time since its merger with erstwhile IA in 2007. Earnings before interests, taxes, depreciation and amortization (EBITDA) of the airline is expected to be positive with a cash surplus of Rs. 25 crores in 2012-13 and Rs. 1000 crores by 2013-14. The airline is likely to turn profitable by 2018. Government shall infuse additional capital of Rs. 30,000 crores into the airline by 2020 and equity capital of Rs. 6,750 crores in 2012-13. It has already infused Rs. 3,200 crores between 2009 and 2012.Things have become brighter now for AI as there is a rise in passenger revenue of Rs. 680 crores during April-December 2012 compared to the year-ago period and load factor of 70.4% against 68.4% a year ago with a decline in net loss of Rs. 1,110 crores during the period. It is estimated that the airline would earn a profit of Rs. 5,198 crores in 2012-13 and Rs. 3,500 crores in 2013-14. It can be well said that an experienced and professional team in the cockpit is the basic requirement for any airline to be able to withstand stormy skies.

SUGGESTIONS

After analyzing the problems and prospects of AI in this article, following recommendations emerge:

(i) **Role of Government:** AI should be given more autonomy in decision making, i.e. government interference should be minimized. Recently, Government has announced 49% foreign stake in Indian airlines which would be a threat for the national carrier.

(ii) **Focus on network expansion:** The airline should focus on more profitable routes and should create new plans and must expand its operations on international routes.

(iii) **Strengthening the role of Independent directors:** Independent directors play an important role in managing affairs of AI. The airline should appoint independent directors who will bring specialized skills and valuable suggestions for achieving the targets in the turnaround plan and financial restructuring plan for AI.

(iv) **Sound Corporate Governance and appointment of professional management:** AI requires a team of visionary members who can take the airline further in abetter way.The management plays an important role behind success of any airline. They must be held accountable and responsible in functioning of the company. Therefore,AI must focus on sound corporate governance in order to be successful.

(v) **Privatization:** It would be better if privatization is done in AI. It would become free from bureaucracy, though privatization has its limitations too.

(vi) **Win confidence of all stakeholders:** AI should focus on minimization of operational cost, and maximization of customer satisfaction. Staff should treat their customers in a cooperative and polite manner. It should provide good working conditions and fair payment to its employees.

QUESTIONS

1. What lessons Air India should draw from IndiGo Airlines?

2. Compare and contrast the reasons of success of IndiGo and failure of Air India.
3. What were the problems faced by Air India since its merger with Indian Airlines?
4. If you are the consultant to Air India then what advise you would give to them particularly in terms of governance.

REFERENCES

Claessens, S. (2006). Corporate Governance and Development.The World Bank Research Observer, 21, 91-122.

Fernando, A.C. (2009). Corporate Governance: Principles, Policies and Practices. Dorling Kindersley (India) Pvt. Ltd.; New Delhi.

Khanna, T., Kogan, J. and Palepu, K.G. (2006). Globalization and Similarities in Corporate Governance: A Cross-Country Analysis.The Review of Economics and Statistics,88, 69-90.

Khanna, T. and Palepu, K.G. (2004). Globalization and Convergence in Corporate Governance: Evidence from Infosys and the Indian Software Industry. Journal of International Business Studies, 35, 484-507.

Kumar Manglam Birla Committee Report on Corporate Governance (2000). www.sebi.org.

Margaret, B. (1995).Ownership and Control: Rethinking Corporate Governance for the Twenty-First Century.Brookings Institution, Washington, D.C.

Monks, R.A.G. and Minow, N. (2008).Corporate Governance.4th Edition.John Wiley.

Panchali, J. (2003). Excellence in Corporate Governance. AMonograph. Indian Institute of Capital Markets.

Reed, A.M. (2002b). Corporate Reforms in India. Journal of Business Ethics, 37, 249-268.

Reed, D. (2002a). Corporate Governance Reforms in Developing Countries.Journal of Business Ethics, 37, 223-247.

Sen, D.K. (2004). Clause 49 of Listing Agreement on Corporate Governance Times. The Chartered Accountant, 806-811.

Sharma, J.P. (2011).Corporate Governance, Business Ethics and CSR. 1stEdition. Ane Books Pvt. Ltd.

Sharma, J.P. and Sethi, P.(2009).Impact of Postal Ballot Mechanism in Improving Shareholders' Participation in Corporate Decision Making: A Research Study.Chartered Secretary, XXXIX,159-170.

Siddiqui, J. (2010). Development of Corporate Governance Regulations: The Case of an Emerging Economy, Journal of Business Ethics, 91, 253-274.

Som, L.S. (2006). Corporate Governance Codes in India. Economic and Political Weekly,41,4153-4160.

Vera-Munoz, S.C. (2005). Corporate Governance Reforms: Redefined Expectations of Audit Committee Responsibilities and Effectiveness. Journal of Business Ethics, 62, 115-127.

Wallace, P. and Zinkin, J. (2005). Corporate Governance: Mastering Business in Asia.John Wiley.

❑❑❑

CHAPTER - 38

Information and Communication Technology Initiatives in Agricultural Research and Development - Research Needs

R. Nagarjuna Kumar[1], B.Sailaja[2], G.R.Maruthi Sankar[3], S.R.Meena[4], N.Showri Raju[5] and Ravi Kumar[6]

[1, 3, 5 and 6]Central Research Institute for Dryland Agriculture, Santoshnagar, Hyderabad.

[2]Directorate of Rice Research, Rajendranagar, Hyderabad.

[4]Central Institute of Arid Horticulture, Bikaner, Rajasthan.

E-mail:rnagarjunakumar@yahoo.com

ABSTRACT

This paper broadly deals with salient applications of Information Technology in various areas related to Agriculture Research, Government's digital initiatives, Indian Council of Agriculture Research IT initiatives in agriculture research as step, towards reaching agriculture knowledge and technology to small holders (Resource-Poor-Farmers). The present paper identifies new emerging areas of usage of computer application in Horticulture research and development.

INTRODUCTION

The horticultural sector is facing the challenges of dwindling land resources, increasing biotic and abiotic stresses, indications of factor productivity decline, threatened loss of bio-diversity, new IPR regime etc, (Adiguru and Mruthyunaja, 2004). Further, Indian agriculture has come under significant adjustment pressure from market liberalization and globalization. Farmers need reliable and timely information about best practices of production, processing, marketing, input and output prices, financial markets and risk-covering institutions. Existing public extension system has become outdated and ineffective in spite of the fact that it has been a catalyst in successfully heralding the Green Revolution in the country. This is partly due to an inadequate use of new means of information dissemination (Adhiguru *et al.*, 2003). The public extension system follows a top-down approach and has become less interactive, more time-consuming and costly and fails to meet the expectations of those involved in the agricultural production and other involved in the value chain. Therefore, a new extension system re-oriented to meet the information needs of the farmers should be put in place across the country by using ICT.

Information and Communication Technology (ICT) in India

Telephone

Telephone Subscribers (Wireless and Landline): 343.87 million (August 2008)

Cellphones: 305.24 million (August 2008)

Land Lines: 38.63 million (August 2008)

Yearly Cellphone Addition: 83 million (2007)

Monthly Cellphone Addition: 9.16 million (August 2008)

Teledensity: 29.83% (August 2008)

Projected teledensity: 500 million, 40% of population by 2010.

Internet

The total Internet subscribers in India currently stands at around 42 million.

Highlights of Indian Broadband (Ex. 256 Kbps download) subscribers:

Broadband connections have continued growth since beginning on 2006. At the end of August 2008 total broadband connections in the country have reached 4.73 million. However, the definition of broadband is pretty constrained in India compared to other countries. A 256 kbps always on connection is the definition of broadband in India compared to 2 Mbps in other countries

Here is a brief on how broadband grown in last few months.

Mar 06	Jun 06	Sep 06	Dec 06	Mar 07	Jun 07	Jul 07	Aug 07
1.35 M	1.57 M	1.82 M	2.10 M	2.34 M	2.42 M	2.47 M	2.56 M

6 per cent of total internet subscribers have broadband in India.

(*Source* http://www.zdnetasia.com/insight/specialreports/india, http://en.wikipedia.org/wiki/Communications_in_India)

Areas of ICT Convergence

Application of ICT in support of agricultural and rural development falls into five main areas, as outlined by Don Richardson (FAO, 1996). These are:

- Media networks
- Research and Education
- Community development
- Small and medium enterprises development and
- Economic development of agricultural producers.

Some Horticulture development services that can be provided in the developing world using ICT are (Meera, 2004)

- Websites established by agricultural research institutes, making the latest information available to extension workers and obtaining the feedback.
- Online services for information, education and training, monitoring and consultation, diagnosis and monitoring.
- The facilitation of interaction among researcher's extension workers, and farmers.
- Tele-education for farmers.
- Feed back services where experts respond to queries on specialized subjects for greater efficiency in delivering services for overall agricultural development.
- Up-to-date information supplied to farmers as early as possible, about subjects such as market information, weather forecasting input supplies, credit availability, packages of practices, etc.
- Creation of databases with details of resources of local villages, site-specific information systems, expert systems etc.
- Providing Networking facility to Connect Rural Villages to share the databases.
- Provision of early warning systems about disease/pest problems, information regarding rural development programmes and crop insurances, post harvest technology etc.
- Facilitation of land records and online registration services.
- Services providing information to farmers regarding farm business and management.

- E-commerce for direct linkages between local producers, traders, retailers and suppliers.

Methods of Information Technology usage in Agriculture

- Opening cyber café's or information centers for farmers.
- Providing Internet access to extension personnel and farmers.
- Hosting web sites by major agricultural institutions.
- Providing efficient market information, agricultural development through Internet.
- Providing up to date weather conditions through on line services.
- Providing user feedback, interactions among the scientists, extension personel and farmers through e-mail.
- Using multimedia to provide consistent high quality training.
- Use of Geographical Information systems (GIS) by extension agencies to provide up to date information on current condition related to weather, crop, probable pest outbreak, land requirements.
- Use of teleconferencing in training of workers in different areas.

Government Initiatives on Agriculture ICT in India (Digital Initiatives)

According to the National IT Task Force (1999) recommendation (No.79), "the Government shall take all necessary steps to boost IT for agriculture and integrated rural development". The Ministry of Agriculture and National Informatics Centre (NIC) also emphasized informatics for Agricultural development in the national conference on "Informatics for Sustainable Agricultural Development (ISDA-95)". Many follow up actions (ICT projects: AGMARKNET, DACNET, etc) were taken up, to provide relevant agricultural information in rural areas, helping farmers to improve their labor productivity, increase their yields, and realize a better price for their produce. The initiatives based on the recommendations of ISDA-95 Conference (Informatics for Sustainable Agricultural Development) includes:

- Establishment of about 100 Million Internet connections and One Million Information kiosks by 2008 with the participation of public and private sector.
- Promotion of development of Indian Languages Content over Internet
- Re-engineering of the Government process leading to "electronic Governance"

- Launching of "Mass Campaign of IT Awareness" (IT-Yatras) etc.
- AGRISNET: An infrastructure network unto block level agricultural offices facilitating agricultural extension services and agribusiness activities to usher in rural prosperity.
- AGMARKNET: With a road map to network 7000 Agricultural produce wholesale markets and 32000 rural markets.
- ARISNET: Agricultural Research Information System Network.
- SeedNET: Seed Informatics Network.
- CoopNet: To network 93000 Agricultural Primary Credit Societies (PACS) and Agricultural Cooperative Marketing Societies to usher in ICT enabled services and rural transformation.
- HORTNET: Horticultural Informatics Network.
- FERTNET: Fertilisers (Chemical, Bio and Organic Manure) Informatics Network facilitating "Integrating Nutrient Management" at farm level.
- VISTARNET: Agricultural Extension Information System Network.
- PPIN: Plant Protection Informatics Network.
- APHNET: Animal production and Health Informatics Network networking about 42000 Animal Primary Health Centers.
- LISNET: Land Information System network linking all institutions involved in land and water management for agricultural productivity and production systems, which has now evolved as "Agricultural Resources Information System" project during the Tenth Plan being implemented through NIC.
- AFPINET: Agricultural and Food Processing Industries Informatics Network.
- ARINET: Agricultural and Rural Industries Information System. Network to strengthen Small and Micro Enterprises (SMEs).
- NDMNET: Natural Disaster Management Knowledge Network.
- Weather NET: Weather Resource System of India.

Indian Council of Agriculture Research (ICAR) initiatives on ICT in Agriculture

The ICAR web-site has been designed including Organization, Research Activities, Agricultural Research Information System (ARIS), International Linkages Publication Offices, National Agricultural Technology Project (NATP), and State Agricultural Universities.

A major initiative has been taken by developing Agricultural Research Information System (ARIS) in order to modernize and bring information management culture in National Agricultural research System (NARS).The basic infrastructure required for linking all ICAR institutes and State Agricultural Universities were already developed under National Agriculture Research Project (NARP II) by creating LAN (Local Area Network) and providing E-mail connectivity. ARIS news provides a much needed forum for exchange of ideas and highlight of the implementation of ARIS programme.

Some of the main initiatives for agriculture development using Networking are

As the majority of Indian populace is in rural areas, networking them can be the most effective solution to bring them on to the main stream of information domain which only privileged urbanites has access to so far. Several community information systems have been operational zed in the recent times with multiple uses and increased simplicity to endear the rural masses. Some of such systems are

TARAhaat

It is a portal created in the simplified format to connect Indian villager to the rest of the world. TARAhaat provides training and management support to its network of franchised TARAkendras to enable them to provide standardized services and also acts as a central provider of the products and services needed, adapting them to meet the local needs of each region. TARAhaat was launched as a pilot in late 2000 in Bundelkhand, Madhya Pradesh and Uttar Pradesh. In 2001, TARAhaat expanded its operations into Punjab. TARAhaat has 22 centers and is in the midst of a major expansion in Punjab, and in the region.

Functions

Supply online information of market, agrofrorestry, fertilizers, crops, chemicals usage, insects and diseases, loan schemes, soil, tractor maintenance

Gyandoot

On January 1, 2000, Dhar district began the new millennium with installation of low cost, self-sustainable and community owned rural Intranet project. Computers in 20 village centres in ten Blocks of the district were wired through an Intranet (presently there are 34 such wired village centres). Local rural youth act as entrepreneurs for running cybercafes-cum-cyberoffices on commercial lines. Computers in the network have been established in *Gram*

Panchayats (Village Committee). They have been called *Soochanalayas* (Information Kiosks). The *Soochanalayas* provide user-charge-based services to the rural people. This Intranet system has been named Gyandoot (Messenger of Informant)

Services and facilities

The rates of grains and vegetables at nearby manuals, copies of revenue maps, information about land records can be obtained from this project. It also provides E-mail facility, Vermin-compost booking.

MAHA-AGRINET

It is started in Maharashtra. MAHA-AGRINET based on Internet framework. All the information, services, programs should be delivered through website. MAHA-AGRINET has set a target to establish about 10000 INFORMATION CENTERS at local level covering entire state and reach up to 1 crore farm families

Services that will be provided to the users can be classified as follows,

- Information Services.
- Consultancy / Expert advice Services.
- Educational Services.
- Marketing Services.
- E-Governance Services.
- Communication Services.

MSSRF Initiatives

In an experiment under Information Village Research Project in electronic knowledge delivery to the poor, M.S Swaminathan Research Foundation (MSSRF) has connected ten villages near Pondcherry in southern India by a hybrid wired and wireless network that facilitates both voice and data transfer, and have enabled the villagers to get information that they need and can use to improve their lot.

The *bottom up exercise* involves local volunteers to gather information, feed it into an Intranet and provide access through nodes in different villages. Value addition to the raw information, use of the local language (Tamil) and multimedia (to facilitate illiterate users) and participation by local people right from the beginning are the noteworthy features of the project. Most of the operators and volunteers providing primary information are women, thus giving them status and influence. All centers evolved themselves to meet the information demands made by the community.

A considerable part of information is accessed from the local sources. All the databases are in Tamil except one on below-poverty-line families which is an official document in English. Rural Yellow Pages have also been created, and people are allowed to insert advertisements like knowing who is renting a tractor and at what price.

e-Chaupal

It is a unique web-based initiative of ITC's international Business Division in Central India and caters to Soya growers regarding all information, products and services required in Soya farming. The Soya kiosks facilitate supply of high quality farm inputs and purchase of Soya at the doorsteps of the villagers. The project has started 23 tele-centers in Hoshangabad district of Madhya Pradesh and has around 600 kiosks in Central India. The project has been selected for the study as the huge private sector investment in e-chaupal has revolutionized Agricultural Commodity Marketing in India

Initiatives at CIAH, Bikaner

Establishment of Local Area Net work (LAN) and Internet facility with VSAT

Local Area Network (LAN) established by linking Server with all the systems available in the Institute for sharing computer resources and databases efficiently. Inter net facility developed through V-SAT (Very Small Aperture Terminal). CAB CD ROM is also connected to all systems through LAN to access on line Research Abstracts.

Website developed

Web-Site developed as per DARE format for the Institute and hosted at the Institute Server. This can be browsed at the http://www.ciah.ernet.in. This web-site provides overview of Institute related information, describes origin and objectives of on going projects, technologies developed and transferred. The web-site is designed using Microsoft Front page and sub menus are designed using Java Script and Active Server Pages. Hindi version of home page is also designed by downloading Hindi fonts from CDAC web-site. Website is updated with latest information. Institute quotations and Tenders and Advertisements are placed on the website.

Services of website

- Technical Information related to current projects.

- Weather Service.
- Email.
- National Agricultural Events.
- Linkages to other Agricultural Institutions.
- Searching of different sites.

Information System for Arid Fruit crops developed

Over the years huge amount of information on arid fruit crops has been collected by various researchers. However, the information regarding fruit crop varieties, cultivars developed, pest, diseases management, etc. generated from various studies by different researchers is scattered. The information related to fruit crops need to be consolidated. With this intention developed Software entitled Information System for Arid Fruit Crops.

Other Initiatives

Table 1 : Some innovative ICT-based initiatives in Indian agriculture

Initiatives	Sponsor (organization)	Important features	Subject matter focus
Public Sector:Cyber extension project	National Institute of Agricultural Extension Management (MANAGE), Hyderabad	Village information centers, institutional support to other ICT projects	Post harvest processing, women and child welfare
Agricultural Technology Information Centers(ATICs)	Indian Council of Agricultural Research (ICAR)	Call centers, expert system, researchers-farmers linkage	Agronomic practices, technologies, inputs
Agricultural Gateway of India	National Academy of Agricultural Research Management (NAARM) (ICAR), Hyderabad	Portal, links to other sites/ portals on agriculture	Profile of agricultural research and extension organizations
Help-line service	Chandra Shekhar Azad University of Agriculture and Technology (CSAUAT), Kanpur	Helpline service through telephone, researcher-farmers linkage	Cultivation practices, plant protection, new technologies
Warna Wired Village Project	NIC. Warna Cooperative Complex, Warna (Maharashtra)	Wide area network, Computer booths	Cultivation practices, pests and diseases, marketing, processing
Rural Information Kiosks	EID Parry, Tamil Nadu Farmers managed	Farm practices, Farm advisory,	

Contd.

	kiosks, portals, public-private partnership in applying ICT innovations & content development	market intelligence, weather	
I-kisan portal	Nagarjuna group, Andhra Pradesh	Portal in regional languages	Agricultural practices, plant protection, animal husbandry, weather
Computer on wheels	Pingali Rajeswari-entrepreneur, Andhra Pradesh	Internet on motor bikes, portals, remote area, resource poor	Market, weather, plant protection, animal health
Drishtee Telecenters (Rajasthan)	Jaipur (Rajasthan)	In the village a local village becomes akiosk owner as a self employment opportunity, mostly financed by some of the government sponsored scheme, leading to anew IT-literature generation in the country side, with about 45,000 kiosks	The services provide information related to land records, Virtual Bidding Market Place,Market Information System
Janmithra (Rajasthan)	Jhalawar (Rajasthan)	Provide encumbrance certificates and valuation certificates. The rural internet provides e-governance, e-education, e-health, and e-commerce services	Services are provided to the people through community Information centers.

Source : Das, P (2005)

E-Extension through KVKs: A Case of the KVK of Babhaleshwar, Ahamednagar District of Maharashtra

During 1999 wide area network (WAN) is established at KVK Babhaleshwar by linking ten different institutions through wireless radio frequency among institutions within 5 KM radius. Inter net facility developed through V-SAT (Very Small Aperture Terminal). KVK has developed its website with different modules like crop cultivation package in vernacular language, government schemes, weather and market information etc. The audio format of the practices and services were also developed (Das, 2005).

Services provided

- Technical Information related to farming practice.
- Weather Service.
- Email and Voicemail.
- National Agricultural Events.
- Linkages to other Agricultural Institutions.
- Video conferencing.
- Development of Crop CD.

Impact Analysis of e-Extension at KVK of Babhaleshwar

During a period of three years from its inception about 32500 farmers has been benefited from e-Extension service of the KVK. About half of the farmers have visited the IT centers 2-5 times, about one-fourth 6-9 times and about one-fifth more than 10 times during the period of three years. As far as the extent of use of various IT tools by the farmers are concerned, 51.32% preferred intranet and internet browsing, 21.82% local information, and 14.48% participated in video conferencing, the remaining 5.67% enquired through e-mail/voice mail.

IMPACT OF ICT INITIATIVES ON AGRICULTURE

The impact of some of the initiatives is presented below based on the experiences of farmers, as reported by them (Adhiguru *et al.*, 2003).

1. Yield Gain and Reduction in Cost of Cultivation

It has been found that both I-kisan and Help line initiatives improved the access to information for farmers and they could use improved varieties, adopt innovative pest and nutrient management practices at critical stages of crop growth and reduce frequency of application of agro-chemicals. As a result, crop yield gain was realised to the tune of 4-5 per cent. Additionally, there was reduction in cost of cultivation by 14 per cent and three per cent in the case of I-kisan and Help line initiatives respectively

2. Reduction in Transaction Cost

Generally, for receiving information or any technical knowledge on crop cultivation, farmers go to a nearby talk headquarters where they can meet officials in the Department of Agriculture or get advice on purchasing agro-inputs from private dealers.

The ICT-enabled initiatives could change this scenario and the farmers could get technical advice by visiting kiosks located in their village or nearby village and save on transaction costs as well. The transaction cost incurred by the farmers was worked by computing variables like distance traveled, labour hours involved per visit, cost equivalent of labour hours, and traveling cost per visit. It is very clear from that through ICT enabled services, a farmer could save his traveling time and transaction costs by more than 80-90 per cent.

3. Time Saving

According to a study (UNESCO, 2001), the users in the three knowledge centers of MSSRF, Pondicherry have saved a travel distance of around 100,000 km, and 4000 hours amounting to imputed value of Rs.16, 000 Time is a valuable commodity for the landless laborers and women in the rural areas (particularly during working seasons) and therefore time saved means money-earned.

RESEARCH NEEDS

Informatics for agricultural development requires coordinated inter-sect oral approach and application of appropriate information technology (IT) tools (Malhotra, 2004). This requires design and development of agricultural resources information system using state-of-the-art IT tools, as given below, to facilitate effective agricultural planning and development:

- Developing statistical software for Analysis of agricultural research data
- Developing simulation models
- Data warehousing (Data Bases & Model Bases)
- Expert Systems & Knowledge Bases
- Geographical Information System (GIS)
- Bioinformatics

Analysis of Agricultural Research Data

There is urgent need to develop software for data analysis for agriculture research, modify the existing packages by the addition of new statistical procedure for data analysis, to make them compatible with the new operating systems and with Graphical User Interface (GUI). Software development for generation of designs for various experimental settings along with randomized layout of generated design and analysis of the data generated, analysis of sample survey data, plant breeding data analysis and bioinformatics, etc.

Modeling and Simulation of Agricultural Systems

To manage our scarce agricultural resources or to estimate the effects of future climatic change on agriculture, we first need to develop an integrated tool that will simulate observed crop growth in wide variety of environments and under wide variety of management practices. The Decision Support System for Agro-technology Transfer (DSSAT) allows users to combine the technical knowledge contained in crop growth models with economic considerations and environmental impact evaluations to facilitate economic analysis and risk assessment of farming enterprises. Some of the areas that need attention are forecasting of yields in various production systems, forecasting systems for outbreak of crop pests and diseases, environment degradation, ground water contamination, water resource management, climate change, crop-water relationships etc.

Establishment of Data Warehouse

The data warehouse addresses the growing need of knowledge for enterprise-wise data access. It functions as a core for decision support processing at the strategic management level, separate from day to day operational data. The design and construction of data warehouse includes granularity of data, partitioning of data, meta-data, lack of credibility of decision support system (DSS) data, the system of record and migration etc. Data ware housing involves the entire information delivery process from access and transformation of data from different operational sources, through the process that makes it available for decision making, to the exploitation of the retrieved data via range of decision support tools.

Expert System

There is a need for transferring expert knowledge instantly at the level of farmer's field to benefit the entire agricultural community. To solve this problem Expert systems (ES) has been identified as powerful tool for extension. Expert system is also known as knowledge based system, a special computer program designed to simulate the problem solving behavior of an expert in a narrow domain or discipline. ES unite the accumulated expertise of individual discipline e.g., plant pathology, entomology, soil science, metrology etc., into a frame work that best addresses the specific, in-site needs of farmers (Bheemappa, 2005). Expert systems combine the experimental knowledge with the intuitive reasoning skills of multi discipline specialists to aid farmers in making the best decisions for the development of horticulture crops.

The main objectives to develop Expert systems are

- To enhance the performance of agricultural extension personnel and farmers
- To make farming more efficient and profitable
- To reduce the time required in solving the problems and performing the routine tasks of extension workers.

Geoinformatics

Geoinformatics is an interdisciplinary field requiring capture, integrating, analyzing, managing and depicting geospatial information. Geoinformatics technologies include Geospatial information systems (GIS), Global Positioning System (GPS), Remote Sensing (RS) and ICT.

Geoinformatics has potential application in the agricultural resource management through precision agriculture to ensure optimum use of the agricultural resources. Geoinformatics has proven as powerful tool for studying the natural resources and help in vocational features, extent of coverage, monitoring the resources and in generating modeling for probable scenarios, which assists in optimizing resource utilization

The geospatial database can be integrated with simulation models to form user oriented decision support systems for local planning, resource management, evaluation of limitations and potentials of soils, crop production strategies, spatial modeling, and production forecasting, spatial surveys.

Bioinformatics

It is the study of information content and information flow in biological systems and process. It has evolved to serve as the bridge between observations (data) in diverse biologically-related disciplines and the derivations of understanding (information) about how the systems or processes the function, and subsequently the application (knowledge).Bioinformatics is an interface between biological and computational sciences (Naredrasinh, 2005).

Some specific areas that fall within the scope of Bioinformatics

- Sequence assembly
- Database design and maintenance
- Sequence(gene) analysis
- Proteomics
- Pharmacogenomics

Information and communication technologies are essential for progress in Bioinformatics. Data mining and online analytical processing extended to this science would assist the researcher by discovering suitable patterns and relationships that could shape subsequent investigations. Information Technology would bring the power of modeling, simulation of systems into bioinformatics research.

Constraints in the Use of ICT

- Lack of content in local language
- Lack of skilled persons for disseminating agricultural information
- Technical constraints
- Economic constraints
- Insufficient basic Infrastructure
- Irregular internet connectivity
- Lack of clear policies

Suggested strategies for effective utilization of ICT

1. Content development: Generic and indigenous knowledge, success stories in local language to meet local needs.
2. Unified dissemination: Research and development institutes to develop synergy in content development and delivery (*e.g.* interlinking of websites).
3. Capacity development programmes: Regional/intermediary institutions may identify emerging training needs and impart training for various stakeholders.
4. Bridging the divide: Strategic deployment of ICT to address socio-economic dividers (age, gender, land holding, geography) is essential.
5. Every village a knowledge centre: Improve connectivity by using wireless, low-cost technologies, low-power alternatives.
6. Enable intermediary organizations: Better e-linkage among rural institutions, extension agents, local NGOs, and producer associations to improve their delivery efficiency.
7. Emphasis on gender equity: Providing women-oriented content, easy access, capacity building, and involvement in indigenous knowledge acquisition and management.

8. Strengthen monitoring and feedback: Deploy ICT in community knowledge gathering and eliciting people's feedback for research/ development projects and democratic governance.

9. Attract private investments: Create a congenial environment for higher investments by private sector in telecommunications and information kiosks.

10. Low-cost training institutes: Schools and panchayat offices can impart ICT trainings.

REFERENCES

Adhiguru, P, and Mruthyunjaya. (2004). Institutional innovations for using Information and Communication Technology. Policy Brief 18, National Centre for Agricultural Economics and Policy Research, New Delhi.

Adhiguru, P, Mruthyunjaya, and P.S. Birthal. (2003). Project on "Innovative Institutions for Agricultural Technology Dissemination: Role of Information and Communication Technology", National Centre for Agricultural Economics and Policy Research, New Delhi.

Statistics of ICT http://en.wikipedia.org/wiki/Communications_in_India, http://www.zdnetasia.com/insight/specialreports/india.

Digital Initiatives in ICT-http://www.digitalopportinity.org.

ICT Initiatives-informatics for sustainable agricultural development (ISD-95), http://agmarket.nic.in

Richardson, D. (1996). The Internet and rural development: recommendations for strategy and activity –final report. Rome: Sustainable Development Department of the Food and Agriculture Organization of the United Nations http://www.fao.org/sd-dimensions

Meera, N, Anita, J, Rao, D.U.M. (2004). Information and Communication in Agricultureal Development: A Comparative Analysis of Three project from India from AgREN website : www.odi.org.uk/agren

TARAhaat.com- http://www.tarahaat.com

Gyandoot-http://www.gyandoot.nic.in/gyandoot/internet.html

Maha-agrinet-http://agri-maha.nic.in

MSSRF-www.msrf.org

E-Choupal-www.itcportal.com, www.echoupal.com

Das, P. (2005). Book chapter of-Extension strategies for human Resource Development by Hirevenkangoudar, L.V, Manjunath L, Hanchinal S.N, Angadi J.G, Chandargi D.M p231-261, ISBN : 81-8321-017-1.

Malhotra, P.K. (2004). Proceedings of XIV National Conference of Agricultural Research Statisticians 17-19, November. pp157-164.

Narendrasinh Chuhan, Myradhavj Jhala, Joravasinh Sarvalya. (2005). Book of Information Technology for Agricultral production, Education and Management. pp152-171.

❑❑❑

Section 6
IPR and Social Issues

CHAPTER - 39

Intellectual Property and Knowledge Management: Infringement, Misappropriation, and Enforcement

Radha Yadav[1], Madhu Kamle[1], Showkat Ahmad Lone[1], and Jasdeep Chatrath Padaria[1*]

[1]Biotechnology and Climate Change, National Research Centre on Plant Biotechnology (NRCPB), Pusa Campus, New Delhi, India-110012

E-mail: jasdeep_kaur64@yahoo.co.in

ABSTRACT

Intellectual property rights (IPR) have, in recent years, emerged as perhaps the most important aspect of legal system as far as protection of inventions is concerned. Intellectual property rights have been created to ensure protection against unfair trade practices. The protection of intellectual property rights (IPR) could be a means to acknowledge a creator for something new or it could be means to recover the financial investments of a financer. IPR ensures that the knowledge, innovation and capital involved in the development of a product/ technology are compensated with highest rewards, insufficient protection of IP will lead to fewer rewards and even some of the inventions will be driven to extinction. As a result the innovators may conveniently relocate to regions where they can protect the IP they develop, the latter will result in intellectual loss to a particular country. Knowledge management on the other hand, emphasizes the challenge behind effective management of innovation systems by providing protection to databases, learning tools and sharing process that innovators have developed over a period of time. Effective Knowledge management provides platform for sharing of technologies through licensing and cross-licensing agreements between different countries. The chapter deals with the fundamentals of intellectual property, its types, the applications of different categories of intellectual property in the area of science and technology including biotechnology, literature and arts, and the commercial value of intellectual property assets. Moreover, protecting traditional knowledge through the intellectual property rights and identification, documentation transmission revitalization and promotion of cultural heritage by traditional knowledge has been discussed.

1. INTRODUCTION

Intellectual Property Rights system has been operational world over for centuries in one form or the other. With advancements in commercialization, this system has become all the more important. Intellectual Property (IP) systems have existed in societies with the purpose of promoting social welfare through the motivation of innovation, research and creativity. Intellectual property (IP) is defined as creation of human mind including ideas, knowledge, design, inventions, innovation and creativity etc which has commercial value. Intellectual Property Rights (IPR) ensures that human intellect is protected legally as physical property. Intellectual property rights are the exclusive rights which are granted to a person for novel innovation and invention in any field. The World Intellectual Property Organization (WIPO), established as a specialized agency of United Nations in 1974 is dedicated to promote the protection of intellectual property throughout the world (Mansfield, 1986). Trade environment is changing at a fast pace world over due to extensive global competition, high innovation risks, short product cycle, rapid changes in technology, high investments in research and development (R&D), production and marketing and need for highly skilled human resources. Simultaneously geographical barriers to trade among nations are collapsing due to globalization, and a multilateral trade system. Many products and technologies are simultaneously marketed and utilized in many countries. Therefore the complexities of global trade are on an increase as more and more variables are introduced in the system leading to an immense increase in uncertainties. In order to save our existing traditional knowledge in terms of agricultural, scientific, technical, ecological, medicinal, and biodiversity-related knowledge the concept of 'Knowledge Management' has come into existence. Knowledge management is a systematic method of compiling and drafting of already existing traditional knowledge and its management through intellectual property rights in order to save the infringement. Thus knowledge management can be broadly defined as intellectual property rights (IPR) issue related to traditional knowledge. IPR encourages people to come forward with innovative ideas, designs, inventions etc which in turn drives economic growths and competitiveness and creates a legal means to appropriate knowledge. Whereas knowledge management (KM) deals with the management of knowledge-related activities (Wiig, 1997; Civi, 2000) such as creating, organizing, sharing and using knowledge in order to create value for an organization. It involves the support of a technological infrastructure, a change in organizational culture and the management of different types of knowledge. KM is an emerging field that has gained considerable attention, predominantly from the industrial community. This is evidenced by the significant number of organizations embarking on various KM programs in their quest to enhance their competency and organizational performance. The importance of KM has been widely promoted and recognized and few organizations are truly capable of leveraging and managing knowledge in their organizations. Yet implementing KM still remains a challenging task for organizations at a large in a contemporary society.

Intellectual property rights is used as a collective term for protecting inventive works of different aspects or innovativeness / invention/ creativity in any field may be science, literature, industry, art, agriculture etc. These are:

1. Patents
2. Copyright
3. Trademark
4. Industrial designs
5. Layout designs of Integrated Circuits
6. Geographical indications
7. Registration of Plant variety
8. Trade secrets

1.1 Patents

Patent is an important Intellectual Property Right granted by government to inventor or creator for his novel invention. Patent consist of a set of exclusive rights granted to patentee for a limited time period. Patenting creates a legal situation in which the inventions can normally be utilized (manufactured, used, sold, and imported) with the authorization of the owner of the patent, thereby protecting patenting rights (WIPO, 2013). The criteria for patenting an invention vary from country to country. The first act related to Patent was passed by the Federal Government of the United States in 1790 and is termed as the first Patent Act. First patent was issued to Samuel Hopkins of Vermont for a potash production technique under Patent Act on July 31, 1790.

In India, the first legislation related to patents was the Act VI of 1856. This legislation was aimed to encourage the inventors to disclose the secrets of their inventions. The act was modified in the year 1957 since it was enacted without the approval of the British Crown. In 1859 a fresh legislation known as Act XV of 1859 was introduced based on the United Kingdom Act of 1852. This legislation in addition to features of previous legislations also offered exclusive privileges to useful inventions and the period of priority was extended from 6 months to 12 months. This act allows the assignees to make application and publication in India and United Kingdom to ascertain novelty. The legislations governing the procedure of granting and validity of patents were modified and some new acts were introduced from time to time, the details of such modifications are given in Table.1.

Table 1 : Description of some Indian Patent Acts

Indian IPR acts	Year
The first legislation in India relating to patents was the Act VI of 1856, it was based on the British patent law of 1852.	1856
The Act modified as Act XV; patent monopolies called exclusive privileges (making. Selling and using inventions in India and authorizing others to do so for 14 years from date of filing specification).	1859
The patents & designs protection Act.	1872
The protection of inventions Act	1883
Consolidated as the inventions & designs Act	1888
The Indian patents & designs Act	1911
The copyright Act (amended in 1983, 1984, 1992, 1994 & 1997)	1957
The copyright rules	1958
The patents Act (act 39 of 1970) came into force on 20th april 1972	1972
On march 26, 1999 patents (amendment) Act, (1999) came into force from 01-01-1995	1999
International copyright order	1999
Information technology (IT) Act	2000
Semiconductor integrated circuits layout design Act	2000
Geographical indication of goods (registration and protection) Act (protect basmati rice, Darjeeling tea, and such other goods that are native to India)	2002
Patents (amendment) Act	2002
Communication convergence Act	2002
Trademark's bill and designs bill	2002
Protection of plant varieties and Farmers' rights Act	2002
E-commerce Act	2002
The patents (amendment) Act 2005 effective from ist january 2005	2005

A certain set of universal criteria's are specified for any invention to be patentable. These include invention, novelty, non-obviousness (inventive) and public morality (order public), usefulness. The invention must be novel such that claimant must ensure that the subject matter of invention is different from anything that is available as public knowledge. Anything that has been published or sold in open market comes under the domain of public knowledge. Since scope of public knowledge is worldwide, therefore same invention cannot be patented in different countries.

For any invention to be patentable, it is essential that the invention is not obtained by ordinary skill and therefore is not something obvious. It must have novelty with respect to the way it was obtained, the procedures followed or in terms of its applications. Governments have the right to refuse a patent for an invention that is against public morality and injurious to public health. Moreover, the well established nature must not be affected during the process and the use of invention. Natural substances including diagnostic, therapeutic and surgical methods, plants and animals (other than microorganisms), and biological processes for the production of plants or animals (other than microbiological processes) are not patentable.

1.1.1 Procedure for patenting

Any invention can be patented by submission of application legal requirements to the concerned patent office and by payment of a stipulated patent fee on regular basis.

The application of patent is filed in a prescribed format and is accompanied by a provisional and complete specification of the invention. The Indian patent office is administered by the Office of the Controller General of Patents, Designs & Trade Marks (CGPDTM), India situated in Mumbai. The headquarters of Patent office is at Kolkata with branches in Chennai, New Delhi and Mumbai. Patent is granted for a specified period in a particular country and different forms of intellectual property rights have different period of protection duration. In India Patent is effective for a term of 15 years from the date of filling application form. Whereas in US current patent term is extended 20 years from the earliest filling date instead of 17 years from the issue date.

1.1.2 What cannot be patented

All inventions are not patentable. Most of the patent offices provide the list of exclusion containing the inventions which are not patentable.

- An invention which is frivolous, or which claims anything obviously contrary to well-established natural laws.

- An invention, the primary or intended use or commercial exploitation of which could be contrary to public order or morality or which causes serious prejudice to human, animal or plant life or health or to the environment.
- Inventions relating to atomic energy and the inventions prejudicial to the interest of security of India. This law falling within section 20(1) of the Atomic Energy Act, 1962
- A presentation of information.
- Plants and animals in whole, or any part thereof, other than microorganism, but including seeds, varieties and species and essentially biological processes for production or propagation of plants and animals.
- A method of agriculture and horticulture
- Mere discovery of new form of a known substance, which does not result in the enhancement of the known efficacy of that substance, or mere discovery of any new property, or mere new use of known substance, or mere use of known process, machine or apparatus unless such known process results in a new product or employs at least new reactant.
- Mere arrangement or re-arrangement or duplication of known devices, each functioning independently of one another in a known way.
- A mathematical or business method or a computer program *per se* or algorithms.
- Mere discovery of a scientific principle or the formulation of an abstract theory (or discovery of any living or non-living substances occurring in nature).
- A substance obtained by a mere admixture, resulting only in the aggregation of the properties of the components thereof, or a process for producing such substance.
- Any process for the medicinal, surgical, curative, prophylactic, diagnostic, therapeutic, or other treatment of human beings, or any process for a similar treatment of animals to render them free of disease or to increase their economic value or their products.
- A mere scheme or rule, or method of performing mental act, or method of playing game.

- An invention which, in effect, is traditional knowledge, or which is an aggregation or duplication of known properties of traditionally known component or components.
- Topography of integrated circuits.

1.2 Copyright

Copyright is another form of IPR which defines a legal set of exclusive right granted by the government to creator or producer for creative expression work such as musical, art, literary and cinematographic works etc. Like other Intellectual Property Rights, a copyright is also applicable to expression of new idea or information that is substantive and discrete. The creative works that are to be protected by copyright must have originality. Originality refers to the adequate skills, labor and the judgment which are spent to create the work. Initially copyright was accepted by the government only to restrict the printing or making the duplicate of literary works but now the main purpose of copyright laws is to promote the creation of new works by giving rights and profit to authors. The copy right act encompasses a wide range of creations includes literary works as books, brochures and newspapers, theatrical works, oral presentations, choreographic works, vocal and instrumental music, drawings, paintings, buildings and sculptures, designs, photographic works and computer programs.

The first federal copyright act was the Copyright Act of 1790 instituted in the United States. International copyright agreements standardize many aspects of national copyright laws. Whereas the first Indian copyright act was passed only in 1957. The copyright license ensures a number of benefits to the holder as:

- It protects the creation from copying and reproduction of work which is neither patentable nor can be protect as trade secret. No body can import or export, sell or assign, display work publically and create derivative works without the permission of right holder.
- It helps the holder to communicate about commercial value of work.
- Government rewards the copyright holders in the form of recognition.
- The holder gets financial benefits in the form of payments

In India Copyright protection is obtained from Registrar of Copyright, New Delhi. It arises automatically and in the UK one does not have to register the copyright in the work before it is protected.

1.2.1 Rights granted by the copyright to owner

With the power of copyright, an owner has the right and freedom to make copies of his work, lend the work to the public and perform or play the work in public. The communication of work to the public can be through broadcasting or electronic transmission. The ownership of copyright arises automatically and is also transferrable through an assignment or license. The copyright Act grants a right to copyright owner to transfer his rights either wholly or partially by assignment or license, even exclusive license. After assignment of property in case of tangible property owner losses his rights over it but in case of intellectual property the owner can enjoy the property after assignment depending upon the rights assigned and transferred. Under UK law, no one can register the copyright in work before it is protected. The creator of work is recognized as the first owner of copyright in Indian law. Copyright ownership in case of computer generated works is granted to the person responsible for carrying out all the arrangements necessary for the creation of work. Copyright ownership in collaborative research is held jointly based on the agreement between partners that regulates the partnership and the owner rights in such cases are clearly distinguishable.

The Copyright protection periods depends on the type of work. Works related to literary, drama, music and art are protected for life time of the owner and 70 years from the year of end in which author dies.

Computer generated works are protected for 50 years from the creation of work date. Works related to sound recordings are protected for 50 years from the end of year of publication. Broadcast related works are protected for the 50 years from the end of year of broadcast. Published editions of typographical arrangement are protected for 25 years from the year of first publication.

1.2.2 Infringement of copyright

An infringement of the exclusive right of a patent owner involves the unauthorized exploitation of the patented invention by a third party. The making of the invention in particular, and its development for industrial application, usually involve considerable expense for the applicant and for the future owner of the patent for invention. The patent owner thus wishes to recover this expense through exploitation of the patented invention, in particular through the sale of products that incorporate the invention. Once the patent rights are granted by the government they are not automatically enforced and it is up to the patentee to bring an action usually under civil law, for any infringement of his patent rights. There are two kinds of infringement related to copyright: primary infringement and secondary infringement. Primary infringement refers to when exclusive rights of an author are performed partly without the permission, consent or authorization of author. Acts like selling, reproducing, making derivative works, communicating to public and distributing the work to damage the ownership are the examples of secondary infringement.

1.3 Geographical Indications

Geographical indications (GI) of products are defined as that aspect of intellectual property which corresponds to a specific geographical location or origin (e.g. an own, region, or country). The geographical indication act certifies that the certain quality, traditional methods of preparation and reputation of products are due to its geographical origin. GI highlights the geographical origin of a good and the characteristics derived from it. As an element of Intellectual Property Right, GIs are covered under articles 1 (2) and 10 of the Paris Convention for the protection of Industrial property. Geographical indications are covered under article 22(1) of the WTO Agreement on the Trade Related Aspects of Intellectual Property Rights (TRIPS) Agreement. Trade Related Aspects of Intellectual Property Rights (TRIPS) is a part of the Agreements concluding the Uruguay Round of GATT negotiations. India, as a member of the World Trade Organization (WTO), enacted the Geographical Indications of Goods (Registration & Protection) Act, 1999 has come into force with effect from 15th September 2003 (Geographical Indications registry). GIs includes the agriculture product, natural products or products manufactured or processed having a reputation and quality which are attributable to the place of origin, environment and other inherent natural and human factors. Geographical indication an element of IPR grants the protection of such goods by legal registration. GIs are the national property it cannot be granted to any individual. Associations of persons or producers or an organization or authority representing the interest of the producers of goods are granted to GI through registration. The legal benefits of GIs include: protection of goods or products of specific geographical origin; prevention of unauthorized use of registered GIs and the economic benefits under GIs include: increase in the market visibility and enhancement the economic prosperity of producers of goods; GIs act as quality mark which in turn enhances export and revenue of a product.

The registration of Geographical indication is valid for ten years but it may be renewed from time to time for a period of 10 years at a time by the payment of renewal fees. In India the GI office is located in Chennai and comes under the purview of Department of Industrial policy and promotions, Ministry of Commerce and Industry. By the virtue of its existing geographical and biological diversity, a number of Indian products have been recognized and protected under GI (Table 2).

Table 2 : A few GIs of India

Place/Item	Geographical Indication
Mango	Alphonso
Dehradun	Basmati Rice
Agra	Petha
Kancheepuram	Silk
Kashmiri	Saffron
Darjeeling	Tea
Malihabad	Dashehari mangoes
Chanderi	Saris
Solarpur	Chaddar
Solarpur	Terry Towel
Bikaneri	Bhujia
Kullu	Shawl
Kota	Doria
Basmati	Rice
Bhavani	Jamakkalam
Mysore	Silk
	Betel Leaf
	Sandalwood oil (word & Logo)
	Sandal soap (word & Logo)
	Traditional Paintings

1.3.1 Infringement of GI

The confutations or falsifications infringe the Geographical Indications. The remedies are same for the infringement of Geographical Indications as in case of infringement of Trademark. Geographical Indications of Goods (Registration and Protection) Act, 1999 carry a penalty with imprisonment for a term which may not be less than six months but may extend upto three years and with penalty charges which may not be less than INR 50,000 (approx. US$ 1075) but may extend to INR 2, 00,000 (approx. US$ 4300).

1.4 Plant Variety Protection Act (PVR)

The Plant Variety Protection Act of 1970 statute in the United States is an intellectual property. The Plant Variety Protection Act grants exclusive rights to breeders to have control over new, distinct, uniform, and stable sexually reproduced or tuber propagated plant varieties. Protection of Plant Varieties and Farmers' Right Act (PPV&FR Act) was enacted through Trade Related Aspects of Intellectual Property Agreement (TRIPs) in year 2001. For any plant variety to be protected under PVP act, it is essential that four major following requirements are accomplished:

(a) **New**, meaning that it has not been commercially exploited during a certain period before the application;

(b) **Distinct**, meaning that it is clearly distinguishable from any other variety whose existence is a matter of common knowledge;

(c) **Uniform**, meaning that the plants of a variety should be uniform in the relevant characteristics, subject to the variations that may be expected from the particular features of its propagation;

(d) **Stable**, meaning that the variety should remain unchanged in its relevant characteristics over a period of repeated propagation;

(e) Have a **suitable denomination**, meaning it must have a name by which it is designated.

Any person, farmer, group of farmers or community of farmers, university or publicly funded agricultural institution and successors of a breeder are eligible to apply to be the breeder of the variety, if the new variety under question qualifies all the stipulated criteria (section 16 of the PVP act). The complete application with all necessary details can be filed at the Office of the Registrar, Protection of Plant Varieties and Farmers' Rights Authority either directly or through to agents.

The applicant must submit quality of the variety to be protected along seeds with the prescribed fee for conducting the tests for confirming the standards of variety as per the specified standards of regulation. The Registrar will issue a certificate of registration to the applicant on acceptance of application and if opposed the application has been rejected under the Act.

The certificate of registration issued by the registrar is valid for different periods according to variety under consideration. In the case of trees and vine it is 18 years from the date of registration of the variety while for extant varieties registration is valid for 15 years from the date of notification. Duration of registration is valid for only 5 years from the date of registration of the variety in case of other crops. The applicant can apply for the review and renewal of registration for the remaining term on the payment of prescribed fee to the Registrar. Export, import and selling of any variety without the permission of original owner of variety is infringement of the rights of owner under the Plant Variety Protection Act. Infringement of any right under the Plant Varieties and Farmers' Rights attracts both Civil and Criminal action. A criminal action under the Act entails punishment up to two years and fine of INR 50,000.

1.4.1 Farmer's Right

A farmer who has bred or developed a new variety is eligible to register his variety under the Protection of Plant Varieties & Farmers' Rights Act (PPVFRA), 2001 in the same manner as a breeder of a variety. According to the PPVFRA *"The farmer shall be deemed to be entitled to save use, sow, re sow, exchange, share or sell his farm produce including seed of a variety protected under this Act in the same manner as he was entitled before the coming into force of this Act.; Provided that the farmer shall not be entitled to sell branded seed of a variety protected under this Act."* A farmer who is engaged in the conservation of genetic resources of land races and wild relatives of economic plants and their improvement through selection and preservation shall be eligible to register his variety for recognition and reward from the 'Gene Fund', provided that material so selected and preserved has been used to donate genes of varieties registered under the Act.

The gene fund is a central government undertaking fund that is collected from:

(a) the benefit sharing received in the prescribed manner from the breeder of a variety or an essentially derived variety registered under this Act or propagating material of such variety or essentially derived variety, as the case may be;

(b) the annual fee payable to the authority by way of royalty under sub-section (1) of section 35;

(c) the compensation deposited in the Gene Fund under sub-section (4) of section 41;

(d) the contribution from any national and international organisation and other sources.

The Gene Fund shall in the prescribed manner be applied for meeting—

(a) any amount to be paid by way of benefit sharing under sub-section (5) of section 26;

(b) the compensation payable under sub-section (3) of section 41;

(c) the expenditure for supporting the conservation and sustainable use of genetic resources including in-situ and ex-situ collections and for strengthening the capability of the Panchayat in carrying out such conservation and sustainable use;

(d) the other expenditures of the schemes relating to benefit sharing, framed under section 46.

1.5 Trade Secret

According to the Uniform Trades Secrets Act, 1970 the trade secret can be defined as: "The Information, including a formula, pattern, compilation, program device, method, technique, or process, that: (i) derives independent economic value, actual or potential, from no being generally known to, and not being readily ascertainable by proper means by, other persons who can obtain economic value from its disclosure or use, and (ii) is the subject of efforts that are reasonable under the circumstances to maintain its secrecy." Thus any type of data, process, program device, method and information can be referred as Trade Secret till it is kept as secret and involved in economical benefits to the owner.

According to the Trade Related Aspects of Intellectual Property Rights (TRIPS) Agreement, for any information to be termed as trade secret, it should have following characteristics.

- The trade secrets information should be secret and not generally known and readily accessible to public.
- Information should also have commercial benefits for its owner.
- The information must be the subject of reasonable efforts of the owner to keep it a secret.

Trade Secret protection has more advantage over other forms of intellectual property like Patent, Trademark and Copyrights because other types of protection have element of uncertainty as compared to Trade Secret. Trade Secret can be maintained for last as long as the information remains secret. It is easy to create and control the Trade secret right which has enhanced the value of Trade Secret over other rights like patent etc. A number of information's are protected under trade secret act. Example

"Energion" is a trade mark given to fermented milk product produced by a dairy company. The "Energion" is an ideal trade mark as it consists of a combination of words that suggest that the product is a source of energy. It is not clearly descriptive of the product (milk), nor is it deceptive (milk is, in fact, rich in energy). Furthermore, it is important to register the trade mark at your national trademark office, in order to obtain protection in this country. Furthermore, and if one intends to export the product and ensure that protection is granted broad, the trade mark must be registered in each of the countries where the goods will be distributed.

1.7 Industrial Design

Design as per the Indian Act means the features of shape, configuration, pattern, ornament or composition of lines or colors applied to any article -

whether in two dimensional or three dimensional or in both forms - by any industrial process, whether manual, mechanical or chemical means, separately or combined, which in the finished article appeal to and are judged solely by the eye. It does not include any mode or principle of construction or anything which is in substance a mere mechanical device. In this context an article means; any article of manufacture and any substance, artificial, or partly artificial; and includes any part of an article capable of being made and sold separately. Stamps, labels, tokens, cards, etc cannot be considered an article for the purpose of registration of design because once the alleged design i.e., ornamentation is removed only a piece of paper, metal or like material remains and the article referred to ceases to exist. An article must have its existence independent of the designs applied to it. So, the design as applied to an article should be integral with the article itself. For any design to be registered and protected under Industrial Design Act, the design should be new or original, not previously published or used in any country before the date of application for registration. The novelty may reside in the application of a known shape or pattern to a new subject matter. However, if the design for which the application is made does not involve any real mental activity for conception, then registration may not be considered. Further, the design should relate to features of shape, configuration, pattern or ornamentation applied or applicable to an article. Thus, designs of industrial plans, layouts and installations cannot be registered under the Act. It is essential that design should be applied or applicable to any article by any industrial process as a result designs of artistic nature such as painting, sculptures and the like which are not produced in bulk by any industrial process are excluded from registration under the Act. The features of the designs in the finished article should appeal to and are judged solely by the eye. Thus the design must appear and should be visible on the finished article, for which it is meant. Any design in the inside arrangement of a box, money purse or almirah may not be considered for showing such articles in the open state, as those articles are generally put in the market in the closed state. Any mode or principle of construction or operation or anything which is in substance a mere mechanical device, would not be a registrable design. For instance, a key having its novelty only in the shape of its corrugation or bend at the portion intended to engage with levers inside the lock it is associated with, cannot be registered as a design under the Act. However, when any design suggests any mode or principle of construction or mechanical or other action of a mechanism, a suitable disclaimer in respect thereof is required to be inserted on its representation, provided there are other registrable features in the design. Moreover, the design should not include any trademark or property mark or artistic works. It should be significantly distinguishable from known designs or combination of known designs and should not comprise or contain scandalous or obscene matter.

The total term of a registered design is 15 years. Initially the right is granted for a period of 10 years, which can be extended, by another 5 years by making an application and by paying a fee of Rs. 2000/- to the Controller before the expiry of initial 10 years period. The proprietor of design may make the application for such extension even as soon as the design is registered.

1.7 Trade Mark (Brands)

A Trade Mark is a visual symbol that distinguishes the goods or services of one enterprise from those of the competitors. A reference to goods will imply services also, unless the context prohibits it. Trade Marks are at the centre of global business today as they are the major source of product differentiation and non-price competition in a modern, market driven economy. Consumers associate certain values in terms of performance, durability, price, after-sales service etc in the goods sold under specific brands, which may be among the greatest assets of the enterprise.

Trademarks are a class of intellectual property with the purpose to protect the name of the product rather than the invention or idea behind the product. *A trademark can be defined as a sign that individualizes the goods of a given enterprise and distinguishes them from the goods of its competitors.* Trademarks can be owned by individuals or companies and need to be registered at a governmental agency, referred to as the Trademarks Office. When a trademark is used in connection with services, it is sometimes referred to as a "service mark". Trademarks are generally not distinctive and generic merely descriptive of the goods and services they represent e.g. a generic word as "vegetable" cannot be registered as a trademark of a supermarket, since it is certainly descriptive of items which all supermarkets sells. On the other hand, the word "vegetable" might well serve as a trademark for bicycles since it has little or nothing to do with bicycles. Trademarks should preferably not be geographical or primarily a surname. Thus, "Paris" cannot serve as a trademark for perfume. In many countries, trademarks which comprise mere letters and/or numbers (i.e. the proposed trademark cannot be pronounced as a word or words or just has too few letters) or are surnames are considered to be indistinct.

A trade mark which consists of at least one of the following essential characteristics can be registered.

a) The name of a company, individual or firm represented in a particular or special manner;

b) The signature of the applicant for registration;

c) One or more invented words;

d) One or more words having no direct reference to the character or quality of the goods except the exceptions listed in the next section

e) Any other distinctive trade mark

f) A trade mark which has acquired distinctiveness by use over a prolonged period of time.

A part of trade mark can be registered separately in addition to a whole trade mark if it satisfies the requirements of registration of a trade mark. The Act also provides for registration of the same or similar trade mark by more than one proprietor in the case of honest concurrent use or other special circumstances.

In 1940, the British Government of India passed the Trade Marks Act for uniform and systematic registration of trade marks in India, and the act came into force on June 1, 1942. It was replaced by the Trade and Merchandise Marks Act, 1958, which came into effect from November 25, 1959. In 1995 as India joined WTO as an original member it was obligatory to bring the Indian law in consonance with TRIPS and make necessary changes in the trade mark law. Hence new Trade Mark Act, 1999 came into force. The Act of 1999 makes important departures from the Act of 1958 in two major aspects:

- Shape of goods was recognized as a trade mark
- Trade Marks were granted for services also.

The Registration of Trade Marks is done in Mumbai where the Trade Marks Registry is situated and houses the office of registrar. There are branch offices of the Registry at Calcutta, Delhi and Chennai with separate jurisdictions.

Controller General of Patents and Designs also functions as the Registrar of Trade Marks. The Register of Trade Marks contains the record of all registered trademarks, with names, addresses and description of proprietors and users, assignments and transmissions, and conditions and limitations and the name of registered users.

Any person who claims to be a proprietor of a trademark can apply to the Registrar of Trade Marks for its registration. The application may be made in the name of an individual, partners of a firm, a Corporation, any Government Department, a trust or joint applicants claiming to be the proprietor of the trade mark.

Application in the prescribed form needs to be filed in the office of the Trade Mark Registry within whose territorial limits the principal place of business of the applicant, or the first applicant in the case of joint applicants, is situated. The Registrar is required to classify goods and services in accordance with the international classification for registration of trade marks. A single application is sufficient for registration of a trade mark for different classes of goods and services; however, the fee is payable for each class separately. Every application for registration of a trade mark shall contain a representation of the mark in the place provided in the form for the purpose. Five additional representations of the mark have to be supplied with the application. The application can either be accepted completely or accepted subject to amendments or rejected. Soon after acceptance, the application is advertised in the Trade Marks Journal to provide the public an opportunity to oppose the registration. Any person may, within three months from the date of the advertisement or within such further period not exceeding one month, give notice in writing to the Registrar of opposition to the registration. Thus it is possible that an application is accepted and later, before registration, the acceptance is found to be in error. In such cases the Registrar has the power to withdraw the acceptance after hearing the applicant.

1.7.1 Advertisement

When the procedure for registration, including the opposition, if any, is satisfactorily complete, the Registrar is mandated to register the mark.

The registration of a trade mark is for a period often years, but it may be renewed from time to time indefinitely.

If a person, who is not the owner of a registered trade mark, uses the same trade mark, or a deceptively similar trade mark without permission from the owner in the course of trade, he infringes the trade mark and is liable to be sued for legal remedies by the rightful owner. No action for infringement is available in respect of unregistered trademarks; however, common law rights for action against 'passing off' are not affected. The exclusive rights of the trademark owner can be exercised by means of an infringement action. The trademark is infringed if, owing to the use of an identical or similar sign for identical or similar goods, there is a risk or a likelihood of the public being misled. The test is not a hypothetical one, but has to deal with the reality of infringement in the marketplace. If a trade mark has a reputation in India, the use of a mark identical with or similar to it, on goods or services which are different, constitutes infringement as such use, without due cause, would take unfair advantage of a reputed trade mark or harm its distinctive character. The Act prohibits adoption of a registered trade mark by another person as trade name, i.e. the name of an enterprise. A suit for infringement of registered trade mark can be filed in the district court within whose territorial jurisdiction, the plaintiff instituting the suit or proceeding actually and voluntarily resides or carries on business or personally works for gain.

1.8 Layout Design of Integrated Circuits

Layout designs (topographies) of integrated circuits are a field in the protection of intellectual property. Like other forms of intellectual property, *IC layout designs are creations of the human mind.* They are usually the result of an enormous investment, both in terms of the time of highly qualified experts and financially. There is a continuing need for the creation of new layout-designs which reduce the dimensions of existing integrated circuits and simultaneously increase their functions. The smaller an integrated circuit, the less the material needed for its manufacture, and the smaller the space needed to accommodate it. Integrated circuits are utilized in a large range of products, including articles of everyday use, such as watches, television sets, washing machines, automobiles, etc., as well as sophisticated data processing equipment. The possibility of copying by photographing each layer of an integrated circuit and preparing masks for its production on the basis of the photographs obtained is the main reason for the introduction of legislation for the protection of layout-designs.

In United States intellectual property law, a mask work is a two or three-dimensional layout or topography of an integrated circuit (IC or "chip"), i.e. the arrangement on a chip of semiconductor devices such as transistors and passive electronic components such as resistors and interconnections. The layout is called a *mask* work because, in photolithographic processes, the multiple etched layers within actual ICs are each created using a mask, called the photo mask, to permit or block the light at specific locations, sometimes for hundreds of chips on a wafer simultaneously. Because of the functional nature of the mask geometry, the designs cannot be effectively protected under copyright law (except perhaps as decorative art). Similarly, because individual lithographic mask works are not clearly protectable subject matter, they also cannot be effectively protected under patent law, although any processes implemented in the work may be patentable. So since the 1990s, national governments have been granting copyright-like intellectual property rights conferring time-limited exclusivity to reproduction of a particular layout.

1.9 Intellectual Property on Integrated Circuits (IPIC) Treaty:

In 1989 in Washington, D.C. a Treaty on Intellectual Property in respect of Integrated Circuits (IPIC Treaty) is open to States Members of WIPO or the United Nations and to intergovernmental organizations meeting certain criteria. The Treaty has been incorporated by reference into the TRIPS Agreement of the World Trade Organization (WTO), subject to the following modifications: the term of protection is at least 10 (rather than eight) years from the date of filing an application or of the first commercial exploitation in the world, but Members may provide a term of protection of 15 years from the creation of the layout-design; the exclusive right of the right-holder extends also to articles incorporating integrated circuits in which a protected layout-design is incorporated, in so far as it continues to contain an unlawfully reproduced layout-design; the circumstances in which layout-designs may be used without the consent of right-holders are more restricted; certain acts engaged in unknowingly will not constitute infringement. The IPIC Treaty (signed at Washington on May 26, 1989) is currently not in force, but was partially integrated into the TRIPS agreement.

Article 35 of TRIPS in Relation to the IPIC Treaty states: All Members agree to provide protection to the layout-designs (topographies) of integrated circuits (referred to in this Agreement as "layout-designs") in accordance with Articles 2 through 7 (other than paragraph 3 of Article 6), Article 12 and paragraph 3 of Article 16 of the Treaty on Intellectual Property in Respect of Integrated Circuits and, in addition, to comply with the following provisions. Article 2 of the IPIC Treaty gives the following definitions:

(i) 'integrated circuit' means a product, in its final form or an intermediate form, in which the elements, at least one of which is an active element and some or all of the inter-connections are integrally formed in on a piece of material and which is intended to perform an electronic function,

(ii) 'layout-design (topography)' means the three-dimensional disposition, however expressed, of the elements, at least one of which is an active element, and of some or all of the interconnections of an integrated circuit, or such a three-dimensional disposition prepared for an integrated circuit intended for manufacture.

Under the IPIC Treaty, each Contracting Party is obliged to secure throughout its territory, intellectual property protection of layout-designs (topographies) of integrated circuits, whether or not the integrated circuit concerned is incorporated in an article. Such obligation applies to layout-designs that are original in the sense that they are the result of their creators' own intellectual effort and are not commonplace among creators of layout designs and manufacturers of integrated circuits at the time of their creation. The Contracting Parties must, as a minimum, consider the following acts to be unlawful if performed without the authorization of the holder of the right: the reproduction of the lay-out design, and the importation, sale or other distribution for commercial purposes of the layout-design or an integrated circuit in which the layout-design is incorporated. However, certain acts may be freely performed for private purposes or for the sole purpose of evaluation, analysis, research or teaching.

1.10 Knowledge Management

Knowledge is an intangible asset and is produced, tracked, managed and accounted for innovation systems. The respective roles of knowledge and intellectual property management, their relation and the potential of each in a broadened perspective on knowledge flows in innovation remains unclear and is not well defined. "*Knowledge management is can be defined as the configuration and control of operational knowledge processes in such a way as to promote the yield and pleasure of knowledge as a factor of production*" (Noordegraaf, 2001). Inventors, innovators, venture capitalists, companies, governments and civil society all have a stake in the management of knowledge and recognize the magnitude of the challenge behind any demand for effective management of innovation systems. Thus formal law-based systems for intellectual property management have come to the fore, demonstrating that innovation is indeed occurring. Knowledge management involves the management of data and information on one side and management of the knowledge of employees on the other side. Documents and employees – all are carriers of knowledge. The method or approach of managing data and managing employees are distinctively different. The content of knowledge in a particular set of data or in a particular document is constant whereas knowledge of organizational employees is ever changing. The value of Knowledge Management relates directly to the effectiveness (Bellinger, 1995) with which the managed knowledge enables the members of the organization to deal with today's situations and effectively envision and create their future. Without on-demand access to managed knowledge, every situation is addressed based on what the individual or group brings to the situation with them. With on-demand access to managed knowledge, every situation is addressed with the sum total of everything anyone in the organization has ever learned about a situation of a similar nature. It is important to identify and implement the approach which would make a more effective organization.

According to the Barclay and Murray (1997) the knowledge management is a business activity. Wherein knowledge management and intellectual capital are part of the same activity. Accordingly, the knowledge component of the activities of an organization deal with tangible element of a business and is reflected in the strategy, policy and activities. There is a direct link between the organization's intellectual capital – tangible (on record) as well as intangible (skills and personal knowledge) – and positive business results (Fig 1).

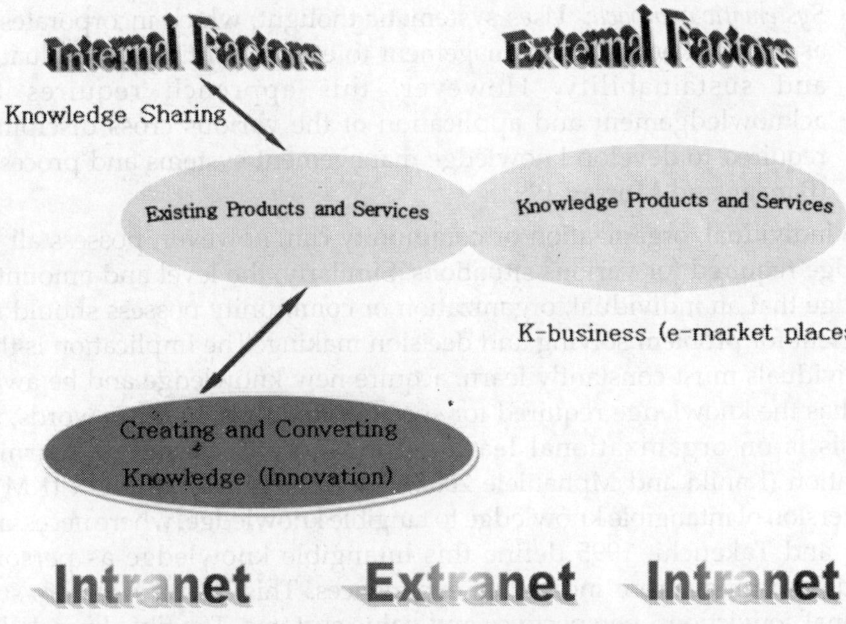

Fig. 1 : General shifts in knowledge management focus

1.10.1 Technologies for knowledge management

Knowledge management is the deployment of a set of tools and techniques that are used to help organizations manage the two knowledge cycles more effectively. Over 100 such techniques have been identified, which can be grouped according the part of the knowledge cycle they augment (many tools can contribute to one or more phases). The value of Knowledge Management relates directly to the effectiveness (Bellinger, 1995) with which the managed knowledge enables the members of the organization to deal with today's situations and effectively envision and create their future.

1.10.2 Frameworks for knowledge management

In the development of frameworks for knowledge management, one of three approaches are generally used namely the mechanical, the cultural or the systematic approach.

- *Mechanical approach*: Focuses on the application of technology as facilitator for access to information.
- *Cultural approach*: Emphasizes innovation and creativity, which is important to the learning organization. New ways of doing things force organizations to follow a holistic approach in their relationship with the environment.

- *Systematic approach*: Uses systematic thought, which incorporates all aspects of knowledge management to ensure continuous evaluation and sustainability. However, this approach requires the acknowledgement and application of the various cross disciplines required to develop knowledge management systems and processes (Barclay and Murray 1997).

No individual, organization or community can, however, possess all the knowledge required for various situations. Similarly, the level and amount of knowledge that an individual, organization or community possess should not be sufficient for problem solving and decision making. The implication is thus that individuals must constantly learn, acquire new knowledge and be aware of who has the knowledge required for specific situations. In other words, the emphasis is on organizational learning and how to become a learning organization (Kaniki and Mphahlele 2002). Knowledge management (KM) is the conversion of intangible knowledge to tangible knowledge, where necessary. Nonaka and Takeuchi, 1995 define this intangible knowledge as personal knowledge resulting from individual experiences. This includes factors such as personal convictions, perspectives and value systems. Tangible knowledge, on the other hand, is knowledge that can easily be conveyed in formal language. This is done by means of mathematical and scientific formulas, manuals and specifications. This type of knowledge is easily conveyed between groups and individuals.

1.10.3 Prerequisites for knowledge management

Knowledge management in a broad sense is a critical aspect of globally distributed work processes (cf. Holden, 2001, Holden, 2002). However, there are certain specific questions which extend domestic intra-organizational processes. These need to cover processes as well as strategies between distributed organizations. They need to take global knowledge exchange and distribution into account. This leads to a variety of additional Influencing factors, barriers and challenges in global settings. Prerequisites of knowledge management comprise sharing of expertise, knowledge mapping, knowledge workers and value creation.

1.10.4 Major Challenges of knowledge management

1. Lack of Expertise Sharing
2. Attaining Expertise
3. Handling Tacit Knowledge
4. Legal Issues

Knowledge management covers a broad spectrum of activities and operates at many levels, from the individual to the enterprise, between enterprises (as in virtual organizations). Additionally, effective knowledge management is the result of a holistic approach, addressing not only technology solutions, but also people, processes and links into core business activities. Table 1 represents some of the key elements of knowledge management across these two dimensions.

Table 3 : Elements of Knowledge Management

	Processes/Strategy	Processes/ Methods	People/ Skills	Technology
Governments (inc. EU)	Stimulation Good practice Regulation	Guidance Standards	Qualification and Skills	Interoperability standards
Intra-organization	Collaborative associations	Collaboration methods and standards	Skills development	E-business networks
Organization	Knowledge-based business	Best practice KM processes	Personal development programmes, e-learning	Corporate portals
Teams	Tasks and outcomes	Virtual working	Team roles	Collaborative workspace
Individuals	Career/life planning	KM specialties	Professional development	ICT/Internet proficiency

1.11 Emerging Issues in Intellectual Property

Intellectual property finds wide range of applications in almost all aspects of science and technology, literature and the arts. However following two areas, Biotechnology and Traditional Knowledge are now discussed extensively at the global arena.

1.11.1 Biotechnology

Biotechnology due to its innovations finds applications in fields ranging from health care, agriculture, food processing, bioremediation, forestry, enzymes, chemicals, cosmetics, energy, paper making, electronics, textiles and mining. These applications have resulted in significant economic activity and development. Biotechnological inventions are creations resulting from inventive efforts, investment and extensive research carried out in sophisticated laboratories. The involvement of higher investments in biotechnological research creates an obvious need for protection of outcome of this research which is usually in the form of products or technologies. The patenting of biotechnological inventions has led to many controversies. For example, the modified microorganism created by Chakrabarty was able to convert xenobiotic (hydrocarbons in oil spills) in oceans to lesser toxic compounds. The recognition of these modified microorganisms as patentable by the United States Supreme Court was a landmark decision. The court ruled that the invention resulted from the inventor's efforts and was not directed to the existing natural phenomenon. However, patenting of biotechnology innovations has been accompanied by controversy. Policy makers of all countries need to discuss the laws on patentability of biotechnological inventions keeping in view the public interests, such as the environmental or medical safety of products, efficacy of products, and unfair competition that may occur in the assertion of patent rights. The association biotechnology with legal and regulatory systems makes it an evolving component of intellectual property law.

1.11.2 Traditional knowledge

Indigenous knowledge may be defined as knowledge that has been created and developed over a period of time. Indigenous knowledge represents generations of creative thoughts and actions within a particular community in an eco-system generated to keep abreast of the ever-changing agri-ecological and socio-economic environment (Kaniki and Mphahlele 2002). It may, therefore, be seen as the sum total of the knowledge and skills of the inhabitants of a certain geographical area. These skills and knowledge have been shared for generations and have been adapted by every new generation to meet its unique requirements and environmental conditions. Indigenous knowledge is unique to a given community and culture. Furthermore, it is dynamic and based on innovation and practical experiment. It is also called local knowledge or traditional knowledge and stands in strong contrast to Western, scientific and modern knowledge that is continuously being developed by research institutions and universities.

According to the World Bank (1998), indigenous knowledge has the following Characteristics:

- It is local, because it is anchored in a specific community, established within the boundaries of broader cultural traditions and developed by a specific community;

- It is intangible knowledge and consequently not so easily codified;
- Conveyed orally
- Experimental knowledge rather than theoretical knowledge
- Learned by repetition
- Changes continuously, is created and recreated, discovered and lost, even though outsiders consider it to be static.

Indigenous knowledge is not only the production of artifacts for the tourism market: it also concerns the development of existing technology, including the production of jewellery, copper work, fishing methods, medicine, etc. The potential of such knowledge must, however, be repackaged to ensure participation by the community and to make a contribution to world development (Odora Hoppers and Mahlanghu, 1998). However, it is important to have safeguards in place to prevent the potential exploitation of this indigenous knowledge by industry.

2. CONCLUSION

Intellectual property rights (IPR) have, in recent years, emerged as perhaps the most important S&T policy instrument. With its growing presence, however, it has also been subjected to intense criticism. The current patent system is practically inaccessible to indigenous peoples and communities, primarily because of their lack of funds, but also because often they have not received the education that is necessary to manoeuvre within the extremely complex legalities of the patent system.

REFERENCES

Barclay, R. and Murray, P. 1997. What is knowledge management? [Online]. Available http://www.media-access.com/whatis.html

Bellinger, G. 1999. Principles of a knowledge leveraging community infrastructure. [Online]. Available WWW: http://www.systems-thinking.org/klcip/klcip.htm.

Demarest, M. 1997. Understanding knowledge management. Journal of Long Range Planning 30(3):374-384.

Encarta. World English Dictionary. Bloomsbury Publishing: London, 1999.

Fao/links. 2005. The utilization of indigenous knowledge in range management and forage plants for Improving livestock productivity and food security in the maasai and barbaig communities (nelson kilongozi, Zabron kengera, samwel leshongo).Available online at http://www.fao.org/sd/links/documents_download/nelson_41.pdf

Kaniki, A.M. and Mphahlele, M.E.K. 2002. Indigenous knowledge for the benefit of all: can knowledge management principles be used effectively? SCESAL Conference, Carnival City, Kempton Park, 20-21 April.

Mansfield, E. (1986) "Patents and Innovation", Management Science, vol. 32:2, pp.173-81.

Nonaka, I. and Takeuchi, H. 1995. The knowledge-creating company: how Japanese companies create the dynamics of innovation. New York: Oxford University Press.

Odora Hoppers, C. and Mahlanghu, M.P. 1998. A comparative study of the development, integration and protection of indigenous knowledge systems in the third world. Pretoria: HSRC.

Patent statistics for decision makers 2012 - Draft agenda. 2012. OECD Conference Center, Paris France.

❑❑❑

CHAPTER - 40

Emerging IPR Issues in Plant Biotechnology

Meenakshi Prajneshu[1] and Chayanika Pragya[2]
[1]*Deshbandhu College, New Delhi-110019*
[2]*Opera Solutions, Sector 16A, Noida-201301*

1. INTRODUCTION

Science and Technology are vital for developing low-input and high-output agriculture and pharmaceutical. India needs frugal use of natural resources and diversification of agricultural activities. Transgenic technologies are highly misunderstood. Genetically modified crops are a result of them. In fact genetic modification of crops for human use is going on since their domestication. By introduction of Bt cotton in 2002, yields have doubled. American bollworm can no longer threaten Indian cotton crops. Insects can develop resistance to Bt gene or some virus attacking the crop needs more research. RNA-mediated gene suppression may aid the development of patent strategies that will support the next generation of genetically modified crops and enhance scope of patenting. Many fancy Organic farming, which will need 40 percent more agricultural land for present number of people on earth although it is ever increasing. Biotechnology has revolutionized agriculture, healthcare, industrial processing, environmental sustainability and is also a revenue generator. India is poised for a tremendous growth in BT sector. NanoBT has now entered into furthering the useful research on faster pace. It has scientific and technical pool of human resources, rich biodiversity, large agricultural and market base for new BT products and world recognition as a producer of low cost, high quality bulk drugs and formulations. Issues surrounding Intellectual Property Rights and BT inventions are varied but interrelated. Basic research has to be transferred to applied field and the resultant is to be commercialized. In some countries, plant varieties are protected by *sui generis* system. Post genome research has added fuel to the fire; new innovative fields, like 'Bioinformatics' with plenty of biology information and new processing methods have emerged. BT uses four tools of IPR, viz. Patents, Trademarks, Trade secrets and Copyright. At present, its contribution to the World's patenting activity is less than three percent. As such there is a necessity to amend the IP laws to give better protection to R&D, and better enforcement of IP, technology transfer and licensing arrangements. Biotech industry in India is flourishing more in pharmaceuticals, particularly in healthcare. There is an urgent need for harmonization of administration and centralization of the patenting process in accordance with WIPO diktats.

2. HISTORY OF PLANT IMPROVEMENT

Cultivation of Plants: Plants were put in to cultivation since prehistoric time. Crops were not domesticated as we see them today. Initially, they were very close to their wild relatives. Shift from their areas of origin brought about mixing of additional germplasm. For example, present day sugarcane crop (*Saccharum officinarum*) is a derivative of five *Saccharum* species (*S. barberi, S. officinarum, S. robustum, S. sinensis, S. spontaneum*) all native of old World. *S. robustum* and *S. spontaneum* occur wild even now. Wheat, a very important cereal crop probably originated from ancient wheats and related wild grasses by natural crossing. Primitive man was growing many crops, like banana, onions, flax, hemp, garden pea, and oats. Since early times, human beings are trying to improve their crops mainly by selection which was a hit and trial method without any awareness of inheritance of characters.

Plant Breeding Programmes: These are concerned with improvement of economically important plants to increase agricultural production through developing new varieties which combine many desirable and beneficial characters. This is achieved by introduction of variations, artificial selection and plant introduction. Variations arise by mutations, polyploidy and hybridization. Hybrids are known for their vigour; they could be achieved by single cross, double cross and three way cross. For example, three genetic lines A, B and D are involved in the origin of hexaploid wheat *Triticum vulgare*. F1 hybrid is obtained by crossing A and B, then it is crossed to D (Fig.1). Conventional breeding has given way to fast improvements by way of BT.

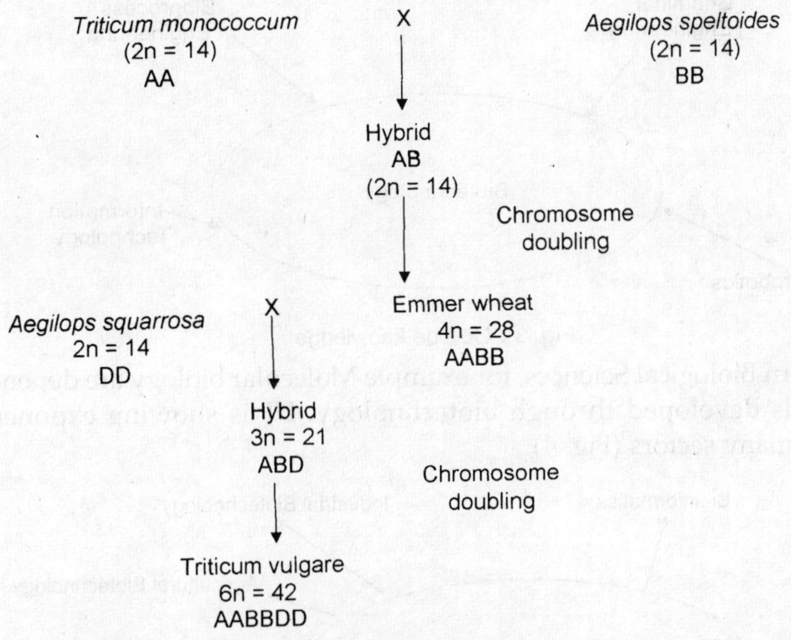

Fig. 1 : Origin of hexaploid wheat

Biotechnology: Traditional BT is selective breeding of plants and animals to fermentation of beer and organic treatment of sewage. Modern BT is a field of applied biology. It makes use of living organisms in engineering, technology, genetic engineering, medicine, cell and tissue culture, immunology, recombinant DNA technology, etc. According to CBD, Biotechnology is "any technological application that uses biotechnological system of living organisms, or derivatives thereof, to make or modify products or processes for specific use". BT is dependent on pure biological sciences and also outside knowledge (Figs. 2 and 3).

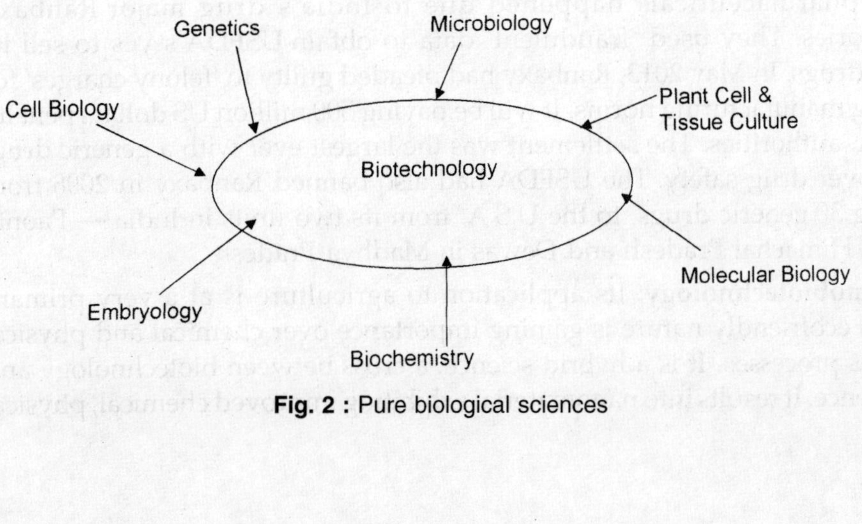

Fig. 2 : Pure biological sciences

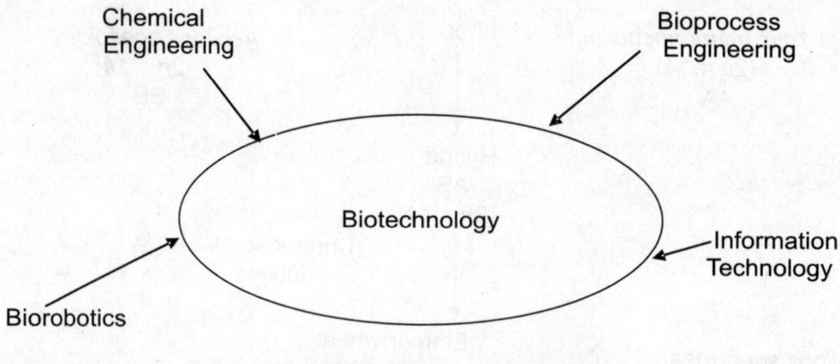

Fig. 3 : Outside knowledge

Modern Biological Sciences, for example Molecular biology are dependent on methods developed through biotechnology. BT is showing exponential growth in many sectors (Fig. 4).

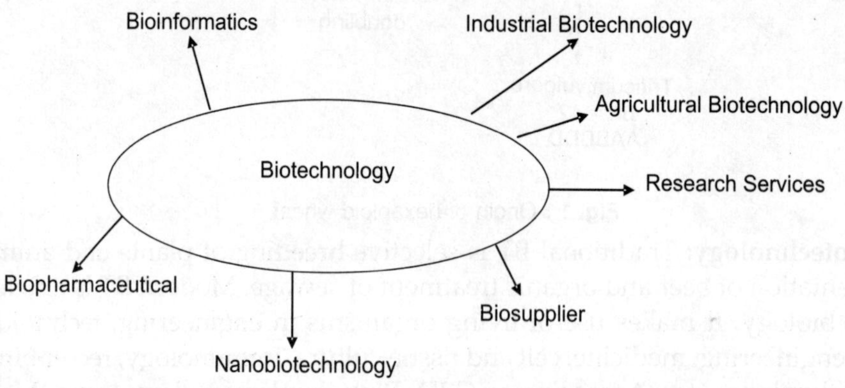

Fig. 4 : Growth of BT in various sectors

BT is an emerging sphere in India on a world level. Large scale investment is also taking place for the purpose of R&D in this field. A major setback to Indian pharmaceuticals happened due to India's drug major Ranbaxy Laboratories. They used 'fraudulent' data to obtain USFDA's yes to sell its generic drugs. In May 2013, Ranbaxy had pleaded guilty to 'felony charges' for violating manufacturing norms. It will be paying 500 million US dollars penalty to U.S.A. authorities. The settlement was the largest ever with a generic drug-maker over drug safety. The USFDA had also banned Ranbaxy in 2008 from shipping 30 generic drugs to the U.S.A. from its two units in India — Paonta Sahib in Himachal Pradesh and Dewas in Madhya Pradesh.

Nanobiotechnology: Its application to agriculture is at a very primary state. Its ecofriendly nature is gaining importance over chemical and physical synthesis processes. It is a hybrid science, a cross between biotechnology and nanoscience. It results into nanomaterial exhibiting improved chemical, physical and biological properties. It explains the material and devices in exceptionally great details. Plant extracts along with metal salt solution form nanoparticles of different sizes. These can help faster seed germination and further growth, can deliver genetic material into plants and can provide controlled sites for the application of pesticides and fertilizers.

3. TYPES OF IPR USED BY BT

Patent: A newly invented product or process is protected under it. Patentee has a legal right to make, sell and prevent others from using the patented invention without his/her authorization. Legal systems in various countries are developing their own responses. The definitions and interpretations are varied. In many countries, scientific theories, discoveries of materials or substances already existing in nature, and method for the medical treatment of human and animals are not regarded as inventions. Medical products and devices are patentable. Intellectual Property system is in a constant state of evolution with advances in technology, like Information technology and Biotechnology. Changes in socio-economic and cultural conditions are also compelling the system to change. For example, patent protection for biological materials, *sui generis* system for plant varieties and topographies. Patents are generally not renewed beyond a maximum of 20 years but there is always some catch, like 'evergreening' employed by multinational companies. A new product or process to be patentable should be technical in nature and should meet the following criteria:

(i) *Novelty:* To be novel, the invention has to show some new characteristic, which is not known in the body of the existing knowledge. This body of existing knowledge is called 'prior art'. The matter disclosed in the specification is not published before the date of filing of patent application

(ii) *Inventive Step:* Non-obviousness. Invention is not obvious to a person skilled in the art in light of prior publication/knowledge/ document. For example, a claim was applied for an isolated DNA sequence encoding a mature human IL-3 protein having a proline residue at position 8 of the mature polypeptide, said protein possessing bone marrow proliferation-inducing activity in a human bone marrow proliferation assay. It was found that there was only one variation in the amino acid sequence which does not normally change the activity and function of the protein. The applicant could not give any evidence that the protein coded by the claimed DNA was any different from the prior art in its chemical properties. Thus, the inventive step cannot be acknowledged and the claim was rejected.

(iii) *Industrially Applicable:* Usefulness. Invention should possess utility, so that it can be made or used in an industry. For example, a Claim was applied on a V28 protein (V28) having a function as a receptor (of a kind known as 7 TM). The use disclosed in the application was speculative, i.e. it was not specific, substantial and credible and as such is not considered industrially applicable.

(iv) *Disclosure:* Inventors have to disclose all technical information about their invention

In addition, an invention must be accepted as 'patentable' under law.

Trademark: It is a distinctive sign, which identifies certain goods or services as those produced or provided by a specific person or enterprise. These are sign or combination of signs used to identify origin or source of a good or service. They have a variety of shapes (2 and 3 dimensional) and forms. Simple word or phrase, a company's name, a number, letters, combination of colours, an image; sometimes sound and smell form Trademarks. In some countries, registration for marks is not necessary but registration protects them from being copied or unauthorized use. They are not limited in time; registration can be renewed every ten years.

Copyright: It is a legal term describing rights given to creators for their literary and artistic work. Its primary objective is not to reward authors but to promote progress of science and useful arts. For example, an artistic label was copyrighted by Hawkins cookers but another cooker manufacturing company started using this label, which is infringement of copyright.

Trade Secret: Includes private proprietary information or physical material that allows a definite advantage to the owner. Here secrecy to a trade secret is the most important factor, for example, the formula used for making aerated drink by Coca Cola company. If the information claimed to be a trade secret is available through any legitimate means and is obtained in this way, then it is no longer secret and becomes ineligible for protection.

4. HISTORY OF INDIAN PATENT SYSTEM

1856	The Act (vi) of 1856 on protection of inventions based on the British patent law of 1852. Certain exclusive privileges granted to inventors of new manufacturers for 14 years
1859	The Act modified as Act (xv); Patent monopolies called exclusive privileges (Making, selling and using inventions in India and authorizing others to do so for 14 years from date of filing specification)
1872	The Patents & Designs Protection Act
1883	The Protection of Inventions Act
1888	Consolidated as the Inventions & Designs Act

Contd...

1911	The Indian Patents & Designs Act
1972	The Patents Act (Act 39 of 1970) came into force on 20.04.1972
1999	On 26.03.1999, Patents (amendment) Act (1999) came into force from 01.01.1995
2002	The Patents (amendment) Act 2002 came into force from 20.05.2003
2002	Hon'ble Calcutta High Court, gave a decision in 'Dimminaco AG v. Controller of Patents and Designs' case which broadened the grant of patents to inventions where the end product of the claimed process contained living microorganisms.
2005	The Patents (amendment) Act 2005 effective from 01.01.2005

India is a member state of WIPO, an organization responsible for protecting intellectual property throughout the World. India is a member of following Treaties, Conventions and Organizations in respect of patents:

- WTO to supervise and liberalize International trade from January 1, 1995. Administers 28 agreements; TRIPS is one of them.
- Convention establishing WIPO to develop balanced and accessible international IP system. Created in 1967; governs 23 treaties on IPRs
- The Madrid Agreement for International filing of registration application for Trademarks
- The Berne Convention for Copyright protection
- Paris convention for protection of industrial property from December 7, 1998.
- PCT for protection of patent internationally from December 17, 1998.
- Budapest Treaty for microorganism patent from December 17, 2001.

Under Indian Patent Act 1970, there was less allocation for R&D; process patents were encouraged rather than new product development. It had negative impact on patent system as no emphasis was given to product innovation. Later improvement was done in the Act (1999, 2002 and 2005); it allots longer patent term, i.e. 20 years. In U.S.A., it is 17 years. Now biochemical, biotechnological and microbiological processes are included within the scope of chemical processes for the grant of patent. The definition of "invention" is also changed to "any new product or process involving an inventive step and capable of industrial application". It has deleted the word "manner of manufacture". Product patents are granted now and there is better compliance and enforcement mechanism. Biotechnological Patent claims in India can contain products, like agrochemicals, known component along with new chemical entities, new products derived from natural resources, new drug molecules, new products resulting through biotechnological, microbiological and biochemical processes, microorganisms, and pharmaceutical preparations. For example, in 2002, Calcutta High Court decided against Dimminaco in a case (Dimminaco AG v.

Controller of Patents and Designs). This was related to a process for the preparation of a live vaccine for protecting poultry from Bursitis infection. The Controller of Patents had refused their application for the vaccine involved processing of certain microbial substances and contained gene sequence. According to court the said claim was not patentable because the claimed process was only a natural process without any manufacturing activity and the end-product contained living material. Many other BT works are non-patentable, like whole plants and animals and their parts thereof, any process for manufacture of living entities, transgenic plants and animals or their parts, biological organs, tissues, cells, viruses, gene sequence, DNA sequence without disclosing their function, methods of crossing and breeding, any biological material or method of making capable of causing prejudice to human, animal or plants, process for cloning human and animals, any invention which in effect is traditional knowledge, and any method of treatment such as medicinal, surgical, curative, prophylactic, diagnostic and therapeutical for human or animal. Some other important Indian Acts are: The protection of Plant Variety and Farmer's Rights Act, 2001 and Biological Diversity Act, 2002.

5. EMERGING ISSUES SURROUNDING PATENTS AND BIOTECHNOLOGICAL INVENTIONS

(i) Legal standards in respect of the scope of patent protection for inventions in the field of BT

(ii) *Patentable subject:* Substances isolated or derived from naturally occurring living organisms are "inventions" or "discoveries"

(iii) *Appropriate application of the patentability requirements:* New, inventive step, industrial applicability and disclosure. Public disclosure of full scope of the patented invention, defining breadth of the claims which are supported by disclosure of invention is a cornerstone of patent system

(iv) *Licensing and other issues related to the exploitation of patents:* India, being a developing nation, needs to avoid all kinds of monopolistic practices by compulsory licensing. There are provisions in Indian legislation (Protection of Plant Variety and Farmer's Rights Act, 2002) comprising provisions for compulsory licensing procedures. Government enforces licensing in case of any fear of malintention of protection holder with respect to production or pricing of the product against consumers welfare

(v) BT in plants requires broad range of comprehensive research, which may be covered by a broad patent granted at an early stage of innovation. The number and breadth of patents granted to early fundamental research have raised concerns about patent thickets and royalty stacking

(vi) Public-private partnership to generate revenue and protect investments

(vii) Facilitating the transfer of technology from basic research to applied research

(viii) Commercialization

(ix) Access to genetic resources and benefit sharing. Conservation and preservation of the environment (including protection of biodiversity). There is a BD Act, 2002 in force which provides a mechanism for access to the genetic resources and benefit sharing accrued therefrom (subject to approval of NBA). To facilitate access and benefit sharing and to prevent any unauthorized use of the biological resources of India applications in the field of biotechnology and other new subjects within the Patent Office have become essential in order to establish uniform and consistent practice (Manual of Patent Office Practice and Procedures).

(x) Moral and ethical dimensions.

6. ISSUES CONCERNING RELATIONSHIP BETWEEN PATENTS AND OTHER FORMS OF INTELLECTUAL PROPERTY

(i) In Plant BT, plant varieties are protected by a *sui generis* system in many countries

(ii) Bioinformatics is characterized by biological information and its processing methods

(iii) Copyright in BT includes DNA sequence data, which may be published. Using wobble in the genetic code, an alternative sequence coding for the same protein can be prepared without infringement. One is not allowed to copy a BT book but the idea given in the book can be used for any purpose without violating copyright

(iv) Trade Secrets in BT include cell lines, hybridization conditions, merchandising plans, customer lists, etc. They have unlimited duration and are not required to satisfy more difficult conditions as laid down by patenting system

(v) Trademarks are borne on laboratory equipments. Certain vectors useful in recombinant research are known by their trademarks

(vi) Example of IP is the development of crop varieties, which are protected through PBRs (not available in India)

(vii) Through PBRs, plant breeder who develops the variety enjoys exclusive right for its marketing. Further breeding or re-plantation is permitted to the buyer (i.e. farmer)

(viii) In some countries, genetic material (plants and animals) are patentable. In such cases, the buyer is not allowed to save and use the seed for cultivation. For use, a fee should be paid to the patent holder

(ix) These rights affect positively as well as negatively to the conservation of PGR and AGR

(x) Patenting life forms, i.e. transgenic plants will restrict free exchange of genetic material

(xi) In U.S.A., patented pharmaceuticals are subjected to regulatory purview of FDA before clinical use. Even insecticides, pesticides, etc. require EPA permits. Countries, like U.S.A., Netherlands, Germany, U.K., Denmark and Switzerland are involved in patenting in BT in India. Vitiligo is a skin pigmentation disorder causing white patches. Hakeems (Unani system doctors) of India are treating it with extracts of melon since long. EPO intended to give patent on this to a Spanish Company but had to decide otherwise because of great digital documentation work (TKDL) done by C.S.I.R., India by enumerating details and traditional knowledge of 2,00,000 Indian useful plants (Prior art)

(xii) Focus of patenting activity is mostly for healthcare and industrial enzymes

(xiii) There is low level of patenting in agriculture and environment. Huge work is done in Agri-biotechnology in India; it needs a comprehensive and intensive IPR protection to identify various inventions

(xiv) Diagnostic methods are non-patentable. In 2012, American Supreme Court disregarded a judgment of the Executive Branch about granting patents for biomarker based diagnostic methods. BIO and numerous *amici* have warned about its negative consequences. According to them, irrationally restricting the ability of innovation to protect invention that are important for ailment cure, medical breakthrough, and other technologies that can make our lives safer, healthier and cleaner environment will be detrimental to growth in this field.

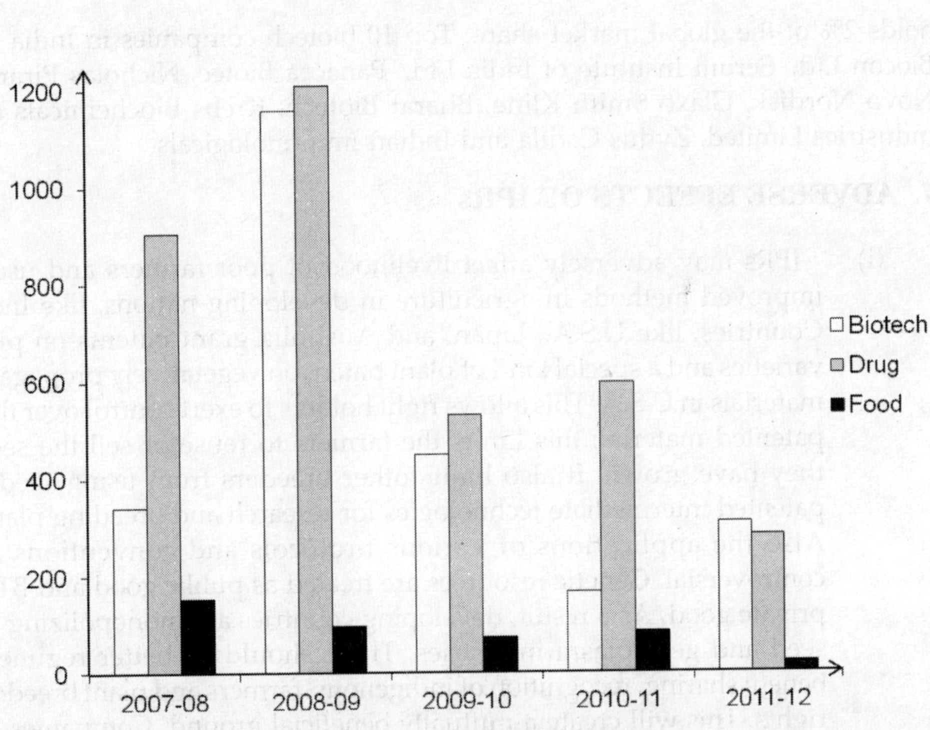

Fig. 5 : Patents granted in India related to BT during 2007-08 till 2011-12

Table 1 : Patents granted in India in some new fields related to BT during 2011-12

FieldsCountry	Biomedical	Biochemistry	Bioinformatics	Agriculture
India	0	9	0	1
Foreign	24	29	0	1

Protection for BT can be achieved by any of four tools of IPR discussed above. As technology is developing fast, trade secret approach may be used. Cost of secrecy is more than that of obtaining a patent but its enforcement is much costlier. Secret may get exposed or disclosed. So rights may be preferred. The Biotech industry is one of the fastest growing knowledge-based industries in India. However, as exhibited in Fig. 5, this trend is not reflected in the number of patents granted during the last five years or so. Further, as reported in Table 1, patenting activity in India in some new fields related to BT during 2011-12 is alarmingly low, which is a cause of serious concern. Biotechnology has the potential to play a major role in rapid economic development. India has skills, knowledge, R&D facilities, and cost effectiveness. With comparative advantages and presence of some top companies in the market, India has got the potential to come out as one of the key players in the World biotech sector. Currently, it holds 2% of the global market share. Top 10 biotech companies in India are: Biocon Ltd., Serum Institute of India Ltd., Panacea Biotec, Nicholas Piramal, Novo Nordisk, Glaxo Smith Kline, Bharat Biotech, Krebs Biochemicals and Industries Limited, Zydus Cadila and Indian Immunologicals.

7. ADVERSE EFFECTS OF IPRs

(i) IPRs may adversely affect livelihood of poor farmers and use of improved methods in agriculture in developing nations, like India. Countries, like U.S.A., Japan, and Australia grant patents on plant varieties and a special kind of plant patent on vegetatively propagated materials in U.S.A. This allows right holders to exert control over their patented material; this limits the farmers to reuse or sell the seeds they have grown. It also limits other breeders from using seed or patented intermediate technologies for research and breeding plants. Also the applications of various protocols and conventions are controversial. Genetic resources are treated as public good and BT as private good. As a result, developing countries are monopolizing the seed and germplasm industries. There should be better regime of benefit sharing, recognition of indigenous, farmers and plant breeders' rights. This will create a mutually beneficial ground. Companies are trying to hold dominant position in the market by selling seeds with terminator genes, i.e. farmer is restricted from using them multiple times

(ii) *Plant diversity and nature balance:* Diversity and selection are two main tools used by farmers in feeding the nation. Diversity enables growth of a species in diverse geographical, environmental and other external conditions. American law is clear that no form of IP can be used to obtain protection over these. India needs to enact such laws

(iii) *Food security:* Misuse of IP rights is crippling innovations in BT. The real use of BT is to enhance global health and nutrition. IP is a legal regime; it has become so suffocating that many scholars, engineers and scientists are desperate to find newer ways to create

(iv) *Costlier drugs:* Under TRIPS agreement, nations are allowed to grant compulsory licenses to make generics, if most people cannot afford patented drugs. Drug-patent related decisions generally go in favor of domestic generic drug companies. In 2012, IPO overruled German drug firms' objections to allowing Natco Pharma to produce a generic version of cancer medicine Nexavar. Glivec is blockbuster anticancer drug used to treat myeloid leukemia. It costs Rs. 1,20,000 per month whereas Indian generic equivalent costs only Rs. 8500 per month. India is a thriving generic market and a low cost global supplier. Novartis' request for 'ever-greening' of Glivec patent is denied by IPO. Supreme court of India (April, 2013) also upheld the decision stating that it is only a new form of existing drug Imatinib. This has given way for more generic companies to enter the Indian market and has helped Pharmaceutical firms, like Ranbaxy, Cipla and Natco to carry on their business

(v) *Human health:* Glyphosate is the World's best selling herbicide developed by Monsanto. Higher levels of plant oestrogen are produced when members of Bean family (leguminosae) are grown in the presence of this herbicide. Glyphosate treatment of cereals results in residues of herbicides in animals feeds, like milk, meat and eggs. These may disrupt development of reproductive system of children when consumed by them

(vi) *Seeds with stacked genes to produce transgenic crops:* Such seeds may be good for insect bio-control but homology in genes might bring in unpredictable changes in pollen and eggs by duplication, translocation, etc. of a crop.

8. ROADMAP FOR BT IN INDIA

- Ensure equitable and sustainable system of living, development, patent law and TRIPS
- Local, regional, national and global level accountability for governmental and intergovernmental institutions
- Work for analyzing Bio-piracy BT
- Invest on products which have home grown advantage
- Diversity in Indian plants and human sub-races may hold key to disease mechanisms and cures
- Rewards for innovators
- Increase in BT fund for drug discoveries, healthcare, agriculture, environment, animal husbandry, etc.
- Skilled manpower trained in India and abroad
- Clinical trials at reduced rates
- With product patents, multinational firms may collaborate with local firms. This will boost Indian R&D and industry will go global in true sense.

9. ABBREVIATIONS

AGR	Animal Genetic Resources
BD	Biological Diversity Act
BIO	Biotechnology Industry Organization
Bt	*Bacillus thuringiensis*
BT	Biotechnology
CBD	Convention on Biological Diversity
CSIR	Council for Scientific and Industrial Research
EPA	Environment Protection Agency
EPO	European Patent Organization
FDA	Food and Drug Administration
IP	Intellectual Property
IPO	India Patent Office
IPR	Intellectual Property Rights
NBA	National Biodiversity Authority
BR	*Plant Breeders Rights*
PCT	Patent Co- operation Treaty
PGR	Plant Genetic Resources
R&D	Research and Development
TKDL	*Traditional Knowledge Digital Library*
TRIPS	Trade Related Intellectual Property Rights
USFDA	U.S. Food and Drug Administration
WTO	World Trade Organization

REFERENCES

Acharya, N.K. (2012). Text Book on Intellectual Property Rights, 6th Edition. Asia Law House, Hyderabad.

Anonymous (2013). Guidelines for Examination of Biotechnology Applications for Patent. Intellectual Property India, Office of the Controller General of Patents, Designs and Trademarks, India, pp. 22.

Chi-Ham, C.L., Clark, K.L. and Bennett, A.B. (2010). The intellectual property landscape for gene suppression technologies in plants. Nature Biotechnology, 28, 32-36.

Kochhar, S.L. (2011). Economic Botany in the Tropics. 4th Edition. MacMillan Publishers India Ltd., Delhi.

Mashelkar, R. A. (1999). Economics of Knowledge. 16th Dr. Deshmukh Memorial lecture. India International Centre, New Delhi.

Mathur, H. (2008). Compulsory licensing under Section 92A: Issues and concerns. Journal of Intellectual Property Rights, 13, 464-72.

PPVFR (2001). The Protection of Plant Varieties and Farmer's Right Bill. Lok Sabha, India.

Prajneshu, M. (2005). Intellectual property rights in biotechnological inventions. In "Advances in Biotechnology. Trivedi, P.C. (Ed.), pp. 379-93. Agrobios, India".

Prajneshu, M. and Gupta, V.K. (2001). Traditional knowledge database: IPR and opportunities for R&D. Journal of Intellectual Property Rights, 6, 449-58.

Sengupta, A. (2013). Two decades of struggle. Economic & Political Weekly, 48 (32), 43-45.

Singh, H.R. and Singh, P.R. (2013). Entertainment network Vs. Super cassette industries: Compulsory licensing in the copyright demystified. Journal of Intellectual Property Rights, 18, 201-11.

www.wipo.net

www.fbae.org

www.plant-molecularbiotechnology.info-intellectual-property-protection.htm

www.ipindia.nic.in/ipr/patent/journal-archive-2008

❑❑❑

CHAPTER - 41

Importance of Intellectual Property Rights and Knowledge, Patenting, Indigenous, Traditional Knowledge and Knowledge Management Challenges

Asim Ray[1] and Suman Patel[2]
[1] *Assistant Professor*
SRM University, NCR Campus, Delhi Meerut Road, Ghaziabad
UP-201204, India
Fax: 01232-234308
[2] **Dr. Suman Patel, Scientist**
CSIR-National Institute of Science, Technology & Development Studies (NISTADS)
Council of Scientific & Industrial Research (CSIR)
Dr. K.S. Krishnan Marg, New Delhi 110 012, India
*Email : *asim.ray2012@gmail.com, *sumanitrc@gmail.com*

INTRODUCTION

Intellectual Property Right (IPR) is described as a generic legal term for patents, copyrights, and trademarks, making the feasibility for legal rights to protect ideas, the expression of ideas, and the inventors and creators of such ideas (Brown, 2003). Two types of rights, first, associated with patents and second, associated with copyrights are included into the current IPR regimes. The social purpose behind the IPR is to reward the originator of an invention. Intellectual property serves as a strong foundation of the modern information economy since it promotes software, life sciences, and computer industries, and has becomes a part of most of the products we consume today (Gallini and Scotchmer, 2002).

IPR can be divided into two broad areas :

(1) Copy right which deals with rights fo authors of literary and artistic work and

(2) Industrial property right which consist of protectionof distinctive seigns in particular trade mark and geographical indication and to stimulate innovation.

Unique, traditional, local knowledge that exists within and developed around specific conditions of individuals indigenous to a specific geographical location or area has been defined as indigenous knowledge (Louise, 1998). It includes know, how, skills, innovation, practices and learning that is associated with the traditional life style of the community. Patent serves as a protector of traditional knowledge and its objective is to preserve the right of the traditional knowledge holder against the third party. Knowledge management (KM) is the ability of an organization to create, share and use the collective knowledge of its products, processes and people (Fontaine and Lesser, 2002). KM provides the possibility of a viable alternative for firms in order to create and maintain competitive advantage in turbulent. This article discusses the importance of IPR and Knowledge, Trade Related Aspects of Intellectual Property Rights (TRIPS), patenting, indigenous, traditional knowledge, Tradeitional Knowledge Digital Library (TKDL), Traditional Knowledge Resource Classification (TKRC) and also highlights KM challenges today.

Today, research in the area of stem cells in regenerative medicine is influenced by the Government policies. For example, patent on stem cells and stem cell research is dictated by U.S. Patent laws (Zachariades, 2013). Human embryonic stem cells (hESCs) and pluripotent stem cells and methods of making or using such cells are patentable in the United States but not in the European Union (EU) according in context with issues of intellectual property (IP) law (Zachariades, 2013). However, trade secrets are suggested as options available in the protection of innovations in the stem cell field.

Intellectual Property Right (IPR) and Knowledge

Property that generate from peoples creative talent and abilities is known as intellectual property. With the emergence of knowledge based-industries, IPR was initiated as an economic mechanism to provide the inventors a temporary monopoly in turn for the disclosure of technical knowhow to facilitate the ongoing innovation (Cowan and Harison, 2001). IPR is a composition of ideas, inventions and creative expression that gives their owner right to exclude others from access (Erstling, 2009). Use of symbols, particular words, logos, or other markings that indicate the source of a product or service is provided with the help of trademark. Another method 'trademark secret' helps to keep an invention as a secret and rather than disclosing it (Brown, 2003).

In the knowledge based economy intellectual property system is an important aspect of nation's public policymaking and encourages investment in innovation, and entrepreneurial spirit. IPR are largely territorial right except of copy right (Erstling, 2009). Knowledge based products are described as intangible, non-excludable and non-rivalrous goods. Protection for patents is given for 15-20yrs and for copyrights is for a longer duration-the author's lifetime plus an additional 50-70 yrs. IPR regimes also include other components like licensing and trade secrecy. The production and application of patented inventions is made possible by other firms upon licensing on the basis of royalty fees. Licensing may be either exclusive-granted only a single firm permits to use inventions. On the other hand it may also be non-exclusive-may allow several companies to exploit its applications. Thus, technological advances and creative art may be well protected by patent and licensing methods (Cowan and Harison, 2001). This strategy in fact maintains the continuity of the innovations e.g. development of personal computer, Internet and recombinant gene technologies etc. Figure 1 describes the IPR and its categories.

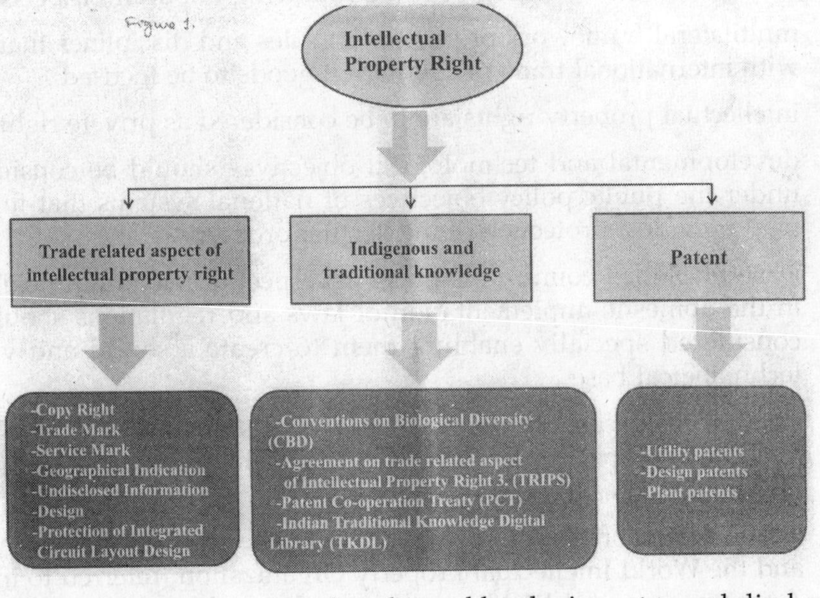

A balance between monopoly achieved by the inventor and disclosure of the technical knowledge is maintained by the IPR legislation in order to maximize social welfare. Like any other property IPR can be assigned, gifted, sold and licensed. At the same time IPR can hold in many countries. What is known to public cannot be protected through IPR. Patents, copyrights, industrial designs, integrated circuit (IC) layout design and trade secrets are associated with something new (Erstling, 2009). Also, trade secrecy has been made to avoid inadvertent technology transfer to rival firms. This is done on the basis of contracts between companies and employees (Cowan and Harison, 2001).

According to World *Trade Organization* (WTO), IPR are the right given to a person over the creation of their mind. They usually give the creator an exclusive right over the use of his or her creation for a certain period of time (Erstling, 2009).

Literally work such as books and musical composition, painting, computer programmed are protected for a minimum period for a 50 year after the death of the author. Trademark and geographical indications have indefinite life provided these are renewed after a stipulated time by paying official fees. Trade secrets also have an infinite life but they do not have to be renewed. The trade secret has the advantage that they never expire however; special measure has to be taken in order to maintain its secrecy. For example, the formula for Coca Cola is a trade secret of all time (Coca-Cola Bottling Co. of Shreveport, Inc. v 1983 & 1985).

Trade related aspect of intellectual property right (TRIPS)

TRIPS Agreement-This recognizes the following important aspects-

a. multilateral framework of principles, rules and disciplines that deal with international trade in counterfeit goods to be focused

b. intellectual property rights are to be considered as private rights

c. developmental and technological objectives should be considered under the public policy objectives of national systems that in turn may provide a protection of intellectual property

d. least-developed country members in respect of maximum flexibility in the domestic implementation of laws and regulations should be considered specially enabling them to create a sound and viable technological base

e. strengthened commitments to resolve disputes on trade-related intellectual property issues through multilateral procedures to be given importance so as to reduce tensions

f. establishment of a mutually supportive relationship between the WTO and the World Intellectual Property Organization (referred to in this Agreement as "WIPO") and also other relevant international organizations

The general agreement on TRIPS under the Uruguay round mention seven intellectual property rights (Erstling, 2009)-

1. **Copy Right-**Copy right is the exclusive legal right of author of literary and artistic work. Books and other writing musical composition, painting, sculpture are protected by copy right. Right of the performer-actor, singer, musician producer of the sound recording and broad casting organization are also protected by this act.

2. **Trade Mark–**Trade mark are design and name which distinguish goods and services of one under taking from those of other. The basic purpose is to ensure fair competition and enabling the consumer to make informed choice between various goods and services. Trade mark may consist of the drawing symbol, three dimensional sign or color. A well known trademark is a mark which is known to the substantial segment of public who uses such goods and services. Associate trade mark resembles each other; owner is same and also applied to same types of goods and services. A readymade garment company can use associate marks for shirts and trousers. Any symbol, word or series of words, logo, or other marking that provides the source of a product or service has been defined as a trademark.

3. **Service Mark-**Mark used to represent service such as banking, communication, education, financing, insurance, chit fund, real state, transport storage, material, boarding, lodging, construction, repair, conveying of news or information are known as service mark .

4. **Geographical Indication (GI)-**Geographical identification identify such goods as agriculture goods, natural goods or manufactured goods as origination or manufactured in the territory of the country or a region or a locality in that region where a given quality reputation or other characteristic of good is attributable to its geographical origin. According to TRIPS agreement property protected under GI will be given protection in domestic and internal market.

5. **Undisclosed Information-**Undisclosed information is generally known as trade secret. It may include a technique or process that provides the owner with an advantage over competitors. It may include new product plan, product costing, best material to use sources of material, accounting information employees record credit rating of customer, production informers. The owner can exploit a trade secret as long as it remains secret.

6. **Design-**Design means, configuration pattern ornament or composition of line or color-whether applied in two dimensions or three dimensions or in both forms by any industrial process or mean but it does not include any mode or principal of construction.

7. **Protection of Integrated Circuit Layout Design-** It provides protection for semi conductor IC layout design. Layout design includes a layout of transistor and other circuitry element.

Indigenous and Traditional Knowledge

Indigenous knowledge has been defined as unique, traditional, local knowledge that exists within and developed around specific conditions of individuals indigenous to a specific geographical location or area (Grenier, 1998).

Specific characteristics of indigenous knowledge include-

a. they are cumulative i.e. represent generations of experiences, careful observations and trial-and-error experiments
b. they are dynamic since it add new knowledge continuously, adapts external knowledge meeting the suitability of local situation

Sharachchandra (1991) describes "Sustainable Development" (SD) as an emerging latest development catchphrase since past few years and its fundamental impact depends on removal of politically expedient fuzziness in favor of intellectual clarity and rigor. Indigenous knowledge is essential for sustainable development that includes agricultural and natural-resource development. This is possible by proper utilization and management of conservation of natural resources so as to meet basic human needs like food, water, shelter, clothing and fuel not only for present but also future generations (Grenier, 1998).

Nature of Traditional Knowledge

Traditional knowledge may include agricultural, environmental and medicinal knowledge. Traditional knowledge includes knowhow, skills, innovation, practices and learning that is associated with the traditional life style of the community. Traditional knowledge may be communicated orally. Traditional knowledge is the part of the custom and culture of traditional community. Tradition knowledge is often restricted to certain community member. There is a link between the traditional knowledge and patent system. Traditional knowledge bears the similarity of intellectual property right but the way is different.

Usefulness of Traditional Knowledge

The protection of traditional knowledge is motivated by economic, social and environmental interest. Some local communities depend on traditional knowledge for their livelihood which is derived from their local ecosystem. This provides opportunity for economic development. Some traditional product like plant based medicine, health product, cosmetic and non-wood forest product are source of export revenue. Traditional method of farming and natural resources management of biodiversity is environmental friendly and hence can preserve bio diversity of plant and animals.

Patent as a Protector of Traditional Knowledge

Biopiracy can be defined as an exploitation of traditional knowledge by multinational companies without the consent of knowledge holder (Erstling, 2009). Patent is helpful in protecting biopiracy. Patent granted for neem, turmeric, the Enola-bean are the example of unjust result (Moyer-Henry, 2006). Three international agreements-Conventions on Biological Diversity (CBD),

Agreement on trade related aspect of Intellectual Property Right (TRIPS), Patent Co-operation Treaty (PCT) protect the traditional knowledge holder.

CBD-The objective of the CBD is the conservation of biological diversity and fair and equitable sharing of benefit which is relevant to patent protection and TK (Moyer-Henry, 2006). Bonn guideline encourages mutually agreed terms of benefit according to degree of contribution "encourage the disclosure of the country of origin ... of traditional knowledge, innovations and practices of indigenous and local communities in applications for intellectual property right.........(Erstling, 2009).

PCT-It is a tool to acquire patent by a single application in every PCT member country where they seek protection. The PCT process is divided into two phases-

1. International Phase
2. Nations Phase

National law should fulfill the requirement of international application (Erstling. 2009). The objective of the protection is to preserve the right of the traditional knowledge holder against the third party. A challenge to the protection is the difference in national and regional requirement. Generally traditional knowledge is communicated orally and used locally. This is a limitation to protect the traditional knowledge.

Following are the guidelines for defensive protection

1) Disclosure should be publicly available and contain publication date
2) Content of disclosure is important. The publication should describe the innovative or technological concept behind traditional knowledge

Data Base for Traditional Knowledge-Information about the traditional knowledge should be available in public. Traditional knowledge data base is an effective way to achieve the objective of public availability.

Indian Traditional Knowledge Digital Library (TKDL)-This takes the reference of centuries old TK from ancient text in Sanskrit, Urdu, Persian, or other inaccessible language. It presents the data in English, French, and German. India has traditional way to treat disease which is described in ancient literature. This is rarely understood by common man. Department of Indian System of Medicine and Homeopathy has created a Traditional Knowledge Digital Library which was initiated in 2001. This is an inter-disciplinary task force that consist of Ayurveda, Yoga, and Naturopathy, Unani, Sidhha, and Homeopathy-AYUSH. Traditional Knowledge Digital Library is a project between Council of Scientific and Industrial Research (CSIR), Ministry Of Science And Technology and Department of Ayurveda, Yoga and Naturopathy, Unani, Sidhha and Homeopathy. South Africa, African Regional Industrial property organization (ARPIO), Mangolia, Nigeria, Thailand, Malaysia has developed own TKDL. Tables 1 describes examples of IPR categories that include-trademark, trade secret, patent and TKDL etc.

Table 1 :

Category	Example	Reference
Trademark	Bristol-Myers Squibb's Claim to the word "Taxol" as the name of its anticancer i.e. trademark Taxol®	Editorial (1995), Chesnoff, 1995, Khan, 1995
Trade secret	Coca Cola	Coca-Cola Bottling Co. of Shreveport, Inc. v 1983 & 1985
Patent	WO2007014467A1-Diagnosis and treatment of mood disorders	Meyer, 2007
TKDL	Basmati Rice (Oryza sativa Linn.), Neem (Azadirachta indica A. Juss.), Turmeric (Curcuma longa Linn.)	Gupta, 2009

Traditional Knowledge Resource Classification (TKRC)

It has gained an international recognition. This is developed for Indian System of Medicine- Ayurveda, Unani, Siddha and yoga by using modern classification. TKRC has created greater awareness by using information technology on TKRC making the knowledge available to patent examiner in a language which is understood by them. India has successfully fought against turmeric and basamati patent granted by (United States Patents and Trademark Office (USTPO) and Neem patent granted by European Patent Office (EPO).

Benefit Sharing-Disclosure of traditional knowledge source ensures that patent applicant has obtained consent of traditional knowledge holder. In traditional based invention traditional knowledge holder is eligible for ownership. An invention should be original work of the person named to be as inventor. Biological Diversity Act 2002 states that invention based on genetic material of Indian Origin should obtain informed consent of National Biodiversity Authority and impose benefit sharing fees or royalties.

Challenges of Protection-Traditional knowledge are generally collective. Community ownership is extension of joint ownership. Traditional knowledge holder does not apply western scientific method. TRIPS or PCT does not impose rules. Patent applications are published after eighteen months following which its ability to maintain confidence diminishes in the application process. Patent law requires novelty. If the patent examiner is unable to access the invention the patentability is questionable.

Patent

Patent is a legal protection given to a new invention considered to be as a property that can be gifted, inherited, assigned, sold or licensed and gives the holder exclusive right to use or sell the patented product (IPR Bulletin, 1999; IPR Bulletin, 2003). Patent has also been described as a government-given, time-limited right to exclude others from practicing an invention. In other words, with the help of patent, an inventor can provides a method to prevent the innovations using the legal force of the state (i.e., courts)-anybody else using the patented technique or making, selling, using, or importing the patented product (Brown, 2003).

Criteria for new inventions to be patentable (Cowan and Harison, 2001; Brown, 2003):

a. **Utility:** Technical knowledge in the patent filed must possess technical exploitation in its applicability Either it should be mentioned explicitly in patent filed or it should be potentially possibly by industry. It means that the invention should possess some known use i.e. any use will do, so long as it is functional and not solely aesthetic.

b. **Novelty:** Invention that has not been described or disclosed previously is considered as "Novel". Patents will be granted only for those inventions if they carry originality, when compared with other existing body of knowledge. It may also include new uses of a known invention.

c. **Non-obviousness:** The inventions in the patent file should be approved by a 'person skilled in the art' i.e. official practitioner who possesses necessary knowledge and skill.

"Non-obviousness" have been described as the invention that is sufficiently different from previously published work (patents, papers, reviews; the so-called "prior art").

Mazzoleni and Nelson (1998) outlined the main theoretical benefits of patenting in terms of economics and public policy formulation:

a. Patent anticipation motivates scientists and researchers for useful invention as they are rewarded for their discoveries in terms of financial incentives and reputation gains ("invention motivation" theory).

b. Patents serve as mechanisms for inventors to disclose their inventions that in turn reduce secrecy, facilitate wide knowledge dissemination about the inventions and their uses and ensures access of researchers to new inventions ("invention dissemination" theory).

Patent period is for 20 years from the date of filing application but may be accompanied with provisional specification in case of delay expected in submitting specific description of invention, patent application (IPR Bulletin, 1999; IPR Bulletin, 2003).

Three types of patents have been described under US law (Brown, 2003):

a. **Utility patents-**It includes any invention or discovery of a new and useful (or a new and useful improvement of any) composition of matter (e.g., a new chemical compound or mixture of compounds), process (e.g., an industrial or technical procedure or method), product, or machine.

b. **Design patents-**It protects only the appearance of an article.

c. **Plant patents-**It covers the "invention" (by crossbreeding) or discovery of new plants, including cultivated mutants, hybrids, and seedlings. Patent application is then submitted by the inventor if they find the inventions are novel or has utility over the existing technology and also the inventor has to "reduce to practice" the invention if not done earlier.

Patent prosecution & First-to-File or First-to-Invent

This has been described as the whole process for obtaining a patent in a fairly straightforward way. After documentation of the inventions, the inventor takes this material to a patent agent or patent attorney who conducts a search of the prior art. Their responsibility is to check all the published literature and all previously granted patents. Both form and substance of the patent is the examined by the patent office. However, a patent is not granted immediately. This application is then challenged by the patent office for being insufficient or inadequate in some manner. Clarification or explanation of the queries made by the patent office has to be provided by the inventor and eventually the patent application is rejected or allowed. Unlike most countries, Under US patent law, an inventor has a one year grace period after the first public disclosure or publication to file a patent application. Patent is given to the first person who invents it even if two or more inventors come up with the same invention and submit patent applications claiming that invention. However, in the United States and the Philippines, the patent goes to the person first to file a patent application (the first-to-file system) when more than one inventor comes up with the same invention and applies for a patent (Brown, 2003).

Knowledge Management (KM) and Challenges

Knowledge has been defined as a fluid mix of framed experience, values, contextual information, expert insight and grounded intuition (Asoh *et al.*, 2002). KM has been defined as the ability of an organization to create, share and use the collective knowledge of its products, processes and people to increase workplace productivity and reduce activities that "reinvent the wheel" (Fontaine and Lesser, 2002). Knowledge provides an environment of and framework for evaluating and incorporating new experiences and information which is originated in the minds of knowers (Davenport *et al.*, 2000, Asoh *et al.*, 2002). KM is associated with communicating and using both knowledge and information and it often involves a number of soft issues that forms an environment in which knowledge and information are created as well as exchanged (Asoh *et al.*, 2002). In fact it deals with performance of the right organizational or business actions possible by its dedicated to more intentional means of people creating and sharing knowledge-data, information, and understanding in a social context (Asoh *et al.*, 2002). World Bank, an international organization possesses an active involvement in KM.

Strategic and economic analysis is essential tool for corporate knowledge management. The objective of the knowledge management is to provide right information to right people at right time. Knowledge should be shared by all people. Communication system for transferring the knowledge is restructured after which analysis of available knowledge in the company is done. Efforts are taken to develop the critical knowledge. Determination of critical knowledge depends on the culture of the firm. Knowledge is a major economic challenge in future. Knowledge has economic value which can increase productivity. We can consider different tools for knowledge management. The knowledge is shared in face to face interaction and co-operative work .Some part of the knowledge is transferred in less structured way. This is possible through experience sharing. Tacit knowledge may be transferred with the help of modeling tools. Model can graphically represent the tacit knowledge. Net work map can represent the theoretical concept in a better way. A picture worth is more than thousand words. Database management systems (*DBMSs*) are technical data base management consisting of huge amount of data. Knowledge is available through documentation which may be available in electronic form.

The IBM Institute for Knowledge-Based Organizations has identified a number of challenges when implementing knowledge management programs (Fontaine and Lesser, 2002)-

a. Failure to align knowledge management efforts with the organization's strategic objectives
b. Creation of repositories without addressing the need to manage content
c. Failure to understand and connect knowledge management into individuals' daily work activities
d. An overemphasis on formal learning efforts as a mechanism for sharing knowledge
e. Focusing knowledge management efforts only within organizational boundaries.

It is suggested that right culture is important for KM success that may be possible by storytelling (Denning, 2000). According to Steve Denning, Chief

Knowledge Officer (CKO) of World Bank KM is about 90% cultural change and 10% technology. Thus, cultural change is biggest challenge that KM faces today. In the new economy, KM aims to provide on line, real time access to knowledge, information and data throughout the organization and to its customers in that order (Asoh *et al.*, 2002). KM provides the possibility of a viable alternative for firms in order to create and maintain competitive advantage in turbulent and thus helps in coping with the influences of various technologies and the globalization of world trends and economies today (Asoh *et al.*, 2002).

According to Fontaine and Lesser, 2002, few common pitfalls that should be avoided for successful implementation of KM are-

- failure to align knowledge management efforts with the organization's strategic objectives
- creation of repositories without addressing the need to manage content
- failure to understand and connect knowledge management into individual's daily work activities
- an overemphasis on formal learning efforts as a mechanism for sharing knowledge
- focusing knowledge management efforts only within organizational boundaries

Knowledge Economy

Society has transformed through many phases from an agrarian economy to knowledge economy. Major features are use of technology, role of knowledge in creation of value, less use of capital, high competence of worker and low commiditization of the work force.

Human Capital-In knowledge economy most important asset is human capital. In the technology industry, linkage between human capital and value creation is indisputable. Other forms of capital have a small role to play.

Decision in knowledge based organization-In knowledge economy, democratic principle are applied for decision making at all level. Decision making process includes both top-down and bottom-up features. It is easy to improve the quality of decision. In knowledge based organization cooperative may make sense for decision making process.

Autonomy and Individual freedom-knowledge play a significant role in creation of value. Creative thinking is the basis of value system. Policies should reflect a high level of individual freedom and economy. Repetitive and mechanical task which aim to increase standaredization and reduce flexibility need to be discouraged.

Obsolesce and knowledge economy-In knowledge economy sources of advantage like market share, economics of scale is irrelevant. Speed of obsolesce in knowledge economy is very high and always determined by smarter ideas.

In knowledge economy, comparative advantage like market share, economics of scale and barriers to entry are only for short time span. Knowledge allows its participant recognition and reward for unique talent.

Basic requirement for knowledge economy-An educated and skilled populatin is requied for knowledge economy. Information infrastraucture ranging from radio to internet is required for effective communication. A regulatory envoronment that supports entrepreneurship, investment in information and communication technology, a network of research centers, university, think tanks, private enterprise and community group is necessity to tap the global knowledge and make it reliable in local context.

"The idea of knowledge driven economy is not just a description of high tech industries. It describes a set of new sources of competitive advantage which can apply to all sector, all companies and all regions from agriculture and retailing to software and biotechnology" (New measures for the New Economy report by Charles Leadbeater, June, 1999).

Economic success is increasingly based upon the effective utilization of intangible asset such as knowledge, skills and innovative potentials as the key resource for competitive advantage. The term knowledge economy is used to describe this emerging economic structure (CESRIC, 2005).

CONCLUSION

IPR is the midpoint of a modern company's success or failure. That is, success of an organization mainly depends on how it applies knowledge management tools and techniques to reduce costs, better serve their customers and gain a distinct competitive advantage in the marketplace. An invention must fulfill the criteria of patentability before its patent declaration. Intellectual property protection in context with stem cell research need an attention as it remains a question of patentable subject matter. Policies regulating stem cell research is a focus in near future. Knowledge has become a major economic challenge for the future. It is important for any innovative organization to create, capitalize and share its knowledge capital.

ACKNOWLEDGMENTS

We acknowledge the Council of Scientific and Industrial Research (CSIR), New Delhi, India and SRM University, NCR Campus, Delhi Meerut Road, Ghaziabad, UP-201204, India for providing the facility and support in completing the manuscript.

CONFLICTS OF INTEREST

The authors declare that there are no conflicts of interest.

REFERENCES

Grenier, L. (1998). Working with Indigenous Knowledge. Ottawa, ON, Canada: KIG 3H9.

University of Victoria. (1998). The Role of environmental degradation in population displacement. Canada: Steve Lonergan. 4, 5-15.

Sharachchandra, M. L. (1991). Sustainable development: A critical review. World Development, 19 (6), 607-621.

Moyer-Henry K. (2008). Patenting Neem and Hoodia: Conflicting Decisions Issues by the Opposition Board of the European Patent Office, Biotechnology Law Report, 27 (1):1-10.

Erstling, J. (2009). Using Patents to Protect Traditional Knowledge. HeinOnline-15 Texas Wesleyan Law Review, 295, 295-333.

Asoh, D., Belardo, S., and Neilson, R. (2002). Knowledge management: issues, challenges and opportunities for governments in the new economy, Proceedings of the 35th Hawaii International Conference on System Sciences: 1-10.

Davenport, T.H., and Prusak, L. (2000). Working Knowledge: How Organizations Manage What They Know. Paperback ed., Boston, Harvard Business School Press.

Denning, S. (2000). The Springboard: How Storytelling Ignites Action in Knowledge-Era Organizations. Paperback ed., Butterworth Heinemann, Boston.

Fontaine, M., and Lesser, E. (2002). Challenges in managing organizational knowledge. Somers, NY, 10589, U.S.A.

Cowan, R., and Harison, E. (2001). Intellectual property rights in a knowledge based economy. MERIT Infonomics Research Memorandum Series.

Rose, A.K. (2002). Do we really know that the WTO increases trade? National Bureau of Economic Research. NBER Working Paper No. 9273. 1050 Massachusetts Avenue Cambridge, MA 02138.

Coca-Cola Bottling Co. of Shreveport, Inc. v. The Coca-Cola Co., 563 F.Supp. 1122 (D.Del. 1983).

Coca-Cola Bottling Co. of Shreveport, Inc. v. The Coca-Cola Co., 107 F.Supp. 288 (D. Del. 1985).

Editorial. (1995). Names for hi-jacking. Nature. 373 (6513), 370.

Chesnoff, S. (1995). The use of Taxol as a trademark. Nature 374 (6519), 208.

Khan, N.U. (1995). Taxol trademark. Nature. 374: 400.

Meyer, J.H., and Ginovart, N. (2007). Diagnosis and treatment of mood disorders. WO2007014467A1.

Gupta, V.K. (2009, July). Conference on Intellectual Property and Public Policy and Issues, Geneva.

Gallini, N., and Scotchmer, S. (2002). Intellectual Property: When Is It the Best Incentive System? National Bureau of Economic Research. MIT Press. ISBN: 0-262-60045-5.

IPR Bulletin. (2003). Technology Information, Forecasting and Assessment Council. 9, 10.

IPR Bulletin. (1999). Technology Information, Forecasting and Assessment Council. 5, 8.

Brown, W.M. (2003). Intellectual property law. Molecular Biotechnology.23, 213-224.

Mazzoleni-Roberto., and Nelson-Richard-R (1998). Economic theories about the benefits and costs of patents. Journal-of-Economic-Issues. 32, 1031-1052.

Robert Harding, (2013). India's patent ecosystem-encouraging strong patents or discouraging innovation? Nature Reviews/Drug Discovery. 12, 732-733.

Zachariades. N.A. (2013). Stem cells: intellectual property issues in regenerative medicine Stem Cells and Development. 22 (1), 59-62.

□□□

CHAPTER - 42

Technology Mediated Participatory Planning for 21st Century

Brajaballav Kar & R. N. Subudhi
School of Management, KIIT University Bhubaneswar
Email: brajkar@gmail.com, rabisubudhi@gmail.com

INTRODUCTION

Mass production was the hallmark for improvement of productivity in early 20th century. Subsequently the productivity development was driven by the use of information technology and related concepts like Entrepreise resource planning (ERP), Customer relationship Management (CRM), Business Process Reingineering, TQM etc. These technologies and concepts were instrumental in collection, codification, analysis, decision making and execution of decision which translated to better coordination and profitability. The ability to harness synergy out of the information systems, coordinated team and goal orientation helped in executing strategies with sharpness, proactively identifying customer need, responding to social context and competitive scenario with alacrity. As it stands now, with internet and multimedia technologies it is faster to form organization, reach out to the stakeholders. Technology mediation has improved the productivity and quality of economic activities. It has still lot more options to come in the 21st century.

Sovereign state performances from different parts of the world have been going through a different set of social and performance context. Over last couple of decades multiple social issues have surfaced. Issues like "rich and poor divide", "increase of least developed countries (LDCs)", have forced a thinking about the efficacy and efficiency of governance processes. The social and economic context in multiple countries gave rise to the Millenium Development Goals (MDG) of the UN. Governments in most of the countries have short life span than before, and are now elected with lower margins. The recent Jasmine revolution has eliminated entrenched dictators, almost without bloodshed vastly due to the use of technology like, social-e-media platforms. Regional aspirations have become strong, vociferous and demanding. Splintering of USSR, Sudan, Unification of Germany, Iraq, overthrowing of monarchy in Nepal and closer home in India, there is clamour for more states. In a multi-party democracy, few national parties have got splintered into or have given rise to multiple regional political parties to represent the local aspirations. Governments are now grappling with economic crisis. Democracy as the form of the government, ironically, has not been able to live upto the expectations. On different facet, recently the issues like wikieleaks and exposure of snooping of different governments on its own citizens, have indicated the lack of trust of people.

By and large, these issus indicate that the governments are not able ***to manage the information base*** to be proactive towards the need and aspirations of the people. The governance structure and systems are not delivering to the differential objectives of multiple stakeholders. Legislating new laws becomes even more difficult because of complexity, interrelatedness with the existing laws. People are not participating in the buying in process of any program, to make it successful.

Why Participatory Planning

In a democratic system stake holders have multiple world views, and usually the problems are complex. In such a scenario, any solution arrived at must have the requisite sustainability and acceptance. Without the adequate acceptance, the different aspects of problems and possible solutions, keep getting iterated in a loop. Participatory planning establishes legitimacy of the solutions arrived at and this becomes the base of the execution success. Dash (2007) proffers the argument that "wicked" design problems are best addressed through collective observations. In case of unstructured, complex social problems, such process adds to individual's capability to synthesize and communicate.

Another argument of participatory planning is that, it increases social capital. Menzel et al (2011) had persued a pre-post design for trust in institution as an element of social capital and observed that trust is impacted by the process quality. In case of resource and time constraints, the participatory process quality becomes more important than the degree of participation.

Takeshi (2006); described the case of Indonesia, where in new order regime of Suharto's collapsed in 1998, after about 3 decades, and the democratic process made decentralization an imperative, through participatory planning process. The government to be more transparent, accountable and responsive, the planning process is to start at local level. The author opines that the aforementioned objectives can be achieved by citizens' ***participation in the decision-making process***.

Though participatory planning model is advocated by many, there are concerns as well. Krek (2005) in his paper questions its assumption and existence. He sites lack of empirical research and argues that if the cost of educating oneself about any issue is significantly higher than its ignorance, then citizens are more like to choose rational ignorance. He sites the prisoner's dilemma to highlight the individual potential benefit versus group benefit. So there exist possibility of free riding in the planning process as well, if the benefit is significantly less than the investments.

Technology interventions for Participatory Planning:

In the subsequent sections this paper discusses possible technology mediations that can be used to further the participatory planning and execution processes to bring out the desired outcomes.

A few necessary tools, with brief description:

1. Web 2.0

Web 2.0 has made the internet based interaction processes bidirectional more interactive and more intense, the role played by social networking softwares in terms of building shared information base, opinion and shared understanding, has immense potential to contribute for effective participatory planning. Blogs, wikie, social networking sites etc are creating, modifying and disseminating various multimedia rich microcontents to develop shared understanding and information. McLoughlin and Lee (2007) espoused the usability of this technology even to be used in pedagogical models where in participants can have own volition and direction for learning.

2. Cybernetics

As mentioned in wikiepedia "cybernetics" is a multi and trans-disciplinary approach for exploring different regulatory systems. The structures, constraints, and possibilities of such systems are also the part of cybernetics. It is used to study and understand social systems as well. In a closed loop system the signal and feedback forms a "circular causal" relationship.

Asiegbu (2011) indicated that national economy should have its economic cybernetic system to solve economic problems. These issues are characterized by unstable open systems, uncertainties (chaos), interdependence and autocatalytic process. Cybernetics can be used to study the components of structure and function of the economy. In a dynamic and complex system the control of processes are maintained by information movements and transformations.

In their article, Espinosa, Harnden and Walker (2004) have indicated that democracy is in crisis because of trust deficit and low level of involvement of citizens. Qutoting the UN survey (2003), they indicate that 60% of the general public dont trust their government. The reason for such disbelief has been indicated in cybernatic language, as open loop system and time delay of feedback. Though in a complex governance process the delay and disconnection is, to an extent natural, there has to be acceptable degree of responsiveness. The Viable System Model (VSM) framework by Stafford Beer (1984) has been discussed to understand the patterns of sustainability. The model was derived to understand the minimum set of invariants that can permit the maintenance of a particular identity in a dynamic environmental condition. VSM like neural networks, require a proper balance between autonomy and cohesion, instead of hierarchical approach. It is recursive at different level of social organization, thus a viable system always will have another viable system in tandem. Ontologies of VSMs will shape the interactions and develop adapative behaviour at different levels of atomicity. Thus it will shape consciousness, over time, at different recursive levels.

In VSM terms, a "democratic decision making mechanism" balances "regulatory views", "exploratory views", "internal views" and "external views". The decision making mechanism should give (i) access to knowledge and information though transparent mechanism, (ii) autonomy to air the views (iii) design the plan collectively (iv) decide the issues to be managed at that level (v) authorise participants to act as agreed.

However there are issues in terms of literacy and communication level that needa to be addressed for larger participation. At this point, technology has the ability to support cybernetic forms of governance, which makes the government real time. It also requires the structures processes and practices to be rebuilt.

3. Multi-criteria decision making

Planning in general and participatory planning in particular being complex, requires adequate theoretical and technological support base. Vassilev V, *et al* (2005) have analysed the existing set of methods and technologies available. Most of the issues in planning, control and analysis can be categorised as multi-criteria decision making. Such problems can be divided into discrete multicriteria or continuous multi-criteria problems. In discrete multicriteria problems, the specified alternatives can be tabulated and evaluated. In continuous multi-criteria problems, finite number of constraints in form of function are there, which can generate infinite feasible solutions (optimization problems). At present, various techniques like multiattribute utility (value) theory methods, outranking methods, interactive algorithms method etc are available to handle complexities of planning. These set of theoretical and technological support base would prove immensely helpful in the participatory planning process.

4. Open source softwares: Freeware

The greatest participatory planning, collaboration and execution success can be indicated as the development of open source softwares. The nature and extent of applicability of such open source softwares are quite vast. These also have driven down the market cost of the licensed softwares, generated shared wealth. It builds the innovation platform of the society as a whole and transforms the cultural competitive landscape.

Participatory Planning Models

There are many models indicated for participatory planning. Stratigea & Papadopoulou (2013) have indicated "analytical participatory scenario planning", "Focus Groups" and "Future Workshop participatory tools". The article indicates "LIPSOR framework" consisting of five discrete parts where in (i) "Key drivers and questions are identified", (ii) key actors are identified (iii) expert–base is explored to get information/opinions (iv) 'plausible scenarios' are identified considering all scenarios and (v) scenarios are evaluated and actions are identified. Similarly, Devine (2002) has indicated "Participatory Planning Through Negotiated Coordination" as a model of participatory planning

In a complex and novel problem situation a systems approach with systems thinking gets deployed. Decision is supported by resources like scientific data, information, knowledge and wisdom, at the same time there are issues of such decisions actually being translated to action. This could indicate the differences in cognition and socio-cultural context of actors or knowledge entities. Thus methodologically or epistemologically the knowledge has to be co-created to take the advantage of tacit knowledge base of the stakeholder.

Viability of the participatory planning process is an important consideration for longterm sustainability. The models for a project, problem or issue based structure would be unsuitable in the long run. In this context we propose a "team revitalization" process, which would fill the gap between out going and incoming participatory planning team. The issue of voluntary process of participation has to compensate for the requirements of the objective. This would determine the tenure of the planning and execution process. Ability of the society to choose the optimal solution will be reflected through the participatory planning team and this process itself needs to be revitalized. In the absence of a revitalization, the process would stop, thus demoralizing and disbanding of the remaining members. Similar would be the case for continual leadership role in such teams. The leadership role in the team also needs replenishment in its own volition. The participatory process components with the revitalization is depicted in figure-1 below:

Resource

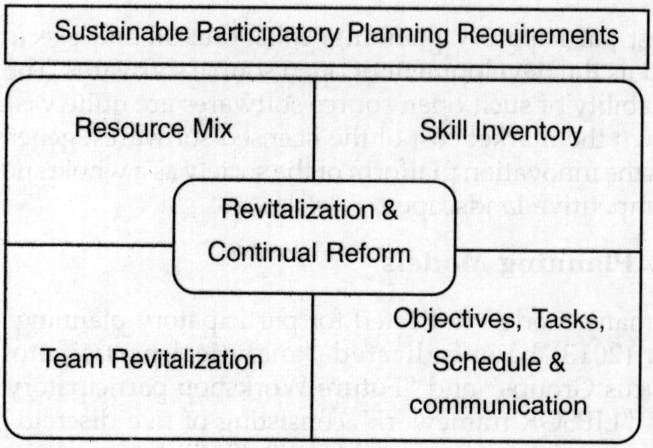

Figure 1 : Revitalization & Continual Reform for sustainable Participatory Planning

DISCUSSION AND CONCLUSION

Participatory planning as a model for inclusiveness, shared growth, information dissemination and long term orientation is here to stay. As discussed in the article, the open source software development is one of the most important evidence of such planning and execution model for the common goal and good. Pertinent issue therefore is how the governance mechanism is adopting, scaling up and promoting such process. Given the performance expectation of citizens from its government and the state of trust deficit, the decentralization and participatory planning as a method will indicate the way forward. Current issues of open loop governacne and unexplainable delay in the system can be addressed through participatory planning process.

Use of technolgoy will bring relational orientedness to governance, handle the planning complexity, close the feedback loop, transcend the geographical and time barrier. It is not a specific technology perse but a suite of technologies based on the information and communication technology (ICT) framework.

One of the assumptions in participatory planning though, people would like, participate and contribute in the process effectively. Second caveat would be longevity and continuity of such participatory planning process. Process would be carried out by participants on a continual and voluntary basis. Thus the team needs to get revitalized from possible attrition. If such attrition in terms of person, skill base and intent is not replenished, the participatory planning process would get setback. Paticipatory planning and execution team and the leadership role need to be regenerated for viability.

The swiftness of change in terms of technology, complexity and universalness of issues, and demand for good governance by the citizens, cutting across state barriers, necessitates participatory planning and execution. Technology mediated participatory governance will make governments and governance process real time and online.

REFERENCES

Asiegbu,BC(2011). Control of National Economies In the Age of Information Technology and Dynamism: A theoretical Perspective of Economic Cybernetics, Journal Of Contemporary Research In Business, Institute Of Interdisciplinary Business Research, VOL 3, No. 8.

Beer Stafford (1984), The Viable System Model : Its Provenance, Development, Methodology and Pathology, The Journal of the Operational Research Society. Vol. 35, No. 1 (Jan., 1984), pp. 7-25.

Dash, D.P. (2007) "Self-observing collective: An exemplar for design research?", Kybernetes, Vol. 36 Iss: 9/10, pp.1277 – 1285.

Devine P(2002) "Participatory Planning Through Negotiated Coordination" Science and Society, Vol 66, No 1, 72-85

Espinosa A., Harnden R. and Walker J (2004); "Cybernetics and Participation: From Theory to Practice", Systemic Practice and Action Research, Vol. 17, No. 6, December 2004; DOI: 10.1007/s11213-005-1230-0

Krek A (2005), "Rational Ignorance of the Citizens in Public Participatory Planning", Paper published in the conference proceedings of CORP, Vienna

McLoughlin, C and Lee, M (2007); "Social software and participatory learning: Pedagogical choices with technology affordances in the Web 2.0 era", Proceedings ascilite Singapore.

Menzel, S., Buchecker, M., and Schulz, T.' (2013) Forming social capital- Does participatory planning foster trust in institutions?, Journal of Environment Management.

Stratigea A. & Papadopoulou CA (2013), "Foresight Analysis at the Regional Level - A Participatory Methodological Framework" Journal of Management and Strategy Vol. 4(2) Sciedu Press 1 ISSN 1923-3965 E-ISSN 1923-3973.

Subudhi, RN (2013), "Knowledge Management and the Changing Need of IT Applications", in Ed. Roy, AK: 'Information and Knowledge Management: Tools, Techniques and Practices', New India Publishing Agency, New Delhi, ISBN: 978-93-81450-62-8.

Takeshi, I.(2006); "The Dynamics of Local Governance Reform in Decentralizing Indonesia: Participatory Planning and Village Empowerment in Bandung, West Java" Asian and African Area Studies, 5 (2): 137-183.

Vassilev V, Genova K and Vassileva M (2005); "A Brief Survey of Multicriteria Decision Making Methods and Software Systems", Bulgarian Academy Of Sciences, Cybernetics & Information Technologies · Volume 5, No 1, Sofia.

Internet References

Simon Wild, "Technology is revolutionising participatory planning– what will you do?" http://www.simonwild.me/2013/08/29/technology-is-revolutionising-participatory-planning-what-will-you-do/ accessed on 25-Dec-2013

Feedback/ querries can be mailed to the first author at: brajkar@gmail.com

❑❑❑

